FURNITURE

FURNITU

Judith Miller

DK

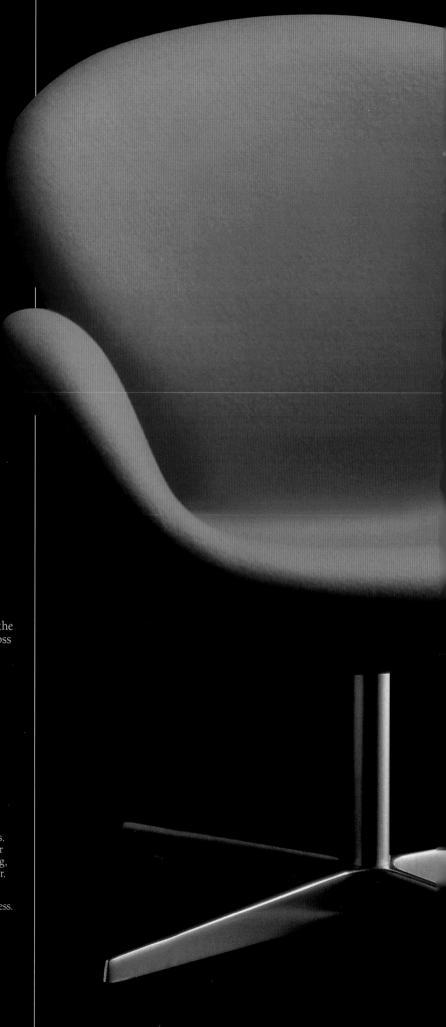

LONDON, NEW YORK,
MELBOURNE, MUNICH AND DELHI

A joint production from **DK** and
THE PRICE GUIDE COMPANY

DORLING KINDERSLEY LIMITED
Senior Editor Angela Wilkes
Senior Art Editor Karla Jennings
Editors Corinne Asghar, Kathryn Wilkinson,
Jane Laing, Margaret Parrish
Art Editors Anna Plucinska, Lee Riches, Ted Kinsey
Managing Editor Julie Oughton
Managing Art Editor Heather McCarry
Art Directors Carole Ash, Peter Luff
Publishing Director Jackie Douglas
Production Melanie Dowland
DTP Designer Adam Walker
Picture Research Sarah Smithies
Picture Library Neale Chamberlain
Jacket Editor Carrie Love
Jacket Designer Nicola Powling
US Editor Christine Heilman

THE PRICE GUIDE COMPANY LIMITED
Senior Managing Editor Anna Southgate
Managing Editor Cathy Marriott
Editorial Assistants Jessica Bishop, Sandra Lange
Karen Morden, Alexandra Barr
Publishing Manager Julie Brooke
Digital Image Co-ordinator Ellen Sinclair
European Consultant Martina Franke

While every care has been taken in the compilation of this guide, neither the
authors nor the publishers accept any liability for any financial or other loss
incurred by reliance placed on the information contained in *Furniture*.

First American Edition, 2005
Published in the United States by
DK Publishing, Inc., 375 Hudson Street,
New York, New York 10014

The Price Guide Company (UK) Ltd
info@the priceguidecompany.com

05 06 07 08 09 10 9 8 7 6 5 4 3 2 1

A Cataloging-in-Publication record for this book is available from the Library of Congress.

ISBN 0-7566-1340-X
Colour reproduction by Colourscan, Singapore

Printed and bound in China
by Leo Paper Products

Discover more at
www.dk.com

FOREWORD

"A chair is a very difficult object. A skyscraper is almost easier. That is why Chippendale is famous."

LUDWIG MIES VAN DER ROHE

Anyone who has ever admired the proportions of a Chippendale chair or the finely carved pediment of a Queen Anne highboy will know there is no skill to match that of a cabinet-maker. There is an immense sense of achievement in bringing a furniture design to fruition; from the first sketch on paper to selecting the wood, working the surfaces until smooth, and adding final touches such as handles and escutcheons, a craftsman takes pleasure in each step of the process. This sense of satisfaction is a lasting one when you consider that a finely constructed desk or table will last many lifetimes and bring pleasure to all who use it.

Furniture styles have changed so much through the centuries. At times designers have been inspired by the past; at other times they have fixed their sights firmly on the future. Whether you are delighted by the simple form of a Shaker cabinet or the exuberance of a Belter sofa, furnish your home in the traditional Chippendale style or the futuristic designs of the Memphis Group, there is much to learn from seeing furniture from around the world placed in context as it is in this book. However, while designs and fashions change, one thing remains the same: the enthusiasm and creativity of furniture-makers.

David Kirkley

CONTRIBUTORS

Jill Bace   Expert in European Decorative Arts, Lecturer at the Wallace Collection and the V&A Museum, London   *Arts and Crafts, Art Nouveau, Art Deco*

Dan Dunlavey   Writer on antiques and collectables   *Ancient Furniture, Mid-19th Century*

Dr Henriette Graf   Furniture Historian and Lecturer at the Technical University of Munich   *Early 18th Century, Late 18th Century, Early 19th Century*

Albert Hill   Writer and curator specializing in 20th- and 21st-century design   *Modernism, Mid-Century Modern, Postmodern and Contemporary*

Scott Nethersole   Art Historian and lecturer on the History of Furniture   *Early 19th Century*

Anne Rogers Haley   American furniture consultant and researcher   *17th Century, Early 18th Century, Late 18th Century*

Jeremy Smith   Senior Furniture Expert and Deputy Director, Sotheby's London   *17th Century, Early 18th Century, Late 18th Century, Mid-19th Century*

CONSULTANTS

Liz Klein   New-York-based consultant and collector's agent specializing in 20th-century decorative arts   *Arts and Crafts, Art Nouveau, Art Deco, Modernism, Mid-Century Modern, Postmodern and Contemporary*

Nicolas Tricaud de Montonnière   European specialist   *Early 18th Century, Late 18th Century, Early 19th Century, Art Deco*

Christopher Claxton-Stevens   Norman Adams, London   *1600–1760*

Silas Currie   Rowley's Fine Art Auctioneers, Ely, Cambridgeshire   *1600–present*

Laurence Fox   Evergreen Antiques, New York   *Scandinavia 1700–1900*

Beau Freeman   Samuel T Freeman & Company, Philadelphia   *America 1600–1840*

Yves Gastou   Galerie Yves Gastou, Paris   *Art Nouveau, Art Deco, Modernism, Mid-Century Modern, Postmodern and Contemporary*

Willis Henry   Auctioneer, Willis Henry Auctions Inc., Massachusetts   *Shaker Furniture*

Maître Lefèvre   Maison de Ventes Beaussant-Lefèvre, Paris   *France 1600–1900*

Marcus Radecke   European Furniture Dept, Christies, London   *Italy, Spain, and Portugal 1600–1900*

David Rago   Consultant and auctioneer, Rago Auction Center, Lambertville NJ.   *American Arts and Crafts*

Patrick van der Vorst   Director and Head of Continental Furniture Department, Sotheby's, London   *Italy, Spain, and Portugal 1600–1900*

Jean-Jacques Wattel   Pierre Bergé et Associés, Paris   *Art Nouveau, Art Deco, Modernism, Mid-Century Modern, Postmodern and Contemporary*

PRICE BANDS

Some of the pieces of furniture in this book are accompanied by a number that gives an indication of value:

1 $200–1,000   **2** $1,000–2,000   **3** $2,000–4,500   **4** $4,500–9,000

5 $9,000–18,000   **6** $18,000–36,000   **7** $36,000–90,000

8 $90,000–180,000   **9** $180,000–450,000   **10** $450,000 upward

Previous page: **The Swan** This lounge chair was designed by Arne Jacobsen for the Royal Hotel, Copenhagen. The chair has a molded, synthetic inner shell with red fabric upholstery and stands on an aluminum, swiveling base. *1958. H:33½ in (85 cm); W:29¼ in (75.6 cm); D:25 in (63.5 cm).*

Opposite page: **Boston highboy** This highboy from Massachusetts has a maple case and a white pine interior. The case is japanned and has Queen Anne-style brass handles, escutcheons, and cabriole legs. *c. 1747. H:70¼ in (178.4 cm); W:39⅝ in (100.6 cm); D:30 in (53.3cm).*

CONTENTS

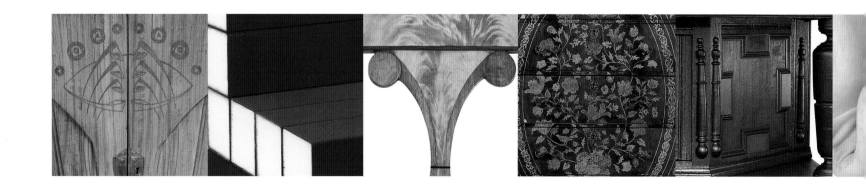

INTRODUCTION

The story of furniture is inextricably linked with the story of our civilization. From Roman day beds to Louis XV armchairs, and from Neoclassical desks to Postmodern storage units, the furniture people have used in their homes has always reflected the aspirations, fashions, and technology of the time.

I was born into the "Formica Generation" of the 1950s. My parents were proud to say they had thrown away the old Victorian furniture they had inherited and replaced it with the latest modern designs. I, however, spent many happy hours wandering through the grand stately homes in the Scottish Borders where we lived, many of them designed by Robert Adam and his sons. I think it was in

Paxton House near Berwick that I was first struck by the wonderful furniture made by an 18th-century craftsman named Thomas Chippendale. It was the beginning of a long and exciting journey of discovery.

Since then I have been able to study furniture in a huge variety of styles and in a wide range of countries, from French Art Nouveau in the Musée d'Orsay, Paris, to the American Furniture Collection in Williamsburg, Virginia, and Modernist pieces in the Bauhaus Museum in Berlin. All of them have added to my fascination with furniture.

Being able to identify a piece of furniture requires an understanding of how it was made, what is was made from, and who it was made for. Most of the grand

furniture that we see today was made for the aristocracy, who wanted to show off their wealth and good taste. By the mid-19th century, however, furniture was more affordable and the middle classes could furnish their homes in the latest styles. This book shows not only the masterpieces created for the finest homes, many of which are now in museums, but also the less expensive, everyday furniture designed for more modest settings.

While furniture design has evolved over time, certain forms, such as the klismos chair, have often been revived. Some styles also spread across continents: the excavations at Pompeii and Herculaneum, for example, inspired French Empire furniture, the designs of Hepplewhite and Sheraton, and American Federal furniture.

There are many fine specialist books on furniture, but I always felt the need for one that would provide a definitive overview of world furniture. This book looks at the evolution of styles from the earliest times to the end of the 20th century, and is illustrated with 3,000 photographs. Each chapter investigates a specific period, setting the development of styles within a social and political context. It provides an overview of furniture design and a guide to the key elements of decorative style, then shows how furniture developed from country to country, including features on styles, designers, and movements. Finally, themed collections of pieces from different countries are analyzed and compared and include price bands, where possible, to give collectors an indication of value. Some pieces are accompanied by a letter code identifying the dealer or auction house that is selling or has sold them.

I hope that this magnificent and comprehensive book will fire your imagination, just as that first piece of Chippendale fired mine, and will give you a lifelong interest in the styles, techniques, and history of this fascinating subject.

Judith Miller.

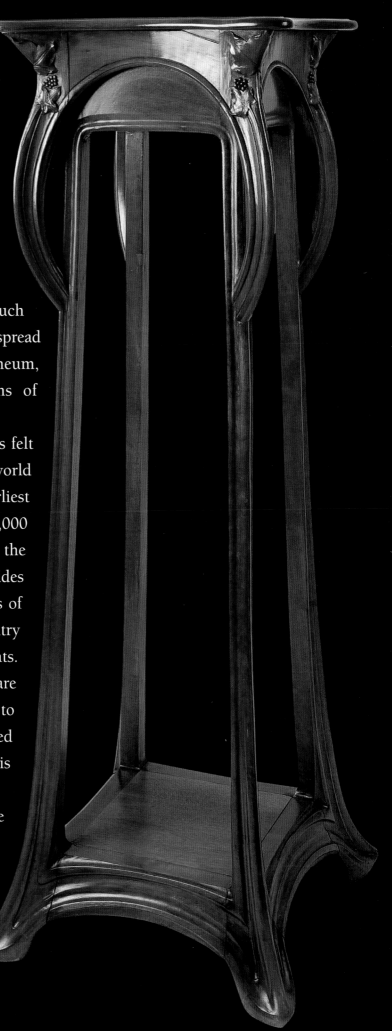

PERIOD STYLES

Developments in furniture design have always been subject to various factors—economic and political change, technological advances, necessity, status, and fashion. Not all countries have experienced exactly the same influences, nor are the features of any one style seen in all the furniture made at that particular time. However, each period style does have its own defining characteristics, whether it is the overall shape of a piece, how it is decorated, or the materials used, which make it easier to identify as belonging to one era rather than another.

Renaissance

Originating in Italy in the 14th century and finding expression throughout Europe over the following 200 years, Renaissance means "rebirth." The style was inspired by a renewed interest in ancient Greece and Rome. Taking their lead from architects, furniture-makers applied Classical features, such as columns, cornices, and pediments, to their work, producing symmetrical, architectural pieces. Popular motifs included vases, putti, and caryatids.

Renaissance sgabello chair (see p.29)

Baroque

An expression of wealth and power, the Baroque style was sculptural and theatrical. Drawing on Classical and Renaissance motifs, designers produced elaborately carved furniture on a grand, architectural scale, using exotic materials and techniques such as marquetry, *pietra dura*, and velvet upholstery. Evident in its purest form in Rome around 1600, the style was adopted by other European countries as the century progressed, with varying degrees of exuberance.

Italian Baroque cabinet (see p.37)

Gothic armchair (see p.166)

Gothic

Influenced by medieval ecclesiastical architecture, Gothic-style furniture has enjoyed a number of revivals. The first emerged in Britain from the mid-18th century, when furniture-makers such as Thomas Chippendale applied Gothic architectural elements, such as cusped arches, ogee curves, and quatrefoils, to their designs. The style was revived during the 19th century and had a considerable influence on the Arts and Crafts Movement.

Chinoiserie

Chinoiserie was a style that developed from the European fascination with the exotic porcelain, lacquerware, and other forms of decorative art imported from China and Japan, from the 17th century onward. Derived from *chinois*, the French word for "Chinese," the style developed in its own right as European designers created their own fanciful interpretation of exotic Asian styles and motifs. The result was a style that lasted in various forms for about 200 years, combining ornament from China and Japan, sometimes with both styles evident in one piece. Characteristic of the style was the use of exotic motifs such as pagodas, dragons, and lotus blossoms, stylized landscapes, Chinese men, imitation lacquerwork known as japanning, and luxurious materials.

Lacquered commode in the Chinoiserie style (see p.170)

Georgian chest of drawers (see p.179)

Georgian

Georgian is a term used to describe furniture made in Britain from 1715 to 1811, during the reigns of Georges I, II, and III. Early Georgian furniture was primarily made from walnut, and incorporated a number of the Rococo features prevalent at the time, such as serpentine curves, C- and S-scrolls, and claw-and-ball feet. Late Georgian pieces were mostly made from mahogany, and displayed the rectilinear shapes and Neoclassical ornament that became popular toward the end of the 18th century.

Rococo commode *(see p.73)*

Rococo

By the beginning of the 18th century, furniture designers began to reject the heavy formality of the Baroque style and sought to create a lighter, more feminine look. Emerging in France, the Rococo style dominated European design for the first half of the 18th century and made much use of curvaceous *bombé* forms, asymmetrical ornament, and the cabriole leg. Popular motifs included C- and S-scrolls, naturalistic foliage, and rocaille, which often took the form of elaborate gilded mounts.

Louis XV

The French interpretation of the Rococo style was named after the early 18th-century monarch Louis XV. The style was influenced by a more informal, intimate, and comfortable way of life, with an emphasis on the interior as a harmonious whole. Color schemes were either rich and vibrant or pale and gilded, and new forms, such as the *duchesse* (chaise longue), the *bergère* (armchair), and delicate *bonheurs-du-jour* (lady's desks) reflected the increasing influence of women in society. Gilt-bronze mounts and japanned surfaces imitating Asian lacquerwork were also popular decorative features.

Queen Anne chair *(see p.116)*

Louis XV giltwood *bergère (see p.78)*

Queen Anne

A more understated form of Rococo design emerged in Britain, influenced, in part, by prevailing trends in the Low Countries. Furniture forms during this period (1700–15) were more restrained than elsewhere in Europe, and elegant proportions were considered more important than decoration. Pieces tended to be made of lightly carved wood—usually walnut—and had very little additional ornamentation. Characteristic features included the cabriole leg, claw-and-ball feet, and vase-shaped back splats on chairs. The style was adopted with considerable success in North America from about 1725.

Neoclassical

Popular during the second half of the 18th century, Neoclassicism was a reaction against the Rococo style and was linked to a renewed interest in ancient Greece and Rome. Furniture-makers were inspired not only by the rectilinear shapes of Classical architecture, but also by its decorative details, such as the Greek key and Vitruvian scrolls. Applied ornament, often gilded, took the form of laurel swags, urns, and medallions.

Neoclassical *secrétaire (see p.177)*

Gustavian armchair *(see p.155)*

Gustavian

The Gustavian style was a restrained version of French Neoclassicism that was unique to Sweden during the reign of Gustav III (1746–92). Characterized by light colors and rich silk damasks, it was based on Neoclassical elements, such as friezes, fluting, and laurel festoons, but the furniture was painted rather than gilded. Klismos-style chairs upholstered in silk and oval-backed chairs with straight, fluted legs were typical. Entire rooms were decorated in the Gustavian style and often had paneled walls embellished with tall giltwood-framed mirrors.

Federal wall mirror *(see p.247)*

Federal style

Taking its name from the creation of the Federal constitution in 1787, the Federal style was an American form of Neoclassicism, based primarily on British forms. Furniture was predominantly made of mahogany, and was light in style, with a sparing use of ornament. Typical motifs included the American eagle, carved scrolls, bellflowers, swags, and shells. Late Federal pieces began to reflect the influence of Empire style, with applied ormolu mounts and brass banding.

Empire mahogany-veneered commode (see p.200)

Biedermeier

Biedermeier was a more restrained version of the Empire style and developed in Germany, Austria, and Sweden during the first half of the 19th century. Principally a middle-class interpretation of the high French style, Biedermeier furniture was simple, classical, comfortable, and practical. The majority of pieces were rectilinear, and Classical motifs and the saber leg were common features. Although many pieces were made from mahogany, light-colored native woods such as walnut, cherry, birch, pear, and maple were also used, often punctuated with ebonized highlights. Biedermeier furniture was visibly hand-crafted, adding to its homely appeal. Chairs and sofas were usually upholstered in pale fabrics to match the overall light color schemes that were a prominent feature of Biedermeier interiors.

Biedermeier walnut-veneered commode (see p.217)

Empire

A form of late Neoclassicism, the Empire style dominated European furniture design in the first half of the 19th century, originating in France under Napoleon. The style was inspired not only by ancient Greece and Rome, but also by ancient Egypt. Rectilinear forms took on grand proportions and were often embellished with brass or gilt mounts, or with sumptuous fabrics. Designers used architectural elements, such as pediments and columns, on case pieces, and saber or splayed legs on seating. Popular motifs included swags, laurels, and medallions, as well as sphinxes and Napoleon's personal emblems: the crown and the bee. The style directly influenced the Regency style in Britain, the Empire style in the United States, and the Biedermeier style in Germany.

Art Nouveau

This decorative style flourished in Europe, particularly France and Belgium, at the turn of the 20th century. In a reaction against the historical revivals of the mid-19th century, designers sought to create a "new art." The style was characterized by sinuous, asymmetrical lines and was primarily inspired by nature, although there were variations from one country to another. It echoed many of the decorative motifs of the Rococo style 200 years before and was also influenced by Japanese art.

Art Deco table by Ruhlmann (see p.293)

Modernism

Pioneered by the Bauhaus School in Germany in the wake of World War I, Modernism was a rejection of all historical styles. Expressed initially through architecture, the movement spread, and furniture designers embraced manufacturing processes with renewed verve. Forms became predominantly stark, geometrical, and stripped of all ornament—being functional was all-important. Preferred materials included glass, laminated wood, and tubular steel, and new designs included the cantilever chair.

Art Nouveau lady's desk (see p.349)

Art Deco

Coined in the 1960s, "Art Deco" is a term used to describe a decorative style that blossomed at the end of World War I. Essentially of French origin, and inspired by influences as diverse as Neoclassicism, the discovery of Tutankhamen's tomb, and Cubism, Art Deco furniture was large, geometric, and sumptuously decorated. Typical motifs included stylized sunbursts, chevrons, and abstract geometric patterns. Art Deco also developed in Central Europe, the Far East, and the United States, where streamlined pieces were particularly successful.

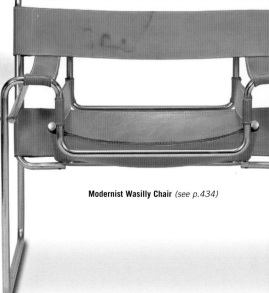

Modernist Wasilly Chair (see p.434)

Victorian armchair
(see p.277)

Historicism

The second half of the 19th century was a time of historical revivals. Epitomized by the Victorian interior in Britain, reproductions of earlier pieces in the Gothic, Renaissance, and Rococo styles were mass-produced, in line with industrialization. There was a greater emphasis on comfort, reflected in curvaceous forms and deep-buttoned upholstery.

Aesthetic Movement

Evident in Britain and the United States toward the end of the 19th century, this was a short-lived movement advocating "art for art's sake." Designers were influenced by the decorative arts of Japan, but also by Gothic, Moorish, and Jacobean styles. Pieces borrowed elements from all these styles and were often ebonized to create a lacquered effect .

Aesthetic Movement rosewood cabinet *(see p.326)*

Arts and Crafts cube chair
(see p.338)

Arts and Crafts Movement

A forceful rejection of the mass-produced, shoddy furniture produced as a result of the Industrial Revolution, the Arts and Crafts Movement championed good design, skilled craftsmanship, and the finest traditional building materials, as part of an ideal of the good life. The style associated with the movement developed in Britain and the United States during the second half of the 19th century and lasted well into the 20th century. Designers worked with native woods—predominantly oak—and produced simple, geometric pieces based on traditional vernacular forms, such as the settle. Additional forms of decoration were sparingly used, the idea being that the grain of the wood, often quartersawn, was sufficiently decorative in itself.

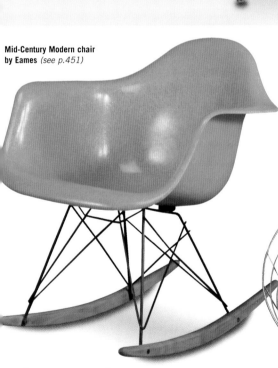

Mid-Century Modern chair by Eames *(see p.451)*

Pop

Pop is a term used for design of the late 1950s and 1960s that exploited popular culture. Furniture could be made very cheaply and took the form of gimmicky, brightly colored pieces, often inspired by the space age and designed predominantly for a young audience. Characteristics of Pop are bright, molded plastics and organic, amorphous forms.

Postmodern Mollusc desk *(see p.519)*

Pop wire-cone chair
(see p.480)

Mid-Century Modern

Mostly associated with designers working in the United States and Scandinavia after the end of World War II, Mid-Century Modern furniture was a natural extension of Modernism, but designers had a looser, altogether more sculptural approach to furniture. They continued to make use of the latest technological advances, which now included the production of molded plastics, foam padding, and lightweight aluminum frames. Characteristic of the period was the experimentation with innovative, often organic, shapes and a bolder use of color.

Postmodern

Peaking in the 1980s, Postmodernism was a style that rejected the ideals of Modernism and promoted the creation of eclectic, distinctive furniture. First expressed in architecture, the Postmodern style was interpreted in a variety of ways by furniture-makers. Some borrowed motifs from different historic styles and incorporated them into a single piece, often made from a mixture of expensive and inexpensive materials. Others produced "High Tech" pieces, or minimalist, unadorned designs using rudimentary materials such as clear acrylic and wicker.

ANCIENT FURNITURE
4000 BCE - 1600 CE

ANCIENT EGYPT

ANCIENT EGYPTIAN FURNITURE is better documented than that of other ancient civilizations, and it was obviously very well regarded in its day. Indeed, excavations at sites in Mesopotamia and farther afield have shown that furniture of Egyptian origin was also exported and given in tribute to foreign dignitaries.

The ancient Egyptian world-view included a complex set of beliefs regarding the afterlife. The Egyptians believed that one aspect of the eternal soul, *ka*, was the double of the physical body, freed at the moment of death but able to return to the corpse at will. This aspect of the soul required sustenance in order to continue to exist, and this is why the burial chambers of Egyptian dignitaries were filled not only with food, but also with ceremonial and household furniture that represented the highest achievements of Egyptian craftsmen. Being perishable, wooden frames did not always survive interment. However, gold casings and ivory inlays, found on tomb floors, have enabled Egyptologists to recreate the furniture.

SECRETS FROM THE TOMBS

Reconstructions of artifacts found in the tomb of Queen Hetepheres have revealed an elaborate canopy

bed, a carrying chair, and other items including numerous boxes. The tomb of Tutankhamen, who was born c. 1340 BCE and died more than 1,000 years after Hetepheres, contained artifacts designed specifically for the burial site: his funerary couch, for example, is carved in the form of Ammit, the eater of the dead, a god with the head of a crocodile, the body of a leopard, and the hindquarters of a hippopotamus. Tutankhamen ruled for less than ten years, and much speculation surrounds the circumstances of his death.

When Howard Carter discovered Tutankhamen's tomb in 1922, there were immediate consequences for the decorative arts. Art Deco furniture, in particular, reflected the influence of ancient Egyptian forms and decorative motifs, just as furniture of the French Empire period had done following Napoleon's triumphant entry into Egypt in 1798.

DOMESTIC FURNITURE

Depictions of items in everyday use by the more affluent members of society have been preserved in paintings and carvings. The most common item of furniture documented was the stool—both three- and four-legged types, with varying degrees of decoration.

The folding stool, constructed from a pair of wooden frames and a slung leather seat, originated in the Middle Kingdom and became a staple of ancient interior design, from Aquae Sulis to Constantinople. Another kind of stool in common use had a concave seat, supported by four upright legs linked with stretchers and reinforced with diagonal braces.

Golden Throne This throne from Tutankhamen's tomb has a wooden frame wrapped in gold and silver sheets with inlaid, semiprecious stones, and lion's head and paw decoration.

Low, straight-legged tables were used to display water vessels or the faience vases so treasured by Egyptians. Stands designed specifically for vases were constructed from timber poles terminating in a collar that supported the vessel.

Beds were usually made of wood, although metal and ivory were also used. Woven cord was suspended between the two sides of the frame to support a mattress of folded linen. There was no uniform height: many beds were low, although some were high enough to require a low step or mounting board.

WOODS

Timbers available to ancient Egyptians included native sycamore fig, acacia, and sidder, a hardwood also known now as "Christ's Thorn." These were supplemented by woods imported from Middle Eastern trading partners, such as cypress and Lebanese cedar, which were also used for boat construction.

CONSTRUCTION AND DECORATION

The arid climate curtailed the growth of trees, so large pieces of lumber were hard to come by. This led to a certain amount of ingenuity on the part of

Copy of a wall painting This painting from the Tomb of Rekhmira, 1475 BCE, shows an Egyptian youth constructing a chair using a bow drill to bore a hole in the seat.

TIMELINE 4000 BCE–31 BCE

Sphinx in front of King Khafre's pyramid, which is in the desert region of Giza, Egypt.

c. 4000 BCE The Egyptians discover papyrus, the precursor to modern-day paper, and guard the secret closely for thousands of years.

c. 3150 BCE The earliest known hieroglyphs, found in a tomb at Abydos, date from this period. Originally used as an accounting tool, these symbols developed into a complete and complex written language.

c. 3100–2125 BCE The Old Kingdom sees the introduction of the 365-day calendar in Egypt, as well as the construction of some of the most enduring monuments ever created by man.

c. 2630 BCE The world's first major stone structure, the Step Pyramid of King

Ruins of Karnak temple complex and obelisk, Luxor, Thebes, Egypt.

Djoser, is built at the necropolis of Saqqara.

c. 2560 BCE The Great Pyramid of Khufu, or Cheops, is built from some two million blocks of stone.

It remains the tallest building on Earth for more than 4,000 years.

c. 2540 BCE Most authorities date the construction of the Great Sphinx to this period, during the reign of King Khafre, although some controversial theorists contest the Great Sphinx may be 12,000 years old.

c. 2040–1640 BCE Egypt is reunited under the Middle Kingdom and trade with foreign nations is resumed.

The painting on the domed lid depicts Tutankhamen hunting lions in the desert.

4000 BCE–1600 CE

Painted box This box from Tutankhamen's tomb has a domed lid above a rectilinear case and is decorated all over with exquisite painted images of Tutankhamen in heroic pursuits. *c. 1347–1337 BCE.*

This panel depicts a chariot-borne Tutankhamen defeating the Nubian army.

Egyptian carpenters, who developed many of the sophisticated paneling and joining methods that have been used ever since.

Dovetails, mortise-and-tenon joints, and even tongue-and-groove were well known, alongside more primitive techniques involving pegging and lashing. Some workshops specialized in complex intarsia designs, often painstakingly constructed from tiny slivers of the most valuable timbers. Sloppy seams or poor-quality wood were frequently masked with veneer, gesso, and paint.

Surface decoration was an important consideration, and the finest furniture was sheathed in silver or gold leaf. Carved and applied decoration could be just as elaborate. The legs of a folding stool often terminated in ducks' heads or, for a higher-ranking member of

society, lion's paws. Among the finest examples known to have existed are stools with goose-head terminals, inlaid with ivory eyes and neck feathers. Upholstery was usually limited to rolls of linen or other fabrics. Furniture was also painted and, in fact, the ancient Egyptians sowed the embryonic seeds of Western art that continue to flourish and develop today. The "frontalist" style, in which figures are depicted with the head in profile and the torso facing outward, was a defining characteristic of ancient Egyptian culture.

Bed from the tomb of Tutankhamen This bed has a rectangular wooden frame sheathed in gold leaf, and a mat of woven cords. The bed has a headrest and is supported on animal-shaped legs, which terminate in paws. *c. 1567–1320 BCE.*

Valley of the Kings, which contains the tombs of many pharaohs, including that of Tutankhamen.

c. 1470 BCE Thutmose I decrees the extension of the massive Karnak temple complex, including the erection of a mighty obelisk, which still exists.

c. 1550–1070 BCE The warrior kings of the New Kingdom aggressively defend Egypt from foreigners and embark on a program of consolidation and an expansion of power.

c. 1540 BCE The Egyptian kings abandon the necropolis at Memphis and begin to construct tombs in the Valley of the Kings. Thutmose I was the first of around 60 figures to be interred here.

This wooden stool has lion supports and a lattice design. *c. 715–332 BCE.*

c. 1300 BCE The Biblical account of Moses leading the Israelites from Egypt, as related in the Book of Exodus, dates from this period.

1279–1213 BCE The 66-year reign of Rameses II is characterized by great building projects such as the Ramessuem tomb complex, decorated with exaggerated accounts of the king's achievements.

31 BCE Egypt and Greece are incorporated into the Roman Empire following the defeat of Anthony and Cleopatra's naval forces at the Battle of Actium.

Statue of Rameses and his daughter from the Karnak temple complex.

ANCIENT GREECE AND ROME

THE CITY-STATES OF ANCIENT GREECE fostered a golden age of culture that was far more sophisticated than that of Egypt. A more personal spirit of inquiry and curiosity prospered, and humankind began to seek scientific and philosophical solutions to the fundamental conundrums of life. The Minoans of ancient Crete were great record-keepers, although more substantial evidence of their culture has proved elusive, limited to excavations of palaces. The Palace of Minos, when excavated, revealed a mighty stone throne, proving that Europeans have been using chairs for 4,000 years.

THE GREEK HOUSE

The average Athenian male spent very little time at home, but devoted his attentions to civic activities at the Agora, religious commitments, and the Gymnasium. As a result, there was not a great need for furniture. A typical house consisted of two pillared courts—the *andronitis*, or men's apartment, and the *gynaeconitis*, or women's apartment, which was used as a general living room. Surrounding these courts were small cells used as sleeping quarters. The most important furnishings were the hearth, at which offerings were made to the goddess Hestia, and an altar to Zeus. Seating furniture, tables, and beds were made predominantly from

wood, and our knowledge of them is limited to depictions on vases, paintings, and carvings.

ANCIENT AND ENDURING MODELS

The *diphros okladias* was a direct appropriation of the Egyptian X-frame stool, and was certainly in use as long ago as the Aegean period. A more original Greek stool design was the *bathros*, consisting of a flat, square top supported on four legs. Similarly, the Greeks made use of Egyptian-style chairs for many years until they developed the klismos, a design of extraordinary longevity that is still encountered to this day.

Regarded by the Greeks as a feminine piece of furniture, the klismos has four curved legs that bend under the seat of the chair before sweeping back outward as they reach the floor. The shaped back, called a stile, displays an awareness of

Roman strongbox This strongbox is made of bronze with plaster relief decoration. Such boxes were used to hold important household items, especially ladies' cosmetics and jewelry.

ergonomics. There is evidence that the ancient Greeks also used stools that were specifically designed to support infants.

Tables were usually constructed with three legs to aid balance on the uneven earth or plaster floors of the Greek home. The Greek word *kline*, root of the English "recline," was used to describe both beds and couches, which were used while eating. The poor made their beds on the ground, while wealthier Greeks had wooden, bronze, or ivory bedsteads on which they arranged animal skins, woolen cloths, and linen. *Kline* were raised on legs at a height that allowed the occupant to reach the dining table. A number of these couches would be present in the *andron*, or dining room, of the richest Greeks. Some were constructed from valuable imported wood, or decorated with marquetry designs or precious metal inlays.

The furniture of Etruria is known only through excavation, as no Etruscan texts survive. Immigrants attracted to the area bought with them knowledge from the flowering civilizations of Greece, Egypt, and Asia Minor. Forms from all over the ancient world, such as the Egyptian X-chair and the Greek *kline*, thus found their way to the Italian peninsula before the advent of the Roman Empire.

THE CONFLUENCE OF TWO CULTURES

Hellenistic influence spread east into Asia Minor and west into Magna Grecia, the Italian peninsula. This

Etruscan sarcophagus This terra-cotta sarcophagus depicts the dead couple lying together, supported on a mattress and pillows, on a low couch raised on carved, square-section legs. Quite often, couches were wide enough for two people. *c. 525 BCE.*

TIMELINE 1250 BCE–80 CE

1250 BCE Accounts of the wars fought by the Achaeans (a coalition of Greek forces) against the Trojans may be based on events that occurred at this time.

Chair from a tomb in Salamina, Cyprus. *8th century BCE.*

753 BCE This is the date most commonly given for the founding of Rome by Romulus and Remus, descendants of Aeneas, the defeated hero of Troy.

c. 530 BCE Pythagoras founds a mystical order at Croton, devoted to learning and spiritual contemplation.

Bronze Roman tripod from Praeneste. *7th century BCE.*

c. 500 BCE The development of the Ionic column represents a refinement of ancient Greek architecture.

480 BCE The Greeks win a decisive victory at the Battle of Salamina, thwarting Persian efforts to conquer all of Europe.

432 BCE The Greek Parthenon is completed.

Ionic capital at the top of a column, part of the Parthenon, Athens.

323 BCE Alexander the Great dies, having spread the Hellenistic civilization across Europe and south Asia.

expansion led to a clash between Greece and Rome in southern Italy around 280 BCE. The decisive Battle of Actium in 31 BCE ushered in the period of *Pax Romana*, and spelled the end of Greek independence from Rome. Integration was swift and fruitful on both sides, and Roman influence on the Greek world eventually resulted in a rejection of asceticism in favor of a more gleeful conspicuous consumption. The people of Rome were famous *bon viveurs*—so much so that Rome was forced to make periodic legislation against more extravagant trends, such as superfluous culinary largesse and the fashion for sheer, silk fabrics. This decadence, a marked contrast to the austerity of ancient Greece, was reflected in the furnishing and decoration of Roman homes, which became increasingly sumptuous through luxury imports from Asia Minor. Furniture was made in a greater variety of forms than ever before, and decorative elements grew more refined.

ROMAN FURNITURE

The basic Roman table was circular, and was usually set on tripod legs for extra stability. The feet were regularly carved to mimic animals' feet, such as lions, just as they had been in Egypt and, later, Greece. The monopodium—a table supported by a single central pillar—was a later innovation, inspired by Eastern furniture, while a half-moon table, known as the *mensa lunata*, was designed to be used alongside a crescent-shaped sofa.

Hospitality was a salient feature of Roman life and, as a receptacle for food, the table was therefore an important possession. Maple and African citrus, and in particular the roots, were especially prized woods that were used for the best tables.

The Latin *sella* was a chair, of which there were many types. The *sella curulis* was a chair of state and was another descendant of the Egyptian X-chair, although it was not collapsible and had a thick, cushioned seat. The *sella curulis*, or curule chair, was an extremely potent symbol of power, and depictions of these chairs can be seen on Roman coins. Beds became grander than those used in ancient Greece, both in size and opulence. Steps were needed to climb onto the highest bedsteads. Gold and silver feet, and veneers of precious woods and even tortoiseshell, displayed the wealth of the owner. One furniture innovation that the Romans never quite developed to fruition was the glass

A Greek vase This vase is painted with images of women. One of them is sitting on a klismos chair, which has outswept front and back legs.

mirror. The glass manufacturers of Siddon, a port city in present-day Lebanon, failed to become as popular as the polished silver mirrors that were in widespread use.

312 BCE The construction of the *Via Appia,* the famous Roman road, begins under Appius Claudius Caecus.

C. 50 BCE The military campaigns of Julius Caesar extend the Roman Empire into France and Germany. He launches the first Roman invasion of Britain.

64 CE Fire rages through Rome for a week, destroying much of the city. Nero oversees the reconstruction on a grander scale than ever before.

Statue of Julius Caesar (100–44 BCE).

79 CE The Roman town of Pompeii is destroyed following an eruption of Mount Vesuvius. The rediscovery of Pompeii and nearby Herculaneum in the 18th century gave modern scholars a great insight into Roman society.

80 CE Titus inaugurates the Colosseum in Rome with a calendar of games lasting

for 100 days. The three-tier structure was able to seat at least 50,000 spectators.

Colosseum The first stone amphitheater built in Rome. *70–82 CE.*

ANCIENT CHINA

THE BEGINNINGS OF CIVILIZATION in China are unknown. What is certain is that by the 18th century BCE, most of modern China was ruled by a single, militaristic dynasty known as the Shang, who had already developed a complex system of writing and a sophisticated agrarian economy.

A TRADITIONAL AESTHETIC

Wooden furniture was made in China from the earliest times. Furniture excavated from ancient Chu sites dating back to c. 250 BCE shows that wooden furniture and lacquer decoration have been in continuous use in China for many hundreds of years. However, it was not until the rise of international trade, great cities, and a wealthy elite that cabinet-makers made the great aesthetic advances that would characterize their art.

The golden age of furniture production in China began during the Ming dynasty (1368–1644), when the ideal was simple furniture with clean lines and sparse decoration that was limited to latticework and open or relief carving.

During the early years of the Qing dynasty (1644–1912), this ideal remained entrenched. However, as China grew wealthy in its stability, the decorative arts began to reflect a new attitude of confidence and prosperity. Pieces of furniture became larger and heavier, while always retaining a fundamental, simple purity. The rich carving

so celebrated in the Ming period never fell from fashion, but was transformed into something far more expressive and used ever more liberally. Chair backs or legs were often carved from top to bottom with detailed, naturalistic designs. Linear styles gave way to a more fluid approach that incorporated graceful curves and shapes.

Domestic furniture remained utilitarian and unassuming; beaded or beveled edges and simple inlays of light metal provided an aesthetic respite from the plain, flat surfaces. Pieces made for royal use were more sumptuous: mother-of-pearl, porcelain, enamel, and even precious stones were often used as decoration on the most important palace furniture.

POPULAR WOODS

Expendable furniture was made from cheap bamboo, but Chinese cabinet-makers prized indigenous hardwoods such as rosewood above all others. These were generally sourced from the warmer areas of southern China, although imports from Indonesia and other southeast Asian nations supplemented home-grown stocks. Burr woods were also popular, but were usually used sparingly, due to cost and scarcity. The most coveted timber of all was zitan, an extremely dense and attractive variety of sandalwood that was literally worth its weight in gold.

Horseshoe chair This chair is made from huanghuali wood in a simple shape in which the back rail and arms form a continuous semicircle. The meticulous craftsmanship and construction makes use of mortise-and-tenon joints. c. 1550–1650. H:38¼ in (97 cm); D:19¾ in (59 cm) (seat).

BEAUTIFUL, PRACTICAL CONSTRUCTION

Furniture components were joined by the mortise-and-tenon method—the dowels, nails, and, eventually, glues that were employed so widely in the West rarely, if ever, found favor in China. Wherever possible, curved components were cut from a single piece of lumber, so that they were completely seamless. Craftsmen disguised seams and placed them in less visible areas to avoid detracting from the beauty of a piece.

Aside from the aesthetic considerations, mortise-and-tenon joints are particularly suited to Chinese furniture for a more practical reason. The changeable and humid climate prevalent in much of the country causes wood to shrink and expand regularly. The widespread use of lacquer as a decorative treatment on furniture also had a practical application; the all-over covering helped to provide the piece with resistance to insect infestation.

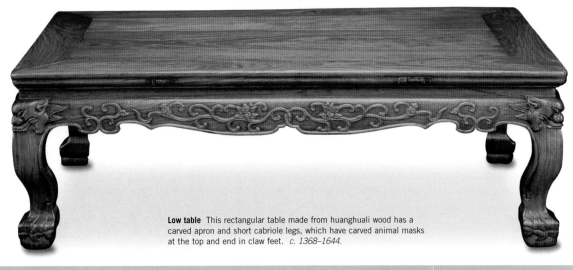

Low table This rectangular table made from huanghuali wood has a carved apron and short cabriole legs, which have carved animal masks at the top and end in claw feet. c. 1368–1644.

TIMELINE 2800 BCE—1516 CE

c. 2800 BCE The *I Ching* or *Book of Changes* reputedly dates from this period and is traditionally accredited to Fu Hsi, the mythical first Emperor of China.

c. 1600–1040 BCE The Shang dynasty are the earliest Chinese people to leave textual evidence of their existence, in the form of "oracle bones." Shang rulers practiced

Genghis Khan

human sacrifice and expanded the borders of China to more or less their present extent.

c. 470 BCE The "Analects," a posthumous collection of Confucius' teachings and dialogues, becomes the most important Chinese philosophical text.

c. 210 BCE Qin Shi Huang, ruler of the short-lived Qin

The Great Wall of China winding across a hilly region of China.

dynasty, consolidates defensive walls into the beginnings of the Great Wall. He is later buried with an army of 7,000 terra-cotta soldiers.

c. 50 BCE Trade along the Silk Road between China and the West

begins in earnest, paving the way for ever-greater cultural and commercial exchange between China and the rest of the world.

25 CE Buddhism is brought to China by immigrants from Persia and India. The religion goes on to experience

Terra-cotta soldiers at the tomb of Quin Shi Huang

THE CONVENTIONS OF USE

The way the Chinese used their furniture was governed by long tradition. It was not the custom to set aside a single area of the home for dining—as people did in the West—and dining tables were often portable, so that they could be moved to different parts of the house. Convention dictated that no more than eight to ten people should be seated around a dining table, so that everyone had access to the dishes of food placed in the center. If this number was exceeded, diners were split into smaller groups. They usually sat at stools with built-in footrests to keep their feet off the floor.

Due to the Chinese custom of sitting or reclining on the floor when reading or writing, lower tables were preferred for these activities. Armchairs were not widely used. They were considered symbols of power, so each family had just one, reserved for use by the head of the household.

The Chinese scholar, an esteemed member of society who devoted his time to the study of time-honored texts, traditionally amassed various treasures that were significant to his calling. Among these numbered fine pieces of rosewood furniture, such as a desk and chair used for reading. Examples of scholars' furniture from the Ming and Qing periods are museum pieces today.

Furniture was generally arranged around the edge of a room, against the walls, in marked contrast to the Western penchant for informal clusters of furniture.

Reverse painting on glass This painting of a Chinese interior depicts a bamboo table decorated with fretwork, a bed, a ceramic rest, and a low table.

The case contains two paneled doors.

The base of the cupboard contains three narrow drawers.

Ming Dynasty cupboard This simple, elegant cupboard is made of huanghuali, a relative of rosewood that was very popular for high-quality Ming Dynasty furniture. *Late 16th century. H:56 in (142.3 cm) W:21⅝ in (54.9 cm).*

times of State sponsorship and vicious repression.

610 CE Emperor Yang orders a massive extension of the Grand Canal, begun during the Wu dynasty. As a result of these works, the canal stretches more than 1,000 miles across China.

868 CE A Chinese translation of the Sanskrit *Diamond Sutra*, found in a sealed cave in Dunhuang, dates from this period.

Blue and white vase from the Ming Dynasty.

It is the oldest dated printed material known to exist.

1271 CE Marco Polo sets out on his journey to the Court of Kublai Khan. On his return to Italy, he maintains that he spent 17 years in Khan's service and traveled extensively throughout China.

1279 CE Kublai Khan, grandson of the great warrior Genghis, inaugurates the Mongol Yuan dynasty, the first nonindigenous dynasty to rule China. Mongol dominion over China continues until the Ming dynasty took power in 1368.

1368–1644 CE The Ming dynasty rules China, reaching a peak of power and influence at the beginning of the 15th century. The period as a whole is one of the

Marco Polo

most prosperous in China's history.

1406 CE Construction of the Forbidden City begins in Beijing. This extensive complex of buildings and courtyards houses emperors of the Ming and Qing dynasties.

1516 CE The Portuguese begin to use the town of Macau in southern China as a staging port for trade, thus establishing the first European settlement in the Orient.

THE MIDDLE AGES

4000 BCE–1600 CE

WHEN ODOACER, CHIEFTAIN OF THE HERULI, overthrew the last of the Western Roman Emperors in 476 CE, it spelled the end of more than 600 years of Roman dominion over Western Europe. The ensuing territorial disputes resulted in a violent dislocation of the region's Classical inheritance, which naturally influenced the arts and, therefore, furniture.

Although the Empire persisted in the East—centered on Constantinople—its Greek Hellenistic tradition was now tempered by the Christian ideals of the Roman rulers. Christianity also informed the culture of the West, influenced by an increasingly powerful papacy. The perpetuation of the Roman Empire in Byzantium, which flourished from the end of the eighth century, created stability. The old Classical aesthetic was fused with Eastern influences, becoming more linear and taking on abstract, geometric decoration. In Byzantine interiors, mosaic was brighter and more colorful than its Roman precursor and was used as a wall decoration more often than on the floor.

BYZANTINE FURNITURE

The Byzantine furniture trade distinguished between the joiner, who made standard items for the general consumer, and the cabinet-maker, whose more architectural designs expressed the aspirations of a thriving and proud culture. The Egyptian X-frame chair abounded, complete with terminals depicting the heads and feet of animals, although it was made of heavier timber than ever before, and sometimes even fashioned from metal.

Chairs remained symbols of power and, as such, they were often monumental in both size and status—more akin to grand thrones than modern chairs. Sophisticated desks with adjustable lectern tops for reading revealed a greater appreciation of function. Dining tables were very low in deference to the Classical manner of eating while reclining, supporting the diner on one elbow—a practice which is still followed in much of Asia Minor. The most common item of furniture was the chest. Lavish examples incorporated intarsia work or inlays of stones, ivory, and precious metals. Their more humble cousins were coffers with simple, flat, hinged lids that also served as beds or benches.

FURNITURE IN THE WEST

The coffer, or chest, was also the most common item of furniture in Western Europe. A basic wooden box constructed from six timber boards

Two panels from a triptych on wood These two panels painted by the Master of Flemalle (probably Robert Campin) depict John the Baptist with Heinrich von Werl and Saint Barbarara in medieval interiors. *1438.* *Each panel: H:39¾ in (101 cm); W:18½ in (47 cm).*

nailed together, or even a hollowed log, it was often the only piece of furniture owned by many people. The landed gentry, on the other hand, usually owned coffers by the dozen, filled with clothes, coins, and other trappings.

Many landlords had itinerant lifestyles because an often-scattered population forced them to spend a lot of their time traveling between different parts of their estates. A great deal of furniture was therefore made to be portable. Tapestries, wall hangings, and cushions were usually removed and taken from one house to another. Chests designed for the safe transport of goods had curved lids to drain away rain water, and were seldom decorated except, perhaps, for a leather cover. Those that doubled as home furnishings had more comfortable flat lids and some also had feet, or even legs.

GROWING CONSTRUCTION SKILLS

As joiners steadily developed more sophisticated carpentry skills, chests were better made. The hutch chest, first recorded in the 13th century, used a primitive kind of dovetail joint reinforced with a dowel peg, making it much stronger and more durable than anything that had gone before. This superior strength did away with the need for iron banding, leaving the entire surface of the chest free for carved decoration.

The Coronation chair This chair in Westminster Abbey was made for Edward I to enclose the Stone of Scone, which was seized from the Scots in 1297. *c. 1300.*

TIMELINE 476–1352

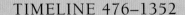

476 The fall of the Roman Empire in the West is precipitated by migrating hordes of Goths and Vandals, fleeing from the Huns.

c. 850 Anglo-Saxons, invited to Britain by the Celts to help fend off Viking marauders, establish

St. Mark's, Venice The building was completed in 1096 but decorative work continued until the 19th century.

themselves as dominant communities in Mercia, Northumbria, and Wessex.

910 William the Pious establishes an abbey at Cluny, France, which becomes one of the largest, most influential monastic orders of the Middle Ages.

1066 The Norman Conquest of Britain is sealed when Duke William of Normandy defeats King Harold's forces at Hastings.

1095–1270 A series of Crusades are fought in retaliation against the persecution

Illuminated Flemish manuscript that depicts St. Thomas. *c. 1276.*

of Christian pilgrims to the Holy Land.

c. 1100 The completion of the Basilica of St. Mark's in Venice marks one of the defining achievements of the Byzantine architectural style.

c. 1200 The art of manuscript illumination flourishes across Western Europe, with the production of elaborate picture Bibles containing vignettes framed with Gothic architectural devices.

The tracery decoration is similar to the design of Gothic church windows.

A geometric frieze design runs along the top of the decorative panel.

The hinged top is undecorated.

Carved coffer This French coffer is made of walnut and is richly carved with flamboyant tracery reminiscent of the reticulated tracery seen in the windows of Gothic cathedrals. *Late 15th-century.*

A molded base supports the coffer.

THE GOTHIC STYLE

The Gothic style—the dominant aesthetic of the Middle Ages—was perceived as the antithesis of the civilized Classical world. It was a Norman innovation, fusing Carolingian and Burgundian artistic traditions with Islamic elements from Saracen Sicily. The greatest achievements of Gothic art were the cathedrals of northern Europe, and elements from this ecclesiastic architecture formed the basis of Gothic furniture design.

The Gothic style was based on the replacement of the rounded Romanesque arch with the innovative pointed arch, a feat of engineering that meant that churches could be larger, since the weight of a church roof could be supported on a framework of open-work piers and ribs, instead of massively thick walls. This architectural structure was reflected in the elaborate tracery of cathedral and church windows, and the trefoil and quatrefoil motifs used lent themselves equally well to the decoration of benches and tables. The upright press developed as a place to store priests' robes, and began to replace the chest as the preferred receptacle for clothing.

Another innovation of the Gothic period was the cupboard, its name derived from its original function, which was to display valuable silver-plate (cups) in wealthy households. Regional variations in the style included a predilection for linenfold paneling among English and Flemish craftsmen.

With the exception of Italy, where the prevailing fashion remained Romanesque, the Gothic style dominated Europe until the 15th century, and lingered even after the Renaissance sought to reject it in favor of a return to the Classical tradition.

MEDIEVAL INTERIORS

Contrary to the common perception of Gothic style as stuffy and dark, the interiors and furniture of the period were remarkably light and colorful. Furniture-makers usually made do with native woods—oak in England and northern Europe, pine and fir in the Alps, fruitwoods in the Mediterranean. Surviving medieval furniture made from oak invariably looks very dark because of its acquired patina, but newly cut oak is much lighter. In addition, many items of furniture were painted in bold hues, including primary colors and gold tones. Chests in particular were often painted. Although relatively few examples survive today, it is still possible to see traces of medieval painting on the ceilings and walls of many churches and cathedrals, which were originally decorated in the same way.

11th-century Byzantine-style fresco of Christ, evangelists, and angels. The fresco is in the Benedictine Basilica Sant' Angelo in Formis, Italy.

1248 King Ferdinand III of Castille, later canonized by Pope Clement X, liberates Seville from the Saracens, converting the city's great mosques into cathedrals dedicated to the Virgin.

c. 1250 Henry III orders the reconstruction of Westminster Abbey in the Gothic style. It has been the site of

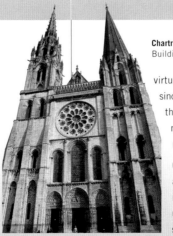

Chartres Cathedral, France. Building begins in 1194.

virtually every coronation since 1066, and is also the resting place of more than 12 English monarchs.

c. 1260 The cathedral at Chartres in France is completed and ushers in a new standard of Gothic

Church coffer made in France. This molded oak coffer has fretwork and paneling. *End of 15th century.*

design that is much imitated all over Europe.

1347–1352 The infamous "Black Death" plague ravages Europe, leaving 25 million dead in its wake.

RENAISSANCE ITALY

4000 BCE–1600 CE

THE INSTIGATORS OF THE ITALIAN Renaissance realized that they were entering a new, modern era even as they helped to lay its foundations. Leonardo Bruni was the first to present a tripartite view of history comprised of antiquity and the modern age, separated by an intervening middle period, or "dark age," characterized by the neglect of Classical knowledge and accomplishments.

A SPIRIT OF INQUIRY

In the 14th century, the affluent city of Florence in Tuscany emerged from a period of civil strife and pestilence into an age of unprecedented prosperity. The peculiarly Italian urban culture, and the republican attitudes of Florentines in particular, predisposed them to the emerging philosophy of civic humanism that informed Renaissance thinking. The universities and merchant classes began to reappraise the science, philosophy, art, and design of ancient Greece and Rome, and Florence's great wealth brought many artists to the city—all seeking

commissions from merchants eager to display their success and good taste. The same spirit of scientific inquiry that led to remarkable discoveries by Copernicus, Vesalius, and Galileo also pervaded the arts. Andrea Palladio recommended architectural proportions that were based on models from the Classical world, and Filippo Brunelleschi clarified the laws of linear perspective. Artists jettisoned the elongated, stylized figures of medieval painting in favor of more accurate depictions of the human form, facilitated by advances in anatomy. A new realism, fused with the humanist principles of the age, took root within the fine and decorative arts.

THE EXPLOSION OF PATRONAGE

All these developments influenced the furniture of the period. The middle classes built sumptuous town houses and *palazzi*, and began to fill these opulent living spaces with furniture and decorative artworks that reflected their status. The greatest families, such as the Medici of Florence, the Montefeltro of Urbino,

Maiolica Plate Maiolica is the term used to define the characteristic white-glazed pottery of Renaissance Italy. The milkiness came from a tin oxide that was added to the glaze. This plate depicts a Maiolica painter at work. *c. 1510.*

and the Farnese of Rome, engaged the finest designers and craftsmen to produce monumental items of furniture in marble, inlaid with semiprecious stones and decorated with family crests and emblems.

MARRIAGE CHESTS

The *cassone*, or marriage chest, was one of the most prized objects in any home and, as such, no expense was spared in its beautification. The side panels were often covered with colored or gilded gesso, built up into relief patterns or sculpted to depict Classical figures and scenes. The best painters and sculptors in Italy were commissioned to work on these chests, and those that survive today exhibit a richness of decoration that is equaled only by the religious art of the day. The increasing secularization of the arts now made it acceptable for people to display objects with lavish surface decoration in their homes.

DECORATIVE WORK

Furniture, often made from walnut or willow, was decorated with marquetry and inlays of ivory, stone, or precious woods such as ebony, or ornate, grotesque carvings. Grotesque ornament—the word derives from the Italian *grottesco*—sought to provoke a sense of uneasy fun by blurring the boundaries between the natural and human-made worlds. A seat carved

The lilies in the design of the inlay are Farnese family emblems.

The table top is inlaid with marble and semiprecious stones.

At the center of the table top are two large alabaster panels.

The table top rests on three massive, carved, marble piers, which bear the arms of Cardinal Alessandro Farnese.

Marble and alabaster table This table was made for the Palazzo Farnese in Rome, after a design by architect Giacomo Barozzi da Vignola (1507–73). *H:37¾ in (96 cm); W:150 in (381 cm); D:66¼ in (168 cm).*

TIMELINE 1324–1570

View of the Palazzo Pitti, Florence, as seen from the bell tower of Santo Spirito.

1324 Marco Polo dies in Venice, with debate still raging about the accuracy of his tales about his Asian journey. His writings later

influenced Renaissance cartographers and explorers.

1418 Filippo Brunelleschi wins a competition to design the cupola for the cathedral of Santa Maria del Fiore in Florence. His model was inspired by Greek and Roman construction techniques.

1420 After a sojourn in Avignon, the papacy

returns to Rome, bringing with it the power, influence, and wealth needed to reverse the city's long decline.

1429 The "Gates of Paradise," the magnificent doors created by Ghiberti for the Baptistry of San Giovanni in Florence, are installed.

Gates of Paradise, Baptistry of San Giovanni The doors feature 28 gilded bronze panels carved with scenes from the Bible.

Marble statue of David by Michelangelo, which is more than twice life-size.

c. 1440 Work begins on the Palazzo Pitti, first commissioned by Luca Pitti in an attempt to outshine the residence of his arch-rivals, the Medici family.

1469 Lorenzo "The Magnificent" di Medici

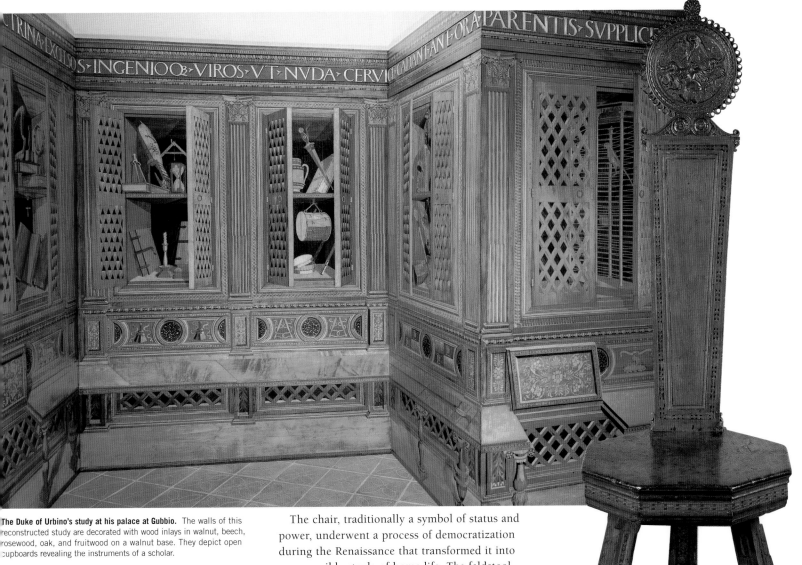

The Duke of Urbino's study at his palace at Gubbio. The walls of this reconstructed study are decorated with wood inlays in walnut, beech, rosewood, oak, and fruitwood on a walnut base. They depict open cupboards revealing the instruments of a scholar.

in the form of an open clam shell is both whimsical and unsettling. Decorated furniture was placed in equally decorative interiors, where walls also featured audacious trompe l'oeil designs that looked like windows, doors, shelves, or vistas.

ARCHITECTURAL INFLUENCE

Renaissance art, like the Gothic style of the Middle architecture, and the use of columns—one of the most characteristic features of Greek and Roman building—was now incorporated into furniture design. Caryatids—columnar supports in the shape of female figures—were especially prevalent.

The chair, traditionally a symbol of status and power, underwent a process of democratization during the Renaissance that transformed it into an accessible staple of home life. The faldstool, or X-chair, made from two pairs of short beams intersecting at a central joint and linked by a stretcher, became common. The most luxurious examples were covered with a thin layer of silver, or upholstered with velvet, but most of them were more modest. The basic form of the faldstool originated in antiquity, and a leather seat slung between two X-frames was used in Renaissance Italy just as it had been in ancient Greece. A side chair called the sgabello chair was basically a stool with an octagonal seat and a long decorated back splat. Sometimes the back splat could be removed to turn the chair into a stool.

Sgabello chair This chair, from 15th-century Florence, is made of carved and inlaid walnut. *1489–91.*

ascends to power in Florence. His unprecedented patronage of the arts contributes to the flowering of the city during subsequent years.

1498 Leonardo da Vinci completes *The Last Supper,* considered by many to be his most perfect achievement.

1504 Michelangelo completes *David,* after three years' work. The sculpture was hewn from a single block of marble called *The Giant.*

Greek sculpture, the work of Rhodian sculptors. This marble piece features the Trojan priest Laocoon. *c. 50 BCE.* H:72½ in (184 cm).

1506 The rediscovery of the Laocoon group, a lost Greek sculpture, provokes jubilant scenes in Rome, and it is escorted to the Vatican amid the pealing of the city's church bells.

1532 Niccolo Machiavelli's political masterpiece, *The Prince,* written as a guide to statecraft for aspiring rulers, is published posthumously.

1543 Copernicus describes his heliocentric model of the heavens in *De Revolutionibus Orbium Coelestium.*

1570 Andrea Palladio publishes his seminal work *I Quattro Libri dell' Architettura,* laying out in detail the architectural principles that go on to make him a master of the art.

Andrea Palladio

RENAISSANCE EUROPE

A COMBINATION OF HUMANIST intellectualism and high-society patronage eventually brought Renaissance ideals to France and northern Europe, just as it had done south of the Alps. The French claim on Naples, and its wider ambitions on the Italian states in general, led to a number of military campaigns and intermittent rule over portions of the peninsula. This served to increase intellectual and artistic commerce between France and the centers of Renaissance thought, such as Florence and Rome.

RENAISSANCE SPREADS TO FRANCE

Continued papal rule over the enclave of Avignon further promoted Italian influence within France. Many of the artists commissioned to work on the great frescoes of the Palace of the Popes came from Siena. This tradition was enthusiastically continued by François I when he invited Italian luminaries such as Benvenuto Cellini, Francesco Primaticcio, and

Gallery of François I, Château de Fontainebleau The gallery has 12 narrative frescoes, sculptural relief borders, and carved walnut wainscoting. The greatest decorated gallery built in France, it introduced the Italian Mannerist style to France. *c. 1533–40.*

Niccolò dell'Abbate to decorate the interiors of his new château at Fontainebleau.

A distinct school of art evolved around the prolonged activity at the château, and the Fontainebleau style was subsequently exported throughout northern Europe. This was essentially a French interpretation of Italian Mannerism: a high style that looked to the work of earlier Renaissance artists rather than to nature for stylistic cues.

The Château de Chambord, a castle built in the Loire valley by Francis I, is perhaps the finest example of Renaissance architecture in France. French Renaissance furniture was shaped to a large extent by architectural developments. Jacques Androuet du Cerceau published works that included furniture designs. Many of his engravings of architectural embellishments and details were modified for decorative use in furniture. He drew his inspiration from antiquity, and was particularly fond of acanthus leaves, plumes, and armorial motifs. Exotic and fantastical beasts were favorite themes for carved decoration. Walnut replaced oak as the favored timber for furniture, the tight grain lending

A *Caquetoire* or "gossip" chair This chair, made from carved walnut, has a solid X-frame with a rectangular back rail and carved scrolling arms. The seat is made of leather. *16th century. H:33½ in (85 cm); W:19¾ in (50 cm); D:23¾ in (60 cm). BEA*

itself particularly well to relief carving. Human figures, often in the form of caryatids, are found more often on French furniture than on any produced elsewhere during the same period.

GERMAN-SPEAKING COUNTRIES

The ideals of the Italian Renaissance first reached the German-speaking countries through artists such as Albrecht Dürer, who had visited Italy. However, a more direct influence on the design of furniture came from the *Kleinmeister*, the designers of ornament, based in Nuremberg, Westphalia, and the Low Countries, who produced engraved or woodcut patterns inspired by Classical antiquity and Italian examples. Their patterns, composed of running floral motifs, birds, animals, naked figures, urns, and trophies, were adopted by a variety of craftsmen and cabinet-makers.

However, the existence of powerful guilds in cities such as Berlin meant that new types of furniture were much slower to develop as the approved

TIMELINE 1455–1588

Engraving of Johannes Gutenberg in his workshop showing his proofsheet.

c. 1455 Johannes Gutenberg publishes his 42-line Bible at Mainz, the first book to be printed using movable type.

1494 Charles VIII sends an army to capture Naples. It succeeds but is later pushed back by an alliance of Venetian, Milanese, and papal forces.

1525 Giovanni de Verrazano sails to the Americas. He claims Newfoundland for the French crown.

c. 1530–1560 The Fontainebleau School,

Martin Luther

originally founded by Francis I to decorate his new Fontainebleau château, helps to spread Renaissance ideals.

1534 The "Day of the Placards" occurs: towns in northern France are deluged with leaflets condemning the Roman Catholic mass, in sympathy with the Protestant theologies of Martin Luther and John Calvin.

The Louvre palace in Paris In 1546, work began to transform the former fortress into a luxurious royal residence. Today the building is known as a world-famous art gallery.

designs that apprentices had to master rarely altered. The cities of Nuremberg and Augsburg, which did not have guilds, became famous for their furniture-makers, such as Peter Flötner and Lorenz Stöer, who published woodcut designs for intarsia panels popular in Augsburg furniture decoration.

NEW STYLES

The structural developments of Renaissance furniture included the evolution of the throne chair, which had usually had a chest base in the Middle Ages, into a lighter style that was supported by pillars around a bottom rail. Open chair arms became more popular, reflecting the trend toward lighter furniture. The French *caquetoire* (gossip) chair was created as a reaction to changing fashions, and had a wide, trapezoidal seat that was designed to accommodate flowing skirts. Upholstery became more common, although the majority of chairs and benches still had hard, wooden surfaces.

New types of case furniture developed, such as the dresser that evolved from the medieval sideboard and was constructed from various combinations of pillars, shelving, and cabinets enclosed with doors. The cabinet, used in medieval Europe to store and display silver-plate, now became more opulent. The treasures of a Renaissance household usually included jewelry and various artistic trinkets, requiring numerous, small drawers for their safe storage. These drawers were often lined with fine cloth to protect the contents. Cupboards in southern Germany, which had originally been created by placing one chest on top of another, developed into a more useful storage space without a frieze dividing the top and bottom half, although the old form remained popular after 1600.

Long dining tables were still made from a simple top on trestles, as in the Middle Ages. There were no fixed dining areas in noblemen's houses, so tables needed to remain portable.

Cupboard after Peter Flötner This massive, elaborately carved, two-part, paneled cupboard from southern Germany is architectural in form. Decoration is in the Renaissance style and features allegorical figures on the upper doors, a central leaf-carved frieze, and lower doors with stylized urns and foliage.

1539 The Edict of Villers-Cotterêts makes French, rather than Latin, the official language of France.

1543 The Flemish anatomist Andreas Vesalius publishes *De Humani Corporis Fabrica*, the first text to contradict theories presented by Galen in the second century.

1546 Work begins on Pierre de Lescot's new design for the Louvre. Francis I begins to collect paintings—still housed there today—that include Leonardo da Vinci's *Mona Lisa*.

Château de Chambord, built between 1519 and 1547. It is one of the finest examples of French Renaissance architecture.

1547 The Château de Chambord in the Loire valley, commissioned by Francis I in 1519, is completed. It is thought that Leonardo da Vinci may have visited and been involved in the design.

1552 Ambroise Paré, a great surgeon, publishes the results of his investigations into vascular ligation, which reduced the need for the painful and dangerous cauterization of wounds.

1555 Nostradamus, royal physician to Charles IX, publishes the first of ten collections of 100 mystical quatrains, claiming they prophesy future events.

Nostradamus

1562 A massacre of Huguenots at Vassy sparks religious civil war until the 1598 Edict of Nantes.

1588 Michel de Montaigne publishes the third edition of his *Essais*, which go on to have a great impact on French and English literature.

17ᵀᴴ CENTURY
1600-1700

POWER AND GRANDEUR

THE 17TH CENTURY WAS AN AGE OF GREAT WEALTH AND EMPIRE-
BUILDING, EPITOMIZED BY A STRUGGLE FOR POWER THROUGH
TRADE, WARFARE, AND THE CREATION OF POLITICAL ALLIANCES.

Bronze statuette of Louis XIV,
the Sun King, on his horse.

DURING THE 17TH CENTURY, successive Popes commissioned architects and artists to build magnificent new buildings and monuments in Rome, to complete the redevelopment of the city. New churches were erected, palazzos rebuilt, and fountains and statues constructed, creating a dramatic symbol of the power and wealth of the Catholic Church.

This theatrical, sculptural expression of grandeur and luxury was expressed in architecture, painting, the decorative arts, and even music, and became known as the Baroque style. Rulers and artists came from all over Europe to admire the city and its works of art, then returned to their own countries, where they created their own interpretations of the new, anti-Classical style. Spain, Portugal, and Germany were strongly influenced by the Baroque style, but in northern countries, such as the Low Countries and England, the style was quieter and more restrained.

EXPANSION OF TRADE

At the beginning of the 17th century, profitable trading companies were established by the Dutch and the British, opening up new markets in the Far East and creating colonies. European rulers sought exotic foreign treasures to display in their palaces, and the resulting increase in trade led to the establishment of a wealthy and powerful merchant class, which lavished vast sums of money on substantial residences to ensure that they were in keeping with the latest fashions. Inspired by the influx of exotic materials, craftsmen created flamboyant new designs, primarily for the Courts of Europe.

THE SOVEREIGN STATE

During the first part of the 17th century, Europe was divided by bloodshed. By the middle of the century, many countries had gained independence from their former rulers. The Treaty of Westphalia in 1648 brought an end to the long war between Spain and the Low Countries and ended the German phase of the Thirty Years' War. The Dutch Republic was officially recognized, as was the Swiss Confederation, and 350 or so German princes were granted sovereignty. The Holy Roman Emperor was left with diminished power. This recognition of absolute sovereignty for territories changed the balance of power in Europe. As countries gained independence, rulers and artists worked to forge their own national identities.

ABSOLUTE POWER

Louis XIV personified the concept of absolute power. When he became the King of France in 1661, he moved his court to the Palace of Versailles and embarked on an ambitious plan to glorify France and his monarchy through art and design. He ruled as an absolute monarch, and the grandeur of his monarchy inspired other European rulers. Versailles came to symbolize Louis XIV's authority in matters of art, and France became the principal producer of luxury furniture and other objects.

In 1685, however, Louis XIV revoked the Edict of Nantes, which had granted tolerance to Protestants in France. As a result, many skilled artists and craftsmen fled the country for the protection of the Low Countries, Germany, England, and eventually North America. French-trained artisans thus worked for monarchs in other countries, ensuring the dissemination of elaborate French design throughout Europe by the end of the century.

Castle Howard, England Begun in 1699, Castle Howard is considered one of England's finest Baroque mansions. It was the creation of the patron, Charles Howard, 3rd Earl Carlisle, and two architects, Sir John Vanbrugh (1664–1726) and Nicholas Hawksmoor (1661–1736).

TIMELINE 1600–1700

1601 Gobelin family of dyers sell their factory in Paris to Henri IV, who sets up 200 workmen from Flanders to make tapestries.

1602 Dutch East India Company, the first modern public company, founded in Java.

1607 Jamestown, the first English settlement in North America, established in Virginia.

1608 Samuel de Champlain founds a French settlement at Quebec.

Statue of Samuel de Champlain

1609 Tin-enameled ware made at Delft.

1618 Beginning of Thirty Years' War. Dutch West African Company founded.

1620 Pilgrim Fathers land at Plymouth, Massachusetts.

1621 Dutch West India Company founded. The company later acquires the North American coast from Chesapeake Bay to Newfoundland.

1630 Paul Vredeman de Vries issues two volumes of furniture designs.

1640 Secession of Portugal, amalgamated with Spain for 60 years since 1580.

1642 English Civil War begins.

Bureau Mazarin (see p.36). GK

1643 Louis XIII of France dies. France is ruled under the Regency of Cardinal Mazarin until Louis XIV comes of age in 1661.

1648 Thirty Years' War ends with the Treaty of Westphalia, and Holland gains independence from Spain, becoming a Dutch Republic.

1649 Charles I beheaded and England declared a Commonwealth under the Protectorate of Oliver Cromwell.

1651 Dutch settle at Cape of Good Hope.

Carved giltwood fauteuil This elegant armchair is the epitome of Louis XIV style. The frame is made of elaborately carved giltwood, with carved Classical motifs, including satyrs, shells, and rosettes. The seat and chair back would originally have been covered in silk or tapestry. *c. 1710.*

Galerie des Glaces, **Versailles** The Palace of Versailles is dominated by the *Galerie des Glaces* (Hall of Mirrors), created to reflect the magnificence of Louis XIV's monarchy. The sumptuousness was originally heightened by fabulous silver furniture, 41 sparkling chandeliers, and gilded candlestands.

1660 Charles II returns from exile as King of England. The new court encourages a revolution in English taste.

1661 Louis XIV becomes King of France.

1662 Charles II's marriage to Catherine of Braganza opens up trade with Goa, the principal source of mother-of-pearl. Louis XIV begins to build the Palace of Versailles.

ng Charles II

1663 The Great Fire of London destroys most of the medieval buildings in London, leading to a vast rebuilding program. Furniture manufactory to supply the French royal palaces started at the Gobelins workshops in Paris.

The Palace of Versailles

1670 English settlement in Charles Town (Charleston) South Carolina.

1682 The Palace of Versailles becomes the royal residence of France. The first weaving mill is established in Amsterdam.

1683 The first German immigrants settle in North America.

1685 Edict of Nantes revoked by Louis XIV. French Protestants flee to the Low Countries and England. All Chinese ports opened to foreign trade.

1688 William III of Holland and his wife Mary accede to the English throne. Plate glass is cast for the first time at Colbert's mirror glass factory in Paris. Stalker & Parker publish *A Treatise of Japanning and Varnishing*.

Plate featuring William III

1697 Peter the Great of Russia sets out on a year-and-a-half journey to study European ways of life.

BAROQUE FURNITURE

Two quite different types of furniture were made during the 17th century: formal furniture for staterooms and palaces, and simpler pieces intended for domestic use.

Traditionally, the aristocracy had moved from one home to another, according to the seasons, but now residences became more permanent. Furniture no longer had to be portable, and substantial pieces were designed for specific rooms, and even for particular positions within rooms. Interiors were very formal, and people began to consider rooms as integrated interiors when commissioning furniture. As well as grand salons, wealthy homes had more intimate, private rooms that required smaller pieces of furniture.

LAVISH STYLE

At the beginning of the century, the Italian Baroque style was dominant in much of Europe. Baroque furniture was designed on a grand scale and intended to impress. Pieces were architectural in form, with dramatically carved sculptural elements and lavish decoration, which drew on Classical or Renaissance-style motifs.

As the century progressed, trade, especially with the Far East, provided furniture-makers with a wealth of exotic new materials, including tortoiseshell, mother-of-pearl, ebony, and rosewood. Furniture was imported from other countries, including

Late 17th-century Dutch walnut armchair The chair seat and carved oval back are made of cane, which was a fashionable and affordable import from India.

lacquerware from the Far East and caned furniture from India, and European craftsmen created their own versions.

KEY PIECES

Most grand, formal rooms had a console or side table intended almost purely for display. The finest examples had *pietra dura* tops (*see p.39*) and carved and gilded sculptural bases. Advances in glass-making meant that larger mirrors could be made, and it was fashionable to place a matching mirror above each console table in a room. The design elements of the mirrors and tables were repeated in the architectural features of the room, such as door architraves, windows, and fireplace surrounds, creating an integrated sense of design. Pairs of *girandoles* or candlestands were placed in front of mirrors, so that their light was reflected in them, illuminating rooms that would otherwise have been dark.

The largest chairs were still reserved for the most important people. Chairs with high backs, sometimes upholstered for greater comfort, were highly desirable. Wing chairs were first used in France in the middle of the century, a precursor to the *bergère* (*see p.77*). The armchair shape was extended to create the sofa or settee. In 1620, an upholstered settee was commissioned for the great house of Knole, in Kent. This settee had a padded seat and back, held in position by ties on the posts. The design is still known as a Knole settee.

Silks and velvets, usually made in Italy, were phenomenally expensive, and only royalty and the wealthiest aristocracy were able to afford upholstered furniture. Cane, imported from India by Dutch traders, became popular because it provided a less expensive method of covering chair backs and seats.

THE AGE OF THE CABINET

Replacing the carved buffet popular in the previous century, the cabinet, or cabinet-on-stand, became an object of desire in wealthy households. Cabinets were primarily intended for display—a response to the new passion for collecting among the wealthy, and the need to house all of the rare and wonderful objects they had acquired. Rather than just a

German "silver" table Made by Albrecht Biller in Augsburg for the Dresden Court, this table is made of walnut covered with chased and gilt silver. It is one of the few surviving examples of the hugely expensive silver furniture of the period. *c. 1715. H:31½ in (80 cm); W:47 in (120 cm); D:32 in (81 cm).*

repository for special collections, however, the cabinet itself became the showpiece, as skilled craftsmen created large-scale versions that were works of art in their own right, using precious materials. Rare panels of *pietra dura*, lacquer panels from the Orient, and veneers of ebony and ivory were all incorporated into architecturally inspired cabinets. It was the ultimate expression of wealth.

DECORATIVE ELEMENTS

The wealthiest patrons commissioned *pietra dura* tabletops or panels for their cabinets. It was also fashionable to insert exotic, patterned, lacquer panels from Japanese and Chinese cabinets into European furniture. This was, however, prohibitively expensive, so innovative craftsmen developed their own methods of imitating lacquerwork, such as japanning (*see p.39*). As well as actual lacquered objects, a fashion developed for Oriental scenes, known as *chinoiserie*.

Cabinet-makers became skilled at veneering, using exotic hardwoods and inlays. The Low Countries, in particular, produced exquisite floral marquetry. French boullework (*see p.54*) created a sumptuous decorative veneer for tables and cabinets using detailed brass and tortoiseshell marquetry.

By the end of the century, French furniture design was highly influential. Louis XIV's palace at Versailles set the style for the fashionable world. Changes in furniture style were avidly watched and interpreted by craftsmen in Great Britain and the rest of Europe. The finest French pieces, such as tapestries from the Gobelins workshops or cabinets by Boulle, were highly sought-after in the homes of the wealthy.

BUREAU MAZARIN

The earliest known example of the bureau Mazarin was made in 1669 by Pierre Gole, who became cabinetmaker to Louis XIV. It is sometimes referred to as a writing table, but contemporary engravings also show similar pieces being used as dressing tables. The term "bureau Mazarin" was coined in the 19th century to reflect the importance of Cardinal Mazarin, who ruled France during Louis XIV's Regency. Cardinal Mazarin's employment of foreign craftsmen had a significant influence on the design of French furniture in the 17th century.

Cardinal Mazarin (1602–61)

French bureau This piece is made of native fruitwoods inlaid with floral marquetry and engraved brass. *c. 1700. H:31 in (79 cm); W:44½ in (113 cm); D:25½ in (65 cm). GK*

CABINET-ON-STAND

Made for the Grand Duchess of Tuscany, this piece exemplifies Italian Baroque. The myriad drawers and compartments satisfied the growing interest in collecting. The fashion for architectural detail is shown in the columns and the balustrade, and the miniature sculptures reflect the prevailing interest in Classical forms. The naturalistic figures and paintings show a move away from the Mannerist style of the Renaissance.

Italian cabinet This massive piece is made of ebony, and is decorated with *pietra dura* panels and gilded bronze. The stand consists of four elaborately carved gilt figural supports, known as caryatids. *c. 1677.* H:140¾ in (352 cm); W:101½ in (254 cm); D:29½ in (74 cm).

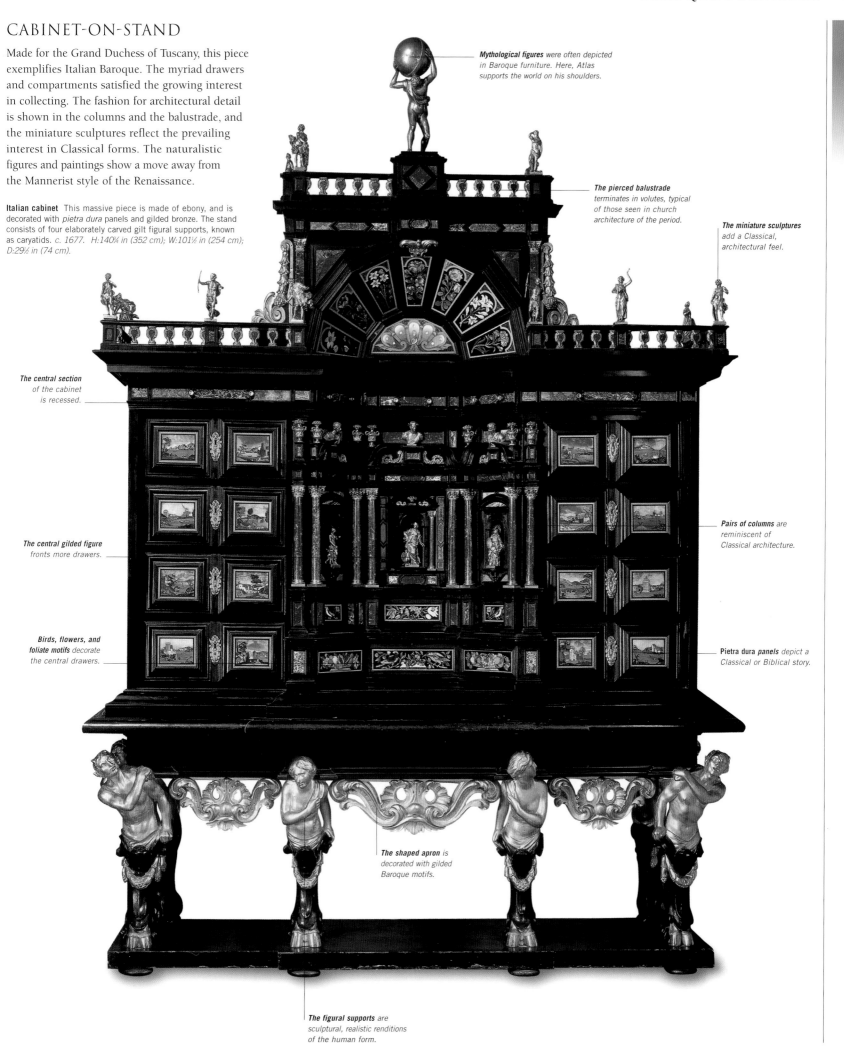

Mythological figures were often depicted in Baroque furniture. Here, Atlas supports the world on his shoulders.

The pierced balustrade terminates in volutes, typical of those seen in church architecture of the period.

The miniature sculptures add a Classical, architectural feel.

The central section of the cabinet is recessed.

Pairs of columns are reminiscent of Classical architecture.

The central gilded figure fronts more drawers.

Birds, flowers, and foliate motifs decorate the central drawers.

Pietra dura panels depict a Classical or Biblical story.

The shaped apron is decorated with gilded Baroque motifs.

The figural supports are sculptural, realistic renditions of the human form.

ELEMENTS OF STYLE

The Baroque style used elaborate decoration and precious materials to create spectacular displays of wealth. Chairs, tables, and cabinets were embellished with ornate carving, gilding, and finely detailed marquetry. Rich colors, fine tapestry, marble, and semiprecious stones, set in scrolling designs, or arabesques, contributed to the sense of status and drama.

17th-century carved chair

Turned oak baluster

Floral marquetry panel

Carved chair

The elaborately pierced splat of this English side chair shows the influence of the engraved designs of Daniel Marot (*see p.45*). This piece exemplifies the exquisite wood-carving skills demanded of the carvers of the era. The florid pattern and tall, formal shape are typical of the grandiose Baroque style.

Turned wood

Created by applying cutting tools to a rotating wooden surface, turned wood was a popular feature of the vernacular furniture of the period, such as the heavy oak baluster of this colonial court cupboard. Turned wood was also seen on legs, posts, and rungs. As the century progressed, these turnings became less heavy in appearance and more columnar.

Marquetry

The practice of arranging small pieces of veneer into an intricate design became a specialty of the century, particularly in the Low Countries, and was much sought-after. Veneers were made of exotic woods such as mahogany, as well as native fruitwoods, including cherry and plum. The veneers were used in their natural colors or stained in bright shades.

Gilt gesso detail on tabletop

Detail of gilded mirror

Detail of a silver table

Gilt gesso

Originating in Italy, gilt gesso became fashionable in France and England. A design was carved in wood, then coated with layers of gesso (a mixture of glue and powdered chalk). Once the gesso had hardened, the design was re-carved and gilded. This technique was used to decorate mirrors, chests, and tables.

Verre églomisé

This technique imitated the sumptuous effect of gilded glass, and was often used to decorate mirrors. The design was actually painted on the underside of the glass, rather than on the front. The glass was prepared using a base of egg white and water and then gilded. Once dry, the design was engraved into the gilding before the surface was painted.

Silver furniture

Owning silver furniture epitomized the phenomenal wealth of the privileged few. The exuberant Louis XIV of France ordered suites of solid-silver furniture to furnish his palace at Versailles. Other rulers, such as Charles II of England, imitated this lavish display of wealth with wooden furniture pieces covered with thin sheets of silver.

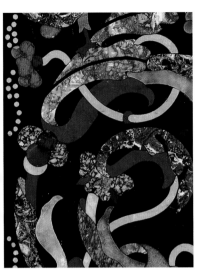

Detail of *pietra dura* table top

Pietra dura

Pietra dura literally means "hard stone." Pieces of highly polished colored stones, such as marble or lapis lazuli, were arranged in a mosaic pattern. This technique originated in Florence and was mainly used to decorate table tops and cabinet panels. The designs could be formal or naturalistic, and commonly featured animals, birds, flowers, or landscapes.

Sun King emblem in gilded, carved wood

Emblem of Louis XIV

Louis XIV of France (r. 1661–1715) was renowned for the brilliance and theatricality of his court at Versailles. Known as the Sun King, his personal emblem was a sun with rays of streaming light, echoing Apollo, the Greek god of light. This motif was used to decorate many pieces of furniture and architectural features used at the court.

Bronze desk mount

Ormolu mounts

This term, from the French *or moulu*, meaning "ground gold," describes the technique of gilding with bronze using mercury. Decorative details were cast in bronze, then gilded with mercury before being mounted onto furniture. Ormolu mounts were often used to protect the edges of veneered pieces. In cheaper imitations the bronze was cast, finished, and then lacquered.

Boullework in tortoiseshell and brass

Boullework

This form of marquetry is named after the French cabinet-maker André Charles Boulle (*see p.54*), who was arguably its finest exponent. Boullework combines materials like an intricate puzzle, using materials such as brass, ivory, ebonized wood, and tortoiseshell to create the effect of a painting in marquetry. Brass on a tortoiseshell ground is a popular combination.

Brass drop-ring handle

Drop-ring handles

This brass drawer pull is typical of the type found on 17th-century furniture. Although the level of carving varied from simple circles to florid swags, the basic design of the drop-ring was found on both simple cabinet drawers and ornate pieces designed for the finest residences. Brass was popular for all furniture detailing at this time.

Gold and black japanning on cabinet

Japanning

The process of japanning uses layers of varnish or shellac to imitate the Asian lacquerwork that was coveted during the 17th century. True Japanese and Chinese lacquerwork was difficult and expensive to obtain, so japanning was developed by European artisans, who used the technique to decorate the wood and metal of cabinets, mirrors, and screens in the fashionable style.

Detail of tapestry wall hanging

Tapestry

Country houses and palaces across Europe used tapestries for decoration, both to cover walls and to upholster chairs. Woven with wool and silk or linen, they were usually pictorial in design. Many tapestries originated from the Low Countries (in particular, Brussels), England, and also Paris, where the Gobelins workshops produced designs for Versailles.

Carved detail of oak trestle table

Carved wood

Wood-carving became a specialized skill during the 17th century. Elaborate designs decorated chests, chairs, and tables. Low-relief carving, such as the stylized flower motif shown above, was used to decorate hardwoods, such as oak. Softer woods allowed carvers to create more detailed patterns, such as those seen on French and Italian furniture.

ITALY

BY THE EARLY 17TH CENTURY, Rome was once again the seat of a powerful Papacy and entered a period of unprecedented prosperity. Architects, sculptors, and artists all strove to create a city that reflected the glory of the Catholic church, creating new buildings, monuments, and paintings on a grand, theatrical scale. The aristocracy instigated vast building programs, creating palazzos that became renowned throughout Europe for their ornate displays of wealth and pomp. The influence of Rome spread throughout the cities of Italy, turning the country into the fountainhead of the Baroque movement.

GRAND FURNITURE

The new architectural grandeur demanded impressive furnishings. Formal 17th-century Italian furniture was sculptural and architectural. It was grand in scale and featured three-dimensional carvings of foliage and human figures that were heavily influenced by sculpture. The makers of opulent palace furniture were often sculptors by training rather than cabinet-makers, and this had a profound effect on the development of the Baroque style. In the state apartments and galleries of palazzos, sumptuous sculptural furniture, such as grand console tables and cabinets, were displayed alongside ancient sculptures, and were regarded in much the same light—as works of art to be looked at rather than used.

The *stippone*, or great cabinet, was mainly produced in the Grand Ducal Workshops in Florence (*see p.42*). Thought to have been derived from the Augsburg cabinet (*see p.46*), it was architectural in appearance and scale, and had numerous small drawers for housing collections. Cabinets were embellished with costly materials, such as ebony, *pietra dura* (*see p.42*), and gilt bronze. Around 1667, Leonardo van der Vinne, a cabinet-maker from the Low Countries, became the director of cabinet-makers at the Grand Ducal Workshops and may have introduced floral marquetry techniques.

Stateroom furniture also included console tables with massive marble tops and *pietra dura* inlays, and heavily carved gilt bases, often featuring human figures or foliage. Chairs had high backs and were frequently upholstered with rich materials, such as the fine silks and velvets made in the city of Genoa.

AGE OF LEARNING

With the new buildings and the interest in humanist learning, many wealthy

GILDED FRAME

This gilded, carved picture frame depicts the legend of Paris. It was made by Filippo Parodi, perhaps the best-known Genoese carver of the late 17th century, who worked in Bernini's studio. As well as the sculptural-style figures, the frame includes foliage and shell motifs, which were very popular throughout the 17th century. The portrait is by Pierre Mignard and shows Maria Mancini. *Late 17th century.*

ANDREA BRUSTOLON

Design for a carved mirror frame, Brustolon annotated this drawing to explain the symbolism in the carvings: valor, virtue, and the triumph of love. *c. 1695.*

THIS VENETIAN CARVER WAS RENOWNED FOR FANTASTIC CARVED FURNITURE.

Andrea Brustolon (1662–1732) was a pupil of the Genoese sculptor Filippo Parodi. Originally trained as a stone-carver, Brustolon took up wood-carving and created many types of furniture, ranging from frames to tables and stands. He is best known for his extravagantly carved chairs, which were designed more as works of art than as comfortable seating. Few pieces have survived, but several of his drawings have.

It is likely that Brustolon traveled to Rome during his apprenticeship. In keeping with the Roman style of the time, Brustolon's furniture is naturalistic and often allegorical, with figural supports, exuberant foliage, and animals. Parodi's influence is evident. Brustolon's drawing for a mirror is very similar to Parodi's gilded picture frame (shown left).

The high back is typical of the Baroque style.

Detail of carving

The legs, arms, and stretchers are ornately carved with foliage and animals.

Armchair This armchair is made of boxwood, which has no pores, so is easy to carve. The decorative woodwork simulates tree branches combined with foliage and naturalistic renderings of animals. The upholstery is not original. *Late 17th century.*

WALNUT ARMORIAL *CASSONE*

The raised lid is carved with a design of beads, leaves, and a fish-scale pattern, while the front and ends of the *cassone* (chest) retain Mannerist features typical of the Renaissance period—strapwork decoration and segmented panels. The *cassone* stands on paw feet and bears the coat of arms of the the Guicciardini family from Florence. These chests were often given as wedding presents. *Late 16th century. H:24 in (61 cm); W:68½ in (174 cm).*

patrons now had important libraries, thus requiring a new form of furniture: built-in bookcases. Influenced by architecture, these bookcases often had pilasters or columns, and sometimes featured statues or carved urns on the cornice.

GRAND BEDS

Late 17th-century Italian beds were an expression of the upholsterer's art, making use of the fine textiles that were produced locally: usually no wood at all was visible. A tester, often draped in silk or damask, would be supported from above the head, and upholstered panels surrounded the mattress. This type of bed remained popular until the end of the 18th century, so it is difficult to date individual examples with any certainty.

EASTERN INFLUENCES

Meanwhile, the Venetians were producing lacquered furniture, a skill that local craftsmen learned through the city's trading links with the East. Green and gold lacquer became a specialty of Venice until the 18th century. Good-quality wood was not available locally, which may explain the popularity of techniques such as lacquering, which covers the surface of the wood completely, allowing the craftsmen to make the most of the materials available to them.

VERNACULAR STYLES

In Italy there was a huge difference between the furniture made for daily use in the ordinary rooms of a palazzo or villa and that on display in the state apartments. Utilitarian furniture, such as stools, x-framed chairs, *cassone* (chests), and tables, were made by carpenters or joiners, using local walnut or fruitwood.

St. Peter's, Vatican, Rome The *Baldacchino* (canopy), the high altar, and the chair of St. Peter by Giovanni Lorenzo Bernini epitomize the Baroque taste for grandeur in design, scale, and materials.

FLORENTINE CONSOLE TABLE

This table is made of carved and gilded wood, and the top is supported by kneeling mythological figures known as harpies. The figures are muscular, in keeping with the bold, masculine Baroque style. The theme is borrowed from contemporary Roman designs, although these harpies are more restrained than examples from Rome. *c. 1700.* H:45 in (115 cm); W:71 in (180 cm); D:32 in (82 cm).

WALNUT TABLE

The octagonal tabletop rests on triform supports, which terminate in male terms (stylized human figures) carved with scrolling foliage, on paw feet. The tops of the supports have a square panel centered by a wine glass and an illegible inscription. *Late 16th century.* H:31¾ in (81 cm); W:47½ in (120 cm).

FLORENTINE CABINET

This cabinet, produced at the Grand Ducal Workshops in Florence, is decorated with *pietra dura* panels depicting mythological scenes. The architectural influence on Italian Baroque furniture design can be seen in the use of pilasters, arched panels, and pediments, and in the structural form of the piece. Mythology was a common theme for decoration, and the meanings would have been widely understood. *1670.* H:42½ in (108 cm); W:35½ in (90 cm).

LION COMMODE

The commode is made of walnut with exquisite inlays of ivory and mother-of-pearl, depicting images of Vanity, Justice, and other allegorical figures, surrounded by putti, flowers, leaves, cartouches, and volutes. The sides are sloped and decorated with inlay and gilding. The front of the commode is bow-shaped and has three drawers and iron fittings. The front feet are shaped like crouching lions. *c. 1680.* H:37 in (94 cm); W:157 in (45 cm); D:28¾ in (72 cm).

PIETRA DURA AND SCAGLIOLA

FLORENTINE TABLE TOPS AND CABINET PANELS INLAID WITH RICHLY COLORED, SEMIPRECIOUS STONES WERE HIGHLY COVETED BY WEALTHY PATRONS DURING THE 17TH CENTURY.

PIETRA DURA (hard stone) involves making a mosaic of hard or semiprecious stones. The manufacture of pietra dura was just one of the trades that supplied furniture-makers from the Renaissance. Scagliola created a similar effect at considerably less cost.

Originating in Italy, the full name, *commesso di pietre dure*, describes stones that are fitted together so closely that the seams are invisible. This mosaic is glued to a slate base for stability. The elaborate process of creating pictures from stone has remained the same for centuries. *Pietra dura* was used for table tops and provided a good contrast with the gilt console bases typical of the time. The rich colors and floral or naturalistic pictures not only displayed the expensive materials; the dedicated craftsmanship required to complete such work was admired and coveted by royal and aristocratic patrons.

TEAMWORK

The finest workshops produced *pietra dura* in teams. An artist or sculptor prepared the design; then other craftsmen chose the stones, polished them, and cut them into fine slices. Tracings of the design were used to cut the stones into the right shapes, and these were then carefully glued and pieced together in position on a base. If the design was particularly delicate, it would be lined with slate. Finally, the stones would be polished with abrasive powders.

THE GRAND DUCAL WORKSHOPS

These Florentine workshops, situated in the galleries of the Uffizi Palace, were preeminent in developing *pietra dura* furnishings. Other workshops sometimes poached Florentine artisans so that they could teach their skills elsewhere. In 1588, Ferdinand I de'Medici made them the court workshop, making furniture as well as mosaics. The works were commissioned for the Grand Duke's residences as well as for important European families. Products ranged from cabinets and tabletops to boxes and architectural features.

Henri IV and Louis XIII of France established their own royal workshops under the Louvre Palace in Paris (see p.50).

PIETRA DURA TABLE, CHARLECOTE PARK, ENGLAND
The center of the table is made of an oval of onyx surrounded by floral patterns of rare and beautiful jaspers. The rest of the slab is inlaid with arabesque patterns of marble and semi-precious stones. The piece is said to have been taken from the Palazzo Borghese in Rome by Napoleon's army. 16th century.

PIETRA DURA DETAIL
This detail of a pietra dura parrot eating fruit demonstrates the variety of color and texture in the semiprecious stones used. The panel is one of six from a cabinet purchased for Charlecote Park in England.

MATERIALS

PIETRA DURA USED A VARIETY OF HARD AND SEMIPRECIOUS STONES, CHOSEN FOR THEIR COLOR OR INTEGRAL PATTERN.

 Jasper is an opaque variety of chalcedony, occurring in a variety of colors.

 Lapis lazuli is a blue opaque stone, sometimes flecked with white, that has been used since ancient Egyptian times.

 Malachite is a semiprecious stone. It has light and dark green bands, which give it a unique ornamental quality.

 Marble is highly valued for its colors and textures. The most famous marble comes from Carrara, near Florence.

 Chalcedony is translucent gray in its pure form, but also comes in colors ranging from apple green to orange-red.

 Porphyry is an igneous rock composed of large crystals. There are many types found within rocks such as granite.

 Agate is a banded form of chalcedony, prized for the beautiful patterns and bands visible when the stone is sliced.

Floral motif | Foliage detail | Bird motif

Onyx cabochon shape | Lapis lazuli detail | Jasper strapwork | Curved ribbon detail

FLORENTINE CABINET
This wooden cabinet, produced at the Grand Ducal Workshops in Florence, has pietra dura panels depicting mythological scenes. The architectural influence on Italian Baroque furniture design can be seen in the structural form of the piece. 1670. H:42½ in (108 cm); W:35½ in (90 cm).

SCAGLIOLA TABLE TOP
Designed by Pietro Antonio Paolini in Florence, this exquisite table top demonstrates how scagliola could be used to create realistic effects, with its trompe l'oeil–style rendition of a violin, a Renaissance drawing, a map and book, flowers, and birds. 1732. W:56 in (142 cm); D:26¾ in (68 cm).

SCAGLIOLA

Scagliola is false marble. The first documented examples of it appeared at the end of the 17th century in Germany and in Italy. *Pietra dura* panels and table tops, especially from the Grand Ducal Workshops in Florence, were prohibitively expensive, so less wealthy patrons were eager to find an alternative and commissioned craftsmen to create an imitation: scagliola.

Black and white perspective designs were popular at the time, and scagliola proved the perfect medium for realizing these. Illusions of marble pictures, engravings, trompe l'oeil, ebony and ivory inlay, and paint effects were all possible. Scagliola reached the height of perfection in the 18th century, both in furniture and architectural use, in such vast spaces as the interior of the Great Hall at Stowe, in Buckinghamshire, England.

THE TECHNIQUE

Scagliola is produced by grinding the mineral selenite into a powder and mixing it with colored pigments and animal glue to produce a plasterlike substance. As with *pietra dura*, a drawing is transferred to a stone slab, on which it is engraved. Unlike marquetry or *pietra dura*, which are both inlaid, the liquid scagliola is poured into the engraved hollows in the stone, then left to set.

Additional effects, such as veining or different color variations, are achieved by adding chips of marble, granite, alabaster, porphyry, or other stones to the mixture, or by engraving and filling the hardened plaster a second time. Once the plaster has finally hardened, it is polished with linseed oil to create the desired finish.

THE LOW COUNTRIES

DURING THE FIRST HALF of the 17th century, the northern provinces became a major maritime power. The city of Amsterdam grew prosperous, and the influx of exotic goods and materials brought from the Far East by the Dutch East India Company made this city a haven for artists and craftsmen.

Traditional manufacturers flourished in the southern Netherlands, which was still under Spanish Hapsburg rule at this time. Flemish craftsmen were known in particular for their luxurious tapestries, weavings, and stamped or gilt leather, used both for upholstery and wall hangings.

POPULAR STYLES

Early 17th-century furniture from the Low Countries was generally simple, although more elaborate pieces were made for wealthy patrons. For much of the century, the four-door court cupboard was the most important piece of furniture in wealthy homes. Usually made of oak, it was often decorated with intricately carved figures, or intarsia panels depicting architectural scenes. Walnut became the timber of choice after 1660 and was often embellished with inlays or exotic veneered panels. In Holland, the "arched" cupboard with two, long paneled doors remained fashionable.

LUXURIOUS CABINETS

As in Italy, the Augsburg cabinet was influential. Early in the century, Flemish craftsmen in Antwerp made small table cabinets veneered in imported ebony, and they began to use new and exotic imports as veneers, perhaps influenced by the Northern provinces' trade with the East. Table cabinets gave way to cabinets-on-stands, decorated with ebony, mother-of-pearl, and tortoiseshell veneers. Later cabinets had carved stands with legs made from

The Linen Cupboard, Pieter de Hooch, 1663. This interior shows a typical wealthy merchant home of the age, with its large two-door oak cupboard, housing the highly prized household linen.

The interlacing "seaweed" marquetry is more frequently seen on English furniture.

Gold lacquer is used against a black lacquer background for greater impact.

The polished skin of a ray fish reflects the trend for seeking unusual inlays to embellish furniture.

The flat cross-stretchers linking the turned, squared baluster legs are typical of 17th-century furniture.

CABINET-ON-STAND

The cabinet is made of oak, and then veneered with a variety of woods: walnut, palm, and purple wood, with lacquer and ray-skin panels forming part of the inlay. The cabinet stands on six turned, squared baluster legs joined by flat stretchers. A wealthy status symbol for its time, this cabinet is the earliest known example of Dutch furniture

made using lacquer panels and polished ray-skin cut from an earlier Japanese coffer. The original piece is likely to have been imported to the Netherlands by the Dutch East India Company, but was probably no longer fashionable. The desirable exotic materials from the East would then have been removed and used to decorate a new, more fashionable, piece of furniture. *1690–1710. H:79½ in (202 cm); W:62½ in (158.5 cm); D:21¼ in (54 cm).*

GILTWOOD PIER TABLE AND MIRROR

One of a pair of tables, each with a matching large mirror above. This heavily carved gilt table has a serpentine marble top and scrolled serpentine-paneled legs joined by a cross-stretcher. In the center is a carved urn. The coat of arms of the original owner is carved into the top of the mirror frame. *Late 17th century. H:32 in (81.5 cm); W:48 in (122 cm); D:27 in (69 cm).*

gilded caryatids or ebonized wood.

Later in the century, craftsmen such as Jan van Mekeren, a cabinet-maker in Amsterdam, decorated large cabinets-on-stands and tables with intricate floral marquetry, inspired by the still-life floral paintings popular at the time. The contrasting colors of ebony from Madagascar, purple amaranth from Guyana, rosewood from Brazil, and sandalwood from India were combined to create marquetry of consummate skill. Exported to France and then England, these cabinets provided inspiration for cabinet-makers there, who developed their own styles of veneering.

EVERYDAY PIECES

Floral marquetry was not just used to embellish cabinets; side tables were occasionally decorated in the same way. More typical of the Low Countries, however, were tables and cupboards decorated with a wealth of naturalistic carving.

Chests of drawers were often made of oak, stained or polished to resemble ebony. Ebony or stained pearwood was used for moldings.

Chairs tended to be rectangular with low or high backs. They were usually made of walnut and upholstered in leather, velvet, or cloth, with brass studs. As the century advanced, inspired by imports from India, chair seats and backs were made of cane. The legs were linked by stretchers. The artist Crispin van den Passe's *Boutique Menuiserie*, published in Amsterdam in 1642, showed elements of Mannerism in chair design, but it also included simpler chairs, with straight backs, double stretchers, and carved arms terminating in dolphins.

FRENCH INFLUENCE

Toward the end of the century, the dazzling furniture of the court at Versailles became a new source of inspiration, compounded by an influx of Huguenot designers and craftsmen, such as Daniel Marot (see below) fleeing religious persecution in France. The French influence soon became evident as Dutch furniture became more sculptural and less rectangular. Based on Marot's designs, chairs now had tall, richly carved backs with crested back-rails.

17TH-CENTURY DOLLHOUSE

This dollhouse was commissioned by Petronella Oortman, a wealthy woman from Amsterdam. She ordered porcelain objects from China and had the city's furniture-makers and artists decorate the interior. Costing as much as a townhouse along the canal, this was not a toy for children. Its importance for the historian is in the design and placement of the furniture. *1686–1705. H:102 in (255 cm); W:75¾ in (189.5 cm); D:31¼ in (78 cm).*

DUTCH OAK AND MARQUETRY TABLE

This table is typical of Low Countries design, with square baluster legs and flat stretchers. Designed to stand against a wall, only the visible surfaces are decorated with marquetry. *1690–1710. H:30¼ in (77 cm); W:39 in (100 cm); D:27¾ in (69.5 cm).*

DANIEL MAROT (1661–1752)

MAROT FLED TO THE LOW COUNTRIES TO ESCAPE RELIGIOUS PERSECUTION. HIS DESIGNS WERE INFLUENTIAL IN BRINGING FRENCH STYLE TO THE REGION.

A Parisian-born Protestant, Marot became architect and designer to the Stadholder, later William of Orange. He decorated the apartments at the new Het Loo palace, and followed William to England in 1694. Marot is best known for his engraved designs for interiors and furniture, which had a great influence on cabinet-makers of the period. His most lavish designs are for great four-poster state beds (see below), but he designed all types of furniture. His best-known designs for elaborately carved chairs with high backs were widely copied.

Design for a Bedchamber with a State Bed, from Marot's *New Book of Apartments,* 1703. Note the high-backed chairs against the walls and the four-poster state bed.

The high back with a pierced and heavily carved splat is typical of Marot's designs.

The seat is wider at the front than the back, but the upholstery is not original.

The legs are carved with bellflowers and rosettes.

One of a set of 12 salon chairs from a design by Marot. The carved top rail is decorated with double scrolls and sprays of acanthus leaves. The seats have a carved apron of pierced foliage and rosettes, and the design is echoed in the stretchers. *1686–1705. H:49¼ in (123 cm); W:20¾ in (52 cm); D:20½ in (51 cm). PAR*

GERMANY AND SCANDINAVIA

The end of the Thirty Years' War in 1648 marked the beginning of German federalism. From then on, Germany was made up of small sovereign states ruled by wealthy princes. The most powerful nation in the Baltic area was Sweden. By 1660, under Charles XI, it had reached the height of its power.

INFLUENCES
Styles of furniture varied from one part of Germany to another, because each principality had its own court. The Bavarian electors built the Residenz in Munich with a style and luxury that made King Gustav Adolf of Sweden jealous. Following an exile in Brussels, Elector Max II Emanuel (1680–1724) returned to Bavaria with expensive Antwerp furniture. During his second exile, in France, he became familiar with the French Baroque and sent Bavarian craftsmen to France to study and bring the style back home.

In Germany, by the beginning of the 18th century, the heavy, opulent Baroque style was making way for the curvaceous Rococo forms that reached their creative high point in church and castle interiors. Partly due to the guild system, the German cities were a little behind in development, generally taking the lead from the masterpieces.

PRINCELY CABINETS
In 1631, the city of Augsburg sent an ebony cabinet decorated with precious materials to the King of Sweden as a peace offering. Augsburg was the stronghold of furniture design, and such a high number of intarsia cabinets were imported to Spain that in 1603 King Philip III introduced a ban on the importation of Augsburg goods. Curiosity cabinets, embellished with fine inlays of silver, ivory, amber, and precious stones, or with colored engravings and porcelain plaques, were sought by noblemen and emulated throughout Europe. Augsburg also produced opulent embossed and engraved silver furniture for export.

KARL VI WRITING DESK

This writing desk from Austria is made of ash veneered with maple, and decorated with marquetry in plum and myrtle woods. The desk has a long central drawer and a pull-out writing slide flanked on either side by two smaller drawers. The top section of the desk consists of an arrangement of six drawers. The piece stands on six, square tapered legs, which are carved and partly gilded. The legs are joined by curved and interwoven stretchers. *c. 1700. H:41½ in (104 cm); W:57½ in (144 cm); D:28½ in (71 cm).*

TYROLEAN CABINET-ON-STAND

These cabinets were intended to house collections of rare objects. The intarsia decoration (pictorial inlay using different woods) was influenced by engravings from pattern books by the Dutch ornamental painter Hans Vredeman de Vries. The perspective view of a portal with a well or fountain in the foreground and the architectural view in the background were all taken from *Various Architectural Forms* (1560). *c. 1700. H:60½ in (154 cm); W:50¾ in (129 cm); D:22 in (56 cm).*

Detail of carving

TRAVEL CABINET

This ebony cabinet from Southern Germany is decorated with ivory inlay. The fall front opens to reveal 10 small drawers flanking a central section with a lockable door. All of the surfaces are decorated with ivory foliate inlay, and the case stands on flat ball feet. *17th century. H:18¼ in (46.75 cm); W:21¼ in (54 cm). LPZ*

TABLE CABINET

This *Kunstkabinett*, or table cabinet, originates from Eger, Bohemia, which was renowned for the use of sculptural relief marquetry or intarsia panels. The cabinet has a stepped top with a sliding lid. The two doors conceal small drawers of various sizes surrounding a vaulted central compartment with columns and a detachable cover. These relief-carved marquetry panels, showing various mythological scenes, are typical of the work of Adam Eck. *c. 1640. H:20 in (51 cm); W:23 in (58.5 cm); D:11 in (28 cm).*

VERNACULAR STYLES

In Germany and Scandinavia, massive, architectural wardrobes with heavy cornices, known as *Schränke*, remained popular in upper-middle-class houses throughout the century. These had two doors over two drawers. In the north they were usually made of oak and were often heavily carved; in the south they were more likely to be made from local fruitwood or walnut. The chest was an important household item well into the 18th century.

Upholstered armchairs with carved top rails were made for the heads of households. These had turned arms and curled, almost scrolled feet.

In Sweden and Germany, suites of stools, chairs, and armchairs were upholstered in leather, or occasionally in imported silk. In less grand homes, it was common to find stools and benches set around long plank tables.

DECORATIVE EFFECTS

German craftsmen were renowned for their use of walnut veneer and, later, for ebony. Eger, Bohemia, was well-known for cabinets using sculptural relief or intarsia panels.

Furniture decorated with boullework (*see p.54*). became popular in southern Germany at the end of the century. Augsburg craftsmen mastered the technique, and produced fine examples of the style.

Berlin became renowned for japanned furniture, especially for the cabinets, tables, *guéridons*, and cases for musical instruments with japanned decorations on a white ground designed by Gerhard Dagly. In Paris his pieces were described as "Berlin" cabinets. Cabinets decorated with red and blue lacquer from Dresden and Brandenburg were also highly coveted abroad.

The Baroque Schloss Biebrich, south of Wiesbaden
This three-winged palace on the banks of the Rhine is a magnificent example of the Baroque style, with its bold color scheme and carved statues looking down from the roof.

SWEDISH GILDED MIRROR FRAME

This gilt-bronze beaded frame, attributed to Burchard Precht, is decorated with *verre églomisé* (an ancient glass-gilding technique). The pattern depicts gold foliage on a red ground. *c. 1700. H: 55 in (140 cm); W: 31 in (79 cm).*

TILED TABLE

This small table from Friesland is similar to Scandinavian furniture and has a top made from blue and white Delft tiles. It has flat stretchers, turned, spiraled legs, and bun feet. *Early 18th century. H:36½ in (92 cm).*

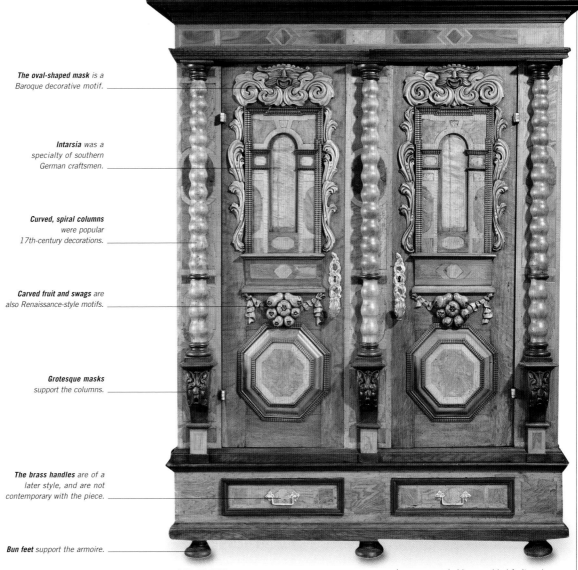

The oval-shaped mask is a Baroque decorative motif.

Intarsia was a specialty of southern German craftsmen.

Curved, spiral columns were popular 17th-century decorations.

Carved fruit and swags are also Renaissance-style motifs.

Grotesque masks support the columns.

The brass handles are of a later style, and are not contemporary with the piece.

Bun feet support the armoire.

ARMOIRE

This exceptional 17th century armoire, a *Fassadenschrank* from southern Germany, is made of walnut, maple, oak, and ash. The molded cornice is positioned above an inlaid frieze and a pair of doors with architectural carvings, surrounded by a molded fruit and mask pattern. The doors are flanked with three ball-pattern carved columns. The lower section of the armoire has two drawers, and the whole piece stands on flattened bun feet. *H:94½ in (240.5 cm) W:44 in (112 cm) D:23½ in (60 cm)*

ENGLAND

DURING THE REIGN of James I, most furniture was made of oak and was limited to joint stools, chests, chairs with plain or spiral turned legs, and long trestle tables. Decoration was confined to elaborate carving on chairs, chests, and settles. The aristocracy of Wales and Scotland tended to follow the lead of the dominant English court style.

FOREIGN INFLUENCES

During Charles I's reign, craftsmen from France, Italy, and the Low Countries came to work on state apartments and grand houses. Influenced by designs from the Low Countries, English furniture was more restrained than Italian Baroque pieces.

Upholstered furniture was made for grand residences. Chairs generally had low, square backs, upholstered with tapestry or leather, and armchairs had seat cushions and padded arms covered with upholstery. Settees were occasionally made as part of a suite with matching chairs.

THE RESTORATION

Furniture was mostly made of plain woods such as oak, ash, elm, or beech under Oliver Cromwell, whose government did not condone lavish displays of ornament, but the situation changed after the restoration of the monarchy in 1660. Charles II had spent his exile in Europe and brought back the latest fashions to England.

Court life under Charles II was less formal, creating a demand for small folding tables, card tables, and gateleg dining tables. Walnut became the most popular wood, and techniques such as veneering and caning were fashionable. Caned furniture with twist-turned frames was considered quintessentially English.

REBUILDING LONDON

A massive building boom after the Great Fire of London in 1666 led to specialization within the woodworking trades. Cabinet-makers made case furniture, tables, and stands, while joiners—and the wood-carvers and gilders who worked with them— concentrated on architectural features, bedsteads, and mirror frames. Chair-making also became a specialist craft.

Trade between the Low Countries and England increased after the accession of William III and Mary in 1689. The European influence on furniture was compounded by the arrival in England of French Huguenot craftsmen, some of whom became cabinet-makers to the royal household.

SKILLED CRAFTSMANSHIP

Cabinets were now veneered with walnut, yew, maple, holly, olive, beech, and fruitwoods. Burr woods were especially desirable. Some woods were cut across the grain to create an "oyster" veneer. The most elaborate forms of veneering used floral, seaweed, or arabesque marquetry.

Other cabinets were japanned, to imitate lacquer, or were covered in patterned gesso to create a raised, gilded appearance. Chests-on-stands were replaced by bureau-cabinets, often topped with domes or pediments intended for the display of expensive porcelain. Clothes presses and livery cupboards were commonplace, as were chests of drawers and kneehole desks.

Tables ranged from oak trestles to grand console tables. These were often designed to stand beneath large, ornate mirrors. High-backed chairs with caned seats and backs were popular, as were chairs in the style of Daniel Marot (see p.45), which had long, carved or pierced back splats.

As the century drew to a close, fine furniture was no longer made solely for grand palaces. Simpler, well-crafted pieces were also being made for wealthy city merchants and the landed gentry, paving the way for the elegant styles prevalent in the 18th century.

Needlework casket Embroidered in colored silks on a satin ground, the casket depicts romantic courtly scenes. Typical of similar caskets of the age, this one has many compartments, some secret. *Mid-17th century. W:11½ in (29.5 cm). BonK*

HIGH-BACKED SIDE CHAIR

Made of imported walnut, this chair, with its carved and pierced back splat, is similar to engravings published by Marot. It has cabriole legs terminating in "horse-bone" feet, but has stretchers. *c. 1710. H:47½ in (121 cm). PAR*

HALL CHAIR

This chair is based on the Italian *sgabello* design. The oak is carved and painted, with a shell-shaped back and pendant mask with swags on the front. *c. 1635. H:43½ in (110.5 cm); W:27 in (69 cm); D:26 in (66 cm).*

The fall front conceals drawers and pigeonholes.

The drawers are decorated with cross-banded veneer.

Locks on the drawers indicate that the bureau would have held valuable items.

The shaped back-plate and bale handles are engraved.

Ball-and-bracket feet were used at the beginning of the 18th century.

MARQUETRY BUREAU

This bureau is veneered in burr maple, but is stained to look like tortoiseshell. Burr woods such as elm and maple were often stained to resemble more expensive materials. The bureau has rosewood and kingwood cross-banding and metal stringing. The fall front encloses an array of drawers and pigeonholes. The lower section has two short and two long drawers supported on ball feet. *c. 1710. H:38 in (95 cm); W:28½ in (71 cm); D:20¾ in (52 cm). PAR*

JAPANESE LACQUER CABINET ON ENGLISH STAND

Designed to stand against a wall, this cabinet is only decorated on the front. Such fine lacquered pieces would have been great status symbols. The imported Japanese cabinet rests on an English William-and-Mary-style giltwood stand. *Late 17th century. H:37½ in (98.5 cm); W:22½ in (57 cm); D:6 in (15 cm).*

Arched pediment.

The central carving is in the shape of a shell.

The insides of the doors are paneled with borders of burr yew wood and cross-banded with padouk wood.

The fitted interior contains shelves and small drawers and pigeonholes arranged around a central cupboard.

Each brass lock plate is engraved with a winged figure blowing a horn.

The drawer fronts each have a different design of carved gesso work.

The feet are in the shape of lion's claws.

RARE PAINTED AND INLAID CABINET

This cabinet is made of pine, painted, and inlaid with precious mother-of-pearl—an imported material from the Western Pacific. The design of the lower cabinet is inspired by imported styles, but the upper section is architectural in design. This piece was probably made in London. *c. 1620.*

BUREAU-BOOKCASE

One of a pair, this is a very rare and fine example of a bureau-bookcase. It is attributed to the partnership of London cabinet-makers James Moore and John Gumley, and is decorated with carved and gilded gesso incorporating strapwork with scrolling foliage and floral detail. An arched pediment with a carved shell sits above arched doors with beveled glass, which open to reveal a fitted interior. The lower part, with a sloping fall front, encloses a bureau interior. The base contains drawers with drop-ring handles. *c. 1720. H:94½ in (240.5 cm); W:44 in (112 cm). MAL*

FRANCE: HENRI IV AND LOUIS XIII

THE EARLY 17TH CENTURY was a time of increasing prosperity in France, after a long period of war. Henri IV ruled a country in which styles had changed little since the Renaissance. Eager to encourage new skills, however, he established a workshop for craftsmen in the Louvre Palace in 1608. The craftsmen he employed were Italian and Flemish (French craftsmen were sent to serve an apprenticeship in the Low Countries) and, protected by royal patronage, they were allowed to work in Paris without being subject to the punitive membership restrictions of the medieval guild of joiners and furniture-makers.

TRADITIONAL FORMS

Most furniture was made of oak or walnut during the reign of Henri IV. The massive double-bodied cupboard, with an upper section that was narrower than the lower section, doors with geometric paneling, and bun feet continued to be popular well into the 17th century. Tables had elaborate, heavy bases and chairs were architectural in form, which made them rather stiff and uncomfortable.

FOREIGN INFLUENCES

After Henri IV's death in 1610, his Italian wife Marie de Medici was appointed regent to the young king.

During her reign, there was a building boom in Paris, and the nobility and a growing middle class began to furnish their apartments in grand style.

Marie was influential in furniture design. She employed many foreign craftsmen, including Jean Macé, a cabinet-maker from the Low Countries, who probably first used veneering in French furniture design, and Italian craftsmen, who introduced boullework (see p.54) and *pietra dura* inlays (see p.42). In particular, Marie de Medici encouraged the manufacture of cabinets inlaid with ebony, which were made in Paris from about 1620 to 1630.

GRAND DESIGNS

Furniture during the reign of Louis XIII was monumental and heavy in style. The cabinet, usually on a stand and housing numerous small drawers, was the most important piece of furniture of the time. Generally made of walnut or ebony, it was decorated with panels, columns, and pilasters.

Ebony-veneered cabinets made late in Louis XIII's reign are embellished with flat relief carving, carved flowers, and twisted columns. They were inspired by the Augsburg cabinets made in Germany (see p.46), which used ebony and other exotic materials in a decorative fashion.

PROVINCIAL CUPBOARD

The top section of this carved walnut cupboard has two doors decorated with molded paneling and is crowned by a molded cornice. There is a long drawer in the center of the frieze, which is flanked by two short drawers. The frieze is supported by four spiral-turned columns and a recessed cupboard in the lower section. The whole cupboard is supported on a molded plinth base and four bun feet.
Early 17th century. W:43⅓ in (110 cm).

ARMOIRE

This armoire originates from the Grenoble region. The pediment and the center of the two paneled doors are profusely inlaid with floral marquetry of various woods, depicting flowers and leaves. The panels also bear the monogram and coronet of the Barras de la Penne family. The panel design is continued on the sides. The armoire would originally have been supported on either turned feet or a molded base. *Early 17th century. H:82½ in (209 cm).*

The cupboard or buffet was popular at this time, especially in the provinces. This form slowly evolved into an armoire, which was used for storing linens, rather than for the display of expensive household items, such as silver plate or ceramics. Fall fronts were added to cabinets, as seen on the typical *vargueños* (*see p.56*), producing an early form of bureau.

Small tables intended for the less formal rooms of a house were made in many shapes, but were mostly oblong, with turned legs. Dining tables now had tops that could be extended, either with hinges or by the use of telescoping leaves. The table bases were usually turned, and H-stretchers provided a popular method of linking the table legs.

Chairs became more comfortable toward the end of Louis XIII's reign, as seats grew lower and wider, and the backs of the chairs became higher. There was a greater emphasis on textiles in Louis XIII furniture, although upholstery was so expensive at this time that only the finest pieces of furniture were covered with textiles. Cushions were used for additional comfort on wooden seats, and chairs made for the upper classes were often covered with fashionable upholstery. Velvet, damask, needlework, and leather were all used. The fabric was fixed into place with rows of brass tacks, which also served as a decorative element of the chairs. Fringe was added below the back seat rail and along the lower chair rail as an extra embellishment. Armrests were usually curved and sometimes incorporated an upholstered pad. Chair legs were carved in a sculptural way, similar to the elaborate legs of Brustolon's chairs (*see p.40*), or they were turned.

DECORATIVE DETAIL
The Low Countries, especially Flanders, had a strong influence on French furniture of the period. Two features typical of Louis XIII furniture were inspired by Flemish furniture: the heavy, molded paneling in geometric patterns and elaborate turning on legs and stretchers.

Turning was an essential feature of Louis XIII furniture, both in formal and vernacular pieces. It was now no longer used simply for legs and stretchers, but also to create decorative details on cupboards and cabinets. A piece of furniture would often feature more than one turned design.

OAK CHEST

This heavily decorated chest has a plain top, attached to the case by interior hinges. The three heavily carved panels on the front of the case are divided by stylized pilasters. The base of the chest contains a long, shallow drawer, which is decorated with carved, architectural elements. The piece stands on straight feet. *Late 16th century. W:33½ in (85 cm). EDP*

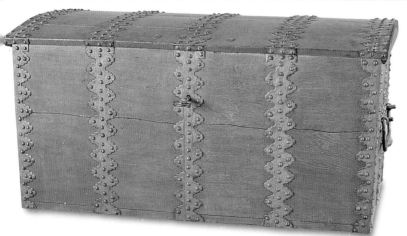

OAK CHEST

This chest is made of oak and is decorated with five gilded and studded metal straps, cut in a wavy pattern over the front, back, and domed lid. The piece has two gilded handles on either side to allow the piece to be carried. The chest retains its original lock and key. Unlike many chests of the period, this piece does not have feet. *Early 17th century. H:29½ in (74 cm); W:56 in (142 cm); D:27½ in (69 cm). PIL*

The seat back is embellished with a gold thread pattern.

The chair arms are scrolled in shape.

A turned H-stretcher joins the legs.

Baluster legs are typical of the period.

LOUIS XIII DINING CHAIR

This carved armchair is one of an impressive set of 12 side chairs and two armchairs, which may have been added to the set at a later date. It has an arched, padded back and seat, covered in close-nailed velvet and decorated with gold thread. The exposed frame is made of walnut and consists of scrolled arms on turned supports and baluster legs, which are typical of the period. The legs are linked by turned H-stretchers. *17th century.*

FRANCE: LOUIS XIV

IN THE SECOND half of the 17th century, the reign of the flamboyant Louis XIV, known as the Sun King, led to the creation of sumptuous palaces and furnishings that were emulated throughout Europe.

In 1662, a year after becoming king in his own right, Louis installed many of Europe's finest craftsmen in the former tapestry workshops of the Gobelin brothers on the outskirts of Paris. Modeled on the Grand Ducal Workshops in Florence (*see p.42*), these centers of excellence created furniture and fixtures for the royal palaces and were responsible for developing a unified design style that celebrated the glory of the king.

ROYAL SPLENDOUR
In 1682, Louis moved the French court into the Palace of Versailles. His favorite designer was Charles Le Brun, whose exuberant designs greatly impressed the King. Le Brun was responsible for many of the greatest rooms in Versailles, including the Hall of Mirrors (*see p.35*). Louis took a personal interest in the decoration and furnishing of his palace, and much of the furniture was embellished with visual references to him. The most common motifs were two interlaced "L"s, the fleur-de-lys, and the sunburst, Louis XIV's personal emblem.

THE EDICT OF NANTES
In 1685, Louis revoked the Edict of Nantes, thereby ending religious tolerance for Protestants. Many French designers and craftsmen, including Daniel Marot and Pierre Gole, fled abroad. This exodus helped spread the influence of French design to the rest of Europe and North America.

POPULAR STYLES
Louis XIV furniture was an expression of the wealth and power of the king, and lavish materials were used, such as exotic woods, silver and gilt, *pietra dura* panels, imported lacquer, and boulle marquetry. Motifs drew on Renaissance decoration, including mythological creatures, grotesques, arabesques, and flora and fauna.

Etiquette changed and comfort became more important. Chair backs were lower and most seats had a wooden frame with leather or cloth upholstery fixed in place with brass-headed nails. The *fauteuil*, an armchair with open sides, became popular, as

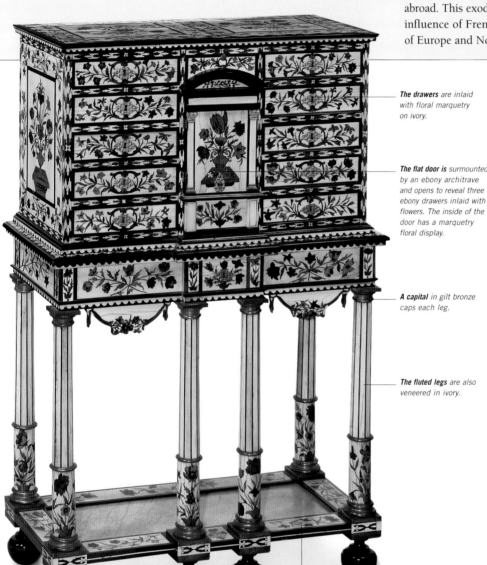

The drawers are inlaid with floral marquetry on ivory.

The flat door is surmounted by an ebony architrave and opens to reveal three ebony drawers inlaid with flowers. The inside of the door has a marquetry floral display.

A capital in gilt bronze caps each leg.

The fluted legs are also veneered in ivory.

The stretchers are flat and are decorated with floral marquetry.

IVORY-VENEERED CABINET-ON-STAND

This piece is attributed to the Dutch cabinet-maker Pierre Gole (c. 1620–84) for the *Cabinet Blanc* (the White Room) in the Palace of Versailles. Veneered with ivory, which acts as a background for floral marquetry in tortoiseshell and various woods, this cabinet is testament to the technical expertise of the maker. The upper section consists of a series of drawers on either side of a central recess. Within the recess, enclosed by doors, are three more drawers, all profusely inlaid with marquetry on ivory. The cabinet stands on six fluted legs, also veneered in ivory, which have ball feet and are joined by flat stretchers. *c. 1662. H:50½ in (126 cm); W:33 in (84 cm); D:15½ in (39 cm).*

CARVED GILTWOOD *FAUTEUIL*

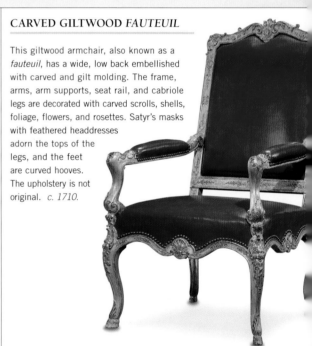

This giltwood armchair, also known as a *fauteuil*, has a wide, low back embellished with carved and gilt molding. The frame, arms, arm supports, seat rail, and cabriole legs are decorated with carved scrolls, shells, foliage, flowers, and rosettes. Satyr's masks with feathered headdresses adorn the tops of the legs, and the feet are curved hooves. The upholstery is not original. *c. 1710.*

LOUIS XIV GILTWOOD *CANAPÉ*

The shaped arms and supports of this gilded *canapé* are wrapped with carved acanthus leaves and have strapwork decoration. The six scroll legs with matching decoration are joined by a double X-stretcher surmounted by urn finials. The *canapé* would originally have been upholstered in needlework or figured velvet. *c. 1700. H:36 in (91 cm); W:62½ in (159 cm)*

did the *canapé* or couch. The arms and legs of chairs incorporated more carved detail than previously, displaying the carver's skills and showing that he was familiar with the latest designs.

Guests were received in the bedroom. The finest beds had a plume of feathers, known as *panache,* at each corner, and a balustrade separated the occupant from the visitors. Louis XIV's bed (*see left*) was raised on a dais.

Toward the end of the century, the buffet, a two-tiered cupboard with four

Part of a Gobelin tapestry This panel depicts Louis XIV in his formal bedroom receiving visitors, according to the etiquette of the time. Note the state bed and the sumptuous surroundings. *c. 1670. H:72 in (180 cm); W:84¼ in (210.5 cm).*

doors, two above and two below, evolved into the *armoire*, which had two tall doors. The chest, or coffer, was replaced by the commode, a case piece on short legs with either doors (two) or drawers, which became more formal toward the end of the century.

The console table was very popular and was generally heavily gilded. It was decorated on three sides, but not at the back, since the table was usually placed against a wall.

Smaller tables, often made of fruitwood, were sometimes painted. Their uses varied: some of them held candlesticks or writing paper; others were used as informal dining tables.

RED BOULLEWORK COMMODE

The top of the commode is inlaid with designs in the style of Louis XIV's chief designer, Jean Bérain (*see p.55*), showing human figures, birds, arabesques, and foliage. The rope twist handles are ormolu (*see p.39*) and the handle

plates have Renaissance-style male masks. Elaborate escutcheons are set down the center and pierced swags of flowers beneath female masks and shells decorate the rounded shoulders. Scroll-shaped mounts terminate in hoof feet. *17th century. H:33 in (84 cm); W:46½ in (118 cm); D:26½ in (67.5 cm). PAR*

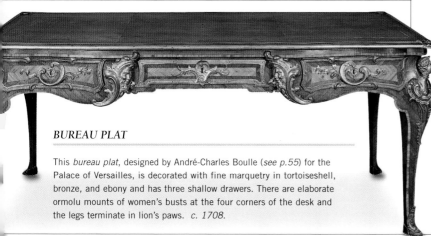

BUREAU PLAT

This *bureau plat,* designed by André-Charles Boulle (*see p.55*) for the Palace of Versailles, is decorated with fine marquetry in tortoiseshell, bronze, and ebony and has three shallow drawers. There are elaborate ormolu mounts of women's busts at the four corners of the desk and the legs terminate in lion's paws. *c. 1708.*

LOUIS XIV *CABINET EN ARMOIRE*

This *contre-partie* cabinet is veneered with brass, pewter, and tortoiseshell and decorated with foliage and strapwork patterns. The breakfront cornice sits above a frieze inlaid with engraved roundels. The central door is inlaid with caryatids and foliate urns. The lower section has two long drawers above cupboard doors. The interior is decorated with marquetry and mirror-glass and contains various drawers. *c. 1680. H:86½ in (220 cm); W:57 in (145 cm); D:23½ in (60 cm).*

BOULLE MARQUETRY

THIS ELABORATE MARQUETRY, USUALLY BRASS INLAID INTO TORTOISESHELL OR EBONY, OR VICE VERSA, WAS NAMED AFTER ANDRÉ-CHARLES BOULLE, CABINET-MAKER TO LOUIS XIV.

MATERIALS

MANY EXOTIC MATERIALS WERE USED AS INLAYS IN BOULLE MARQUETRY.

Bone and horn Bone is naturally pale, while horn varies from white to black. They were painted or dyed to imitate other materials.

Ivory This expensive, hard, white material comes from the teeth and tusks of animals. Traditionally the terms applies to elephant tusks.

Metal The most common metal in Boulle marquetry was brass. Copper, pewter, and silver were also used.

Tortoiseshell This was usually the shell of the Hawksbill turtle. The shell becomes malleable in hot water.

Mother-of-pearl Rare in Boulle marquetry, this hard material cut from the lining of shells has an iridescent, lustrous sheen.

PREMIÈRE-PARTIE
This form of boulle marquetry has brass inlaid into a dark background, usually made of ebony or tortoiseshell. This is one of a pair of cabinets from the Chateaux de Versailles and Trianon, each with two doors decorated with marquetry depicting the seasons of fall and spring. Late 17th century. H:44 in (112 cm); W:35½ in (90 cm); D:17 in (43 cm).

BOULLE MARQUETRY originated in Italy during the 10th century, where it was known as *tarsia a incastro*, meaning a combining of materials. Italian craftsmen are thought to have introduced the technique to France in around 1600 when they produced work for Marie de Medici, Henri IV's second wife. Pierre Gole, a cabinet-maker from the Low Countries, is also credited with first using the technique in France.

MATCHING PAIRS

Furniture decorated with boullework was often made in pairs, mainly because the process of cutting out the materials resulted in two complete sets of the marquetry design. Boulle marquetry was very time-consuming, and making one set of designs, the *première-partie*, also produced an opposing set, the *contre-partie*. The examples most commonly seen are pairs of matching cabinets (*see above and right*).

CONTRE-PARTIE
The second part of the pair is decorated with the reverse form of boulle marquetry. This is created when dark marquetry, usually made of ebony or tortoiseshell, is inlaid into a brass or pewter background. Late 17th century. H:44 in (112 cm); W:35½ in (90 cm).

Arabesque scrolls were very popular motifs on boullework pieces.

Chinoiserie motifs were European interpretations of the Orient, rather than authentic designs.

Red tortoiseshell is created by dyeing the shell or pasting reflective foil underneath.

The top of this commode has a tortoiseshell and brass panel set within a molded and chased border.

Brass inlaid designs were often highlighted by engraving and etching designs into them.

The bérainesque designs include figures, birds, arabesques, scrolling, and foliage.

LOUIS XIV COMMODE, ATTRIBUTED TO BOULLE
This intricately decorated commode has two short and two long drawers, all with similar decoration to the top, rope-twist ormolu handles, and elaborate escutcheons. Pierced swags of flowers beneath female masks and shells decorate the shoulders, which develop into scrolls at the bottom and terminate in hoof feet.   17th century. H:33 in (84 cm); W:46½ in (118 cm); D:26½ in (67.5 cm). PAR

THE TECHNIQUE

To create boulle marquetry, a design was first drawn up. Any wood being used, such as ebony, was cut into thin slices to form a veneer—a decorative surface area. Tortoiseshell was flattened, then polished and sometimes painted on the underside for color. Any other materials were flattened in the same way, then cut into sheets the size of the marquetry pattern.

The tortoiseshell was then glued to a sheet of metal, such as brass or pewter, and wedged between two sheets of wood, like a sandwich. The design was glued to one side of the "sandwich" and the pattern was cut out of both the tortoiseshell and metal with a fretsaw. When the materials were separated from each other, the pieces of tortoiseshell and metal were sorted to form two marquetry sets: the brass details were set into the tortoiseshell background, known as the *première-partie*; and the tortoiseshell details were set into the brass background to form a reverse pattern, known as the *contre-partie*.

Once the marquetry veneer had been applied, the brass was engraved to add depth and detail. It was then rubbed down with sharkskin, which has a texture similar to sandpaper, and polished with a mixture of charcoal and oil. This process filled in the hollows of the engraving, making the design more pronounced.

The inner and outer panels of doors were frequently decorated in the same way. Sometimes Boulle used a mixture of both types of boullework on the same piece of furniture. The parts not decorated with boulle were often veneered in ebony, creating a striking contrast to the rest of the piece.

FINISHING TOUCHES

Boullework furniture was usually finished with gilded and engraved bronze mounts (known as *ormolu, see p.39*). This was partly to protect the edges, legs, feet, and locks, which were the most vulnerable areas, and partly for decoration. The mounts were not usually made by the cabinet-makers themselves, but by specialist foundries, which cast and shaped the metal before it was gilded.

ANDRÉ-CHARLES BOULLE (1642–1732)

CABINET-MAKER TO LOUIS XIV, ANDRÉ-CHARLES BOULLE WAS RESPONSIBLE FOR MANY OF THE INTERIOR FIXTURES AND MUCH OF THE FURNITURE AT THE PALACE OF VERSAILLES.

Born in Paris, Boulle trained as a cabinet-maker, an architect, a bronze-worker, and an engraver and obtained the royal privilege of lodging and working in the Louvre. Perhaps his most spectacular work was the design and creation of the mirrored walls, parquetry floors, inlaid paneling, and boullework furniture at the Palace of Versailles. As well as Louis XIV, his patrons included many French dukes, King Philip V of Spain, and the electors of both Bavaria and Cologne.

Boulle excelled at the marquetry that eventually took his name, although he was not the only cabinet-maker developing this technique. His later designs were influenced by those of Jean Bérain, an engraver who was also working at the Louvre, and it is often difficult to tell the work of the two craftsmen apart. Bérain usually incorporated swirling scrolls (arabesques) alongside figural images. His designs also have a more fanciful element than those of Boulle, with small grotesques and monkeys among the scrolling patterns. Very few pieces of furniture can definitely be attributed to Boulle himself.

Boulle was largely responsible for the development of new types of furniture, including the bureau and the commode, designs for which were published under the title *Nouveaux Desseins de Meubles* (New Designs of Furniture) and became widely known.

Louis XIV Boulle commode
This commode is one of a pair made for Louis XIV's bedchamber at Trianon. It is veneered with ebony inlaid with brass. *17th century.*

JEAN BÉRAIN (1638–1711)

A draftsman, designer, painter, and engraver from the Low Countries, Jean Bérain was appointed designer to Louis XIV in 1674. His Louvre workshop was near that of Boulle, for whom he created many designs. During Louis XV's reign, Bérain provided designs for furniture, weapons, theatrical costumes and sets, and even funeral processions.

Marquetry patterns with arabesques, scrolled foliage, or fanciful scenes were features of his work, and, like André Boulle, he was inspired by Renaissance and Classical designs. The term "bérainesque" was coined to describe designs based on his inimitable style.

SPAIN AND PORTUGAL

AT THE BEGINNING of the 17th century, Spain was very powerful and ruled over Portugal and many other parts of Europe. By the end of the century, however, Spain had lost much of its wealth and power, whereas Portugal, now independent from Spain, was enjoying a period of peace and economic stability.

Spain and Portugal were separated from the rest of Europe by the Pyrenees, so influence was predominantly North African, or Moorish. Both countries also had strong economic and political ties with the East, and Oriental and Indian influences can be seen in Iberian furniture. Indo-Portuguese

furniture was made in Goa for Portuguese clients, and also by Indian craftsmen working in Portugal, mainly in Lisbon. Toward the end of the century, the influence of Portuguese furniture had spread to Britain and the Low Countries because of strong trading links between the countries. The Spanish practice of placing furniture in specific places in a room was also widely adopted.

SPANISH FURNITURE
The Spanish nobility led a relatively nomadic existence, so furniture had to be portable. Most furniture was made of local walnut. Cabinets, or *vargueños*,

had handles on the sides so that they could be lifted on or off stands. During the 16th century, *vargueños* had been luxury items, but they became more common during the 17th century. Early-17th-century *vargueños* often had geometric decoration, but later in the century they featured architectural motifs and twisted Baroque columns. As in northern Europe, cabinet-makers began to incorporate exotic ebony veneers and ivory and tortoiseshell inlays. Chests were replaced by cupboards or trunks. Trunks usually had domed tops, covered in velvet or leather, with pierced metal mounts and elaborate stands.

The folding Renaissance X-frame chair was still popular. Toward the end of the century, craftsmen made their own versions of Louis XIV fauteuils. These had high, shaped backs and elaborately carved stretchers with interlaced scrolls and turned legs. They were usually upholstered in fabric or stamped leather, and the upholstery was fastened in place with decorative brass studs. Spanish chairs usually had scrolled feet rather than the ball feet typical of French chairs.

Plain trestle tables, often covered with textiles, remained popular. Spanish side tables had turned legs and distinctive, curved, iron stretchers

Small drawers were used to hold either rare items or papers.

Elaborate metalwork is often found on Portuguese or Indo-Portuguese furniture.

This marquetry pattern is known as "seaweed" or "arabesque" (named after the interlacing designs and dense arabesques).

The spiral-turned legs and stretchers are typical of Portuguese furniture.

INDO-PORTUGUESE BUREAU

This bureau is made of walnut and inlaid with ivory. The shape of the piece is basically the same as a bureau Mazarin (*see p.36*) with drawers set into a box frame at the back of the writing surface. *17th century*.

INDO–PORTUGUESE CABINET-ON-STAND

The cabinet-maker used native woods—teak and rosewood—for the carcass of this *contador*, which was then inlaid with ebony and ivory. The bottom

panels have a seaweed marquetry design. The rosewood stand has turned, spiral legs and stretchers, and terminates in bun feet. The cabinet was made in India, probably in Goa. *Late 17th century. H:49½ in (126 cm); W:37½ in (95 cm); D:18 in (46 cm).*

Ring-pull drawer handle

Detail of marquetry

SPANISH CARVED ARMCHAIR

This walnut chair has square, rather than turned, legs, and a pierced front stretcher. The chair is upholstered in velvet embroidered with gold thread. *1615–25.*

joined to the cross-bars between the [ta]ble legs. Many of these tables could [b]e folded, making them portable. [A]nother type of side table had turned, [c]olumnar legs joined by low stretchers [an]d an overhanging top.

Spanish and Portuguese beds [d]iffered from those in the rest of [E]urope. Heavy bed curtains were not [p]opular, since Spain and Portugal have [a] warm climate, so the bedsteads [t]hemselves were decorative and often [h]ad triangular, carved backboards with [t]urned columns or spindles.

PORTUGUESE STYLES

As in Spain, Portuguese furniture remained traditional until mid-century. Chestnut was the most popular native wood, but as the century advanced, imported Brazilian rosewood, or palisander, became popular—the first American tropical wood to be used by European cabinet-makers. Rosewood is easy to work, and cabinet-makers produced turned legs and stretchers in bulb and saucer shapes and lavishly turned and decorated bedsteads.

Cupboards and vast chests of drawers, originally intended for monastic churches, were the most highly decorated pieces of Portuguese furniture at first, with carvings that imitated the geometric decoration on Moorish tiles. The mid-century cabinet or *contador* was one of the most characteristic pieces of Portuguese furniture. A *contador* was a cabinet placed on a highly elaborate stand, which was decorated to match the upper cabinet.

High-backed chairs were similar to Spanish versions, with stamped and gilded leather upholstery held in place by brass studs. This remained the standard covering for seats and backs well into the 18th century.

In about 1680, a new type of chair developed. It had a high, shaped back, turned legs and arms, and a heavy, scrolled front stretcher. The ancient motifs of shells and garlands often decorated the backs of the chairs.

Furniture made by Portuguese craftsmen in the colonial empire contained elements of European and local styles. In Goa, European-style, low-backed chairs were made in indigenous ebony. The heavy, spiral-turned stretchers used on colonial Portuguese, or Indo-Portuguese chairs, chests, tables, and bed frames drew inspiration from Indian cabinet-making traditions.

CARVED SPANISH SIDE TABLE

[T]his plain, rectangular table is made of walnut [a]nd rests on trestle supports in the form of [fl]uted square legs. Tables were made in a [si]milar style for centuries, although the style of [d]ecoration often reveals the age of a piece. The [st]rapwork decoration on the stretcher is typical [o]f styles seen during the Renaissance, but it has the relatively shallow carving typical of the 17th century. These tables were found in urban and rural homes, and were often used as stands for cabinets. *17th century. H:31¾ in (80.5 cm); W:58¼ in (148 cm); D:37 in (94 cm).*

Ivory inlay detail

INDO–PORTUGUESE CABINET

The top and sides of this rectangular cabinet-on-stand are inlaid with ivory in a geometric stringing pattern. The two doors open to reveal 15 long and short drawers. The central wide drawer has a steel lockplate, inlaid all over with stylized leaf sprays within geometric borders. The stand is English and dates from around 1760. *Early 18th century. H:45 in (114 cm); W:26½ in (67 cm); D:16¾ in (42.5 cm).*

SPANISH *VARGUEÑO*

This cabinet is made of walnut, decorated with bone, ivory, gold sheet inlays, and paint. This type of furniture was produced in the southern Spanish city of Vargas. The fall front is decorated with intricate iron mounts, typical of the Spanish decorative tradition. The top section opens to reveal drawers and pigeon-holes. The bottom section displays strong Arab influences, including the geometric inlay pattern. *Early 17th century. H:59 in (150 cm).*

EARLY COLONIAL AMERICA

DURING THE 17TH CENTURY, the American colonies (excluding the Canadian provinces) were governed by Britain. Between 1630 and 1643, about 20,000 English men and women emigrated to colonial America seeking opportunities in a new land. Design influences came from the styles the colonialists favored from home.

While the southern colonies were largely populated by the English, New York and the middle colonies were mainly settled by German, Dutch, and Scandinavian immigrants.

Most activity was concentrated in the port towns, especially on the eastern seaboard, where the fashionable commodities of the new arrivals were enthusiastically embraced. Boston became the center of colonial trade. However, it took time for these furniture developments to reach the rural outlying areas of the colonies.

Many of the early settlers with woodworking skills were joiners rather than cabinet-makers (although the term "cabinet-maker" became more common as the century progressed). No formal reception furniture was made in America. Colonial American furniture resembled the vernacular furniture made in Europe, rather than Baroque court styles.

DOMESTIC STYLES

Chests and simple tables were common in colonial homes. Chests were mainly used for storing expensive textiles, such as the finest household linens. Most homes had two principal rooms, and the furniture was simple and functional. Chests, or blanket chests as they were known in the colonies, had a lid that lifted to reveal a single space for storage and often a "till" on the side—an additional, smaller storage space with a cover. Many cupboards were of simple plank construction, but others had tongue-and-groove paneling with carved and painted decoration.

Red oak joint stool A standard form of vernacular furniture, the joint stool was common in colonial America, where European settlers greatly influenced furniture design. *c. 1640. H:20¾ in (52 cm); W:17⅜ in (43.5 cm); D:13¾ in (34.5 cm).*

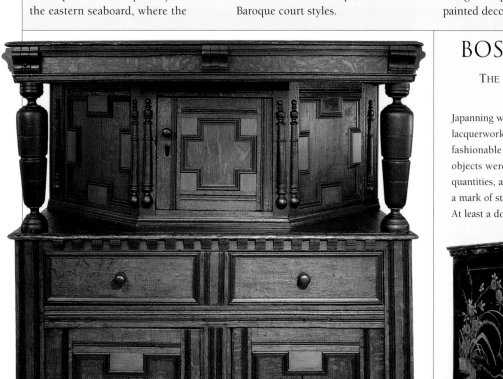

RED OAK AND RED MAPLE COURT CUPBOARD

This cupboard, made in the Boston area, has architecturally inspired, ebonized, applied pilasters, turned baluster supports, and geometric, framed panels. The panels in the top section are recessed, leaving a surface on which the owner can display silver or ceramics.

The top would have been covered with fabric, probably imported. The lower section has two drawers above two cupboard doors. The timbers used are indigenous, common to the woods of New England. This type of cupboard was made in New England for longer than its counterpart survived in the Low Countries or England. *1667–1700. H:152½ in (387 cm); W:126 in (320 cm); D:59 in (150 cm).*

BOSTON JAPANNED FURNITURE

THE CRAZE FOR ALL THINGS "ORIENTAL" REACHED THE COLONIES, ESPECIALLY THE PROSPEROUS SEAPORT OF BOSTON.

Japanning was the art of imitating Oriental lacquerwork. English merchants imported fashionable commodities, and japanned objects were brought to Boston in great quantities, as these items were considered a mark of status for wealthy colonials. At least a dozen Boston japanners were working by the first half of the 18th century. Usually, American japanning was done on white pine. Imitating lacquerwork required ingenuity: vermilion was applied to the surface with lampblack to achieve the effect of tortoiseshell.

Flowers, birds, and landscapes are typical decorations on japanned furniture.

Oversized animals are depicted among the trees and temples.

The base can be separated from the top of the cabinet.

The turned legs and flat stretchers are typical of the colonial style.

High chest of drawers This chest is made of maple and pine and is made up of two pieces: a top section of drawers and a stand on legs. *1710–30. H:62½ in (156.25 cm); W:39½ in (98.75 cm); D:21¼ in (53 cm).*

Case pieces included the cupboard or "court cupboard"), which is closely related to the English buffet. It served similar purpose in the New England colonies—the display of silver plate—nd would have been covered with an xpensive textile. Later cupboards had drawers below, rather than doors. hese evolved into chests with two r three drawers, and, by the 18th entury, became chests of drawers in he style that we recognize today.

Chairs and stools, made by joiners nd completed by upholsterers, were roduced in Boston from around 1660. Daybeds and couches were also made, out only for the wealthy. By the early 18th century, these were being exported to other colonies. Great chairs were important household items. These high-backed chairs had a turned front stretcher. Some were upholstered in leather, the brass tacks anchoring the leather serving as decoration; others had a simple rush seat. Sometimes these chairs are called Brewster chairs, named after one of the prominent Puritan elders.

The linen cupboard, or *kas*, a typical Low Country or German piece, was made in New York and New Jersey, but rarely in New England or the south. Usually made of local woods, the *kas* mirrored popular architectural styles and was often painted. Early examples had ball feet, while later cupboards had bracket feet.

Little Southern furniture from this period survives, owing to the hot, humid climate, but historians do know of several forms. Southern joint stools were made in walnut rather than the traditional oak favored in England and the rest of the colonies. Carved chests were used, and some joined chests made of walnut survive. A carved chest made specifically for church use by Richard Perrot dates from the late 17th century. Chairs were made of turned wood, with leather or rush coverings.

NATIVE WOODS

Owing to the different climates of the colonial states, the types of wood used varied tremendously. Furniture-makers in the north used maple, oak, pine, and cherry, while those in the middle and southern colonies used tulipwood, cedar, southern pitch pine, and walnut.

Immigrant joiners and craftsmen along the eastern seaboard gradually began to use local woods because they were less expensive than imported timbers. The choice of wood is important in determining the origin of colonial furniture, especially since the style of many pieces closely resembles English furniture of the time.

OAK CHEST

This chest from Massachusetts is made of red and white oak. Chests like this were common in the best rooms of houses. This chip-carved floral and leaf design is closely related to English vernacular work, particularly chests made in the Devon area of England. This piece would originally have been painted blue and red, since color was a very important feature in the 17th-century American interior. *1676. H:32¼ in (80.5 cm); W:50½ in (126 cm); D:23 in (57.5 cm).*

OAK AND MAPLE GREAT CHAIR

This leather-upholstered "great chair" with a low back is virtually identical in shape to upholstered chairs made in London at the time. It was made in Boston, Massachusetts. Such examples are extremely rare today. Oak and maple were both common in the northern colonies, so furniture made from these would have been fairly common in the area. The cushion is an authentic reproduction of the type of luxurious textile that would have been used on the chair to increase its comfort. Brass tacks were used not only to fasten the leather covering in place, but also for decorative effect. The wooden frame is relatively simple, with turned front legs and a stretcher to add decoration. *1665–80. H:39¼ in (99.5 cm); W:23¾ in (59.5 cm); D:16¾ in (42 cm).*

Fruit motifs on the doors represent fertility and marriage.

Pendants and festoons resemble European Renaissance motifs.

Painted decoration simulates the carved designs popular in Europe at the time.

GUMWOOD *KAS*

The cupboard, *kas*, or *schrank* was brought to New York by German settlers from the Rhine valley. Like all settlers, they made furniture in the style to which they were accustomed. This painted example features *grisaille* decoration rather than the more usual carving. The quince and pomegranate paintings on the doors represent fertility, so this cupboard may have formed part of a bridal dowry. The ball feet of earlier examples have been replaced with simpler bracket feet, and the piece is much smaller in scale than previous cupboards. This is a simplified version of the traditional, imposing examples seen in Germany. *1690–1720. H:61½ in (156.2 cm); W:60¼ in (153 cm); D:23 in (58.4 cm).*

CASE PIECES

ONE OF THE most common forms of case furniture in the 17th century was the cupboard. At the beginning of the century, most cupboards had an open area above a closed lower section, but gradually, the form changed so that both sections were enclosed.

Generally, the upper portion had two doors, while the base had doors or drawers below, depending on the use of the piece. By the end of the century, this style had evolved into the armoire, or wardrobe, which had two long doors from top to bottom.

Many armoires were influenced by architectural designs. They were often massive, highly decorated pieces with overhanging cornices. The carving gradually became less detailed, and by the end of the century, the principal decoration took the form of simple geometric patterns on the doors. These armoires had a lower section containing drawers, and most of them had ball feet. The common terms for them were *kas* (in the Low Countries), or *schrank* (in Germany).

Two-part cupboards made in urban areas were less imposing. The cornice was smaller and decoration was provided by veneers of different colored woods rather than carving.

DUTCH OR FLEMISH CUPBOARD

Made of oak, this cupboard is carved and embellished with architectural elements and caryatids. With its framed panels and ball feet, this cupboard retains many features of the Renaissance *buffet à deux corps*. *Early 17th century.*

Detail of carving

CABINET-ON-STAND

This cabinet is actually made up of a Spanish cabinet on top of a late English, mahogany base. The upper section has ripple molding, ebony banding, ivory stringing, and metal mounts surrounding tortoiseshell and painted panels. The pierced metal escutcheon on the base would have been added to provide a visual link to the top section. *Early 18th century. H:68½ in (174 cm). L&T* **5**

Pierced metal escutcheon

DOWER CHEST

Probably made in New York, this chest with a drawer below shows an early stage in the development of the chest of drawers. It has geometric, raised fielded panels on the front and sides. The drawer has two inverted sections with diamond-shaped decoration. Turned ball feet support the front, while the back has simple plank supports. It was probably made as a wedding, or dower, chest. *c. 1715.*

Carved figures *appear to support the top of the cupboard.*

The framed panels *are typical of early-17th-century cupboards.*

Ball feet *were popular on all types of cupboards.*

Fluted columns *were common architectural features.*

ARMOIRE

This armoire from Madeira is made from mahogany and laurel, both native woods of Madeira. The armoire has geometrical, fielded panels on both sets of drawers and on the sides of the piece. The top and bottom sections are separated by two narrow, central drawers. *17th century.*

LOW COUNTRIES CUPBOARD

This two-door cupboard has a writing slide. It is decorated with floral marquetry in walnut, rosewood, and fruitwoods, which were popular on cupboards from the Low Countries. The piece stands on flattened ball feet. This form is also known as a *buffet à deux corps*. *Late 17th century. H:72 in (183 cm). LPZ* **5**

SWEDISH CUPBOARD

This cupboard displays Germanic influences, with its architectural features, carved panels, and long drawers. The upper section consists of two doors carved with a raised geometric design within square panels. The base has two drawers with an elongated, carved panel design and simple cast-metal pulls. The turned feet are flattened and very wide. *Late 17th century. H.67¼ in (168 cm).*

RUSSIAN CUPBOARD

This pine cupboard has features typical of the architecture of the period, with applied split balusters dividing the two doors, top and bottom, from each other. The large hinges that hold the doors in place form part of the decoration. Large architectural pieces remained desirable in Russia longer than in the more fashionable societies of France and Italy. *Early 18th Century. H:55½ in (141 cm); W:30¾ in (78 cm); D:18½ in (47 cm).*

GERMAN CUPBOARD

This simply decorated walnut cupboard from the Brunswick area has a heavy architectural cornice and moldings, but the overhang is smaller than it would have been on earlier pieces. The decoration is provided by veneers and bronze fittings. The two doors sit above three full-width drawers. The piece is supported by ball feet. *Early 18th century. H:84 in (213 cm); W:54¾ in (139 cm); D:20 in (51 cm). AMH* **5**

CUPBOARD

This massive cupboard is made of walnut. It has an overhanging cornice that is stepped in the center, with a heavy, applied geometric design positioned in the center of the doors. The flat pilasters that flank the two doors are capped with carved cherub heads, reminiscent of Renaissance-style architectural motifs. The cupboard stands on six flattened, turned ball feet. *Early 18th century. WKA* **6**

SWISS WARDROBE

This wardrobe is made of a softwood covered with walnut veneer, and the front and sides are decorated with rounded fielded panels. The molded base mirrors the shape of the overhanging cornice. The piece is supported on six turned ball feet. Swiss furniture is similar in style to German pieces of the period. This wardrobe was made in Zurich. *1701. H:92 in (230 cm); W:87½ in (219 cm); D:34 in (85 cm). LPZ* **5**

GERMAN WARDROBE

Made in Saxony, this walnut and burr-walnut wardrobe retains the stepped-back square cornice popular on early 17th-century pieces, but it overhangs the later, two-door wardrobe form. The piece is decorated with carved molding and flat pilasters, as well as veneers applied in geometric patterns and bands. Like many large pieces of the time, it stands on six ball feet. *c. 1710. H:96¾ in (242 cm); W:90 in (225 cm); D:33¼ in (83 cm). VH* **6**

CABINETS

IN ITS SIMPLEST FORM a cabinet is a piece of furniture with drawers or compartments for storage. Until the 17th century, collector's cabinets for precious items were owned only by the wealthy, and were viewed by a select number of people in private rooms. Dutch cabinets were also used for storing linen, and were important status symbols in the Low Countries.

As the century progressed, however, the cabinet become a grand piece of furniture that dominated a room, a showpiece both for the consummate skill of the cabinet-maker, and for the exotic materials used, including ivory, amber, ebony, *pietra dura*, and

exquisite marquetry panels. Cabinets from Augsburg, Antwerp, Naples, or the Orient were especially coveted.

There were many types of cabinets—from Iberian *varguenos*, which were originally portable writing desks, to exotic Oriental pieces. Imported lacquer cabinets from the Far East were immensely fashionable. In England, carvers created ornate gilt stands to display the cabinets.

Still-life and floral paintings in the Dutch style were reproduced in marquetry, and actual paintings were incorporated as panels on cabinets.

Colonial pieces incorporated stylistic scenes from their native sources.

Detail from door panel

CABINET-ON-STAND

This cabinet from the Low Countries is made of oyster walnut and decorated with marquetry. It has a molded cornice above paneled doors. The stand has a long frieze drawer on spirally turned legs and ebonized bun feet. *H:82 in (208 cm).*

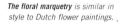
The floral marquetry is similar in style to Dutch flower paintings.

The cabinet stand is decorated with marquetry.

CABINET-ON-STAND

This oak-veneered cabinet from Amsterdam is attributed to Jan van Mekeren. The exquisite marquetry panels are made from diverse imported woods, including kingwood,

tulipwood, rosewood, ebony, olive wood, and holly, reflecting the naturalistic still-life paintings of flowers popular at the time. The squared legs and flat stretchers of the stand are also decorated with floral marquetry. *1700–10. H:70¼ in (178.5 cm).*

LACQUERED CABINET

This exquisite cabinet has a floral pattern on the inside of the doors that reflects the style of Dutch paintings of the period. The elaborately carved and gilt stand would have been made in England after the piece was imported. *c. 1680.*

QUEEN ANNE CABINET

Rather than having a stand, this English black and gilt japanned cabinet is supported by a chest of drawers on ball feet. The brass hinges on the upper case continue the Oriental theme of the piece. *c. 1700.*

GERMAN TABLE CABINET

This inlaid collector's table cabinet is made of a number of woods, some stained to provide additional color. It originates from the town of Neuwied, which was famous for exquisite marquetry. The cabinet has two doors, which

open onto eight small drawers and a central architectural tabernacle door. The front of each drawer depicts a richly painted landscape scene with stylized birds and animals. This small cabinet would have been placed on top of a table or a stand. *17th century. H:14¾ in (36.5 cm); W:17¾ in (44 cm); D:11½ in (29 cm).* 3

Columns imitate Bernini's style

VARGUEÑO-ON-STAND

The fall flap of this Spanish writing cabinet conceals carved drawers and small cupboards. The tiny columns give an architectural feel and imitate spiral Baroque columns. The cabinet sits on a stand with spirally carved and fluted supports. *17th century. H:59½ in (151 cm); W:44 in (112 cm); D:17¾ in (45 cm).*

AUGSBURG CABINET

This cabinet is is made from indigenous walnut, elm, maple, and fruitwood, and is decorated inside and out with intarsia, depicting architectural and floral motifs. The two-door base is similar to a buffet. *c. 1600. H:63¾ in (159 cm); W:45 in (112 cm); D:18 in (45 cm).* **7**

PORTUGUESE OR COLONIAL CABINET-ON-STAND

One of a pair, this cabinet is veneered in tropical rosewood, sometimes called jacaranda. The body is decorated with an inlaid "seaweed" pattern of arabesques and the front has an arrangement of paneled drawers with pierced-brass mounts. The stand contains a paneled drawer and has bobbin-turned tapering legs, joined by carved stretchers, which are typical of the Portuguese style. This piece may have been made in Portugal or in the Portuguese colonies in India. *17th century. H:60½ in (154 cm).*

GERMAN CABINET

This ebony and pine cabinet is finely carved with cartouches and flowers. The design incorporates a number of red-brown tortoiseshell panels. The top of the cabinet has one drawer above a richly carved plinth. Behind two doors, the architecturally inspired interior of the lower section has one central door with two small drawers above and below, and is flanked on either side by columns with Corinthian capitals and a further five drawers, one above the other. *c. 1700. H:35½ in (90 cm); W:38½ in (98 cm); D:16½ in (42 cm).* **4**

FLEMISH CABINET

Panels depicting a variety of rural landscapes have been set into this ebony cabinet from Antwerp. The piece has a rectangular hinged top, and two doors at the front. The interior has nine drawers around a columned door with a broken-arch pediment, behind which is a mirrored interior. The rippled ebony moldings framing the painted panels are typical of those seen on picture frames of the period. This piece is attributed to Isaac van Ooten. *17th century. H:39¾ in (101 cm); W:41¾ in (106 cm); D:15 in (38 cm).*

TABLES

ONE OF THE MAJOR innovations in 17th-century furniture design was the console table, which was found in the formal reception rooms of fashionable residences. Console tables were made to display wealth, and were not intended for any practical use. They were typically heavily carved and gilded. Roman console tables often had massive supports that were very architectural in design.

Utilitarian tables were made for private, family rooms and for less wealthy homes. Large utilitarian tables with rectangular plank tops above turned legs joined by stretchers are often described as "refectory" tables, named after the monastery dining halls in which they were commonly used. Stools or benches were used for seating. Massive, bulbous turnings of the legs become less pronounced toward the end of

the 17th century, while Louis XIV's influence is evident in the turnings, which were more square in shape and were often carved.

Smaller tables for different purposes appeared in the 17th century, largely because houses were being designed with rooms for specific uses, demanding new types of furniture. This coincided with the new fashion for coffee-drinking and the growing trend for small, portable pieces.

Some tables could be adjusted in size by the use of drop leaves and extendable tops. This was not a new development; records of tables that could be raised and lowered date back to the 14th century.

Center tables became popular. These were finished on all four sides (rather than having a plain side to face a wall), and would have been placed in the center of a room.

ITALIAN TABLE

This Italian refectory table would probably have been used in a large, rural home, or even a monastery. Such a large table would not have been moved often. The frieze is decorated on all four sides with carving, indicating that the table was intended to stand in the center of a room. The eight legs are composed of heavy, bulbous turnings, which suggests the table originates from early in the century. Wide, flat stretchers connect the legs both side-to-side and front-to-back. *Early 17th century. H:42 in (105 cm); W:138 in (350 cm); D:38 in (96 cm).*

TUSCAN TABLE

Instead of having turned supports and exterior stretchers, this walnut refectory table has waisted square supports. A flat central stretcher is pegged into the main supports and the platform feet, making the table more comfortable to sit at than those that have stretchers around the edge. The stretchers are pegged into place, probably indicating that the table could be dismantled for storage or moved to a new location if required. *17th century. H:32¼ in (82 cm); W:138 in (350.5 cm).*

The frame of the table is covered in carved, gilded gesso.

The cipher of the owner is positioned in the center.

The squared, tapered legs indicate the date of the piece.

CONSOLE TABLE, LONDON

Attributed to the cabinet-maker James Moore, the oak and pine frame of this console table is decorated with gesso and gilt. The elaborate carving incorporates scrollwork and shells on the top and apron, and acanthus leaves on the

square, tapered legs. The central flat section of the stretcher may originally have held a vase. The patron, Richard Temple, Baron Cobham, had his cipher added to the central part of the design. Small console tables would have been placed against the walls in formal rooms. *c. 1700.*

FRENCH TABLE

This substantial table is made of fruitwood. It has a rectangular top slightly overhanging a frieze. The narrow drawers in the case are decorated with fielded front panels. There are carved roundels at the junctions where the legs

are pegged into the frame below the top provide additional decoration. The six turned legs are quite straight with molding at the tops, but without the earlier balusters. The stretchers connect to the legs at square bases, and the piece terminates in ball feet. *Late 17th century.*

GATELEG TABLE

This English, William-and-Mary-style table is made of oak. The gateleg mechanism allows the top to fold down. The bobbin-turned legs are joined by square stretchers. This style was popular well into the 18th century, so such tables are difficult to date. *Late 17th century. H:39½ in (70 cm); W:27½ in (100.5 cm). EP*

ENGLISH TABLE

This English refectory table is made of oak. The low stretchers indicate that the table has probably been reduced in height, which happens when the legs suffer termite or water damage. It was possibly made for a manor house in Cornwall. *17th century. H:30¾ in (78 cm); W:80 in (203 cm); D:26¾ in (68 cm). L&T* **3**

ENGLISH TABLE

This Charles II table has a deep frieze without drawers, and carving that incorporates a Tudor rose. The cup-and-cover supports are typical for its date, but the four-plank top was added later. Reeded cross-stretchers are positioned between chamfered block feet. *c. 1665. W:19 in (302 cm). FRE* **2**

FLEMISH TABLE

This center table is made of oak inlaid with ebony. The legs have massive bulbous turnings, and the top has a pull-out flap on each side to extend the length of the table. The table has square stretchers above flattened bun feet. *Mid-17th century. H:29½ in (75 cm); W:44½ in (113 cm); D:28 in (71 cm).*

SWISS TRESTLE TABLE

This small table has a plain top, but the visual interest is provided by the highly decorative lower section. The slender, turned legs are complemented by the wavy pattern of the trestle. The piece terminates in pad feet. *17th century. H:38 in (95 cm); W:30½ in (76 cm); D:25¼ in (63 cm).*

RUSSIAN EXTENDABLE TABLE

This table is made of oak, decorated with carving and inlay. The top has a pronounced overhang and is made of two layers; the bottom layer pulls out to extend the top. The stretchers are set quite high on the legs. This piece would have been made for an aristocratic home. *Early 18th century. H:28 in (71 cm).*

SPANISH TABLE

A more vernacular version of a refectory table, this one lacks wooden stretchers but instead is supported by chamfered leg supports and a turned iron rod. Metal supports were a popular feature of furniture from the Iberian peninsula.

There are a number of narrow drawers under the table top, indicating that this table would have belonged to a relatively affluent home. A more basic table would have had a flat top. Spanish furniture was often easy to take apart, reflecting the Spanish taste for moving house according to the season. *17th century.*

SPANISH TABLE

This sturdy table has a single drawer in the case, separated visually into two sections, and decorated with fielded panels. It has turned baluster legs decorated with carved acanthus leaves, that fit directly into the case.

The legs are connected with three carved stretchers. The absence of a front stretcher allows a chair to be pulled up to the table, and may indicate that the table was used for writing. *17th century.*

CHAIRS

DURING THE 17TH CENTURY, chairs, as opposed to stools and benches, were only found in the homes of the wealthy. The chair evolved from the simple joint stool. Changing fashions, the import of exotic examples, and the introduction of new materials and techniques meant that this was a crucial time in the chair's development.

There were two major types of chairs: the low chair with a rectangular back, and the high-backed chair. The low chair or "back stool" is often referred to as a Cromwellian, Jacobean, or Farthingale chair. The introduction of smaller, private rooms to the 17th-century home meant that chairs were used in more different ways. High-

backed chairs, particularly those with caned seats and backs, were often used in halls and along the walls. By the end of the century, several variations of the high-back were being made.

The most elaborate high-backed chairs were designed by Daniel Marot for the French court. These chairs were made in suites, and were used in the bedchamber.

Upholstered chairs were signs of great wealth and status, as the materials used to cover the seats and backs was incredibly expensive. In Spain and Portugal, stamped-leather upholstery was popular. Cane seats were fashionable by the end of the century.

MEXICAN ARMCHAIR

The shape of this chair is similar to high-backed chairs popular in Spain. The piece would have been made for an important member of society. The imported leather is gilt and painted with a floral design popular in marquetry and paintings. *17th century.*

ENGLISH ARMCHAIR

This English chair is made of oak and is upholstered on the back and seat in an expensive *gros point* needlework. When the chair was made, it probably had a fringe along the seat rail. The chair has turned bobbin legs. *1650–80.*

CARVED ARMCHAIR

This type of chair, made of solid ebony, was imported by the Dutch East India Company from India, Ceylon, and the East Indies. Carved on all surfaces, it has turned legs, terminating in small bun feet. This chair inspired Horace Walpole's furniture for his London house in the 18th century. *Late 17th century.*

Ebony is a very hard wood, and carving it required great skill from the maker.

The cane seat is a typical feature of Indian furniture.

Turned stretchers were popular.

ENGLISH SIDE CHAIR

This chair is made of indigenous beech, and has been japanned with Chinese symbols. It shows an early use of the caned seat, and illustrates the appeal of Oriental design. The curved legs resemble the cabriole legs popular in the 18th century. *c. 1675.*

CARVED ENGLISH SIDE CHAIR

This carved, tall oak chair has a pierced back and stretcher, and is the epitome of the Baroque style. The seat is upholstered in tapestry and has a shaped apron. This chair resembles designs by Marot (see p.45), which showed similar chairs in bedchambers. *17th century.*

EW ENGLAND SIDE CHAIR

pholstered in imported leather, this chair is ade of native maple. This form is properly rmed a "back stool" and is very similar to nglish examples, although these would have een made of oak. *1650–90. H:36 in 91.5 cm); W:18¼ in (46 cm) D:17¼ in (44 cm).*

SPANISH ARMCHAIR

This Spanish chair is made from walnut and would have been made for an important client. The owner's status is indicated by the heraldic symbols carved onto the wooden chair back. Originally the seat would have been covered with a cushion. *17th century.*

GERMAN ARMCHAIR

This impressive-looking high-backed armchair has a relatively plain frame, which is decorated with some relief carving. It is covered on the back and seat with elaborate upholstery. The piece sits on straight square feet with vats. *17th century. H:50½ in (126 cm). NAG*

SPANISH CHAIR

This solid walnut chair is decorated with carved rosette motifs, used all over the front of the chair. The back comprises two rows of spindles separated by a central rail, and the spindle design is continued with another row below the chair rail. *17th century.*

PANISH ARMCHAIR

his walnut armchair has a wide, high, arched ack and deep scrolled arms. The stamped eather upholstery, held in place by brass tacks, s typical of Iberian furniture of the period, as re the turned stretchers and carved, arched ain stretcher. *17th century.*

AMERICAN ARMCHAIR

This armchair is made of maple and red oak, two woods that are common in New England. The shape and style make it difficult to distinguish from English examples without identifying the wood. *1695–1710. H:53¼ in (135 cm); W:24 in (61 cm); D:27½ in (70 cm).*

ENGLISH SIDE CHAIR

This English walnut chair is a less expensive interpretation of a high-backed chair, with its caned seat and back. The turned legs are joined by carved stretchers, and the medial stretcher is arched. Originally the seat would have had a cushion. *1695–1705.*

FRENCH CHAIR

This is one of a pair of fauteuils. The front legs are turned, and linked with H-stretchers. The seat and back are covered with tapestry depicting characters from the Old Testament. *Late 17th century. H:49¼ in (123 cm); W:27½ in (69 cm); D:23¾ in (62 cm). BEA*

EARLY 18TH CENTURY

1700-1760

EXUBERANT LUXURY

IN THE EARLY 18TH CENTURY, COUNTRIES VIED WITH EACH OTHER TO EXPAND THEIR EMPIRES, AND THE ARISTOCRACY EMPHASIZED ITS POSITION WITH LAVISH DISPLAYS OF WEALTH AND LUXURY.

THE FIRST HALF of the 18th century was a time of transition, as the absolutist rule of monarchies diminished, paving the way for the rise of the wealthy middle classes. The end of the War of Spanish Succession in 1713 changed the balance of power in Europe, and ushered in a period of relative peace. This and greater wealth gave the aristocracy more time to pursue their interests in education, science, and the arts.

SHIFTING POWER

By the start of the century, Italy had lost much of its power and was no longer the cultural

leader of the western world. The influence of the Low Countries and Spain had also waned. France became politically less influential after the death of Louis XIV in 1715, so the stage was set for new powers to emerge. Great Britain was building its empire, not only expanding its American colonies, but establishing a stronger presence in India and throughout Asia. The resulting trade meant that the aristocracy and an increasingly wealthy merchant class indulged their tastes for expensive country houses and foreign travel, leading to a golden age of British design later in the century.

NEW BUILDING

Following extensive travels to the cultural centers of Europe, Peter the Great of Russia westernized his court and began building the city of St. Petersburg, using the finest European craftsmen and designers. Portugal grew wealthy on the spoils of the abundant diamonds and emeralds mined in its colony of Brazil. As a result, the Portuguese embarked on a massive program of palace-building and redecoration designed to glorify the monarchy, just as Louis XIV of France had done years before.

The accession of Frederick the Great of Prussia in 1740 heralded the Prussian rise to dominance in northeastern Europe. Meanwhile, across the Atlantic, America began to emerge from the shadow of Great Britain and the Low Countries and started to develop a national identity and style of its own.

AGE OF REASON

While Europe was mostly free from widespread wars,

An Italian giltwood girandole mirror c. 1770. H:34 in (86.5 cm). NOA

this was, nonetheless, a time of great change. It was the beginning of the Age of Enlightenment when writers and philosophers appealed to human reason and began to challenge traditional views on the church, the monarchy, education, and science. Louis XIV's concept of the monarch as God's representative on Earth was replaced by more liberal views, resulting in a wealth of radical new ideas in the sciences and a burst of creativity in the arts.

CHANGING STYLES

The more liberal cultural climate, compounded in many countries by an influx of craftsmen and designers from France, following the Revocation of the Edict of Nantes, ushered in a period of social change. As well as lavish royal palaces, smaller mansions were built for the minor aristocracy and the rising middle classes, and there was an increased demand for more informal, elegant, and comfortable interiors.

The grandeur and austerity of the Baroque style gradually gave way to the more eclectic tastes of the early 18th century, resulting, in many countries, in the lighter, more delicate Rococo style that originated in France. Rooms were now decorated with wood paneling, delicate, swirling stucco work, and pale colors highlighted with gilding and mirrors.

Exterior of the south facade of the Palacio Nacional, Queluz, Portugal
Work on the palace began in 1747, and it was designed both as a lavish display of wealth, and, as was fashionable, as a comfortable family home. It is often referred to as the "Versailles of Portugal."

TIMELINE 1700-1760

1703 Peter the Great lays the foundations of the city of St. Petersburg.

1707 England and Scotland united as Great Britain.

1709 Roman ruins discovered at Herculaneum, Italy.

1710 Jakob Christoph Le Blon invents three-color printing. Kaolin clay found in Germany, allowing porcelain to be made for the first time at Meissen.

Peter the Great

1714 Queen Anne of England dies. She is succeeded by George Louis, Elector of Hanover, as King George I.

1715 Louis XIV of France dies. He is succeeded by Louis XV (who was five years old) under the regency of Philippe, Duc d'Orléans.

French commode
This commode made of exotic inlaid woods is an exquisite example of Régence furniture. GK

1715 English translation of Palladio's *Four Books of Architecture* published.

1718 England declares war on Spain. New Orleans founded in America by the French.

1719 France declares war on Spain. Ireland declared inseparable from England.

1720 France prohibits the export of walnut, with repercussions for English cabinet-makers. German architect Johann Balthasar

Neumann starts work on the Residenz, a Rococo palace for the prince-bishops of Würzburg.

1721 Great Britain abolishes taxes on wood imported from the American colonies.

1723 The teenage Louis XV becomes King of France.

The Residenz in Würzburg

The Throne Room of the Palacio Nacional in Queluz, Portugal This room is the epitome of Rococo style, with its light stuccoed ceiling decorated with gilded, scrolling garlands and foliage. Glass-paneled doors, mirrors, and chandeliers reflect glittering light and add to the impression of exuberant luxury.

Giltwood console table This marble-topped Italian table continues the use of 17th-century motifs such as masks and strapwork, but is smaller in scale, reflecting the 18th-century taste for lighter, more feminine furniture. The carving incorporates Classical elements such as the acanthus and guilloche. *c. 1745. H:37½ in (95.5 cm); W:58½ in (148.5 cm); D:31 in (79 cm).*

1727 George I of England dies and is succeeded by his son, George II. William Kent publishes *The Designs of Inigo Jones*.

1729 Baltimore founded in America. North and South Carolina become crown colonies.

1730 Height of Rococo period in European art and architecture.

1732 Georgia, last of the 13 colonies, founded in America.

George II

1734 François de Cuvilliés designs the Amalienburg Pavilion for the gardens of the Nymphenburg Palace near Munich.

The circular hall of mirrors at the Amalienburg Pavilion, designed by François Cuvilliés.

1738 Excavation of Herculaneum begins.

1740 Accession of Frederick II of Prussia.

1741 Bartolomeo Rastrelli builds the Summer Palace, St. Petersburg.

1748 Roman ruins are discovered at Pompeii.

1751 Tiepolo paints ceiling of Würzburg Residenz.

Neptune and Amphrite An intricate mosaic from a wall of a house in Herculaneum, Italy, depicting the mythological King and Queen of the sea.

1753 Foundation of British Museum, London. Thomas Chippendale opens his first furniture shop.

1755 Lisbon earthquake kills 30,000 people.

1756 Great Britain declares war on France. Porcelain factory founded at Sèvres, France.

1759 Josiah Wedgwood founds his English ceramics company.

ROCOCO FURNITURE

IN THE FIRST HALF of the 18th century, furniture design was mainly influenced by France, and it was here that the Rococo style reached its height in the exuberant pieces of Juste-Aurèle Meissonier, Nicolas Pineau, and François de Cuvilliés. Meissonier decorated Louis XV's bedchamber with fantastic, asymmetrical designs featuring waterfalls, rocks, shells, and icicles. The new style took its name from the French word for rockwork: *rocaille* (rococo in Italian). Its features included flowers, arabesques, C- and S-shaped scrolls, cupids, Chinese figures, and scallop shells. Pineau, a Parisian wood-carver and interior designer, was Meissonier's contemporary. Their engravings influenced all the decorative arts and were copied in other publications and by other craftsmen, spreading the Rococo style far and wide.

In keeping with the latest demands for more informal and comfortable interiors, new types of rooms were designed for specific functions: drawing rooms (salons) both large and small where people could converse; and rooms for music, games, and reading. Reflecting the increasing social importance of women, the boudoir also first appeared at this time. Rococo design included all the elements of a room, not just the furniture, to create an integrated interior. The decorative features of the furnishings would mirror those in the wood paneling, doors, and chimneypieces.

THE NEW STYLES

Rococo furniture was interpreted in many different ways throughout Europe and America, but they all had certain features in common. Pieces of furniture were smaller, lighter, and more curvaceous in form than earlier styles, often with curved cabriole legs and pad or claw-and-ball feet. Women, such as Louis XV's mistress, Madame de Pompadour, were very influential and coveted small, decorative pieces that were suitable for intimate salons and appealed to the 18th-century taste for informality and leisure.

Many new types of chairs appeared, reflecting the demand for greater comfort and the interest in conversation. The high-backed chair, typical of Louis XIV's reign, gave way to chairs with a lower, slightly shaped back, a lighter frame, and visible wooden framework, including arched crest rails. Upholstered furniture was more widely available than before. Stretchers disappeared or were reduced to two cross-pieces in X-formation with restrained molding, although they were still occasionally used in Scandinavian and Spanish furniture.

Apart from console tables, which remained much the same, tables changed in various ways. Free-standing tables no longer had cross-stretchers, and baluster and pedestal legs were replaced by cabriole legs with a double S-curve. Scrolled or ogee bracket feet were common. Commodes first appeared at the beginning of the century, while the chest of drawers was added to a frame and then placed on top of another chest to produce a chest-on-chest. Many similar storage pieces developed, often designed for specific uses and positions within a room. By mid-century, many chests had built-in writing surfaces.

Mirror frames were the most flamboyant expression of early-18th-century style (*see pp.118–21*). This relatively new discipline allowed makers to indulge their wildest tastes, since frames did not have the same practical restrictions as other forms of furniture.

DECORATIVE INFLUENCES

Decoration was derived from Classical architectural motifs, Oriental patterns, and, in England, from Gothic designs. Oriental screens and lacquerwork were popular throughout the period. In colonial ports, japanning continued into the 1740s, while in France and England, lacquer panels were cut out of 17th-century furniture and incorporated into mid-18th-century pieces. Motifs depicting Chinese figures and willow trees appeared in all the decorative arts, but particularly in mid-century mirror frames, when the Rococo style was at its peak.

This **chest-on-chest** is typical of the English style. It has a pierced cartouche at the center of the pediment, and flowers and fruit suspended from griffin's beaks either side of the upper drawers. The writing surface is behind the bottom drawer. The lower case comprises three drawers. *c. 1725. H:88¾ in (222 cm). PAR*

This **duchesse brisée** has sumptuously upholstered cushions and a stool to support the legs. A new desire for comfort made the upholstered chair more popular.

This **bureau cabinet** has a typically English shape, but the inlay around the drawers, the construction, and the decoration suggest it was made by a German maker. *c. 1725. H:97 in (246.5 cm). PAR*

IMMIGRANT CRAFTSMEN

There is a long tradition of immigrant craftsmen disseminating styles and techniques. Not only had many Huguenot craftsmen left France following the Revocation of the Edict of Nantes, but many other craftsmen went abroad to work for European monarchs. In turn, monarchs sent their own craftsmen to Paris to learn the latest styles. As a result, many pieces have characteristics of more than one country. They adhere to the style popular in the country they were designed for, but use techniques more common to the maker's country of origin.

This **bureau plat** is attributed to Jean-Pierre Latz, a German working for Louis XV. German makers were renowned for their fine marquetry. *c. 1740. H:31½ in (80 cm); W:56½ in (143.5 cm). PAR*

THE COMMODE

Commodes first appeared at the beginning of the century at the court of Louis XIV. The form was quickly adopted by other countries and adapted to their particular needs. The term itself comes from the French word for greater convenience, *commodité*. The two-drawer commode on tall legs was the first version, but by the Régence it usually had three or more drawers on short feet (*commode à la Régence*).

During Louis XV's reign, the two-drawer chest on two curved legs with curved sides was favored. The facade was treated as a single decorative unit and the division between the drawers was ignored. Commodes were frequently made with a matching pair of corner cupboards known as *encoignures*. Pieces with a vertical curve were known as "*bombé*," while horizontal curves were called "serpentine."

This two-drawer commode is covered with black lacquer and decorated with chinoiserie motifs and fine floral bouquets and leaves. It has a cambered form with a curved apron and stands on high curved legs. This fine-quality piece was made in France and would have been the work of a very important maker. *c. 1750. W:38½ in (96.5 cm). GK*

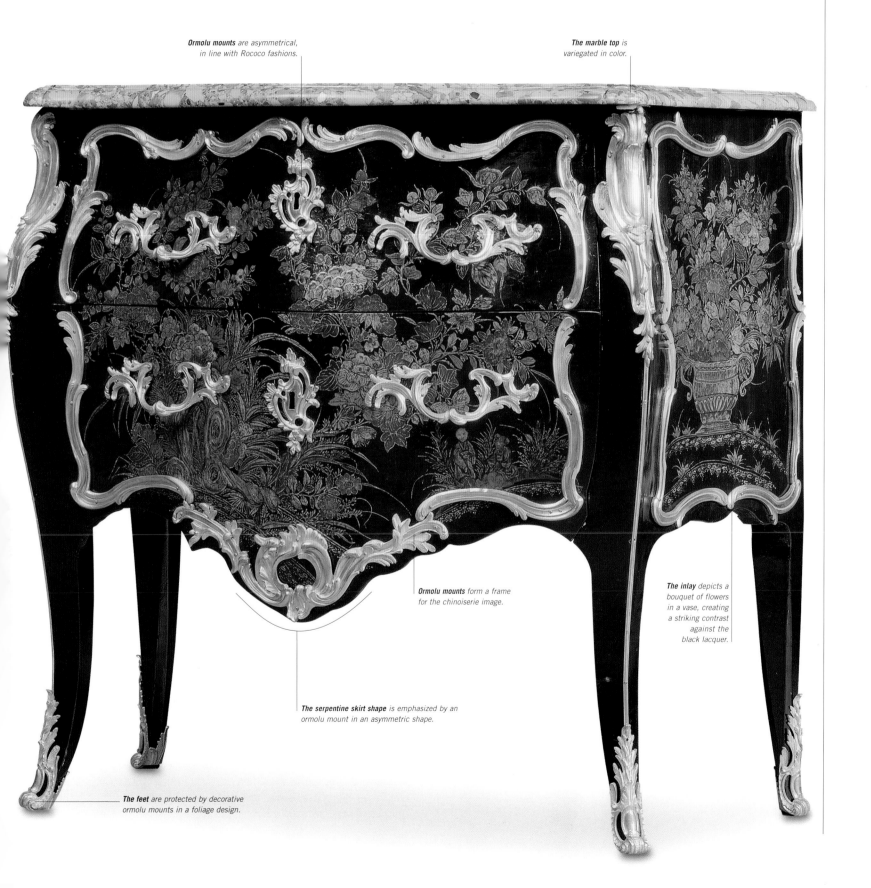

Ormolu mounts are asymmetrical, in line with Rococo fashions.

The marble top is variegated in color.

Ormolu mounts form a frame for the chinoiserie image.

The inlay depicts a bouquet of flowers in a vase, creating a striking contrast against the black lacquer.

The serpentine skirt shape is emphasized by an ormolu mount in an asymmetric shape.

The feet are protected by decorative ormolu mounts in a foliage design.

ELEMENTS OF STYLE

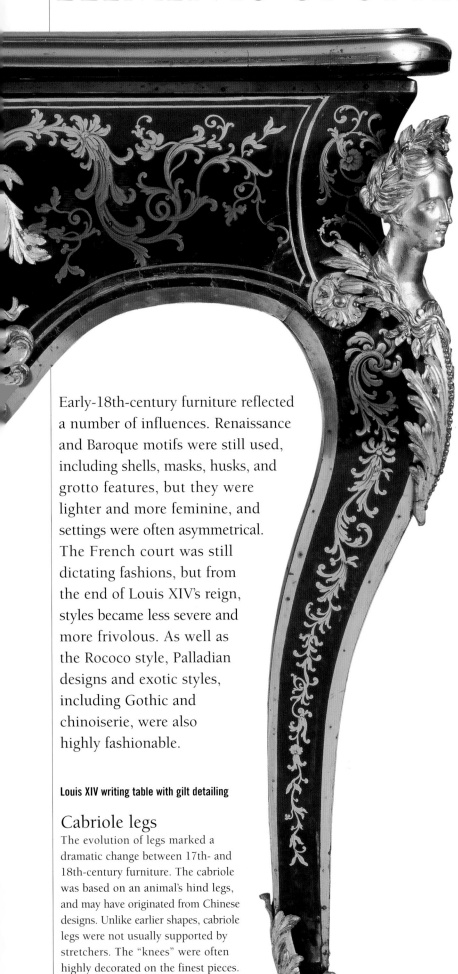

Early-18th-century furniture reflected a number of influences. Renaissance and Baroque motifs were still used, including shells, masks, husks, and grotto features, but they were lighter and more feminine, and settings were often asymmetrical. The French court was still dictating fashions, but from the end of Louis XIV's reign, styles became less severe and more frivolous. As well as the Rococo style, Palladian designs and exotic styles, including Gothic and chinoiserie, were also highly fashionable.

Louis XIV writing table with gilt detailing

Cabriole legs
The evolution of legs marked a dramatic change between 17th- and 18th-century furniture. The cabriole was based on an animal's hind legs, and may have originated from Chinese designs. Unlike earlier shapes, cabriole legs were not usually supported by stretchers. The "knees" were often highly decorated on the finest pieces.

Leather stamping on Portuguese hall chair

Stamped leather
Fine leather upholstery was made in Spain and Portugal and exported throughout Europe. It was often embossed or stamped with patterns, and also decorated with paint or gilt. Leather was used not only for upholstery but also for wall coverings, although this latter use became less popular in the 18th century.

Carved and gilt shell on Italian console table

Shell motif
The shell was used as early as the Renaissance, and represented Venus and love. During the Rococo period, shell motifs were used on tables, case furniture, chairs, and mirror frames. Rococo shells used curves to represent movement. This Italian shell curves under and sideways, and has incised gilding to add a sense of movement.

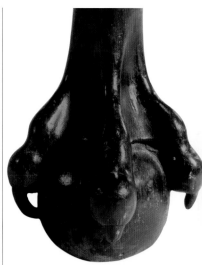

Claw-and-ball foot on English tea table

Claw-and-ball feet
This carved foot was usually the terminus for a cabriole leg. The design may be derived from the Chinese motif of a dragon's claw clasping a pearl. Early pieces tended to have wide-spaced claws, revealing much of the ball beneath, but on later pieces the ball was almost entirely hidden by the foot. At the start of the 18th century, pad feet were more common.

Female mask mount on commode

Ormolu mounts
Mounts made of cast bronze, with a fire-gilt finish, were integral to formal French furniture. Originally designed to protect veneer, mounts were also decorative. The mounts were fixed in place with pins. Craftsmen used the Classical Palladian and Rococo motifs of the time, as well as traditional motifs such as this Renaissance masque.

Detail from the top of a Régence commode

Floral marquetry

Elaborate pictorial designs in wood inlays were used as a decorative feature of furniture throughout the 18th century, although English cabinet-makers discarded marquetry in favor of carved ornament around 1730. The floral motif, derived from Dutch and Flemish paintings, remained popular in European furniture throughout the period.

Walnut side chair with solid back splat

Chair splat

The back splat of a chair is a good indicator of the chair's date and country of origin. A solid splat, as shown in this example, generally indicates a date between 1720 and 1740; the carved embellishments and rosettes suggest that this chair is closer to the later date. Pierced splats appeared later, when, generally, the back became squarer in shape.

Japanning on *secrétaire* cabinet

Chinoiserie

Trade with the Orient provided numerous designs and techniques suitable for furnishings—known as chinoiserie. Oriental figures and scenes adorned everything from porcelain to carved mirrors, while japanning, the European version of Oriental lacquer, was popular throughout the century. This scene is one of many similar panels on a rare, white-japanned, English bureau-bookcase.

C-scrolls on a tripod table base

Tripod table base

Cabinet-makers combined elements of different styles to great effect during the 18th century. Here, the central upright finial combines an acanthus plant base with a pine-cone top—both symbols from the ancient world. The tripod support is fashioned from elongated C-scrolls terminating in carved foliage—elements defining Rococo. A fluted column serves as a support for the table.

Carved putto

Mythological figures

Mythological figures, such as this putto, decorated all sorts of furniture, and sometimes referred to a specific place. Cabinet-makers in Naples, for instance, used the symbol of Neptune in their work, which referred to their city. Cherubs and putti reflected the increasingly feminine influence on furniture design.

Needlework panel from seat of Louis XV chair

Needlework

Thomas Chippendale stated that the backs and seats of his French design chairs "must be covered with Tapestry, or other sort of Needlework." French needlework was more formal than English designs. In England, pastoral scenes in *gros point* or *petit point* were popular. Unlike other needlework, tapestry was created on a loom.

Carved and gilt wooden table leg

Carved wood

Softer woods such as pine, beech, or lime wood were easier to carve than oak or walnut, so were particularly suited to the elaborately curved designs of the 18th century. Generally, these cheaper, "inferior" soft woods were covered in gesso and gilt. The carving under the gilt-gesso layer was incised to give greater definition.

Escutcheon on American mahogany chest

Escutcheons

Decorative keyhole surrounds often embraced fashionable styles more recognizably than the pieces of furniture themselves. This gilt metal cast plate was designed as an asymmetrical piece of foliage with an S-curve on the base, which is typically Rococo. Tiny gilt brass pins attach the plate to the case.

FRANCE: THE RÉGENCE

WHEN LOUIS XIV DIED in 1715, he left the throne to his young great-grandson, the future Louis XV, who was not legally permitted to become king for another eight years. Therefore, Philippe, Duc d'Orléans, was appointed regent from 1715 to 1723, a period known as the Régence.

The Duc d'Orléans moved the court to his Parisian home, the Palais Royal, where he initiated a more informal court style. He hired the architect Gilles-Marie Oppenord to supervise the massive interior redecoration of the Palais Royal. Oppenord, the son of a cabinet-maker, had lived in the Louvre and then trained in Italy, where

he studied architecture and copied Classical monuments. He designed the *Salon à l'Italienne* at the Palais Royal, with paneled walls and doors influenced by the innovative decorative paneling, known as *boiserie*, which Robert de Cotte had used in the Louvre during Louis XIV's reign. Oppenord's flamboyant, sinuous designs incorporated naturalistic carved flowers, leaf fronds, mythical figures, and mischievous animals, and the carving was deliberately asymmetrical, with decoration flowing freely over the edges of the panels. This extravagant, curvilinear style foreshadowed the blossoming of French Rococo.

Charles Cressent worked as both a sculptor and a cabinet-maker for the Duc d'Orléans, and carried out many of Oppenord's designs. Cressent made grand, marble-topped commodes with ormolu mounts, elegant writing desks, and many other pieces in the Rococo style. He also made furniture for Dom João V of Portugal and Charles Albert, Elector of Bavaria.

THE NEW STYLE SPREADS

The Court's move to Paris meant that Paris became fashionable, and the French nobility began to prefer city life to the isolation of their country residences. They refurbished their

grand homes in Paris and built new ones, and the merchant classes followed suit. Rooms remained sparsely furnished, with most of the furniture arranged symmetrically around the walls, to show off the highly polished wooden parquet floors. Furniture followed the significant changes to design and elements of Régence style that the refurbishment of the Palais Royal had introduced. Instead of having straight legs, cupboards, tables, and chairs were now slightly curved,

COMMODE "A FLEURS"

This large commode is made from walnut, veneered in exotic woods, and inlaid with ivory. The workmanship is exquisite, with a detailed floral and foliage pattern running across the shaped drawers. The imagery on the top of the commode is asymmetrical and depicts a vase of flowers with a bird to one side. The piece has three long drawers with bronze mounts, and stands on short cambered legs.
c. 1710. W:52 in (130 cm). GK

Simple bale handles with circular backplates serve as drawer pulls.

The escutcheons have a stylized shell and foliage design.

The edge of the top is decorated with an ormolu mount.

Short cambered legs covered in ormolu mounts support the case.

The shell and foliage mount relates to the elaborate marquetry of the piece.

The side panels are veneered with diamond-shaped panels decorated with inlaid flowers.

CARVED MIRROR

The arched mirror glass has an elegant giltwood frame, carved with flowers, foliage, and scallop shells. At the top is a female mask, carved in relief, on a cartouche of wave motifs and scrolling acanthus. At the base is a carved scallop shell and foliate sprays. *c. 1720. H:87 in (221 cm); W:51½ in (31 cm).*

CONSOLE TABLE

This Parisian table has a *brocatello siciliano*—colored marble-top resting on a gilded openwork apron, carved with a central mask, flowers, and leaves. The four cambered scroll supports are joined by a similarly carved cross-stretcher. *c.1730. W:55¼ in (138 cm). GK*

choing the contour of a crossbow (contour à l'arbalète). Veneers, including boullework (see p.55), were still popular, and thin bronze inlays were used to frame drawers, panels, edges, corners, and legs of furniture.

The commode evolved from the chest of drawers, and had curved legs and an exaggerated curved case, described as bombé. Pairs of commodes with pier glasses, or console tables, often flanked windows, and stools were designed to fit window embrasures. The most popular variation was the commode developed by Cressent. This piece had two drawers—one above the other—a serpentine front, and a shaped apron, supported on cabriole legs. The bureau Mazarin was replaced by the bureau plat—a writing table with three shallow drawers. These pieces were usually veneered in expensive woods and had ormolu mounts on the edges of the cases and feet, forming "shoes" known as sabots.

FASHIONABLE INFLUENCES

The new interest in salons, where people could gather for conversation, was led largely by women, and meant that elegant, less formal rooms became popular. Women also influenced chair design. This had changed little until about 1720, when the fashion for hooped skirts led to chair arms being shortened. Chair backs were lowered to accommodate the elaborate coiffures of the day. A desire for greater comfort brought about the creation of the bergère, an armchair with upholstered panels between the arms and seat. The fauteuil, an upholstered armchair with open sides, had many variations: the fauteuil à la Reine rested against the paneled wall of a room; while the smaller fauteuil en cabriolet could be moved to the center of a room. In reception rooms, the shapes of sofa and chair backs echoed the wall paneling, and the seating was upholstered in matching fabrics, usually costly woven silks.

COMMODE

This cherrywood, three-drawer commode originates from southwestern France. The main decoration of the piece is provided by the color of the polished wood, but the shaped sides and apron of the case are carved with cartouches, foliage and rocailles. The piece terminates in scroll feet. The escutcheons and drawer pulls are made of brass, and the locks are asymmetric in design; typical of the Rococo style. Early 18th century. H:39¼ in (98 cm); W:49¼ in (123 cm); D:39½ in (99 cm). ANB

TAPESTRY-COVERED FAUTEUIL

This walnut armchair has padded arms with scrolling carved supports. The cabriole legs are joined by a cross-stretcher and have outward-pointing toes. c. 1715. H:42 in (107 cm); W:29 in (73.5 cm); D:36 in (91.5 cm). PAR

PAINTED COMMODE CHAIR

This provincial chair is made of beech and has a cane seat and back, curved arms, and gently sweeping legs. The whole piece is painted, and has a floral decoration in relief on the front. c. 1760. H:35½ in (90 cm). CDK

ORNAMENTAL MOUNTS

ORNAMENTAL MOUNTS WERE USED AS DECORATIVE DETAILS ON FURNITURE, AND ALSO SERVED TO PROTECT THE EDGES AND VENEER OF A PIECE.

A mount is an ornament attached to furniture. Generally, mounts were made of gilt bronze, or ormolu. The term ormolu means "ground gold" and is derived from the French term bronze doré d'ormoulu.

Molten bronze was poured into a sand cast and the resulting rough bronze was cleaned and cut, then burnished or polished. Next, the finished surface was decorated with mercury and gold. Mercury gilding provided exquisite mounts, but the process was highly toxic.

Charles Cressent worked as a sculptor and ébéniste for the Regent, Philippe II, Duc d'Orléans, and created some of the finest ormolu of the period. His gilt-bronze mounts decorated his signature commodes, and featured naturalistic female figures, known as espagnolettes. These figures resemble the women in the paintings of Jean-Antoine Watteau (see p.78).

On larger case pieces such as commodes and bureaus, the design of ormolu mounts often signaled a change in fashion. Due to the small size of the mounts, ormolu makers could create mounts to reflect the latest fashions.

Commode "aux bustes de femmes" The bombé form of this kingwood commode is enhanced by the gilt-bronze mounts. Cast as female busts, they follow the curves. Gilded mounts have also been used to give shape to the scroll feet. c. 1720. H:52 in (130 cm). GK

Escutcheon   **Ormolu mask**

FRANCE: LOUIS XV

THE PREVAILING STYLE during Louis XV's reign (1723–74) became known as Rococo, and was fashionable from about 1730 to 1765. The style was a composite of influences, including exotic Chinese design, *rocaille*, based on shell-lined grottos; and fanciful arabesque and grotesque motifs popularized by Jean Bérain (*see p.55*).

Craftsmen in France worked within a strictly controlled guild system. Between 1743 and 1751, they had to stamp their initials on their work, followed by the letters J.M.E. (*juré des menuisiers et ébénistes*). As a result, much French furniture can be attributed to specific makers.

LE STYLE MODERNE

With origins in Régence design, Rococo, also known as the *style moderne*, ignored the rules of Classical architecture and was, essentially, a fantasy style with scrolls, shells, grotesque ornament, and foliage rendered in an unnaturalistic style. Ormolu mounts and carved decorations were very popular.

The style became sought-after by the French nobility and spread through Europe, owing to the influence of artisans such as Juste-Aurèle Meissonnier, a designer of gold and silver items. Along with Jean-Baptiste Pillement, Meissonnier developed the

genre pittoresque (the original term for Rococo). Pillement's engravings were used for marquetry as well as textiles and ceramics, and featured Oriental motifs including stylized Chinese figures, swirling foliage, and flowers.

DECORATIVE INFLUENCES

The sculptor and architect Nicolas Pineau published designs for carved decoration for walls, ceilings, fireplaces, console tables, and torchères, which were widely used by cabinet-makers such as Charles Cressent. These engravings spread the Rococo influence across the continent.

The paintings of Jean-Antoine Watteau introduced a new decorative feature, the *fête galante*. These garden scenes, showing aristocratic couples in amorous pursuits, were depicted in marquetry, painted furniture, and tapestries and textiles.

COMFORT AND INFORMALITY

New styles accommodated the desire for comfort and intimate conversation,

The brass gallery prevents items on the top from falling off the table.

The interior of the desk reveals the original color, protected from daylight.

The adjustable, silk-covered writing surface is supported by a bracket.

The cabriole legs are pierced and decorated with ormolu mounts.

SECRÉTAIRE À ABATTANT

This serpentine-fronted *secrétaire* is veneered in tulipwood, inlaid on the diagonal. The upper section opens to reveal a writing surface and six drawers. Ormolu banding frames the marquetry panels. The sabot feet have scrolling foot mounts. *c.1758. H:45 in (114 cm); W:39½ in (93 cm); D:15½ in (39 cm). PA*

LADY'S WRITING TABLE

This lady's writing table was made for Madame de Pompadour, Louis XV's mistress, by the German-born maker Jean-François Oeben. It is made of oak and veneered with mahogany, kingswood, tulipwood, and various other woods, and it is decorated with gilt-bronze mounts. The top displays marquetry patterns reflecting

Madame de Pompadour's love of the arts, including a vase of flowers, as well as designs representing architecture, painting, music, and gardening. Elements from the owner's coat of arms are included on the gilt-bronze mounts on each corner. When the top slides back to reveal the workings of the writing table, the surface area is almost doubled. *c. 1762. H:27½ in (69.8 cm); W:32¼ in (81.9 cm).*

CARVED GILTWOOD BERGÈRE

This is part of a four-piece suite. All the woodwork is carved with flowers and foliage. The bergère has a shaped rectangular back with a carved and shaped back rail, and is upholstered with silk damask. The curved seat rail leads into cabriole legs. *c. 1745. H:38½ in (97.5 cm); W:28 in (72 cm); D:26½ in (67 cm). PAR*

Interior of the Château de Bataille This elegant reception room is furnished in the comfortable, feminine style favored by wealthy French patrons of the period. Gilding and upholstery are much in evidence.

while existing forms evolved to fit new decorative schemes. Console tables were usually gilt or painted, and were highly carved, often in a softwood, such as pine. Motifs included foliage, shells, and C- or S-scrolls.

Chairs were designed to sit against walls, and reflected the paneling and architecture of the room. The upholstered sofa, or *canapé*, was, essentially, an elongated arched-backed *fauteuil á la Reine* (see p.52). Like bergère chairs, *canapés* were decorated in light Rococo colors, such as sea green, pale blue, yellow, lilac, or white, and enriched with gilt. Carved flowers often adorned chair frames.

WORK-RELATED FURNITURE
Wide writing tables, bureaux, were used in the bedchamber. They usually had three drawers at the front and back, although the back drawers were false. The decorated backs indicate that the pieces were designed to be used in the center of rooms. Homes often had rooms dedicated to work. The desk, or *secrétaire*, evolved from the medieval *escritoire* to become a case piece with a fall front.

THE COMMODE
Commodes were the most prestigious and expensive pieces of furniture and were lavishly ornamented. They were used in different rooms, including the bedchamber, although they were not used in reception rooms until later in the century. *Commodes à encoignures* (corner cupboards) had display shelves at either end. The *commode en console* appeared around 1750, and had a single drawer and long legs, designed principally in the Louis XV style. The *commode à vantaux*, which had two tiers of drawers behind two doors, was most popular during the reign of Louis XVI (1774–92).

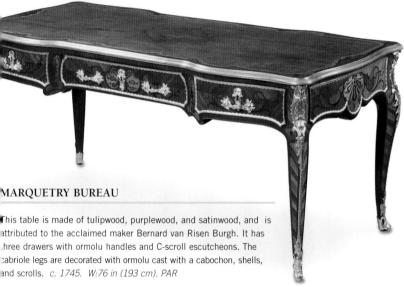

MARQUETRY BUREAU
This table is made of tulipwood, purplewood, and satinwood, and is attributed to the acclaimed maker Bernard van Risen Burgh. It has three drawers with ormolu handles and C-scroll escutcheons. The cabriole legs are decorated with ormolu cast with a cabochon, shells, and scrolls. *c. 1745. W:76 in (193 cm). PAR*

MARBLE-TOPPED COMMODE
This commode has two drawers, decorated with kingwood marquetry inlaid on a tulipwood ground. The central spray of flowers is positioned within a pierced ormolu cartouche. Pierced scroll and foliate mounts run down the cabriole legs and end in Rococo sabots. *c. 1750. W:42½ in (108 cm). PAR*

RED LACQUER ARMOIRE
This is an example of a two-door armoire, which began to replace the four-door buffet during the second half of the 18th century. This piece shows the fascination for lacquerwork and Chinese decoration that was rife throughout Europe at the time. The bright vermilion lacquerwork is decorated with floral motifs and butterflies in the Chinese style. The stand has a shaped apron, decorated with a gilt motif, and terminates in bracket feet. *c. 1750. H:62¾ in (157 cm); W:55¼ in (138 cm); D:22 in (55 cm). PAR*

ITALY

DURING THE FIRST HALF of the 18th century, most of the Italian states came under the control of Spain and Austria. Only Venice, Genoa, and Lucca remained independent, although the republics of Venice and Genoa declined in power and population.

ITALIAN ROCOCO

Italy was no longer a cultural leader in Europe. The noble landowners who built large palazzos were conservative on the whole, and the Baroque style was favored for longer than elsewhere. The only concession to changing

fashions, however, was that furniture for the main reception rooms was now conceived as an integral part of the interior.

Gradually, during the second quarter of the 18th century, as interiors became less formal, the lighter and more graceful Rococo style became more prevalent, reaching the height of its popularity from 1730 to 1750. Italian Rococo furniture was mainly influenced by French Régence and Louis XV styles, but it was embellished with decorative lacquerwork, colorful paintwork, and extravagant carved

details. Styles of furniture varied considerably from one region to another. Craftsmen in Piedmont were strongly influenced by neighboring France, and Genoese furniture was renowned for its skillful construction. Furniture from Lombardy was more sober and severe, whereas Venetian furniture was theatrical and colorful.

NEW FORMS

Italian chairs were often inspired by the French *fauteuil*, but had higher, fan-shaped backs, which were ornately carved and often gilded. Unpainted furniture was usually made of walnut, but fruitwoods were also common.

Side chairs, in the English style, had pierced splats with a central carved and pierced cartouche, and restrained cabriole legs. Some had flat stretchers. These chairs were often upholstered over the seat rail, rather than having slip-in seats. Caned examples also existed and more vernacular versions had rush seats.

Sofas, stools, and daybeds followed French fashion, although long settees with joined chair backs looked more like English examples. These settees were designed for specific reception rooms, such as the ballroom or the long rooms that ran from the front to the back of a palazzo.

SICILIAN COMMODE

This painted commode with its two drawers, subtly curved sides, and shaped legs, reflects the cabinet-maker's knowledge of French fashion. The paintwork on the panels of the sides and drawers is a simplified interpretation

of the arabesques, scrollwork, and foliage decoration seen on French commodes, and is influenced by the designs of French *ébénistes*, such as Jean Baptiste Pillement, who developed the *genre pittoresque* (*see p.78*). Paint is also used to simulate an expensive marble top. *c. 1760. W:60¼ in (153 cm). GK*

CARVED CONSOLE

This console has only two legs, since its back would be attached directly to the wall in a reception or state room. It is made of carved and gilded lime wood that was originally silvered. It features a grotesque mask flanked

by scrolling foliage—a popular motif from the 16th century until the mid-18th century—but the carving on this table is less ponderous and the face less threatening than on earlier examples. *c. 1720–30. H:40 in (101 cm); W:65 in (165 cm); D:33 in (84 cm). LOT*

PIETRO PIFFETTI (1700–70)

CABINET-MAKER TO THE KING OF SARDINIA, PIETRO PIFFETTI WAS ARGUABLY THE FINEST ITALIAN CABINET-MAKER OF THE 18TH CENTURY.

The illustrious artisan Pietro Piffetti was trained by the architect Filippo Juvarra, which is reflected in his very sculptural furniture. Piffetti worked with Juvarra to create dazzling rooms, with every surface covered in lavish Rococo decoration.

At a time when much Italian work was considered inferior in quality to French furniture, Piffetti was a virtuoso among the artist-craftsmen of Italy. His work is renowned for its detail and quality, even rivaling the great *ébénistes* of France.

Piffetti's furniture included highly intricate marquetry work in exotic woods and precious materials such as tortoiseshell, mother-of-pearl, and engraved ivory. His effusive style was more decorative than practical, and he became known for his "confectionery furniture". This frivolous style featured theatrical motifs, including scrolls and marquetry, and was the zenith of the flamboyant Rococo period.

Chest of drawers with bookshelves This imposing piece is decorated with Piffetti's characteristic marquetry in ivory and mother-of-pearl. The scenes are based on engravings of the siege of Troy. *c. 1760. H:123¼ in (308 cm).*

Serpentine commode with scrolling foliate arabesques in mother-of-pearl and ivory inlay. It has gilt-bronze handles and escutcheons. *c. 1735. H:39 in (99 cm); W:53¼ in (135.5 cm); D:24¼ in (64 cm).*

Most tables had attenuated, curved legs. Console and side tables were still heavily carved and gilded. The marble tops were inserted or framed rather than resting on top of the table. Tables were now made for specific rooms: the *trespoli*, for example, was for use in a bedroom, where it would support a dressing mirror. *Guéridons*, small tables often made in pairs, were popular and tended to have a single, rounded, carved support above a tripod base. Larger tables had carved stretchers, often with a cartouche or decoration at the junction in the middle.

Writing tables had been used since the 16th century, but new forms now appeared. The bureau, or bureau-cabinet, became quite common. The sides of a bureau were often squared and the central section serpentine in shape. Bureaux were veneered in complex geometric shapes, generally of walnut, or tulipwood in Genoa, or decorated with lacquer and paint.

The *credenza*, or cupboard, was made of fruitwood and had elongated bracket feet that extended from the front of the piece around to the side.

The bureau-bookcase, inspired by English versions, often had an exaggerated crest on top. The lower case had serpentine drawers, squared at the ends, and short bracket feet. Bureau-bookcases were usually made of walnut veneers, or were lacquered, gilded, and painted.

The French-style commode was also popular, though Italian versions often had shorter legs. While they rarely had gilt-bronze mounts, they were generally lacquered, and adorned with intricate veneer and paint.

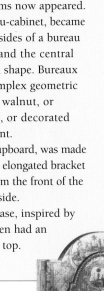

ARMCHAIR

This chair, probably from Genoa, is derived from the French *fauteuil à la Reine* but its back is wider at the top and the crest-rail cartouche is more exaggerated. The upholstery is not original. *c. 1760.* H:37 in (94 cm); W:23⅝ in (60 cm). GK

BUREAU

This walnut bureau is inspired by an English kneehole desk, but its slope and upper drawer overlap the smaller drawers. It has wider, shorter, bracket feet, and its geometric veneer is more flamboyant. H:41 in (104 cm); W:47 in (119 cm). GK

Japanned panels depict pastoral scenes.

The central mirror hides shelves and drawers.

Red japanning covers the whole piece.

The slope opens to reveal pigeonholes and drawers.

Classical landscapes in lacca contrafatta—*lacquerwork*— cover the visible surfaces.

The canted corners and sides terminate in scrolled acanthus and carved feet.

BUREAU-CABINET

This extravagant bureau-cabinet made in Rome for Pope Pius VI is decorated with japanning, lacquerwork, and gilding. The figures on the top represent the four seasons. *Early 18th century.* PAR

ITALY: VENICE

DURING THE 18TH CENTURY, Venice faded as a trading republic and was politically isolated from the other regions. However, the cosmopolitan Venetian Republic excelled as the capital of taste, fashion, and luxury, rivaling the reputation of Paris.

A GRAND PALAZZO

The grand palazzi faced directly onto the larger canals, and it was here that the finest furnishings were enjoyed by Venice's wealthiest citizens. Huge antechambers measured about 120 ft (36 m), and special furniture was created for these rooms. A long *bergère* with an upholstered back, the *pozzetto*, was designed to be placed against the walls, as was the exaggerated *divani da portego*, a long settee.

Bedchamber from the Sagredo Palace, Venice, c. 1718.
The furnishings relate to the overall architectural theme. The sculptural quality of the ceiling is reflected in the ornately carved headboard.

The family bedchambers and associated rooms were furnished in luxurious velvet and damask, often fringed or laced with gold. The floors were laid with marble or scagliola (*see p.43*), and the frescoes on the skirting boards and ceilings added more color. At times, the overall effect could be overpowering, and the furniture and decoration competed for prominence.

FURNITURE STYLES

Much Venetian furniture was brightly painted or decorated with lacquer, silver, or gilt, and ornately carved.

Venetian design was the embodiment of the effusive Rococo style, which remained fashionable in Venice after its popularity had waned elsewhere. Although the furniture retained the sculptural qualities of the Baroque, the carving was lighter and more delicate. Scrolls, serpentine outlines, and *bombé* shapes were common. Cabriole legs were often decorated with Rococo carving. New types of furniture included girandole mirrors, and *guéridon* tables that had a candlestand base supporting a marble top. Even large pier tables had carved and pierced frames that were gilded or painted in the Rococo style. In addition to pier mirrors or glasses placed over pier tables (*see p.120*), other mirrors were introduced that often contained colored panels of glass interspersed with the mirror glass.

Chests of drawers ranged from the French commode to smaller pieces such as the *cassettoncino*, typically with three serpentine-shaped drawers with square ends. These were often veneered in walnut, and supported on ball or bracket feet. Pairs of small chests, *comodini*, painted or veneered in walnut, had a single door, sometimes with a drawer above, and were raised on short, curved or scrolled feet. Another popular form was a small, *bombé*-shaped, two-door chest.

In addition to the grand *pozzetto* and *divani da portego*, the Venetians created carved, lacquered armchairs with shaped crest and seat rails.

As well as painted or lacquered furniture, pieces made solely of walnut or walnut veneer were fashionable, including summer versions of the long *pozzetto*, with caned backs and seats.

LACQUER

Lacquerwork was highly popular in Venice, and was used to adorn everything from commodes to armchairs. Chinoiserie designs imitated imported Far Eastern lacquer, but Venetian craftsmen incorporated whimsical floral motifs, often with foliage. It often took 20 layers of varnish to complete the lacquer process. Although the outsides of pieces were effusively decorated, the interiors were often relatively plain. Light colors were popular for lacquer, especially yellow, gold, and blue.

VENETIAN COMMODE

Venetian cabinet-makers favored lacquered furniture throughout the 18th century. This Venetian two-drawer, black-lacquered commode is inspired by Louis XV styles, but is wider and bulkier than French examples. There are two long drawers and the drawer division is emphasized by gilded molding. The legs are less sinuous than French examples and the case lacks ormolu mounts. The black lacquer is highlighted with a delightful series of Chinoiserie motifs with landscapes, fantastic creatures, and stylized flora. *c. 1750. GK*

The sides of the cupboard are canted.

The triangular top is made from Levanto Rouge marble.

The carcass is decorated with Rococo motifs.

The cupboard door is decorated with Chinoiserie motifs.

Five cabriole legs support the piece.

CORNER CUPBOARD

One of a pair, this polychrome cupboard is decorated all over with sprays of flowers and scrolling foliage on a light blue-green background, and carved with stylized shells and *rocaille*. The marble top sits above a concave molded frieze. The cupboard door depicts an Oriental figure, but the interior of the cupboard is plain. The sides are canted and the piece terminates in five short cabriole legs, one of which still retains its paper label. *Mid-18th century. H:34 in (86 cm); W:25½ in (65 cm); D:21½ in (54.5 cm).*

GILDED PIER TABLE

This pine table is gilded and silvered. The top is painted to simulate marble: the rear edge is so realistic it appears to have the mason's saw marks where the unfinished marble would be placed against the pier. The exaggerated scroll of the legs is emphasized by inner knee scrolls. The table has an interlaced stretcher with a central carved cartouche, and the legs terminate in stylized hoof feet. *c. 1760. H:36½ in (93 cm); W:53½ in (136 cm); D:26 in (66 cm). JK*

UPHOLSTERED ARMCHAIR

One of a pair, this armchair is made in the style of a French design, although the cartouche-shaped back is wider and higher than those on French examples. The frame of the back is molded and the central cartouche more exaggerated than is typical of French chairs. The frame is carved all over rather than highlighted with carved floral elements. The scrolled legs and pierced seat rail illustrate the Rococo love of fluid curves and movement. *c. 1745.*

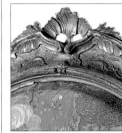

Detail of the crest rail

LACCA POVERA

THIS INNOVATIVE DECORATIVE TECHNIQUE, WHICH IS NOW OFTEN REFERRED TO AS DÉCOUPAGE, ORIGINATED IN VENICE IN THE MID-18TH CENTURY.

Lacca povera (poor man's lacquer) is also known as *arte povera* (poor man's art), or *lacca contrafatta* (fake lacquer). In mid-18th-century Venice, the taste for lacquerwork was so great that artists developed *lacca povera* as an alternative in order to meet the demand. This new, and relatively inexpensive, technique evolved alongside traditional lacquerwork.

THE TECHNIQUE

Craftsmen used engravings to decorate furniture and other objects. These images were often obtained from specialist firms who produced sheets of engravings especially for *lacca povera* decoration. These were then colored, cut, and pasted onto a prepared surface. Several layers of varnish were applied to create a surface that resembled the high-gloss effect of traditional lacquerwork, and the best examples resembled imports from the Orient. Initially, craftsmen favored Chinoiserie designs, but European motifs

also became popular, as seen on this bureau-bookcase. The influence of the painter Jean Watteau (*see p.78*) and the designer Jean Bérain (*see p.55*) can be seen. The printed scenes varied from extravagant *rocailles* to maritime and pastoral themes. On the finest *lacca povera*, details were picked out in gilt or engraved once the varnish had dried. The most common color for the background was red. Rare white *lacca povera* is now highly prized. Desks, chairs, tables, cabinets, and screens were all decorated using this technique.

DÉCOUPAGE

The center of professional production was Venice, but the technique became popular throughout Europe. In France the technique was renamed découpage, from the French word *couper*, meaning to cut. This skill was taught to ladies in the 18th century, and was mainly used on smaller, decorative objects, as it is today.

Decorated interior.

Detail of the *lacca povera*.

Bureau-bookcase This piece is profusely decorated with *lacca povera* on a cream ground depicting mythical beasts, lions, camels, Classical gods and Father Time, and floral and heraldic motifs. *1735. H:82½ in (210 cm); W:40 in (102 cm); D:21½ in (55 cm). MAL*

Gilt moldings with arabesque decoration surround the doors.

The mirror plates on the doors are replacements.

The upper section opens to reveal drawers and pigeon holes.

The slant-front desk and narrow drawer are part of the upper section.

The lower drawers depict period carriage scenes and pastoral landscapes.

GERMANY

GERMANY AT THIS TIME was made up of over 300 principalities, loosely bound into the Holy Roman Empire. Only three of the German states were large enough to compete as powers on a European scale: Bavaria, Saxony, and Brandenburg-Prussia. The princely rulers vied with each other for power and prestige, building magnificent Baroque palaces and Rococo pavilions at enormous cost.

FRENCH INFLUENCE

The most clearly defined German styles of the time were Bavarian and Frederician Rococo. Under the patronage of Maximilian II Emanuel, Elector of Bavaria, and King Frederick the Great of Prussia, architects and cabinet-makers were encouraged to take inspiration from France.

A French designer of particular significance was François Cuvilliés, who was employed by the Elector of Bavaria. Cuvilliés's spectacular interiors at the Residenz and the Amalienburg Pavilion in Munich represent the height of German Rococo. Swirling, gilded, carved wood decorations covered the walls and furniture of Cuvilliés's interiors, with motifs ranging from pure rocaille to sculptural figures, masks, and animals.

GERMAN ROCOCO

Early-18th-century German furniture was heavier in style than French or Italian pieces. Commodes and cabinets, in particular, were massive and were decorated with typical Rococo motifs, such as scrolls, shells, cartouches, and fantastic foliage. Enormous bureau-bookcases were serpentine in shape and had scrolled legs and tiny scrolled feet. Glass-fronted display cabinets were painted in pale Rococo colors, such as white and gilt, and decorated with shells, foliage, and scrolls. Commodes had exaggerated curves.

As in France, furniture, usually carved and gilded or painted, was designed for an integrated interior. Special rooms or themes, such as the garden, often influenced the decoration. The desire for informality inspired new types of furniture. Fire screens, couches and settees, writing tables, and carved and gilded console tables were made for the wealthy.

Typical 17th-century furniture, such as the two-part cupboard and the wardrobe, was still made well into the 18th century. Carving tended to emulate French *boiserie* paneling, and great emphasis was placed on the woods chosen for veneers. Walnut, engraved ivory, fruitwoods, sycamore, and green-stained softwoods were used for both marquetry and veneers. Lacquerwork was still popular, and exquisite cabinets and tables, often made in Berlin, were decorated with fashionable chinoiserie patterns and *fêtes galantes* (see p.78).

Unlike French furniture, which is usually stamped with the maker's name, German furniture of this period is rarely attributed to specific makers. This is because in Germany at this time, the best cabinet-makers were employed by the royal courts and worked directly for their employers. They lived in the grounds of palaces, had workshops there, and were often salaried.

THE UTILITY OF SPLENDOR

These Court workshops (which housed carpenters, sculptors, plasterers, upholsterers, and gilders) now delivered complete arrangements for newly refurbished state apartments. During the 18th century, simple rooms evolved into specific ones designed for a particular activity. Antechambers tended to be very sparsely furnished, perhaps with just a pier table. In the formal entertaining room—the focus of Court events—the prince's armchair would be raised on a carpet-covered platform. Although by far the most elaborate chair in the room, its style would be matched by the remaining chairs. Desks and commodes could be found in private reception rooms.

The *chambre de parade* became the highlight of social activity, where the nobility would meet and converse or play cards. From around 1720, these rooms had large, floor-to-ceiling windows. These allowed light to flood into the room; the light was then reflected in huge mirrors on the facing walls. In the wealthiest homes, furniture was gilded, as were the candleholders on mirror frames and the elaborate paneling on the walls and ceilings.

FRANÇONIAN COMMODE

This commode has a carcass of lacquered lime wood, and is decorated with carved and gilt moldings and escutcheons. The drawers are edged with curving rocaille borders and the escutcheons are surmounted by shells and scrolling foliage. The curved apron has a shell in the center. The scrolled feet are also typically Rococo. It was probably commissioned by the Prince-Bishop of the Würzburg Residenz in Franconia and is, unusually for German furniture, attributed to specific cabinet-makers: Johann Wolfgang van der Auvera and Ferdinand Hund. *c. 1735. H:31½ in (80 cm); W:57 in (145 cm); D:24¾ in (63 cm). PAR*

Detail of japanning

CABINET-ON-STAND

This cabinet-on-stand, which possibly originates from Berlin, is covered in red and black japanning, decorated with gold. The interiors of the doors are covered with black japanning and open to reveal ten drawers, painted to resemble the work of the celebrated French artist Jean- Antoine Watteau who painted elaborate parties held outdoors, known as *fêtes galantes*. The front and sides of the piece are decorated with similar patterns. The stand has a shaped apron and elegant, slim cabriole legs, also decorated with red japanning and gold. *Early 18th century. H:18 in (46 cm); W:35½ in (90 cm); D:15¾ in (40 cm).*

CONSOLE TABLE

This elegant console table has a red and white rounded marble top. The frame of the table consists of highly carved wood, which has been gilded and painted. The intricate, open-work frieze depicts floral and foliate motifs, and leads into similarly styled cabriole legs. *Early 18th century. H:26¾ in (92 cm).*

The open pediment is carved with volutes.

The cabinet interior

The mirrored doors have beveled glass plates.

The fall front is serpentine in shape.

The concave drawers have canted and rounded edges.

Detail of the locks

Gilt-metal and ormolu mounts decorate the whole piece.

Detail of seat rail

GARDEN CHAIR

Made of carved, gilded, and painted linden wood, this chair is part of a suite of "garden furniture" made for the Schloss Seehof in southern Germany. The frame and legs are decorated with carved trellis, leaves, and flowers. The seat is covered in green velvet, completing the garden theme. *1764. H:44 in (112 cm).*

The inside of the doors

DRESDEN BUREAU-CABINET

This imposing cabinet is made of rosewood and burr elm and decorated with ormolu and gilt-metal. It has a volute-carved open pediment above mirrored doors, framed by foliate and rocaille clasps. The fitted interior has 15 walnut-lined drawers around a central compartment flanked by Classical-style columns. The compartment is decorated with an ivory, ebony, and rosewood parquetry floor and mirrored sides and back. The fall front opens to reveal seven drawers arranged around a central mirrored compartment. The four concave-fronted drawers are decorated with gilt volutes, cabochons, rocaille, and foliage. The piece stands on a stepped and molded plinth. *c. 1740. H:93 in (236 cm); W:54½ in (141 cm); D:31 in (79 cm).*

ROCOCO INTERIOR

THE ELABORATE DESIGN OF THIS SUMPTUOUS HUNTING PAVILION DISPLAYS THE SPLENDOR OF GERMAN ROCOCO INTERIOR STYLE AT ITS VERY BEST.

Gilded cherubs playing musical instruments adorn the walls of the grand pavilion.

Musical instruments were popular motifs, both as interior decoration, and also on pieces of furniture.

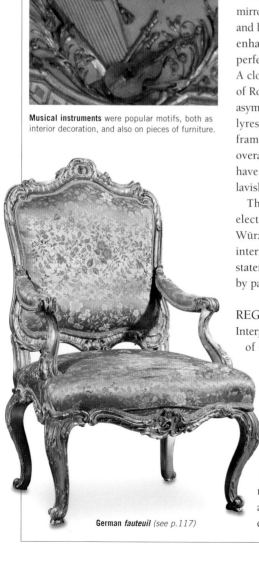

German *fauteuil* (see p.117)

BY THE SECOND quarter of the 18th century, modern French manners, and with them the delicate, playful design of the Rococo, were the height of fashion. The aristocracy and the upper middle classes aspired to status and a refined lifestyle, inspired by the court of Louis XIV.

A HOME FIT FOR A KING

It was against this backdrop that Max Emanuel, the elector of Bavaria, redesigned his Munich Residenz and extended his summer palace at Nymphenburg. He employed Joseph Effner, who became the chief court architect and furniture designer, and the French-educated architect François Cuvilliés. Both were influential in introducing the light, intimate Rococo style to the elector's estates. Their designs cast aside the formality of Baroque architecture in favor of a freer, more intimate feel. In 1735, Cuvilliés started work on the Amalienburg pavilion in the palace gardens of Nymphenburg. Built as a hunting lodge for Electoress Amelia, the interior became the epitome of Bavarian Rococo.

The magnificent centerpiece of the Amalienburg, the mirror room, is ringed by ornately framed silver-gilt mirrors and lit by elaborate chandeliers. The pale bluish-green walls enhance the feeling of delicacy and light and provide a perfect backdrop to extensive silver stucco decoration. A closer look at the applied design work reveals an array of Rococo motifs and scenes; naturalistic birds fly above asymmetrical floral swags hanging from borders of cherubs, lyres, and scrolling leaves. Expansive paneled mirrors, framed by shells and S-curves, reflect and multiply the overall effect of movement and vivacity. This room would have been used for entertaining, including banqueting and lavish celebrations.

The Amalienburg style spread through Germany. The elector of Mainz transformed the interior of his Baroque Würzburg Residenz with an almost overwhelming Rococo interior. Ornate stucco was added to Balthasar Neumann's staterooms, including an elaborate mirror room enhanced by painted portrait cartouches.

REGIONAL VARIATIONS

Interpretations of Rococo varied greatly from one region of Germany to another. The furniture produced to compliment fashionable interiors was particularly diverse. Although many pieces were fairly conservative in form, as a result of the influence of the guilds, decoration was elaborate, and typically included naturalistic motifs and scrolling lines. Furniture from Munich was often heavily carved and gilded. Although inspired by a French movement and diverse in style, Rococo furniture at the highest end of the market, and the interiors of the Amalienburg, Würzburg and other fine palaces, are distinctly German in their elaborate nature and grand scale.

THE LOW COUNTRIES

WHEN WILLIAM, Prince of Orange and King of England, died in 1702, he left no adult heir. For the following 45 years, the Low Countries were ruled by councillor pensionaries and regents. The first half of the 18th century was a period of stability. Dutch trade and shipping maintained the levels reached during the 17th century, and money was ample.

SOMBRE DESIGN
Furniture design reflected the prevailing attitude of conservatism and there was little innovation. Many forms imitated British examples, the major differences being not in design, but in the choice of woods and the use of marquetry. While marquetry was no longer fashionable in Great Britain, it continued to flourish in the Low Countries.

Chairs were similar to British designs, although the seat rails tended to be more serpentine in shape, and some chairs had a serpentine blocked seat rail with a shaped lower central section. Settees were also similar to British models, with high backs and wings with curved armrests, but stretchers remained fashionable well into the 1740s, unlike in Great Britain.

SIGNATURE PIECE
The bureau-cabinet, which developed in England around 1700, was common throughout much of the 18th century. Versions with two doors were often fitted with mirrors, a feature that was used throughout the century.

The china cabinet was also popular. Similar in shape to the bureau-cabinet, the upper section had glazed doors in front of display shelves. There were several different designs for the lower section, each distinctive of furniture from the Low Countries. If the piece had straight sides, the corners were chamfered and extended outward in heavy, overgrown scrolls. Otherwise, the lower section was designed in a *bombé* shape. Drawers were rounded, blocked, or serpentine.

Both the bureau-bookcase and the china cabinet illustrated the desire in the Low Countries for versatile, dual-purpose furniture. Generally, the upper case was used to display books or ceramics, while the drawers in the lower section provided storage for household linens, or even clothes.

UNIQUE ELEMENTS
The commode did not become popular until the middle of the century. It was similar to British examples until about 1765, tending to have four drawers or doors covering shelves. The choice of wood, the use of imported mounts, and the heavier shape of commodes from the Low Countries help to differentiate them from British versions. Burr walnut was the veneer of choice in the Low Countries. It was not until the 1730s that mahogany—a wood commonly used in British furniture—was used in Rotterdam, a city in which British influence was particularly strong. From the mid-18th century, the Low Countries exported ornamental mounts to Britain.

As there was no reigning monarch, the highly ornate styles of the French court were not as influential in the Low Countries as elsewhere in Europe, and British design was the style of choice.

Dutch armchair, made in a typical George II style, but decorated with floral marquetry. The cabriole legs terminate in claw-and-ball feet, but as with many mid-century pieces, the chairs lack stretchers. *c. 1750. DN.*

DUTCH COMMODE

This mahogany, serpentine-shaped commode is influenced by English style, having two doors that open to reveal an interior fitted with shelves. This piece has little decoration, although originally the case may have been embellished with ormolu mounts and escutcheons. The pierced gilt-brass gallery at the back is a later addition. The piece stands on outswept bracket feet. *c. 1770. H:35 in (89 cm). DN.*

CHEST OF DRAWERS

The four-drawer chest of drawers is veneered with figured and burr walnut, which has subsequently been framed in bands of tulipwood. The top and the waved apron are also shaped to reflect the curves of the case. The chamfered corners of the chest extend into heavily scrolled sides and legs and terminate in scrolled feet. This style is typical of furniture from the Low Countries. *c. 1750. H:32¼ in (82 cm); W:34¼ in (87 cm); D:21 in (53 cm).*

GILTWOOD MIRROR

This mirror is made up of two pieces of plate in a frame with asymmetrical cartouches at the top and base. Its pilaster sides are wrapped in foliage. C-scrolls flank a pediment with two carved birds. *c. 1760–70. H:71 in (180 cm); W:38 in (97 cm).*

BUREAU-BOOKCASE

This bureau-bookcase, of softwood and oak, is veneered in walnut, with rosewood fillets. The lower case has a serpentine front, *bombé* shape, and sits on high volute feet. It is crowned with a phoenix and has an interior mirror. *c. 1760. H:114 in (290 cm). LPZ.*

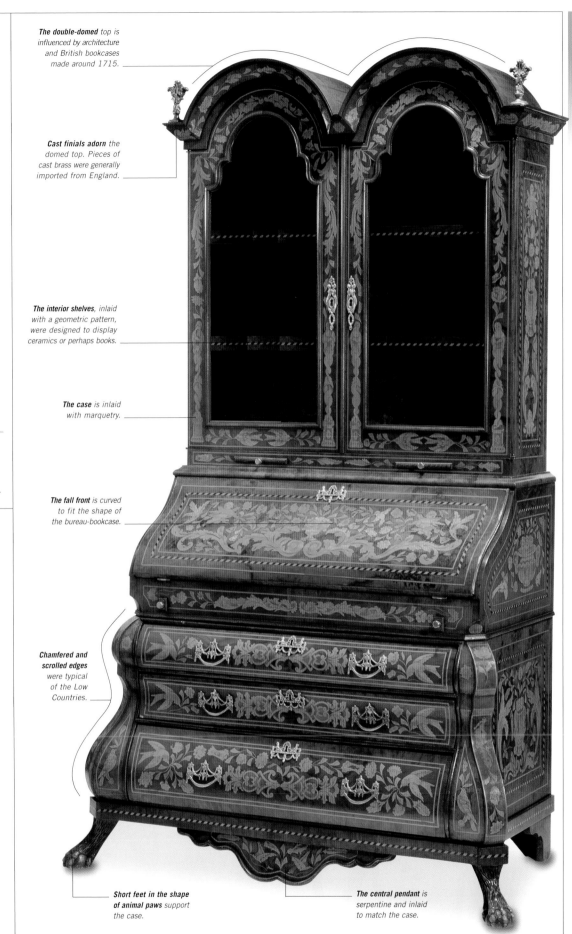

The double-domed top is influenced by architecture and British bookcases made around 1715.

Cast finials adorn the domed top. Pieces of cast brass were generally imported from England.

The interior shelves, inlaid with a geometric pattern, were designed to display ceramics or perhaps books.

The case is inlaid with marquetry.

The fall front is curved to fit the shape of the bureau-bookcase.

Chamfered and scrolled edges were typical of the Low Countries.

Short feet in the shape of animal paws support the case.

The central pendant is serpentine and inlaid to match the case.

BUREAU-BOOKCASE WITH FLORAL MARQUETRY

This bookcase is typical, in both shape and design, of furniture from the Low Countries. As a bureau-bookcase, it serves the triple purposes of providing a writing surface, a display cabinet, and storage. The piece has graduated drawers below a serpentine fall front: each drawer gradually increases in size from top to bottom. Covered in floral marquetry and some pictorial marquetry depicting exotic birds, cherubs, urns, and scrolling foliage, this bureau-bookcase also has chinoiserie-style escutcheons. The attached curved scrolls are often seen on case furniture from the Low Countries. *18th century. H:81½ in (207.5 cm). FRE.*

SPAIN AND PORTUGAL

STYLE DEVELOPMENTS IN Spain and Portugal were influenced by royal marriages and also by the success of Louis XIV of France. Philip V of Spain's marriage to Italian-born Elizabeth Farnese and his son's marriage to the daughter of Dom João V of Portugal both brought stylistic influences from abroad.

THE LEGACY OF VERSAILLES

Philip V remained in awe of the achievements of his grandfather,

Louis XIV, while Italian influence came from his wife's use of architects and painters from Italy, notably Filippo Juvarra and Giovanni Battista Sacchetti.

Dom João V's reign coincided with the discovery of gold and diamonds in colonial Brazil. He used his fabulous wealth to develop a national monarchy modeled on the absolute rule of Louis XIV, and, like Louis, wanted art and literature to glorify his rule as sovereign. To this end, he spent vast sums on Parisian furniture, and commissioned

Charles Cressent (*see p.76*) and Juste-Aurèle Meissonnier (*see p.78*) to design furniture. He ordered his marital bed from Holland, made to a design by Daniel Marot (*see p.45*).

A STYLE OF ITS OWN

Furniture from the Iberian peninsula was unique. Although inspired by designs from France, Italy, and—through trade links—England, it also incorporated colonial references and materials, such as Brazilian hardwoods, jacaranda, pausanto, and rosewood. Portuguese furniture was

particularly heavy due to the density of the woods used. Japanning, which had gone out of favor in France and England, was still popular, and English cabinet-makers capitalized on this, exporting cabinets japanned in vivid colors such as scarlet, yellow, and gold to their wealthy clientele.

Chairs were based on the French *fauteuil*, with high backs, leather upholstery, and carved upper rails with a central stylized shell. They often had gilt carving, ball-and-claw feet, and square stretchers. The fashion for pannier dresses, with their wide skirts, led to a demand for chairs with broader seats, and arms that curved

A central cartouche is positioned on the carved frieze.

The stretchers are joined by ornate foliate carving.

The cabriole legs are decorated with carving.

Scroll feet support the piece.

SPANISH CONSOLE TABLE

One of a pair, this ornate console table is carved, gilded, and silvered. It has a serpentine, faux marble top, above a carved frieze decorated with *rocaille* and foliage, and a cartouche at its center. The top is mounted on carved cabriole legs, joined by a cross-stretcher. The carving is less flamboyant than that found on Italian pieces of the period. The curve of the leg is not very pronounced, and is heaviest where the leg meets the table frame. *c. 1750.* H:30¾ in (78 cm); W:50 in (127 cm); D:24¾ in (63 cm).

SPANISH WARDROBE

This fruitwood *armario* is a vernacular piece. The cornice is decorated with small, tooth-shaped blocks, known as "denticulation." It is less heavy than earlier styles. *Early 18th century.* H:73 in (185.5 cm); W:49 in (124.5 cm). MLL

PORTUGUESE TABLE

This drop-leaf table is made of jacaranda. The end drawer has a brass lock and drawer pull above a carved apron. The table stands on six slender, cabriole legs—two of which swing out to support the leaves. *Mid-18th century.* H:30⅓ in (77 cm); W:40½ in (103 cm).

CONSOLE TABLE

This Portuguese carved mahogany console table has an inset marble top above a serpentine frieze. The corners are carved with stylized shells, and the whole table is decorated with *rocaille* and foliage. The piece stands on cabriole legs and terminates in claw-and-ball feet. *Early 18th century.* H:34¼ in (87.5 cm); W:45¼ in (115 cm).

The Royal Bedroom in the Hall of Don Quixote, Palacio Nacional, Queluz, Portugal Rococo-style elements include the parquet floor, parquetry decorated bed, and the French-inspired *boiserie* room decoration.

outward. These chairs usually had an English-style splat, with gilt edges, which flowed into a carved upper rail and stiles. The legs were cabriole and had gilt leaves carved on the knees.

The 18th-century folding chair was similar to earlier versions with straight legs, but its stretchers were either flat or turned. The chair back was now shaped, with a central carved shell or a vase-shaped back splat.

In Portugal, Brazilian rosewood was often used, and the upper panel and seat were upholstered in leather, stretched across the top of the rear legs, to allow the chair to fold inward. The settee, made up of a number of chair backs, was more common than the French *canapé*.

Cupboards, commodes, and bureaux were large and relied on the grain of the wood for decorative effect. Scrolled feet, while in proportion, were wider and lower than on furniture made elsewhere in Europe.

Portuguese pier tables were usually made of carved and gilded pine or rosewood. Rococo motifs were applied around the rectangular frame of the matching mirror that was positioned above the table. Portuguese tables were often larger than Italian versions. Multipurpose tables, with tops that lifted to reveal various surfaces for writing and playing cards, were a specialty of Portuguese cabinet-makers.

Ormolu mounts and veneering were not often used on Spanish furniture of this period, but elaborate, often engraved, brass and silver mounts were a common feature of Portuguese furniture.

GILT LEATHER

GILT LEATHER WAS ORIGINALLY AN ISLAMIC TECHNIQUE AND IS OFTEN CALLED "SPANISH LEATHER" ON ACCOUNT OF THIS ORIGIN. "SPANISH LEATHER" IS EMBOSSED OR PUNCHED WITH PATTERNS, PAINTED, AND GILDED.

Gilt leather was used for wall hangings and chair covers during the 17th century, and by the 18th century it was being used for writing tables, bed backs, and chair backs. While leather was used on every type of seat, from the basic folding chair to the formal throne chair, it was particularly useful on hall chairs because it was easy to clean. The gilt leather used was made of calfskin that had been punched with patterns, or embossed to create a raised pattern on the leather. The pattern was then painted in vibrant colors and details were picked out in gilt. Noble families often incorporated their coat of arms into the design.

The embossed leather upholstery on the seat and back is original.

Detail of painted and gilt leather

Portuguese chair This leather-upholstered chair may have been used for ceremonial purposes, which could explain the lack of wear. *c. 1720. H:41 in (104 cm). JK*

PORTUGUESE COMMODE

This marble-topped commode is one of a pair and closely follows French style: the *bombé* shape of the commode, and the arrangement of three drawers mounted above shaped feet with imported ormolu mounts. The case is covered in parquetry, similar to that found on French pieces. This fine piece would have been made for a very wealthy client. *c. 1715. H:35 in (89 cm); W:55 in (139.5 cm); D:28 in (71 cm). PAR*

SPANISH DINING CHAIRS

These dining chairs are thought to be part of a set supplied to King Ferdinand VI (r. 1746–59). English Chippendale-style furniture was popular in Spain and Portugal. Unlike British chairs of this style, which were usually mahogany, these chairs are made of walnut. Decorative highlights are created by gilding some of the carved areas, a feature known as parcel gilt. The legs are linked by stretchers with a shaped upper edge. *Mid-18th century.*

SCANDINAVIA

IN THE EARLY 1700s, Sweden, previously the dominant Protestant power of continental Europe, had lost major lands and its position in the Holy Roman Empire.

However, by 1727, plans for a grand royal palace in Stockholm, which had first been drawn up in the 1600s, were reinstated. The design for the palace's facade remained Roman Baroque, but the interior followed the French Rococo style. During this project, French and Italian sculptors, painters, and craftsmen worked in Stockholm and many pieces of French furniture were imported. The French style also influenced the nobility's choice of furniture, although British and Low Country designs were also widely imitated by chair and cabinet-makers. The Scandinavian use of indigenous softwoods led to much of the furniture being painted, and gave Scandinavian furniture a distinctive look of its own.

NORWAY AND DENMARK
Norway remained part of Denmark during the 18th century, and was closely linked to northern Germany. Furniture-makers were heavily influenced, therefore, by the German form of Rococo, and the guilds in both Denmark and Norway were based on the system in Germany. Furniture was also influenced by designs from Great Britain and the Low Countries, mainly because of of the large amount of furniture being imported.

SCANDINAVIAN CHAIRS
Chairs were made in a variety of styles and were often painted. Side chairs had cabriole legs and a solid splat, often with a "keyhole" pierced through the upper section, just under a central shell carving in the crest rail. Like British examples, the stiles were curved, becoming straight at the junction of the back legs. Designs tended to be conservative, and, in Denmark especially, high-backed chairs with stretchers remained popular well into the 18th century.

Between 1746 and 1748, the government banned the import of chairs that had been made abroad. This stifled innovation and meant that less fashionable styles of British chairs like those seen in the reign of George I remained popular.

Toward the middle of the century, chairs like the French *fauteuil*, but with low upholstered backs and turned legs, became popular. Sofas in the shape of two or three chairs placed together were common, as were stools with legs and carving that matched that of the chairs. Sometimes these pieces were

Marble tops were often used on expensive console tables.

Lion's heads were popular motifs throughout the 18th century.

The cabriole legs are decorated with half-human, half-bird figures.

The center of the frame is heavily carved with natural motifs.

Scroll feet support the piece.

A stylized shell motif with a foliate clasp forms the cartouche.

SWEDISH GILT TABLE

Influenced by Louis XV tables, this gilt table is made of *Griotte Svedois*: a type of cherry wood, covered in layers of gesso and gilt. The top is made of marble, further indicating that this would have been an extremely expensive piece of furniture. The table is heavily carved with half-human, half-bird figures depicted on the tops of the cabriole legs, which terminate in scroll feet. This magnificent table may be the work of a French-trained carver working in Stockholm. *c. 1760. H:39 in (99 cm); W:22 in (56 cm); D:34⅔ in (88 cm). GK*

SWEDISH CUPBOARD

This cupboard shows how the standard Germanic form was adapted to suit changing fashions. Its upper case shows the influence of Low Country style, and is less heavy than earlier architectural models. Its curved cornice has less of an overhang. The drawers and doors are cross-banded with veneer and the grain of the veneer gives movement to the piece. Bracket feet, rather than turned balls, support a base with straight drawers, which shows the influence of British style. *c. 1760. H:88½ in (225 cm); W:61½ in (156 cm). BK*

ainted, but solid beech or walnut hairs were also made. Elongated, pholstered sofas appeared in the 750s. These were often painted in ght colors, with gilt details.

ABINET-MAKERS

Massive linen cupboards were odeled on northern German xamples. These were made with eavy cornice moldings and bun feet for ome time, but gradually, bracket et—as shown in the engravings of hippendale and others—replaced he bun feet and the ornices became lighter nd less pronounced.

Chests of drawers were influenced by the commode: a typical version had four drawers on slightly curved legs terminating in animal feet. The facade was sometimes blocked, making it similar to pieces from the Low Countries. A new form of furniture, the glazed cabinet, mounted on a frame with slender turned legs, was popular for displaying collections of Chinese porcelain.

The cabinet-on-chest was an important piece in Scandinavia during this time. Massive in size, it incorporated a chest of drawers in the lower section with either one or two doors

above. These doors opened to reveal numerous small pigeonholes or shelves. The pediment was architectural in design, and later versions had pierced, carved, and gilt decorative features. The guilds that existed in Stockholm until the late 18th-century required a master cabinet-maker to make a cabinet-on-chest before he could be admitted, thus perpetuating the form.

Tables ranged from carved pine and gilded pier and console tables with marble tops, to dressing tables with three drawers below a top on cabriole legs.

High-style pier and console tables followed elaborate French fashions and were heavily carved and gilded with expensive marble tops. Dressing tables tended to be based on English examples, and some were decorated with japanning. The fashion for tea tables, card tables, and small portable tables also followed English and French trends.

WEDISH ARMCHAIR

ne of a pair, this chair is French in design but has shorter abriole legs than most French examples. Its staid shape onsists of a square back, slightly shaped crest rail, and rms set straight outward. Its carving is restrained, and the pholstered seat has no additional cushion. *c. 1750–60. BK*

PAINTED DRESSING TABLE

This elegant dressing table is covered in red japanning. The molding on the drawers and the drawer pulls are picked out in gilt, and the decoration beneath the central drawer is also gilt. Two pendants flank a central kneehole. The piece rests on slender cabriole legs. *Mid-18th century.*

LONGATED SWEDISH SOFA

esigned by Johan Erhard Wilhelm, this sofa is painted in a ght color. The carved decoration is highlighted in gold, and eatures sinuous foliate and floral motifs beneath a geometric ieze. The back, side, and seat cushions are covered in a pale naterial with gold stripes, giving the whole piece a restrained,

quintessentially Scandinavian look. It is typical of Swedish furniture with its solid back—rather than one formed of numerous chair backs, which was common in English settees. These elongated sofas were made for reception rooms and were often made en suite with chairs. *c. 1760. BK*

DANISH WALNUT CABINET-ON-CHEST

This cabinet-on-chest, with gilt fretwork on top of the cornice, is architectural in character. The carved and gilt-mirrored door gives the illusion of an actual mirror hanging on a wall. The serpentine lower case has three drawers above a pierced base and rests on scroll feet. *c. 1750. H:91 in (231 cm); W:42½ in (108 cm); D:9¼ in (23.5 cm). PAR*

BRITAIN: QUEEN ANNE AND GEORGE I

THE MAIN CHANGE TO FURNITURE during the reign of Queen Anne (1702–14) was the increased use of walnut-veneered oak for less expensive pieces. The cabriole leg, another dramatic development of the early 18th century, was introduced in Great Britain during this time. The Dutch-style chair with a rounded back, solid vase-shaped splat, and cabriole legs with pad feet is widely known as a Queen Anne chair, and continued to be made long after her death.

Case furniture and chairs made during the reigns of Queen Anne and George I (1714–27) are often veneered with walnut and are sometimes crossbanded or featherbanded. This change and the waning popularity of elaborate floral marquetry began around 1700 in England. Spiral, baluster-turned supports were also replaced by cabriole legs. On cabinet pieces, bun feet were common until around 1725, when bracket feet became prevalent.

One of the most popular case pieces was the bureau-bookcase, which developed from the writing cabinet with a fall front. Walnut bureaux and bureau-bookcases suited architectural interiors and were placed against the wall between windows. Less expensive versions were made of oak.

Dressing tables, or lowboys, now usually with three drawers, were used in bedchambers and, like bureau-bookcases, stood between windows. Dressing tables were usually made of walnut, either solid or veneered, but some were made of pine and were japanned. A few dressing tables were still made with turned legs and stretchers, but cabriole legs became more common as time went on.

GEORGE I
During the reign of George I, war with France, and the resulting animosity toward the French, inspired the British to develop their own style of furniture rather than follow French fashions. With a growing empire and valuable trade links, Great Britain grew wealthy and the merchant classes became increasingly powerful and influential.

ARCHITECTURAL INFLUENCES
The Classical style of ancient Greece and Rome was the height of fashion. In 1715, the Scottish lawyer and architect Colin Campbell published *Vitruvius Britannicus*, surveying the growth of the English country house. The architects and designers who read the book created the Palladian style o[f]

GEORGE I KNEEHOLE DESK

This top of this walnut dressing table/writing desk is decorated with crossbanded veneer, and the long drawer at the top of the desk is featherbanded. Six smaller drawers flank the central kneehole, which has both a frieze drawer and a cupboard door. *c. 1725. H:28 in (70 cm); W:27½ in (69 cm); D:19¼ in (48 cm). L&T*

WILLIAM III SIDE TABLE

This walnut table has a single drawer with simple brass drop pulls. The piece is supported on turned baluster legs and joined by a cross-stretcher. The legs are typical William-and-Mary style. This piece would probably have belonged to a wealthy merchant. *c. 1700. H:27 in (68.5 cm); W:35¾ in (91 cm); D:21 in (53.5 cm). NOA*

CENTER TABLE

This small portable table is covered with gilt gesso incised with a low-relief design of C-scrolls and foliage. It has gently curved cabriole legs and pad feet. This table would have belonged to a very wealthy household. *c. 1720. H:30¾ in (78 cm); W:34 in (86.5 cm); D:22 in (55.5 cm). PAR*

UPHOLSTERED SOFA

The two-seater sofa has a beech frame and walnut cabriole legs with shells carved on the knees. The upholstery has been replaced, but the sofa would originally have been covered with imported silk damask or needlework, which was used on the finest pieces. *c. 1720. W:55½ in (141 cm). L&T*

CHEST OF DRAWERS

This George I-style oak chest of drawers has a molded rectangular top above two short and two long drawers, and has double-beaded molding on the carcass and petition rails. The ring handles are not original. The piece stands on stile feet. *c. 1700. H:33½ in (85 cm); W:37 in (94 cm); D:22 in (56 cm). DN*

e 1720s to 1740s (*see p.96*), and this
fluenced furniture design.

HE AGE OF WALNUT

rly Georgian furniture was usually
ade of walnut or decorated with a
alnut veneer, although gilt gesso
rniture was also popular. Marquetry
as no longer
shionable,
though inlaid
binets were still
ported from the
ow Countries.
stead of relying
inlays for
coration,

English cabinet-makers emphasized
the decorative features of the wood
itself, such as the burrs and root
timbers of walnut, which provided
swirling patterns of timber.

Wooden furniture was decorated
with single carved motifs, such as
scallop shells, often on the knees of
legs or in the center of seat rails. By
about 1710, corner blocks on the
interior frames of chairs and tables
meant that they no longer needed
stretchers, so craftsmen could make
cabriole legs more curved. Feet
developed from the pad foot to the
slightly scrolled foot, and subsequently
to the claw-and-ball foot.

CHANGING TRENDS

Seats became more rounded, or
"compass'd," and broader, and backs
became lower and spoon-shaped,
making chairs more comfortable.
This chair may have been based on
imported Chinese designs. Settees and
sofas became more common. The
settee was basically an armchair
extended to seat two or more people,
with a back in the same style as those
used for single chairs. A sofa was a
wide seat with an upholstered seat and
back. Upholstery was still extremely
expensive, and could only be afforded
by the very wealthy. Little original
upholstery survives from this period.

Walnut chests-on-chests became
more architectural and decorative
during the first quarter of the century.
They often had pediments, fluted
pilasters, and shaped bracket feet.
Featherbanding was also popular.

The fashion for letter-writing made
desks very popular, and the secrétaire
chest-on-chest was created in response.
The top drawer of the lower section
had a fall front that opened to reveal a
writing surface, drawers, and numerous
small pigeonholes.

The popularity of gambling created
a demand for card tables, as well as for
small tea tables and stands for holding
refreshments during games.

APANNED SIDE CHAIR

e frame is decorated with japanning. The
ned back and stretchers are typical of early-
8th-century chairs, but the caning now flanks
vase-shaped splat and the stretchers are no
nger turned. *c. 1725. H:44½ in (113 cm). PAR*

/ALNUT ARMCHAIR

his George I chair has a solid back splat and
tspread arms terminating in scrolls. The
briole legs are carved with shells and husks,
d have trefoil feet. *c. 1725. H:39¾ in (101
m); W:23½ in (60 cm); D:23½ in (60 cm). PAR*

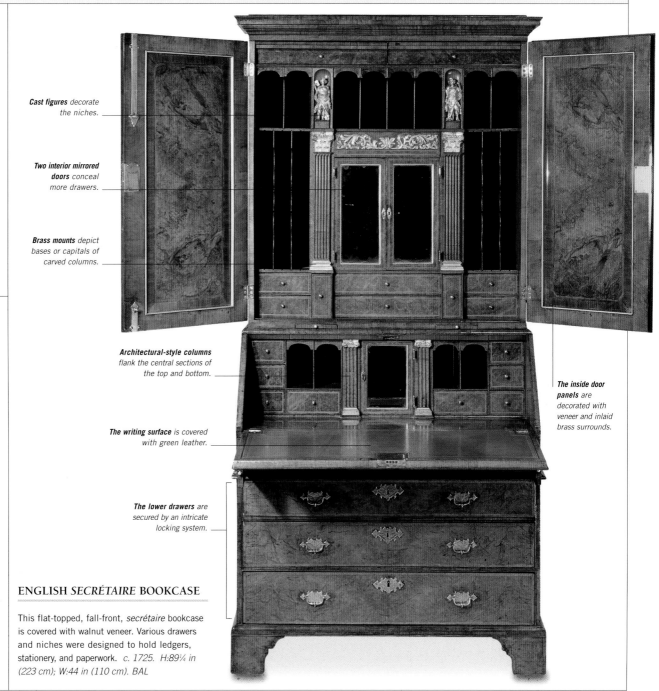

Cast figures decorate
the niches.

*Two interior mirrored
doors* conceal
more drawers.

Brass mounts depict
bases or capitals of
carved columns.

Architectural-style columns
flank the central sections of
the top and bottom.

The writing surface is covered
with green leather.

The lower drawers are
secured by an intricate
locking system.

*The inside door
panels* are
decorated with
veneer and inlaid
brass surrounds.

ENGLISH *SECRÉTAIRE* BOOKCASE

This flat-topped, fall-front, *secrétaire* bookcase
is covered with walnut veneer. Various drawers
and niches were designed to hold ledgers,
stationery, and paperwork. *c. 1725. H:89¼ in
(223 cm); W:44 in (110 cm). BAL*

BRITAIN: PALLADIANISM

THE BRITISH PALLADIAN style is named after the Italian Renaissance architect Andrea Palladio (1508–80), who published drawings of ancient Classical architecture. This style was popular in England from the 1720s to the 1740s, especially among educated, well-traveled aristocrats such as the Earl of Burlington, who built Chiswick House near London in 1725. Burlington's mansion is now regarded as the epitome of the Palladian style.

This was the golden era of the English country house, and many fine examples were built and furnished in the Palladian style, incorporating Classical motifs and rigid symmetry.

PALLADIO'S INFLUENCE
Palladio applied the mathematical precision of ancient structures to his work. His buildings, such as the Villa Rotunda near Venice (based on the Pantheon in Rome), are geometrically balanced structures. In 1570, he published *I Quattro libri dell' architettura* (*The Four Books of Architecture*), which influenced architecture for centuries.

The architect Inigo Jones (1573–c. 1652) studied Palladio's designs during a trip to Italy. On his return to England, he built the Banqueting House at Whitehall (1619–22) and the Queen's House in Greenwich (1635)

in the Palladian style. However, the influential architect Christopher Wren adopted the Baroque style, popular in Continental Europe, when he designed new buildings in the wake of the Great Fire of London, and it was not until the early 18th century that Palladianism was widely adopted in England.

ELEMENTS OF THE STYLE
Ancient Classical architecture was often at its best in large, public areas. The same is true of Palladian architecture, which was mostly designed for entrance halls and reception rooms. To fit such grand spaces, furniture had also to be grand. Large-scale architectural

Villa Almerico Capra, known as the Villa Rotonda, built 1566–70 by Palladio This symmetrical building, with its central dome and Classical columns, was much admired by British architects

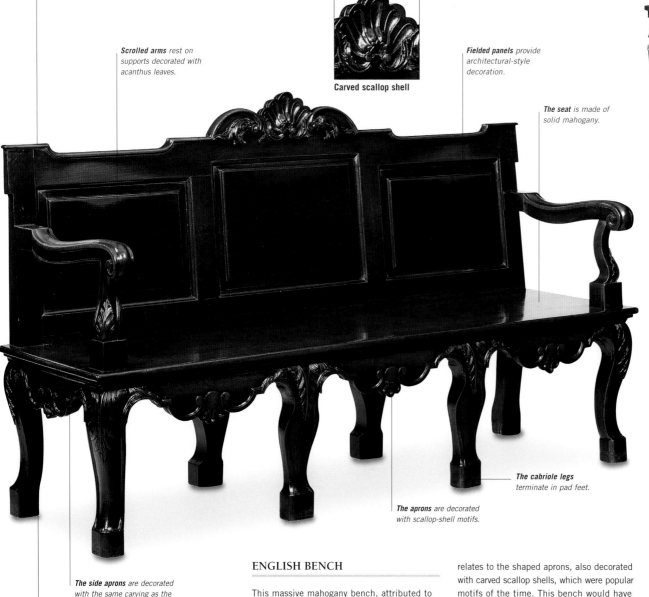

Scrolled arms rest on supports decorated with acanthus leaves.

Carved scallop shell

Fielded panels provide architectural-style decoration.

The seat is made of solid mahogany.

The cabriole legs terminate in pad feet.

The aprons are decorated with scallop-shell motifs.

The side aprons are decorated with the same carving as the front of the piece.

ENGLISH BENCH

This massive mahogany bench, attributed to the architect William Flitcroft, would have been made to enhance a grand hall. The rectangular-field back panels are derived from architectural motifs. The scallop shell above the center panel

relates to the shaped aprons, also decorated with carved scallop shells, which were popular motifs of the time. This bench would have echoed the design and architectural details in the great hall for which it was commissioned. *c. 1730. H:43 in (108 cm); W:73 in (185 cm); D:23 in (59 cm). PAR*

MAHOGANY COMMODE

This commode is architecturally inspired: th pilasters on the sides and front are headed wit lion's masks, with "bodies" of carved fish scale and acanthus. *c. 1730. H:32 in (81 cm); W:43 in (109 cm); D:20 in (51 cm). PAR*

GILTWOOD CONSOLE TABLE

The carved, gilded eagle and the heavy marble top are architecturally inspired. The table is attributed to William Kent, and is typical of his style. *Early 18th century. H:39½ in (89.5 cm); W:31 in (78 cm); D:19 in (48 cm). PAR*

features, including pediments, pilasters, and fielded panels, were applied to side tables, seating furniture, and large overmantel frames. Acanthus leaves and Greek keys were popular decorative motifs.

Symmetry was crucial: many pieces were too heavy to be moved and were designed to fit in a particular place. Tables were often made in pairs with matching mirrors, which were designed to be positioned above them.

One of the paradoxes of this style is that although Palladian buildings were quite plain, many were furnished in the florid Rococo style, which appeared at the height of Palladianism.

WILLIAM KENT

The English landscape gardener and architect William Kent revived interest in Jones's and Palladio's work, promoting a severe architectural style based on ancient Classical tenets. At Holkham Hall in Norfolk, Kent was one of the first English architects to plan a complete interior and exterior design. Before the excavations at Pompeii and Herculaneum from 1738, no one had seen real ancient Roman or Greek furniture, so Kent designed furniture in his own version of an ancient style. His designs also reflected Italian Baroque taste, influenced by his studies in Italy.

Kent's furniture, or that attributed to him, tends to be large in scale, with decorative features inspired by ancient Classical designs. Kent is particularly associated with marble-topped side tables, supported on carved and gilt eagles. Vitruvian scroll decorations were also common in Kent's work.

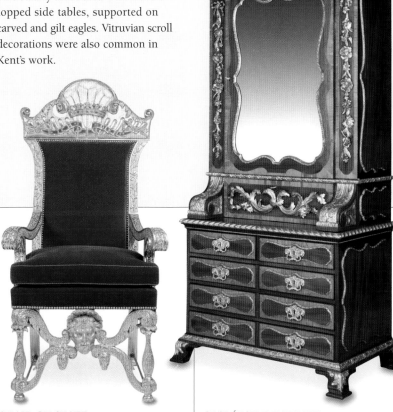

JOHN VARDY (1718–65)

THIS ARCHITECT AND FURNITURE DESIGNER HELPED TO POPULARIZE PALLADIAN TASTE DURING THE MID-CENTURY BUILDING BOOM.

Design for a bedroom mirror This combines the symmetry of the Palladian style with the lighter carving popular with Rococo designers.

John Vardy rose from a humble background to become one of the most important British designers. Vardy's book *Some designs of Mr Inigo Jones and Mr William Kent*, 1744, was instrumental in popularizing the Palladian style. However, he was also a respected architect and designer in his own right.

One of Vardy's most famous projects was Spencer House in London, one of Great Britain's most important Palladian mansions. As well as designing the building, Vardy also created furniture for the house. These pieces were symmetrical, in the Palladian style, but also displayed more florid, Rococo traits. This combination of roles and styles was typical of the architect/designers who were influential in Britain at this time.

CHAIR OF STATE

This chair was designed by Kent for the Prince of Wales' residence at Kew. It includes motifs from ancient Greece and Rome, such as the central mask. The pediment incorporates the Prince of Wales' emblem. *1733. H:56 in (142 cm). HL*

SECRÉTAIRE CABINET

Made in mahogany, olive wood, and padouk, this bureau-bookcase is decorated with parcel (part) gilding. The pediment echoes the style of a Greek temple. *c. 1745. H:85 in (191 cm); W:40½ in (103 cm); D:23½ in (60 cm). PAR*

The guilloche molding under the marble table top reflects Greek architectural motifs.

Pier table This gilt table has a marble top and serpentine legs carved with acanthus leaves. The sides are decorated with carved fish scales. *c. 1745. H:15¾ in (39 cm); W:53¾ in (136.5 cm).*

MARBLE-TOPPED SIDE TABLE

Carved from pine and then gilded, this table would have been one of a pair, or perhaps four, matching tables. The marble top is supported by stylized mythological torsos, inspired by ancient Greek statuary. Such figures were used as supports from the Renaissance to the Rococo period. The carved and gilt scallop shell, female mask, scrolls, and garlands are also Classical motifs. *c. 1735. H:35 in (89 cm); W:56 in (143 cm); D:31 in (79.5 cm). PAR*

THOMAS CHIPPENDALE

THE NAME CHIPPENDALE HAS BECOME SYNONYMOUS WITH 18TH-CENTURY LONDON, AND WITH THE VERY BEST IN BRITISH FURNITURE DESIGN OF THE PERIOD.

THOMAS CHIPPENDALE IS arguably the most famous furniture designer of all time. The description "Chippendale" has become a generic term applied to furniture made in London between about 1750 and 1765, and has come to represent timeless design excellence. As well as his impact on English furniture, Chippendale was hugely influential around the world, especially in the American colonies, where his designs were widely copied. Chippendale is most famous today for his chairs. The typical Chippendale chair had a carved and pierced back splat, a serpentine top rail, carved knees, cabriole legs, and claw-and-ball feet. The elegance of Chippendale's furniture challenged the French claim to be the greatest furniture designers of the age.

ST. MARTIN'S LANE

Thomas Chippendale was one of a number of brilliant craftsmen working in the vicinity of St. Martin's Lane in London in the middle of the century. London was a vibrant capital for craftsmen, with a host of patrons, architects, and designers working together. Cabinet-makers copied each other's wares, new craftsmen appeared on the scene, and new designs were published.

YELLOW DRAWING ROOM, HAREWOOD HOUSE
Two large mirrors designed by Chippendale, incorporating elaborate scrolls, fronds, and swags, dominate the drawing room of this imposing stately home in Yorkshire.

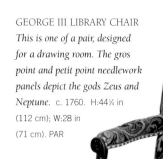

GEORGE III LIBRARY CHAIR
This is one of a pair, designed for a drawing room. The gros point and petit point needlework panels depict the gods Zeus and Neptune. c. 1760. H:44¼ in (112 cm); W:28 in (71 cm). PAR

Ormolu mounts decorate the edges of each panel.

Each pedestal contains a cupboard.

The frieze is decorated with rosette medallions.

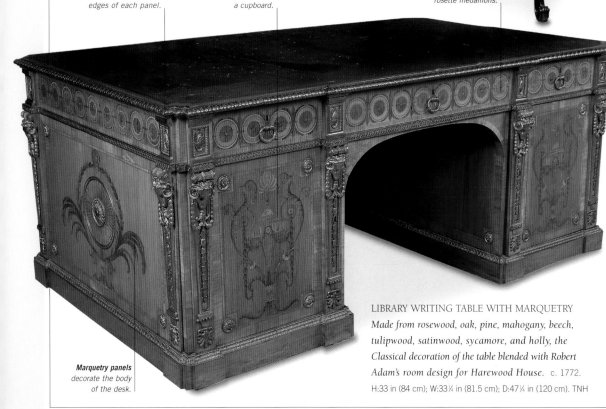

Marquetry panels decorate the body of the desk.

LIBRARY WRITING TABLE WITH MARQUETRY
Made from rosewood, oak, pine, mahogany, beech, tulipwood, satinwood, sycamore, and holly, the Classical decoration of the table blended with Robert Adam's room design for Harewood House. c. 1772. H:33 in (84 cm); W:33¼ in (81.5 cm); D:47¼ in (120 cm). TNH

KEY DATES

1718 Thomas Chippendale is born into a family of joiners and carpenters in Yorkshire, England.

1748 Chippendale is married. He is well established in London as a cabinet-maker by this time.

1753 Chippendale and his financial partner, James Rannie, lease three buildings on St. Martin's Lane in London. These buildings were occupied by Chippendale, and later his son, for 60 years.

1754 First edition of *The Director* is published. All furniture known to be the work of Chippendale was commissioned after this date.

1755 Fire breaks out at Chippendale's warehouse, but within the year he is advertising his trade as both a cabinet-maker and draftsman.

1766 Chippendale's warehouse employs approximately 50 specialist craftsmen.

1769 Chippendale attempts, unsuccessfully, to import 60 unfinished chair frames from France.

1779 Thomas Chippendale dies.

DESIGNS & STYLES

THE WORK OF CHIPPENDALE PROVIDES A SNAPSHOT OF THE FASHIONS OF THE TIME.

Chippendale's furniture ranged from pieces for the grandest reception rooms to domestic styles. For Harewood House in Yorkshire, he supplied a library table, an elm chopping block for the kitchen, and a deal table for the laundry. Harewood still contains one of the largest Chippendale collections in the world. Chippendale provided a complete interior decoration service, supplying (and often designing) curtains, chimneypieces, and wallpaper. He also made furniture specifically for particular architects, such as Robert Adam, to complement the style of each room.

This English armchair is similar to the "French Chair" design in *The Director* (above). The overall shape is Rococo, but the carved elements, such as the guilloche motif, are Classically inspired. PAR

THE MOST FAMOUS CABINET-MAKER

What sets Thomas Chippendale apart from other cabinet-makers of the time is that so many of his designs have survived. This is partly due to the enduring popularity of his style, but Chippendale's place in history is also thanks to the success of *The Gentleman and Cabinet-Maker's Director* (often referred to simply as *The Director*). This book was intended to cultivate the patronage of the aristocracy, although the instructions were meant for cabinet-makers, who were invited to copy the designs. The engraver Matthias Darly was Chippendale's chief collaborator on the book.

By the time *The Director* was published, Chippendale was a master cabinet-maker. The increasing demands of running a successful business meant that Chippendale no longer actually made any of the furniture himself; instead, he directed and administered his London workshop of approximately 40 men. He also subcontracted work to the best suppliers for mounts and marquetry panels. *The Director* brought financial backing that allowed Chippendale to expand his business and become the leading furniture-maker of the day. His success also prompted fellow cabinet-makers to produce their own pattern books (*see p.138*).

EXOTIC INSPIRATION

Chinoiserie was very popular in the 1740s, and Chippendale produced a large number of designs inspired by the motifs used on traditional Chinese pieces. As the liking for chinoiserie developed, lacquer details were no longer sufficiently exotic on their own, so Chippendale designed furniture with pagoda surmounts, little bells, galleries of fretwork, and wood carved to represent interlaced bamboo. These were, of course, flights of fancy rather than representations of authentic Oriental furniture. One of the most famous commissions of "Chinese Chippendale" was a suite of green and white japanned furniture created for actor David Garrick's villa on the Thames river. Chippendale's pieces were designed for the villa's best dressing room and the Chinese bedroom.

GOTHIC ELEMENTS

The mid- to late 18th century saw a revival in Gothic motifs and taste, inspired by the architecture and furniture of the Middle Ages, and Chippendale also published designs to satisfy this fashion revival. Gothic Chippendale furniture included decorative details such as pointed arches, finials, and panels with quatrefoil motifs.

SERPENTINE COMMODE
This piece has two oak-lined drawers and a mahogany-lined top drawer, with an olive, gilt-tooled, leather writing slide. Finely carved acanthus leaves, flanked by paterae and hung with bell flowers, overlay the molded and shaped angles. c. 1770.
H:33½ in (85 cm); W:53¼ in (135 cm); D:24¾ in (62 cm). PAR

BRITAIN: GEORGE II

GEORGE II'S REIGN (1727–60) signaled a period of peace and prosperity. Trading posts established by the East India Company in Calcutta and Madras were expanded, so by the time of George II's death in 1760, England was confirmed as a commercial power.

THE AGE OF MAHOGANY

Imported from the British colonies in the West Indies and Honduras, mahogany became the favored wood for fine cabinet-making in Britain by the early 1730s. In response to a blight on walnut trees, the French had stopped exporting walnut in 1730, and besides, mahogany had many advantages. Cabinet-makers wanted to make the most of the wood's rich color, which combined well with gold, silver, and bronze. The hardness of the wood also made it possible to create delicate pieces with pierced decoration and carving. This led to the creation of a British style based on mahogany, using less elaborate decoration than the French Rococo.

FASHIONABLE PURSUITS

Bureaux of all sorts were popular during this time, and chests of drawers and commodes "in the French taste"—with three drawers on feet—were made for fashionable patrons.

Tables ranged from grand, gilt pier tables with marble tops, used in formal reception rooms, to mahogany tilt-top tables with tripod bases and scalloped

edges, suitable for the fashionable pursuit of taking tea. Small portable tables were used in many rooms for a variety of purposes, ranging from playing cards to sewing or drawing.

Grand dining rooms were furnished with large sets of chairs, which often had carved and pierced back splats and upholstered slip seats fitted into a seat frame. These chairs had carved claw-and-ball feet, pad feet, or even, occasionally, scrolled feet.

ROCOCO INFLUENCE

Although the Rococo style was most influential in Continental Europe, British designers of the time were responsible for creating some of the movement's more extreme flights of fancy. The Rococo style affected the decoration of furniture as well as the shape. Large case pieces and beds were decorated with carved C-scrolls and foliage or other natural motifs, and some pieces had scrolled feet. The fashion for asymmetrical scrolls and curves was also evident on smaller furnishings, such as torchères, mirror frames, and tables.

The most famous English exponent of the Rococo style was Thomas Chippendale (*see p.98*), although it was just one of the design styles he embraced during his career.

Thomas Johnson, a respected English wood carver and furniture designer, published his engravings: *Designs for Picture Frames, Candelabra, Ceilings, &c* (1751), and *One Hundred and Fifty New Designs* (1761), for small tables and stands, wall sconces, clocks, frames, and other small decorative objects. His designs were wildly extravagant and epitomized the *genre pittoresque* decoration of Louis XV style (*see p.78*). He incorporated elements of the three most popular motifs of the time in his work: Chinese, Gothic, and Rococo. Johnson created elaborate pieces using *rocaille*, stalactites, foliage, birds, and other natural motifs. Some of the designs were so highly stylized that the wood was not strong enough to support the intricate carving.

Tripod table Made of mahogany, this tilt-top table would have been called a claw table in early inventories. The metal catch snaps into place when the top is lowered down onto the tripod base. *c. 1755. H:27½ in (70 cm); D:26¾ in (68 cm). PAR*

GILTWOOD PIER TABLE

The frame of this marble-topped, giltwood pier table is exuberantly carved with Palladian motifs, including acanthus foliage and scrolls. The bearded mask in the center is flanked by eagle's heads, hung with a festoon of oak leaves and acorns, and has a pierced apron below. The cabriole legs are carved with putti and terminate in scroll feet. The table is possibly by Matthias Lock. *c. 1740. H:45½ in (115.5 cm); W:50½ in (128 cm); D:27 in (68.5 cm). PA*

GILES GRENDEY (1693–1780)

THIS LONDON-BASED CABINET-MAKER RAN A THRIVING EXPORT BUSINESS OVER MANY YEARS FROM HIS WORKSHOP IN ST. JOHN'S SQUARE.

Grendey's printed label noted that he "Makes and Sells all Sorts of CABINET GOODS, Chairs, Tables, Glasses, etc." His workshop, employing numerous craftsmen, supplied both high-quality goods and well-made but simple furniture for less wealthy clients, but he was most renowned for his export business, mostly to Spain. He famously supplied a suite of red japanned furniture to the Spanish Duke of Infantado, which comprised at least 77 pieces: the largest recorded suite of English furniture. A Grendey label causes great excitement among dealers and experts, but genuine Grendey pieces are extremely rare.

Side chair This beech chair, japanned in scarlet, is overlaid with gilt chinoiserie. The chair combines earlier design elements—the solid splat and turned stretchers—with cabriole legs with claw-and-ball feet, pierced crest rail, and squared seat. *c. 1735. H:41½ in (105.5 cm). PAR*

Armchair Made of mahogany, the shell motifs on the splat and the crest rail are carved rather than gilt. The carving shows the large-scale motifs sometimes used by Grendey. *c. 1740. H:39¾ in (101 cm); W:25 in (63.5 cm). PAR*

CHEST OF DRAWERS

This mahogany chest has a serpentine front with a similarly shaped top. Four graduated long drawers are flanked by chamfered corners carved with cartouches and pendant flowers, and there is a slide-out writing surface. The handles are typical of the period, without backplates or elaborate escutcheons. The exquisite carving on the corners makes this a very fine, rare piece. *c. 1755. H:34 in (86 cm); W:44 in (112 cm); D:26 in (68 cm). PAR*

ARMCHAIR

This style of mahogany armchair is usually described as a "Gainsborough," after the artist, who often included the style in his paintings, and would have been made for a library or reception room. The seat and back have been reupholstered in silk damask, similar to the original fabric, which would have matched that on the walls of the room. The cabriole legs are too heavy to be construed as Rococo. *c. 1755. H:39 in (100 cm); W:30½ in (77.5 cm). PAR*

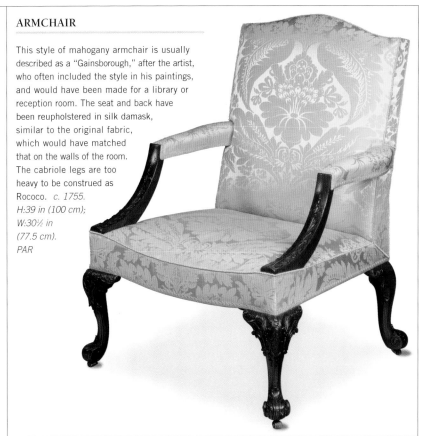

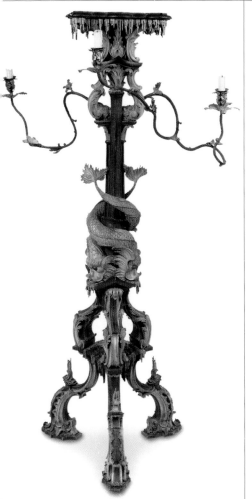

CARVED PINE CANDLESTAND

This stained pine and gilded candlestand is entwined with carved branches and dolphins and has iron candle branches. The naturalistic carving and scrolled base are typically Rococo. *c. 1758. H:62 in (157 cm). TNH*

The fitted interior is very simple in style.

The writing surface retracts when not in use.

The simple ring brasses are reminiscent of the earlier William-and-Mary style.

The cabriole legs are decorated with carved leaves.

The shaped apron is decorated with brass.

The feet are scroll-shaped.

WALNUT BUREAU-ON-STAND

This bureau-on-stand is unusual for English furniture. Made of walnut instead of the more typical mahogany, it sits on a carved, Rococo base terminating in scroll feet. *c. 1735. H:37¾ in (96 cm); W:29 in (74 cm). MAL*

AMERICA: QUEEN ANNE

QUEEN ANNE'S NAME is not only associated with British furniture, but also describes a style of furniture made in the American colonies, after her death, from about 1720 to 1750, depending upon the region.

By the early 18th century, British-trained cabinet-makers working in Boston were producing sophisticated furniture for the wealthy. Newspapers carried advertisements announcing the arrival of craftsmen conversant in the latest fashions. Furniture was also imported in great quantity, and included cane-backed chairs and lacquered trays, and mirrors from England, the Low Countries, and Spain.

INFLUENCE OF THE HOMELAND
Furniture made in the colonies did not imitate court styles, but was similar to furniture made for the middle classes in Great Britain and the Low Countries, because the settler communities consisted primarily of merchants, servants, and tradesmen, although some high-end pieces were produced.

By 1725, most furniture-makers were second- or third-generation Americans, who interpreted traditional designs in new ways, but the influence of their ancestry meant that designs varied between regions. These differences were also due to the woods available in the colonies.

THE CHOICE OF WOODS
During this time mahogany became more popular, although in the middle colonies, walnut remained the wood of choice into the 1780s. Maple was often used in New England, and furniture made in the mid-18th century often emphasized the curved grain of the wood. Cherry was popular in Connecticut, although other local woods were also used.

FURNITURE STYLES
Seating became more comfortable, but textiles remained prohibitively expensive, so upholstered furnishings were rare. Leather was often used to

upholster slip seats. Queen Anne chairs generally had balloon-shaped seats and solid, vase-shaped splats. The stiles were rounded and the crest rails were often decorated with carved shells. As the century progressed, turned legs with stretchers evolved into cabriole legs, but some makers favored turned legs long after they had gone out of fashion.

Early chests of drawers tended to be veneered, but by the 1750s many were made of solid wood. Ball or bun feet favored in the early 18th century were replaced by bracket, then claw-and-ball feet. On high chests of drawers, turned legs became cabriole

HIGH CHEST OF DRAWERS

This high chest, originating from Boston, is veneered in both tiger maple and burr maple. The decorative pattern of the wood is enhanced by the use of crossbanding around each drawer

of the upper section, which gives the appearance of two drawers instead of one long drawer. The turned "cup-and-vase" legs are joined with flat, shaped stretchers, and are typical of the work of Boston cabinet-makers. *c.1715. KEN*

CHEST OF DRAWERS

This chest of drawers, made in Boston, is referred to as William and Mary, although it was made in the first quarter of the 18th century. Its burr walnut veneer imitates the oyster veneer pattern used on British examples. *1700–20. KEN*

FALL-FRONT BUREAU

This bureau from Boston is made of mahogany with pine secondary wood. The piece consists of various drawers behind a fall-front, and nine lower drawers with brass escutcheons. The piece sits on paw feet. *c. 1750. H:44 in (112 cm); W:41 in (104 cm); D:21 in (53 cm). BDL*

MAPLE DINING TABLE

Made in the Boston area, this table is made of black-painted maple. It has a scrubbed, hinged oval top, with demi-lobe leaves. The apron has a single drawer for storage. The vase-and-reel

turned gatelegs terminate in claw-and-ball feet and are joined by similarly turned stretchers. When not in use, the leaves were closed and the table could be placed against the wall. *c. 1715. H:29 in (73.5 cm); W:59 in (150 cm open); D:48 in (122 cm). NA*

and cornice drawers disappeared. Bonnet-top pediments became more fashionable (although flat tops remained popular) and an extra drawer appeared in the upper section.

Dressing tables also served as writing tables in bedchambers. They were often made *en suite* with high chests and were one of the most expensive objects in a household. The tripod base snap table—so called because the metal catch under the top snapped into place—was made in all the colonies. This had a round or square top and was easily moved for dining, cards, or writing. Turned-leg dining tables with folding side flaps, known as gateleg tables, were a staple item in most households. These tables remained popular until the 1750s and are often difficult to date.

As in Europe, tea tables were popular. The finest versions were made of mahogany and had elegant cabriole legs terminating in pad feet, and later, claw-and-ball feet.

REGIONAL VARIATIONS

While less wealthy areas favored indigenous woods, New England and the southern colonies followed British fashions, and New York was influenced by the Low Countries. New York chair-makers preferred square claw-and-ball feet and rarely used medial stretchers. The high chest was unfashionable in New York, where the wardrobe or chest-on-chest was preferred. Boston cabinet-makers used block-front facades on bureaux and chests of drawers. This distinctive feature may have originated from Indo-Colonial furniture from Goa and Madeira, which would have been familiar to New England merchants.

MAPLE ARMCHAIR

This armchair, in the style of the School of John Gaines, was made in Portsmouth, New Hampshire. The pierced scrolled crest with molded shoulders and a vase-form splat are typical features of furniture made in this area. *c.1730–40. NA*

SIDE CHAIR

This side chair was made in Philadelphia. It has a mixture of Queen Anne and Chippendale features. The back splat is solid, in the Queen Anne style, but its stiles and seat are shaped, and the chair has cabriole front legs, following the Chippendale style. *FRE*

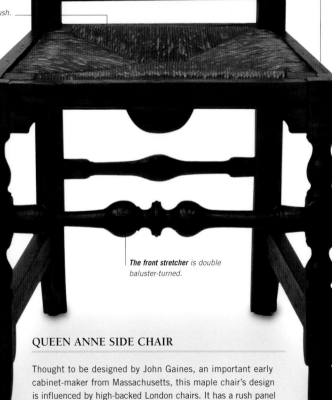

The crest rail is elaborately carved and pierced.

The back splat is of a solid vase form.

The seat is made of rush.

The front stretcher is double baluster-turned.

QUEEN ANNE SIDE CHAIR

Thought to be designed by John Gaines, an important early cabinet-maker from Massachusetts, this maple chair's design is influenced by high-backed London chairs. It has a rush panel and seat, a new solid vase-shaped splat, turned stretchers, and "Spanish" feet. *Early 18th century. NA*

TRAY-TOP TEA TABLE

This tea table is made of mahogany. The molded edge of the table top is designed to keep expensive implements used during tea-drinking from falling on the floor. The piece has slender cabriole legs, terminating in pad feet. *1740–60. KEN*

DRESSING TABLE

This dressing table comes from Salem. The case is decorated with walnut veneer, and the piece has William-and-Mary style features in the form of turned legs and flat stretchers. *1710–30. H:30 in (76 cm); W:34 in (86 cm); D:22 in (56 cm). NA*

AMERICAN CHIPPENDALE

The description "Chippendale," when applied to American furniture, refers to stylistic features, rather than indicating that a piece was made by Chippendale. American Chippendale furniture was made from around 1745 to 1775, primarily in Philadelphia.

From the 1730s, Philadelphia welcomed immigrant craftsmen who brought with them new ideas and European fashions, which resulted in a more exuberant style than New England furniture. Some of the most fashionable Philadelphian furniture was made by immigrants such as Scottish-born Thomas Affleck.

PREDOMINANT FASHIONS
Interior fashions popular in Europe, such as placing pairs of pier tables against the wall with mirrors positioned above them, were scaled down to suit smaller colonial homes.

Slab tables with marble tops were highly prized, using expensive materials and elaborate carving. In general, less expensive versions were made in New England and in the South, but the frames were not as finely carved and the legs were stocky. Dining tables, with or without drop leaves, were popular throughout the colonies. These were made in various woods including mahogany, walnut, and maple. In less grand houses, tavern tables were common. These stood on cabriole legs and one or two pieces of wood were attached to the frame by wooden pegs: the top overhung the frame. Card and gaming tables were extremely popular. These also generally had cabriole legs, the knees carved with shells or flowing foliage, and terminated in pad or claw-and-ball feet. Most had four legs with the rear two legs swinging outward to support the top leaf, but five legs were favored in New York.

By about 1745, side or dining chairs usually had pierced backs, rather than the solid splats common in Queen Anne furniture. Chippendale chairs generally had a squared seat with an upholstered slip seat that fitted into the frame. The most expensive versions were upholstered over the frame. Side chairs were often made in sets, sometimes with armchairs. Upholstered easy chairs offered greater comfort, but the expense of textiles

The top is made of imported marble, which is shaped to fit the frame.

A carved chinoiserie figure sits within an asymmetrical cartouche.

The cabriole legs are elaborately carved with C-scrolls.

Intricate scroll feet support the piece.

PHILADELPHIA SLAB TABLE

This mahogany slab table was probably made by a foreign-born cabinet-maker. The backboard is made of yellow pine and the corner braces are of walnut. The elaborate decoration would have been designed to order for a wealthy client. *c. 1770. H:32¼ in (82 cm); W:48¼ in (122.5 cm); D:23¼ in (59 cm).*

CARD TABLE

This New England mahogany table has a central drawer to hold playing materials. When opened, square corners, hollowed out to hold a candlestick next to each player, are revealed. The piece rests on cabriole legs with carved knees and ball-and-claw feet. *c. 1760. W:32½ in (82.5 cm). NA*

SLANT-FRONT DESK

This mahogany desk from the Boston area has 12 traditional, square, blocked drawers. However, it also has fashionable elements, such as the claw-and-ball feet and Chinese Chippendale brasses. The central shell motif is echoed in the carved pendant on the front rail. *c. 1770. W:40 in (102 cm). Pook*

SLANT-FRONT DESK

This mahogany desk has brass handles at the sides for carrying. The wooden drawer pulls may be replacements. This classic desk shape was produced by the Newport cabinet-maker John Townsend. Its carved block and shell, used in the interior, is unique to furniture from Newport. *18th century. H:42 in (107 cm). NA*

WING ARMCHAIR

This mahogany armchair was made in Massachusetts. It has a serpentine crest, canted back, shaped wings, and rolled arms, and is upholstered in velvet, although it would originally have been a woolen textile. The turned front stretcher is recessed, and the front legs terminate in claw-and-ball feet. *c.1765. NA*

meant that only the very wealthy could afford them. Wing armchairs protected the occupants from drafts.

OTHER FURNITURE

The chest of drawers and the high chest, often with a matching dressing table, remained popular. However, by the 1760s, these had been superseded by the clothes or linen press, a fashionable English form. Chests of drawers usually had four graduated drawers and stood on bracket or claw-and-ball feet, but the commode was rarely seen. New forms furnished fashionable abodes, including basin stands, candlestands, and kettle stands.

DECORATIVE STYLES

Decoration tended to be similar to that used on European furniture, with carved shells, foliage, and trailing husks. However, colonial furniture tended to be less ornate. Gilt furniture was not found in the colonies, with the exception of mirrors, although gilt highlights were sometimes applied to interior carving, finials, and claw-and-ball feet. Painted furniture was popular outside the port towns and reflected the styles of the craftsmen's home countries. The Pennsylvania German community produced highly decorative, painted furniture, particularly dowry chests.

Woods, carving techniques, and the style of furniture all help to identify where a piece was made. In Newport, Rhode Island, the Goddard-Townsend school of cabinet-makers produced shell-carved, blocked bureaux and secretary bookcases that are immediately identifiable. Newport cabinet-makers also favored claw-and-ball feet hollowed out under the claw tenons. New York cabinet-makers carved squared, claw-and-ball feet with deeper webbing over the ball.

WOODS

Mahogany was favored by urban cabinet-makers, although maple and cherry were popular in New England. Walnut, from Pennsylvania and Virginia, was still used after the introduction of mahogany. Secondary woods tended to be indigenous: white pine, birch, tulipwood, cedar, yellow pine, and sycamore. Wood was plentiful in the colonies, so veneers were not common. Solid woods were also less susceptible to changes in climate.

PHILADELPHIA CANDLESTAND

This mahogany candlestand has a tilt-top, birdcage mechanism. The turned support extends to a compressed ball and a tripartite, cabriole base, terminating in slipper feet. *Early 18th century. H:20¼ in (51.5 cm). FRE*

PHILADELPHIA LOWBOY

This mahogany lowboy has inset fluted quarter columns on the case. Shell, vine, and foliate carving decorates the center drawer, apron, and cabriole legs. *1796. H:31 in (77.5 cm); W:36 in (90 cm); D:21½ in (53.75 cm). NA*

SIDE CHAIR

This walnut chair is similar to the Queen Anne style. The solid vase splat and trifid feet are typical of Philadelphia Queen Anne chairs. The projecting ears, cabriole legs, and squared seat reflect the Chippendale style. *c.1745. NA*

SIDE CHAIR

This mahogany chair, attributed to Thomas Affleck, has a carved crest rail, fluted stiles and knees, and a pierced splat. The front legs have scrolls under the seat and terminate in claw-and-ball feet. *c. 1765. H:37 in (94 cm). BDL*

PHILADELPHIA HIGH CHEST

This mahogany high chest is clearly derived from the Chippendale pattern books, although the date of the piece is toward the end of the period. The gilt-brass escutcheons and the quality of the carving indicate the Chippendale influence. The pediment follows the design of a desk and bookcase illustrated in Chippendale's *Director*, while the carving on the central lower drawer is taken from a chimneypiece tablet design by Thomas Johnson. *1762–75. H:91¾ in (233 cm); W:45½ in (113.5 cm); D:25 in (62.5 cm).*

AMERICA: SOUTHERN STATES

THE SOUTHERN STATES of Maryland, North and South Carolina, and Virginia were British colonies along the eastern seaboard of America, whose societies were centered on large plantations.

The largest southern city in the early 18th century was Charles Town (known as Charleston) in South Carolina, a port where rich merchants aspired to recreate British fashions. The wealthy plantation owners traded with their compatriots in Great Britain and employed native craftsmen to build their houses in the latest style. Imported furniture, pattern books, and immigrants all introduced new styles of furniture to the area.

NEW FORMS
As in New England, types of furniture developed in pace with changes in housing and with the growth of the middle class. In larger houses, rooms were now designated for specific purposes, such as rooms for dining, libraries, steward's rooms, and bedrooms.

The clothes press, which usually had drawers at the bottom, was related to the European armoire and was common, while the high chest of drawers—so popular in the north—was rarely seen in the southern states.

Tables ranged from round and square tilt-top tables, breakfast tables, and card tables, to dining tables and sideboard or slab tables. The sideboard table usually had a marble top, making it suitable for use in the dining room. If made with a wooden top, it also had a cover to protect it from wet objects. These tables were based on British furniture and were copied from imports or drawings.

Dressing tables, which were also used for writing or reading, were closely related to British examples and rarely had the same arrangement of drawers as those originating from New England. The southern versions either had one long drawer at the top of the table, or two square drawers flanking a central long drawer. The legs tended to have pad, rather than claw-and-ball, feet.

Chairs varied from simple side chairs with turned stretchers and backs, and rush seats, to sumptuous wing armchairs with claw-and-ball feet. Corner chairs, known as smoking chairs, were made for gentlemen in Maryland, Virginia, and North Carolina. These had curved backs, which were sometimes upholstered in leather.

The Chippendale-style chair was made by both rural and urban

WALNUT ARMCHAIR

This Maryland chair is inspired by Chippendale or similar pattern books. It has a serpentine crest with scrolled ears, a pierced back splat, carved shell details, and cabriole legs. *1755–70. H:41½ in (105.5 cm); W:32 in (81 cm). SP*

MAHOGANY LINEN PRESS

This linen press was made in Eastern Virginia. The upper case fits into the molded top of the lower case. It has stop-fluted corner columns, a dentil cove cornice, and ogee bracket feet. The two doors, when open, reveal a yellow pine fitted interior with a number of pigeonholes. *c. 1760. H:72½ in (184 cm); W:36½ in (93 cm); D:21 in (53.5 cm).*

TEA TABLES

THE FASHION FOR TAKING TEA CREATED A MARKET FOR LOCALLY MADE TEA TABLES.

By the early 18th century, wealthy Americans had taken up tea-drinking, and as a result, Southern cabinet-makers made tea tables using predominantly European methods.

Square tables often had rectangular tops with slightly beveled edges, as well as straight, turned legs ending in "button" feet, and rails with curved lower edges.

The middle classes picked up on the trend for taking tea, and by 1750, rural Southern cabinet-makers and craftsmen were making tea tables in vernacular styles from black walnut, cherry, and maple. The craftsmen reinterpreted the designs favored by the rich to suit local tastes and their own abilities. Styles tended to be a combination of William and Mary and Queen Anne.

By 1760, round tea tables had become popular. These typically had baluster and column shafts sitting on tripod bases. Slipper feet were designed with a pronounced ridge on the top edge and a large pad underneath. The table top usually sat on a shaped, solid block rather than on a birdcage device popular on earlier tables.

Mahogany tray-top tea table This table has a shaped bulging skirt and cabriole legs, which have acanthus-carved knees and end in claw-and-ball feet. *1740–60.*

SLAB OR SIDEBOARD TABLE

This Virginian dining table has a marble top and unusual legs with bifurcated knees. The ball-and-claw feet are all forward-facing and have pronounced webbing. *1745–60. H:25½ in (65 cm); W:27 in (69 cm); D:18½ in (47 cm).*

craftsmen. The detail of the pierced splats varied, but all the chairs had a squared seat and shaped back legs. The seat was usually narrower than on British examples.

LOCAL MATERIALS

Historically, Southern furniture has often been confused with furniture from Great Britain or New England. Examining the types of wood that have been used is generally the best way to determine the origin of a piece. In most cases, it is the secondary woods, not visible to the eye, that help identify the region of origin. Secondary woods used in the southern states included tulipwood—particularly for drawer linings in both mahogany and walnut furniture—gumwood, yellow pine, and bald cypress, which is resistant to decay and so particularly suited to the South's hot and humid climate. Primary woods, the wood on show, included mahogany, which was imported and used in Charles Town in the 1730s, and walnut, which other southern towns preferred.

SIDE CHAIR

This is one of a pair of chairs made of walnut and yellow pine. The crest rail has a shell motif centered above a carved splat. The front cabriole legs terminate in trifid feet. *Mid-18th century. H:40 in (100 cm); W:20 in (50 cm).*

OVAL-TOP DINING TABLE

This Virginian table, based on a British design, has drop leaves and could be moved easily and stored against the wall. The shape of the legs and use of yellow pine indicate its Southern origin. *1690–1740. H:32 in (81 cm); W:48 in (122 cm).*

SECRÉTAIRE BOOKCASE

This mahogany secretary bookcase is believed to be the earliest known piece of American furniture with this pattern of chinoiserie Gothic mullions. This piece is similar in construction to four other case pieces made in Charleston. The carved rosettes on the pediment are typical of the Charleston style. *c. 1760. H:97¾ in (244 cm); W:43½ in (109 cm); D:24¼ in (60.5 cm).*

The mullion pattern is a Chinese railing design interpreted in a Gothic pattern.

The prospect door is flanked by carved document drawers.

The fall front is supported on lopers that pull out of the case when needed.

Simple brass bale handles are attached to the drawer fronts.

Shaped bracket feet support the case.

NEW FORMS

DURING THE 18TH CENTURY, the desire for a more relaxed and informal life became increasingly important among the wealthy and leisured classes, creating a demand for new types of furniture.

The growing popularity of writing and playing games, in particular, influenced furniture design, and many new kinds of writing tables and desks were created. These were usually intended for bedrooms, rather than being placed in a reception room. In addition to writing tables specifically intended for correspondence, writing surfaces were skillfully incorporated into other small tables, including dressing tables.

Game tables evolved in response to the popularity of board and card games, and the most elaborate versions incorporated different surfaces for playing a variety of games. The 18th-century fascination for novelty furniture with secret devices led to the creation of ordinary-looking tables that opened to reveal hidden writing or game surfaces.

Kettle stands and tea tables were designed to accommodate the new fashion for drinking tea and coffee. Like other small occasional tables, these were light and easy to move, so that they could be placed against the walls of a room when not in use, as convention demanded.

Comfort became much more of a priority during the 18th century, particularly in light of the greater interest in conversation and informal social gatherings. Powerful women, such as Louis XV's mistress, Madame de Pompadour, were influential patrons and held salons, where guests met to discuss literature, science, and the arts. New types of chairs, sofas, and settees were shaped with gently curved backs, and had padded and upholstered seats, backs, and arms, to make them more comfortable, despite the high cost of textiles. Design books featuring these new forms of furniture often contained special sections indicating how people should use them and giving the proper dimensions.

KETTLE STAND

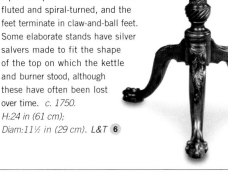

This English mahogany kettle stand has a solid gallery to stop the kettle from sliding off, and a column on top of a tripod base. The column is fluted and spiral-turned, and the feet terminate in claw-and-ball feet. Some elaborate stands have silver salvers made to fit the shape of the top on which the kettle and burner stood, although these have often been lost over time. c. 1750. H:24 in (61 cm); Diam:11½ in (29 cm). L&T **6**

ENCOIGNURE "À FLEURS"

This Louis XV corner cupboard is decorated with rosewood inlays of flowers and foliage. It has a quarter-circle marble top above a two-door case, a shaped apron, and short cabriole legs. Bronze mounts and sabots provide additional decoration. c. 1750. H:37¼ in (93 cm); W:30½ in (76 cm); D:21¼ in (53 cm). GK **4**

Green baize-lined surface for playing cards.

The inner surface is inlaid with a board for backgammon and other games.

The shaped cabriole legs terminate in pad feet.

GEORGE II GAME TABLE

Made of mahogany, this table has four legs, one of which swings back to provide support for the leaves. Inside the triple-hinged top is a baize-lined card-playing surface with squared recesses on the corners to hold candlesticks, and an inlaid surface for playing backgammon and other games. c. 1740. H:34 in (85 cm). NA **4**

BUREAU DRESSING TABLE

This rare piece has one long drawer above three short drawers at each side. There is a cupboard and a small drawer in the recess. The desk is richly japanned with gold chinoiseries on a green background, and has brass mounts and bracket feet. c. 1720. H:33¼ in (83 cm); W:31¼ in (78 cm); D:19¼ in (48 cm). MAL

ENGLISH WRITING TABLE

Made of mahogany, this writing table has tall cabriole legs rather than the short legs found on a bureau dressing table. The top of the desk has a leather-covered writing surface. Two of the front legs swing out to support the frieze drawer, to reveal slides and compartments. *c.1745. HL* **7**

FRENCH LADY'S WRITING BUREAU

This small Louis XV secrétaire is veneered in kingwood and satinwood parquetry and has five drawers and cabriole legs. The restrained use of ornamental ormolu mounts marks this out as a mid-century, rather than an early-century, piece. *c. 1750. H:38½ in (96 cm); W:40½ in (101 cm); D:20¾ in (52 cm). GK* **5**

FRENCH LADY'S WRITING BUREAU

Known as a *secrétaire en pente* (secrétaire with a slope), this bureau is decorated with black lacquer. The decoration is quite sparse, which is typical of the Japanese style. This piece is stamped with the initials of the acclaimed ébéniste Jean-Pierre Latz. *c. 1750. H:39¼ in (98 cm). GK* **9**

CHINESE GAMES TABLE

This rare Padouk table from Canton has a square top made in two pieces, which are hinged so that they open out. Support for the extended top is supplied by lopers concealed in the apron.

The interior contains several game surfaces, including one for backgammon. The cabriole legs have carved knees and terminate in claw-and-ball feet. The piece would have been made for export. *c. 1775. H:32¾ in (82 cm); W:55½ in (139 cm) (open); D:28 in (70 cm). MJM*

GEORGE II DRAWING TABLE

When closed, this mahogany table looks like an ordinary card table. However, the double fold-over top opens to reveal a surface for cards as well as a drawing or writing slope with two

drawers below and a tray for writing utensils. The piece has square, chamfered legs, which were introduced around this time. Unlike writing desks or card tables, architect's tables have a covered writing surface that can be adjusted. *c. 1760. H:36¼ in (90.5 cm). L&T* **4**

ENGLISH SETTEE

The back-splat design for this mahogany settee is based on two chair backs. The seat is upholstered in a flamestitch pattern. This medieval design was a favored textile of the period, and was used for curtains and bedhangings. The piece terminates in cabriole legs and claw-and-ball feet. *c.1755. NOA*

FRENCH CANAPÉ

This Louis XIV tapestry-covered walnut canapé is part of a suite. The original Beauvais tapestry is worked in vivid colors, depicting bold flowers, foliage, birds, and squirrels. The piece has eight cabriole legs that are carved with shells and foliage. *c. 1715. H:44 in (112 cm); W:68 in (173 cm); D:36 in (91.5 cm). PAR*

PAINTED ITALIAN SETTEE

This small, upholstered settee is based on the design for a French chair, but the Italian maker has added floral carving at the top of the legs and in the center of the chair rail. It is slightly bulkier than a French settee and the leg curve is more exuberant. *c. 1760. H:35¼ in (88 cm); W:51 in (130 cm). NAG* **4**

COMMODES

THE COMMODE BECAME popular in France around 1700, and the shape is now synonymous with the 18th century. Initially, the width was always greater than the height, sometimes exaggeratedly so, and the commode was a curved, *bombé* shape, often with slightly splayed legs.

Fashionable commodes had marble tops to match the marble of chimneypieces. They were often surmounted by a pier glass and either faced the chimneypiece or stood between the windows in reception rooms. As other countries created their own versions, commodes became more varied in form and decoration, and

were used in different rooms. Louis XV commodes usually have three large drawers, but the upper drawer is sometimes divided into two half-drawers. The drawer divisions were often disguised in French furniture. Louis XV commode cases were generally made of oak or walnut and veneered, and ormolu mounts were used to protect the veneers.

Louis XVI commodes were less curved and had shorter legs shaped like spinning tops (*toupées*). They were made of walnut and had veneers in exotic woods such as tulipwood, violet, or satinwood, enhanced with ebony and mahogany parquetry.

ITALIAN COMMODE

This Milanese commode is decorated with ivory marquetry set into olivewood and crossbanded veneers. The drawer divider, molding, frame, and legs are stained to resemble ebony. The marquetry top depicts mythological goddesses. *c. 1760. H:40¼ in (102 cm). LT* **6**

AMERICAN COMMODE

This marble-topped commode is made of mahogany, white pine, and chestnut, with brass drawer pulls and escutcheons. The commode is extremely rare in colonial furniture. *c. 1760. H:34¾ in (88.3 cm); W:36¾ in (93.3 cm); D:21½ in (54.6 cm).*

The top is made of marble.

The locks are decorated with gilt bronze.

Intricate veneers create elaborate parquetry.

Fine marquetry shows a bird-and-flower pattern.

The curved shape echoes Louis XV style.

SWEDISH COMMODE

This three-drawer commode by C. G. Wilkom has the short legs of Louis XVI commodes but not the fashionable *toupée* feet. The exaggerated curve at the top of the case is unusual. *c. 1776. H:31½ in (79 cm); W:32¼ in (80.5 cm); D:45 in (46 cm). BK* **5**

PARISIAN COMMODE

The two-drawer shape was standard in Louis XV design. The front of the piece is decorated with illusionist marquetry depicting a bouquet of flowers with birds, and the sides are covered with veneer made into a geometric pattern, known as parquetry. The front is made *sans*

traverses, meaning that the divide between the drawers is subtle, creating a unified pattern, although the drawers have dropped over time. The legs and body are curved, but less so than in many Louis XV pieces. Like much Louis XV furniture, ormolu mounts protect the feet and veneer. *c. 1760. H:34 in (85 cm); W:51¼ in (128 cm); D:24 in (60 cm). GK* **7**

The gilt bronze mounts are for both protection and decoration.

CURVED SWEDISH COMMODE

Although it is inspired by the French commode, the drawer divisions of this Swedish piece are emphasized by the banded inlay framing the drawers, and the placing of the escutcheons and handles. *c. 1750. H:33¼ in (83 cm); W:41¼ in (103 cm); D:19½ in (48.5 cm). BK* **5**

PROVINCIAL FRENCH COMMODE

abinet-makers from the provinces imitated Parisian fashions,
ut often used cheaper materials. This commode from Bordeaux,
ade in walnut rather than veneered with precious woods, has
ubtle incised frames around the handles and escutcheons.
he paneled sides and feet form an S-shaped curve.
. 1760. W:49¾ in (124.5 cm). SL **3**

GERMAN COMMODE

This French-style commode, made by the German cabinet-maker
Matthäus Funk, accentuates the divisions between the two
drawers more dramatically than most French pieces, using
gilding to emphasize the bottom of each drawer. The mounts
and the grain of the walnut provide decoration. c. 1760.
H:41½ in (104 cm); W:24½ in (61 cm); D:18 in (84 cm). GK **7**

PROVINCIAL DRESDEN COMMODE

This oak commode is an early Saxon example. It has a
serpentine front and carved bottom, typical of the commode
form. The escutcheons are very simple in design, and the
commode has simple French bracket feet, rather than the
cabriole legs found on more elaborate examples. c. 1750.
H:34¾ in (87 cm); W:50 in (125 cm); D:26½ in (66 cm). BMN **3**

PAINTED ITALIAN COMMODE

his two-drawer commode is decorated with paintings of
ristocrats in an idealized landscape, similar to the Rococo
aintings of Watteau (see p.78). Stylized leaf patterns adorn the
kirt, sides, and legs. The shape of the legs resembles the curved
abriole style of Louis XV, but is less pronounced. c. 1765. H:36 in
90 cm); W:46½ in (116 cm); D:25½ in (64 cm). GK **6**

ENGLISH CHIPPENDALE-STYLE COMMODE

This mahogany bombé commode has three oak-lined drawers.
The chased gilt brass Rococo swing handles and escutcheons are
not original. The piece has a Rococo carved frieze and foliage
carving on the front molded serpentine corners. The front legs
are decorated with leaf sprays emanating from cartouche carved
feet. Mid-18th century. H:38 in (97 cm). WW **7**

GERMAN COMMODE

This fine serpentine bombé walnut and fruitwood commode is
decorated with exquisite marquetry and parquetry. The locks,
drawer pulls, and feet are decorated with gilt bronze mounts.
This piece may have been made by the famous Spindler
brothers, court ebénistes to Frederick the Great. c. 1765.
H:35½ in (89 cm); W:64 in (160 cm); D:25¼ in (63 cm). NAG

FRENCH COMMODE

his walnut commode has a serpentine front and a shaped
pron. As is typical of French commodes, the top is made
f marble. The three drawers have decorative brass pulls and
eyholes. The piece terminates in cabriole legs and rests on
croll feet. Mid-18th century. H:36½ in (91 cm); W:48½ in
121 cm); D:24 in (60 cm). PIL **4**

PROVINCIAL GERMAN COMMODE

This serpentine commode is veneered in walnut with banding
around the drawers and veneer flitches of different colors.
The escutcheons are Rococo in style with asymmetrical pierced
attachments. Like most provincial commodes, it does not have
a marble top, but is veneered. The legs are slightly cabriole in
shape. c. 1750. W:50¾ in (127 cm). BMN **5**

TURKISH CHEST OF DRAWERS

This chest of drawers is influenced by different sources. It
incorporates the serpentine shape of the commode as well as the
massive shape and drawer configuration of library table designs
published in 18th-century pattern books. Columns and elaborate
carving add to the decorative features. c. 1750. H:18¾ in
(47 cm); W:36¾ in (92 cm); D:18½ in (46 cm). **5**

HIGHBOYS

HIGHBOYS AND LOWBOYS first occurred in England, but by 1730 highboys were almost exclusive to colonial America. Both pieces were intended for use in the bedroom, and were often made to be used together.

A lowboy, known in Great Britain as a dressing table, had drawers below a fixed top, and long legs to allow easy access to the drawers and to enable someone to sit comfortably at it. Lowboy drawers did not have locks, which indicates that items stored in them were not as valuable as those stored in the upper part of a highboy, which did lock. A mirror would often be hung above or placed on top of a lowboy.

Known as tallboys in England, highboys consisted of chests placed on top of lowboys. These imposing pieces were highly prized in America as symbols of wealth, and remain an important part of American cultural heritage. Each region had its own style, influenced by local materials and the cultural origin of the makers.

Flat-topped highboys were used to display ornaments, and cabinet-makers also made high chests with shelves on top which stepped inwards to display ceramics and other treasures. Toward mid-century, shaped tops became fashionable, and the finest pieces had carved pediments and finials.

ENGLISH HIGHBOY

This provincial George I highboy is made of oak and ash. The upper section has a flat cornice above two short drawers and three long drawers. The lower section has an arrangement of five drawers. It has fashionable cabriole legs but also has the "bat-shaped" brass escutcheons and handles popular at the beginning of the century. *c. 1720. MAL*

MASSACHUSETTS HIGHBOY

Made on the north shore of Massachusetts in native figured maple, this highboy is similar to English pieces of the period. Its flat projecting cornice may have been used to display prized pieces of ceramics or glass. The cabriole legs and Queen-Anne-style brass escutcheons indicate that this piece was made mid-century. *c. 1750. H:72¾ in (185 cm). NA* **4**

This pediment shape is known as a "bonnet top."

The urn-shaped finials display a Classical influence.

The central motif is a carved shell, which is repeated on the lowboy.

The brass escutcheons are etched.

Lowboy drawers do not have locks

Cabriole legs support the piece

The carved shell echoes the motif at the top of the piece.

BOSTON HIGHBOY AND LOWBOY

The japanned case of this Boston highboy is made of maple, while white pine is used for the interior supports. Its brass escutcheons are Queen Anne style in shape but with earlier-style engraving. Highboys like this were made in Boston as late as 1747, and this highboy's cabriole legs help to date it as a later example. Made with a matching lowboy, this highboy is one of only eight known japanned Boston highboys, with cabriole legs. *1747. H:70¼ in (178.5 cm); W:39¼ in (100.5 cm); D:20¾ in (53 cm).*

The japanned motifs are repeated from the highboy.

The turned pendants are carved and gilt, matching those on the highboy.

CONNECTICUT HIGHBOY

This highboy is made of cherrywood, a material favored by Connecticut cabinet-makers. The tapering scroll feet are a variation of a type known as Spanish feet, which were popular on American furniture. Connecticut pieces often incorporated features such as double Spanish feet and triple molded cornices. *c. 1730. H:76 in (193 cm). NAO*

PENNSYLVANIA HIGHBOY

This highboy is decorated with reeded quarter columns on the sides of the upper and lower base, and carved shells in the center of its cabriole legs. Trifid feet (which have three toe-shaped sections) were generally used only in New Jersey and Pennsylvania. *c. 1730. H:75 in (190.5 cm); W:42 in (107 cm); D:23 in (58.5 cm). NAO*

THE POUDREUSE AND COIFFEUSE

THE HIGHBOY AND LOWBOY DREW INSPIRATION FROM FEMININE FRENCH FURNITURE DEVELOPED FOR POWDERING HAIR AND APPLYING MAKEUP.

The French word *poudreuse* means "powder" or "dust." When applied to furniture, it refers to a table originally used as a place to powder hair. These fashionable French pieces evolved into dressing tables, lowboys, and ultimately highboys. A *poudreuse* usually had a marble top, which opened to reveal a mirror that could be raised on a rack. Beneath the mirror were compartments for powder and wigs.

As the fashion for face makeup grew, the *poudreuse* evolved into a larger piece, called the *coiffeuse*. Ladies' *coiffeuses* were often decorated with floral marquetry.

By the late 18th century, a *coiffeuse* with a writing surface and inkwell had been developed for use by gentlemen.

Paris Coiffeuse concealed compartments and a leather writing slide. This piece was intended for use in a lady's dressing room. *c. 1760. H:33⅜ in (86 cm); W:18½ in (47 cm); D:29 in (74 cm). GK*

French Coiffeuse with three false upper drawers and a mirror which is revealed when the central portion of the top is lifted. *c. 1750. H:27½ in (70 cm); W:32¼ in (82 cm); D:20 in (50 cm). NAG*

ENGLISH DRESSING TABLE

This mahogany dressing table has four drawers that pull out. Unlike French examples, these drawers are not divided into compartments. *c. 1750. H:28 in (71 cm); W:29 in (76 cm); D:18½ in (47 cm). PooK* **5**

WALNUT LOWBOY

This Delaware Valley piece has four equal-sized drawers positioned in pairs—a configuration favored by the middle American colonies. Its cabriole legs terminate in Spanish feet, a common characteristic of furniture from this area and New Jersey. *c. 1760. H:31 in (79 cm). PooK* **6**

NEW YORK HIGHBOY

This highboy is made of walnut, a wood used and favored by New York cabinet-makers in the 1720s and 1730s. Its proportions are particular to the New York region: it has a smaller upper section with four long drawers (the single top drawer appears to be split), and a lower case with three drawers. *c. 1730. H:41 in (104 cm). NA* **3**

CONNECTICUT HIGHBOY

This Chippendale-style tall chest is made of cherry. The upper section has a curved pediment flanked by terminals and has six drawers. The lower part is made up of one long drawer and short drawers on either side of a central fan-carved drawer. The piece has turned pendants and cabriole legs. *c. 1750. H:72 in (180 cm). PooK* **6**

PHILADELPHIA HIGHBOY

Highboys from Philadelphia were often highly carved and elaborately decorated. The upper section of this mahogany piece has a swan-neck pediment with floral terminals, which were popular in England. The urn and flame finials, and the acanthus carved on the cabriole legs, are typical Neoclassical motifs. *c. 1760. H:81½ in (206 cm). S&K* **3**

NEW ENGLAND LOWBOY

The case and top of this piece are veneered in figured walnut. The single long drawer—in this example fitted with compartments—over three short drawers is an arrangement typical of the New England style. The highly arched skirt is decorated with pendant finials, and the piece rests on cabriole legs. *c. 1735. W:32½ in (82.5 cm). FRE* **5**

TABLES

CHANGING SOCIAL CUSTOMS at the beginning of the 18th century created a need for many new types of table. The fashion for entertaining small groups of people led to a demand for light, portable tables that could be arranged wherever required. Specific tables were made for playing cards, taking tea, and writing letters.

The card table was primarily a British innovation. In the early part of the 18th century, the card table was basically a square table with a hinged top that folded back. The rear leg swung back to support the open top. Since card tables were stored against the wall, only the front skirt and legs were carved. The top often had hollowed-out corners for holding cards, chips, or candlesticks.

Writing tables were often fitted with a velvet or leather writing surface. Lady's writing tables were small, with a sloping top and a drawer for storing writing materials. These tables could also be used for embroidery or needlepoint. Men's writing tables, which were known in France as *bureaux plats*, were larger and had flat tops and a storage drawer.

Both console tables and pier tables were created as part of the design for an integrated interior. A console table usually had supports at the front only, because the back was attached to a wall. Pier tables were also designed to be positioned against the wall, but these were usually smaller, and had four legs. Traditionally, they stood between two windows or doors, and often had matching mirrors, known as pier glasses, above them. Both types of table were often elaborately decorated with carving and gilt, and had decorative marble tops, but the designs were generally lighter than the Baroque style favored in the 17th century, and they incorporated the asymmetric, natural motifs of the Rococo style.

Pedestal tables were columnar and had three splayed legs. The style of the tabletops varied. These tables were often used in dining rooms as tea tables for holding china and crockery.

Tripod candlestands generally had small, rounded tops. Larger tripod tables were often called tea tables, and the finest examples had scalloped tops with molded edges and elaborately carved columns and feet.

SWISS CONSOLE TABLE

This gilt table, probably made in Bern, has a marble top above a carved, pierced frame with Rococo scrolls, foliage, and asymmetrical shells. The apron and stretcher are both carved with an asymmetrical cartouche. *c. 1765. H:32¼ in (83 cm); W:14½ in (36 cm). GK* **4**

GERMAN PIER TABLE

This small pier table displays both Rococo and Neoclassical elements. The top is made of marble and sits above a frieze, decorated with a stylized Greek key motif. It is supported by four carved, scrolled legs. *c. 1760. H:35 in (89 cm); W:18 in (46 cm); D:32 in (81 cm). GK* **5**

GERMAN OAK TABLE

This imposing oak table is made in the Franconian Baroque style. It is veneered in walnut and the shaped top is inlaid with damson, cherrywood, and maple wood in a geometric marquetry pattern within a crossbanded surround. A shallow frieze, which is also crossbanded, leads into carved cabriole legs with scroll feet. The legs are joined by flat, shaped stretchers. The piece terminates in ball feet. *18th century. W:55¼ in (138 cm). BMN* **6**

FRENCH RÉGENCE *BUREAU PLAT*

This bureau is made of ebony with brass inlays. It has a serpentine bronze-framed top above three drawers at the front and blind drawers at the back. The piece is decorated with ormolu and sabot mounts, and has cabriole legs. *c. 1720. H:29 in (74 cm); W:59 in (150 cm). GK* **3**

The top is covered with inset gold leather.

The legs are cabriole-shaped.

The corners and sides are decorated with ormolu masks.

Ormolu mounts in the shape of animal hooves protect the feet.

ENGLISH SIDE TABLE

This small, vernacular side table is made of oak and fruitwood. It has one narrow frieze drawer above an undulating, shaped apron. The table stands on turned, slightly tapering legs, and terminates in pad feet. *c. 1750. H:27½ in (69.5 cm). DN* **1**

ICILIAN SIDE TABLE

his table is made of gilded pine with a marble top. The frieze
faced with glass panels painted on the underside to simulate
ue-gray onyx. Neoclassical symbols, such as egg and dart,
ay leaf moldings, and lion's masks, provide decoration. The
pered legs have acanthus plumes and are faced with glass
anels. *18th century.* H:38½ in (96 cm) W:50½ in (126 cm). TNH

GILTWOOD SIDE TABLE

This French Régence side table is heavily carved and covered
with gilt. The top is made of *rosso antico* marble. The frieze and
cabriole legs are elaborately decorated with carvings of pierced
foliage surmounted by nymphs' heads. The table was bought by
an English gentleman for his country house. *c. 1725.* H:33 in
(84 cm); W:43 in (110 cm); D:28 in (72 cm). MAL

GILTWOOD SIDE TABLE

This marble-topped giltwood table, which may be of German
origin, has an ornately carved frieze and apron, which are
enlivened with Rococo flames and swags of flowers on each
side. The cabriole legs have carved knees decorated with large,
bearded masks. *18th century.* H:32 in (80 cm); W:50 in
(124.5 cm); D:28 in (70 cm). HL **7**

ENGLISH TEA TABLE

his George II tea table has a mechanical
oncertina action, which means that when
ne two-part hinged tabletop is open, it reveals
ompartments for holding games. The piece
ands on cabriole legs and terminates in claw-
nd-ball feet. *c. 1750.* W:38 in (96 cm). DN **3**

GERMAN TABLE

This simple table, which has one small drawer
underneath an inlaid floral marquetry top, is
decorated with more marquetry over the shaped
frieze and cabriole legs. It is small enough to
move easily, and would have fulfilled many
uses. *c. 1760.* H:38 in (95 cm). BMN **3**

LOUIS XV WRITING TABLE

This small French writing table has a raised,
pierced brass edge around the top. The sides
and feet are decorated with ormolu mounts. The
escutcheons are asymmetrical in typical Rococo
style. *c. 1750.* H:29 in (72 cm); W:24 in
(60 cm); D:16½ in (41 cm). BK **4**

AMERICAN TEA TABLE

This vernacular table is made of painted maple.
The rectangular top has a molded edge
projecting over a shaped skirt with a drawer.
The corners of the frieze continue into sharp
edges down the cabriole legs, which lead into
pad feet. *c. 1740.* H:27½ in (70 cm). NA **5**

TILT-TOP TABLES

THESE VERSATILE TABLES WERE IDEAL FOR THE
NEWLY FASHIONABLE PASTIME OF DRINKING TEA.

Tilt-top tables had three parts: the top, a "birdcage"
mechanism that allowed the top to tilt and revolve, and a
columnar support with a tripod base. The top folded flat,
so that the table could be stored against a wall.

The top had a lip around the edge, to protect items on
the table, such as valuable porcelain cups. The birdcage,
named after its appearance, was used in England but was
more popular in America. An iron catch was fitted to the
underside of the top and birdcage, to lock the top in place.
The column was anchored to the birdcage with a removable
wedge. The various parts of the table were purchased from
different craftsmen, then assembled by a cabinet-maker.

Tilt-top tables from Philadelphia are considered the best
examples of colonial cabinet-making. The finest ones are
made of solid mahogany, which makes it difficult to
distinguish them from English examples.

Detail of mechanism

Birdcage

Philadelphia tilt-top tea table This fine table has a
birdcage support, a scalloped edge, a tripod base,
and claw-and-ball feet. The top is made from a
single piece of figured mahogany. *c. 1765.* H:48 in
(122 cm); W:35 in (89 cm). SP

CHAIRS

EARLY IN THE CENTURY, Queen Anne-style chairs had a solid, narrow splat, usually of a vase or baluster shape, which fitted into the center of the back rail. The frame tended to be straight and narrow, with rounded shoulders, and the seat was rounded or balloon-shaped with an upholstered seat.

Queen Anne chairs were usually made of walnut, although vernacular versions were made of elm or oak. They had slightly cabriole legs and pad feet. The earliest versions had flat or turned stretchers.

During the second quarter of the 18th century, squared seats became more common. The seat rails were shallower and often shaped, and sometimes had carved or applied shells in the center. Chair backs had serpentine crest rails terminating in scrolls or volutes and the back splat was wider. The upper section of the back splat sometimes had scrolled ears close to the intersection with the top rail. On very fine examples, splats were sometimes carved at the edges.

The knees of cabriole legs were now more pronounced and frequently carved with shells or husks, or had carved volutes attached below them. Most chairs still had pad feet, but claw-and-ball feet first appeared in about 1725 in Great Britain and around 1740 in the American colonies.

Chinese furniture-makers produced chairs that were similar in style for the lucrative European market.

The back splat is solid and an inverted baluster shape.

Carved roundels echo the decoration on the crest rail.

Shell motifs are often found on cabriole legs of the period.

ENGLISH SIDE CHAIR

This is the ultimate example of a George I side chair. The solid, inverted baluster-shaped back splat slips into a shaped shoe. Rounded shoulders form a continuous S-shape to the stiles, which terminate in volutes. Carved shells adorn the center of the crest rail and appear on the shaped knees. The balloon-shaped seat is upholstered in needlepoint. The front of the seat rail has a cartouche in the center. The cabriole front legs have claw-and-ball feet while the back legs have block feet. This type of chair was copied all over Great Britain, Europe, and the colonies, with chair-makers drawing on various elements depending on their clientele. *c. 1720. H:41½ in (105.5 cm); W:22½ in (57 cm); D:24 in (61 cm). PAR*

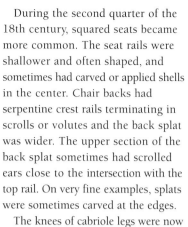

ENGLISH SIDE CHAIR

This is an early example of a Queen Anne side chair. The back splat is solid, the shoulders and stiles are slightly curved, and the slip seat is balloon-shaped. The chair is attributed to John Yorke on the basis of the design and construction. *c. 1710. H:45 in (114 cm); W:21 in (53.5 cm); D:23 in (58.5 cm). PAR*

CHINESE ARMCHAIR

This open-style armchair, made of solid padouk, incorporates a variety of different elements. The solid splat is shaped but the stiles below the shoulders remain straight. The splayed cabriole legs are shorter than those seen on European examples. *c. 1740. H:43 in (109 cm). B&I* **5**

AMERICAN SIDE CHAIR

This walnut chair from Massachusetts displays a mixture of styles. It has the slim back splat and turned stretchers popular at the beginning of the century, while the square slip seat and curved legs are more typical of the mid-century. It represents a transition between Queen Anne and Chippendale styles. *c.1745. NA* **4**

PERUVIAN ARMCHAIR

This mahogany chair reflects the Rococo style. The crest rail has asymmetrical central carving. The sinuous molding continues from the crest rail down the stiles and onto the arms. The cabriole legs have C-scrolls on the knees. The splat may be a later replacement. *c. 1750. H:48 in (122 cm); W:23¼ in (59 cm). TNH*

ANTONESE SIDE CHAIR

he wide, undulating shoulders of this chair
nd the unusually wide splat indicate that the
air is of non-European origin. The crest rail
d back stiles are made from one piece of
od, which is typical of Chinese furniture.
*1730. H:41¾ in (106 cm); W:20½ in
3 cm); D:20¾ in (53 cm). MJM*

INTERPRETING THE FRENCH STYLE

A MOVE AWAY FROM THE FORMALITY OF THE BAROQUE INTERIOR LED TO A DEMAND FOR MORE COMFORTABLE FURNITURE,
AND THE FRENCH LED THE WAY WITH THE *FAUTEUIL*, ONE OF THE MOST ICONIC PIECES OF THE 18TH CENTURY.

During the 18th century, the European nobility and the
increasingly influential middle classes sought more elegant
surroundings and rooms in which to entertain and
converse, and with this came more comfortable furniture,
which invited visitors to linger.

This desire for a more sociable environment led
to the development of new chair styles. French
craftsmen created the *fauteuil*, an upholstered
armchair with open sides. This feminine-
looking piece influenced the development
of chairs around the world, and allowed
the occupant to entertain in comfort.

Compared to the heavy-looking, high-
backed chairs of the 17th century,
these armchairs were lighter and
more refined in shape, reflecting
the fashion for feminine
furnishings. They were often
decorated in the same style as
the room's other furnishings,
using similar color and fabrics.

The seat and back of the
fauteuil were upholstered
to make the chair more
comfortable. The armrests
were also padded and covered

in the same fabric. The arms were set farther back around a
quarter of the length of the side-rail in order to accommodate the
large, hooped skirts that were fashionable with aristocratic
ladies from around 1720.

Decoration was often asymmetrical in the Rococo style,
incorporating shells and rocaille. Raised on cabriole legs, the
entire frame of the chair was a mass of graceful curves.

Usually painted in pale blues, greens and yellows
to match the color scheme of the interior,
the exposed framework might also have
gilt decoration to emphasize both shape
and carved detail.

Cabinet-makers all over Europe strove
to emulate and surpass the talents of
their French counterparts in meeting
the demands of their wealthy
clients, many of whom were
hungry for furniture in the
French taste. Interpretations
of the *fauteuil* were plentiful
throughout the continent,
and the *fauteuil* became
the seating style of choice
for the most fashionable
European homes in the
early 18th century.

Italian armchair Inspired by the *fauteuil*, this Italian
example has a higher, more oval back with intricate
gilt carving. The pastel paint reflects the French
fashion for more subtle surroundings. *c. 1750.
H:37 in (94 cm); W:24 in (61 cm). PAR*

WEDISH ARMCHAIR

he back splat of this mahogany chair is
nusual in that it terminates into a back
tretcher rather than into the seat of the chair.
stylized carved shell decorates the crest rail
nd serpentine apron. This chair also has
rned stretchers, even though they were no
nger fashionable at this time. *c. 1755. BK* 4

German chair This chair emulates those of
contemporary French cabinet-makers, whose
influence can be seen in the ornate, rocaille
carving and the pale colors of the floral-
embroidered silk upholstery. *NAG*

English armchair Essentially French in style, the
later date of this armchair by Ince and Mayhew
is evident from the square, tapering legs and
Neoclassical decoration, which were fashionable
from the 1760s. *c. 1770. H:38½ in (98 cm). PAR*

French fauteuil The elegance of the gentle curves
is emphasized by the gilt decoration. The shell
motifs on the crest rail and the knees are typical
of the period. *c. 1750. H:38 in (96.5 cm);
W:27½ in (70 cm); D:24 in (61 cm). PAR*

EVOLUTION OF MIRRORS

FOR MANY YEARS THE MIRROR WAS A RARE AND VASTLY EXPENSIVE ITEM, AND TODAY IT IS DIFFICULT TO APPRECIATE JUST HOW PRIZED AND IMPORTANT MIRROR GLASS ONCE WAS.

AT THE END of the 17th century, a mirror about 40in x 36in (1m x 90 cm) would have cost the equivalent of $36,000 in today's currency. The earliest mirrors were handheld, but by the 18th century, the mirror had become an essential part of the fashionable home.

A BRIEF HISTORY

Mirrors have been used for thousands of years. They were believed to foretell the future and to bring bad luck, especially when broken. Many people thought that to see your reflection was to see your soul, and for years the Church was against the use of mirrors.

The earliest known mirror was made of bronze, and ancient civilizations also used silver, gold, tin, steel, obsidian (volcanic glass), and rock crystal. Curved glass mirrors, made by cutting a sphere in two, were produced during the Middle Ages, but it was not until the 15th century that it was possible to create flat, colorless glass, known as "crystallo." This technique created relatively small pieces of glass.

VENETIAN GLASSMAKERS

Crystallo, or crystalline glass, and blown glass were developed in Venice. The Venetian workshops were the only places producing glass mirrors before the mid-17th century. The commercial importance of this discovery prompted the Venetian authorities to forbid glassmakers to move from their headquarters on the island of Murano on pain of death.

DEVELOPMENTS IN EUROPE

Although some Venetian glassmakers were seduced into setting up workshops, principally in Germany and the Low Countries, it was not until around 1663 that Murano's supremacy was challenged. Louis XIV of France established a glassworks at Tourlaville, while in England, a glassworks was set up at Vauxhall to produce mirrors for the court of Charles II.

At the end of the 17th century, Bernard Perrot, working at Tourlaville, developed the casting method, which made it possible to create larger sheets of glass. The glass was translucent but not transparent, since minerals in the sand affected the result. Artisans cut, ground, engraved, polished, and silvered the glass, using mercury to produce a reflective surface. In 1835, real silver was used for the first time, relieving the makers of the hazards of mercury poisoning.

ENGLISH GILDED EASEL MIRROR
This mirror was designed to be placed on a table. Mirror backs were often covered with softwood, to protect the glass and metal from being oxidized by the light. c. 1725. H:31¼ in (78 cm). NOA

Chinoiserie mask

Foliage motifs

Female masks

Marble fire surround

GEORGE II CHIMNEYPIECE
This giltwood mirror, attributed to Matthias Lock, has an elaborately carved frame with Rococo details of fruit, leaves, birds, scrolls, and chinoiserie elements. c. 1755.
H:236 in (590 cm); W:86 in (215 cm).

MIRROR BOX
This stunning box mirror has a number of architectural elements, including the broken pediment and the two marble columns flanking the mirror plate. The piece is inlaid with precious stones. This mirror was once owned by Marie de Medici.

CARVED, GILDED GIRANDOLE
This is one of a pair of fine giltwood girandoles after a design by Thomas Johnson, published in 1758. The gilding and candles helped to reflect more light around a room.
1760. H:48 in (120 cm); W:21¼ in (53 cm). NOA

VENETIAN OVAL MIRROR
This oval-shaped glass is typical of Italian design and uses etched and applied glass to frame the central oval mirror. Its Venetian origin would have made it highly coveted. Whole teams of artisans were needed to create mirrors like this.
1800–15. H:39 in (100 cm). DC

CHANGING FASHIONS
The production of larger sheets of glass enabled mirrors to become the focal point of the room, and to reflect light around what were previously very dark homes. The *Salle des Glaces* at the Palace of Versailles (*see p.34*) must have made a powerful impact on those who had never seen anything other than a small hand mirror.

In England, 1700–40 marked a golden age of mirror production while the 20 percent tax on mirrors was temporarily abolished. Large mirrors were designed to be placed over the mantelpiece, and long pier glasses were made, often in pairs, to fit between windows in grand houses. Fashionable country homes were furnished with fine mirrors. In 1703, John Gumley produced 10-ft- (3-m-) high mirrors decorated with blue glass for Chatsworth.

From about 1725, English design was inspired by Palladian architecture (*see p.96*), often mirroring architectural details of the house in the frame. Oval mirrors were also very popular.

FRAME DESIGN
Due to their size and the versatility of frame carving, mirrors were among the first household objects to reflect fashion. At the turn of the 18th century, lacquer panels or japanning were sought after. Later, fashion favored elaborately carved Rococo frames, including asymmetrical mirrors with chinoiserie, C-scrolls, and foliage.

KEY DATES

20th century BCE Hand-held polished bronze mirror.

6th century Etruscan hand mirror.

1291 Venetian Republic requires glassworkers to move to the island of Murano.

1448 Term "crystalline glass" appears in the inventory of René d'Anjou.

1571–92 Venetian craftsman, Jacopo Verzelini, sets up glassworks in the City of London.

1612 *L'Arte Vetraria*, by Antonio Neri, about the processes of glassmaking, published in Florence.

1618 Sir Robert Mansell obtains patent to set up a London glasshouse employing Venetian glassmakers.

1665 Nicholas du Noyer sets up a glasshouse employing 200 workers in Paris.

c. 1670 Bernard Perrot invents casting technique, making it possible to create larger sheets of glass.

1676 George Ravenscroft invents lead crystal glass by adding lead oxide to glass.

1678 Patent granted to John Roberts' "invention of grinding, polishing and diamonding glass plates for looking glasses…by the motion of water and wheels."

1719 *Real Fábrica de Coina*, probably Portugal's first mirror factory, established by John Beare.

MIRRORS

NOWHERE WAS THE influence of Rococo style stronger than in mirror design. It was difficult to produce big sheets of glass, so large mirrors were often made of several pieces of glass. Eighteenth-century glass tends to be thin with shallow bevels. Many pattern books were published at the time, and as a result, many pieces show influences from other countries.

In the early part of the century, mirror frames were usually made of carved gilt or silvered gesso on a wooden base, and then walnut was used with giltwood until the start of the Rococo period, when carved giltwood and mahogany took over. Costly materials such as colored and etched glass were sometimes included. Candelabra were often attached to the base of frames (known as *girandoles*) to reflect light into dark rooms and cast dancing shadows on the walls.

Frames were made from softwoods such as pine and fruitwoods, making it possible to carve curves, scalloped shells, and ornate cartouches with relative ease. The joints were gessoed and painted with gold or silver leaf. Popular motifs included shells, acanthus leaves, egg-and-dart molding, and cresting, often depicting birds with outstretched wings. Bird motifs were popular in America. It is difficult to distinguish American mirrors from the English ones that were imported in large quantities, partly because the American and European species of spruce, which were often used in the frames, are very similar.

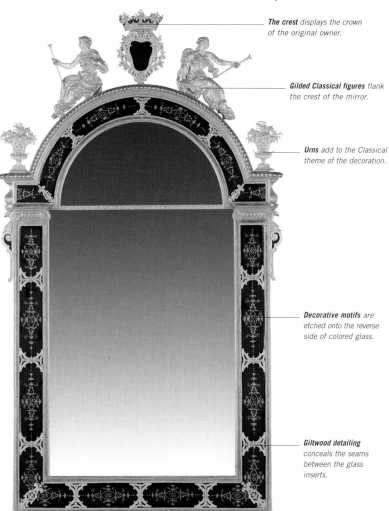

The crest displays the crown of the original owner.

Gilded Classical figures flank the crest of the mirror.

Urns add to the Classical theme of the decoration.

Decorative motifs are etched onto the reverse side of colored glass.

Giltwood detailing conceals the seams between the glass inserts.

PIER MIRROR

This elegant mirror would have been placed above a pier table and was probably one of a pair. Pier mirrors were designed to hang between the windows in a drawing room. Since it was difficult to manufacture large mirrors, two plates of glass are joined by a gilt wooden frame. The cobalt-blue etched glass inserts were designed to glow in candlelight, and were created by *églomisé*, where the design is etched on the back of the glass. Classical forms were fashionable, as seen by the trumpet-bearing maidens on the top of the mirror. Frames were more influenced by fashion than larger items of furniture, so they are good indicators of contemporary styles. *c. 1735. H:78¾ in (197 cm); W:46¾ in (117 cm). MAL*

ENGLISH PIER GLASS

This mirror is a fine example of the Palladian style. with a central mask set into the crest. Decorated with carved and gilded gesso, this pier glass is a rare find because it still retains the original candle arms, which are often missing from pieces of this period. *c. 1720. H:47½ in (119 cm); W:26½ in (66 cm). NOA*

MIRROR WITH PAINTED FRAME

This highly colored Venetian mirror frame is reminiscent of Italian painted furniture of the time, but it also has elements of Louis XV style in the scrolled feet and curvaceous frame. The frame is painted and has highlights picked out in gilt. *c. 1760. H:29¼ in (73 cm); W:17½ in (44 cm). GK* 2

GERMAN MIRROR

This south German wall mirror frame is made of carved and gilded wood. The foliate carving winds around the frame to make a curvaceous rectangular shape. The crown and pendant are typical of the asymmetrical Rococo style. *Mid-18th century. H:53¼ in (133 cm); W:24¾ in (63 cm). BMN* 3

ENGLISH MIRROR

One of a pair, this walnut mirror features a gilt carved phoenix flanked by a broken pediment terminating in carved and gilt foliage. The birds on the crests of the two mirrors face in different directions, indicating that the mirrors were originally placed next to each other. *c. 1740. H:41½ in (104 cm); W:21¾ in (54.5 cm). NA*

⎡ERMAN MIRROR

the early 18th century, Germans continued to
⎡vor designs that were no longer fashionable in
⎡ance or England. The pelmet in the cresting
⎡d the heavy design features are similar to
⎡te-17th-century styles, but the scrolling
⎡liage decoration is typical of the Rococo
⎡yle. *c. 1760. H:28 in (70 cm). GK* 2

ENGLISH CARTOUCHE MIRROR

This cartouche-shaped mirror is a good example
of the English interpretation of Rococo. C-scrolls
and curved foliage were very popular motifs in
all Rococo pieces, but the carving of this mirror
frame is less ornate than that on French pieces
of the period. *c. 1760. H:35½ in (89 cm);
W:(max) 18¾ in (47 cm). NOA*

ITALIAN GIRANDOLE MIRROR

This Italian late Rococo mirror is strikingly
similar to English and French designs of the
time. It is made of carved and gilded soft wood.
A candle holder is positioned at the base of
the glass. Mirrors incorporating candle holders,
girandoles, were popular in the Rococo period.
c. 1770. H:34½ in (86.5 cm). DL 3

ENGLISH GEORGE II MIRROR

This beveled mirror frame is made of carved
giltwood and red lacquer. The pierced giltwood
frame is carved at the top with scrolling foliate
cresting, flanked by two bird's heads. The frame
is decorated with birds, flowers, acanthus leaves,
strapwork; and a cartouche at the base. *c. 1735.
H:40 in (101.5 cm); W:26 in (66 cm). PAR*

⎡TALIAN OVERMANTEL MIRROR

⎡his large mirror uses many different sizes of
⎡late in the frame. The joints are disguised
⎡y carved, gilt fillets across the larger pane
⎡f glass and scroll elements along the sides.
⎡⎡any smaller pieces of glass alongside the
⎡ain mirror reflect additional light. *c. 1750.
⎡:76½ in (191 cm). DN* 5

AMERICAN CHIPPENDALE MIRROR

This mirror is a fine example of Chippendale
style. Made of highly polished mahogany, it
lacks the gilt decoration of many pieces of the
period. The interior of the frame surrounding
the glass is double-molded and both the crest
and base are serpentine-shaped with delicate
ears. *Mid-18th century. FRE* 2

AMERICAN CHIPPENDALE MIRROR

This mirror frame in the Chippendale style is
made of walnut with parcel gilding. The crest is
decorated with a foliate design. It is attributed
to John Elliott of Philadelphia, who both made
and imported mirror frames. Many British
Chippendale-style frames were exported to the
colonies at this time. *NA* 3

ENGLISH CHIPPENDALE MIRROR

Mirrors of this design, often without a gilt bevel
surrounding the plate, were exported in large
numbers from England, spreading the
Chippendale style. This frame is made of pine
veneered in walnut and parcel gilt. The candle
holders are decorated with leaf motifs. *c. 1750.
H:45½ in (114 cm); W:24½ in (61 cm). NOA*

LATE 18TH CENTURY
1760-1800

A NEW CLASSICISM

THE SECOND HALF OF THE 18TH CENTURY WAS A PERIOD OF IMMENSE REVOLUTIONARY CHANGE AND A RENEWED INTEREST IN CLASSICAL ARCHITECTURE AND DESIGN.

Transitional *fauteuil à la reine* This giltwood armchair is carved with berried laurel leaves and rosettes. *c. 1775. H:40½ in (103 cm). PAR*

DURING THE EARLY YEARS of the 18th century, an agricultural revolution slowly spread across Britain, Europe, and the Americas. Farmers enclosed the old open, mixed fields of crops and pasture, and used new and intensive methods of farming as well as experimenting with new breeds of livestock. These changes increased food production, thus pushing down prices, but also drove farm workers off the land into the rapidly expanding towns.

In 1760, a second revolution got under way in Britain as inventors and engineers developed new machinery powered by coal and water. The steam engine and pump, mechanical spinning machine, blast furnace, and other inventions revolutionized the manufacture of textiles and eventually led to the mass production of furniture and other household goods. Methods of working changed, too, as people who had previously worked at home in rural cottage industries now lived together in towns and cities and worked long hours in vast factories.

THE ENLIGHTENMENT

Alongside and informing both these revolutions was the cultural revolution known as the Enlightenment, a philosophical attempt to rationalize the replacement of customs, traditions, and religion with reason and natural law. Philosophers, scientists, astronomers, explorers, and surveyors questioned the boundaries of their world and pursued new ways of thought that influenced two of the most important political revolutions in history: the American Revolution of 1776 against British colonial rule, which led to the independence of the United States of America; and the French Revolution of 1789, which overthrew the monarchy and introduced new ideas of liberty, equality, and fraternity.

NEOCLASSICISM

Just as the Enlightenment philosophers looked back to the ordered Classical world for inspiration—to understand how humankind fitted into a universe of laws and reason—so, too, did designers, giving birth to the movement we now call Neoclassicism. The term itself did not appear in print until 1861 in a review of a painting, but it is generally used to refer to the style of art, architecture, and design that was concerned with the ideals of the Classical world and flourished in the late 18th century.

The intellectuals and travelers of the period revered the Classical world of the ancient Greeks and Romans. With the discovery of ancient Roman villas and their furnishings in Pompeii and Herculaneum after 1738, the craze for the Classical world was unleashed. It began with the application of decorative Classical motifs and the principal of symmetry to architecture. Various artists and architects published great tomes illustrating the ancient world, thus creating a demand for a more accurate Classicism rather than just a reworking of Italian Renaissance and Baroque architecture. It then spread to interior design, notably furniture, as well as to painting, pottery, glass, and tapestry, totally transforming the environment and style of the period.

Somerset House, London This is a fine example of a symmetrical Neoclassical building. It was designed by Sir William Chambers between 1766 and 1786.

TIMELINE 1760–1800

George III

c. 1760 The Age of Enlightenment, embodied in works by Voltaire, Diderot, Rousseau, and Hume.

1760 George III crowned king of Britain.

1762 James Stuart and Nicholas Revett publish *Antiques of Athens*, raising public interest in Classical antiquities, and influencing design styles.

1762 Accession of Catherine the Great to the Russian throne, extending European influence in Russia.

1762 English government declares war on Spain over colonies in Europe; Spain declares war on Portugal.

1763 Treaty of Paris ends Seven Years' War between France and England.

The American eagle

1767 Jesuits expelled from Spain and all Spanish colonies by Charles III.

1769 Josiah Wedgwood relocates his pottery to Etruria in Staffordshire.

1773 Robert and James Adam, Scottish architects, publish *Works in Architecture*, instigating a major Classical revival in architecture and the decorative arts.

1776 The US Declaration of Independence. The eagle is adopted as an American emblem on furniture.

The world's first iron bridge This bridge was erect over the Severn River at Coalbrookdale in Shropsh England in 1779.

Room in Syon House, London Syon house was remodeled by the British architect Robert Adam in around 1765. This room is richly decorated and exhibits the Neoclassical influence with the golden statues supported on marble columns that circle the room.

Giltwood console table One of a pair, this table has a painted satinwood top and a painted tablet in satinwood at the center of the carved and gilt frieze, which has gilt swags below. The table is supported on turned and fluted, tapering legs. c. 1770. W:38⅝ in (98 cm). PAR

779 First iron bridge is erected at Coalbrookdale in Shropshire.

780 David Roentgen becomes a member of the Paris Guild of *Ébénistes*.

1783 End of American Revolution war. The Treaty of Paris recognizes the new United States, and Britain accepts American independence.

The Argand lamp allowed more oxygen to the flame and so increased brilliance.

1783 Louis XVI orders a suite of furniture for Marie Antoinette costing 25,356 livres.

1784 End of the Anglo-Dutch war.

1784 Invention of the Argand lamp revolutionizes lighting and interiors.

1788 First British settlement founded at Botany Bay in Australia.

1788 George Hepplewhite publishes the *Cabinet-Maker*

Wolfgang Amadeus Mozart

and Upholsterer's Guide.

1789 The French Revolution begins with the storming of the Bastille.

1789 George Washington becomes the first president of the United States.

c. 1790 High point of European orchestral music with compositions from Mozart, Haydn, and Beethoven.

1792 Trial of Louis XVI; French Republic proclaimed.

1793 Louis XVI and Queen Marie Antoinette executed; Roman Catholicism banned in France; Reign of Terror begins; Holy Roman Empire declares war on France.

1796 James Wyatt begins building Fonthill Abbey in Wiltshire, England, for the writer William Beckford.

1799 Napoleon Bonaparte becomes Consul.

Napoleon Bonaparte

NEOCLASSICAL FURNITURE

THE HEART OF NEOCLASSICAL DESIGN lies in ancient Greece and Rome. It was initially inspired by architecture, since there were no examples of ancient furniture until after the excavation of Pompeii and Herculaneum in the mid-18th century. Thus, early Neoclassical furniture tends to use architectural motifs adhered to in standard furniture forms, such as acanthus leaves, swags and foliage, guilloche bands, and scrolls. The use of these motifs was not new, as they were employed as ornament in both the Renaissance and Baroque periods. What was new was how the motifs were adapted, added to, and incorporated within the decorative schemes encountered through travel on the Grand Tour (see p.132) and the discoveries made in ancient sites.

INTRODUCING THE STYLE

France was the first country to embrace Neoclassical design, although it was not until the 1770s that the final vestiges of Rococo were erased from

the decorative library. The French barometer of taste, the Comte de Caylus (1692–1765), was instrumental in introducing Classicism, including Classical furniture, to France, publishing in 1752 the first of seven volumes of *Recueil d'antiquités égyptiennes, étruscanes, grecques et romaines*, in which he discussed and illustrated the tastes and styles of the ancient world.

Neoclassical furniture tends to be rectangular and lacks curves. This did not happen all at once, since larger pieces often remained in stock after fashions had changed and cabinet-makers adapted the Rococo forms by applying Neoclassical decoration. In this French transitional style, serpentine shapes were gradually straightened and cabriole legs evolved into turned or tapered legs. Chair backs were rectangular or oval with turned legs, often fluted in reference to Classical architectural columns.

DIFFERENT INTERPRETATIONS

Throughout the Neoclassical period, building booms influenced the production of furnishings. More palaces were built in Russia in the second half of the 18th century than in any other European country. These new buildings, and refurbished older buildings, required new furniture, as most of the existing pieces lacked sufficient pomp and majesty for Catherine the Great's court. Most Russian furniture was imported from Paris, as Russian taste tended to emulate French style. The German *ébéniste* David Roentgen (see pp.142–43) made furniture specifically for his Russian clientele that was far more flamboyant than French court furniture.

ADAM STYLE

The Neoclassical style in England—home to the innovative architecture of Robert Adam—adapted some French forms such as the commode and the "French chair." Adam's furniture complemented the light colors used in his interiors and textiles, and painted decoration featured more than

Parisian *guéridon* Made of rosewood, kingwood, and sycamore, this table is inlaid with musical instruments and has a brass gallery. *c. 1775. H:29 in (74 cm); W:19¼ in (49 cm); D:15 in (38 cm). GK*

in its French counterparts. Greek vase paintings greatly influenced Adam, and he often used painted panels in his work; these might be the central panel of a *demi-lune* or rectangular commode, or a centered roundel at the top of a pier glass flanked by carved maidens and urns.

Thomas Chippendale also worked in the Neoclassical style, producing a pair of rectangular pedestals with urns, a sideboard table, and wine cooler for the dining room at Harewood House (see p.98). For this commission he used circular inlaid medallions on the pedestals with carved swags and rams' heads above, to match the other pieces.

TRANSMITTING THE STYLE

The pattern books published by George Hepplewhite and Thomas Sheraton simplified Adam's designs for the mass market. Their designs were hugely influential particularly in the US. Furniture in this style is termed Federal after the new US government and often features the official symbol of the American eagle.

Swedish furniture from this time is referred to as Gustavian after King Gustav III who admired the work of the French cabinet-makers so much that he invited them to work in Sweden. When he could not afford to pay them, they returned home, but left their furniture style as a lasting legacy. Danish furniture was simpler and often made from darker woods. Decoration was limited to dentil molding, the Greek key motif, and rosettes.

European furniture fashion tended to follow French or English taste: in Spain, the north was inspired by English styles, while in the south, French styles were dominant.

English lady's writing desk The satinwood and yew tambour shutter opens to reveal a fitted desk interior. Beneath this is a long drawer with a frieze. The scrolling foliage pattern, brass ring pulls, and etched wyverns are all typical Neoclassical motifs. The desk has square, inlaid, tapering legs and brass feet on casters. *c. 1775. H:37 in (94 cm); W:32½ in (82.5 cm). PAR*

SIGNATURE STAMPS

Parisian guild restrictions drawn up by the French *Parlement* in 1751 stipulated that cabinet-makers and chair-makers had to mark their work. Each master had his own stamp, and an impression of this *estampille* in lead was kept by the guild. From 1743, many artisans had, in fact, already been stamping their pieces, with an iron stamp in the form of their name. Some, like the chair-maker Georges Jacob and his sons, merely used their surname. Others used their initials, like the cabinet-maker Robert Vandercruse La-Croix, with his stamp R.V.L.C.

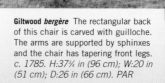

Georges Jacob's stamp Stamped on the underside of the back rail of the *bergère* shown is JACOB, the *estampille* for the chair-maker Georges Jacob (1739–1814). He received his mastership in 1765.

Giltwood *bergère* The rectangular back of this chair is carved with guilloche. The arms are supported by sphinxes and the chair has tapering front legs. *c. 1785. H:37¾ in (96 cm); W:20 in (51 cm); D:26 in (66 cm). PAR*

A NEOCLASSICAL COMMODE

This harewood and marquetry commode represents the zenith of 18th-century cabinet-making. It has been attributed to various London furniture workshops, including those of John Cobb and William Vile, and William Ince and John Mayhew, both workshops competing with Chippendale. The marquetry is of the finest quality and may have been supplied by a specialist maker. The top panel is more freely designed than the door panels, indicating that they might have been made by two different makers.

This piece is more decorative than functional and would have been used in the drawing room, a French practice introduced by the French cabinet-maker Pierre Langlois and quickly taken up by Robert Adam. Up until about 1760, commodes had only been deemed fit for use in the bedroom.

Harewood and marquetry commode The serpentine-shaped top of this commode is inset with a circular panel, inlaid with a marquetry design. The serpentine front is fitted with doors, behind which are shelves. The commode is supported on splayed bracket feet with cloven-hoof ormolu mounts. Both the top and sides are decorated with ormolu fluted and beaded banding. *c. 1760.* H:36 in (91.5 cm); W:46 in (117 cm); D:22 in (56 cm). PAR

The serpentine top and sides *are trimmed with ormolu fluted and beaded banding.*

This circular panel *is inlaid with a marquetry design of flowers and gardening tools.*

This diaper pattern *repeats the parquetry pattern on the sides of the commode.*

The splayed bracket feet *have ormolu mounts in the shape of animal hooves.*

Rococo influences *can still be seen in the curvaceous shape of the commode.*

The oval door panels *are inlaid with a striking design of flaming urns with ram masks on tripod stands.*

Oval panels *on the sides of the commode feature intricate geometric parquetry.*

ELEMENTS OF STYLE

The decorative details of Neoclassical furniture were inspired by ancient Greece and Rome, and there was a marked move away from the asymmetrical exuberance of the Rococo period toward a more restrained, symmetrical, and linear style. Architectural details, such as friezes and swags, were used to decorate chair rails and tables and the shapes of legs were influenced by Greek columns. Many Classical motifs had symbolic meanings. Grecian urns were particularly popular, although designers chose to ignore their symbolic funerary use and concentrate on the pleasing symmetry of their shape.

Swag of laurel leaves

Greek urn on a mahogany cabinet

French-style armchair

Oval chair backs

Oval and shield-shaped chair backs became increasingly popular from the 1760s onward, especially in France. The frames of these sumptuous chairs were usually gilded and carved with Classical motifs, including acanthus. The finest armchairs were upholstered with costly silks and damasks.

Swags

The swag is a decorative motif inspired by hanging garlands of laurel leaves, ribbons, or budlike motifs known as husks. They were based on Classical Roman stone examples, which were themselves copies of the garlands that decorated altars and temples.

Greek urns

Urns were carved, incorporated in marquetry patterns, or applied as sculptural relief to furniture. They were based on the shape of ancient Greek vases, which were often used to hold human ashes. The motif was popular on Louis XVI and Adam-style pieces. Often the urns incorporated Classical mask heads and swags.

Gilded mask motif on a frieze

Intarsia panel on a German cabinet

Friezes

A frieze is a horizontal band used to decorate case furniture, chairs, or tables. Architectural details taken from friezes at the tops of Classical columns were often copied. These included Vitruvian scrolls, Greek key motifs, egg-and-dart molding (which symbolized life and death), and lines of small beads, known as beading.

Intarsia

Cabinet-makers working in the Neoclassical style took advantage of the flat surfaces on rectilinear furniture to create elaborate three-dimensional intarsia inlays. Designs ranged from complex architectural scenes, which were particularly popular on Italian and German pieces, to simple ribbon-tied bouquets.

Anthemion frieze on a *demi-lune* commode

Oval inlaid shell motif

A carved ram's head

Parquetry detail on a cabinet

Anthemion

The stylized floral motif of the anthemion is based on the ancient Greek representation of the honeysuckle flower and leaves. It was mainly used horizontally as a repeated motif, often alternating with carved acanthus, palmettes (palm leaves), or lotus leaves, to form a frieze. Single motifs were sometimes also used on vertical panels.

Decorative inlays

Delicate inlaid designs were particularly popular as decorative veneers on tables and case furniture. Many motifs, such as shells and flowers, were inspired by nature, but fans and vases were also popular. The maker required a great deal of skill to create the intricate inlays used on the finest examples of Neoclassical furniture.

Ram's head

The motif of a ram's or goat's head was used in antiquity to decorate altars, probably as a sacrificial representation. Robert Adam first used them on English furniture. Carved ram's heads were a popular decoration on tripod table knees, and as objects from which to hang swags.

Parquetry

Cabinet-makers took advantage of the increased availability of exotic woods with a strong grain, such as kingwood, tulipwood, and satinwood, to create striking veneers. Parquetry, which used geometric patterns made up of cubes, lozenges, trellis, or trellis patterns with dots in the center, was particularly popular and reflected the interest in symmetrical, rectilinear designs.

Detail of a gilt table leg with husk carving

Oval brass handles with solid backplates

Inlaid satinwood table top

Cameo of a Roman emperor

Columnar legs

In a move away from the curved cabriole leg, based on an animal's leg, which dominated furniture design earlier in the 18th century, the legs of tables and chairs frequently looked like miniature Greek and Roman columns. Often tapering and fluted, they sometimes had additional decoration, such as the carving above.

Brass handles

Supplied by specialist craftsmen, brass handles were made in many shapes during the second half of the 18th century, but unlike Rococo pieces they tended to be symmetrical in shape, usually oval or circular. Handles and escutcheons were often embellished with Classical decoration, such as wreaths of laurel leaves.

Satinwood

The period from 1765 to 1800 is sometimes referred to as the Age of Satinwood. This light yellow wood from the West Indies had a silky sheen and satinlike markings, hence its name. Because it was expensive, it was mostly used as a veneer. Many satinwood furniture pieces were created from designs by Robert Adam.

Classical figures

Classical imagery of all types was widespread in the second half of the 18th century. The motifs often appeared on friezes or in the center of doors or panels. Cameos, in which figures were shown in profile, were particularly popular. The medallion above is typical of the type of decoration used by the Adam brothers.

ITALY

THE ITALIAN STATES retained their separate identities during the late 18th century. These rival regions assimilated the Neoclassical style at different times: Rome, Naples, Turin, and Genoa gradually moved toward Classical forms, while Venice was much slower and only embraced Neoclassical designs toward the end of the 18th century.

INFLUENCES

France, and to a lesser extent Britain, provided the main sources of Neoclassical design. However, the Neoclassical style was also directly influenced by Italy's ancient sites and contemporary archeological discoveries.

In 1757, the first volume of eight, *Le antichità di Ercolano esposte,* was published in Naples, describing the discoveries at Herculaneum. The illustrations of ancient motifs and decorations such as palmettes, beading, ribbons, cameos, lion's heads, pelts, and feet subsequently appeared in painted decoration and furniture. The colors seen at Herculaneum—red, green, blue, and white—also became very popular in painted furniture.

Giovanni Battista Piranesi's *Diverse Maniere d'Adornare i Cammini* illustrated a more sumptuous version of Neoclassicism. His designs were not only influential in Rome, where they were refined and used by the architects furnishing several rooms at the Vatican, but also throughout the rest of Europe.

FURNITURE TYPES AND MATERIALS
Commodes had rectangular cases, inspired by Louis XVI shapes, but their legs were distinctly Italian, with their sharply tapered shape in an exaggerated triangle, and recessed necks.

Vernacular wardrobes or *armadios* were made in plain walnut, but more decorative versions were painted and gilded, or inlaid with intarsia marquetry in rare woods including rosewood. The French *encoignure* or three-cornered cabinet also appeared in Italian furniture for the first time.

Desks were heavily influenced by French design and writing tables were the most popular form. The *secrétaire à abattant* was often inlaid with Classical scenes or panels, and the slant-top secretary, although similar to English models, was also decorated with inlay or figured veneers.

Table tops were specimen marble, *pietra dura,* or scagliola in Neoclassical designs. Sometimes they were made from Roman marble or material painted to resemble marble. The legs and aprons of pier and console tables were carved in low relief and usually painted and gilded. Late-18th-century

VENETIAN GIRANDOLE

This carved and gilded girandole has a rectangular form with pierced cresting centered by a C-scroll cartouche engraved with a flower and leaves. The plate is engraved with an image from the Zodiac and the frame is carved and gilded with flowers and leaves in a symmetrical design. *c. 1750.*

GILTWOOD SIDE TABLE

This Louis XVI-style gilt side table from Turin has a semicircular marble top above a frieze carved and gilded with an interlaced guilloche and quatrefoil decoration. It has stocky, tapering legs encircled with carved swags and small ball feet. Attributed to Guiseppe Maria Bonzanigo. *c. 1780. D:43⅓ in (110 cm). GK*

GENOESE COMMODE

With a design derived from the French commode, this painted and gilded example is one of a pair designed for the Palazzo Saluzzo. The shaped top sits on a case with two drawers, *sans transverse.* The four cabriole legs are also painted and gilded. *c. 1760. H:35 in (89 cm); W:48½ in (123 cm); D:22½ in (57 cm). BL*

VENETIAN SALON TABLE

In the style of Louis XV, this salon table has a marble top, with coloring that matches the light-green and gilt decoration of the frame. The serpentine frieze is carved in panels with foliage and scrollwork. The frame is supported on four sinuous cabriole legs. *c. 1760. W:38¾ in (98 cm). GK*

WRITING TABLE

This provincial writing table may have been made in the Duchy of Parma. The rectangular top is inlaid with burr wood. The shaped base is fitted with four drawers, one on each side. The tapering, slightly cabriole legs are a continuation of the frame. *c. 1790. H:30½ in (77.5 cm); W:42½ in (108 cm); D:29 in (74 cm). BRU*

onsole tables generally had four egs and were round, rectangular, r *demi-lune* in shape and no longer ad serpentine fronts.

Many Italian chairs were based on rench and English designs, such as he open-splat back chair and the *auteuil*. However, sculptural, throne-ke chairs were still made. The main eatures that distinguished Italian chairs rom other European chairs were their ainted decoration, the contours of he chair back, which usually had a ronounced outward curve, the flaring rms, and the overall proportions, vhich were generally more exaggerated. The interlacing circular splat, a

sunburst rosette decoration, was another Italian feature. Sofas had either all-over upholstery, open backs with an upholstered seat, or were caned.

Native woods such as walnut, olive, and pine were used for furniture, but the scarcity of good-quality lumber meant that much Italian furniture was painted and had decoration inspired by Neoclassical designs.

REGIONAL DIFFERENCES
In Turin, furniture for the royal palaces was made by Giuseppe Maria Bonzanigo, who was inspired by the French forms of the 1770s. Bonzanigo's work is said to represent the best Italian

Neoclassical furniture ever made, and he is celebrated for the quality of his wood carving, particularly of light wood and ivory, which is known as microsculpture.

In Rome, bold, highly sculptured furniture was produced. The Roman Neoclassical architect and craftsman Giuseppe Valadier restored many of the city's ancient monuments as well as making furniture, including tables with thick marble tops, veneers, and gilded edges.

Lombardy was renowned for cabinet-making. One of the regions most talented *ebenista* was Giuseppe Maggiolini (*see p.205*) who decorated

items with marquetry, parquetry, carved medallions and flower-heads, and inlays.

Venice still produced the largest, most lavish, and expensive mirrors. While the frames became rectilinear, the scrollwork remained Rococo. Here, bulbous forms remained popular, but painted pieces incorporating Neoclassical motifs, show the gradual acceptance of the style.

ROLL-TOP BUREAU

This transitional roll-top bureau is made of indigenous walnut and fruit voods. The lower section is rectangular in shape and has one central rawer flanked on either side by three shorter drawers. The desk is upported on short, tapering legs. Similar to French examples, it was robably made in Piedmont or Lombardy. *c. 1780. W:58 in (145 cm). GK*

NORTH ITALIAN COMMODE

This early fruitwood and ebonized commode has a divided and hinged top and a false top drawer, with a fitted and veneered interior. The drawers have elaborately carved handles and escutcheons, and bone and ivory stringing; parquetry paneling decorates the top, sides, and front. The bracket feet have leaf cast mounts. *1700–50. W:63 in (160 cm). L&T*

VENETIAN ARMCHAIR

This armchair is reminiscent of the Baroque tradition of sculptural carving. The frame has a carved central cartouche containing a coat of arms and is flanked by boldly carved sides above down-scrolled arms. The molded seat frame has a central pierced apron. The baluster legs are joined by a flat cross-stretcher on ball feet. *c. 1795. H:56 in (140 cm). GK*

The central cartouche contains a coat of arms.

Bold scrolls make up the arms and terminals.

Stylized acanthus leaves are carved on the arm support.

A pierced apron decorates the chair frame.

A flat cross-stretcher connects the legs.

THE GRAND TOUR

TRAVEL ACROSS EUROPE TOOK IN THE ART AND
CULTURE OF THE GRECO-ROMAN WORLD AND
HELPED TO DEVELOP THE NEOCLASSICAL IDEAL.

EUROPEAN TRAVEL AIMED at furthering the Classical
education of young aristocrats and gentry first
became popular in the late 16th century. Such a
journey came to be referred to as the Grand Tour
after 1670, when the term was first used in the
French translation of Richard Lassels' *Voyage or
Compleat Journey through Italy*.

DESTINATIONS OF THE GRAND TOUR

"All our religion, all our arts, almost all that sets
us above savages, has come from the Shores of
the Mediterranean." So wrote Dr. Samuel Johnson,
author of the first English dictionary, explaining
why learned men should visit Italy.

Travelers arrived in Italy via the seaports of
Genoa, Livorno, or Civitavecchia, or, carried in a
chair, crossed the Alps to Turin. Depending on the
season, they visited Florence, Rome, Naples, and
Venice. Florence offered the opportunity to see the
Medici collection of antiquities, while Venice beckoned
travelers with its festivals. However, as the study of
Classical antiquity was the purpose of most Grand
Tours, Rome was the focal point, since it contained
the largest number of ancient sites. From Rome,
travelers went south to Naples to visit the ancient
sites of Pompeii and Herculaneum and walk up
Mount Vesuvius, as well as inspect the remains of
the various Greek colonies in the region.

Such journeys were expensive and often arduous,
but they gave the privileged tourist an opportunity
to see at first hand the monuments of Greco-Roman
antiquity, the Italian Renaissance, and the Classical
Baroque. Paintings and sculptures were also studied,
mainly in private collections, because public
museums were rare at this time.

THE PARTICIPANTS

Grand Tour travelers tended to be young aristocrats
with a knowledge of Greek and Latin literature,
accompanied by a teacher or guardian, although art
students also visited the sites. The numerous and
wealthy upper classes of Britain were pioneers in
travel for pleasure and enlightenment, but travelers
also came from Denmark, the German states, Poland,
Russia, Sweden, and North America. Tours by royalty
were documented in the Italian press, particularly
the Roman *Diari Ordinario*.

Tourists were often helped by the numerous
influential foreigners who had settled in Florence,
Rome, and Venice. They acted as agents for the
travelers, directing them to the sites and aiding
them in the acquisition of souvenirs, for which they
often received payment.

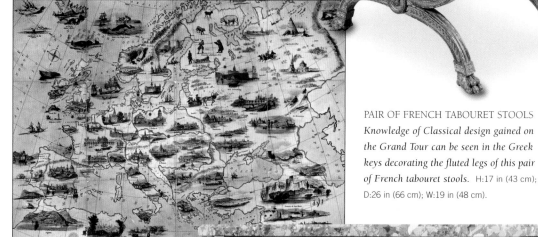

MAP OF THE GRAND TOUR
*This hand-colored lithograph of a map
is taken from* The Travellers, or A Tour
Through Europe *by W. Clerk, published
in London in 1842.*

PAIR OF FRENCH TABOURET STOOLS
*Knowledge of Classical design gained on
the Grand Tour can be seen in the Greek
keys decorating the fluted legs of this pair
of French tabouret stools.* H:17 in (43 cm);
D:26 in (66 cm); W:19 in (48 cm).

CLASSICAL SOUVENIR
*This model of ruins from the forum in Rome
is made from Siena marble. Copies of ruins
were popular souvenirs and continued to be
so well into the 19th century.*

PARISIAN *SECRÉTAIRE À ABATTANT*
*This secrétaire has marquetry panels depicting
Classical ruins with figures highlighted in inlaid
ivory.* c. 1775. H:55¼ in (140 cm); W:36 in (91.5 cm). PAR

THE RUINS OF HERCULANEUM

THE EXCAVATION OF THE RUINS FOUND AT THE FORMER ROMAN TOWN OF HERCULANEUM IN THE MID 18TH CENTURY SUBSEQUENTLY HAD A HUGE IMPACT ON EUROPEAN FURNITURE DESIGN.

Herculaneum is an ancient town at the foot of Mount Vesuvius in the Bay of Naples. In Roman times, Herculaneum and its neighbor Pompeii were fashionable places with fine villas. However, the eruption of Mount Vesuvius in 79 CE buried both towns completely in volcanic ash, preserving the residents and their homes as they were, complete with architecture and furnishings. Herculaneum was rediscovered in 1709, but major excavation of the site did not begin until 1738, under the patronage of the King of the Two Sicilies.

The rediscovery of Herculaneum had a great effect on European design and created a heightened awareness of Classical antiquities. While ancient furniture was unearthed—such as a tripod table with animal feet—it was the discovery of wall paintings depicting Roman furnishings that had a greater impact and resulted in many imitative designs. The colors used at Herculaneum and Pompeii, such as rich reds, also inspired interior designers.

Roman fresco from Herculaneum Several items of furniture are depicted, including a three-legged table with animal legs, and chairs on which the couple reclines. *50–79 CE.*

THE ALLURE

The Grand Tour also offered the opportunity to acquire antiquities. Excavations of "new" ruins received funding from non-Italians, particularly the British, often in an attempt to discover pieces that could be taken home. Italy's pleasant climate and low cost of living were also appealing—especially since tours sometimes took as long as eight years.

Participants traveled through Europe—although not to Greece, which was largely inaccessible to foreigners—examining, measuring, and drawing Classical architecture. Many royals and aristocrats employed artists to document their visit. Others sponsored visits for professional men, like the architect Robert Adam, who published engravings of his observations. The Society of Dilettanti, established in London in 1743, funded expeditions that resulted in accurate drawings, and such prints fueled interest in ancient objects, while for those who could not afford such a trip, the publications brought Classical images into their homes.

SPREADING THE NEOCLASSICAL IDEAL

The Pope and other Italian rulers presented their royal tourists with gifts, while other tourists were eager to purchase mass-produced souvenirs such as tapestries, small mosaics, and prints of Giovanni Battista Piranesi's paintings of Roman views.

Some of the souvenirs were on such a scale that they required Italian artisans to install them at the traveler's residence. Englishman Sir Francis Dashwood attempted to create an entire Roman villa, complete with mosaic floors. Travelers returned with pieces of buildings or statuary, which designers, including Robert Adam, made use of.

These souvenirs helped to spread the Neoclassical ideal. However, it was probably Piranesi's romantic paintings of antiquity—representing the theatricality of ancient ruins rather than their reality—that had the greatest impact on Neoclassical design.

Classical-style side table This English table is made in the Classical style. An Italian trellised, specimen-marble top sits above carved swags, foliage, and a medallion of a Roman Emperor. The tapering legs have carved palmettes in laurel wreaths. *c. 1760. W:66½ in (169 cm). DN*

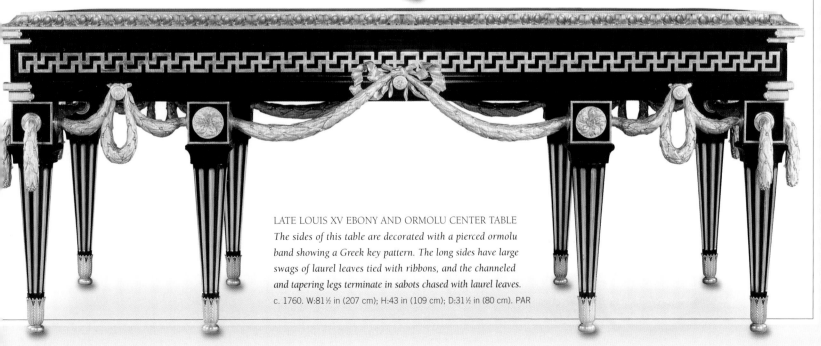

LATE LOUIS XV EBONY AND ORMOLU CENTER TABLE
The sides of this table are decorated with a pierced ormolu band showing a Greek key pattern. The long sides have large swags of laurel leaves tied with ribbons, and the channeled and tapering legs terminate in sabots chased with laurel leaves.
c. 1760. W:81½ in (207 cm); H:43 in (109 cm); D:31½ in (80 cm). PAR

TRANSITIONAL FURNITURE

FRENCH FURNITURE MADE BETWEEN ABOUT 1760 AND 1775 IS
KNOWN AS "TRANSITIONAL," AND DISPLAYS CHARACTERISTICS
OF BOTH THE ROCOCO AND NEOCLASSICAL STYLES.

FRENCH TRANSITIONAL FURNITURE reflects the
transition from Rococo to the Neoclassical style.
The reaction against Rococo started in about 1750 in
France. The curator of the King's drawings, Nicolas
Cochin, who had spent two years in Italy, was put in
charge of the redecoration of the royal chateaux and
was highly critical of the Rococo style. In 1768,
Jean-François de Neuffroge published a book about
architecture that was also clearly against Rococo, and
in the same year Jean-Charles Delafosse, a designer
and architect, published a book containing designs
for furniture and ornaments in the Transitional style.

A HYBRID STYLE

Transitional pieces usually incorporate features
of both Louis XV and Louis XVI furniture. The
sinuous Louis XV style gradually gave way to the
rectilinear shapes, tapering lines, and restrained
decoration of the Neoclassical style. Transitional
commodes were rectangular in shape, rather than
curved, but they still had short, cabriole legs, like
Louis XV commodes. The most characteristic
example of the Transitional style was the breakfront
commode. This retained the swelling, serpentine
shape of earlier forms, but the central front façade
protruded. Chairs no longer had curved, but oval
backs and cabriole legs were replaced by straight,
fluted legs.

The decoration of Transitional furniture also
combined elements of both the Rococo and
Neoclassical styles. Some motifs harked back to
the Louis XIV style, and featured acanthus leaves,
gadroons, palmettes, lion masks, and trophies. Floral
designs proliferated under Louis XV and were still
used on Transitional pieces. As the influence of
Neoclassicism grew, Greek key motifs, interlaced
scrolls, and parquetry became more common.

EMINENT CABINET-MAKERS

The cabinet-maker Louis Joseph Le Lorain furnished
the Paris town house of Lalive de Jully, who was
highly influential at the French Court, with furniture
inspired by the Greek style. Under the influence of
Madame de Pompadour, the King's personal office
was decorated completely in the Transitional style,
with furniture made by Jean-François Oeben in 1760
and Jean-Henri Riesener in 1769.

PARQUETRY AND ORMOLU COMMODE
*This rectangular tulipwood and lemonwood
commode, stamped M. Carlin (maître, 1766),
has a marble top with a molded edge and canted
corners. The single frieze drawer is overlaid with
a band of ormolu guilloche. Below are two drawers
decorated* sans traverse *with parquetry. The apron
has a pierced ormolu cartouche and the cabriole
legs end in leaf and claw sabots.* c. 1770. H:24½ in
(62 cm); W:39¼ in (100 cm); D:21½ in (54 cm). PAR

LOUIS XV *SECRÉTAIRE À ABATTANT*
*This gilt-bronze mounted tulipwood, kingwood,
amaranth, and parquetry desk has a curved fall
front, which opens to reveal an interior fitted with an
arrangement of compartments and drawers.* c. 1765.

COMPARE AND CONTRAST

is helpful to compare Louis XV and Louis XVI eces of furniture, to understand the transition om the first style to the second. Louis XV is the pitome of Rococo and is characterized by the use f swirling scrolls, shell and flower motifs, rocaille, nd asymmetry. Louis XVI, on the other hand, Neoclassical in style and features shapes and otifs inspired by Greek and Roman architecture, urel leaves, swags, and rosettes.

Louis XV furniture is characterized by serpentine shapes, curves, and cabriole legs, whereas Louis XVI pieces have straight lines, geometric shapes, and turned, tapering legs.

Light colors highlighted with gilding were typical of Louis XV furniture, as were veneers of colorful, exotic woods, such as kingwood. Lacquer, including imitation japanning, was also popular, as were ormolu mounts. Louis XVI

furniture, on the other hand, relied on the grain of woods such as mahogany for decorative effects, and carved details replaced ormolu mounts as decorative features.

Styles of furniture changed slowly, as it took cabinet-makers a while to adopt the latest fashions and they frequently had to adapt existing stock in order to sell it.

LOUIS XV

Pierced and scrolled mounts protect the veneer edges.

he ormolu escutcheons are decorated with asymmetrical foliage.

The case is bombé shaped.

The splayed bracket feet are cast with C-scrolls and foliage.

The curved apron has a central, shaped drop.

The shaped top rail is carved with pomegranates.

The cartouche-shaped back is a feature of Louis XV chairs.

The lower arms have curved edges.

The seat and armrests are covered in close-nailed gros and petit-point tapestry.

The base decoration is of trailing foliage.

The scrolled feet are decorated with leaf carving.

OUIS XV COMMODE This kingwood, tulipwood, d parquetry commode is of bombé form and has a rpentine-fronted marble top above two short and two ng drawers inlaid with strapwork cartouches and set

with foliate and C-scrolled escutcheons. The drawer handles are cast with scrolling foliage. The sides of the case are inlaid with cube parquetry and the front has a shaped apron. The commode stands on splayed bracket feet. FRE

LOUIS XV FAUTEUIL This armchair has a cartouche-shaped back, padded arms, and serpentine-fronted seat. The channeled and C-scroll carved frame is decorated with flower-heads and scrolling foliage. The chair has cabriole legs terminating in scroll feet. PAR

LOUIS XVI

The rectangular top has straight sides.

The drawers have Neoclassical motifs of stylized paterae, and carved ribbon decoration around the locks.

The case sides are straight.

The square, tapering legs do not have ormolu mounts.

The base has straight edges.

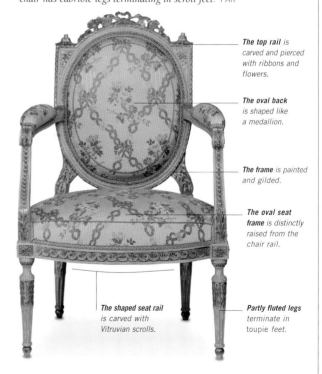

The top rail is carved and pierced with ribbons and flowers.

The oval back is shaped like a medallion.

The frame is painted and gilded.

The oval seat frame is distinctly raised from the chair rail.

The shaped seat rail is carved with Vitruvian scrolls.

Partly fluted legs terminate in toupie feet.

OUIS XVI PROVINCIAL COMMODE
his rectangular wooden commode has a molded top and raight sides. Its four long drawers are decorated with eoclassical carved swags of drapery and ribbon bows,

and paterae at the outer edges. The short legs are square and tapering, in contrast to the splayed legs of the piece above, and do not have ormolu mounts, because it is a provincial piece. c. 1780. W:55 in (137.5 cm). FRE

LOUIS XVI FAUTEUIL

This painted armchair has a medallion-shaped back with a carved top rail. The seat rail is decorated with Vitruvian scrolls and it has partly fluted legs with toupie feet. c. 1785. H:37 in (94 cm); W:24½ in (62 cm). PAR

LOUIS XVI

WHEN LOUIS XVI and his Austrian wife Marie Antoinette came to the French throne in 1774, many German craftsmen, including prominent cabinet-makers such as Adam Weisweiler and Jean-Henri Riesener, moved to France in the hope of royal commissions. Their hopes were fulfilled, and in the years before the Revolution they supplied the royal household with sumptuous furniture that was both Rococo and Neoclassical in style.

Commissions also came from wealthy French households—who demanded fashion and luxury—and European monarchs who held French design and quality in high regard.

DEVELOPING STYLE

Furniture styles evolved gradually at this time. Pieces from the early years are often referred to as "Transitional" because they contain elements of both Rococo design and the Neoclassical style (see pp.134–35). As time went on, however, the Neoclassical elements became more pronounced.

In the 20 years or so before the French Revolution in 1789, English taste began to influence the French, and this trend can be seen in furniture designs. Mahogany was now used frequently, particularly when trade with America increased at the end of the Revolutionary War, and the wood could be easily imported from the West Indies.

DECORATION

Different styles of marquetry developed as a method of decoration. Pictorial designs became more prominent than the loosely arranged floral decorations of previous eras. Landscapes and architectural compositions were very popular, as were vases or baskets of flowers. Parquetry, a geometric form of marquetry, was another common decorative feature.

Later in Louis XVI's reign, Riesener became one of the most important cabinet-makers. Around 1780, he abandoned marquetry and started to produce much plainer furniture that relied on well-figured veneers for its decorative effect. One truly French aspect of furniture design of this period was the use of delicately detailed porcelain plaques from the Sèvres factory, which were set into

pieces of furniture as a decorative feature. Mounts were often elaborate and of fine quality, particularly those made by foundries such as Gouthière and Thomire.

Boullework was still favored, as was furniture that incorporated pieces of painted and foiled glass known as verre églomisé, or Chinese or Japanese lacquer panels, often reused from late 17th- or early 18th-century pieces. Painted furniture was also popular.

NEW DEVELOPMENTS

Chairs, which had previously been fairly rounded in shape, became more rectilinear and had tapering legs. Since rooms were now smaller than they had been, furniture was made on a correspondingly smaller scale. Women were now more influential in society than they had been before and so light, elegant pieces, such as bonheurs-du-jour and delicate worktables, were designed specifically for female clients.

In the late 18th century, banks and security were not what they are today, so elaborate desks with secret compartments and hidden drawers were popular with the wealthy. These had intricate locks to enhance security.

EFFECTS OF THE REVOLUTION

After the French Revolution, the furniture-makers' guilds were disbanded and the quality of French furniture began to decline as a result. The market for high-quality pieces dwindled as the nobility fell victim to the guillotine and the country became impoverished by war. Furniture became simpler in design and was decorated with plain veneers, rather than marquetry. The war made it harder to import exotic woods, so furniture-makers often used local fruitwoods instead.

The Neoclassical style found favor with the new government of France and continued to develop during both the Directoire and Consulate periods that followed (1795–1804). It was only when Napoleon came to power in 1804 that fine-quality, highly decorated pieces of furniture became fashionable once again.

The single frieze drawer has two drop-ring handles.

The escutcheons are carved in the shape of flowers and branches.

The top is made of gray and white marble.

The legs terminate in ormolu toupie feet.

The apron is decorated with ormolu ribbing.

LOUIS XVI *COMMODE À VANTAUX*

This is one of a pair of rectangular commodes surmounted by a gray and white marble top. The case is veneered in flame mahogany, and the frieze contains one long drawer, which is paneled with ormolu to look like three smaller drawers. The lower section has two drawers, designed to look like three, which open to reveal three long drawers with ring handles. The legs terminate in ormolu *toupie* feet. The piece is attributed to the Paris-based maker, Godefroy Dester. c. 1785. H:36¾ in (93 cm); W:52½ in (133.5 cm); D:22¼ in (56.5 cm). PA

BUREAU À CYLINDRE

This fine *bureau à cylindre* (roll-top desk) is made of mahogany veneer on oak and soft wood. The top of the piece is made of gray and white marble and sits above three narrow drawers. The curved upper section slides back to reveal a fitted interior consisting of shelves and drawers, and gives access to the leather-covered writing surface, which can be extended. Beneath this are two pairs of side drawers and one longer drawer above the kneehole. The piece stands on four fluted legs. c. 1789. H:48½ in (121 cm). LPZ

PARISIAN SUITE

These seats have rectangular backs with arched top rails and cut-out corners, decorated with guilloche patterns. The arms consist of reeded columns headed by paterae and finials, and are overlaid with carved acanthus leaves leading to padded armrests. The front and sides are similarly carved. The frames are supported on tapering, spiral-fluted legs. *c. 1780. Canapé: H:38½ in (96.5 cm); W:78¼ in (195.5 cm). Fauteuils: H:38½ in (96.5 cm); W:26 in (65 cm). PAR*

ECTANGULAR MIRROR

his mirror has a carved and erced giltwood frame. The crest decorated with two birds in leaf arlands and the base has a beaded eze. *H:45¼ in (115 cm). BEA*

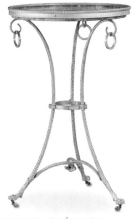

BRONZE *GUÉRIDON*

Inspired by Roman paintings, this table is made of gilded bronze with a marble top mounted in brass. A stretcher joins three claw feet on casters. *c. 1785. H:32½ in (81 cm). GK*

PARISIAN *GUÉRIDON*

This table is inlaid with satinwood and sycamore, and decorated with ormolu. The piece stands on cabriole legs. *c. 1770. H:31½ in (79 cm); D:17½ in (44 cm). PAR*

ERGÈRE

his fruitwood chair has a simple axed frame. The crest and seat rail re carved with foliage. Turned and uted tapering legs support the frame. *1780. GK*

PARISIAN *ENCOIGNURES*

This pair of corner cupboards has gray marble triangular tops set on similarly shaped cases. Elegantly veneered door fronts that open to opposite sides are inlaid with flowers in swagged, Classically shaped vases. Stylized ormolu columns sit above the inlaid canted corners, which terminate in slightly flared feet. The shaped bases are decorated with a single ormolu mount. *c. 1790. H:35¼ in (88 cm). GK*

PARISIAN *SEMAINIER*

This style of chest is named after the French word for week, *semaine*. The chest was designed to store a week's supply of clothes. This elegant piece is veneered in tulipwood and purple-wood inlaid in a geometric chevron pattern. The drawers are decorated with ormolu beaded borders and ribbon and foliage escutcheons, with an ormolu back plate and laurel ring pulls. *c. 1780. H:64 in (160 cm); W:32½ in (81 cm). PAR*

ENGLISH PATTERN BOOKS

FURNITURE PATTERN BOOKS HELPED TO BRING THE VERY BEST OF LONDON DESIGN TO AN AUDIENCE OF TRADESMEN AND EAGER CLIENTS.

PATTERN BOOKS REVOLUTIONIZED the way furniture fashions were disseminated. Much of the modern understanding of Georgian furniture originates from the designs illustrated in pattern books, and the golden trio of British design; Thomas Chippendale, Thomas Sheraton, and George Hepplewhite, owe the longevity of their reputations more to their published works than to the furniture itself. Pattern books were published for many reasons: to introduce new fashions; to assist in the pricing of work; to impress wealthy patrons; and, ultimately, to acquire new clients. The London cabinet-makers William Ince and John Mayhew, publishers of *The Universal System of Household Furniture* (1759–62), even translated their volumes into French in order to target the lucrative market across the Channel.

Some of the pieces illustrated in pattern books already existed, such as Robert and James Adam's pieces, and work by Chippendale, and Ince and Mayhew. Many designs were not meant to be slavishly copied, but rather were intended as a guide for other makers. In the "French Chairs" plate, illustrated right, the chair could be either an arm or side chair and Chippendale designed a variety of choices for leg designs.

Other cabinet-makers were actively encouraged to recreate the designs themselves. Some publications included dimensional drawings and most included heights of the furniture and instructions for when these should be altered—a change that was dependent upon the room for which a piece of furniture was intended.

Thomas Sheraton's two volume *The Cabinet Dictionary* (1803) ensured that nothing was left to chance in the implementation of his instructions. The book included perspective drawings, measurements, the type of wood or paint to be used, a description of types of furniture, and even instructions on where the furniture should be placed.

It is a curious fact that despite his immense fame, no actual pieces of furniture can be attributed to George Hepplewhite. His notoriety is entirely due to his published works, and he only became famous after his death, on the publication of *The Cabinet-Maker and Upholsterer's Guide* in 1788. This book was intended to be of use to both craftsmen and clients. Hepplewhite was a great advocate of the Adam style, and it is thanks in no small part to Hepplewhite's publication that Adams' work continues to be so well known today.

MAHOGANY BUREAU-CABINET
Desks and bookcases were made in two parts: the upper section with either doors or glazed panels behind which were shelves to contain books; and a lower section below the sloping writing front that contained drawers or clothes-press shelves. They were originally intended to be used in bedchambers, but during the course of the 18th century were used in other parts of the house. In the American colonies, such an expensive piece of furniture would have been displayed in the grandest room. NA

FRENCH CHAIRS, PLATE XX
THE GENTLEMAN &
CABINET-MAKER'S DIRECTOR
Chippendale drew the upholstered chair to display multiple interpretations. It could be an arm or side chair. The feet could be scroll or trifid in shape and the carving could be adapted depending on the skill of the chair-maker or the tastes of the patron. PAR

CHIPPENDALE'S *THE GENTLEMAN
CABINET-MAKER'S DIRECTOR*
This was not the first pattern book to be
published but it was unique in that it was
the first-ever publication to concentrate
solely on furniture. Moreover, it was
singularly comprehensive—illustrating
all contemporary forms, along with
examples of Gothic, Chinese, French, and
Rococo variations. The Chippendale chair
is probably the most emulated of all
Chippendale's designs, where the same
basic form was interpreted in a number
of different ways.

A BRIEF HISTORY OF DESIGN BOOKS

Few English furniture designs were printed before
1715. Daniel Marot's publications, which first appeared
in 1702 (*see p.45*), were widely used in England and
contained ideas for all branches of the decorative arts,
including interior design and furniture arrangements.
English furniture designs also first appeared in
architectural publications, and designs for chimneypieces, pier tables, and mirror frames within an
architectural framework were common. In 1735, the
Engravers' Copyright Act protected designers from
being copied by their competitors—although
plagiarism continued.

From 1740, two or three furniture pattern books
appeared each year, right up until the end of the
century. Thomas Chippendale's *The Gentleman and
Cabinet-Maker's Director* of 1754 was the first pattern
book to focus solely on furniture, and set the standard
for the subsequent range of pattern books that were
published from the 1760s. The book also helped to
establish Chippendale's name and his distinctive style
of furniture for posterity, a power that Sheraton's later
publication also possessed.

CHIPPENDALE CARVED CHERRYWOOD SIDE CHAIR
*This chair from Philadelphia has a serpentine crest rail with a
central carved ornament above a carved and pierced splat and
fluted uprights. The square, tapering, drop-in seat has a seat rail
with a centered shell ornament. The acanthus carved cabriole
legs have claw-and-ball feet. The chair takes its basic form
from the illustration from the pattern book (see left), in this
instance in a Rococo interpretation.* c. 1770. H:39½ in (100 cm).

THOMAS SHEARER'S LONDON BOOK OF PRICES

THIS INFLUENTIAL DESIGN BOOK, PUBLISHED BY LONDON CABINET-MAKER THOMAS SHEARER IN 1788,
FEATURED DESIGNS BY BOTH SHEARER HIMSELF AND BY GEORGE HEPPLEWHITE.

The Cabinet-Maker's London Book of Prices was a practical
trade manual and contained tables of prices to assist in
calculating the cost of labor. It was compiled for the
London Society of Cabinet-Makers by journeymen
working in London and Westminster and was originally
produced not as a pattern book, but as a guide to prices.

The first edition contained only 20 plates but had
extensive text and an index to types of furniture. Seating
furniture, mirrors, and upholstered beds were excluded,
as they were made by specialist craftsmen rather than
cabinet-makers. It was not until the 1793 edition, greatly
enlarged, that a complete set of rules for calculating costs
for all furniture was published. This had over 250 pages
and addressed pricing in more detail. Approximately
1,000 copies were printed, most of which were used
in workshops. *The London Book of Prices* remained a
standard work well into the early 19th century.

Calculating the cost of an item, particularly from a
journeyman's point of view, was not easy. Journeymen
were paid either a daily wage or "by the piece." The cost
of lumber and materials was usually borne by the master,
but the journeymen had to cost all the extras. They

submitted their calculations to the master, and this book
was intended to eliminate grievances between the two.
The London Book of Prices gives us a snapshot of Georgian
furniture designs. It shows which styles of furniture were
complicated to make, and which less so.

**Chest of drawers by Thomas Shearer, *The
Cabinet-Makers' London Book of Prices*, Plate 17**
The design for this serpentine-fronted chest
of drawers has been used to create the piece
shown at left. It has a molded edge over four
long graduated drawers flanked by three short
graduated drawers on fluted bracket feet.

English chest of drawers This chest of drawers
is inspired by a design from Shearer's book
(above). The parquetry top would have added
significantly to the price of the piece. c. 1790.
H:36½ in (91.5 cm); W:47 in (117.5 cm); D:61 cm.

GERMANY

NEOCLASSICAL STYLES came later to the German states than other European countries. This was partly the result of German guild restrictions, which primarily sought to protect those craftsmen who were not privileged enough to work in a Court workshop. By restricting the numbers of workshops in a city in order to guarantee work for all the masters, the guilds made it extremely difficult for foreign craftsmen to settle, so their influence was, at times, found to be lacking. Also, the conservatism of the middle classes meant that new fashions were less readily accepted.

The Spindler brothers were leading cabinet-makers who made furniture for Frederick II. They were famous for their use of floral marquetry, and continued to make Rococo-style commodes up until the late 1760s. At the height of their career, the two-drawer serpentine commode on long legs was popular, a shape that had already become passé in France. Commodes made for use outside court circles were less formal and resembled a chest of drawers with three or four drawers. However, despite this simplicity, these commodes still favored Rococo styling with curvilinear fronts and veneers in walnut, rather than mahogany.

Abraham Roentgen and his son, David, were the most famous German cabinet-makers to embrace the Neoclassical style. However, the furniture Abraham Roentgen initially produced was strongly influenced by the English Queen Anne and Low Countries designs. Much of the Roentgens' early furniture was made in walnut, as mahogany became fashionable in German cabinetwork much later than in Britain and France. Both enjoyed a tremendous following at all the German Courts of their time.

NEOCLASSICAL FURNITURE
It was not until the 1770s that the early Neoclassical style, or *Zopfstil*, became accepted. As in France, where enthusiasm following the excavations of Pompeii and Herculaneum had led to the emergence of the *goût grec* style, German designers began to seek inspiration in the ancient Greco-Roman world. The term *Zopfstil* itself derives from Classical braided friezes

(*der Zopf* translates as "braid") and hanging swags.

The *Zopfstil* continued to apply many of the decorative features seen in the marquetry of the late Rococo style: acanthus-shaped mounts, bay leaves, swags, medallions, triglyphs, and lion's and ram's heads. Initially, furniture was similar to that of the Louis XVI style, albeit with more exaggerated proportions. From the middle of the 1780s, however, furniture forms became lighter, more refined, and had very little decoration.

This shift was partly due to the increasing influence of the middle and merchant classes in matters of design. Although the Neoclassical style was popularized by Abraham and David Roentgen, their patrons remained exclusively at Court, while the Baroque and Rococo styles continued to have a greater influence on cabinet-makers in the provinces.

As elsewhere in Europe, the use of Neoclassical design was initially restricted to the application of decorative elements to traditional forms. Marquetry had never fallen from favor in the German states and it was still used in the latter half of the 18th century. However, designs became more geometric and, rather than completely covering a case, often focused on the center of a piece.

POPULAR FORMS
The cylinder bureau, which was devised by Francois Oeben at the courts of Louis XV and Louis XVI, the flat desk with a functional top with drawers or doors, and the commode were popular pieces. Legs were mostly fluted columns or conical squares. Commodes tended to have two or three drawers and square, tapered legs. The china cabinet remained popular, but, again influenced by French fashion, became rectangular, with restrained ornament. Seating furniture also followed French examples with oval or square backs, painted or gilt seat frames, and tapered legs.

Toward the end of the century, imported mahogany became the most favored wood. Brass-mounted furniture with well-figured mahogany veneers became popular, although regional woods such as walnut or cherry wood were also used.

The urn is a typical Neoclassical element.

The gallery is carved.

A swagged medallion surmounts the secrétaire.

The veneer has been laid on the diagonal.

Rococo marquetry includes floral and musical motifs.

The brass lock is integral to the architectural design.

The gilded bronze fittings are original.

ROLL-TOP *SECRÉTAIRE*

This pine *secrétaire* from Munich has a geometric veneer in walnut, fruitwood, and maple. The carved gallery has a central medallion of an emperor surrounded by laurel leaves. The upper section has architectural marquetry across two large doors, with drawers and pigeonholes inside. The roll-top desk front has marquetry flowers and musical instruments in a marquetry border. The lower drawers have similar marquetry. The desk stands on short, fluted, tapering legs. *c. 1775.* H:91¼ in (233 cm) W:45⅔ in (116 cm); D:25½ in (65 cm). BAM

ET OF SIX AUSTRIAN CHAIRS

e beech frames of these Neoclassical chairs
e painted green and white. The rigid, square
cks are channeled and have a rectangular
plet in the center of the top rail. The seats
e also square with stiff upholstery, raised and

squared at the edges. Each chair rail mimics
the chair back, with a central tablet. The frames
are supported on fluted, tapered legs, also
painted green and white. The gilding and paint
would have reflected the overall design of the
room for which the chairs were made. *c. 1780.
H:37 in (92.5 cm). LPZ*

SOUTHERN GERMAN COMMODE

This Louis XVI-style commode has a rectangular
and architectural pine case with a veneer in
walnut, plum, maple, and oak. The central
medallion-and-garland motif is thought to have
been influenced by the work of David Roentgen.

The handles on the two drawers, constructed
sans traverse, are in the form of four different
bronze portraits on a silver ground. The case
is set on four squared, tapering legs.
Attributed to Cornelius Pentz. *c. 1785.
H:33½ in (85 cm); W:48¾ in (124 cm);
D:24¾ in (63 cm). SBA*

Carved dolphin detail

WALNUT SALON TABLE

This round tilt-top table *aux dauphins*
(with dolphins) rests on a hexagonal
column surrounded by three carved
dolphins that are painted green and
partly gilded. The table is supported on
a tripod base with casters. *H:32¼ in
(82 cm); W:39 in (100 cm). GK*

ER COMMODE

his pine, squared commode is veneered
th cherry, plum, and maple woods in a
ometric pattern. Below the rectangular
p is a frieze containing a drawer, and
o further drawers, flanked by inlaid flat
lumns. Slightly flared feet support the
ase. *c. 1795. H:47¾ in (119.5 cm). SLK*

SWISS CABINETS

This pair of rectangular-shaped cabinets
is designed in the style of Louis XVI. They
are made of walnut and veneered with cherry
and local fruitwood. The tops slightly overhang
the bases and the friezes are decorated with

Neoclassical-style ormolu mounts. Each
cabinet is glazed on three sides—opening
to the front with a single-lock escutcheon—
and is fitted with three shelves. The cases
are supported on short, tapered legs, which
terminate in metal casters. *c. 1800. H:60¾ in
(154 cm). GK*

DAVID ROENTGEN

THE FINEST, MOST INNOVATIVE AND COMMERCIALLY DRIVEN CABINET-MAKER OF THE 18TH CENTURY CREATED FURNITURE THAT REMAINS UNPARALLELED IN QUALITY.

It is unlikely that David Roentgen would have achieved his level of fame without the influence of his father, Abraham, who produced furniture combining superb craftsmanship with technical complexity. David began as Abraham's apprentice, and took over his Neuwied workshop, near Koblenz, Germany, in 1768.

Increasingly influenced by French design, David traveled to Paris in 1774 to present a desk to Queen Marie-Antoinette. Realizing that his work was old-fashioned, he began to study the latest Neoclassical styles he saw in the city. By the late 1770s, his furniture showed the results of this study in its more austere shapes, the decoration

SECRÉTAIRE EN COMMODE BY ABRAHAM ROENTGEN
The oak and maple body of this piece is surmounted by an adjustable top. The top drawer contains a leather-covered, sliding writing surface and nine small drawers. 1755–60.
H:34¾ in (87 cm); W:54½ in (136.5 cm); D:26½ in (66.5 cm).

Satinwood stringing

Molded ormolu edge

Book rest

Sliding writing surface

Patera

Interior drawers

Ormolu-ribbed panels

PARISIAN ARCHITECT'S TABLE
When closed, this piece appears to be a typical writing table with a single drawer. But when the mahogany top is lifted up on a double-ratchet mechanism, a book-rest springs forward. c. 1785.
H:31 in (80 cm); W:43 in (109.5 cm). PAR

KEY DATES

David Roentgen

1743 David Roentgen born in Herrnhag.

1757 Works in his father Abraham's workshop in Neuwied.

1768 Takes over father's workshop.

1770 Roentgen delivers a table to Frederick the Great of Prussia.

1774 Presents a desk to Queen Marie-Antoinette in Paris, where he also acquires engravings of the latest fashions.

1779 Sets up a depot in Paris.

1780 Joins Paris Guild of *Ébénistes*.

1783 Visits Russia to sell a *secrétaire* to Catherine the Great, later making four subsequent trips to St. Petersburg.

1785 Receives title of *Ébéniste-mécanicien du Roi et de la Reine* from Louis XVI of France.

1789 Outbreak of French Revolution threatens his business.

1791 Appointed Court Furnisher to Frederick William II of Prussia.

1793 Abraham Roentgen dies.

1795 Paris stock is liquidated by France's revolutionary government and much of the furniture provided to the court and aristocracy is sold at official auctions.

1807 David Roentgen dies in Wiesbaden.

CONSTRUCTING AN OCCASIONAL TABLE

DAVID ROENTGEN PERFECTED A STANDARDIZATION OF PARTS IN HIS ELEGANT FURNITURE THAT ALLOWED IT TO BE TAKEN APART, SHIPPED SAFELY TO CLIENTS, AND THEN EASILY REASSEMBLED.

Although Roentgen's primary workshop was in Neuwied, he also had warehouses in three major European cities. He therefore developed a process of disassembly that allowed him to ship furniture safely and efficiently.

The table below illustrates this feature. It breaks down into eight separate components: the top and its frame, the drawer and shelf, and the four legs. Once taken apart, the pieces were put into a special packing case, which helped to protect the veneer.

Taking the table apart also saved space and made the piece easier to handle during shipment, while standardization of the process saved valuable time during manufacture.

As Roentgen was often away soliciting orders for months at a time, he relied on his foreman to load wagon trains, find coachmen, sort out horses, and documents, and ensure that orders were completed. This could be complicated: a single shipment to Russia often contained more than 50 pieces of furniture.

reduced to veneering in plain timbers, usually mahogany, with gilt-bronze or brass mountings. Such was his success in Paris that he joined the Guild of Ébénistes. His stamp was D.ROENTGEN, although most of his pieces were unstamped.

Roentgen set up depots for his furniture in Paris, Berlin, and Vienna, enabling him to promote his designs, gain commissions, and supply furniture more quickly without losing control of his Neuwied workshop. This innovative thinking and commercial acumen also allowed him to keep up with the latest fashions, through pattern books and prints.

ROENTGEN'S FURNITURE

Initially, Roentgen worked in wood, which he engraved, but by the late 1760s he was using stained and tinted woods. After 1770, delicate pictorial marquetry became a specialty of his workshop, the designs for which were often taken from paintings by Januarius Zick. This resulted in extraordinarily realistic renditions of floral sprays, arrangements of garden utensils, musical instruments, and, after his first trip to Paris, pastoral idylls and architectural scenes.

Toward the end of the 1770s, Roentgen was producing a range of furniture in the Louis XVI style. He was also noted for his writing desks, produced in the later years of the Neuwied workshop, which featured ingenious mechanical devices that were operated by moving a section of the piece (see pp.174–75).

In 1783, Roentgen visited Russia with his first consignment of furniture, which included dressing tables, chests of drawers, a revolving armchair, and desks at which one could write seated or standing. Following this visit, he received several commissions from Catherine the Great. Roentgen's main customers were the French king and court. Louis XVI had purchased a writing table in 1779 and subsequently appointed David Ébéniste-mécanicien du Roi et de la Reine; he was already cabinet-maker to Queen Marie-Antoinette.

Over the next ten years he supplied the French court with furniture that was noted both for its intricate marquetry and its ingenious mechanical construction.

In 1791, Roentgen was appointed Court Furnisher to Frederick William II of Prussia, and by this time he was recognized as the most celebrated cabinet-maker in Europe. However, the French Revolution seriously weakened his business and he never regained his former status. David Roentgen died in Wiesbaden while on his travels in 1807.

Top **Drawer**

Leg **Frieze** **Undertier**

German occasional table This table, one of a pair, was specially constructed to be taken apart easily. The legs unscrew and the ormolu galleries on both the top and around the undertier can be removed. *1780–90. H:29¼ in (74 cm); W:22½ in (57 cm); D:15 in (38 cm).*

CAMORE AND MARQUETRY *TABLE À ÉCRIRE*
is ormolu-mounted writing table has a spring-loaded frieze
awer enclosing a leather-lined slide and four small drawers.
o additional spring-loaded drawers each contain an inkwell
d two drawers. The square, tapering legs end in spade feet and
sters. *1775–80. H:30 in (78 cm); W:29½ in (75 cm); D:21 in (51 cm).*

GERMAN LADY'S *SECRÉTAIRE*
Rectangular in shape, the front flap opens to form a writing surface. The geometrical nature of the case is emphasized by ormolu bands that highlight the rectangular central panel. The square, tapering legs are inlaid with ormolu-ribbed panels. c. 1790.

RUSSIA

CATHERINE THE GREAT became Empress of Russia in 1762 and ruled until 1796. Her reign marked a golden age of Russian culture, during which St. Petersburg, built in the first half of the 18th century, became a prominent European capital. Catherine's predecessor, Empress Elizabeth I, had commissioned architects to build magnificent Rococo palaces and pavilions, but Catherine promoted the Neoclassical style, both in architecture and furnishings. During her reign she commissioned the building of the two Hermitages next to the Winter Palace in St. Petersburg. Both were built in the austere Neoclassical style, with colonnaded facades, the first as a pavilion where Catherine could relax and the second to house the Empress's library and growing art collection. Following Catherine's example, the aristocracy built imposing new mansions in St. Petersburg and grand homes on large country estates.

NEOCLASSICAL STYLE
Furniture styles became more severe, but lighter. Russian Neoclassical furniture is rectilinear and decorated primarily with symmetrical motifs and geometric patterns, but it is larger in scale and often more brightly decorated than similar styles elsewhere in Europe.

Commodes, tables, and chairs were influenced by French examples and were often made of mahogany with gilt, bronze, or brass mounts. Elaborate tables were designed to be placed in the center of a room, rather than against a wall, and were therefore decorated on all sides. Elegant brass-enriched dining chairs were fashionable in the 1790s and could be found in most of the palaces and in the collections of the Russian elite. Some had trellis-pattern backs with mounts attached to the joins of the pattern, and legs inlaid with reeded brass.

INNOVATIVE DESIGNS
Mechanical furniture was popular in Russia. The inventive German cabinet-maker David Roentgen visited St. Petersburg five times between 1783 and 1789, and

PARCEL-GILT ARMCHAIR

This mahogany, maple wood, and parcel-gilt armchair has scrolled finials and swan-shaped supports under its scrolled arms. The padded back and seat are covered in silk. *c. 1800. H:43¾ in (111 cm); W:31½ in (80 cm).*

DINING CHAIR

One of a set, this mahogany side chair has a five-piece vertical splat above an upholstered seat. The frame is supported on square, tapering legs joined by a stretcher. The frame is embellished with brass mounts. *c. 1800.*

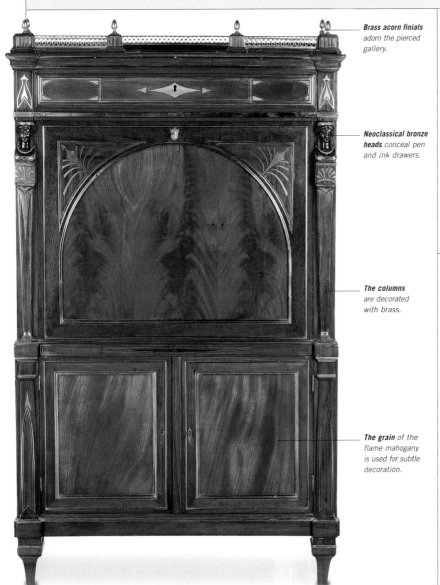

Brass acorn finials adorn the pierced gallery.

Neoclassical bronze heads conceal pen and ink drawers.

The columns are decorated with brass.

The grain of the flame mahogany is used for subtle decoration.

FALL-FRONT WRITING CABINET

Made of flame mahogany and inlaid with brass, this writing cabinet has a flat top and a pierced gallery with finials. Below is a frieze with a central drawer, flanked by panels inlaid with arrowheads. The fall front opens to reveal a fitted interior and is flanked by Neoclassical bronze heads. The lower section of the piece has two doors with brass surrounds, flanked by panels inlaid with an arrowhead. The plinth base has tapering, block feet. Attributed to Heinrich Gambs. *c. 1790. H:63½ in (161 cm); W:38¼ in (97 cm); D:17⅞ in (45 cm). BLA*

SECRÉTAIRE-CABINET

The upper section of this ormolu-mounted and brass-inlaid mahogany *secrétaire*-cabinet has a frieze of scrolling foliage and satyrs. Below this are two doors enclosing an interior fitted with three shelves. The doors on either side are decorated with circular medallions and enclose more shelves and three secret drawers. A *secrétaire* drawer encloses a writing surface, four small drawers, and a central shelf, above two small drawers. The tapering legs terminate in sabots. *Late 18th century. H:67 in (170.5 cm); W:58½ in (148.5 cm); D:31¼ in (79.5 cm).*

...pplied many intriguing pieces of ...rniture to Catherine the Great, ...cluding desks at which she could ...rite either standing up or sitting ...own, cabinets in which she could ...splay her medals and gems, and a ...volving armchair. The pieces that ...oentgen produced for his Russian ...ients were more elaborate and ...stentatious than those that he ...oduced for his French and German ...trons, and were made from woods ...at resembled the native Russian ...arelian birch.

DECORATIVE FEATURES

Private factories and estate workshops were set up in St. Petersburg and around Russia, to create furnishings for the new palaces and mansions. Russian craftsmen became highly skilled and created fine pieces of furniture decorated with marquetry and gilding, influenced by both French and German designs. The Classical motifs of sphinxes, griffins, dolphins, lions' heads, acanthus, rosettes, and swags were common, and fine brass inlays were used to imitate Classical columns. Table cabinets were decorated with exotic inlays of ivory and bone, and porcelain plaques from the Wedgwood factory in England were set into furniture panels.

TRADITIONAL STYLES

Vernacular furniture remained traditional and was usually made of oak. Armchairs based on monastic furniture, benches, and tables, sometimes with extending leaves, were simple and differed little from the pieces in peasant homes.

Brass-inlaid mahogany mirror The mirror frame has a Greek-key brass inlay and gilt mounts on the corners. c. 1790. H:43½ in (110.5 cm); W:23¾ in (60.5 cm). EVE

MAHOGANY CENTER TABLE

This table from the Winter Palace in St. Petersburg has a raised surface in the center. Embellished with brass inlay, the apron has a Wedgwood panel depicting Hercules and Deianeira. With ormolu mounts, the table is supported on tapering, square-section legs. 1790–1800. W:59½ in (149 cm). GK

MAHOGANY BUREAU

...e upper section of this mahogany bureau has ...hinged top with a red gilded leather writing ...rface above two drawers. The lower case has ...additional, sliding, green-felt writing surface ...ove four drawers. The interior is fitted with five large shelves. The bureau has gilt-bronze mounts, with swags over the keyholes and simple circular pulls on the drawers. It is supported on bracket feet. The desk was intended for an architect or similar, and enables the user to stand while working. c. 1800. W:46½ in (116 cm). GK

TULA FURNITURE

MADE OF SPARKLING CUT STEEL, THE FURNITURE PRODUCED BY TULA'S IMPERIAL ARMORY EPITOMIZES 18TH-CENTURY RUSSIAN DECORATIVE ARTS.

Founded in 1712, the Imperial Armory at Tula came to the fore under Catherine the Great, supplying not only weaponry but an eclectic range of cut-steel objects. Tula furniture represents the very best of Russian decorative arts in the 18th century. Tula's armorers used an extraordinary diversity of metal-working techniques. They cut steel into diamond facets that sparkled like jewels, colored and chased the surface, and used nonferrous metal inlays. The table pictured below is regarded as the finest example of Tula furniture.

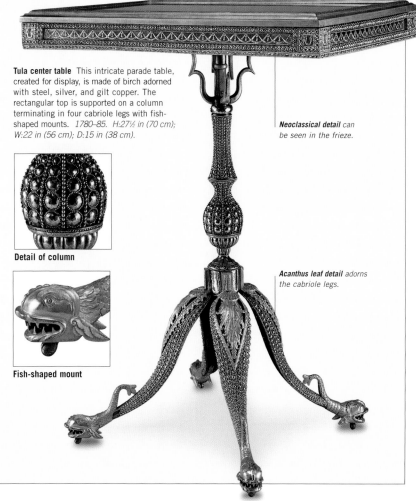

Tula center table This intricate parade table, created for display, is made of birch adorned with steel, silver, and gilt copper. The rectangular top is supported on a column terminating in four cabriole legs with fishshaped mounts. 1780–85. H:27½ in (70 cm); W:22 in (56 cm); D:15 in (38 cm).

Neoclassical detail can be seen in the frieze.

Detail of column

Fish-shaped mount

Acanthus leaf detail adorns the cabriole legs.

LOW COUNTRIES

THE NETHERLANDS underwent a variety of political changes in the late 18th century as Spanish and Austrian rule was ceded to revolutionary France in 1795, and the Netherlands was renamed the Batavian Republic. Despite these changes, several areas of commerce continued successfully: agriculture, the money markets of Amsterdam, and trade with the East Indies all prospered and provided income for furniture and building.

The established trade links also facilitated the import of exotic woods such as mahogany and American satinwood.

IMPORTED FURNITURE BAN
While wood continued to be imported, the import of finished furniture was banned in 1771, largely due to the excessive popularity of French and British furniture. This ban meant that Dutch cabinet-makers lacked

competition and an environment in which new ideas were readily generated. This led to the provincial nature of much late 18th-century furniture and—to satisfy demand—the imitation of French Louis XVI pieces. Andries Borgen was known for this type of work.

APPLYING THE NEW STYLE
The rectilinear styling of Louis XVI furniture was applied to Low Countries case furniture. Cabinets were also inspired by British designs, as pediments became less heavy, and later examples incorporated a stylized swan's neck or a broken pediment.

Canted corners were common and, while cases swelled out at the base, they were not as broad as previous examples. Feet became square and sharply tapered. Glazed panels, rather than solid wooden doors, were used on cabinets designed to display collections of ceramics. Smaller case pieces such as the commode kept their signature shape but had a lighter, more geometric feel.

In the last quarter of the 18th century, a new type of case furniture, the low buffet or sideboard cabinet, was introduced. This piece was similar to a commode, but had a hinged top that opened to reveal an enclosed cistern.

BONHEUR-DU-JOUR

The rectilinear case of this *bonheur-du-jour* has an upper section with three cupboards above a writing surface and five drawers. It is decorated throughout with Neoclassical motifs and the square, tapering, gilded legs have *toupie* feet.

Detail of handle pull

MARQUETRY COMMODE

This mahogany commode has a shaped top over a case with four drawers, flanked by canted corners that curve outward toward the base. The commode is profusely inlaid with satinwood, fruitwood, and walnut marquetry. It is supported on bracket feet. *c. 1790. H:32 in (81.5 cm). FRE*

DEMI-LUNE CARD TABLE

The top of this table is inlaid with butterflies, flowers, and cornucopia. When opened, floral marquetry is revealed. It has two pivoting drawers in the frieze, and inlaid tapered legs. *c. 1785. H:35 in (89 cm); W:17¼ in (44 cm); D:30 in (76 cm).*

SIDE CHAIR

One of a set of eight, this Dutch mahogany chair has an oval padded back and seat upholstered in striped gray velvet. The top rail has a stylized urn motif. The chair stands on turned, tapering, fluted legs. *1775–1800.*

CENTER TABLE

The top of this mahogany oval table is echoed by its inlaid, oval shell *patera*. Square, tapered legs support the case and terminate in brass casters. *c. 1800. H:29½ in (75 cm); W:14½ in (37.5 cm). RGA*

GATELEG TABLE

This mahogany, oval, drop-leaf table has one drawer in the frieze. It stands on tapering legs terminating in pad feet. *Second half of the 18th century. H:29 in (74 cm); W:49½ in (126 cm); D:36 in (91.5 cm).*

r washing glasses. On some examples, number of shelves were attached to e lid, which fell open on lifting the d. On other models, additional flaps ere fitted under the lid and could be pened to provide more surface space. The innovative buffet was just one xample of metamorphic furniture at had a dual use and could be ansformed when elements such as ace-saving cupboards and fold-over ps were opened up—particularly

suitable for small Dutch townhouses. Chairs had either an oval or a rectangular back, as in France. However, mahogany was preferred for the frame, while the carved decoration and set of the arms was characteristic of the Netherlands.

Despite these details, even in the Neoclassical period, Dutch furniture remained largely unchanged from the previous 50 years, although a more refined sense of proportion is evident.

DECORATIVE FEATURES

Local cabinet-makers continued to excel in the art of marquetry, using exotic woods such as rosewood, satinwood, or ebony. During the second half of the century, marquetry designs began to incorporate Classical motifs such as the stylized fan, urn, and trophies.

Despite the Dutch appreciation of French style, the angular, contrasting geometric shapes of the marquetry and

the minimal use of ormolu mounts— except in keyhole escutcheons and handles—gave their furniture a distinctive Duch character.

Decorative inlays remained popular, and as furniture became more rectilinear in the 1780s, lacquer was again used for decoration on cupboard doors, table tops, and cabinet fall- fronts. These lacquer panels were often combined with light woods to provide a strong color contrast.

Checkered inlay is a typical Dutch feature.

The centerpiece is a reused Chinese lacquer panel.

Ribbons and tassels are popular motifs of the period.

The fall front folds down to provide a writing slide.

MARQUETRY *SÉCRETAIRE À ABATTANT*

ade of satinwood, walnut, sycamore, and fruitwood, and decorated th parcel-gilt black lacquer and marquetry, this desk has a fall front closing a fitted interior with three pigeon holes, a central door, and four awers. The mounts on the frieze door are inset with porcelain plaques. 780. H:55½ in (141 cm); W:34 in (86.5 cm); D:16½ in (42 cm).

The supports are square and tapering.

FLORAL MARQUETRY DISPLAY CABINET

This solid oak piece with maple marquetry is made in two parts. The upper section has a central carved-and-scroll swan's-neck pediment, and glazed doors. The lower section has drawers. It has carved feet to the front. Essentially Baroque in style, the single concession to Neoclassicism is the carving on the apron. *c. 1795. H:94¾ in (241 cm). BMN*

OAK CHEST

This rectangular chest has a hinged top with a molded edge. It has ebonized detailing, and the two panels at the front are inlaid in fruitwood with stylized fans and a central urn. Two drawers are set below the panels. The case is supported on tapering, channeled feet. *c. 1790. W:58¼ in (148 cm). DN*

BRITAIN: EARLY GEORGE III

George III came to the throne in 1760, and British furniture-making reached its zenith during his 51 year reign. British design was highly influential, owing to the publications of key designers whose names have become synonymous with Georgian furniture.

The key style of this period was Neoclassical, which was largely introduced to Britain by James Stuart and Robert Adam in the 1760s (*see pp.152–53*). Thomas Chippendale also played a role in the development of the movement, and worked alongside Robert Adam on a number of occasions. However, the designers George Hepplewhite, who published

his *Cabinet-Maker and Upholsterer's Guide* in 1788, and Thomas Sheraton, whose *Cabinet-Maker and Upholsterer's Drawing Book* came out between 1791 and 1794, are also strongly associated with the style and helped to spread the Neoclassical ideal. Important furniture-makers included Gillows of Lancaster, Ince and Mayhew, George Seddon, and John Linnell.

ADOPTING A NEW STYLE

By about 1765, the Rococo style was waning, and its typical decorative details, such as carved foliage and C-scrolls, had become passé. The main change ushered in by the Neoclassical

movement was the introduction of symmetrical designs. New decorations made use of Classical ornaments such as urns, rosettes, swags of husks, and bellflowers. Other popular motifs included vases, Greek keys, laurel wreaths, palmettes, sphinxes, anthemion, and guilloche.

At first, Neoclassical decoration was applied to existing Rococo furniture shapes. However, these soon began to show the influence of Neoclassicism, and became more refined and rectilinear in shape, with symmetrical lines and fewer curves.

DECORATIVE FEATURES

The way in which furniture was decorated also changed. Carved decoration was pronounced at first, but as the century progressed it became shallower, and was finally replaced by inlaid woods in imitation of earlier carved decoration. These inlays were made from a greater

GILTWOOD ORNAMENTAL MIRROR

The upper part of this gilt frame contains an oil painting of a pastoral scene. The sides are carved with rushes bound with ribbons and palm brackets. The cresting is centered by a trophy of Cupid's bow, tied with ribbons and palm branches. *c. 1775. H:90 in (223 cm); W:69 in (175 cm). PAR*

The grain of the mahogany top is contrasted with lighter sycamore banding and boxwood stringing.

The urn design is frequently seen on Neoclassical furniture.

Carved, entwined bands of husks run down the legs.

Roundels decorate each side of the spade-shaped feet.

Carved rosette

CARVED SIDE TABLE

The rectangular top of this mahogany side table is inlaid with stained sycamore banding and boxwood stringing. The table has a shaped apron frieze, which is decorated with a large carved central urn flanked by paterae, a pair of smaller vases, and a swag of husks. The two foliate side handles are integral

to the design. The four square-section, tapering legs are headed by paterae and carved with entwined bands of husks, which are frequently used Neoclassical motifs. The carving runs down the length of the legs to spade-shaped block feet, which are decorated with carved roundels. This piece is one of a pair. *c. 1775. H:34 in (86.5 cm); W:44½ in (112 cm); D:23½ in (60 cm). PAR*

ACCORDION-ACTION CARD TABLE

The hinged, crossbanded, serpentine, mahogany table top has a carved border of flowers and leaves. It opens to reveal a baize playing surface. It has reeded, cabriole legs with bead-and-ree carving, foliate brackets, and scrolled toes on square, block fee *c. 1760. H:28½ in (72.5 cm); W:35½ in (90 cm); D:17¼ in (44 cm). P*

riety of woods than previously, cluding satinwood, tulipwood, and sewood. By 1780, carving on case rniture or tables was reduced to a inimum. The grain of the timber inlay became more important. Painting was also a popular corative technique, and was another ay in which Neoclassical designs and otifs could be incorporated into eces of furniture.

FURNITURE TYPES

Linen chests or clothes presses remained popular, as did mahogany chests of drawers. Neoclassical styling sometimes appeared as canted corners and carved, fluted corner columns.

Large dining tables were made from about 1770 onward. The most formal tables had rounded ends with center sections and gatelegs. Additional leaves were made to fit in between. Gateleg tables were sometimes placed side by side to be used as dining tables well into the 1790s. Toward the end of the 18th century, long pedestal dining tables were introduced. These always had extra leaves that could be inserted

to extend them. The pedestal form also became popular for a variety of other types of table, including drum, breakfast, and center tables.

Other tables suitable for dining included the Pembroke table, which was easy to move because it nearly always had casters. It had two leaves on either side of a rectangular center section, and frequently had a drawer or shelf under the top. Pembroke tables were often decorated with exquisite marquetry patterns that could only be seen in their entirety when the table was open.

Armchair designs continued to be influenced by those emerging from

France, and the *fauteuil* adapted well to Neoclassical style. Increasingly, chairs had oval rather than square upholstered seats and backs, and square, tapering legs with spade feet, or columnar legs with fluting.

The shield-back chair was one of five designs popularized by George Hepplewhite, which also included the oval, heart, camel, and wheel. Shaped like a shield, with a double carved crest rail and tapering uprights, the back splat of the shield-back chair was pierced and decorated with typical Neoclassical motifs, such as wheat sheaves or fleur-de-lys. Such chairs tended not to have stretchers.

HIPPENDALE SIDE CHAIR

is mahogany side chair has a shell-carved est with foliate scrolled ears above a pierced d carved back splat. The trapezoidal slip seat raised on cabriole legs with shell-carved ees and claw-and-ball feet. *NA*

EORGE III *FAUTEUIL*

ne of a set of six, this elegant, French-style eorge III painted and gilded *fauteuil* has crolling rails, arms, and legs. It is upholstered silk from a later date, which features a oral design. *L&T*

MARQUETRY COMMODE

This fine George III ormolu, rosewood, satinwood, kingwood, and marquetry commode is serpentine and slightly *bombé* in shape. The top is inlaid with a musical trophy and foliate scrolls. The two doors have ormolu banding and open to reveal shelves within. The side panels are inlaid with vases. The commode has ormolu shoulder mounts and scrolled feet. *c. 1770. H:35½ in (90 cm); W:56 in (142 cm). PAR*

The intricate marquetry depicts a musical trophy and scrolls.

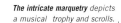

The ormolu mounts run down the sides of the commode to the feet.

Ormolu mounts protect the veneer on the feet and provide decoration.

The doors are framed with contrasting chevron inlays in a lighter veneer.

The sides of the commode are inlaid with Classical vases.

BRITAIN: LATE GEORGE III

AS GEORGE III'S REIGN continued, furniture design evolved. By 1770, Neoclassical styles were being made and soon became the favorite in fashionable circles. However, Rococo styles coexisted with Neoclassical designs for several years, and furniture from this time often has elements of both styles. French influences and Gothic taste can still be seen in some pieces. Furniture that was Neoclassical in shape, for example, occasionally had elements of Gothic-style decoration.

Chinese lacquer also remained popular as a method of decoration for some of the more important pieces of furniture, but overall shapes were straight and elegant.

Many important cabinet-makers worked in the Neoclassical style, including George Seddon, Ince and Mayhew, and John Linnell. Their work, together with that of many other makers, shows how important exotic woods and marquetry were in George III furniture.

INFLUENCE OF THE GRAND TOUR

From the 1750s onward, many of the aristocracy had been going on the Grand Tour of Italy (see pp.132–33). On their return to England, they wanted to build new houses that emulated the Classical architecture, interiors, and furniture they had seen on their travels. As souvenirs, many of these Grand Tourists shipped back marble tops from Italy, and they wanted tables made to match—the obvious style to choose was, of course, Neoclassical.

Cabriole chair design This design, from Plate 10 of *The Cabinet-Maker and Upholsterer's Guide* of 1788 by George Hepplewhite, shows a Neoclassical upholstered chair entitled a "cabriole chair," described as being "in the newest fashion."

SCOTTISH LINEN PRESS

This linen press has rosewood crossbanding around the doors' central mahogany ovals, which are outlined with boxwood stringing. It has graduated drawers, a central inlaid tablet in the shaped skirt, mirrored in the plaque in the cornice, and bracket feet. *c. 1780. H:83 in (211 cm). L&T*

GILLOWS FURNITURE

GILLOWS OF LANCASTER DESIGNED AND MADE A VAST QUANTITY OF FURNITURE FOR THE NOBILITY, THE GENTRY, AND THE GROWING MIDDLE CLASS.

The Gillows firm of cabinet-makers was established in Lancaster, in northern England, around 1730. It made furniture for a varied clientele and opened a London branch in 1769.

Most of the furniture it produced in the late 18th century was of Neoclassical design, without decoration, and followed the designs of Hepplewhite and Sheraton. Pieces were made in fine mahogany or satinwood and took into account the grain of these timbers. After 1770, Gillows

furniture had an austerity reflecting contemporary architecture. Writing, library, and dressing furniture often had ingenious arrangements of small drawers and hidden compartments.

Unlike many 18th-century cabinet-makers, the firm did not publish any of its designs, preferring to keep them exclusive to clients. Gillows consistently produced furniture of high quality, and made pieces for the domestic and export markets well into the 19th century.

Small, lockable compartment

The frieze drawer is fitted with writing implements.

Square, tapering legs are joined by an undertier.

Small *bonheur-du-jour* The upper section has lockable compartments either side of a short drawer. The bowed front has a central frieze drawer, and the square, tapering legs have brass caps and casters.

Forms became lighter and more elegant with straight, square legs, rather than cabriole legs. By about 1780, legs had became square and tapering. Caned seats became popular once again.

Classical emblems often reflected the purpose of the piece of furniture; music rooms would have furniture decorated with musical trophies or Neoclassical figures playing instruments such as lyres.

Some architects such as Robert Adam designed whole rooms, including door fittings, in the Neoclassical style and commissioned Chippendale to make the furniture for specific places within the rooms.

Provincial furniture was also made in the Neoclassical style but was usually simpler and did not have elaborate inlays.

NEW FORMS

Several new types of furniture were first made during this period. Long dining tables became common and the sideboard evolved from two pedestals flanking a serving table to one piece of furniture. Long sets of chairs were made to complement longer tables.

Mirrors increased in size, as the technology evolved to create larger plates of glass. New types of desks were also made. The Carlton House desk, made in 1795 for the Prince of Wales (the future George IV), was named after his London residence. It took the form of a table with raised drawers along the sides and back.

Other new forms of furniture at this time included cylinder desks that closed with tambour tops; dressing tables incorporating elaborate compartments and a folding mirror; and game tables with removable sliders and reversible tops. Smaller items such as tea caddies and sewing boxes were also made in the Neoclassical style.

SHIFTING STYLES

Toward the end of the 18th century, styles became less elaborate and the use of marquetry and inlay decreased. Despite being at war with France, British styles were influenced by the French taste for plainer furniture with the use of well-figured veneers. Changes were subtle, such as square, tapering legs being replaced with turned, tapering legs. Furniture became slightly heavier in form, but was still very elegant.

Nelson's successful campaign in Egypt had an influence on English designers and Egyptian motifs began to appear in English furniture.

The serpentine-shaped table top has a molded edge.

The frieze drawer has a baize-lined writing slide.

The central marquetry design is repeated on each drop leaf.

The tapering legs terminate in brass shoes and leather-lined casters.

Table top

GEORGE III DINING CHAIRS

Part of a set, these mahogany chairs have molded, oval backs. The carved decoration on the chair backs is of wheat ears and paterae, with a flower-head at the top of each upright rail. *c. 1785.* H:36 in (91.5 cm); W:20½ in (52.5 cm); D:20¼ in (53 cm). PAR

Carved anthemion

MAHOGANY CARD TABLE

This card table is in the French Hepplewhite style. The serpentine top opens to reveal a playing surface, above a serpentine frieze. The table is raised on cabriole legs, which have carved knees and terminate in scroll feet. W:40 in (102 cm). L&T

BREAKFAST OR PEMBROKE TABLE

This satinwood table has a serpentine-shaped top inlaid with an oval medallion surrounded by swags and ribbons. The drop leaves have matching veneers and the tapered legs are inlaid with satinwood flutes and bellflowers. *c. 1780.* H:28 in (71 cm); W:14 in (35.5 cm); D:11 in (28 cm). PAR

ROBERT ADAM

THE INTERIORS OF THE SCOTTISH ARCHITECT ROBERT ADAM
BECAME SO WELL KNOWN THAT THE TERM "ADAM STYLE" WAS
COINED TO DESCRIBE HIS DISTINCTIVE LOOK.

ROBERT ADAM began his career by training as an
architect in Edinburgh, under his father William, a
classical architect. Robert spent five years studying
in Italy, drawing the sights frequented by scholars on
the Grand Tour. On his return in 1758 he established
an office in London, where he was later joined by his
elder brother James.

Adam's designs were primarily for interiors, rather
than whole buildings, and he designed every element
of them, to create an integrated whole, from ceilings
and matching carpets down to mirrors and urns.
As a result, his designs included a wide variety of
furniture, including chairs, sofas, commodes, stools,
and mirrors. He also designed console tables,
bookcases, and sideboards as "wall furniture"—an
integral part of his decorative scheme for walls.

Adam did not make furniture himself, but
commissioned established London cabinet-makers,
including Chippendale and Linnell, to make it. In
his first decade in London, Adam developed the
style of decoration that was to remain the dominant
feature of his work throughout his career.

KEY DATES

Robert Adam

1728 Robert Adam born in
Kirkcaldy, Scotland.

1743–45 Adam attends
Edinburgh College.

1746–48 Adam works
with his elder brother John
as an architect's apprentice
to his father, William, until William's death in 1748.

1750 Robert and his brother James begin their first
major commission, Hopetoun House, near Edinburgh.

1754–58 Adam goes on the Grand Tour.

1758 Adam returns from Italy and goes to London.
Becomes a member of the Royal Society of Arts.

1761 Adam is appointed "Architect of the King's
Works," a position he holds jointly with William
Chambers, the architect of Somerset House.

1764 William Adam & Co. established, with offices
in London and Scotland.

1773 The first volume of *Works in Architecture of
Robert and James Adam* is published, (the second
in 1779, the third posthumously in 1822).

1792 Adam dies and is buried in Poet's Corner at
Westminster Abbey, London.

PIER GLASS
*This carved giltwood and gesso pier glass in
the Neoclassical style was made for hanging on
the wall between two windows, with a pier
table below. The margin of the mirror's
frame allows a greater expanse of glass,
with anthemia marking where the
separate pieces are joined.*

"FRENCH-STYLE" ARMCHAIR
This painted and gilded fauteuil *has an oval back,
a half-round seat, splayed rear legs, and fluted front
legs.* c. 1775. H:37 in (94 cm); W:25½ in (65 cm). NOA

ORMOLU-MOUNTED URNS
*Designed by Robert Adam, these
pine, lime, and mahogany urns were
made by John Linnell and have
removable tops. Urns with pedestals
like this were usually made for
dining rooms. The pedestals often
served as plate-warmers and had
metal racks and a small oil burner
at the base.* 1767. H:61 in (155 cm);
W:17½ in (44.5 cm).

ALCOVE AT KEDLESTON
Adam designed the alcove at the west end of the dining room at Kedleston Hall in Derbyshire. He also designed the furniture for it, such as the semicircular sideboard, specifically to fit the given space and echo the filigree design and pastel colors of the alcove ceiling above. Adam frequently designed new shapes of rooms, such as alcoves, galleries, and libraries, to add a sense of movement to an interior.

GILTWOOD SIDE TABLE
One of a pair, this giltwood table has a carved frieze and fluted, tapering legs, the tops carved with plumes and acanthus. The white marble top is inlaid with coloured scagliola decoration of storks and bands of ribbon.
c. 1770. H:34¼ in (87 cm); W:59¼ in (150.5 cm); D:29 in (74 cm). PAR

The most important influence on this style was Roman antiquity, of which he had made many drawings while in Italy. Visits to Herculaneum and Rome inspired him to incorporate tripods, urns, oval medallions, Vitruvian scrolls, Greek keys, anthemia, and many other Classical motifs into his work. Adam also used Renaissance motifs, such as grotesques, chimeras, and sphinxes.

The Italian artist Giovanni Piranesi became a close friend and inspiration to Adam. Many motifs in Adam's designs can be found in Piranesi's drawings of Roman views and fantastic interiors, and while Adam's chimney pieces were not as wild as Piranesi's engravings, many were inspired by them.

EARLY INFLUENCES
The Palladian style had a strong influence on Adam's early work. Armchairs and sofas that he designed for Sir Laurence Dundas—made by Chippendale—had typically Palladian, rectangular backs. However, the sphinxes on the curved seat rails showed the influence of Renaissance grotesques, and the use of anthemia harked back to Classical motifs.

By the late 1760s, Adam had begun to develop a more sophisticated style. His furniture designs became more delicate, the carving less dramatic, and he began to use straight legs. Case pieces were still rectangular, but Adam began to use new shapes in other types of furniture. In 1767, he designed furniture for the dining room at Osterley Park in west London and the dining chairs introduced a new shape of chair back—known as a harp- or lyre-back, inspired by Classical shapes.

THE LATER YEARS
By the 1770s, Adam's fame had grown and he carried out many commissions for the aristocracy. His elegant furniture designs were widely imitated. His tables and chairs had slender, tapered legs and armchairs had oval backs and slender frames. Mirrors were an important feature of his interiors and included simple designs intended to be positioned above pier tables, as well as enormous pieces with slight frames that were designed to cover an entire wall.

COLORS AND DECORATION
Adam's designs were usually for furniture made from light woods, such as satinwood and harewood (sycamore that was dyed gray). Adam favored delicate, painted designs, in soft pastel colors, such as pale green and lilac pink, and gilding.

The intricate, swirling arabesques that he used to decorate ceilings and floors were repeated in the filigree decoration used on his furniture. He also frequently used scagliola, not just on pieces of furniture but also as architectural features of an interior, such as the intricate scagliola columns at Syon House in West London.

GUSTAVIAN

IN SWEDEN, as in Britain, the last 40 years of the 18th century were a golden age of design, and the beginning of a recognizable Swedish furniture style. The term "Gustavian" is used to describe the Swedish Neoclassical style, and refers to the period from about 1755 to 1810.

GUSTAV III
The greatest exponent of the Swedish Neoclassical style was King Gustav III. He spent time at Versailles before being crowned in 1771, and developed a love of the French Neoclassical style. On his return to Sweden, he invited French cabinet-makers to Sweden to

make furniture. When he was unable to pay them, they returned home, leaving behind their furniture. This was copied by the local craftsmen, but in a less ornate style that became known as "Gustavian."

Walnut was often used in these earlier pieces; later furniture was usually made from local woods such as pine and schubirch, and then painted rather than gilded because it was cheaper—Sweden was a much poorer country than France at the time.

Gustav's enthusiasm for Neoclassical design led him to incorporate the style into his ancestral home, Gripsholm Castle. The Grand Cabinet, an official

reception room (see opposite), was lavishly decorated in this way.

NEOCLASSICAL DESIGN
The designs most favored in the Swedish Neoclassical era were light, elegant interpretations of the Louis XVI style. Grand reception rooms were decorated with architectural elements such as pilasters and columns. Others were paneled or painted in Gustavian colors: light gray, blue, or pale green.

In these rooms, the most important item was the faïence stove. In larger rooms, pairs of stoves—often of huge proportions and in Neoclassical style—with brightly painted faïence tiles

graced the spaces usually occupied b[y] pairs of pier tables.

Swedish cabinet-makers decorated their furniture with figured veneers and banding made of mahogany and other tropical woods, such as kingwood, and ebony for sophisticate[d] pieces. High-style furniture used imported gilt mounts in the French style. The mounts never overwhelm[ed] the furniture, but were discreetly use[d] on the sides of case pieces and at the ends of legs. Intricate marquetry, with typical Neoclassical motifs such as urns, reflected the influence of Britis[h] fashions in some Gustavian furnitur[e] although it was less common.

The marquetry swags are set within an ebony border.

The table top is inset with specimen marble squares.

The table legs are joined by a flat cross-stretcher.

GUSTAVIAN ARMCHAIR

This painted and gilt chair has a splat in the form of entwined "Gs," to represent Gustav III. The upholstered seat rests on a decorated frieze above a carved apron with gilt foliage decoration. c. 1780. Bk

OCCASIONAL TABLE

The top of this satinwood Neoclassical table is decorated with different colored marbles. The frieze is decorated with marquetry swags, and there

is a single drawer for storage. Strips of ebony are inlaid into the legs to imitate Classical columns. The table was designed by George Haupt, and was probably made for serving coffee. 1769. H:29½ in (75 cm); W:17 in (43 cm).

GILTWOOD CONSOLE TABLE

The marble top of this table rests above a guilloche-decorated frieze. The tapering legs are joined by flat stretchers, on which a decorative urn is centered. c. 1780. H:30¾ in (77 cm); W:36¼ in (92 cm); D:18½ in (47 cm). Bk

PAINTED CABINET

This painted side cabinet is made in two parts. The upper section has leaf-tip carved cornice molding above two fluted panel doors and a niche below. The lower section

of the cabinet has two matching panel doors on square, fluted, and tapered feet. It is painted pale green—a typically Gustavian color. c. 1800. H:101 in (252.5 cm); W:53 in (132.5 cm); D:16½ in (41.25 cm). EVE

FASHIONABLE HOMES

Furniture and floor-and-wall coverings were all designed as part of an integral interior. The most fashionable floor-coverings were inspired by those of Louis XV's carpet factory, the *Savonnerie*. However, floors were often bare, so were paneled to resemble marquetry designs.

Upholstered furniture was covered in red, blue, or green damasks, which matched the wall coverings. Chairs were oval- or square-backed, with turned, fluted legs. Daybeds (*see*

below) and *badkarsoffas*, or bathtub sofas—where the sides of the sofa were the same height as the back and curved to create a bathtub form—were typically Gustavian and proved popular.

LATE GUSTAVIAN FURNITURE

Swedish furniture design became more austere later in the period. The rectilinear two-part cabinet is a provincial example of this.

Gustavian pieces are clearly influenced by European, especially French, styles of furniture. However, Swedish designers interpreted the style in a way that is instantly recognizable as Scandinavian.

The Grand Cabinet of Gripsholm Castle Heavy laurel swags and panels adorn the room, which is furnished with giltwood chairs and benches.

GUSTAVIAN ARMCHAIRS

These white-painted and gilt armchairs are square in form with upholstered seats and backs. The sweeping arms have upholstered elbow rests. The seat rail is decorated in each corner with a gilded rosette and is supported

on tapering, fluted legs. These armchairs are typical of Gustavian furniture in that they are painted and the upholstery is of a pale pink color. However, they are regarded as coarse, provincial examples of the style, even though they were originally made for a sophisticated home. *c. 1790. Bk*

GEORG HAUPT

AS THE PRINCIPAL CABINET-MAKER TO THE SWEDISH ROYAL FAMILY, GEORG HAUPT WAS THE GREATEST EXPONENT OF SWEDISH NEOCLASSICAL STYLE.

The son of a cabinet-maker, Georg Haupt worked in Amsterdam, London, and Paris before finding fame in Sweden. He returned to Sweden around 1768; his work was much in demand, and he became principal cabinet-maker to King Adolf Frederick in 1769.

Most of his furniture designs were inspired by French styles, including commodes, night stands, and *secrétaires*. Haupt was especially famed for his use of exotic tropical woods for veneers. He is also believed to be the first cabinet-

maker after the Rococo period to use birch for veneer. This pale wood was indigenous to Sweden and could be easily stained to create different colors.

Like French marquetry designers, Haupt used geometric formulae: a trellis pattern with centered quatrefoils. His furniture often featured ormolu mounts used in an understated way that was subordinate to the overall design. He produced work of the highest quality, and his masterpiece was a desk given by King Adolf Frederick to Queen Louisa Ulrika.

Detail of inlay

The lower drawers are sans traverse, *meaning they have no distinguishable break in the marquetry design.*

The inlay includes foliage and nautical symbols.

Commode One of a pair, this has a marble top over a conforming case. The side panels are inlaid with a vase shape. Four slightly cabriole legs support the case. *c. 1775. H:33 in (84 cm); W:20 in (51 cm). Bk*

Imported mounts *trail to the feet of the front legs.*

GUSTAVIAN DAY BED

This painted day bed is probably made from pine and has deep, upholstered sides and back. Each end has an arched and scrolled top rail with central foliate carving and curved uprights, above tapering, stop-

fluted legs headed by rosettes. The seat rail is carved with floral motifs. The 20th-century upholstery replaces what probably would have been silk, decorated with much stronger Neoclassical motifs. The pale colors mimic the Swedish Gustavian style. *c. 1780. Bk*

SCANDINAVIA

THE ADVENT OF NEOCLASSICISM coincided with the first emergence of identifiable national styles in Scandinavia. Previously, much of the furniture made in these countries had been a wholesale imitation of British or French design. During the late 18th century, however, designers exploited lighter-colored indigenous woods as an alternative to mahogany—partly out of economic necessity—and a fashion for painting furniture, rather than gilding, developed.

DENMARK

The dining room of A. G. Moltke's palace at Amalienborg, Copenhagen's smartest address, was decorated in the Neoclassical style by the Frenchman Nicolas-Henri Jardin, in 1757. This was one of the earliest incursions of the Neoclassical style into Scandinavia, and was typical of the almost slavish manner in which the Danes and their neighbors emulated French fashions.

The pattern books of English masters such as Hepplewhite and Sheraton were also very influential, particularly in the design of commodes, whose Continental-style parquetry and marble-slab tops were phased out in favor of plainer English veneers. Chairs often had splat backs, a direct appropriation from the English Neoclassical style. In common with the rest of Europe, mahogany became the timber of choice for chairs and case pieces. Furniture was frequently embellished with gilt Neoclassical motifs such as shells, acanthus leaves, and urns.

NORWAY

Norway was administered from Copenhagen until the Napoleonic Wars in 1814. As the dominant member of this union, Denmark exported many manufactured goods to Norway, including furniture.

Neoclassical design emerged in Norway in the 1770s, just as it was gaining popularity in Denmark. Many of the wealthiest Norwegian families had close ties with Britain, and their homes were furnished with imported English furniture, or copies made by local cabinet-makers in the late Georgian style. Alongside mahogany, Norwegian cabinet-makers began to use birch, a light-colored, deciduous wood that was indigenous to Norway and that became synonymous with vernacular furniture.

SWEDEN

Gustav III (see pp.154–55) was responsible for introducing the Neoclassical style to Sweden. Touring in France when informed of his father's death, he completed his visit to Versailles before journeying home to take up the crown, and returned full of enthusiasm for the Neoclassical style he had seen there. George Haupt, who had worked in France and Britain, was a key figure in the development of Swedish Neoclassicism and went on to become the principal court cabinet-maker.

Case furniture made during this period tended to be rectilinear, with tapered legs. Chests had chamfered sides or carved quarter columns, and often incorporated fluted brass mounts and cock-beading in the manner of German commodes. As an alternative to gilding, furniture was often painted in pale colors. British influence can be seen in the adoption of forms such as the tea table and the splat back chair, and the polished mahogany finishes that became popular toward 1790.

FINLAND

Something of a backwater until granted its status as an independent Duchy by the Russians in 1809, Finland was slow to adopt the Neoclassical style that had swept across the rest of Europe. Until around 1770, apprentice cabinet-makers in Finland continued to present elaborate Rococo-style cabinets to the furniture guilds as examples of their most accomplished work.

Neoclassical style did not really flourish in Finland until Carl Ludvig Engel introduced it from Russia in the 19th century, but furniture of the late 18th century did take on some aspects of more fashionable European pieces. Economic depression compelled Finnish cabinet-makers to use local woods such as pine and beech and stain them to imitate the more expensive imported timbers demanded by the Neoclassical aesthetic. In the last years of the 18th century, the Finns began to use veneers of oak, walnut, and finally mahogany.

DANISH CORNER CABINET

This mahogany corner cabinet is in two parts, and is decorated with Neoclassical motifs. The upper section has a molded, fluted pediment, which sits above a carved dentil and Greek-key frieze. Below this, the two panelled doors are flanked on either side and centered with fluting and roundels. They open to reveal a shelved interior. The lower section has a bow-fronted, fluted, frieze drawer above three long drawers, and the whole is supported on squared, block feet. c. 1780–90. H:90 in (228.5 cm); W:45 in (114 cm). EVE

GILTWOOD CONSOLE TABLE

This carved wooden console table has exceptionally fine rosettes and beading. The frieze, legs, and raised plinth are gilded. It has a rectangular marble table top and is supported on four fluted column legs that terminate in square feet. *c. 1800. H:35 in (92 cm); W:31½ in (80 cm); D:17⅓ in (44 cm). GK*

DANISH MIRROR FRAME

This mirror plate is surrounded by an ornate Louis XVI giltwood frame, with a beaded inner edge and a leaf-carved outer edge. The top of the frame is surmounted by a carved ribbon crest. *c. 1790. H:29 in (74 cm); W:21 in (53 cm). EVE*

DANISH COMMODE

The rectangular top of this Louis XVI-style mahogany commode has a molded edge and sits above a similarly shaped case with three drawers, flanked on either side by fluted quarter-pilasters. The case stands on raised bracket feet. *c. 1790. H:28½ in (72.5 cm); W:28 in (71 cm); D:17 in (43 cm). EVE*

SWEDISH TEA TABLE

This tilt-top, tripod tea table has a circular top made from alder root veneer. The turned pedestal leads into cabriole legs, and both parts are made from ebonized birch. The table bears the stamped signature of the maker Jakob Sjölin. *H:28¾ in (73 cm); Diam:33⅓ in (85 cm). Bk*

Classical motifs decorate the tops of the upper cupboards.

The case is made of mahogany.

The locks are made of bronze.

Greek key motifs decorate the frieze.

Bronze details decorate the lower section.

DANISH CUPBOARD

This mahogany cupboard is decorated with bronze ornaments. The piece consists of an upper section with three cupboards, and a larger lower section with two doors. The piece was designed by Caspar Frederik Harsdorff, a noted Neoclassical architect. *Late 18th century.*

SPAIN, PORTUGAL, & COLONIES

SPAIN CAME UNDER French Bourbon rule in the 18th century, and this continued with the ascension of Charles III to the throne in 1759. Previously King of Naples, Charles III brought to Spain both Italian architects and designers, notably the Neapolitan Gasparini, who ran the *Manufactura Real* from 1768. However, although the Italians had some influence on Spanish furniture design, the French style continued to dominate.

Spanish society was largely rural and was conservative about interior design: it was not until 1788, for example, that Neoclassicism was widely accepted. Spanish society was also content with

far fewer items of furniture than was normal in other parts of Europe. Some forms, such as the day bed, did not exist at all, and chests of drawers, sideboards or china cupboards, and commodes were seldom used.

Instead, *vargueño* cabinets—which still represented around half of the furniture made—cupboards, armarios, *secrétaires*, and chests remained the standard case pieces.

Secrétaires either showed an English influence, with straight sides, or were inspired by French or Low Country design, with a *bombé* lower case. However, Spanish examples were more flamboyant and theatrical than

either French or English pieces, and lacquered *secrétaires*, especially in red, were particularly popular.

English-style chair backs, whether a solid splat or pierced, were used on Spanish settees. They usually had a four-chair splat back and a caned seat. Later versions were made of mahogany, but unlike English examples, carved details were gilded.

PORTUGAL
The country's politics and its colonial expansion opened Portugal to influences from both France and England. However, dependence on the English maritime trade and the

influential port-wine merchant communities meant that British influence was often stronger. Northern Portugal tended to follow

SPANISH MIRROR AND TABLE

This elaborately carved mirror frame and demilune table are made entirely of gilded wood. The table has a deep, curved frieze and stands on six splayed legs, which are joined by wavy stretchers. *Late 18th century.*

The roll top has a marquetry scene with foliage surround.

Pull-out slide for writing

The edge is inverted and bowed.

The case stands on short, cabriole legs.

The sides are decorated with an inlaid medallion held by a ribbon.

The overall shape of the case indicates the piece is transitional.

Shaped apron

Neoclassical handles with swags

SPANISH ROLL-TOP DESK

The roll-top front of this desk pushes back to reveal a fitted interior. Below this is a pull-out writing slide, above three long, slightly serpentine drawers. The roll top and side panels are inlaid with medallions containing

a landscape design in the former and an urn with flowers and foliage in the latter. The drawers are inlaid with swags of flowers. The escutcheons bear Neoclassical swag-and-medallion motifs. The case has a serpentine base on short cabriole legs. Signed and dated by Sevilla Jh de Varga. *1786. EGU*

PORTUGUESE CONSOLE TABLE

This ivory-painted and parcel-gilt table has a marble top above a pierced frieze. The table stands on leaf-carved fluted legs, joined by a stretcher centered by a classical urn. *H:38½ i (96 cm); W:46¼ in (117 cm) D:26¼ in (67 cm)*

itish taste, while Lisbon and the ourt were inspired by France. Portuguese furniture also shows the fluence of Italy, the Low Countries, nd East Asia due to trade links and olonial possessions—the latter fueling taste for Asian styles.

The resulting furniture was unique. he exaggerated styles often bore milarities to Italian pieces but were ade from foreign woods such as ahogany or jacaranda, which were rticularly suitable for carving.

The furniture also continued to corporate elements from earlier rtuguese designs such as turned iral legs, though by the late 18th

century these elements had become less prominent.

The English tripod table form was extremely popular in Portugal, due to the style's appearance in the third edition of *The Gentleman and Cabinet-maker's Director* in 1762.

Commodes first appeared in 1751 and by the 1770s were being created in a Portuguese interpretation of Louis XVI style, with rectilinear breakfronts, deep aprons, and handles with embedded medallions.

Portuguese chairs resembled English ones with solid back splats and cabriole legs. However, the use of elaborate curves, scrolled feet, and numerous

C-scrolls was unique to furniture from Portugal. Chairs were often made of rosewood, a denser wood than mahogany, which made them look heavier than their English counterparts, such as Chippendales.

MEXICO

Mexican furniture was originally inspired by European styles introduced in the 16th century. Spain and Portugal introduced the advanced art of furniture-making to their colonies, and soon countries such as Mexico started to produce furniture in their own right. By the 17th century,

Mexican furniture had acquired a distinctive style of its own, which continued to be dominant in the 18th century. It was characterized by massive dimensions and exuberant but rural decoration, often incorporating the use of silver.

The "friary" chair was a continuation of a medieval shape, with a square back upholstered in leather with decorative brass tacks positioned around the edge of the frame. The square seat was also upholstered, and it had straight back supports, which flowed into the legs; the front legs were often carved.

SPANISH COLONIAL ARMCHAIRS

The wooden frame of each chair features repoussé silver plaques, an arched, decorative top rail, an arched, padded back, inscrolled arm terminals, and squared, cabriole legs with claw-and-ball feet. *1780–1800.*

PORTUGUESE CENTER TABLE

his rosewood table has cedar linings. The ctangular top is edged all around with silver ounts. The frame has two drawers to the ont, each with a silver escutcheon and bale andle. The base of the table has exquisitely

turned legs, which terminate in small, turned feet. The legs are joined by similarly turned stretchers. *c. 1760. H:30 in (76 cm); W:52 in (132 cm); D:33 in (84 cm). BL*

CABINET-ON-STAND

This heavily carved and gilded cabinet-on-stand has a carved cornice surmounted by an elaborate asymmetrical carved crest. The paneled doors are decorated with alternate squares of gilt to create a checkered effect.

The whole piece is raised on four caryatids, which are joined by a carved cross-stretcher with an urn at the center. *Late 18th century.*

AMERICA: CHIPPENDALE TO FEDERAL

NOT LONG AFTER the American Congress signed the Declaration of Independence on July 4, 1776, the Revolutionary War began in earnest. While the colonists fought for their independence, they had neither the energy nor the enthusiasm to keep up with British fashions, as they had in the past. And so, while the British embraced Robert Adam's Neoclassical designs, American cabinet-makers continued to develop the Chippendale-style furniture they had been making for the past 30 years.

NEW STYLES

It was only after the war ended in 1783 that the new styles were seen in the US, and they were probably not actually made there until after 1790. For some years, the old Chippendale and new Federal styles were made alongside each other, or even combined. In fact, the new American furniture did not adhere to Adam's Neoclassical designs, but followed the styles seen in the latest British pattern books from George Hepplewhite and Thomas Sheraton, often adding a regional twist to these forms. It did, however, borrow Adam's use of marquetry, caning, painted surfaces, and the use of exotic woods.

A NATIONAL STYLE

This emerging style became known as Federal because it reflected the new identity of the US, which now had a Federal government, a Federal party, and was building a Federal city. Confusingly, the style is sometimes called Sheraton or Hepplewhite, depending upon which style it was based. With the new politics came prosperity, and Baltimore and New York joined Philadelphia, Newport, Boston, Charleston, and Williamsburg as centers of fine furniture production.

Early Federal furniture was restrained in form and shows great attention to detail. Pieces had simple, geometric shapes. Those that were Hepplewhite in style had slender, tapered, square legs, while the Sheraton-style pieces had round, slightly vase-shaped or reeded legs. The feet were usually shaped like spades or arrows.

Early Federal chairs typically had shield, oval, or square backs, or painted finishes. They were upholstered in silk, cotton, or wool, either in plain colors or with Classical, striped, or lattice patterns.

NEW FORMS

As the US became more prosperous, the variety of furniture increased. Traditional candlestands, serving tables, and dining tables were joined by Pembroke tables, side tables, and pier tables, along with small card, sewing, and worktables. These were made from New England, through New York and Philadelphia to the southern States. Dressing tables began to replace lowboys, especially in Maryland, New York, Philadelphia, and Salem. Chests of drawers were made in the latest styles in all the states.

Escutcheons usually matched the pulls on doors and drawers. Where wood, ivory, or bone plates were used, they were inset into the wood. Brass pulls on Hepplewhite-style designs usually had an oval mount and a bail handle. On Sheraton designs, which were popular in Salem, they often had an oblong plate and a bail handle, a rosette with a ring, or were in the form of a lion's head with a ring pull.

In Baltimore, Newport, Salem, and New York, furniture was generally made from mahogany, but maple was favored in Boston. Cabinet-makers used satinwood, ebony, ash, and other contrasting veneers. Baltimore, in particular, was known for its painted gilt glass panels and delicate inlays.

DECORATIVE FEATURES

The grain of the wood often provided the only form of decoration, but some pieces featured carvings in low relief, veneers, inlays, or paint. Carved decoration was confined to the early years of the period, while painted Federal furniture is rarely seen today.

Popular motifs inspired by antiquity included patera, bellflowers, thunderbolts, sheaves of wheat, and vases of flowers. Many pieces of furniture from this period were carved or inlaid with patriotic symbols, including the American Eagle, the symbol of the Federal Union.

PHILADELPHIA SIDE CHAIR

This Chippendale chair has a serpentine crest with a carved central shell. The vase-shaped splat is flanked by shaped stiles. It has cylindrical rear legs, and cabriole front legs, ending in claw-and-ball feet. *1760–80. NA*

PHILADELPHIA SIDE CHAIR

This chair's crest has a carved shell motif and molded ears. The pierced splat has scroll volutes. The shell motif is repeated on the front rail. The chair has cylindrical rear legs, cabriole front legs, and claw-and-ball feet. *c. 1770. NA*

The cupboard doors are crossbanded to look as though there is a drawer above the door.

The demi-lune top is inlaid along the edge for contrast.

The oval, stamped brass escutcheons have bail handles.

Turned and reeded legs were often used by New England cabinet-makers on Federal furniture.

MASSACHUSETTS SIDEBOARD

This Sheraton mahogany *demi-lune* (half-moon) sideboard from Massachusetts is inlaid with various woods. The elliptical top has an inlaid edge. Three crossbanded central drawers are flanked by cupboard doors, which are inlaid to resemble a drawer above a door and open to reveal shelves. The case stands on turned, reeded legs. This design was popularized by English pattern books. *c. 1795. H:36 in (90 cm) W:54 in (135 cm); D:22 in (55 cm). NA*

EW ENGLAND SECRÉTAIRE

:ributed to John Seymour, this Hepplewhite mahogany
:sk has inlaid pilasters and two tambour doors concealing
:eonholes and drawers. The hinged writing surface with
:anded edge is above two drawers, and the square legs
:minate in tapering feet. *1785–95. H:38 in (103 cm).*

NEW ENGLAND BUREAU

This mahogany desk has a fall-front lid that opens to reveal
a fitted interior. The oxbow-shaped case has four graduated
drawers above base molding with a central, concave, carved-
shell drop. The desk stands on short, cabriole legs with claw-
and-ball feet. *c. 1770. H:44¾ in (112 cm). NA*

NEW ENGLAND CHEST OF DRAWERS

This Sheraton carved, mahogany, bow-front chest of drawers has
a D-shaped top with outset rounded corners above four wide
drawers the same shape. The stiles are carved with leaves
above barley-twists and terminate in turned feet. *c. 1790.
W:39½ in (99 cm).*

EW HAMPSHIRE CABRIOLE SOFA

:is small mahogany cabriole sofa comes from the Winslow Pierce
:mily of Portsmouth, New Hampshire. It has an arched, molded
: rail that extends to curved arms with rosette terminals resting

on molded, curved supports. The frame is upholstered and the
seat cushion is covered in a matching fabric. Square tapering
legs at the front terminate in spade feet. This sofa was probably
one of a pair in the Pierce Mansion, Portsmouth. *1790–1800.
W:63 in (160 cm).*

HILADELPHIA CARD TABLE

:is mahogany card table has a rectangular top above a molded
:eze with a single cock-beaded drawer. Pierced frets decorate
: corners of the front legs, which are molded with tapering
:et. When open, one of the rear legs swings back to support the
:p. *c. 1785. W:36 in (90 cm). FRE*

PENNSYLVANIA TABLE

Made of walnut, this simple, Chippendale-style drop-leaf table
from Pennsylvania has a rectangular top and two leaves with
notched corners. The frame has a shaped skirt and cabriole
legs terminating in carved claw-and-ball feet. *c. 1780.
W:41½ in (104 cm). FRE*

RHODE ISLAND CHEST-ON-CHEST

This cherry bonnet-top chest-on-chest is constructed in two
parts: the upper part has twin drawers above three graduated
drawers; the lower part has a case of four graduated drawers,
and stands on a base molding supported on ogee bracket feet.
c. 1770. H:87 in (217.5 cm); W:37½ in (93.75 cm). NA

AMERICA: SOUTHERN STATES

BY THE TIME the Revolutionary War was under way, the southern states of Maryland, Virginia, North and South Carolina, and Georgia were home to some of America's wealthiest people.

EUROPEAN INFLUENCE
Successful trade with Europe had enabled the local planters and merchants to live the lives of a sophisticated elite who kept abreast

of London fashions. By visiting Europe and importing European, and especially British, goods, they were able to give their homes a British feel. Those who did not import the latest London furniture designs could have them copied locally by some of the finest craftsmen in the country. It used to be thought that all good southern furniture originated in Britain, but research over the past

few years has proved that much of it was made in the south, by immigrant British and other craftsmen.

POST-WAR FURNITURE
After the war, southern furniture started to be influenced by furniture from New York and New England; many southern Neoclassical chairs were very similar to New York ones of the same period.

Dining tables were usually simpler in design, following the English taste. Corner tables and other small, drop-leaf tables were used for dining, tea, writing, gaming, and sewing. Cards were a popular pastime in the south

and so many tables were designed for this purpose.

Sofas, which had been expensive to upholster, became more affordable aft the war and many were made by urba and rural craftsmen. However, early examples were likely to be British.

REGIONAL DIFFERENCES
Wealthy families in the coastal areas, who had once furnished their principa rooms with chests, moved them to les important bedchambers and passages using chests of drawers and clothes presses for storage instead.

Inland, in West Virginia, families continued to use chests in the main

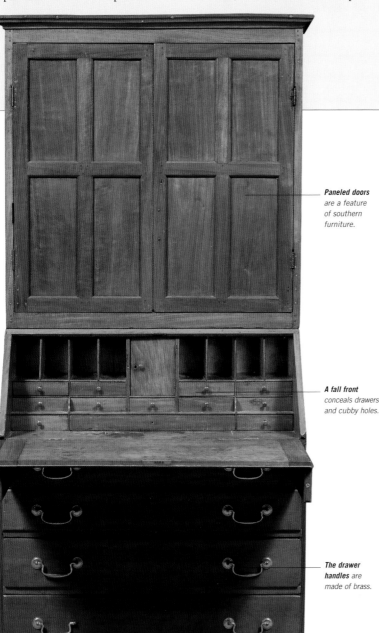

Paneled doors are a feature of southern furniture.

A fall front conceals drawers and cubby holes.

The drawer handles are made of brass.

WRITING OR DRESSING TABLE

This small walnut table with a single drawer has a rectangular top with a large overhang, a typical feature of southern furniture. The brass handle and plate were imported from Britain. *c. 1760. W:32½ in (82.5 cm). POOK*

VIRGINIA CHEST

This mahogany and yellow pine chest has a rectangular top, two-over-four graduated and dovetailed drawers, and ogee feet. *Late 18th century. H:39½ in (100.3 cm); W:39¼ in (99.6 cm); D:20¾ in (52.7 cm). BRU*

SOUTHERN SECRÉTAIRE

The primary wood of this bookcase is walnut, but the poplar and yellow pine interior woods identify this as a southern piece. The upper part is flat-topped with two hinged, paneled doors; doors of this type are rarely seen in the

northern states. The lower section consists of a slant-front desk above four graduated drawers supported on bracket feet. The slant front conceals an interior with drawers and cubby holes flanking a central prospect door. *c. 1770. H:88 in (223.5 cm); W:39 in (96 cm); D:24 in (61 cm). BRU*

SOUTHERN CHEST

This rectangular southern chest is made of pine. It has a flat top with a small overhang. The case retains much of its original painted surface, comprising blue-and-white latticework decoration with painted pinwheels on a salmon-

colored background. It was probably made as a dower chest: a special piece that was designed to hold wedding finery and textiles. The molded base terminates in bracket feet, which are decorated with pierced spurs. *c. 1780. W:39¾ in (101 cm). POOK*

bedchamber and other formal parts of the house. These were often painted, German-American examples.

Desks, rather than *secrétaires*, continued to be made as well as desks and bookcases with wooden or glazed doors to protect the books from the sun and dust.

The British trend for sideboards was also fashionable in the south and, along with buffets and china presses, provided a useful place to display valuable objects.

Bottle cases—a type of free-standing cellaret—were more typical in the south than the north. This was because drinking cider, beer, and wine was seen as a healthy, acceptable way to cope with the intense heat and humidity in the south.

Outside the major towns, people tended to keep to the old, British furniture styles, and so rural craftsmen did not learn the new Neoclassical skills such as inlay-making and veneer-cutting. However, as the number of furniture-makers in the towns grew, competition often forced some of them out into the country. As a result, their skills gradually spread outward.

Southern style The Heyward-Washington House in Charleston, South Carolina, built in 1772, houses a fine collection of Charleston furniture. The dining room is furnished in typical styles and colors.

KENTUCKY CHEST OF DRAWERS

his bow-fronted chest is made of yellow pine ecorated with cherry veneer. The drawers have ock-beading edging. The shaped skirt ends in aring French bracket feet. *c. 1800. H:38½ in 97.75 cm); W:39⅓ in (100.5 cm). BRU*

VIRGINIA CHEST OF DRAWERS

This walnut-on-pine chest is similar to British copies of Chinese cabinets. The top has no overhang or molding, which is rare in American furniture, but popular in Chinese design. *c. 1780. H:36 in (91.5 cm); W:42 in (106.5 cm). BRU*

ENGLISH INFLUENCES

AN ENGLISH-STYLE CHINA TABLE GAVE IMPORTANT CLUES TO A SOUTHERN HOUSEHOLD'S SOCIAL STANDING WITHIN ITS COMMUNITY.

In the late 18th century, tea drinking was a sign of wealth and good taste. As a result, well-to-do families were proud to show off the paraphernalia needed to enjoy this pastime.

China tables were used both to display the ceramic tea set when it was not in use, and to act as a tea table when it was time to take tea. The gallery that ran around the rim of the table protected the precious china from falling off the edge of the table.

These tables originated in Britain, where they were popular. However,

they were less fashionable in America, apart from areas such as Boston and Portsmouth, New Hampshire in the north, and Charleston, South Carolina, and Williamsburg, Virginia, in the south, where the British influence was strong.

China tables were often far more ornate than typical southern American furniture, and were frequently adorned with fretwork and carved decoration. This probably shows their importance both in the social hierarchy and as a focal point in the tea-making ritual of the time.

VIRGINIA SIDE CHAIR

his mahogany chair has a serpentine top rail, nd tapering stiles that continue into squared ack legs. The chair has an elaborately pierced ack splat. *1760–75. H:37 in (94 cm); :21½ in (54.5 cm). BRU*

NORTH CAROLINA DINING CHAIR

This mahogany chair has a simple top rail, tapered stiles, and an upholstered slip seat. The square, beaded legs are joined by H-stretchers. The pierced vase-shaped splat with a cut-out heart is a typical southern detail. *c. 1790. POOK*

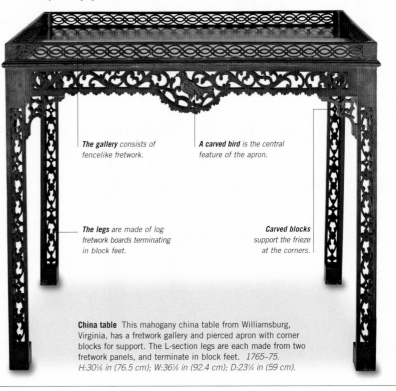

The gallery consists of fencelike fretwork.

A carved bird is the central feature of the apron.

The legs are made of log fretwork boards terminating in block feet.

Carved blocks support the frieze at the corners.

China table This mahogany china table from Williamsburg, Virginia, has a fretwork gallery and pierced apron with corner blocks for support. The L-section legs are each made from two fretwork panels, and terminate in block feet. *1765–75. H:30⅛ in (76.5 cm); W:36⅓ in (92.4 cm); D:23¼ in (59 cm).*

BRITISH INFLUENCES

BY THE LATE 18th century, American furniture styles were once again very similar to those in Britain. This was partly due to the number of British craftsmen emigrating to the colonies, and partly because of the continuing popularity of British pattern books in America. Craftsmen moved to wherever they could find work, taking their designs and techniques with them. As a result, styles were gradually disseminated over a wide area.

Differentiating between a piece of British or American furniture can be difficult, since craftsmen in both countries used similar techniques to create similar styles. Many American craftsmen were technically as proficient as their British counterparts, and their wealthy American customers wanted furniture that was just as elegant and well made as pieces imported from Britain. American Chippendale, which was still being made at this time, was not just a provincial adaptation of the British style but

also an elegant interpretation.

However, the origin of a piece can often be determined by the material used. Mahogany was imported to both Britain and the ports of the east coast of America, for example, so the secondary, or inner wood, used for parts such as drawer linings, often identifies the place of manufacture. Maple and cherry were more commonly used in American furniture, whereas oak and elm were typical of British pieces.

American cabinet-makers developed distinctive pieces of their own, such as a desk-and-bookcase combination in which the secretary drawer protrudes over the others. However, due to the fact that they often followed the same original design as British cabinet-makers, the only clue to where a piece originated is usually buried in the details. American craftsmen often used brass finials, for example, and turned feet on American pieces tended to be higher than those made in Britain.

ENGLISH CHEST-ON-CHEST

This mahogany chest-on-chest is Neoclassical in style. It has a molded cornice above an architectural frieze and chamfered sides designed to look like pilasters on the upper case. The lower case has three drawers and bracket feet. *1760–70. H:73¼ in (183 cm). L&T* **3**

AMERICAN CHEST-ON-CHEST

This Massachusetts piece is made of native maple. The upper case is similar to that of the English example, as it has little carving, but the pulls and molded base are Chippendale in style. The lower case has graduated drawers and high, bracket feet. *c. 1765. PHB* **3**

SIDE CHAIR

Made for a merchant in Massachusetts, this chair is interesting, as it is not possible to tell whether it was made in the colonies or imported from England. The complex back splat is typically English, as is the serpentine, carved top rail. The molded back stiles terminate in raked rear legs, which are typical of Boston furniture. *c. 1760. NA*

The back splat *is wider than typical English examples.*

The lower back *is slimmer than English chairs.*

The chair rail *is wider than English examples.*

The knee *is well carved, but not as wide as on English chairs.*

The rounded, raked-back rear legs *are typical of furniture made in Boston.*

The cabriole legs *are carved and terminate in claw-and-ball feet, which were no longer fashionable in England.*

IRISH DROP-LEAF TABLE

Commonly described as a wake table in Ireland, this mahogany piece has a drop-leaf top with oval leaves supported by a simple frame. The legs swing out to support the table when it is open. *1760–70. H:28¾ in (72 cm); W:55¼ in (138 cm) (open). L&T* **5**

AMERICAN DROP-LEAF TABLE

This large drop-leaf table is made of walnut, indicating that it was probably made in Pennsylvania or farther south, where walnut was common. The oval leaves have molded

edges and the frame is supported on eight square-section legs. The colloquial term in the United States for this type of table is a coffin table, which links it to the Irish wake table above. *c. 1790. H:29 in (73.5 cm); W:88½ in (224.75 cm); D:61 in (155 cm). SL* **3**

NGLISH CHEST OF DRAWERS

is mahogany, serpentine-shaped chest has
matching top with a molded edge. The
aduated drawers have cast brass bail handles.
oth the sides of the chest and the bracket
et, which have large C-scrolls on either side,
e canted. *c. 1765. W:44 in (112 cm). L&T* **5**

AMERICAN CHEST OF DRAWERS

This New England chest is of reverse serpentine
form. The top and drawers are edged with bead
molding. The base has a central pendant,
which is typically American, and C-scroll bracket
feet. The brass bail escutcheons and handles
are English. *c. 1765. H:35 in (87.5 cm). NA* **5**

ENGLISH CHEST OF DRAWERS

Made of mahogany and pine, this bow-front
chest of drawers is veneered with cross-banding.
The drawers are graduated in size and descend
to a shaped apron. The case sits on flared feet.
The brass drawer pulls are simple in design.
c. 1780. W:36¾ in (92 cm). NA **3**

MID-ATLANTIC CHEST

This bow-front mahogany chest has a
rectangular top with a crossbanded veneer
edge. The graduated drawers are emphasized
by further crossbanded veneer. The tapered
legs flare out at the base—known as French
bracket feet. *c. 1790. W:41¾ in (106 cm). SI* **3**

NGLISH TRIPOD TABLE

e top of this mahogany table tilts back when
latch under the table top is released. The
p rests on a turned baluster column, which
joined to a tripod base with a mortise-and-
non joint. The cabriole legs have pad feet.
1770. Diam:36 in (90 cm). DN **2**

PHILADELPHIA TRIPOD TABLE

This mahogany tea table has a dish top
birdcage device, which holds the top onto
the turned base. The claw-and-ball feet are
a typical feature of American Chippendale
pieces, but were no longer fashionable in
Britain. *c. 1770. Diam:33 in (82.5 cm). NA* **6**

ENGLISH DROP-LEAF TABLE

This oval-topped mahogany table is made up of
a rectangular section with two leaves. A hinged
butterfly bracket supports the extended leaves.
Tapering legs end in brass casters. These tables
are known as Pembroke tables. *c. 1780. H:28¾ in
(72 cm); W:46½ in (116 cm) (open). L&T* **4**

MID-ATLANTIC DROP-LEAF TABLE

This mahogany Pembroke table has an oblong
top and hinged D-shape leaves, with a bow-
shaped frieze. The frieze is inlaid with lily-of-
the-valley flowers and the table is supported
on square, tapering legs. *c. 1800. W:32 in
(81.5 cm). FRE* **4**

NGLISH CORNER WASHSTAND

his bow-fronted mahogany piece has a hole
r a basin, flanked by two sunken saucers and
 arched splashback. The shelf has a central
rawer flanked by two false drawers. The splayed
gs are joined by a shaped stretcher. *c. 1790.
:44½ in (111 cm); W:24 in (61 cm). L&T* **1**

AMERICAN CORNER WASHSTAND

The shaped splashback has a small shelf at
the top with a central basin hole. The inlaid
medial shelf has a drawer, and a pierced flat
stretcher joins the splayed legs. *c. 1790–1800.
H:38¼ in (97 cm); W:22½ in (57 cm); D:16 in
(40.5 cm). NA* **4**

ENGLISH DROP-LEAF TABLE

This mahogany table has hinged, drop leaves.
The frieze contains one drawer with a dummy
drawer on the opposite end. The square,
tapering legs are joined by a cross-stretcher.
A hinged, butterfly bracket supports the
leaves. *c. 1790. W:20¼ in (51.5 cm). WW* **2**

MID-ATLANTIC DROP-LEAF TABLE

This mahogany table has hinged leaves, which
are supported by a butterfly bracket. The
beaded frieze has a cock-beaded drawer and a
dummy drawer. The square, tapering legs are
joined by a cross-stretcher near the bottom of
the legs. *c. 1790. W:29¼ in (73 cm). FRE* **3**

GOTHIC

MEDIEVAL-STYLE GOTHIC design, or Gothick, as the 18th-century revival is known, became popular in the 1750s. The style coexisted with Neoclassical but was never the dominant style. The Gothic revival was primarily an English phenomenon, but by the end of the century there were new Gothic-style buildings in France and Germany.

In 1742, the English architect Batty Langley published *Gothic Architecture Improved*, an influential publication that provided Gothic designs for architecture and interiors. He also published Gothic furniture designs. His work was not concerned with historical accuracy, but emphasized the visual, emotional appeal of the Gothic versus the formal architecture of Neoclassical design.

EXPONENTS OF THE STYLE

As with the Neoclassical style, Gothic furniture was based on an idea, rather than on original pieces, and the designs published by Langley, William Kent, Matthew Darley, Thomas Chippendale, and others were romanticized interpretations of medieval Gothic designs. Darley's publication *A New Book of Chinese, Gothic and Modern Chairs* (1750–51) and Thomas Chippendale's *Director* (*see pp.98–99*) both contained interpretations of 18th-century Gothic furniture. The

cabinet-maker Sanderson Miller was also famous for his Gothic pieces.

ARCHITECTURAL INFLUENCE

Furniture in the Gothic style was decorated with applied architectural motifs taken from Gothic architecture. These included tracery, fretwork, arches, and compound columns derived from 12th- and 13th-century Church architecture.

Library furniture was considered particularly suitable for the Gothic style. A magnificent mahogany library table made for Pomfret Castle in London was decorated with carved "rose windows" on the sides, and compound columns flanking the kneehole arches.

The Gothic Windsor chair was very popular. It had a back of three pierced splats carved to look like Gothic window tracery without using standard Windsor spindles; sometimes the bow back was shaped like a pointed arch. Underneath the curved arm support was another row of smaller pierced splats. Some of the finest examples of these chairs were made primarily of yew, although oak, beech, and elm were popular. Windsor chairs were seldom made from just one wood, as the shaped elements required different types of timber.

Gothic furniture remained whimsical throughout the 18th century. Robert Adam made armchairs inspired by the Coronation Chair in Westminster Abbey, with backs shaped like church windows with tracery. Pinnacles sprouted from the top rails and pendants hung from chair rails. Adam combined these Gothic elements with Neoclassical acanthus leaves and tapered square legs.

STRAWBERRY HILL

Horace Walpole, the influential author of the Gothic novel *The Castle of Otranto*, had his country house near London, Strawberry Hill, designed and decorated in the Gothic style. The gallery was fan-vaulted; mirror glass placed between the vaults created a glittering space. The library had trefoil-shaped windows and a three-paneled Gothic window with arches; it was fitted with massive bookcases, complete with crockets and pinnacles, tracery, and arches.

ENGLISH CHEST

This rare, painted and gilt oak chest is in the style of the Gothic medieval painted oak coffers. However, it does not have the wrought iron bands that would be used to hold a medieval chest together. The top of the chest is plain, but the paneled sides and front are decorated with Gothic-style tracery and figure in carved gilt, and the metal escutcheon in the center of the chest is decorated in a similar style. The piece rests on bracket feet. *Mid-18th century. H:26 in (65 cm); D:22¾ in (57 cm). L&T*

GOTHIC CHIPPENDALE

THOMAS CHIPPENDALE APPLIED GOTHIC DESIGN TO CONTEMPORARY FURNITURE IN *THE GENTLEMAN'S & CABINET-MAKER'S DIRECTOR*.

Chippendale was the first designer to use the term "Gothic" in relation to furniture, and his Gothic-style designs for chairs and bookcases were particularly popular. The design of his Gothic chair backs was derived from elements of Church architecture. He combined decorative motifs such as ogee arches, lancets, arcades, crockets, and pointed arches with tracery. These details

combined well with the Rococo scroll motifs, which were still popular at the time. Cluster, or compound, columns were often used as chair legs, although Chippendale's designs indicate that other leg shapes could also be used on Gothic chairs. These chairs were intended for use in halls, passages, or summer houses.

At the time of Chippendale's Gothic designs, follies were popular, and it was fashionable to build them in landscape settings. Gothic-style architecture was a favorite choice, and sometimes furniture was made to match.

English armchair This chair displays typical Gothic elements: quatrefoils across the back rail, arched astragals in the back and under the arms, and pendants under the seat rails. *c. 1775.*

Hall Chair, Plate XVII, *The Gentleman & Cabinetmaker's Director* This design is one of several for use in a hall or a garden room and is an alternative to the realized design on the left. *1762.*

Cologne Cathedral, Germany This is the largest Gothic cathedral in the world. Building began in the 13th century, and it took 632 years to complete. The cathedral displays all the architectural elements that inspired furniture-designers in the late 18th century.

...NG CASE CLOCK

...s standard oak and mahogany clock has
...hic decoration on the case. The door is
...hed and flanked by compound columns,
...ch also decorate the case. The base of
...hood is decorated with pendants. *1770.*

...NGLISH SIDE CHAIR

...s mahogany side chair is actually a music
...ol with a back. The adjustable round seat
...o revolves. The back has pierced Gothic
...hes together with leaf-carved finials. The
...s resemble compound piers. *c. 1800.* DN

ENGLISH BOOKCASE

This mahogany piece is decorated with Gothic,
Chinoiserie, and Neoclassical motifs. The
pierced cresting with a central, scrolled swan's-
neck pediment has Gothic pinnacles at each end
and Chinoiserie lattice decoration. The glazed
doors feature Gothic arched astragals.   *c. 1765.*
H:112¾ in (282 cm); W:101½ in (254 cm);
D:28½ in (71 cm). PAR

The glazed doors *have
Gothic arched astragals
dividing the glass
sections.*

The lattice decoration
is Chinese in style.

**Gothic quatrefoils and
pinnacles** *decorate the
top of the bookcase.*

Acanthus leaf carvings
*decorate each corner of
the paneled doors.*

The plinth base *is
paneled and molded.*

The side doors *conceal three
drawers, while the middle
section has fitted shelves.*

SOUTH AFRICA

CAPE TOWN was established by the Dutch East India Company as a halfway station between Amsterdam and the East Indies in 1652. However, it was not until the late 18th century that the population of settlers in Cape Town reached 3,000—large enough to support a number of local craftsmen.

By the end of the century, settlers were establishing towns outside Cape Town and the more affluent farmers built homes in the gabled Cape Dutch style. The few wealthy settlers who desired European furniture had it imported, and by the 1770s and 80s, large quantities were shipped over from both England and the Low Countries.

Initially, furniture made in South Africa itself showed the influence of Dutch, French, and English design; the Dutch Baroque style continued well into the 18th century, with Neoclassical being largely restricted to decoration.

PATRICIAN AND COUNTRY

By this time, there was a clear distinction between the "patrician" and "country" furniture that was being produced. Patrician furniture encompassed the fine-quality pieces commissioned by and made for the merchant classes, mainly in the areas immediately surrounding Cape Town. The designs closely followed those of French and English cabinet-makers and, although made from indigenous woods, the pieces were finished using exotic woods from the East. Country furniture mimicked these designs but was primarily restricted to local woods, and rarely exhibited the fine craftsmanship found in the city.

South Africa's remoteness meant that there was a significant delay in the technical advances already used by European cabinet-makers. Therefore furniture did not have sophisticated veneering or marquetry until the end of the century, and the mortise-and-tenon joints adopted by European cabinet-makers were seldom employed. Instead, framed panel construction

STINKWOOD CABINET

This cabinet is made primarily of stinkwood with heavy molding. The cornice has a carved acanthus key block and a chevron-pattern inlay runs down the center of the upper section. It has serpentine doors above graduated drawers, and a molded base. The overall styling is still predominantly influenced by Dutch Baroque furniture. *c. 1785. H:110¼ in (280 cm); W:74¾ in (190 cm). PRA*

The serpentine cornice has a central carved cartouche.

A chevron design inlay is created using a combination of satinwood and stinkwood veneers.

The bombé shape is derived from Portuguese and Low Countries furniture.

Carved animal claw feet are common supports for cabinets of this type.

CORNER CABINET

This triangular-shaped corner cabinet, one of a pair, is made from local yellowwood with exotic veneers, including satinwood door panels, amboyna frames, and ebony. It has square, tapering, fluted legs. *c. 1790. H:39½ (100 cm); W:47¼ in (120 cm); D:24¾ in (63 cm). P*

TEA TABLE

This table is made of imported teak. The shape is reminiscent of French styles, although simplified. It has a flat, molded top above a shaped apron with a single drawer, and is raised on cabriole legs. *c. 1790. H:28 in (71 cm); W:34⅔ in (88 cm); D:22 in (56 cm). P*

as common and solid timber was ⋯ed for an entire piece. This timber ⋯as the local stinkwood or yellowwood. ⋯ was not until the end of the century ⋯at fine South African furniture was ⋯ade from imported woods such as ⋯tinwood, partridge, ebony, and teak.

⋯RNITURE TYPES

⋯ the late 18th century, the massive ⋯binet had replaced the Baroque flat-⋯pped cupboard. These cabinets ⋯ually had a serpentine-shaped ⋯rnice, and a serpentine-, blocked-,

or *bombé*-shaped base with serpentine molding, and ball or animal-claw feet. The cabinet was one of the most distinct pieces of Cape furniture and differed greatly in styling from the Neoclassical cabinets made in Europe during this period.

Slant-front desks on stands were also popular, and were known as "Bible desks." Corner cupboards were loosely based on the French *encoignure*. Toward the end of the century, the English-style chest of drawers was adopted, and was thickly

veneered in imported woods such as satinwood, coromandel, and ebony. Stinkwood was used for the case—an often striking color contrast.

Tables with both cabriole and spiral-turned legs were made. Toward the end of the century, gateleg tables, with rectangular or oval tops, were made with tapered legs.

EUROPEAN INFLUENCE

Seating furniture made around the time was also heavily influenced by European trends, particularly English, and sometimes combining stylistic details of several countries in one piece. Ebony chairs with caned seats were often used

by the wealthier residents of Cape Town, or in churches, and showed the influence of the Asian colonies. Caning also appeared on day beds.

Chairs with two back splats and baluster-turned legs and uprights remained popular until the 1780s. English Queen Anne-style chairs, with solid back splats and cabriole legs were made well into the late 18th century, and corner chairs were also fashionable long after they were in Europe. The popularity of the shield-shaped back on chairs and settees was due to the increasing influence of English designs after 1795, when Britain gained control of Cape Town.

⋯DE CHAIR

⋯is stinkwood chair is influenced by English ⋯een Anne chairs with its simple carved crest ⋯l, solid vase-form splat, seat with shaped ⋯ron, cabriole legs, and pad feet. However, ⋯ differs in the overall dimensions. *c. 1750.* *41¼ in (106 cm); W:23⅔ in (60 cm).*

ARMCHAIR

This stinkwood chair is a simplified version of Dutch chair styles with its pierced back splat within a square back, inlaid patera in the center of the seat rail, and inlaid "columns" on the front legs. *c. 1795. H:39 in (99 cm); W:23½ in (59.5 cm); D:17¾ in (45 cm). PRA*

CAPE CHIPPENDALE

THE SUCCESS OF CHIPPENDALE'S *DIRECTOR* WAS WIDESPREAD AND, ALTHOUGH RARE IN SOUTH AFRICA, IT INFLUENCED SOME LOCAL CRAFTSMEN.

Interpretations of furniture inspired by the work of Thomas Chippendale have been documented in South Africa and include the occasional ladder-back settee, some chairs, and a four-seater bench, as well as the sideboard table with a marble top (*see below*). Certainly, Chippendale's designs for Gothic and Chinese-style pieces seem to have inspired at least one cabinet-maker in the Cape region. Although the provenance of such pieces is not always known, all of them would have been intended for use in the homes of wealthy clients.

It is likely that copies of Chippendale's *The Gentleman's and Cabinet-Maker's Director* (*see p.99*) found their way to South Africa with immigrant craftsmen or fashion-conscious merchants, much as they had done to North America (*see pp.104–05*). It is also possible that actual pieces of Chippendale furniture were imported from England to the Cape during the 1770s and 80s, and were subsequently copied by native craftsmen. Perhaps a client commissioned a chair or table in the style of furniture he had brought with him, so that all pieces in any given room matched, as was the fashion of the day.

Teak sideboard table
This table has a marble top, which was probably imported from Europe. It has a simple apron with molded edge, central, carved, entwined C-scrolls, and brackets between the chamfered legs and skirt. *c. 1775. H:33½ in (85 cm); 54⅓ in (138 cm); D:19 in (48 cm). PRA*

⋯ATELEG TABLE

⋯is simple gateleg table is made of stinkwood. ⋯ has a plain rectangular top with wide drop ⋯aves. The extent of the drop leaves provides ⋯very generous top surface when the table ⋯ opened, while making this an extremely ⋯onomical piece to store when it is not in

use. When the table is open, the apron is supported on eight squared and fluted, tapering legs—the fluted decoration is the only concession to the patrician Neoclassical style in what is otherwise a rustic-style piece. The table has a single drawer at one end for storage. *c. 1795. H:30 in (76 cm); W:73¼ in (186 cm); D:54⅓ in (138 cm). PRA*

EUROPEAN CHINOISERIE

FROM THE START of the 17th century, Europeans had been fascinated by rare and exotic objects from China and Japan. The fine silks, porcelain, and lacquerware imported by the East India Company created a demand for Asian designs. The prohibitive cost of these imports inspired European designers and craftsmen to create imitations of the originals. The style was called Chinoiserie, from *chinois*, the French word for Chinese.

Europeans had a vague and romantic notion of Far Eastern culture and Chinoiserie combined fanciful, exotic motifs with luxurious materials. Entire rooms, particularly bedrooms and dressing rooms, were decorated with fantastic landscapes with jagged mountains, golden willow trees, delicate pagodas, dragons, Chinese figures, and exotic birds.

ASIAN SETTINGS
The fashion for Chinoiserie interiors reached its height between 1750 and 1765, overlapping with the Rococo style, which had a similar frivolity and love of asymmetry, but Chinoiserie continued into the 19th century. Interiors often featured genuine Chinese objects, such as painted wallpaper, which had been made for the Western market since the mid-17th century, lacquer screens, or porcelain, but European designers also created their own Chinese-style furnishings.

In 1765, Thomas Chippendale redecorated the State Bedchamber at Nostell Priory in Yorkshire in the Chinese style. He created a suite of green lacquer furniture decorated with Chinese landscapes and figures and a mirror frame featuring the mythical ho-ho bird and a Chinese pagoda.

Genuine lacquer was unavailable in Europe because, although people had imported it, it did not travel successfully, so furniture-makers recreated the style in other ways. European furniture of the period made in the Chinese style was often "japanned" rather than decorated with actual lacquer. John Stalker and George Parker's influential book *A Treatise of Japanning* (1688), provided technical advice for japanning and contained Chinoiserie designs, which were widely copied. Layers of pigmented varnish, usually in gold on black or red, recreated the striking effect of genuine Asian lacquer

ELEMENTS OF STYLE
In the 1750s, Chinese-style pieces began to assume new and more exotic forms of decoration. Designers such as Thomas Chippendale and Ince and

LACQUERED COMMODE

This Louis XV piece has a marble top and is decorated with reused panels of Chinese lacquerware. The curved body depicts a landscape of pagodas and Asian trees in gold and red. The commode has gilt-bronze mounts, escutcheons, and gilded feet. *c. 1760. H:34¾ in (87 cm); W:45¼ in (113 cm); D:20¾ in (52 cm). GK*

LACQUERED *BOMBÉ* COMMODE

This European gilt-decorated lacquer commode is fitted with three drawers. The top is made of wood rather than marble, and the handles and escutcheons are Rococo in style. The edges of the body are decorated with relief carving, and the piece terminates in hoofed feet. *c. 1760. W:47 in (117.5 cm). NA*

LACQUERWARE

THE ASIAN TRADITION OF LACQUERWARE DATES BACK THOUSANDS OF YEARS.

Asian lacquer is derived from the sap of the tree *Rhus vernicifera*, which is native to China, Japan, and Korea. There is evidence that lacquer was used in China and Japan as far back as Neolithic times.

Lacquered surfaces are made up of very thin layers of the product, which are allowed to dry completely before another is added. The result is a hard, glossy surface that is resistant to water and heat, and is even safe for use on food containers.

Asian lacquerware was much sought-after in Europe during the 17th and early 18th centuries. By the middle of the 18th century, the lacquerware was often stripped from its original carcass and veneered onto contemporary French furniture, then further embellished with gilt-bronze.

LACQUERED SCREEN

This Chinese screen is typical of the type that inspired European interpretations of the style. It is decorated with two tones of gold on a red lacquered background and depicts an Asian landscape. It has a flat top and a curved base terminating in simple feet. *c. 1780. H:84¾ in (212 cm). GK*

PAINTED SCREEN

This French screen with interpretations of Asian motifs and design is typical of Jean-Baptiste Pillement's work. The panels show exotic birds and children in an idealized garden landscape. The screen is made from panels of painted canvas attached to a wood frame. *c. 1770. H:76 in (190 cm). GK*

Detail of inlay

Gilded lacquerwork depicts maidens in a pastoral setting. The figures have applied ivory faces.

Chinese oval table
This tilt-top table is decorated with exquisite lacquerwork. The tripod base and table edges are decorated with Greek key motifs. The table has scroll feet. *c. 1780. D:41 in (104 cm). Cato*

ayhew published designs for hinese-style furniture, including airs with pierced latticework backs d pagoda-shaped top rails. The motif interlaced batons appears repeatedly the furniture in Chippendale's *rector*—on chair backs, stretchers, ookcase doors, bed boards, and imney pieces. Few of these elements ere based on actual Asian rniture but, like the Chinese eces made for the European arket, they formed part of the 3th-century European idea of hinoiserie. As trade with Asia creased, the designs became ore accurate.

Although Chinoiserie was popular throughout the late 18th and 19th centuries, it was at the peak of its popularity during the 18th century. Many pieces were embellished with decorative panels: entirely lacquered or japanned Neoclassical furniture is rare.

The principal colors for English lacquerwork were black, a red that

resembled the color of sealing wax, yellow, green, brown, tortoiseshell, and, more rarely, blue. Although Chinese-style motifs were highly fashionable, European pieces were

usually decorated to appeal to European tastes. So motifs were inspired by, rather than copies of, original Chinese or Japanese images. Due to these style differences, it is easy to distinguish between genuine pieces of 18th-century Asian furniture and European interpretations of lacquerwork and Chinoiserie.

ABINET-ON-STAND

is George III cabinet is decorated with Chinoiserie figures d animals. It has gilt-metal engraved hinges on the doors d escutcheon. The interior of the cabinet contains ten small awers. The stand is of a later date than the cabinet. *c. 1760.* :38½ in (98 cm). WW

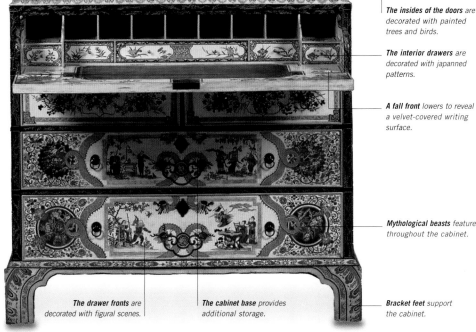

The insides of the doors are decorated with painted trees and birds.

The interior drawers are decorated with japanned patterns.

A fall front lowers to reveal a velvet-covered writing surface.

Mythological beasts feature throughout the cabinet.

The drawer fronts are decorated with figural scenes.

The cabinet base provides additional storage.

Bracket feet support the cabinet.

SIAN-STYLE SETTEE

his George III faux-bamboo settee has a caned back and sides. aning was often combined with faux bamboo frames. The frame nsists of a rectangular back and downswept arms and the seat as a separate squab cushion. The slender legs are raised on en brackets. *c. 1765. W:74 in (185 cm). L&T*

GEORGE I *SECRÉTAIRE*-CABINET

This rare white-japanned cabinet has bow-shaped molding on the cornice. Although this is an early piece, it is an extremely fine example of European Chinoiserie. Mirror-glazed doors open to reveal an array of drawers and pigeonholes. The blue and white discs painted on the interior drawers are inspired by the design of

Asian-style plates. The base has a fitted drawer containing a writing surface and more drawers and pigeonholes. The whole cabinet is decorated with delicately painted figures and patterns on a japanned background. The fine decoration draws its inspiration from genuine Chinese porcelain, rather than from Stalker and Parker's *A Treatise of Japanning* (1688). *c. 1725. H:90 in (228.5 cm); W:43 in (109 cm); D:22 in (56 cm). PAR*

PAINTED FURNITURE

THE PRACTICE OF PAINTING furniture was popular in the Middle Ages but reached its zenith in the second half of the 18th century. In some regions, particularly Italy, painting had never fallen from favor on either formal or vernacular furniture. However, in English and French furniture, painted decoration had been much less common in high-style furniture, unless it was deliberately copying lacquer in the early 18th century, and had generally been used on cheaper furniture.

Furniture was often painted to disguise an inferior type of wood in regions where better-quality imported timbers were prohibitively expensive, as was the case in Italy. Imitation surfaces, or *faux bois*, mimicked the grain of woods: pine, for example, was colored to imitate Spanish mahogany.

French interiors during the reigns of Louis XV and Louis XVI began to feature lighter color schemes in delicate pastel shades, grays, and white. As an alternative to furniture, such as *bergère* frames, which were

waxed to emphasize the grain of the wood, pieces were painted to match a room's overall color scheme.

In England, architects such as Robert Adam also designed color-coordinated interiors. The design motifs used on the painted ceilings of grand rooms were repeated in the textiles and the furniture. At first, this repetition came through the use of lighter woods and marquetry decoration, but as the style developed, furniture such as chairs, pier-glasses, and tables was sometimes painted to match the overall scheme.

Painting had advantages over marquetry, as it allowed more intricate details, such as miniature landscape paintings, to be added to a piece. High-style painted designs were imitated to various degrees in vernacular, regional furniture, which also used painting as a substitute for carved designs. The trend for traditional painted motifs on vernacular furniture was particularly popular with artisans who had traveled to the colonies.

GERMAN CHEST

Primarily made of spruce, this vernacular "farmer's" chest originates from the Franconia region of Germany. The molded lid is decorated with panels and lifts to reveal the interior storage space. The rectangular panel decorations on the front and sides, and the central arched panel around the lock, are painted with brightly colored floral motifs. The chest stands on flattened bun feet. *c. 1800. W:49 in (124 cm). BMN* **1**

AMERICAN DOWER CHEST

This vernacular chest is made of poplar, a wood native to Pennsylvania. The lift lid, with molded edge, covers a case that is supported on bracket feet. The case has a central, salmon and ivory, double-arched tombstone panel enclosing stylized tulips in a double-handled urn. The urn is incised with the maker's name and date. Two similarly decorated panels flank the central image. Painted by Johann Rank. *1798. W:51 in (129.5 cm). POOK* **6**

The white marble semicircular top has a stepped edge with a band of ormolu beading.

The central medallion contains a painted Classical female figure.

The frieze and apron are painted with Neoclassical scrolls and anthemia.

The reeded, tapering legs terminate in bun feet.

ENGLISH COMMODE

This ormolu-mounted, *demi-lune* commode has a front that is divided into three painted panels within borders of gilt waterleaves. Each panel has a circular painted medallion containing a Classical female figure. The two side panels have doors. The case has a giltwood guilloche apron and four reeded, tapering legs with bun feet. Attributed to George Brookshaw. *c. 1790. H:33¾ in (89 cm); W:48 in (122 cm); D:52 in (20.25 cm). PAR*

ENGLISH COMMODE

This *demi-lune* commode has a crossbanded, veneered, satinwood top, which is painted with a seated woman reading. Swag-hung paterae and bellflower borders surround this scene. The *demi-lune* case has a central hinged cupboard door painted with a figure of a courtier writing. Two similarly decorated oval reserves flank the center. The entire case is supported by short, tapering, spade feet. *c. 1790. W:48 in (122 cm). FRE* **5**

WEDISH ARMCHAIR

ade in Stockholm, this armchair has a squared back with a
aped back rail. The open armrests flare slightly to the outside.
e square seat is supported on tapered legs that have cups just
low the juncture of the seat rail. The chair is painted white
th highlights, such as the flutes in the tapered legs, picked out
bright blue. *c. 1790.* BK **2**

FRENCH SETTEE

Known as a *canapé*, this small, upholstered settee has a frame
of beech, a wood often used by French chair-makers. The back
rail encloses the sitters and is supported on turned, tapering
legs. The frame is painted and gilded. Originally, the paint would
have echoed the room for which it was made and complemented
the upholstery. *c. 1760.* W:41½ in (105.5 cm). DL **4**

PARISIAN *BERGÈRE*

This is one of a pair of *bergères* with beech frames. The top
rail is carved with flowers at the center—a motif echoed in the
center of the seat rail and on the knees. The arms are swept
back and are upholstered above the frame, and the chair has a
large cushion. The frame is painted light gray. *c. 1760.* H:37¾ in
(96 cm); W:28¾ in (73 cm); D:24¾ in (63 cm). CHF **6**

NGLISH BUREAU

is slant-front desk is veneered with satinwood
d painted. It has two shorter top drawers over
ree graduated drawers. The base is shaped
d terminates in high, bracket feet. Painted

ribbon-tied foliate swags and scrolling foliage
adorn the drawers. The slant front has a central
painted medallion depicting a Classical female
with two cherubs. This piece is a 19th-century
imitation of a late-18th-century style. *c. 1800.*
H:42½ in (106 cm). FRE **4**

CANADIAN ARMOIRE

This simple pine wardrobe was made in Quebec.
It has a stepped, molded cornice above a pair
of fielded panel doors with hand-wrought rat-tail
hinges. Behind the doors are shelves. Stile feet

support this case piece. The green-blue paint
has faded, but when originally painted would
have made a striking statement. Blue pigment
was very expensive and so the paint would have
cost more than the original armoire. *c. 1790.*
W:54 in (137 cm). WAD

MECHANICAL PIECES

THE SCIENTIFIC advances of the 18th century led to the creation of ingenious pieces of mechanical furniture, which had secret drawers and compartments operated by hidden springs and levers. In France and Germany, in particular, mechanical furniture became an art form during the second half of the 18th century.

Abraham Roentgen is usually credited with introducing mechanical devices to cabinet-makers. Between 1742 and 1750, he perfected the harlequin table, which had secret drawers and compartments.

David Roentgen, his son, also created mechanical furniture, primarily to amuse the nobility. In 1768, he made a bureau-cabinet with a commode-shaped base containing a mechanical device that sounded like a piano.

In France, Jean-François Oeben made mechanical furniture for Madame de Pompadour. He also developed the *bureau à cylindre*, which had a flexible, sliding cover known as a *tambour*. The most elaborate *bureau à cylindre* had candlesticks, clocks, and drawers hidden inside it.

Another French novelty was the *secrétaire à la Bourgogne*. This looked like a table with small drawers, but the top of the table was divided in two. The rear section rose to reveal a set of drawers and the front opened forward to create a writing surface.

The rent table, which appeared in England at about this time, was a circular, revolving table that contained labeled drawers for filing correspondence. Some versions also had a concealed well for holding money. A hinged, locking, central section could be opened by a catch concealed in one of the drawers. Since banks, security boxes, or safes did not exist at this time, desks were a favorite hiding place for valuables, which is why many of them had secret drawers.

Ormolu mounts

FRENCH ROLL-TOP DESK

This bureau has a flexible cylinder, or roll top, made of thin wood slats, which rolls back into the frame so that it is concealed when open. The bureau is inlaid in tulipwood, in a basket-weave pattern, and has rectangular ormolu scrolls and a foliage border. The lower section contains four drawers. The bureau stands on fluted, tapering legs. Stamped by Ferdinand Bury. *c. 1780. H:49½ in (126 cm); W:57½ in (146 cm); D:33 in (84 cm). PAR* 1

The top drawer is divided into compartments for cosmetics.

An easel mirror lies flat when not in use.

The serpentine case stands on shaped, bracket feet.

ENGLISH DRESSING CHEST

Although this chest looks like a standard mahogany serpentine chest of drawers with four graduated drawers on shaped bracket feet, it can also be used as a dressing chest. The top drawer contains an easel mirror, various powder boxes, and divisions for bottles. This drawer is concealed under a brushing slide—a mahogany section that pulls out from the case and fits into a groove on the sides. *c. 1780. H:31½ in (81 cm); W:36¾ in (93 cm); D:23½ in (59 cm). HauG* 5

Floral marquetry

BUREAU À CYLINDRE

This gilt-bronze-mounted satinwood, tulipwood, and burr walnut *bureau à cylindre* has a rectangular top with a pierced gallery above a frieze drawer and a roll-top. The fitted interior has a leather writing surface. The kneehole drawer is flanked on either side by drawers, which, when activated by a spring mechanism, reveal additional drawers. The legs are square and tapering. *c. 1775–80. H:51 in (129 cm); W:44 in (113 cm); D:26½ in (67 cm). DL* 4

CRÉTAIRE À LA BOURGOGNE

e top of this French desk has two sections:
e front opens forward on a hinge and the
ck rises on a spring mechanism to reveal four
awers. The side drawer, right, has a pounce
t and inkwell. *c. 1765.* H:28 in (71 cm);
20 in (51 cm); D:15¾ in (40 cm). PAR **1**

GERMAN COMMODE

The front of this mahogany, cherry, and
pear harlequin table moves forward when
a mechanism is triggered, making the rear
section, with its drawers and compartments,
spring out of the case. It was designed by
Abraham Roentgen. *c. 1755. OVM*

BUREAU PLAT AND CARTONNIER

Veneered in ebony, with a leather writing surface, this French
bureau has a frieze of Vitruvian scroll ormolu mounts. The
front of the bureau has three drawers and the reverse a slide
with drop-ring handles. The *cartonnier* at the end has two
leather-fronted boxes and a clock that contains an intricate
striking mechanism. It has square-section tapering legs and
small bun feet. *c. 1780. PAR*

ENGLISH RENT TABLE

The circular brown leather top of this rent
table has a hinged, locking, central section
that opens with a catch concealed in one
of the drawers to reveal a sunken well. The
frieze contains eight wedge-shaped drawers
with swan-neck handles for correspondence.

The top also rotates on its square plinth base,
which itself contains a cupboard with a single
shelf. This table was made by Gillows of
Lancaster. *c. 1790.* H:30¾ in (88 cm);
D:46 in (117 cm). PAR **1**

NGLISH GAMES TABLE

e top of this mahogany table swivels open,
hile the legs remain stationary, to provide
 inlaid surface for checkers. There are two
awers in the case: the top one is a dummy.
1790. H:29 in (73.5 cm). DL **4**

FRENCH ARCHITECT'S TABLE

The rectangular top of this table lifts up on a
ratchet and has pull-out slides to either side.
This entire section can be raised several
inches by a winding mechanism on the side.
The frieze contains a writing drawer, which opens

to reveal a leather surface. The
table sides have two more pull-
out slides. Stamped by Adam Weisweiler.
c. 1790. H:51 in (129.5 cm); W:34½ in
(87.5 cm); D:21¼ in (54 cm). PAR

FALL-FRONT DESKS

AS FURNITURE MADE especially for writing grew in popularity in the 18th century, different styles were developed. The *secrétaire à abattant*, a tall French writing desk, was first produced in the 1760s in Paris by the cabinet-maker Jean-François Oeben.

The *secrétaire à abattant* looked, from its flat-fronted exterior appearance, like an armoire, or wardrobe. However, its upper section was hinged and, when opened, fell forward to reveal a leather-lined writing surface. The lower section had drawers or doors, behind which were shelves or drawers for storage. In many examples, an additional drawer was located below the cornice of the upper section, often concealed by decoration.

Many *secrétaires à abattant* were tall and narrow. Their rectilinear shape, which was sometimes softened by the use of legs and rounded corners, was Neoclassical in style, and made the earliest ones very influential in furniture design.

High-quality woods were used in the construction and marquetry was often employed, particularly on the fall-fronts, in geometric or Classically inspired designs. Panels of Oriental lacquer were also popular, and during the 1770s and 80s *secrétaires à abattant* incorporating Sèvres porcelain plaques were produced. Neoclassical motifs such as Vitruvian scrolls, keyhole escutcheons of laurel leaves, and inlaid urns were sometimes used.

The design of the *secrétaire à abattant* quickly spread across Europe. In the Low Countries, lacquer and marquetry were sometimes combined with Dutch floral marquetry, while in Germany, Eastern Europe, and Scandinavia, decoration was more restrained. British pieces became particularly good examples of the country's Neoclassical furniture.

ENGLISH FALL-FRONT *SECRÉTAIRE*

This *secrétaire* has tulipwood and satinwood crossbanded inlays. Its fall front and cupboard door are quarter-veneered, with a central oval fan medallion and vase. *c. 1780. H:49 in (124.5 cm); W:31 in (79 cm); D:16 in (40.5 cm). PAR*

FRENCH *SECRÉTAIRE À ABATTANT*

This Parisian marble-topped, harewood *secrétaire* is inlaid with geometric marquetry. Ormolu borders surround its panels. Below the long drawer is a fall front and a pair of doors. *c. 1780. H:48¾ in (124 cm); W:28 in (71 cm). PA*

A pierced ormolu gallery runs around three sides at the top.

The white marble top with canted corners is set into a brass frame.

The side panels are lacquered, decorated with foliage, and inlaid with mother-of-pearl.

The lion's-head mask, here made of gilt bronze, is a common Neoclassical motif.

The doors—inlaid and lacquered with an eagle and a peacock—conceal a safe.

FRENCH *SECRÉTAIRE À ABATTANT*

This Parisian *secrétaire* is covered with black lacquer, with mother-of-pearl decoration, and gilt-bronze mounts. Made by Philippe-Claude Montigny. *c. 1770. H:59 in (149 cm); W:38¼ in (97 cm). PAR*

The apron is centered by a grotesque ormolu mask.

FRENCH *SECRÉTAIRE À ABATTANT*

This kingwood and rosewood veneered desk has a maple inlay and marble top. Under the cornice is a locking drawer that opens, supported by metal hinges, to reveal a fitted interior. The legs are high and tapered. *c. 1780. H:55¼ in (138 cm); W:25¼ in (64 cm); D:14¼ in (36 cm). BMN* **3**

ENGLISH CABINET

This writing cabinet is made of mahogany, the grain of the wood providing its decoration. A writing slide pulls out from the lower case, which has a drawer below. The upper section doors open to reveal drawers and pigeonholes. *c. 1800. H:58½ in (148.5 cm). DL* **5**

OW COUNTRIES *SECRÉTAIRE À ABATTANT*

is mahogany *secrétaire* uses different veneer patterns to create
nament and movement. Its doors are quarter-veneered and
ossbanded. A shell-shaped oval patera adorns the center of
e fall front, and a geometric ribbon inlay decorates the canted
rners of the case. *c. 1790. H:60 in (150 cm). L&T* **3**

FRENCH *SECRÉTAIRE À ABATTANT*

This piece is made of rosewood, kingwood, and other exotic
woods. It has marquetry decoration and gilt-bronze mountings.
Below the cornice is applied ormolu, in a Vitruvian scroll, which
in this piece serves to conceal a drawer. *c. 1780. H:55½ in
(139 cm); W:37¼ in (93 cm); D:18⅞ in (48 cm). GK* **7**

SWEDISH *SECRÉTAIRE*

This *secrétaire* lacks a lower cupboard, but its upper section is a
writing surface that opens in the same way as a French *secrétaire*.
It has a marble top, a geometric brass band across the top, and
decorative inlay on the fall front and side panels. *c. 1780.
H:50 in (127 cm); W:40¼ in (102 cm); D:18¼ in (46 cm). BK* **6**

OW COUNTRIES *SECRÉTAIRE À ABATTANT*

e corners of this Dutch piece are rounded, with etched
cutcheons in the Chinese style as the decorative focal point.
is also japanned, in imitation of Chinese lacquer, with a
esign of idealized landscapes and figures, using two shades of
ld on a black ground. The fall front opens to reveal drawers,
geonholes, and shelves. *c. 1800. H:60½ in (151 cm). GK* **5**

INLAID *SECRÉTAIRE*

The marble top of this *secrétaire* rests above a case with canted
corners. The fall front opens onto a fitted interior with six drawers
and a green leather insert. Below are two drawers, each with
Japanese-style light wood inlays. With gilt-bronze mounts
throughout, this piece stands on fluted, tapering feet with sabots.
c. 1780. H:38 in (97 cm); W:24⅞ in (63 cm); D:17⅓ in (44 cm). GK **7**

FRENCH *SECRÉTAIRE À ABATTANT*

This Parisian piece is made of woods including rosewood and
kingwood, with floral inlays. Decoration comes from its geometric
patterns, as its mounts are limited to the central drop and feet
fronts. Its fall front opens to reveal green, gilded leather. The lower
section doors cover three drawers either side of a large shelf. *1778.
H:55 in (140 cm); W:47½ in (120 cm); D:15¾ in (40 cm). GK* **4**

COMMODES

THE COMMODE EVOLVED slowly during the late 18th century, only gradually incorporating Neoclassical elements into its design. In its early transitional stage, in the 1760s, its shape retained many Rococo features, such as rounded corners and cabriole legs, but the case became more rectangular and the decoration Neoclassical.

However, by the 1770s, the shape of commodes had also been refined, as commodes became plainer and more linear in design, with straight legs. Their angular shape was sometimes augmented by the adoption of a breakfront—the result of inset drawers being placed on either side of protruding drawers—a feature that was particularly popular.

By the 1790s, the French commode generally had two or three short frieze drawers with long parallel drawers below them. Columns of term figures, headed by female masks in Classical or Egyptian garb, flanked the drawers. The columns were also often headed by engine-turned, plain, Tuscan, gilt-bronze capitals. Commodes with three

deep drawers on short feet turned like tops were also common.

In the 1770s and 80s, commodes with sumptuous ormolu mounts and pictorial marquetry were still made for royal households, but decoration became more sparing after 1790. Mounts were rare, and plain ring handles and escutcheons, inspired by simple Grecian design, were used. Transitional commodes used satinwood veneer or mahogany, but as designs became more refined, plain, well-figured wood such as mahogany, or fruitwood for provincial pieces, was used with marble tops. Decoration was provided by molded wood, ebonized columns, and grisaille panels.

In Britain the side cabinet became plainer but was still of good quality. No particular shape was favored, but some designers were influenced by Egyptian campaigns. Italian designers used walnut, olive, and tulipwood, combining a pictorial frieze drawer with two plain drawers. Geometric marquetry was used to emphasize the commode's rectangular shape.

FRENCH COMMODE

This three-drawer walnut commode has a molded top over three graduated paneled drawers and a shaped and molded apron.

Short, scroll feet, each with a block terminus support the case. It is decorated with pierced foliate C-scroll escutcheons and handles. The style of this commode is provincial and rather old-fashioned. *c. 1765. W:54¾ in (139 cm).*

FRENCH *DEMI-LUNE* COMMODE

This mahogany commode has a semicircular or *demi-lune* shape. It contains three central drawers, and curved side doors, which open to

reveal shelves. It has a marble top, gilded bronze escutcheons that are Neoclassical in design, and pulls with swags surrounding them. *c. 1795. H:34½ in (87 cm); W:53 in (136 cm); D:22½ in (57 cm). GK* **4**

The rounded corners of the case are inlaid with three rectangular panels corresponding to the depths of the drawers.

Crossbanded veneers and light boxwood string inlays emphasize the edges of the drawers.

Lion's head brass pulls like these became popular toward the end of the 18th century.

MALTESE COMMODE

This commode has three walnut-veneered drawers. Its skirt is slightly shaped and it has short, cabriole legs with carved toes. *c. 1700. W:50 in (127 cm). FRE* **4**

FRENCH VENEERED COMMODE

This commode has a breakfront shape, created by three short drawers inset either side of three protruding long drawers. It has a molded

white marble top and geometric parquetry veneer, which includes kingwood, tulipwood, and rosewood. The cabriole legs are squared and veneered, and terminate in gilt-metal sabots. *c. 1770. W:51½ in (131 cm). FRE* **3**

ILANESE VENEERED COMMODE

is kingwood-veneered commode has three long drawers, a
aight apron, and square, almost bracket-shaped legs. Its
nt, distinctive color is a result of the inner sapwood of the
ngwood being used for the veneer. Its pulls are Neoclassical
design. *c. 1790. W:74 in (188 cm). Cdk* **5**

ITALIAN COMMODE

This rectangular fruitwood commode has three drawers, the upper
one narrower than the others, and stands on short, tapering feet.
It has a floral inlay, and its central cartouche, outlined in a darker
veneer, is inlaid with birds and flowers. *c. 1780. H:37½ in
(95 cm); W:49¼ in (125 cm); D:26¾ in (68 cm). MAG* **5**

SWEDISH COMMODE

This three-drawer commode has a marble top. Its case has canted
corners, as do the feet, which taper slightly toward the base. Its
side panels and drawers are veneered, and the central drawer
has an inlay of musical instruments *c. 1790. H:34 in (84.5 cm);
W:48¼ in (120.5 cm); D:22½ in (56 cm). Bk* **7**

ITALIAN COMMODE

is rectangular walnut commode has three drawers, the top one
rrower than the two below. Its drawers have floral marquetry
d a central oval inlaid with an architectural scene. Its handles
e lion's-head masks with a circular pull held in each lion's mouth.
1780. W:46¼ in (117.5 cm). DN **4**

ENGLISH CHEST OF DRAWERS

This mahogany chest of drawers is serpentine in shape. It has a
molded edge, four graduated drawers, a molded plinth, and
the piece terminates in four ogee bracket feet. The top drawer
of the chest is fitted as a dressing chest. *c. 1770. W:41½ in
(105 cm). L&T* **5**

GERMAN COMMODE

This commode's rounded, breakfront shape is echoed in the
conforming top, which slightly overhangs the case. It has three
drawers of equal size with Rococo-style drawer pulls. Its base
molding is shaped and the case stands on small bracket feet.
c. 1770. W:54½ in (136 cm). BMN **3**

ARISIAN *À LA GRECQUE* COMMODE

his commode has three drawers, the upper one hidden by an
pplied ormolu entrelac frieze. Its two lower drawers are covered
ith a veneer pattern. The four cabriole legs end in feet ornamented
ith sabots. *c. 1775. H:33⅓ in (84.5 cm); W:48¾ in
24.5 cm); D:22¼ in (56.5 cm). GK* **7**

SWEDISH COMMODE

This breakfront commode, with three small drawers flanking
three larger central drawers, is closely related to French styles.
This one is slightly heavier, particularly in the canted corners
and the marginally tapering legs. *H:35 in (86 cm); W:48 in
(120 cm); D:23 in (57 cm). Bk* **4**

PARISIAN MARBLE-TOPPED COMMODE

This rectangular commode has three drawers, and doors in the
central section, flanked by a single door on each side. It has
rounded pilasters on the sides that connect with its turned
and tapering legs. It has circular escutcheons with swags, and
circular pulls. *c. 1775. W:51¼ in (128 cm). GK* **5**

TABLES

DINING TABLES, although not described as such in Chippendale's *Director*, were a new type of table. During the first half of the 18th century, people tended to sit at small tables to eat, arranged in groups in a dedicated eating room.

Around the 1750s, people began to eat at longer tables. Quite often, these consisted of a central, rectangular gateleg table to which two D-ends were joined to make one long piece. When not assembled as such, the D-ends might be used as pier tables.

For the most part, these dining tables were plain, with either square or tapering legs. This began to change from around 1780, when tables were often supported by pedestals.

Early examples of dining tables, such as those supplied by Chippendale in 1770, had half-round ends and deep, rectangular drop leaves. These were supported, when raised, on gate legs and secured using stirrup clips.

Table legs were influenced by Neoclassical style and became more slender and tapering in shape as the century progressed.

As the passion for games and gambling now pervaded every level of society, large numbers of game tables were made, particularly in England and the American colonies, and these gained popularity in Europe toward the end of the century.

Many game tables had a top that folded back to reveal a baize-lined surface or an inlaid game board, and one or two legs that swung back to support the open top. When not in use, the table would usually be stored against the wall, so the side facing the wall was generally left undecorated.

Pembroke tables were multipurpose, and could be used for dining, games, or as worktables, depending on the occasion. Being small and on casters, they could be moved around a room as required.

Like other occasional tables, Pembroke tables were usually highly decorative. Those made of satinwood or mahogany were often inlaid with Neoclassical designs, although painted decoration was also popular. Marquetry remained fashionable throughout the period.

Dressing tables were often designed like deep tables with drawers. These usually featured ingenious mechanical fittings such as dressing mirrors that rose and fell in slots.

ENGLISH CARD TABLE

This mahogany, D-shaped card table has a fold-over top and baize-lined interior. It is veneered with satinwood banding, with ebony and boxwood string inlay. *c. 1785. H:29 in (74 cm); W:36¼ in (92 cm); D:18 in (46 cm). L&T* **3**

ENGLISH PEMBROKE TABLE

This small mahogany table is intricately inlaid with various woods, including harewood, a veneer from the sycamore tree that is stained to produce a brown-green color similar to kha... *c. 1780. W:37 in (94 cm). DL* **6**

SCANDINAVIAN TABLES

Made of satin birchwood, each table has a *demi-lune* top placed at an angle on a frame above three square-section, tapered legs. The D-shape or *demi lune* is often associated with card tables that were designed to be placed against a wall when not in use. However, these tables are more likely to have been used as side tables because they are too tall to sit at. *c. 1790. W:34¾ in (87 cm). L&T* **3**

The protruding, square corners are also functional, as their concave insides hold counters.

Metal hinges hold the two top sections together.

The escutcheons and handles are made of brass.

Carved acanthus adorns the knees of the table.

The rear legs do not have claw-and-ball feet, as the table was not designed to be seen from all sides.

ENGLISH GAME TABLE

Made from mahogany, this game table has a rectangular top that folds back to reveal a baize-lined playing surface. The concave corners hold counters. *c. 1760. W:35 in (87.5 cm). NA* **3**

SWEDISH PIER TABLE

This table is made of painted and gilded softwood, with a faux-marble top and plinth. Gilt balls top each turned, tapered leg, below which are carved and gilded acanthus leaves and gilt supports. *c. 1790. H:32 in (81.5 cm). DL* **4**

FRENCH TABLE

Made of mahogany, this rectangular table has a single frieze drawer. The square, tapering legs have brass terminals and casters, which allowed the occasional table to be moved easily. *c. 1785. H:28¼ in (71.5 cm). DN* **3**

NGLISH FOLD-OVER TEA TABLE

his mahogany tea table is made in the French Hepplewhite
tyle. The serpentine top has a molded edge and rests on a
erpentine frieze, which is raised on cabriole legs. The legs
re carved at the top of the knees with stylized anthemia.
. 1770. W:40 in (102 cm). PAR

ITALIAN PIER TABLE

This imposing table has a rectangular faux-marble top. The frame is
painted and decorated with applied gilt scrolls and rosettes. The
circular, tapered legs are also painted. Gilding is applied to the
concave sections of the stop-fluted legs. *c. 1780.* H:34½ in (88 cm);
W:43½ in (110.5 cm); D:22 in (56 cm). BL **6**

ENGLISH DRUM TABLE

This table has an inset-leather surface, four frieze drawers,
one of which is fitted with an adjustable writing slope, and four
dummy drawers. The table revolves on a turned central column,
which is set above four inlaid saber legs with brass lion's paw
casters. *c. 1800.* H:28¼ in (72 cm); D:43 in (109.5 cm). RGA **6**

DUTCH OCCASIONAL TABLE

he top of this *demi-lune*-shaped piece is decorated with an
laid urn surrounded by crossbanding. Tambour doors slide
deways to open. It stands on three square-section, tapering
gs decorated with boxwood and ebony stringing. *c. 1790.*
:29½ in (75 cm); W:29½ in (75 cm); D:15 in (38 cm). C&T **2**

FRENCH DROP-LEAF DINING TABLE

This Cuban mahogany table has a rounded, rectangular top with two
D-shaped leaves. It has a plain frieze and six squared, tapered legs
with brass caps and casters. The legs move out to support the open
leaves and additional leaves. Signed Jean-Antoine Brunes. *c. 1795.*
H:29 in (74 cm); W:102 in (255 cm); D:48⅞ in (124 cm). GK **5**

SWEDISH CARD TABLE

This *demi-lune*-shaped table has a frieze and squared legs. It
is very similar to an English card table, apart from the two legs,
which are awkwardly bunched together. One of them swings back
to support the top when opened. *c. 1780.* H:30½ in (77.5 cm);
W:34¼ in (88.5 cm). BK **4**

NGLISH OVAL TABLE

his is one of a pair of French-style tables decorated with
arquetry and parquetry. The oval top has a central panel
ith an inlaid spray of flowers and ribbons and the frieze has
floral inlay. The table has cabriole legs. *c. 1785.* H:25¾ in
55.5 cm); W:23¾ in (59 cm); D:17½ in (44 cm). DN **6**

ENGLISH PIER TABLE

The top of this *demi-lune* table is inlaid with satinwood, rosewood,
ebony, and boxwood. The marquetry features a fan, echoing the
shape of the table. Inlaid paterae are inserted at the tops of the
square, tapering legs, which terminate in spade feet. *c. 1790.*
W:56¼ in (133 cm). DN **5**

SWISS GAME TABLE

This walnut and cherrywood table has a heavy, hinged, fold-over
top, with rounded corners and a brown, gilt-leather inner surface.
The shaped table skirt is carved and the cabriole legs are carved
at the knees and tips. The rear leg swings back to support the
open top. *c. 1780.* H:28⅓ in (72 cm); W:35½ in (90 cm). GK **1**

OCCASIONAL TABLES

IN THE SECOND HALF of the 18th century, occasional tables became more varied in style. They were small and light, and so could be moved into reception rooms as required. Many of these tables were highly decorative, but gradually they became more utilitarian and were often designed for specific purposes.

A passion for games and gambling resulted in a proliferation of card tables. By the end of the century, French card tables were fitted for every sort of game: roulette, chess, backgammon, and *jeu de l'oie*.

A wide variety of writing tables was developed. The larger, portable tables made for writing were called *tables à écrire*. Some were fitted with candle slides that pulled out from the sides.

The newly fashionable custom of gathering to drink tea and coffee required two or even three tables: one table with a gallery around the edge, on which to place the china; a round table at which people sat and conversed; and a kettle stand. In the grandest homes, the kettle stand had a silver salver shaped to fit the top, with a silver coffee- or teapot on top of it.

Worktables first appeared in the second half of the 18th century. Those made for sewing often had tops that lifted up to reveal small drawers for holding reels of thread and other sewing accessories. Some sewing tables had fabric bags hanging beneath them, in which the needlework was kept. These were made from wooden frames covered with fabric that slid into runners in the base of the frames. French sewing tables, *tables en chiffonière*, did not usually have these. Some English worktables were also fitted with a leather surface for writing

The French *table de salon*, meaning "sitting room table." served many purposes. It had an ormolu gallery around the top, with three drawers and a shelf below. The intricate decoration meant it was elegant enough for formal reception rooms.

Many portable tables contained a fire screen, often made of the finest textiles or displaying needlework skills. The screen protected the face and legs of anyone sitting in front of a fire, and was particularly important for ladies who wished to protect their wax-based cosmetics from melting.

FRENCH *TABLE DE SALON*

This satinwood and holly table has a pierced ormolu gallery. The case, three drawers, and shelf are ornately inlaid. The tapering legs end in ormolu sabots. *c. 1780.* H:28½ in (72.5 cm); W:16¼ in (41 cm); D:13½ in (35.5 cm). PAR **1**

ITALIAN FIRE SCREEN TABLE

The entire surface of this olivewood table is veneered. It has a serpentine skirt and slender cabriole legs. The silk-lined fire screen moves up and down at the back of the table. *c. 1780.* H:27 in (68.5 cm). DL **4**

ENGLISH WRITING TABLE

This one-drawer, mahogany table has a leather-inset top. A silk-upholstered, adjustable face screen is fitted at the back. It has square, tapering legs with brass casters. *c. 1790.* W:17 in (43 cm). FRE **2**

FRENCH WORKTABLE

This diagonally veneered, single-drawer table has a cambered top and cabriole legs. It has a drawer in the mid-shelf, and a fire screen at the back. *c. 1760.* H:28⅜ in (72 cm); W:15 in (38 cm); D: 11 in (28 cm). GK **4**

The top is inlaid with flowers and has protruding rounded corners.

The frieze is inlaid to simulate fluting. It has a single front drawer.

The sides are inlaid with crossbanded borders with geometric banding and Neoclassical decoration.

The cabriole legs are gently curved.

The legs terminate in foliate ormolu sabots.

The tambour front slides back to reveal six small, ring-handled drawers.

ENGLISH WORKTABLE

This transitional-style worktable has an inlaid top above a single drawer. The table has a tambour front and an incurved shelf, and terminates in cabriole legs. *c. 1770.* H:30 in (76 cm); W:18¼ in (46.5 cm); D:13½ in (34.5 cm).

ENGLISH KETTLE STAND

This small mahogany stand has a circular top with a brass-lined spindle gallery. The fluted column has a leaf-carved baluster knob above a tripod base, with claw-and-ball feet. *c. 1760.* H:23 in (58.5 cm); D:13 in (33 cm). LT **7**

FRENCH SEWING TABLE

This table has a marble top surrounded by a pierced three-quarter gallery. The parquetry-veneered case contains two drawers. It has a shaped frame, lower shelf, cabriole legs, and ormolu feet. *c. 1765.* H:28 in (71 cm). S&K **1**

NGLISH WORKTABLE

his satinwood table has contrasting ebony
ringing, an inset leather top, and two candle
des. The case has a fitted drawer over a wool
x and is supported on square, tapered legs.
1785. H:22 in (56 cm). GORL **3**

RENCH TABLE

his sycamore, kingwood, and floral marquetry
ble has a Sèvres-style plaque in the top. It
as a pierced brass gallery and mounts, three
awers, and a lower shelf. c. 1780. H:29 in
3.5 cm) W:16½ in (41 cm). GK **7**

BONHEURS-DU-JOUR

A SMALL, FEMININE WRITING TABLE FOR LADIES, THE *BONHEUR-DU-JOUR* WAS FIRST MADE IN FRANCE
IN THE 1760S. ITS NAME REFERS TO THE FACT THAT SUCH PIECES SOON BECAME EXTREMELY POPULAR.

The *bonheur-du-jour* ("pleasure of the day") is a small, light,
elegant desk or dressing table. It is different from other writing
tables in that it has a raised back, like a miniature cabinet, made
up of shelves, drawers, or pigeonholes designed to hold papers,
writing accessories, and sometimes toiletries. Occasionally,
a mirror was also included. The top of the table is usually
surrounded by a brass or gilded gallery, which often served for
displaying small ornaments. Beneath it are drawers, or a small
cupboard. These sometimes have tambour doors that slide into
the case—another example of the technical skill of the cabinet-
maker. The table invariably has long, graceful, slender legs,
occasionally with a shelf attached to them about halfway down.

The *bonheur-du-jour* was made by many of the famous French
cabinet-makers, such as Martin Carlin, who designed 11 of them.
The most exquisite examples, such as Carlin's, were mounted
with plaques of Sèvres porcelain and painted with delicate floral
patterns, or richly decorated with fine marquetry, Oriental lacquer
panels, and ormolu.

Bonheurs-du-jour were valued both for their delicate beauty
and for the skill and ingenuity with which hidden drawers
and compartments were concealed within such a small space.
Originating in France, their popularity soon spread, partly due to
the increased importance of women in society at this time. They
appeared in grand British houses from about 1770 onward.

Louis XV cherrywood *bonheur-du-jour* The
upper section has two doors, and the lower
section holds a long, single drawer. The case
is set on cabriole legs. H:39 in (99 cm);
W:31½ in (80 cm); D:21¼ in (54 cm). PIL **3**

Louis XVI mahogany *bonheur-du-jour* This desk has a
marble top and a brass three-
quarter gallery, with a glazed
upper section and a roll-top
desk element. H:50¾ in
(129 cm); W:31 in (79 cm);
D:9 in (23 cm). PIL

ERMAN GAME TABLE

his provincial walnut, cherry, and native
uitwood table top is supported on tapered
gs. The surface is inlaid with a chess board;
e interior is fitted for backgammon. c. 1780.
:30 in (75 cm). GK **4**

GERMAN DRESSING TABLE

This solid cherrywood table from southern
Germany has a wide, overhanging top above
two small drawers. It stands on tall, tapering
legs. Late 18th century. H:30 in (76 cm);
W:26¾ in (68 cm); D:17½ in (44 cm). BMN **1**

FRENCH WRITING TABLE

The table top has a gilt-bronze-edged frieze and
is inlaid with flower-heads and a ribbon border.
The drawer is fitted with a sliding writing surface,
inkwell, pounce-pot, and pen tray. c. 1780.
H:28¼ in (72 cm); W:24¼ in (61.5 cm). PAR **1**

FRENCH WRITING TABLE

The top is inlaid with lozenges and a central
cartouche. The frieze has a geometric inlay and a
drawer. Each side has a pull-out writing slide.
c. 1780. H:27½ in (69.5 cm); W: 24½ in
(62 cm); D: 15½ in (39.5 cm). PAR **1**

CHAIRS

THE VARIETY OF CHAIRS burgeoned in the mid- to late 18th century, with French styles remaining popular. Although elements of the Rococo style lingered, chairs began to look more Neoclassical and became squarer and straighter. Cabriole legs were rejected in favor of turned, tapered supports, often fluted or decorated with reeding, and oval and rectangular chair backs became more common.

Different types of chair evolved: the *bergère* remained the same stylistically, but the frame was often simply waxed, rather than painted and gilded, as in the first half of the century. Desk chairs and corner chairs, which were popular at the beginning of the period, had shaped backs. The shield back became fashionable toward the end of the century, with the pierced splats incorporating a wide range of Neoclassical motifs. Desk chairs

usually had rounded seat rails and often had an extra leg at the center of the seat rail, making five legs in total.

Corner chairs, like hall chairs, were small and designed to be decorative rather than useful. They were usually rather fragile, as they were not designed for regular use.

At first, chairs were ordered individually, but from the mid-century onward, sets of furniture known as suites became more popular. These varied from small groups of matching chairs to extensive suites that included a number of pieces, such as armchairs, side chairs, *bergères*, window seats, stools, and sofas.

Any decoration on hall and corner chairs was likely to be carved, but more expensive armchairs and their matching side chairs, designed for grander rooms, were often delicately painted or highlighted with gilding.

LOUIS XVI DESK CHAIR

This French tub desk chair has a curved and lightly carved seat rail, and the seat, back, and sides are all upholstered in leather. It has Neoclassical turned and tapered armrests and legs. *c. 1780.* H:32¾ in (82 cm). CdK **3**

QUEEN ANNE CORNER CHAIR

This walnut chair has a crest rail with a raised yoke center, shaped arms, and solid, vase-shaped splats. It has one front cabriole leg and three turned legs, all with slipper feet. *c. 1770–1800.* H:30 in (76 cm); W:28 in (71 cm). BDL

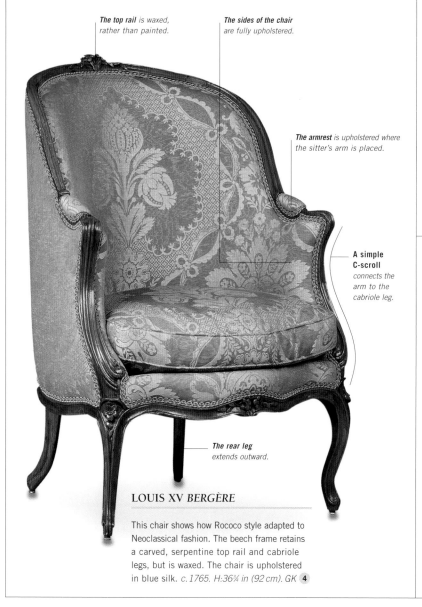

The top rail is waxed, rather than painted.

The sides of the chair are fully upholstered.

The armrest is upholstered where the sitter's arm is placed.

A simple C-scroll connects the arm to the cabriole leg.

The rear leg extends outward.

LOUIS XV *BERGÈRE*

This chair shows how Rococo style adapted to Neoclassical fashion. The beech frame retains a carved, serpentine top rail and cabriole legs, but is waxed. The chair is upholstered in blue silk. *c. 1765.* H:36¼ in (92 cm). GK **4**

SOUTH AFRICAN CORNER CHAIR

This chair is made from native stinkwood and yellow wood. The pierced back splats are reminiscent of Chippendale designs. The square, chamfered legs are connected by stretchers. *c. 1780–1800.* H:33¼ in (83 cm). PRA **3**

NEW YORK CORNER CHAIR

This mahogany chair has a top rail with a raised yoke center, carved knuckle handholds, and vase-shaped splats. The deep seat rail is supported on three cabriole legs with slipper feet and one rear turned leg. *c. 1750.* NA

GEORGE III HALL CHAIR

This mahogany hall chair has a cartouche-shaped back. Within the C- and S-scrolled frame are carved heraldic elements, including an Irish harp and crown. The piece terminates in paneled, tapering legs. *c. 1770.* L&T **2**

GEORGE III HALL CHAIR

One of a set of four, this mahogany chair has a typically Neoclassical oval back. The solid mahogany seat overhangs the front rail. Tapering legs support the frame and a stretcher connects the rear legs. *c. 1780.* L&T **4**

HINESE CORNER CHAIR

is rosewood chair has a central leg with a
ell carved on the knee, and it terminates
a claw-and-ball foot. Attenuated turned
retchers anchor the legs. *c. 1780. H:34 in
6 cm). MJM*

GEORGE III CORNER CHAIR

This provincial oak chair is one of a pair. The
seat is composed of three planks of oak. Turned
spindles connect the seat to the rounded back, a
technique often seen on Windsor chairs *c. 1800.
H:32 in (81.5 cm). DL* **4**

HALL CHAIRS

HALL CHAIRS, AS THEIR NAME IMPLIES, WERE DESIGNED TO STAND ALONG
THE WALLS OF HALLWAYS, RATHER THAN IN RECEPTION ROOMS.

Small, formal, and more decorative than
functional, hall chairs were first named
by Robert Manwaring, a furniture designer,
in *The Chair-Maker's Real Friend and
Companion*, published in 1865.

Thomas Sheraton noted in *The Cabinet
Dictionary* that "chairs such as those that
are placed in halls are for the use of
servants or strangers waiting on
business." These wooden chairs were
usually smaller than side chairs. They
had turned seats and often had the crest
or arms of the family carved or painted
on the chair back. Some chairs were
made with plain backs so that families
could have their own insignia carved or
painted onto the basic chair.

The hall chair first appeared when
Thomas Chippendale illustrated six
designs of chairs for "Halls, Passages, or
Summer-Houses" in his *Director*.

Rival cabinet-makers William Ince
and John Mayhew published three
designs for hall chairs in the "gothic
taste" in their serialized pattern book,
*The Universal System of Household
Furniture* (1759–62). If it was too
expensive to carve the decorative crest
on the back, then it was considered
acceptable to "be painted, and have a
very good effect."

Hall chairs These illustrations are from Thomas
Chippendale's *The Gentleman & Cabinet-Maker's
Director*, 1762 (Plate XVII).

ENGLISH HALL CHAIRS

These mahogany hall chairs have central
veneered tablets, and pierced, waisted
supports. The seats are slightly bowed and
framed with panels. The turned, blocked
legs are joined by cross-stretchers.
c. 1780. L&T **4**

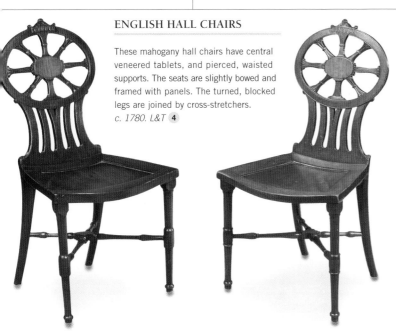

NGLISH HALL CHAIR

his mahogany chair has a balloon-shaped back
at fits into a shoe at the base. The seat is solid
ahogany with a circular lowered section. The
pered legs terminate in squared ends.
1790. H:38 in (96.5 cm). DL **4**

CHINESE HALL CHAIR

This chair was made for export to the West.
The solid splats are decorated with an inlay.
The dish-molded seat is shaped at the edges.
Square, chamfered legs are joined by stretchers.
c. 1760. H:37½ in (95 cm). HL **6**

ENGLISH HALL CHAIR

One of a pair, this mahogany chair is modeled on
the Renaissance *sgabello* chair. It has a shaped,
waisted back and shaped seat. The front support
and seat have indented panels, designed to bear
a crest. *c. 1780. H:39 in (99 cm). DL* **3**

ENGLISH HALL CHAIR

This chair, one of a set of four, has a pierced
wheel back with a central, raised, circular
plaque. The wide, slightly dished seat is
supported on tapered legs, and the front legs
terminate in spade feet. *c. 1770. GorL* **5**

CHIPPENDALE CHAIRS

THE CHAIR DESIGNS that Chippendale created and reproduced in his book *The Gentleman and Cabinet-Maker's Director* (1762) offer a sample of the various design trends in the mid- to late 18th century, such as Rococo, Chinese, Gothic, and Neoclassical. Chippendale's name has become generic for 18th-century furniture and, in particular, chairs, but his designs borrowed from published English and French work. His most original work can be found in his Neoclassical pieces, which he created from 1760 onward, inspired by the interiors of architect Robert Adam.

Despite the variety of influences on his designs, many Chippendale chairs follow a basic pattern, with their stylistic influence being most obvious in their carving. Therefore, while most chair backs had pierced and interlaced splats with carved scrollwork, it is the shape and carving that reveals the predominant influence: cartouche shapes and scrolling acanthus for Rococo, Gothic arches, Chinoiserie fretwork, and interlacing ribbons, or the lyre and fan shapes typical of Neoclassicism. The importance of deep-cut, detailed carving in Chippendale's designs meant that mahogany was most commonly used, although provincial versions were still often made in walnut or fruitwoods.

The top rails of the chairs were usually serpentine in shape, sometimes ending in carved ears, with stiles curving outward. Most of them had squared or trapezoidal seats, and while Chippendale preferred stuff-over upholstery, many cheaper or colonial versions had slip-in seats. Designs often had different front and back legs. The front legs could be cabriole with a claw-and-ball foot, tapered, or straight with stretchers.

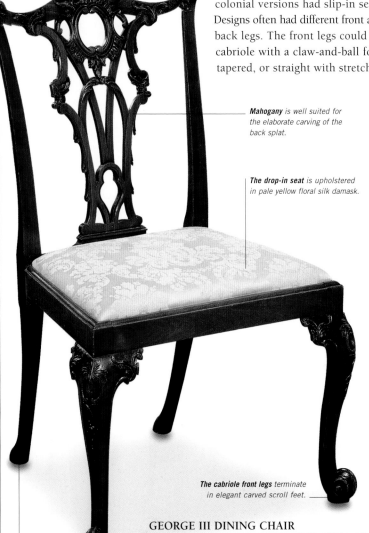

Mahogany is well suited for the elaborate carving of the back splat.

The drop-in seat is upholstered in pale yellow floral silk damask.

The cabriole front legs terminate in elegant carved scroll feet.

Rear legs were often simply chamfered, as these chairs were placed against the wall.

GEORGE III DINING CHAIR

This mahogany chair, part of a set of 11 together with one later copy, has a serpentine top rail above an interlaced, pierced splat headed by C-scrolls carved with leaves. The cabriole legs are flanked by C-scrolls, also carved with leaves, and the legs taper toward scrolled toes. *c. 1775.*

NEW HAMPSHIRE DINING CHAIRS

Each of these mahogany dining chairs has a serpentine top rail with rounded shoulders and flaring stiles with scribed borders. The interlaced back splat includes an inverted heart-shaped cutout. The over-upholstered, seat is a trapezoidal shape and has a serpentine front. The piece is supported on square-molded, chamfered legs. The legs of the chair are joined by recessed box stretchers. The chairs retain an old or original finish, and are attributed to Robert Harold of Portsmouth. *c. 1765–75.* **5**

ENGLISH DINING CHAIRS

The serpentine top rail of each mahogany chair is carved at the shoulders with scrolls and foliage. The pierced, vase-shaped back splats are carved with acanthus and trailing foliage. The curved arms with scrolling ends have downward-sweeping supports, and stretchers join the straight front legs and sweeping back legs. The saddle-shaped seats are covered in red leather with a double row of studs. *c. 177* *Chair: H:37½ in (95 cm); W:24 in (62 cm); D:23½ in (59.9 cm). Armchair: H:37½ in (95 cm W:25½ in (65 cm); D:25½ in (65 cm). PAR*

ENGLISH DINING CHAIRS

These mahogany chairs have serpentine top rails carved with trailing acanthus and side rails with flowers and trelliswork. The pierced, vase-shaped back splats are carved with acanthus and *rocaille*. The curved arms have downward-sweeping supports. The chairs have drop-in seats with egg-and-dart-molding on the seat rails. The square front legs have chamfered back corners and foliate brackets, while the back legs are sweeping. *c. 1760. H:38½ in (98 cm); W:22½ in (57 cm); D:19 in (48 cm). PAR*

OLONIAL INDIAN SIDE CHAIR

is Asian hardwood chair has a serpentine
p rail above a pierced, vase-form back splat.
e shaped seat rail has a padded drop-in seat.
e cabriole legs have acanthus-carved knees.
1770. H:39 in (100 cm); W:28 in (71 cm). MJM

AMERICAN DINING CHAIR

This is one of a pair of fine Delaware Valley
walnut chairs. Each has a serpentine top rail
centered by a carved shell over a pierced, vase-
form splat. The molded seat rail has a drop-in
seat. *c. 1770. P&P*

AMERICAN CARVED SIDE CHAIR

This walnut chair has a serpentine top rail
centered by a carved shell over a pierced, vase-
form splat. It has a molded seat rail, padded
drop-in seat, cabriole legs, and claw-and-ball
feet. *Late 18th century. SI* **4**

ENGLISH DINING CHAIR

This mahogany chair has an arched, molded
top rail and carved shells at the corners of the
uprights, in the center of the pierced splat, and
at the center of the shaped apron. *c. 1770.
H:34¾ in (88.5 cm); W:22½ in (57 cm). PAR*

CHIPPENDALE'S CHAIR DESIGNS

IN THE 1762 EDITION OF THE *DIRECTOR*, 25 PAGES WERE DEVOTED TO
SEATING, WITH OVER 60 SEPARATE DESIGNS FOR CHAIRS AND CHAIR BACKS.

In the notes that accompany his
illustrative plates, Chippendale wrote
that there "are various designs of chairs
for patterns. The front feet are mostly
different, for the greater choice."
Elsewhere, he was more specific, as with
his instructions that chairs should be
upholstered in the same material as the
window-curtains and the height of the
back should seldom exceed 22 in (55 cm)
above the seat—although sometimes
these dimensions could be less to suit
the chairs to the room.

Chippendale felt that "seats look best
when stuffed over the rails and have a

brass border neatly chased; but are most
commonly done with Brass Nails, in one
or two Rows." Despite the number of
designs in his *Director*, not all the chair
patterns that are termed "Chippendale"
are included: the ladder-back design, for
example, does not appear.

Chippendale's designs for chairs and
backs of chairs were perhaps the most
influential of his designs to appear in the
Director. His designs were interpreted by
craftsmen throughout the world, who
followed his instructions to varying
degrees, and so increased the variety
of "Chippendale" chairs.

AMERICAN ARMCHAIR

This mixed wood armchair from Philadelphia
has a serpentine top rail, an urn-shaped splat,
and flared arms with scrolled knuckles. It has a
straight seat rail, a slip seat, cabriole legs, and
pad feet. *Mid- to late 18th century. FRE* **4**

GEORGE III ARMCHAIR

This child's open mahogany armchair has a
serpentine top rail and a ladder-back splat.
The scroll arms have fluted uprights. The
stuff-over seat rests on square, tapering legs.
c. 1790. FRE **1**

GEORGE III SETTEE

This early George III mahogany chair-back
settee has a C- and S-scroll top rail above
two pierced, vase-shaped splats
with an open outscrolled
arm at each end. The
stuff-over seat rests on
chamfered, square- section
legs joined by stretchers.
*W:57¾ in (147 cm).
L&T* **3**

ARMCHAIRS

ARMCHAIR DESIGNS based on the French *fauteuil* shape were still popular in the latter half of the 18th century. The shape of the chair was slow to adopt Neoclassical styling and, until the 1780s, chairs with undulating curves and cabriole legs, like those of Rococo chairs, continued to be made.

However, the shape gradually developed as the fervor for "antique" or Neoclassical designs grew. These changes could be seen in the shape of chair backs: first they became more oval, then they became rectangular and were often flanked by colonettes.

Seats also changed shape and became round rather than rectangular. Toward the end of the century, they became square, to accompany the rectangular chair backs.

Chair legs gradually became straight and tapered. They were often reeded, spiraled, or fluted, the latter being a reference to Classical architectural columns—part of the new craze inspired by Greco-Roman styles.

Further carved decoration was used in the form of rosettes at the tops of the legs, and guilloche or chain motifs around the bowed seat rails.

Many chairs still had painted and gilt decoration, although polished mahogany was more popular in the Low Countries, due to imported timber from its Far Eastern colonies and from foreign trading links.

Coverings for armchairs were varied at this time, and ranged from Aubusson tapestries to silk or needlework. Silk finishes tended to match the wall coverings of the rooms for which the chairs were intended. Horsehair was generally used as a stuffing for upholstered seats.

ENGLISH ARMCHAIR

This armchair has a fanlike back, and the upper section is wider than the lower section. The seat is wider and lower than most French examples. The cabriole legs are connected to the seat rail, but they lack continuous undulation. The frame is painted and gilded and the chair has been upholstered in a silk fabric that has been dated later than the frame itself. *c. 1780.*

PARISIAN *FAUTEUIL*

This carved beech armchair has an oval back, outswept arms, and a wide seat. The seat and back are upholstered in silk. The back and rail are carved with a Neoclassical guilloche pattern, punctuated with a rosette at the top of each leg. The turned, tapered legs are carved with stop-fluting, a pattern representing fluted architectural columns that was typically Neoclassical. *c. 1773. Bk* **5**

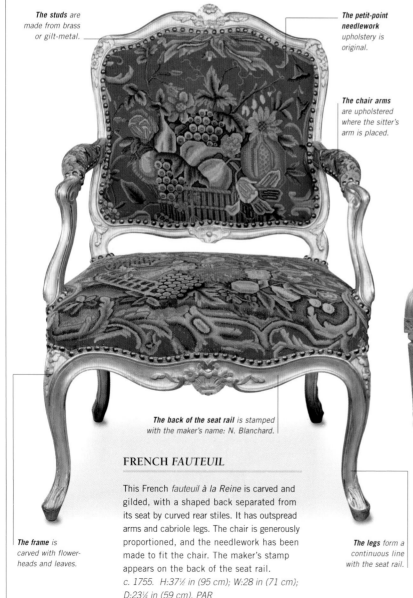

The studs are made from brass or gilt-metal.

The petit-point needlework upholstery is original.

The chair arms are upholstered where the sitter's arm is placed.

The back of the seat rail is stamped with the maker's name: N. Blanchard.

FRENCH *FAUTEUIL*

The frame is carved with flower-heads and leaves.

This French *fauteuil à la Reine* is carved and gilded, with a shaped back separated from its seat by curved rear stiles. It has outspread arms and cabriole legs. The chair is generously proportioned, and the needlework has been made to fit the chair. The maker's stamp appears on the back of the seat rail.
c. 1755. H:37½ in (95 cm); W:28 in (71 cm); D:23¼ in (59 cm). PAR

The legs form a continuous line with the seat rail.

GUSTAVIAN ARMCHAIR

This armchair is in the Gustavian style. The shaped oval back and wide seat are upholstered in fabric with a blue and white Classical design and the chair is supported on a white-painted frame—a typically Gustavian feature. The top rail, arms, and legs are all carved with Neoclassical motifs. The chair is raised on stop-fluted legs, which are also typically Neoclassical. *Bk* **1**

SWEDISH ARMCHAIR

Painted white and gilt in the Gustavian style, this square-backed, upholstered armchair has outswept arms, a rounded seat frame, and turned and tapered legs. The carved decoration is in the Neoclassical guilloche pattern, and rosettes appear above its tapering, columnar legs. Gilt highlights the decoration. This armchair is one of a pair. *c. 1780. Bk* **5**

OUTHERN GERMAN ARMCHAIR

e frame of this armchair is probably walnut
d is neither painted nor gilded. The seat and
ck are upholstered in silk. The rounded back
small compared with its wide seat, and with
her examples of *fauteuils*. The arms are
swept at the ends, widening as they join
e chair rail. The fluted legs terminate in
all button feet. *c. 1780. H:36 in (92 cm).*
MN 2

ENGLISH ARMCHAIR

This *fauteuil* shares many attributes with its
Parisian prototype, including the proportions
of the back and seat. The simple carved floral
motif in the center of the back rail is also very
French in style. However, the arm terminus is
an English interpretation, as are the fluted arm
supports. The tapered, single-flute, columnar
legs are more slender than most French
examples. *c. 1780.* BOUL 4

ITALIAN ARMCHAIR

This armchair incorporates several
Neoclassical elements with its shield-shaped
back, acanthus-carved arms, and the spray of
laurel leaves that decorates the front chair
rail, an element derived from ancient Greece.
The chair is caned, the frame is painted
green and gilded, and it has flat stretchers.
*c. 1790. H:37 in (94 cm); W:24 in (61 cm);
D:24 in (61 cm).* BRU 2

SOUTHERN GERMAN SIDE CHAIR

Although this is a walnut, caned side chair,
its back and seat frame are very similar to the
shape of a French *fauteuil*. The center of its
back chair frame and the seat rail both have
simple, carved floral details. The cabriole legs
are higher than most French examples, and
terminate in stylized paw feet. This side chair
is one of a pair. *c. 1780. H:37 in (92 cm).*
BMN 2

QUARE-BACKED ARMCHAIR

is square-backed armchair is larger than
ost French examples. The square arms
rve down from the upper chair back and
pe toward the legs. These legs are slightly
rned and feature flutes. The starkness of
e design, accentuated by the white paint,
barely relieved by the vibrant red and white
riped silk upholstery. This is one of a pair
armchairs. *c. 1790.* Bk 4

GERMAN SIDE CHAIR

Made of beech, and one of a pair, this chair
has a square back with a pierced center,
reminiscent of Chippendale Gothic designs.
However, the fluted legs show a greater degree
of French influence. Its upholstery is tacked
over the top of the seat, but it leaves the
frame showing. Simple, tapered legs with
a slight flare support the frame. *c. 1785.
H:37 in (92.5 cm).* BMN 2

FRENCH CHAIRS

SUCH WAS THE *FAUTEUIL'S* APPEAL THAT IT WAS COPIED THROUGHOUT
EUROPE. THOMAS CHIPPENDALE PRODUCED NUMEROUS VARIATIONS OF IT.

Parisian furniture was particularly
coveted by the English, but it was the
fauteuil that was imitated across Europe.

In his *Director*, Thomas Chippendale
published ten designs of "French
Chairs," two of which had "Elbows"
(arms). Accompanying the illustrations
is the claim that "The Feet and Elbows
are different," giving chair-makers a
wider range of options. Chippendale's
instructions stated that "some of them
are intended to be open at the Back:
which make them very light, without
having a bad Effect…The Seat is twenty-
seven Inches wide in Front, twenty-two
Inches from the Front to the Back, and
twenty-three Inches wide behind; the
Height of the Back is twenty-five Inches,
and the Height of the Seat fourteen
Inches and an Half, including Casters."

Chippendale also noted his preferences
for upholstery—"Both the back and the
seat must be covered with Tapestry, or
other sort of Needlework"—and that the
backs and seats should be stuffed and
nailed with brass nails.

While the *Director* certainly helped
the popularity of the *fauteuil*, looking at
the variety of chairs from this period,
it is clear that many of Chippendale's
dictates were not followed to the letter.

Plate no. XXIII *The Gentleman
& Cabinet-Maker's Director,* by
Thomas Chippendale. *1762.*

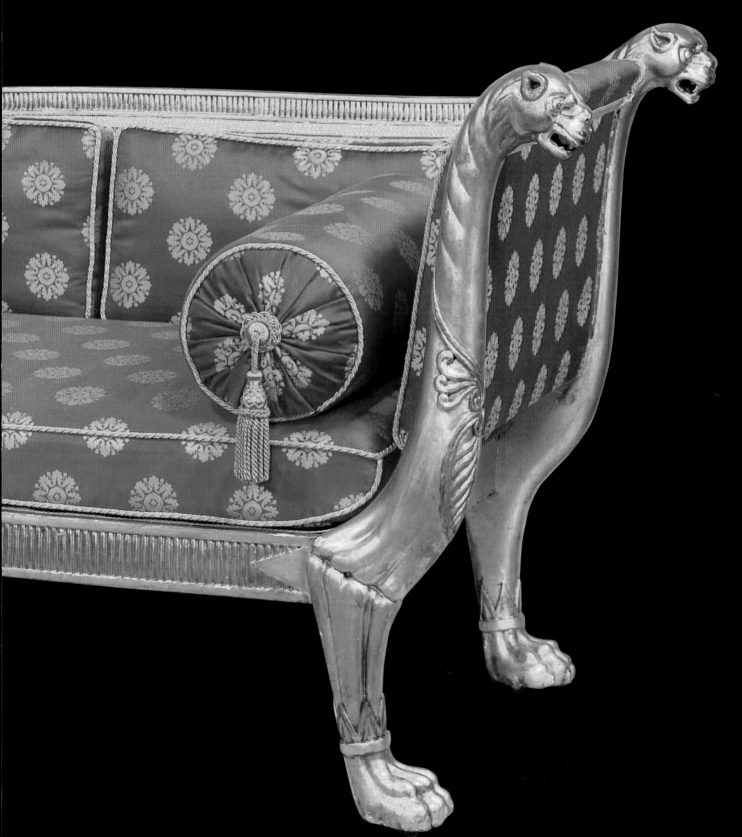

REBELLION AND EMPIRE

THE TURN OF THE 19TH CENTURY WITNESSED VIOLENT REBELLION AND UNPRECEDENTED SOCIAL CHANGE, USHERING IN A NEW WORLD ORDER.

ON JULY 14, 1789, French peasants stormed the Bastille prison in Paris in a gesture that has become a symbol of the beginning of the French Revolution. This national uprising was to have major international consequences, not only political, but more significantly, social. Over the next decade, the *ancien régime* and its absolute monarchy gave way to a new world order.

In January 1793, Louis XVI was executed. The Reign of Terror that followed led to the deaths of around 40,000 people. From 1794, France was ruled by a Directorate of five members, appointed by councils, but in 1797 a young army general, Napoleon Bonaparte, helped the Directorate stage a coup d'état.

The Regency Pavilion, Brighton This elaborate Indian-style palace with domes and minarets was created for the Prince Regent by John Nash. The building took more than 30 years to complete, and the interior decoration mixes Eastern exoticism with British style. *1826.*

EUROPE AT WAR

Although the revolution in France caused great unease in other European countries, it was France, still notionally under Louis XVI, that declared war on the rest of Europe in 1792. The war lasted until 1815 and left many European countries economically exhausted. In conquering other states, France sought to create republics on the French model, thus changing the social order of the continent. Holland, Milan, Genoa, Rome, Naples, and Greece all became republics by 1799.

Britain, meanwhile, remained steadfastly royalist. The Prince of Wales spent lavishly, buying up the spoils of the French Revolution and building exotic palaces. However, the French struck indirectly at the British establishment by helping Irish republicans and by trying to block the route to India through Egypt, a move that had unexpectedly wonderful consequences for the decorative arts, since it inspired a craze for Egyptian design.

Bonaparte became First Consul in 1800 and declared himself Emperor in 1804. He introduced the Civil Code into French law in the same year, having invigorated the French economy by establishing the Bank of France. This prosperity enabled him to combine the luxury of prerevolutionary France with the grandeur of Imperial Rome and ancient Egypt in the decorative arts. The resulting Empire style became the most pervasive decorative influence of the period.

Tea service by Sèvres This porcelain and gilt tea service was a gift from Emperor Napoleon I to his wife, Josephine. The set is decorated with Classical motifs, and is the epitome of Empire style. *1808.*

CHANGE AND RESTORATION

The French empire reached the height of its power around 1810, but it was under strain. French inroads into Spain in 1808 were eroded by a Spanish people supported by the British. Napoleon's Russian campaign in 1812 was disastrous, and there was a revolt the following year against the French in Germany. In 1814, Napoleon abdicated and the monarchy was restored under Louis XVIII. Napoleon mustered one final show of force, but was defeated by the Duke of Wellington at Waterloo and exiled. Europe, however, had changed forever.

Meanwhile, Britain found itself at war with the United States once again; a war that ultimately saw the British burn the White House. By the end of the 18th century, the Americans were very proud of their fledgling nation, and patriotic symbols, including the bald eagle and images of famous Americans, were enthusiastically displayed.

Politics in the 19th century was henceforth dominated by nationalism and liberalism. At the same time, industry and the arts began a process of rapid industrialization and modernization. The modern world was born.

TIMELINE 1790–1840

1791 The *Corporation des Menusiers-Ébénistes* (Guild of Joiners and Cabinet-Makers) is banned.

1793 Louis XVI of France is executed by guillotine: the Reign of Terror begins.

1797 Napoleon wins the Battle of the Pyramids in

A Pennsylvania Federal walnut tilt-top lamp table This piece has a round top inlaid with an eagle holding an olive branch and arrows.

A Wedgwood jasperware vase and cover The molded cover is in the shape of a Pharaoh's head and the body is decorated with Egyptian motifs.

Egypt. The French capture Rome.

1799 Napoleon is made First Consul: the Consulate period begins. George Washington dies.

1800 Washington, D.C. is declared the

capital of the United States; an ambitious building plan is undertaken, modeled on the palace and gardens of Versailles.

1801 Alexander I is made czar of Russia after the execution of Paul I. Architects Percier and Fontaine publish *Recueil des Décorations Intérieures*, including the first known use of the phrase "interior decoration." These drawings set the standard for the Empire style, which spreads throughout Europe.

1803 France and Britain renew war.

The Roman city of Pompeii While Naples was under French rule, excavations at Pompeii were expanded.

France sells Louisiana to the United States to finance the war.

1804 Napoleon crowns himself Emperor of France. Thomas Sheraton publishes the first volume of his *Cabinet Maker,*

The picture gallery at Pavlovsk Palace, Russia
The czar's summer palace near St. Petersburg was redecorated after a fire in 1803 to the designs of Friedrich Bergenfeldt, possibly the finest bronzier of the age. *Early 19th century.*

A giltwood *fauteuil* This chair is carved with stylized flowers and volutes and has arm supports in the shape of sphinxes. It stands on straight legs. *c. 1810. H:38½ in (98 cm); W:30¾ in (78 cm). PAR*

---

upholsterer and *General Artist's Encyclopaedia.*

1806 Napoleon defeats the Holy Roman Empire, which had ruled for almost 900 years. Second British occupation of the Cape of Good Hope.

1808 Joseph Bonaparte usurps the Spanish throne. George Smith publishes *Collection of Designs for Household Furniture and Interior Decoration.*

A Prattware oval plaque The relief is molded with the head of a Classical maiden, decorated in blue, brown, green, yellow, and ocher.

1811 George III is declared mad and the Prince of Wales becomes Regent. The Regency period begins.

1812 The United States declares war on Britain. Napoleon's Russian campaign ends in abject failure.

1814 Napoleon abdicates. Ferdinand VII retakes the Spanish throne: the Ferdinandino period begins in Spanish furniture.

1815 Napoleon is exiled to St.

Cleopatra's needle Made for Thotmes III in 1460 BCE, it was shipped to London in 1878 to commemorate Britain's victory over Napoleon.

Helena after his defeat at Waterloo.

1829 Greece gains independence from the Ottoman Turks.

1834 Victoria crowned Queen in Britain.

French candlesticks These take the form of columns and Corinthian capitals supported on a tripod base.

EMPIRE FURNITURE

A GREAT DEAL OF the furniture produced in Europe, the United States, and South Africa from the time of the French Revolution to around 1830 owes some stylistic allegiance to the French Empire style. The British Regency and German Biedermeier styles (*see pp.206 and 216*) were both highly idiosyncratic and, although indebted to the Napoleonic manner, were influential in their own right. It is one of the ironies of the period that countries so hostile to Napoleon and French rule, including Britain, Germany, and Russia, adopted a style derived from Paris fashions.

NEW CUSTOMERS

The period is also notable for a subtle shift in market from the aristocratic patrons of prerevolutionary France to the bourgeoisie. It is sometimes argued that the rise of the middle-class buyer heralded a decline in the quality of furniture, but the discerning eye will appreciate that fine Empire furniture is of an equal quality to that which preceded it. The Industrial Revolution also affected furniture workshops, which, throughout the 19th century, were increasingly mechanized. This process was aided by the disbanding of the guild system in France early in the Revolution, freeing cabinet-makers and bronze founders from the restrictive procedures formerly enforced upon them.

EXPANDING THE EMPIRE

The Empire style, which was closely tied to the taste of the Emperor Napoleon Bonaparte, was in part disseminated across Europe through members of Napoleon's family, whom he appointed to rule the countries France had conquered, including Spain, Italy, and the Netherlands. However, these were not the only countries to be influenced by the new Empire style, and even Russia, which Napoleon famously failed to conquer, still enthusiastically adopted this fashion.

Empire furniture was a stricter, more austere and truer version of the prerevolutionary Neoclassical style, which had now been abandoned as too ostentatious for the new political climate. The Empire style favored sparsely adorned surfaces punctuated only by Neoclassical or revolutionary gilt-bronze motifs and mounts.

The campaigns in Egypt had engendered a scholarly and decorative interest in the land of the Pharaohs, and sphinx heads and other Egyptian motifs, known as *Egyptiennerie*, consequently often appear in furniture design of the time. The Empire style remained the height of fashion until 1815, when the Emperor was finally exiled for good. Thereafter, it became heavier in proportion and freer of decoration such as ormolu mounts.

However, as the Empire style was taken up in various other countries in Europe, it was combined with the local traditions and techniques. In the Netherlands, this often meant a combination with floral marquetry.

Fauteuil **and footstool** Part of a large suite, these pieces exemplify the French Empire style: the saber back legs, the sphinx-carved front legs and arms, the lion's-paw feet, and the X-form of the stool are all typical features. Attributed to Jacob Frères. *c. 1800. Fauteuil: H:37 in (94 cm); W:25 in (63.5 cm); D:21¾ in (55 cm). PAR*

In Italy, where good-quality timber was hard to com by, furniture was frequently painted and gilded, o retained some of the sculptural qualities associate with Italian furniture. In Russia and the United Sta British Regency style, which had developed in Brita from the francophile Neoclassical designs of Thom Sheraton and Thomas Hope, was as important as Fre Empire, while in South Africa, it was diluted to its most basic forms.

MODIFICATION AND REVIVAL

Around 1820, a squatter version of the Empire sty began to be combined with a confused historicism Materials changed, and light-colored woods (*bois clairs*) became fashionable. This was partly due to the scarcity of mahogany, which the British stopped exporting from their colonies during the Napoleoni wars. This change in fashion varied from country to country. In Britain, by the end of the 1810s, the fir of Bullock and Bridgens led a taste for 17th-century styled oak furniture, although the full flowering of the Gothic revival was still a decade away. A late Regency style, sometimes referred to as the styles of George IV and William IV, lingered on in vernacular furniture reinterpreting Regency forms with an increased clumsiness that anticipated Victorian furniture. In Italy, although the occasional Gothic motif appeared it was largely ignored, while Baroque traditions wer revived in Florence. Other countries looked to their own histories for inspiration as the Empire style wa adapted and modified to suit national tastes.

Federal mahogany sideboard This is typical of American furniture, which was largely influenced by British style: the shaped back panel, bowed front and tapering legs display the Classical influences of the period. *Early 19th century. H:51½ in (131 cm); W:78¼ in (199 cm); D:27¼ in (70 cm). BRU*

FURNITURE SHOWROOMS

From the late 18th century, manufacturers began opening showrooms in London from which to sell their wares. Josiah Wedgwood opened some of these warehouses in the 1780s, while a German visitor to London in 1803 noted the brilliant displays in the city's shop windows. This brought the latest styles to an ever-wider audience, and enhanced the desirability of fashionable furniture.

This commercialism was aided by fashion magazines, such as Rudolph Ackermann's *The*

Repository of Arts, which was published from 1809. While guiding taste, it also promoted certain shops and suppliers, such as Morgan and Sander's, the patent furniture-makers, which had premises off the Strand in London.

In Paris, furniture dealers such as Rocheux, the Treattels, and Jean-Henri Eberts had been operating since the 18th century.

"Messrs. Morgan & Sanders, Catherine St., Strand" This is from a color lithograph, Number 8 of Ackermann's *Repository of Arts*. *Published on August 1, 1809. AR*

A ROYAL FRENCH CENTER TABLE

Center tables became increasingly popular in the early 19th century. Designed to stand in the middle of a room, this piece was intended to be seen from all angles. Consequently, the tessellated marquetry top is decorated on all sides, and the top even swivels. Placed over planks, which make up the top, the veneers include alternating petals of maple and mahogany. The outer border is crossbanded with tulipwood and encloses several thuyawood panels "inlaid" with trophies of Science, Painting, Gardening, Architecture, Music, and Navigation.

Technically the use of the word "inlaid" is inaccurate here, since the trophies and the thuyawood ground are cut from veneers of equal thickness and pieced together (more like parquetry). In other words, the trophies are not laid into a thick piece of timber but are veneered on top of the secondary carcass of the table top. The pentagonal column and the concave-sided plinth are veneered in burr elm. This local light-colored wood, like the maple veneers on the top, is typical of the taste for *bois clairs* during the Empire period.

Equally typical of this style are the ormolu mounts on the column and plinth, depicting winged figures of victory. This choice of subject is of great significance, as the table bears a print label inscribed *Château des Tuileries/1929* and *1047 Salon de la famille du Roi.*

This table was made for Louis XVIII of France by Louis-François-Laurent Puteaux around 1815. The victory figures could, therefore, refer to the restoration of the Bourbon monarchy after the final exile of Napoleon in that year.

An exceptional piece, it is unusual for the period, as most pieces relied on well-figured veneers for decoration rather than parquetry.

A burr-elm and marquetry center table This piece has a circular swiveling top, with a central geometric-inlaid rosette and broad border. It is raised on a pentagonal column and supported on a concave-sided pentagonal plinth. The table rests on bun feet. Made by Louis-François-Laurent Puteaux. *c. 1815.* H:29¾ in (75.5 cm); Diam:55½ in (141 cm). PAR

Table top

The **trophies** of Science, Painting, Gardening, Architecture, Music, and Navigation are divided by green-stained wreaths.

The table top is inlaid with hundreds of triangular pieces of veneer carefully pieced together in a radiating pattern.

The pentagonal column has chamfered corners.

The column is decorated with winged figures of victory.

The plinth is decorated with laurel wreaths cast in gilt-bronze.

ELEMENTS OF STYLE

The two most influential countries in the early 19th century, France and Britain, looked rigorously—almost archaeologically—to the ancient civilizations of Egypt, Greece, and Rome for stylistic inspiration. From the late 1820s, they also began looking to the historical styles of their own countries, and Gothic (and later) motifs started to appear. Rich and diverse materials, often imported from far afield, combined to give furniture both luxurious comfort and a sense of the exotic.

Classical gilt-bronze chariot

Neoclassical motifs

Strict Grecian lines and Classical motifs characterize the decoration of the early 19th century. At times, even the ancient forms of furniture were copied, as in the case of the klismos chair. These motifs often took on a warlike or revolutionary tone, in the case of fasces or trophies of weapons.

Serpent motif

Brass fittings

In Britain, the vogue for brass fittings and inlays was revived during the first two decades of the century. The molded brass rope-twist was fashionable; the serpentine motif is a variation on this, inspired by ancient Egypt. On the Continent, gilt-bronze or ormolu mounts were more popular.

Detail from a brass-inlaid table top

Exoticism

Luxurious, exotic materials, such as calamander or amboyna, brass, ivory, mother-of-pearl, and tortoiseshell were used as veneers and inlays on furniture. Exotic motifs from China and India appeared on Regency furniture, while Empire-styled furniture looked to ancient Egypt and Rome for its influences.

Detail from an armchair

Bois clairs

The British stopped the import of mahogany from its colonies during the Napoleonic wars, so continental craftsmen turned, instead, to local, light-colored veneers, such as bird's-eye maple or walnut. Birch (shown in the example above) was more commonly used in Central Europe than in France.

Upholstered seat on a sofa

Textiles

Upholstery became increasingly important as sofas and chairs became more comfortable and windows were more elaborately dressed. Some rooms were even tented to look like a military camp. Popular fabrics included silks, damasks, and velvet in Regency stripes or Neoclassical motifs.

tail from a *guéridon* top

pecimen marble

pecimen marble tops were imported
om Italy at this time, or were bought
gentlemen on the Grand Tour, and
en placed on stands made in their
me country. Some countries also
ade use of local marble, such as
alachite in Russia, or Derbyshire
ones in England.

Ram's-head capping

Animal motifs

Animal motifs were popular with both
Regency and Empire designers. They
often capped pilasters, or casters, and
were carved, of gilded softwood or
gilt-metal. The swan motif is usually
associated with the Empress Josephine,
while fish motifs appear on a suite of
furniture marking Nelson's victories.

Detail from an Empire chest

Flame veneers

Although luxurious, flame veneers
had been characteristic of British 18th-
century furniture. An appreciation for
richly figured mahogany only entered
the French decorative vocabulary in
the late 18th century. As an essential
feature of the Empire style, this was
disseminated across the Continent.

Detail from a Regency cabinet

Gothic arches

From the late 1820s, most European
countries experienced a revival of
interest in the Gothic style. As a
consequence, features such as pointed
arches and crockets were sometimes
applied to Empire-style furniture.
King George IV, in fact, extended
Windsor Castle in the Gothic style.

etail from an occasional table

enwork

enwork is a type of decoration
panned in black and white, with the
etails worked in India ink. Typical
British design, penwork decorated
arious objects, from a tea caddy
an entire cabinet. Designs often
corporated Chinoiserie. Penwork
as a popular pastime for ladies.

Detail of a parquetry table top

Marquetry

Although large expanses of timber
were increasingly popular, marquetry
remained fashionable. Maggiolini
specialized in this technique in Italy,
while in Britain and France specimen
woods were sometimes arranged on
a table top in geometric parquetry
patterns, almost like specimen marble.

Brass mount

Lion-mask motif

The lion mask was especially popular
in Britain, where the motif was used
on table friezes, as a chute mount on
a side cabinet, or as the capping for
a table leg, to which the caster was
attached. It could also be made in
brass or gilt-metal as a loop handle
support—popular with Thomas Hope.

Detail from a bow front chest

Egyptiennerie

Napoleon's campaigns in Egypt
inspired a fashion for Egyptian motifs.
Furniture on both sides of the channel
was covered in sphinx heads, crocodile
motifs, lotus leaves, and palmettes.
However, designers only used motifs
at this time; Egyptian forms were not
copied on furniture until the 1920s.

FRANCE: *DIRECTOIRE/CONSULAT*

FOLLOWING THE REIGN OF TERROR in France, the *Directoire* was established in October 1795. It was followed by Napoleon's first government, the *Consulat*, which he established after a coup d'état in November 1799, appointing himself as First Consul. This survived until the declaration of the Empire in 1804. The styles that take their names from these political arrangements are difficult to tell apart, and represent a transition between the light, aristocratic Louis XVI style and the proud, austere Empire manner of the early 19th century. However, *Directoire* style or, as it was sometimes known, *le style républicain*, shows the effect of the Revolution on the style of Louis XVI, while the *Consulat* style lays the foundations of the Empire style.

DESIGN INFLUENCES

Directoire style shows the effect of a weakened economy and the position that cabinet-makers found themselves in after the period of the Convention (1792–95). The Revolution had deprived furniture-makers of their traditional patrons; furniture had even been burned beneath a Tree of Liberty in front of the celebrated Gobelins factory. The *Corporation des Menuisiers-Ébénistes* (Guild of Joiners and Cabinet-Makers), which had regulated not only standards but the organization of the industry, had also been disbanded in 1791. As a consequence, the *Directoire* style is simplified, smaller in scale than Louis XVI, and less costly, with minimal decoration and usually no marquetry or parquetry.

In the *Consulat* style, the design became more confident, reflecting France's pride in the new Republic and the slow return to stability and prosperity. The style was formal and rectilinear, and often included symbols of the Revolution such as the Phrygian or Liberty cap, bound fasces, arrows, spikes, clasped hands, and wreaths.

PATTERN BOOKS

In 1801, the architects Charles Percier and Pierre-François-Léonard Fontaine published their *Recueil des Décorations Intérieures*. This became the seminal pattern book of the period, and established them as the chief exponents of the nascent Empire style. The *Recueil* established strict and sober Classicism as the official style of the time: plain mahogany furniture

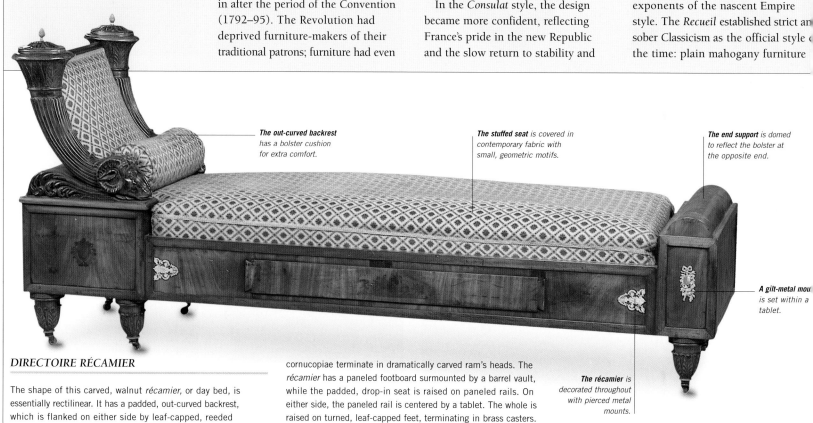

The out-curved backrest has a bolster cushion for extra comfort.

The stuffed seat is covered in contemporary fabric with small, geometric motifs.

The end support is domed to reflect the bolster at the opposite end.

A gilt-metal mount is set within a tablet.

The récamier is decorated throughout with pierced metal mounts.

DIRECTOIRE RÉCAMIER

The shape of this carved, walnut *récamier*, or day bed, is essentially rectilinear. It has a padded, out-curved backrest, which is flanked on either side by leaf-capped, reeded cornucopiae surmounted by finialed paterae. Below, the cornucopiae terminate in dramatically carved ram's heads. The *récamier* has a paneled footboard surmounted by a barrel vault, while the padded, drop-in seat is raised on paneled rails. On either side, the paneled rail is centered by a tablet. The whole is raised on turned, leaf-capped feet, terminating in brass casters. *c. 1800. H:37 in (97 cm); L:82 in (208.5 cm). SI*

DIRECTOIRE COMMODE

This commode is veneered in rosewood, kingwood, and a number of stained tropical woods. The rectangular case has a veined gray-white marble top with rounded corners above three drawers with geometric filets and inlay, and gilt-bronze mounts. It is supported on short, tapering legs. *c. 1800. W:52 in (130 cm). GK*

DIRECTOIRE CHIFFONIER

This small table-chiffonier is made from walnut and has two drawers, with an additional shelf below. The rectangular case has brass filets and is supported on fluted legs joined by a shelf and terminating in small, *toupie* feet. *c. 1800. H:29¼ in (74.5 cm). JR*

ith bold, antique-inspired gilt-bronze ounts became fashionable. Percier d Fontaine owed much to Jean-emosthène Dugoure, who had signed strict Neoclassical interiors r both royal and private residences ring Louis XVI's reign. Percier and ntaine had both studied architecture France and Italy and so had first-nd experience of the ruins of cient Rome. In the very last years the 18th century, they oversaw the ecoration of the Music Room and brary of the Empress's house at almaison, and supervised the design the furniture, which was made by apoleon's favorite furniture-makers,

the Jacob brothers. It was this commission that earned them the role of quasi-court designers.

ANTIQUE MOTIFS

The orators and pamphleteers of the Revolution praised the moral values of the ancient world, which found visual expression in the work of the great revolutionary artist Jacques-Louis David. This filtered into the decorative vocabulary of the *style à l'antique*.

Consulat furniture is full of Greek and Roman devices that became the stock repertoire of Empire designers. The purity of Classical design, epitomized in the work of Jacob-

Desmalter, became a hallmark of the furniture of the period. As in Britain, this was occasionally combined with Egyptian motifs inspired by Napoleon's campaigns and his victory at the Battle of the Pyramids. This was supplemented by Baron Denon's publication, *Voyage dans la Basse et Haute-Égypte*, in 1802. The archaeologist and engraver (who later became director of the Musée

Napoléon at the Louvre) became the leading authority on antiquity, and had a considerable influence both in France and Britain.

This taste for all things Egyptian commonly manifested itself in sphinx heads, which were often used to top pilasters, terminate armrests, or support console tables, as on a fine, mahogany example supplied to the Elysée Palace.

CONSULAT BERGÈRES

Each of this pair of mahogany and mahogany-veneered *bergères* has an upholstered back, side panels, and seat. The chair backs themselves are slightly reclining. The loose cushioned seats are supported on square-section, tapering legs, which are surmounted by stylized Egyptian female heads and terminate in outsplayed, square-section feet. Originally, the chairs would have been covered in silk and would have formed part of a large, similarly styled suite. *Early 19th century. H:36⅔ in (93 cm). ANB*

CRÉTAIRE À ABBATANT

is *Consulat secrétaire à abbatant* is made of lnut and is designed in the Egyptian-revival le. The body of the piece is flanked by yptian female masks above tapering pilasters bronze brasses. The upper section has a gray

marble top above a long drawer. The fall front drops down to reveal a leather-lined writing surface. The lower section consists of three long drawers with lion's mask handles. The *secrétaire* still retains its original bronze mounts. The piece terminates in carved claw feet. *c. 1800. H:60 in (150 cm). CSB*

BUREAU PLAT

The surface of this mahogany desk is faced with gilt-tooled black leather. Below is a long kneehole frieze drawer, flanked by two deeper drawers; all are edged with ebony stringing. At each corner of the frieze is a mount in the form

of a satyr. The table is supported on four octagonal, tapering legs with ormolu collars and ball-shaped sabots. *c. 1800. H:30 in (76 cm); W:65 in (165 cm); D:34 in (86.5 cm). PAR*

FRENCH EMPIRE

NAPOLEON CROWNED HIMSELF Emperor in 1804. From this date until his abdication in 1814, and his final defeat by Wellington at the Battle of Waterloo in 1815, he dominated the European scene. Moreover, his taste, and the Empire style that he cultivated, became omnipresent in Europe.

Already emerging before 1804, this austere style sought to associate Napoleon's Empire with the glories of ancient Egypt and ancient Rome. This aim manifested itself in an almost archaeological interest in Classical motifs, promoted by Percier and Fontaine, whose *Recueil* was republished in 1812. The light style of furniture that prevailed before the turn of the century was now transformed into a truly imperial idiom in keeping with Napoleon's despotic tendencies.

EMPIRE MOUNTS

Neoclassical influences are evident in the ubiquitous bronze *doré* mounts on Empire furniture: griffons, lions, and sphinxes abound. Martial motifs, such as trophies or crossed swords, were especially popular. Some of the best-quality mounts were produced in the workshop of Pierre Thomire. His mounts appear on furniture by Beneman and Weisweiler. Other Beneman pieces are known to have similar, high-quality appliqué details made by Antoine-André Ravario.

EMPIRE MAKERS

The dissolution of the Guild of Joiners and Cabinet-Makers in 1791 meant that craftsmen could now establish workshops comprising several trades in a single location. The workshops of the *ancien régime* were quick to reopen after the Revolution, seeking a wider, often middle-class, clientele, who were sometimes less demanding. Some feared that this might lead to a decline in quality French furniture. However, the finest pieces, made for the Emperor and his circle, reveal the same technical brilliance as items produced in the previous century. Many of the great *ébénistes* had previously worked for Louis XVI, including Bellanger, Beneman, Georges Jacob, Molitor, and Weisweiler. It was also a period of great productivity:

The frieze is decorated with a central gilt-bronze rosette, flanked by palmettes.

The protruding columns have gilt-bronze capitals and bases.

Column base detail

Gilt-bronze rosette

The drawers are decorated with carved, gilt-bronze swing handles.

The escutcheons have Neoclassical ormolu mounts.

This boxlike plinth base is typical of Empire commodes.

MAHOGANY AND MAHOGANY-VENEERED COMMODE

Beneath the rectangular, gray-fossil marble top is a frieze with one drawer. The commode front is slightly recessed, with three drawers flanked by protruding columns ending in rounded feet. *Early 19th century. H:35¼ in (89.5 cm); W:50 in (127 cm); D:23¼ in (59 cm). ANB*

MAHOGANY SETTEE

This ormolu-mounted settee is made of mahogany and has a rectangular, padded back applied with gilt-bronze mounts of figures, hounds, urns, rosettes, and palmettes, above a padded seat. The scrolled arms have carved, gilt leaf-tips. The settee is raised on short, scroll feet carved with leaves. *Early 19th century. W:72 in (180 cm). S&K*

FAUTEUIL DE BUREAU

The mahogany chair has a concave top rail above a pierced, trellis-pattern back. The curved arms are supported on ebonized winged lions. The upholstered seat is supported on a plain seat rail on ring-turned front legs and saber back legs. *c. 1800. H:37 in (94 cm; W:26½ in (67 cm); D:23 in (60 cm). PAR*

tween 1810 and 1811, as much as 7,000 francs was spent on furniture r Imperial residences, and half a illion francs went to Georges Jacob- esmalter alone for furniture made r the Palais des Tuileries. There ere 10,000 workers involved with rniture production in Paris during e first decade of the 19th century, aking pieces for both the local and xport markets. Jacob-Desmalter nployed at least 88 workers, some his Porte Saint-Denis workshop. Upholstery and drapery sometimes verpowered the Empire room. eilings could be tented in strong, sually striped, colors (blues, reds, greens, and yellows) to echo tented military accommodation. The embroidered patterns on chair upholstery were both large and bold.

NOVEL FORMS

Several novel forms also appeared. The *lit en bateau* was very fashionable, often with scrolled ends, raised on a dais, and draped in fabric. It was similar in form to the *récamier*, or day bed, and the *méridienne*, a type of sofa with scrolled ends, one higher than the other. For middle-class homes, the less expensive *lit droit* was popular; it had a headboard under a triangular pediment. For the first time, bedrooms were furnished with a Psyche mirror, or Cheval glass. The small, round *guéridon*, or candlestand, served a variety of functions, and sometimes had metal legs, patinated green to simulate ancient metals, possibly set with a porphyry top.

The commode slowly became more functional and occasionally the drawers were set behind doors. Chairs were often supported by Grecian saber back legs, and had either rectangular or over-scrolled backs. Usually the arms were supported on human or swan forms. Empress Josephine's dressing room at Fontainebleau probably houses the most famous Empire chairs—those with a curved back *en gondole*.

Finally, there were various furniture forms for writing, from the boxlike *secrétaire à abattant* (and its relative the *secrétaire de compiègne*) to the *bureau plat*, which assumed grand and monumental proportions under the Empire.

ARMCHAIRS "AUX TÊTES DE LION"

These chairs are made of mahogany. Each has a simple, rectilinear back, an upholstered seat and back, and armrests terminating in lion's heads. The padded, upholstered seats are supported on saber legs, with those at the front terminating in lion's-paw feet. The chairs are attributed to the maker Jean-Baptiste Demay of Paris. Although lion's masks appear frequently on British furniture of the period, they are a relatively unusual feature on French Empire pieces. *1805–10. H:35⅛ in (91 cm); W:22⅞ in (58 cm); D:18⅛ in (46 cm). GK*

NAPOLEON BONAPARTE

FRENCH FURNITURE EXCELLED DURING NAPOLEON'S ERA DUE TO HIS PATRONAGE AND MILITARY CONQUESTS, WHICH HELPED SPREAD EMPIRE STYLE.

The Empire style was born from a merger of art and political aspirations in a heady, post-Revolution atmosphere of social and economic upheaval. It was largely shaped by Napoleon's powerful personality, and his awareness that formal grandeur had great propaganda value. The new style reflected Napoleon's desire for clean designs that incorporated his preference for masculine and military effects. Popular Empire forms and furnishings include tented beds, camp stools, consoles and the *table de toilette*.

Once Napoleon was crowned Emperor in 1804, he set up a dynamic art and design program, choosing Charles Percier and Pierre-François-Léonard Fontaine to be his official architects and decorators. Their famous pattern book, *Recueil de Décorations Intérieures*, gave furniture pride of place and influenced cabinet-making in much of Europe.

Due to Napoleon's patronage, Paris regained its position as the center for fine cabinet-making, and his military conquests—he installed relatives as rulers in various European countries— helped to spread this art as far as Russia.

Napoleon personally oversaw the establishment of new factories to ensure the highest quality of furniture and bronze production. Through the *Garde-Meuble Impérial*, which was responsible for the furnishings of the Imperial Palaces and oversaw their execution by cabinet-makers and bronze founders, he also refurnished the royal palaces in the

Napoleon Bonaparte

austere, military style that reflected his life in the field. The palaces had been emptied during the Revolution, and some of the contents were auctioned abroad. Bonaparte took over Saint Cloud in 1802, quickly ordering complete suites of furniture. The Palace of Fontainebleau was also redecorated for Pope Pius VII in 1804, and Versailles, St. Germain, and the Elysée Palace, among many others, were all treated to new, Classically-inspired furnishings.

The most famous Napoleonic house was the Château de Malmaison, acquired by his wife, Josephine, in 1799. It was redecorated by Percier and Fontaine, and furnished by the Jacob brothers. The building is covered in the motifs associated with Napoleon: the gilt "N" within laurels, his heraldic device of bees, and the Roman imperial eagle. The Empress Josephine's furniture was often embellished with a swan motif.

TRIC TRAC TABLE

This fine-quality flame-veneered tric trac, or game, table has a removable writing table top with inset brass corners and a baize playing-card surface on the reverse. Each side has one false drawer and one drawer for playing pieces. The table stands on square, tapering legs terminating in brass casters. *c. 1810. H:28 in (71 cm); W:44 in (112 cm); D:22 in (56 cm). MAL*

FRANCE: RESTAURATION

THE *RESTAURATION* STYLE, as its name suggests, refers to the restoration of the Bourbon monarchy from the expulsion and final exile of Napoleon in 1815, until its fall in 1830.

Louis XVIII became King of France in 1815 and was followed in 1824 by Charles X, who finally abdicated in 1830 in favor of the exiled Duc d'Orléans, Louis Philippe. It was a period of considerable political unrest, culminating in the revolutions of 1830 and 1848, which forced Louis Philippe to flee to England.

The market for furniture also changed, with growing interest from the middle classes and the increasing

industrialization of furniture-making due to improved tools and the use of steam. Fortuitously, this coincided with the need to furnish apartments, which, for the first time, the middle classes could rent.

CHANGING STYLES

Empire decoration remained the leading style of furniture, and many of the cabinet-makers who had worked in the Empire style, such as Jacob-Desmalter, Felix Rémond, and P. A. Bellanger, continued to produce furniture with a great deal of success.

However, Napoleonic motifs and mounts gradually disappeared, and the

Empire style was slowly watered down as severity gave way to comfort. Strict linearity eventually relaxed into the occasional curve in a nostalgia for Rococo style. Overall, forms became heavier and more solid, replacing the Empire love of rectilinear elegance. As elsewhere in Europe, furniture became bulkier. Inlays became more common and mounts gradually became smaller, or disappeared altogether.

STYLE DIFFERENCES
Restauration-style furniture can sometimes be difficult to distinguish from the

simpler, more domestic Empire piece (*see pp.200–01*). The surfaces of *Restauration* pieces tend to be even simpler and less decorated than those found on French Empire furniture, which was typically designed to creat an opulent effect.

SECRÉTAIRE À ABATTANT

This flame-veneered mahogany writing cabinet is raised on claw feet and has a molded cornice above a pair of Gothic-carved, glazed doors, enclosing shelves, above drawers. A frieze drawer fitted for writing is set above cupboard doors flanked by scrolls. *c. 1820.* H:76¾ in (196 cm); W:40 in (107 cm); D:23⅝ in (60 cm). PIL

DRESSING TABLE
This is a mahogany dressing table with a swing-frame mirror set above a platform with two small drawers above another drawer. The dressing table stands on C-scroll supports and has a shaped platform base. *c. 1825.* H:70 in (178 cm); W:26¾ in (68 cm); D:17¾ in (45 cm). PIL

CHARLES X DRESSING TABLE
This dressing table is made of burr elm inlaid with amaranth depicting stylized foliage. The top section has an oval mirror wi carved supports in the shape of swans. The table top is made white marble. The lower section consists of a frieze drawer abov two carved consoles. The piece terminates in a shaped platform base and flattened bun feet. *1825–30.* H:30 in (141 cm). BEA

FAUTEUILS AUX DAUPHINS
This set of six mahogany armchairs, made by Pierre-Antoine Bellanger, has straight top rails terminating in carved scrolls. The curved arms are carved with dolphin heads and each chair has a padded, upholstered seat with a plain seat rail and is supported on saber legs. *c. 1815.* H:36½ in (91 cm). GK

BOIS CLAIRS

Restauration furniture was usually made of oak, but it was increasingly veneered in lighter woods, the so-called *bois clairs*. This change in tone began in 1806, when the British blockaded the importation of mahogany to France from its colonies. As a result, local woods became more popular, including walnut, sycamore, ash, elm, yew, plane, beech, and, perhaps most characteristically of all, decorative bird's-eye maple.

Mahogany, being expensive, was reserved for the most lavish interiors, so its use was often an indicator of the high value of a piece of furniture.

Traditionally, the Duchesse de Berry, the daughter-in-law of Charles X, is credited with the introduction of *bois clairs*, but this appears to be an unfounded myth. Mahogany, however, continued to be extensively employed both as a veneer—where the decorative effect of its figure was much exploited—and in the solid.

With the decline in use of mounts, various timbers, particularly ebony, and metals such as brass or pewter, were inlaid instead. However, their treatment was always restrained. Some furniture even included plaques of painted porcelain.

GOTHIC STYLE

Towards the end of the *Restauration* period, the Romantic-revival styles gradually became evident in French furniture design.

These were probably first hinted at in Pierre de La Mésangère's *Collection de meubles et objets de goût*, published between 1802 and 1835 in the *Journal des Dames et des Modes*. Here, La Mésangère adapted the severe, architectural style of Percier and Fontaine to create a simple, domestic style for the middle classes. He also began introducing the motifs that

would dominate the next epoch—Gothic motifs, otherwise known as the Troubadour style.

Unlike the Chinese style, which was completely forgotten in early 19th-century France but played an important role in Britain at the time, the Gothic style did create a small impact. For example, in 1804, the cabinet-maker Mansion the Younger suggested a Gothic-style piece for Napoleon.

However, it was not until the late 1820s and 30s that the pointed arches so typical of the Gothic style started appearing on Empire-style furniture.

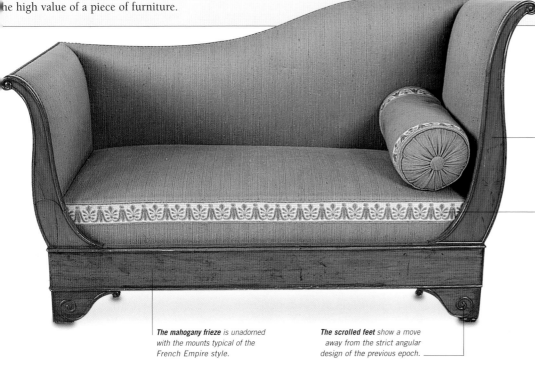

The scrolled side support is only decorated by moldings to the edges.

Detail of bolster

The decorative motifs are Neoclassical in style.

The mahogany frieze is unadorned with the mounts typical of the French Empire style.

The scrolled feet show a move away from the strict angular design of the previous epoch.

MÉRIDIENNE

This mahogany *méridienne* has one end higher than the other, and an elegant, curved, padded back. The frame of the sofa has scrolling sides, a plain frieze, and stands on volute feet. *c. 1820–30. H:34⅔ in (88 cm); W:58¼ in (148 cm); D:26⅛ in (67 cm). PIL*

CIRCULAR CENTER TABLE

This table is made from rosewood inlaid with fruitwood and marquetry. The circular top, and the four frieze drawers below, are raised on a columnar support, which has four splayed legs that terminate in paw feet on brass casters. *c. 1830. H:30½ in 77.5 cm); W:47¾ in (121.5 cm).*

CHARLES X OCCASIONAL TABLE

The top of this oval rosewood table is inlaid with a panel of Gothic tracery and is bordered with a boxwood rolled molding. The frieze has a single writing-slide drawer. The table stands on six turned legs joined by a double-baluster stretcher. *c. 1830. H:28 in (71 cm); W:33 in (84 cm); D:19 in (48 cm). MAL*

MARBLE-TOPPED TABLE

This table has a black-and-gray-veined Saint Anne marble top set above a plain frieze. The massive columnar support is baluster-shaped although it has been faceted. The three scrolled feet are similarly angular and are square in section. *H:28 in (71 cm); Diam:38⅛ in (97 cm). PIL*

ITALY

LIKE MANY OTHER European states, the majority of the Italian states and kingdoms followed the lead of Paris. The greatest French-style furniture and interiors were created during the period of Napoleonic patronage, in the first decade of the 19th century. The French Emperor installed his brothers as rulers in Italy: Joseph became King of Naples and Lucian became Prince of Canino. Napoleon's sisters also created significant interiors in the area: Elisa Baciocchi in Lucca and Florence, Pauline Borghese in Rome, and Caroline Murat in Naples. But it was not just aristocratic patrons who commissioned the cabinet-makers: one of the period's characteristics was the emergence of middle-class buyers. This widening of the market coincided with the beginnings of mechanization and the gradual organization of the workshop—a trend that continued throughout the 19th century.

ITALIAN EMPIRE

In some ways, the French Empire style did not suit Italian furniture-makers. Its emphasis on large expanses of high-quality lumber was a significant problem in an area where this was difficult to find. Also, its rectilinear forms and strict, sober lines seemed antithetical to a furniture tradition that favored sculptural qualities. However, symmetry and balance, with few curves and little ornament apart from Neoclassical gilt-bronze mounts, eventually dominated Italian furniture production. To overcome the problem of poor-quality timber, many pieces were painted—white, pale blue, and eau-de-nil were popular colors. Classical architectural forms were favored, along with motifs from Imperial Rome, such as trophies of instruments or weapons, fasces (banded rods), laurel wreaths, and antique lamps.

FRENCH IMPORTS

The Grand Duchess of Tuscany (one of Napoleon's sisters) actually brought French *ébénistes* to Florence to establish workshops and impart their skills and techniques to the Italians. Mounts were also imported from France. Consequently, it is almost impossible to differentiate between the French Empire furniture in the Palazzo Pitti in Florence and the Italian variants. The Empire style remained in fashion after 1815, sometimes combined with French *Restauration* styles, but the use of mahogany declined in favor of walnut or lighter-colored timber.

During this period, Italy was made up of a patchwork of small states and kingdoms, dominated by Austro-Hungary in the north. Regional diversity was, therefore, far greater than in Britain or France, and much of the furniture produced echoes the traditions for which they are famous: Classical in Rome, Baroque in Florence, and Rococo in Venice. Lombardy produced some of the greatest innovators of the era, particularly Giocondo Albertolli, who trained at the *Accademia di Brera* and who published his influential *Corso elementare d'ornamenti architettonici* in 1805.

The study of Umberto I This shows a room in the Palazzo Pitti in Florence. Under Elisa Baciocchi, Napoleon's sister and Grand Duchess of Tuscany, several rooms in the palace were redecorated to reflect Paris fashions.

CARVED MIRROR

This carved and gilded mirror frame is decorated with masks of grotesques at the corners. The pediment is richly decorated with baskets overflowing with flowers. *c. 1800. H:63 in (160 cm); W:33½ in (85 cm). BEA*

MURANO MIRROR

This mirror has an applied crystal pediment and a frame with C- and S-scrolls at the corners. The oval mirror is surrounded by mirror sections engraved with leaves and divided with molding. *Early 19th century. H:80¾ in (205 cm).*

GILTWOOD SIDE CHAIR

These two Neoclassical giltwood side chairs form part of a set of six Cardinal Fesch chairs; Fesch, a Corsican cardinal, became French ambassador to Rome in 1804. Each chair has a richly carved, domed back depicting a pair of carved griffins above a stylized serpentine floral carving on a punched ground. The upright back supports are in the form of fluted pilasters with a frieze of running husks. The padded seats have fluted seat rails and are raised on gilded lion's-paw legs. *c. 1810. H:44½ in (103 cm); W:22 in (56 cm); D:18 in (46 cm). MAL*

The massive table top is veneered with marble.

The frieze is inset with marble panels that match the table top.

Caryatids support the table top.

Stop-fluted corner

The table legs are inset with marble panels.

ARMCHAIR *AUX TÊTES DE LION*

This mahogany armchair has a gently curved top rail, an X-frame back, and armrests terminating in carved and gilded lions' heads. The X-frame base has gilded paw feet. *c. 1810.* H:33 in (84 cm); W:22⅞ in (58 cm); D:21⅔ in (55 cm). GK

GILTWOOD AND *VERDE ANTICO* SIDE TABLE

This rectangular table has a *verde antico* (old green) veneered marble top above a frieze inset with matching marble panels and fluted corners. The square, tapering legs are also inset with marble panels and are surmounted by carved caryatids, whose hands support the table top. *c. 1800.* H:40½ in (103 cm); W:75½ in (192 cm); D:31½ in (80 cm).

MAGGIOLINI

THE MOST FAMOUS NEOCLASSICAL FURNITURE-MAKER OF THE LATE 18TH AND EARLY 19TH CENTURY, MAGGIOLINI IS ASSOCIATED WITH A PARTICULAR STYLE OF MARQUETRY.

Inset of Classical figure

Giuseppe Maggiolini (1738–1814) made furniture that was austere, boxy, and unpretentious in form, with no carving and few mounts. However, its characteristic pictorial marquetry lent his work a brilliant opulence. Maggiolini used many different types and colors of wood to create his marquetry pictures, shunning stains, artificial coloring, and other tricks to achieve decorative effects. In the tradition of Piranesi and, more recently, the ornamental designer and interior decorator Giocondo Albertolli, he produced marquetry trophies, still-lifes, Chinoiserie, and *caprici*. As a result, his name is used to refer to all work of this type, whether produced in his workshop or not.

Maggiolini started his career as a carpenter in a Cistercian monastery, where he established his first workshop in 1771. He later founded a second workshop in Milan, which was inherited by his son, Carlo Francesco, and Cherubino Mezzanzanica. He crafted some of his most brilliant furniture for the Archduke Ferdinand of Austria, who was the Governor General of Lombardy, and the King of Poland was also one of his clients.

In keeping with the tastes of his age, Maggiolini's furniture is simple in design and follows late 18th-century French prototypes. Its defining difference is the intricate marquetry; in Italy this had a long tradition stretching back to Renaissance intarsia works.

Louis XVI commode This rectilinear, marble-topped piece, from the studio of Guiseppe Maggiolini in Milan, is made from rosewood and several exotic woods with inlays of Classical figures in medallions and interlacing festoons. The commode has three drawers with bronze mounts and is supported on square, tapering legs. *c. 1800.* W:48¾ in (122 cm). GK

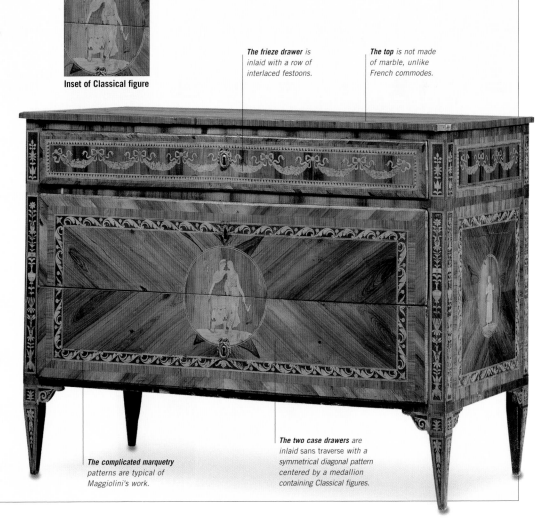

The frieze drawer is inlaid with a row of interlaced festoons.

The top is not made of marble, unlike French commodes.

The complicated marquetry patterns are typical of Maggiolini's work.

The two case drawers are inlaid sans traverse with a symmetrical diagonal pattern centered by a medallion containing Classical figures.

REGENCY BRITAIN

THE REGENCY WAS a clearly defined period in British history. From 1811 to 1820, the Prince of Wales, who later became George IV, ruled instead of his father, who was suffering from porphyria—a form of madness. However, as a furniture style, Regency has come to embrace a wider time frame, from the 1790s to the third decade of the 19th century.

Reflecting the exuberant tastes of the Regent himself, the period begins with his commission of the Neoclassical architect Henry Holland for his London home, Carlton House, in the 1780s, and concludes with the exotic, Oriental confection that is John Nash's

Brighton Pavilion, remodeled for the Prince of Wales between 1815 and 1823. George, the Prince Regent, came to dominate taste in the early 19th century. He and his circle drew on a diverse group of talented architects and artisans, often trained in France, many of whom had worked on Carlton House. These included the architect Charles Heathcote Tatham, the decorators and cabinet-makers Morel and Hughes, and the clock-maker Benjamin Vulliamy.

The Circular Room at Carlton House, London The Prince of Wales's London residence was designed in the finest Regency style. The room is decorated with Neoclassical motifs and furnishings. *1819.*

The padded seat has an upholstered, tasseled bolster cushion for extra comfort and support.

The upholstery is buttoned, woven silk.

The back rail is inlaid in brass with a Greek-key pattern.

Attenuated, elegant S-shapes are typical of Regency furniture.

The front rail and highly scrolled ends are inlaid with trailing foliage and flowers, terminating in floral paterae.

The seat rail is inlaid with a trailing brass foliate motif.

The design of the chaise longue is influenced by the contemporary French form, the méridienne—a type of sofa with scrolled ends, one higher than the other.

Saber legs terminate in lion's-paw feet and casters.

Brass inlay detail

CHAISE LONGUE

This elegant Regency chaise longue is made of rosewood and is profusely inlaid throughout with brass inlay in a foliate design. The frame has a sweeping back rail that is centered with a scrolled hand grip, and has highly decorative scrolled end supports. The generously padded seat and arms are supported on a rectilinear front rail decorated with a foliate motif. The piece stands on outswept saber legs that terminate in lion's-paw feet on casters. *c. 1810. H:34 in (86 cm); L:72 in (183 cm); D:28 in (71 cm). MAL*

URNITURE STYLE

egency furniture is often symmetrical ith clean, rectilinear lines. As such, was inspired by French Empire rniture and the simple late 18th-ntury furniture designs of Thomas heraton. Large surfaces were often eneered in highly figured rosewood d then decorated with gilt-brass ounts of ancient motifs, such as settes, paterae, laurels, and anthemia. he Liverpool cabinet-maker George

Bullock is best known for his use of patterned surfaces; he frequently balanced English timbers, especially oak, with a riot of border patterns featuring stylized flower-heads, lotus leaves, and dot motifs.

The strict Neoclassical taste found its most archaeological expression in the designs of Thomas Hope, which he published in 1807. Not only had he plundered ancient Egypt, Greece, and Rome for decorative ideas, but he also attempted to recreate ancient furniture and interiors. Probably the most typical furniture of this type is the rounded klismos chair—first known to have been produced in ancient

Greece—which has back stiles that rise from outswept saber legs to support an almost semicircular back.

During this period, a wide variety of side cabinets of diverse outlines came to dominate the wall space in drawing rooms, replacing the use of commodes. In the dining room, a similar role was performed by the popular sideboard and chiffonier.

ECLECTICISM

It would be a mistake, however, to see the Regency as simply a curvaceous and light Neoclassical style. It was characterized by endless variety, a freedom of forms, and an eclectic

ornamental vocabulary. George Smith, who published a pattern book the year after Hope, reinterpreted his cold, academic designs by applying Neoclassical motifs to French Empire models that also included Gothic- and Chinese-inspired furniture. Indeed, exotic forms and materials became the hallmark of Regency taste. Smith popularized Hope's designs in his pattern book, introducing them to a wider public.

Smith inspired impressive-looking furniture, with boldly carved leopard's masks or large lion's-paw feet, which anticipated the slightly heavier furniture of the 1820s and 30s.

MALL CENTER TABLE

e surface of this tilt-top table has a painted ene within a laburnum veneer border. It is pported on a rosewood-veneered stem, on a se with scrolled, ribbed feet on brass casters. rly 19th century. D:34 in (86 cm). WW

MAHOGANY STOOL

This Regency mahogany stool has a gently shaped rectangular seat with scrolled ends and light carving on the surface. It is supported on an X-frame base with simple, carved decoration and stretchers. c. 1810. W:20 in (51 cm). DL

DWARF SIDE CABINET

The rosewood and black-lacquer breakfront cabinet has a mottled gray marble top above a frieze with a central female mask. The central cupboard door is inset with a late 17th-century black-lacquer Japanese panel. The curving

sides have open shelves with mirror backs and pierced brass galleries. The whole stands on bold paw feet. Unlike gilt-bronze mounts in France, those on this cabinet are likely to be gilt-brass. c. 1810. H:33 in (84 cm); W:79½ in (202 cm); D:20 in (51 cm). PAR

CARLTON HOUSE WRITING TABLE.

This mahogany writing table has a three-quarter brass gallery and a central, pull-out insert. There are six drawers behind a lift-up flap, two drawers on either side, and two in the frieze, supported on slender, turned legs. c. 1800. H:37 in (93 cm); W:46½ in (118 cm); D:24 in (62 cm). NOA

LIBRARY TABLE

The rectangular top of this rosewood library table is inlaid with a Greek-key border in satinboard and ebony. The frieze has a central pierced ormolu palmette and two drawers. The bowed legs are headed by gilt lion's heads and

terminate in lion's-paw feet, joined by a shaped stretcher. c. 1810. H:29 in (74 cm); W:44¾ in (113.5 cm); D:28 in (71 cm). PAR

BRITISH EXOTICISM

A RICH MIX OF BOTH FOREIGN AND HOME-GROWN
INFLUENCES AFFECTED THE DESIGN OF BRITISH
FURNITURE DURING THE REGENCY PERIOD.

FROM MOGUL DOMES to Islamic arches, Regency
designers drew on a wide variety of exotic sources.
When Napoleon invaded Egypt in July 1798, his
invasion force included not only soldiers, but artists
and poets, botanists, zoologists, and cartographers.
The ensuing publication of *Descriptions de l'Egypt*
established a vogue in France for all things Egyptian.

ANCIENT EGYPT
The Egyptian craze surfaced in Britain following
Nelson's subsequent defeat of Napoleon in 1798 at
the Battle of the Nile. Sphinx heads appeared on the
pilasters of bookcases and side cabinets and lotus
leaves were carved on chair splats and printed on
textiles and wallpaper designs.

Thomas Hope designed furniture based on the
engravings of French Egyptologist Baron Denon,
and Thomas Chippendale the Younger, who had
inherited his father's famous workshop, created a
suite of furniture for Stourhead in 1805, resplendent
with sphinx masks. These pieces were made in
mahogany, but the foreign motifs of the period were
often complemented by the use of highly polished,
unusual, imported timbers: streaky calamander, dark
ebony, or flecked amboyna.

CHINOISERIE REVIVAL
An integral part of the Rococo repertoire in Britain
during the mid-18th century, Chinoiserie enjoyed a
revival in the early 19th century. The Royal architect,

A DWARF GOTHIC CABINET
*This lacquered cabinet has a crenellated
upper section with octagonal corner
towers. A deeper base with a pierced
quatrefoil gallery sits above a pair of
tracery paneled doors flanked by
clasping buttresses. The cabinet
stands on a plinth base.* Early 19th
century. H:67¼ in (168 cm). L&T

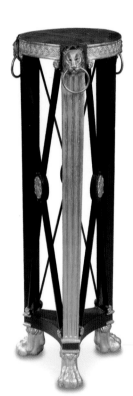

REGENCY *TORCHÈRE* STAND
*This stand is made of bronzed and
gilded wood. Below the top is a
guilloche molded frieze and three gilt
supports, with lion masks, joined by
cross supports with applied rosettes.
The concave base rests on gilt paw
feet.* H:39½ in (99 cm). L&T

A CHINESE EXPORT BUREAU
*This bureau has a fall front above
three drawers, a shaped apron, and
is raised on cabriole legs. All the
surfaces are black and gilt lacquered
with lake scenery and flowers.*
19th century. H:36⅔ in (93 cm);
W:28⅓ in (72 cm). DN

THOMAS HOPE

THE MOST CELEBRATED OF ALL THE REGENCY DESIGNERS, THOMAS HOPE ENCAPSULATED THE LOVE
OF ANCIENT DECORATIVE MOTIFS THAT INSPIRED THE FURNITURE DESIGN OF THE PERIOD.

Thomas Hope came from a wealthy banking family, but established himself as one of the the early 19th century's foremost connoisseurs of furniture and antiquities. He also appears to have designed his own furniture. In 1807, he published a pattern book, *Household Furniture and Interior Decoration,* which showed the interiors, furniture, and individual motifs of his house on Duchess Street in London. The Grecian interiors were archaeological in style and featured both Greco-Roman and Egyptian pieces. Classical X-frame

stools appear in the prints, as do klismos chairs, their large bar-backs decorated with strigules (serpentine flutes) copied from Roman sarcophagi.

Hope is probably best remembered for the masks that appear in his engravings. Inspired by Greek tragic and comic masks, they were repeatedly used on Regency furniture, often as gilt-brass mounts. Some of the furniture from Hope's Surrey mansion, Deepdene, survives, as does his famous collection of antique marbles in the Lady Lever Art Gallery.

Giltwood and bronzed stool This rectangular stool has ends in the form of griffins with gilt wings and heads. The buttoned cushion is upholstered in green velvet and supported on the griffins' outstretched legs. *c. 1810.* H:28 in (71 cm); W:42 in (106.5 cm); D:19 in (48 cm). PAR

Mahogany X-frame chair This has been made according to a Thomas Hope design, which is in the style of the curule chairs of ancient Rome. *1800–10.* H:38 in (96.5 cm); W:23 in (59 cm); D:19½ in (49.5 cm). JK

Circular *guéridon* With its *pietra dura* top, this piece emulates the Empire style of Thomas Hope. It has lion's-head motifs and a tripod base with large, gilded, bronze, claw feet. *Late 19th century.* Diam:43½ in (109 cm). GK

Henry Holland, was profoundly influenced by Sir George Staunton's *An Authentic Account of an Embassy from the King of Great Britain to the Emperor of China in 1797*; and interest in East Asia increased after Napoleon's defeat in 1815, when further British envoys were sent to the new emperor of China, Chia-ch'ing.

Furniture was japanned black with gilt to simulate lacquer—as in the late 17th century—while lacquer cabinets (or lacquer panels reused from early screens) were incorporated into British cabinet work. Oriental bamboo was also echoed in the ring turnings on late Regency chairs. Many pieces of furniture were made out of genuine bamboo, while others were turned and painted to simulate it.

The Prince Regent gave the royal seal of approval to this trend when he furnished several rooms at the Brighton Pavilion with bamboo furniture imported from China. Indeed, this architectural folly became the most famous melting pot of all the exotic styles of the Regency period.

Western styles of lacquer and bamboo furniture were also imported from Canton. The trade in goods from China to Britain had been established since the early 17th century, but the scale of Chinese imports in the 19th century was unprecedented. As well as imported, Chinoiserie-style furniture, Oriental motifs such as dragons appeared on the crestings of convex mirrors, while latticework and Chinese paneling were applied to chair backs, commode friezes, or brass grills on side cabinets or chiffoniers.

STYLES FROM THE SUBCONTINENT

India, as well as China, influenced the decoration of the Brighton Pavilion. Nash was inspired by William and Thomas Daniell's book, *Oriental Scenery,* and included pierced screens, copied from Indian *jails* (perforated stone screens from Madhya Pradesh), in his designs. The interest in India manifested itself more in the importation of Western-style furniture than in the application of Indian motifs to British furniture. Exotic ivory-inlaid rosewood furniture and boxes came from Vizagapatam, and ebony chairs of Regency form were shipped from Ceylon.

HISTORICISM

Toward the end of the Regency period, designers and furniture-makers turned away from exoticism and toward their own traditions for inspiration. The Napoleonic wars and their subsequent victories spawned a surge in nationalist feeling. This, along with the historic novels of Walter Scott, inspired designers such as George Bullock and Richard Bridgens to include Elizabethan and Jacobean motifs in furniture for Abbotsford and Aston Hall in the late 1810s and early 1820s. Gothic motifs were always prevalent, particularly as tracery in glazing bars and in panels for cabinet doors. Pointed arches appeared as early as 1807 in the backs of hall chairs published by George Smith. This furniture, often commissioned by a new breed of antiquarian collectors such as William Beckford, was usually made in oak or other native woods.

BRITISH VERNACULAR

THE VERNACULAR FURNITURE of the first 20 years of the 19th century has more in common with the light, elegant furniture of the late 18th century than with high-style furniture in the style of Thomas Hope. It was usually made of mahogany, either solid or used as a veneer, or the newly popular rosewood. Pieces were also constructed of inexpensive timbers, such as beech, and then painted to simulate rosewood or more exotic woods. Penwork, often the pastime of young ladies, was also used to decorate cheaper woods. Here, once again, the Regency pictorial fascination with surface pattern and large, flat expanses of timber is evident.

It was also during the early 19th century that oak reemerged as a wood suitable for use in public rooms, and it was popularized by the work of George Bullock. However, oak really came to prominence in the antiquarian interiors of the 1820s and 1830s.

SUBTLE MOTIFS
Although plainer than the classic Regency furniture destined for the Prince Regent's circle, furniture made for middle-class homes or country-house bedrooms still displayed all the inventiveness and exoticism of the period. Subtle lotus-leaf carvings evoked the cultures of the Nile, while Greek-key-patterned friezes on tables and bookcases echoed the ancient culture of Athens. Similarly, thin cross-bandings of an exotic timber such as calamander or amboyna were often used on even the humblest furniture. These were contained within boxwood or ebonized stringing, although it was often replaced with ebony on more expensive pieces. Shiny brass was also back in fashion, utilized as inlaid line decoration, cut patterns, or pierced galleries. The cabinet-maker George Oakley is often associated with the use of cut-star motifs in brass.

NEW FORMS
One of the characteristics of the period was the increased variety of furniture types that were made for a range of everyday needs. This is evident in the wide variety of tables designed for specific functions. For example, sofa tables with side flaps, central pedestals, or side standards—

sometimes of Classical lyre form—stood in front of sofas, while library tables, often with leather-inset tops and fixed ends, were designed to be used in libraries. Kidney-shaped, occasional, and worktables (for sewing equipment) were all new types of furniture, as was the nest of tables. Sometimes called *quartetto* tables, these were designed so that three, four, or five tables fitted into one another.

Chiffoniers—a type of side cabinet—were also invented around 1800. Games and dining tables, both Georgian inventions, remained popular and were often designed with central, turned pedestals and reeded, downswept legs.

The so-called Trafalgar chair is probably one of the archetypes of Regency vernacular design (*see p.242*). Its sinewy line, with saber legs at the front and back, epitomizes the gracefulness of the era. These chairs usually had a drop-in seat, although some seats were caned.

Caning, with its overtones of the Far East, came back into fashion at this time, and was used both in seats and in the sides and backs of library *bergères*.

The Davenport desk was another new form of this period. It owes its name to a Captain Davenport, who commissioned the design from the firm of Gillows.

GILLOWS STYLE
Vernacular furniture production in England in this period is dominated by Gillows, which started in Lancashire in the 1830s and later opened in London. Famous for high-quality mahogany furniture, often characterized by carefully matched figured veneers, it is also associated with particular motifs. On furniture, it would frequently gadroon the edges or add lobes to the legs. Unlike designers such as Hepplewhite, Gillows never produced a pattern book, but its Estimate Sketch Books provide a valuable index of its evolving style and are preserved in the Westminster City Archives. Unusually for this period, it frequently stamped its furniture (often on the front upper edge of a drawer) with its name. Although this would become more standard practice later in the century, Gillows is known to have left its mark on furniture from the 1790s.

SCOTTISH CHEST OF DRAWERS

This Scottish, bow-front chest of drawers is made of mahogany and decorated with boxwood stringing. The piece has a reeded, D-shaped top above a shallow frieze drawer with compartments and a writing slide.

Below the frieze are four long graduated drawers flanked on either side by pollard elm panels. The piece has a curved apron. The chest of drawers is raised on tapering, square-section legs with reeded decoration. *Early 19th century. H:43¾ in (111 cm); W:47¼ in (120 cm); D:23¼ in (59 cm). L&T*

GEORGE IV TEA TABLE

This elegant tea table is made of mahogany. The rectangular top has rounded corners and opens out to create a larger surface. The top sits above a flame-veneered frieze with a carved border. The table top is raised

on a baluster column, which is decorated with carved acanthus leaves. The table is supported on four outswept, molded legs decorated with a carved reeded pattern. The legs terminate in brass, leaf-cased terminals and casters. *Early 19th century. W:36¼ in (92 cm). DN*

ENWORK SIDE CABINET

his Regency side cabinet has a shaped back panel with a
arrow shelf supported on miniature columns, set above the
ain shelf. A single drawer is raised on turned, column supports
d a plinth base. All the surfaces are decorated with penwork.
810–20. H:49 in (125 cm); W:32 in (81 cm); D:18 in (45 cm). JK

DAVENPORT DESK

The hinged top of this mahogany desk has a gallery to the rear,
above a small pen drawer. Below this are four graduated side
drawers. The desk front is paneled, with a shaped, crossbanded
border. The case stands on carved and molded bracket feet.
c. 1810. H:33 in (94 cm); W:15 in (38 cm); D:19 in (49 cm). NOA

MAHOGANY TALLBOY

This tall chest of drawers, or tallboy, has a domed, paneled
cornice above six long drawers. All of the drawers are lined with
mahogany and have brass shell ring-handles. The piece stands
on saber legs to the front. *Early 19th century. H:88 in (224 cm);
W:49½ in (126 cm). WW*

ECORATED *BERGÈRE*

is armchair has a richly carved and decorated frame, arm
pports, and legs. The side, back, and seat panels are caned
d have loose cushions. The armrests are padded. The seat is
pported on turned and reeded legs with brass casters. *c. 1810.
36 in (91.5 cm). DL*

Pressed brass handle

Detail of loper

BONHEUR-DU-JOUR

This mahogany and marquetry *bonheur-du-jour* has a
shaped upper section, two matching veneer cupboard
doors, a writing surface, frieze drawer, and tapering
legs with spade feet. *c. 1790. H:41 in (103.5 cm);
W:28½ in (72 cm); D:18½ in (47 cm). NOA*

The shaped gallery
is outlined in
boxwood stringing.

Quarter-veneered doors
are inlaid with an oval
panel and foliage
in satinwood.

The square, tapering leg
is inlaid with boxwood.

The frieze drawer
is fitted with small
compartments for
writing implements.

The loper suggests
a baize-lined
writing surface.

GEORGE IV AND WILLIAM IV

WHEN GEORGE III died in 1820, his scandalous son, who had been ruling as Regent for nine years, became King George IV. Known for his extravagant tastes, the interiors created during his reign, particularly those at Windsor Castle, are some of the most sumptuous in British history. The reconstruction of the apartments on the east and south sides of the Upper Ward of the Castle between 1824 and

1830 was entrusted to the architect Sir Jeffry Wyattville. The furniture and upholstery was supplied by cabinet-maker Nicholas Morel. These heavily gilded interiors have a French flavor.

On George's death in 1830, his brother became William IV. In contrast to the worldly pursuits of his predecessor, William's reign was dominated by the Reform Act, which brought about parliamentary reform.

However, this period also marked an important period of transition between the Regency and Victorian eras. Much of the furniture was still Neoclassical in style, although it was generally heavier than Regency pieces.

TOUS LES LOUIS

The interest in 18th-century French styles dates from the late 1810s, when French furniture became available

after the Revolution. These pieces, especially those with tortoiseshell and brass boullework, were collected by, among others, the Duke of Wellington and the Prince Regent. Sometimes called the Rococo revival, it was known (incorrectly) at the time as the Louis XIV style. The serpentine lines of Louis XV furniture were reinterpreted on furniture typical of Louis XIV or XVI.

The Elizabeth Saloon at Belvoir Castle, created by Benjamin Dean and Matthew Cotes Wyatt in the 1820s, mixed French Rococo furniture and paneling with modern scrolling and gilded English furniture. This opulent

Bolster cushions provide additional comfort.

Carved arm detail

The legs are decorated with foliate carving.

The back of the sofa is decorated with scrolling acanthus carving.

The arms are decorated with leaf motifs.

WILLIAM IV SOFA

The paneled top rail of this elegant mahogany sofa is flanked by scrolling terminals depicting acanthus leaves. The lower arms of the sofa are upholstered to match the back and seat cushion. Two bolster cushions provide added comfort. The piece has leaf-carved urn terminals and is supported on turned and carved tapering feet with brass caps and casters. *Early 19th century. W:80¼ in (204 cm). L&T*

LIBRARY TABLE

This burr-oak and ebony-inlaid rectangular George IV library table has a crossbanded top above a frieze with two drawers. The table top is supported on quadruple-baluster end columns linked by a stretcher. Stamped Holden & Co, Liverpool. *Early 19th century. W:48 in (122 cm); D:24 in (61 cm). MLL*

WILLIAM IV TRIPOD TABLE

This painted tilt-top table has a rectangular top above a single column, which is supported on a tripod base. There is an armorial design painted on the surface of the table. The piece terminates in bun feet. *c. 1835. H:27½ in (70 cm). DL*

le was particularly appropriate
seat furniture with buttoned,
holstered backs or sides and plump,
briole legs. Case furniture tended to
ve rectilinear, classical lines.

The Old French Style was promoted
a series of pattern books from 1825,
cluding publications by John Taylor,
nry Whitaker, and Thomas King.
hn Weale published reprints of
id-18th-century pattern books
Thomas Chippendale's
ntemporaries, including Matthias
ck, Thomas Johnson, and Henry
pland, giving rise to the so-
led Chippendale revival of
e late 1820s and 30s.

LATE REGENCY

Much of the mahogany furniture
of the period was a heavier version
of Regency designs, anticipating
Victorian solidity. Carving was often
Classically inspired and combined
with gadrooning and ribbing. Bun feet
were used on chests of drawers or
plinth supports. Chair and table legs
were often turned and ring-turned
rather than outsplayed or saber-form.
Bedposts were similarly designed,
sometimes with acanthus carving.

allop shell motif

ILLIAM IV MIRROR

is mirror has a rectangular plate
thin a gilt and silvered wooden
me, surmounted by a laurel
eath and carved with berried
rel. The lower section has a
ntral scallop shell motif with a
stle below, flanked by rocaille,
nts, and foliage. One of a pair.
1830. H:52 in (134.5 cm);
31½ in (80 cm). PAR

WILLIAM IV FOUR-POSTER BED

This elegant mahogany bed has a molded
cornice decorated with a carved frieze and
supported on four turned and carved bed posts.
At the foot, the posts are reeded and leaf-
carved, while at the head of the bed the posts
are plain, enclosing a paneled head board
(formerly the foot board). The scalloped
pelmet and drapes are made of a floral fabric.
*Early 19th century. H:107½ in (273 cm);
L:79½ in (202 cm). L&T*

GEORGE IV LIBRARY ARMCHAIR

The upholstered tub back of this library
armchair has a U-shaped front, which has
been faced in mahogany and carved with
reeds and roundels. The chair is supported
on turned and reeded legs that
terminate in brass casters.
The chair is one of a pair.
Early 19th century. DN

LIBRARY TABLE

This tortoiseshell-veneered library table has a molded edge
above a shaped apron, and is supported on cabriole legs.
All of the surfaces are decorated with tortoiseshell and
embellished with gilt-metal mounts. *c. 1830. H:31 in
(79 cm); W:64¾ in (165 cm). HL*

GERMANY: EMPIRE

WHEN NAPOLEON BONAPARTE became ruler of Germany in 1806, he brought the Empire style to the region. Germany and Austria retained close stylistic links with France, as many German craftsmen trained and worked in Paris and became familiar with the Empire style. The grand, Classical motifs used in Empire style furniture, including eagles, mythical creatures, laurel wreaths, and columns, combined with military-style bronze mounts and details, epitomized Napoleon's victories and celebrated his triumphs.

ROYAL INFLUENCES

It was the Bonapartes themselves who really made Empire furniture fashionable in Germany. The Emperor's brother, Jérôme Bonaparte, became King of Westphalia in 1810, and he furnished the Schloss Wilhelmshöhe with Empire-style pieces. These included pieces ordered from Georges Jacob-Desmalter (see p.201), and an imposing desk that was decorated with marble reliefs designed by Friedrich Wichmann. In 1806, Napoleon had a suite of Empire furniture made for his Residenz at Würzburg, Franconia. These pieces were inspired by the work of French architects Percier and Fontaine, whose work Napoleon favored. Their 1801 pattern book, *Recueil de décorations intérieurs comprenant tout ce qui a rapport à l'ameublement*, was well received and highly influential in Germany, inspiring local craftsmen to produce their own publications.

Gilt bronze embellishes the interior fittings.

Fall-front writing surface

The body of the desk is modeled on a lyre.

The applied bronze decoration includes gilded stars and lion's heads.

A rectangular plinth supports the piece.

Carved paw feet

Gilt bronze lion's head

VIENNESE *GUÉRIDON*

This mahogany-veneered and partially carved *guéridon* has an overhanging table top with a gilt-edged round frieze below. The three tapering legs are topped by lions' heads and terminate in a tripartite base with paw feet. *c. 1810. H:40 in (102 cm); W:17¼ in (44 cm). BMN*

BEECHWOOD CHAIR

This chair has a scrolled back and rose-colored upholstery on both the back and seat. The chair has tapering front legs and cabriole back legs. The design is attributed to Leo von Klenze and the chair is thought to have come from the Residenz in Munich. *c. 1818. H:36½ in (91 cm). NAG*

VIENNESE *SECRÉTAIRE*

This exquisite *secrétaire* is made of fruitwood and mahogany. It has a lyre-shaped case which is decorated with partial inlay and gilding. The case has a single arched pediment, flanked on either side by gilded Classical figures. A rectangular, fall-front writing surface opens to reveal a fitted interior with an arrangement of drawers and arched compartments, luxuriously decorated with gilt bronze. The lower section of the *secrétaire* consists of two graduated drawers that are decorated to give the appearance of the strings of a lyre. The whole piece is raised on a rectangular plinth, which is supported on carved paw feet. *c. 1807. H:55½ in (139 cm); W:24¾ in (62 cm); D:16½ in (41 cm). GK*

ERMAN INTERPRETATIONS
rman furniture was often larger
d grander than its French Empire
uivalents. Locally-produced pieces
ided to have heavy columns and be
gidly symmetrical.
Empire furniture was predominantly
style for the nobility and was soon
opted by the rulers of the monarchies
d princedoms that made up the
rman Confederation after the
enna Congress in 1815. These rulers
owed off their power by building
w castles or by lavishly refurbishing
isting ones, and the exuberant
teriors of the palaces were designed
the Empire style.

Anterooms and throne rooms were
furnished with gilded Empire pieces.
Gifted court cabinet-makers produced
various ensembles with matching sofa
tables and console tables based on
French designs or adapted from the
fashion magazines that were popular at
the time. Private rooms were furnished
with mahogany pieces ornamented
with gilt-bronze mounts. Decorative
motifs were influenced by those of
ancient Egypt.
Seating furniture was also directly
inspired by the designs of the ancient
world. The influence of the Greek
klismos chair, for example, can be
seen in the chairs designed by Leo von

Klenze, who worked for the Bavarian
King Ludwig I in Munich and whose
Neoclassical buildings form much of
the city of Munich today.

VIENNESE DESIGN
Vienna was a leading center for the
production of furniture. It was here
that some of the most inventive
designs were developed, including the
lyre-*secrétaire*, which often took on
unusual shapes. Unlike the designers
and craftsmen working in the German

states, Viennese designers favored the
striking contrast of ebonized wood and
gilt bronze and created finely cast and
chased gilt bronze mounts that equaled
the work of French craftsmen.
One of the most gifted Viennese
cabinet-makers was Josef Ulrich
Danhauser. He ran the first Viennese
furniture manufacturers, from 1804
until his death in 1829, and made his
name by decorating his furniture with
wood paste molded to look like
expensive bronzes.

AUSTRIAN CHERRY WOOD TABLE

This table has a rectangular top with rounded
corners, which rests above a single frieze drawer.
The piece is raised on sharply tapering, square-
section legs. *c. 1810. H:30¼ in (77 cm); W:38¾ in
(98.5 cm); D:25¾ in (65.5 cm). SLK*

NORTH GERMAN COMMODE

This rectilinear commode is made from mahogany veneered
with maple. It has canted corners and three drawers with
ebony stringing. The commode is supported on square,
tapering legs. *Early 19th century. H:32⅝ in (83 cm);
W:44⅛ in (112 cm); D:22¾ in (58 cm). BMN*

KARL FRIEDRICH SCHINKEL (1781–1841)

THE MOST INFLUENTIAL GERMAN MASTER-BUILDER OF THE EARLY 19TH CENTURY,
SCHINKEL WAS ALSO A CITY PLANNER AND ARTIST, AND A FAMOUS FURNITURE DESIGNER.

Karl Friedrich Schinkel was born near Berlin,
and originally trained as an architect as one
of the first students at the new Berlin
Bauakademie. He studied under the architect
Friedrich Gilly, whose plans for a monument
to Frederick the Great of Prussia greatly
inspired the young Schinkel.
He traveled to France and Italy, and was
influenced by the Classical-style architecture
and furnishings he saw. His theory was that
new designs should draw on the ancient world
for inspiration, rather than slavishly recreate
it. On his return to Germany, he worked for
the Prussian state, including working as a
stage designer for the National Theater.
One of Schinkel's earliest works was a bed
with bedside table, designed for Queen Louise
for the Charlottenburg castle in Berlin. His
use of light-colored veneers anticipated the
Biedermeier style (*see pp.216-17*). He was not

afraid to experiment with shape and created
pieces designed for specific places within
a room. Typical Schinkel designs are for
architectural secrétaires and comfortable
armchairs. His publication *Vorbilder für
Fabrikanten und Handwerker*
(Role Models for Makers and
Craftsmen) in 1835 had a
widespread influence.
In later years, Schinkel's
work drew less on the
Neoclassical style, and
more on the designs of
the Renaissance.

Schinkel armchair This generously
upholstered armchair has a
curvaceous frame with a high
backrest and is decorated with
motifs from the ancient world.

Schinkel in Naples This oil painting, by Franz Louis
Catel, shows Karl Friedrich Schinkel in Naples in
1824 during his second Italian journey. *1824*

GERMANY: BIEDERMEIER

THE TERM "BIEDERMEIER" covers the wide spectrum of simple, Classical, handcrafted, functional furniture made between 1805 and 1850, which was made at the same time as furniture in the Empire style (*see p.212*). While the nobility furnished their formal rooms with Empire furniture, the more private parts of their houses and mansions were furnished in the Biedermeier style, which was favored by the wealthy middle classes in Germany, Austria, Switzerland, and Scandinavia.

Political unrest in the German states in the early 19th century created a general feeling of uncertainty and increasing poverty. As a result, people withdrew into the privacy of their own homes, and the middle classes in particular began to take an increasing interest in furnishings.

MODEST STYLE
Biedermeier furniture typically had straight lines and lacked decorative carvings. Motifs inspired by Classical designs, such as columns, gables, egg and dart, and bead and reel details were all popular.

From about 1830, designs incorporated scrolled forms: chairs often had splayed legs, sofas had arched backs, and molded cornices were used as ornament for writing cabinets.

POPULAR WOODS
The most fashionable woods for Biedermeier furniture were mahogany, which was imported and, therefore, rather too expensive for this essentially middle-class style, and also less costly local woods such as walnut, cherry,

pear, birch, and ash, combined with dark elm and thuyawood. The grain of the wood was the most important decorative feature. The natural grain of the veneer was emphasized with various pyramidal or fountainlike shapes. Root veneers of acorn, burr-walnut, and elm were also popular because of their varied color and attractive markings. Darker woods were frequently used as borders around diamond-shaped keyholes, block feet, or cornices.

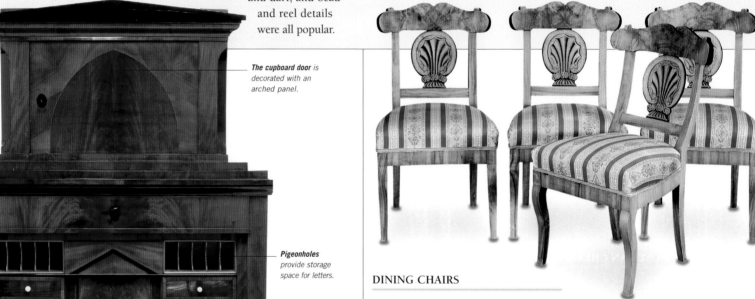

The cupboard door is decorated with an arched panel.

Pigeonholes provide storage space for letters.

The interior drawers have ivory handles.

The fall front opens to form a writing surface.

The bottom part of the cabinet is made up of three drawers.

DINING CHAIRS

These chairs are made of solid walnut wood and walnut veneer. The backs are balloon-shaped and have double baluster splats and a shaped top rail. The tapered, upholstered seats are typical of the period and sit above saber legs. The chairs are upholstered with a Neoclassical-style striped fabric, probably the original fabric, that is decorated with flowers. *1820–30. H:35 in (87.5 cm); W:17¾ in (45 cm); D:18⅛ in (46 cm).*

WRITING CABINET

Covered entirely in cherry-wood veneer, this impressive writing cabinet has a fall front that opens to reveal a fitted interior. The inner compartment consists of 11 small drawers flanking a central tabernacle. The lower portion of the cabinet consists of three large drawers set on simple bracket feet. This practical piece embodies the Biedermeier ethos of comfort and convenience and would have been used in the sitting room, which was the focal point of the home. *c. 1820. H:60½ in (151 cm); W:41½ in (104 cm); D:19½ in (49 cm). KAV*

SOFA

The frame of this elegant sofa is scroll-shaped with a slightly raised back. The shape takes its inspiration from Classical pieces, and is typical of the simple, geometric design that was favored by Biedermeier designers. Ornate carvings and decoration were not part of the Biedermeier style. The sofa is veneered in cherry wood, which has been blackened in places, using a simple inlay of ebony to accent the flat surface of the wood. The upholstered seat is coil-sprung for comfort. *c. 1825. W:74 in (185 cm). KAV*

RESTRAINED INTERIORS

Biedermeier interiors were modestly furnished, and the emphasis was on practicality and comfort, rather than decoration. The furniture was moderate in size, rounded in shape, comfortable, and homey.

Many pieces had a counterpart—another piece that was similar in size—to balance the furnishing of the room. The *secrétaire* with a fall front and the *blender*, which looked like an imitation *secrétaire*, but was designed for use as a linen press or wardrobe, were very common styles.

An overall color scheme was a prominent feature of Biedermeier interiors and frequently light-colored upholstery, curtains, and woods were chosen to create a homey interior with an integrated sense of design.

The advances in manufacturing that occurred during this period did not have much impact until the second half of the century, so early Biedermeier furniture was visibly handmade. Upholstery was generally flat and square, made of silk or horsehair, and wooden surfaces were simply planed and polished with oil.

By the mid-19th century, the style was seen as comfortable but rather dowdy, and was given the name *Biedermeier,* a satirical term that meant "the decent common man." The name was originally used in a German publication for a fictional middle-class character, and was not intended to be particularly flattering.

The style gradually began to decline in popularity and it was only at the beginning of the 20th century that this negative evaluation began to fade, and Biedermeier-style furniture once again became much sought-after. This led in turn to the style being widely copied.

A typical Biedermeier living room, c. 1820–30
This simple Saxon living room is typical of a modest townhouse of the period. The living room was the social center of the home, and great care was taken with the arrangement of the furniture.

DINING TABLE

Made in southern Germany, this simple dining table is veneered in cherry wood with a star pattern on the table top. Some of the veneer is blackened to add visual interest. The single pedestal terminates in a tripartite base. *c. 1830. W:46 in (115 cm). BMN*

WALL MIRROR

This mirror frame is architectural in style and is decorated with cherry veneer. The ebonized columns are edged by gilded bases and capitals, which support a Classical-style cornice and pediment. The central mount shows the goddess Diana. *1820–30. H:67 in (170 cm); W:28 in (71 cm). BMN*

WALNUT-VENEERED COMMODE

This commode has a top with an ebonized border above a frieze drawer. A further two recessed drawers are flanked by turned, ebonized columns with gilded Corinthian capitals and feet. The middle drawer is decorated with floral and figural details. *1820–30. H:33½ in (85 cm). BMN*

GLAZED CABINET

This birch-veneered cabinet was made in Berlin and has a stepped pediment with a flat top. The oval glazed door panel is decorated with fine wooden spokes emanating from a central sun motif. At the base of the cabinet there is a single drawer with a lock. *c. 1820. H:71½ in (182 cm); W:42½ in (108 cm); D:21½ in (54.5 cm). BMN*

THE LOW COUNTRIES

THE COUNTRY OF BELGIUM did not formally exist until 1831. Indeed, in October 1797, after the Treaty of Campo Formio, the region was annexed to France. As a result, the furniture produced there in the early 19th century scarcely differs from the French Empire style. Although the province was struggling economically, those with sufficient financial means ordered their furniture directly from Paris. After 1831, as elsewhere, a series of historical revival styles dominated Belgian furniture design.

The situation in the Netherlands was slightly different, partly because of antagonism toward the French occupation. After the Battle of Jena in 1806, Napoleon gave his brother Louis the throne of the Netherlands. As in Italy, the Empire style was introduced directly by the Emperor's family.

INNOVATION

In 1808, the new King ordered that the 17th-century town hall of Amsterdam be refurbished as a royal residence and had a suite of principal rooms built in the fashionable Empire style. Most of the furniture was supplied to the new French overlords by loyal Dutch craftsmen, including the talented Carel Breytspraak, the son of a German cabinet-maker, who had matriculated to the Amsterdam guild in 1795. His furniture is heavily influenced by the severe Classicism of Percier and Fontaine (*see pp.200–01*), but demonstrates idiosyncratic touches, such as applied moldings around drawers or the use of typically

Dutch tapering feet. He also frequently used canted pilasters on case furniture to reduce the sense of bulk. Much of the seating supplied for the new royal palace was upholstered by Joseph Cuel, including a scrolling day bed commissioned for the bedroom of Queen Hortense.

TRADITION

The Empire style remained popular even after Waterloo, so when King William I redecorated the State apartments of the palace in the Hague, they were conceived in a Napoleonic style.

One of the most important suppliers to the palace was Nordanus, a local cabinet-maker. In 1818, he provided numerous mahogany pieces, some of which were veneered with floral marquetry. Local motifs, such as the fluted friezes and corner chamfering characteristic of 18th-century Neoclassical Dutch pieces, occur on much Dutch Empire furniture.

Classical features still persisted in the Low Countries into the second quarter of the 19th century and, as elsewhere in Europe, furniture was frequently made from light woods, particularly maple or burr-walnut, and was often influenced by both British furniture and the German Biedermeier style. Furniture workshops also became increasingly mechanized as the century progressed.

The *Salon de Boiserie*, Amsterdam Almost all of the painted paneling in this room is decorated with lavishly carved gilding. The room was designed by architects Charles Percier and Pierre Fontaine. *SBA*

DUTCH DINING CHAIR

This elm dining chair has a paneled top rail of joined construction with tapering sides. The felt upholstered seat has brass studding and is raised on a plain seat rail above turned and tapering legs. *Early 19th century. H:33½ in (85 cm). DN*

Brass studs

BELGIAN *FAUTEUILS*

The top rails of these Neoclassical, laminated, black-painted armchairs are decorated in gilt with central twin putti flanking a lyre in husk-decorated borders. The downcurved arms end in gilt ball finials and are supported by gilt cornucopiae headed by leaf tips. The inverted, U-shaped legs of each chair have gilt-metal leaf-tip sabots. Each chair is stamped "*Chapuis.*" *Early 19th century. H:32 in (89 cm). SI*

Detail of marquetry

DUTCH CARD TABLE

The folding top of this walnut table has rounded corners and sits above a rectangular paneled frieze. The table top stands on square-section, tapering legs with gilt-metal feet. The table is decorated throughout with floral marquetry typical of the Low Countries. *Early 19th century. W:32¾ in (83 cm). DN*

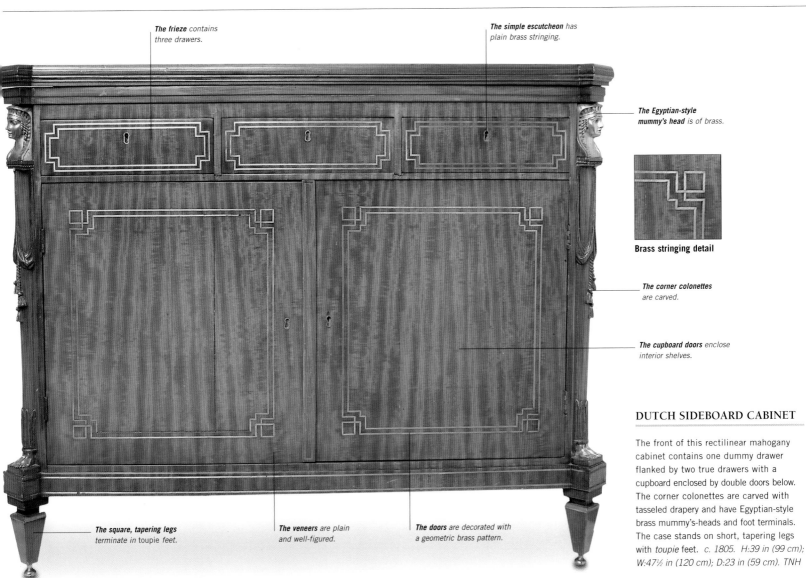

The frieze contains three drawers.

The simple escutcheon has plain brass stringing.

The Egyptian-style mummy's head is of brass.

Brass stringing detail

The corner colonettes are carved.

The cupboard doors enclose interior shelves.

The square, tapering legs terminate in toupie feet.

The veneers are plain and well-figured.

The doors are decorated with a geometric brass pattern.

DUTCH SIDEBOARD CABINET

The front of this rectilinear mahogany cabinet contains one dummy drawer flanked by two true drawers with a cupboard enclosed by double doors below. The corner colonettes are carved with tasseled drapery and have Egyptian-style brass mummy's-heads and foot terminals. The case stands on short, tapering legs with *toupie* feet. *c. 1805. H:39 in (99 cm); W:47½ in (120 cm); D:23 in (59 cm). TNH*

Relief carving

LINEN PRESS

he top section of this mahogany nen press has a pediment crest bove a pair of cupboard doors, hich open to reveal three shelves nd three aligned drawers. The wer section of the press has vo short over two long drawers nd is raised on rectangular et. The linen press is relief- arved with Neoclassical motifs. arly 19th century. H:91 in 231 cm); W:63 in (160 cm); :22 in (56 cm). NA

Escutcheon detail

DUTCH CABINET

This mahogany and rosewood cabinet has two doors crowned by a molded and shaped cornice with a domed pediment and central cartouche. The lower section has a *bombé* base with three long drawers and claw-and-ball feet. *Early 19th century. H:95½ in (239 cm); W:71 in (178 cm); D:24¾ in (62 cm). VH*

SCANDINAVIA

THE GREAT BRITISH VICTORIES of Abukir (1798) and Trafalgar (1805), which opened up trade along the North Sea coastline, suggest that sympathy for Britain and British design could be evident in Scandinavian furniture. This was not always the case. Denmark and Sweden's ambivalence toward France encouraged the British prime minister, Pitt, to destroy the Danish fleet and bombard Copenhagen, creating much animosity toward the British. This affected trade and shipping and left the Danish-Norwegian economy at the point of bankruptcy in 1813.

So, although there are traces of British Neoclassicism in early-19th-century Scandinavian furniture, it was often due either to the residual effect of late-18th-century design, or it had filtered through the influence of north German cabinet-making.

The one positive outcome of these hostilities was that local craftsmen were protected from British competition and were encouraged to develop their own workshops and styles. As in the rest of Europe, the Empire style predominated, although it had marked local characteristics.

DANISH EMPIRE

A traditional preference for simplicity, and the need for frugality as a result of war and financial hardship, gave rise to a version of the prevailing French style called Danish Empire, which was taken up by three of the Scandinavian countries. Although mahogany was favored, and was used in the larger, wealthier cities, it was difficult to obtain due to war. As a result, the Danish Empire style made use of light local woods, such as alder, maple, ash, and birch, which could be polished to look like satinwood. Mahogany furniture did reappear after 1815, and was generally veneered on pine rather than oak pieces.

Danish furniture was often inlaid with contrasting woods, such as citrus, rather than having ormolu mounts. Inlaid lunettes and arched details were popular, as was the occasional pressed brass or giltwood detail.

One of the most distinctive chairs produced in Denmark was the klismos chair, designed by Nicolai Abilgaard in 1800 and now in the Copenhagen Museum of Decorative Arts. Similar

to a chair later designed by the sculptor Hermann Freund (now in the Fredericksborg Castle), it mimics the ancient Greek original.

The Danish custom of using one room as a combined dining room, drawing room, and study at this time resulted in some unique types of furniture. One of these, the *Chatol*, consisted of a cylinder bureau with a retractable writing slide, surmounted by cupboards for storing cutlery and glassware. Another was a divan, which had cupboards in the sides.

HETSCH STYLE

In Denmark, the Neoclassical style lasted into the 1840s, thanks to the late Empire style popularized by Gustav Friedrich Hetsch. Hetsch had studied with Charles Percier in Paris earlier in the century, returning to Copenhagen to direct the porcelain factory. He was also a designer and his works were often scholarly reproductions of antique prototypes. This style, which favored the use of carved appliqués and moldings over mounts, is sometimes confusingly called Christian VIII after the Danish king who reigned from 1839 to 1848.

SWEDEN

Sweden was slightly more francophile in its tastes than Denmark, particularly in Court circles. The furniture in the Yellow Room at Rosendal Castle in Stockholm, created for the king in the 1820s, is closer to true French Empire style than any furniture produced in Scandinavia during the early 19th century. It was designed by Lorenz Wilhelm Lundelius, the leading craftsman in Stockholm.

A famous *secrétaire*, made by Johan Petter Berg in 1811, demonstrates how Swedish cabinet-makers absorbed German heaviness, combined it with Empire motifs (such as white marble pilasters), and added the occasional British reference, such as the Sheraton-inspired inlaid shell.

The Hetsch style eventually arrived in Sweden, but it did not become dominant because Neo-Gothic had taken hold there quite early. Indeed, by 1828, there was already a room decorated in the Gothic style in the Royal palace in Stockholm.

BIEDERMEIER LOVE SEAT

This mahogany, Biedermeier-style love seat has a solid, rectangular form with outswept arms. The back and sides of the seat have brass-molded panels and fan spandrels. The arms have rosette terminals and mahogany facings. The seat rail has brass mounts and is supported on verdigris brackets, carved in the shape of drapery. The piece terminates in massive gilt and verdigris claw-and-ball front feet. The love seat has an upholstered back, sides, and seat. *Early 19th century. W:54¾ in (139 cm). L&T*

SWEDISH *SECRÉTAIRE*

The tall, flame-veneered case of this Swedish Empire *secrétaire* has tapering sides. The upper section of the case has a fall front positioned beneath a shallow drawer. The lower section consists of three graduated drawers; the bottom drawer has a cut-away arched shape. The piece is raised on rectangular block feet. This *secrétaire* is made in the style of furniture from toward the end of the period and is a move away from the Empire style. It was possibly made by J. Reher. *1841. H:57⅛ in (145 cm); W:48 in (122 cm); D:22⅞ in (58 cm). Bk*

DANISH ARMCHAIR

The substantial hooped-back, upholstered backrest of this mahogany armchair is raised on curved supports. The upholstered seat has square, tapered legs at the front and saber legs at the rear. *Early 19th century.* H:30 in (76 cm); W:27 in (68.5 cm); D:23 in (58.5 cm). EVE

LATE GUSTAVIAN ARMCHAIR

This Swedish gilt-and-painted armchair has an upholstered seat and back, a curved top rail with lion's head terminals, and carved, down-sweeping arms. The padded seat is supported on a carved seat rail and is raised on turned and fluted legs at the front and saber legs at the rear. *Early 19th century. Bk*

LADY'S WORKTABLE

This late Gustavian Swedish worktable has an oval, galleried top above a single frieze drawer. The table top is supported on tapering legs terminating in brass caps and casters and joined by a shaped cross-stretcher. *Early 19th century.* H:30½ in (77 cm); W:22 in (56 cm); D:18½ in (47 cm). Bk

The table top is made of marble.

The frieze is carved as a concave molding with foliate paterae carved in high relief.

The winged sphinxes are surmounted by stylized basketwork columns.

The faux marble plinths are decorated with gilt laurel leaves.

The central column is carved with fluting and supported on a circular plinth carved with acanthus leaves.

The faux marble plinth has concave sides.

SWEDISH CENTER TABLE

This outstanding parcel-gilt center table has a marble top supported on a carved frieze above a central column carved with spiral fluting. The table corners are mounted on faux-marble plinths surmounted by sphinxes. The whole stands on a concave-sided plinth. *c. 1820.* H:34 in (86.5 cm); W:58 in (147.5 cm); D:28 in (71 cm). MAL

RUSSIA

FROM THE 18TH CENTURY, Russia had been turning its attention to the West for cultural inspiration, and this continued in the opening decades of the 19th century. However, unlike elsewhere in Europe, the Empire style did not make inroads through the imposition of a member of Bonaparte's family or through French control.

Napoleon's invasion of Russia in 1812 had devastated the land, yet the period is marked by a flowering of the arts and economic recovery. Indeed, the Mikhailovsky, Winter, and Yelagin palaces were supplied with important Empire-style suites during the reign of Czar Alexander I (1801–25).

FOREIGN INFLUENCE

Since the time of Catherine II (r. 1762–96), furniture had been imported from Western Europe, particularly France, but also Britain and Germany. Architects, too, were brought over. By the time of Alexander I (r. 1801–25), architects such as the Swiss Thomas de Thomon, and the Italians Carlo Rossi and Giacomo Antonio Domenico Quarenghi, were introducing the strict Neoclassical style prevalent elsewhere in Europe. They continued the work of Rastrelli, Rinaldi, and the Scot Charles Cameron, in the urban development of St. Petersburg and its outlying palaces.

They provided designs for local craftsmen, which were also taken up by local architects, such as Zacharov.

The furniture for the White Hall of the Mikhailovsky Palace was designed by Rossi and supplied by the Russian Bobkov brothers. Architectural in detail and conception, the pieces epitomized French style and were covered in wreaths, rosettes, and other Empire motifs.

Pavlovsk Palace was rebuilt by the Russian architect Andrei Voronikhin, after extensive damage during the Napoleonic wars. He was also a consummate designer

of furniture. One particular chair—made for the czar's summer residence, Tsarkoye Selo, in 1804—is often associated with his name. It has sphinx monopodiae legs that rise, uninterrupted, into the winged arm supports. Not only does this chair demonstrate the vogue for Empire furniture and ancient Egyptian motifs, but it anticipates Biedermeier chairs, which conceal the link between the arm and the leg. However, the French style was not the only influence on

CENTER TABLE

This center table is made of birch. The circular marble top has a raised rim and reeded edge above a chamfered frieze. The table top is raised on a leaf-clasped column with three anthropomorphic legs and paw feet with sunken casters. *Early 19th century. D:38¾ in (97 cm). L&T*

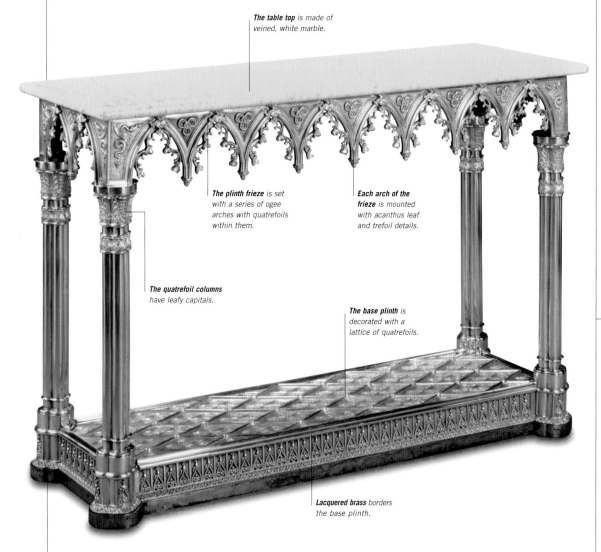

The table top is made of veined, white marble.

The plinth frieze is set with a series of ogee arches with quatrefoils within them.

Each arch of the frieze is mounted with acanthus leaf and trefoil details.

The quatrefoil columns have leafy capitals.

The base plinth is decorated with a lattice of quatrefoils.

Lacquered brass borders the base plinth.

GOTHIC SIDE TABLE

This Gothic-style side table is made of silver alloy and has a veined white marble top. The frieze is designed to look like a series of Gothic ogee arches: these are decorated with acanthus leaves and have a trefoil set within each lunette. The corners of the frieze are embellished with foliate capitals set on slender quatrefoil column stems. The table stands on a rectangular base plinth decorated with an elaborate lattice of quatrefoils. Lacquered brass decoration adds color to an otherwise austere-looking piece. *c. 1820. MAL*

NEOCLASSICAL CONSOLE TABLE

This Empire console table has a rectangular marble top above a richly carved frieze with a stylized rosette at each corner. Each of the four legs is a carved monopodia surmounted by a female head. *Early 19th century. H:31½ in (80 cm); W:44 in (112 cm); D:29½ in (75 cm). Bk*

ussian furniture; England, especially
e designs of Thomas Sheraton, also
ayed an important part.

ATIVE LUMBER

uch fine Russian furniture of this
eriod, with its simplicity, symmetry,
d love of *bois clairs*, is difficult to
stinguish from Central European
eces. Mahogany was probably
ported, but birch came from the
rests near Karelia in Finland. Poplar,
ive wood, and sandalwood were also
shionable, as were inlays in
ntrasting stones. The
arble was often Russian,
ch as that from Siberia

or the famous green malachite, which
could be cut into such thin veneers
that it was used on curved surfaces.

METAL FURNITURE

Timber was frequently gilded and
patinated to simulate metal, particularly
bronze, but some furniture was also
made in metal. A rich tradition of steel
furniture was produced by the Arsenal
at Tula, and some pieces were made
entirely of gilt-bronze. *Guéridons*
might be entirely metal, sometimes

with malachite tops and in-curved
supports with eagles' heads. One of
the most lavish gilt-bronze items was
the dressing table supplied to the
Mikhailovsky Palace. With a blue smalt
(silica glass) table top, the piece is a
riot of antique motifs, from sphinxes
to cornucopiae.

STYLISTIC DIVERSITY

After the mid-1820s, the Neo-Gothic
style became fashionable, along with
a plethora of other revivalist styles,

including Rococo. Later, in the second
quarter of the 19th century, furniture
designers began to look back to Russia's
own traditions and folklore for
inspiration, designing pieces *à la russe*.
These modes were popularized by
architects such as A. Staken-Schneider,
and the Tour furniture shop. Typical
chairs with pierced, rounded backs
survive in the dining room at the
Arkangelskoe, near Moscow. The design
is thought to reflect traditional 17th-
century Russian architecture.

AHOGANY-FRAMED SOFA

is sofa has an ornately scrolled top rail carved
th anthemion motifs and downswept solid arms
th scroll-carved terminals. The seat and back are
holstered and are raised on saber front and rear
gs. *Early 19th century. W:83½ in (212 cm). L&T*

Scroll-carved terminal

CONSOLE DESSERT

This gilt-bronze and brass-mounted mahogany *demi-lune* console
dessert has an upper section with three tiers, each with pierced
galleries, and a frieze with brass fluted stiles. The columnar
supports are joined by a tiered platform stretcher on block feet.
Early 19th century. H:57½ in (146 cm); 58¼ in (148 cm).

EMPIRE ARMCHAIR

This mahogany and ormolu-mounted
armchair has a rectangular paneled
top rail above a pierced back splat
with military motifs. The chair has
distinctive sphinx-head monopodia
legs, and the wings of the sphinxes
form the arm supports. *Early
19th century. Bk*

MAHOGANY
ARMCHAIRS

These mahogany chairs have
carved top rails and leather-
upholstered seats and backs.
The armrests and arm supports
are formed from one sweeping
curve. The tapering seat is
supported on a straight seat
rail. The chairs are decorated
with brass inlay throughout
and supported on saber legs.
*c. 1815. H:37¾ in (96 cm);
W:23⅗ in (60 cm); D:20⅞ in
(53 cm). GK*

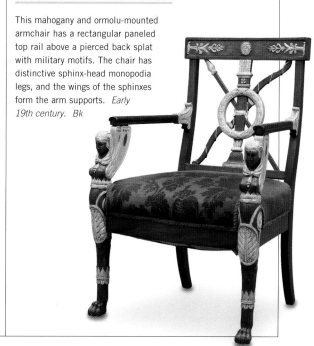

SPAIN AND PORTUGAL

THE FURNITURE OF THE IBERIAN peninsular during the early 19th century was strongly influenced by prevailing styles in other European countries, mixed with the various tastes, techniques, and regional differences that reflect both Spain and Portugal's cultural backgrounds.

The greatest foreign influence was the French Empire style. Spain was dominated by France for a period following the abdication of Charles IV and Ferdinand VII in 1808, when Napoleon's brother, Joseph Bonaparte, introduced a taste for Empire furniture. A similar Francophile furniture style also developed in Portugal, which had come under French rule the previous year.

FERDINANDINO

However, the true flowering of the Empire style in Spain only occurred after Napoleon's fall. It consequently bears the name Ferdinandino, after Ferdinand VII, who reigned from 1814 to 1833. Less sophisticated and clumsier than French pieces, the Spanish variants are usually made of mahogany, with carved gilt decoration instead of gilt-bronze mounts. Classical motifs were preferred, especially figurative devices such as putti or swans. These are epitomized on the typical Gondola chairs, which had legs featuring swans or dolphins. Similarly, the king's desk in the Royal Palace, Madrid, is made of mahogany supported on carved gilt swans.

The Spanish love of walnut, pine, cedar, and olive wood is also evident in pieces with relatively little decoration and few appliqués. Overall, like contemporary Portuguese work, the pieces are heavier than true Empire furniture and often of slightly exaggerated proportions. Spanish pieces from the south also feature an occasional motif echoing Spain's exotic Moorish past.

Although France was the predominant cultural dynamo, British, German, and Italian influences are all discernible in Spanish furniture of this period. The presence of British cabinet-makers on the island of Minorca helped to diffuse the principles of British Neoclassical design, while 18th-century ties with Naples generated Italianate forms.

With the accession of Isabella (1833–70), and the development of the so-called Isabellino style, a more romantic trend emerged in Spain, which revived many of its historical furniture types, particularly Baroque. As such, it corresponded to the style of the Second Empire in France.

PORTUGAL

In the opening years of the 19th century, British Neoclassical style reigned supreme in Portugal. The French occupation introduced a ponderous version of the Empire style, but when power returned to General Beresford in 1811, so did a preference for Regency design. Trafalgar chairs were most popular, while the engravings of Sheraton continued to be influential.

Portuguese furniture production experienced a downturn from this time onward: with the return of João VI from Brazil, political and social instability was accompanied by general economic decline. This reached its peak with the civil strife under Maria II de Gloria (1826–53).

Portuguese furniture is characterized by the use of South American woods, particularly those from the Brazilian forests, such as jacaranda and pausanto. These woods are easy to carve and allow sharp details, so carving is more common on Portuguese furniture than its French or British prototypes. However, the furniture produced in Lisbon tends to be far heavier and altogether simpler than the examples that inspired them. Generally, some fine-quality furniture was produced, such as the mahogany and gilt-brass mounted suite supplied for one of the bedrooms at the Royal Palace of Queluz.

From the 1830s, when Maria II's consort, Ferdinand of Sachsen-Coburg-Saalfeld, began building the Peña Palace, the German Biedermeier style became popular.

Portugal's strong colonial ties with India and the Far East ensured that much colonial furniture was also imported, particularly from Goa and the Malabar Coast. Often simplified versions of European styles carved in Eastern hardwoods, they tend to echo 18th-century styles rather than reflect the latest European trends.

PORTUGUESE COLONIAL CABINET

This cabinet-on-stand is made of white metal-mounted hardwood and ebony. It has a molded, shaped, and arched cornice above two shaped doors with glazed panels, and two short drawers. The cabriole legs are joined by a wave-shaped cross-stretcher with a central urn finial in the center. The cabinet terminates in claw-and-ball feet. *Early 19th century. H:87½ in (222 cm); W:68 in (173 cm); D:24 in (61 cm).*

NEOCLASSICAL SIDE CHAIRS

These side chairs are part of a set of four. They have mahogany frames with parcel gilt decoration. A scrolled top rail sits above a rectangular backrest. The seat rails are plain, but mounted with gilt rosettes. The chairs stand on circular, tapered legs. *Early 19th century.*

DINING CHAIRS

These Spanish chairs are made of walnut and form part of a set of ten dining chairs. Each chair is decorated with mask finials. The seat back comprises two vertical rows of turned spindles—the upper row is of widely spaced, long spindles, and the lower forms a tightly spaced decorative border. The leather seats are attached to the frames with brass studs, and the seat rails are shaped and decorated. The chairs stand on ring-turned, reeded legs, which are joined by an H-stretcher. *Early 19th century.*

MALLORCAN COMMODE

This marquetry commode, one of a pair, is made from mahogany, fruitwood, and rosewood. The rectangular, white marble top rests above a convex frieze drawer, which is inlaid with scrolling leaves, and three drawers, that are inlaid *sans traverse*. The drawers are flanked by canted scrolled angles, which are also decorated with leaf inlay. At the base of the commode is an inlaid concave-fronted drawer above a banded rim and acanthus-carved feet. *Early 19th century. H:41 in (104 cm); W:49¼ in (125 cm); D:24¼ in (61.5 cm).*

Brass lock plates

Brass drawer pulls

The lock plates are made of pierced brass.

Tapered pilasters flank the case.

The drawers are decorated with paneling.

Saber legs support the commode.

SPANISH COMMODE

This rare commode is veneered all over with mahogany. The piece has a molded rectangular top above two narrow drawers, which are flanked by fluted pilasters. The two paneled drawers are carved with geometric relief patterns, and are flanked with tapering pilasters. The drawer pulls and lock plates are made of brass. The piece stands on elegant, saber legs. *c. 1800. H:41½ in (104 cm) W:54 in (135 cm) D:26 in (65 cm).*

SOUTH AFRICA

Thonged seat

NORTH EASTERN CAPE CHAIR

The top rail of this stinkwood chair is inlaid in yellowwood with simple geometric motifs, which are repeated in the two additional back rails. The chair has simple, carved uprights and similarly carved legs joined by an H-stretcher. One of a pair. *1830–40. H:33 in (84 cm); W:18½ in (47 cm); D:15¾ in (40 cm). PRA*

THE DISTINCTIVE FURNITURE of the Cape of Good Hope reflected the styles of the two major colonial powers in the area: Britain and the Netherlands. The various struggles in Europe had also been played out in the colonies, but by 1806 British dominance was assured. In 1820, more British settlers established themselves farther up the East coast. The Cape's position at the midpoint of the trading routes between Europe and the Far East also gave rise to influences from such places as Batavia.

A wide range of furniture was made in the Cape both for the metropolitan homes of Cape Town and the famous white-painted and gabled homesteads of the vineyards. Their forms and motifs were often simplified versions of those in Europe. A slight delay is generally considered when dating colonial furniture. The Empire style, omnipresent in Europe, appears to have had little influence in the Cape, except perhaps in an increased linearity of design. Its preference for highly polished timber and expensive gilt-bronze mounts did not suit the local traditions, lifestyles, or materials.

The most recognizable aspect of South African furniture is the use of local woods, which, unlike mahogany, do not tend to take a glasslike polish to their surfaces. Most characteristic is the combined and contrasting use of stinkwood and yellowwood.

COLONIAL CHAIRS

A wide variety of different chairs were made in the early 19th century. Some so-called "Adam" chairs from the early

Painting in oil on wood This shows typical wall decoration, curtains, and furniture styles of the early 19th century. All the furniture, with the exception of the writing bureau, was made according to the prevalent Neoclassical style. *1815. PRA*

years of the century survive at Groot Constantia. With their upholstered, oval back-panels, this type is luxurious and rare. Far more common are Sheraton and Neoclassical chairs— the latter with pierced vertical splats, caned or thonged (animal hide strips) seats, and tapering, square-section legs that were sometimes fluted. The Sheraton variety, introduced around 1810, had a wide top rail, generally above a second horizontal bar splat and square seat. Later the front leg was either turned or ring-turned. More provincial chairs, the tulbagh, of simplified boxlike form, survived into this period. These shapes are also evident on the rusbank, a Cape type of settee-cum-settle with a chair-back.

TABLES AND CUPBOARDS

D-end dining tables and gateleg tables were also produced during these years. Different timbers were sometimes used for the top, frieze, and legs, which were often tapered and fluted like other chairs of the period. Chests of drawers in the Sheraton style, which were popular in Britain, seem to have been relatively rare in the Cape; South African cabinets tended to favor earlier serpentine lines. However, the monumental armoires, corner-cupboards, and wardrobes, so typical of high-production Cape furniture in the 18th century, seem to have been produced into the early years of the next century.

CAPE OF GOOD HOPE CABINET

This low cabinet is made from amboyna, stinkwood, and satinwood. It has a rectangular top, shaped at the front above two bowed

doors, divided by a fluted pilaster. The canted corners of the cabinet are also fluted and are raised on claw-and-ball feet. *Early 19th century. H:31½ in (80 cm); W:41⅓ in (105 cm); D:24⅓ in (62 cm). PRA*

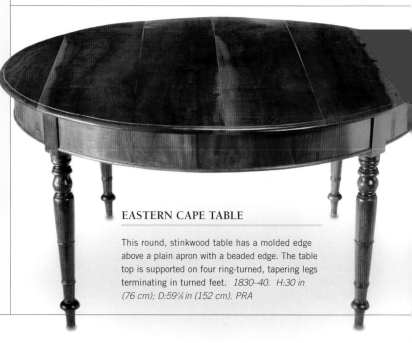

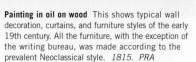

EASTERN CAPE TABLE

This round, stinkwood table has a molded edge above a plain apron with a beaded edge. The table top is supported on four ring-turned, tapering legs terminating in turned feet. *1830–40. H:30 in (76 cm); D:59⅞ in (152 cm). PRA*

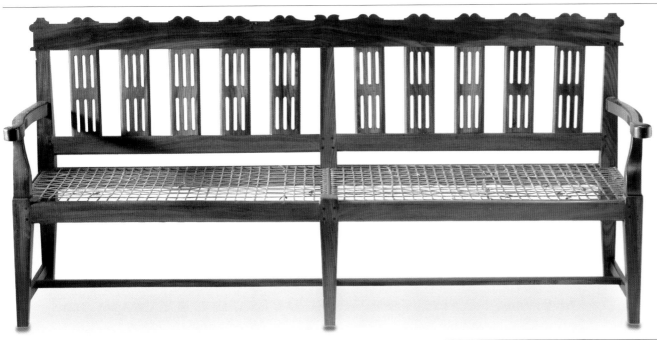

WESTERN CAPE SETTEE

This stinkwood settee has a carved top rail above a seat back comprising a series of evenly spaced pierced panels—ten in total—and gently outswept arms with simple scroll terminals. The settee is supported on tapering, square-section legs joined by H-stretchers. *c. 1800. H:38¼ in (97 cm); W:86⅔ in (220 cm); D:38¼ in (97 cm). PRA*

OUTH WESTERN CAPE HALF-MOON TABLES

hese two half-moon tables, which can be placed together to make he round table, have table tops and aprons made from yellowwood, nd square-section, tapering legs made from the darker stinkwood ith yellowwood inlay. The aprons have a simple molded edge with tinkwood beading. *1810–20. H:29 in (74 cm). PRA*

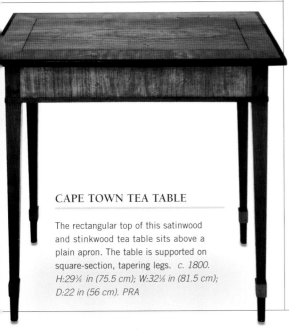

CAPE TOWN TEA TABLE

The rectangular top of this satinwood and stinkwood tea table sits above a plain apron. The table is supported on square-section, tapering legs. *c. 1800. H:29¾ in (75.5 cm); W:32⅛ in (81.5 cm); D:22 in (56 cm). PRA*

The rectangular top is simple and molded.

The two paneled doors have chamfered edges set in a rectangular frame.

A shaped apron rests above shaped bracket feet.

EASTERN CAPE CUPBOARD

This stinkwood and yellowwood cupboard is of simple rectilinear form and has a molded rectangular top above two paneled doors. The panels have chamfered edges and are set within an additional, rectangular frame. The case has a shaped apron and stands on shaped, bracket feet. *1820–30. H:66½ in (169 cm); W:41⅓ in (105 cm); D:17⅓ in (44 cm). PRA*

UNITED STATES: LATE FEDERAL

FOLLOWING THE REVOLUTIONARY WAR, the victorious Americans embraced the Neoclassical movement and made it their own Federal style. This new style was initially inspired by the work of Robert Adam and the pattern books of Sheraton and Hepplewhite, and slender, delicate furniture was produced.

However, in the later stages of the Federal style, cabinet-makers took fresh influences from the ancient Greek and Roman worlds and used them directly in their work. For example, after 1800, chair designs became heavier and were based closely on the ancient Greek klismos model, with a thick, curved top rail and usually a carved horizontal slat at the back. Designs also showed the influence of the latest French styles, or English interpretations of them, and the English Regency style.

NEW YORK CRAFTSMEN

At this time, New York became a center of fine craftsmanship and home to the largest group of cabinet-makers in the country, who started exporting their work to the other states.

One of its best craftsmen was Duncan Phyfe (see p.233), whose name is synonymous with furniture that combines Greek-cross or saber legs, paw feet, harp and lyre backs, and caned top rails, with Neoclassical decoration of swags, cornucopias, wheat sheaves, and thunderbolts.

Another of New York's great cabinet-makers was Frenchman Charles-Honoré Lannuier, who worked there from 1803 to 1819. He worked in the French *Directoire* and *Consulat* styles until 1912, when he switched to the new Empire style, often using decorative motifs base on the art and architecture of ancient Greece and Rome. Lannuier's furniture was marked with his stamp and carried a label written in French and English, which promoted his European training and knowledge of Parisian styles. These labels offer a very useful tool for identifying Lannuier's pieces today, in contrast with Phyfe's furniture, which is very rarely labeled.

SOFAS AND CHAIRS

Late Federal sofas became more delicate and simple in style than previously, and had straight-topped or curved backs and tapered legs. Greek-style couches were designed to serve as day beds. Painted fancy chairs became highly fashionable, and Baltimore was renowned for its

MAHOGANY PEMBROKE TABLE

This Baltimore "Hepplewhite" inlaid table has an oval top and hinged leaves above plinths with fan-inlaid corners. The square tapering legs have a rare five-petal bellflower pendant. *H:28¾ in (73 cm); W:35¾ in (91 cm).*

The top of the chest is bow-fronted to match the case.

The oval panels are inlaid with bellflowers.

The handles are oval and made of brass.

BOW FRONT CHEST OF DRAWERS

This chest of drawers is made of mahogany with inlaid decoration, and comes from the southern US states. It has a bow-shaped top with a line-inlaid edge. The similarly-shaped case consists of four graduated drawers. Each drawer front has oval brass handles and inlaid decoration giving the impression of three panels. An exotic wood tablet at the center of each drawer depicts a swag of bellflowers. The base of the case has a shaped apron, which continues into French feet. *c. 1810. W:41½ in (105.5 cm). FRE*

The shaped apron curves continuously into the splayed French feet.

"SHERATON" WORK TABLE

This inlaid, figured mahogany and birch veneer table has a swelled, rectangular top with round outset corners above two drawers. The ring-turned, tapering, reeded legs have ring cuffs, on brass casters. *c. 1807. H:28 in (71 cm).*

ery elaborate examples of these. Chairs and sofas were often covered with silk or satin decorated with Neoclassical patterns, such as feathers, baskets of flowers, animals, or Classical figures.

TABLES
Drop-leaf, tilt-top, and Pembroke tables continued to be made, as did consoles, side and tea tables, work, card, and center tables, and stands of varying sizes.

Early Federal sideboards were too long for most American houses—some were up to 7 ft (210 cm) long—but by 1820, many smaller, simpler versions had been devised.

DESKS AND DRESSING TABLES
Tambour desks, an early version of the roll-top desk, first appeared in the US at the beginning of the 19th century. The tambour was made up of a series of wooden rods glued to a length of fabric and sometimes had an inlaid motif.

As glass became more widely available, some secrétaires and small desks were made with an upper section with glazed doors. The panes were separated by thin wooden strips, often arranged in complex patterns.

By the late Federal era, dressing tables had become small and rectangular in shape, often with a knee hole. The plain top could be left flat or mounted with a small case of drawers. Urban examples were often painted and gilded or decorated with fabric swags. Rural tables were simpler in design and made from inexpensive wood, which was painted to imitate woods such as mahogany.

STORAGE FURNITURE
Storage furniture ranged from linen presses—some of the finest of which were made at this time—to chests of drawers, chests-on-chests, and chests-on-frames. These last three tended to be flat-topped with bracket feet or turned Sheraton-style legs. They were often decorated with veneers or inlays. Most chests of drawers were made with straight fronts and the drawers were set with oval or rectangular mounts and bail handles. However, pieces were made also with serpentine fronts, and these examples are often said to represent a high point in American furniture-production.

FEDERAL SOFA

This mahogany-framed sofa has a gentle serpentine back and partially upholstered arms. The scrolled wooden armrests continue to vasiform and ring-turned posts, which then become vasiform-shaped, reeded front

legs, terminating in turned feet. Two further front legs are in the same style. The three rear legs are plain and splayed. The sofa is upholstered in yellow scalamandre fabric. *Early 19th century. L:81 in (202.5 cm). FRE*

HEPPLEWHITE'S PATTERN BOOK

THIS GUIDE WAS ONE OF SEVERAL PATTERN BOOKS THAT HELPED TO
TRANSMIT EUROPEAN STYLES TO THE UNITED STATES.

George Hepplewhite's *Cabinet-Maker and Upholsterer's Guide* is one of the best known of the 18th-century British furniture pattern books.

Published by his widow in 1788, two years after his death, its Neoclassical furniture designs had a great influence on American Federal furniture.

They appealed to members of the American upper and middle classes who were looking for new forms to reflect the new politics of the young republic.

Hepplewhite's ideas had been influenced by the work of Robert Adam and are noted for their grace and elegance. They can be seen in particular in the designs for Federal chairs, cabinets, sideboards, sofas, and tables.

FEDERAL ARMCHAIR

This mahogany armchair has gently curving arms that continue to turned supports. The upholstered seat is held in place with brass studs. The chair has tapered front legs and splayed back legs. *Early 19th century.*

CARVED MAHOGANY CHAIR

The back of this chair has flame-birch veneering on the arched top rail and urn-shaped splat, which is flanked on either side by reeded supports. The front legs are tapered and are joined by box stretchers.

Desk and bookcase Plate 40 from George Hepplewhite's *The Cabinet-Maker and Upholsterer's Guide*, 3rd Ed, 1794, Dover Publications, New York.

An inlaid butler's desk and bookcase This has a scalloped cornice beneath urn finials. The trefoil-arch doors and shelves are above a desk with a butler's drawer, a further three drawers, a shaped skirt, and French feet. *H:103 in (257.5 cm). NA*

FEDERAL INTERIOR

FOLLOWING AMERICA'S DECLARATION OF INDEPENDENCE IN 1776, THERE WAS A BOOM IN THE CONSTRUCTION OF BOTH GOVERNMENT BUILDINGS AND GRAND PRIVATE HOUSES.

Maple and ebony armchair This chair has a curved, flat top rail above a pierced back rest and scrolled arms. The cane seat is covered with a fixed cushion. The chair rests on ebonized, ring-turned legs. *c. 1820. H:32½ in (81 cm). FRE*

THE NEWLY FORGED American state saw itself as the scion of the Classical world, heir to the traditions and prestige of Republican Rome. The Neoclassical interior style of Robert Adam was enthusiastically adopted by American architects and designers, in spite of its English provenance.

Wealthy merchants and planters in Charleston, South Carolina, built impressive harbor-front houses. One such figure was Nathaniel Russell, whose residence at 51 Meeting Street, completed in 1808, was one of the most elegant in the town. The decorative scheme included shades of gray and a rich oxblood red, lightened with gilt embellishments. The architraves, mantels, and wainscoting boards were painted in bold monochrome, and the wall hangings included a plain, salmon paper with a lamb's-tongue border first used in ancient Greece. The most striking features are the wide, unsupported staircase that sweeps up in a graceful curve to the second and third floors, and the oval drawing room, shown here. This room was the scene of Alicia Russell's grand wedding ball in 1809. Demonstrations of wealth and confidence are as much a hallmark of the Federal style as the American eagle. Homemakers employed a variety of color schemes, although the walls were generally decorated in light colors, especially pastel shades.

NEOCLASSICAL STYLE

The basic structure of the Federal room closely follows the Neoclassical Georgian model; the overriding impression is one of pleasing symmetry, with the doorways placed centrally and flanked by equal numbers of windows. Public, showcase rooms often occupied unorthodox floor spaces, including hexagonal and circular chambers.

Dentil moldings or balustrades tempered the sparse Classical lines. Banisters and rails were often constructed from iron, since wood did not perform well when cut to the requisite lean proportions. Neoclassical swags, urns, and medallions were applied to cornices and friezes on interior walls. Rather than being carved out of stone, these decorative motifs were hewn from wood or, more commonly, were molded from composition ornament, or "compo." Compo was a mixture of animal glue, resin, and chalk that was malleable when warm but hardened to the consistency of plaster when cool. It was most famously used to create the central ceiling rosette in the dining room at Mount Vernon, George Washington's Virginia home.

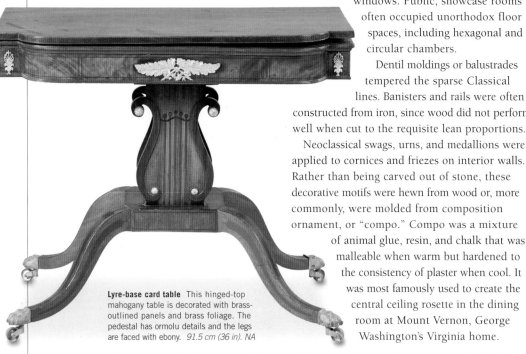

Lyre-base card table This hinged-top mahogany table is decorated with brass-outlined panels and brass foliage. The pedestal has ormolu details and the legs are faced with ebony. *91.5 cm (36 in). NA*

AMERICAN EMPIRE

THE EMPIRE STYLE, which originated in France around 1800, became popular in the United States about 15 years later. This was the start of the Industrial Revolution. Transportation, education, health, and communications were improving rapidly and many people were moving west in search of prosperity and new opportunities.

As industrialization increased, Empire-style furniture was made to suit a variety of budgets—it could be elegant and costly for the wealthy, or plain and affordable for the middle classes. This meant that furniture in one style could be made to suit people of all classes. The style proved to be popular, and country pieces were still being made at the end of the century, when urban cabinet-makers had moved on to newer styles.

CHANGE OF SHAPE

The new style of furniture took the early delicate Federal form and made it huge, bulky, and ornate. Like Federal furniture, Empire pieces were inspired by ancient Greek and Roman forms, but used them more literally while still making furniture suited to life in the 19th century.

Designs started to emphasize the outline rather than the details of a piece, and decoration such as undulating scrolls carved in high relief was applied to heavy, geometric furniture. Cabinet-makers stopped using inlays and started using stenciling, gilded-brass or bronze mounts, or as little decoration as possible.

The cornice is molded.

The side columns are reeded and fluted.

The cuffs and feet are made of brass.

The paneled doors enclose shelves.

DUNCAN PHYFE SIDE CHAIR

This mahogany and ebonized Neoclassical chair has a curved and rolled top rail above *demi-lune* splats, flanked by reeded stiles. The upholstered seat is raised on curved legs, the front ones terminating in claw feet. *1820.*

MAHOGANY BREAKFAST TABLE

This table has a top with shaped, hinged leaves above a single frieze drawer and is raised on leaf-carved baluster-shaped base and platform. The downswept legs end in brass paw caps and casters. *c. 1815. H:28 in (70 cm). FRE*

CLASSICAL ARMOIRE

This impressive, Classical-style armoire is made of mahogany. The piece has a molded architectural-style cornice, which is set above a rectangular case. Two shaped doors, decorated with geometric paneling, open

to reveal an interior fitted with shelves. The case is flanked by elegant, fluted, engaged columns and is supported on short, turned legs with brass cuffs and feet. The piece was probably made in the New York area. *1800–20. H:90 in (228.6 cm); W:62 in (157.4 cm); D:24 in (60.9 cm).*

CHEST OF DRAWERS

This chest of drawers is made of flame-mahogany, and most of the decoration is provided by the color and patina of the wood. The chest has a rectangular top with a molded edge set above a blind drawer. Below this are

three long, graduated drawers, each of which has two gilt-brass ring pulls in the shape of lion's heads. The drawers are flanked on either side by tapering columns carved with lotus motifs. The columns rest on a plinth base, giving the piece an architectural, Neoclassical feel. *W:48 in (120 cm). S&K*

EY DESIGNERS AND INFLUENCES
he new style first flourished in New
ork, inspired by British and French
ublications, and in particular by the
ork of the English designer Thomas
ope. By the 1840s, American
esigners were making their own
esign statements, and John Hall of
altimore published the country's first
esign book, *The Cabinet Maker's
ssistant*, featuring Empire designs.
   The cabinet-maker who was pivotal
 establishing the style in the United
ates was the British-born Duncan
hyfe (*see box*). Another early
xponent was Charles Honoré
annuier (*see pp.228–229*). His

exuberant designs for tables and
chairs, often with gilded caryatids,
were made at his workshop in New
York. However, the more flamboyant
Empire furniture was generally made
in both Boston and Philadelphia.

SHAPES AND DECORATIONS
Empire furniture usually has saber or
curule—X-shaped—legs with large
scroll, ball, or carved animal feet.
Chairs often had solid vase-shaped
splats. Some table tops were made
of marble, while others had heavy
pedestal bases.
   Typical Empire furniture included
klismos chairs, scroll-end sofas and

settees, ornamental center tables,
mirror-backed pier tables, sleigh and
canopy beds, and day beds, such as
récamiers and *méridiennes*. Cabinet-
makers also continued to produce
sideboards, dressing tables, and
pedestal desks. Chests of drawers
were now made with splashboards.
   Roman symbols were especially
important in the decoration of Empire
furniture and included cornucopia,
anthemion and acanthus leaves,
eagles, dolphins, swans, lyres, and
harps. Napoleon's campaign in
Egypt inspired the use of scarabs,
lotus flowers, and
hieroglyphs. Doors

and drawers were furnished with lion's
head mounts, and brass, pressed glass,
or turned wooden knobs.

MATERIALS
Rosewood and richly grained mahogany
or walnut were popular woods, but
maple and cherry were also used.
Vernacular furniture was made from
local woods including pine and birch.
The woods were also used for veneers.
   Chairs and sofas were upholstered
in silk damask with bold, large-scale
Classical designs or stylized flowers,
striped silk, or plain silk or velvet.

DUNCAN PHYFE

DUNCAN PHYFE'S FASHIONABLE AND HIGH-QUALITY FURNITURE HELPED TO ESTABLISH HIM AS
ONE OF THE MOST SUCCESSFUL AND PROLIFIC CABINET-MAKERS IN THE UNITED STATES.

By the end of his life, Duncan Phyfe (1768–1854) had
helped to transform American cabinet-making. His
furniture was based on a series of European styles,
from Sheraton and Regency through to Empire, and
he produced many of these styles simultaneously.
   Born near Loch Fannich, Ross and Cromarty, in
Scotland, Phyfe emigrated to the United States as a
teenager and was apprenticed to a cabinet-maker in
Albany, New York. In 1792, he moved to New York City
and within three years had opened his own store. By
1845, he was one of the richest men in the city.
   Such was the demand for his work that he went on to
employ 100 carvers and cabinet-makers, each undertaking
a specific task, such as turning legs or carving. They
produced a wide range of furniture, especially large and
ambitious pieces for dining rooms, using the best
mahogany and featuring elegant proportions and fine
details, particularly in the carving. Phyfe's customers were
the wealthy of New York and beyond, including the multi-
millionaire fur trader and landowner John Jacob Astor.

Phyfe has now given his name to the generic furniture
made in the Late Federal and Empire styles, which
featured Neoclassical motifs from ancient Greece and
Rome. However, since he rarely attached a trade label to his
furniture, few Phyfe-style pieces can be conclusively
linked to the designer himself.

MARBLE TOP PIER TABLE

This table is carved and stencil-decorated. The top rests on a
cyma-curved apron and frontal columnar supports with gilded
Corinthian capitals and ringed bases on ribbed feet. The mirrored
back is flanked by flat pilasters. The table has a shaped medial
shelf. *c. 1835. W:41 in (102.5 cm). NA*

Phyfe's shop and warehouse This watercolor, black ink, and
gouache picture depicts Duncan Phyfe's shop and warehouse
in New York City. The artist is unknown. *c. 1816.*

"SHERATON" CARD TABLE

This carved mahogany card table has a serpentine hinged
top over a similarly shaped apron, which is decorated with
a carved basket of fruit. The table is raised on turned and
reeded, tapering legs, which are decorated with floral and
foliate carving. *1830. L:37 in (94 cm). NA*

Empire sofa This sofa has a carved top rail and arms, and a caned
seat, back, and arms. The reeded, crossed, curved legs end in
casters hidden in brass paws. *1815–25. L:82 in (208 cm). AME*

EUROPEAN INFLUENCES

THE RELATIONSHIP BETWEEN American, British, and French furniture in the early 19th century is complex, and there is often no easy way to distinguish the origins of pieces. Although the United States was stylistically dependent on the Old World, it still produced some highly original makers, who adapted the Regency and Empire styles in much the same way as European countries diluted the French Napoleonic style. However, it is sometimes only possible to confirm that a piece is American by analyzing the construction timbers.

The American interpretation of styles is best seen in the work of Duncan Phyfe and Charles-Honoré Lannuier. Phyfe's Scottish origin probably encouraged him to adopt Thomas Sheraton's style initially.

Phyfe usually worked in Santo Domingo mahogany, palisander, or purpleheart. He went on to produce pieces in the Empire style before developing the Fat Classical style, which favored sculptural decoration.

Charles-Honoré Lannuier was French and settled in New York in 1803. Having trained in France, he brought with him the Louis XVI style, which evolved into an idiosyncratic form of Empire. His furniture is often difficult to distinguish from the French prototypes, especially since he used costly materials and probably imported gilt-bronze mounts from Paris.

Pattern books produced in Britain and France by Sheraton, Percier, and others disseminated European style to the United States more quickly than in the past, so trends were less delayed.

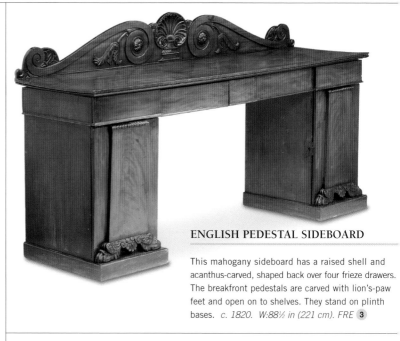

ENGLISH PEDESTAL SIDEBOARD

This mahogany sideboard has a raised shell and acanthus-carved, shaped back over four frieze drawers. The breakfront pedestals are carved with lion's-paw feet and open on to shelves. They stand on plinth bases. *c. 1820. W:88½ in (221 cm). FRE* **3**

AMERICAN PEDESTAL SIDEBOARD

This Classical mahogany sideboard mirrors the Englis version (*above*) having a leaf-carved, shaped backboa and pedestals on a plinth base. The rectangular top stepped and sits above an ogee-molded frieze fitted with drawers. *c. 1840. W:72¼ in (183.5 cm). FRE* **4**

The arms have small, padded elbow rests.

The fluted legs are crowned by carved rosettes.

The upholstery is from a later date, in the 20th century.

DIRECTOIRE BERGÈRE

This French armchair exemplifies the *bergère* design. It has a high, curved back with a top rail sweeping forward to form the armrests, which are padded to provide support for the elbows. The chair has a fully upholstered seat and back, downswept arm supports, and a gently shaped seat rail. The upholstery fabric is not original. The frame of the *bergère* is carved with leaves throughout and is raised on short, tapering, fluted legs to the front and splayed legs to the rear. The front legs are decorated with carved rosettes. *c. 1800. Bk* **3**

ENGLISH CURRICULE CHAIR

The rounded back and arms of this rosewood and beech chair flow in a continuous line, echoing the *bergère*. It is one of a pair designed by Gillows. *c. 1811. H:34¼ in (87 cm); W:21¼ in (54 cm); D:21 in (53 cm). LOT*

AMERICAN TUB CHAIR

Like the curricule chair (*left*), this Federal mahogany armchair shares characteristics with the *bergère*: the upholstered seat, back, and arms, and the continuous line of the rounded back and arms. *Early 19th century. NA* **4**

EORGE IV CARD TABLE

s mahogany, boxwood, and ebony-strung
rd table has a rectangular, crossbanded,
ding top above a plain frieze and ring-turned,
ering legs with brass casters. *Early 19th
ntury. W:35½ in (90.5 cm). DN* 4

AMERICAN CARD TABLE

Made of mahogany and bird's-eye maple, this
card table has rosewood crossbanding and a
hinged top above a serpentine frieze. The ring-
turned, fluted legs end in turned feet. *Early
19th century. H:29 in (73.5 cm). NA* 3

ENGLISH CENTER TABLE

This rosewood table has a circular tilt-top with
a plain, crossbanded frieze. It has an octagonal
spreading pedestal and a concave triform base
with scrolling paw feet. *Early 19th century.
D:54 in (135 cm). L&T* 4

AMERICAN CENTER TABLE

This Empire table has a circular rope-carved
top with a plain frieze and a floral carved and
gilded pedestal. The base and feet are almost
identical to the English example, left.
Early 19th century. D:35½ in (104 cm). L&T 4

NGLISH CELLARET

e rectangular hinged top of this mahogany
laret encloses a divided interior. It is
ported on a rope-turned plinth and raised
ring-turned brass caps with casters. *Early
h century. H:27¼ in (68 cm). L&T* 3

AMERICAN CELLARET

This inlaid cherry-wood cellaret, on a stand, has
a hinged lid and compartmentalized interior.
The cellaret stands on square-section, tapering
legs. *Early 19th century. H:16 in (40.5 cm);
W:13 in (33 cm); D:12½ in (32 cm). BRU* 5

FRENCH *SECRÉTAIRE À ABATTANT*

This Empire-style, mahogany tall chest has
three drawers above a pair of cupboard doors.
The case is flanked by tapered pilasters topped
by gilt-metal female busts. *Early 19th century.
H:64½ in (164 cm). FRE* 3

AMERICAN *SECRÉTAIRE*

This Classical-style *secrétaire à abattant* has
a marble top and a frieze drawer flanked by
figural mounts. The drop front sits above
cupboard doors. *Early 19th century. H:56½ in
(143.5 cm); W:39 in (99 cm); D:18 in (46 cm).*

GENCY SOFA

s mahogany Regency-style sofa has a
med scrolling back and outscrolled arms
h reeded, mahogany fronts. The squab
shion and bolsters are supported on a reeded
t rail with bead-and-reel molded tablets.

The sofa is supported on splayed, reeded
legs with leaf-cast brass caps and casters.
The splayed legs are particularly susceptible
to damage. *Early 19th century. W:90 in
(225 cm). L&T* 3

AMERICAN SOFA

This elegant American sofa has a shaped and
carved top rail and outscrolled arms similar
to the Regency sofa *(see left)*. The back,
arms, and seat are upholstered and raised on
a leaf-carved seat rail. The sofa is supported

on elaborately carved legs that terminate in
paw feet. Compared to the Regency example,
this sofa is proportionally more bulky. *1825.
W:86 in (218 cm). FRE* 1

THE SHAKERS

THE THRIVING COMMUNAL SOCIETY OF THE SHAKERS PRODUCED FINELY CRAFTED BUT SIMPLE FURNITURE, IN ACCORDANCE WITH ITS DEEP RELIGIOUS PRINCIPLES.

The Shakers were a Christian group led by Ann Lee, known as Mother Ann, who emigrated to America from England in 1774. Within 50 years, there were 19 communities, made up of over 5,000 men (Brothers) and women (Sisters). They were celibate and lived separated from the outside world. They shared their resources and were self-sufficient, believing that their work was for the good of their community. Women had the same rights as the men, but they lived apart and only came together for meetings and singing. Since their communities were built on recruits, they often took in orphans.

SIMPLE FORMS

Joseph Meacham, who became their leader in 1784, declared that Shaker buildings, furniture, and clothing should be devoid of decoration and extravagance, so the communities strived for

simplicity in all things. Items had to fit their purpose, and making them was another way in which they could praise God. The result was fine craftsmanship devoid of superfluous decoration such an inlays, turning, or carving. Wood was smoothly finished, with no tool marks left on the finished piece.

The Shakers took the simple forms of 18th-century design, such as the ladder-back chair, trestle table, cupboard, and chest of drawers, and adapted them to suit their way of life. All their furniture was made from pine, maple, cherry, walnut, butternut, poplar, and birch woods found on their own property.

Furniture was often painted or stained red, red-brown, yellow, or dark blue. Although decorative painting was forbidden, Brothers and Sisters were allowed to paint their buildings and certain utilitarian items. Boxes were frequently painted red or yellow, for example.

Shaker furniture was based on simple Neoclassical designs. Common items included slat-back chairs, plain and sewing tables, candlestands, benches and stools, and low-post beds. Chests had complex drawer arrangements and were made on simple, geometric lines. All these items were quick and inexpensive to make. The Shakers used traditional construction techniques, such as mortise-and-tenon joints that were often pegged, nailed, or dovetailed. Drawer and cupboard pulls were usually turned wooden knobs. Chair seats might be caned or made from woven tape.

CUPBOARD-OVER-DRAWERS
This case piece has two hinged cupboard drawers set above an arrangement of ten short over two long graduated drawers with turned knobs. It is made from pine and boss wood with its original finish. It is from Mount Lebanon, New York, and is attributed to Brother Amos Stewart. WH

SHAKER ROCKING CHAIR
The chair is made of solid beech that has been stained a darker color. It has a gently curved frame, a cane seat, and sweeping armrests.
H:41 in (104 cm); W:24 in (61 cm); D:29½ in (74 cm).

CHEST OF DRAWERS
This piece is made of butternut and poplar, with pine as a secondary wood. It has a finely-beveled top board above six dovetailed and lipped drawers, with cherry-wood threaded knobs. The case has inset paneled ends and stands on arched feet. W:43 in (109 cm). WH

SIMPLE HOMES

SHAKER FURNITURE AND INTERIORS REFLECT THE
UTMOST SIMPLICITY FOR WHICH THEY STRIVED.

Shakers lived in dormitories, two to a room, which usually
contained two single beds on wheels, with a candlestand
and iron candleholder between them, and two ladder-back
chairs, fitted with small tilters. These were turned, wooden
balls with flat bases that fitted into hollows at the base of
the back chair legs. The balls were attached to the legs by
leather thongs and helped to keep the chairs in balance.

The roommates usually shared a cupboard-over-drawers.
The top cupboard held bonnets or hats and the drawers
clothes. Sometimes there would be another small cupboard
at the bottom for shoes. Pegs and pegboards
surrounded the walls of every Shaker room.
These were used for hanging an occasional
piece of clothing on a wooden hanger or for
hanging up chairs while the room was being cleaned. A
small mirror would hang on a holder attached to the peg
rail. No decoration was allowed in the room.

Shakers led a very ordered life, and rooms and the pieces
of furniture made for them were often numbered so that if
a piece was moved it could be returned to its rightful place.
These numbers can still be found painted on the
undersides of chairs and tables.

Sewing Room This room in
the Centre Family Dwelling
at Pleasant Hill was built by
Shakers in the 19th century.
It was sparsely furnished
in the simple Shaker style
with two ladder-back rocking
chairs and a round stand.

Shaker round stand The small, circular top of this table
is raised on a turned column and legs in the form of
intersecting crescents. The piece is probably made of
cherry wood and was used for setting down small objects.
1820–30. H:25¼ in (64 cm); Diam:15¾ in (40 cm). AME

Elder's rocking chair This chair is made
from tiger maple and has its original finish.
It has curvilinear arms, a taped seat, and
tall finials and is from Mount Lebanon,
New York. *c. 1840.* H:44 in (112 cm). WH

COMMERCIAL SUCCESS

Due to the Shakers' productivity,
they started selling their surplus
products to people outside their communities. They
made chairs that were sold in sizes from "0" (the
smallest child's chair) to "7" (a large adult rocking
chair). Ladder-back rockers could be ordered with a
shawl bar across the top of the back, so that people
could hang a shawl on them for warmth.

When other manufacturers began copying their
products, the Shakers put a trademark decal on the
inside of their rockers or on the back of the bottom
slat of the ladders, to show that the chair was a
genuine Shaker product.

The Shakers reached the height of their success in
the mid-1800s. After the Civil War, the United States
started to shift to a more industrial and urban society
and it became more difficult for the Shakers to find
converts. After 1900, communities started to close
their doors. A number of them have since been
reopened as museums.

TAILORESS' COUNTER

*This chest of drawers was used for storage and as a sewing
table. It has a curly maple top set over four short and two long
drawers with maple stiles and rails and curly maple drawer
fronts. The sides and back of the case are paneled pine and the
legs are turned.* 1820–30. H:45 in (114 cm); D:24 in (61 cm). AME

NORTH AMERICAN VERNACULAR

IN THE EARLY 19TH CENTURY, pioneers were building new towns and settlements across North America. Like many of the families who had been living in the colonies for the past 200 years, these pioneers needed furniture that was practical rather than fashionable. Vernacular pieces dating back to this time are considered some of the most interesting made in the United States and Canada, because rural makers began imitating more sophisticated pieces.

The cabinet-makers and wood-workers in small settlements rarely learned skills such as veneering, which were being used in the larger towns

and cities. However, as urban cabinet-makers moved to find work, some trends began to have an impact on country furniture, and the traditional styles favored in rural areas were influenced by newer designs.

STYLE INSPIRATIONS

While the United States tended to be influenced by British styles, parts of Canada, which had originally been French, were influenced by French designs. When Britain took over the French colonies in 1760, the local craftsmen continued to make furniture in the modified French style they had been using for decades. Slowly, the

Neoclassical style that was popular in the United States and Britain started to catch on, although cabinet-makers trained in French techniques still used them to make the new British- and American-style furniture.

The Federal style, which had developed in urban America at the end of the 18th century also appealed to rural craftsmen, and their interpretation of its simple shapes, decorated with brightly colored paint, was popular for decades.

The quality and design of vernacular furniture across North America were usually determined by the skill of the maker, the materials on hand, and

the taste and budget of the clients. Many pieces seemed to be unaffected by the latest fashions, or were a very simple interpretation of them. However, even inexpensive vernacular pieces made by urban craftsmen often mimicked the fashions of the time. Sometimes elements of different styles were combined. Later in the century, for example, a Victorian chest might have incorporated late Empire features, such as scrolled feet.

VERNACULAR STYLE

Although basic in both design and construction, vernacular furniture was rarely crudely made. Details were often

LOW BUFFET

This carved and painted pine buffet has a rectangular top above fielded panel sides. The case contains a pair of short drawers above lozenge-carved doors, and is raised on stile feet. *W:54 in (137 cm). WAD*

Escutcheon detail

NEW MEXICAN CHEST

This pine carved chest has seven panels on the front with rosettes and stylized lions of Leon Province in Spain, and pomegranates in low relief. The side panels are decorated with large rosettes. Vernacular styles took longer to

change style, so pieces like this were common in the 1900s. *Late 18th century. H:19 in (48.3 cm); W:24 in (61 cm); D:18 in (71 cm).*

The bedding is made from a simple woven textile.

The mortise-and-tenon joint is exposed.

Each bed end has two rows of turned spindles.

The sabre leg is a rustic interpretation of the style.

NEW MEXICAN DAY BED

The design for this pine day bed was influenced by the pieces that came to New Mexico via the Santa Fe trail. This rustic-style piece has exposed joints. The bed would have been used for the sick or dying. *AME*

SINGLE-DRAWER STAND

The top of this Federal stand is inlaid with a geometric design and has rounded corners. The piece has a single drawer set below the top. The stand is raised on square, tapering legs. *c. 1810. H:28½ in (72.5 cm). FRE*

eavier than those found on more
fined and expensive pieces, but
ey were always elegant.

Craftsmen used local lumber, such as
ne, ash, hickory, birch, oak, maple,
d fruitwoods including cherry and
ple, and decorated them with stains
paint rather than the veneers
vored by city furniture-makers.
any of these painted pieces have
ow achieved the status of folk art
d are, therefore, highly prized.
Legs and spindles were often turned,
d pediments and skirts frequently
d cut-out details. Seats were
nerally carved, or were made from
sh, splints, tape, or cane.

Different parts of the furniture
were usually joined using a mortise-
and-tenon construction, but they
were also sometimes pegged, nailed,
or dovetailed.

DOMESTIC PIECES

Common types of vernacular furniture
of the early 19th century include slat-
back chairs. Stools, benches, and
settles were also made, as well as
low-post beds and cradles.

Dry sinks—which were usually
made by simply nailing together
boards to make a place for washing
dishes—were a necessity before
indoor plumbing was available.

Cupboards were often built to fill
a particular space and rarely had feet.
Sometimes they were made from scrap
lumber and then decorated with
colored stains, sponging, or graining.
The doors were fastened with shaped
wooden, brass, or iron latches, and
had turned wooden knobs or porcelain
pulls. Escutcheons usually took the
form of either brass or iron plates,
or keyhole surrounds.

Six-board chests were among the
earliest American pieces, and they were
sometimes decorated with molding,
carving, or paint. By the early 19th
century, they were made from paneled
oak or pine and were gradually
superseded by chests of drawers.

Other common pieces of vernacular
furniture included drop-leaf, tea, work,
sewing, and other small tables, as well
as chests and hanging racks.

HUTCH TABLES

THESE QUAINT CHAIR-TABLES ARE TYPICAL OF THE TYPE OF VERNACULAR
AMERICAN FURNITURE MADE DURING THE EARLY 19TH CENTURY.

The hutch table was one of the first
pieces of multipurpose, space-saving
furniture in the United States. It was
basically a table with a round top that
could be swung back to create a chair
with a circular back. Some hutch tables
also had a drawer or cupboard built into
the base, to provide useful storage space.

These chair-tables were first made in
the 17th century in rural areas of the
East Coast colonies, but their popularity
in the countryside continued until the

mid-19th century. They were made from
local woods such as pine, maple, oak,
birch, and fruitwoods.

Hutch tables were variously decorated
according to the styles that were popular
when they were made: fashions reached
rural communities later than they reached
cities, and these were adopted on a more
modest scale. A plain hutch table, for
example, might indicate that it was
influenced by the Federal style popular
in the early 19th century.

RUSH-SEAT SIDE CHAIRS

These three Neoclassical side chairs from the
mid-Atlantic states are made from tiger maple
and have rush seats. The outswept back of
each chair has a shaped center rail, which is
flanked, top and bottom, by rectangular rails.

The turned legs are joined by a number of
stretchers, the one at the front being double
and more elaborate than those at the sides and
back. The rush seats were probably original,
although it is likely that the upholstered
cushions were added later for increased
comfort. *c. 1825. H:33½ in (84.5 cm).*

This piece is plainly
styled and lacks
decoration, indicating
that it is vernacular.

The shelf doubles as
a chair seat when the
table top is raised.

The table top lifts
up to transform the
piece into a chair.

*The four turned
legs* are joined by
cross-stretchers.

A hutch table This piece has birch
arms, a pine seat, and is painted
red. *c. 1800. W:50 in (127 cm). PS*

NEW MEXICAN CHAIR

This is a simple, low chair made from yellow
pine. The only decoration is provided by
geometric chip carving on the apron and back
slats. The legs are linked by turned stretchers.
Early 19th century. H:15⅓ in (39 cm). AME

CANADIAN ARMCHAIR

This armchair is made of birch and has three
salamander-shaped slats, which are flanked
by block-and-urn turned stiles over a rush
seat. The chair is raised on similarly turned
legs joined by stretchers.

WINDSOR CHAIRS

THE WINDSOR CHAIR is often associated with country timbers and provincial manufacture (particularly around High Wycombe, England). However, its origins were far from provincial. The Duke of Chandos had japanned Windsor chairs in his library at his Middlesex home, Canons, and there were mahogany examples in the library of St. James' Palace in the early 18th century. However, by the early 19th century, they were restricted to humbler homes or taverns.

Windsor chairs were only ever produced in Great Britain and North America, but British and American Windsor chairs often display different characteristics. While the seat (generally a saddle type) is central to the construction of both, with the

elements of the back, legs, and arms all mortised into it, they were made in different timbers. In Britain, ash, yew, and fruitwoods were used, with elm for the seat and, occasionally, beech for the turnings. In North America, hickory, chestnut, oak, ash, and sometimes maple were favored, with tulip, poplar, and pine for the seats.

There are also some stylistic differences between the two types. For instance, the use of a splat was more typically British, while the low-back Windsor chair was entirely American until the 1840s. Similarly, the Neoclassical Windsor chair, sometimes called an "arrow-back" on account of the spear or arrow shape that constitutes the back sticks, was never produced in Great Britain.

AMERICAN WRITING-ARM CHAIR

This high-back Windsor chair from Connecticut has an arched top rail, a mid-rail with an arm and a writing paddle with drawer, a saddle seat with a drawer beneath, reel-turned legs, and an H-stretcher. *1797. NA* **3**

AMERICAN COMB-BACK CHAIR

This chair, from Philadelphia, has a serpentine top rail with scrolled ear terminals, a yoked mid-rail with scrolled knuckle-arm terminals, a saddle seat, outsplayed legs, and an H-stretcher. *NA* **5**

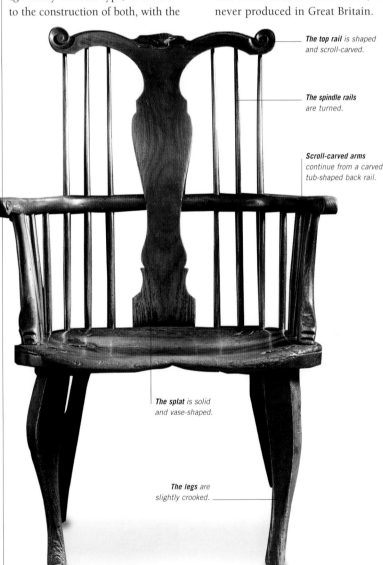

The top rail is shaped and scroll-carved.

The spindle rails are turned.

Scroll-carved arms continue from a carved tub-shaped back rail.

The splat is solid and vase-shaped.

The legs are slightly crooked.

GEORGIAN WINDSORS

Each of these yew armchairs has a hoop back and arms with a Gothic pierced splat and spars. The elm saddle seats are supported on cabriole legs terminating in pad feet and joined by hoop stretchers. *1750–70. L&T* **4**

FAN-BACK WINDSORS

Each of this pair of English elm, walnut, and fruitwood fan-back Windsor armchairs has a shaped seat supported on turned legs joined by an H-stretcher. The chairs bear traces of their original paint finish. *c. 1770. H:40 in (101.5 cm); W:24¾ in (63 cm); D:18 in (46 cm). RY*

CROOKED LEG WINDSOR

This is an early English Windsor chair made of fruitwood, ash, and elm. It has a ram's horn- and shell-carved top rail that terminates in scrolled ears. The central back rail curves forward to provide the scroll-carved arms, while

the solid, vase-shaped, central splat is flanked by elegant, turned spindle rails. There are three main spindles that continue from the top rail to the seat, and extra spindles in the lower section. The shaped seat is supported on four crooked legs. *c. 1750. H:38 in (96.5 cm); W:26¼ in (66.5 cm); D:23 in (58.5 cm). RY*

HILADELPHIA WINDSOR

is Windsor armchair has a top rail with a tterfly and seven spindles with bamboo rnings above a shaped seat. The seat is pported on tapering legs joined by stretchers. *1800. Seat: H:17½ in (44.5 cm). AAC* **1**

AMERICAN BOW-BACK WINDSOR

This mahogany and painted armchair has an arched, molded top rail, nine flaring spindles, down-curved arms over raked bamboo supports, a squared, shield-form seat, and raked bamboo turned legs with an H-stretcher. *NA* **1**

AMERICAN WINDSOR SIDE CHAIR

This side chair has a bow-shaped back with nine spindles above a saddle seat. The seat is supported on splayed legs with bamboo turnings and is joined by an H-stretcher. *H:18 in (45.75 cm). AAC* **1**

GOTHIC WINDSOR CHAIR

Made from ash and elm, this chair has a lancet-shaped back with pierced splats. The chair seat is shaped and supported on cabriole legs with a hooped stretcher. One of a set of four. *Early 19th century. L&T* **3**

WINDSOR SETTEES

DESIGNED VIRTUALLY AS AN ELONGATED CHAIR, THIS TYPE OF SETTEE
WAS ONLY PRODUCED IN GREAT BRITAIN AND NORTH AMERICA.

There is little agreement on the differences between a settee and a sofa and indeed, the preferred term seems to be largely dictated by current fashion. However, "settee" generally designates a particular type of furniture made in the late 18th and early 19th century that was much more closely related to chair, rather than sofa, design.

Often conceived as a chair extended to seat two or more people, its origins lie in the chair-back settee of the mid-18th century and the settle. Consequently, it might have a caned seat and back, or a

pierced back with splats, just like a chair, rather than the complete upholstery of a sofa. The Cape rusbank was a simplified variation of this type of furniture.

Windsor settees are peculiar to Great Britain and North America. They are constructed in the same way as Windsor chairs, with a wooden seat into which the back, arms, and legs are mortised. The backs are either of a continuous form, running into the arms with vertical splats, or take the form of a series of chair backs.

An English Regency settee This beech piece was overpainted in verdigris and gilt. The back of the settee has four lattice backs with musical trophy panels below an outscrolled top rail and down-scrolled arms. The caned seat is supported on turned front legs with brass caps and casters. *Early 19th century. W:73 in (185 cm). L&T*

A Philadelphia bow-back Windsor settee
This black- and gold-painted settee has bamboo turnings. There are 29 spindles below the curved top rail and the downswept arms are on modified

S-curved supports. The seat is supported on bamboo turned legs joined by swelling H-stretchers. *W:79 in (197.5 cm). NA* **6**

An American arrowback, painted Windsor settee
This has a flat top rail and scrolling arms set above a planked seat. It has turned legs and turned panel stretchers. *Early 19th century. H:77½ in (194 cm). FRE* **1**

CHAIRS

ALL THE CHARACTERISTICS OF Regency and Empire furniture, from the Neoclassical motifs—often on pierced backs—to the choice of timbers, are displayed on early 19th-century chairs.

One of the most typical types of chair of the period is the Trafalgar chair, which was made in Britain and used for dining. The chair had two horizontal splats—one usually of bar form, the lower one sometimes a rope-twist, set above a caned or drop-in seat. Caning, with all its exotic overtones, was revived again during this period, particularly on British or Cape furniture. During the first two decades of the century, the front and back legs were usually of saber form, but turned or ring-turned legs, which are structurally stronger, were used later.

These chairs, and many that they inspired, were often made of solid mahogany or rosewood, with veneered panels on the bar back. Beech was used, and was often painted; light-colored woods were favored outside Britain. Chairs from this period rarely had stretchers.

One type of armchair, inspired by Georges Jacob, had a rectangular, scrolled, upholstered back and open arms with straight supports, often carved with sphinx heads or female masks. It also had turned and tapered front legs. These more comfortable *fauteuils* might be used in the drawing room, while Regency *bergères*, which had caned backs, sides, and seats, were probably made for the library. These chairs had squab cushions, often covered in leather and buttoned. Other pieces might be upholstered in silk or velvet. Needlework was rare, although a suite of furniture from the Winter Palace in Russia was covered in tapestry, in a mixture of wool and silk.

ENGLISH LIBRARY ARMCHAIR

This mahogany armchair has a reeded frame and arm supports. The sides, back, and seat are caned and have loose cushions. The turned and reeded legs have brass casters. *Early 19th century.* W:24¾ in (63 cm). DN **3**

FRENCH *RESTAURATION BERGÈRE*

The crest of this maple *bergère en gondole* is inlaid with a flower-head and stylized leaves, and the arms have carved leaf tips. The leather slip seat is supported by a carved seat rail on cabriole legs. *Early 19th century.* NA **3**

ENGLISH TRAFALGAR CHAIR

This Regency mahogany dining chair has a plain top rail and a rope-twist back rail. The needlework-covered drop-in seat is supported on a plain seat rail and saber legs. One of a set of four. *Early 19th century.* DN **3**

FRENCH *DIRECTOIRE* CHAIR

This is one of a pair of *Directoire* side chairs, each with a rectilinear back rail and splat inlaid with brass musical instruments. The upholstered stuffover seat is supported on saber legs. *c. 1800.* H:32 in (81 cm). **2**

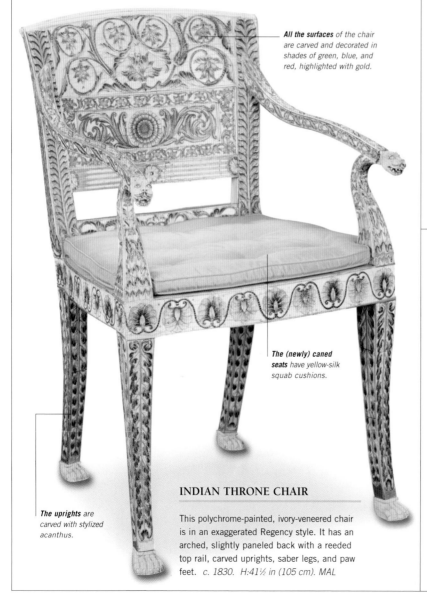

All the surfaces of the chair are carved and decorated in shades of green, blue, and red, highlighted with gold.

The (newly) caned seats have yellow-silk squab cushions.

The uprights are carved with stylized acanthus.

INDIAN THRONE CHAIR

This polychrome-painted, ivory-veneered chair is in an exaggerated Regency style. It has an arched, slightly paneled back with a reeded top rail, carved uprights, saber legs, and paw feet. *c. 1830.* H:41½ in (105 cm). MAL

SWEDISH BIEDERMEIER ARMCHAIR

This birch open armchair has a stepped yoke backrest with a decorative oval inlay and scrolled armrests. The drop-in seat has a plain seat rail and is raised on saber legs. *c. 1825.* W:22½ in (57 cm). EIL

CHINA TRADE ARMCHAIR

This Asian hardwood armchair has a Greek-key carved top rail and a shaped, carved back rail. The cane seat rests on a reeded seat rail above slender reeded legs joined by an H-stretcher. *Early 19th century.* H:33½ in (84 cm). MJM

RENCH *RESTAURATION* CHAIR

is walnut and fruitwood side chair has a
ntly reclining back with a rectangular top
d back rail. The padded seat is supported on
plain seat rail above stylized cabriole legs.
rly 19th century. H:31½ in (80 cm). ANB **4**

GERMAN BIEDERMEIER CHAIRS

These Biedermeier mahogany-veneered dining
chairs were made in Berlin. Each chair has
a bar top rail, a solid, shaped back rail with a
central oval, and elegant, slightly sweeping
uprights. The shaped caned seats are set

within a curved frame with a rounded seat rail
and are supported on four outswept saber legs.
*1820-30. H:33¼ in (84.5 cm); W:18⅛ in
(46 cm); D:16¾ in (42.5 cm). BMN* **10**

AMERICAN FEDERAL SIDE CHAIR

This mahogany side chair has a molded and
rope-carved shield back around an urn, Prince-
of-Wales feathers, draped swags, and leaves. The
serpentine seat rests on reeded, tapering legs.
Early 19th century. H:38½ in (98 cm). FRE **1**

MERICAN GONDOLA CHAIR

his is one of a pair of Neoclassical figured
ahogany gondola chairs, each with a curved
ack and vasiform, solid splat, a padded slip
at, and downswept stiles continuing into
aped saber front legs. *c. 1830. S&K*

ITALIAN GONDOLA CHAIRS

These six dining chairs are made of walnut
and are designed in the Neoclassical style.
Each chair has an unusual fluted, rectangular
backrest positioned above a pierced, stylized
leaf border. The cane seats have an applied

roundel at each side and are supported on
plain seat rails. The chairs are raised on
saber legs. The elegant sweeping uprights
give the chairs their characteristic shape,
which is reminiscent of the style of the
gondola boats found in Venice.
Early 19th century. NA

GEORGE III SHIELD-BACK CHAIR

This mahogany armchair has a shield-shaped,
curved back, outlined with guilloche molding,
with five reeded splats, curved downswept
arms, a bowed seat rail, and reeded, tapering
front legs. *c. 1800. H:37½ in (95 cm). PAR*

USSIAN OPEN ARMCHAIR

his birch open armchair has a stepped yoke
ackrest, with carved fan detail, and slender,
crolled armrests. The upholstered seat is
ised on saber legs. It is one of a pair.
arly 19th century. H:36 in (91.5 cm). EVE **4**

AMERICAN DINING CHAIRS

These eight Neoclassical-style dining chairs are
made of mahogany. Each chair has a flat
curved top rail carved with a foliate pattern
and a slender horizontal splat, also decorated
with leaf carving, plus a rosette. The seats

are upholstered with black Naugahyde and
are showing considerable signs of wear. The
seats are supported on plain seat rails and
raised on saber legs. The armchairs have gently
curving supports. The set comprises two
armchairs and six side chairs, and is attributed
to Anthony Quervelle. *c. 1820. FRE* **3**

SWEDISH GUSTAVIAN SIDE CHAIR

This white-painted side chair has a shield-
shaped back with a solid, carved splat. The
padded seat is supported on a molded seat
rail and is raised on stop-fluted legs joined by
an H-stretcher. *Early 19th century. Bk* **2**

NEW DEVELOPMENTS

IN THE EARLY 19TH century, many different forms of furniture were developed for specific purposes. Previously, furniture was placed against the wall and had to serve multiple functions, but this had gradually changed through the 18th century, and by the early years of the next century, more specialized pieces were made. The same period saw the rise of novel patent furniture. Thomas Morgan and Joseph Sanders of London specialized in the "Patent Sofa-Bed & Chair-Bed." They also made a celebrated type of armchair that hinged over to form library steps.

Not only were new forms of furniture developed, but old types were revitalized after taking forms derived from ancient Egypt, Greece, and Rome. For example, a cellaret, or wine cooler—an 18th-century invention—might be reconfigured in the form of an ancient sarcophagus.

New types of furniture were made for the dining room. The sideboard was still a relatively new invention. Often of rectangular form with a bowed front, it usually had two compartments separated by a drawer.

These might contain shelves or even a cellaret drawer. They frequently had a brass railing at the back, although they are now usually missing. British sideboards are generally made of mahogany with brass or ebonized stringing. Side cabinets and chiffoniers, both developments of the commode, were also new. They often had a pair of doors with brass grilles backed with pleated silk.

The cheval mirror, or Psyche glass, was a new piece of bedroom furniture. It consisted of a large single mirror held within a plain frame on a pivot, through which it was attached to the uprights of its stand. This was generally set on splayed legs with casters, so that it could be moved around easily.

Other new types of furniture, such as campaign furniture, reflected the military turbulence of the period. Campaign furniture was specially designed to be portable and easy to dismantle (*see pp.280–81*).

In similar vein, the *chaise à l'officier* (officer's chair) was made in France. It had arm supports, but lacked elbow rests, to enable a man wearing a sword to sit down with relative ease.

ENGLISH CELLARET

This Sheraton mahogany, arched-top cellaret has a domed lid above a rectilinear case with central oval panels and geometric inlay, set on rope-twist legs. *c. 1800. H:27 in (68.5 cm); W:17½ in (45 cm); D:17½ in (45 cm). NOA*

AMERICAN TAMBOUR SECRETAR

This desk has a rectangular upper section with tambour doors that open to reveal a fitted interior. The lower section has two long drawers raised on square-section legs with tapering feet. *c. 1795. H:40½ in (103 cm). NA* **6**

ENGLISH REGENCY SIDE CABINET

The shaped top of this parcel-gilt rosewood side cabinet is outlined with satinwood stringing. The frieze beneath contains five drawers, each

with lion's-mask ring handles. The cupboard below have front grilles, and there is a cent shelf. The cabinet has gilt-wood lion's-paw fe *c. 1805. H:37½ in (95 cm); W:69 in (175 cm), D:26 in (66 cm). PAR*

AMERICAN D-SHAPED SIDEBOARD

The rectangular top of this satinwood and figured maple sideboard has a bowed front above a conforming case with an arrangement of drawers and cupboard doors. The reeded legs have ringed cuffs. *1800–05. W:74 in (188 cm). NA* **6**

Each of the drawers and cupboard doors has banded and satinwood-inlaid borders.

The central cupboard doors are flanked by bottle drawers and additional cupboard doors.

The stiles each have an inlaid diamond motif set over a diagonally segmented column with a Gothic arch crest.

AMERICAN KLISMOS CHAIR

This mahogany chair has a curved, rectangular top rail with scroll carving, and a shaped, carved back rail. The seat is supported on saber legs. *c. 1815. H:33¾ in (86 cm); W:17½ in (44.5 cm); D:18 in (46 cm). BDL*

EGENCY WATERFALL BOOKCASES

ch mahogany bookcase has a three-quarter
llery above four graduated shelves and a
gle drawer with ivory handles. The cases
ve brass carrying handles at the sides.
rly 19th century. W:21 in (53 cm). L&T **5**

AMERICAN WORKTABLE

This Classical mahogany astragal-end worktable
has various compartments. It sits on a reeded
urn pedestal on four splayed, carved legs, which
end in brass feet and casters.
Early 19th century. H:29¼ in (73 cm). NA **6**

ENGLISH DAVENPORT DESK

The hinged top of this pollard oak desk has a
three-quarter spindle gallery enclosing two real
and false drawers, flanked by a pen drawer and
slides above four side drawers. *Early 19th
century. W:20 in (51 cm). BonS* **4**

NEW MATERIALS

A RANGE OF EXOTIC MATERIALS FROM INDIA OR OTHER COLONIES WERE
OFTEN USED TO ADD DECORATION TO SMALLER ITEMS OF FURNITURE.

Many previously rare materials became
more widely available early in the
century. Brass inlays were used in British
furniture, although they had been used
from around 1740 to 1760. Similarly,
mother-of-pearl was increasingly used
throughout the 19th century, particularly
on small objects such as tea caddies.
Exotic woods and materials, such as
amboyna or ivory, were imported from the
colonies, and lacquer cut from Chinese

screens was still used as a veneer. On the
Continent, the embargo on mahogany led
to an increased use of light-colored local
timbers, the so-called *bois clairs*. In
Britain, pieces were often completely
japanned in a technique called
penwork. Other popular decorative
techniques in Britain were Tumbridgeware
(wooden inlay in small geometric designs)
or straw-work (pieces of straw arranged
in patterns to look like marquetry).

The tilt-top has a
lacquered surface.

Ebonized parcel-gilt table The papier-mâché top
has painted Oriental figures and rests on a turned
leaf-carved support, triform base, and paw feet.
Early 19th century. H:28¼ in (72 cm). DN **3**

ENGLISH CHEVAL MIRROR

This Regency mahogany cheval mirror has a
crossbanded rectangular frame supported on a
ring-turned frame. It has outswept legs with
brass paw terminals and casters. *Early 19th
century. H:67 in (170 cm). DN* **2**

A mirror is revealed
when the table
top is opened.

The rosewood veneer
is inlaid with mother-
of-pearl.

Penwork decorates
the surfaces of this
occasional table.

**A turned baluster
column** supports
the oval table top.

Biedermeier sewing table
This sewing table is veneered in
rosewood and inlaid throughout with
mother-of-pearl. The top opens to
reveal a fitted interior and mirror.
*c. 1830. H:30 in (76.5 cm); W:19 in
(48 cm); D:16 in (40.5 cm). BMN*

**English penwork oval-top
occasional table** This
piece has a turned
baluster column support,
a triform base, and is
decorated with penwork.
c. 1825. CATO **6**

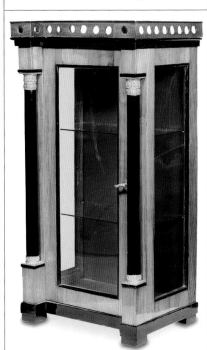

SOUTHERN GERMAN VITRINE

Veneered with part-ebonized cherry wood, this
vitrine has three glazed sides flanked by
protruding column stiles with gilt-metal
capitals. A front-opening door reveals two glass
shelves. *c. 1825. H:35¾ in (91 cm). BMN* **3**

MIRRORS

MIRRORS, LIKE PICTURE FRAMES, are decorative, so are rarely subjected to much wear. As a result, they are often gessoed and gilded. Painted examples from this period also exist, as well as Empire pier glasses, which often have mahogany frames and ormolu mounts.

From the late 18th century, larger plates became available, so early 19th-century mirrors with a divided plate became less common. Although not new, convex plates became especially fashionable in Britain and the United States, and were used in dining rooms to give servants an all-around view of the table. The convex mirror plate was usually framed by an ebonized and reeded slip with a gilt frame echoing the shape of the mirror. The frame was

often surmounted with an eagle or similar motif and frequently had candle arms attached to it.

Also fashionable was the use of *verre églomisé*, in which glass was back-painted in black and then engraved with a design before gilding. *Verre églomisé* plates were frequently inserted above normal plates. Mirrors with a more rectilinear design were also popular, particularly those intended to stand above pier tables between windows. From the late 1820s, revival styles led to the reintroduction of Chippendale-style mirrors in Britain; these are often difficult to distinguish from the 18th-century originals. In Florence, boldly carved foliate frames were introduced in imitation of the Baroque originals.

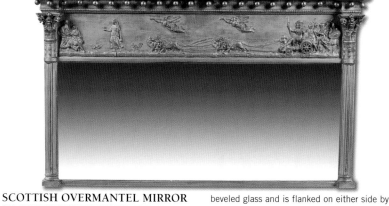

SCOTTISH OVERMANTEL MIRROR

This Regency giltwood and gesso overmantel mirror has a molded cornice with ball decoration above a deep frieze depicting a scene with angels playing trumpets flying over a chariot being drawn by lions. The mirror has

beveled glass and is flanked on either side by slender, reeded, Corinthian columns. The wide landscape format of the mirror means that it was probably an overmantel mirror and would have been intended to hang over a fireplace. *Early 19th century. H:35⅞ in (91 cm); W:63¾ (162 cm). L&T* **3**

The acanthus leaves are pierced and scroll-carved.

The guilloche motif is stylized.

ITALIAN WALL MIRROR

This rectangular giltwood wall mirror has a carved softwood frame featuring guilloche and stylized, scrolling acanthus leaves. The whole frame has been covered in white gesso and then given an undercoat of red paint, before

being gilded. The ornate, sculptural form of the mirror frame is reminiscent of the Baroque style of the 17th century, and harks back to the designs of Andrea Brustolon and the work of the Genoese carver, Filippo Parodi *(see p.40). Early 19th century. H:26½ in (67 cm); W:23⅓ in (59 cm). Cato* **3**

AMERICAN LOOKING GLASS

This simple, late Neoclassical maple looking glass has a rectangular mirror plate set within a relatively unadorned rectangular frame. The top and sides of the mirror frame have corner blocks joined by half-section balusters with

gilded and molded ends. Like the mirror above, this type of overmantel mirror is sometimes erroneously referred to as "Adam," perhaps because of its rectilinear Neoclassical styling, or perhaps because such mirrors frequently featured in Robert Adam interiors. *c. 1835. H:20 in (51 cm); W:83¾ in (85.5 cm). SL*

REGENCY MIRROR

This giltwood mirror has a molded cornice with ball decoration above a panel with a shell cresting flanked by latticework. Columns flank both sides of the mirror. *Early 19th century. H:43½ in (109 cm). L&T* **3**

ENGLISH PIER GLASS

With a concave cornice above a ring-and-leaf frieze, this giltwood and gesso pier glass has 11 plates of varying sizes divided by astragals and flanked by half-columns. *Early 19th century. W:46¾ in (117 cm). L&T* **4**

AMERICAN *GIRANDOLE*

[Th]is giltwood and ebonized *girandole* has a [co]nvex mirror plate with a reeded slip. The [fra]me is decorated with carved leaves, has four [ca]ndle arms, and is surmounted by the Federal [ea]gle. *c. 1825. H:52 in (132 cm). FRE* **5**

ENGLISH WALL MIRROR

The circular, mirrored plate sits within a reeded ebonized slip and a ball-molded frame. The frame is surmounted by a dragon flanked by two sea serpents. Below is a leaf-carved apron. *c. 1815. H:46 in (115 cm). FRE* **4**

OVAL MIRROR

This mirror is set within a molded gadrooned frame, surmounted by a painted figure of Neptune. At the base is a giltwood figure of Triton, and foliate arms that end in candle nozzles. *W:44 in (112 cm).*

ENGLISH GILTWOOD MIRROR

This simple Regency giltwood mirror has a convex mirror plate within a circular leaf-molded and reeded border. It might originally have had candle arms or cresting. *Early 19th century. D:22¾ in (58 cm). DN* **1**

[A]MERICAN LOOKING GLASS

[Th]is Classical mahogany and carved giltwood [lo]oking glass has an architectural pediment [ab]ove a carved eagle tablet and a mirror plate [fla]nked by colonettes. *Early 19th century. [H:]47 in (190.5 cm); W:24¼ in (61.5 cm). SL* **2**

REGENCY LOOKING GLASS

This carved and gilded looking glass has a molded, projecting cornice above a carved frieze, with a *verre églomisé* tablet, and reeded pilasters. *Early 19th century. H:43 in (109 cm); W:24½ in (62 cm). FRE* **2**

AMERICAN GILTWOOD MIRROR

This Federal mirror has a broken pediment with ball decoration above a *verre églomisé* panel depicting Hope with an anchor, flanked with festoons. The columns have spiral beading. *Early 19th century. H:32 in (80 cm). NA* **3**

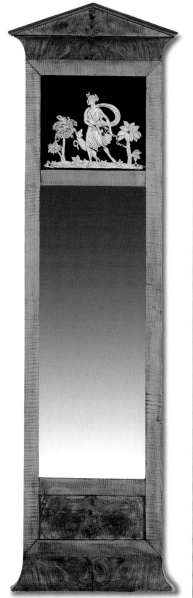

[A]MERICAN LOOKING GLASS

[Th]is tall, narrow, carved mahogany looking [gl]ass frame has a molded cornice above a [ve]neered frieze. The mirror plate is flanked by [pr]ojecting blocks linked by carved urns and [sl]ender pilasters. *c. 1825. FRE* **1**

AMERICAN LOOKING GLASS

The molded cornice of this giltwood mirror is hung with ball decoration above a wreath-and-acanthus molded frieze. Below this is a tablet. The colonnettes are rope-turned. *c. 1800. W:30¼ in (77 cm). SI*

IRISH OVAL MIRROR

This oval mirror, one of a pair, has its original plate set within a copper frame, which is decorated with applied, alternating blue and clear crystal facets. *Late 18th–early 19th century. H:41¼ in (105 cm). L&T* **5**

BIEDERMEIER PIER GLASS

The rosewood-veneered frame of this southern German pier glass has an architectural pediment above an ebonized panel depicting the goddess Diana in gilded brass. *c. 1820. H:44⅛ in (112 cm); W:13 in (33 cm). BMN* **3**

CHESTS OF DRAWERS

THE CHEST OF DRAWERS is limited in scope by the rectangular shape of its drawers. While its more elaborate cousin, the commode, might contrive to contain them within serpentine or *bombé* shapes, the chest of drawers shows little stylistic development.

With the exception of plain British pieces, which often bowed at the front, chests of drawers tended to be boxlike in the early 19th century. Meanwhile, the status of the commode as the seminal item of drawing-room furniture was on the decline. Also on the wane were chest-on-chests and highboys, although the occasional bowed example does survive.

A smaller version was developed resembling a miniature highboy and similar to the French *semainier*. Called the Wellington chest after the famous commander, its drawers were locked by a hinged pilaster to one side.

A particular type of French Empire chest of drawers was popular throughout Europe. It was rectangular, usually with a marble top, below which was a projecting frieze drawer supported on either side by a pair of architectural columns. Set back were two or three drawers above a plinth base. The piece in flamed, or plum pudding, mahogany was decorated with Neoclassical ormolu mounts, particularly on the frieze drawer and around the capital and column bases.

Another type of chest, which had its origins in the Louis XVI style, also featured a marble top, but, instead of the projecting upper drawer, all the drawers were flush. The piece had a more delicate look, possibly because it was raised on square-section, tapering legs. It was especially popular in Italy, and was known to be produced by Maggiolini, sometimes in walnut.

Due to their widespread use and relatively simple carcass construction, chests of drawers had a huge range of surface decoration, from veneering in exotic timber to painting, which was useful for disguising cheaper woods.

Inlays of walnut and other stained woods create a strong, geometric design.

Escutcheon and geometric inlay detail

A straight frieze emphasizes the rectilinear shape of the case.

Short, tapering legs support the case.

The side cabinet has two large front cupboard doors.

NORTH ITALIAN SIDE CABINET

This side cabinet, or commode, has a slightly overhanging top above a straight frieze, and a rectilinear case with two large cupboard doors at the front. The front and sides of the cabinet are richly decorated with inlays of figured walnut and other contrasting, stained woods, forming a strong, colorful geometric design. The cabinet is supported on short, tapering legs. *c. 1800. H:40½ in (102.5 cm); W:53⅛ in (135 cm); D:24⅞ in (63 cm). GK* **5**

AMERICAN CHEST OF DRAWERS

This Federal inlaid chest of drawers is made of mahogany. The piece has a rectangular top with an applied, inlaid edge that rests above four long, graduated drawers, each one with crossbanding, stringing, and a beaded edge, and brass, oval drawer-pulls. The case is supported on a molded base with straight bracket feet. Although American, the design closely follows British prototypes. *Early 19th century. W:39¾ in (101 cm). NA* **3**

AMERICAN EMPIRE CHEST OF DRAWERS

This Empire carved mahogany and mahogany veneer chest of drawers is stamped "Wm Palmer/Cabinet Maker/Catherine St./New York." The molded top is set over three outset short drawers, with carved attached columns flanking four drawers. The case sits on leaf-capped hairy-paw feet. *Early 19th century. W:45½ in (123.2 cm). SI* **2**

FRENCH COMMODE

This case of this provincial commode is made of walnut, and the piece is designed in the Empire style. It has a rectangular, dark-gray marble top that is set above a deep, rectangular frieze. The three drawers have glass handles and matching escutcheons and are flanked by ogee scrolls. The piece is supported on block feet. *Early 19th century. H:35½ in (90 cm); W:43⅓ in (110 cm); D:20½ in (52 cm). MAR* **3**

ITALIAN COMMODE

This Neoclassical walnut and marquetry commode has a marble top above a frieze drawer inlaid with foliate swags and flaring urns. Below are two further drawers, similarly inlaid *sans traverse* and centered by a panel inlaid with two maidens and a cupid. The sides are decorated to mirror the front, and the case is raised on square, tapered legs. *c. 1800 (the marble top is later).* W:53 in (132.5 cm). FRE **4**

SWEDISH COMMODE

This rectangular top of this late Gustavian commode has canted forecorners above three long drawers. The drawers are flanked by fluted and canted sides, and the commode is raised on short, tapering, fluted legs. The whole commode is painted in a typical Gustavian pale gray. *c. 1820.* H:33½ in (85 cm); W:45 in (140 cm); D:18 in (46 cm). EVE **4**

ITALIAN PARQUETRY COMMODE

This walnut and parquetry inlaid commode has a top with projecting concave front set above four corresponding long, graduated drawers. It stands on bun feet and the case and drawer fronts are inlaid throughout with geometric walnut, mahogany, and boxwood panels. *Early 19th century.* H:36¼ in (92 cm); W:49¼ in (125 cm); D:25½ in (65 cm). L&T **3**

DANISH MAHOGANY COMMODE

This Danish Louis XVI commode has a rectangular top above a fluted frieze drawer and return with roundel corners. The three lower drawers are flanked by fluted quarter pilasters. The commode is raised on bracket feet. *Late 18th century.* H:31 in (78.5 cm); W:30½ in (77.5 cm); D:18 in (45.5 cm). EVE **4**

BIEDERMEIER COMMODE

This southern German commode is veneered in cherry wood and partly ebonized. The rectangular top overhangs the case and has an ebonized edge. There are three drawers: the top has a bowed decoration, and the bottom two are flanked by ebonized columns. The case has saber feet. *1820–30.* H:36⅝ in (93 cm); W:54⅛ in (130 cm); D:25½ in (65 cm). BMN **3**

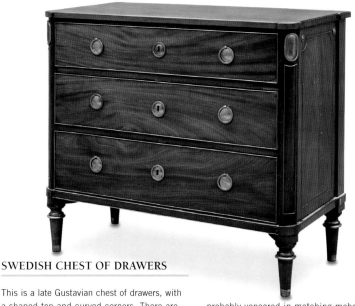

SWEDISH CHEST OF DRAWERS

This is a late Gustavian chest of drawers, with a shaped top and curved corners. There are three graduated drawers with brass roundels and the case stands on turned, tapering feet. It is probably veneered in matching mahogany. *Early 19th century.* H:33 in (84 cm); W:37½ in (95 cm); D:18½ in (47 cm). Bk **5**

SOFAS

SOFAS IN THE EARLY 19th century reached new levels of comfort. Except for the rusbank in the Cape, they were nearly always entirely upholstered, often in silk damask. As a result, the antique motifs that were frequently used on the open backs of chairs of this period were confined to the uprights and top rails of sofas. Similarly, because of their weight, the use of splayed legs was less common on sofas than on chairs. At the beginning of the period, the sofa sides tended to be straight or were carved with Neoclassical motifs such as sphinxes. Later, they began to scroll outward; the sides of a William IV sofa, for example, were often S-shaped.

During the early 19th century, there was a revived interest in the day bed and chaise longue. These elegant pieces had a scrolling form and were specifically designed for reclining. They were intended for use in a drawing room or lady's bedroom and often had outsplayed legs with brass cappings and casters.

Typically of French *Restauration* design, the *méridienne* is a type of canapé with two scroll arms, one higher than the other. In Denmark, where people still dined on sofas, *méridiennes* usually had cupboards on the sides where utensils and glasses could be stored. Because of the nature of their use and the ease with which they could be chipped, sofas were more often made from plain wood rather than completely created in gilt.

As the upholstered surfaces of sofas are particularly susceptible to wear and tear, it is unusual to find pieces from this time with their original fabrics. Authentic textiles included velvets, silks, damasks, and chintzes. Sprung seats were introduced in this period, bringing a new level of comfort to seating furniture.

MÉRIDIENNE

This *méridienne* sofa is typical of its kind, in having one end slightly higher than the other, and is probably French. It is veneered with rosewood and the plinth, supports, and feet are decoratively inlaid with stylized arabesques and scrolling foliate motifs in a lighter wood. The seat, back, and sides of the piece are generously padded and upholstered in a Neoclassical striped fabric in light green, cream, and gold. The scrolling supports and plinth are supported on volute feet. *c. 1830. H:34⅔ in (88 cm); W:58¼ in (148 cm). BEA*

The sphinxes have female heads and wings, which form the armrests of the canapé.

The molded top rail has carved lions' heads at the corners.

The canapé has four straight legs at the front and four saber legs at the back.

The squab cushion provides extra comfort.

Carved sphinx detail

FRENCH EMPIRE *CANAPÉ*

The padded back of this three-seater *canapé* has a straight, molded top rail, which continues down to form two of the back legs. The front legs and arms are carved in the form of Egyptian sphinxes and terminate in lion's-paw feet. The *canapé* seat and back are upholstered in tan suede with black and tan piping and braid. Attributed to the Jacob brothers, this is part of a large suite comprising two *canapés*, six armchairs, and a pair of stools. *c. 1800. H:37 in (94 cm); W:62 in (157 cm); D:22½ in (57 cm). PAR*

SWEDISH SOFA

This large, wide, solid sofa has a gently shaped top rail with simple molding and applied, gilded rosettes at the center. The form of the sofa is almost entirely rectilinear, with rectangular padded armrests and eight wide, square-section legs standing on block feet. The seat is upholstered in a striped fabric and is supported on a deep, plain seat rail decorated at intervals with applied rosettes. The sofa is based on a design by Carl Fredrik Sundvall for Skottorp, a manor house in Blekinge, Sweden. *c. 1820. W:113¾ in (284 cm). Bk* **4**

ENGLISH REGENCY CHAISE LONGUE

This simulated rosewood and gilt-metal mounted chaise longue has a scrolled three-quarter back and ends and saber legs. *Early 19th century. W:80 in (200 cm). L&T* **3**

WEDISH PAINTED SETTEE

his late Gustavian painted and upholstered
ettee has a rectangular back with three loose
ushions. The side panels have circular turned
upports, flanking central cross-form supports
bove a frieze with Neoclassical decoration.

The upholstered cushion seat is supported on
a carved laurel-leaf frieze and raised on 16
slender, circular, turned legs with long leaf
banding. *1800–10. H:35 in (89 cm); W:75 in
(195.5 cm); D:28 in (71 cm). EVE* **5**

AMERICAN SHERATON SOFA

This small, inlaid mahogany and flame birch
sofa has a sloping top rail with a central raised
tablet. The tablet has a contrasting ellipse
within an inlaid outline. The edge of the top
rail is capped with reeding, which continues

on the downsloping arms. Each arm rests on
a reeded baluster support and is supported on
tapering, reeded legs. The legs are headed by
inlaid panels and terminate in spade feet.
Early 19th century. H:37 in (94 cm). NA **5**

MERICAN NEOCLASSICAL SOFA

his carved mahogany sofa, from the mid-
tlantic states, has a shaped top rail with
-shaped corners, and back-scrolled arms. The
pholstered back, sides, and seat are raised
n a bolection seat rail, which is supported

on lion's-paw feet, richly carved with foliage
at the knees. The upholstery is not original.
Early 19th century. W:85 in (212.5 cm). FRE **1**

AUSTRIAN BIEDERMEIER SOFA

This Viennese sofa has a walnut-veneered,
partially ebonized frame, and an upholstered
seat, arms, and back. It has a high, straight
back and outswept, scrolling arms, and is
raised on four splayed legs. The upholstery

has a striped, floral design. It has a notably
lighter effect than the Anglo-French examples.
*1820–30. H:37½ in (95 cm); W:75½ in
(192 cm); D:26½ in (67.5 cm). BMN* **2**

NGLISH REGENCY SOFA

he rectangular back of this rosewood-framed
egency sofa has a leaf-carved cresting above
quare, upholstered arms with molded
rminals. The sofa has a squab seat and is
aised on a channel-molded seat rail. The

whole stands on turned, reeded, tapering feet
with brass caps and casters. *1820–30.
W:85¼ in (213). L&T* **3**

DANISH DAY BED

This Danish Louis XVI elmwood day bed has
a rectangular, upholstered seat between
outscrolled, vertical, slat armrests. With a
bolster cushion at either end, the day bed
is raised on six square, tapered, and fluted

legs. Unlike a chaise longue, a day bed does
not have a back. *c. 1800. H:29½ in (75 cm);
W:78 in (198 cm); D:26 in (66 cm). EVE* **4**

DESKS

DESKS GENERALLY TENDED TO BE of two forms: flat- or slant-topped. Neither of these types were new in the early 19th century. Of the former, which were generally intended for a library, several outstanding examples survive. The Jacob brothers of France provided Napoleon with a flat-topped desk for his study at the Tuileries, which is now at Malmaison. A type of mechanical bureau plat, the boxlike top slides back to expose the working surface. It is supported on side pylons formed from paired lion monopodia painted and gilded to simulate bronze.

A late Empire "Ferdinandino" style desk in mahogany survives in the Spanish Royal Palace in Madrid. With a leather top, which is typical of flat-topped desks of the period, it is supported on gilt swans linked by a platform stretcher. Chippendale the Younger's desk for Sir Richard Colt Hoare at Stourhead demonstrates a British variation of this type. Unusually,

the top of the desk is rounded and has Egyptian mask pilasters running around all sides.

Slant-fronted bureaux were still produced, particularly in provincial centers in Britain and the United States. The cylinder bureau, which had a rounded fall that pushed upward into the carcass of the piece, remained popular on the Continent, particularly in the north. The *chatol* in Denmark was a variation with a cabinet above it. Similar bureau-cabinets were produced in Britain, as was a much smaller desk called the Davenport. In some instances the slant provided the actual writing surface rather than covering it, while others were made with a piano-top style. They are thought to be named after a version made by Gillows for a Captain Davenport. Other small desks, such as the *bonheur-du-jour*, were in vogue on both sides of the channel. The *secrétaire à abattant* continued to be popular, especially in France.

AMERICAN SLANT-FRONT DESK

This Federal maple and tiger-maple slant-front desk from New England has a molded slope front with a fitted interior and four long graduated drawers. There is a molded base and the case sits on French feet. The secondary wood is white pine. *c. 1800. H:44 in (112 cm); W:41 in (104 cm; D:19¼ in (49 cm). SI* **3**

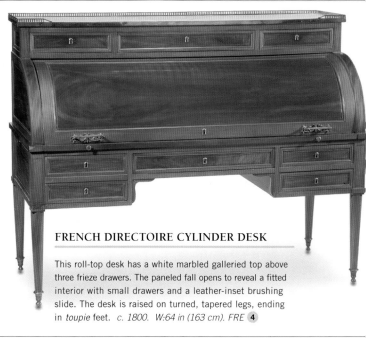

FRENCH DIRECTOIRE CYLINDER DESK

This roll-top desk has a white marbled galleried top above three frieze drawers. The paneled fall opens to reveal a fitted interior with small drawers and a leather-inset brushing slide. The desk is raised on turned, tapered legs, ending in *toupie* feet. *c. 1800. W:64 in (163 cm). FRE* **4**

Each side panel has a lion's head brass ring pull.

The frieze has three drawers.

The ebony inlay takes the form of leaf sprays and geometric motifs.

Arched bracket lion's paw foot.

Detail of inlay

ENGLISH REGENCY DESK

This shaped rectangular pedestal desk has a black gilt-tooled leather writing surface and is decorated around the edges with ebony inlay depicting sprays of leaves and geometric motifs. The frieze has three drawers to the front above

a kneehole, flanked on either side by a door enclosing three drawers. The reverse of the desk has three conforming frieze drawers and cupboard doors enclosing a shelf. The case stands on eight arched bracket lion's-paw feet. *c. 1820. H:31½ in (80 cm); W:60 in (152.5 cm); D:42 in (106.5 cm). PAR*

ITALIAN LIFT-TOP DESK

This desk has a lift-top with iron strap hinges and lock that folds back to reveal a fitted interior. The desk is supported on canted, scrolled ends with carved supports. *Early 19th century. H:35 in (89 cm); W:43 in (109 cm). BRU* **3**

Carved shell motif

Interior drawer detail

AMERICAN FEDERAL DESK

The slant front of this Federal cherry-wood clerk's desk encloses a fitted interior of four drawers and valanced compartments on both sides of a central, shell-carved, prospect door flanked by two document drawers. Below is a single long drawer. *Early 19th century. H:41½ in (103 cm). S&K* **2**

Reeded drawer detail

SWEDISH PAINTED DESK

This is a late Gustavian painted desk, with a wide overhanging rectangular writing surface above three reeded frieze drawers. Each pedestal has three graduated short drawers, again reeded, and is raised on a narrow plinth with block feet. *1800–20. H:30¾ in (78 cm); W:51½ in (131 cm); D:20¼ in (51.5 cm). EVE* **4**

Gilt-metal mounts

FRENCH CLERK'S DESK

This mahogany desk has a three-quarter gilt-metal gallery and a leather inset slope. There is a gilt-metal mounted frieze with a drawer above a grille door and sides with folio divisions, flanked by turned columns. The desk is raised above a platform with square supports on bun feet. *H:48 in (122 cm); W:36½ in (93 cm). DN* **4**

BIEDERMEIER CYLINDER BUREAU

This German walnut-veneered cylinder desk has a frieze drawer above the roll-top and two long drawers below. The front opens to reveal a fitted interior with six small drawers and compartments. The case is supported on square-section tapering legs. *c. 1820. H:49½ in (126 cm); W:47⅝ in (121 cm); D:24¾ in (63 cm). WKA* **4**

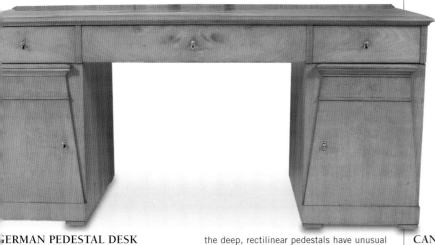

GERMAN PEDESTAL DESK

This pedestal writing table is covered with cherry wood veneer. The rectangular top has a higher, molded edge to the back and sits above one long and two short frieze drawers with locks. On either side of the kneehole, the deep, rectilinear pedestals have unusual tapered doors with applied molding above, which give the piece an architectural feel. The interiors of the pedestals are fitted with shelving. The whole piece is supported on a plinth base. *c. 1825. H:32½ in (82.5 cm); W:72⅞ in (185.5 cm); D:28⅓ in (72 cm). SLK* **6**

CANADIAN DROP-FRONT DESK

This rare Quebec pine desk has a fall front, which opens to reveal a fitted interior. On either side of a central cubbyhole are three wide, graduated drawers, and above it is a series of pigeonholes. The case has three long drawers and is supported on a molded plinth. The exterior of the desk has been stripped, but still bears traces of its original paint finish. *c. 1820. W:48½ in (123 cm). PER* **4**

TABLES

THE EARLY PART OF THE 19TH century is characterized by the development of many different types of furniture that were designed for specific tasks. The sofa table, which was developed around 1800, is one example. Intended to stand directly in front of a sofa, it provided a support for reading, writing, sketching, and similar tasks. Although the sofa table was an English invention, it was widely copied on the Continent.

Sofa tables were usually veneered in mahogany or rosewood and were often banded in exotic timbers or outlined in brass stringing. Closely related to the Pembroke table, the sofa table has a flap at either end—unlike the center, writing, or library table—although they all share the same basic function.

The sofa table also usually has two frieze drawers, which are sometimes set opposite dummy drawers. It is supported on end standards linked by a stretcher. Alternatively, it may be supported on a central pedestal, often with splayed legs on later examples,

with brass cappings and casters.

Console tables traditionally stand against a window pier beneath a high mirror that reflects light around the room. Consequently, the back of the table is usually unfinished, since no one ever sees it. Consoles are often screwed directly into the wall so they do not have back legs. If they do, the legs are purely functional and do not match the more elaborate, decorative forms of the front legs.

Serving tables and hall tables are often similar in shape to console tables, but they are usually longer and were often intended to stand against a windowless wall.

Although smaller, card and tea tables (the former does not have a baize lining) are often similar in style to sofa tables, and have identical decoration, veneers, and construction timbers. Their fold-over tops are usually supported on a swing leg, or they are supported on a central pedestal so that they can pivot.

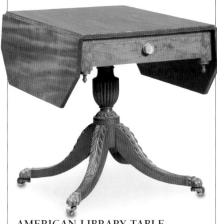

AMERICAN LIBRARY TABLE

This Neoclassical mahogany table has a hinged rectangular top with drop leaves, a drawer and an opposing dummy drawer, a pedestal base, and outsplayed legs on casters. *Early 19th century. W:35 in (87.5 cm). NA* **3**

AMERICAN PIER TABLE

The rectangular marble top of this American Empire-style table rests above a molded frieze with carved scrolls supported on turned columns. Below the tabletop is a framed mirror. *c. 1815 W:39 in (100 cm). FRE* **5**

FRENCH WORKTABLE

This rosewood worktable has a crossbanded rectangular top above two drawers and opposing dummy drawers. It has lyre-shaped trestle supports joined by a turned stretcher and saber legs. *W:22 in (57 cm). L&T* **4**

AMERICAN CLASSICAL TABLE

This table has a rectangular top with canted corners above a conforming frieze. It is supported on fluted cylindrical columns on an incurved rectangular plinth joined to shaped, downswept legs. *W:36 in (90 cm). NA* **3**

The sofa table is decorated throughout with brass inlay.

The lyre-shaped supports are a recurrent motif of late Neoclassical design.

The "strings" of the lyre are made from brass.

REGENCY LIBRARY TABLE

This fine rosewood writing or library table has a rectangular top with gently rounded corners, the whole of which is surrounded by a pierced gallery. There are two short drawers set into the frieze, both of which have round brass handles.

The table top is raised on elegant twin lyre-shaped supports with brass "strings" in the center. The supports terminate in brass-capped paw feet, and are joined by a central, turned stretcher. This typical form of Regency table was also produced with two flaps, to be used as a sofa table. *c. 1820. H:30 in (76 cm). FRE.* **5**

EMPIRE CONSOLE TABLE

This table has a rectangular marble top above a frieze drawer. There are front consoles with paw feet and two rear pilasters on a plinth base. *Early 19th century. H:33⅞ in (86 cm); W:31 in (79 cm); D:18¾ in (47.5 cm). L&T* **3**

FEDERAL TABLE

This mahogany table has a rectangular top above two graduated frieze drawers, and turned legs joined by a stretcher and terminating in outswept feet. *c. 1810. H:32 in (81 cm); W:33 in (84 cm); D:20 in (51 cm). BDL*

ANISH EMPIRE SOFA TABLE

his fruitwood-inlaid, ebonized, and parcel-gilt mahogany sofa
ble has a rectangular top and D-shaped drop leaves above a
eze with a fruitwood drawer. The end supports are flanked by
itwood and ebonized bird-head supports. *1810–20. H:30½ in
*7.5 cm); W:33 in (84 cm); D:59½ in (143.5 cm). EVE **5**

AUSTRIAN TABLE

Veneered in cherry wood, this table has a rectangular top above
a frieze with a single drawer. The table top is supported on two
elaborately-carved lyre supports with upturned ends, joined to
each other by a turned stretcher. *c. 1830. H:30⅓ in (77 cm);
W:39 in (99 cm); D:28¾ in (73 cm). SLK **4**

CHINESE EXPORT CENTER TABLE

This highly decorative, Regency-style, black lacquer table has a
rectangular top with rounded corners. The frieze has two front
drawers and two dummies at the back. The splayed end- supports
rest on a plinth with bun feet. *c. 1830. H:29½ in (75 cm);
W:48 in (122 cm); D:24 in (61 cm). PAR*

COTTISH REGENCY CONSOLE TABLE

e rectangular top of this mahogany console table sits above
n ogee frieze. The table top is supported on palmette-carved,
crolling front console legs, which terminate in bun feet. The
quare-section back legs are paneled and have square, block
et. *c. 1820. W:58 in (148 cm). L&T*

GERMAN CARD TABLE

This mahogany table has a rectangular top with molded sides
and rests above a frieze flanked by carved scrolls. It is supported
on a column with a carved base, four splayed legs carved with
stylized swans, and scroll feet. *c. 1820. H:30⅓ in (77 cm);
W:43⅓ in (110 cm); D:21⅖ in (55 cm). SLK **4**

BRITISH CONSOLE TABLE

This William IV mahogany console table has a rectangular slate
top raised on a base with a frieze. The table top is supported on
a pair of elaborately scrolled and leaf-carved console legs with
paw feet at the front. The back legs take the form of rectangular-
section, paneled pilasters. *c. 1830. W:72 in (183 cm). L&T **4**

GEORGE IV CARD TABLE

e rectangular top of this pedestal card table has a narrow brass
lay and rounded corners. It is supported on a sturdy octagonal,
pering column with a nulled collar, a round platform, and four
utswept legs that end in brass terminals and casters.
arly 19th century. W: 36 in (91 cm). DN **3**

AMERICAN NEOCLASSICAL CARD TABLE

The rectangular, hinged top of this mahogany table has a bowed
center section above a conforming apron with a brass-outlined
panel and central applied brass foliage. It sits on a lyre-form
pedestal with brass strings, on outsplayed legs with brass paw
toes and casters. *Early 19th century. W:36 in (91.5 cm). NA **4**

REGENCY SOFA TABLE

This rosewood sofa table has satinwood crossbanding. Below the
rectangular top there is a frieze with two drawers and rounded
drop leaves. The table sits on rectangular-section supports on
inlaid saber legs terminating in anthemion-cast brass caps and
casters. *Early 19th century. W:57½ in (146 cm). L&T **4**

OCCASIONAL TABLES

THE SMALL-SCALE OCCASIONAL table truly stands out. Many examples were also portable and could be moved around a room to serve a variety of functions, although often they had a specific use. In this case, a table could be brought out when required and then moved back to the walls or out of the room. Because occasional tables might be seen from all sides, they were usually veneered on the back, unlike side tables.

Occasional tables are often associated with leisure or with ladies' activities. Worktables, for example, were given considerable attention by Sheraton and were largely an invention of this period.

Intended to hold sewing apparatus, worktables often have a silk work bag that slides out from beneath the upper surface. Others have a rising lid

with compartments. Some are even equipped with a rising screen for use in front of the fire. Small and fragile, worktables are often made in exotic wood, either with marquetry or painted details.

Other types include those for gaming (often with a marquetry chess and backgammon board) and reading stands. These were known from the mid-18th century and had a ratcheted slope, sometimes inset with leather if the table was also to be used for drawing. Small, circular *guéridons* in France were often used to hold candelabra or perfume burners. *Quartetto*, or nests-of-tables, were also an invention of the period. Elaborate examples with cut-brass decoration and exotic wood were made by George Oakley, and others with ring-turned supports and veneers by Gillows.

REGENCY WRITING BOX

This bird's-eye maple and ebony string writing box has a hinged slope with a leather inset, a drawer, and dummy drawer. The ring-turned, ebonized legs are joined by a C-scroll stretcher. *c. 1810. H:33¾ in (86 cm). DN* **3**

BIEDERMEIER SIDE TABLE

This solid beech and beech-veneered side table has a round frieze with an overhanging circular top. It is raised on three saber legs, joined lower down by an additional, circular shelf. *1820. H:30⅔ in (78 cm). BMN* **2**

Brass ring pull

INLAID STAND

This stand is from the southern US states and has a rectangular top with rounded corners and a band of double string inlay. It is raised on inlaid, tapered legs below bird's eye maple panels. The single drawer has three interior compartments. *H:28½ in (72.5 cm); W:26¼ in (66.5 cm); D:18¼ in (46.5 cm). BRU* **7**

The inset table top is made of white marble.

Verre églomisé vignettes in black and gold depict repeating motifs of flaming torches and crossed quivers.

The turned tapering legs are carved with spiral flutes.

SWEDISH SIDE TABLE

This fine-quality, giltwood side table has an inset table top made of white marble, which is set above a giltwood frieze carved with laurel leaves and with recessed panels incorporating black and gold *verre églomisé* vignettes. There

are additional panels above the legs and at the center of the frieze. The turned, tapering legs are carved with low-relief laurel above a band of Greek key pattern, and then carved with spiral flutes below. The legs terminate in baluster feet. *c. 1810. H:32 in (81.5 cm); W:32 in (81.5 cm); D:20 in (51 cm). MAL*

CONSOLE TABLE

Made in Franken, Germany, this console table is veneered in mahogany. It has a rectangular marble table top above a frieze drawer and stands on square, tapering legs. *H:33 in (84 cm); W:33 in (84 cm); D:19¾ in (50 cm). SLK* **5**

SHERATON GAME TABLE

This mahogany game and worktable has a rectangular top with chamfered corners and a chessboard inlaid in its surface. It stands on square, tapering legs. *c. 1790. H:29 in (73.5 cm). DL* **4**

WEDISH SIDE TABLE

This gilt-metal, mounted, mahogany side table Karl Johan has a circular top above a frieze. The circular stem ends in a tripartite base with rolled feet. *H:31 in (79 cm); Diam:17½ in 4.5 cm).* EVE

OCCASIONAL TABLE

Inlaid with brass, this French Empire mahogany table has a circular top featuring an inset marble and pierced-brass gallery. It has a fluted column support ending on a tripod base. *Early 19th century. H:31¼ in (79 cm). SI* **1**

PATTERN BOOKS

THE VOGUE FOR SMALL OCCASIONAL TABLES WAS ENCOURAGED BY VARIOUS PATTERN BOOKS PUBLISHED IN THE LATE 18TH AND EARLY 19TH CENTURIES.

The use of pattern books by furniture makers was well-established by the end of the 18th century, when Thomas Sheraton published *The Cabinet-Maker and Upholsterer's Drawing Book*. Hugely significant in disseminating the Neoclassical Regency style in England and the US, this book included many designs for occasional tables, from pot cupboards to urn stands. Although this was not particularly new—Chippendale and Ince and Mayhew had included such objects in their pattern books of the 1750s and 60s—the lightness and variety of Sheraton's examples was innovative.

Sheraton's next book was his *Cabinet Dictionary*, published 1803, which, possibly influenced by Thomas Hope, included some Egyptian designs. The influence of French furniture is also evident in the inclusion of the small writing desk known as a *bonheur-du-jour*. Sheraton never completed his final massive volume, *The Cabinet-Maker, Upholsterer, and General Artist's Encyclopaedia*, although it was published, incomplete, in 1805. In this late title, contemporary developments in France, notably the post-revolutionary styles, were particularly evident.

OUTH AFRICAN TEA TABLE

This stinkwood tea table has a rectangular top with rounded corners, a plain frieze, decorative, contrasting inlays, and slightly tapering legs. *790–1810. H:28 in (71 cm); W:33½ in 5 cm); D:19⅔ in (50 cm). PRA*

ITALIAN BEDSIDE COMMODE

Made of olive wood and tulipwood, this crossbanded, bedside commode has a lift-up lid above a fall front and fitted interior. It has square, tapering legs. *H:31 in (79 cm); W:20½ in (52 cm); D:14 in (35.5 cm). Cato* **3**

Sheraton prototypes These designs are for an urn stand (*left*) and pot cupboards (*center and right*), taken from *The Cabinet-Maker and Upholsterer's Drawing Book* (3rd edition). *1794.*

IEDERMEIER SEWING TABLE

This sewing table from Weimar is veneered cherry wood with ebony stringing. The overhanging table top has rounded corners. The rounded case has two drawers and saber gs. *c. 1830. H:30½ in (77 cm). BMN* **3**

FEDERAL WORKSTAND

This figured mahogany workstand has a rectangular-shaped top supported by half-round colonettes and two drawers. It stands on rounded, tapering, ring-turned legs ending in ball feet. *c. 1820. H:28 in (71 cm). FRE* **1**

ITALIAN TABLE

This Neoclassical inlaid fruitwood table *en chiffonière* has a three-quarter gallery, two drawers with chevron banding, and square-section, tapering legs. *Early 19th century. H:27 in (65.5 cm). SLK* **1**

WORKSTAND

This Massachusetts Sheraton mahogany workstand has a rectangular top with cut corners and two compartmented drawers. The ringed pilasters lead into tapering, reeded legs with ringed cuffs. *H:28¾ in (73 cm). NA* **4**

PAINTED FURNITURE

TWO TYPES OF PAINTED furniture were evident in the early 19th century. One could be characterized as high style: that is furniture produced in the fashionable Empire or Regency manner, which, instead of being veneered in mahogany, rosewood, or *bois clairs*, was painted. This was particularly common on seating furniture, which might have been made out of cheaper materials and then painted to simulate rosewood or calamander. Similarly, pieces might be painted to look like marble, while boxes, music stands or small pieces were decorated with penwork.

The second category comprises more provincial pieces, particularly the rustic furniture produced in Russia, Scandinavia, the Tyrol (Austria), or southern Germany, around Bavaria. These naive case pieces (often wardrobes or chests) are frequently entirely covered in bright patterns, relieved only by the occasional painting of flowers or landscapes. A good collection is preserved in the Skansen, Stockholm. Many of these items of furniture are signed and dated.

ITALIAN CORNER CABINET

This corner cabinet has two quarter-circle shelves above two cupboard doors and stands on shaped bracket feet. The whole cabinet is painted with floral motifs on a yellow ground. *1810. H:30 in (76 cm). SS* **3**

GUSTAVIAN CHAIR

This white-painted side chair, one of a pair by Melkior Lundberg, has a simple oval back with a solid, vase-shaped splat. The tapering seat has a carved seat rail and is raised on stop-fluted legs. *Early 19th century. Bk* **3**

The later date at the top suggests this cupboard was given as a wedding gift to a child of the original recipients.

Most of the decorative panels are filled with painted floral displays, while the one in the center of the door portrays a young couple.

The raised plinth base is fitted with a drawer.

Detail of floral pattern

MARRIAGE CUPBOARD

The arched, molded cornice of this pine cupboard sits above a case with canted corners and a single door with three shaped, decorative panels flanked by additional painted panels. The base of the cupboard has a single drawer and stands on bun feet. All of the surfaces of the cupboard are painted. In some rural communities, it was traditional to make a wedding gift of this type of cupboard. It could then be re-dated and given as a gift to the next generation. *c. 1830. H:77½ in (197 cm); W:46 in (117 cm); D:20½ in (52 cm). RY*

Painted detail

PAINTED PINE CHEST

This central-European painted chest is decorated throughout with flowers in scroll-edged panels with a cream ground on a pale blue border. The piece has a rectangular top above four scrolling front drawers with red-painted stiles and turned corner pilasters. The chest has a paneled back and stands on red painted, turned feet. The drawers are graduated in size. *Early 19th century. W:40¾ in (103.5 cm). WW* **3**

MARBLE-EFFECT STOOL

This beech stool with a mahogany seat has been painted all over with purple and gray mottling to simulate yellow Siena marble. The seat is carved to simulate fringed drapery falling over the sides in folds. The massive rectangular legs have been designed as tapering fluted columns, headed by detached roundels enclosing florets. After a design by C. H.Tatham. *c. 1800. H:18 in (46 cm); W:24½ in (62 cm); D:18½ in (47 cm). TNH*

AMERICAN STAND

his elegant painted stand is made of rosewood. It has a
ctangular top that sits above an ornately decorated frieze
th a single drawer. The case is raised on turned and tapering
gs that terminate in turned feet. *Early 19th century.*
·31 in (77.5 cm). NA **4**

AMERICAN CUPBOARD

This green-painted walnut cupboard has a dovetailed splash
panel with scrolled cut-outs set above two dovetailed drawers
and two framed, paneled doors. The case stands on shaped
bracket feet. *Early 19th century.* H:54 in (137 cm); W:44 in
(112 cm); D:17 in (43 cm). BRU **2**

CANADIAN CHINA CABINET

This china cabinet has a yellow-painted scrolling crest flanked by
finials set above a pair of glass doors, which open onto a blue,
shelved interior. The lower section of the cabinet has three short
drawers above a pair of cupboard doors, and stands on bracket
feet. *Early 19th century.* H:89 in (226 cm). WAD

FANCY FURNITURE

PARTICULAR TO THE UNITED STATES, ELABORATELY PAINTED FANCY FURNITURE WAS WIDELY PRODUCED
DURING THE LATE 18TH CENTURY AND FIRST HALF OF THE 19TH CENTURY.

Fancy Furniture, a particular type of painted furniture,
was produced in the United States on the eastern
seaboard from the late 18th century to the second
half of the 19th century. Although other pieces
were made, it was primarily chairs that were
decorated in this way.

Sometimes called Hitchcock chairs, after
Lambert Hitchcock, their most famous
producer, the shapes of these pieces were often
inspired by the designs of Thomas Sheraton
(*see p.138*). With turned legs joined by spindle
stretchers and bar backs, they were essentially
provincial pieces, similar in style to Windsor
chairs (*see p.240*). Light, portable, and frequently
with rush or caned seats, fancy chairs are
characterized by their elaborate painted
surfaces, which were often black with gilt
highlights. The backs were hand-painted and
decorated with stenciling. The style of the

*The scrolled
backboard and
frieze drawer have
a similar painted
floral decoration.*

Dressing table and chair
This is a New England
yellow-painted and
decorated dressing table
with putty-grained top and
barber-pole turned legs,
together with a companion
chair. *Early 19th century.*
H:38 in (95 cm). NA **3**

decoration varied from Neoclassical to
more naturalistic designs, including floral
motifs and even landscapes.

From his factory in Connecticut,
Hitchcock produced his furniture on an
assembly line, and it was often stenciled
with the name of the factory. The Irish
brothers John and Hugh Findlay produced
similar painted furniture in Baltimore,
including some furniture that they made
for the White House in 1809, although
these pieces were destroyed by a fire
during the War of 1812.

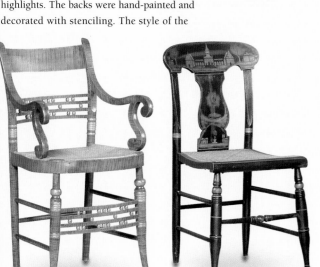

Sheraton-style chairs These two fancy-painted
and decorated chairs comprise an armchair with
faux graining and a fiddle-back side chair with
landscape decoration and cane seat. *Early 19th
century.* NA **1**

DIRECTOIRE SEMAINIER

An elegant piece with its original painted finish, this French
semainier is made from cherry wood and oak with a marble
top. The chest has a simple, molded frieze set above six drawers
and stands on square-section tapering legs. *c. 1810.* H:59½ in
(151 cm); W:41 in (104 cm); D:17½ in (44.5 cm). RY

MID-19TH CENTURY
1840-1900

TURMOIL AND PROGRESS

UNREST AND REVOLUTION BETWEEN 1840 AND 1865 GAVE WAY TO
STABILITY, EXPANSION, AND INDUSTRIAL PROGRESS, WHICH BENEFITED
AN EMERGING MIDDLE CLASS KEEN ON FASHIONABLE FURNITURE.

IN 1837, QUEEN VICTORIA ASCENDED the British throne, just as the Chartist movement was gaining momentum. Increasingly vehement demands for suffrage were met with similar cries from the disaffected working classes across Europe and even greater tumult further afield in the Americas and East and South Asia. In 1848, revolution erupted across Europe: from Paris to Vienna huge swaths of the angry populace vented their dissatisfaction, sending tremors of panic through the political elite.

The Opium War was fought and won in China in 1840, and further unrest was to follow in East Asia. The Indian Mutiny in 1857 brought about the final collapse of the East India Company, forcing the British Crown to formally take charge of the administration of the subcontinent. The American Civil War raged from 1861 to 1865, disrupting the economy and pitting state against state.

REBUILDING FROM THE ASHES

The turmoil of these chaotic years eventually gave way to a period of relative stability. The two great European unification movements of the 19th century finally succeeded: the Kingdom of Italy was created in 1861 and Germany, under the Machiavellian direction of Otto von Bismarck, took shape in 1871. In 1869, two Herculean engineering projects were completed—the Suez Canal and the Union Pacific railroad.

The preservation of the Union in the United States paved the way for a period of unprecedented expansion. In the East, Japan was finally encouraged to open its ports to the West for a limited time at the end of the Edo period and, under the leadership of Emperor Meiji from 1868, it slowly emerged from years of isolation and plowed huge investment into its infrastructure and businesses.

DOMESTIC CONSEQUENCES

Until around 1860, the majority of European furniture-designers were content to rehash historical styles, and relied excessively on surface decoration in lieu of innovative design. The florid, feminine Rococo revival, which emanated from France, and the heavy, masculine Gothic revival, which became the British national style,

Gothic chair The Gothic revival was evident in all styles of furniture. The arched back of this hall chair, with rosette roundels, and the arcaded seat rail are typical features of the style. *L&T*

were adopted almost universally. Neoclassical revivals flourished at various points in many countries. Colonial traders brought fine hardwoods, including excellent mahoganies, to Europe, and the Industrial Revolution introduced new materials, such as cast iron, to the manufacturing base.

Industrialization also brought better-equipped factories and, as the production of household goods became more mechanized, they became more homogenous. A redistribution of wealth in favor of the middle classes created huge demand for fashionable furnishings. From 1860, a new confidence breathed life into the furniture industry, assisted by exhibitions that became showcases of 19th-century European aspiration. Nations began to assert their individuality, looking to their own past for inspiration.

West facade of the Rijksmuseum, Amsterdam Designed by Pierre Cuypers to house the national art collection, the building opened to the public on July 13, 1885. It is a combination of Romanesque, Gothic, and Dutch Renaissance styles.

TIMELINE 1840–1900

1840 In Britain, Victoria marries Albert of Saxe-Coburg. The British practice of deporting its convicts to Australia ends.

1841 China cedes Hong Kong to the British. David Livingstone begins his explorations of Africa.

1842 The Austrian designer, Michael Thonet, receives a patent for his steam-bending process. His bentwood furniture proves a phenomenal success in the ensuing years.

Bentwood chair This classic piece was designed by Michael Thonet in 1859.

1848 Revolution in France sparks similar scenes in cities across Europe, marking the beginning of the end of European absolutism.

1851 The Great Exhibition of the Industries of all Nations is held in Hyde Park in London.

1852 Queen Victoria officially opens the new Palace of Westminster (also known as the Houses of Parliament). It was designed by Sir Charles Barry and his assistant A. W. N. Pugin, although work continues until 1868.

1853 Japan is compelled to open its ports to foreign trade for the first time in generations by Commodore Perry.

The Palace of Westminster Sir Charles Barry designed the building along Classical lines, and it was built between 1836 and 1868. The Gothic details were designed by A. W. N. Pugin.

Drawing Room of Osborne House, Isle of Wight With its mixture of Neoclassical, Rococo, and Empire elements, this drawing room is typical of the Victorian era. Bought in 1845 by Queen Victoria and Prince Albert, the original house was demolished, and by 1848 a new three-story pavilion with flag tower and wings was built in its place.

1861 Abraham Lincoln becomes president of the United States. The secession from the Union of 11 southern states marks the American Civil War, which leaves 600,000 dead.

Bismarck statue This monument to the first German chancellor, Otto von Bismarck, stands in Berlin. It was designed in 1896 by Reinhold Begas.

1861 Italy is unified and the former King of Sardinia becomes King of Italy. Venice and Rome become part of the new kingdom in 1866 and 1871.

1871 Bismarck steers the German states to a union dominated by Prussia, following successful wars with both France and Austria.

1874 The Paris Opera House, designed by Charles Garnier, is completed, representing one of the centerpieces of Hausmann's newly reconstructed Paris.

The Palais Garnier Located at the *Place de l'Opéra* in Paris, the *Palais Garnier* was designed in traditional Italian style, inspired by Italian and French villas of the 17th and 18th centuries.

1886 The Statue of Liberty is unveiled in New York harbor, ten years later than planned.

1899 The Boer War begins in South Africa.

The Statue of Liberty Designed by French sculptor Frédéric-Auguste Bartholdi, the statue stands on a pedestal designed by the American architect Richard Morris Hunt, and funded by the United States.

REVIVAL STYLES

THE AGE OF INDUSTRIALIZATION wrought a great deal of change on the furniture industry. Factories and division of labor made furniture more accessible than ever before, while aggressive colonization and feverish trade with Asia introduced new materials to the West and changed the attitude of countries such as India and Japan to cabinet-making.

AN ECLECTIC AGE

Despite these powerful influences, the mid-19th century failed to produce a distinctive and recognizable idiom of its own. Instead, the period was dominated by the revival of styles that had previously been fashionable. Foremost among these were the Gothic

Louis XVI-style mirror In this carved and gessoed giltwood mirror, the oval beveled mirror plate sits within a mirror surround, separated by a beaded frame. The outer frame has egg-and-dart molding, foliage, and a pierced crest. *c. 1880. S&K*

style, rooted in the spectacular church architecture of the Middle Ages, and the aspirational Rococo, which had developed in 18th-century France. Despite being polar opposites in terms of the philosophies that lay behind them, these two styles would frequently feature in the same room—even, sometimes, in the same piece of furniture.

This plethora of styles was augmented by the addition of various Classical trophies to the decorative canon. The grand Neoclassical designs of the previous century enjoyed periodic revivals, and Grecian, Roman, and Egyptian themes were never far from the public consciousness, thanks to frequent and well-publicized archaeological discoveries. Even the most visionary designers of the period—men such as A. W. N. Pugin and Michael Thonet—worked within these derivative constraints.

International exhibitions, beginning with the Great Exhibition of 1851 held in the Crystal Palace, London, did much to promote this wide range of styles to the world during the second half of the 19th century. Not only did they attract thousands of visitors, but their lavishly illustrated catalogs reached many more potential patrons and furniture-makers, ready and able to copy them.

MATERIALS AND FORMS

Revival styles took different manifestations from country to country, but certain staple forms were common to all. The balloon-back chair was a standard design between 1830 and 1860, when the cheaper bentwood chair finally forced it out of favor. Display cabinets grew in popularity, as many people cultivated arcane and extensive collections of trinkets. Plush, velour tapestry and braid seat covers added a feminine touch and fulfilled the general desire for comfort within the home.

Mahogany and walnut were the most prevalent timbers used in furniture-making, although the revival styles often made use of oak and ebony. Mahogany, rosewood, and teak were imported by powerful Western nations from their colonial interests around the world, creating plentiful supplies of exotic timbers for craftsmen to work with. Novel materials replaced wood altogether in some furniture—papier-mâché,

Oak chair Designed by A. W. N. Pugin, this is a version of the Glastonbury chair, a medieval folding chair owned by the Bishop of Wells. It retains the Gothic shape and construction of the original chair, but does not fold. *1839–41. H:33½ in (85 cm); W:21 in (53.5 cm); D:24½ in (62 cm).*

originally used to make tables, trays, and small boxes, became a fashionable material for chairs and even beds, and cast iron was manipulated to produce pieces of interior and garden furniture.

COST OF INDUSTRIALIZATION

Fine furniture had never before been available to so many people. Machines cut veneers far thinner than were ever achieved by hand and made short work of intricate dovetails and dowels. Even the carving process was automated, and many craftsmen found themselves downgraded to simple finishers. As costs dropped and productivity soared, the middle classes were able to fill their homes with fashionable furnishings that would have been prohibitively expensive to the previous generation.

Unfortunately, the quality of the furniture suffered. With the exception of the finest craftsmen, there was a noticeable degeneration of artistry. In Victorian Britain, a liking for pattern and ornament resulted in cluttered rooms, which, together with the decline in quality, led to a backlash at the end of the century with the Arts and Crafts Movement (*see pp.320–45*).

ANTLER FURNITURE

An interest in the woodsy outdoors combined with a love of excess conspired to create a demand for antler furniture in 19th-century the US. Members of the deer family, such as moose and elk—all abundant in the northern states—naturally shed their antlers every year, and these became prized as table legs, chair backs, lamp stands, and all manner of decorative objects. Antler lamp stands were invariably combined with shades fashioned from deer hide.

This type of furniture was also popular in Austrian and German hunting lodges for its obvious associations. Tables with antler legs were favored as were antler

chandeliers. Antler furniture is a rare example of a rustic, vernacular form of furniture becoming widespread and popular at a time when the industry was dominated by historical revival styles. It is also typical of the kitsch furniture of the period, in which making a decorative statement sometimes seemed to override considerations of comfort, harmony, or good taste.

Dining chairs Each of this set of four oak and antler-horn chairs has an oval upholstered back, supported by an antler frame. The stuffover seat of each chair is raised on antler supports. *L&T*

WALNUT AND MARQUETRY

Walnut had fallen out of favor as a material for cabinet-making after about 1740, owing to a walnut shortage in Europe following the freeze of 1709. Mahogany became more widespread, but walnut enjoyed a renewed surge of popularity in the Victorian period. A light brown color, walnut can have a very dark grain and has long been prized for its handsome figuring. It is also easy to carve. These qualities made walnut an ideal ground on which to practice the Dutch art of marquetry—a very popular surface decoration in the mid-19th century.

Colonial interests in the tropics, especially in the Caribbean and Asia-Pacific regions, provided European countries with numerous exotic and attractive specimen woods. Talented craftsmen were quick to exploit the decorative potential of these woods and incorporated them into complex intarsia designs, such as those incorporated in this walnut side cabinet (right). Boxwood and ebony were combined with less well-known timbers, such as snakewood, jelutong, and Burmese teak, lending those pieces a sumptuous decadence that set such furniture apart from the rest.

Each cantered corner has a scrolled, shell-cast mount.

The curved frieze is centered by a mount cast with putti.

The pierced, chamfered, tapering corner buttress mount has shell-, flower-, and leaf-cast decoration.

The oval marquetry medallion depicts birds perched on flowering sprigs on an ebony ground.

The spandrels contain foliate, scrolled marquetry.

Side cabinet This walnut, marquetry, and gilt-brass mounted cabinet is serpentine in outline. The glazed upper part has foliate-, scrolled-, shell-, and flower-cast mounts with glazed, arched, paneled side doors enclosing a mirrored back and shelf. The projecting lower part has a frieze centered by a mount with putti and flanked by oval marquetry. Below this is a pair of cupboard doors centered by oval marquetry medallions within ornate-cast border mounts. The sides have conforming decoration, flanked by pierced, chamfered, tapering corner buttresses with gilt-brass cast mounts. *c. 1870.* H:61 in (155 cm); W:39¼ in (100 cm); D:20½ in (52 cm).

The shaped apron is centered by a pierced and scroll-cast foliate mount.

A ribbon-cast and reeded cartouche mount surrounds each bordered medallion.

ELEMENTS OF STYLE

Decorative features in the 19th century were drawn from the same historical sources that pervaded architecture and the fine arts—Gothic, Rococo, and Neoclassical styles all enjoyed a global revival at this time. Increased mechanization meant that furniture could be produced from previously unused materials, such as coal and glass. It also allowed elaborately inlaid or carved furniture to be made more easily and cheaply. Improved transport and communication enabled many more people to adopt new ideas, production methods, and materials.

Corner of Louis XV-style writing table

Decorative inlay from a bedside cabinet

Louis XV style

The delicate colors of the marquetry work and the restrained gilt metal mounts on this table hark back to the French Louis XV style. The mid-19th-century interpretation was softer and more delicate than the original opulent Louis XV style. The mounts on the corners of this Louis XV-style writing table are machine-made, helping to reduce the cost of the piece.

Neoclassical urns

An archetypal Classical motif, the urn was a consistent decorative feature used during the Neoclassical revivals that punctuated the 19th century. This example is inlaid into the body of the furniture, although carved urns were just as prevalent, especially in chair backs. The lightweight proportions of the handles are typical of 19th-century design style.

Inlaid table top with kingwood veneer

Eclecticism

This Fortner table features brass, mother-of-pearl, and rosewood inlaid into a kingwood veneer. The German-made table carries influences from a variety of historical periods: the central medallion is inspired by Gothic motifs; the scrolling designs are pure Rococo; and the symmetry of the overall design of the table top is more Neoclassical in style.

Mahogany and marquetry center table

Dutch marquetry

The Dutch were among the first to develop the technique of marquetry in Europe during the 18th century. During the 19th century, Dutch craftsmen continued to produce some of the best examples of wooden intarsia design, typically with floral themes and using different colored woods. Sometimes bone or shell were used, stained bright colors to contrast with the wood.

Decorative ivory inlay work on rosewood

Engraved ivory inlays

The profusely engraved ivory inlay that covers this Collinson and Lock center table is similar to the work of Italian craftsmen of the same period, and is essentially Renaissance revival in style. The putti, figures, urns and formal leaf border are Classical decorative forms. The use of rosewood as a foil for the ivory detail is also typical of the Renaissance revival style.

Painted lyre back of Regency-style chair

Ceramic plaque on a jasper ware panel

Fine engraved mounts on red tortoiseshell

Needlepoint garden scene

Painted chair backs

The practice of painting furniture had dwindled by around 1825 but was resurrected, along with the lyre back, as part of a Regency revival in about 1850. During the late Victorian period, some considered Regency furniture superior to contemporary styles, and cabinet-makers such as Gillows catered to this taste, producing furniture that equalled the original pieces in quality.

Wedgwood plaques

The Bacchanal figure on this Wedgwood jasper ware panel on a cabinet by Lamb of Manchester is taken directly from the ancient Greek tradition, although her long flowing robes are probably a Victorian addition. The architectural Greek revival style was spurred by the archaeological discoveries of Mycenae and Troy by Heinrich Schliemann.

Boullework

This Napoleon III serpentine, marble-top cabinet features *première-partie* boullework on a red tortoiseshell ground. These intricate patterns and the fine engraved mounts stem directly from the work of André-Charles Boulle, cabinet-maker and sculptor to Louis XIV, whose work was much imitated by furniture-makers during the 19th century in France.

Needlepoint upholstery

The Medieval tradition of covering chairs with needlepoint upholstery was revived by the Victorians. Such tapestries were generally rich in detail, like this formal scene depicting lovers in a garden. The red, gold, and blue palate used in the design is inspired by Italian Renaissance decoration. Upholstery was worked in *gros* and *petit point* needlework.

Panel of screen decorated with scraps

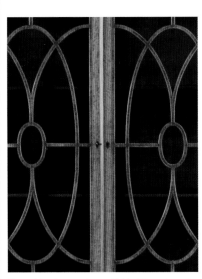

Glazed bookcase doors divided by astragals

Italian black slate table top with *pietra dura*

Louis XVI–style romantic ormolu mount

Scrapwork

The Victorians used scraps—embossed and printed paper images—in the creation of Christmas and Valentine's Day cards. Once used, it was the custom to collate these pieces of printed ephemera in scrapbooks. Sometimes the scraps were used to decorate folding screens as shown here. This was a leisure activity primarily for middle-class ladies.

Astragal molding

The panes of glass in these bookcase doors are divided by graceful, interlacing, semicircular, convex molding, known as astragal molding. Their curving lines represent a more rounded version of the Neoclassical style, providing an illustration of how contemporary fashions influenced the revival styles that were popular during this period.

Pietra dura

Pietra dura is an Italian mosaic technique that uses semiprecious stones and marbles to create multi-colored inlaid designs, most frequently depicting flowers, birds, and fruit. Originating in 16th-century Florence, it was a popular, if expensive, embellishment to 19th-century furniture. Here, the mosaic is thrown into relief by the black slate ground.

Ormolu mounts

Ormolu mounts were cast in bronze, then gilded with mercury to make them resemble gold. This mount is set on ebonized wood, providing a decorative contrast. The romantic theme recalls the Rococo and Neoclassical styles prevalent during the reign of Louis XVI. Faces were a popular motif on mounts, and this girl's hairstyle is typical of the 19th century.

GRAND EXHIBITIONS

THE GREAT INDUSTRIAL NATIONS OF THE WORLD HOSTED IMPRESSIVE EXHIBITIONS, PROVIDING IMPETUS TO THEIR MANUFACTURERS AND EXCITEMENT FOR THEIR SUBJECTS.

EUROPEAN CRAFTSMEN had appreciated the value of trade exhibitions for many years. The medieval *Büchermeß*, held in Frankfurt to celebrate and stimulate the embryonic book trade, and the Imperial Trade Fairs held in 16th-century Leipzig are two early examples. The RSA (The Royal Society for the encouragement of Arts, Manufactures & Commerce) was established in Britain in 1754 and provided platforms for the exhibition of industrial and artistic artifacts. However, the Great Exhibition of the Works of Industry of All Nations, held in London's Hyde Park in 1851, was a far more ambitious project.

A NEW KIND OF FESTIVAL

The brainchild of Albert, the Prince Consort, the Great Exhibition was the first truly international exhibition and a grandiose expression of the confidence of Victorian Britain. Prince Albert's plan was for a great collection of works in art and industry, "for the purposes of exhibition, of competition, and of encouragement." The imposing Crystal Palace housed the event, which featured in excess of 13,000 articles,

ETRUSCAN-STYLE SIDE CABINET

This amboyna, ebony, Wedgwood, and ivory side cabinet, designed by Lamb of Manchester, has a carved, shaped pediment, above a red marble slab. The lower part has a glazed door enclosing shelves, with a further door on either side. The cabinet stands on a plinth base. Below the carved pediment is a jasperware panel with a bacchanal in relief. The central, glazed door is flanked by fluted rods intertwined with ivy leaves. The jasperware plaque on each of the lower cabinet doors is centered by a naked nymph with a shaped border. 1867. H:72½ in (184 cm); W:82 in (208 cm); D:20 in (51 cm)

BARBER OF SEVILLE PIANO

This French gilt-bronze and tulipwood bombé piano is in Louis XV manner. The sides and top of the piano are quarter-veneered and crossbanded, and divided by finely inlaid, foliate marquetry. The lid is outlined with a gilt-bronze molded border. The piano stands on cabriole legs, richly ornamented with asymmetric acanthus and caryatid mounts. c. 1890. H:40½ in (103 cm); W:55 in (140 cm); D:78¾ in (200 cm).

NEW YORK'S CRYSTAL PALACE

New Yorkers crowd the street outside the New York Crystal Palace during the 1853 World's Fair. The building was modeled on the original Crystal Palace in London. It burned down just five years later.

THE CRYSTAL PALACE

DUBBED "THE CRYSTAL PALACE" BY *PUNCH* MAGAZINE, THE VENUE FOR THE GREAT EXHIBITION OF 1851 WAS ESSENTIALLY A COLOSSAL GREENHOUSE BUILT OUT OF GLASS, WOOD, AND IRON.

The panoply of fantastic wares on display at the Great Exhibition demanded an equally spectacular setting. The Commissioners for the Exhibition raised a total fund of £230,000 (about $24 million in today's terms) of which £120,000 was to cover the cost of the building. Joseph Paxton (1801–65), head gardener to the Duke of Devonshire, won the commission to design the venue with his plans for an audacious glasshouse. The Crystal Palace represented a pinnacle of Victorian engineering—from conception to completion, the entire project took only nine months. Tests were carried out during construction to prove to doubters that the

structure could withstand the vibrations of a large crowd walking inside it. The finished structure covered almost 20 acres (8 hectares) and towered to more than 100 feet (30 meters) at its transepts, which were extended to accommodate a cluster of Hyde Park's elm trees.

After the Great Exhibition had run its course, the structure was dismantled and rebuilt on Sydenham Hill in south London, where it housed a large number of successful exhibitions. In 1911, the site played host to the Festival of Empire, and John Logie Baird established his television studios there in 1933. The Crystal Palace was lost forever when it was destroyed by fire in 1936.

made by 14,000 companies from nations across the world. The exhibits included every kind of art, as well as those from industry and the natural world. Each of the participating countries mounted their own series of courts, exhibiting their best pieces.

The Great Exhibition was an enormous popular success. More than 6 million people visited the Crystal Palace in the six months from May 1851 during which its doors were open. The prestige it lent to British designers and manufacturers inspired a rash of similar fairs across the world, beginning in Dublin the very next year. However, with the exception of Pugin's display in the Medieval Court, the British furniture on display at the Crystal Palace in 1851 won but scant critical praise. It was the French entries that received most of the prizes.

Many of the entries at the Great Exhibition of 1851 went on to form the basis of the collections at the South Kensington Museum. A. W. N. Pugin's Gothic cabinet and Angiolo Barbetti's Renaissance cabinet were both bought by the museum, which itself was financed by the profits made from the Great Exhibition. Later renamed the Victoria and Albert Museum, it still displays these pieces today, alongside pieces from subsequent world's fairs.

THE INTERNATIONAL WORLD STAGE

Two years later, in 1853, New York hosted an international exhibition based on the British model, even down to the construction of a "New York Crystal Palace" off Fifth Avenue. Despite serious problems—a leaking roof damaged the attractions and doused visitors with rainwater—the event was a boon for the American manufacturing base.

In France, 1855 brought the *Exposition Universelle*. Queen Victoria and Prince Albert bought an ebony display cabinet by Grohé Frères, and a table and cabinet by Edouard Kreisser in Louis XVI style.

There were three more exhibitions in Paris, and three more in London before the end of the century. In the 1867 Paris Exhibition, the Thonet Brothers won a gold medal for their Number 14 bentwood chair (*see p.277*). The most memorable part of the 1889 Paris Exhibition was the Eiffel Tower, which was built as the fair's grand entrance. Large-scale trade fairs were also organized in Vienna, Sydney, Kyoto, Philadelphia, Cape Town, and Melbourne.

As an indication of what the general public was buying at any one time, these grand exhibitions are not particularly useful tools. Many of the companies that submitted pieces for display seized the opportunity to showcase their most flamboyant and technically complicated achievements, rather than items that were in general production. These events were, after all, competitive, with esteemed judges awarding prizes for the best entries in various classes. However, the exhibitions did help to communicate ideas and styles to the world. Many of the designs exhibited spawned cheaper imitations, and some, such as Thonet's bentwood furniture, was, in fact, mass-produced and transported all over the world.

Sideboard This totara knot and boxwood sideboard is by Johann Martin Levien. The crest is flanked by dragons. It has a boxwood panel that is carved with foliage, nymphs, and satyrs and flanked by medallion portraits of Queen Victoria and Prince Albert, one signed by Lovati. The lower section consists of a drawer and pedestals resting on a plinth base. *1851.*

French center table This kingwood table was made by François Linke with bronzes by Leon Messagé. The Louis XV-style table has a parquetry top above a serpentine frieze with female masks. The stretcher is decorated with two putti sitting by a water vessel. *H:31½ in (79 cm); W:70 in (175 cm); D:38 in (95 cm).*

Fire at the Crystal Palace Fire broke out on the evening of November 30, 1936. Although the structure was mostly glass and iron, the dry floorboards and flammable exhibits meant that 500 firemen could not contain the fire. By the morning, all that remained of Paxton's amazing glass construction was a mass of twisted steelwork and smoldering ruins. Sir Winston Churchill commented: "This is the end of an age."

FRANCE: LOUIS-PHILIPPE

LOUIS-PHILIPPE WAS THE LAST monarch to be recognized by the people of France. Descended from the House of Orléans, he faced opposition from the Legitimists who wished to see a Bourbon regain the French throne, as well as from Republicans and those in the Napoleonist camp. Aware of the deep divisions that troubled his nation, Louis-Philippe strove to restore unity during his 18-year reign (1830–48). He adopted the populist title "King of the French" and founded the Museum of French History, which he dedicated to "All of France's glories." The king was also a significant patron of the arts, and his love of architecture can be seen today in the buildings he commissioned at Versailles.

A HAPPY DISARRAY OF STYLES

Furniture of the period reflected Louis-Philippe's reconciliatory agenda. Revivals of various historical styles remained popular, despite often having close associations with the Bourbon monarchy. Fashionable citizens and those wishing to show off their new-found wealth would furnish their dining rooms in the Renaissance style and their living rooms with pieces imitating Louis-XIV taste. An altogether different tenor was struck by exponents of the Cathedral style, or *gothique troubadour*, which harked back to the Gothic era. Characterized by deep carving and molding, frequently incorporating devotional motifs, the Cathedral style was architectural, and its heavy aspect suited to darker woods such as oak. There was a move away from the lighter woods that were popular during Charles X's reign (1824–30),

Swan-carved uprights, each incorporating a scroll, support a rectangular mirror.

Only two of the five small platform drawers are real.

The frieze drawer is inlaid with stylized Neoclassical anthemia.

WALNUT TABLE

This walnut drop-leaf dining table features additional leaves (totaling five when fully extended). The table top is supported on six turned legs, which terminate in casters. *c. 1840.* W:118 in (300 cm) (max). DC

Carved lotus leaves

Stylized anthemion inlays flank the mirror back and echo the inlaywork of the frieze drawer above.

The mirror back reflects two of the pilasters.

Each pilaster is carved with lotus leaves.

DRESSING TABLE

This elegant ebony-inlaid dressing table is made of satinwood and decorated with foliate scrolls. The upper section has a rectangular mirror flanked by carved upright supports in the form of swans. Below the mirror are two real and three dummy drawers. The lower section of the dressing table has a dish top above a frieze drawer, which is raised on lotus leaf-carved pilasters supported on a shaped platform base and raised on turned feet. The back of this section is covered with mirror glass. This piece is more reminiscent of the style of furniture prevalent during the reign of the last Bourbon king, Charles X (reigned 1824–30), with its light wood veneers. *c. 1840.* H:58 in (147 cm). SI

GUÉRIDON

This *guéridon* (French candlestand) has a marble top with a recessed center. This top is supported on a baluster-shaped column, which terminates in a tripod base. The lion's-paw feet at the ends of the base rest on casters. *c. 1840.* H:30¾ in (78 cm); D:31½ in (80 cm). BEA

and manufacturers favored walnut and more exotic hardwoods such as mahogany and rosewood, which were imported from France's colonies.

REFRESHING AND MODEST
Simple and sturdy, the Louis-Philippe style displayed a confidence that did not require excessive surface decoration. Instead, cabinet-makers asserted their assurance through large, bold forms with simple lines. Where materials other than wood were incorporated into the body of a piece, they were designed to blend into and complement the whole. Gilt-metal mounts depicting mythological or grotesque figures and marble table tops were employed to bring out the colors and textures of the woods, sometimes accentuated with flame veneer. Industrial cutting techniques reduced the amount of labor required in the manufacture of furniture. This resulted in a greater availability of pieces. New forms included the *canapé borne*, or "sociable sofa," which consisted of an upholstered seat with central cushions, allowing users to sit facing opposite directions, and a whole range of pieces made from wood and wrought and cast iron for furnishing the *jardins d'hiver*, or conservatories.

The Apartment of the Count de Mornay Painted by Eugène Delacroix, this scene depicts a room decorated and furnished in typical Louis-Philippe style. Furniture became slightly heavier and plainer in form during this period of France's history. Central to the Count de Mornay's room is a sofa, which later became known as the *canapé borne*.

MAHOGANY COMMODE

This Louis-Philippe mahogany commode has a rectangular, gray, fossilized marble top with rounded corners, which rests on top of a concave frieze drawer. Below this drawer are three long drawers all featuring matching flame mahogany veneers. The case stands on a plinth supported on four square, bun feet. *c. 1840. W:52¼ in (132 cm). L&T*

BREAKFRONT BOOKCASE

The upper section of this walnut breakfront bookcase has a raised central door with applied shaped moldings, flanked by corresponding doors with lower panels. The three doors of the upper section are divided by ring-turned columns with octagonal turrets and finials. The lower section of the bookcase follows the style of the upper section: the central door has an applied circular cusp panel and is flanked on either side by a door with arched paneling. The whole stands on a plinth base. *c. 1840. H:109 in (277 cm); W:81 in (206 cm); D:25¼ in (64 cm). L&T*

Cast ram's-head bracket

Tablet frieze

LOUIS-PHILIPPE VITRINE

This walnut and gilt-brass vitrine has mahogany banding, and boxwood and ebony stringing. It is raised on a plinth with flattened, bun feet. The rectangular top has canted angles. The single glazed door has a frame inlaid with specimen woods and applied rosettes. *c. 1840. W:37 in (94 cm). L&T*

FRANCE: 1848–1900

"BOULLE" CABINE

This Louis XIV-inspired
cabinet is decorated with
première-partie boullewo
on a red tortoiseshell
ground. The black, shape
rectangular marble top h
molded serpentine edges
The conforming front has
frieze above a door, cente
with an oval panel and
flanked by outset rounded
stiles with figural chute:
The shaped skirt is cente
with an espagnolette and
raised on disc feet. c. 18
H:42½ in (108 cm);
W:42¾ in (108.5 cm);
D:17½ in (108.5 cm). SI

IN CONTRAST TO THE reconciliatory
stance adopted by Louis-Philippe,
Napoleon III sought to align himself
firmly with the Classical past as part
of his consolidation of power. Designs
from the reign of Louis XIV, the Sun
King, were appropriated along with
forms and decorative motifs from the
reigns of Louis XV and Louis XVI.
Napoleon III had promised France
glory, and he hoped to provide this
at least in part by reminding it of a
golden age. There was also a pan-
European revival of interest in the
Classical and Renaissance periods.

The Salon de Musique This music room at the
Chateau de Compiègne has an eclectic mix of
17th-, 18th-, and 19th-century furniture that
is typical of interiors of the Second Empire.

LUXURY AND COMFORT
Dark woods, especially mahogany and
ebony, were used in abundance by the
cabinet-makers of the time. Newer
materials such as cast iron, turned
out by foundries all over newly
industrialized France, and papier-
mâché, provided a contemporary twist.
Precious materials such as gilt bronze
heralded the wealth and status of the
owner and loaned visual interest to
a piece, as did inlays of ivory and
mother-of-pearl, which provided a
dramatic contrast to the dark wood.
A revival of the intricate veneering
and marquetry work as practiced
by André-Charles Boulle in the
time of Louis XIV further added to
the sumptuous decadence that is a
hallmark of Second Empire furniture.
Comfort was a high priority.
Upholstery became far more prevalent
due to the widespread availability of the

coiled spring. Tapissier chairs, named
for the richly embroidered upholsteries
with which they were covered, became
staples of fashionable salons. The
1850s saw the introduction of new
forms to the canon of French cabinet-
making, including the round,
upholstered ottoman known as the
pouffe, which is still in use today.
The dos-à-dos and the boudeuse, or
courting chair, also date from this
period. In such seating, the occupants
sat beside each other but facing away
from each other, divided by an
S-shaped seat rail.

ANTIQUARIAN NATIONAL STYLE
Architectural elements, such as
columns and pediments drawn from
Greco-Roman buildings, provided the
Classical and Renaissance look that
pandered to the Emperor's desire to
root his regime firmly in the glorious
past. Egyptian motifs provided a similar
link but were the consequence of
French archaeologist Marcel Dieulafoy's
avid interest in architecture. Many
19th-century designers were heavily
influenced by his studies of excavated
Egyptian and Middle-Eastern buildings.
All these ingredients combined to
produce a national style that became
more extreme toward the end of the
century, as shown by the kingwood
vitrine opposite.

LOUIS XVI TABLE

Almost an exact copy of
an 18th-century piece, thi
rosewood, marquetry-inlai
gilt-metal mounted side
table has a fitted frieze
drawer. The table top is
raised on gilt-metal caryati
legs. The legs are joined by
a pierced platform stretche
with a bowl at its center,
and stand on spiral, tapere
feet. 1880. W:34 in
(86.5 cm). GorB

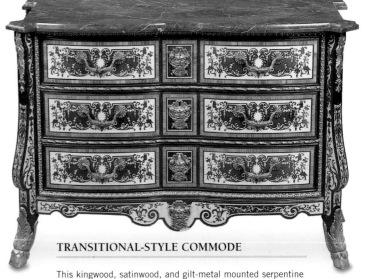

TRANSITIONAL-STYLE COMMODE

This kingwood, satinwood, and gilt-metal mounted serpentine
commode has a marble top with outset corners. The three long
drawers have inlaid panels, each centered by a grotesque
mask motif. The capped, splayed legs are joined by a shaped
apron and have hoof feet. c. 1900. W:44½ in (113 cm). SI

ONVERSATION SEAT

is Louis XV-style giltwood and upholstered conversation seat
covered in a red and gold striped fabric. The piece has a
rpentine back with a shell surmount and stands on molded,
briole legs. *c. 1890.*

125 in (317.5 cm). SI

Serpentine crest rail

There are upholstered armrests at each seat division.

The center section of
the conversation seat
is for three people.

The serpentine seat rail
mirrors the design of
the top rail.

Each end section seats
an additional person.

KINGWOOD VITRINE

he tapering ogee top of this serpentine vitrine has a central
artouche above a pair of glazed doors and sides, enclosing a
irrored interior. Below is a single central door inspired by
ouis XV style with a *vernis martin bombé* panel of lovers.
:80 in (203 cm); W:53 in (135 cm); D:20½ in (52 cm). L&T

GABRIEL VIARDOT

THE FRENCH TASTE FOR *JAPONISME* WAS ALREADY ENTRENCHED WHEN
DESIGNER GABRIEL VIARDOT BEGAN WORKING IN THE ASIAN STYLE.

Gabriel Viardot was an expert wood-carver and was
already operating his own business when he took
over the reins of the family furniture business in
1861. Records show that in 1885 Viardot employed
around 100 men at his premises on Rue Amelot in
Paris. His renown was such that he was invited to
adjudicate at the *Expositions Universelles* held in Paris.
He also submitted his own pieces for exhibition and
was the recipient of a series of awards, including a
gold medal in 1889. The Viardot name is most closely
associated with furniture in the Japanese style, but
he also produced Vietnamese-style work—Vietnam
was one of Napoleon III's most prized colonies.

The furniture created by Viardot was solidly
constructed, typically from beech or walnut, with
decorative motifs drawn from the East. Grotesque
masks, very much a feature of mainstream French
furniture, were adapted so that they took on an
Eastern countenance. Carvings depicting dragons
and demons were inspired by Asian mythology and
tradition, and the frequent use of lacquer coating
was a direct influence of Chinese style. Viardot's
juxtaposition of European and Eastern forms
resulted in the creation of very distinctive pieces
that bridged the gap between exotic imports and
more prosaic homespun furniture.

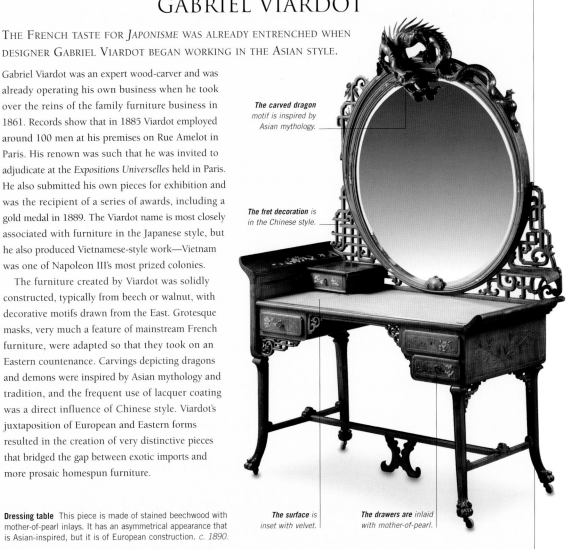

The carved dragon
motif is inspired by
Asian mythology.

The fret decoration is
in the Chinese style.

Dressing table This piece is made of stained beechwood with
mother-of-pearl inlays. It has an asymmetrical appearance that
is Asian-inspired, but it is of European construction. *c. 1890.*

The surface is
inset with velvet.

The drawers are inlaid
with mother-of-pearl.

ITALY

DESPITE A NEW NATIONALISTIC fervor that eventually resulted in the creation of the modern Italian state in 1861, furniture production in mid-19th-century Italy was a fragmented affair, concentrated around the cities of Rome, Milan, Venice, and Florence, in the north. The poorer states and kingdoms of the south of Italy, with the exception of Naples, seemed content to continue using simpler, vernacular forms of furniture.

PERSISTENT FRENCH INFLUENCE
Until the Risorgimento movement gathered pace, climaxing in the revolutions of 1848, Italy lived in the cultural shadow of France, its more powerful neighbor to the north. The prominence of the Rococo and Empire styles in Italy is a direct consequence of this relationship and, despite a wave of anti-French feeling following Napoleonic occupation during the early 19th century, this influence persisted. The growing importance of Piedmont as the cultural and political apex around which the emerging Italian state revolved only served to protract this lingering Francophilia. The Rococo-revival style was, therefore, one of the most prominent in mid-19th-century Italy. Fussy forms such as the *canapé en cabriolet*, a padded sofa, were richly carved and enveloped in gilt. Side tables with pierced and scrolled detail were covered with marble tops in a typically Italian twist. The grotto or fantasy style, originating in medieval France, was one that Italian craftsmen had adopted with relish. Meticulously detailed representations of timber and

CANAPÉ EN CABRIOLET

Executed in the Rococo style, the frame of this elaborate sofa is made of gilded wood. The backrest is composed of three cartouche-form padded backs set in conforming frames with pierced C-scroll crests, giving the appearance of three *fauteuils* joined together. The out-curved arms at each end have padded elbow rests to provide additional comfort. The serpentine-fronted stuffover seat with similarly pierced rails continues into cabriole legs with scroll toes. The whole piece is decorated with carved flower-heads and foliage. The *canapé* would have been part of a salon suite with chairs, armchairs, and stools all designed to match one another. *c. 1860. W:77 in (196 cm). S&K*

CONSOLE TABLE

This Rococo-style console table has a serpentine marble top, raised on a fluted, carved scrolling frame made of gilded wood. The frame is decorated with foliate designs, and the heavy cabriole legs are joined by a pierced strapwork stretcher. *Mid-19th century. H:35 in (89 cm); W:48 in (122 cm); D:24 in (60 cm). L&T*

MICROMOSAIC

BEAUTIFUL "ETERNAL PAINTINGS" OF INTRICATE ENAMEL MOSAIC WERE MADE
BY ITALIAN CRAFTSMEN TO DECORATE TABLE TOPS AND TRINKET BOXES.

Micromosaic was developed within the Vatican in the 17th century as an alternative means of decorating altars with devotional tableaux. The paintings in the vast basilica of St. Peter's had been damaged by damp, and the enamel tesserae used in micromosaic overcame this problem. They became known in Rome as *la vera pittura per eternita*, meaning "eternal paintings."

The technique is an evolution of the ancient architectural mosaics developed in the Greco-Roman period. An image is built up using tiny components, or *tesserae*, of different-colored enamel or glass. Each *tessera* is a thread about ⅛ in (3 mm) long with a diameter slightly wider than a hair. The thread is pushed into the putty of the mosaic base, leaving the end visible. The attention to detail and level of expertise involved in their creation are remarkable— the finest examples include 5,000 *tesserae* per sq in (775 per cm²).

European gentlemen on the Grand Tour would purchase trinkets, such as boxes and jewelry, decorated with micromosaic as mementoes of their time in Rome. The wealthiest tourists brought home table tops made by craftsmen operating in workshops in the Vatican. Typically, these table tops depicted scenes from antiquity or famous Roman vistas. They were highly prized throughout Western Europe as fine-art objects. Other tables might have plain marble tops with panels of micromosaic incorporated within them.

There is a collection of micromosaic artifacts in the Gilbert Collection Museum in London and another in the Hermitage Museum in St. Petersburg, Russia.

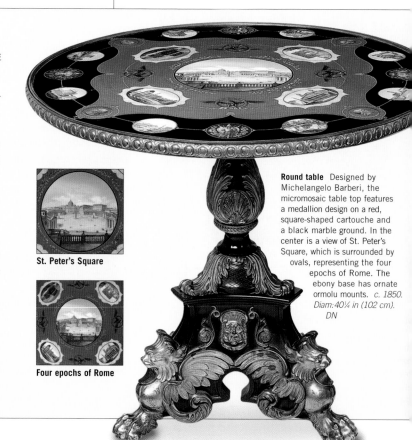

St. Peter's Square

Four epochs of Rome

Round table Designed by Michelangelo Barberi, the micromosaic table top features a medallion design on a red, square-shaped cartouche and a black marble ground. In the center is a view of St. Peter's Square, which is surrounded by ovals, representing the four epochs of Rome. The ebony base has ornate ormolu mounts. *c. 1850. Diam:40¼ in (102 cm). DN*

ell forms characterized this look, hich was particularly indebted to e work of French designer Bernard lissy (1509–90). Although examples fantasy furniture from the mid-19th ntury are generally considered ferior to earlier pieces, it was evertheless a popular revival style.

ALIAN TRADITIONS

he Renaissance revival was more presentative of Italian history, and

the quality of furniture made in this style by Italian craftsmen demonstrates the high esteem in which it was held. The Florentine cabinet-maker Andrea Baccetti and the Sienese wood-carver Angelo Barbetti both produced particularly fine pieces in the Renaissance style. Archaic forms, such as the settle and architectural wall mirrors, were made in walnut, with deep carving depicting Classical and grotesque forms.

Blackamoors, an 18th-century Venetian invention, remained popular well into the 19th century, either as bases for *torchères* or as decorative *objets* in their own right. Venetian glass-makers continued to produce mirrors of the highest quality. Particularly fine examples of mirrors with intricately etched glass frames

speak of the greatness of the glass-masters of Murano. Elaborate decorative techniques, such as micromosaic, provided a forum for the most accomplished artisans to demonstrate their proficiency.

In the later 19th century, the regional Italian furniture industry began to flourish, and regions such as Brianza and Pesaro, which are famous today for their fine work, started to develop the infrastructures and traditions that would ensure their future success.

ALL MIRROR

his Renaissance-style walnut wall mirror has a oken pediment carved with cherub heads and female head. The oval mirror plate is flanked carved caryatids with further cherub heads elow. *Mid-19th century. H:59¼ in (148 cm). L&T*

AHOGANY ARMCHAIR

his elaborately carved grotto-style armchair is ade of mahogany. The seat and back combine form a huge, hinged scallop shell, linked by nate arms and splayed legs. *c. 1890. H:37 in 94 cm). B&I*

The stiles are inlaid with arabesques.

The drawers have molded surrounds.

Frieze drawers feature stiff, dull, mechanical inlay work.

Turned, gilt-metal supports support the upper case

Slender, turned baluster legs support the stand.

Gilt-bronze finial

Bronze figure

A pierced, flattened **cross-stretcher** connects the legs of the stand.

CABINET-ON-STAND

This ebony and black-lacquered cabinet-on-stand is inlaid all over with ivory in a fine foliage pattern in imitation of the Baroque style of the 17th century. A narrow central door is flanked on either side by three drawers—one above the

other—and has a further three drawers, arranged side by side, below. The upper case has a gilt-bronze carrying handle on either side. It is supported on a similarly decorated stand with turned legs, joined by a carved, flat cross-stretcher. *Mid-19th century. H:65 in (165 cm); W:44 in (112 cm); D:14½ in (37 cm). BEA*

EARLY VICTORIAN BRITAIN

BRITISH FURNITURE DESIGN during the early Victorian period was confused. The prevalent styles were overlapping attempts at recreating looks from three key historical eras—the Greek, the Gothic, and the Rococo.

In reality, the actual forms of the furniture created at this time were largely standard and had little basis in the eras they purported to emulate. Rather, the "design" of a piece of furniture was all about the surface and the applied decoration it carried.

GOTHIC, ROCOCO, AND GREEK
Victorian Gothic was a masculine style based on idealized notions of Tudor furniture. New cupboards, chests, tables, and chairs were created by piecing together fragments of older furniture from grand houses.

A. W. N. Pugin (see box, below right) led a move toward a more authentic interpretation of the Gothic style. This was at least partially successful: his work on the interiors of the Houses of Parliament prompted Gillows to

introduce a range entitled "New Palace Westminster," which was distinguished by the use of roundels incorporating a Tudor rose or thistle at the conjunction of the legs and stretchers.

The feminine Rococo taste was widespread throughout fashionable drawing rooms because of George IV's particular interest in the revival. The florid decoration was structural—incorporated into the shape of the furniture rather than added to the surfaces. The heavy use of gilding was

The library at Tyntesfield House, near Bristol Many of the rooms in this house were rebuilt in Gothic-revival style by businessman William Gibbs, who bought the original Regency-Gothic house in 1843.

Each oval porcelain plaque is painted with a French courtly lady.

The canted stiles are mounted with free-standing ormolu figures of Shakespeare and Milton.

Thuyawood panels are inlaid into an ebonized ground.

The legs are mounted with gilt-bronze moldings and Sèvres floral plaques.

The mirrored back serves to reflect ornaments placed on the shelves.

The center drawer has a hinged, leather-lined adjustable writing slope.

Casters made from brass are fixed to turned feet.

BREAKFAST TABLE

This early Victorian mahogany breakfast table has a round, tilt-top with a molded edge. The table top is supported on a lappet-carved column and collar, which stands on a circular platform supported by paw feet. *c. 1840. Diam:51½ in (131 cm); H:29¾ in (74 cm). DN*

PAPIER-MÂCHÉ TRAY

This painted and gilt papier-mâché tray has a curvilinear-shaped outline and a deep concave rim decorated with gilt penwork leaves. The main panel is painted with a Himalayan mountain landscape, containing figures crossing a waterfall. *c. 1840. H:31 in (81.5 cm); W:24½ in (62 cm). L&T*

BONHEUR-DU-JOUR

This Louis XVI-style *bonheur-du-jour* of part-ebonized thuyawood is ormolu-and-porcelain-mounted. The upper section has a tall, central, mirror-backed display cabinet with a three-quarter gallery flanked by similar, but lower,

cabinets, each with a central porcelain plaque. The outset lower section has an *entrelac* frieze with three drawers above mirror-backed shelves. It is raised on turned, tapered, and fluted legs on casters. The piece is a mix of Victorian and French Court styles. *1860. H:58¾ in (149 cm); W:47½ in (120.5 cm); D:22¼ in (56.5 cm). SI*

Sèvres floral plaque

ondemned by architects, as it as used by many manufacturers o conceal shoddy construction.

The Greek style, informed by Henry haw's 1836 *Specimens of Modern urniture*, was simple and solid, efreshingly free from the extraneous ecoration that was a feature of much arly Victorian furniture.

RIED AND TESTED IDEAS

he stagnant state of the industry an be demonstrated by the fact at the same edition of the *London abinet-Maker's Union Book of Rules*,

a depository of patterns used by the trade, was in print continuously between 1836 and 1866. This situation was exacerbated by a new middle class who did not want to appear uneducated: the majority of people would rather rely on tried-and-tested ideas than risk committing a gaffe. Whereas the wealthy consumer of the 18th century would commission furniture tailored to his exact requirements, the aspiring Victorian gentleman had to make do with whatever stock was available in the showroom of his chosen retailer,

which generally consisted of rounded forms, such as the balloon-back chair, a staple of early Victorian design. The gradual mechanization that characterized the Victorian furniture industry led to a separation of the roles of designer and manufacturer, at least in urban centers.

The traditional role of the furniture-maker persisted in the provinces, as did many vernacular forms. In Lancashire, for example, ladder-back chairs were produced in stained ash instead of the mahogany fashionable in London.

Pockets of craftsmen throughout Britain created Windsor chairs with idiosyncratic features typical of the region in which they worked.

Niche markets arose in provincial cities as craftsmen in certain areas developed expertise in specific fields. Birmingham was a center for the production of metal bedsteads, forged in furnaces fueled by the coal and iron that were cheap and abundant in that industrial hub. Farther east, Nottingham and Leicester were renowned as centers for cane and wicker furniture.

IBRARY CENTER TABLE

he octagonal, revolving top of this table is urfaced with green leather outlined by tooled nd gilt lilies and centers on a lobed marquetry anel. The shaped border is inset with floral prays and clusters of fruit, alternating with

Asian scenes framed by Rococo cartouches. The table has four frieze drawers and rests on a concave-sided central support. Four splayed, inward-scrolling feet and the shape of the apron reflect Louis XV influence. Ebony, tulipwood, mahogany, pine, and cedar are all used. *1840. H:30 in (76 cm); D:60 in (152 cm). LOT*

BALLOON-BACK DINING CHAIR

This balloon-back dining chair has a pierced scroll splat and is raised on acute cabriole legs. The upholstered seat is covered in green velvet. This style of dining chair was a popular early Victorian form. *GorB*

SHOW-FRAME ARMCHAIR

The back rail of this mahogany chair is carved and terminates in carved scrolls, where it meets the upholstered arms. The seat and back are padded. The chair is supported on carved, cabriole legs with brass casters. *DN*

A. W. N. PUGIN (1812–52)

PUGIN'S DEDICATION TO AUTHENTIC GOTHIC DESIGN WAS INFORMED BY HIS RELIGIOUS BELIEF AND HAD A PROFOUND INFLUENCE ON OTHER DESIGNERS.

Engraving of Pugin

Pugin's relationship with his father, a French aristocrat who fled Paris during the Revolution, was instrumental in the future direction of his career. Pugin senior worked for John Nash as chief draftsman, and instilled in his son a respect for architectural style and decoration. Father and son drafted two volumes on Gothic design, which fueled the Victorian penchant for works in this style.

Conversion to Catholicism in 1834 galvanized Pugin's admiration for what Victorians knew as the "middle-pointed" style, dating from the period between 1280

and 1340, when great cathedrals were built and the faithful expressed their devotion through the decorative arts. From the late 1830s, Pugin published works extolling the virtues of this "pure" Gothic style as distinguished from the bastardized attempts created by so many of his contemporaries.

In contrast to prevailing mid-Victorian taste, Pugin was concerned with coherence in his interiors. This philosophy is evident at the Palace of Westminster (Houses of Parliament), for which Pugin provided furnishings as well as assisting with the building's design. Pugin's work for the Medieval Court at the Great Exhibition in 1851 was one of his last commissions. The following year he became mentally ill and died at home.

Oak table, made for Horsted Place, Sussex This table is an example of the simpler Gothic-style furniture designed by Pugin especially for more modest houses. The carved decoration and use of chamfered, or beveled, edges is drawn from church woodwork. *1852–53. H:30 in (76 cm); W:45 in (114 cm); D:29½ in (75 cm).*

LATE VICTORIAN BRITAIN

THE LATER VICTORIAN PERIOD saw a growing distinction between general "trade" furniture and what came to be known as "Art Furniture"—that is, furniture made by firms that retained architects and specialist designers.

PARALLEL INDUSTRIES
Cabinet-makers in London's West End, and their downmarket counterparts in the East End, continued to employ the cabriole legs and rounded backs that had already been made for many years. Newer developments in furniture included a proliferation of corner and mantelshelves for displaying decorative objects, and

the adoption of a gallery of turned spindles, from the French style. Art Furniture, in whatever guise it took, tended to adhere to certain structural or philosophical principles, leaving the manufacturers who plowed the trade furrow to concentrate on such lesser concerns as comfort, practicality, and—most of all—affordability.

That British furnishers were operating on a two-tier basis can be demonstrated by the way they reacted to overseas influences. The gradual emergence of Japan from its isolationist shell led in a great deal of interest in Japanese culture and aesthetic traditions in all spheres of the arts, including the

furniture industry. Trade furnishers responded by churning out "Anglo-Japanese" pieces, adding fake Japanese decoration to existing Victorian forms. Exponents of Art Furniture, meanwhile, took a more studious and disciplined approach. The influential designer Christopher Dresser visited Japan in 1876 and became a champion of authentic Japanese style. Similarly, the designer Edward Godwin made close studies of Japanese art and carefully incorporated what he learned into

his furniture designs, as evident in his striking juxtapositions of horizontal and vertical pieces. Bamboo became very popular because it was very sturdy yet cheaper than exotic hardwoods.

NEW STYLE FROM THE PAST
A perennial favorite of historically-minded furniture-designers, the Gothic style was as widespread as ever during the late Victorian period. Among its principal exponents was Bruce Talbert, a practitioner of the "Early English"

Brass corner clasp

LATE VICTORIAN WRITING TABLE

This top of this writing table is lined with green leather and framed by a brass edge molding. The serpentine frieze, containing two narrow drawers, is faced with panels of floral marquetry, crossbanded in tulipwood and set into a zebrawood ground. *H:30 in (76 cm); W:40 in (101 cm); D:22 in (56 cm).*

Renaissance-revival panels are fitted into each side cupboard door.

A mirror backs the upper display section of the cabinet.

A molded architectural cornice frieze overhangs the two cupboards.

A glazed cupboard door allows ornaments to be seen.

SIDE CABINET

This inlaid Adam-style side cabinet is made of mahogany with satinwood banding, and was designed by Gillows. The upper section of the cabinet has a consoled reverse-breakfront cornice with a central beveled mirror below. The mirror is flanked by

cupboards on either side, each with a grotesque-inlaid door in the Renaissance style. The deeper, lower section of the cabinet has three drawers in the frieze, above a central glazed door; on either side of the glazed door is an open shelf. The whole stands on bracket feet. *Late 19th century. H:69¾ in (177 cm); W:60 in (152 cm). L&T*

CHAMBER CUPBOARD

This Gothic-revival pedestal cupboard has a galleried top and stands on a chamfered plinth. The door has a central harewood panel with stylized flowers and circular rosettes. *1865. H:33 in (84 cm); W:14½ in (36 cm); D:15¼ in (39 cm). LOT*

DINING CHAIR

One of a set of 21, this walnut chair has a curved back rail, solid splat, and upholstered bow-fronted seat. The Greek-revival chair is supported on turned, tapering legs. *c. 1880. H:33¼ in (87 cm). DN*

style, who arrived in London in 1865. His predilection was for honestly constructed furniture of the Gothic school. He celebrated mortise-and-tenon joining and despised the use of glue for, as he stated: "Glue leads

The Drawing Room of Cragside House, Northumberland
The marble chimneypiece is a spectacular example of Renaissance-revival style. Added to Cragside by architect Richard Shaw in 1883–84, the carving includes putti, swags, arabesques, and strapwork.

to veneering and veneering to polish." Rather than commit the sin of veneering, he offset the dark wood bodies of his work with decorative panels of contrasting colors.

REGIONAL FURNITURE-MAKERS
A number of provincial furniture centers flourished. Gillows of Lancaster built on an established reputation for quality furniture and continued to expand during the mid-19th century. Lancaster port provided Gillows with steady supplies of Caribbean mahogany. Shipyards also provided Gillows with commissions to furnish luxury yachts, the most

prestigious of which were the Royal Yacht *Victoria and Albert* and *Livadia*, constructed for Czar Alexander II.

Wylie and Lochhead of Glasgow employed craftsmen to make furniture for their department store as well as for the grand liners that were built on the Clyde. Established in 1829, by 1870 Wylie and Lochhead made, upholstered, and sold furniture for the middle classes of Glasgow and beyond.

High Wycombe, Buckinghamshire, was one of many centers of Windsor chair production. Chair bodging—the rural practice of making various parts of chairs—eventually spawned a number of chair factories.

GEORGIAN REVIVALS

HIGH-QUALITY REPRODUCTIONS OF 18TH-CENTURY, NEOCLASSICAL-STYLE FURNITURE WERE PARTICULARLY POPULAR DURING THE 1870S.

Many Victorians turned their backs on contemporary furniture design and imitated the 18th-century Neoclassical style instead. Many of the great cabinet-makers of that period had bequeathed the industry detailed pattern books, making it easy to recreate their products. In 1867, Wright and Mansfield made a cabinet designed by Crosse, which is credited with sparking the interest in Neoclassical decoration and style. It has a satinwood carcass, and incorporates marquetry in various woods, with giltwood mounts and Wedgwood plaques. The cabinet is now at the Victoria and Albert Museum in London.

Reproductions of 18th-century pieces by Chippendale, Sheraton, Hepplewhite, and Adam were pervasive during the

second half of the 19th century. Many of them were of very high quality and, now that they have aged, can be difficult to distinguish from the originals.

The look was characterized by profuse use of inlay and banding. Satinwood was highly prized for its pleasing color, useful for contrasting banding, and gilt lacquer provided an alternative to the dark colors of the Gothic style. Cameo carving featured Classical motifs, such as urns, shell, and acanthus. The style was such a success that unscrupulous sale rooms would apply fake Neoclassical ornaments to plain 18th-century furniture. Popular at various times throughout the 19th century, the Neoclassical revival style was especially fashionable during the 1870s.

Chippendale mahogany open armchair This chair has a splat with pierced, interlaced strapwork headed by acanthus sprays. It stands on cabriole front legs with carved acanthus knees and claw-and-ball feet. *c. 1900. D:30 in (12 cm). Bon*

Adam-style gilt wall mirror The beveled rectangular plate is flanked by panels with ribbon-tied husk pendants, and surmounted by an urn, anthemion, and floral swag design. *Late 19th century. H:49½ in (124 cm). L&T*

Sheraton-revival satinwood, semi-elliptical commode
This commode is painted with swags of flowers and female figures within ovals in Neoclassical style. The commode has a frieze drawer above a central paneled door and stands on square-section feet. *Late 19th century. H:37¼ in (93 cm); W:39½ in (98.5 cm). DN*

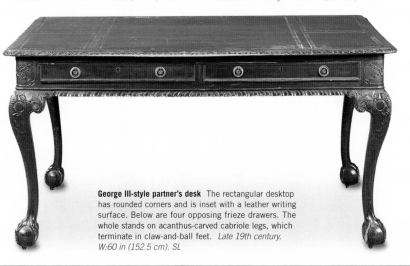

George III-style partner's desk The rectangular desktop has rounded corners and is inset with a leather writing surface. Below are four opposing frieze drawers. The whole stands on acanthus-carved cabriole legs, which terminate in claw-and-ball feet. *Late 19th century. W:60 in (152.5 cm). SL*

CAMPAIGN FURNITURE

SPECIALLY DESIGNED TO BE ERECTED AND DISASSEMBLED IN A FEW
MOMENTS, THE FURNITURE PRODUCED FOR OFFICERS TO TAKE ON
CAMPAIGN WAS AS FASHIONABLE AS THAT MADE FOR THE HOME.

AS STARTLINGLY INCONGRUOUS as
the idea seems today, the military
gentleman of the Victorian period
would not countenance the idea of
a foreign posting without taking his
drawing room suite. Indeed, it appears
that the 19th-century mindset detected
nothing even faintly risible when Thomas
Sheraton boasted in his 1803 *Cabinet
Directory* that the addition of his stylish,
collapsible furniture to one's kit bag
"should not retard rapid movement, either
after or from the enemy." Among the
"absolutely necessary" articles he produced
for use on campaign were elegant dining
tables that would seat as many as 20 guests.

A LONG TRADITION OF COMFORT
Campaign furniture, or "knockdown" furniture
as it was often called, has its roots in the campaigns
of the Napoleonic wars (1800–15). Among the most
popular examples from this initial period of production
was the Wellington chest, named after the legendary
Duke. Available in a variety of sizes, it featured a
hinged, lockable bar that extended from the frame
to secure the drawers.

During the reign of King George III (1760–1820),
campaign furniture was commissioned almost
exclusively by the wealthiest officers from the upper
classes and was luxurious. Fine upholstery, leather
lining, and intricate hidden compartments combined
to make this furniture just as comfortable and
elaborate as that produced for use in the home. Soon
it was not just merchant officials and military officers
who bought such furniture but also seafarers and
families emigrating to start a new life abroad.

GOOD BUSINESS SENSE
By the mid-Victorian period, campaign furniture
was a well-established and sophisticated feature of
the best cabinet-makers' repertoires. Of course, the
most important feature of campaign furniture was
that it should be easily transportable. Whereas most
ordinary furniture was held together with dovetail
or mortise-and-tenon joints, it was crucial that
knockdown furniture could be quickly erected
and taken apart with the minimum of fuss.

WILLIAM IV CAMPAIGN CHAIR
*This dining chair, one of a set of four, has hinges at
the front and back rail, which allow it to be folded
neatly once the upholstered seat and two long bolts
have been removed.* c. 1835. H:34½ in (87.6 cm);
W:18 in (45.7 cm); D:16 in (40.6 cm). CCA

CAMPAIGN *SECRÉTAIRE* CHEST
*Two drawers side-by-side sit below a carved,
three-quarter gallery and above the* secrétaire *drawer of this
camphorwood chest, which features brass-bound corners and
contains a further four short drawers and three long drawers,
all with sunken handles.* 1835–40. H:58¼ in (148 cm); W:41¾ in
(106 cm); D:18¾ in (48 cm). L&T

The iron supports can
be dismantled.

The cotton canopy is white
to reflect the sunlight.

The column supports are
reeded and baluster-turned.

The slatted base
is lightweight and
can be folded.

REGENCY CAMPAIGN BED
*This mahogany campaign bed, made by John Durham of
London, has a rectangular headboard, downswept half-sides,
reeded baluster-turned posts, an arched tester, slatted base,
and six ring-turned legs.* c. 1810. W:76 in (193 cm). S&K

The turned legs are on casters so
that the bed is easy to move.

Brass hinges connect the
sections of the slatted base.

Most examples used screws, which did away with the need for specialist tools. Brass mounts, placed strategically in areas that were subject to bumps and knocks, especially the corners, helped to protect the furniture while it was in transit. A Victorian brass-bound chest of drawers succeeded the Wellington chest as a campaign furniture staple. Composed of two parts, it was a simple matter to separate the top and bottom sections, which could then easily be carried with the aid of brass handles sunk into the body of the wood. Much campaign furniture was meant for use in the tropics, and cabinet-makers used materials that were suited to extremes of heat and humidity. Canvas seats were more comfortable in these conditions than wooden or upholstered examples, and cane furniture was far lighter and better suited to tropical climates than solid wood.

FASHION ON THE FRONT

Although campaign furniture was generally less fussy than that used in the home, expatriates and those on overseas assignments strove to keep up with the latest London fashions. The insular and competitive nature of life on camp was such that people would attempt to trump the efforts of the next man by acquiring the most extensive suite of furniture in the most up-to-date design. Furthermore, it was important for the colonialists to establish their perceived superiority over their charges. By displaying the wealth and sophisticated fashions of the seat of empire, an unspoken message might be conveyed to the "barbarous" natives. As a result, a typical officer's domicile might be furnished with a sofa, a dining table complete with six chairs, and two library or armchairs, all specifically designed for an itinerant lifestyle. Styles tended to lag slightly behind fashions at home, and pieces were often made in the country in which they were intended for use.

COLONIAL FOLDING CHAIR
This teak folding armchair is strengthened with brass strapping. Brass-capped bolts hold the sections together, to allow it to fold, and the stretchers and back rails are pegged. General Philip Henry Sheridan (1831–88) used such a chair during the Plains Indian wars (above). 1875–1900. H:29 in (73.6 cm). CCA

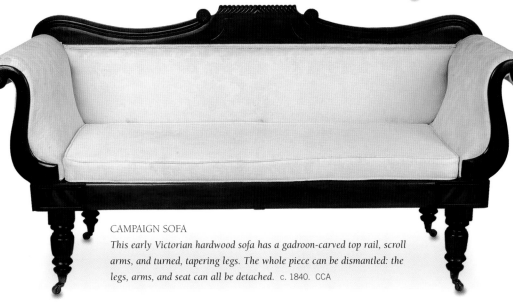

CAMPAIGN SOFA
This early Victorian hardwood sofa has a gadroon-carved top rail, scroll arms, and turned, tapering legs. The whole piece can be dismantled: the legs, arms, and seat can all be detached. c. 1840. CCA

THE BRAMAH LOCK

JOSEPH BRAMAH'S PATENT CYLINDER LOCK LED THE FIELD IN SECURITY AND WAS FITTED TO MUCH OF THE KNOCKDOWN FURNITURE TAKEN ABROAD BY BRITISH OFFICERS AND MERCHANTS.

Campaign chest This chest has a hinged lid and metal carrying handles. The chest has the typical Bramah lock, which remained unchanged for over 100 years. CCA

The Bramah lock

Locksmiths competed strenuously to come up with the most secure devices. In 1784, Joseph Bramah, an ingenious Yorkshireman whose curiosity took him into the realms of hydraulics and printing, patented a lock that still bears his name today. After a professional locksmith managed to crack Bramah's first design, he improved the mechanism and defiantly offered a 200-guinea prize to the first person that could successfully defeat it. The improved Bramah lock had 494 million possible permutations, and included dummy notches cut into the mechanism to foil the unscrupulous, not to mention persistent, lock-picker. The substantial prize went unclaimed for more than 50 years until a flamboyant American locksmith named Alfred Charles Hobbs caused a sensation by defeating both Bramah's patent lock and the Chubb Detector in 1851.

TRAVELING GAME TABLE
This early Victorian mahogany table has a top formed from its storage box. The top is marked with rosewood and boxwood veneers for chess and is supported by a telescopic column on tripod legs. c. 1840. H:28½ in (72.3 cm); W:15½ in (39.4 cm); D:13 in (33 cm). CCA

GERMANY AND AUSTRIA

THE GERMAN-SPEAKING world developed its own style years before the modern German state took shape. Although the Biedermeier style had evolved from the Neoclassical movement, particularly the Empire look that emerged from Napoleonic France, it was distinctly Germanic. Its popularity was such that Biedermeier furniture never quite disappeared in the 19th century and a number of popular revivals occurred, particularly in the 1860s. At the same time,

Germany and Austria embraced the same eclectic historicism that was popular throughout Europe during the mid-19th century.

ROCOCO REVIVAL
The Rococo revival was met with particular favor in Vienna, a city whose conservative nature was such that the court had never relinquished the original Germanic *Rokoko* of the 18th century, and so there was a seamless progression to the revival

style. New processes and technologies ushered in by the Industrial Revolution made it possible to recreate Rococo forms from published patterns at a fraction of the original cost and in less time, making them accessible to a wider market. Machines cut much finer veneers and carved Rococo ornament for application to carcasses constructed from local woods.

One of the pinnacles of the Rococo-revival style was the refurbishment of the Palais Liechtenstein in Vienna,

which made a lasting impression on public taste. Michael Thonet (*see pp.284–85*), who assisted Peter Hubert Desvignes in this mammoth task between 1837 and 1849, went on to revolutionize the furniture industry in his adopted Austria with his mass-produced bentwood furniture.

Other accomplished masters included Anton Pössenbacher, whose lavish carved and embroidered chairs for King Ludwig II represent the zenith of Bavarian Rococo.

The base contains four drawers.

The handles and escutcheons are intricately carved.

Carved details resemble Classical columns.

SIDE CHAIRS

These two chairs are from a set of six Biedermeier-style, walnut-veneered and polished side chairs made in Austria. The curved crest rail is supported on flat supports above a rounded, upholstered seat with lightly sweeping legs. *c. 1900. H:35⅞ in (91 cm). GK*

PRESS CUPBOARD

This massive cupboard is made of oak, and is decorated with architectural-style motifs. The design is completely symmetrical, in keeping with the Neoclassical style. The upper section of the cupboard consists of a molded cornice, which projects above a carved frieze. Pilaster supports are positioned either side of two framed doors, which are designed

to resemble those found in Classical architecture. Below this are four narrow drawers. The lower section of the cabinet consists of two small cupboards with heavily inlaid and carved doors, also flanked by fluted pilasters. The whole piece is supported on a base that contains a further four drawers. Such an impressive piece would have belonged to a wealthy household. *Late 19th century. H:100½ in (251 cm); W:89 in (223 cm); D:27 in (67 cm). VH*

GAMES TABLE

This Louis-Philippe-style mahogany games table has a molded table top above a serpentine apron with carved finials at the corners. The rectangular table top opens up to reveal a playing surface, supported on a baluster column and four cabriole legs with floral carving. *1850–60. H:30¾ in (78 cm); W:33 in (84 cm); D:16½ in (42 cm). BMN*

UNIFICATION AND RENAISSANCE
The reworking of historical styles was characteristic of German and Austrian furniture design at this time. The same Gothic, Rococo, and Renaissance revivals that informed furniture design in Paris and London diffused through the continent far more quickly after the development of an integrated rail network in the mid-19th century. After the eventual unification of the German states under Bismarck in 1871, there was a general reappraisal of the roots of German culture, creating a fusion of traditional vernacular design with these wider European trends.

Just as the US embraced the Neo-Renaissance style after winning its independence from Britain, German designers developed a particular affinity for the style following the Franco-Prussian war in 1871. Known as the *Gründerzeit*, this style continued to be popular into the 20th century, remaining fashionable in some circles in parallel with the more radical *Jugendstil*. New wealth, industrialization, overseas trade, and colonial acquisitions all contributed to a burgeoning confidence in the new German state.

GOTHIC STYLE
The German Gothic revival, a lighter and fussier aesthetic than its British counterpart, often featured boullework—a product of Louis XIV's France rather than of the medieval period. The German version of the Gothic style was more elaborate, making use of multiple colors where the original French version had been predominantly monochrome. A carved oak bookcase designed in Gothic style by Austrian cabinet-makers Bernardo de Bernardis (1808–68) and Joseph Cremer (1808–71) was displayed at the Crystal Palace exhibition in 1851, and afterwards it was presented to Queen Victoria by Emperor Franz Josef.

DINING TABLE
The round surface of this exquisite intarsia dining table is richly decorated with rosewood, brass, and mother-of-pearl inlaid into a kingwood veneer. The table top is supported on a solid oak-carved frame with three cabriole legs, which terminate in brass casters. The table is the work of Franz Xavier Fortner (1798–1877). The table top design brings together influences from three different historical styles. The overall symmetry of the design is Neoclassical, the scrolling motifs resemble those popular in the Rococo period, and the central medallion of the table takes the Gothic style as its inspiration. *c. 1840. H:30¼ in (77 cm); D:52¼ in (133 cm). BMN*

PORCELAIN MOUNTS

GERMANY MAY NOT HAVE BEEN AT THE CUTTING EDGE OF EUROPEAN FURNITURE DESIGN IN THE MID-19TH CENTURY, BUT THE PORCELAIN MOUNTS PRODUCED WON INTERNATIONAL ACCLAIM.

Porcelain plaque

Ever since Meissen produced the first European porcelain, Germany has been a market leader in the ceramics industry. During the mid-19th century, enterprising cabinet-makers undertook to harness this resource and combine it with their own stock-in-trade. Cabinets decorated with porcelain mounts were not an entirely new concept—Asian craftsmen had been making furniture with applied ceramic plaques for centuries, although their minimalist designs were a far cry from the elaborate models produced in Germany. In France, Sèvres plaques had been used to adorn cabinets on occasion, but it was in Germany that the most celebrated examples were made.

The carcasses of these cabinets were roughly constructed from pine in Renaissance forms. An ebony veneer or, more usually, a coat of black paint provided a suitably dark ground on which to mount elaborate porcelain plaques, pillars, and feet: the dark wood acted as a foil to the richly decorated white ceramic. The best examples, many of which came from the Meissen factory, were hand-painted with scenes taken from 17th-century paintings with antiquarian or folk themes. The public appetite for these cabinets was vast, and William Oppenheim won widespread acclaim for an example he exhibited in Paris in 1878 for the Royal Dresden factory.

Ebonized cupboard This piece is richly decorated with Meissen porcelain mounts, the most prominent being the oval panel on the cupboard door. They have chased gilt-metal borders and depict courting couples. The cupboard has a rectangular top with conforming gallery and is flanked by four polychrome, floral-decorated detached columns above turned, bulbous feet. *c. 1880. H:52½ in (133.5 cm). FRE*

THONET'S BENTWOOD

THONET'S DEVELOPMENT OF THE BENTWOOD CHAIR—ONE OF THE MOST SUCCESSFUL PRODUCTS EVER CONCEIVED—HAD AN ENORMOUS INFLUENCE ON THE COURSE OF FURNITURE DESIGN.

MICHAEL THONET (1796–1871) WAS BORN in Boppard-am-Rhein, a picturesque town that was then part of Prussia, now part of Germany. He trained as a cabinet-maker and set up a workshop in his home town as soon as he finished his apprenticeship. However, it was not until he was in his thirties that he began to experiment with steaming laminated wood veneers in order to create bentwood furniture. At first, he was only able to use this process to produce component parts, such as chair backs, which he incorporated into pieces constructed from more orthodox, straight, wooden elements. Still, his work was innovative, and Thonet's exhibit at an 1841 Koblenz trade show attracted the attention of Chancellor Metternich, who invited him to Austria to make some furniture for the Palais Liechtenstein.

Michael Thonet (center), surrounded by his five sons

TORTUOUS CURVES
To prevent the beech from splitting when it was bent violently into shape, a metal strip was attached to each end of the piece of wood before it was steamed.

ROCKING CHAIR
The frame of this beech Thonet rocking chair exemplifies the Thonet technique of using single pieces of wood to create elaborate, elegant, curved structures. The seat and back of the chair are each made from a simple green fabric sling. c. 1880. H:33½ in (88.5 cm). QU

BENTWOOD CHAISE LONGUE
Inspired by Arts and Crafts styling, the sinuous lines of the frame and arms of Thonet's chaise longue are created from long pieces of bent, solid, laminated beech. The seat is made of woven cane. Suitable for the conservatory or the garden, this recliner appealed to the taste for more rustic styles of furniture in the late 19th century, although it was, in fact, industrially produced. It is the precursor of Le Corbusier's chaise longue, designed in 1928, which used tubular steel instead of bent wood for the frame (see pp.432-33). 1883–84.

GEBRÜDER THONET

FROM FAMILY BUSINESS TO GLOBAL CORPORATION, GEBRÜDER THONET BECAME PHENOMENALLY SUCCESSFUL.

Gebrüder Thonet was established in 1853. The runaway success of the company's bentwood furniture led to rapid growth, and within 20 years it had offices in London and New York. Expansion within continental Europe continued apace and, by the end of the 19th century, Gebrüder Thonet was operating more than 50 factories. Collaborations with eminent designers and architects, such as Josef Hoffmann, Otto Prutscher, and Emile Guyot, kept the firm at the forefront of new trends. In 1922, Gebrüder Thonet became part of the Thonet-Mindus holding company, employing 10,000 staff under the direction of Leopold Pilzer, who established Thonet Industries, Inc. in New York. Throughout the latter half of the 20th century, a steady focus on innovation and contemporary design has sustained the company's identity, and Thonet remains a world leader in industrial furniture design.

The bending process Steamed until pliable, the solid wood is bent into shape. The men have to work in perfect unison with each other as they manipulate the wood, opening and closing a series of clamps to keep control.

Chair No.14 This classic bentwood chair is perfectly shaped, elegant, and light. Designed by Thonet in 1859, 50 million were sold by 1930. The currently available No.214 is its direct descendant. *H:25¼ in (64 cm); W:17 in (43 cm); D:20½ in (52 cm).*

The component parts Only six pieces of wood make up the backrest, seat, and legs of chair No.14.

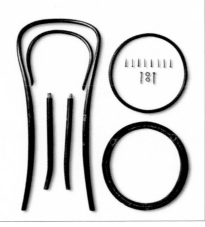

VERSATILITY AND SIMPLICITY

By 1842, Thonet had perfected his steam-bending process, and in July of that year he was granted an international patent that protected his "chemical mechanical methods" from imitation. The extravagant curlicues of the bentwood furniture he produced for the interiors of the grand Rococo staterooms at the Palais Liechtenstein are a testament to the versatility of his invention.

Once softened through immersion in steam or boiling water, the wood (beech was particularly suitable) could be molded into almost any shape with the aid of a press. A single piece of timber could be manipulated to form the back legs, uprights, and top rail of a chair. Thonet's process meant that furniture could be constructed from far fewer members and did away with the need for dovetails, tenons, or any kind of joint; simple screws and nuts would suffice to hold the parts together.

In 1853, Thonet set up his own furniture company—Gebrüder Thonet—with his five sons (Franz, Michael, August, Josef, and Jacob), and designed a factory in Vienna to produce furniture that could be packed flat for shipping and assembled at its destination. Before long, Thonet's bentwood furniture was being exported all over the world.

WORLD-BEATING DESIGN

Mid-19th-century Vienna was famous for the lively political and cultural debate that found its focus in the city's cafés, and these establishments proved the ideal testing ground for Thonet's new bentwood chairs. Light yet durable, their distinctive but understated style and modest cost made them a hit with the hospitality industry. Thonet's first large-scale commission was to supply chairs to Vienna's *Daum* coffeehouse in the late 1850s, and the world-beating "No.14" chair was developed for this purpose. It was so successful that before the turn of the century more than 15 million No.14 chairs had been made and sold throughout Europe. This was functional furniture for the masses rather than furniture as a signifier of wealth, and the industrial production lines in Thonet's factories across central Europe were turning it out in huge quantities.

THE CONTRIBUTION LIVES ON

When compared to the convoluted decoration of so much mid-19th-century furniture, the bentwood designs of Thonet and his sons are positively spartan. Le Corbusier commemorated this refreshing aspect of Thonet's *oeuvre* in 1925 when he used the No.14 chair as part of his hugely influential *l'Espirit Nouveau* exhibit, espousing his rejection of decoration in favor of function. It is unlikely that John Henry Belter (1804–63) would have had so much success with his carved laminate furniture in New York had Thonet not laid the foundations before him. Thonet's legacy has endured well into the modern age—he precipitated Charles and Ray Eames's mass-produced office chairs (*see pp.456-57*), and, of course, the modern flat-pack domestic furniture industry.

SETTEE NO.2

A single length of bent wood forms both the back rail and the back legs of this settee. The back is constructed from just three lengths of bent wood, curled and intertwining to form a symmetrical pattern. The wickerwork seat is supported within a beech wood frame and stands on tapering legs. This Thonet settee bears the company's stamp. c. 1888. W:46¾ in (117 cm). DOR

LOW COUNTRIES

THE NEOCLASSICAL REVIVAL persisted in the Netherlands under the auspices of the Waterstaat ministry, who presided over church construction until 1875. This "Waterstaatstjil" was primarily inspired by Grecian temple forms and became firmly entrenched in the Dutch consciousness, informing furniture design throughout the mid-19th century.

HISTORICISM BY NUMBERS
The interiors of many Catholic churches constructed at this time were decorated in an approximation of the Baroque style, although many of the features were false: plaster vaulting and walls painted to look like marble were common. This falsification was also a feature of Willem II Gothicism, an early Dutch Gothic-revival style that was championed by Pierre Cuyper among others.

Despite having studied under Viollet-le-Duc, the architect of so many sympathetic restorations, Cuyper's work was more of a pastiche than a genuine representation of the Gothic era. Native oak was used to construct Gothic-revival furniture, often with a similarly scant regard for the fundamental principles of the Gothic style.

INFLUENCES FROM THE EAST
The Dutch enjoyed their privileged position as the only Western people to trade with the Japanese until the 1850s. They imported lacquer furniture inlaid with fine pieces of shell, and restrained, plain versions of Western forms such as chairs, tables, and high cabinets finished in the finest lacquer.

Other colonial interests in the region, particularly in Indonesia, provided the Netherlands with fine exotic hardwoods. These were often quite different from the woods used elsewhere in Europe, where they were imported predominantly from the Caribbean and Africa. Dutch cabinet-makers used satinwood from the East Indies to create copies of 18th-century Neoclassical furniture, with slim, tapering legs, metal mounts and fine inlays, and stringing made from contrasting timbers.

A PASSION FOR MARQUETRY
The main centers of furniture production in Belgium were Antwerp and Malines. Many of the craftsmen active in these areas were very adept in marquetry techniques, a perennially popular form of surface decoration in the Low Countries. Apart from the appearance of Neoclassical elements in the late 18th century, the distinctive style of Dutch marquetry did not change much from the early 18th century to the end of the 19th century. Ebony, kingwood, satinwood, and other fine and exotic timbers were used to create intricate and arresting floral designs, often in a variety of colors.

This practice was not limited to new furniture—demand was such that these same craftsmen adapted older pieces of plain walnut furniture and made them more saleable through the application of their art. Table tops, drawer fronts, back splats, friezes, and skirts were all considered appropriate places for marquetry design. However, with the advent of mass production in the late 19th century, the quality of the marquetry work deteriorated.

Brass, ebonized, and tortoiseshell mirror This wall mirror has raised foliate brass decoration centered and surmounted by a mask motif. The beveled rectangular plate sits within a brass and ebonized frame, which in turn is surrounded with a further paneled and molded tortoiseshell frame. The piece is Baroque in its overall appearance. *Late 19th century. SL*

CORNER CABINET

This satinwood corner cabinet is painted to simulate marquetry decoration and has leaf-cast, gilt-brass mounts. The shaped triangular top is centered by an oval panel of oak leaves and has padouk banding. It sits above a frieze of scrolling roses issuing from a basket of fru below which is a single door centered by a putti mask in a panel. The case is raised on pyramidal legs with small, brass bun feet. Predominantly Neoclassical in style, the central mount is distinctly Rococo in design. *Late 19th century. W:35½ in (89 cm). L&T*

MARQUETRY CABINET

The rectangular top of this mahogany and marquetry cabinet sits above a single, long ogee frieze drawer, below which is a pair of doors, flanked on each side by a pilaster. The case is supported on a plinth and turned feet.

All the surfaces of the chest are richly decorate with a marquetry design of baskets, flowers, and birds. The molded frieze drawer is typical 19th-century designs. The marquetry on the doors is a little awkward but still identifiably Neoclassical in style. *Mid-19th century. W:38¼ in (97 cm). L&T*

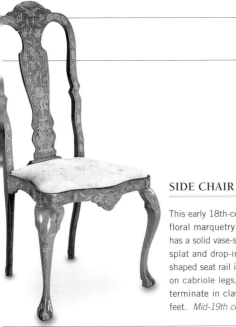

SIDE CHAIR

This early 18th-century-style floral marquetry side chair has a solid vase-shaped back splat and drop-in seat. The shaped seat rail is supported on cabriole legs, which terminate in claw-and-ball feet. *Mid-19th century. DN*

[R]ECTANGULAR SIDE TABLE

[Th]is ebony and floral marquetry side table takes inspiration from the [la]te 18th century. The table top is centered with marquetry birds on an [ur]n and has a molded edge above a frieze drawer of similar decoration. [Th]e table top is supported on spiral-turned legs, joined by a flat cross-[str]etcher, and terminating in bun feet. *H:28¾ in (73 cm). DN*

[O]VAL CENTER TABLE

[Th]is Neoclassical-style oval center table is made of mahogany and [de]corated with marquetry. It is inlaid throughout with scrolling foliate [de]signs, and the table top is centered by a flowering urn design. The piece [is] raised on slender, square, tapering legs, with tiny, brass bun feet. *[c.] 1880. W:38 in (96.5 cm). FRE*

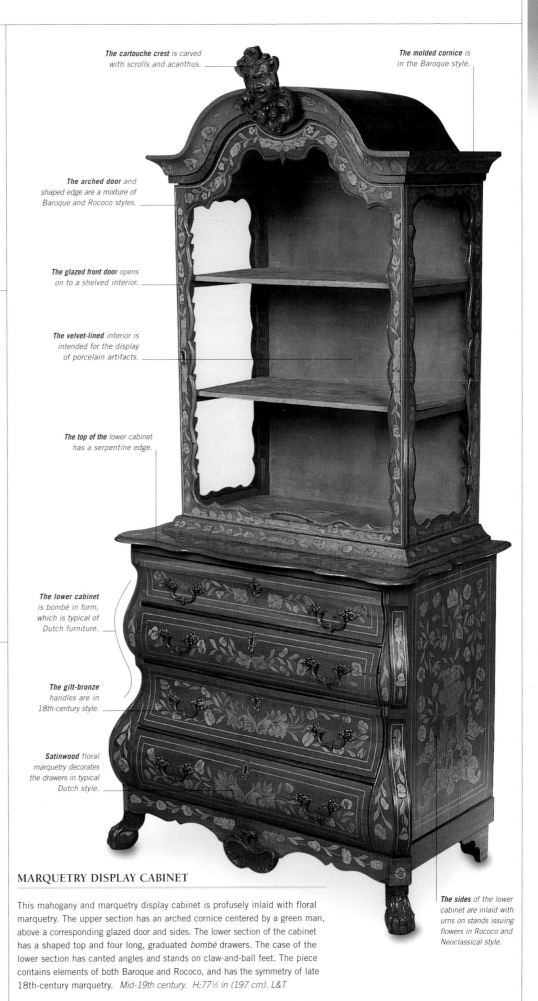

The cartouche crest is carved with scrolls and acanthus.

The molded cornice is in the Baroque style.

The arched door and shaped edge are a mixture of Baroque and Rococo styles.

The glazed front door opens on to a shelved interior.

The velvet-lined interior is intended for the display of porcelain artifacts.

The top of the lower cabinet has a serpentine edge.

The lower cabinet is bombé in form, which is typical of Dutch furniture.

The gilt-bronze handles are in 18th-century style.

Satinwood floral marquetry decorates the drawers in typical Dutch style.

The sides of the lower cabinet are inlaid with urns on stands issuing flowers in Rococo and Neoclassical style.

MARQUETRY DISPLAY CABINET

This mahogany and marquetry display cabinet is profusely inlaid with floral marquetry. The upper section has an arched cornice centered by a green man, above a corresponding glazed door and sides. The lower section of the cabinet has a shaped top and four long, graduated *bombé* drawers. The case of the lower section has canted angles and stands on claw-and-ball feet. The piece contains elements of both Baroque and Rococo, and has the symmetry of late 18th-century marquetry. *Mid-19th century. H:77½ in (197 cm). L&T*

SPAIN AND PORTUGAL

ON THE IBERIAN PENINSULA, styles from countries that had close relationships with Spain and Portugal, especially Morocco, were fused with a dominant French aesthetic. This resulted in distinctive, solid furniture peppered with lighter touches.

SPANISH FUSION

"Isabellino" furniture was the Spanish interpretation of the French Second Empire style. Richly decorated with contrasting colors, it was more exuberant than its French counterpart, and its symmetry allies it more closely with the Baroque than with the Rococo revival that swept across the rest of

Europe. Pieces made for the court of Isabella II (1833–68) were the most sumptuous of all and set the agenda for the aspiring merchant classes.

The use of mother-of-pearl inlays, frequently in geometric patterns, was very widespread. Other fashionable decorative elements included mounts of bronze or gilded wood, and painted decoration applied directly to the timber. Classical motifs, including carved putti and acanthus leaves, were also commonly used.

Openwork carving often made use of themes drawn from Morocco, Spain's closest neighbor to the south, and one that has lent a distinctive

Islamic twist to the Spanish decorative arts for centuries. Moorish forms and decoration, such as woven upholstery and turned spindles, were widespread throughout Spain during this period. In fact, Moroccan influence was by now so well established that it broadened to include elements from other Islamic cultures.

Isabella II's bedroom at the Palacio Real, Aranjuez The solidity of the dark wood furniture and fittings is offset by the sumptuous gilded carving that adorns the bed.

PORTUGUESE CENTER TABLE

This center table is made of rosewood and is in the style of those popular in the late 17th century. The rectangular table top has brass mounts at the corners and the frieze is fitted with drawers and dummy drawers. It stands on bulbous, twist-carved legs joined by twisted stretchers. *c. 1880.*

PORTUGUESE SIDE TABLE

This side table is made of stained walnut. Beneath the plain top is a single frieze drawer. The overall form, with its H-stretcher and central uprights, is 17th-century French but the style of carving gives it a Portuguese provenance. *Late 19th century.*

SPANISH MOORISH DRESSING TABLE

This walnut and ebony dressing table is inlaid with intarsia. The cabinet is surmounted by an arched mirror, at the base of which are two small drawers. A frieze drawer sits above a pair of paneled doors, which enclose a fitted interior. The case stands on block feet with casters. *Mid-19th century. H:76¾ in (195 cm). L&T*

SPANISH CABINET

The parquetry top of this tortoiseshell, mother-of-pearl, and walnut cabinet has projecting corners. The case has seven drawers, flanked by freestanding columns, and arranged around a central door and two drawers below. The Moorish influence is apparent in the Arab-style design. *Mid-19th century. W:45½ in (114 cm). L&T*

PORTUGUESE COMMODE

This is one of a pair of carved Rosewood *petite* commodes. The exaggerated waisted shape is a very common Portuguese form during this period. The ball-and-claw feet on cabriole legs are taken from mid-18th-century English designs. *Late 19th century.*

Cyrillic script betrays the central sian provenance of some Moorish rniture constructed in Spain at this me. Carpets used as upholstery were urced from the Tekke of Turkestan, r example. Heavy silver adornments ere another decorative element orrowed from this part of the world.

The drawing-room suite, usually omprising a sofa and a pair of rmchairs, became extremely popular Spanish homes during this period. he occasional table continued to enjoy e popularity it had won in the earlier Fernandino" period. Around 1870, ter a period of civil war that followed e end of Isabella's reign, designers began to seek inspiration in traditional Spanish furniture from the 16th and 17th centuries.

PORTUGUESE ASSIMILATIONS

The Portuguese had suffered greatly at the hands of Napoleon's forces but had been impressed by a system of government that freed them from the yoke of a repressive monarchy. Rebellion and civil war plagued the reigns of Maria II, Pedro V, and Luis I, the rulers of Portugal during the mid-19th century.

French influence had declined after liberation from Napoleon, and designers began to follow the work of British cabinet-makers more closely. As a result, features such as the cabriole leg and paw foot became widespread in Portuguese furniture. Another important outside influence came from Germany. The Portuguese embraced the fading Biedermeier style through Maria II, who had a number of German consorts.

Toward the end of the century, Spain began to embrace styles based on the more distant past of their own peoples, while Portugal embarked on an enduring affair with designs from the João V period (1706–50). Rosewood continued to be the favored wood because of Portugal's colonial interests.

LATIN AMERICAN NEOCLASSICISM

The thriving Latin colonies in Central and South America had never been exposed to the French Empire style that had pervaded Europe and from which the bulk of European mid-19th-century furniture had developed. The widespread diaspora of patterns originally drawn by 18th-century masters, such as Chippendale and Hepplewhite, did reach these distant western outposts and were the basis for a Latin American Neoclassical revival. Latin American furniture in the mid-19th century was, therefore, far closer to British forms than that produced on the Iberian mainland.

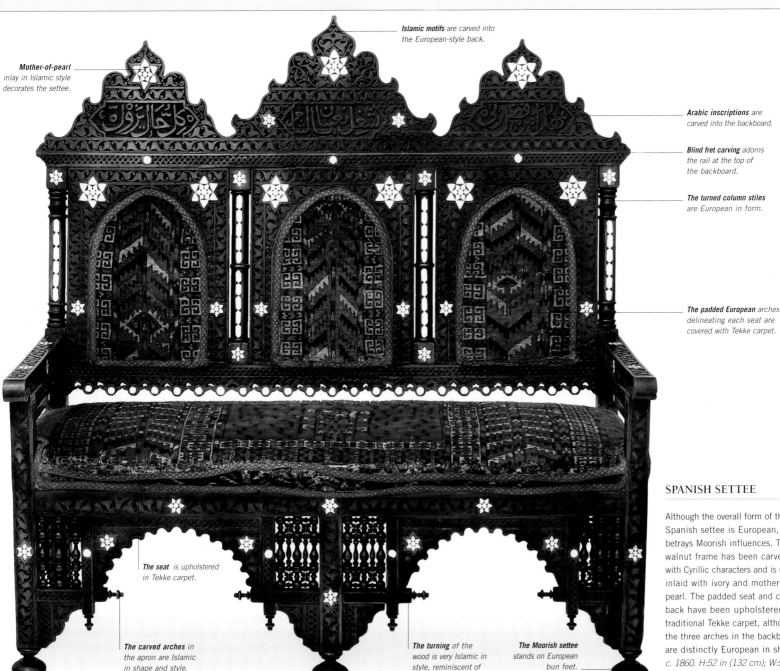

Islamic motifs are carved into the European-style back.

Mother-of-pearl inlay in Islamic style decorates the settee.

Arabic inscriptions are carved into the backboard.

Blind fret carving adorns the rail at the top of the backboard.

The turned column stiles are European in form.

The padded European arches delineating each seat are covered with Tekke carpet.

The seat is upholstered in Tekke carpet.

The carved arches in the apron are Islamic in shape and style.

The turning of the wood is very Islamic in style, reminiscent of Muslim screens.

The Moorish settee stands on European bun feet.

SPANISH SETTEE

Although the overall form of this Spanish settee is European, it betrays Moorish influences. The walnut frame has been carved with Cyrillic characters and is richly inlaid with ivory and mother-of-pearl. The padded seat and chair back have been upholstered in traditional Tekke carpet, although the three arches in the backboard are distinctly European in shape. *c. 1860. H:52 in (132 cm); W:53 in (135 cm); D:23½ in (60 cm). JK*

SCANDINAVIA

THE SCANDINAVIAN COUNTRIES emerged from a period of economic strife in the 19th century, eventually finding the confidence to channel the historical revivals of the period into a distinctive regional style.

DANISH TASTE

In Denmark it was the Late Empire, or Christian VIII style, first popularized by the architect Gustav Friedrich Hetsch (1788–1864), that held sway in the mid-19th century. It expressed a rigid Classicism through applied ornament carved with urns, acanthus leaves, and similar motifs. Some of this decoration was not carved but instead was made from sawdust pressed into molds, an economical innovation that illustrates how the profession embraced new technologies.

The improvement of the Danish economy in the 1830s was spurred on by a series of four national trade and industry exhibitions. The displays at these exhibitions were reviewed by a consortium of the cultural, scientific, and artistic elite put together by Hetsch himself. Under the watchful eyes of these arbiters of taste, who included the physicist H. C. Ørsted, the Danish furniture industry managed to avoid some of the creeping vulgarization that afflicted so many other European nations. Although there was a certain lowering of standards among the mass-market trade, the best practitioners maintained very high standards.

Cabinet-makers in Copenhagen actually enjoyed a boom that echoed that of 18th-century London, with master craftsmen beginning to combine workshops with grand exhibition spaces in which they could both display and sell their wares. C. B. Hansen, the court chair-maker, was among the first of these newly successful furniture-makers.

SWEDEN AND NORWAY

Swedish furniture in the mid-19th century was still dominated by the Gustavian style, which had emerged more than half a century earlier. Imitations and reproductions of the Rococo and Neoclassical forms produced during that time also remained extremely important.

The very light, off-white stains and painted finishes that are hallmarks of Gustavian furniture were ideally suited to Swedish interiors, as maximizing

DANISH SAFE

This steel, two-door safe has a stepped top with two reeded finials and an overhanging cornice molding with leaf-tip borders. The two cabinet doors have Neoclassical and foliate decoration and are flanked by circular pilasters raised on paw feet. *Mid-19th century. H:65 in (165 cm); W:27 in (68.5 cm); D:22 in (56 cm). EVE*

SWEDISH ARMCHAIRS

Each one of this pair of Swedish Empire-style, beech or fruitwood, painted open armchairs has a rectangular, padded, and leaf-tip-bordered backrest, a spool-turned cross-form splat, and downswept armrests raised on curved supports. The upholstered seat is raised on circular, tapered legs, which are decorated with leaf banding. *1880. H:36½ in (92.75 cm); W:22½ in (57 cm); D:20½ in (52 cm).*

SWEDISH CENTER TABLE

This Gustavian-style painted table has a rectangular top above a bead and leaf-tip frieze with swags. Acanthus leaves adorn the tapering fluted legs. *Mid-19th century. H:31 in (78.8 cm); W:34¾ in (88.25 cm); D:24¾ in (62.8 cm).*

DANISH ARMCHAIRS

These armchairs are part of a suite of Danish painted furniture, which includes a settee and four side chairs. Each armchair has an upholstered rectangular backrest with laurel-leaf carving between rows of bead carving. The drop-in upholstered seats with a leaf-and-vine frieze and rosette corners, are raised on turned and fluted legs headed with fish-scale carving. *Late 19th century. H:40 in (101.5 cm); W:27 in (68.5 cm); D:25 in (63 cm).*

DANISH WORKTABLE

This Empire-revival walnut worktable has an oval top above a frieze drawer. Supported on two tapering legs, it is headed by gilt wings and has outswept feet. *c. 1870. H:29½ in (75 cm); W:23¾ in (60.5 cm); D:15 in (38 cm).*

the available light was a boon in Scandinavian countries. The *bois-clair* look, a remnant of the Gustavian style, remained a firm favorite, at least for base furniture and chairs. Woods that could not be stained to achieve a light finish were often painted white or pale gray, or sometimes parcel gilt.

A version of the Danish style pioneered by Hetsch was adopted in Sweden for a time, but failed to survive the first half of the 19th century. Instead, the Swedish were quicker to embrace the Gothic-revival style that had been so successful in Britain. Hansen was one of the pioneers of the Swedish Gothic revival,

employing a much lighter touch than his British counterparts, to correspond to the pale Scandinavian palette.

Norway enjoyed a growing economy during the mid-19th century, and the laying of the first railroads and a growing merchant shipping fleet helped to increase internal and external trade. Despite a growing nationalistic feeling, Norwegian furniture of the period was largely based on Swedish and British models. However, some of the vernacular furniture produced did carry a recognizably Norwegian aesthetic in the form of brightly painted folk art roses and other traditional details.

A SCANDINAVIAN AESTHETIC

The Neoclassical, Gothic, and Rococo revivals dominated Scandinavian interiors as they did throughout Europe. Denmark and Sweden produced a great many salon suites in these revival styles, consisting of a sofa and four side chairs, sometimes also including a pair of armchairs. The popularity of these suites was such that they could be found in most fashionable middle-class homes.

Much of the furniture of this period was made from painted soft woods, such as pine or beech, and drew inspiration from French, Russian, and German designs. From about 1870, a

Biedermeier revival began, and lighter birch wood was used. Forms remained simple and veneers became thinner and plainer in design.

Toward the end of the 19th century, the Scandinavian furniture industry began to assert a distinct regional identity with the enthusiastic uptake of a starker, Modernist aesthetic. Lilla Hyttnäs, the cottage inhabited by the great Swedish artist Carl Larrson from 1888, became the archetype for austere but homey interiors throughout Sweden. The textile and furniture designs of his wife Karin helped to introduce an abstract aesthetic to the wider Scandinavian consciousness.

The downswept arms are molded.

The upholstery is covered with a silk damask material in an early 19th-century design.

Walnut and parcel-gilt griffins decorate each arm.

Eight turned, tapering legs support the sofa.

The sprung seat is fully stuffed over the frame.

Paterae are applied to the faces of the side rails.

DANISH PEDESTAL CUPBOARD

This tall, oval, pedestal cupboard is made of walnut with inlaid ebony decoration. The curved door encloses three shelves, which are intended to store hats. *c. 1860. H:56 in (142 cm); W:24½ in (62 cm).*

SWEDISH SOFA

This Swedish sofa is made of walnut highlighted with parcel-gilt, and is based on a late 18th-century design. The straight, rectangular top rail and the faces of the side rails are decorated with paterae and beading. The arm supports are carved

in the shape of griffins and give the piece a very Neoclassical appearance. The pale blue silk damask upholstery is similar in style to patterns popular at the beginning of the 19th century. The piece stands on eight turned, tapered legs decorated with gilt banding. *Late 19th century. W:71¾ in (182 cm).*

RUSSIA

WHILE RUSSIA'S SERFS scraped out a meager existence tied to the land, the affluent society centered around the Imperial court in St. Petersburg enjoyed an extremely high standard of living that was reflected in the grand furniture they commissioned.

EUROPE'S MELTING POT

St. Petersburg was a cosmopolitan city in the mid-19th century, with strong ties with France, the Low Countries, and the German and Italian states. Craftsmen from each of these areas flowed into the Russian capital, bringing with them ideas and designs from across Europe. French influence, in particular, was very

strong. Many of these journeymen were masters of their professions—Leo von Klenze, for example, was Court architect to Ludwig I of Bavaria before he designed interiors for the New Hermitage. He continued to champion the Russian Empire style well into the mid-19th century with his malachite and marble furniture. Russian rule over Finland meant that there was a free exchange of information between the two countries, and many Finnish craftsmen plied their trades in St. Petersburg. As a result, the dominant Russian style of the period was an amalgam of fashions from many different places. The heavy

aspect of polite Russian furniture, designed for use in large spaces, was complemented by grand mounts of gilded wood or brass, featuring Classical motifs drawn from the European tradition.

Among the peculiarly Russian specialties of the period was metal furniture, which was used more frequently here than elsewhere in Europe. The Tula Imperial Armory, an important weapons foundry, became famous for its iron furniture, such as the dressing room suite on display at the Pavlovsky Palace Museum. Carl Fabergé, jeweler to the Imperial Court from 1884, designed a

handful of superb items of furniture that exerted an enormous influence on the fashionable elite. These high-fashion pieces were the exception, however, as a general decline took place in the Russian furniture industry during the late 19th century. Increased mechanization was the death knell for many craftsmen who could not compete with the new factories in

Four scroll and foliate ormolu cartouche mounts decorate the malachite table top.

Tiny pieces of malachite are fixed to a base to create a mosaic pattern.

The oval top of the malachite table is shaped and stepped.

Gold scrolls decorate the baluster stem.

The central malachite column is vase-shaped.

Gold foliate sabots decorate the scroll legs of the table.

A foliate motif carving completes the base of the baluster.

The glass bun feet were added in the late-19th century.

ROUND-BACKED ARMCHAIR

Carved out of mahogany and upholstered in velvet, this armchair with a rounded back was made at the Melzer factory for the Alexandria Palace in Peterhof. *Late 19th century. H:32 in (81 cm); W:21½ in (55 cm); D:17¾ in (45 cm)*

SILVER-MOUNTED TABLE

The top of this Louis XVI-style Fabergé table ha[s] a beaded silver border. The drawer is applie[d] with a silver laurel wreath with ribbon cresting. The fluted legs are joined by a silver-mounted stretcher. *Late 19th century. H:27⅝ in (70.2 cm[)]*

MALACHITE TABLE

The shaped, stepped oval top of this Alexandre II malachite low table is mounted with four scroll and foliate ormolu cartouches. Beneath the table top, a baluster stem, ending in a foliate motif carving, is flanked by four scroll legs on scroll and foliate sabots. The table stands on glass bun feet, which were added at a later date. The malachite used to create this table

was mined at Yekaterinburg in the Ural Mountains. Malachite from the same source was also used to create the Malachite Room at the Winter Palace in St. Petersburg (*see above right*). Russian craftsmen from the Peterhof and Yekaterinburg works used the Russian mosaic technique to cover large surfaces; they cut pieces of malachite into ⅛-in- (3-mm-) thick slices and attached them to a base to produce an attractive overall pattern. *c. 1860. H:26 in (66 cm); W:39⅓ in (100.5 cm); D:29¾ in (75.5 cm).*

rms of output or cost. In these
ctories, machine-cut pine carcasses
ere covered with very thin machine-
ut hardwood veneers before finally
eing finished by hand. In this way,
rniture that appeared to equal the
uality of that created by the artisan
as produced far more cheaply.

Winter Palace interior Designed by Alexander Bryullov, the Malachite Room was rebuilt in 1837 as a drawing room for Alexandra Fyodorovna, the wife of Tsar Nicolas I. The richly gilded furniture was produced by the workshop of Peter Gambs from sketches by Auguste de Montferrand.

PHOLSTERED ARMCHAIR

om a suite of furniture made for the Winter
alace in St. Petersburg, this carved and gilded
mchair is upholstered in crimson silk. It was
eated in the Louis XV style. *1853. H:36 in*
2 cm); W:19¾ in (50 cm); D:18¾ in (48 cm).

GOTHIC CHAIR

This Gothic-style, high-backed chair carved
out of walnut was designed by E. Gambs for
the Gothic Study of the Golitsyn-Stroganov
estate in Maryino. *Mid-19th century.*
H:48½ in (123 cm); W:25¼ in (64 cm).

Roll-top curved lid

Carved, gilded swans

CYLINDER BUREAU

ne drum-shaped case of this mahogany desk
supported by two shaped legs with carved
nd gilded swans at the top and partly gilded
aw-and-ball feet at the bottom. The legs are
ined by a flat, carved cross-stretcher. The

desk has a fitted interior, containing shelves
and compartments for letters and writing
equipment, and a leather writing slide. A series
of wooden slats attached to a single piece of
cloth composes the roll-top lid, which retracts
to the back. *Late 19th century. H:37⅓ in*
(95 cm); W:34¼ in (87 cm); D:17¾ in (45 cm). GK

MAHOGANY BOOKCASE

This two-door glazed bookcase has a broken
pediment with a brass molded edge and brass
fluted decoration to the central frieze. The
doors have well-figured mahogany frames with
central glazed panels and boldly modeled

brass astragals. The doors have canted corners
with brass flutes, surmounted and supported by
brass square paterae. The sides are inset with
panels, bordered by brass lines. The whole
stands on a plinth, supported on square,
tapering legs, terminating in brass sabots.
c. 1840. H:82 in (208 cm); W:56 in (143 cm).

UNITED STATES

A RENEWED RUSH of immigration from northern Europe swelled the US population in the mid-19th century. After the Civil War (1861–65), the victorious North was imbued with new vigor and wealth as the tide of industrialization swept across the states.

APPROPRIATIONS FROM EUROPE

The American Empire style reached its zenith around 1840, when the tide of fashion turned in favor of plain surfaces. Heavy furniture in mahogany and rosewood veneers dominated the later American Empire period.

The Empire manner was gradually ousted from its central position in American taste by an influx of European craftsmen, who helped to disseminate the Rococo-revival style. The Classical motifs of Empire furniture gave way to emblems drawn from the natural world, and rounded Rococo forms replaced the earlier architectural structures. The development of laminate veneers greatly aided the practitioners of the Rococo revival, led by German-born New Yorker J. H. Belter (*see pp.296–97*). Some American designers, such as Alexander Roux, eschewed the use of laminated bentwood in favor of a more authentic Rococo look. Roux was a French immigrant whose elaborately carved pieces featured decorative motifs drawn from hunting, such as grouse, dogs, and deer.

The Gothic style also remained popular during the second half of the 19th century. Examples of solid dark wood furniture crowned by cathedral-style trefoils and quatrefoils could be found in many middle-class homes.

HOMEGROWN INGENUITY

George Hunzinger, a German who arrived in the United States in 1855, devised ingenious space-saving, mechanical furniture. He amassed more then 20 patents during his career, for furniture that folded, extended, collapsed, or converted. William Wooton, a native of Indiana, secured a patent for an equally clever, but altogether more immutable form in the 1870s. The Wooton Patent Secretary was a large desk that concealed innumerable small drawers and compartments for the storage of documents and chattels.

A NEW AMERICAN RENAISSANCE

Renaissance forms were rediscovered after the Civil War and incorporated into a new, distinctly American look. The 1876 Philadelphia Centennial Exhibition was a statement of the nation's confidence and marked the culmination of the Renaissance revival. Luminaries of the Gilded Age, such as J. P. Morgan, commissioned grand houses designed in the Renaissance style. The Centennial also spawned an interest in a revival of American colonial furniture forms.

The American people had long been fascinated with Egyptology, and a number of exhibitions of ancient Egyptian artifacts drew vast crowds during the latter half of the 19th century. It is therefore no surprise that Egyptian motifs found their way onto furniture of the period. Actual Egyptian forms were rarely used. Instead, lotus, sphinx, and other emblems were applied to Renaissance-revival furniture.

The Pennsylvania Academy of the Fine Arts The current building was designed in the popular Gothic-revival style by American architect Frank Furness (1839–1922). The Academy opened in 1876.

CHIPPENDALE-STYLE CHAIR

This mahogany side chair with an upholstered drop-in seat has an openwork splat, shaped top rail, and scrolled ears. Elegant cabriole legs terminate in claw-and-ball feet. It is one of a set of six chairs. *c. 1900. H:39 in (100 cm). BRU*

GOTHIC-REVIVAL ARMCHAIR

This walnut armchair has a carved and pierced crest. The back is flanked by spiral spindles and stiles. The ring-turned arms terminate in ball-turned hand-holds, and the seat is raised on spiral-turned legs. *H:46½ in (118 cm). SL*

CHEST-ON-CHEST

This Colonial-revival chest-on-chest is made from mahogany. The upper section of the chest consists of an outset gadroon-carved top, two molded frieze drawers, and three graduated drawers. The lower section has two long drawers positioned above a gadroon-carved base and the piece is supported on claw-and-ball feet. The overall form is based on a mid-18th-century original. The legs are inspired by a mid-18th-century form, while the molded top drawer is 19th century in style. *Mid-19th century. H:60 in (152.5 cm). S&K*

EA TABLE

his tea table or card table is an exact copy of a late 18th-entury piece, with a top that opens out to provide a larger urface. Made from mahogany, the table is inlaid with boxwood. he frieze is inlaid with an urn motif, and the table is raised on quare, tapering legs. *Mid-19th century.*

TRIPLE-ARCH SOFA

This Renaissance-revival, laminated walnut, triple-arch sofa is influenced by Louis XV style. It has a pierced foliate, scroll-and-grape clustered frame, centered by a carved mask crest. The tufted back of the sofa is in three sections above a padded serpentine seat with a floral-carved apron on cabriole legs. *c. 1865. W:80 in (200 cm). S&K*

terior detail

etail of crest

etail of drawers

VOOTON DESK

his imposing variation of the fall-front desk has an elaborate, omed pediment. Two lockable, hinged front panels open to veal an extensive, complex arrangement of interior drawers and ivisions. The writing surface, also hinged, lifts from horizontal o vertical so the panel doors can close. The doors are also fitted ith shelves and divisions. *Late 19th century.*

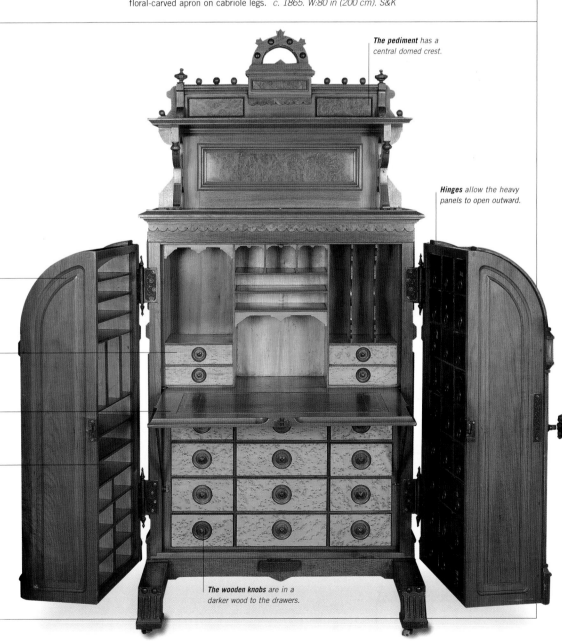

The pediment has a central domed crest.

Hinges allow the heavy panels to open outward.

The panel doors are as deep as the desk itself.

Two small drawers flank either side of a central recess.

The writing surface is hinged so it can be raised when locking up the desk.

Panel doors are fitted with shelves and divisions.

The wooden knobs are in a darker wood to the drawers.

BELTER AND THE ROCOCO REVIVAL

BELTER WAS THE STAR OF THE AMERICAN ROCOCO REVIVAL—HIS FURNITURE COMBINED TECHNICAL WIZARDRY WITH TRADITIONAL SKILL AND WON HIM THE ADORATION OF NEW YORK'S GLITTERATI.

JOHN HENRY BELTER (1804–63), as he came to be known, was born Johann Heinrich Belter, near Osnabrück in present-day Germany. He was trained in the art of wood-carving in Württemberg, a town steeped in the traditional Black Forest traditions of hewing complex designs from the native hard woods. Belter left his homeland for the US, arriving in New York in 1833. Within six years he had become a naturalized citizen of the United States, and was in business as a cabinet-maker in his newly adopted city as early as 1844. It was not long before his name, like that of Thomas Chippendale, became synonymous with the type of furniture he produced.

A SINGULAR TALENT

Unlike many of his contemporaries in the furniture business, Belter only ever worked within one idiom. Somewhat fortuitously, but also due in no small part to Belter's own great skill, the Rococo-revival style in which he excelled remained in vogue throughout his career and long after his death. His great triumph, and the exclusive feature of his work that kept him in the vanguard of the competition, was the series of breakthroughs he made in the lamination process.

LOVE SEAT
Asymmetrical in design, this small, upholstered love seat has a carved, laminated satinwood frame. The crest of the frame is richly carved with fruits and foliage, and the pierced back rail sweeps down gently, in sections, to meet the seat rail. The whole is supported on elegant cabriole legs, which terminate in brass casters. c. 1855. H:40 in (101.5 cm); W:40 in (101.5 cm); D:40 in (101.5 cm). AME

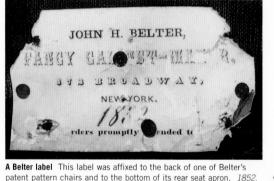

A Belter label This label was affixed to the back of one of Belter's patent pattern chairs and to the bottom of its rear seat apron. *1852.*

Belter bedstead Made of laminated rosewood, the footboard of this bedstead is bent and decorated with a small carved panel. An elaborate carved Rococo-style crest adorns the headboard.

BELTER PATENTS

AT THE TIME BELTER WAS WORKING, THE US PATENT OFFICE WAS PROCESSING THOUSANDS OF APPLICATIONS A YEAR TO HELP FOSTER A CLIMATE OF INNOVATION.

The distinctive style in which John Henry Belter worked would not have been possible without his innovative technical and methodical achievements. A patent effectively acted as a limited monopoly sanctioned by the state, and could prove extremely lucrative if used wisely. Although Belter was successful in securing a number of patents during his career, he apparently failed to exploit them to their full potential, since he never became very wealthy. It seems likely that some of Belter's rivals, including Charles Baudouine of New York, infringed his copyright in their imitations of his work.

The first of Belter's patents was granted in 1847. His "machinery for sawing arabesque chairs" made it possible to cut intricate curves through his tough laminate boards. This was followed in 1856 with a far more specific application to patent a laminate bedstead. Belter was evidently very proud of this item, boasting that its simple two-piece construction allowed for swift disassembly in case of fire and had no recessed joints to harbor bed bugs. Two years later, Belter belatedly patented refinements he had made to his laminate and cutting processes. An ingenious central locking device provided the basis for Belter's final patent in 1860, through which he sought to protect a mechanism that secured multiple drawers at the turn of a single key.

Belter fashioned strong laminate panels by affixing thin strips of wood together, the grain in each layer lying perpendicular to that of the layer below. This practice enhanced the natural strength of the wood, rendering it extremely resistant to cracking or splitting. Rosewood was especially fashionable at the time—Belter sourced his from Brazil and India—but he also worked in oak, mahogany, and other hard woods, sometimes ebonizing them.

DRAMATIC CURVES

A typical Belter piece might be constructed from a series of eight-ply laminate boards, although he sometimes used up to 16 layers of wood. Additional panels carrying carved decoration were often glued on to the frame of a piece of furniture. These panels had been bent under extreme pressure with the application of steam to produce the dramatic curves that are a hallmark of Belter's *oeuvre*, along with tight "C" and "S" scrolls. The hardiness lent to wood by Belter's lamination process enabled him to produce elaborate open crestings and aprons.

High-backed chairs provided him with an ideal canvas for his carving skills. Naturalistic depictions of flowers and fruits—vines were a favorite—feature alongside more Classical motifs such as scrolls. It is often only the quality of the carving and the audacity of the openwork that show that a piece came from his workshops. Belter's furniture was of a consistently high quality, and he was patronized by some very wealthy New York clients. He also designed a table in ebony and ivory for display at the 1853 "Exhibition of the Industry of All Nations."

EXCLUSIVE TO A FAULT

Belter's refusal to cater to the mass market left him open to rivals who had no such qualms and made small fortunes selling a diluted version of Belter's pieces to aspiring, less wealthy consumers. Despite this, however, Belter was not unsuccessful. In 1854, he had his own five-story factory erected on Third Avenue, on the Upper West Side of Manhattan. Two years later, he was joined in business by his brother-in-law, John H. Springmeyer. In 1861, William and Frederick Springmeyer also came aboard. When Belter succumbed to tuberculosis in 1863, the Springmeyers continued in business. It is a testament to the singular skill of John Belter that they were unable to survive for more than four years, despite the unabated popularity of the Rococo-revival style that the firm had made its own. Belter's absence was felt sharply, and in 1867 the company was forced into closure.

ROSEWOOD SETTEE
This Louis XV-style twin-seater sofa has a scroll-carved top rail, padded back and seat, and cabriole legs. The angled ends encourage users to turn toward each other.
H:42 in (106.5 cm);
W:62 in (157.5 cm);
D:34 in (86.5 cm).
BRUD

850S AMERICAN INTERIOR
elter-style furniture is prevalent in this home. The furniture and rnishings are influenced by Louis XV style and Rococo taste.

DRESSING TABLE
This mahogany dressing table has an oval mirror, surmounted by an ornately carved crest, and a shaped white marble top. he serpentine apron has carved acanthus at the corners and is supported on cabriole legs, terminating in scroll feet. The legs are joined by a pierced and carved cross-stretcher with a carved finial at its center. It was made by Prudent Mallard, New Orleans. Mid-19th century. AME

JAPAN

HAVING REMAINED almost completely isolated from the rest of the world for several hundred years, Japan entered a period of momentous and unprecedented change in the mid-19th century, instigated by the *Kurofune Raiho* (visit of the black ships) in 1853. Commodore Perry's American fleet effectively forced the Tokugawa government to reopen Japanese ports to international trade.

THE NEW ORDER

Japan had been a rigid feudal society, steeped in conservatism and slow to change. In 1868, after a short civil war, the last Shogun was overthrown and

the Meiji Emperor—Mutsuhito, who ruled from 1867 to 1912—was restored, promising modernization. Japanese industries developed at an astounding rate, and its citizens began to turn their backs on many aspects of their traditional past and adopt Western attitudes and customs.

Changes were gradual at first. Although it became fashionable among the wealthy elite to add rooms with a Western theme to their houses, these were generally areas in which to

Six-panel silk and paper screen This screen is decorated with a stylized landscape scene depicting wildlife—predominantly birds—in their natural habitat. *c. 1880. H:62½ in (156 cm). NAG*

DISPLAY CABINET-ON-STAND

This rosewood display cabinet is from the Meiji period (1867–1912). It has an elaborately carved pediment and stand, both featuring representations of birds and vegetation. The cabinet also has a number of inlaid gold lacquer

panels. Some of the panels slide open to reveal numerous interior shelves and compartments. The relief-carved ivory, bone, mother-of-pearl, and lacquerwork depict figural scenes, floral arrangements, and birds. The whole cabinet is of very fine quality. *Late 19th century. H:90½ in (230 cm); W:65⅜ in (166 cm).*

TWO-FOLD LACQUERED SCREEN

Consisting of two lacquer panels, this hinged screen from the Meiji period has carved rosewood and mahogany surrounds and a similarly carved rosewood and mahogany frame. The face of the screen is inlaid with

ivory and mother-of-pearl, and depicts an anthropomorphic battle of frogs, including a commander, infantry, standard-bearers, and trumpeters. The back of the screen is decorated with flowering cherry trees in *togidashi* (lacquerwork). *Late 19th century. H:74 in (188 cm); W:67¾ in (172 cm).*

entertain guests, rather than living spaces. Traditional Japanese furniture, rectilinear and plain, was the product of a culture in which people sat on the floor to eat and converse. Cabinets and tables therefore had very short legs. The case furniture in many houses was limited to a large chest for storing bedding, a smaller chest, and a stand for a mirror.

Modular living spaces were divided by a paper screen, typically consisting of two to six panels, and often decorated with paint or simple inlays of ceramic or wood. The joints in the lacquer frame were sometimes disguised with metal mounts. Lacquer was by far the most common form of surface decoration—usually in black, though sometimes in red.

EXPORT FURNITURE

The greatest changes within the furniture industry were those that catered to the export market. The unsurpassed quality of Japanese lacquer was widely known in the West, and craftsmen began to construct cabinets and screens with gold lacquer grounds, elaborately inlaid with precious natural materials, including ivory and mother-of-pearl, to form designs with Japanese motifs such as dragons or Samurai. This kind of crowded decoration was anathema to Japanese taste but very popular in the West, and business was brisk.

The export market also benefited from a renaissance among Japanese woodworkers. Although intarsia techniques had been widely understood in Japan for more than 1,000 years, they had fallen into disuse owing to the preference for lacquered furniture. A process known as *Ran Yosegi*, or "random parquetry," in which mosaics of different woods were assembled to draw attention to their various textures and colors, established the Hakone region as the preeminent center of intarsia work in Meiji Japan. Later, craftsmen began to adapt Kimono designs for use on furniture, and the process became more refined as it was mechanized.

Japanese expertise in manipulating wood extended to the art of carving. Again, this was an alien concept to most Japanese, and the bulk of carved furniture produced in Japan at this time was sent to international exhibitions and sold abroad. Friezes and crests were carved with scenes adapted from shrines and temples. Traditional Japanese symbolic motifs, such as ripped leaves signifying autumn, delighted Western consumers and found a ready market.

DECORATIVE IRON CASKET

The cover of this iron casket by Ryuunsai Yukiyasu is inset with a copper panel decorated in silver and gold relief with a basket of flowers and insects. The sides depict aquatic scenes, flowering trees, and Mount Fuji. The inner rim is ornamented with wisteria and grape vines. *c. 1870. W:7¼ in (15.5 cm). WW*

FOLDING CHAIR

This red-lacquered priest's folding chair is from the Edo period (1603–1867). The back is gold-lacquered and carved with *manji* diaper and a trellis of repeated *manji* motifs. Originally *manji* was a Sanskrit symbol that has come to represent Buddhism in Japan. *Mid-19th century. H:36½ in (93 cm).*

The black-lacquered base provides a perfect foil for the gold and silver panel scenes.

The panels on the front and sides of the cabinet are slightly recessed.

The cabinet is furnished with engraved metal mounts.

There is an arrangement of five shallow and four deep drawers behind each cabinet door.

The roundels depict stylized rural and landscape scenes in gold, silver, and colored lacquerwork.

The shaped saber feet are mounted in metal.

COLLECTOR'S CABINET

This unusual lacquered cabinet has been made as two stacking parts. The front and sides have recessed panels decorated with roundels on a deep gold ground. The roundels show various scenes in gold and silver, and display a variety of techniques, including lacquerwork. The upper section of the cabinet has two doors, which open on to a fitted interior containing ten shallow and eight deeper drawers. The lower section has two deep drawers. The whole stands on shaped saber feet. *c. 1900. H:52 in (132 cm); W:58⅜ in (149 cm); D:33 in (84 cm).*

INDIA

UNTIL THE 19TH CENTURY, artistic depictions of domestic Indian interiors tended to portray very little furniture. A low, canopied bed, a small dressing table, and a chest were quite often the only pieces present in such images. The throne chair, a staple form in most world cultures, was a symbol of prestige and had more currency as a ceremonial object than as a piece of domestic furniture.

Even the wealthiest of the Indian elite had very sparsely furnished homes until the 19th century, when they became influenced by European colonialists, whose opulent lifestyles they eagerly imitated.

A UNION OF TWO TRADITIONS
The ease with which Indian wood workers turned their hands to producing furniture in European forms was astounding. Fanny Parks, a British traveler, published a journal in 1850 that included an account of how an Indian carpenter constructed a table from a model she had made from river mud.

The Dutch had encouraged Indian craftsmen to make furniture for export during the 17th century, establishing a tradition that was to flourish as the British consolidated their grip on the subcontinent. As more and more British citizens arrived in India,

demand for furniture that was similar to that which they had used at home increased steadily.

From the mid-19th century, a new style of furniture that came to be known as Anglo-Indian began to evolve. Indian cabinet-makers were quick to adopt British forms, such as the cabinet-on-stand, or the armchair, but they transformed them into something entirely new through the application of decorative elements drawn from their own culture. The use of surface decoration was profuse; it is not uncommon for every available surface of a table to feature

elaborate openwork carving or intricately patterned inlays.

A WEALTH OF RESOURCES
The practitioners of the Anglo-Indian style had a huge creative resource

MAHOGANY *JARDINIÈRE*

This Anglo-Indian *jardinière* has profuse leaf-and-scroll carving. The circular well has a gadrooned edge and is supported on a turned, baluster column and three stylized bird consoles. The concave triform base has paw feet. *Mid-19th century. H:30¼ in (77 cm); Diam:17 in (43 cm). L&T*

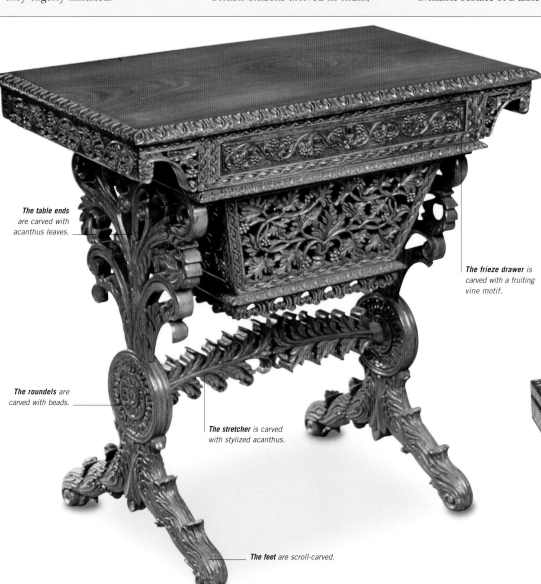

The table ends are carved with acanthus leaves.

The roundels are carved with beads.

The stretcher is carved with stylized acanthus.

The feet are scroll-carved.

The frieze drawer is carved with a fruiting vine motif.

QUILL BASKET

This Anglo-Indian quill basket is of tapering, rectangular form with a deep, flat lid. The quills—typically porcupine—are spaced at regular intervals to form the sides of the basket. The black lacquered surfaces have decorative ivory inlay. *c. 1860. W:9⅞ in (25 cm). SS*

WORKTABLE

The rectangular top of this early Victorian Anglo-Indian rosewood worktable has an egg-and-dart molded edge above a carved frieze drawer with pierced brackets. Below the frieze

is a tapering, pierced wool bin. The worktable is supported on pierced and carved trestle supports joined by a similar stretcher. The overall form is British, but the carving and wood are Indian. *Mid-19th century. H:30 in (76 cm); W:30½ in (78 cm); D:17¾ in (45 cm).*

Fruiting vine motif

vailable to them in the shape of ndia's diverse and rich cultural reritage. Devotional carvings from acred sites, such as the Buddhist nonuments at Sanchi, were incorporated into furniture design.

The great natural bounty of India had an equally important role to play. Although timber from the Far East vas imported, the majority of Indian urniture was constructed from teak, osewood, ebony, and padouk, all of

which was harvested locally. Ivory was widely available and craftsmen used it frequently as an inlay material, carving it with intricate designs before applying dark shellac varnish to enhance the decoration. It was not unheard-of for chairs and other smaller items to be hewn from solid ivory. Even elephant or rhinoceros feet were incorporated into some of the more outlandish furniture designs of the mid-19th century.

STYLES OF DECORATION

Cheaper alternatives to ivory-inlaid furniture were pieces decorated with penwork. Regional centers throughout India soon developed their own specialties. The town of Vizagapatam became famous for its wood and quillwork ornamental boxes, while Baharampur—notable as the flashpoint of the Indian Mutiny in 1857—was renowned for the skill of its carvers. The care taken by Indian

craftsmen was most evident in the ornament of the furniture they created. By contrast, hidden areas, such as the tops of cabinet doors, would often be finished somewhat roughly and bear visible tool marks.

MINIATURE CHESS TABLE

his Vizagapatan, ivory-and-bone veneered miniature chess table as an octagonal top with an inlaid chessboard and an applied ligree border. The table top is supported on a baluster column rith a studded knop on a conforming octagonal base with carved aw feet. *Mid-19th century. Diam:10 in (25 cm). L&T*

COLONIAL OCCASIONAL TABLE

This striking table has been made from the hide and skin of a rhinoceros. The square top is made from glass and has a brass edge. It is laid on a wooden base above three curved supports, which terminate in three rhino feet. *Mid-19th century. H:30⅓ in (77 cm); W:24⅓ in (62 cm); D:24⅓ in (62 cm). L&T*

IVORY-VENEERED ARMCHAIR

The padded back of this armchair has a scroll-carved, ivory-veneered frame with tablet cresting. Padded open arms with carved, reeded terminals extend above a cushioned seat. The seat rail has a medallion and foliate boss above a pierced scroll apron. The cabriole front legs end in collared paw feet. *Mid-19th century.*

OSLER GLASS FURNITURE

THE ELABORATE GLASS ORNAMENTS AND UNUSUAL FURNITURE MADE BY THE HIGHLY SUCCESSFUL OSLER GLASSWORKS COMPANY IN BRITAIN WERE ESPECIALLY FAVORED BY INDIA'S ELITE.

The glassworks of F. & C. Osler was one of the most successful in Victorian Britain. Founded in Birmingham at the beginning of the 19th century, the firm rose to such prominence that its crystal was shipped all over the British Empire. In Britain, Osler's most prestigious commission was to construct the enormous centerpiece fountain for the Great Exhibition at the Crystal Palace in 1851. The project took eight months to complete and used 4 tons of crystal glass. It was joined at the exhibition by a massive chandelier that held 144 candles, which was also made by Osler. The firm's reputation for delivering monumental glass objects spread far and wide, and they established a showroom in Calcutta to cater for their customers on the subcontinent.

Osler glass was shipped to the Himalayas for use in the construction of Seto Durbar's magnificent crystal hall in Nepal, completed in 1893 but destroyed by fire in 1933.

The wealthy rulers of India were smitten with Osler's grand designs and willingness to undertake the largest of projects. In Hyderabad, the Falaknuma Palace is home to 40 Osler chandeliers, which are among the largest in the world, each incorporating about 140 arms.

The company's most famous patron was Maharana Sajjan Singh of Udaipur in Rajashtan, India's northwestern desert kingdom. He commissioned Osler to supply him with an enormous array of vessels, trinkets, and ornaments in finest crystal. Most audacious of all, his order also included tables, chairs, sofas, and even a bed, thought to be the only one ever made from pure crystal glass. Singh died before Osler's shipments arrived at the Grand City Palace, and the crystal languished in packing crates for years. In more recent times, the whole ensemble has been arranged and is on display in the Fateh Prakash Palace in Udaipur.

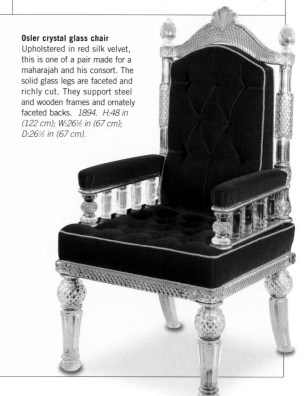

Osler crystal glass chair
Upholstered in red silk velvet, this is one of a pair made for a maharajah and his consort. The solid glass legs are faceted and richly cut. They support steel and wooden frames and ornately faceted backs. *1894. H:48 in (122 cm); W:26½ in (67 cm); D:26½ in (67 cm).*

CHINA

WOODWORKING AND cabinet-making were advanced industries in the China of the late Qing dynasty (1644–1912). Although most authorities agree that the best Chinese furniture was made before the 19th century, traditional methods and forms persisted well into this period of greater communication and trade with the West.

A PERIOD OF DISTRESS

By the mid-19th century, China was home to British, American, Russian, Japanese, German,

Italian, and French colonies. Foreign influence in China was further extended when, in the aftermath of the first Opium War (1839–42), China was compelled to open five of its ports, including Canton and Shanghai, to foreign trade. This number was increased in 1860 following another Chinese military defeat. Far from being a welcome addition to the cultural diversity of China, these foreign incursions were resented by the majority of the populace.

More pressing matters dominated the political and social landscape during this period. China was beset with internal rebellion, famine, and drought—a series of calamities that conspired to wipe out 60 million people in the next 12 years.

Western powers were quick to help the Qing dynasty during these periods of crisis, yet their primary aim was always to open up Chinese markets to the West to improve Western economies. Consequently, Chinese furniture of the mid-19th century, although predominantly based on Ming and early Qing ideals, bore the

stamp of Western influence to a greater extent than ever before.

A MIX OF OLD AND NEW

The last years of the Qing dynasty, though troubled, did produce some fine furniture. A deep reverence for the past kept the traditions and monumental forms of the early Qing period in production. Concurrent with this, there was a general softening of the strict rectilinearity that had previously characterized Chinese furniture. Rounded forms, such as spoon and horseshoe backs, began to proliferate, as did peculiarly European

A pierced medallion is centered above the panel.

The top rail is curved into a horseshoe shape to simulate bamboo.

The back is inset with a Chinese lacquer panel.

A cane seat is fitted into the rosewood seat frame.

The turned legs simulate the appearance of bamboo.

HORSESHOE ARMCHAIR

This is one of a pair of rare horseshoe armchairs made of *huanghuali*, the Chinese name for rosewood. It has a U-shaped, bamboo form, a carved top rail, a cane seat, and a lattice splat. The top rail and legs have been carved to simulate the appearance of bamboo. *S&K*

ANGLO-CHINESE CENTER TABLE

This Anglo-Chinese center table is made from amboyna and ebony and has three drawers— one long and two short—with dummy drawers at the back. It is raised on carved ebony

trestle supports, terminating in claw feet. The supports are joined by an ebony stretcher. Although it was made in 1840, the design of the table is closer in style to examples from about 1810. *c. 1840.*

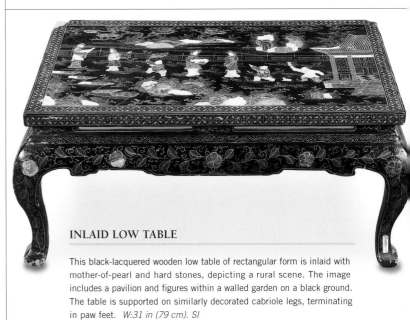

INLAID LOW TABLE

This black-lacquered wooden low table of rectangular form is inlaid with mother-of-pearl and hard stones, depicting a rural scene. The image includes a pavilion and figures within a walled garden on a black ground. The table is supported on similarly decorated cabriole legs, terminating in paw feet. *W:31 in (79 cm). SI*

hapes, such as the breakfront. ontinuity came in the shape of plant tands, low tables, screens, and a ariety of other forms that had been opular in China for many years.

Cabinet-makers continued to use cquer to decorate a great deal of the urniture, although the quality Ming cquer furniture was never surpassed. hree predominant styles of lacquer ecoration date from this period. The ost common were *daqi*, a thick cquer coating applied to a paste ndercoat, and *tulqi*, a thin wash ainted directly on to the wood. Less

common and more elaborate was *miaojin*, which incorporated gold-colored highlights on a ground of black and colored lacquer.

Another traditional decorative element, the ceramic plaque, enjoyed something of a revival toward the close of the Qing period due to the work of porcelain masters, such as Liu Xiren, who worked in Jiangxi province.

ELABORATE DECORATION

The persistent admiration for Chinese furniture was due in no small part to the quality of the exotic woods

available to craftsmen. Hardwoods, particularly rosewood, were ideally suited to the profuse pierced and carved decoration practiced by so many cabinet-makers. Huali, a type of rosewood, was found to fade to an attractive golden color after prolonged exposure to light, and furniture with this hue became known as *huanghuali* during the late Qing period. Hard stones, either in the form of decorative inlays or inset marble table tops, appealed to the European taste and became staples of more ornate Chinese furniture of the period.

The export market was a prime source of commissions and revenue for many cabinet-makers, particularly those in the newly opened city ports, such as Shanghai. European markets demanded that this export furniture look as Asian as possible, with the result that decoration that might be rejected as overexuberant by the Chinese was carried out on some furniture purely to satisfy Western buyers. Intricately inlaid figural landscapes containing pavilions and other typically Chinese features are hallmarks of this new direction taken by Chinese craftsmen in the second half of the 19th century.

LANT STANDS

hese intricate plant stands are made of rosewood and have aped tops with polished marble insets. The tops are supported profusely carved frames and shaped legs, which are joined by retchers and headed by mask motifs. The stands terminate in nimal-paw feet. *c. 1900. SI*

NEST OF TABLES

This set of four hardwood tables graduates in size, fitting one inside the next, making the tables easy to store when not in use. Each table has a tray top and a decorative pierced apron set above shaped legs, which are joined by similarly shaped stretchers. *Largest: H:28 in (71 cm). L&T*

SPOON-BACK NURSING CHAIR

This Burmese, carved hardwood nursing chair features ornate, pierced, carved decoration throughout. The shaped back has a deep, carved surround with bird and foliage motifs. The padded drop-in seat has a similarly carved seat rail and is supported on cabriole legs molded as rampant lions. *c. 1900. SI*

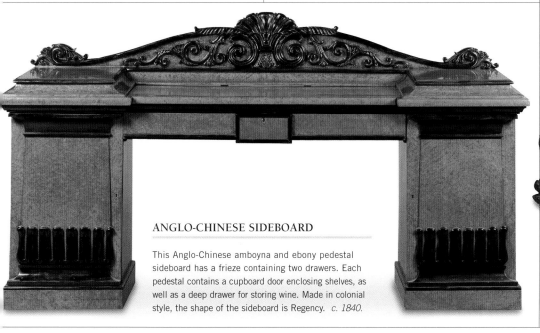

ANGLO-CHINESE SIDEBOARD

This Anglo-Chinese amboyna and ebony pedestal sideboard has a frieze containing two drawers. Each pedestal contains a cupboard door enclosing shelves, as well as a deep drawer for storing wine. Made in colonial style, the shape of the sideboard is Regency. *c. 1840.*

NEW STYLES

FURNITURE THAT DEBUTED during the mid-19th century was imbued with the innovative spirit, social mores, and the whimsy of its age. Metamorphic furniture allowed cabinet-makers to show off their technical expertise. The German-born American cabinet-maker George Hunzinger pioneered the design of functional, mechanical pieces in the United States, and many manufacturers soon followed suit.

Stephen Hedges patented a desk in 1854 that converted from an elegant side table to an *écritoire* combined with a seat. It became known as the Aaron Burr desk after an article appeared in the *New York Herald* in 1911, stating that Burr had challenged the presidential candidate Alexander Hamilton to a duel in a letter written at one of them. In fact, Hedges had patented the ingenious desk 50 years after the duel and 18 years after Burr's death, but the desk became forever known as the Aaron Burr desk.

Various collapsible and extendible forms, including dining tables and buffets, proliferated as people became enamored with their ingenuity and space-saving qualities.

SOCIAL MORES

The fashion for lavish entertaining gave rise to the cocktail cabinet, which contained crystal decanters and perhaps a cigarette case or humidor. The wealthy displayed their valuables in a glass-topped *bijouterie*—the name is derived from the French word for "jewelry." The Sutherland table, named for Queen Victoria's Mistress of the Robes, was used for taking tea and playing cards. A precursor of the coffee table, it was never very popular.

The repressive morality of the period conspired to create the *dos-à-dos* and the conversation suite. Both these seat forms enabled courting couples to become acquainted in what was regarded as a seemly manner.

CONVERSATION SUITE

This upholstered suite in Louis XV manner comprises four independent buttoned sections—two long sides and two short ends—arranged back-to-back with each other. The angled ends of each section make it easy for a person seated with another in one of the long sections to turn toward a person seated in the adjacent smaller section and converse. The sections are supported on rosewood scrolling feet and casters: a 19th-century innovation allowing ease of movement around the room. *Late 19th century. L&T* **4**

SHOW-FRAME SOFA

This early Victorian show-frame sofa is made from rosewood. It has two high-backed, rounded ends and a lower back section with spirally fluted supports. The seat, back, and scroll arms are upholstered in green raised fabric. The seat is supported on carved legs with ceramic casters. The sofa is a combination of styles: the twist decoration is Jacobean, while the cabriole legs are inspired by Louis XV style. *c. 1850. W:181 cm (71¼ cm). DN* **3**

The exterior surface of the desk has a simple panel with beading.

The hinged top opens to reveal a seat and a drawer.

The seat is upholstered in leather, fixed to the wood with rivets.

The underside of the desk bears the patent label "by Stephen Hedges."

Lockable drawer

The scroll feet terminate in brass casters.

AMERICAN AARON BURR DESK

This ingenious, space-saving design was patented by Stephen Hedges. The long, oval top of an unassuming mahogany side table is hinged so that it can fold back on itself, and the case of the desk is also hinged to open at the front. When both are opened, the table is transformed into a writing desk with a drawer to one side and a leather upholstered seat to the other. The piece is supported on cabriole legs and scroll feet on casters for portability. *1854. H:29¼ in (74.3 cm); W:33¼ in (84.5 cm); D:25½ in (64.8 cm). POOK* **4**

METAMORPHIC OAK CHAIR

This chair converts into a set of library steps. The chair seat is hinged near the front so the chair back swings up and over the seat to become the rear support for the steps, which double as the back legs of the chair. *Late 19th century. WW* **1**

GOTHIC-STYLE CHAIR

This walnut chair features Gothic-style, needlework upholstery and Jacobean twist carving. The tall back is framed by barley-twist columns above a spreading seat. The high back and low legs make this a new form. *L&T* **1**

MAHOGANY COCKTAIL CABINET

This cabinet has a divided, hinged top, which encloses a rising interior with crystal decanters, glasses, and a cigarette box. It is supported on square-section, tapering legs with brass caps and casters. *c. 1900. W:23¼ in (59 cm). L&T* **2**

MAHOGANY *BIJOUTERIE* CABINET

The circular hinged top of this cabinet is inset with beveled glass. The cabriole legs have gilt mounts, terminate in hoof feet, and are joined by a shaped stretcher. *Late 19th century. H:30⅛ in (76.5 cm); Diam:17⅞ in (45 cm). L&T* **3**

BIJOUTERIE CABINET

This mahogany and gilt-metal mounted cabinet has a serpentine top with floral marquetry, inset with glass. The case is supported on slender cabriole legs, which are united by an undertier. *W:25 in (63.5 cm). WW* **1**

SCOTTISH DINING TABLE

The top of this extending dining table has *demi-lune* ends and boldly molded edges above a plain frieze. The table top is raised on turned and tapering legs with fluted decoration, ending in brass caps and casters. The table is extended by using a winding mechanism operated by a key. The mechanism was invented in 1835 but became popular later in the century. It can use up to six extra leaves. *Late 19th century. W:185 in (460 cm). L&T* **5**

ENGLISH ROSEWOOD CARD TABLE

The serpentine top of this Victorian table opens out and swivels to provide a playing surface. It has a molded edge, enclosing a round baize lining, and rests on four scroll supports with a central finial and scroll legs with recessed casters. *Mid-19th century. W:36¼ in (92 cm). DN* **2**

scrolled bracket

scrolling foot with caster

ENGLISH MAHOGANY BUFFET

The top of this buffet has molded angles and a counterbalanced undershelf. Beneath that lies a third shelf. On opening the buffet, the bottom shelf slides down the supports at each end of the table, the middle shelf remains in place, and the top opens out to form the upper tier. It is raised on paneled trestle supports and scrolled console brackets. *c. 1860. W:48 in (120 cm). L&T* **3**

SUTHERLAND TABLE

This burr walnut, oval, drop-leaf table has a veneered top over twin, carved, baluster uprights with carved cabriole supports on casters, joined by a turned stretcher. It has a swinging action to each side. *W:35⅞ in (91 cm). BAR* **1**

CHESTS OF DRAWERS

MANY OF THE CHESTS made and sold in this period were direct descendants of their 18th-century counterparts. The chest was still in widespread use, both in the bedroom as a clothes store and in the salon, very often for display purposes only. Examples with specialized uses, such as music cabinets and folio chests, augmented the range of commodes, cabinets, and vitrines already found in the home. The traditional low, broad chest was frequently of very fluid form, incorporating serpentine, *bombé*, or bow-front curves reminiscent of 18th-century styles. Elaborate commodes were rare, however, and, in the drawing room, were often replaced by credenzas, or side cabinets.

CONTRASTING STYLES

A more contemporary look was provided by a new generation of tall and slender, rather elegant, filing cabinets, precipitated by the best-selling Wellington chest. These filing cabinets tended to be less fussy than the more old-fashioned chests of drawers, particularly those in the Rococo-revival style, which were often excessively ornamented. Profuse use of gilt-metal mounts, sabots, and inlays combined with marble tops, carved skirts, friezes and aprons, and intricate marquetry decoration often made these very busy items of furniture. Neoclassical and Gothic forms sat alongside chests in the Rococo style, although these labels often referred to little more than token applied decoration, used by cabinet-makers to distinguish an otherwise plain piece of furniture.

FAVORED WOODS

Tropical hardwoods, such as mahogany and rosewood, were frequently used for chests, although Dutch cabinet-makers often substituted walnut for their marquetry-decorated pieces, and cherry wood was sometimes used in the United States.

ITALIAN PARQUETRY COMMODE

This kingwood parquetry commode is of *bombé* form and has a molded Siena marble top above two chequer-veneered drawers. Each drawer has a flower-head motif centered over the escutcheon plate. The same motif appears on the sides of the case. It is raised on square cabriole legs, terminating in sabots. Although almost an exact copy of an 18th-century piece, its excessively slender legs reveal its 19th-century origins. *W:47 in (117.5 cm). FRE* **3**

The gilt-bronze *corner mounts are Louis XV in style.*

The top *of the commode is made of breche d'Alep marble.*

The division *between the two drawers is disguised by the sans transverse marquetry.*

The gilt-bronze *apron mount is Rococo in style.*

Each cabriole leg *terminates in a gilt-bronze sabot.*

FRENCH COMMODE

This 18th-century-style commode has a molded, veined marble top above a Rococo-style, rosewood- and walnut-veneered *bombé* case with polished, gilded, bronze mounts. The front of the piece is inlaid with colorful marquetry, and shows an asymmetrical floral pattern. The case is set on cabriole legs. It is an accurate copy of a Louis XV commode and uses expensive materials. However, this mid-19th-century example was constructed by machine rather than by hand. *H:33⅞ in (86 cm); W:41¾ in (106 cm); D:23⅔ in (60 cm). VH* **6**

DUTCH CHEST OF DRAWERS

The molded top of this Dutch, Empire-style, walnut and marquetry tall chest of drawers has an outset frieze drawer. Below this are five equal-sized drawers, decorated *sans traverse* with fine floral marquetry inlaywork, which exhibits a mixture of mid-18th- and late 18th-century styles in its overall design. The oval border is Neoclassical in inspiration, while the floral design within it is asymmetrical and, therefore, more Rococo in style. The case is supported on tapering, square-section feet. *1880. W:41 in (104 cm). SI* **3**

ANGLO-INDIAN WELLINGTON CHEST

Made of the distinctively striped coromandel wood—a type of ebony from the Coromandel coast of India—this Wellington chest also features surface carving typical of the subcontinent. *c. 1880. H:36 in (90 cm); W:18 in (45 cm); D:10½ in (26.5 cm). JK* **5**

FRENCH FILING CHEST

This late Louis XVI-style ebony and brass filing chest has a molded edge above eight drawers. The drawers have leather fronts and brass catches and are supported on a plinth base. *c. 1900. H:65⅓ in (166 cm); W:22 in (57 cm). DN* **4**

BRITISH WELLINGTON CHEST

The molded top of this figured maple chest protrudes above its frieze. Beneath the frieze are seven graduated drawers, flanked on either side by a locking flap. At the top of each flap is an applied scroll-leaf decoration. *c. 1860. H:48 in (122 cm); W:22 in (56 cm); D:16½ in (42 cm). L&T* **4**

GERMAN COMMODE

This mahogany commode has a protruding rectangular top above four flame-mahogany veneered drawers. The front of the case has canted corners, with a carved scroll and acanthus top and bottom. The case is supported on carved scroll, bracket feet. *c. 1850. H:32¼ in (82 cm); W:32¾ in (83 cm); D:19¼ in (49 cm). BMN* **1**

FRENCH COMMODE

This bowfront kingwood commode has a molded, veined marble top. The four drawers have veneered fronts, and are divided and flanked by brass-lined flutes. A veneered herringbone pattern is on each side. The commode has a shaped apron with gilt mounts and stands on bracket feet. *c. 1900. W:32 in (82 cm). L&T*

BRITISH CHEST OF DRAWERS

This rectilinear chest of drawers has two short above three long, equal-sized drawers. Each drawer is decorated with laurel swags, and the long drawers also feature a central carved rosette. The chest is supported on a shaped plinth base. *Late 19th century. W:44¾ in (113.5 cm). DN* **1**

GERMAN COMMODE

This small commode is made from solid mahogany and veneered in various exotic woods. There is a single frieze drawer below the molded top and two additional, *bombé*-form drawers decorated, *ans traverse*, with flowers, figures, and rocaille. *c. 1900. H:25¼ in (64.5 cm); W:24⅛ in (62 cm); D:12⅝ in (32 cm). WKA* **1**

Painted side panel

AMERICAN CHEST OF DRAWERS

This chest has been grain-painted in ocher and yellow with dark green moldings and recessed side panels. The backboard is dark green with the initials "A" and "M" in gold and copper. The chest has two short above four long drawers. Each side panel is stenciled with a vase of flowers. *c. 1863. W:39 in (99 cm). FRE* **6**

AMERICAN BUTLER'S CHEST

This cherrywood chest has paneled sides and four dovetailed drawers with glass handles. The top drawer has a drop front with spindle columns and opens onto a fitted interior with four drawers, eight cubbyholes, and a central prospect door. *Mid-19th century. H:46 in (117 cm); W:42 in (107 cm); D:21½ in (54.5 cm). BRU* **2**

BUFFETS AND SIDEBOARDS

THE VICTORIAN PENCHANT for formal social gatherings made the buffet and the sideboard very important items of furniture in more affluent households. Both were used in the dining room to display food and house crockery. They differed in that the buffet was a rather grand superstructure with two or more tiers, similar to the kitchen dresser, whereas the sideboard was a less imposing, single-tiered cabinet.

DIFFERING STYLES

A wide variety of shapes were popular during this time, incorporating elements from various periods and styles. Arched tops and backs became more common as forms in general grew more rounded, although the traditional rectangular shape certainly persisted. The range of leg shapes used included cup and cover, square, tapering, and cabriole—all very different in style.

Woods used for buffets and sideboards tended to vary just

as they had in the late 18th century. Although these pieces of furniture were often made of mahogany or oak, many carried veneers of burr timbers.

From the mid-19th century, people wanted everything in a room to match in style and material. As a result, in many houses, all the furniture in the dining room, including the buffet or sideboard, would be made of a single wood, such as oak or walnut.

DESIGNED FOR STORAGE

As well as displaying and serving food, the buffet was used to store cutlery, dinnerware, and even decorative *objets*. Victorian households were cluttered environments, and the sideboard was a reflection of this. They were peppered with various compartments, cupboards, and drawers, each with their own specific purpose and many fitted with locks. Buffets in the grandest houses could be exceptionally large, with an average height of more than 6 ft (183 cm).

FRENCH LOUIS XV-STYLE BUFFET

This Louis XV-style, cherry and burr walnut buffet has a molded, gently arched top above a frieze carved with a flowering basket. The upper section of the buffet has a number of open shelves for displaying cups, plates, and decorative objects. These open shelves are

flanked by a pair of decorative serpentine paneled doors. The lower section of the buffet two small frieze drawers and two further large paneled doors carved with swirling foliate decoration. The buffet has an ornamental shaped apron and is raised on short, slightly cabriole legs. *Late 19th century. H:84 in (213.5 cm). SI* **2**

A twin-handled urn finial surmounts the central curve of the shaped backboard.

A carved coat-of-arms of family antiquarian interest is applied to the center of the backboard.

The apron is composed of intricate strapwork carving.

Cup-and-cover gadroon supports surmount the pedestal feet.

Each of the plinth bases is carved with paterae.

BRITISH SIDEBOARD

This early Victorian, possibly Anglo-Indian, oak sideboard has an elaborately shaped backboard surmounted by a number of finials and with an urn at its center. Below the urn is an applied, carved coat of arms. The stepped, rectangular

top of the sideboard has a carved edge, above a gadrooned guilloche frieze and an elaborately carved strapwork apron. The sideboard is raised on carved cup-and-cover legs with gadroon supports above plinth bases carved with paterae and pedestal feet. *H:67⅓ in (171 cm); W:84⅔ in (215 cm); D:29½ in (75 cm). L&T* **4**

BREAKFRONT SIDEBOARD

This British mahogany breakfront sideboard is simply decorated with satinwood banding and boxwood and ebony stringing. Two square, bowed doors flank the two graduated central drawers. The case stands on six square,

tapering legs, terminating in spade feet. This elegant piece is Neoclassical in style and was probably based on a Sheraton example of around 1780. The deep cupboards would have been used for storing wine, and the frieze drawers for storing silver or cutlery. *Late 19th century. W:66¼ in (168 cm). DN* **2**

TALIAN POLYCHROME CREDENZA

his painted cabinet has a rectangular top with a coved center
ction and ends. The conforming case has three small drawers
ove three cupboard doors, all opening to shelved interiors. The
se is supported on a molded base with bracket feet and is
inted with arabesques, swags, flowers, birds, figures, and masks
a crackle ground. *c. 1900. W:67¼ in (168 cm). S&K* **3**

RITISH MAHOGANY SIDEBOARD

is mahogany sideboard has a scrolling, arched backboard
at is centered by a cabochon with mask surmount. The
verse breakfront top contains ogee frieze drawers and
e four arched paneled doors enclose both sliding trays
d shelves. The whole sideboard is raised on a plinth base.
79½ in (202 cm). L&T **3**

FRENCH OAK BUFFET

The upper section of this oak buffet stands on turned supports and has a
molded cornice above two glazed doors, which open on to a shelved
interior. The doors are flanked by fluted pilasters. The rectangular top of
the lower section has two frieze drawers above two cupboard doors with
applied carved decoration showing a Classical urn filled with flowers. It
stands on squashed bun feet. *Late 19th century. H:74 in (188 cm). SI* **1**

ANGLO-INDIAN CABINET

The shelved upper section of this rosewood bookcase
cabinet has leaf-molded cresting above twin doors with
elaborate pierced and carved panels, flanked by scrolling
brackets. The lower section has two long, carved frieze
drawers above two similarly carved doors. The piece
stands on carved bracket feet. *W:41 in (104 cm). L&T* **5**

NGLO-INDIAN SERVING TABLE

e backboard of this hardwood serving table is elaborately carved
th anthemion, acanthus, and birds. The rectangular top has
ld, leaf-carved edging and rests on carved brackets with foliate
twork to the back and sides. The table has a curved support with
rved paw feet. *Mid-19th century. W:48 in (122 cm). L&T* **4**

BRITISH PEDESTAL SIDEBOARD

This fine George III-style mahogany, satinwood, and marquetry
sideboard was made by Wright and Mansfield. The pedestals of
the desk contain cellaret drawers for storing wine. The decorative
motifs are strongly Neoclassical in manner, inspired by Robert
Adam's (1728–92) delicate interpretation of the style. The

elongated urns centered on each of the pedestals also serve
to indicate their contents. Lightly drawn swags and striking
anthemion motifs are used to define the individual drawers and
cupboards, and to accentuate the essential symmetry of the
piece with its carefully balanced use of curved and flat surfaces,
sinuous lines, and geometric shape. *c. 1880. H:36¼ in (92 cm);
W:86 in (218 cm); D:71 in (28 cm).*

CHAIRS

CHAIR DESIGN HAD NEVER been so diverse as in this eclectic age. The different styles seen in other types of furniture also existed in chairs. Elements from the popular revival styles—from Classical acanthus carvings to Gothic arches and all points in between—combined to create a multifarious riot of forms.

Chairs were often designed to complement other pieces in a room, but were also influenced by fashion, which resulted in the design of low, wide seats to accommodate full skirts.

COMFORT FIRST

An emphasis on comfort was at the core of many mid-19th-century chair designs, especially those that emanated from France, where padded arms, seats, and backs were *de rigueur* components of the Rococo- and Neoclassical-revival styles. In Britain, the easy chair was thickly padded in fabric or leather and

provided a respite from the more ascetic oak chairs in the Gothic style. There was a renewed interest in the designs of Chippendale, Sheraton, and Adam toward the end of the century.

Two separate interpretations of the Rococo style—the bentwood laminate styles of the Thonet and Belter factories on the one hand, and the padded giltwood offerings of French workshops on the other—both enjoyed popularity. Classical motifs such as urns, acanthus, and festoons were equally prolific. Asian and Anglo-Indian furniture expanded the canon of Western decorative arts to include elements from these two ancient Eastern cultures.

Salon suites also became popular in middle-class homes during this period. The suite typically comprised a sofa, a chaise longue, four side chairs, a lady's armchair, a gentleman's armchair, and a stool—all in the Louis XV style.

FRENCH OPEN ARMCHAIRS

These open armchairs are made of white-painted wood and each have a flower-carved crest and apron. The seat, arms, and back are upholstered in a pale fabric decorated with a floral and foliate pattern. In each case, the

serpentine seat is supported on painted (formerly gilt) cabriole legs. The chairs are Louis XV in style and make an interesting contrast to the armchairs shown below. *c. 1880. DN* **2**

FRENCH OPEN ARMCHAIRS

Each one of this pair of giltwood open armchairs has an upholstered back, arms, and seat. The frame of each chair is carved with a scroll, ribbon, and swag crest and stiff lead

borders. Each chair has fluted, finial-surmounted supports and tapering legs, which terminate in brass casters. The chairs are Louis XVI in style. *c. 1900. H:40½ in (103 cm).* **3**

A carved top rail adorns the top of the shield seat back.

The shield back is carved with anthemions and acanthus motifs.

The upper side of each serpentine arm is carved with a guilloche motif.

The square, tapering legs with bellflowers terminate in spade feet.

A Neoclassical tablet is centered on the carved seat rail.

BRITISH ARMCHAIR

This mahogany shield-back armchair has been made in the manner of 18th-century interior designer Robert Adam. The shield back has a carved top rail, an inlaid satinwood border, and

applied, carved decoration showing Classical motifs, including swags, laurel leaves, and urns. The upholstered seat has a carved seat rail and is supported on leaf-carved, square-section legs, terminating in spade feet. *c. 1860. CATO* **7**

GERMAN CHAIR AND ARMCHAIR

This solid mahogany chair and armchair are designed in the Empire style, with scrolled top rails and upholstered backs and seats. The supports, armrests, and seat rails are inlaid

with bronze decoration. The arm supports are giltwood sphinxes, while the cabriole legs have carved and gilt griffin heads and paw feet. *c. 1880. H:40¾ in (103.5 cm). WKA* **3**

AMERICAN SIDE CHAIRS

This pair of Rococo-revival, laminated, rosewood side chairs each has a shaped, molded back, enclosing scrolling devices. The upholstered seats have a flower-carved rail and are supported on cabriole legs. *1850. H:32¾ in (83 cm). FRE* **1**

BRITISH EASY CHAIR

This George III-style, mahogany, upholstered easy chair has a curved crest above rolled arms and is raised on cabriole legs with claw-and-ball feet. The chair has rose and beige silk damask upholstery. *c. 1900. H:39 in (97.5 cm). S&K* **1**

BRITISH GENTLEMAN'S CHAIR

This walnut-framed gentleman's easy chair has a Morocco-leather buttoned back and seat with studded decoration and outscrolled arms. It is a good example of a chair with coil springs. The chair is raised on turned front legs and casters. *1890–1900. L&T* **3**

Carved splat panel

CHINESE ARMCHAIRS

These red-lacquered elm armchairs from Shangxi Province each have a scrolling top rail and a paneled splat carved with an animal and objects. Each panel seat with a carved seat rail is supported on square-section legs with stretchers. *c. 1880. SI* **1**

BLACK FOREST HALL CHAIRS

Each one of this pair of chairs has a stained and carved frame inlaid with hunting scenes on the back and seat. The waisted, pierced, scrolling back rises above a shaped serpentine seat, which is supported on cabriole legs. *L&T* **2**

BRITISH OPEN ARMCHAIR

The rounded back and seat of this armchair in George I style are upholstered with *gros* and *petit-point* woolwork. The walnut frame has shepherd-crook arms and shell-carved cabriole legs, terminating in claw-and-ball feet. *DN* **3**

ANGLO-INDIAN OPEN ARMCHAIR

This Empire-style armchair has a shaped top rail, a square-section back rail, scrolled arms, and cabriole legs. Every surface is covered with *sadeli* work decoration set within ivory and ebony borders. *c. 1900. WW* **1**

ITALIAN ARMCHAIR

This lime and walnut armchair has an oval back with an upholstered panel framed by carved, gilt surrounds. The seat has a molded crest rail and is supported on cabriole legs. *c. 1840. H:39 in (99 cm); W:26 in (66 cm); D:20 in (51 cm). LOT*

BRITISH SIDE CHAIR

The caned, shield-shaped back of this Sheraton-style, painted satinwood side chair is surmounted by a medallion depicting a female figure. The seat is raised on square, tapering legs, which terminate in spade feet. *c. 1900. SI* **1**

SOFAS

THE MAJORITY OF 19th-century sofas were designed either for comfort or for formal seating. The fluidity of the revival styles during this period allowed for a certain poetic license in the designs.

COIL-SPRING UPHOLSTERY

The French fashion for upholstering their luxurious *canapés* with sumptuous, overstuffed seats and padded backs soon spread across Europe. The increased thickness of the upholstery was the result of the introduction of coiled springs. These were, in themselves, quite deep, but they also required a thick layer of padding to prevent them from piercing the seat cover. Deeply set buttons were used to hold both the springs and the padding in place, and became a feature in themselves.

The fabrics used to cover these upholsteries were often extremely expensive, making it necessary to

shield furniture from direct sunlight, hence the Victorian reputation for gloomy interiors. Both *petit* and *gros point* were popular.

The confidante, or *tête-à-tête*, evolved from the standard French *canapé* as a slightly less formal design, allowing couples or parties to sit together and converse while facing each other. These were fairly variable forms, as were many of the Rococo-revival, show-frame sofas, chaises longues, and daybeds made at this time. They contrasted with Neoclassical- and Empire-revival styles, which made greater use of flat planes and regular angles.

Toward the end of the period, influences from the Middle East and the Orient began to infiltrate sofa design in the West. Turkish-style daybeds, Chinese bamboo frames, and the no-nonsense Arts and Crafts aesthetic started to reverse the trend for decadent, comfortable seating.

Cushion tassels

Scrolled leg

BRITISH WINDOW SEAT

This mahogany, Regency-revival-style window seat has an upholstered back, outswept sides, and seat. The frame of the window seat is carved with acanthus and is supported on scroll legs with paw feet. *c. 1900. W:49½ in (126 cm). D*

BRITISH SHOW-FRAME SOFA

This early Victorian, Rococo-revival, show-frame sofa is made of rosewood and has a generously upholstered seat, arms, and back. The serpentine seat is supported on scroll-carved cabriole legs, terminating in ceramic casters. *c. 1850. W:72 in (183 cm). S&K* **2**

The lion's heads are supported on turned columns.

The arched top rail above the panels is inlaid with floral marquetry.

The seat back has scroll-topped supports.

The cabriole legs terminate in claw-and-ball feet.

Each seat is concave-fronted with a marquetry-inlaid apron.

The base of the chair back is galleried, with turned spindles.

DUTCH HALL BENCH

The triple concave-shaped back of this mahogany and marquetry-decorated bench has a molded crest and a carved lion's head at each seat division. The sweeping arms terminate in carved heads. The shaped seat

has a similarly shaped apron and is raised on four carved cabriole legs to the front and two slightly sweeping, square-section legs to the back. The entire bench is profusely decorated with marquetry inlay, depicting flowers, leaves, urns, birds, and insects. *W:64½ in (164 cm). HAD* **3**

FRENCH DAY BED

This carved walnut and upholstered day bed is designed in the Louis XVI style. The reeded and scroll arms carved with leaves and the loose cushion seat are covered in a beige fabric and raised on turned and stop-fluted legs, joined by

a rope-carved apron. This piece would have been made for an alcove and placed parallel to a wall. It may originally have had a canopy of matching fabric suspended above it. *W:81½ in (207.5 cm). FRE* **2**

FRENCH BENCH

This carved oak and walnut bench has a galleried back with carved panels, depicting dragons, figures, and cherubs. It has square arms above a solid seat and is supported on spiral-turned legs. *W:54½ in (138.5 cm). FRE* **2**

FRENCH *CANAPÉ*

This Louis XVI-style walnut *canapé* has a carved crest rail above a padded back. The cushioned seat is supported on fluted, tapered legs, which end in peg feet. *c. 1900. W:50 in (125 cm). DN* **2**

Gilt-brass molding

BRITISH SETTEE

This mahogany, Empire-revival settee has a scrolled crest rail, upholstered seat and back, and padded arms. The frame of the settee has Neoclassical gilt-brass applied moldings throughout and is supported on turned legs. *Late 19th century. L&T* **3**

Tapestry detail

FRENCH SOFA

This is one of a pair of Napoleon III-style ebonized sofas. The back is in three sections and has a central shaped, rectangular, upholstered panel flanked by two similarly upholstered oval panels in carved gilt frames.

The padded seat is supported on six turned and fluted legs, terminating in pad feet. The sofa is attributed to Charles-Guillaume Diehl. The tapestry upholstery was probably made by the prestigious Aubussan company. *BK* **6**

AMERICAN SETTEE

This carved walnut settee has an undulating back and a crest rail carved with flowers and grapes. The padded, upholstered arms scroll outward and show William IV influence. The padded, upholstered seat has a similarly carved serpentine apron and has additional side cushions. The whole settee is supported on slightly cabriole legs. Chairs and sofas featuring elements of ornate, naturalistic carving in the Rococo-revival style were very popular in the United States, particularly between 1830 and 1865. *W:70 in (175 cm). S&K* **1**

BRITISH SETTEE

This walnut, tub-shaped settee has an upholstered back, armrests, and seat. Originally, it was almost certainly part of a salon suite. The settee has a pierced back and is supported on turned legs, terminating in brass casters. Neoclassical in style, it was probably inspired by Sheraton's furniture designs, combining the simple geometric forms of the pierced back with the gentle, curving contours of the seat and upholstered back shape. *c. 1900. GorL* **2**

TABLES

AN ABUNDANCE OF table types, each designed for a specific use, was made in the mid-19th century. Many of these were suited to popular pastimes of the period, such as playing cards. The general trend was for smaller, more portable tables in greater numbers.

TABLES FOR EVERY PURPOSE

Pier tables, originally used as early as the 16th century, became popular again as householders sought to fill their homes with more furniture than ever before. The card table was another popular addition to many homes; unobtrusive when not in use, when required for playing cards, the top of the table was opened to reveal a baize-lined playing surface. The worktable, designed to store needlework accoutrements or writing utensils, frequently incorporated a hanging bag as was previously the fashion. Despite the introduction of gas and oil lighting,

the *torchère* remained a very popular fixture on which to stand candlesticks.

A MIXTURE OF STYLES

Tables of all kinds were produced in a wide range of historical and cultural styles. Tables in the Rococo style were covered with extravagant "C" and "S" scrolls and rested on cabriole legs, whereas fluted, tapering legs were found on Classical- or Renaissance-style tables. A softening and rounding of contours was expressed in the West by the use of serpentine shapes and undulating moldings, but Asian forms remained steadfastly rectilinear.

French and Italian console tables often had marble tops, a fashion that was exported to many countries, especially Britain and the United States. Center and side tables often had tripod legs. Such tables frequently featured foldaway tops so that they could be put away easily when not in use.

CHINESE SIDE TABLE

This beech wood side table originates from the Shuzhou province. It has a rectangular top positioned above three drawers and an apron carved with simple roundels. The table top is raised on square-section legs, with carved bracket supports and terminates in spade feet. The back of the table is left undecorated as the piece is designed to stand against a wall. *c. 1850. W:45½ in (115.5 cm). S&K* **1**

CONSOLE TABLES

This pair of Louis XVI console tables is possibly Italian. Each one is gilded and has a shaped, mottled brown-black and white marble top with canted corners and coved sides set above a similarly shaped base. The bowed front of each table is decorated with a frieze hung with leafy swags on either side of a Classical figural medallion. Each table is supported on Neoclassical-style fluted, tapering legs carved with leaves and drapery. The tables were probably designed to stand in piers—the spaces between two windows—possibly with matching gilded mirrors hung immediately above them. *W:45 in (112.5 cm). S&K* **4**

Scrolling brasswork is inlaid on a red tortoiseshell ground.

The table top has a shaped apron frieze.

Each cabriole leg features a gilt-bronze mount at its head.

The serpentine platform base has a red tortoiseshell ground.

Acanthus and scroll mounts decorate the base of each leg.

Bun feet support the shaped undertier.

FRENCH CONSOLE TABLE

This Louis XV-style boullework and ebonized serpentine console table is decorated with gilt-metal mounts, which are similar to the earlier *Régence* style in appearance. All the surfaces of the table are inlaid with scrolling brasswork

on a red tortoiseshell ground. The table top has a shaped apron and is supported on cabriole legs headed by putti and acanthus leaves. The legs are joined by a shaped undertier, below which are bun feet. The table probably had an elaborate mirror in similar style above it originally. *c. 1860. W:51½ in (131 cm). SI* **2**

CHINESE LOW TABLE

This rectangular low table is made of *huanghuali* wood (rosewood). It has a cleated top, which is positioned above an ornate frieze carved with stylized scroll motifs. The table top is supported on straight legs with angular, scroll-carved terminals. *1880. W:35½ in (90.5 cm). DN* **2**

AMERICAN PIER TABLE

his is one of a pair of Classical, arble-top pier tables. It has a ctangular, ogee-molded top on conforming apron above crolled supports, which are ainted with acanthus leaves nd ornamented with applied ltwood gadrooning. The ctangular base has a sloping, adrooned skirt with a mirror ack. It sits on claw feet. *Late 9th century. W:43½ in 10.5 cm). FRE* **6**

ENGLISH *JARDINIÈRE*

This Victorian amboyna and ebony *jardinière* is rectangular in form with rounded ends. The top lifts off to reveal a well for plants. The table top has metal-beaded borders and simulated ivory inlay, with a molded edge above a frieze set with green jasper-type round plaques with Classical figures. The case is supported on fluted, turned, tapering legs with ceramic casters joined by a shaped cross-stretcher centered with a turned finial. *1860. W:35½ in (90 cm). DN* **3**

BRITISH TRIPOD TABLE

he marquetry-decorated circular top of this ripod table has a carved, molded edge and raised on a fluted, turned, and carved stem upported on three acanthus-decorated legs ith scroll toes and original brass casters. . *1860. Diam:22 in (56 cm). HamG* **2**

BRITISH TEAPOY

The molded-edge, hinged lid of this early Victorian rosewood teapoy has canted corners over a deep, ogee-molded frieze, and is raised on a baluster upright, with a spiral-turned knop, on double C-scroll supports with brass casters. *c. 1840. W:20½ in (52 cm). BAR* **1**

ENGLISH WORKTABLE

This Sheraton-revival, painted satinwood worktable has an oval, hinged top decorated with putti, flowers, ribbons, and bows above a drawer on turned, tapering legs, which are joined by a cross-stretcher. *1900. H:30 in (76 cm); W:19¼ in (49 cm). DN* **3**

GERMAN TRIPOD TABLE

This carved walnut and inlaid tripod table is from the Black Forest. The shaped oval top is inlaid with oval panels of stags and is raised on a turned column support, ending in three foliate carved cabriole legs. *c. 1860. H:30½ in (76 cm). FRE* **1**

MONGOLIAN TABLE

his low, Asian-style table is made from vood decorated with polychrome. It has a rightly decorated rectangular top above molded and carved apron and two carved nd flaps. The table top is supported on four circular-section legs, which are joined by a straight central stretcher. The table is decorated with a broad geometric border and 18th-century designs. Originally, this piece would probably have been used as a dining or occasional table. *Mid-19th century. W:25¼ in (64 cm). SI* **1**

ITALIAN *TORCHÈRE*

This is one of a pair of Venetian *torchères*, which were painted some years after they were originally made. The scrolling support of this one incorporates a male Blackamoor torso and is raised on a white overpainted and gilt tripod base. *H:38½ in (98 cm); W:14⅛ in (36 cm). L&T* **2**

ITALIAN *TORCHÈRE*

This elegant, carved, walnut *torchère* stand is one of a pair crafted in Renaissance-revival style. It has a shaped square top resting on a columnar carved support in the shape of a winged caryatid. The *torchère* is raised on a carved, scrolling tripod base. *1880. SI* **3**

GARDEN FURNITURE

THE FLORAL CHINTZES AND NATURALISTIC DECORATION OF MID-19TH-CENTURY INTERIORS SPILLED INTO THE GARDEN IN THE FORM OF SPECIALLY DESIGNED FURNITURE.

BOTANY WAS A HOUSEHOLD SCIENCE in the 19th century, appealing to the rational, genteel, pious, and relentlessly self-improving Victorian mindset. Its popularity inspired an unprecedented interest in gardening that permeated the social strata. Jane Loudon's 1840 publication *Instructions in Gardening for Ladies* advocated the pastime as one eminently suited to the disposition of the fairer sex, and was a runaway success. The terrarium, invented in 1827 by Dr. Nathanial Ward, allowed people to grow exotic plants in a cold climate—even on a windowsill— and protected delicate specimens from harsh urban environments. The abolition of glass tax in 1845 made conservatories more affordable, and they became fashionable settings in which to entertain one's guests.

Gardens of the period were generally bright and bold, with vast beds planted with swaths of colorful plants very much in vogue. Garden ornaments took many forms, but were rarely subtle. The era that witnessed the introduction of the garden gnome to Britain also saw householders hang brightly colored glass globes, called gazing balls, as decorative additions to their gardens. Urns, statues, birdbaths, obelisks, and even life-sized reproductions of animals, all in metal or stone, populated the gardens of the wealthy. The same ostentatiousness was at work in garden furniture design of the period. Where garden chairs and tables had been relatively restrained early in the century, they became increasingly elaborate as the 19th century progressed. Simple, wrought-iron forms gave way to industrial cast iron that mimicked the triumvirate of styles—Greek, Gothic, and Rococo— that dominated interiors.

IRON CHAIRS FROM IRONBRIDGE

Cast iron was far cheaper than wrought-iron or bronze and was ideally suited to use in the garden, owing to its strength and resistance to rust. A number of iron foundries across Europe had been engaged in the production of garden furniture for some time when the Darby family, owners of a large iron works at Coalbrookdale in Shropshire, turned their attention to the manufacture of iron products. Taking their lead from companies such as Val d'Osne in France, they built the Coalbrookdale

TRAINED TREE
Heinrich Weber's engraving shows a more unusual approach to garden furniture. Instead of buying a canvas sunshade for your garden table and chairs, it suggests creating a natural, yet rather formal, sunshade by training the branches of a tree over an umbrella-shaped trellis. The table and chair are cast iron. c. 1850.

Fig. 573.
Schirmartig gezogener Obstbaum.

WINTER GARDEN
This engraving by Georges Remon from Intérieurs Moderne *shows an elaborate French conservatory. The fountain, trelliswork, and palm trees serve to bring the garden inside, where bentwood chairs share the ample space with cast-iron tables and chairs.* 1900.

VAL D'OSNE CAST-IRON CHAIR *This green-painted cast-iron garden chair has a Gothic cast-diamond back and a honeycomb seat. The cast diamonds have quatrefoils at their center. Pierced stretchers join the legs at the front and sides.* L&T

CAST-IRON GARDEN SEAT
The back of this green-painted, cast-iron garden seat for two features a lily-of-the-valley design. The seat is a scrolling vest, and there is leaf decoration on the legs. It may have been made by the American A. J. Mott Foundry. Late 19th century.

SWAN GARDEN BENCH
This garden bench with its simple board seat and back is transformed by the cast-iron ends formed in the shape of swans. There are traces of old white and orange paint and repainting in places. H:38 in (96.5 cm); W:72 in (183 cm); D:28 in (71 cm). BRU

Company into the preeminent manufacturer of garden furniture of the mid-19th century. Its most popular designs are still in production today. The process was an industrial one: iron was cast from molds in a variety of different shapes, and then pieced together to produce furniture of various styles. At the Great Exhibition in London in 1851, the company won a Council Medal, and Queen Victoria purchased a statue of Andromeda made by them. The centerpiece of Coalbrookdale's 1851 exhibit was its new range of Nasturtium chairs and benches, which epitomized garden furniture design of the period. The ironwork was elaborately pierced with floral designs and scrolling to give a Rococo look, yet the actual construction of the furniture was simple and suited to mass production.

RUSTIC FURNITURE

A vernacular tradition of handcrafted garden furniture persisted in tandem with the industrial cast iron aesthetic. Local craftsmen fashioned and sold basic wooden benches and chairs, as well as more elaborate novelty forms. Unfortunately, few examples now survive due to wood's tendency to rot, especially when exposed to the elements. In the United States, a celebrated form of rustic timber furniture started to gain popularity in the later part of the 19th century. Named for the mountain range—now a national park—in upstate New York from which it originates, Adirondack furniture used native timbers, such as oak, cherry, butternut, birch, and walnut, and often included the bark. It echoed the local Great Camp style of architecture in that it assimilated the natural contours of the branches and roots from which it was fashioned.

KEW GARDENS

MORE THAN 300 YEARS IN THE MAKING, THE ROYAL BOTANIC GARDENS AT KEW ARE THE CULMINATION OF EFFORTS BY DOZENS OF ENGINEERS, SCIENTISTS, AND GARDENERS.

The first gardens at Kew Park were laid out by the Capel family during the late 17th century. In 1772, George III inherited the Gardens from his mother and, by the end of the 18th century, many of the monuments and buildings familiar to generations of visitors were in place. The development of the Royal Botanic Gardens at Kew coincided with a revival of interest in Classicism, itself a consequence of the vogue among the landed classes to go on the Grand Tour. Expeditions by botanists throughout Britain's expanding Empire unearthed myriad newly discovered plants, which were brought back and exhibited at the Gardens under the "kind superintendence" of Sir Joseph Banks, whom George III had established there in 1773. Banks, who became President of the Royal Society in 1778, established the Gardens as the

British center for economic botany. His death in 1820 coincided with George III's, and Kew Gardens lost its direction for 20 years.

Between 1841 and 1885, father and son William and Joseph Hooker held consecutive directorships of the Gardens and contrived a renaissance in its fortunes. Among the developments they oversaw were the construction of the iconic Palm House and the Temperate House—the largest surviving mid-19th-century glass structure in the world. William Nesfield, a watercolorist turned landscaper, designed a new arboretum for the Gardens as well as the cedar-lined Broad Walk and the *parterres* around the Palm House. The Victorian obsession with botany bequeathed the world an educational and recreational landmark—Kew Gardens became a World Heritage Site in 2003.

The Palm House This was built between 1844 and 1848 by Richard Turner, with Decimus Burton as architectural consultant. Light but strong wrought-iron "ship's beams" were used to create a vast 50-ft (15.2-m) open, pillarless span.

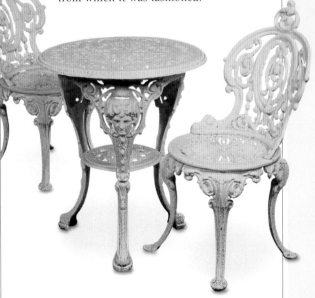

CAST-IRON GARDEN CHAIRS AND TABLE
Each of these chairs has a pierced scroll back and circular pierced seat on four scrolling legs. The table has a solid top and stands on three scrolling legs. There is a lady's mask at the top of each table leg. 1880. Chair: H:34 in (86 cm). L&T

ARTS AND CRAFTS

1880-1920

REFORM AND REACTION

THE INDUSTRIAL REVOLUTION TURNED THE WORLD UPSIDE
DOWN, BUT WHILE SOME REVELED IN URBAN PROSPERITY, OTHERS
YEARNED FOR A SIMPLER LIFE BASED ON TRADITIONAL VALUES.

IT IS DIFFICULT to overestimate the dramatic
changes in society that had come about by
the start of the 20th century. The Industrial
Revolution transformed Great Britain from a
land of rural husbandry to a highly mechanized
urban economy in less than a century. The
railroad, the telegraph, and later the telephone
effectively shrank the country and accelerated
the pace of life to a new, terrifying level.

THE SELF-MADE MAN
These social changes brought a new powerful
class to the fore—middle-class industrialists
who earned their prosperity, rather than
inheriting it. Urban life offered the opportunity
to "move up in the world." Consequently,
community spirit was often overridden by
a focus on individual success.

Gamble House, Pasadena, California
This house, including the furniture,
was designed by the architects Charles
and Henry Greene in 1908 for
David and Mary Gamble of the
Proctor & Gamble company.

THE DECLINE OF RURAL LIFE
Mechanization meant that the world of work
was no longer ruled by the changing seasons
or the setting of the sun. While cities and towns
became the centers of the new world, rural
communities became marginalized. Country
life was considered backward and inferior.

THE DESIRE FOR CHANGE
In a world that was spinning faster and faster,
eventually people began to demand a slowing
of pace and a return to the less mechanized
society of just a few generations before. Under
the tutelage of its founding father, William
Morris, the Arts and Crafts Movement used a
desire for the simplicity and craftsmanship of the
Middle Ages to reject the dehumanizing effects
of industrialization and mass production.
Morris and his followers
championed the revival of
traditional craftsmanship
and good-quality
materials, emphasizing
the importance of the
home and artistic,
individually crafted wares
as part of integrated
interior design.

Gustav Stickley vice cabinet
This piece has a hinged
lid, a single drawer, and
a lower cabinet. c. 1909.
H:24 in (61 cm). DRA

SPREADING FAR AND WIDE
The Arts and Crafts Movement soon became
highly influential, and its effect permeated
every area of design, from textiles to glass and
ceramics. Once Arts and Crafts designs became
known in the United States in the 1870s and
80s, American designers interpreted the style
in their own way, drawing inspiration from the
Shaker Movement and the crafts of the American
Indian nations. The American Movement
focused on the use of natural materials, and
houses were built from local wood and stone,
to blend in with the surrounding landscape.

Following the pioneering example of William
Morris, architects, designers, artists, and
craftsmen around the world adopted variations
of the Arts and Crafts style, in the spirit of
social and artistic reform. Ultimately, the
success of the Arts and Crafts Movement itself
was relatively short-lived in Great Britain,
because the designers' insistence on handcrafted
furnishings proved prohibitively expensive.
However, by promoting the revival of traditional
handicrafts, a return to simple, honest social
values, and the importance of art and beautiful
objects in everyday life, the Arts and Crafts
Movement set the stage for the far-reaching
design movements that followed during the 20th
century, from Art Deco to Modernism.

TIMELINE 1880–1920

Richard Wagner

1881 William Morris
sets up his Merton
Abbey Works.
1882 A.H. Mackmurdo
founds the Century
Guild. Richard
Wagner's last opera
Parsifal is staged.
1883 Arthur Lazenby
Liberty opens his retail emporium in
London. Brooklyn Bridge completed in New
York. Fabian Society founded in London.

First underground train
(Tube) runs in London.
1884 Henri de Toulouse-
Lautrec settles in
Montmartre in Paris,
where he paints and
draws cabaret stars,
prostitutes, barmaids,
and clowns.

Poster by Toulouse-Lautrec
This poster promotes a Paris
appearance of the Irish
performer May Belfort. *1895*

1887–89 Arts and
Crafts Exhibition Society
founded, with Walter
Crane as its first
president. The Eiffel
Tower is designed and
erected for the Paris
Exhibition of 1889.
1888 C. R. Ashbee
forms the Guild of
Handicraft in the East
End of London.

1890 William Morris establishes the
Kelmscott Press, producing handmade
books using handmade paper, in line
with his philosophy.
1890–91 Louis Sullivan designs the
Wainwright Building in St. Louis.
1893 *The Studio* magazine started by
Charles Holme. World Exhibition held
in Chicago.
1895 Sino-Japanese War. Marconi
invents radio telegraphy.

Morris and Co. ebonized-walnut armchair The chair has a reclining back, turned spindle sides and stretchers, curved back legs, and upholstered arms and cushions. *c. 1865. H:36¼ in (92 cm).*

Interior of Wightwick Manor, Staffordshire, England This manor, designed by Edward Ould, was furnished in the Arts and Crafts style. The house contains many Morris wallpaper and fabric designs.

William Morris

1896 William Morris dies.

1896 Spanish-American War. First modern Olympics held in Athens.

1897 The first Arts and Crafts Exhibition in Boston. Paris Metro opens.

1901 Gustav Stickley publishes his *Craftsman* magazine. Frank Lloyd Wright addresses the Arts and Crafts Society in Chicago with a speech on "The Art and Craft of the Machine."

1902 The Guild of Handicraft moves to the Cotswolds.

1903 First flight by the Wright Brothers.

Plate from Omega Workshops

1905 Architect Hermann Muthesius publishes his three-volume *Das Englische Haus* on English housing and design.

1908 Ford produces the first Model T car in the United States.

1913 The Omega Workshops, the last of the Arts and Crafts groups, established by Roger Fry in Bloomsbury, London.

1914 World War I begins.

1915 A German U-boat sinks the

R.M.S. Lusitania

passenger liner *Lusitania* in the Irish Sea.

1918 Lytton Strachey publishes his landmark biography *Eminent Victorians*.

ARTS AND CRAFTS STYLE

LAMENTING THE INFERIOR quality of mass-produced furniture and the abandonment of handcraft skills, a new generation of architects and craftsmen aimed to create soundly constructed furniture by hand, using fine materials in solid, simple forms that were both attractive and functional. Inspired by the ideas of William Morris (*see pp.332–33*) and the writer John Ruskin, furniture-makers created a new style that was as much a social statement as an artistic one, championing the individual craftsman and rejecting the mechanized world of the late 19th century.

The new movement was named after the Arts and Crafts Exhibition Society, one of a number of groups promoting a return to traditional skills. Many of the furniture-makers who adopted the style originally trained as architects. This was key to the creation of Arts and Crafts furniture, in which simplicity was paramount, and designers let the materials and techniques of cabinet-making dictate shape and decoration. High-backed chairs, rectangular benches, square cabinets-on-stands, desks, and bookcases all reflected architectural influences.

With an emphasis on the vernacular, oak was the favored wood. The distinctive grain and finish of the wood was appreciated for its natural beauty. Elaborate metal hardware, such as hand-hammered strap hinges and drop handles, was used as ornamental features on cupboards and cabinets. Cut-out patterns in the shapes of hearts, rectangles, and circles were another distinctive feature, as were elaborately turned stretchers and seat rails, and deliberately exposed construction details, such as mortise-and-tenon joints or corbels.

AN ADAPTABLE STYLE

The furniture was not exclusively vernacular, and many designers produced fine-quality pieces for their wealthy clientele. Richer woods—mahogany, walnut, satinwood, and ebony—were used and often enhanced with exquisite inlays of ivory, silver, mother-of-pearl, and colorful fruitwoods.

Although essentially a British movement, interpretations of the style varied between countries. However, the unifying principle was a distrust of industrialization and mass production.

In the United States, the ideals promoted by Ruskin and Morris were translated into a more robust version of Arts and Crafts furniture. American craftsmen created solid oak furniture in rectilinear forms that mirrored the very best of British craftsmanship and design. However, unlike their British counterparts, American furniture-makers valued the role of the machine in manufacturing their designs, and they used mechanized processes to produce chairs, cabinets, and cupboards in the Arts and Crafts style.

An occasional table Made of mahogany, this table has an octagonal top above three twin tapering supports linked by a lower tier. H:27½ in (69 cm). L&

THE AESTHETIC MOVEMENT

The Aesthetic Movement that developed in the 1870s coincided with the Arts and Crafts Movement and also aimed to produce well-designed, fine-quality furniture. Considering beauty as more important than practicality, in striking contrast to the Victorian taste for clutter, Aesthetic designers were influenced by the stark simplicity of Japanese designs rendered in dark woods with minimal decoration and arranged in pale, uncluttered interiors.

ENDURING IDEALS

Although by the late 1920s, Arts and Crafts furniture had fallen from favor, simple, practical design, good construction, and native materials remained popular features in furniture design until World War II. The Arts and Crafts style was rediscovered in the 1970s by collectors who appreciated elegant simplicity, fine materials, and handcrafted design. The influence of this revolutionary, idealistic movement continues to be felt today.

Late Victorian kneehole desk This desk has an ebonized finish and parcel-gilt decoration in the Aesthetic Movement style. The top has a molded edge above nine mahogany-lined drawers. The desk once belonged to Edward Austen Knight, brother of the novelist Jane Austen. c. 1880. W:48 in (122 cm). DN

A music cabinet This cabinet was made by C. R. Ashbee for The Guild of Handicraft. It is made from pine and has elaborate brass hardware and a Moorish-style cut-out base. c. 1899. H:49 in (124 cm). CR

CRAFTSMEN'S GUILDS

The medieval concept of the craftsmen's guild, which formed a cornerstone of the Arts and Crafts philosophy, flourished in the last two decades of the 19th century. Recognizing that artists working on their own could not effect meaningful change, a burgeoning number of groups emerged that championed the Arts and Crafts ideals. The first guild to be founded was A. H. Mackmurdo's Century Guild; other influential guilds that followed were the Art Worker's Guild and C. R. Ashbee's Guild of Handicraft, founded in 1888.

Craftsmen at work This photograph was taken in the Guild of Handicraft's metalwork shop at Essex House. The guild moved to Chipping Campden in 1902.

THE STICKLEY CHAIR

In the 19th century, the rocking chair enjoyed enormous popularity in the United States. Both stylish and functional, it was enthusiastically adopted by American Arts and Crafts furniture-designers such as Gustav Stickley, who produced many rocking chairs at his Craftsman Workshops, including this example.

Made of quarter-sawn oak, it boasts a time-worn, fumed surface finish and a lustrous dark patina. These effects were created by applying chemicals that reacted with the wood.

This rocking chair is an ideal prototype of the Arts and Crafts philosophy, which aimed to produce well-made, sturdy, and comfortable furniture by hand, and was often based on traditional designs.

Leather upholstery for drop-in seats and cushions, and construction features used for decorative effect such as exposed tenons, vertical slats, and short corbels beneath the flat chair arms, typically highlight Stickley's Craftsman furniture.

The top back slat is pinned to the back upright for added strength and visual beauty.

The seat is covered in padded leather for comfort and support.

The front leg support ends in a tenon through the front of each arm, serving both as supporting joinery and decorative detail.

Side slats between the arms and seats were a hallmark of Stickley's designs. These, like the rest of the chair, are covered with a rich, fumed finish.

Gustav Stickley Arts and Crafts rocker *(no. 323)* The chair has five vertical slats and short corbels beneath flat arms. The finish is original, although color has been added to the tops of the arms, and the leather upholstery has been replaced. The chair is branded on the back stretcher. *c. 1880–1920.* H:40 in (101 cm). DRA

ELEMENTS OF STYLE

Traditional materials, fine craftsmanship, and attention to detail were all key features of the Arts and Crafts philosophy, and this was reflected in the furniture. Most pieces were essentially simple in structure and their beauty relied partly on the intrinsic color, warmth, and fine grain of high-quality woods such as oak or mahogany, often enhanced with decorative cutouts, carved designs, and bold marquetry or inlays of contrasting timbers. Details of construction, such as hardware and joints, were frequently exposed or even exaggerated to form decorative features in their own right, and upholstery was covered with rich, specially designed textiles inspired by nature.

Marquetry detail

Marquetry

Since they believed that the inherent beauty of the wood was sufficient decoration in itself, Arts and Crafts furniture craftsmen used marquetry sparingly. They rejected elaborate designs and exotic materials such as metals, ivory, and bone in favor of simple wood veneers, which detracted from neither the purpose of the piece nor its beauty.

Exposed tenon

Exposed construction

Arts and Crafts furniture-makers strongly believed that part of the beauty of an object was to be found in the way it was made. Construction features that would normally be concealed, such as mortise-and-tenon and butterfly joints, exposed or keyed tenons, pegs, dovetails, and corbel supports, were turned into decorative features in their own right.

Mahogany occasional table

Handcrafted pieces

William Morris was opposed to mechanical production, believing that it lowered the standard of furniture-making. Handcrafted furniture, often based on traditional vernacular forms, became a hallmark of the Arts and Crafts Movement.

Machine-turned table legs

Machine processes

Not all Arts and Crafts designers, particularly those in the United States, believed that furniture should be entirely handcrafted. Steam-powered machinery was used not only to make cutting, sawing, and planing easier, but also to create various decorative elements, such as carved work, veneers, and turning.

***Pietra dura* decoration**

Oriental motifs

The Aesthetic Movement celebrated art for art's sake and the sophisticated techniques discovered in designs created by Japanese artisans. Oriental-inspired asymmetric designs and subtle colors featuring flowers, birds, and insects embellished not only textiles but also furniture, including oak and mahogany tables and cabinets.

etail of a chair back

apanese influence

Designers of the Aesthetic Movement were much inspired by the Japanese ceramics, lacquers, metalwork, and extiles that they saw at international xhibitions. Impressed by the implicity, geometry, and abstraction of apanese pieces and the high standard f craftsmanship, Aesthetic designers used Oriental motifs in their work and trove to emulate Japanese design.

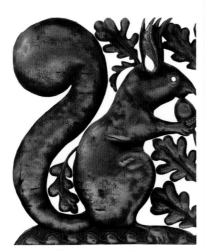

Squirrel motif on a brass fender

Traditional metalwork

Machines could not compete with the finely wrought, complex, pierced designs for handcrafted metal wares, including furniture fittings and fire dogs, which were created by Arts and Crafts designers. Nature was the most important source of inspiration, and the plant and animal motifs were often influenced by medieval stonework, plasterwork, and ironwork.

Strap hinges

Handcrafted hardware

Exposed metal hinges, usually made of copper or brass, were inspired by medieval furniture. Strap hinges were used to add abstract, understated decorative motifs. The hinges were frequently hand-hammered to illustrate construction techniques, and the metal was sometimes chemically treated to produce a rich patina, as if weathered by time.

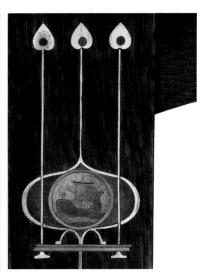

Exotic inlay on a table leg

Rich inlays

More sumptuous pieces were inlaid with designs using colorful exotic woods, leather, or metals such as copper and pewter, set against a background of maple, solid or veneered oak, or mahogany. Such designs brought a light, sophisticated dimension to the rather heavy and ponderous, but nonetheless well-constructed, Arts and Crafts style.

arved detail of an oak leaf

Carved wood

While Arts and Crafts designers ejected elaborate carving, sturdy, olid, and relatively simple furniture vas frequently "signed" with a single, eeply carved decorative motif, such s a flower-head, a simple pattern of n oak leaf, or the mouse used as a ignature in later years by the vorkshop of Robert Thompson.

Detail of oak corbel

Wood grain

Arts and Crafts cabinet-makers accentuated the grain of woods to decorative effect. Oak was particularly appreciated for its natural beauty, its rich, warm color, and the pleasing quality of its grain. In the United States, quarter oak was favored: its tiger-striped figuring became a feature of American Arts and Crafts.

Morris & Co. "Compton" printed cotton

Stylized nature

William Morris's rediscovery of vegetable dyes and his handmade block-printed wallpapers and fabrics inspired Arts and Crafts designers to produce bold patterns in rich, natural colors for upholstery, curtains, wall hangings, and wallpaper. The designs were often based on stylized, interlacing wildflowers, leaves, birds, and animals.

Heart motif

Vernacular traditions

Most Arts and Crafts designers sought inspiration in traditional country furniture and tended to shun elaborate embellishments on their designs. Simple shapes cut out of the wood that formed chair backs and table supports were a common feature. Hearts were a popular motif, but squares, circles, and trefoils were also used.

BRITAIN: THE AESTHETIC MOVEMENT

AESTHETICISM, THE BELIEF that art and beauty were to be pursued for their own sake, became the foundation of the Aesthetic Movement, which developed during the 1870s and 80s. It gained support from designers who were reacting against the dark, cluttered interiors popular with many Victorians.

The Aesthetic Movement was essentially a British phenomenon, although it did inspire some American designers. It had much in common with the Arts and Crafts Movement with which it overlapped, but it was not concerned with the social and moral values of art.

Many of the theories of Aesthetic design had been set out during the preceding two decades by the British designers Owen Jones and Christopher Dresser. They believed that nature, combined with the best designs from disparate cultures and periods, should be reworked and blended into a new harmonious whole.

THE JAPANESE STYLE

Museum collections and exhibitions all provided design inspiration for the Movement. Great Britain had already been introduced to Japanese art in 1862, and this had a huge influence on Aestheticism. Visitors were

captivated by the simple furnishings in uncluttered, light-colored settings.

E. W. Godwin, the most innovative designer of the Aesthetic Movement, adapted Japanese decorative and architectural elements into his Anglo-Japanese furniture, which was often ebonized to resemble Asian lacquer furniture. Designs comprised symmetrical arrangements of horizontal and vertical lines, and decoration was restrained.

Manufacturers of cheaper furniture applied decorative Japanese fretwork to standard shapes, especially bedroom

furniture. More expensive pieces featured embossed-leather paper panels or sections of carved boxwood and geometric marquetry.

Asian design forms were Westernized, while Western forms were orientalized, often with Japanese motifs such as dragonflies or fans.

The 1870 International Exhibition in London introduced the Aesthetic Movement to a wider audience. Design objects were soon sold through shops such as Liberty & Co., while furniture could be seen in showrooms such as Morris & Co. in London. Word also

EBONIZED CHAIR

This chair has a beaded top rail and stylized foliate tops on the fluted uprights. The cross rail has turned bobbins and the front supports have wreathed and turned banding. The back and seat are upholstered. *DN*

REVOLVING CHAIR

This mahogany chair, by James Pedal and attributed to E. W. Godwin, has a curved back with fine slats. The curved shape of the seat is echoed in the legs below. *c. 1881.* *H:34 in (86.5 cm). PUR*

ROSEWOOD CABINET

This fine-quality rosewood and calamander cabinet was made by furniture manufacturers Collinson & Lock, and designed by the architect T. E. Collcutt. The top has a gallery pierced with trefoils and vaulted side sections.

There are quarter-circular open shelves to both sides of the central fielded panel cupboard, which is supported on turned columns. The base has a further fielded panel cupboard with Aesthetic brass door furniture, and open shelving on both sides. *1870–80.* *W:62¼ in (158 cm). DN*

CORNER CABINET

This walnut, ebonized, and gilt corner cabinet is by Gillows of Lancaster, designed by Bruce Talbert. A single drawer is set above a door with inset and gilt-tooled leather panels and flanked by open shelves. The cabinet is raised on turned and tapering legs. *1870–80. H:37¾ in (96 cm). L&T*

pread through interior decorating anuals such as Charles Locke astlake's *Hints on Household Taste*.

OTHER DESIGN STYLES
nspiration also came from Classical nd Moorish sources, as well as acobean and Gothic furniture. The othic style was popularized by the cottish designer Bruce Talbert. Called rt Furniture, it was often ebonized, ith decorative moldings, painted anels, inlays, and mirror-backed to eflect the objects displayed.

By the mid-1870s, the Queen Anne tyle was in vogue. Furniture became ore delicate with finer detailing.

New materials became fashionable, including rattan and cast-iron, and designers mixed media, incorporating painted or *cloisonné* panels, ceramic tiles, or stamped leatherwork into the furniture.

The typical Aesthetic interior consisted of Art Furniture placed among Japanese-style pieces such as embroidered textiles, vases and fans, and displays of peacock feathers.

Metalwork details are typical embellishments on Anglo-Japanese furniture.

The lacquer and ivory panels reflect the Japanese Shibayama style.

The writing surface is inlaid with tooled leather.

Glazed doors reveal interior shelves.

An elaborate H-stretcher joins the legs.

Slender legs and stretchers and decorative fretwork provide an Oriental flavor.

WALL CLOCK

his wall clock contains many elements ssociated with Aesthetic Movement furniture, cluding the dark finish, galleried shelves, nd fine spindle supports. *c. 1880.* H:32 in 81 cm). TDG

WRITING CABINET

The influence of Japan is clearly evident in this mahogany writing cabinet by Gillows. The *Shibayama*-style ivory panels are inlaid with a picture of a warrior and flowering branches. The molded top has a pierced, silvered gallery.

The upper section has glazed doors and sides and typical drop handles above a slide-out writing surface inlaid with tooled leather. The drawer is stamped "Gillow & Co. 1668" and bears the maker's label. *c. 1880.* H:51½ in (131 cm). L&T

AMERICA: AESTHETICISM AND REVIVALS

THE ENTHUSIASM FOR Japanese art that inspired Great Britain's Aesthetic movement crossed the Atlantic in the 1870s. Philadelphia hosted an international exhibition in 1876, where a Japanese Bazaar helped fuel American interest in Japanese design.

Japanese design and motifs seemed to particularly inspire various furniture designers around New York; the firm of A. & H. Lejambre was an enthusiastic exponent of the Anglo-Japanese style.

Luxurious materials and expert craftsmanship were the cornerstones of American Aesthetic furniture. One of the most influential champions of the American Movement during the 1870s and 80s was Herter Brothers. It produced superbly crafted, well-designed Art Furniture with a discreet Oriental influence, and catered to a wealthy clientele.

RENAISSANCE REVIVAL

Herter Brothers was also renowned for its furniture in the Renaissance Revival style—exuberant carving was a hallmark of its work. Other makers associated with this revival style include Berkey & Gay of Michigan and Prudent Mallard of New Orleans.

Renaissance Revival furniture was generally built on a large scale and combined rectilinear shapes with Neoclassical motifs such as veneered panels and columns. Walnut was commonly used, with ash or pine favored for less expensive pieces. Chairs and sofas were upholstered with silk or woolen fabrics decorated with symmetrical Neoclassical designs.

Mass-production, and the trend for designers to combine historic styles in their own experimental way, created numerous revival movements in the late 19th century. Although the Rococo Revival was on the wane, the Gothic Revival continued to inspire designers such as Frank Furnace. The style took decorative elements such as Gothic

CHURCH PEW

This oak church pew designed by Frank Furnace has molded armrests, with turned supports and applied geometric design, enclosing a simple plank seat and back. *c. 1870–80. FRE*

Geometric carving

SIDE CHAIRS

These chairs (a pair) are made from inlaid and parcel-gilt ebonized wood, with upholstered seats. They have molded, rectangular top rails, with three inlaid-and-gilt panels, above fret-carved splats.

TIFFANY STAND

This Tiffany & Co. bronze stand has a circular top centered with a medallion relief decorated with Classical figures. The piece is raised on three ribbed legs, and the base is accented with scroll-and-leaf decoration. *Early 20th century. H:31½ in (80 cm). SK*

The back panels are upholstered in red leather.

Brass studs provide a decorative edging to the upholstery.

Carved mask detail   **Detail of arm support**

Neoclassical motifs, such as columns, were very popular on Herter Brothers furniture.

HERTER BROTHERS SOFA

The turned frame of this elaborate, large sofa is heavily carved with female masks and musical instruments on the top rail, reflecting the Renaissance style. The apron is decorated with a Greek key motif. The three back panels and the seat are upholstered in red leather. The sofa stands on eight short, bulbous legs. *1870–90.*

rches, tracery, quatrefoils, and trefoils o create a medieval look on ashstands, cabinets, and bookcases.

MOORISH CRAZE

he enthusiasm for the exotic Moorish tyle of the 1880s and 90s—also revalent in Great Britain—was opularized in the US by Tiffany & Co. s furniture was simple in shape but ith prolific decoration and had typical Moorish features such as horseshoe rches and delicate floral inlays.

Louis Comfort Tiffany, like other xponents of the Aesthetic style, was nspired by a variety of cultures and eriods. He also shared the Arts and

Crafts Movement's appreciation of fine craftsmanship. These influences can be seen in the interiors of Mark Twain House in Hartford, Connecticut, which Tiffany and his company, Associated Artists, helped to decorate.

COLONIAL REVIVAL

The Colonial Revival style was also in vogue after 1876. Inspired by the United States' colonial heritage, it reintroduced furniture styles popular in the 18th century. These tended to be narrower and more delicate than the originals, and included pieces such as gateleg tables and carver chairs made in oak, mahogany, and walnut.

COTTAGE STYLE

At the same time, Cottage style furnishings in simple, painted pine became popular with the working classes.

Eastlake furniture, the American version of Art furniture, was prevalent during the 1880s and 90s, with its rectilinear forms, spindled galleries, and turned uprights.

Renaissance-inspired decoration was also fashionable and appeared on furniture made by firms such as John Jelliffe.

DISPLAY CABINET

This elegant cabinet is made of mahogany. Two winged, mythical creatures adorn the top above a large alcove decorated with a carved shell motif. Open shelving flanks the central section, featuring mirrored panels, galleried shelves, and columnar supports. The lower section is decorated with stained glass.

CHARLES LOCKE EASTLAKE

THE WRITINGS OF ENGLISH ARCHITECT CHARLES LOCKE EASTLAKE HELPED TO SHIFT FASHION AWAY FROM OVERLY ORNATE INTERIORS IN FAVOR OF FURNISHINGS WITH SIMPLE DESIGN AND QUALITY CRAFTSMANSHIP.

Born in Plymouth, England, Charles Locke Eastlake studied architecture before turning to journalism. In 1868, he wrote the famous *Hints on Household Taste in Furniture, Upholstery and Other Details* based on articles he had initially written for the *Cornhill Magazine* and *The Queen*. *Hints* became a popular and influential handbook, and featured Gothic-inspired decoration and design as championed by architect-designers such as George Edmund Street and Norman Shaw.

The hallmarks of Eastlake's design philosophy— honesty of materials and construction, rectilinear forms, ornament, and sharp geometric patterns—were instrumental in driving Victorian fashions from favor, but found even greater success in the United States, where six editions of *Hints* appeared between 1872 and 1879. The American Eastlake style for furnishings—said to be "Eastlaked"—had the same rectilinear forms as the English version but was more ornate, using materials such as ebonized cherrywood and drawing on a range of Moorish, Arabic, and Asian styles. As such, it often bore

little relation to Eastlake's own principles and instead came to be associated with a mass-produced, shabby version of Gothic Revival taste.

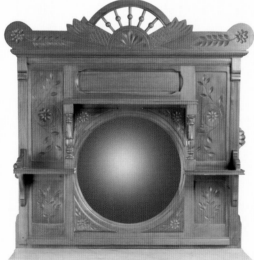

TRIPOD TABLE

This *pietra dura* tripod table has a circular top with an inlaid floral spray and molded edges. The top rests on cluster-columns, which are mounted on turned, splayed feet. *H:30 in (77 cm). S&K*

An Eastlake walnut and burr-walnut side cabinet This cabinet has a white marble top and has three frieze drawers. The four central drawers are flanked by narrow cupboards with molded decoration on the doors. *H:54 in (137 cm). S&K*

An Eastlake carved walnut *chiffonier* The upper section of this *chiffonier* has a circular mirror and three open shelves. Below the marble top are three drawers over two paneled doors. *c. 1880. H:81¾ in (207.5 cm). S&K*

BRITAIN: ARTS AND CRAFTS

THE ARTS AND CRAFTS Movement believed that good design could change and improve people's daily lives. Inspired by the example set by William Morris (*see pp.332–33*), Arts and Crafts designers endeavored to breathe new life into traditional methods of craftsmanship and to produce functional furniture that was simple in design and true to the materials used.

Morris based his social and aesthetic philosophy largely on the medieval ideal, which celebrated the role of the craftsman and the establishment of workers' guilds. A number of Arts and Crafts guilds were set up in Great Britain in the 1880s, including Ruskin's short-lived St. George's Guild; A. H. Mackmurdo's Century Guild, whose craftsmen designed houses as well as furnishings in a collaborative spirit; C. R. Ashbee's Guild of Handicraft (*see p.335*); and the Art Workers' Guild, which brought together artists, architects, designers, and craftsmen in the name of decorative unity.

Much Arts and Crafts furniture was austere, architectural in form, and had little surface decoration. It often incorporated exposed constructional features into the design—beautifully cut dovetails, for instance, enhanced the natural beauty of the wood—while striking grain effects or figured wooden panels were considered decoration enough. Strong vertical and horizontal lines reflected the movement's emphasis on simplicity and fitness for purpose.

Gold-tooled leather

CABINET-ON-STAND

This cabinet was designed by C. R. Ashbee and made by the Guild of Handicraft. The plain sycamore case rests on a stand made of walnut. Inside the cabinet are cedar drawers with gold, tooled Morocco leather. The sharp contrast between the interior and exterior was inspired by the Spanish *vargueño* and Ashbee employed this to great effect in a number of his cabinet designs. The cabinet's wrought-iron fittings were probably added after 1906.
c. 1905. H:54¾ in (139.2 cm); W:42¼ in (107.2 cm); D:24¾ in (63.2 cm).

The plain oak exterior is contrasted with a painted red interior.

Long metalwork strap hinges are used for decoration.

An open stand supports the cabinet.

The legs are joined by stretchers.

KELMSCOTT OAK CABINET

This oak cabinet was designed by C. F. A. Voysey to hold *The Kelmscott Chaucer*, as illustrated by the metal lettering on the front. Further decoration comes from the large metalwork strap hinges. *c. 1890.*

Fabric detail

WALNUT ARMCHAIR

This walnut armchair, designed by E. Punnet, has slatted sides and a solid bow-front seat. The shaped back is decorated with a stylized heart cutout. The back is upholstered in a floral and foliate textile. *c. 1903.* H:32 in (82 cm). PUR

LEADING DESIGNERS

Key designers such as Ernest Gimson, C. R. Ashbee, Charles Rennie Mackintosh, and C. F. A. Voysey were also architects and so were able to approach their work in an integrated style. Like their Aesthetic counterparts, Arts and Crafts designers borrowed extensively from other cultures and periods: Japanese design, Celtic and medieval motifs, and even Indian carpets were used. Symbolism also played an important role, and motifs such as hearts often featured in their work.

Key furniture associated with Arts and Crafts interiors include medieval pieces such as settles, dressers, long tables, and benches. These all reflected the movement's ideal of the home and communal living.

Morris & Co.'s version of a light, adaptable Sussex chair inspired many Arts and Crafts designers to come up with variations such as simple rush seats and ladderback chairs.

POPULAR IMITATIONS

Although the furniture made by the Arts and Crafts Movement was intended to be "good citizen's furniture" aimed at the middle classes, the handcrafted pieces were often prohibitively expensive. Responding to a need for affordable, fashionable furnishings, British firms such as Heal's and Liberty & Co. produced popular imitations of Arts and Crafts furniture. However, while they brought a diluted version to a wider public, these companies ultimately contributed to the demise of the guilds and hastened the decline of the Arts and Crafts Movement.

OAK SETTLE

This oak revival piece is paneled on the front and sides. The arms are open with horizontal slats, as is the back rest on which flowering plants are carved. The piece is supported on four block feet. The charm of the traditional oak settle captivated William Morris, who instigated its revival in the late 19th century. *c. 1900. H:42 in (107 cm); W:43 in (111 cm). L&T*

LIBERTY & CO.

ESTABLISHED IN 1875, THE CUTTING-EDGE STORE LIBERTY & CO. MET THE DEMAND FOR AFFORDABLE ARTS AND CRAFTS-STYLE FURNITURE.

Arthur Lazenby Liberty, founder of the pioneering London department store Liberty & Co., recognized the commercial potential of Art furnishings, and in 1883, established a Furnishing and Decorating workshop under the direction of Leonard F. Wyburd. Charged with supplying affordable furniture for fashionable interiors, Wyburd developed a style that married commercial concerns with the Arts and Crafts design vocabulary. Liberty's cabinet-making studio borrowed liberally from renowned Arts and Crafts designers, turning out a range of clean-lined chairs and country-style oak and mahogany furniture, often with elaborate strap hinges and metal handles, inlaid decoration, and leaded glass panels.

By 1900, Liberty & Co. was celebrated across the globe as a leader in the production of artistic yet moderately priced furniture in the fashionable Arts and Crafts style.

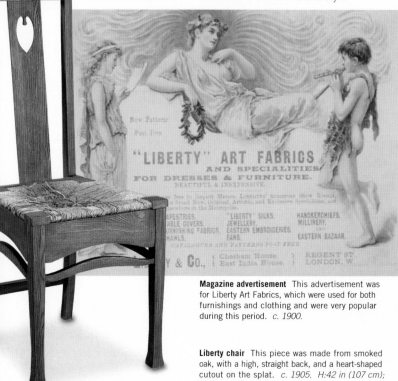

Magazine advertisement This advertisement was for Liberty Art Fabrics, which were used for both furnishings and clothing and were very popular during this period. *c. 1900.*

Liberty chair This piece was made from smoked oak, with a high, straight back, and a heart-shaped cutout on the splat. *c. 1905. H:42 in (107 cm); W:17 in (45 cm); D:14 in (37 cm).*

OAK TABLE

This sturdy oak table has a circular, molded top and heart-shaped piercings on its four tapering supports. It is linked by cross-stretchers with exposed pegs. *c. 1900. H:26 in (67 cm). L&T*

HALL CHAIR

This early C. F. A. Voysey chair has five vertical back slats, paddle arms, and tapering legs and back posts. This rare piece has a burgundy leather seat and retains its original dark finish. *c. 1895. H:55 in (140 cm); W:27 in (68.5 cm).*

WILLIAM MORRIS & CO.

THE FOUNDING FATHER OF THE ARTS AND CRAFTS MOVEMENT, WILLIAM MORRIS EXTOLLED THE VIRTUES OF TRADITIONAL SKILLS IN THE QUEST TO PRODUCE SIMPLE, WELL-MADE OBJECTS.

ONE OF THE MOST prolific designers of the late 19th century, William Morris took a stand against the low standards of mechanical production methods and the decline of time-honored craftsmanship. He campaigned for the revival of traditional skills and aimed to create quality, handcrafted objects that were both useful and pleasing to the eye. With a team of artist friends, including Dante Gabriel Rossetti, Edward Burne-Jones, Ford Madox Brown, and Philip Webb—who had designed, built, and furnished Morris's Red House in Kent—Morris and his design firm, Morris, Marshall, Faulkner & Company, promoted integrated decorative schemes influenced by medieval ideals, which made extensive use of local and natural materials and traditional crafts.

EARLY INFLUENCES
Trained as an architect, Morris first designed furniture for the rooms he shared with Edward Burne-Jones at 17 Red Lion Square in London. His most inspired designs, such as the early Throne chairs painted with scenes of Sir Galahad, featured narrative themes that were drawn from nature or from the romantic legends of the Middle Ages. Popular in the 1860s, this type of painted furniture, which reflected the influence of William Burges and was an early example of Morris's more formal furniture, featured in the company's display at the International Exhibition of 1862. Other sources of inspiration included 17th-century furniture and Oriental woodwork.

Morris believed that there were two distinct types of furniture: practical everyday furniture and grander, more formal furniture. The former needed to be solid, well made, and well proportioned. The latter was intended for more important rooms and had to be useful as well as aesthetically pleasing, with carving and inlaid or painted decoration to make it more elaborate and elegant.

From 1861, Philip Webb worked exclusively for the Morris firm, creating furniture that was monumental and sturdy, and featured exposed joints and hinges. Webb favored plain oak, often stained green or black but occasionally decorated with painting, gesso work, or lacquered leather. His early enthusiasm for Gothic design eventually gave way to other influences, such as the Queen Anne and Japanese styles.

THE LONDON WORKSHOPS
Furniture made up a significant portion of the Morris, Marshall, Faulkner & Company business, and as the company became more successful, it moved to larger workshops in London. In 1875, it became Morris & Co., and produced stained glass, as well as

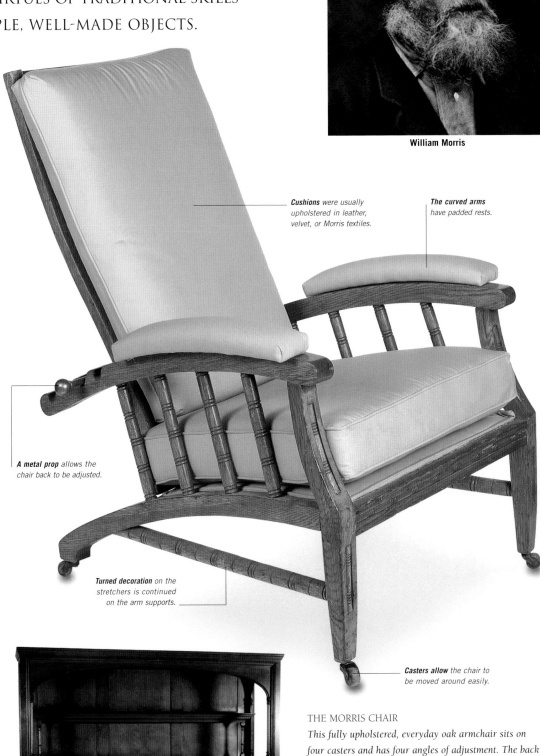

William Morris

Cushions were usually upholstered in leather, velvet, or Morris textiles.

The curved arms have padded rests.

A metal prop allows the chair back to be adjusted.

Turned decoration on the stretchers is continued on the arm supports.

Casters allow the chair to be moved around easily.

THE MORRIS CHAIR
This fully upholstered, everyday oak armchair sits on four casters and has four angles of adjustment. The back legs and arms curve in parallel and are united by turned spindles. 1890. H:40 in (101 cm). GS

WALNUT SIDEBOARD
The plain solid top has fluted details, with arched pane supported by turned, knopped columns. The three frieze drawers, with field panels and cupboards below, have t original brass drop pulls. The piece was designed by Phil Webb. c. 1890. W:61 in (156 cm). DN

MORRIS TEXTILES

MORRIS REDEFINED DOMESTIC INTERIORS BY CREATING DISTINCTIVE TEXTILE DESIGNS IN VIBRANT COLORS, WHICH ARE STILL HIGHLY SOUGHT-AFTER TODAY.

Throughout his life William Morris was fascinated by textiles, considering them to be an essential part of the decoration and comfort of a home. Dismissing machine-made fabrics as mediocre and uninspiring, his love of pattern and textures led him to experiment from the beginning of his career with the design and techniques of textile production. His experiments with natural vegetable and animal dyes produced "aesthetic" colors, such as madder red,

"Tulip and Rose" textile design by William Morris
The design was registered on January 20, 1876.
H:37 in (94 cm); W:33 in (84 cm). Wrob

peacock blue, russet brown, soft yellow, and sage green, which brought his intricate plant-based designs to life.

Morris & Co. produced textiles with a highly individual style, based on flat, well-balanced, and integrated patterns of intertwined flowers, fruits, and foliage—roses, honeysuckles, tulips, strawberries, pomegranates, acanthus, and ivy—as well as bird and animal motifs in a palette of rich, glowing hues. Although he sought inspiration from the past and was enamored of art and cultures from around the world, Morris created a range of fresh, modern designs that significantly influenced the work of a number of textile designers working in the Arts and Crafts style.

Morris & Co. grew in reputation and successfully fulfilled the middle-class demand for fashionable and stylish furnishings. Its woven and printed textiles—made of wool, cotton, linen, hand-woven silk, and sometimes embellished with delicate embroidery—were used for upholstery, as well as for curtains, wall panels, wallpapers, carpets, and tapestries. Morris's textiles paved the way for a lighter, cleaner style of furnishing that finally superseded the Victorian penchant for heavy drapery and upholstery in dark colors.

Three-fold draft screen This screen is made from mahogany with floral panels in colored silkwork. The top is shaped and surmounted by finials with a pierced frieze at the base. c. 1890. H:74 in (187 cm). L&T

SETTEE DESIGNED BY GEORGE JACK FOR MORRIS & CO.
This piece has an upholstered back, seat, and armrests in fabric featuring a design of intertwined flowers. The chair has open-rod sides and turned supports terminating in casters. c. 1900. 37 in (94 cm). PUR

sturdy furniture crafted in oak or occasionally in mahogany with satinwood inlay decoration, authenticated with the "Morris & Co." stamp.

The Sussex chair took pride of place among the everyday designs. Based on a traditional country chair, Webb's 1880s design had an ash frame with a handwoven rush seat and turned, vertical spindles, but was reproduced with an ebonized finish in various forms, including an armchair, corner chair, and settee. Other designs with lasting appeal were the spindle-backed Rossetti chair and the Morris chair.

THE LATER YEARS

Morris & Co. moved to Merton Abbey in 1881. When the American George Jack was appointed chief designer in 1890, the furniture shifted toward a more sophisticated taste. Jack favored 18th-century furniture design and introduced more exotic woods, such as walnut and mahogany. Large buffets and dressers were now embellished with marquetry in sumptuous woods, glazed doors, and pierced carving.

Morris died in the fall of 1896. Right up until his death, he rejected the use of machines, although, ironically, this meant that only the very wealthy could afford his handmade pieces. The company finally closed its doors in 1940.

THE COTSWOLD SCHOOL

THE COTSWOLDS PLAYED HOST TO A NUMBER OF CHAMPIONS
OF THE ARTS AND CRAFTS MOVEMENT WHO ESTABLISHED
WORKSHOPS FOSTERING THE ARTIST-CRAFTWORKER IDEAL.

INSPIRED BY THE EXAMPLE set by William Morris,
late 19th-century designers and craftworkers in
Great Britain aspired to leave the city and move to
the countryside. Such a move meant more space for
workshops and a lower cost of living that allowed
furniture and decorative household wares to become
more affordable.

A popular location for such a move was the
Cotswolds, a series of rolling limestone hills and
wooded valleys in Gloucestershire. Among the first
to decamp to this idyllic landscape was the architect
and designer Ernest William Gimson, who, together
with a group of skilled craftsmen that included the
Barnsley brothers, Sidney and Ernest, moved in 1893
to Pinbury Manor in Ewen, near Cirencester. Here,
they aimed to leave behind their urban way of life
and adopt the lifestyle of self-sufficient countrymen,
rearing their own animals, growing their own food,
and setting up their own workshops. Ernest Barnsley
moved into the manor house, while the two brothers
set up home in the workers' cottages. All three
enthusiastically became part of the local community
and were quick to cultivate working relationships
with local artisans.

Gimson set about producing ladder-back chairs
and decorative plaster panels, Ernest Barnsley began
to restore the manor house, as required by their
rental contract, and Sidney Barnsley—who worked
independently—mastered carpentry skills, ultimately
becoming an accomplished cabinet-maker.

SITTING ROOM AT RODMARTON MANOR
*This Gloucestershire manor was built and
furnished by Ernest Barnsley and the Cotswold
craftsmen in the Arts and Crafts style. Work on
the house started in 1909, and the project took
20 years to complete.*

AN OAK COMPENDIUM
*This piece, attributed to the Cotswold School,
incorporates a chest of drawers, a bookcase,
and a wardrobe, with paneling effect.* H:79 in
(197 cm). FRE

The back of the settle
swings over on a pivot
to form a table.

OAK MONK'S BENCH

*Made by Sidney Barnsley, this bench is based on a traditional
form that originated in late medieval times. It combines a settle
and table. The back can be tilted forward to create a table.
Medieval designs were associated with communal living and
were regularly used in Arts and Crafts interiors.* c. 1925.
H:27 in (70 cm); W:60 in (152 cm); D:27 in (70 cm). DP

Oak runners sit either side of
the armrests when the back
of the settle is lowered.

Plain, paneled construction
is typical of Barnsley's
tables and chairs.

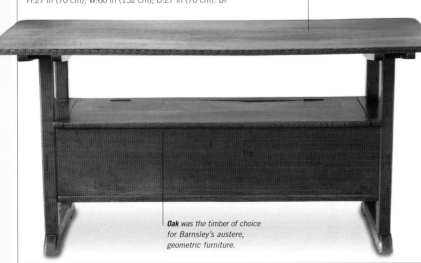

Oak was the timber of choice
for Barnsley's austere,
geometric furniture.

Decoration is sparse and
consists of exposed
joints and chamfering.

CONTINUING THE TRADITION

FOLLOWING IN THE FOOTSTEPS OF THE COTSWOLD MASTERS, SOME CRAFTWORKERS REJECTED
THE MACHINE AND ADOPTED THE VALUES OF THEIR ARTS AND CRAFTS PREDECESSORS.

Improvements in industrial technology after 1910 made
it possible to produce furniture that was both well
designed and affordable, in novel materials. In contrast,
the handmade furniture produced by the Arts and
Crafts Movement had become out of reach to all but
the very wealthy, so was generally eschewed in favor
of mass-produced pieces. Nevertheless, this did not
signal the end of handcrafted furniture altogether.

The 1920s witnessed another high-profile crafts
revival. Among its champions were Edward Barnsley,
son of the Arts and Crafts pioneer Sidney Barnsley, who
created simply designed wooden furniture produced
largely by hand using traditional 18th- and 19th-
century carpentry techniques; and Robert
"Mouseman" Thompson, who signed every
piece of furniture with his trademark carved
mouse. His interest in traditional tools and
methods led him to produce handcrafted oak
furniture, inspired by 17th-century designs and
characterized by uneven, rippled surfaces created
with an adz—a cutting tool with an arched blade.

The eventual marriage between handwork and
machine was achieved by the English furniture
designer and manufacturer Gordon Russell, who
set up his woodcraft workshops in Broadway in 1919.
Initially he continued the handicraft tradition, but
with the establishment of Gordon Russell Ltd. in 1923,
he married the machine with good carpentry and
joinery, believing that the two could happily coexist.
He eventually chaired the wartime Utility Design
Panel to design and manufacture affordable furniture
in a more simple, modern style. Traditional
handcraftsmanship continued with designers such as
John Makepeace, a British craftsman who pioneered
a Craft Revival in the late 1970s (see p.519).

Carved lattice splats

Thompson's trademark mouse

An oak desk chair Designed by Robert Thompson, this
piece has carved lattice splats on octagonal baluster
supports, and the original uprights. H:31 in (80 cm);
W:23 in (60 cm); D:21 in (53 cm). DP

Flat cross-stretchers join the
octagonal baluster supports.

A light oak dressing table
This piece, by Gordon
Russell, has five drawers,
all of which have walnut
handles. c. 1929. H:33 in
(84 cm); W:50 in (127 cm);
D:18 in (47 cm). DP

AESTHETICS OVER STYLE

In 1902, the team moved from Pinbury Manor to
Daneway House in the nearby village of Sapperton,
where they established a more formal commercial
furniture workshop. Sidney Barnsley produced
austere furniture mainly in oak, only occasionally
decorated with a simple gouged ornament or a small
amount of inlay. Ernest Gimson and Ernest Barnsley
set up a successful, albeit short-lived, company
that, at its height, employed ten highly skilled
cabinet-makers. These craftsmen included the
Dutch immigrant Peter Waals, whose work was
distinguished by simple, uncluttered design
and attention to the nature of the wood itself.

For the Cotswold School, style was generally less
important than the use of traditional techniques
and materials. The furniture created by Ernest
Gimson shows a detailed understanding of
materials and techniques, such as timbers
specially treated to highlight the grain. Oak,
walnut, and black and brown ebony were
favored by Gimson for his elegant, clean-lined
furniture. A number of pieces were decorated
with elaborate inlays of holly, fruitwood, ivory,
abalone shell, and silver—a favorite decorative
motif was checkered banding around drawers and
doors—highlighting the Arts and Crafts' love affair
with both luxury and austerity.

PAST, PRESENT, AND FUTURE

C. R. Ashbee's Guild of Handicraft was established
in 1888 in emulation of Ruskin's medieval-style
Guild of St. George, in order to train and employ
local craftworkers. In 1902, it moved to the village
of Chipping Campden in Gloucestershire, where
it soon became a local tourist attraction. Gimson's
craft studio was equally celebrated, with designers
journeying from London to see, at first hand, the
craftsmen at work.

Both Ashbee and Gimson were first and foremost
architects, for whom furniture was an important part
of their interior designs. Both revived long-forgotten
techniques, often achieving results through a
mixture of trial and error, but neither was
backward-looking. As Gimson described his
involvement with the Arts and Crafts Movement:
"I never feel myself apart from my own times by
harking back to the past; to be complete we must
live in all tenses, past, future as well as present."

This enterprising Cotswold community of
designers, craftworkers, and artisans eventually
disbanded with the outbreak of World War I in
1914, when the younger members of the group
were called up for war service and the older
craftsmen turned their attention to producing
goods in aid of the war effort. Gimson remained
in the Cotswolds and attempted to rekindle the
craft movement toward the end of the war with
the formation of the Association of Architecture,
Building, and Handicraft in 1917. Ill health,
however, prevented him from pursuing this new
venture, and he died in 1919.

AMERICA: ARTS AND CRAFTS

THE ARTS & CRAFTS MOVEMENT flourished in the United States in the first quarter of the 20th century. The inaugural American Arts and Crafts Exhibition was held in Boston in 1897, and this, along with the establishment of Arts & Crafts societies based on British models, introduced the work of prominent British designers to the American public. The American Arts and Crafts Movement quickly gained ground, initially in New York, Chicago, and California, before spreading farther afield.

Gustav Stickley of Syracuse, New York, was one of the first designers to combine Arts and Crafts design with American vernacular styles to create the Craftsman or Mission style of sturdy oak furniture (*see p.339*), named after the simple furniture found in the California missions.

Also based in New York, the Roycroft craftworkers produced basic Mission-style furniture, which they sold by mail order.

Another significant designer was Charles Limbert of Grand Rapids, Michigan. Clearly influenced by the Glasgow School (*see pp.366–67*) and by Charles Rennie Mackintosh (*see pp.364–65*), Limbert designed chairs in geometric forms decorated with cut-out squares or heart-shaped patterns.

ARCHITECT-DESIGNERS
By far the most influential designer of this era was the avant-garde architect Frank Lloyd Wright. A founder member of the Chicago Arts and Crafts Society in 1897, Wright designed buildings in which the interiors and furnishings were integral parts of the design, often built into the structure of the building or made using the same, predominantly local, materials. On the West

The dining room at Gamble House, California
The interior of this house was designed by Charles and Henry Greene using simple, sparse furniture. *1908–09.*

The overhanging top softens the severity of the rectilinear form.

The case is made of fumed oak.

The hinges and slights are made of copper.

This cut-out shape is typical of Limbert's decoration.

VICE CABINET

This rare Limbert cabinet has two doors and copper hardware. The oak has been fumed with ammonia to give it a rich reddish color. The cut-out sides are evocative of church furniture. *1880–1920. H:32½ in (82.5 cm). DRA*

LAMP TABLE

This circular oak table is by the Roycroft community of craftsmen and bears their signature cross and orb. It has a cross-stretcher and Mackmurdo style feet. *c. 1880–1920. D:30 in (76 cm). DRA*

BOOK TABLE

This oak table was made by L. & J. G. Stickle It has vertical slats on all sides and still has its original finish, although this has worn away in parts. *c. 1880–1920. H:29 in (74 cm DRA*

CUBE SETTLE

This quarter-sawn oak settle has vertical back slats and slatted crosswork under the arms. The uprights are decorated with a floral pattern fruitwood inlay and are capped with hammered metal fittings. *W:67 in (170 cm). DRA*

oast, architects Greene and Greene
ere working in a similar vein,
lfilling commissions such as the
amble House (see left), for which
ey designed the furniture, light
xtures, and textiles.

Both architects were also influenced
y the Far East, and their designs
veal a synergy with the surrounding
ndscape, as well as a love of
orizontal lines and geometric form.

USING TECHNOLOGY
In their bid to create affordable,
handcrafted, artistic furniture that
was also profitable, the American Arts
and Crafts designers encountered
challenges similar to those faced
by their British counterparts.

Unlike the British, however, they
found a way to accommodate the
modern factory system—for while
the Americans aimed to create the
appearance of handcraftsmanship,
they also succeeded in reducing
production costs by taking advantage of
available technology—a fundamental
difference between the American and
British movements.

In his search for a simple, honest,
and moderately priced furniture style
that would appeal to the middle-class
market, the innovative furniture-maker
Gustav Stickley used steam-powered
or electric woodworking machines to
prepare the lumber, which was then
hand-finished by craftsmen.

Frank Lloyd Wright also
championed the machine over
handcraftsmanship: in a powerful
speech to the Chicago Arts and
Crafts Society in 1901 entitled "The
Art and Craft of the Machine," Wright
stressed the benefits of using machines
to produce affordable furniture for a
wider audience.

A STYLE FOR THE MASSES
Across the United States, furniture
companies introduced their own
lines of Arts and Crafts furniture. The
Grand Rapids Bookcase and Chair Co.
is one such example: they produced
the Lifetime or Cloister style, so called
because it combined craftsmanship in
the medieval tradition with modern
machine techniques.

Ever since the late 19th century, the
Arts and Crafts philosophy and style
have remained at the heart of the
American consciousness, esteemed
by all who value elegance, honest
construction, native materials,
and practicality.

ARREL CHAIR

ne of Frank Lloyd Wright's most important
esigns, produced until the 1930s, this oak
hair has curved arms that are echoed in the
upports and vertical back slats. *First made in
904. H:30 in (76 cm); D:19½ in (49.5 cm). CAS*

OCKING CHAIR

his oak L. & J. G. Stickley open-arm rocking
hair has a drop-in seat cushion. It has six
rtical back slats and it still has its original
nish and maker's label. *c. 1907. H:40 in
01.5 cm). DRA*

CHARLES ROHLFS

A KEY PLAYER IN THE AMERICAN ARTS AND CRAFTS MOVEMENT, DESIGNER CHARLES ROHLFS
IMAGINATIVELY COMBINED ART NOUVEAU–STYLE DECORATION WITH CLEAN-LINED, RECTILINEAR SHAPES.

The son of a cabinet-maker, New York-born
Charles Rohlfs trained at Cooper Union before
turning to furniture design around 1889. Following
a successful period creating elaborately pierced and
carved Gothic-style oak furniture, Rohlfs established
a small studio in Buffalo. Here, he and his assistants
produced a range of custom-built furniture using
craftsman techniques for decorative effect—exposed
mortise-and-tenon joints, dovetails, and chamfering,
along with metalwork strap hinges and brass
nailheads—that all reflected the influence of
the British Arts and Crafts Movement.

Rohlf's highly original designs for desks, small tables,
chairs, and storage cabinets embraced a number of exotic
influences, from the Gothic and Moorish to Scandinavian
traditions. Solidly constructed in oak or occasionally mahogany,
his elongated, rectilinear pieces typically had a warm, rich patina
and were decorated with elaborately carved, cut-out patterns,
Gothic ornament and lettering, or sinuous, nature-inspired,
whiplash-and-tendril motifs in the Art Nouveau style.

Double pedestal desk and chair This desk has four drawers to one side and
a bookshelf to the other. A high-backed, swiveling desk chair completes
the set. *c. 1902. W:60 in (152 cm).*

Rohlfs' superbly crafted furniture won him admirers on both
sides of the Atlantic—especially following the Turin International
Exhibition of Modern Decorative Art in
1902. Before retiring in the mid-1920s,
Rohlfs completed many prestigious
commissions, including furniture for
Buckingham Palace in England.

Carving detail

A rare Rohlfs oak settee This piece is decorated
with unusual carvings and a signature mark on
the front. This style foreshadows the curvilinear
Art Nouveau style. *c. 1900. W:45 in (114 cm).*

GUSTAV STICKLEY

THE FIGUREHEAD OF AMERICAN ARTS AND CRAFTS, GUSTAV STICKLEY CREATED SOLID, PLEASING, HANDCRAFTED FURNITURE THAT SET NEW STANDARDS IN DESIGN.

Stickley's trademark

GUSTAV STICKLEY was the oldest of five brothers, all of whom were involved in the country's burgeoning furniture industry. However, it was ultimately Gustav whose fame rested on his vision as a designer of American Arts and Crafts furniture. Having trained as an architect, he worked in his uncle's chair factory, developing his skills as a craftsman. Making and selling reproduction furniture was followed in 1898 by a visit to Europe, where he discovered the writings of John Ruskin and William Morris (*see p.332*), and the furniture of contemporaries working in the Arts and Crafts style. On his return to the United States, he established the Gustav Stickley Company in Eastwood, New York, producing simple, solid furniture inspired by the designs of William Morris.

FUNCTIONAL FURNITURE

Stickley rejected the extravagant curves and decoration of Victorian furniture in favor of clean, geometric lines and solid forms. This conviction was illustrated by the Craftsman range of functional furniture made in American white oak that he introduced in 1900. His furniture was widely praised at the Michigan trade show in 1900, and further exposure for his designs came from his illustrated catalog. Stickley renamed his business United Crafts and adopted a joiner's compass as his trademark. However, by 1904, the studio, which was home to a guild of apprentices dedicated to learning cabinet-making, metal-working, and leather-working, was known as The Craftsman Workshops.

Stickley's aim was to create "furniture that shows plainly what it is and in which the design and construction harmonize with the wood." His workshop produced well-made, comfortable furniture by hand from thick pieces of solid, quarter-sawn oak and, later, from mahogany and silver-gray maple. Construction features were amalgamated into the design of the furniture, which was then covered with fumed finishes in a rich, dark patina. Stickley's innovative designs combined craftsmanship with

Inlaid floral patterns on the back slats emphasize the vertical structure of the chair.

OAK DROP-FRONT DESK
Designed by Harvey Ellis, this fruitwood desk has a hinged flap with an inlaid floral design. c. 1910. W:30¼ in (77 cm). GDG

Inlays in colorful fruitwoods and metals are typical of Ellis's designs.

Leather upholstery covers the seat.

Simple, square legs continue to become the chair's uprights.

The rails and stretchers are light and refined.

OAK ARMCHAIR
This dark-stained oak armchair by Harvey Ellis has a stylized plant-form inlay on the slats of the back splat, and a leather-covered drop-in seat pad. The foliate decoration adds a characteristic lightness to this solid and geometrical chair. c. 1910. H:44 in (112 cm). GDG

CUBE CHAIR *This oak chair has a spindled back and sides.* c. 1905. W:29 in (72.5 cm). DRA

mechanized techniques. Colonial furniture inspired many shapes, but his adjustable reclining chair was prompted by a Morris original, and the spindle-backed chairs made from 1905 owed much to the designs of Frank Lloyd Wright.

A LIGHTER STYLE

A successful collaboration with the architect and designer Harvey Ellis began in 1903. The pair adopted a lighter, more sophisticated style that relied on small sections of oak covered with a pale brown patina. The collaboration only lasted until Ellis's death in 1904, but Stickley continued his partner's subtle approach, using understated patterns of flowers or *Jugendstil*-type designs (*see p.372*) inlaid with metals or stained timber.

Stickley's furniture became more widely available in the United States in the next decade and was popular among the middle class, but competition and changing tastes ultimately drove him into bankruptcy. His factory closed in 1916.

THE LOUNGE AT CRAFTSMAN FARMS
The collection of buildings that formed the Craftsman Farms Project in New Jersey illustrates Stickley's philosophy of using natural building materials in harmony with the environment. This ideal was carried through to the interior design, as can be seen in the exposed timber and furniture in this lounge.

THE CRAFTSMAN MAGAZINE

IN 1902, STICKLEY LAUNCHED THE HIGHLY INFLUENTIAL *THE CRAFTSMAN* MAGAZINE, A VEHICLE FOR PUBLICIZING BOTH HIS DESIGNS FOR DECORATIVE ARTS AND HIS PHILOSOPHY OF GOOD DESIGN.

The first issue of Gustav Stickley's *The Craftsman* was priced at 20 cents and was dedicated to the work of William Morris. Throughout his career, Stickley used the journal to promote his own work, through illustrated examples, and advance his design beliefs, which centered on the need for handcrafted furniture made with honest materials and sturdy construction. Stickley's Craftsman, or Mission, furniture—which *The Craftsman* magazine illustrated—was constructed according to his three basic principles of design: that the object affirmed the purpose for which it was intended; that there was sparing use of applied decoration; and that it was perfectly suited to the medium in which it was executed.

Like William Morris, Stickley was a visionary who did not confine his energies and activities to a single field. In 1908, he developed the Craftsman Farms Project in New Jersey, in an effort to establish a utopian guild. Aiming to both inspire and report on new directions in the decorative arts, *The Craftsman* published a detailed account of this project, as well as charting Stickley's design and production of his own dwellings in Syracuse.

The Craftsman proved to have enormous influence, and its advertisements promoting the Arts and Crafts Movement reached a wide, enthusiastic audience across the United States. Stickley's innovative work throughout his long career—including his writings in *The Craftsman*—was largely responsible for a renewed appreciation of handcrafted, high-quality furniture in the United

States, and the elevation of the status of both the craftsman and the designer.

Stickley enjoyed commercial success, mainly as a result of the sale of furniture franchises across the United States. However, his ill-judged decision to open a retail outlet in New York City led to his being declared bankrupt in 1915, and the closure of *The Craftsman* the following year. However, Stickley's financial misfortune failed to overshadow the enormous impact of his achievements in the field of American Arts and Crafts design, which *The Craftsman* had so successfully promoted.

Cover of *The Craftsman* This was the design journal that Stickley published from 1902 to 1916.

Interior room design This sketch is from a rare copy of *Craftsman Homes* by Gustav Stickley.

CHAIRS

SIMPLE FORMS WERE a hallmark of the Arts and Crafts chair, which broke away from the various historical styles that dominated the Victorian era. This period was largely marked by the production of well-proportioned chairs, where function was paramount. They were often based on vernacular designs such as the Sussex chair—with its handwoven rush seat and simple, turned, vertical spindles—and Ernest Gimson's sophisticated version of the rush-seated ladder-back chair, or the sturdy Mission pieces being produced by Gustav Stickley in the United States.

Local woods—predominantly oak— were favored on both sides of the Atlantic, with quarter-sawn oak being a particular trademark in the United States: the exquisite tiger-stripe grain of the wood was considered the only necessary decoration. By nature a very light wood, oak pieces were frequently stained, ebonized, or fumed to give them a richer color.

Rush seating was popular on communal or dining chairs, while leather was often used for armchairs, or fabrics inspired by medieval designs. Decoration was usually limited to cutouts in heart or geometric shapes, satinwood inlays, or vertical spindles; construction features provided the main decoration.

DRAWING-ROOM CHAIRS

These chairs are made from ebonized and gilded wood and are upholstered in patterned moquette. Each chair has a stylized fan crest and is raised on fluted, tapering legs. *1870–80. MLL* **2**

BEECH CHAIRS

These Aesthetic Movement ebonized-beech chairs have rush seats. The corner chair is in the style of E. W. Godwin with a curved top rail and Japanese-style lattice slats. The side chair has a spindle-filled back. *1870–80. L&T* **1**

Upholstery loop detail

The exposed tenons on the flat arms add a decorative element.

The corbel, which helps to support the arm, also serves as a decorative feature.

The quarter-sawn oak has been chemically treated to render a rich, fumed finish.

SLATTED OAK CHAIR

This Gustav Stickley quarter-sawn oak chair is of a typically sturdy and functional design. The flat, open arms have vertical slats and are supported at the front by short corbels. There is no additional decoration, which was in keeping with the philosophy of the Arts and Crafts Movement, as was the simple, solid design. Quarter-sawn oak was prized for its tiger-stripe grain, and was a distinctive feature of American Arts and Crafts furniture. The chair has a fumed finish. *c. 1900. H:42½ in (108 cm). DRA* **3**

SUFFOLK CHAIRS

This pair of ebonized-elm Suffolk chairs is by Morris & Co. The backs have spindles and horizontal rails, and each chair has open armrests above a rush seat. The turned legs are linked by stretchers. *c. 1870. L&T* **2**

PIERCED CHAIR

This oak chair, one of six, is by Stickley Bros. The three vertical slats on the chair back have heart-shaped piercings. The square legs are joined by stretchers and end in Mackmurdo feet. *H:39½ in (100.5 cm). GS* **5**

ENGLISH SIDE CHAIR

This walnut chair, which is attributed to Heal's, has a curved top rail, a shaped and heart-pierced splat, tapering uprights, and a rush seat, raised on tapering supports. *c. 1890. H:41¾ in (106 cm). DN* **1**

ENGLISH ARMCHAIR

This oak Arts and Crafts armchair has scrolled ears, high, downswept arms, a tall, woven cane back, and a trapezoidal caned slipseat. The turned legs are joined by an arched stretcher. *H:29 in (73.5 cm). FRE* **1**

TALL-BACK CHAIR

This chair, one of a pair of Arts and Crafts chairs, has cube-topped posts and a cross-spindled back. The upholstery is in leather, and is decorated with a winged griffin. *H:57½ in (146 cm). DRA* **2**

AMERICAN DINING CHAIR

This chair is one of a set of six Limbert side chairs. The chair has two vertical back slats and an inset seat. The finish is original, but the chair has been reupholstered in green vinyl. *H:36¼ in (92 cm). DRA* **3**

SIDE CHAIR

This chair is one of a harlequin set of four Arts and Crafts chairs by William Birch of High Wycombe. The chair is made of oak and has a solid shaped back, turned uprights, and a rush seat. *DN* **1**

PADDED CHAIR

This Arts and Crafts oak open armchair was possibly retailed by Heal's in London. It has a padded back and seat and a pierced splat. The chair is raised on square legs with turned feet. *DN* **1**

ENGLISH ARMCHAIR

This armchair, one of a pair of Arts and Crafts armchairs, is made of elm and has a slatted back. The open arms have upholstered rests and the drop-in seat is raised on square, tapered legs. *L&T* **1**

TABLES

TABLES PRODUCED BY Arts and Crafts designers in the late 19th century tended of be of heavy, solid construction and were frequently based on traditional vernacular forms, sometimes dating as far back as the 16th and 17th centuries.

Plain and simple shapes, straight lines, and the emphasis on the natural grain of fine timber—usually oak—formed the cornerstone of Arts and Crafts designs. Quarter-sawn oak was particularly favored in the United States for its remarkably striking, tiger-stripe grain.

The designs for the table tops were often inspired by those found on medieval pieces and tended to be geometric in shape. The legs were usually square or square-tapering, and were usually joined by stretchers, an undertier, or both. Sometimes the legs terminated in wide, square feet, which are often referred to as Mackmurdo feet.

Decoration was sparing and was usually restricted to exposed joints, geometric cut-out patterns, or restrained inlaid designs in metal, ivory, or occasionally in high-colored exotic woods. In line with the medieval and rural sources of inspiration, designers often stained or fumed pieces to make them look old. Popular forms included joined side tables, trestle dining tables, card tables, and library tables.

Although tables produced by the Aesthetic Movement's designers were also often based on popular geometric shapes, they tended to be more delicate than the solid Arts and Crafts tables. Simple tabletops were raised on elegant turned or tapering legs. There also tended to be more decoration, including partial gilding, mother-of-pearl inlay, and spindled stretchers. Many had a Japanese influence, seen in the ebonized wood, delicately turned supports, and octagonal table tops.

LIMBERT CHALET TABLE

This solid-looking octagonal oak chalet table was made using simple, traditional construction methods. The four sturdy legs are united by cross-stretchers, which are held in place by exposed, keyed through-tenons. Limbert pieces bearing heart- or spade-shaped cutouts—as can be seen on the legs of this table—have become particularly popular with collectors. The finish is original. *c. 1910. D:45 in (114 cm). DRA* **3**

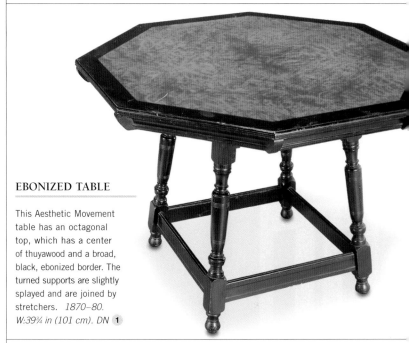

EBONIZED TABLE

This Aesthetic Movement table has an octagonal top, which has a center of thuyawood and a broad, black, ebonized border. The turned supports are slightly splayed and are joined by stretchers. *1870–80. W:39¾ in (101 cm). DN* **1**

The table top is circular and overhangs the frame.

The gently arched apron is typical of tables produced in Charles Limbert's studio.

Oak was favored by Limbert for his furniture designs.

A cross-panel shelf and splayed legs are characteristic of Limbert's work.

LIMBERT LIBRARY TABLE

This oval oak library table with cut-out, flaring, plank sides was made by Charles Limbert. It has a circular, overhanging table top and a gently arched apron, which softens the straight lines on this superbly made table. Construction features, such as the corbels set under the table top, serve as one of the only decorative elements. The solid legs are splayed, and are joined by a cross-panel shelf toward the base of the table. The piece bears a branded mark of a craftsman at his worktable. *W:30 in (76 cm). DRA* **3**

OCTAGONAL TABLE

This ebonized Aesthetic Movement table has a top inlaid with calamander and a molded edge. The legs are curved and are joined by wheel-like stretchers with a central wreathed column. *1870–80. H:28½ in (72.5 cm). DN* **5**

OAK CENTER TABLE

This table, designed by Sir Robert Lorimer, has a paneled octagonal top with exposed peg joints and an uneven surface created with an adz. The table rests on four writhen columns linked to a plain apron above, rising from curved stretchers and stepped, block feet. *c. 1900. W:33¾ in (86 cm). L&T* **4**

LAMP TABLE

This lamp table by the American company Lifetime has a circular overhanging top and a small lower shelf. The four legs are joined by over-arched cross-stretchers. Simple and functional, this piece is unmarked and has been refinished. *H:29¼ in (74 cm). DRA* **2**

EBONIZED TABLE

This small Aesthetic Movement table has a square top, in the manner of the architect and designer E.W. Godwin, for the famous shop Liberty & Co. of London. The undertier is supported by turned supports and fine rods extending from the stretchers. *H:25¾ in (65.5 cm). DN* **1**

LIBRARY TABLE

This solid Arts and Crafts single-drawer library table, designed by Limbert, is made of brown oak. The corbeled top has serpentine ends and the flared sides have square cutouts. The table also has an undershelf. *1880–1920. W:30 in (76 cm). DRA* **4**

PAGODA TABLE

This rare Limbert table has flaring sides, typical arched aprons, and corbels set under the square top. Its name and stylized form suggest an Asian influence. The base has decorative geometrical cutouts and the top bears the company's paper label. *W:34 in (86.5 cm). DRA* **5**

AESTHETIC CARD TABLE

This ebonized card table, attributed to Gillows of Lancaster, has a hinged, rectangular top, which opens on to an interior lined with green baize. The delicate spindled apron has quarter-roundels at each end and spindled stretchers. *1870–80. H:35¾ in (91 cm). DN* **1**

CIRCULAR TABOURET

This Arts and Crafts–style tabouret table is made of oak. It has a plain, circular top and is supported by four rectangular legs. The legs are raised on a cross-shaped base and are joined by cross-stretchers positioned toward the base of the legs. *D:24 in (61 cm). S5* **1**

DINING TABLE

This Limbert extension dining table has a circular top and a pedestal base with shoe feet. Two leaves can be added to the table to increase the size. The piece has been refinished and restored and is branded with the Limbert mark. *D:54 in (137 cm). DRA* **3**

OCTAGONAL EBONIZED TABLE

This small Aesthetic Movement table is in the style of E. W. Godwin. The influence of Oriental design is shown in the delicate turned supports and the octagonal top. The design is further enriched with gilded detailing. *1870–80. H:26¾ in (68 cm). DN* **1**

CABINETS

THE CABINET WAS ONE of the most important pieces of furniture in the Arts and Crafts home. With its large, solid shape, the cabinet offered a challenge to the skills and imagination of the craftsman.

In line with William Morris's ideal of formal furniture, cabinets were often based on the massive, Gothic style of the 13th century. Oak, mahogany, and ebonized wood were favored for large buffets, dressers, and sideboards, and deliberately exposed joinery and copper hinges were used to decorative effect, along with painted plaques featuring medieval themes, inset panels of glass, copper, brass or embossed leather, gesso work, or inlaid marquetry.

The taste for Art Furniture, derived from both Japanese and medieval design, led to cabinets with clean, straight lines, display shelves, and slender, turned supports. Carved decoration was eschewed in favor of medieval-inspired coved tops, galleries of turned spindles, and painted panels featuring either human figures or floral motifs.

In the United States, cabinets were produced in a sturdy, undecorated, rectilinear form in oak and mahogany. Others produced by commercial factories were "Eastlaked," and combined Gothic shapes with more intricate detailing. It was not unusual, at this time, for pieces to combine elements from more than one style.

WALNUT SIDEBOARD

This buffet sideboard is by Maple & Co. of London, and incorporates Arts and Crafts, Aesthetic, and Renaissance Revival elements. The spindles at the back of the galleried top are a recurring feature of Arts and Crafts furniture. The central pad is carved with pomegranates and there is an arcaded panel of sunbursts and sunflowers below—typical of Renaissance Revival. The lower section has twin-paneled, carved doors, and is raised on turned feet with brass caps and casters. *H:59½ in (151 cm); W:60¼ in (153 cm). L&T* **2**

A broken pediment tops the cabinet.

Open shelves for display are a popular feature of large cabinets.

Decorative wood carving was a distinctive feature of Eastlake furniture.

Marquetry using colorful, exotic woods or metals was a popular form of decoration.

EASTLAKE CABINET

This solid rosewood and marquetry side cabinet is in the Eastlake style, named after architect Charles Locke Eastlake. The upper section of the cabinet features a carved broken pediment set above mirrored panels and open shelves. The side shelves are decorated with marquetry, using exotic wood inlays. The lower section of the cabinet has two astragals and glazed central doors, flanked by rounded, carved, open shelves, and is similarly decorated with marquetry. *Late 19th century. H:95 in (237 cm). S&K* **2**

DISPLAY CABINET

This Arts and Crafts satinwood cabinet is in the style of George Walton, an interior designer and architect who collaborated with Charles Rennie Mackintosh. The structure is solid with straight lines and has little in the way of additional decoration. The twin glazed doors have applied astragals and enclose a glass shelf flanked by two further bowed glazed doors. There is a drawer and additional display space below. The cabinet is set on slender legs, joined by a lower shelf located near ground level. *W:66¼ in (168 cm). L&T* **4**

MAHOGANY BUFFET

Flower motifs feature on the top carved panel, cupboard doors, and metal drawer pulls of this Arts and Crafts mahogany buffet. The mirror is flanked by panels pierced with hearts—a typical Arts and Crafts motif. *H:71¼ in (181 cm). DN* **2**

OAK SIDEBOARD

This oak sideboard is made in the style of Bruce Talbot. The central roundel is carved with a songbird in holly and the cupboard doors are carved with sunflower motifs. *W:72 in (183 cm). DN* **1**

SIDE CABINET

The Glasgow company Frances and James Smith manufactured this Aesthetic Movement walnut side cabinet. It is designed in the style of Daniel Cottier and is decorated with gilded panels painted with flowering plants. *1870–80. W:72 in (183 cm). L&T* **3**

Gilded and painted panels

MIRRORED SIDEBOARD

This large Limbert sideboard has a mirrored backsplash and two drawers above three shorter drawers that are flanked by cupboards. There is also a large linen drawer with brass drop pulls near the base. *H:60 in (152.5 cm). DRA* **4**

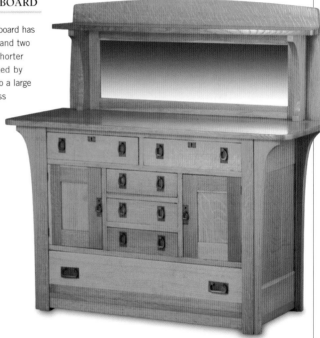

OAK SIDEBOARD

The upper section of this Arts & Crafts sideboard has astragal-glazed doors and an open shelf, while the lower section has a rectangular tip above two drawers and three doors. *H:76¼ in (194 cm); W:67¼ in (171 cm). L&T* **3**

RECTANGULAR SIDEBOARD

The decorative iron hinges on this oak sideboard are unmistakably Arts and Crafts in style. The tongue-and-groove doors reflect earlier rustic forms. *H:72 in (183 cm). L&T* **3**

Decorative iron hinges

ART NOUVEAU
1880-1915

AGE OF TRANSITION

THE TURN OF THE 19TH CENTURY WAS A PERIOD OF CHANGE AND UNCERTAINTY. TRADITIONAL VALUES WERE IN A STATE OF FLUX AS PEOPLE LOOKED FORWARD TO THE CHALLENGES OF A NEW CENTURY.

WMF pewter dressing table mirror
This mirror is decorated with floral and foliate motifs, and a reclining, garlanded maiden in a flowing robe. *c. 1905. H:20½ in (52 cm). AN*

THE FINAL DECADE of the 19th century was marked by political turbulence on one hand and modernization on the other. France was rocked by political scandal in 1894 and its latest form of government, the Third Republic, continued to expand its colonial empire in Africa and Asia, while dealing with poverty, industrial unrest, and political discontent at home. Great Britain vied with France in building up its empire, whereas the Habsburg Empire, which covered much of Central and Eastern Europe, was declining in power and had to contend with mounting domestic pressure for change. A newly united Germany, however, was growing in stature and influence, as was the affluent United States.

This was a time of great industrial progress, and cities and towns were expanding rapidly. Scientific and medical discoveries were opening up new opportunities, and psychologists such as Freud and Jung published influential new theories about dreams and the role of the subconscious mind.

The upper and middle classes were enjoying a period of relative peace and prosperity, but there was increased poverty among the working classes, particularly in the cities. As the century drew toward its close, there was a certain atmosphere of malaise and uncertainty about the future that was reflected in art, literature, and music.

STYLE OF THE AGE
The sentiments that gave birth to the Arts and Crafts Movement in Great Britain in the 1880s—essentially a backlash against revivalism and the poor-quality, mass-produced goods produced as a result of the Industrial Revolution—were also responsible for kick-starting a new form of artistic expression that began to emerge in Europe in the 1890s—Art Nouveau.

Taking its name from the shop opened by Siegfried Bing in Paris in 1895, what lay at the heart of this style was the determination to break with the tired historicism of the past and forge a new form of art in keeping with the spirit of the age—hence the term *Art Nouveau*, meaning "new art." All over Europe, artists and craftsmen founded groups and workshops to provide a forum for young artists to show their work. Unlike previous artists, they drew no distinction between the fine arts and the decorative arts, believing that all the arts should be integrated.

THE NEW ART
By the end of the century, Art Nouveau had become a recognizable style and was evident in every form of the arts, from architecture and interiors to posters, glasswork, ceramics, jewelry, and sculpture, as well as in furniture. Unlike the art of previous periods, Art Nouveau could literally be seen on the streets. Buildings in Brussels, Paris, Budapest, and Vienna were a visual expression of this modern form of art, providing a striking contrast to the heavy grandeur of most revivalist 19th-century buildings, and billboards in Paris were covered in the latest Art Nouveau posters.

Cast-iron gate. Designed by the architect and furniture designer Hector Guimard, this sinuous gate stands at the entrance to the Castel Béranger, a block of flats for which Guimard designed both the exterior and interior, allowing his imagination free reign. *c. 1890.*

TIMELINE 1890–1915

Oscar Wilde

1890 Vincent Van Gogh paints his last masterpiece, *Cornfields with Flight of Birds.*

1891 Oscar Wilde publishes his novel *The Picture of Dorian Gray.*

1894 The Dreyfus Affair in France. Aubrey Beardsley's

Yellow Book magazine is published.

1895 The Lumière Brothers open a movie theater in Paris. Siegfried Bing opens his gallery *L'Art Nouveau* in Paris. Guglielmo Marconi invents the wireless telegraph or radio.

1896 The first modern Olympic Games are held in Athens; Giacomo Puccini's opera *La*

Guglielmo Marconi radio

Bohème premieres.

1897 The Vienna Secession is established in Vienna, Austria.

1898 Marie and Pierre Curie discover polonium and radium.

1899 Scott Joplin's *Maple Leaf Rag* launches a craze for ragtime music in the United States. A peace conference at The Hague establishes an International Court of Arbitration.

1900 The *Exposition Universelle* opens in Paris, and the Secessionist Exhibition in Vienna. Giacomo Puccini's opera *Tosca* premieres in Rome. Freud's *The Interpretation of Dreams* is published in Vienna, causing a sensation.

1901 Queen Victoria dies, and is succeeded by Edward VII.

Queen Victoria

Victor Horta staircase The sinuous contours of Horta's wrought-iron staircase complement the dramatic wall decorations and mosaic floor in the entrance of the Hotel Tassel in Brussels, an outstanding example of Art Nouveau architecture. Horta designed the house and its interiors for Tassel, a professor at Brussels University and a connoisseur of Japanese art. *1893–95.*

Louis Majorelle lady's desk Made from mahogany and oak in Nancy, France, this lady's desk is typical of Art Nouveau, with its kidney-shaped writing plate and top with graceful, curving, wing-shaped ends. It is decorated with floral marquetry of different tropical woods.
c. 1905. H:44 in (110 cm). QU

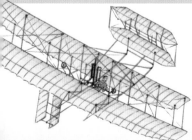

Wilbur and Orville Wright's plane

1902 Turin hosts the *Prima Exposizione d'Arte Decorativa Moderna.*

1903 Wilbur and Orville Wright complete the first crewed airplane flight.

1903–11 The Municipal House, an iconic Art Nouveau building, is built in Prague by Osvald Polívka and Antonín Balsánek.

1905 Work begins on Josef Hoffmann's Palais Stoclet in Brussels. The Simplon tunnel in Switzerland is completed.

1907 A landmark exhibition of Cubist paintings by Pablo Picasso and Georges Braque opens in Paris. Josef Hoffmann designs the Fledermaus cabaret in Vienna.

1909 Futurism is launched by the Italian artist Filippo Marinetti.

1911 The first nonstop flight from London to Paris.

1912 *The Titanic* sinks on its maiden voyage.

1913 *The Rite of Spring* by Igor Stravinsky debuts.

1914 World War I begins. Charlie Chaplin makes his first silent movie.

1915 Albert Einstein publishes his *General Theory of Relativity.*

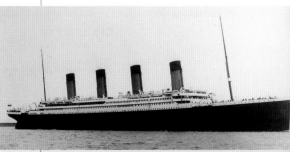

The Titanic

ART NOUVEAU FURNITURE

A TRULY EUROPEAN STYLE, there is no single artist or designer whose work embodies Art Nouveau. The style itself was known by a variety of names across Europe—*Le Style Moderne* in France, *Jugendstil* in Germany, *Secession* in Austria, *La Stile Liberty* in Italy, and *Modernista* in Spain—and the style embraced all of the decorative arts in equal measure.

A COHESIVE STYLE

Art Nouveau was a movement born of the desire of a number of brilliant artists and designers to make something beautiful, functional, and above all, new.

Interiors in the 19th century were often made up of various styles and historical revivals, sometimes in the same room. Art Nouveau was a reaction against this confusion, and a rejection of the mass-produced furniture born of industrialization. Taking the lead from William Morris (*see pp.332–33*), architects, artists, and designers placed more emphasis on craftsmanship and artistic inspiration. Rooms were designed to work as a whole, from the architecture to the furniture, and even the smallest decorative details.

DIFFERENT INTERPRETATIONS

The most striking feature of Art Nouveau style was its diversity. Each country had its own interpretation of the new style. In France and Belgium, designers created sinuous, fluid shapes based on flowers, foliage, and marine life, and it is this interpretation that is generally thought of today as Art Nouveau.

In Great Britain, Germany, and Austria, more linear designs used geometric shapes. Designers also experimented with materials such as bentwood and aluminum. In Spain, Antoni Gaudi worked with dazzling vitality, using organic shapes and an extravagant use of plant-inspired motifs. Much of his furniture was made for his extraordinary, sculptural buildings such as Guel Palace in Barcelona.

NEW INSPIRATIONS

Art Nouveau designers didn't entirely reject the styles of the past. French designers in particular were heavily influenced by the asymmetry and fine craftsmanship of the the Rococo style (*see pp.68–121*). Many designers drew on the decorative vocabulary

Curving bentwood chaise longue This piece was made by German designer Michael Thonet. It is made from beechwood that has been steamed and bent into shape, which is a hallmark of Thonet's pioneering furniture. The seat and back are made of cane work. *c. 1890. W:157½ in (46 cm). DRA*

of the natural world. The sensuous female form, so beloved of the poetic Symbolist movement, was another popular motif. Designers also looked east for inspiration to Japan. Simple, elegant designs inspired by nature were enthusiastically adopted by many Art Nouveau designers, and motifs including cherry blossoms, waterlilies, and dragonflies were often used.

THE END OF AN ERA

The individuality of Art Nouveau was ultimately its undoing. It was a movement that burned brightly, fueled by the creativity of a few brilliant designers creating their own artistic expressions. Such intensity could not be sustained, and after 15 years, Art Nouveau floundered as innovation turned to cliché and the onset of World War I killed the creative and decadent spirit that gave birth to the movement.

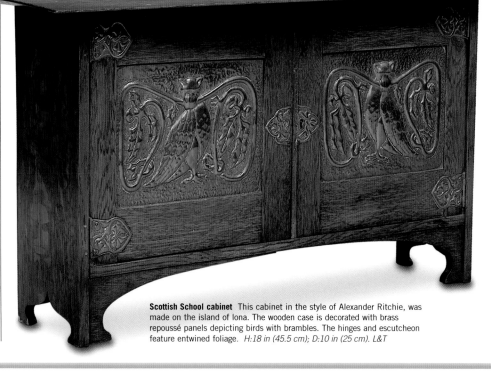

Scottish School cabinet This cabinet in the style of Alexander Ritchie, was made on the island of Iona. The wooden case is decorated with brass repoussé panels depicting birds with brambles. The hinges and escutcheon feature entwined foliage. *H:18 in (45.5 cm); D:10 in (25 cm). L&T*

GILT-BRONZE MOUNTS

Art Nouveau furniture designers often looked for inspiration to the reign of Louis XV (*see pp.78–79*) and the work of the celebrated *ébénistes* working in the Rococo style. The mid-18th century fashion for furniture rendered in luxurious woods and decorated with finely-crafted mounts of gilt bronze was embraced by cabinet-makers including Louis Majorelle. Majorelle embellished the legs, feet, handles, and keyholes of tables and case furniture with nature-inspired motifs, from flower blossoms and waterlilies to leaves and berries.

Lily-pad feet

Lily buds

Louis Majorelle carved mahogany cabinet This cabinet has carved gilt-bronze decorative mounts at the top, sides, and on the feet modeled as waterlily stems, buds, flowers, and leaves. The embellishments are reminiscent of Rococo gilt decorations. *H:79 in (200 cm). CSB*

The gallery is pierced with a foliate motif.

The asymmetrical arrangement of shelves is supported on stylized branch elements.

The back of the vitrine is lavishly decorated with a marquetry pattern of leaves rendered in bird's-eye maple and other exotic woods.

Gallé's marquetry is of the highest quality and echoes the finest work of the 18th-century French ébénistes.

The legs of the vitrine are embellished with leaf-shaped mounts of gilt-bronze.

Organic designs feature on Gallé's furniture, such as these carved cherry flowers.

VITRINE BY EMILE GALLÉ

This vitrine is a stunning example of the marquetry decoration favored by Emile Gallé of the *Ecole de Nancy* (*see pp.356–57*) and his contemporaries. Made of walnut, the piece is lavishly veneered with marquetry composed of bird's-eye maple and other exotic woods in an asymmetrical pattern of leaves and foliage. The Art Nouveau taste for organic, nature-inspired motifs is also epitomized by the Japanese-style cherry flowers carved in relief on the cresting and apron, and the delicate leaf-shaped mounts in gilt bronze decorating the slender legs of the vitrine. Motifs drawn from nature, including scrolling plants and flower blossoms, such as waterlilies, fruits and vegetables, and insects, were captured in breathtaking detail.

The pierced gallery and apron detailing are asymmetrical—a feature popular on 18th-century Rococo furniture. The unusual arrangement of the interior shelves also takes up the asymmetrical theme.

Emile Gallé walnut vitrine This fine vitrine has carved and pierced cresting and an apron of Japanese cherry flowers. The glazed single door and sides enclose an asymmetrically-stepped, two-tier interior, and bird's-eye maple and exotic wood leaf marquetry. *c. 1900. H:59¼ in (148 cm); W:25¾ in (64.5 cm); D:18½ in (46 cm). MACK*

ELEMENTS OF STYLE

Art Nouveau designers sought inspiration from the natural world. From Nancy to Glasgow, nature was interpreted in a host of different and distinctive ways. Sensuous, flamboyant designs with scrolling shapes and whiplash curves were popular, as were more abstract shapes and motifs. Across the genre, embellishments based on natural motifs—foliage, flowers, and insects—were rendered in an array of rich materials: expensive timbers such as walnut, rosewood, and mahogany for relief carving; exotic woods, ivory, and precious metals for marquetry and inlays; and mounts of gilt bronze for decoration.

Rear of an inlaid cabinet

Louis XV influences

A number of designers took inspiration from the Rococo style, which flourished in 18th-century France under Louis XV (*see pp.78–79*). Art Nouveau designers reinterpreted its asymmetry, swirling, curving lines, and stylized plant and floral decorations. This cabinet epitomizes the style, with its sinuous shapes, exotic inlay, and bronze mounts.

Detail of a fireplace

Female figures

The motif that remains most closely associated with Art Nouveau is that of the beautiful maiden with long, flowing hair. This cast-iron design is typical of the Glasgow School and Margaret Macdonald Mackintosh style (*see pp.366–67*). The maiden's head is cast in high relief, has flowing hair and stylized floral details, and is part of a geometrically balanced design.

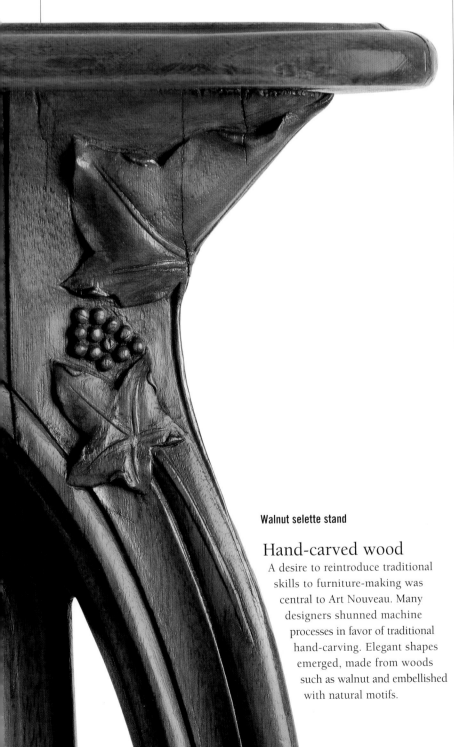

Walnut selette stand

Hand-carved wood

A desire to reintroduce traditional skills to furniture-making was central to Art Nouveau. Many designers shunned machine processes in favor of traditional hand-carving. Elegant shapes emerged, made from woods such as walnut and embellished with natural motifs.

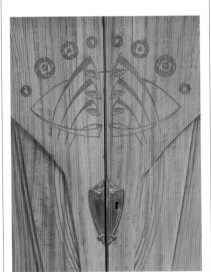

Cupboard door detail

Fixtures and detailing

This detail of a Patriz Huber lemon-mahogany, polished cupboard has characteristic Art Nouveau fixtures and detailing. The understated copper key plate is gently curved with simple, embossed foliate detailing. The cupboard is partly carved with gently curving lines and also decorated with geometric flower-bud and foliate motifs.

Duck head arm support

Stylized nature

In France, the two main centers of Art Nouveau furniture production—the Nancy and Paris schools—pioneered the fashion for curvilinear furniture designs that looked to nature for inspiration. This stylized duck head is a good example of how natural motifs were cleverly incorporated into furniture design.

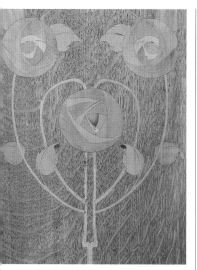

arquetry on an oak cabinet

Art Nouveau marquetry

lthough marquetry was widely used, esigns varied tremendously. This ose-tree example is closely associated ith Charles Rennie Mackintosh and he Glasgow style (*see pp.364–67*). he design is both stylized and mmetrical, combining long, straight nes with gentle curves. It is more inimal and restrained than the rench marquetry style.

Carved walnut bed-end

Relief carving

This type of carved decoration rises above the surface background. This detail of a carved walnut bed-end, designed by Louis Majorelle (*see p.357*), shows an intricately carved daffodil motif flanked by graceful, gently curving fielded panels. It is typical of the French style of Art Nouveau, which often applied organic motifs to furniture.

Detail of a chair back

Sinuous lines

The curved splats on the back of this chair and the curving arms on the unusual, cantilevered supports are typical of the Paris School, which favored distinctive, curved, and sculptural chair backs and minimal applied decorations. This style of curved wood is carved from a single piece, as opposed to using the bentwood technique (*see p.375*).

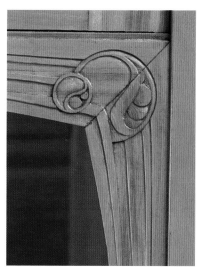

Carved detail of a cupboard

Abstract motifs

The Art Nouveau credo that architecture, decoration, and furniture should be united into a cohesive whole inspired some designers to develop a spare, linear style that moved away from the sensuous interpretation of nature toward simple, elegant shapes and geometric patterns. This carved detail is curved but simple in design and moving toward abstraction.

etail of a two-tier table

Whiplash curves

he scrolling design of the supports f this two-tiered, rosewood table by mile Gallé is typical of the whiplash urves favored by French and Belgian esigners, and is exemplified in the rchitecture of Victor Horta (*see p.360*). nspired by nature, the sinuous curves e, in fact, stylized renditions of lant tendrils.

Detail of an inlaid sideboard

Exotic materials

This roundel is a tour de force of embossed and inlaid metalware by Italian designer Carlo Bugatti (*see p.362*). Influenced by Japanese, Moorish, and Egyptian design, the banding in embossed brass encloses a geometric pattern resembling winged insects in a pale wood, ebony, silver, ivory, and brass inlay.

Repoussé clock face

Repoussé metalwork

This technique was common in Arts and Crafts and Art Nouveau. Relief decoration was produced by hammering from the underside, causing the decoration to project outward. This design is influenced by natural motifs, Liberty's Celtic revival, and Charles Rennie Mackintosh's heraldic designs (*see p.364*).

Floral and foliate gilt mount

Gilt-bronze mounts

Many French furniture-makers designed finely wrought, decorative mounts of gilt-bronze or wrought iron. This decorative detail echoes the Rococo preference for warm, lustrous woods enhanced by nature-inspired mounts in gilt-bronze. Popular natural motifs were flower-buds, waterlilies, and orchids.

PARIS EXPOSITION

THE LAVISH INTERNATIONAL EXHIBITIONS WERE IMPORTANT PROMOTIONAL VEHICLES FOR THE ART NOUVEAU MOVEMENT.

INTERNATIONAL EXHIBITIONS, known as *Expositions Universelles*, World Fairs, or Great Exhibitions, were lavish forums that sought to present, in specially constructed pavilions, the diversity of human civilization. Following the first major exhibition in 1851 at Crystal Palace in London (*see pp.268–69*), these events were acknowledged as important tools for showcasing cultures and ideas. International exhibitions helped to influence the development of Art Nouveau, for in addition to having their work presented on the international stage, designers were affected by what they saw at the exhibitions, including art from around the world.

The vast repertoire of ideas and designs displayed at exhibitions from around 1889 culminated in the year 1900, when Art Nouveau reached its pinnacle and enjoyed its greatest success at the *Exposition Universelle* in Paris.

THE *EXPOSITION UNIVERSELLE*
This view looks across the Seine River toward the Eiffel Tower and the Globe Céleste. The Eiffel Tower was designed in 1889 by the structural engineer Alexandre Gustave Eiffel, and was the winning proposal in a building design competition to commemorate the French Revolution's 100th anniversary. Eiffel's radical creation was the central focus of the Paris Exhibition site in both 1889 and 1900.

Carved crest

MAHOGANY-FRAME ARMCHAIR
This rare chair by Edouard Colonna has a scroll carved, crested, padded back above molded arms with knuckle-scroll terminals, cabriole legs, and a low, upholstered back. The chair was part of a suite, including a settee and side chair, exhibited at the Siegfried Bing stand at the 1900 Paris Exposition Universelle. c. 1900. MACK

SILVER-PLATED WALL MIRROR
This mirror by Georges De Feure was exhibited at the 1900 Paris Exposition. The relief-molded scene depicts a woman in profile wearing a long, flowing dress, in an elaborately stylized landscape setting within a molded oak frame. 1900. H:14¼ in (36 cm); W:17¾ in (45 cm). MACK

Knuckle-scroll terminal

Cabriole leg

SIEGFRIED BING

PERSONIFYING THE ENTREPRENEURIAL SPIRIT OF ART NOUVEAU, SIEGFRIED BING, AND HIS SHOP, L'ART NOUVEAU, PLAYED A PIVOTAL ROLE IN THE DEVELOPMENT OF THE STYLE.

Siegfried Bing

Born in Hamburg in 1838, the art collector and dealer Siegfried Bing moved to Paris in 1871. Following travels to East Asia a few years later, he opened a shop called *La Porte Chinoise* specializing in the sale of Oriental objects. After a visit to the United States to report on architecture and design for the French government, Bing opened the doors of his new Paris emporium in December 1895. Named *L'Art Nouveau*, it sold the works of leading Art Nouveau craftsmen, including Emile Gallé, Henri van de Velde, and Louis Comfort Tiffany.

It was in France that Art Nouveau became most firmly established. Paris was highly influential, and Bing's shop became the focus of attraction. The inaugural exhibition at the gallery and shop caused a sensation—not all of it favorable—but the success of the venture was ensured. *L'Art Nouveau* eventually expanded to include workshops and studios. The master cabinet-maker was Léon Jallot, who worked

designs created by Eugène Gaillard, Edouard Colonna, and Georges De Feure. However, Bing personally selected the designs that were made into finished pieces.

La Maison de L'Art Nouveau had a brief life, remaining open for a mere nine years before finally closing in 1904, but Bing's imaginative displays, in both his shop and at international exhibitions, became renowned among artists, designers, and manufacturers, and also achieved notoriety with politicians, collectors, and museums.

Bing dealt in modern works of art, but he promoted the idea of amalgamating all aspects of the arts. At *L'Art Nouveau*, he sold a wide range of goods, from textiles and ceramics to glass and silverware—all showcasing the best that the new style had to offer. The international style of Art Nouveau thus amounted to more than simple a group of enthusiastic artists and designers creating works of art in a single, identifiable idiom.

FRENCH INFLUENCE

It was the French who held sway, as neither the Belgian Henri van de Velde (*see p.360*), nor the Scottish contingent led by Charles Rennie Mackintosh (*see pp.364–67*), were represented, and the Germans gave a weak showing. Art Nouveau was generally seen as a French movement, an expression of French refinement and extravagance.

While the Exhibition was largely monopolized by neo-Rococo, neo-Baroque, and exotic styles, there was nonetheless a celebrated array of Art Nouveau buildings, including the *Pavillon Bleu* Restaurant by Gustave Serrurier-Bovy, the *Loie Fuller Pavilion* by Henri Sauvage, and the *Pavillon Bing*. Hector Guimard's spectacular station entrances greeted visitors who arrived at the site on the new Métropolitain subway. Imaginative international displays, such as the Finnish Pavilion, showed that other countries were accomplished promoters of their versions of the Art Nouveau. The *Union Centrale des Arts Décoratifs*, the *Pavillon Bing*, and the spaces dedicated to the department stores *Le Louvre*, *Le Bon Marché*, and *Le Printemps*, were all private initiatives at the *Exposition*. Along the *Esplanade des Invalides*, the Decorative Arts Pavilions exhibited hundreds of different interpretations of Art Nouveau.

INTERIOR STYLE

At Siegfried Bing's Pavilion at the 1900 *Exposition*, Art Nouveau enjoyed its greatest success. Bing's exhibits demonstrated how great his influence on interior design had become.

Immediately apparent in the six rooms of Bing's Pavilion was the sense of a consistent, unified look. Instead of an eclectic collection of furniture, textiles, and ornaments inspired by a host of different historic styles, as preferred in the Victorian era, these rooms promoted a single, cohesive design theme that was reflected in wall colors, floor surfaces, furniture, and fixtures in equal measure. Georges De Feure designed the dressing room and boudoir, Edouard Colonna the drawing room, and the vestibule, bedroom, and dining room were created by Eugène Gaillard. Although Bing's Pavilion was scarcely mentioned in the Parisian papers, it became a benchmark against which designers and collectors outside France judged the unified approach to interior design.

On the heels of the *Exposition Universelle* in Paris came the 1902 *Prima Esposizione d'Arte Decorativa Moderna*, held in Turin, which saw Art Nouveau at its final peak of international influence.

By the end of the decade, Art Nouveau was no longer an exhibition sensation. Its role as a modern global style had diminished considerably, and its commercial viability had been lost. However, the *Exposition Universelle* brought a new era of art and design to the world, and for the 51 million people who passed through its doors, it must have been a truly remarkable experience.

The Siegfried Bing Pavilion at the Paris *Exposition* In an attempt to create a *Gesamtkunstwerk* (a complete artwork), Bing enlisted three promising, although relatively unknown, designers to collaborate on the design: Georges De Feure, Edouard Colonna, and Eugène Gaillard. The dining room was designed by Gaillard.

Walnut dining chair Designed by Gaillard, this chair was exhibited at the Siegfried Bing Pavilion at the 1900 Paris *Exposition*. The original leather seat and back of this dining chair are decorated with sinuous forms, an example of his success in flat pattern design. Gaillard's design is inspired by nature, and, like the branches of a tree, the carved walnut frame appears to grow. The sculptural form of this chair was an excitingly novel design at the exhibition. 1899–1900. H:37 in (94 cm); W:18¾ in (47.5 cm).

FRANCE: THE NANCY SCHOOL

MANY OF THE FINEST WORKS of French Art Nouveau were created at the *Alliance Provincale des Industries d'Art*, or *École de Nancy*, in the province of Lorraine. It was founded in 1901 by the innovative furniture and glass designer Emile Gallé, and was based on the example set by the English Arts and Crafts guilds. A design school and workshop that was profoundly influenced by the Symbolist movement in art and literature, the enterprise was intended to modernize technical training in both the decorative and applied arts.

The natural world inspired and informed the artists and craftsmen who gathered around the brilliant Gallé at the *École de Nancy*, and the school gave a coherent identity to the diverse craftsmen working there.

Among those who ran the Nancy school with Gallé were some of the finest craftsmen and designers of the day, including Louis Majorelle, Eugène Vallin, Victor Prouvé, and the Daum brothers, Auguste and Antonin.

BOTANICAL INSPIRATION

In addition to history of art and Symbolist poetry and literature, Gallé's rich influences included the study of local flora and fauna—cow parsley, thistles, insects, and so on—which was to furnish him with creative inspiration for shapes as well as decoration. His romantic vision of nature, a delight in plants, animals, and other living creatures, and a passionate faith in the mystery of creation lay at the heart of his most inspired designs.

FURNITURE STYLES

Gallé's emotional connection with the vitality of nature and his love of symbolism resulted in highly original, imaginative furniture that seemed to breathe with life.

Tables and cabinets were made from richly colored or exotic woods, including rosewood, maple, walnut, or fruitwoods such as apple or pear. The pieces stood on carved supports in the shape of dragonfly wings, or boasted cornices featuring carved creatures such as snails, moths, and bats. Decorative bronze mounts resembled insects, and fruitwood inlays in extravagant compositions depicted natural motifs, including flower blossoms, leaves, fruit, ears of corn, snails, and butterflies.

ARMCHAIRS

These mahogany chairs by Louis Majorelle have rectangular padded splats, stuff-over arms on unusual, sweeping, reverse-curved supports, and stuff-over seats on molded legs. This is a graceful variation on the traditional chair style with gently curving lines. *c. 1900.* *H:40½ in (103 cm). MACK*

ROSEWOOD AND WALNUT VITRINE

This rosewood and walnut vitrine by Emile Gallé is inspired by organic motifs. The upper section has glazed doors with carved foliage surrounds extending to a central support to form a heart motif. The back is decorated with fruitwood leaf-form marquetry. *c. 1900. H:62 in (158 cm); W:31½ in (80 cm); D:19 in (49 cm). MACK*

TABLE LAMPS

This is an unusual pair of glass and bronze lamps made in Nancy by Daum Frères and Louis Majorelle. The tapering, gilded, bronze shaft has a flower motif in high relief and three raised supports for the domed, mushroom-shaped shades. The lamp shades are made of clear flashed glass with powder inclusions in rose, greenish-yellow, and dark violet. They are signed "Daum Nancy" and have a Cross of Lorraine on the rim of the shade. *c. 1904. H:25¼ in (63 cm). VZ*

Many of Gallé's pieces were unique, and were signed and frequently engraved with verses by Victor Hugo, Paul Verlaine, or Charles Baudelaire.

LOUIS MAJORELLE

The other great furniture designer working at Nancy—Louis Majorelle – turned his back on the Louis XV taste, which had been the staple of many established workshops, and created some of the finest pieces of Art

Giltwood *Aubépine* table by Louis Majorelle
This occasional table has a circular marble top above a molded gilt frieze. The tapering molded legs are decorated with foliate carving. *c. 1900. H:32 in (81 cm). L&T*

Nouveau furniture. Although his desks, tables, chairs, and bedroom suites lack the symbolic poetry found in the works of Gallé, his finely crafted furniture is beautiful in its own right.

Majorelle established several workshops so that he could increase his output. He was a trained cabinet-maker, and although much of his furniture incorporated some machine-made parts, the quality was superb. Majorelle's furniture was usually made

of dark hardwoods such as mahogany and rosewood, with fluid outlines and massive, sculptural gilt-bronze mounts shaped as orchids or water lilies, alongside delicately carved, inlaid, or marquetry decoration in fruitwoods, pewter, or mother-of-pearl. He also collaborated with the Daum brothers, who were famous for their glassware, to produce a wide variety of decorative lamps with glass shades and elegant bronze or iron mounts.

NEST OF TABLES

These Emile Gallé tables *Aux Magnolias* are made of fruit- and rootwoods and decorated with magnolia and butterfly design inlays, and carved branch patterns on the legs of the largest tables. *c. 1900. H:28½ in (71 cm). GK*

ARMCHAIRS

This pair of *Marrons d'Inde* armchairs by Louis Majorelle have splats with exotic wood marquetry, bent and curved arms, tapering legs, and stuff-over upholstered seats. *1905–10. H:41½ in (105 cm); W:22 in (55 cm). QU*

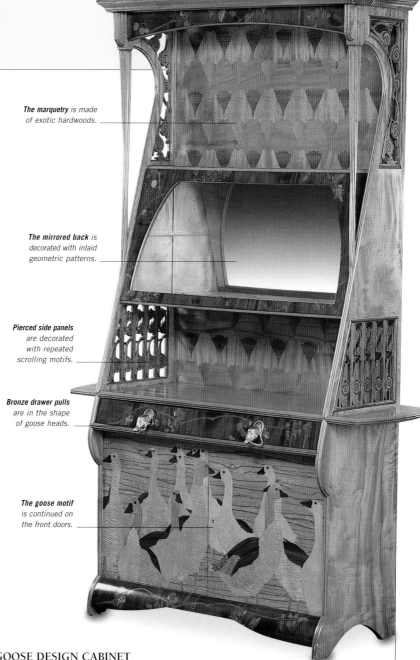

The marquetry is made of exotic hardwoods.

The mirrored back is decorated with inlaid geometric patterns.

Pierced side panels are decorated with repeated scrolling motifs.

Bronze drawer pulls are in the shape of goose heads.

The goose motif is continued on the front doors.

DISPLAY CASE

Made from mahogany and makasar, this display case by Louis Majorelle rests on curved diagonal legs. The doors have distinctive blossom ornaments. *c. 1920. H:50 in (125 cm); W:33½ in (83.75 cm); D:18 in (45 cm). QU*

TWO-TIER TABLE

This rosewood occasional table by Emile Gallé has three out-splayed supports and scroll legs with carved hoof feet. The table is decorated with floral marquetry. *c. 1900. H:30 in (77 cm); W:21 in (53 cm). MACK*

GOOSE DESIGN CABINET

This sumptuous, blonde mahogany, goose-design cabinet by Louis Majorelle is decorated with marquetry, pierced wood, and exotic timbers. The piece has pierced side panels, a frieze drawer with bronze goose-head drawer

pulls, and cupboards inlaid with exotic wood showing a gaggle of geese. A superb designer and highly skilled technician, Majorelle created flamboyantly luxurious pieces of unrivaled quality. *c. 1900. H:97 in (246.5 cm); W:61 in (155 cm). CALD*

FRANCE: THE PARIS SCHOOL

THE DEVELOPMENT OF the Parisian thread of French Art Nouveau is distinguished by a group of forward-looking individuals who formed artistic groups to experiment with new forms, and who were supported by a circle of entrepreneurs. The most important patron was the influential dealer Siegfried Bing (*see p.355*). An enthusiastic collector with a special interest in Oriental art, Bing played a crucial role in *Le Japon Artistique*, a publication that was instrumental in popularizing Asian art in 19th-century Europe, before he moved on to promote Art Nouveau.

AN ENTERPRISING ENDEAVOR
Key to the success of the "new art" in Paris was Bing's transformation of his antique shop in Paris into the gallery *L'Art Nouveau* in 1895. He dedicated this to exhibiting a host of decorative objects, which embodied the new directions in art while also being inspired by French tradition. He assembled a group of innovative artists—not only from France but also Henri van de Velde of Belgium and American Louis Comfort Tiffany—and showcased their latest works. Bing succeeded in bringing Art Nouveau to a wealthy, fashion-conscious clientele and was joined in this endeavor by the German art critic Julius Meier-Graefe, who established *La Maison Moderne* in 1898. His aim was to offer more affordable decorative wares in the Art Nouveau style, made using industrial methods.

THE PARIS AND NANCY STYLES
Although both the Paris and Nancy Schools pioneered the new, curvilinear, organic furniture style, the leading designers of both schools—Hector Guimard in Paris and Louis Majorelle and Emille Gallé in Nancy—each drew inspiration from nature in a very different way. At the *École de Nancy*, the style was much more exuberant and florid: the finely crafted pieces had sculptural shapes and were richly veneered in exotic woods, with mother-of-peal inlays, marquetry, and gilt-bronze mounts.

The Parisian strand of Art Nouveau was lighter and more restrained, and owed much to the work of the architect and furniture designer Hector Guimard.

One of a talented group of cabinet-makers, Guimard—who was a disciple of Victor Horta in Belgium and is best remembered for his Paris Metro entrances—was one of the most innovative and progressive. His bold and energetic three-dimensional furniture designs were imaginative, sculptural evocations of the natural world. At first these were made in solid mahogany, but later he used a soft pearwood that was easier to model.

DECORATIVE INSPIRATION
Although the decoration favored by the Paris School took its inspiration from nature, it was stylized. Other furniture designers who were part of Siegfried Bing's influential gallery and retail shop, and who formed the core of the Paris School of Art Nouveau, included Eugène Gaillard, the Dutchman Georges De Feure, and German-born Edouard Colonna.

ROCOCO INFLUENCE
Gaillard's robust, dynamic furniture looked back to the 18th-century Rococo style of Louis XV for inspiration, and included pieces such as the magnificent display cupboard in walnut that was shown at the 1900 International Exhibition in Paris (*see pp.354–55*), as well as light and airy tables and chairs with sinuous decoration in aquatic plant patterns.

The slender and refined gilded wood furniture created by De Feure was delicately carved with plant motifs and combined with silk fabrics. His sophisticated designs drew inspiration from the 18th-century French tradition of furniture-making, especially the Louis XVI style.

Colonna's furniture was a quieter version of Art Nouveau. Its simple forms and scrolling, decorative patterns were carved with a light and delicate hand.

The top rail carving is inspired by asymmetric Louis XV furniture designs.

The leather upholstery is embossed with a floral pattern.

Brass studs fix the leather upholstery to the frame.

The carved legs terminate in flared, square-section feet.

WALNUT-FRAMED CHAIR

This carved walnut chair was designed by Eugène Gaillard. The chair has a distinctive pierced, asymmetric floral and foliate carved frame decorated with sinuous curves and plant tendril carving on the back. The chair seat and back are upholstered with the original floral embossed brown leather, which is fixed in place with brass studs. The chair stands on flared feet. This style was influenced by leading Paris School artist-craftsmen such as Hector Guimard. *c. 1905. H:42 in (107.5 cm). MACK*

OAK SERVER

more restrained Art Nouveau style is shown
this oak and purple-heart server designed
y Léon Jallot. The piece has an arched,
ised back with pierced, stylized leaf motifs
bove two frieze drawers and open shelves.
1910. H:49¼ in (125 cm); W:48¼ in
122.5 cm). CAL

DESK CHAIR

This Tony Selmersheim desk chair is made
from padouk, a type of rosewood. The chair
has a wavy top rail above a cartouche-shaped
padded back with inscrolled arms and a
padded seat. The piece stands on gently
splayed tapering legs. c. 1902. H:30 in
(76 cm); W:23 in (58.5 cm). CAL

MAHOGANY SIDE TABLE

Designed by Camille Gauthier and Paul
Poinsignon, this table has a concave rectangular
top with delicate, floral-motif fruitwood
marquetry. It sits above an arched frieze with
daffodil-design marquetry, on spiral-carved,
tapering legs. c. 1900. H:29 in (74 cm);
W:32 in (81 cm); D:24 in (60.5 cm). MACK

LIBRARY SELETTE

This mahogany selette by Tony Selmersheim
has a square top and molded edge, with
a bookshelf compartment above an offset
square-shaped lower tier. The piece stands
on out-splayed molded legs united by a
cross-stretcher. c. 1910. H:53 in (135 cm);
W:35 in (90 cm). MACK

WALNUT SELETTE

his two-tier walnut selette stand was designed
y Edouard Diot. Beneath a flat top, distinctive,
elicately curved supports decorated with carved,
visting floral motifs extend from the upper
er via open supports. The piece rests on out-
played carved feet. 1902. H:53½ in
36 cm). CAL

LINKS WITH ARCHITECTURE

ARCHITECTURE PLAYED A KEY ROLE IN THE DEVELOPMENT OF THE
PARIS SCHOOL, ESPECIALLY THE DESIGNS OF HECTOR GUIMARD.

In the 1890s, public and private interiors
in France underwent a period of radical
change, reflecting a burgeoning interest
in modern materials, nature-inspired
decorative motifs, and imaginative forms
of Art Nouveau. One of the most original
French Art Nouveau architects, Hector
Guimard, was celebrated for his sinuous,
decorative, wrought-iron entrances for
the Metro stations in Paris.

Guimard made his mark as an architect
with a distinctive block of flats he built
in Paris between 1894-98, which was
known as Le Castel Béranger, located at

16 rue de la Fontaine. Both the exterior
and interior of the flats boast bold,
abstract ornament. He used variegated
color on the facade, and built an
interior courtyard to allow more light
into the apartments.

Guimard understood the need to
create brightly colored living spaces
that were open and full of light. With
the Castel Béranger, he demonstrated
how the decorative arts, in a wide range
of materials, could successfully work
together with architecture to create a
unified, modern theme.

Entrance to Boissière Metro station This is one of
the curvaceous cast-iron Paris Metro entrances
designed by Hector Guimard. 1899–1904.

Le Castel Béranger flats in Paris Designed by
Hector Guimard, both the exterior and interior of
the flats feature his fanciful designs. 1894–98.

GLASS-FRONTED CABINET

This cabinet is made of lemonwood and
satinwood and carved with foliate motifs.
The stained glass cabinet doors contain
simple, swirling foliate designs in colored
glass. The piece was designed by Edouard
Colonna for Siegfried Bing. 1900.
H:83 in (211 cm); W:57 in (145 cm). CALD

BELGIUM

IN LATE 19TH-CENTURY Europe, Art Nouveau reached its creative peak in Belgium. Its success there was largely due to the fact that people were encouraged to explore fresh, exciting ways of looking at the arts.

The same, spirited Art Nouveau message that called for a cohesive, unified interior—so successfully accomplished elsewhere in Europe—took root in Belgium in the work of a number of innovative artist-architects, such as Victor Horta, Henri van de Velde, and Gustave Serrurier-Bovy.

The Belgian version of Art Nouveau had much in common with its French counterpart. Both embraced free-flowing, sinuous, sculptural furniture, and had a rich vocabulary of decorative motifs in organic shapes—plants, flower blossoms, trees, butterflies, and insects—all drawn from the natural world.

HENRI VAN DE VELDE
Henri van de Velde won universal acclaim for the design of his own home near Brussels—Bloemenwerf—where furniture, carpets, and wall coverings combined to create a harmonious whole. He forged strong links with France by showcasing and selling his furniture at prestigious retail shops in Paris, including Siegfried Bing's L'Art Nouveau and La Maison Moderne, owned by Julius Meier-Graefe. Widely celebrated

throughout Europe, van de Velde was influenced by the writings of William Morris and believed that art should always follow organic form—a theory that underlined his furniture designs. Echoing nature's subtle curves and lines, they were rendered in light-colored, native woods such as walnut, beech, and oak, and had minimal decoration. Despite van de Velde's theories, function was key to his sturdy yet elegantly simple cabinets, tables, and writing desks.

VICTOR HORTA
Another Belgian pioneer of the Art Nouveau style was the architect and designer Victor Horta, who designed spectacular buildings such as the splendid Hotel Tassel in Brussels. His interiors coalesced into harmonious and integrated ensembles, from wall paneling, ceilings, and door frames to furniture and metalwork fixtures, using an exciting range of new materials, such as iron and glass.

The cross-fertilization between French and Belgian Art Nouveau resulted in Horta's energetic, curving style—with its signature whiplash curves—influencing Parisian designers such as Hector Guimard. His expensive furniture was skillfully crafted in luxurious woods such as maple, mahogany, and fruitwoods, and lavishly upholstered in fabrics such as velvet and silk.

GUSTAVE SERRURIER-BOVY
Like van de Velde and Horta, Gustave Serrurier-Bovy adopted many familiar Art Nouveau decorative motifs to complement his furniture, including plants and flowers, sinuous curves, and high-wrought mounts of pewter or brass. Determined to produce well-designed furniture for everyone, Serrurier-Bovy was also inspired by the English Arts and Crafts Movement, as seen in his robust, rectilinear furniture and in his preference for oak.

The influence of these highly original Belgian designers reached beyond their national borders to set the cultural standard for Art Nouveau furniture throughout much of Europe.

The Musée Horta This building was originally built by Victor Horta as his own studio and residence. This view shows the integrated interior, with both the staircase and glass dome featuring his characteristic whiplash curves. 1898.

COIFFEUSE

This mahogany *coiffeuse* was designed by the artist-architect Gustave Serrurier-Bovy as a piece of bedroom furniture. The mirror is composed of three panels, contained within a gently curving frame. The table section has two pairs of drawers above and two drawers below. The elegant, curved lines of the top of the piece are echoed in the arched stretchers joining the legs, and the arch at the front of the table, which creates the kneehole. 1899. H:74 in (188 cm); W:54 in (137 cm); D:22½ in (57 cm).

BED FRAME

This bed frame has a bold, curvilinear shape and is made from stained oak. It was designed by Henri van de Velde. The head and foot-boards have bowed and arched profiles and pairs of raised and fielded, shield-shaped panels. The piece terminates in splayed feet, which form part of the overall curved shape, and rests on brass casters. Henri van de Velde believed that art should follow an organic form, and this influenced the shape and decoration of his furniture. c. 1897–98. W:80 in (203.5 cm). QU

SIDE CHAIR

This mahogany chair was designed by
Victor Horta and illustrates his use of
sumptuous materials and curving
style, as shown in the design of the
chair back, legs, and stretchers.
The seat is covered with a
generously upholstered
cushion. *c. 1901.*
H:37½ in (95.2 cm).

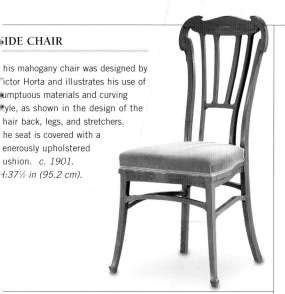

WALNUT TABLE

This walnut occasional
table has an overhanging
circular top, arched apron,
and curving, cabriole legs
that terminate in stylized
feet. The piece was
designed by Henri
van de Velde. *c. 1916.*
H:27¼ in (69.25 cm). QU

MAHOGANY SCREEN

This mahogany screen, designed by Gustave Serrurier-Bovy, has
three glass panels that create strong vertical lines. In contrast, the
top of the piece is sinuous in shape. While the glass in the lower
half of the screen is original, the upper pieces are replacements.
1899. H:63 in (159.8 cm).

MAHOGANY VITRINE

The rectangular, tiled top of this mahogany vitrine has
a sinuous, carved surround, above an open recess and
cupboard with glazed door. The side has small shelves
and carved brackets. The piece is in the style of the
work of Victor Horta. *c. 1900. W:35 in (90 cm).*

The copper key mounts are
simple and unobtrusive.

The table top has a
distinctive kidney shape.

The three raised shelves
emphasize the curved
form of the bureau.

Two doors on either side frame
one open compartment.

Rounded brass shoes on
conical legs emphasize
the curved design.

LADY'S BUREAU

Designed by Henri van de Velde and made by H. Scheidemantel in Weimar, this bureau
design is typical of the work of van de Velde. The curved lines of the wood are used to
create an unusual and organic shape, avoiding applied, inlaid, or elaborate decoration.
The only detailing is the unobtrusive copper key mounts and the brass shoes. *c. 1903.*
W:49¼ in (123 cm). QU

MAHOGANY AND MIXED-WOOD TABLE

This side table is made of mahogany decorated with marquetry.
The top is inlaid with a floral decoration above a short drawer,
and the cupboard is inlaid with a daffodil design. The supports
are embellished with sinuous tendrils and brass hardware.
c. 1902. W:25 in (63.5 cm). CAL

ITALY AND SPAIN

LAVISH, HIGHLY ORIGINAL furniture created by designers working in Spain and Italy represented the most exotic form of Art Nouveau.

Italy called the style *Stile Liberty*, after the London shop at the forefront of the movement, or *Stile Floreale*, due to the nature-inspired decoration that characterized the movement. Italy had a rich tradition of decoration based on nature, from Roman mosaics to the grandiose style of Baroque (*see pp.40–41*). The new style—on display at the 1902 International Exhibition of Modern Decorative Arts in Turin—was taken up by artisans such as Ernesto Basile, a master of *Stile Floreale*; the prolific designer and cabinet-maker Carlo Zen; and Eugenio Quarto. Quarto's exquisitely carved pieces were praised for appealing to Italian tastes and modern living needs, rather than replicating northern European Art Nouveau designs.

CARLO BUGATTI

However, it was Carlo Bugatti who held pride of place as a designer of extraordinary originality. Bugatti established workshops in Milan in 1888, where he created an eclectic interpretation of Art Nouveau, based on flowers, animals, and plants, Egyptian, Byzantine, and Moorish influences, Japanese art, and fantasy.

The handcrafted furniture produced in Bugatti's workshop—desks, cabinets, chairs, and settees—was not well constructed but had a rustic, imaginative charm. The furniture often combined useful features, such as tables with built-in cabinets, and chairs that incorporated lamps. Pieces used a wide range of sumptuous materials, including silk, leather, and vellum for upholstering chairs and covering boxes and tabletops, and ebony, bone, mother-of-pearl, and metals, which were used as inlays.

The range of Bugatti's influences can be seen in his use of soft, warm colors, textiles, and strips of beaten or pierced metal evocative of North Africa, and the distinctive shield backs, crescent legs, and pinnacle and minaret shapes inspired by Islamic motifs. Bugatti caused a sensation with the furniture he designed for particular settings, such as the prize-winning Moorish interior he created for the Italian Pavilion at the 1902 Turin International Exhibition of Modern Decorative Arts.

While Bugatti's early furniture was robust, with lively, complex patterns, he later developed a more restrained style that depended on a palette of pale colors and serpentine curves, influenced by the Parisian Art Nouveau designers.

SPAIN AND GAUDI

A band of Catalan architects, led by Antoni Gaudi in Barcelona, brought the Art Nouveau style to Spain. A daringly original designer, Gaudi created idiosyncratic furniture that embraced nature with its sinuous shapes and lavish use of decorative flower and plant motifs. Gaudi's furniture featured several practical elements, such as cupboards that incorporated small tables. He often worked in oak, and much of his furniture was created for his sculptural buildings, such as Casa Mila and the Guell Palace. Other Spanish champions of Art Nouveau included cabinet-makers Gaspar Homar and Juan Busquet, who were known for their fantastic furniture.

ITALIAN CHAIR

This Italian side chair was designed by Giacomo Cometti and is made of carved oak. The sinuous carving on the back of the chair is confined to the splat, and the basic shape of the chair is uncluttered by ornate decoration. The upholstery is attached to the seat with small brass studs. *c. 1902.*

SPANISH CABINET

This corner cabinet is made of oak. It has a round top with two curved glazed doors at the front. The doors are divided into six panels of glass by sinuous wooden partitions. The interior of the cabinet has two shelves, and the piece stands on three legs. *1904–05.* H:90½ in (230 cm).

ITALIAN SIDEBOARD

This Italian carved oak sideboard was designed by Giacomo Cometti. The sideboard is decorated with sinuous brass mounts carved with floral and foliate motifs, which are typical of the low-relief metalwork favored by Cometti. The upper section consists of a central cupboard and drawers flanked by open storage. The lower section contains a marble-topped cupboard. Cometti was an artist-turned craftsman who originally trained as a sculptor. He was heavily influenced by the English Arts and Crafts Movement. *c. 1902.*

Parlor, designed by Agostino Lauro True to the concept that the room should be designed as a unified whole, all the elements of this parlor follow the same sinuous styling. The built-in bookcases are an integral part of the wall design and the furniture echoes the curves of the paneling.

MEDITERRANEAN ARMCHAIR

This striking "Calvet" armchair is made entirely of oak. The piece was designed by Antoni Gaudi and has a heart-shaped back. The rounded seat rests on gently curving cabriole legs. *c. 1900. H:37½ in (95 cm).*

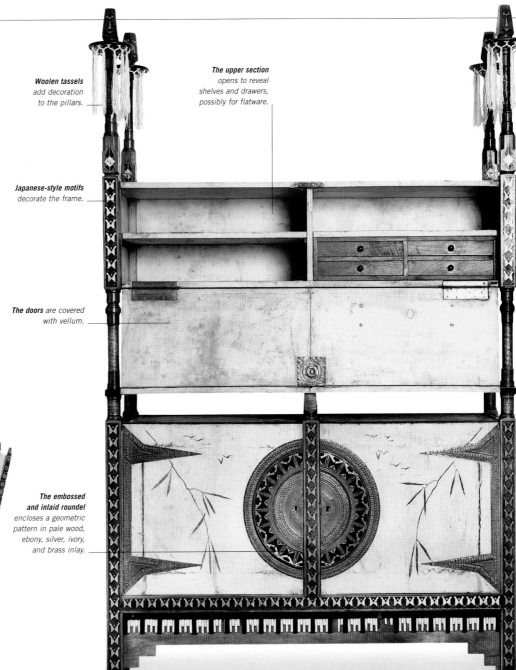

Woolen tassels add decoration to the pillars.

The upper section opens to reveal shelves and drawers, possibly for flatware.

Japanese-style motifs decorate the frame.

The doors are covered with vellum.

The embossed and inlaid roundel encloses a geometric pattern in pale wood, ebony, silver, ivory, and brass inlay.

NUTWOOD ARMCHAIRS

This pair of dark stained armchairs was designed by Carlo Bugatti. Each chair is decorated with inlaid pewter and embossed copper banding. The seat and back are upholstered in natural leather and further embellished with woolen tassels. *c. 1900. H:46¾ in (118.7 cm). DOR*

ITALIAN INLAID SIDEBOARD

Made by Carlo Bugatti, this sideboard shows Japanese, Moorish, and Egyptian influences. The doors are covered with vellum, and the upper door is hinged and drops down to reveal shelving and small drawers. The whole piece is contained within a four-pillar construction; the frame is made of brown stained and

polished nutwood with tops and inlays, and the boxes are made of softwood, covered with parchment and Japanese-style painted motifs. The piece is also decorated with lavish inlay materials, including brass, silver, ebony, and ivory. This imaginative combination of wood, metal, parchment, and vellum results in an idiosyncratic style. *c. 1900. W:60 in (154.4 cm). VZ*

PRAYER BENCH

This prayer bench, designed by Antoni Gaudi, has a curved back, with flat armrests and a slightly bowed seat. The bench is supported on slender and elegant curving legs, which are linked by stretchers. *Early 20th century.*

OCCASIONAL TABLE

This mahogany occasional table by Carlo Bugatti has a top inlaid with pewter and bone and circular marquetry, and sides with stylized florets and roundels. The legs feature embossed bronzed coverings. *Early 20th century. H:15¾ in (40 cm). L&T*

CHARLES RENNIE MACKINTOSH

STRAIGHT LINES WITH GENTLE CURVES AND GEOMETRIC DECORATION TYPIFY THE ELEGANTLY ATTENUATED FURNITURE BY ONE OF SCOTLAND'S MOST RESPECTED DESIGNERS.

BORN AND EDUCATED in Glasgow, Charles Rennie Mackintosh won many prizes as a student, including the prestigious Alexander Thomson Traveling Scholarship, which took him to France, Belgium, and Italy. His career as an architect began in 1889 when he joined the firm of John Honeyman and Keppie, rising to partner 12 years later, and remaining there until 1914. Mackintosh turned his back on the widespread preference for the Classical tradition, cultivating instead an interest in Gothic architecture as well as that of his native Scotland.

Whereas furniture design in most parts of Great Britain was dominated by the Arts and Crafts style, a new design movement flourished in Glasgow. Mackintosh was heavily influenced by the journal *The Studio*, which illustrated the work of innovative artists and designers, and he started to design furniture, textiles, and interiors. Encouraged by Francis Newbury, the progressive director of the Glasgow School of Art, Mackintosh teamed up with the artist Herbert MacNair and the sisters Frances and Margaret Macdonald to form "The Glasgow Four." Together they created distinctive designs for furniture, textiles, metalwork, and posters that became known as the Glasgow Style (*see p.366*).

ARCHITECT AND FURNITURE DESIGNER

Among Mackintosh's architectural achievements were the design and furnishing of the Glasgow School of Art in 1897; a number of Glasgow tearooms for Miss Kate Cranston in collaboration with the decorator George Walton; and several private houses. Furniture was minimal, emphasizing spatial effects and giving the rooms an almost poetic atmosphere.

Mackintosh designed furniture in his own name and also provided designs for the Glasgow furniture-makers Guthrie and Wells. Chairs particularly caught his imagination, and he designed a variety of original styles in which the back was the main focus of attention. The furniture for Miss Cranston's tearooms included the first of his signature high-backed chairs, in this case with an oval-shaped top rail.

EBONIZED SYCAMORE CHAIR
This chair has a distinctive geometric trellis back resembling a stylized tree extending to the lower stretcher. The drop-in seat is upholstered in a plain fabric. The piece was designed for Miss Cranston's "Hous'hill." 1904. H:28¼ in (72 cm). L&T

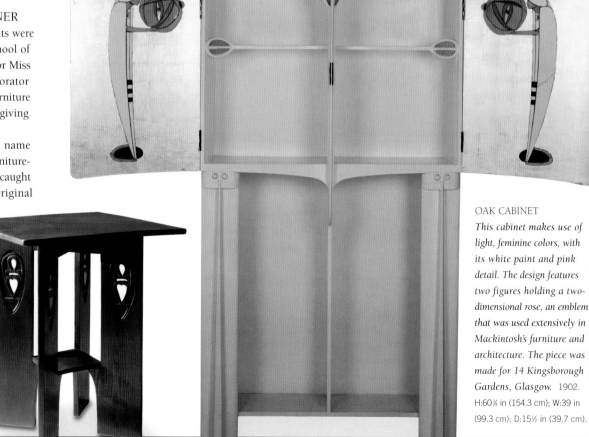

OAK TABLE
This table is of characteristic rectilinear design with bold, straight lines and a cut-out heart motif on each of the supporting legs. The table was designed for the Billiard Room at Miss Cranston's Argyle Tearooms. 1897. H:28 in (71 cm); W:24 in (61 cm); D:24 in (61 cm).

OAK CABINET
This cabinet makes use of light, feminine colors, with its white paint and pink detail. The design features two figures holding a two-dimensional rose, an emblem that was used extensively in Mackintosh's furniture and architecture. The piece was made for 14 Kingsborough Gardens, Glasgow. 1902. H:60¾ in (154.3 cm); W:39 in (99.3 cm); D:15½ in (39.7 cm).

MACKINTOSH INTERIORS

AMONG HIS MANY ACHIEVEMENTS, CHARLES RENNIE MACKINTOSH IS BEST REMEMBERED FOR DESIGNING BUILDINGS WITH DECORATIVE INTERIORS THAT WERE CREATED AS PART OF A SINGLE, COHESIVE THEME.

In 1896, Mackintosh won the competition to design the new Glasgow School of Art. Mackintosh not only produced the architectural design for the school but also designed the interiors, in collaboration with Margaret Macdonald. The design, which successfully blended clean, rectangular shapes with the languid, delicate curves of Art Nouveau, covered everything

from mantlepieces, lighting fixtures, and carpets to furniture and crockery.

In 1897, Mackintosh received the first in a series of commissions from Kate Cranston to decorate her chain of Glasgow tearooms, a collaboration that continued until 1917. For the Buchanan Street rooms, Mackintosh's input was restricted to the production of wall murals—the interiors and furnishings were designed by George Walton. However, for the next commission—the Argyle Street Tearooms—these responsibilities were reversed, and Mackintosh produced his innovative, rectilinear chair designs. Mackintosh went on to create unified decorative schemes for tearooms in Ingram Street and at The Willow in Sauchiehall Street, where the architecture and interior design combined to create serene atmospheres. Furniture was restrained in both shape and decoration and exhibited his signature "light feminine" and "dark masculine" color schemes. The importance that Mackintosh placed on total design meant that he even designed the teaspoons and waitresses' dresses for The Willow's *Room de Luxe*.

While Kate Cranston was Mackintosh's most consistent patron, others who bought into his ideal of integrated interiors included the Wiener Werkstätte's primary financial backer, Fritz Warndorfer, for whom he designed a music room, and the publisher Walter Blackie, who commissioned Hill House near Glasgow.

The House of an Art Lover, Glasgow Mackintosh's geometric interior features a suite of white high-backed chairs and a square dining table. The geometric shapes of the furniture are echoed in the wall panelling.

A SOPHISTICATED STYLE

The principles that lay at the heart of the Arts and Crafts movement, such as careful attention to fine craftsmanship and using the nature, beauty, and color of wood for decorative effect, mattered little to Mackintosh. Instead, his sophisticated furniture designs, which were sometimes even structurally unsound, were inspired by E. W. Godwin's work and were based on bold, straight lines combined with gentle curves. Mackintosh's favorite woods included oak and beech, and while rich "dark masculine" tones of gray, brown, and olive were used, he favored a palette of "light feminine" white and pastel shades, similar to the colors found in the paintings of American artist James McNeill Whistler.

Decoration was sparing and featured geometric shapes such as rectangles and squares; curved, rounded inlays in metal, pink or amethyst-colored glass, mother-of-pearl, or enamel; and intricate flower motifs such as the rose, derived from Japanese patterns and Celtic art. Elegant chairs had attenuated backs, cupboards were crowned with broad projecting cornices, and tables had long, tapered supports. Mackintosh's interpretation of Art Nouveau was in marked contrast to both the luxurious sensuality of the French and Belgian Art Nouveau and the robust, masculine style found in English Arts and Crafts furniture.

GAINING RECOGNITION

Although Mackintosh's pure, rectilinear style was largely ignored in the rest of Great Britain, it was widely admired throughout Europe and had a great influence on artists in Germany and Austria. When Mackintosh exhibited his furniture at the 8th Secessionist Exhibition in 1900 in Vienna, his work made a lasting impression on contemporary Austrian designers: Koloman Moser and Josef Hoffmann, in particular, appreciated his confident, rational style, and decorative schemes.

Mackintosh left Glasgow for London in 1914, and his last years were devoted to a few modest architectural projects, painting, and textile designs. A memorial exhibition, after his death, in Glasgow in 1933 stimulated interest in Mackintosh's designs for buildings, interiors, and furniture, and finally gave him the recognition he deserved. In the 1950s, a revival of interest in Art Nouveau sparked a reappraisal of Mackintosh's furniture designs, and today he is acknowledged as an influential forerunner of the Modern movement (see pp.416–47).

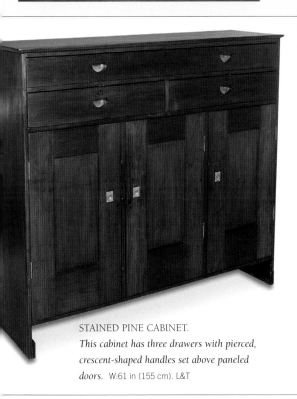

STAINED PINE CABINET.
This cabinet has three drawers with pierced, crescent-shaped handles set above paneled doors. W:61 in (155 cm). L&T

CABINET ON STAND
This oak rectilinear cabinet has two doors with central glazed panels, and the frame has three square-section vertical supports at either end, joined by two stretchers at floor level. Midway up is a shelf with a raised edge on three sides. 1900. H:55½ in (141 cm). Qu

THE GLASGOW SCHOOL

AT THE HEART OF the Art Nouveau movement in Scotland, the Glasgow School of Art sowed the seeds of an artistic revolution.

The enterprising director, Francis Newbery, and his wife Jessie, were instrumental in taking the Glasgow School of Art beyond its traditional role as an institution for formal instruction in painting. A great admirer and champion of the teachings of William Morris, Newbery urged his students to learn as much as they could from the Arts and Crafts and Art Nouveau movements. He set up art studios where artist-craftsmen provided a "technical artistic education" in a broad range of commercial crafts, including bookbinding, woodcarving, ceramics, stained glass, and metalwork.

KEY DESIGNERS

An influential team of designers and architects closely associated with the Glasgow School included Charles Rennie Mackintosh, J. Herbert MacNair, and the sisters Margaret and Frances MacDonald. Known as "The Glasgow Four" or "Four Macs," they created furniture and interior decoration inspired by Arts and Crafts ideology, but which developed as a movement in its own right and was celebrated around the world as the "Glasgow Style". This style incorporated natural imagery together with a strong, psychological identification with the city—then booming economically and culturally—powered by its engineering and industrial skills.

It was a decidedly Scottish and occasionally modest interpretation of Art Nouveau. Simple, geometric furniture designs were decorated with stylized patterns of flowers, plants, animals, figural patterns, and Celtic-style decoration. These were shown in unusual colors drawn from local scenery, such as

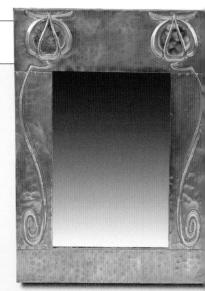

A Glasgow School hammered brass mirror This piece has a repoussé, stylized, floral motif design with long, flowing tendrils ending in a swirl, and a circular bud design with striking blue enamel centers. *c. 1900–10. H:23¼ in (59 cm). GDG*

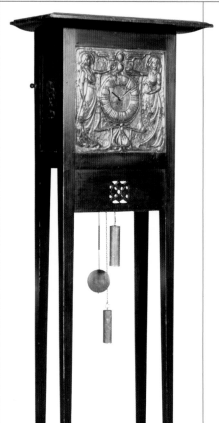

STANDING CLOCK

The stained beech case has foliate piercings. The brass dial, designed by Margaret Thomson Wilson, depicts two female figures—one holding a galleon—touching a stylized hourglass above sinuous plant forms. *c. 1900. H:80½ in (206 cm). L&T*

HALLSTAND

This arched rectangular mirror is set in a shaped and pierced oval frame fitted with coat pegs above a shelf. The piece is made of ebonized wood. It has a glove drawer and a shaped, foliate upright supporting a stick stand. *H:75½ in (192 cm). L&T*

ARMCHAIR

This stained beech chair has an elongated splat inlaid with stylized plant forms, a U-shaped top rail and arms, an upholstered panel seat, and square, tapering, stretchered legs. *H:58 in (147.25 cm). L&T*

TABLE CABINET

This *Bijouterie* table and cabinet by James Herbert MacNair is made of stained beech. The glazed, hinged top is flanked by sliding *demi-lune* display boxes. It has square, tapering legs. *c. 1901. H:30½ in (77 cm). L&T*

SETTLE

This stained beech settle by Sir Robert Lorimer has a rectangular solid seat and back. The back is carved with five roundels enclosing leafy plant forms and bears the inscription: "*Blessit be simple life without end Reid.*" *W:59¾ in (152 cm). L&T*

heathery purple, misty grays, and soft green. The Glasgow style won international acclaim, especially at the 8th Secessionist Exhibition in 1900 in Vienna, and exercised a potent influence on the architects of industrial design in Germany and Austria. The rooms furnished by the group for the 1902 Turin International Exhibition of Modern Decorative Arts focused on controlled line, eschewing serpentine curves, and favoring symmetrical flowers,

The Glasgow School of Art This building was designed by Charles Rennie Mackintosh in 1896 and is regarded as one of his most notable architectural achievements.

elongated figures, and intricate linear designs in glass, metal, and enamel.

THE ROSE EMBLEM

Nature always inspired the Glasgow Four and was occasionally approached from a scientific perspective. Even the group's emblem—the two-dimensional rose, which was designed by Mackintosh and featured frequently on its architecture and furniture—was

inspired by a cabbage cut in half. Other talents associated with the Glasgow School were Ernest Archibald Taylor, lauded for his clean, elegant, and highly refined designs in the style of Charles Rennie Mackintosh; George Walton, with his delicate and subtle designs for furniture, textiles, and glass; and Talwin Morris, who worked in a variety of media, from furniture to textiles, metalwork, and glass.

Geometric floral design

Molded hinges and handles display intricate foliate designs.

Elaborate wooden inlays depict stylized geometric floral designs.

Rectangular and arched fielded panels decorate the front.

The pierced wooden plinth has a curved geometric pattern.

HALLSTAND

This hallstand is made of stained oak. It was designed by Wylie and Lochhead and shows the influence of Mackintosh. The molded cornice above a central beveled plate is flanked by repoussé copper panels showing stylized briar roses. Decorative supports in the form of flower stems add to the overall design. *H:79 in (197 cm); W:73 in (186 cm); D:12½ in (32 cm).* L&T

MAHOGANY CUPBOARD

This inlaid cupboard is made from mahogany and consists of elegant, vertical lines embellished with a projecting and molded cornice. It is raised on a plinth. In contrast to the simple lines of the piece, the fielded, paneled door is inlaid with florid, geometric, stylized flowers, plant forms, foliage, and stems, and is flanked by similarly inlaid panels.

The molded hinges and handles are elaborately decorated with foliate motifs. The plinth is pierced at the front and sides with a repeating heart-shaped pattern that echoes the inlaid design. The cupboard was possibly designed by J.S. Henry, a Glasgow wholesale company that often supplied furniture to Liberty and Co. and worked with leading designers such as George Walton. *H:82¾ in (210 cm); W:59 in (150 cm).* L&T

BRITAIN

BRITISH FURNITURE DESIGNERS took the basic themes of Art Nouveau and interpreted them in two different ways: some experimented with a more understated version of the flowing, feminine lines popular in France and Belgium; others, most famously Scotland's Charles Rennie Mackintosh (see pp.364–65), favored the restrained, rectilinear style seen in Germany and Austria. In fact, the Viennese Secessionists later drew inspiration themselves from the bold, architectural furniture that Mackintosh designed. Interestingly, the Art Nouveau movement in Great Britain also evolved from the stylized forms of Aesthetic period furniture (see p.326).

WELL-CRAFTED FURNITURE
Toward the end of the 19th century, the quality of British furniture had started to decline, as mass-production enabled manufacturers to churn out hundreds of identical pieces at affordable prices for the growing middle class.

The work of William Morris and the Arts and Crafts movement had started to reverse this by championing furniture handmade by craftsmen. The trend was continued by designers and craftsmen working in the Art Nouveau style, who, despite using machines to produce their furniture, also put a premium on quality.

Many British Art Nouveau furniture-makers used satinwood or walnut as well as mahogany for their designs. Some of the most spectacular examples of their work are display cabinets or cupboards that feature intricately cut and inlaid designs.

SHAPLAND AND PETTER
Although perhaps best known for their work in the Arts and Crafts tradition, the firm of Shapland and Petter produced elaborate, high-quality furniture in exotic woods such as mahogany. Based in Barnstaple, Devon, they also made oak pieces decorated with good-quality carving, color-stained panels, or stylized copper panels, as well as ceramic roundels made locally by the Brannam pottery works.

Their team of designers remained anonymous, but Shapland and Petter supplied stores across Great Britain,

including Marsh Jones and Cribbs in Leeds, and Wylie and Lochhead in Glasgow. Their work also sold abroad. Although their furniture was mass-produced, it was of very high quality.

DECORATIVE INLAYS AND MOTIFS
Shapland and Petter, together with the architect and designer Ernest Gimson, used inlays of ivory, silver, abalone shell, mother-of-pearl, and fruitwoods to decorate their designs.

As in France and Belgium, motifs from the natural world—stylized peacock feathers, snowdrops, and lilies—were worked in marquetry or metal inlays; designs for decorative hinges and door pulls were often inspired by the sinuous, whiplash lines favored by Continental makers.

The Glasgow firm of Wylie and Lochhead also made pieces in this style, sometimes combining elements with the angular look favored by Mackintosh and the Glasgow School.

ARTS AND CRAFTS HYBRID
Some of the designers and craftsmen who had been working in the Arts and Crafts style—including Charles Frances Annesley Voysey and Charles Robert Ashbee—were influenced by Art Nouveau motifs, and combined them with a more sturdy Arts and Crafts form to create a hybrid look.

Voysey, for example, used decoration sparingly, preferring to let the grain and beauty of the woods he used speak for themselves. However, when he occasionally used metal mounts or panels, these were often in a flowing style inspired by Art Nouveau.

The London store Liberty & Co. (see right) helped to popularize Art Nouveau by championing the work of the most innovative designers, such as Voysey and Mackintosh, and also by commissioning commercial imitations. Much of Liberty's furniture was made in oak and mahogany, and the designs they commissioned from Leonard F. Wyburd and E. G. Punnett for oak cupboards, tables, and chairs are among the store's most widely recognized items of furniture. Liberty furniture was known for its simple construction, symmetrical design, and the restrained use of decorative motifs, and it was often marked "Liberty & Co." on a rectangular plaque.

UPHOLSTERED ARMCHAIR
This mahogany armchair has distinctive, horizontal, slatted arms and a drop-in seat. The top rail is inlaid with a band of five stylized seedpods. The seat and back are upholstered in a floral fabric. *L&T*

OCCASIONAL TABLE
This table has a shaped lower tier beneath the hexagonal lobed top. There are three elaborately pierced supports, each terminating in a pair of slender, curved legs. *H:28¼ in (70.5 cm). L&T*

LIBERTY & CO.

THIS EMPORIUM ON LONDON'S REGENT STREET WAS FOUNDED IN 1875, AND WAS AT THE VANGUARD OF THE NEW STYLE.

In 1883, Liberty & Co., already famous for its Oriental wares and Art Nouveau fabrics, opened a Furnishing and Decorating Studio under the direction of Leonard F. Wyburd. The Studio's aim was to meet the growing demand for fashionable, decorative, and affordable furniture that incorporated the design vocabulary of Art Nouveau. The furniture borrowed freely from pioneering designers such as C. F. A. Voysey and Charles Rennie Mackintosh, who also contributed designs. By 1887, Liberty was selling a highly successful range of simple chairs and country-style oak furniture embellished with inlaid decoration, elaborate strap hinges, leaded glass panels, and tiles, bringing Art Nouveau furniture to a wider audience.

A signature Liberty & Co. ivorine plaque

Copper mirror This piece is decorated with embossed repoussé stems, each supporting a blue bud-shaped "roundel," or pottery disc. *c. 1900. W:25 in (64.5 cm). PUR*

Walnut dressing table The table has original hinged copper handles. The simple construction and restrained decoration are typical of Liberty & Co. *H:71 in (180 cm). L&T*

CORNER CHAIR

Specifically designed to stand in a corner, and a direct descendant of the corner chairs of the late 18th century, this chair has backs on two sides of the square rush seat. The molded top rail is supported by shaped splats. The chair is raised on turned legs, linked by parallel stretchers, and ending in bulbous feet. *L&T*

WRITING DESK

The pierced gallery at the back of this mahogany desk, and the embossed copper panels depicting owls and stylized plants, place this piece firmly in the Art Nouveau period. The desk is thought to be the work of either Shapland & Petter or Wylie & Lochhead—both highly regarded furniture manufacturers. *H:46½ in (118 cm); W:41¾ in (106 cm). L&T*

DISPLAY CABINET

This ornate and curvaceous mahogany cabinet features marquetry decoration of flowers and whiplash tendrils. This fashionable technique was used extensively on expensive furniture during the period. The cabinet doors, positioned below the oval mirror, are made of leaded glass decorated with a tulip pattern. *H:70¾ in (177 cm). L&T*

The door and drawer fittings are handmade.

A central tabernacle provides open storage.

The marquetry panel has a stylized and geometric floral design.

The door hinges, handles, and escutcheon are decorated with bold geometric motifs.

The wooden case was made by machine.

WARDROBE

This mahogany wardrobe is a high-quality combination of traditional craftsmanship and machine technology typical of its maker, Shapland & Petter. A decorative feature is made of the plated metal-hammered door and drawer hardware, and the central cupboard door is inlaid with distinctive foliate motifs. *H:82¾ in (210 cm). DN*

EDWARDIAN BRITAIN

WHILE SOME EDWARDIAN households embraced the latest Art Nouveau forms, many returned to the furniture styles of the past and the latest Classical revivals. Designs from various historical periods were dusted off and reworked by companies throughout Great Britain. Inspiration ranged from the distant past—Renaissance, Elizabethan, Jacobean, and even Gothic—to the more recent Neoclassical work of Sheraton, Hepplewhite, and Robert Adam. The result was comfortable rather than cutting-edge, and less cluttered than the Victorian ideal.

Art Nouveau and Revival furniture were made in parallel to satisfy the needs of the less adventurous Edwardians as well as those who subscribed to the latest fashions.

REVIVAL FURNITURE

The Revival trend had started in the late 19th century after a new series of interior design books, aimed at the middle classes, reignited the fashion for the three great names of British Neoclassical furniture. Then, in 1897, Sheraton's *The Cabinet-Maker and Upholsterer's Drawing Book* and Hepplewhite's *The Cabinet-Maker and*

Upholsterer's Guide were reprinted and the Revival was confirmed. The result was a fusion of the work of these three designers, adapted to suit smaller Edwardian rooms and a desire for comfort. It was also a rejection of the heavy, somber furniture popular in Victorian times.

Revival furniture was often made from light mahogany, satinwood, or satin-birch, and decorated with stringing, crossbanding, and wooden inlays of fans or shells, set with bone, or painted with flowers and foliate scrolls. Decoration was often elaborate. Sometimes pieces were made from less exotic and expensive wood and

painted to resemble satinwood.

Some designers slimmed down Sheraton's designs to make them more delicate. This occasionally went too far and resulted in pieces that were spindly and out of proportion.

Others took the path of true imitation and aimed to recreate Sheraton and other Neoclassical designers exactly. Some of these pieces are so faithful to the original that it takes an expert to tell them apart. Gillow of Lancaster and Edwards

SIDE CHAIR

This is one of a pair of Sheraton Revival satinwood side chairs. The pierced, oval back is centered by a portrait of a young girl, and the seat is covered with caning. The front legs are turned. *Early 20th century. DN*

Glass shelves reflect the light and emphasize the objects inside.

Glass panels allow treasured objects to be displayed.

Painted swags and medallions are Classically inspired.

The casing and legs are slender and delicate.

SATINWOOD VITRINE

The elegant proportions of this cabinet are characteristic of the Edwardian era, when furniture became more slender and delicate. Influences were diverse, but the painted swag decoration, medallions, and motifs typical of

the period are Classical in style. The cornice and pediment are decorated with portrait-style paintings. Vitrines did not become common until the second half of the 19th century. This one bears a label from Maple & Co. *Early 20th century.* H:29¾ in (73 cm); W:53½ in (136.5 cm). MLL

OCCASIONAL TABLE

This circular table is made from mahogany and has satinwood banding and floral marquetry. The square tapered supports are united by stretchers. *Early 20th century.* D:26 in (66 cm). GorL and Roberts of London are among the best of these furniture-makers, but many other firms made inexpensive copies for the mass-market. Many pieces were not marked by the makers, so attributing them can be difficult.

A STEADY DEMAND

Despite the volume of furniture made, much Edwardian furniture was of good quality. However, veneers were sometimes used to disguise poor construction. There was a great demand for desks; bookcases; chests-of-drawers; display cabinets; commodes; side, dining, and other chairs; tables including dining, occasional, and dressing; marble-topped washstands; bedside cupboards; and wardrobes that were frequently part of a bedroom suite.

Sofas were often based on Sheraton and Hepplewhite styles, but were less overblown than Victorian examples. Manufacturers made suites of chairs with matching sofas, usually from mahogany, but sometimes walnut or satinwood. Seats were often upholstered in silk or damask, while the backs and sides were caned.

PRINCIPAL MAKERS

Important names in Edwardian furniture included Waring and Gillow and Maple and Co. Maples was based on Tottenham Court Road, London, and was the largest furniture store in the world. It made its own furniture

for sale at home and abroad, and drew its customers from both the middle and upper classes and even royalty—Czar Nicholas of Russia furnished his Winter Palace with furniture from its workrooms. Maples also furnished British Embassies, even going so far as to arrange for a grand piano to be carried up the Khyber Pass on packhorses.

For those whose taste did not fit in with either the Revival or Art Nouveau movements, there was an opportunity to furnish their homes in an exotic manner using the new bamboo and wicker furniture, or pieces with a Moorish or Japanese influence.

Elaborate drop handle

Classical inlay motif

LADY'S WRITING DESK

Probably made by Maple & Co, this rosewood and marquetry compact lady's writing desk, or *bonheur-du-jour*, has a raised, galleried back with lidded interior compartments. The inset-leather writing surface sits above three frieze drawers and the piece is raised on slender legs. *c. 1905. W:40 in (100 cm). FRE*

ROLLTOP DESK

The lid of this satinwood marquetry-decorated piece opens to reveal a mechanical interior. Initially introduced in the 18th century, the rolltop desk was reinterpreted during the Art Nouveau period to meet changing tastes. *Early 20th century. W:37½ in (95 cm). DN*

TWO-TIER *ÉTAGÈRE*

This *étagère* is made of inlaid mahogany and satinwood banding. The top is formed from a later glass-based tray, and the piece stands on square, swept supports. *Étagères* were used for displaying objects or serving food. *Early 20th century. W:36 in (91.5 cm). GorL*

DISPLAY CABINET

This impressive mahogany cabinet has crossbanded decoration and astragal-glazed panels and a door. The cornice is centered with an architectural pediment and the base is decorated with fiddleback mahogany-and-satinwood lozenges on the central door and canted sides. The cabinet stands on slender legs. *Early 20th century. W:37½ in (95 cm). DN*

GERMANY

GERMANY TOOK LONGER to embrace the changes in decorative arts seen elsewhere in Europe. This was largely because it was still preoccupied with the prevailing *Historismus* style, where design was centered on an interpretation of historic elements.

However, through the influence of the Belgian designer Henri van de Velde—who worked on a number of high-profile projects in Germany—and the innovative work of gifted German artists such as Richard Riemerschmid, Peter Behrens, and Franz von Stuck, the Art Nouveau style became popular. This style was known in Germany as *Jugendstil*

(Youth Style)—a name associated with the popular review *Die Jugend*—and it subsequently flourished throughout Germany during the last decades of the 19th century.

Jugendstil embraced both Symbolism and a preoccupation with nature and natural shapes. It was applied to everything from architecture to furniture and simple household objects. Each element had to work as part of the whole in terms of form and design: a concept called *Gesamtkunstwerk*. The aim was to make the home a unified work of art: practical, simple, dignified, and beautiful.

Many of the exponents of *Jugendstil*

were painters who turned to the decorative arts as part of a reaction against the stifling historicism of the fine arts. Munich was home to some of these designers, and came to be the city at the heart of the movement.

INNOVATIVE DESIGNERS

Early advocates of *Jugendstil* included Hermann Obrist, who was inspired by the Symbolists' emotions and the plant world, and architect August Endell, who played a pivotal role throughout the development of Munich's Secessionist movement by seeking to echo the spirit of his Austrian

contemporaries. Endell designed boldly proportioned, clean-lined furniture in materials such as elm or forged steel, and paid considerable attention to decorative detail.

Among the furniture designers in the Munich group were Richard Riemerschmid, Bruno Paul, and the architect Peter Behrens.

Behrens was also one of the founding members of the *Vereinigte Werkstätten für Kunst im Handwerk* (United Workshops for Applied Art). His furniture combined traditional rectilinear shapes with restrained curves. Richard Riemerschmid, a talented designer, painter, and

The six-panel circular top is repeated in the six C-scroll supports underneath the table.

The six veneered fields bring out the decorative quality of the wood surface.

The pedestal is urn-shaped.

Six C-scroll supports stand on a plain circular foot plate.

SIDE CHAIR

This chair by Peter Behrens was designed for the poet Richard Dehmel's house in Hamburg. Made of white painted wood, the chair is geometric in design, with bold cut-out shapes on the back, and has straight legs. *c. 1903. H:37½ in (95 cm).*

CIRCULAR DINING TABLE

This oak pedestal dining table was designed by Peter Behrens and made by *Vereinigte Werkstätten für Kunst im Handwerk*, Munich. It has a paneled top above an urn-shaped pedestal. The six C-scroll supports underneath the table repeat the symmetry of the six-panel circular top. The circular foot plate also repeats the

shape of the circular table top. With Richard Riemerschmid, Behrens was the first industrial designer, designing specifically for mass production. With this piece, Behrens moved away from his earlier elaborate and curvilinear Art Nouveau style, toward a simpler style reliant on the quality of the wood, and simple shapes and proportions. *c. 1900. W:40¾ in (102 cm). QU*

YELLOW LACQUERED CUPBOARD

This pinewood cupboard was designed by Gertrud Kleinhempel and made by Dresdner Werkstätten. Two of its four doors are pierced with heart motifs, and it is divided horizontally with three rows of rectangular, black-and-white scenic panels. *c. 1900. H:73 in (185 cm). QU*

architect, was also linked to the workshops. His furniture followed Behrens' example but was also influenced by Celtic origins, which played a role in Germany's decorative traditions. His simply shaped furniture used wood in its natural state and color, with the grain its most distinctive decorative feature. Bruno Paul, another protagonist of *Jugendstil*, developed comfortable, rectilinear designs called *Typenmöbel*, which he was able to mass-produce. They were a forerunner of the industrial furniture production of the 1930s and 40s.

Germany also spawned a host of artists' guilds, established in an effort to realize the ideals of the British Arts and Crafts movement.

THE DARMSTADT COLONY
The most notable of these guilds was founded in 1899 by Ernst Ludwig, Grand Duke of Hesse, and was based at Darmstadt. Largely the vision of the Austrian architect and designer Josef Maria Olbrich, the Darmstadt colony included public buildings and residences that were designed, built, and furnished for various artists.
    Some of the most celebrated examples of the German "new

art" could be found at Darmstadt in the house that Peter Behrens designed for himself. The interior, furniture, and decoration created a unified whole.
    By the beginning of the 20th century, Germany had embraced industrial production and increasingly turned its attention to improving the quality of mass-produced, industrial products. This signaled the death knell for Art Nouveau, with its ideals of hand-craftsmanship, freedom of artistic creation, and refined decoration.

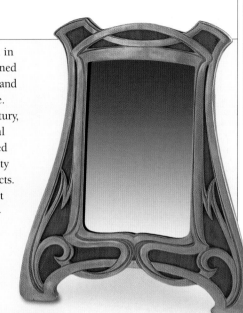

Pewter picture frame The frame has a curvaceous, waisted shape with sinuous and interlaced stylized plant motifs rising from the feet. *c. 1905. H:9½ in (24 cm). TO*

DINING CHAIR

This is a poplar dining chair that comes from a set of nine, designed by Peter Behrens. It is lacquered and has a leather seat. *c. 1901.*

BEECH FRAME ARMCHAIR

This beech chair was designed by Marcel Kammerer and made by Thonet of Vienna *(see p.375)*. The bentwood frame is stained mahogany, and the stuffed seat and buttoned back are covered in brown leather. *c. 1910. H:32 in (81.5 cm). DOR*

SIX-DRAWER COMMODE

This stained pine commode, designed by Richard Riemerschmid, has a rectangular top with a three-sided backsplash. The six drawers have nickel-plated pulls. *c. 1905. H:51½ in (130.5 cm). QU*

LEMON MAHOGANY CUPBOARD

This Patriz Huber cupboard is polished and partly carved. It has inlays of different exotic woods and copper mountings. The top has faceted glazing and shelves on either side. *c. 1900. H:80 in (200 cm). QU*

COUCH TABLE

This mahogany table, designed by Richard Riemerschmid and made by Dresdner Werkstätten, has a hexagonal top, a round second tier, and curved legs. *1905. H:27 in (69 cm); W:20 in (51 cm); D:20 in (51 cm). QU*

OAK FRAME ARMCHAIR

This oak chair by Otto Eckmann has square-section arms, rails, legs, supports, and stretchers, with the latter two bowed. It has a brass-riveted, leather-upholstered back and seat pads. *c. 1900. H:37½ in (95 cm). QU*

AUSTRIA

VIENNA WAS PARTICULARLY receptive to the desire for innovation that swept across Europe in the last 25 years of the 19th century. This recognition of the need for change signaled the approaching demise of the Austro-Hungarian Empire, which collapsed at the end of World War I. Austria founded its own distinctive version of Art Nouveau, and established a new set of stylistic ideals.

The Vienna art establishment was challenged by a group of artists, architects, and designers, who, in 1897, founded the "Secession" under the chairmanship of Gustav Klimt. This movement protested against the conservative teachings of its masters and campaigned for modernity, heralding the beginning of one of Austria's most creative periods.

BOLD DESIGNS
Sculptors and artists were active in the Secession, as were the architects and interior designers Otto Wagner, Adolf Loos, and Josef Maria Olbrich, and furniture designers Josef Hoffmann and Koloman Moser. This enterprising group created bold furniture designs for the new century. The Secessionists rejected the flamboyant naturalism of French Art Nouveau, preferring the linear furniture designs created by the Scottish architect Charles Rennie Mackintosh (see pp.364–65), who was widely admired in Vienna. Austrian designers were more influenced by the British Arts and Crafts movement of the late 19th century than by French or Belgian Art Nouveau.

NATURAL INSPIRATION
The Secessionists were inspired by the geometry of nature. The curving, sinuous plant forms popular with the French and Belgian Schools were rejected in favor of rectangles and squares. The Secessionists based their designs on a spare, geometric style,

The case is oak, furnished and polished, with maple inlays.

The panels of the glazed door form a geometric pattern with the low shelf.

The brass embossed panels with knight motifs were inspired by Klimt.

DISPLAY CABINET
This mahogany display cabinet is part of a dining-room set designed by Otto Wytrlik of Vienna. Note the straight lines of the design and the simple veneered walnut finish and brass hardware. c. 1901. WKA

BLACK-PAINTED CUPBOARD
Designed by Adolf Loos, this functional cupboard is made from softwood, painted black and then varnished. It has distinctive twin two-over-three glazed doors and brass hardware. c. 1908. H:56 in (142.25 cm). WKA

DISPLAY CABINET
This oak cabinet was made in Vienna. It is almost square in shape and rests on a framed plinth. The glazed central door is flanked by flat-panel doors with geometric-pattern oak figuring and maple inlays. The open shelf in the center is flanked by brass panels embossed with a scene depicting a harpist and a knight. The design of these panels was influenced by Gustav Klimt's Beethoven Frieze. The embossed panels were probably created for this piece by Klimt's brother, Georg. c. 1905–10. H:72 in (183 cm). QU

VIENNESE SERVING TABLE
This serving table is made of stained oak with brass handles. It has a removable top with glass inlay, and hinged sides with faceted glass panels to allow access to the shelves. c. 1905. H:31 in (77.5 cm). DOR

CIRCULAR TABLE
This small, circular-topped, beech bentwood table is of a very simple design with no additional decoration. It has two circular undertiers, and the piece stands on slightly splayed supports. H:29½ in (75 cm). DN

sing simple shapes and linear
atterns and new materials such
plywood, aluminum, and bent
eechwood. Their furniture was
esigned for uncluttered interiors.

EY FIGURES
he most distinguished Secessionists
ere Josef Hoffmann and Koloman

Moser, co-founders of the Wiener
Werkstätte in 1903. Hoffmann created
a purer, more linear version of the Art
Nouveau style producing furniture
in a simple, geometric form that was
elegant and restrained, thereby forging
a link between Art Nouveau and
Modernism. Hoffmann was a designer
for the firm established by the German,

Michael Thonet (see below).

More colorful than most Viennese
furniture of the time, Kolomon Moser's
tables, cabinets, and chairs were linear
but lavishly embellished. In fact,
decoration often took precedence over
form, with luxurious woods, such as
rosewood, used for veneers and
decorative inlays.

ADOLF LOOS

The architect Adolf Loos was a key
member of the Secessionist movement.
Better known for his philosophical
writings than his buildings, Loos
wrote an essay, "Ornament and
Crime," in which he opposed the
highly decorative style of Art Nouveau.
Instead, he advocated that reason, not
passion, should determine the way
that people designed.

The Secessionist's linear, geometric
interpretation of Art Nouveau paved
the way for the geometric shapes and
spare style later favored by the
Bauhaus and the Modern movement
of the 1930s.

ARCHWOOD TABLE AND CHAIRS

his round table and chairs were designed
nd made by the company of Portois & Fix in
enna. The chairs are made of larch wood
nd the backs are carved in an elaborate floral
attern. The seats are upholstered in a floral
fabric. The table is made of nut wood, with
a red-brown leather skiver on the top. The
profiled legs are decorated with floral carving,
and there is a shelf about halfway down the
legs. All of the pieces bear the manufacturer's
stamp. *c. 1900–05. H:42 in (106.5 cm)
(table). DOR*

BENTWOOD CHAIR

Armchair "No.25," made by Mundus of Vienna,
is made of dark-brown stained beech, with
an open backsplat decorated with stylized,
scrolling plant stems and a canework seat.
c. 1910. H:36 in (91.5 cm). DOR

FOOTSTAND

This three-legged footstand was designed by
Adolf Loos. It has a mahogany-stained, beach
top, which is carved into a bowl shape. The
piece stands on splayed mahogany legs.
c. 1905. H:17½ in (44 cm). DOR

GEBRÜDER THONET

IN AUSTRIA, THE EVOLUTION OF ART NOUVEAU FURNITURE OWES MUCH
TO THE TRAILBLAZING DESIGNS OF CRAFTSMAN MICHAEL THONET.

In his small furniture workshop,
Michael Thonet perfected the bentwood
technique—marrying forward-looking,
elegant design with industrial
production—that ultimately exploded
onto the international stage. In 1849,
Thonet established the Gebrüder Thonet
company, setting up a host of factories
across Eastern Europe. In the following
decades, the company achieved
tremendous growth and success as it
paved the way for the industrial mass-
production of functional, inexpensive
and robust furniture that contributed to
the fashion for minimal ornamentation.

Toward the end of the 19th century,
Thonet's signature bentwood furniture

with its sinuous, elegant curves
inspired a number of celebrated
Art Nouveau architects and
designers, including Charles Rennie
Mackintosh and Henri van de Velde.
The reputation of the
Thonet Brothers attracted
a collection of visionary
talents who designed
furniture for the firm,
among them one of the
pioneering founders of
the Wiener Werkstätte,
Josef Hoffmann, along
with Otto Wagner, Adolf
Loos, Koloman Moser,
and Otto Prutscher.

Wall mirror This piece is made from carved
bentwood to create a simple, elegant effect.
The wood has been steamed and then bent
into shape, and this technique is a hallmark
of Thonet's furniture. *H:21 in (53 cm);
W:39½ in (100 cm). CSB*

Gebrüder Thonet catalog The catalog for
L'industrie Thonet bears the subtitle "From
handcraftsmanship to mass production:
bentwood furniture."

Guéridon This small table is made of beech
wood and consists of a plain top above an
ornate bentwood base, decorated with oval
motifs. *H:30 in (75 cm); W:32 in (80 cm);
D:24 in (60 cm). CSB*

WIENER WERKSTÄTTE

THE DESIRE TO MAKE SIMPLE, FUNCTIONAL OBJECTS THAT WERE ALSO WELL DESIGNED MOTIVATED A TRIO OF DESIGNERS TO CREATE THE WIENER WERKSTÄTTE IN 1903.

THE PAINTER, DESIGNER, and book illustrator Koloman Moser, the architect and designer Josef Hoffmann, and the painter and designer Carl Otto Czeschka established the Wiener Werkstätte (Viennese Workshops) for the applied and decorative arts. The Wiener Werkstätte rejected the sweeping curves and floral motifs of Art Nouveau and, instead, followed the example set by similar workshops in Germany and Great Britain. These aimed to elevate the role of the artist-craftsman by integrating the skills of the artisan with those of the designer. It is a measure of the Wiener Werkstätte's considerable commercial success that it influenced taste throughout the decorative and applied arts until it closed in 1932.

Initially, the Wiener Werkstätte was sponsored by the enlightened industrialist and financier Fritz Warndorfer, who took the title of commercial director, with Moser and Hoffmann in artistic charge. A skilled team of craftsmen worked across a broad spectrum of the decorative arts, including handmade metalwork, furniture, textiles, the graphic arts, fashion, jewelry, leatherwork, and the theater.

PROGRESSIVE DESIGN

By 1905, after Hoffmann and Moser had deserted the Secessionists, the Wiener Werkstätte became the center of progressive design, employing a host of talented artists and designers, including Otto Prutscher and Michael Powolny. Over 100 people worked there, including 37 *Meister*, skilled craftsmen, and artisans who were given their own individual marks. The company brochure claimed that all of its products were designed by Hoffmann and Moser, and the distinctive objects were celebrated for their level of technical expertise in periodicals such as *Deutsche Kunst und Dekoration* and the special summer edition of *Studio* in 1906.

The different interests and skills of the architects and designers produced a style that was constantly evolving. Contemporary trends in architecture, such as the work of founding member Josef Hoffmann, who designed the *Palais Stoclet* in Brussels and the *Purkersdorf Sanatorium*, were reflected in furnishings made at the Wiener Werkstätte. Furniture had rigorous, well-defined, vertical and horizontal outlines, smooth surfaces, and linear patterns. Geometric shapes, such as open-centered rectangles, spheres, circles, and the "Hoffmann square," were used on ceramics, furniture, cutlery, and graphic ornament, and were combined with rich, colorful materials for a luxurious look.

SECESSION HOUSE, VIENNA *The Secession House was designed by Josef Maria Olbrich and used by Secession artists. The building's spare, geometric style is typical of the Secession movement, which pioneered striking, linear designs. 1897–98.*

J. & J. KOHN

JACOB AND JOSEF KOHN BECAME RECOGNIZED ACROSS EUROPE AS LEADING MANUFACTURERS OF SIMPLE, WELL-DESIGNED, AND WELL-MADE FURNITURE AIMED AT A MIDDLE-CLASS CLIENTELE.

The company that the brothers Jacob and Josef Kohn established in Vienna in the late 19th century had an extensive output. Among the goods manufactured was unpretentious furniture inspired by an artistic tradition based on the modest, Neoclassical Biedermeier style of the early 19th century (*see pp.216–17*), which, according to Josef Hoffmann, was "the last period…to offer a valid expression of art." The artists of the Wiener Werkstätte tried to emulate the achievement of the Biedermeier movement by energizing middle-class taste and liberating homes from mass-produced revivalist styles, and they were aided in this mission by J. & J. Kohn.

Kohn's reputation was enhanced by its collaboration with Josef Hoffmann, and it manufactured a number of his furniture designs, including his adjustable armchair in 1901, and the chairs for the bar of the *Cabaret Fledermaus* in 1907. The company also specialized in light, durable, and functional bentwood furniture that was perfected and popularized by Michael Thonet (*see p.375*). Kohn carried out the prestigious commission for the bentwood dining chairs made of laminated beechwood and decorated with circular motifs, which were designed by Hoffmann in 1904–05 for the Purkersdorf Sanatorium, Austria's most fashionable retreat for wealthy Viennese.

Josef Hoffmann chair This *Cabaret Fledermaus* chair is made of stained beechwood, with turned legs, ebony ball brackets under the curved top rail and seat rails, and an upholstered, drop-in seat. *c. 1905. H:29½ in (75 cm). DOR*

Dark-brown stained beech settle This piece by J. & J. Kohn is made in the style of Josef Hoffmann. Its three splats are each pierced with a rectangular panel of circles, and rise within a triple-arch framework. *c. 1906. W:49 in (125.5 cm). VZ*

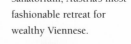

Dark-stained beech table This table was made by Thonet for the *Cabaret Fledermaus*. Its circular top and base are joined by pairs of turned posts, which are united top and bottom with ball brackets. *c. 1905. H:40 in (101.5 cm). QU*

CABINET BY KOLOMAN MOSER *This* Die Verwunschenen Prinzessinnen *cabinet shows a strong geometric influence and is almost triangular in section, with doors centered by circular lockplates.* c. 1900. H:67½ in (171.25 cm); W:21 in (53.25 cm); 12¾ in (32.75 cm).

BEECHWOOD CHAIR. *Designed by Koloman Moser for the Purkersdorf Sanatorium's entry hall, the frame of this geometric chair has bold, vertical rungs, with a checkerboard woven seat.* c. 1901. H:28¼ in (72 cm); W:26 in (66.25 cm).

HOFFMANN'S FURNITURE

Josef Hoffmann attempted to champion art for the people, with function, quality, and artistic merit his overriding concerns. The furniture he created for the Wiener Werkstätte was primarily made in mahogany, limed oak, and beechwood.

His style was characterized by rectilinear lines and smooth surfaces stained by rubbing dye into the wood, a technique that highlighted the grain. Hoffmann's sophisticated designs for chairs, tables, and cabinets had a formal purity and simplicity, and they were carried out with great craftsmanship.

The influence of Charles Rennie Mackintosh *(see pp.364–65)*, whose work was highly valued in Vienna, is clear. However, although he was influenced by the elegant, linear style of Mackintosh, Hoffmann emphasized volume in his work more than the line preferred by Mackintosh. His furniture often featured the square and the cube. The simple classicism of the early 19th-century Austrian Biedermeier style also influenced Hoffmann's designs *(see pp.214–17)*.

THE IMPORTANCE OF AESTHETICS

In spurning what they considered to be second-rate, mass-produced wares, in rejecting the flamboyant, sensuous spirit of the French and Belgian Art Nouveau movements, and by turning their backs on historicism, the Wiener Werkstätte movement allied itself with the aims of the English Arts and Crafts designers *(see p.330–33)*, who sought to produce simple, well-made household objects.

However, unlike their English counterparts, the aims of the Wiener Werkstätte designers were primarily aesthetic rather than social, and they designed luxurious goods for a wealthy and discerning clientele. They tried to liberate middle-class taste from mediocrity by bringing fine craftsmanship to the modern interior, and in the process established Vienna as a sophisticated and cosmopolitan European capital that was at the forefront of the Art Nouveau movement.

NEST OF BENTWOOD TABLES *These four tables are attributed to Josef Hoffman. The sides of the largest table are decorated with a cut-out square design called the Hoffman square.* c. 1905. H:29 in (74 cm); W:22 in (55.5 cm); D:16¾ in (42.5 cm).

MAHOGANY ARMOIRE *This impressive piece has two wide doors that are inlaid with exotic woods and mother-of-pearl in an elegant geometric design. It belongs to a bedroom suite, which also includes a bed and two nightstands.* c. 1900. W:48 in (122 cm). FRE

TABLES

ART NOUVEAU DESIGNERS transformed the functional table into works of art, with motifs inspired by the natural world. A table embellished with dragonflies or sculpted leaves, for example, might take on the form of a tree, with its support shaped like a trunk, and feet resembling roots.

Those working in the French and Belgian style of Art Nouveau, such as Louis Majorelle and Emile Gallé, created tables with tapering, sinuous legs; serpentine-shaped tops; and carved decoration or marquetry patterns of flower blossoms, trees, or fruit. These were rendered in veneers of precious and exotic woods.

The Glasgow School, led by Charles Rennie Mackintosh and other like-minded designers, including Josef Hoffmann and Koloman Moser, offered a radical contrast. They favored tables with rectangular, geometric proportions, narrow, elongated lines, and decorative cut-out motifs such as squares and spheres.

In England, tables mirrored historic styles, exotic Japanese or Moorish designs, or favored simple construction and functional, aesthetic design, as seen in the work of C. F. A. Voysey and Charles Ashbee.

In Spain and Italy, tables were often incorporated into sofas or other pieces of furniture, or had practical features such as built-in cabinets.

The Japanese style was popular with its simple designs, asymmetric forms, undulating lines, use of lacquer or lacquer lookalikes, and a love of nature, often appearing as typical Japanese motifs such as dragonflies.

Many innovative types of tables appeared, such as the tripod, tier, and the nest of tables, while decorative features such as the arched stretcher showed how new techniques pushed wood to limits never seen before.

LACQUER TABLE NEST

This nest of four Secessionist, black-lacquered tables is attributed to Josef Hoffmann. Each table has a rectangular top with rounded edges supported by turned, spindl filled supports leading to platfor stretchers. The largest of the fou carries two sphere-turned carvin handles. The Japanese influence is displayed in both the materials used and the form of this nest.
H:30¾ in (77 cm). L&T **2**

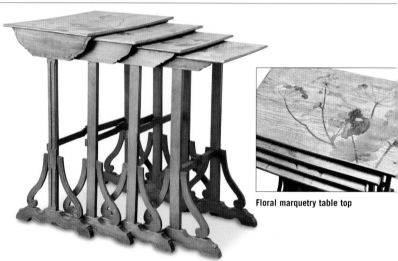

Floral marquetry table top

MARQUETRY TABLE NEST

This nest of four occasional tables was designed by Emile Gallé. They are constructed from mahogany and various other hardwoods with high-grade veneer. The tops and side moldings of the tables are supported by frames with elegant scroll curves at the bases. Each of the rectangular table tops is decorated in marquetry using various fruitwoods with a different floral scene. The largest of the tables bears the signature "Gallé" within the marquetry. *c. 1900. H:28½ in (72.5 cm). VZ* **3**

Raised edges prevent items from falling off.

Brass handles allow the table to be easily moved around the room.

The second tier has a molded edge.

Sculptural design with W-shaped table sides

MARQUETRY TWO-TIER TABLE

This two-tier nutwood and mahogany occasional table by Louis Majorelle is of double-framed construction. It has decorative carving, and each of the two tiers is embellished with floral marquetry. The top tier also has applied brass handles. *1900. H:34 in (86.5 cm); W:23½ in (59.5 cm). VZ* **5**

BEECH TABLE NEST

This nest of four "968" tables is made of beech. They were designed by Josef Hoffmann and produced by J. & J. Kohn of Vienna (see p.376). The tables are raised on slender, tapering legs, joined on three sides by stretchers. The largest of the tables has handles and trellis splats on the sides. Each of the smaller units slides into place on runners, which store the tables in a hanging position. The table nest has a mahogany stain and the remains of an original paper label underneath. *1905. H:29¾ in (75.5 cm). QU* **3**

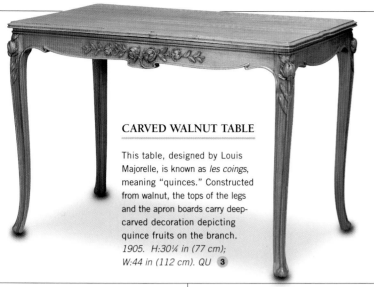

CARVED WALNUT TABLE

This table, designed by Louis Majorelle, is known as *les coings*, meaning "quinces." Constructed from walnut, the tops of the legs and the apron boards carry deep-carved decoration depicting quince fruits on the branch. *1905. H:30¼ in (77 cm); W:44 in (112 cm). QU* **3**

GLASS-TOPPED TEA TABLE

This French tea table, from the *École de Nancy*, is constructed from walnut, brass, and glass. It has a tray top with a raised edge to prevent items from falling off. Below the tray top is an additional shelf with fold-down sides. These offer more table space but can be folded away when not in use. *c. 1900. W:31½ in (79 cm). FRE* **2**

THREE-TIER TABLE

his small Austrian bentwood three-tier table designed in the manner of Josef Hoffmann. has a rounded square top supported on splayed gs. Two undertiers with wooden balls at the ints provide additional storage. *H:29½ in 5 cm). DN* **1**

FRETWORK OCCASIONAL TABLE

This J. S. Henry occasional table has a shaped top above an elaborate fretwork frieze. It is supported on slender, tapering, cabriole legs with pad feet that are linked by a lower tier. The maker's label is still attached. *H:28¼ in (72 cm); W:20¾ in (53 cm). L&T* **2**

PINE WORKBOX

This stained pine artist's workbox is from the Scottish School. The rectangular top has a twin-hinged lid, which opens to reveal an interior fitted with compartments for materials. The pegs used for joining are visible at the sides. *H:30¾ in (78 cm). L&T* **2**

ROSEWOOD STAND

This rare rosewood and marquetry stand was designed by Emile Gallé. The lobed top is inlaid with floral decoration and butterfly motifs. The four molded legs are united by an elegant arched stretcher. *H:41½ in (105 cm). CSB* **5**

EXAGONAL TABLE

iginally sold by Liberty & Co., this hexagonal ble has a molded top raised above square, pering legs, which are linked by distinctive erced stretchers halfway up the legs. e piece terminates in simple, pad feet. 28¾ in (73 cm). L&T* **2**

GILT SIDE TABLE

This opulent, giltwood side table with relief-molded decoration was designed by Louis Majorelle. A mottled-orange marble top is set within a leaf-and-berry carved slip, with a wavy frieze below. Arched stretchers link the legs. *H:30¾ in (78 cm). MACK* **6**

BRASS FRAMED TABLE

The elegant brass tripod of this Richard Müller-designed table bends toward the center at the top. The plain, circular table top is made from mahogany. Two triangular mahogany tiers provide additional storage. *1902. H:30 in (76 cm). VZ* **3**

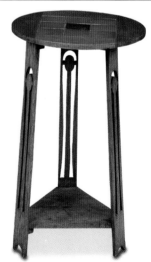

TILED OCCASIONAL TABLE

This occasional table is made of oak. The circular top features a red and green tiled insert in a geometric pattern. The three tapered supports are pierced with decoration in the manner of the Glasgow School. *H:24 in (61 cm). L&T* **1**

CASE PIECES

THE CABINET CONTINUED to be one of the most expensive and impressive pieces of useful furniture in European houses. Both decorative and functional, cabinets were used as writing chests, for locking away precious jewels, for storing important papers, and for the display of small, treasured collectibles.

Art Nouveau cabinets were made in a variety of styles. The Anglo-Japanese cabinets, such as those designed by E. W. Godwin, were embellished with brass mounts and painted decorations.

Charles Rennie Mackintosh, C. F. A. Voysey, and E. W. Gimson combined simple designs and an attention to the details of fine craftsmanship with the use of rich woods such as oak, walnut, satinwood, and mahogany.

These designers influenced the design of cabinets in the Art Nouveau style in Europe, especially the austere, geometric style favored in Germany and Austria.

In contrast, French cabinets were more sensuous in their design, with Rococo and Oriental elements combined to produce asymmetrically shaped pieces, decorated with curvilinear plant, flower, and vegetable motifs. Louis Majorelle created superbly crafted cabinets of extraordinary luxury, in fine-quality woods. These pieces were often embellished with finely wrought gilt-bronze or wrought-iron mounts, or included decorative inlays of mother-of-pearl or metal.

ENGLISH HALLROBE

The top of this hallrobe supports Classical carved panels. The paneled front is adorned with stylized copper hinges and handles and the interior is fitted. This piece was made by the prominent commercial furniture manufacturer, Shapland and Petter.
c. 1905. H:82 in (209 cm). PUR **4**

SCOTTISH BOOKCASE

This oak bookcase, by leading furniture-maker Wylie and Lochhead of Glasgow, is in the style of the Scottish school. The intricate floral panels are in stained glass and flanked by angular, stylized, copper, repoussé panels, above a long drawer and a bottom cabinet.
c. 1900. H:72 in (183 cm). PUR **5**

Carved circular supports are decorated with a twisting tendril and rootlike design.

The cabinet body is made from walnut with marquetry in exotic hardwoods.

The marquetry incorporates floral motifs.

FRENCH CABINET

This elegant cabinet is made of walnut. It is decorated with a marquetry design depicting a clematis and a bird, executed in exotic hardwoods. The top section provides open storage, which is accessed via a rounded opening, surrounded by relief carving. The piece was made by Louis Majorelle. His sinuous and fluid style, evident here, was inspired by 18th-century Rococo furniture. c. 1900. H:67 in (170 cm); W:28 in (71 cm). CALD

VIENNESE SIDEBOARD

This impressive walnut veneer sideboard is by the school of Josef Hoffmann. The piece is decorated with intarsia. The symmetrical, clean design is typical of Hoffman, and the linear style reveals the influence of Charles Rennie

Mackintosh. The upper section is enclosed behind glazed doors that form a geometric pattern. The mirrored central section is supported by rounded columns. The base has a marble top and contains cupboards and a drawer. The plinth and the handles are made of brass. c. 1902. H:70 in (178.5 cm). DOR **9**

TAINED-GLASS CABINET

he straight lines and gentle curves of this abinet are typical of the Glasgow School, as the stained-glass window depicting a pastel-olored flower design. The piece has a broad, rojecting cornice, which was a feature of any Glasgow School cabinets. *W:42¼ in 07 cm). GDG* **5**

DINING ROOM CABINET

This walnut veneer and brass dining room cabinet is part of a set by Otto Wytrlik. The matching table, stool, pair of commodes, four armchairs, and two further chairs are solid, dark pieces with strongly geometric lines, and would have given the room a masculine look. *c. 1901. WKA* **5**

VENEER CUPBOARD

This small mahogany veneer cupboard from Austria is raised on four slender legs. The two cupboards, two drawers, and shelves all have nickel hardware. The distinctive top cupboard has three sides of paneled glass with ornamental silver decoration. *c. 1900. H:64½ in (164.5 cm); W:32¾ in (83.5 cm). DOR* **3**

MUSIC CABINET

Anglo-Japanese influences are evident in this mahogany music cabinet decorated with stylized, floral, stained-glass panels. The fine, string ebony and boxwood inlay is enriched with delicate floral carvings. The arched apron is reflected in the curved pediment. *c. 1895. W:49 in (125 cm). PUR* **4**

NLAID CABINET

his ornate mahogany display cabinet is laborately inlaid in copper, pewter, and pecimen woods with decoration of stylized ower-heads and leafy tendrils. The central anel is mirrored and flanked by two glass oors opening onto glass shelves. *:81½ in (207 cm). L&T* **4**

MAHOGANY CABINET

The shaped, raised back, and molded finials of this highly decorative display cabinet have whiplash-style foliate and floral marquetry inlays. The leaded and stained-glass panel doors are decorated with a floral design, and are enclosed by marquetry panels. *H:64 in (164 cm); W:42 in (107 cm). L&T* **3**

FLORAL CABINET

This mahogany display cabinet, attributed to the Scottish designer Ernest Archibald Taylor, has silver-plated repoussé decoration on the glass. The architectural form is decorated with a butterfly centerpiece and floral designs in sycamore and tulipwood inlay. *c. 1903. H:69 in (175 cm). PUR* **5**

OAK BOOKCASE

This bookcase cabinet has a projecting dentil cornice above three open compartments, flanked by pierced decorative brackets. The twin doors, enclosing adjustable shelves, have leaded clear glass panels with stained-glass decoration on the top. *H:76½ in (195 cm); W:56 in (143 cm). L&T* **3**

CHAIRS

WHEN IT CAME TO the chair, Art Nouveau designers let their imaginations run wild. Designers from Glasgow to Nancy used the chair to illustrate and promote the Art Nouveau ideal.

Breaking free from traditional methods of design and construction, designers experimented with flowing, abstract shapes influenced by nature, and bending or elongating wood into sculptural pieces.

The Scottish architect Charles Rennie Mackintosh left an indelible mark on Art Nouveau furniture, especially with his ground-breaking chair designs. Well proportioned, with attenuated backs imparting an almost ecclesiastical appearance, his cube-based chairs decorated with geometric cut-out patterns were enormously influential, especially on designers

working in Germany and Austria, who embraced this more linear approach.

The French strand of Art Nouveau produced a contrasting style, with its sinuous, organic, fluid chair designs, which were made by Louis Majorelle and Hector Guimard in exotic woods. These were often lavishly decorated with intricate inlays, marquetry, and carved botanical motifs on top rails, legs, and aprons.

A taste for the exotic also provided another decorative and extremely influential outlet in chairs—from Japanese and Moorish-inspired designs to bizarre seat furniture created by Carlo Bugatti and Antoni Gaudi using a variety of materials. Bugatti and Gaudi used imaginative combinations of wood and metals, embellished with materials such as leather, vellum, and silk.

BENTWOOD CHAIR

This beech chair, made and signed by Austrian manufacturer Thonet, has a flowing bentwood frame made of bent rods, which curves without the use of carving and joints. It has a shaped seat rail and a reversed, heart-shaped back that sweeps below the seat to form stretchers. The triangular seat is made of cane, although it is not original. The chair terminates in three legs. *c. 1900. H:32 in (81.5 cm); W:24 in (62.5 cm); D:23 in (60 cm). Qu* **3**

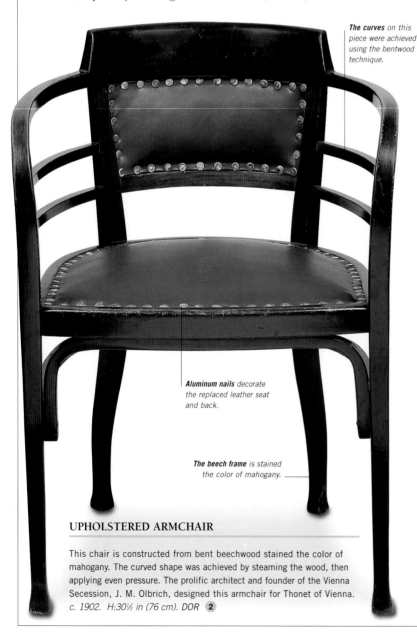

The curves on this piece were achieved using the bentwood technique.

Aluminum nails decorate the replaced leather seat and back.

The beech frame is stained the color of mahogany.

UPHOLSTERED ARMCHAIR

This chair is constructed from bent beechwood stained the color of mahogany. The curved shape was achieved by steaming the wood, then applying even pressure. The prolific architect and founder of the Vienna Secession, J. M. Olbrich, designed this armchair for Thonet of Vienna. *c. 1902. H:30½ in (76 cm). DOR* **2**

ARMCHAIR

This mahogany armchair has an upholstered crest, a slat back and carved arms. The seat and back panel are upholstered in velvet. The slat back forms a back leg and the piece terminates in bun feet. *c. 1900. H:37 in (94 cm). FRE* **1**

LAYERED WOOD CHAIR

This is one of a set of four chairs made in the style of the early Vienna Secession. The chair is made of cut beechwood and layered wood, which is stained in two shades. The seat is covered black leather, but is not original. *c. 1900. H:39½ in (99 cm). DOR* **3**

ARMCHAIR

This stained beech and elm chair was probably made by Wylie & Lochhead of Glasgow. The curved top rail sits above three splats. The seat is inlaid with boxwood lining. The legs are joined by double stretchers that terminate in upholstered, paneled feet. *L&T* **1**

SLAT-BACK ARMCHAIR

This Viennese slat-back armchair is constructed from veneered and polished nutwood massif. The design is accredited to Josef Hoffmann. A low, D-shaped stretcher unites the straight legs near the base of the chair. *c. 1905. H:34 in (86.5 cm). DOR* **3**

ENTWOOD SIDE CHAIR

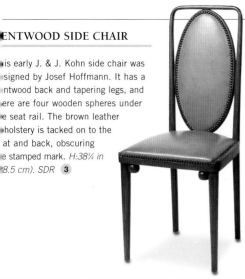

This early J. & J. Kohn side chair was designed by Josef Hoffmann. It has a bentwood back and tapering legs, and there are four wooden spheres under the seat rail. The brown leather upholstery is tacked on to the seat and back, obscuring the stamped mark. *H:38¾ in (98.5 cm). SDR* 3

ARMCHAIR

This is one of a pair of mahogany armchairs designed by J. S. Henry. The tall, upholstered back has sinuous leaf finials, curving open arms, and an upholstered pad seat. The seat is supported on turned and tapering legs linked by an arched stretcher at the front and straight side stretchers. *L&T* 3

SIDE CHAIR

This is one of a pair of side chairs made of oak. The back of the chair has curvilinear rails linking tapering uprights above a drop-in seat. Square-section, tapering legs terminate in pad feet. *L&T* 1

MARQUETRY ARMCHAIR

Designed by Louis Majorelle, the back splat of this mahogany armchair is decorated in marquetry depicting branch and leaf designs. The chair has molded "U"-shaped crinoline arms that have distinctive duck's-head terminals. The seat is upholstered in velvet. *MACK* 6

UPHOLSTERED ARMCHAIR

This mahogany armchair, designed by G. M. Ellwood, has a tapering back containing an oval upholstered panel and elegant vertical splats. The piece has open upholstered arms and an upholstered seat. The legs terminate in tassel-carved feet. *L&T* 3

ARMCHAIR

This stained mahogany armchair features distinctive, wavy, horizontal splats positioned above and below the rectangular paneled back. The downswept, open arms and upholstered panel seat are raised on turned, tapered legs. *L&T* 1

CANED-SEAT ARMCHAIR

This is one of a pair of "Model 511" chairs by Thonet, constructed from bent beech. The splat is pierced with holes, with parallel slats below. The back continues in a curve down to the feet. The seat is made of woven caning. *c. 1904. 41¼ in (104.5 cm). HERR* 3

DESK CHAIR

This mahogany desk chair by Louis Majorelle has open arms featuring galleries of tapered spindles. Red-leather upholstery on the back and seat is fixed to the frame with studs. The twisted form of the legs emphasizes the sinuous, feminine design. *MACK* 7

OPEN ARMCHAIR

This carved walnut armchair designed by Henri Rapin has a wing back and bold scrolling terminals. The tapering legs lead to splayed spade feet. The heavily patterned upholstery is not original. *1910. H:30½ in (77.5 cm); W:22 in (56 cm). CAL* 5

CURVED DESK CHAIR

This Louis Majorelle carved mahogany desk chair (part of a desk set) has molded arms leading into sweeping, reverse-curved supports. The chair has a distinctive, low upholstered back. The front legs are cabriole in shape. *c. 1903. H:31 in (80 cm). CSB* 8

ARMCHAIR

This armchair was designed by Josef Maria Olbrich and made by Josef Niedermoser of Vienna. The frame is black-varnished maple, the chair is upholstered with yellow leather covers, and the feet are metal. *1898–99. H:32 in (81.5 cm); W:22¾ in (58 cm). QU* 3

ART DECO
1919–1940

FROM BOOM TO BUST

ORIGINATING IN FRANCE, THE ART DECO STYLE BLOSSOMED IN THE UNITED STATES, MIRRORING THE MOOD OF LIBERATION AND FANTASY THAT PERMEATED A FRAGILE BUT BRAVE NEW WORLD.

English two-tier table This Art Deco occasional table is constructed from chrome and laminate, and mounted on a circular walnut base. *c. 1928. H:29½ in (75 cm); W:14¼ in (36 cm); D:14¼ in (36 cm). JK*

AS THE WORLD EMERGED from the shadow of World War I, the rhythms of jazz and the fantasy world of Hollywood captured the imagination of people eager to celebrate liberation. A colorful cocktail of wit, fantasy, new materials, and luxury, Art Deco in both its "high" French style and its "streamlined" American mode fitted the mood. Alongside Bauhaus, it was the prevailing decorative style for furniture, sculpture, ceramics, metalwork, and glass, as well as architecture and interior design, throughout the 1920s and 30s.

NEW LUXURY

Producing luxuries for the masses now became the central activity of the economy, especially in the United States. The number of cars on

American roads rose from half a million in 1914 to 26 million in 1929, one for every five of the population. By 1929, two-thirds of Americans had electricity, and sales of electrical goods rocketed. Movie palaces, dance halls, sports stadiums, and luxury hotels sprang up as the leisure industries flourished. Both the artifacts and the architecture exhibited the Art Deco style: geometric shapes inspired by the Cubist movement together with a range of exotic, stylized floral, and folk motifs.

STREAMLINED TRAVEL

Travel became faster and more luxurious, whether on ocean liners such as the *Normandie*, airships such as the *Graf Zeppelin*, or trains drawn by streamlined engines such as the *Mallard*. Not only was Art Deco the style for luxury transportation interiors, but the principles of aerodynamic design were reflected in the Art Deco taste for streamlined forms. New, light-reflecting materials, such as tubular steel, chrome, and mirror glass, were adopted, especially in bars, dance halls, and movie theaters.

In economics and politics, the year 1929 marked a fault line dividing the interwar years in two. The 1920s were boom years for the American economy. Skyscrapers, such as the Chrysler Building and the Empire State Building

in New York, were the most striking embodiment of growing prosperity. But the 1920s boom was fueled by easy credit and speculation. By 1929 share prices had lost any relationship to real values. When the Wall Street crash came in October 1929, thousands of investors lost their shirts. The United States entered the Great Depression with unemployment shooting up to 14 million over the next three years. The New Deal, introduced by President Franklin D. Roosevelt in 1933, restored a little optimism, but the climate was turbulent.

The American economic slump brought mass unemployment and financial crisis to Europe in the early 1930s. Germany's fragile democracy disintegrated and in 1933 Adolf Hitler was appointed German chancellor. This, and aggressive regimes in Japan and Italy, led to a second global conflict.

Yet progress did not end just because boom turned to bust, and Art Deco held its own well into the 1930s. The movement encapsulated both the period's technological progress and a form of escapism from the mounting political and economic troubles. Eventually, however, Art Deco was superseded by Modernism, with its focus on functionalism and the machine.

Office and factory for the Hoover company This 1933 landmark London building by architects Wallis, Gilbert, and Partners has an American-style glazed Art Deco façade and a striking, brightly colored, Egyptian-style faience over its entrance.

TIMELINE 1919–1940

The Bauhaus School was founded at Weimar in 1919 by Walter Gropius. He promoted a new functional style of architecture. The Nazi regime closed the School in 1933.

1919 The Treaty of Versailles is imposed on Germany by the Allied Powers.

1920 Cecil B. De Mille brings French designer Paul Iribe to Hollywood to design the sets and costumes for the historical movie drama *The Affairs of Anatol*.

1922 Tutankhamen's tomb and treasures are discovered by Howard Carter in the Valley of the Kings, Luxor, Egypt.

1923 The first UK-to-US wireless broadcast takes place between London and New York.

The Charleston dance The flapper-girl style epitomized the hedonistic jazz age. Independent and irreverent, flapper girls wore makeup, dispensed with corsets, and delighted in risqué behavior.

Hyperinflation in Germany brings about the collapse of the German economy.

1924 The fashion illustrator Erté becomes head of the Art Department at Hollywood's MGM studio.

1925 The *Exposition Internationale des Arts Décoratifs et Industriels Modernes*, which was originally planned for 1915, is held in Paris. *The Great Gatsby* by F. Scott Fitzgerald, *The Trial* by Franz Kafka, and *Mein Kampf* by Adolf Hitler are published.

This Art Deco *torchère* has a twisted wooden shaft painted a creamy yellow, and topped with a stepped brass lamp shade. *H:67 in (107 cm). FRE*

The interior of the entrance hall of Eltham Palace The interior was commissioned from Swedish designer Rolf Engströmer. It is completely lined with Australian blackbean veneer with marquetry panels by the Swedish artist Jerk Werkmäster. The colors of the large circular rug by Marion Dorn reflect the tones of the marquetry panels. The hall is bathed in light, which floods through the concrete, glass-domed roof. *1930s.*

1926 John Logie Baird invents television.

1928 The *Graf Zeppelin* makes the first transatlantic flight.

1929 The New York Stock Market on Wall Street crashes, precipitating the Great Depression of the 1930s.

1930 The Chrysler Building in New York City is completed in May. Designed by William Van Alen, it is the world's tallest human-made structure until the completion of the Empire State Building a year later.

1932 *Brave New World* by Aldous Huxley is published.

Blackfaced actor Al Jolson starred in the first movie with sound—*The Jazz Singer*—which premiered in 1927.

1933 Radio City Music Hall is built in New York by Donald Deskey and Associated Architects.

1934 MOMA holds the Machine Age exhibition, marking the midpoint of the Industrial Design movement in the US.

1935 *Bluebird*, driven by Malcolm Campbell, reaches 300 mph (480 km/h). The movie *Top Hat*,

The Chrysler Building The dramatic use of stainless-steel sunbursts symbolized the march of progress.

The *Normandie* This French luxury ocean liner was launched in 1932. Its interiors were designed in the "high-style" Art Deco.

with Ginger Rogers and Fred Astaire, is released, together with the Marx Brothers' *A Night at the Opera.*

1939 Hitler invades Poland on September 1, starting World War II in Europe.

ART DECO FURNITURE

IN THE YEARS FOLLOWING World War I, furniture designers followed two distinct courses: one was founded on tradition—Art Deco—and the other's driving force was functionalism—Modernism.

Much of the most sophisticated Art Deco furniture created was shown at the *Exposition Internationale des Arts Décoratifs et Industriels Modernes*, which opened in Paris in the spring of 1925. Originally planned for 1915, but postponed because of World War I, the Exhibition reflected a prewar aesthetic and embodied the desire of France to reestablish itself as the center for the production of stylish luxury goods. Although the term "Art Deco" is derived from the title of this Exhibition, it was not actually used to identify a style until 1968 when Bevis Hillier's book *Art Deco of the*

Skyscraper vanity unit
The thick dark lines on this vanity unit emphasize the stylized geometric forms that characterize Art Deco style. The mirror towers over the wooden structure, recalling the silhouettes of Manhattan's tallest buildings. *1930s. H:61 in (155 cm).*

20s and 30s was published. He defined two main strands of Art Deco: "The feminine, somewhat conservative style of 1925, chic, elegant, depending on exquisite craftsmanship and harking back to the 18th century; and the masculine reaction of the 30s, with its machine-age symbolism and use of new materials like chrome and plastics."

TRADITIONAL ART DECO

Traditional Art Deco evolved out of Art Nouveau and was born in France. Designers following this path subdued the flowing lines and naturalistic decoration characteristic of Art Nouveau to create a more restrained, geometric style of furniture with graceful proportions and stylized motifs.

Furniture-makers, such as Émile-Jacques Ruhlmann (*see p.393*) and Paul Follot (1877–1941), favored the use of luxurious materials to enhance simple, stylized, and abstract forms. Exotic woods with distinctive markings and decorative grains—macassar ebony, burr walnut, and sycamore—created rich, lustrous veneers. Unusual materials, including lacquer, ivory, and shagreen (imitation sharkskin), were used for marquetry and inlays. Decorative motifs employed included baskets of stylized flowers and geometric sunbursts. The hard surfaces of highly polished woods were often juxtaposed with brightly colored and richly decorated upholstery.

MODERNIST ART DECO

Many American designers were inspired by the flamboyance of French Art Deco. Using new materials, such as Bakelite and aluminum, designers, such as Donald Deskey, who designed the interior of Radio City Music Hall in New York, mixed the French Art Deco style with elements of the more functional, rectilinear Bauhaus style, to create a Modernist form of Art Deco. Paul Fuller's iconic Wurlitzer jukebox designs, with their use of brightly colored plastic, geometric grille, chromium plate, and dramatic lighting, also combined French style with new-found technology. Specifically American references, such as the skyscraper motif, appeared in the Deco-inspired furniture of the Viennese-born New York designer Paul T. Frankl and the German-

Folding screen This French, four-paneled folding screen is an exquisite example of Art Deco design. Either side of each panel has rosewood and fruitwood parquetry surfaces in different geometric designs. *H:73 in (185 cm). CSB*

born Californian designer K.E.M. Weber. In the land of the automobile, the influence of car styling became increasingly strong in American Art Deco furniture designs. Known as Streamlined Moderne, slick torpedo-style curving was used on a huge range of objects, from radios to desks.

The Art Deco fountain and chevron motifs were seen repeatedly in the escapist Hollywood movies of the 1930s, with their backdrops of luxury Art Deco-styled hotels, nightclubs, skyscrapers, and ocean liners. Such films did much to advertise the American Art Deco style to the world, and to link it forever with ideas of fantasy, glamour, and sexual liberation.

COCKTAIL CABINETS

With the introduction, in the 1920s, of a new social pastime—the cocktail party—a new piece of furniture was created, inspired by the 18th-century sideboard with its ice drawers and fitted decanter cabinets. Intended for storing all the accoutrements associated with the making of cocktails, the cocktail cabinet contained fitted shelves and bottle holders. It often took the external form of a traditional writing desk, while its modern interior was frequently a flamboyant, conversation-making piece of furniture veneered with a host of exotic woods,

equipped with lights, and lined with mirror glass. Far from its original intention as a piece of furniture designed for writing, the cocktail cabinet added a more frivolous and decadent note to the fashionable interior that chimed with the contemporary taste for luxury and glamour, which persisted throughout the Jazz Age and the Great Depression.

Cocktail cabinet This semicircular cabinet in walnut, supported by tapering legs, was designed by H&L Epstein. The cabinet opens to reveal a mirrored, shelved bar. Manufacturers at the upper end of the market concentrated on these high-quality veneered pieces. *1930s. H:64 in (162.5 cm). JAZ*

TRADITION AND LUXURY

Designers working in the traditional, sophisticated Art Deco style that developed in Paris and became fashionable during the 1920s and 30s frequently looked back to the 18th century for inspiration. This basis for their work can be seen in the design of the chairs below, which boast curving, wooden frames that recall the serpentine shapes often found in Rococo furniture. With outlines reminiscent of 18th-century French *bergères*, these chairs form part of a three-piece parlor suite.

Suites of matching furniture, such as a sofa, two chairs, and a cabinet, created to fit in with the overall interior decorative scheme of a room, were favored by designers of the Art Deco period. The form of these Art Deco suites often echoed the architectural structure and paneling of a room, as had been the case in the 18th century.

The purity of shape, harmonious proportions, refined decoration, and use of lavish materials that characterized the furniture created by the celebrated French *ébénistes* of the late 18th century, such as Jean-Henri Riesener and Jean-François Leleu, also characterized the furniture of the craftsmen creating pieces in the fashionable "high style" of French Art Deco. These sumptuous armchairs reflect the 18th-century tradition and the taste for luxury. The rich color of the burr wood with its distinctive markings is enhanced by the sumptuous, cream-colored leather upholstery, while the Art Deco desire for comfort and simplicity is underscored by the generous proportions and graceful form of the "Cloud" design.

Parlor suite This three-piece parlor suite consists of a sofa and two armchairs. The sofa and armchairs are encased in a bentwood shell terminating in molded feet set on casters. The pieces are all upholstered in cream leather in the curvaceous "Cloud" design. *W:30 in (76 cm). FRE*

The ample proportions and harmonious lines underscore the simple beauty and emphasis on comfort that were hallmarks of the Art Deco style.

The curving bentwood shell recalls the shape of an 18th-century French bergère.

The richness of the wood is heightened by the contrasting, luxurious, cream-colored leather upholstery.

The shape of the chair embodies the luxury of the period, implied by the idea of lounging on a cloud.

The undulating wooden frame looks back to the serpentine shapes of the 18th-century French Rococo style.

The feet of the chairs have casters so the chairs can be easily moved around the room.

Burr wood of maple or ash was among the woods favored by Art Deco furniture-makers.

ELEMENTS OF STYLE

There is a host of distinctive features associated today with the Art Deco style. Every branch of the decorative arts—from furniture and textiles to ceramics and metalware—was affected by the fashion for exotic materials and handcrafted techniques, a continuation of the sumptuous Art Nouveau style of the late 19th century. Designers drew on a wide range of ornamental motifs, from folk art and stylized baskets of fruit to Egyptian-style motifs and patterns inspired by the treasures discovered in 1922 in Tutankhamen's tomb. Rectilinear shapes and geometric designs reminiscent of African tribal art and Cubist paintings were also a key element of Art Deco. This aspect of the style recalled the work of the Wiener Werkstätte (*see pp.376–77*).

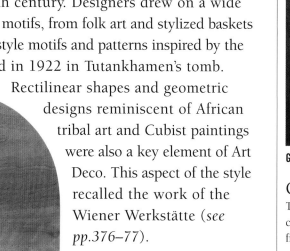

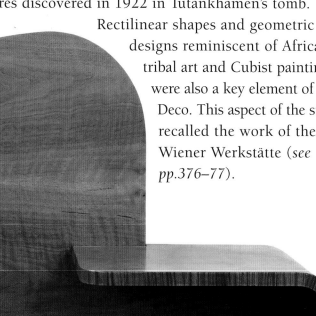

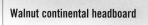
Walnut continental headboard

Multipurpose designs
For designers and decorators working in the Art Deco style, the objective was to create simple, uncluttered interiors. This aim was realized with built-in furniture, such as wardrobes and washstands, and with multipurpose pieces, such as a sofa that incorporated a table, or a headboard with side cupboards and a lampstand.

Geometric design on a wool rug

Geometric textiles
The decorative designs featured on carpets, fabrics, and tapestries were frequently inspired by the flat exotic patterns and geometric motifs drawn from Africa, Asia, Cubism, and folk art. Dynamic geometric schemes for upholstery, curtains, and rugs were often made up of overlapping blocks of color or abstract patterns of squares, zigzags, chevrons, and triangles.

Table edge with geometric ivory banding

Ivory inlay
Ivory inlays were frequently used to embellish cabinets, tables, and chairs. The pure white color formed a rich contrast to the warm, lustrous tones of mahogany and macassar ebony wood veneers. Ivory was often used to enhance the drawer pulls of a cabinet, the elegant outlines of a chair leg, or the edge of a table top with delicate geometric banding.

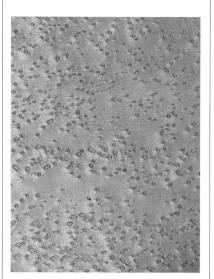
Close-up of bird's-eye maple surface

Bird's-eye maple
A timber native to northern Europe, Canada, and the United States, bird's-eye maple is a variety of maple. Its light brown markings consist of rings that resemble the eyes of a bird. It was a fashionable veneer for furniture during the late 18th century, and found favor once again in the 1920s with furniture designers working in the French Art Deco style.

Armrest carved with leaves

Low-relief carving
Following on from Art Nouveau, designers used hand carving to create sumptuous, richly decorated furniture. The crests of cabinets, the rails or arms of chairs, and the aprons of tables were often carved in shallow, low relief with stylized patterns of berries, leaves, flower bouquets, or garlands of fruits and plants, or curving spirals, tassels, sunbursts, and beading.

Dressing table with floral marquetry design

Floral marquetry

Of all the decorative motifs found on Art Deco furniture, it is flowers that dominate. Stylized flower designs reminiscent of the pre–World War I Art Nouveau style were adopted for marquetry veneers by artisans working with both luxurious and more modest materials. The motifs were often less flamboyant than those used previously, or even severely geometric in taste.

Etched, glazed cupboard doors

Decorative glass

Glass played a key part in Art Deco furniture. Massive, architectural cabinets made from rare and lustrous woods were often lightened by fitted panels made of plain or colored glass. These were frequently pressed or etched with designs featuring stylized geometric patterns of sunbursts, triangles, chevrons, or flower baskets, garlands, and foliage.

Table top featuring *verre églomisé*

Verre églomisé

The technique known as *verre églomisé* is one in which the back of a glass panel is painted with a layer of gold or silver leaf, which is then engraved and covered with a protective film of varnish or glass. Furniture designers of the 1920s and 30s often embellished their pieces by setting glass panels enriched with *verre églomisé* into tables, cabinets, and cupboards.

Veneered table top in geometric design

Veneering

The fashion for veneered furniture, especially favored by cabinet-makers working in the Art Nouveau style before World War I, was also widely employed by Art Deco furniture designers. Thin layers of colorful and precious woods were arranged in a broad range of decorative patterns, from naturalistic flower sprays to abstract, geometric designs.

Rosewood crossbanding

Rosewood inlays

Rosewood was widely used for decorative crossbanding on Art Deco furniture. An evenly grained hardwood, ranging in color from light hazel to reddish-brown, it forms a subtle but decorative counterpoint to contrasting timbers when thin strips are cut across the grain and inlaid along the edge of a drawer, table top, panel, or cabinet door.

Lacquered table with stylized design

Lacquerware

Jean Dunand, Eileen Gray, and Maurice Jallot made their furniture more opulent with inlaid lacquer panels. Screens, chairs, tables, and cabinets were also sometimes made entirely of glossy black or brightly colored lacquer, featuring stylized flowers, exotic animals, and abstract geometric motifs recalling sumptuous 18th-century French designs.

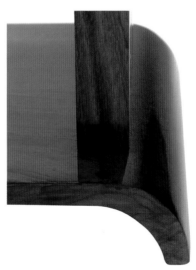

Base of a side table

Geometric forms

Many Art Deco designers favored geometric forms. Emile-Jacques Ruhlmann was influenced by the rectilinear, Neoclassical shapes of the late 18th century in the design of his cabinets, cupboards, and writing desks. American designers, such as Donald Deskey, were inspired by the geometric forms of the Industrial age and the designers associated with Bauhaus.

Stylized acorn back splat

Decorative splats

The central vertical panel of an open-backed chair has traditionally been used as a canvas for decorative designs. Many Art Deco chairs were made from rich timbers and boasted splats featuring carved motifs of stylized arrangements of foliage, fountains, baskets of flowers or fruit, drapery, or, alternatively, patterns of geometric shapes.

1925 PARIS EXHIBITION

THE PARIS *EXPOSITION INTERNATIONALE DES ARTS DÉCORATIFS ET INDUSTRIELS MODERNES* OF 1925 MARKED A DEFINING MOMENT FOR WHAT WAS IDENTIFIED IN THE 1960S AS ART DECO STYLE.

ORIGINALLY PLANNED FOR 1915 in response to Germany's growing international commercial success, the *Exposition Internationale des Arts Décoratifs et Industriels Modernes* was postponed when World War I broke out in 1914. When the Exhibition finally opened its doors in April 1925, its main aim was to reassert France's position as the world's arbiter of taste and the unrivaled center for the production of luxury goods. It also hoped to persuade French manufacturers to embrace the "modern," and work with decorative artists to produce artifacts of "real originality." As a result, the Exhibition gave a new generation of decorative artists, as well as those already well established, an opportunity to exhibit their work.

LUXURIOUS "GOOD TASTE"

Most European countries took part in the exhibition, although Germany was conspicuously absent, and the French section took up two-thirds of the 55-acre (23-hectare) site. The United States also declined to participate, as its Secretary of Commerce, Herbert Hoover, believed that it would be impossible to meet the entry requirements laid out in the Exhibition's charter, which stated that displays should make no reference to past styles and called for examples of "new and original inspiration" that personified the modern lifestyle. In fact, this prerequisite was not fulfilled by the majority of the exhibits, which reflected a prewar aesthetic and a continuation of the Art Nouveau style. Nonetheless, the Exhibition was considered by most to be a resounding success, drawing 16 million visitors from around the globe.

A large part of the French section was composed of pavilions exhibiting the work of eminent, established French designers, such as the furniture designer Émile-Jacques Ruhlmann and the glass-maker René Lalique. Whole interiors and room sets were also on display, showing furniture, textiles, carpets, and other household wares in harmonizing styles. These were presented by the design studios of the major Parisian department stores—Primavera at *Printemps*, La Maîtrise at *Galeries Lafayette*, directed by Maurice Dufrene (1876–1955), and Pomone at *Au Bon Marché*. These extravagant displays were set against the backdrop of the Eiffel Tower, which was transformed into an ultra-modern advertisement

ROBERT BONFILS'S POSTER FOR THE PARIS EXHIBITION
This poster shows some of the key characteristics of Art Deco. The stylized basket of flowers is reminiscent of much Art Deco inlay work and the female figure and antelope were often used in metalwork as a symbol of speed.

BERGÈRE
This rare Paul Follot armchair, one of a pair, has an arched, ribbed, upholstered back above a U-shaped seat rail, and scroll arm terminals. The tapering feet are ebonized and fluted. c. 1920.
H:32 in (81.25 cm); W:20 in (51 cm). CAL

COFFEE TABLE
This mahogany table by Rosel has carved, semicircular legs and feet, which support a glass top. The racks within the construction of the crossbar and post are made of ebony with mother-of-pearl applications. c. 1925. H:25½ in (65 cm); W:30 in (76 cm); D:30 in (76 cm). QU

ROSEWOOD AND MAHOGANY *SECRÉTAIRE*
This secrétaire by Léon Jallot has a bow-fronted case with a fall front and a sycamore interior. It has mirror-cut, mahogany crotch veneers, slightly splayed legs, and a hand-incised signature on the back. H:45 in (114 cm); W:34½ in (88 cm). CAL

ÉMILE-JACQUES RUHLMANN (1879–1933)

RUHLMANN'S WORK REPRESENTS THE FINEST EXPRESSION OF ART DECO, AND THE MOST SUMPTUOUS AND ACCOMPLISHED PIECES PRODUCED IN FRANCE DURING THE 1920S AND EARLY 1930S.

Ruhlmann

Born in Paris in 1879 to Alsatian parents, Ruhlmann first exhibited his work at the 1913 *Salon d'Automne*, and continued to produce lavish designs throughout the war before establishing a partnership in 1919 with Pierre Laurent in Paris: Les Établissements Ruhlmann et Laurent. Ruhlmann's reputation as a furniture-maker *par excellence* was sealed by his extravagant display at the 1925 Paris Exhibition. His deluxe furniture—which was aimed at a sophisticated and very wealthy clientele—was inspired by the work of the finest 18th-century French *ébénistes*, such as Jean-Henri Riesener. Ruhlmann insisted upon the highest standards of craftsmanship

from his workmen for the simple and elegant cabinets, writing desks, dressing tables, and chairs he designed. Early pieces tended to be delicate with slender, tapering legs, while later pieces were sturdier. Ruhlmann used the rarest and most exquisite materials, such as veneers of palisander, macassar ebony, burr walnut, Cuban mahogany, and amaranth. These were enriched with tortoiseshell, silver, horn, or ivory inlays, featuring stylized flower baskets, garlands, or geometric motifs, or embellished with leather, parchment, or sharkskin paneling. Drawer pulls sometimes featured elegant silk tassels, and fabrics were often designed specially for individual pieces of furniture. Exorbitant prices did nothing to deter demand for his work, as owning a piece of Ruhlmann furniture was a huge status symbol.

for Citroën cars. Most exhibits conformed to an "official taste," with adaptations of historical or traditional styles lavishly ornamented with a host of motifs, including stylized flowers, figures, and animals, and geometric patterns, such as zigzags and chevrons.

Nowhere was this tendency more in evidence than in Ruhlmann's majestic pavilion, the *Hôtel d'un Collectionneur*. Ruhlmann was responsible for the overall design of the interiors of this pavilion, which featured work by several of his preferred designers and craftsmen. Within it, André Groult's (1884–1967) *Chambre de Madame* contained chairs inspired by 18th-century designs and wall-coverings in bold and colorful patterns. Veneered with pale green sharkskin, the sumptuous suite of elegant furniture brought to mind the sinuous lines of Art Nouveau. Jean Dunand's (1877–1942) *Fumoir* featured streamlined black and silver lacquered furniture together with brightly colored screens and fabrics inspired by African art.

CONTRASTING MODERNIST STYLE

These lavish examples of what later became known as "high-style" Art Deco were in marked contrast to the few displays mounted by Modernist designers. At the pavilion *L'Esprit Nouveau*, for example, the Swiss-born architect Le Corbusier (see pp.432–33) promoted his vision of minimalist architecture and affordable furnishings for the middle classes. Although this style made a powerful impression, it was not until the 1930s that its influence really began to be felt.

CONSOLE TABLE
Designed by Raymond Subes, this wrought-iron table has a demi-lune top above scrolling supports on a curved solid base. The scrolling supports and stepped geometric decoration are typical of Art Deco design. H:39½ in (100.5 cm); W:50½ in (128 cm).

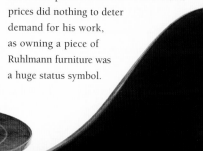

Table with rotating top
This elegant circular table, signed by Ruhlmann, is made from amboyna and ivory. Its rotating circular top rests on a central support decorated with stepped geometric panels and an arching base. Like many of Ruhlmann's pieces, the exotic wood veneer is the main form of decoration. *c. 1929.* W:29⅓ in (74.5 cm). DEL

Armchair This unsigned Ruhlmann armchair is made of burr amboyna with ebony detailing, gilt metal sabots, and brown velvet upholstery. It appears to be the first model of the macassar ebony and ivory chair that Ruhlmann designed for Jacques Doucet in 1913. *c. 1913.* H:39⅓ in (100.5 cm); W:27 in (68.5 cm). DEL

Rosewood cabinet This signed *demi-lune* cabinet by Ruhlmann has a pull-out shelf above a central recess and drawer carved in medium relief. The two curved side doors are inlaid with ivory and the whole cabinet is raised upon fluted spindle legs. *c. 1919.* W:50¾ in (129 cm). DEL

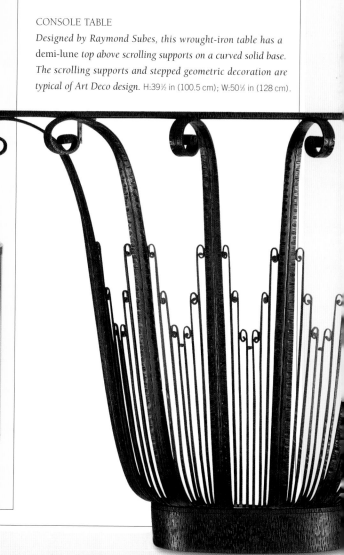

FRANCE

FRANCE, ESPECIALLY PARIS, was the hub of the lavish, or "high-style," strain of Art Deco. The sumptuous, graceful furniture that was created in the 1920s by Émile-Jacques Ruhlmann (*see p.393*) set the tone for this version of the style.

DUAL INSPIRATION

Using a host of exotic woods for decorative veneers, and embellishments made of colorful and expensive materials, ranging from ivory to lacquer and from leather to sharkskin, Ruhlmann and his colleagues—who included Paul Follot, André Groult, Jules Leleu, Léon-Albert Jallot, and Louis Süe and André Mare at the

Compagnie des Arts Français—sought inspiration from the opulent furniture crafted by the fine cabinet-makers of the 18th century, such as Jean-Henri Riesener and Adam Weisweiler.

Ruhlmann and his associates were also influenced by Art Nouveau (1880–1910). They took the sinuous lines, organic forms, and naturalistic motifs of that movement and restrained and stylized them, giving their pieces a more geometric form. Their

Wrought-iron gates designed by Edgar Brandt
The stylized water fountain of these fine gates has swirling stems of leaves and pierced flowers, and vines run along the bottom. *c. 1924. H:51 in (129.5 cm). SDR*

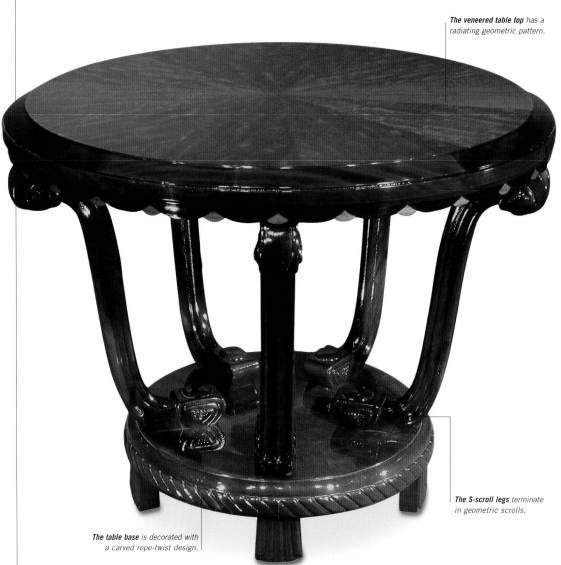

The veneered table top has a radiating geometric pattern.

The table base is decorated with a carved rope-twist design.

The S-scroll legs terminate in geometric scrolls.

CENTER TABLE

This center table, designed by Maurice Dufrene, has a veneered table top supported by ornately molded S-scroll legs. The table top is made from several different pieces of wood, which meet at the center of the table. The contrasting patterns and textures of the woods used form the main decorative feature of the table; seen from above, they create a subtle, radiating geometric pattern. The molded block feet are carved and support a small circular level with a carved rope design around the outer edge. A center table was designed to be primarily ornamental rather than functional—to furnish the space in the middle of the room where it would also be the center of attention. *c. 1925. H:27 in (68.5 cm); D:36 in (91.5 cm). MOD*

DEMI-LUNE SIDE TABLE

This Louis Süe and André Mare bird's-eye maple and mahogany *demi-lune* table has a broad crossbanded top above a thumb-molded edge and a single frieze drawer. The table is supported on cabriole legs. *H:31 in (79 cm); W:48 in (122 cm). CAL*

AMBOYNA CABINET

This amboyna cabinet has two central doors flanked by five small drawers on each side, each of which is decorated with ivory handles and inlay. The cabinet was designed and stamped by Paul Follot, and its symmetry and restrained style typify the elegant French Art Deco style. *c. 1925. W:60¼ in (153 cm).*

xquisitely crafted Art Deco cabinets, ables, and writing desks were much oveted by an exclusive and wealthy lientele who sought status. Their vork was extensively displayed at the 925 Paris Exhibition (*see pp.392–93*), ringing it to the attention of a much vider public.

UXURIOUS MATERIALS

allot—who worked with his son Maurice—and Leleu favored a rich palette of warm woods, such as walnut, palisander, and amboyna, enhanced vith understated marquetry created vith ivory, eggshell, shagreen, or nother-of-pearl. This often featured

signature Art Deco motifs, such as stylized garlands or baskets of flowers. Süe and Mare created luxurious, theatrical furniture in the Louis-Philippe style, and the decorating firm of Dominique produced stylish and sophisticated furniture in woods such as ebony and sycamore, upholstered in colorful silks, leather, and velvet.

The most exotic form of French Art Deco was realized in the innovative furniture created by Eileen Gray, Jean Dunand, and Pierre Legrain. Both Gray and Dunand exploited the popularity of Oriental art by creating distinctive lacquered screens, tables, cabinets, and chairs, in which the lacquer was

often combined with other luxurious materials, such as tortoiseshell, eggshell, animal skins, and metal, to create a rather dramatic impression. Legrain was one of several designers inspired by African art.

TOWARD MODERNISM
After 1925, some of the most committed French traditionalists, such as the

Jallots, slowly began to adapt to the changes brought about by both the machine age and the introduction to furniture design of new materials, such as metal and glass. As a result, their later Art Deco designs are distinctly more Modernist in appearance They set the stage for the Modernist furniture created by designers such as Pierre Chareau and Francis Jourdain.

ILT-METAL TABLE

his table by René Prou is rectangular in shape and has elegant abriole legs reminiscent of the early 18th-century Rococo style. he table is made of gilt metal and has a decorative pierced frieze f linked circles below the table top. *c. 1937. GYG*

MACASSAR CHAIR

This luxurious ebony and rosewood macassar chair, designed by Paul Follot, is one of a set of four. Each chair has a stylized acorn back within a "theater drape curtain" arched back, carved by Laurent Malcles. *H:32 in (81.25 cm); W:20 in (51 cm). CAL*

SOLID ROSEWOOD OFFICE CHAIR

This rare Edgar Brandt chair was one of a set designed for Brandt's own offices. The arched high back extends above boldly scrolling J-shaped arms. The tapering legs terminate in gilt sabots. *c. 1932. H:43½ in (110.5 cm); W:27 in (68.5 cm). CAL*

BUTTON-BACKED CHAIR

One of a pair of square button-backed chairs by Marc du Plantier, this chair has square-section legs at the front and saber legs at the back. The legs are made from painted wood and terminate in parchment sabots. The chair is newly upholstered in calfskin. *c. 1935. GYG*

ABLE BAR

his Jules Leleu sycamore and mahogany table bar has a ectangular top above a rectangular section column. The fall ront encloses a bar compartment with a single drawer below, ocated in the column. Its interior is veneered in contrasting nahogany. *H:24 in (61 cm); W:33½ in (85 cm). CAL*

LOW ROSEWOOD STOOL

This low stool is made of rosewood embellished with zebrano banding. The seat cushion is upholstered in a fabric that is typical of an Art Deco printed pattern, with overlapping geometric shapes, inspired by abstract art. *c. 1928. H:14 in (35 cm); W:18 in (46 cm). JAZ*

THE UNITED STATES

ALTHOUGH THE UNITED STATES did not participate in the 1925 Paris Exhibition, the Exhibition was still hugely influential in the US. Many American designers, including Eugene Schoen, visited it, and it was covered by American newspapers and magazines. Also, the following year, a tour of more than 400 objects that had been displayed in Paris was organized by Charles Richards, director of the American Association of Museums. He had been impressed by the Exhibition and hoped to initiate

"a parallel movement" in the United States by mounting the tour.

New York department stores, such as Lord & Taylor and R. H. Macy Company, also helped to publicize the Art Deco style by putting on exhibitions in the late 1920s of Art Deco furniture by leading Parisian designers. Eugene Schoen emulated his French contemporaries by creating pieces in rare and exotic woods, incorporating marquetry and inlays, colored lacquers, and subtle carvings. His forms were architectural, with

their clean lines and restrained, stylized decoration, and his cabinet-making was of the highest quality.

A NEW DIRECTION

A parallel Art Deco movement did blossom in the United States, but it developed along different lines from those of Europe. A handful of innovative designers, such as Paul Frankl, K.E.M. Weber, and Josef Urban, who were born in Europe, combined the French Art Deco style with those of the Bauhaus (see p.386) and the Wiener

Werkstätte in their designs. Instead of producing expensive luxury pieces, they created well-crafted, functional pieces that could be mass produced.

Donald Deskey, the principal interior designer for New York City's Radio City Music Hall, created dramatic, highly charged furniture. It combined the luxurious elements of French Art Deco with the more functional and rectilinear features of the Bauhaus style, which made full use of the latest technology. Deskey used the rare woods, lacquer, and glass loved by

Screens with two or three panels were popular with Art Deco furniture designers.

The stylized zebras are painted in black and tan on an ivory ground.

Signed and dated Robert W Chanler 1928.

CHINA CABINET

This simple, rectilinear cabinet was designed by Paul Frankl. The limed, slate-gray base and case of the lower section provide a striking contrast to the three ivory doors with semi-circular brass pulls. On top of this is is an unadorned china cabinet with a limed ivory finish. The three shelves of the cabinet are enclosed by two sliding glass doors. *W:72 in (183 cm). DRA*

PAINTED SCREEN

This dramatic, three-paneled wooden screen by Robert Winthrop Chanler features two zebras locked in combat, painted in black and tan on an ivory background. The back of the screen is decorated with diagonal stripes in black with silver foil, in imitation of a zebra's stripes.

The screen is signed and dated in the lower right corner. Chanler's screens were greatly admired, and this example was commissioned by the Broadway composer Kay Swift and her husband. Screens were popular during the Art Deco period, and this particular piece is of the utmost luxury, as emphasized by the use of silver foil. *1928. H:78 in (198 cm). SDR*

MAPLE DESK

Eugene Schoen designed this unusual maple desk for Schieg Hungate and Kotzian. The heavy rectangular desktop, with molded sides, sits on block feet. The supporting table underneath, which has a semicircular cutout, carries the desktop section. *c. 1935. W:45 in (114 cm). AMO*

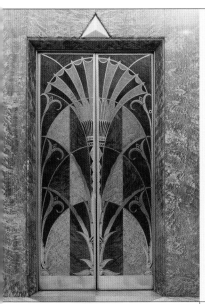

French designers but combined them with modern materials, such as aluminum and Bakelite, to embellish his opulent furniture designs.

NEW MATERIALS AND MOTIFS

It was modern materials that ultimately beguiled American Art Deco furniture designers. At the celebrated Cranbrook Academy of Art in Michigan, the Finnish-American architect Eliel Saarinen produced elegant pieces of furniture made from rich

Elevator doors These doors in the Chrysler building in New York City, designed by William Van Alen, represent the height of American Art Deco. The abstract fountain motif and surrounding geometric patterns lead the eye upward. *1928–30.*

wood veneers and natural materials, occasionally used in conjunction with innovative materials, such as steel and polished metal.

American designers welcomed the machine age with open arms. They decorated their furniture with machine motifs, such as interlocking cogs and wheels. They celebrated speed and dynamism with the increasingly streamlined look of their furniture inspired by automobiles, ocean liners, and locomotives, and motifs based on dramatic bolts of lightning. They made bold use of Cubist-inspired geometric shapes and jazzy abstract patterns, and included iconic American motifs based

on the modern city and way of life, such as the skyscraper.

The industrial designer K. E. M. Weber established a Californian version of Art Deco. His distinctive furniture was mostly made from metal and glass and often had skyscraper-like features. Weber created sleek, functional furniture for private commissions as well as designs intended for mass production, using new materials such as chromed metal, sprung steel, and laminated wood. He also designed lavish Art Deco furniture for dazzling Hollywood movie sets, which were largely responsible for transmitting the American Art Deco style to the world.

PAINTED CHAIR

This William L. Price painted chair has molded legs and an intricately carved backrest. It was designed for the dining room at Traymore Hotel, Atlantic City, New Jersey, which was demolished in 1972. *c. 1915. H:34 in (85 cm).*

COMMODE

Designed by John Widdicomb for a department store, this commode has a geometrically inlaid top above a single long drawer, with stylized inlay. The twin inlaid and figured panel doors enclose three drawers. *H:44 in (111.75 cm). FRE*

PAUL FRANKL (1887–1958)

PAUL FRANKL WANTED TO DESIGN A MODERN FORM OF FURNITURE THAT EXPRESSED THE "NEW SPIRIT MANIFEST IN EVERY PHASE OF AMERICAN LIFE."

Born in Vienna, the architect and engineer Paul T. Frankl fled Europe and settled in New York in 1914 at the outbreak of World War I. At first, he designed and manufactured furniture based on a formal European tradition, but by the mid-1920s, inspired by the architect-designers Le Corbusier and Walter Gropius, he devoted his attention to producing practical and economical modular furniture.

It was in 1925 that Frankl really came into his own as a furniture designer with his renowned range of custom-made furniture inspired by the New York skyline and the skyscrapers that soared above his New York gallery. Typical Frankl "skyscraper" designs, which frequently evoke the pure lines found in the work of the Dutch painter Piet Mondrian, include tall, stepped chests of drawers, cabinets, and bookcases boasting an architectonic, rectilinear form. They were made from oak or California redwood and were sometimes

embellished with a lacquer finish in black, red, or pale green, edged with silver leaf. He also designed "skyscraper" writing desks and dressing tables with mirrored tops. Designed to be affordable, the "skyscraper" furniture was not always of the highest quality standard. Frankl also supplied lacquered tables, chairs, and cabinets for the Oriental-style interiors that became fashionable in the period between the two world wars.

"Skyscraper" chest This rare Paul Frankl chest is asymmetrical, with long and short drawers, a single cabinet, a pull-out enameled shelf in red and black, and geometrically shaped brass pulls. *H:56 in (142 cm); W:36 in (91.5 cm); D:21½ in (54.5 cm). SDR*

STEEL STOOL

One of a set of four patinated steel stools, this stool has an upholstered, padded seat and a pierced apron cast with scrolling foliage. The stool has turned supports, linked by stretchers, with a maker's label. *L&T*

ILLUMINATED BAR

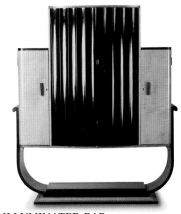

Made from black lacquer with an exotic wood veneer, this illuminated bar has a central cabinet with fluted doors and a mirrored interior. It sits on a U-shaped base. *H:64 in (162 cm); W:55¼ in (140 cm); D:19 in (48 cm). SDR*

STREAMLINING

SYMBOLIZING AN AGE OF PROGRESS, CHANGE, AND MODERNITY, THE STREAMLINED FORMS OF ART DECO HELPED TO REINVIGORATE THE AMERICAN ECONOMY.

ART MODERNE, AS THE AMERICAN form of Art Deco is also known, had always been inspired by city life, from the outline of the skyscraper to the sharp-edged designs reminiscent of syncopated jazz rhythms. It had always embraced the machine age in its use of industrial motifs and new materials. Then, in the 1930s, it made its final and perhaps greatest contribution to Art Deco with the concept of streamlining.

The Great Depression that swept across the country after the Wall Street crash of 1929 left in its wake a crippled economy in need of rejuvenation and a public whose confidence had been shattered. Embracing both new technology and innovative materials, streamlining had a tremendous impact on American architecture and the decorative arts, as well as giving the economy a much-needed boost.

DYNAMISM AND GLAMOUR

It was in the area of transportation that streamlined designs were first developed and popularized. From the early 1930s, great strides were made in the design of all modes of transportation, especially train locomotives and cars. The contoured lines, slick torpedo curves, and smooth horizontal surfaces that were meant to decrease air resistance and reduce turbulence became a glamorous symbol of the modern spirit. The industrial designer Norman Bel Geddes did much to popularize the streamlined style with his book *Horizons* (1932), which was full of striking images of streamlined trains, planes, and cars.

The dynamic qualities that were linked to speed and technological progress captured the imagination of a public eager to move away from the Depression era and into a bold new, brighter future, and the

COFFEE TABLE
This split-level coffee table by Donald Deskey has a large, rectangular Bakelite table top above a smaller, rectangular level. The two are supported on elegant, J-shaped nickel legs.
c. 1925. H:18 in (45.75 cm); W:28 in (71 cm); D:14 in (35.5 cm). MSM

FILING CABINET
One of a pair, this Donald Deskey cabinet is made from black lacquer and rosewood and has nickel and bronze hardware. Inspired by industrial developments, Deskey's work has much in common with that of the Bauhaus (see p.426). c. 1945. H:55½ in (141 cm); W:16½ in (42 cm). AMO

STREAMLINED SOFA
This sofa with end tables by Paul Frankl is made from black lacquer and black leather and has nickel-plated speed bands, derived from the "speed whiskers" that often decorated trains and cars.
H:50 in (127 cm); W:88 in (223.5 cm). MSM

DECORATIVE HOUSEHOLD OBJECTS

PAYING LITTLE REGARD TO FUNCTION, MANY PRODUCT DESIGNERS APPLIED THE SOFT CURVES AND HORIZONTAL BANDING OF STREAMLINING TO A HOST OF HOUSEHOLD OBJECTS.

Every type of household object—from tableware to lamps and from the accoutrements of the jazz age, such as the cocktail shaker, to the radio—was given the streamline treatment in 1930s America. Their shapes echoed the smooth, egg-shaped outlines of the contemporary railroad car or the glamorous ocean liner and were often decorated with horizontal decorative stripes, or "speed whiskers."

The idea was to create traditional, everyday objects in the new, streamlined style, creating a demand for merchandise in the new "modern" style,

which would, in turn, stimulate the beleaguered economy. Raymond Loewy's refrigerator design for Sears in 1934 embodied the style superbly, with its gently rounded corners and horizontal stripes. Many designers experimented with streamlined forms in tableware made of metal. Russel Wright broke new ground in 1931 with his cylindrical cocktail shaker and spherical cups made of spun chrome-plated pewter. Meanwhile, the chrome-plated brass "Normandie" water pitcher designed by German-born Peter Müller-Munk in 1935 emulated the shape of an ocean liner.

Extendable Bakelite lamp The shape of this lamp emulates the dynamic "lightning bolt" form typical of Art Deco streamlining. *1940s. H:18 in (45 cm). ROS*

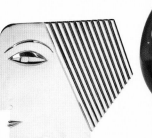
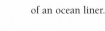

Chrome sculpture of a woman's face by Karl Hagenauer This sculpture has stylized features, including hair patterned like the "speed whiskers" that decorated trains and cars. *H:21 in (53.5 cm); W:17 in (43 cm). SDR*

Fiesta pitcher The shape of the pitcher is echoed by a pattern of sleek, streamlined curves. *H:7 in (18 cm). K&R*

French poster advertising the *Nord Express* The power and speed of the streamlined locomotive is dramatically expressed in this iconic poster. Designed by A.M. Cassandre (1901–68), the poster is mounted on Japanese paper. *1927. H:41¼ in (105 cm).*

CURVED DESK
This desk was designed by Donald Deskey for Widdicomb. It has black lacquered surfaces and two veneered side panels with chrome detailing. It was designed as part of a suite. c. 1935. W:52 in (132 cm). HSD

streamlined style was soon adopted by interior and product designers. The interiors of hotels, gas stations, diners, and shops were all given the streamlined treatment. Streamlining was also strikingly evident on the glamorous sets of 1930s Hollywood movies, such as *Grand Hotel* (1932).

As the 1930s progressed, streamlining was adopted more frequently in the design of a broad array of consumer wares—from every kind of furniture to all manner of new household appliances. The clean lines and powerful forms made a strong statement. Practical, everyday objects, such as the vacuum cleaner, stove, and radio, made of new materials, such as Bakelite, plastic, rubber, vinyl, aluminum, and chrome-plated steel, brought a sense of glamour and modernity to familiar pastimes and household chores. They also served to domesticate the machine, cleverly concealing its moving parts and removing any awkward protrusions with its smooth surfaces.

Streamlined products were to a certain extent "the technological result of high-speed mass production," as Harold Van Doren pointed out. Gently curved forms with no surface decoration were easy to manufacture using plastic moldings and pressed-sheet steel, and assembly-line techniques. However, they were also affordable and hugely popular. With streamlining, American Art Deco finally arrived.

BRITAIN

DURING THE FIRST HALF of the 1920s, most British furniture designers remained loyal to the principles of the Arts and Crafts Movement (see p.330), but occasionally used decorative elements inspired by French Art Deco in their work. One of London's most successful retailers and manufacturers, Heal & Son, produced Arts and Crafts designs made from sycamore, oak, or limed oak, quietly embellished with some Art Deco features. The furniture was essentially machine-made but was finished by hand.

RESTRAINED STYLE

Gordon Russell's furniture designs of the 1920s exhibited the more traditional Art Deco style. He adopted motifs, such as sunbursts and chevrons, and used exotic materials such as ivory and macassar ebony. Exhibiting to great acclaim at the 1925 Exhibition in Paris, Russell rejected the opulence favored by his French counterparts, and displayed a cabinet that celebrated the simplicity of traditional Georgian design with a minimum of decoration.

The 1925 Paris Exhibition influenced Heal's designer J. F. Johnson. From 1926 to 1927, he displayed a range of bedroom furniture made from macassar ebony and influenced by the high Parisian Art Deco style of Émile-Jacques Ruhlmann (see p.393). In 1928, Waring & Gillow, who provided luxury furniture for ships and hotels,

displayed fine furniture in the high Art Deco style in an exhibition called "Modern Art in French and English Furniture and Decoration." The exhibition marked the launch of their Department of Modern Art, which was headed by the Russian émigré Serge Ivan Chermayeff. Although Chermayeff favored the use of opulent veneers, he soon moved away from the French Art Deco style toward a more Modernist aesthetic. His sofas and coffee tables were geometric in form and the upholstery and carpets featured geometric patterns. His designs were widely copied, using less expensive materials, and were mass-produced for the middle-class home.

A TASTE FOR LUXURY

Fashionable Art Deco furniture made of sumptuous, expensive materials, and echoing traditional shapes—albeit with a Modernist twist—was also created in Great Britain by Betty Joel and Sir Edward Maufe. Maufe had won a medal at the 1925 Paris Exhibition for his mahogany, camphor wood, and ebony writing desk, which was gessoed and gilded with white gold, and featured silk tasseled handles. Betty Joel's prestigious and exclusive clientele included the King and Queen and Louis Mountbatten.

By the 1930s, Gordon Russell was producing more Modernist pieces, developing a successful range of good-quality, mass-produced furniture that made use of new materials such as tubular steel. Sir Ambrose Heal was also firmly aligned with the Modernist movement. However, elements of Art Deco persisted in Great Britain. The sunburst motif and stepped tiling could be seen in many suburban houses, and household objects, such as radios, telephones, and vacuum cleaners, exhibited the streamlined style of American Art Deco (see pp.398–99). In 1933, Maurice Adams produced the archetypal streamlined cocktail cabinet in ebonized mahogany with metal casing and chromium mounts.

The lobby of the former Daily Express building on Fleet Street, London The lobby was designed in 1932 by Robert Atkinson and was inspired by Hollywood movie sets. It features a starburst ceiling with a silvered pendant lamp and a huge silver and gilt plaster relief panel along one side.

OAK BOOKCASES

This pair of Betty Joel bookcases is made from Australian silky oak. Each bookcase is asymmetrical, with random open and enclosed shelves and two cupboard doors. The circular door handles contrast with the rectangular and square shapes of the cupboards and shelves. The bookcases stand on fluted square feet. Each one bears the following label on the base: "Token Hand-Made Furniture by Betty Joel, made by J. Emery at Token Works Portsmouth 1932." W:36¼ in (92 cm). L&T

BURR MAPLE TABLE

This Epstein table is part of a set, made up of a table and eight chairs (see below). The table is crafted from burr maple, one of the most expensive woods of the time, and has a rectangular top with rounded corners. The U-shaped base is a typical feature of Epstein's work and was much used by Art Deco designers. It gives a modern twist to the traditional pedestal base of a table. c. 1932. W:78 in (198 cm). JAZ

DINING CHAIR

This chair by Epstein is made of burr maple and is one of eight designed to accompany the table above. The chair is simple in form, has lightly splayed legs, and is upholstered in cream. c. 1932. H:35 in (89 cm). JAZ

MIRROR

This Art Deco mirror, by Whytock and Reid of Edinburgh, has a shaped, rectangular red-lacquered frame. The stylized plant motifs in the crested molding are highlighted in gilt. H:39¾ in (101 cm). L&T

CHEST OF DRAWERS

This English chest of drawers, made from walnut, has black-lacquer banding around the drawers and the edges of the case that accentuates its rectilinearity. The distinctive, slender drawer handles are attached vertically in juxtaposition to the horizontal, rectangular drawers. *c. 1930. W:48 in (123 cm). JAZ*

NEST OF TABLES

These three tables are made from amboyna and satinwood with a decorative inlay. Each table top has a geometric sunburst design, made from contrasting woods, and a molded edge. The tables are supported on tapering splayed legs and have molded pad feet. *c. 1925. H:27 in (68 cm); W:31 in (79 cm). JAZ*

TUB CHAIR

This squat, geometric tub chair, one of a pair, has a U-shaped framework with a curved back and arms that are veneered in oak from top to bottom. The back and apron of the chair, and the loose cushion seat, are upholstered in a striped fabric. The other chair of the pair has a slightly taller back. *L&T*

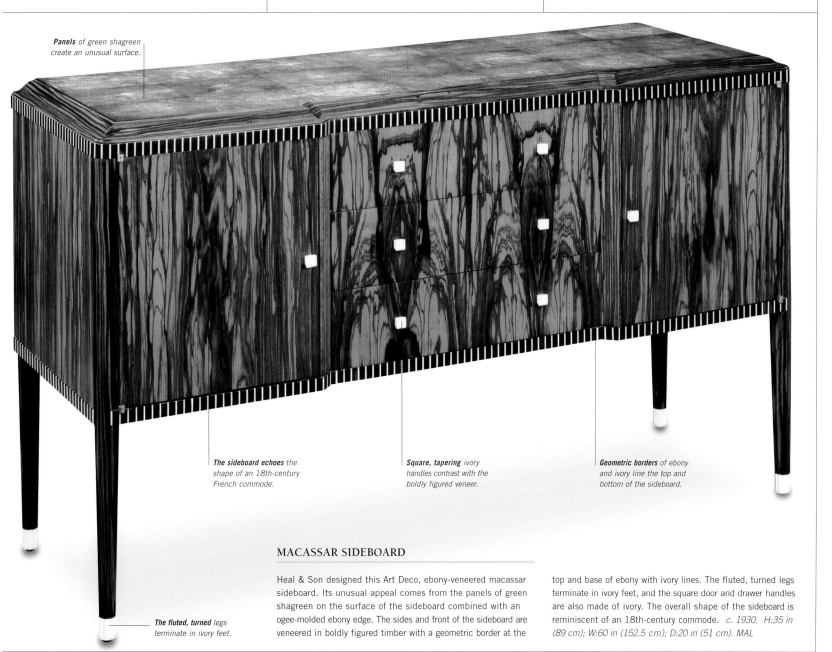

Panels of green shagreen create an unusual surface.

The sideboard echoes the shape of an 18th-century French commode.

Square, tapering ivory handles contrast with the boldly figured veneer.

Geometric borders of ebony and ivory line the top and bottom of the sideboard.

The fluted, turned legs terminate in ivory feet.

MACASSAR SIDEBOARD

Heal & Son designed this Art Deco, ebony-veneered macassar sideboard. Its unusual appeal comes from the panels of green shagreen on the surface of the sideboard combined with an ogee-molded ebony edge. The sides and front of the sideboard are veneered in boldly figured timber with a geometric border at the top and base of ebony with ivory lines. The fluted, turned legs terminate in ivory feet, and the square door and drawer handles are also made of ivory. The overall shape of the sideboard is reminiscent of an 18th-century commode. *c. 1930. H:35 in (89 cm); W:60 in (152.5 cm); D:20 in (51 cm). MAL*

ART DECO INTERIOR

ART DECO, WITH ITS BLEND OF MODERNITY AND EXOTICISM, FOUND A SHOWCASE IN A NEW MUSEUM IN PARIS—THE CITY WHERE THE STYLE WAS BORN.

IN 1931, AN Art Deco design was chosen for the ambitious new *Musée des Colonies* (now renamed the *Musée des Arts d'Afrique et d'Océanie*) which was built specially for the Colonial Exhibition, to glorify the relationship between France and its colonies. The original plans for the building, incorporating motifs from North African architecture, were rejected in favor of Albert Laprade's clean, modern design inspired by European Classicism.

The exterior of the museum was decorated with an enormous stylized frieze designed by the prominent Art Deco sculptor Albert Janniot. The interior also became a spectacular showcase for Art Deco design, as well as for art and artifacts from Africa and Asia.

Although the rooms designed to display colonial artifacts were kept fairly plain, two oval rooms were lavishly decorated and were used as reception rooms. The *Salon de l'Afrique* celebrated contributions from the African colonies, while the magnificent *Salon de l'Asie*, also known as the *Salon Lyautey*, was dedicated to the arts of Asia.

THE SALON LYAUTEY

Designed by Eugène Printz, and with frescoes by André-Hubert and Ivanna Lemaitre, the *Salon Lyautey* remains a fine example of 1930s French Art Deco. The majestic parquet floor, with its radiating geometric design typical of the era, is made of Gabonese wood, with highlights of ebony and rosewood. The rich coloring of the floor, enhanced by the dark draped curtains, sets the tone for the whole room. In keeping with the Art Deco fascination with exoticism, the dramatic frescoes depict Asian figures, scenes, and deities and dominate the room.

The furniture, which was also designed by Printz, is typically Art Deco: bold and simple in form with clean, lines and minimal ornamentation. The doors of the Salon and most of the furniture are made of patawa (palmwood), a vividly patterned wood much favored by Printz. The beauty of the two imposing desks lies in the figuring of the palmwood as much as in their sleek, curved forms. The dramatic outlines of the uplighters, which resemble exotic trees, echo the curves of the desks and the armrests of the matching chairs.

The overall effect is striking; the blend of natural materials, modern shapes, and Asian-inspired frescoes creates an impression of exoticism, whilst remaining distinctly French. The *Salon Lyautey* is both a lasting momento of Art Deco and a monument to a European empire on the point of decline.

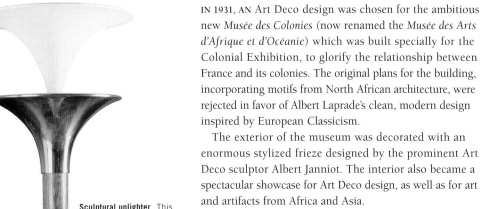

Sculptural uplighter This distinctive lamp, designed by Eugène Printz, is made of palmwood and has a trumpet-shaped top. The shelf near the base of the lamp serves as an occasional table.

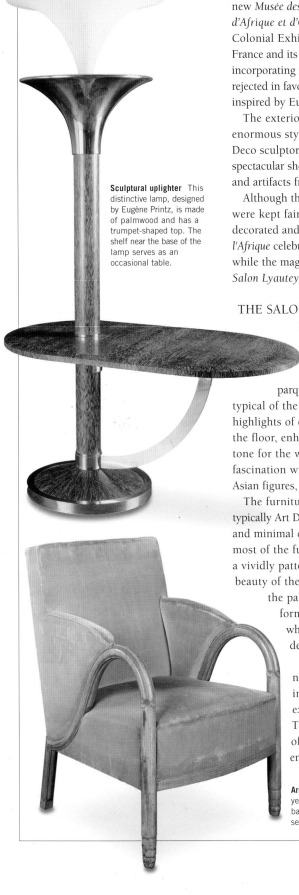

Armchair This colonial-style armchair, upholstered in a golden-yellow fabric, has a curved bentwood frame and a rectangular back. The upholstered armrests create fan shapes between the seat back and the curved arms, which continue into the legs.

EUROPE

TREMENDOUS UPHEAVALS came about in Europe in the wake of World War I. The need for change was keenly felt by architects and designers from Italy to Belgium and the Netherlands, and from Germany to Scandinavia.

At the heart of this longing for change lay a functionalist ideology and a desire for art to accommodate the exciting technological advances of the early 20th century. Mass-produced, functional furniture designs became the order of the day, a philosophy that was realized by Alvar Aalto in Finland and with the formation in 1919 of the Bauhaus by Walter Gropius. Internationally acclaimed, the Bauhaus sought to

bring together the talents of creative artists, designers, and craftspeople, to create prototype designs suitable for industrial mass production (see p.426).

Although the Modernist Bauhaus style prevailed in Germany during the 1920s and 1930s, there were also architects and designers working in a more decorative manner. Using vibrant colors, and drawing on the Rococo and Biedermeier styles for inspiration, German Art Deco furniture exhibited Asian touches in its use of lacquer, together with Cubist detailing. Bruno Paul's "Room for a Gentleman," shown at Macy's department store in New York in 1928, was typical of the

restrained form of Art Deco that was pursued by these German designers. The room contained lacquered furniture with inlay work, and a rug with a geometric design. Many German and Austrian—mainly Jewish—designers emigrated to America in the late 1920s and early 1930s, and joined Paul Frankl (see p.397) in developing the Art Deco style there.

NORTHERN EUROPEAN TRENDS
It was in the Netherlands that the concept of abstraction was first applied to furniture design. At the helm of this revolutionary artistic idea was the avant-garde De Stijl group, formed

in 1917 by the painters Theo van Doesburg and Piet Mondrian. The functionalist furniture designed by the group was conspicuously absent from the 1925 Paris Exhibition. The Dutch pavilion there was designed by J. F. Staal, a member of the Amsterdam School, which favored the use of theatrical, expressionist, and Asian motifs in furniture designs. Among the exhibits was furniture by C. A. Lion Cachet, designed for a Dutch ocean liner. He used dark tropical woods inlaid with ivory and lighter woods in traditional-shaped pieces with Asian decoration and parchment panels. Jaap Gidding's theater and movie theater

ITALIAN COFFEE TABLE

This fine Italian coffee table has a rectangular glass-topped surface on tapering plank legs. It has been crafted from bird's-eye maple and ebony veneer. Exotic wood veneers, such as the ebony used in this piece, were commonly used in European Art Deco furniture. The dark ebony highlights the simple geometric structure of the coffee table. *W:39¼ in (99.5 cm). SDR*

SWEDISH CHAIR

This Swedish Art Deco chair is upholstered in brown leather and supported on tapering legs, with two slightly splayed rear legs, and curvilinear arm rests. The backrest has a central panel with burr wood and satinwood details. *c. 1920. W:24 in (61 cm). LANE*

BELGIAN BRIDGE CHAIR

This bridge chair is one of a pair designed by De Coene Frères. The curved armrests form a continuous "U" shape with the bowed seat frame. The chair is upholstered in a red, checked fabric and has tapering front legs. *c. 1930. H:32¼ in (82 cm). LM*

BELGIAN DESK

Designed by De Coene Frères, this Belgian desk has four drawers, tapering legs, and nickel feet, and is covered in black lacquer. The sleek black design demonstrates a relinquishing of unnecessary decoration in favor of pure functionality. *c. 1930. W:68 in (172.5 cm). LM*

SWISS DESK

This Swiss walnut desk has a rectangular top with rounded corners. The central drawer and two flanking cabinets have decorative "English-style" handles, and the whole piece is raised on square feet. The grain of the walnut has been highlighted, providing additional visual interest. *c. 1925. W:58 in (145 cm). VH*

interiors also followed the French Art Deco style. The Tuschinski movie theater in Amsterdam (1918–21) was typical, with its decorative, opulent interior, and special light effects.

In Scandinavia, Art Deco took a more classical turn, with an emphasis on elegance, proportion, luxurious materials, and hand-crafting. In 1930, British writer Morton Shand defined the Swedish restrained Neoclassical style prevalent at the 1925 Paris Exhibition as a "line characterized by its slender and almost elfin grace." Exhibiting a similar style, Otto Meyer's and Jacob Petersen's graceful, curving chairs crafted out of sycamore and mahogany were superbly set off by the batik wall-covering of Ebbe Sadolin in the Danish pavilion.

ITALIAN BALANCE

Italian furniture designers struggled to find a balance between the demand for classical elegance and the language of the sophisticated modern style. Although ill at ease with the display of sumptuous luxury that was the hallmark of French Art Deco, Italian cabinets, tables, writing desks, and chairs made full use of the beauty of lustrous local and exotic woods. Many of them were embellished with bronze mounts, or lightly carved or inlaid patterns of flower baskets, garlands, or geometric motifs that were typical of Art Deco.

The Italian version of Art Deco reached its fullest expression in the hands of the innovative architect Gio Ponti. He successfully managed to combine the functional, geometric, spare structure promoted by the Wiener Werkstätte designers with the sophisticated and elegant refinements of the French Art Deco style.

ITALIAN CABINET

This rectangular Ulrich Guglielmo cabinet has two doors and is supported on a square plinth lined with goat parchment. The doors have ivory mounts and the plinth is veneered with kingwood. Round ebony knobs, with gilded bronze mountings and keys, are attached to the 14 interior drawers. *c. 1930. H:60 in (150 cm). QU*

Mirror glass is commonly used as a decorative feature of Art Deco furniture.

The burr wood veneer makes a boldly luxurious statement.

The strict geometric shape of the buffet is highlighted by the warm color of the burr wood veneer.

The rectilinear structure of the buffet is emphasized by the austere placement of the doors and drawers.

The ivory inlay used for the drawer pulls is a typical Art Deco detail.

ITALIAN BUFFET

The shelf structure of this Italian buffet is characteristic of Art Deco design, combining clean lines and asymmetry with a luxurious and decorative burr wood finish. The shelf structure contains a mirror on a case with four small drawers and a twin cabinet door enclosing an adjustable shelf. Subtle, inlaid handles are attached to the four drawers and the cabinet doors. The geometric shape is typical of Italian Art Deco, which took its lead from the Wiener Werkstätte. The use of exotic lumber is more typical of the French style. *W:70 in (177.75 cm). FRE*

WALNUT EASY CHAIR

This continental walnut easy chair is upholstered in cream, a popular color in Art Deco furniture design. The chair has broad, curving armrests, each supported on three vertical fluted rods, and molded sledlike block feet. *DN*

INDIA AND EAST ASIA

ALTHOUGH THE Art Deco style had its origins and greatest success in the West, it also found voice in the East.

INDIAN GLAMOUR
Despite a strain of social conservatism and an economy that remained sluggish and underdeveloped, Indian designers welcomed the aesthetic ideals and stylish visual viewpoint promoted by the fashionable modern taste for Art Deco favored by the colonialists. Appreciation for, and support of, the Art Deco style was also fostered by designers who had emigrated to India from Central and Eastern Europe, taking with them an

astute knowledge of the style, along with a calculated eye to receiving patronage from wealthy, cultivated, and influential benefactors.

At the heart of the Art Deco style in India was Mumbai (then called Bombay), the center of international communication and a thriving port. Here, the mercantile classes and the Westernized ruling communities came together with the development of the Back Bay area between 1929 and 1940. The Development Trust insisted that all the buildings conform to the same architectural style to ensure "uniformity and harmony of design." The style was an elegant, streamlined, yet decorated

form of Art Deco. By the end of the 1930s, Bombay had nearly 300 movie theaters, all of which were glamorous Art Deco palaces, both inside and out. The sophisticated and luxurious residences commissioned by wealthy Indian princes also reflected the Art Deco style. The furniture often combined the "high-style" French Art Deco with native decorative traditions.

EAST ASIAN AFFINITY
During the 1920s and 1930s, a lot of the Japanese and Chinese architecture, interiors, and furnishings were inspired by the Art Deco style. Much of Art Deco's inspiration—simple design,

spare, nature-inspired decoration, and the use of sumptuous, exotic materials such as lacquer, ivory, and mother-of-pearl—came from the traditions of East Asia in the first place, so there was already an affinity between the two.

Throughout Japan, and especially in Tokyo, economic and industrial development after World War I was accompanied by democratization and cultural change. Western ideas were promoted through exhibitions and

CHINESE JADE TABLE SCREEN

This large Chinese screen has a striking central panel made of jade, which is carved to depict a pavilion and figures under pine trees. The panel is set within a fretwork frame. *c. 1930. H:21 in (53.5 cm). S&K*

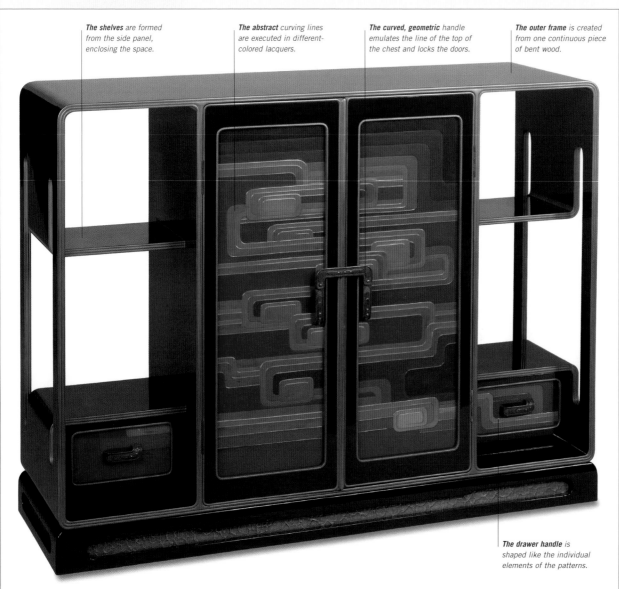

The shelves are formed from the side panel, enclosing the space.

The abstract curving lines are executed in different-colored lacquers.

The curved, geometric handle emulates the line of the top of the chest and locks the doors.

The outer frame is created from one continuous piece of bent wood.

The drawer handle is shaped like the individual elements of the patterns.

JAPANESE CHEST

This boldly curving, geometric chest features a trailing smoke design in gold and colored lacquer. It was designed by the leading Kyoto lacquer artist Suzuki Hyosaku II, who was a member of *Ryukeiha Kogeikai* (the Streamline School Craft Association). Continuous pieces of bent wood create the outer frame, the frames of the two central doors, and those

of the two outer drawers. The upper shelf above each drawer is formed from a piece of wood cut out of the side of the chest and bent horizontally. Black lacquer is used to define the outer rim of each of the doors and to set off the abstract design that decorates them. The curving, asymmetrical patterning in shades of red, orange, and gold blend with the overall streamlined form of the chest as well as contrast with its symmetry. *1937. H:32¾ in (83.5 cm); W:44¼ in (112.5 cm); D:12 in (30.5 cm).*

CHINESE HARDWOOD CABINET

The case of this cabinet is rectangular in outline with rounded corners. Two paneled doors open onto two sections, one with two shelves. The case stands on molded bracket feet. *c. 1930. H:49 in (124.5 cm). S&K*

publications, and by Western designers themselves. The Tokyo earthquake of 1923 left a devastated city ripe for renewal, and many of the new buildings reflected the Art Deco style. Numerous movie theaters, cafés, and dance halls were built, their interiors filled with modern materials such as aluminum, glass, and stainless steel.

In China's thriving metropolis of Shanghai, the spirited Art Deco style was appropriated and assimilated with

The Umaid Bhawan palace, Jodhpur, India
This bathroom is typical of the palace's interior in its use of streamlining, bold curves, and luxuriant materials. The architect, Henry Vaughan Lanchester, brought the state architect G. A. Goldstraw to Jodhpur to ensure the integrity of the design.

enthusiasm by Chinese architects and designers. Known as the "Paris of the East," Shanghai was a prosperous and cosmopolitan city of business and pleasure. The American Art Deco style dominated in the new high-rise hotels, apartment blocks, offices, department stores, cafés, and restaurants.

The 12-story Cathy Hotel, built by Palmer & Turner in 1932, set the tone, with its green pyramidal roof and Art Deco features. The Grand Theater, designed by Czech-Hungarian émigré Laszio Hudec, was a monument to Hollywood glamour with its sparkling Art Deco interior, complete with a marble lobby and neon lighting.

JAPANESE SCREEN

This wooden screen was designed by Ban-ura Shogo. The spare, asymmetric pattern of flowers and foliage was created with different-colored lacquers and is typical of Japanese design. It provides a decorative foil for the geometric shape of the screen. *1936. H:35¾ in (91 cm); W:43 in (109 cm); D:12¼ in (31 cm).*

ECKART MUTHESIUS (1904–89)

IN HIS DESIGNS FOR THE MAHARAJAH OF INDORE, ECKART MUTHESIUS SUCCESSFULLY MARRIED THE SIMPLE AND FUNCTIONAL WITH THE MORE DECORATIVE AND FANCIFUL FRENCH ART DECO STYLE.

Nowhere was the desire for the fashionable and the modern better demonstrated than in the luxurious palaces designed by Western architects for the wealthy and sophisticated Indian princes.

One such palace, built with an eye for practical considerations as well as for the latest style, was built by the German architect Eckart Muthesius. Commissioned in 1930 by the Oxford-educated Maharajah of Indore, Yeshwant Rao Holkar, Muthesius designed an air-conditioned, "U"-shaped palace known as Manik Bagh. Containing private apartments, as well as a large ballroom, a banqueting hall, and guest rooms, it had a steel frame, concrete walls, and a wooden roof.

Muthesius was personally responsible for designing all the interiors and created a stylish and modern palace of Art Deco, resplendent with sparkling golden-yellow walls. Nearly all of the fixtures that he designed, from

floors and window frames to light fixtures, switches, and door handles, were ordered from companies in Germany and shipped out to India. The furniture was bought from some of the best French designers, mainly from the *Union des Artistes Modernes.*

Muthesius furnished the palace with lavish pieces made from sumptuous materials. The Maharajah's study contained fine macassar ebony furniture by Émile-Jacques Ruhlmann, while his bedroom featured an armchair by Eileen Gray and a chaise longue by Le Corbusier, covered in leopardskin. The beds in the palace were made of aluminum and chrome, and the deep leather armchairs had frames of chrome-plated band iron and built-in reading lamps. There were also plush carpets by Ivan da Silva Bruhns, and silverware by Jean Puiforcat.

JAPANESE RADIO

This wooden hyperbolic radio was designed by Inoue Hikonosuke. Lacquer was a favorite material for Japanese designers working in the Art Deco style. The powerful stylized flower shapes of luminous gold highlighted with silver foil stand out against the glossy black-lacquer background. *1934.*

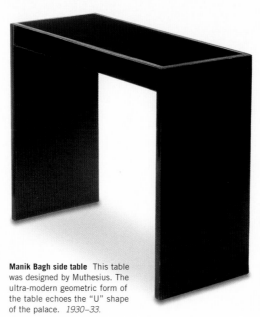

Manik Bagh side table This table was designed by Muthesius. The ultra-modern geometric form of the table echoes the "U" shape of the palace. *1930–33.*

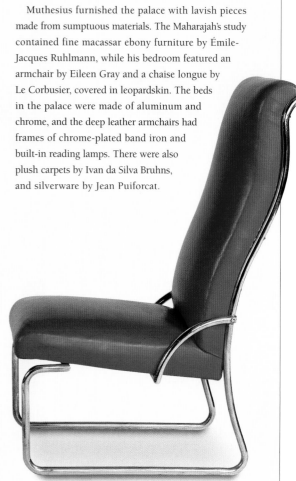

Tubular steel side chair This chrome-plated chair is covered in brilliant red vinyl and was commissioned by Muthesius for Manik Bagh. *1930–33. H:39½ in (100 cm).*

THE SUITE

SPECIALLY DESIGNED MATCHING SETS OF ELEGANT AND LUXURIOUS FURNITURE BECAME AN INTEGRAL FEATURE OF THE ART DECO INTERIOR.

MATCHING PIECES OF FURNITURE have had a long and rich tradition. From the second half of the 18th century onward, fashionable rooms in French houses were frequently designed as integrated interiors and were furnished with large and elaborate suites of furniture. In the mid 19th century, rooms became more densely furnished and the desire for comfort among the growing middle classes led to the creation of new furnishings that were often produced as elegant, machine-made matching sets.

ELEGANCE AND COMFORT

In the 1920s and 1930s, designers working in the Art Deco style also responded to the demand for integrated interiors. They aimed to make a bold visual statement while also providing comfort.

French Art Deco designers created luxurious suites of furniture. Each piece of furniture was embellished with a sumptuous material, such as shagreen or animal skin, lacquer, or an exotic veneer, and matching upholstery. Émile-Jacques Ruhlmann exhibited a complete set of furniture for the "residence of a rich art collector" to great acclaim at the 1925 Paris Exhibition. Paul Follot created suites in the 18th-century style and Jules Leleu designed luxury suites for embassies, ministries, and ocean liners. André Groult created a spectacular bedroom suite veneered in green galuchat (ray skin) and upholstered in pink satin, which was exhibited as the "Chambre de Madame" in the Ambassade Française pavilion at the 1925 Paris Exhibition. This extravagant ensemble caused a sensation.

FROM ART DECO TO MODERNISM

Suites of Art Deco furniture were also designed in Great Britain. Betty Joel produced room sets in the style of Ruhlmann, while Syrie Maugham created beige and white color schemes featuring mirror glass and silvered wood. It was the more Modernist style that took hold, however. In 1929, Serge Chermayeff designed a comfortable, but practical, suite of living-room furniture for Waring & Gillow. The room featured geometric sofas upholstered in Cubist-inspired patterned fabric, set around a hexagonal coffee table and rug, also decorated with geometric patterns.

BEDROOM SUITE
Coordinating suites of furniture for bedrooms were particularly popular during this period. The centerpiece of the room was usually the bed, which was surrounded by a host of chests of drawers, dressing tables, wardrobes, and so on, all geometrically shaped and made from the same materials, as here.

Chest of drawers This has a compartmented blind drawer. Below this are three long drawers, with distinctive long metal handles. *W:45¾ in (114 cm). S&K*

Bedside table The table contains a blind drawer, above a cupboard that is formed to look like a drawer. *H:26 in (65 cm). S&K*

Gentleman's tall chest of drawers This piece has a blind top drawer containing an adjustable mirror, above five graduated drawers. The bottom drawer is cedar-lined. The chest is flanked by a cedar-lined hanging compartment. *H:56 in (140 cm). S&K*

Pedestal desk This desk has a blind, compartmented center drawer, flanked by two small blind drawers, set over two banks of two deep drawers. *W:48 in (120 cm). S&K*

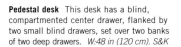

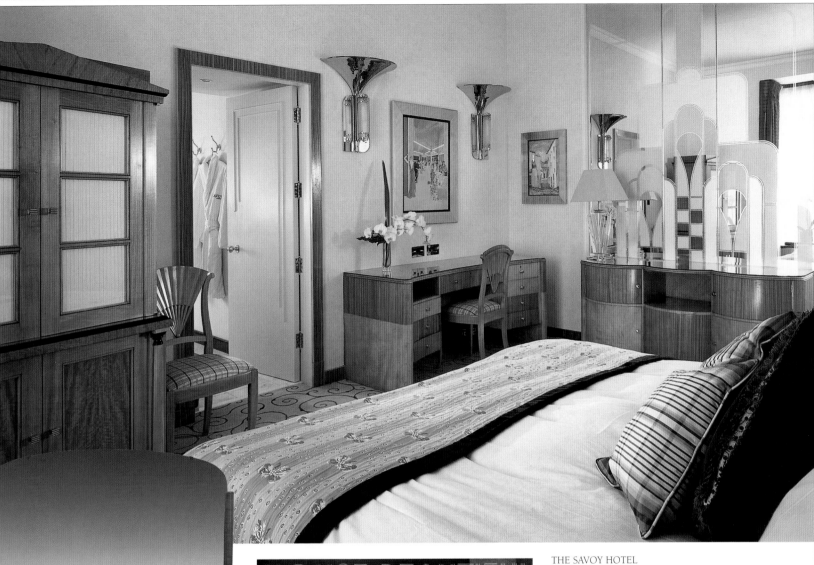

Bedroom mirror This mirror is one of a pair. It has a simple rectangular design with a gently arched top and bottom, and wooden strips at the sides. *W:39¾ in (101 cm). S&K*

THE SAVOY HOTEL

This well-appointed room in the Savoy Hotel, London, has a pastel decor and is complemented by original Art Deco furnishings, including the curvaceous bedroom suite.

AMERICAN SUITES

In the United States in 1928, at the American Designers' Gallery, ten designers contributed complete, integrated room sets. Among them was Donald Deskey, who designed a "Man's Smoking Room," with elegant, rectilinear furniture, often decorated with geometric motifs, and made from new materials such as chrome-plated steel, glass, and Bakelite. Paul T. Frankl (*see p.397*) displayed an entire room full of his furniture shaped like miniature skyscrapers at the same exhibition.

Also in 1928, at Macy's department store in New York, Bruno Paul integrated Oriental and Western traditions in his "Room for a Gentleman." The Japanese screen-style windows were a perfect complement to the plush armchairs and veneered sideboard. The following year, in *Good Furniture* magazine, Paul stated that "the whole interior is more important than any of its parts."

Norman Bel Geddes did much to popularize the American streamlined Art Moderne look. His suites of furniture, characterized by horizontal lines and rounded corners, were frequently made of machine-age materials, such as enameled metal.

STREAMLINED GEOMETRY

The October 1935 issue of House Beautiful *shows an elegant Art Moderne interior on its cover. The red upholstery stands out from the clean white lines of the curved chairs, which are grouped symmetrically around a rectangular black backgammon table.*

CHAIRS

ART DECO CHAIRS tended to delight in the taste for comfort and luxury. They boast generous proportions and were made from luxurious and inviting materials. Many chairs were designed as part of a salon suite that included a sofa and several chairs. Whether shaped in clean lines based on traditional forms or in more avant-garde, abstract forms, chairs were created to be both comfortable and pleasing to the eye.

LUXURY AND EXOTICISM

The French designers Émile-Jacques Ruhlmann, Süe et Mare, and Paul Follot often based their chair designs on 18th-century forms, such as the *bergère* and the *fauteuil à la reine*. With shaped backs, slender tapering legs terminating in delicate sabots of ivory or bronze, and graceful, scrolling arm supports, these chairs were made from sumptuous lumbers, such as mahogany, rosewood, and macassar ebony, and were often decorated with carving or inlays of exotic materials, including lacquer, tortoiseshell, sharkskin, and mother-of-pearl.

Upholstery played an important part in Art Deco chair design. Luxurious materials, such as the finest leather, exotic animal skins, and velour were used, and vivid colors and geometric or exotic patterns prevailed. The set designs and costumes of Serge Diaghilev's *Ballets Russes*, Cubist and Fauve paintings, and African, Asian, and folk art were all key decorative influences.

By the 1930s, many Art Deco chairs were designed along more geometric, abstract lines, with simple contours, and were made from new materials, such as laminated wood, tubular steel, chromed metal, aluminum, and vinyl.

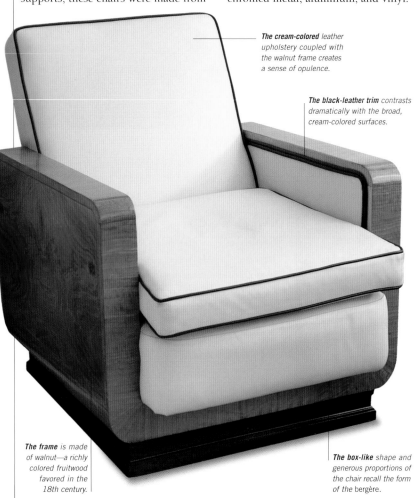

The cream-colored leather upholstery coupled with the walnut frame creates a sense of opulence.

The black-leather trim contrasts dramatically with the broad, cream-colored surfaces.

The frame is made of walnut—a richly colored fruitwood favored in the 18th century.

The box-like shape and generous proportions of the chair recall the form of the bergère.

BRITISH WALNUT CHAIR

Part of a three-piece suite, this comfortable and luxurious armchair was produced by Hille & Co., who were manufacturers of reproduction furniture. The chair has a U-shaped walnut frame that forms armrests with gently rounded corners, and is supported on a square, molded, block base. The seat and the matching cushion are upholstered in fine cream leather and have a contrasting narrow black-leather trim. The U-shaped frame was a popular feature of many Art Deco pieces of furniture. *c. 1928. W:72½ in (184 cm). JAZ* **5**

FRENCH DESK CHAIR

This mahogany desk chair, by Maurice Dufrene, has an arched tub back and padded seat. The armrests end in bold scrolls and the seat is raised on scrolling, tapering legs. *c. 1920. H:28 in (71 cm); W:26 in (66 cm). CAL* **5**

SWEDISH CLUB CHAIR

This Swedish club chair is boxlike in shape and has rounded wooden armrests. The back, seat, and sides of the chair are upholstered in matt black leather with brass rivet details on the arms. *W:25¼ in (64 cm). LANE* **3**

FRENCH DINING CHAIR

This elegant tall-backed dining chair is one of a set of six designed by Maurice Jallot. The chair is padded and upholstered in red, with elliptical detailing, and has tapering, slightly splayed legs. *1940s. LM* **5**

ENGLISH C-SHAPE ARMCHAIR

One of a pair of open armchairs, this has prominent, reverse C-shape armrests on squat saber legs. The avant-garde Cubist and Futurist movements influenced the pattern of the upholstery. *c. 1930. BL* **3**

AMERICAN D-SHAPE CHAIR

One of a pair of chairs designed by Paul Frankl, the armrests are curved and finished in black lacquer. The seat is upholstered in black vinyl with red piping. *c. 1927. H:26¾ in (68 cm); W:24 in (61 cm); D:30 in (76 cm). MSM*

FRENCH NIAGARA CHAIR

One of a set of four, this chair was designed by Maurice Dufrene. The "Niagara" patterned upholstery sits within a plain molded frame, on distinctive, stepped, "falling water" legs. *H:37 in (94 cm); W:19 in (48.25 cm). CAL* **6**

FRENCH ARMCHAIR

This armchair is one of pair designed by Pol Buthion. It has a chrome and red-lacquered wooden frame and flat paddle arms. The seat and back are upholstered in dark brown fabric. H:33 in (84 cm). CSB **6**

FRENCH LACQUERED ARMCHAIR

This armchair is one of a pair by Francisque Chaleyssin and is made from black-lacquered wood. The seat, back, and tubular arms are upholstered in brown and beige velvet. H:33½ in (85 cm). CSB **5**

FRENCH ARMCHAIR

This armchair is one of a pair designed by Soubrier. It has an arched back and is upholstered in a diamond-patterned fabric. The chair stands on block feet. H:31 in (79 cm); W:26 in (66 cm); D:29 in (74 cm). MOD **6**

FRENCH MAHOGANY SIDE CHAIR

One of a pair, this Jules Leleu chair has an arched back, inverted heart base, and stepped, scroll arm terminals. The tapering legs terminate in gilt-bronze sabots. c. 1930. H:29 in (73.65 cm); W:25 in (63.5 cm). CAL **6**

AMERICAN V-SHAPED CHAIR

One of six mahogany dining chairs designed by Paul Frankl and produced by Johnson Furniture Co., this armchair has a distinctive V-shaped upholstered back and curved mahogany arm rests. H:31 in (79 cm). FRE **2**

BRITISH CURVED CHAIR

Tapering splayed legs support this sycamore chair, attributed to Hille and Co. The padded seat and arched tub back are upholstered in a geometrically patterned fabric, with one curving side. c. 1930. H:27¼ in (69 cm). TDG **1**

FRENCH DINING CHAIR

This Léon and Maurice Jallot dining chair has an ebonized frame and legs. The seat and back are upholstered in green leather, above sides mounted with three chrome rails. c. 1930. H:33 in (84 cm); W:24 in (61 cm). CAL **5**

FRENCH CHAIR

This black-polished and upholstered chair is one of a pair by Alfred Porteneuve. It has slender, flattened arms and tapering legs, which end in bronze sabots. 1940s. H:35 in (89 cm); W:21 in (53.35 cm). CAL **6**

FRENCH ROSEWOOD CHAIR

This Süe et Mare rosewood side chair has an upholstered arched back above a padded seat. The carved frame has feather detailing and the cabriole legs terminate in scroll feet. c. 1925. H:39 in (99 cm); W:20 in (51 cm). CAL **5**

AMERICAN CHAIR

This mahogany dining chair is part of a dining suite comprising eight chairs. It has a solid, rectangular back and a padded seat upholstered in striped fabric. The chair is supported on tapering, splayed legs. FRE **3**

BLACK-LACQUERED CHAIR

Designed by De Coene Frères, this Belgian black-lacquered armchair has a framed, square, padded back and seat upholstered in green leather. The armrests are flattened and the tapering legs terminate in nickel feet. LM

FRENCH GAME CHAIR

One of a pair, this Dominique cherry armchair is late for the period, but its square form, Aubusson upholstery, and tapering legs are all Art Deco in style. 1945. H:31 in (78.75 cm); W:24 in (61 cm). CAL **5**

TABLES

AFTER WORLD WAR I, designers working in the Art Deco style created tables of extraordinary richness and originality, continuing the Art Nouveau tradition in a less flamboyant manner.

TRADITIONAL FORMS

Many Art Deco furniture designers based their designs on traditional table forms, such as the early oak trestle table and the drop-leaf designs of the 18th century. They used richly figured lumbers, such as walnut, yew, and mahogany, and decorated their tables with crossbanding in exotic woods, such as ebony and tulip wood.

Émile-Jacques Ruhlmann and Jules Leleu created writing tables, dressing tables, and pier tables that echoed the forms favored by the French *ébénistes* of the 18th and 19th centuries. They used exotic materials, such as lacquer and expensive wood veneers, and their tables often featured decorative details, such as drawer pulls of ivory, slender legs terminating in sabots of gilded bronze, and table tops covered with leather, sharkskin, or marble.

The Irish-born designer Eileen Gray designed finely crafted and exquisitely lacquered tables whose abstract shapes were frequently defined by different-colored lacquers and costly inlays of foil and mother-of-pearl.

BOLD INNOVATIONS

The furniture designers who followed a more Modernist Art Deco path, such as Marcel Coard and Pierre Chareau in France, and Donald Deskey in the United States, made tables for a wide variety of uses in bold geometric shapes, such as cubes, cylinders, and pyramids. They used innovative materials characteristic of the machine age, including mirror glass, chrome, and tubular steel, and interpreted traditional forms, such as the tilt-top table, with great ingenuity.

Pierre Legrain combined luxurious and machine-age materials with severity of form in a striking low table entitled "Python," which he designed in 1928 for Pierre Meyer. Made entirely of wood, the long, rectangular top and two supports are entirely sheathed in snakeskin. The supports fit into a rectangular base, which is the mirror image of the top, but is veneered in nickel plate. Two nickel-plated ovoid discs encircle the square supports, completing the symmetry of the design.

Geometric form

Maker's label

FRENCH SIDE TABLE

This rosewood side table, designed by Michel Dufet, is composed of geometric forms, which are characteristic of the Art Deco style. The circular rosewood surface has a glass top, and is placed on two rectangular supports. The whole table is supported on a lipped tray base. Furniture designers who favored the Modernist thread of the Art Deco style created all kinds of tables with strong geometric outlines, including interlocking circles, triangles, and cubes. *c. 1930. H:23½ in (59.5 cm). CAL* **6**

OCCASIONAL TABLE

This 12-sided table is decorated all over with mirrors to create an unusual, completely mirrored surface. The table top is supported by slightly tapering square legs. *c. 1930. W:20 in (51 cm). L&T* **1**

WALNUT TABLE

This geometric occasional table is made from walnut and has an octagonal, crossbanded top that is raised on a rectangular column. The column is centered on a square, spreading base. *H:22 in (55 cm). L&T* **1**

The stepped top of the table is a distinctive Art Deco feature.

The octagonal shape of the table top is innovative and striking.

The substantial apron adds strength to the table design.

The central support links the two table legs.

The overhanging top is reminiscent of early trestle and refectory tables.

The two box-shaped table legs replace the usual four supports at either end.

BRITISH DINING TABLE

This solid, architectural table is from a table and six chair set designed by H&L Epstein. Made from walnut, the table top is octagonal in shape, with black-lacquered banding running around the edge. Two rectangular block legs with block feet, connected to each other by a rectangular panel, support the table top. The crossbanding around the edge and the thick inlaid band of crossbanding across the table top add a subtle but decorative touch to the distinctive markings of the walnut veneer. *c. 1935. W:72 in (183 cm). JAZ* **6**

FRENCH MAHOGANY TABLE

This Lucie Renaudot rosewood, mahogany, and ivory-inlaid side table, has a circular top with ivory dentil edging. The stepped, square-section legs are united by a square undertier. *c. 1925. H:27 in (68.5 cm); D:23½ in (59.5 cm). CAL* **6**

MIRROR TABLE

This table is made from walnut and has a circular top, attached to tapering square legs that support the whole table. The table top is covered with a mirrored surface. *c. 1930. D:23 in (58.5 cm). TDG* **1**

BELGIAN LYRE CONSOLE TABLE

Designed by De Coene Frères, this Belgian lyre console table stands on a lipped tray base. The base supports a highly polished lyre-shaped frame, a popular feature of the Art Deco style. The frame in turn supports a narrow, rectangular table top. *c. 1930.* H:29½ in (75 cm). LM **3**

BELGIAN COFFEE TABLE

This rosewood coffee table, designed by De Coene Frères, is veneered in walnut and has two legs made of chrome tubing. Two crossed, lipped tray bases support the U-shaped structure. The chrome tubular legs reinforce the rectangular table top, which has rounded corners. *c. 1930.* H:24½ in (62 cm). LM **3**

FRENCH U-SHAPED TABLE

This graceful French side table has a rectangular top with a stepped edge. It is supported by a tulip-shaped structure, rather than conventional legs, with decorative chrome detailing at the base. The table has been restored and piano-varnished, hence its glossy black appearance. *c. 1930.* SWT

BRITISH DRUM TABLE

This sturdy oak drum occasional table is designed in the style of Betty Joel. A broad central oak cylinder supports three circular table tops, each arranged one above the other. *c. 1935.* D:24 in (61 cm). TGD **2**

BRITISH QUARTETTO TABLE

The quartetto table is designed by H&L Epstein and is made from burr maple. The set of four small tables of graduated size nest together and are supported on square legs. *c. 1930.* H:22 in (56 cm); D:30 in (76 cm). JAZ **3**

CHROMIUM TABLE

This chromium-plated occasional table has a circular top inset with a black glass panel above three curved supports. The supports are attached to a circular ebonized base on flattened bun feet. H:20 in (51 cm). L&T **1**

MAPLE CONSOLE TABLE

This console table has a maple top with a molded mahogany edge, and a single drawer at the front. The two U-shaped supports are united by a stretcher beneath and have arched feet. W:37 in (94 cm). FRE **1**

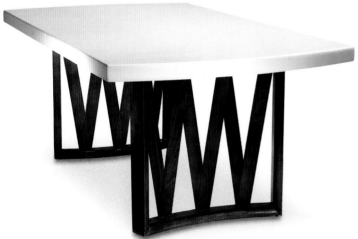

AMERICAN DINING TABLE

This extension dining table, designed by Paul Frankl, has a white rectangular gesso top with gently bowed edges and two 12-in- (30.5-cm-) long leaves that rest on two curved mahogany supports. Each of the mahogany supports incorporates three V-shaped slats. The robust, architectural nature of this piece is typical of Paul Frankl's furniture designs, which reflected trends in contemporary architecture. The chevron pattern of the supports is reminiscent of key design elements on the Chrysler Building *(see p.387).* H:29 in (73.65 cm). FRE **3**

DINING TABLE

This elegant dining table is part of a table-and-eight-chair set. The table has a simple rectangular top, with pull-out extensions. A pedestal base, with two C-shaped supports, carries the solid table top. The eight chairs that accompany the dining table have solid backs with upholstered seats. The graceful interaction of interlocking arcs and rectangles adds a powerful three-dimensional and distinctively avant-garde element to the shape of the conventional rectangular dining table. W:61½ in (156 cm). FRE **3**

CABINETS

THE CLEAN LINES and geometric shapes of Art Deco cabinets gave free reign to the prevailing taste for luxurious finishes. The cocktail cabinet made its first appearance in the jazz age. Featuring mirrored interiors and door panels, it contained enough shelving to house all the accoutrements for making cocktails.

REFINED OPULENCE
French furniture designers, such as Paul Follot and Emile-Jacques Ruhlmann, created cabinets that were veneered in a wide range of exotic lumbers, including amboyna, bird's-eye maple, mahogany, zebrawood, rosewood, and sycamore, which were admired for their distinctive markings and lustrous sheen. Understated and refined decorative features adorned their cabinets. Crossbanding was used as edging along the top of a cabinet and delicate marquetry flower

bouquets appeared sparingly. Drawer pulls were defined by their contrasting shapes or finishing material. Decorative motifs were created from rare and expensive materials, such as ivory, shagreen, tortoiseshell, and wrought iron. Oriental lacquerwork in strong colors was also used by some cabinet-makers, especially Jean Dunand and Eileen Gray.

CLEAN LINES
Furniture-makers working in the Modernist strand of Art Deco, such as Sidney Barnsley in Great Britain and Paul Frankl and Eliel Saarinen in the United States, created streamlined cabinets in geometric shapes. These designers still used lacquerwork and exotic veneers, but they combined them with modern materials, such as Bakelite, mirror glass, and tubular steel. Ivory, metal, and chrome were used to provide decorative details.

BRITISH DISPLAY CABINET

This stylized display cabinet is veneered in walnut. The upper section of the cabinet is circular in form, with two glazed doors enclosing two glazed shelves. The cabinet is raised on a paneled base and has block feet. *H:43 in (109 cm); W:73½ in (187 cm). L&T* **1**

BRITISH DISPLAY CABINET

This unusual display cabinet, possibly veneered in walnut, is carried on two deeply grooved triangular supports that resemble a fish's fins. The cabinet itself is circular and has two minimally decorated glass doors, which enclose four wooden shelves. *BW* **1**

BELGIAN SIDEBOARD

This Belgian sideboard is crafted from mahogany, and veneered with rosewood. The shape recalls the forms of late 18th-century commodes. The minimalist design of this rectangular sideboard consists of two simple

doors with understated bronze handles, and the whole piece is raised on short, circular bronze feet. The clean-lined, geometric shape of the piece is complemented by the distinctive vertical figure of the lustrous rosewood veneer used all over the case. *c. 1935. W:94 in (235 cm). SWT* **5**

The stepped top of the cabinet is a distinctive Art Deco feature.

The cabinet is veneered with coromandel, an unusual variety of ebony.

The rectangular shape of the cabinet recalls 18th-century French commodes.

The handles are painted red to look like lacquerwork.

The bracket feet are similar to those on late 17th- and 18th-century case furniture.

BRITISH SIDE CABINET

This rectangular side cabinet, flanked with a further two slim cabinets, is veneered with coromandel, a variety of ebony sometimes known as zebrawood because of its distinctive striped markings. Below the stepped top, there

is a central drawer and the main cabinet, which has two doors. Two cabinets make up the outer sides. The bracket feet and the door and drawer handles are painted red, the only obvious form of decoration. The cabinet was designed by Whytock and Reid of Edinburgh. *H:30½ in (77 cm); W:55 in (140 cm). L&T* **1**

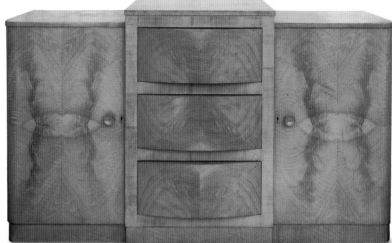

BRITISH SIDEBOARD

This sideboard, designed by M. P. Davis of London, is crafted in bleached mahogany. The three central drawers are flanked by two side cabinets, of a slightly lower height, which have small, circular mahogany handles. The central

pull-out drawers are slightly protruding, arching outward. The strongly marked, distinctive figure of the mahogany veneer gives the geometric sideboard a rich opulence that needs no additional ornament—a characteristic common of much Art Deco furniture. *c. 1929. H:38 in (96 cm); W:64 in (162 cm). JAZ* **3**

FRENCH SIDE CABINET

This side cabinet is made from mahogany, with amboyna veneering and a stylized ebony inlay. The three drawers have circular metal handles and the whole cabinet is raised on tall, cylindrical, tapering legs. *c. 1935. H:31 in (78 cm); W:18½ in (46.5 cm); D:13 in (32 cm). SWT*

FRENCH COMMODE

Designed by Süe et Mare, this rectilinear, mahogany-veneered commode is a good example of their understated yet luxurious style. The two cabinet doors have subtly stylized circular handles, and the legs and the lower edge of the cabinet are lightly embellished with carving. The cabinet is raised on four slightly tapering, molded legs. *c. 1919. H:35 in (89 cm); W:45 in (114.3 cm). LM* **5**

BURLED MAPLE CONSOLE

This rectangular burr maple console has four centrally placed drawers with nickeled brass handles. These are flanked by a pair of cupboard doors with circular wooden handles. The whole console is supported on two rectangular side panels. Beneath the cupboards and drawers there is a lower shelf that connects the two side panel supports. *W:47 in (119.4 cm). FRE* **1**

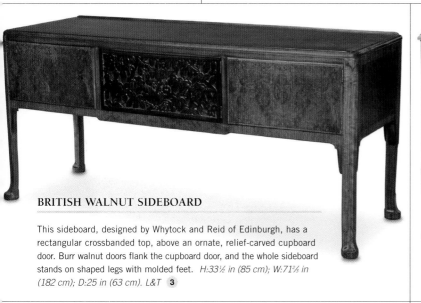

BRITISH WALNUT SIDEBOARD

This sideboard, designed by Whytock and Reid of Edinburgh, has a rectangular crossbanded top, above an ornate, relief-carved cupboard door. Burr walnut doors flank the cupboard door, and the whole sideboard stands on shaped legs with molded feet. *H:33½ in (85 cm); W:71⅔ in (182 cm); D:25 in (63 cm). L&T* **3**

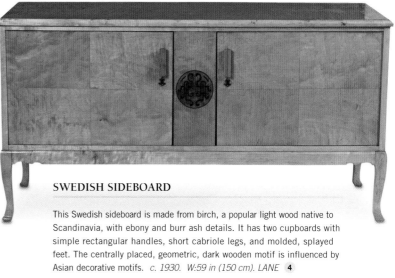

SWEDISH SIDEBOARD

This Swedish sideboard is made from birch, a popular light wood native to Scandinavia, with ebony and burr ash details. It has two cupboards with simple rectangular handles, short cabriole legs, and molded, splayed feet. The centrally placed, geometric, dark wooden motif is influenced by Asian decorative motifs. *c. 1930. W:59 in (150 cm). LANE* **4**

FRENCH SIDEBOARD

This mahogany sideboard is a good example of French Art Deco, with its simple elegant forms, rectilinear design, and high standard of craftsmanship. The cabinet has four cabinet doors, decorated with narrow horizontal bands of chrome and a central circular feature. The whole sideboard is raised on a pedestal block base. It is typical of Art Deco styling in combining fine woodwork with chrome details. *c. 1925. W:65 in (165 cm). JAZ* **3**

BRITISH SIDEBOARD

Designed by H&L Epstein, this fine rectangular maple sideboard has rounded corners and a stepped top. The central section is made up of two drawers with circular, molded handles above a cupboard with a decorative vertical, slatted-wood design. Two more cupboards with molded oblong wooden handles flank the central section of the sideboard. The whole sideboard is set on a block base. *c. 1935. H:41 in (104 cm); W:60 in (152 cm). JAZ* **3**

MODERNISM

1925-1945

A NEW AGE

WORLD WAR I AND THE RISE OF INDUSTRY AND TECHNOLOGY BROUGHT ABOUT RADICAL CHANGES IN SOCIETY THAT WERE REFLECTED IN MODERN DESIGN.

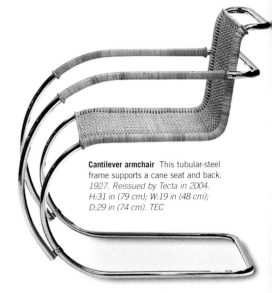

Cantilever armchair This tubular-steel frame supports a cane seat and back. *1927. Reissued by Tecta in 2004. H:31 in (79 cm); W:19 in (48 cm); D:29 in (74 cm).* TEC

THE EFFECTS OF World War I on the nations of Europe and North America were considerable. People were psychologically scarred by the atrocities of the war, and the economies of many countries were in ruins. Homelessness, too, proved a major problem, as bombs had destroyed large areas of housing. Indeed, such was the devastation that many had witnessed, it was inevitable that some would question the cultural values that had caused the war in the first place. It is no coincidence, then, that the period after World War I saw some of the most radical cultural shifts the world had seen in centuries.

The interwar years must be considered a new dawn, too, in terms of industry. During the years leading up to World War II, industry became an integrated part of civilized societies, although many still resented its existence. Allied to the march of industry were the technological breakthroughs that occurred during this era: the car, the telephone, electricity, and air travel all became relatively common aspects of daily life.

Such rapid and momentous advancements inevitably had their side effects. For many, this progress was seen as a license to dream of a new, utopian future, while for others, it was a worrying sign of moral degeneration.

Mass production, in particular, was changing society and was a direct cause of the growth of the leisure industry. Mass production meant cheaper products, and long days of labor became increasingly unnecessary, giving many an unprecedented amount of free time. The prospect of national and international travel also became more realistic, and a spirit of adventure took hold of many people's imaginations.

This optimism was short-lived, however, as the interwar years were also a time of economic turmoil. In 1926, Great Britain was rocked by the General Strike, while the Wall Street crash of 1929 ushered in the Great Depression in the United States. By the mid-1930s, poverty was a grave concern. A sense of disillusionment descended across Europe and North America, as it became clear that widespread industrialization was not the panacea some had painted it as. This increasingly sour climate proved the ideal breeding ground for extremist political parties. Promising to bring drastic change to the everyday lives of citizens, these parties took advantage of the economic instability and uncertainty that many felt in the face of cultural changes brought on by the rise of industry and technology. The National Socialist Party of Germany would, of course, prove the most powerful of these factions, as it was Adolf Hitler's rise to power in the 1930s that eventually sparked World War II.

Villa Savoye, Poissy-sur-Seine This is an early and classic example of Modern architecture. Typical of what became known as the International Style are the strip windows, flat roof and deck, and rectilinear lines of the design. Designed by Le Corbusier and Pierre Jeanneret. *1929–30.*

TIMELINE 1925–1945

1925 Le Corbusier presents *Pavilion de l'Esprit Nouveau* at the *Exposition des Arts Décoratifs et Industriels Modernes* in Paris. Chromium becomes commercially available. Marcel Breuer designs his first tubular-steel chair. Josef Stalin comes to power in USSR.

1925–26 The Bauhaus moves from Weimar to Dessau.

1926 Mart Stam designs a tubular-steel cantilever chair. Italy becomes

Josef Stalin

a one-party state under Benito Mussolini. General Strike in Britain.

1927 The first transatlantic telephone call is made. An electronic television system is developed in the US. Charles Lindbergh makes the first solo flight across the Atlantic.

1928 Penicillin is discovered by Alexander Flemming.

1929 The Wall Street Crash cripples the American economy. Ludwig Mies van der Rohe completes the German pavilion at the *Exposición Internacional* in Barcelona. *Die Wohnung* exhibition in Stuttgart is organized by *Deutscher Werkbund*. The Museum of Modern Art (MoMA) opens in New York City.

Paimio chair by Alvar Aalto

1929–33 Alvar Aalto creates a range of fixtures for the Paimio Sanatorium.

1930 The Swedish Functionalism exhibition is held in Stockholm and sparks debate.

1931 *Wohnbedarf* store opens in Zurich; the catalog gives Modern designs international exposure. Empire State

Interior of the Schroeder House, Utrecht, the Netherlands Built of steel, wood, and concrete, this early Modernist house is a composition of abstract planes. The movable walls make it possible to transform the upper floor from a single space into a series of rooms. Furnishings and design by Gerrit Rietveld. *1924–25.*

Gerrit Rietveld's Beugelstoel The chair has a lacquered plywood seat and back, which curves over the aluminum frame to provide stability. *1927. H:23½ in (59.75 cm); W:15¾ in (40 cm); D:23 in (58.5 cm).*

Building is opened. Collapse of banks in Central Europe results in major recession.

1931–32 The Bauhaus moves to Berlin after the National Socialists force the school out of Dessau.

1933 National Socialist Party closes the Bauhaus. First annual Triennial exhibition held in Milan. **Empire State Building**

Hitler becomes German chancellor.

1934 Wells Coates designs London's Isokon Flats, which become a magnet for Modernists in Britain. "Machine Art" exhibition at MoMA in New York.

1936 SLR camera is developed in Germany. Spanish Civil War begins (ends 1939).

1939 Gino Sarfatti founds the Arteluce

lighting company in Milan, helping to establish Italy's reputation as the leader in lighting design.

1939 World War II begins. The first successful jet airplane is flown in Germany.

1939–40 Organic Design in Home Furnishings competition held at MoMA; designs include a plywood chair by **SLR camera, 1936**

Charles Eames and Eero Saarinen. World's Fair held in New York.

1940 Roosevelt elected for a third term in office.

1942 First nuclear reactor built in USA.

1945 United Nations is established. World War II ends.

Franklin D. Roosevelt

MODERN DESIGN

THE STRIPPED-BACK, EXPOSED STYLE of much Modern furniture had already been experimented with by designers years before it became common across Europe in the 1930s. Adolf Loos, an Austrian architect, wrote his influential text "Ornament and Crime" as early as 1908, and the designers of the *Wiener Werkstätte* (*see p.367*) produced a few stark, minimal designs long before the outbreak of World War I. These early efforts, however, seem tentative compared with what followed. In the aftermath of the war, many designers gave up decoration for good, developing a severe, anonymous style that valued structure over surface.

Although the Modernists' reductionist style was certainly intended as an aesthetic affront to what had gone before, it also had more practical aims. It was a considered attempt by designers to develop a new language for industrially manufactured furniture. Previously, manufacturers had preferred to reproduce old styles, making their mass-produced furniture rather duplicitously appear hand-crafted. A new generation realized the absurdity of this and proposed a style that fearlessly articulated the processes by which furniture was made. Thus, they hoped, mass-produced furniture would finally be afforded the dignity it deserved, especially considering the urgent need for inexpensive furniture at the time.

It was in Germany, which was particularly hard hit by World War I, that the most significant advances in furniture design were made in the interwar years. In an earnest attempt to produce viable prototypes for industrial production, students and staff at the celebrated Bauhaus school (*see p.426*) instigated a new approach to design that was mimicked, with varying degrees of success, the world over.

Black-and-white desk The desk's steel case has alternating black-and-white drawer fronts and a glass top. A chrome leg supports the black-stained ash desktop. *By Marcel Breuer in 1932. Reissued by Tecta in 2004. H:27 in (69 cm); W:63 in (160 cm); D:24 in (61 cm). TEC*

Child's NE60 stool This simple stacking stool is made from lacquered birch. The circular, linoleum-covered seat rests on rectangle-section legs that curve in under the seat. Designed by Alvar Aalto for Artek in 1932–33; this example is a reissue. *H:13⅜ in (34 cm).*

MATERIALS OF MASS PRODUCTION

It was not only the forms of furniture that came under scrutiny from Modernists at the Bauhaus and beyond, but the materials as well. Tubular steel, plywood, and plate glass—all little explored in terms of furniture design before 1925—were introduced in the interwar years as the materials to take furniture forward. Indeed, metal, which had none of the mystical, emotional qualities of wood, soon came to symbolize the ruthless, reforming character of Modernism. First used by a few pioneers in the late 1920s, these materials would eventually become a common, if controversial, sight across the developed world by the end of the 1930s.

As well as throwing up new materials and processes with which designers could work, the relentless march of industrialization also provoked a shift in lifestyles. Leisure became an increasingly prominent feature of family life and, as such, the formality and structure of day-to-day existence began to loosen. Designers responded by concentrating increasingly on lounge chairs aimed not only at the affluent elite, but also at the working classes. Chaises longues became increasingly popular and designers took inspiration from the folding furniture found on ocean liners. The lightness of furniture also became a key feature, as the concept of a fluid space filled with multipurpose furniture made its presence felt.

When considering the breadth of the innovations that occurred in furniture design in this era, it is worth remembering that this was a period of unprecedented communication between countries. The telephone and advances in the travel industry made it easier than ever before for designers to keep abreast of developments elsewhere. The use of tubular steel spread rapidly after the initial experiments made by Marcel Breuer at the Bauhaus in 1925, and, by 1934, some American academics were referring to an International Style that encompassed developments in architecture and the decorative arts. Of course, each nation developed its own idiosyncrasies—the Scandinavians, for instance, steered clear of tubular steel, preferring the warmth of wood in their harsh climates—but overall it was an era of standardization, a time when feats of audacious craftsmanship became firmly unfashionable.

Designers of the interwar years attempted to let the processes of manufacturing guide the shapes of their furniture. The simple, angular shapes of much tubular-steel furniture of this period expresses the way it was made, while the more organic lines of plywood furniture reflect the gentle bending done to produce it. The furniture of Modernist designers, while certainly ideologically motivated in its rejection of all that their predecessors held dear, was also largely inspired by nothing more radical than mere common sense.

THE CHAISE LONGUE

In the 1920s and 30s almost all the major Modernist designers created a chaise longue. Mies van der Rohe, Walter Gropius, and Alvar Aalto all produced their take on the chaise longue ("long chair"). Le Corbusier designed his B306 chaise longue with Pierre Jeanneret and Charlotte Perriand, while Marcel Breuer produced versions in tubular steel, plywood, and aluminum. He even made one with wheels, to be dragged outside when it was sunny.

Originating in 16th-century France, the chaise longue differs from the day bed, or *récamier*, in that users lie on their backs, not sideways. Modernists were smitten with the idea of healthy living, and chaises longues were in vogue due to their association with sanatoriums and bracing ocean-liner voyages.

A couch on wheels This chaise longue by Marcel Breuer has a chrome frame and cane seat. *c. 1928–30. This is a 2004 Tecta reissue. H:24¾ in (63 cm); L:73¼ in (186 cm); D:24 in (61 cm). TEC*

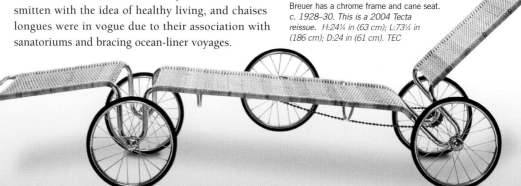

EASY CHAIR

The forms, materials, and mechanisms of industry provided significant inspiration for all designers of the Modern era, but never is this more apparent than in the work of Jean Prouvé. The *fauteuil de grand repos*, or easy chair, created by the French designer in 1928 almost appears to be ripped from the interior of a car, plane, or train. The long, low shape of the chair, too, reminds one even more of a form of vehicle. Never one to spare a thought for those with more delicate aesthetic sensibilities, Prouvé produced furniture as if he were building a functional machine. The crudely sprung adjustable seat is proof that Prouvé thought primarily on a practical level, using whatever means necessary to make the chair comfortable. First shown to the public in 1930 at an exhibition of work by the members of the UAM (*Union des Artistes Modernes*), the *fauteuil de grand repos* has recently been refined by the Tecta furniture company in Germany and put back on the market.

The seat is made of canvas, a material that had previously been used exclusively for portable military or nautical furniture.

The chair's structure is exposed, allowing the sitter to see how the chair was made.

The long, sloping back of the chair gives it an unexpected elegance.

Padded armrests offer additional comfort.

Steel armrests provide leverage when sitters push the seat forward or pull it back.

Obscured ball bearings allow the seat to move back to a reclining position.

Springs beneath the seat provide comfort and also ease the seat's movement.

Side sections are of varnished steel, a material borrowed from the automobile industry.

A bar at the rear of the chair provides the structure with added strength.

Jean Prouvé's *fauteuil de grand repos* The chair is made from varnished steel. It is upholstered with horse hair and covered in canvas. The seat is adjustable. *1930. H:37 in (94 cm); W:26¾ in (68 cm); D:42½ in (108 cm).*

ELEMENTS OF STYLE

There is the sense that the Modern era of furniture was a period of cleansing the palate. Furniture forms became remarkably stark after World War I, with stylistic flourishes occurring only very rarely and even then with great understatement. The skills of the hand-craftsman became increasingly marginalized as designers were awed by the capabilities of the machine. The arrival of new technologies and new materials in the field of furniture design also gave rise to new forms and techniques that soon spread across Europe and North America. Particular emphasis, too, was placed on lowering the cost of furniture production, since World War I had left many countries economically shattered. Furniture acquired a lean quality in the Modern era that had never been seen before, and has never been seen since.

Starburst-patterned table

Birch
While many Modernist designers adopted the new-found materials of the industrial age—glass and metal—some, particularly in Scandinavia, turned to birch, which suited the fashion for light-colored furniture. Birch is lightweight and easily stripped into layers, so it is ideal for plywood.

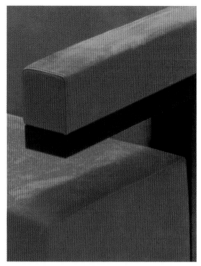

Wooden frame and upholstered armrest

Plain surfaces
In their constant effort to align their work with industrial methods of production, Modernist designers almost entirely abandoned the notion of surface decoration on their furniture. The decreasing use of solid wood, too, dictated the decline in decorative carving and ushered in an era of streamlined simplicity.

Tubular-steel chair

Tubular steel
The strength, affordability, and pliability of tubular steel made it the ideal material for Modern furniture. The fact that it produced such lightweight furniture was also of crucial importance at a time when many people had lost their homes in World War I and were living in temporary housing.

Chrome-plated legs and armrests

Chrome-plating
While surface decoration may have been outlawed by Modern designers, many of them were drawn to the shiny effect of chrome-plating on the dull surface of tubular steel. Americans, in particular, were enamored of the technique of chrome-plating and used it to dazzling effect in their furniture designs.

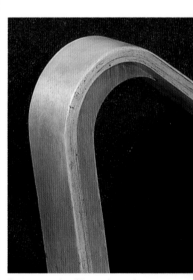

Armrest made of bent plywood

Bent plywood
Plywood is made by bonding thin strips of wood together. When it is softened by steam, plywood can be bent easily. It is inherently more flexible than solid wood and was adopted by Modernist designers who recognized that it could eradicate the need for numerous joints on a piece of furniture.

Detail of buttoned-leather seat back

Leather and hide

Leather was much appreciated in the Modern era for its versatility and ready availability; as such, it became a very popular material and was widely used by furniture designers. Hides were often employed to add an exotic element of to furniture designs, particularly when designers were trying to appeal to more affluent clients.

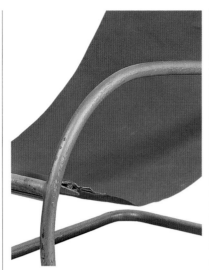

Detail of tubular-steel chair frame

Curvaceous lines

The process of producing both tubular-steel and plywood furniture often involves a great deal of bending, especially if one is attempting to avoid welding or joining. Allowing this action to inform the shapes of their furniture, many Modernist designers created works that incorporated flowing, curvaceous lines.

Heavy plate-glass table top

Glass

Glass appealed to furniture designers of the Modern era because of its associations with both architecture and industry. Its transparency, and thus its integrity, was appreciated, too—as was the fact that glass could provide the sort of clean, concise lines that many furniture designers wanted to create.

Structure of seat back in plain view

Exposed structures

With surface decoration considered superfluous, the structure of Modern furniture became all-important, for stylistic as well as functional reasons. Designers equated exposed structure with integrity and rationality and saw the stripped-back style as a way to minimize the use of costly materials and create an egalitarian style of design.

Cantilevered chair base

Cantilevering

Cantilevered chairs, which did away with the accepted notion that a chair needs to have four legs, were the most obvious expression of the reductionist tendencies of the Modernist style. The sinuous shape of a cantilevered chair also achieved the purity of form that many Modernist designers were constantly striving to create.

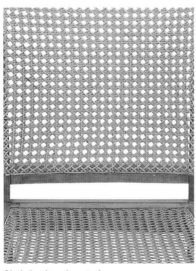

Chair back and seat of woven cane

Cane

Of all the pre-Modern furniture admired by Modernist designers, none received more praise than the mid-19th-century work of Michael Thonet (*see p.284*). Many adopted Thonet's use of cane, recognizing it as lightweight and inexpensive. The decorative effect of cane is expressive of its construction, which also appealed to Modernists.

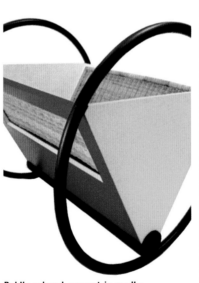

Boldly colored, geometric cradle

Geometric forms

In an era when many designers were seeking to align themselves with industry and steer clear of whimsical associations with nature, it seemed an obvious move to employ geometric forms. The use of geometric shapes, often rendered in primary colors, was also a response to the new forms of abstract art of the time.

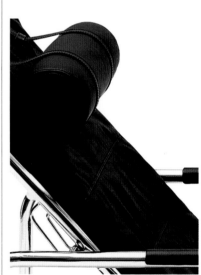

Detail of black leather headrest and seat

Black

In an effort to distance themselves from the decorative designs of their predecessors, many Modernist designers abolished color from their furniture. The use of black deflected attention away from the furniture's surface to its structure. Black leather was a favorite, and plywood was often painted to hide the wood's grain.

GERRIT RIETVELD

KNOWN FOR MODERN CLASSICS SUCH AS HIS FAMOUS RED-AND-BLUE CHAIR AND ZIGZAG CHAIR, DUTCHMAN GERRIT RIETVELD WAS ONE OF THE MOST INFLUENTIAL DESIGNERS OF THE 20TH CENTURY.

GERRIT RIETVELD WAS BORN the son of a cabinet-maker in Utrecht, Netherlands, in 1888. His early years, working in his father's workshop and as a goldsmith's draftsman, gave no indication that he would later become one of the most influential and uncompromising furniture designers of the 20th century. Initially, he planned to become a painter, but pressing financial needs and the birth of the first of his six children in 1913 pushed him to take up the family profession.

Even as the first works emerged from Rietveld's furniture studio, he appeared to be producing pieces reluctantly. The chairs seemed defiantly inelegant when compared to those of his contemporaries, and even Rietveld himself referred to his furniture works as "studies." If we look at Rietveld's celebrated Red-and-Blue chair, of which an early, unpainted version was made in 1918, it certainly has the appearance of being unfinished—as if the chair is waiting to have the overlapping bars of its structure cut down to size.

MONDRIAN ET AL.

It was the startling nature of Rietveld's designs that brought him to the attention of a radical group of artists, architects, and thinkers who went by the name of De Stijl. Led by Piet Mondrian and Theo van Doesburg, De Stijl expressed "a new spirit," one that overlooked the charms of nature in favor of a rigorous, abstract approach to design.

Rietveld, in turning his back on refined hand-craftsmanship, clearly intrigued Mondrian and van Doesburg. On seeing Rietveld's work, van Doesburg proclaimed that it held a particular form of beauty, an "unspeaking elegance like that of a machine." Rietveld's work, unlike that of his contemporaries, articulated only its construction and made no attempt to seduce by aping natural forms.

So closely did this approach mirror the aims of De Stijl that it is often assumed that Rietveld constructed the Red-and-Blue chair, and other similar works, while a member of De Stijl. Indeed, this chair is often described as "a 3-D Mondrian painting": the strong line definitions and geometric shapes of the seat and back suggest that they are merely fragments of a larger structure that continues beyond the actuality of the

GERRIT RIETVELD
The designer and architect is preoccupied with a model of his design for the Schroeder House. Built in 1924, the house conforms to De Stijl ideals. The walls on the upper floor of the house can all be removed to make a single space, rather than a number of rooms. Rietveld designed not only the house, but also the furnishings that went in it.

CRATE DESK
This desk is part of a range of furniture that also included an easy chair, a table, a bookcase, and a stool. It is made of identical strips of pine, which have been fixed together and painted white. By Metz & Co. 1934. H:28 in (71 cm); W:39½ in (100 cm); D:23½ in (59.5 cm).

ZIGZAG CHAIR
This cantilevered chair is made from four rectangles of oak. The seat and back are dovetailed and the zigzags are reinforced with wedges. 1934. H:27¾ in (70.5 cm); W:14¾ in (37 cm); D:14¾ in (37 cm). BonE

END TABLE
This end table consists of four sheets of lacquered wood. The asymmetry of the table's design, with the square tabletop above two end-on rectangular sheets of wood and the circular base, gives the piece a precarious look, and yet the pieces are well balanced and the table perfectly stable. Designed for the Schroeder House. 1924. H:22¾ in (58 cm); W:19¾ in (50 cm); D:19¾ in (50 cm).

MONDRIAN

AS A LEADING MEMBER OF THE DE STIJL GROUP, PIET MONDRIAN LAID DOWN MANY OF THE FOUNDATIONS FOR THE GROUP, WHICH PROMOTED A RIGOROUS, ABSTRACT APPROACH TO ART AND DESIGN.

The De Stijl group, of which Gerrit Rietveld was a member, is probably best recognized today by the geometric paintings of Piet Mondrian. Where Rietveld, who was working in his father's furniture workshop at the age of 12, was essentially a practical man, Mondrian was more cerebral. In 1917, inspired by the Cubist work he had seen in France, Mondrian wrote "Abstraction as Representation of the Pure Spirit." It was a dense, polemical text that laid the foundations for the De Stijl movement, which was started in the same year.

Although Mondrian was always clear that the "new spirit" of De Stijl should be "manifested in all the arts without exception," he was, understandably, concerned primarily with painting. Mondrian stressed repeatedly in his writings, and expressed in his pictures, the belief that a painting should "aim to express equilibrium and harmony *as purely as possible*" (his italics). By "purely," he meant without recourse to the representation of nature. A painting of a tree, he argued, was primarily enjoyed as a harmonious composition of color and line, so why paint a tree when you can paint pure color and line instead?

Mondrian called this approach "a new plasticity," and with it he attempted to express a standardized, universal beauty of the sort rarely found in what he described as the capricious world of nature. Mondrian's writings—and paintings, too—clearly emboldened his fellow De Stijl members and clarified for many of them the way in which they should go forward. Rietveld, in particular, gained direction and momentum from the ideas of Piet Mondrian, and without his input would have certainly left a far fainter impression on the history of Modern design.

Large Composition with Red, Blue and Yellow, 1928. Oil on canvas. Piet Mondrian. Stefan T. Edlis Collection. © 2005 Mondrian/Holzman Trust c/o HCR International, Warrenton, Virginia, USA. *1928. H:48½ in (123 cm); W:31½ in (80 cm).*

Rietveld's Red-and-Blue chair This is the three-dimensional equivalent of Mondrian's art. Designed in 1918 mostly for visual effect, it is made from dyed pine wood and plywood. This example is by Cassina. *c. 1980. H:40 in (101.5 cm); W:20½ in (53 cm); D:27 in (68.5 cm). BonBay*

chair. This similarity with Mondrian's work, however, was entirely serendipitous. Although it was his contact with De Stijl designers that prompted Rietveld, in 1923, to paint the Red-and-Blue chair in red, black, yellow, and blue, he came up with the chair's form independently.

In 1924, by this time a committed member of De Stijl, Rietveld completed his first major architectural work, the Schroeder house in Utrecht. It was a building based on strict De Stijl principles. Curves of any sort were absent, and the house became something of a celebration of "the tensed line," which, according to Mondrian, "most purely expresses immutability, strength, and vastness."

Almost all the furniture and fixtures for the house were designed by Rietveld, and it is interesting that among them were some tubular-steel chairs. The dining chairs owe a clear debt to the tubular-steel designs of Marcel Breuer (*see p.434*). Breuer is known to have greatly admired the work of Rietveld, to the extent that he adopted the Dutchman's geometric approach to chair design when tackling the Wassily chair, his first work in tubular steel. It is intriguing, then, to see Rietveld follow the younger man with metal designs of his own.

A RETURN TO WOOD

Rietveld's experiments with bent tubular steel were short-lived, and he soon returned to his favored medium of wood. In 1932, inspired once again by Breuer, and by the work of Dutch architect Mart Stam, Rietveld designed a wooden cantilever chair. He approached the problem of the cantilever chair in a typically no-nonsense style, resulting in the stark forms of the Zigzag chair. Despite having such a severe, angular silhouette, the Zigzag chair still manages to charm, thanks to its sheer simplicity.

In the 1930s, the Dutch economy was in a seemingly endless slump and, in response, Rietveld produced a series of low-cost furniture designs. Never one to err on the side of luxury, Rietveld's 1934 range of Crate furniture appears amazingly minimalist even by today's standards. Some of his most avid supporters took their time to appreciate these rudimentary designs. "A crate represents a method of carpentry aimed straight at its goal," Rietveld argued, "and the plain materials of which it is composed often make it stronger than its precious contents." Consisting of a desk, a stool, a bookcase, a low table, and an easy chair, Rietveld's Crate collection was, perhaps, his most explicit snub to the craftsman's skills he learned as a boy.

During the 1940s and 50s, Rietveld continued to work in the raw, reductionist idiom that he had established. By this time, however, design had somewhat overtaken him and, while he created exceptional pieces (many still in production today), he rarely made the impact that he had in his earlier career. In 1954, Rietveld designed the Dutch pavilion at the *Venice Architecture Biennale,* and in 1963 he started work on the Van Gogh Museum in Amsterdam. A year later, though, he was to die in his hometown of Utrecht, leaving behind him a remarkable legacy.

BAUHAUS

DURING ITS SHORT LIFESPAN, THE BAUHAUS BECAME THE MOST IMPORTANT DESIGN SCHOOL OF THE MODERN ERA, AND ITS IDEAS CONTINUE TO RESONATE.

NO NAME LOOMS LARGER in the history of Modern furniture than that of the Bauhaus. Founded by Walter Gropius in Weimar, Germany, in 1919 and dismantled by the Nazis in 1933, this avante-garde school for art, architecture, and design was the most important institution of the era. Now known for its severe, industrial aesthetic, the Bauhaus was, in its early days, concerned with crafts. It was Gropius's radical idea that the school contain many disciplines, all of equal status. "Let us create a new guild of craftsmen without the class distinctions," he wrote. The "building of the future will combine architecture, sculpture, and painting in a single form...and will one day rise toward the heavens from the hands of a million workers as the crystalline symbol of a new and coming faith."

This spiritual rallying cry was reflected in the teachings of the most important tutor of the school's early years, Johannes Itten. Itten initiated a preliminary course for newcomers that became the precursor to the

WASSILY CHAIR
This chair has a bent, tubular-steel frame, leather slings for the back, seat, and armrests, and a sled base. Designed by Marcel Breuer, this chair was revolutionary in its use of industrial materials. 1925. H:28⅓ in (72 cm); W:31⅛ in (79 cm); D:27½ in (70 cm). SDR

THE BAUHAUS BUILDING

WALTER GROPIUS'S VISION FOR THE BAUHAUS—TO ALIGN ART WITH INDUSTRY—IS REFLECTED IN THE BAUHAUS BUILDING IN DESSAU.

Walter Gropius

In 1925, having been forced out of their original location in Weimar for political reasons, the Bauhaus moved to Dessau. This change mirrored a shift in the school's outlook, with director Walter Gropius now wanting to cast the Bauhaus as a research center dedicated to producing prototypes for industry.

To reinforce this point, he and Adolf Meyer designed a building for the Bauhaus that borrowed heavily from the architecture of factories. Gone was any evidence of the hand-craftsmanship or decorative touches that had adorned the first building designed under the umbrella of the Bauhaus (the wooden Haus Sommerfeld, built in 1921). Instead, the new building used vast expanses of industrial-looking glass and steel. The word "Bauhaus" appeared on the facade in the new Universal typeface, designed by Herbert Bayer, a Bauhaus tutor.

Before the Dessau building was erected, the Bauhaus had achieved a certain degree of recognition throughout the world, although it was nothing compared to the attention it received after the building went up. Walter Gropius's and Adolf Meyer's design proved to people that the Bauhaus meant business, and was not just another idealistic art school. Sadly, the Nazis closed the school in 1933, and the building fell into disrepair, only being renovated in recent years.

Form study This is a Bauhaus model for a building proposal during the Weimar years. *c. 1920. MOD*

Gropius's and Meyer's industrial-looking masterpiece for the Bauhaus School
The dominant feature of this building was its steel-and-glass facade. It was testament to the Bauhaus belief that form should follow function.

ADJUSTABLE TABLE

This painted ash table, designed by Erich Brendel at Bauhaus Weimar, has four flaps and additional foldable tops stored within the table base, making it possible to extend the table in a number of ways. A shelf sits within the base and the table stands on casters. First designed in 1924, the table was reissued by Tecta in 1985. H:28 in (71 cm); W:22/58 in (56/147 cm); D:22/58 in (56/147 cm). TEC

foundation courses now found at all art schools. Students were taught the value of interdisciplinary study and allowed to experiment in new areas. In 1923, Laszlo Moholy-Nagy joined the Bauhaus. The Hungarian had little time for mystical idealism and encouraged Gropius to adopt a practical approach. Gropius received similar advice from Theo van Doesburg, a De Stijl founder, who suggested that the machine be adopted by architects and designers, as crafts were becoming outdated.

Gropius's chance to redefine the Bauhaus came in 1924, when the school moved to Dessau. He launched the new-look Bauhaus in 1926 under the banner of "Art and Technology: A New Unity." Students worked in laboratories, not workshops, creating prototypes for industrial production. The aim was "the methodical removal of anything that is unnecessary," and so the look that we now associate with the Bauhaus was born.

PIONEERS IN DESIGN

At this time, Gropius also took the bold step of asking his most talented students to become tutors. Perhaps the most important of these was Marcel Breuer, whose pioneering work with tubular steel revolutionized the forms of furniture and became his legacy.

Another student-turned-teacher was Marianne Brandt. With Christian Dell, she dominated the metalwork department, producing designs that were mass-produced and affordable—and among the few Bauhaus products to make money.

The role of women within the Bauhaus can be viewed from conflicting angles. While the most talented women were given the credit they were due, most were confined to the weaving workshops. It is worth noting, however, that the weaving workshop, under Gunta Stölzl, was the school's most successful workshop.

BAUHAUS AFTER GROPIUS

In 1928, Hannes Meyer became director of the Bauhaus. Meyer stressed the social responsibilities of the school, but fell foul of the authorities because of his left-leaning views. In 1930, the Bauhaus appointed its final director, the architect Mies van der Rohe. Although many think of him as a major figure within the school, he was only there to oversee its sad decline and fall. The Nazi Party objected to the liberal tendencies of the Bauhaus and shut it down in 1932. Mies van der Rohe attempted to reestablish the school in Berlin, but in 1933 it was closed for good.

By 1937, most of the students and staff had scattered across Europe and America. Wassily Kandinsky settled in France, Marcel Breuer in Britain, and Paul Klee in Switzerland. Laszlo Moholy-Nagy, who fled to the United States along with Walter Gropius, Mies van der Rohe, and Josef Albers, established a New Bauhaus in Chicago that ran 1937–46. Although the school had closed, the ideas and innovations of the Bauhaus continued, and still continue, to shape the future of art, architecture, and, in particular, furniture design.

DESK LAMP

An opaque glass globe sits at the top of a nickel-plated metal column and base. This simple lamp became known as the Bauhaus lamp, so closely did it embody the theories of the school. Designed by Wilhelm Wagenfeld. 1923. H:14¼ in (36 cm); D:7⅛ in (18 cm).

Frosted glass for the shade ensures that the lamp produces a gentle light.

The hemispherical shape is in keeping with the simple forms of the lamp.

The prominent use of metal gives the lamp an industrial look.

The use of prefabricated parts makes the lamp inexpensive to produce.

The metal, disc-shaped base is in line with the simple, industrial look of the lamp.

BAUHAUS CRADLE

Designed by Peter Keler while at Bauhaus Weimar, this cradle was inspired by Wassily Kandinsky. Its form is geometric, with blue-painted circular rockers and red-and-yellow painted triangular sides. The sides are lined in wicker. Originally designed in 1922, this example is a Tecta reissue from 2004. L:38⅖ in (98 cm); D:35¾ in (91 cm). TEC

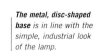

GERMANY

OF ALL THE COUNTRIES in Europe, Germany was the most committed to Modern design. The reasons for this are many, but can be boiled down to two: first, World War I had a particularly destructive impact on Germany, thus kindling a desire among the people to move on; second, the central ideas of Modernism—most significantly, the union of art and industry—had their origins in the existing cultural heritage of the *Deutscher Werkbund* (DWB), formed in Munich in 1907.

EARLY INFLUENCES
Founder members of the DWB, such as Richard Riemerschmid, Josef Maria Olbrich, and Peter Behrens, aimed to engender discussion between designers and manufacturers. The DWB's members were incredibly active in making their voices heard—they gave lectures, mounted exhibitions as far afield as the United States, and published books and magazines. "The German ideal for the future," wrote Friedrich Naumann, a prominent DWB member, "is to become a highly educated machine people." By 1914, however, a split had occurred between those who saw the future of design as a process of standardization and others who were reluctant to lose the individual, artistic approach to design.

STANDARDIZATION
It was the desperate need for economically viable products in the wake of World War I that eventually brought the DWB down on the side of standardization. In 1924, the DWB published "Form without Ornament" and in 1925 it relaunched the influential journal *Die Form*. It was the ambitious *Die Wohnung* (The Dwelling) exhibition in Stuttgart in 1929, however, that proved the DWB's high point. The exhibition featured a housing project that was built by architects and designers including Le Corbusier, Walter Gropius, Mart Stam, and J.J.P. Oud. It was the furnishings as much as the architecture that caused shock waves. This was the first time that tubular-steel furniture had been seen by a wider public, and the event persuaded many manufacturers to work with avant-garde designs.

Despite the international flavor of *Die Wohnung*—participants came from the Netherlands, Belgium, Sweden, Austria, and France—Germany made a strong showing. In buildings designed by Peter Behrens and Mies van der Rohe, the furniture of the Stuttgart-based brothers Heinz and Bodo Rasch could be found. Their cantilevered Spirit of Sitting chair was a

SIESTA MEDIZINAL CHAISE LONGUE

This chair has a solid beech frame and a birch-plywood-slatted seat, back, and footrest. There is a tension adjustment bracket to one side. The design of the chair is such that the user can adjust the positions of the three separate supports, simply by shifting his or her body weight, and without the chair losing balance. Designed by Hans and Wassili Luckhardt. *c. 1937.* H:44½ in (113 cm). BonBay

Exposed screws and joints accentuate the functionality of the chair.

The slight kink in the chair's back, and bent slats, give better support to the sitter's back.

The surface of the wood is left unpainted and undecorated, a further indication of the functional nature of this chair.

Hinges are used to allow the sitter to shift the chair from an upright to a reclining position.

A built-in footrest allows the chair to function as a chaise longue.

CLUB CHAIR

The exposed frame of this chair is made from solid oak and is held together by screws. The seat and chair back are upholstered and covered in a hand-woven wool fabric. Designed by Erich Dieckmann for the *Bauhochschule* (Building Academy) in Weimar. *1926–28* H:27¾ in (70.5 cm); W:24½ in (62 cm); D:29¾ in (75.5 cm). WKA

SIDEBOARD

This dark-stained birchwood sideboard has a rectangular case and stands on a plinth with four short, square-section legs. It has two short drawers above a hinged, fall-front door, which opens to reveal a fitted interior. Attributed to the *Deutsche Werkstätte*. *c. 1935.* QU

alking point of the event, as was the refreshingly plain furniture of Erich Dieckmann and Ferdinand Kramer.

In Berlin, another pair of brothers, Wassili and Hans Luckhardt, were also breaking ground with their unadorned style—their ST14 cantilevered, tubular-steel and plywood chair (1931) being, perhaps, their best-known work.

MODERNISM EMBRACED

One of the most notable features of Modernism in Germany is just how widespread the movement was. Berlin, Stuttgart, and Munich have already been mentioned, while Weimar and Dessau proved important centers of Modernism as well, by being home to the Bauhaus. Hamburg, too, had a thriving Modern community, while in Frankfurt the local authorities embraced Modernism enthusiastically.

A slew of housing projects in the Modern style went up in Frankfurt in the years following World War I. In 1926, Ferdinand Kramer designed a range of simple, plywood furniture suitable for the new houses. It was made in workshops set up in disused army barracks. Also in 1926, the Austrian architect Grete Schutte-Lihotzky developed the Frankfurt Kitchen, which was a scientifically researched standardized unit that could be fitted into kitchens at minimal cost. Revolutionary at the time, the idea later became commonplace.

THE MOVEMENT'S DECLINE

Adolf Hitler's rise to power in 1933 signaled the decline of the Modern era in Germany. Although in favor of the Modernist ideals of efficiency and cleanliness, Hitler was troubled by the non-Germans involved in the movement. A select few German Modernists worked for the Nazi government, while schools such as the Bauhaus (accused of "cultural Bolshevism") were closed. Although Germany was the breeding ground for many of the greatest ideas and developments of the Modern era, it was in other countries that the full range of the style was eventually explored.

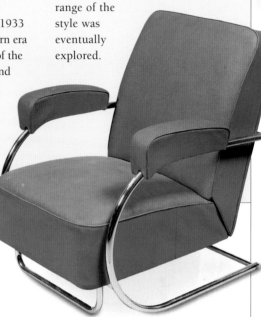

CANTILEVER CHAIR

In its original condition, this cantilever chair has a metal frame within the green, upholstered seat and back. The arms of the chair are made from chrome-plated tubular steel and have padded elbow rests. Designed by Hans and Wassili Luckhardt. *c. 1930. L:68¾ in (175 cm). DOR*

LUDWIG MIES VAN DER ROHE

ONE OF THE MODERN ERA'S BEST-KNOWN DESIGNERS AND ARCHITECTS, LUDWIG MIES VAN DER ROHE WAS RESPONSIBLE FOR CREATING SOME OF THE PERIOD'S MOST ICONIC FURNITURE AND BUILDINGS.

Ludwig Mies van der Rohe, the son of a stonemason, was born in Aachen, Germany, in 1886, and was the man who coined the famous phrase "less is more." Mies, as he is more commonly known, was an architect and furniture designer whose dedication to Functionalism was allied with an instinct for graceful form. This combination, and his exacting eye for detail, has made his furniture among the most enduring of the Modern era.

Although many associate Mies with the Bauhaus, he was only involved with the School at the very end of its lifespan. Such iconic designs as the Barcelona chair (created for the king of Spain) and the cantilever chair were developed in his architectural office in Berlin, some years before he became director of the Bauhaus in 1930. It is perhaps because Mies had little interest in low-cost designs (he insisted on using only the best-quality materials) that he steered clear of the Bauhaus and its more egalitarian agenda for so long.

In 1938, Mies moved to Chicago to escape the Nazi regime, and, although he almost completely stopped designing furniture, he did go on to design two of North America's most revered Modern buildings—the Farnsworth House in Illinois (1946–50) and the Seagram Building in New York City (1951–58).

Barcelona table The X-shaped base of the table is made from chrome-plated steel and supports a heavy plate of glass. *1929. H:18⅛ in (46 cm); W:39 in (100 cm); D:39 in (100 cm). Bk*

Barcelona chair The simple-looking design consists of chromium-plated steel cross-frames, which support buttoned-leather cushions on leather straps. *H:29⅛ in (74 cm); W:29½ in (75 cm); D:29⅞ in (76 cm). SDR*

OCCASIONAL TABLE

The circular top of this occasional table has a geometric, rosewood-marquetry surface and is supported on nickel-plated tubular uprights, which extend to form stretchers. The table was designed by Josef Albers for his colleague Wassily Kandinsky. *c. 1933. D:31 in (79 cm).*

FRANCE

IN 1925, THE FRENCH opened a grand international exhibition entitled the *Exposition des Arts Décoratifs et Industriels Modernes* (Decorative and Modern Industrial Arts Exhibition). Although the exhibition promised to showcase the modern and industrial arts, it instead highlighted just how much the French still favored opulence and decoration. Instead,

it was the Russians and a young, Swiss-born architect named Le Corbusier who showed the public the inspiring new designs the organizers had promised.

The Russian designer Konstantin Melnikov's Soviet Pavilion was a striking design in the Constructivist style, while Le Corbusier's *Pavillon de l'Esprit Nouveau* was a stark exercise in rational geometry. Perhaps most shocking to the public was the sparse interior of Le Corbusier's pavilion, which looked like a

prison cell compared to the lavish pavilions designed by designers such as Emile-Jacques Ruhlmann (*see p.404*).

With his high-profile pavilion design, Le Corbusier laid down a challenge to the French, and slowly some designers started to respond.

UNION OF MODERN ARTISTS

By 1929, a group of French architects and designers had come together to fight the rising tide of Art Deco. Calling themselves the *Union des Artistes Modernes* (Union of Modern Artists, or UAM), they counted Eileen Gray, Charlotte Perriand, Jean Puiforcat, and Jan

and Joel Martel among them. Their first president was Robert Mallet-Stevens, an architect whose heavily geometric buildings led to the group's style being dubbed "the great nudity."

Although the influence of the Bauhaus was clear, the UAM kept a careful distance from activities in Germany. In the wake of World War I, there was bad blood between the neighbors, so no matter how much they admired the works of Marcel Breuer, Walter Gropius, and Mies van der Rohe, UAM members did not admit as much.

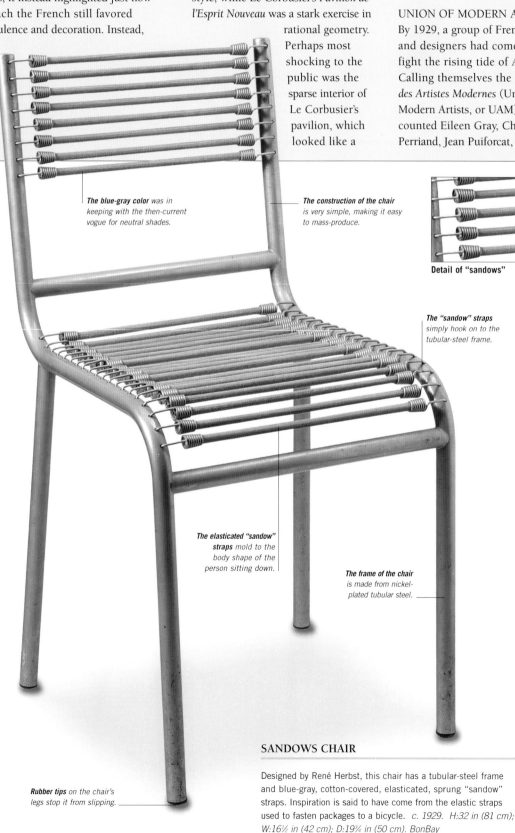

The blue-gray color was in keeping with the then-current vogue for neutral shades.

The construction of the chair is very simple, making it easy to mass-produce.

Detail of "sandows"

The "sandow" straps simply hook on to the tubular-steel frame.

The elasticated "sandow" straps mold to the body shape of the person sitting down.

The frame of the chair is made from nickel-plated tubular steel.

Rubber tips on the chair's legs stop it from slipping.

SANDOWS CHAIR

Designed by René Herbst, this chair has a tubular-steel frame and blue-gray, cotton-covered, elasticated, sprung "sandow" straps. Inspiration is said to have come from the elastic straps used to fasten packages to a bicycle. *c. 1929. H:32 in (81 cm); W:16½ in (42 cm); D:19¾ in (50 cm). BonBay*

PLYWOOD CHAIR

This is an early design for a chair by Jean Prouvé. The molded plywood seat and back are screwed to a solid, dark-stained wooden frame. The durable plywood seat has waterfall edges. The chair can be used in a domestic or a commercial setting. *1942. BonBay*

RECTANGULAR CHAIR

This Modern chair is of strict rectangular construction with prominent feature screws. The back panel, seat panel, arms, and floor-level stretchers are made of ebonized wood. The panel legs and uprights are fashioned from figured oak. Attributed to Robert Mallet-Stevens. *c.1930. BonBay*

There were, at any rate, considerable discrepancies between the Modern styles in Germany and France. Although the French embraced materials such as tubular steel and plate glass, they used them with greater grace and elegance than the Germans, who preferred to keep their designs unerringly concise.

The second UAM president, René Herbst, was among the first in France to experiment with tubular steel. A advocate of low-cost mass production, which he said would "provide a healthy home for every family," he was also active at the affluent end of the market, designing, in 1930, a Paris apartment for the Prince Aga Khan.

A close friend of Herbst, and a member of UAM, was the architect and designer Pierre Chareau. It was Chareau who designed an icon of the Modern era, the *Maison de Verre*. Built from glass bricks and exposed iron beams in 1928, the house caused a stir in Paris. It was some time later that Chareau translated his bold approach into furniture design. After years of designing luxurious furniture, he eventually developed a leaner style. Chareau's desks of wood and bent-iron strips appeared almost mechanized.

This mechanical aesthetic, startling enough in the work of Chareau, was taken to even further extremes by Jean Prouvé, who was younger than many UAM members. "In my opinion," Prouvé once said, "furniture design requires the same procedure as any other building construction," which is perhaps why his designs appear so robust. Based in the small town of Nancy, the prolific Prouvé took an energetic and fearless approach to furniture design. If French designers were accused of shying away from the raw vocabulary of industry in the early interwar years, Prouvé's work was inarguable proof that their attitudes changed considerably.

TEA TABLE

This tea table, or coffee table, was designed by the French furniture designer Jean Prouvé. Its simple design consists of an oak-veneered tabletop positioned above three legs that are fashioned from solid oak; the legs taper fairly sharply toward the bottom. The table top is supported beneath by a lacquered iron frame in a reddish-brown color. *1934. H:13½ in (34.5 cm); Diam:37⅓ in (95 cm).*

MB 405 DESK AND SN 3 STOOL

This L-shaped rosewood desktop is raised on a wrought-iron frame, which supports additional shelving above and below the desktop. The stool has a rectangular rosewood seat above a wrought-iron frame, where the back leg bends under the stool to provide extra stability for the two front legs. *c. 1927. Desk: H:36¾ in (93.4 cm); W:63½ in (161.2 cm); D:40½ in (102.8 cm). Stool: H:14 in (35.6 cm); W:19¾ in (50.2 cm); D:15¾ in (40 cm).*

EILEEN GRAY

ARCHITECT AND FURNITURE DESIGNER EILEEN GRAY CREATED REDUCTIONIST PIECES OF FURNITURE THAT ARE SOME OF THE MOST REMARKABLE OF THE MODERN PERIOD.

Born in Ireland in 1878, Eileen Gray was to make her name in France. Having studied at the Slade School of Art in London (as one of its first female students), Gray headed for Paris in 1907. When she arrived, she was greeted by a city enjoying a rich period of creativity.

Gray began to work for a Japanese craftsman, Seizo Sugawara, from whom she learned lacquering. Her early furniture designs were heavily inspired by Sugawara and appeared as a luxuriant mix of Art Deco with Japanese overtones.

In 1922, Gray opened her own gallery in Paris—Galérie Jean Désert. Her work became a favorite of the intellectual classes, although she soon tired of making exclusive furniture. An encounter with the De Stijl group made her question her own design style as well.

A pivotal year in Gray's life was 1927; it was then that she drifted away from Paris and began work on a house in southern France. Known as E1027, the house was incredibly radical for its time. Built with an open-plan interior, it also gave Gray the opportunity to reappraise her approach to furniture.

The furniture designs that Gray created for E1027 are among her most successful. Viewing items of furniture as components in the larger "machine" of the house, she developed an immensely practical style that was the very definition of form following function. The economy of line and flexibility of such pieces as the E1027 side table and the *Transat* chair make them among the most remarkable works of the Modern era.

Throughout the rest of her long life (she died in 1976), Gray worked in this Reductionist style, although her ability to give a sense of singular refinement to her work never deserted her.

Eileen Gray

Blocs screen An ingenious design, this screen consists of 28 black-lacquered panels that pivot on rods to open and close holes in the screen. *1923. H:74½ in (189 cm); W:53½ in (136 cm); D:¾ in (2 cm).*

Bibendum chair Padded, tirelike rings form the back and seat of the chair, which is covered in fabric. The base is chrome-plated steel. *1929. H:28⅔ in (73 cm); W:34½ in (87.5 cm); D:32⅔ in (83 cm).*

LE CORBUSIER

LE CORBUSIER'S BOLD, MINIMALIST ARCHITECTURE AND INDUSTRIAL-LOOKING FURNITURE UNIQUELY CAPTURED THE FORWARD-LOOKING IDEALS OF THE EARLY MODERNISTS.

IF ONE MAN WERE SAID TO EPITOMIZE the spirit of the early Modern movement in architecture and design, it would be Le Corbusier. With his famous statement, "The house is a machine for living in," he encapsulated the Modernists' utopian desire for efficiency, economy, and a radically contemporary lifestyle.

Although an architect first and foremost, Le Corbusier was too energetic to restrict himself to the slow process of erecting buildings. He instigated the artistic movement known as Purism (a form of Cubism), was a prolific writer, and designed some of the most important furniture of the 20th century.

Le Corbusier's approach to design reflected his wider ideas, one of which was that industry should be accepted into daily life. His writings, for instance, extolled the virtues of industrial designs such as the grain silo. In an era when Art Deco was the dominant force (see pp.386–415), he was understandably viewed with suspicion.

THE EARLY YEARS

Although Le Corbusier became a French citizen in 1930, he was born in La Chaux-de-Fonds, Switzerland, in 1887. His first architectural project, which was completed at 18 under his real name—Charles-Edouard Jeanneret—was a house in La Chaux-de-Fonds. The Le Corbusier moniker came later, in the 1920s. Lecorbesier was the name of one of his forefathers, so it is thought that this is where he took the name from.

Le Corbusier's early years in Paris, where he settled after World War I, were spent writing such progressive tracts as the "Contemporary City for Three Million Inhabitants." Printed in 1922 in L'Esprit Nouveau—a reivew magazine Le Corbusier created with the painter Amédée Ozenfant in 1920—this magnificent vision of the future showed just how ambitious he was.

MINIMALIST STYLE

In 1925, having persuaded the organizers of the Paris Exposition des Art Décoratifs et Industriels Modernes to grant him an exhibition site, Le Corbusier built his Pavillon de L'Esprit Nouveau with his cousin Pierre Jeanneret. The bare walls and bold, geometric lines of the structure prompted outrage. "We find nothing but inadequate fittings, metal furniture, glass tables, cold lighting, and pale colors," wrote a shocked reviewer.

Inside the pavilion, the interior was sparsely furnished with Thonet's bentwood No. 9 and No. 14 chairs (see p.375), which Le Corbusier thought possessed "a nobility of their own." Still, Le Corbusier

LE CORBUSIER

The artist is in his studio in Rue Jacob, Paris. A prolific writer, he also co-founded and produced the influential design journal L'Esprit Nouveau. 1931.

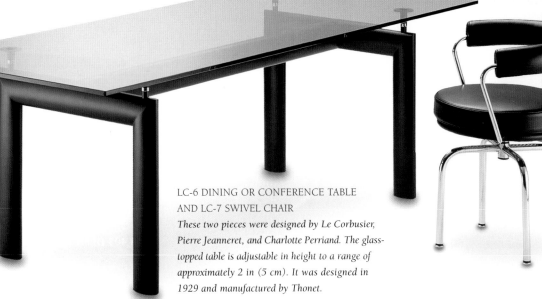

LC-6 DINING OR CONFERENCE TABLE AND LC-7 SWIVEL CHAIR

These two pieces were designed by Le Corbusier, Pierre Jeanneret, and Charlotte Perriand. The glass-topped table is adjustable in height to a range of approximately 2 in (5 cm). It was designed in 1929 and manufactured by Thonet.

BIOGRAPHY

Le Corbusier

1887 Born Charles-Edouard Jeanneret in La Chaux-de-Fonds, Switzerland.

1905 Completes his first architectural project: a house in La Chaux-de-Fonds.

1910–11 Travels to Germany, where he meets members of the Deutscher Werkbund.

1917 Opens his own architecture office in Paris.

Early 1920s Changes name to Le Corbusier.

1922 Publishes the progressive tract "Contemporary City for Three Million Inhabitants" in L'Esprit Nouveau.

1925 Builds Pavillon de L'Espirit Nouveau for the Exposition des Art Décoratifs et Industriels Modernes.

1928 With Pierre Jeanneret and Charlotte Perriand, develops forward-looking range of furniture that includes the B306 chair and the Gran Confort chaise longue.

1930 Becomes a naturalized French citizen.

1950–55 Builds chapel in Ronchamp.

1965 Dies in Cap Martin.

JEANNERET AND PERRIAND

ALTHOUGH THEY WERE NOT AS FAMOUS AS LE CORBUSIER, PIERRE JEANNERET AND CHARLOTTE PERRIAND INFLUENCED SOME OF HIS MOST RENOWNED DESIGNS.

When correctly credited, the less famous names of Pierre Jeanneret and Charlotte Perriand often appear alongside the furniture designs of Le Corbusier. Although it must be assumed that Le Corbusier led the way in the design of these items, they must, nonetheless, be considered a collaborative effort.

Pierre Jeanneret was a cousin of Le Corbusier who had worked with the architect since 1922. Charlotte Perriand was offered a position by Le Corbusier after he saw an exhibition of her anodized-aluminum and chromed-steel furniture.

It was Perriand's specialist knowledge that gave Le Corbusier the confidence to develop a range of furniture that, debuting in 1927, would include such renowned designs as the B306 chaise longue and the *Gran Confort* range.

The trio's furniture designs were first seen by the public as part of a mockup of a modern apartment exhibited at the *Salon d'Automne* (Autumn Salon) in 1929. Incorporating such features as concealed lighting, sliding doors, and modular storage units—things that were not to become commonplace for many years—it proved to be the high point of the trio's collaboration.

Perriand left Le Corbusier's office in the late 1930s and went on to forge a successful career as an independent architect and designer. She spent much of the 1940s collaborating with companies in Japan, although she briefly returned to work with Le Corbusier in the 1950s, helping him with the interiors of his *Unité d'Habitation* (Living Unit) in Marseille.

Perriand and Jeanneret were to work together again in 1940, when both teamed up with Jean Prouvé to produce a series of prefabricated aluminum structures that were intended as temporary housing. Jeanneret, who assisted Le Corbusier throughout his career, also briefly made a name for himself as an independent furniture designer with the production of the birch Scissor chair that, in 1947, became one of the first items to appear in the catalog of Knoll, the celebrated American manufacturer of furniture.

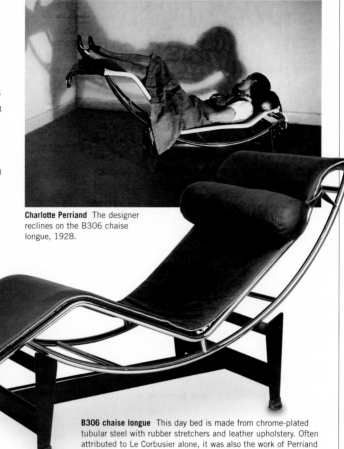

Charlotte Perriand The designer reclines on the B306 chaise longue, 1928.

B306 chaise longue This day bed is made from chrome-plated tubular steel with rubber stretchers and leather upholstery. Often attributed to Le Corbusier alone, it was also the work of Perriand and Jeanneret. Designed in 1928, this is a Cassina reissue from the 1960s. *H:28¼ in (70.5 cm); L:64 in (160 cm); W:19¾ in (49.5 cm). QU*

recognized the irony of using 75-year-old designs in such a brazenly contemporary structure. By 1925, he knew that his next project would be to create furniture for his radical architecture.

The arrival of Charlotte Perriand was just the catalyst he needed. In 1927, Perriand, Pierre Jeanneret, and Le Corbusier devised a range of designs that were industrial-looking, yet surprisingly comfortable. The resplendent B306 chaise longue looked more like a piece of equipment than a luxury item of furniture. The slight *Basculant* chair was an economical design that used the bare minimum of materials. The cube-shaped *Gran Confort* armchair was the trio's take on the club chair, although in this case the chair's structure appeared on the outside. Produced in 1928, these designs made full use of tubular steel, the material popularized by Marcel Breuer. Ironically, it was Thonet—the maker of Le Corbusier's beloved bentwood chairs—that produced these designs.

Le Corbusier's crusade to turn the world into a symphony of mechanical existence continued unabated until the advent of World War II. After this, he struggled to stick to his hard-edged aesthetic views in the face of such destruction. After the war, Le Corbusier developed a softer, although no less impressive, style (his chapel in Ronchamp, built from 1950 to 1955, being a good example). In his later years, Le Corbusier's attention turned increasingly toward urban planning, and his early interest in furniture, unfortunately, rarely resurfaced.

GRAN CONFORT

This sofa, model LC2 was produced as part of the Gran Confort *range by Le Corbusier, Perriand, and Jeanneret. It has a chrome-plated tubular-metal frame and leather cushions. Designed in 1928, this example is a Cassina reissue from the 1980s.* W:66 in (167.5 cm). FRE

TUBULAR STEEL

ORIGINALLY USED ONLY IN INDUSTRY, TUBULAR STEEL WAS EMBRACED BY DESIGNERS AS THE IDEAL MATERIAL FOR MODERN FURNITURE AND A NEW KIND OF LIFESTYLE.

TUBULAR STEEL WAS a truly Modern material. Not long after it emerged as a viable material for domestic furniture construction in the mid-1920s, it became a symbol of the new era of the interwar years. Industrially manufactured, easily cleaned, lightweight, and, of course, with a striking metallic gleam, it was ideal for a forward-looking lifestyle.

A method for manufacturing tubular steel was patented in 1885 by two Germans, Max and Reinhard Mannesmann. The technique involved passing a short, heated stick of steel through a piercing machine, thus producing a tube. By 1921, a more advanced technique had been developed that produced more pliable tubes with thinner walls.

GERMANY LEADS THE WAY

It was some years before furniture designers thought of using this slimline tubular steel. At the time, tubular steel was largely used in the central heating systems of industrial plants. It was only when the automobile industry and bicycle manufacturers began to use the material that tubular steel became visible in everyday life. The first experiments with domestic tubular-steel furniture—by Marcel Breuer in Germany and Mart Stam in the Netherlands—were in 1925.

Breuer's first tubular-steel design was the Wassily chair, created in 1925 for the flat of artist Wassily Kandinsky, a Bauhaus tutor. The stout outline of the Wassily chair is clearly modeled on the English club chair, although Breuer appears to have dissolved the entire bulk of the club chair, leaving just the skeleton.

In 1925–26, Breuer developed tubular-steel chairs and tables for the Bauhaus canteen, although it was only in 1927 at the *Die Wohnung* exhibition in Stuttgart that tubular-steel furniture gained wider exposure.

Not long afterward, the furniture manufacturer Thonet began to produce tubular-steel designs across Europe. It was fitting that Thonet took on these designs, since it was the German company's innovations in functional, inexpensive bentwood furniture in the mid-19th century that pushed many Modernist designers toward the use of tubular steel.

DEVELOPMENTS FARTHER AFIELD

Although Germany was the launching pad for tubular-steel furniture, it soon appeared in other countries. Mart Stam introduced the material to the Netherlands, and by 1930 many Dutch designers were using tubular steel. Gerrit Rietveld was briefly smitten by it, even making a tubular-steel version of his Red-and-Blue chair. Willem Gispen, a designer who had worked in a florid style, became a champion of tubular steel. "Seeing the social changes in the world around me",

BREUER'S INSPIRATION

Marcel Breuer had the idea of using tubular steel for furniture while riding his bicycle, which had tubular-steel handlebars. Sheet steel was also a favored material at the Bauhaus, and was used for jewelry and lamps as early as 1923.

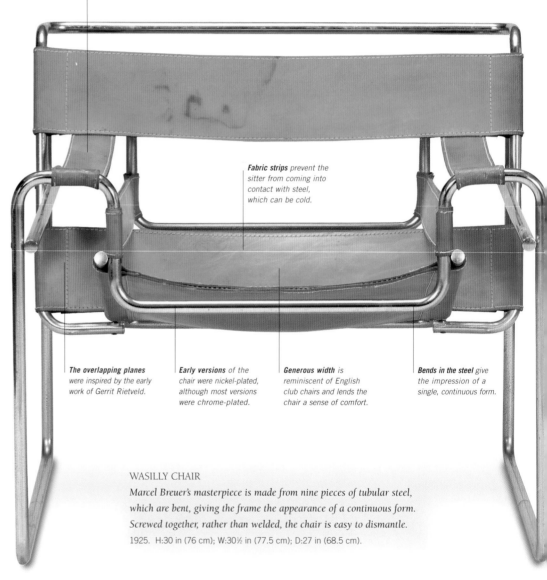

The armrest appears substantial but is little more than a strip of fabric.

Fabric strips prevent the sitter from coming into contact with steel, which can be cold.

The overlapping planes were inspired by the early work of Gerrit Rietveld.

Early versions of the chair were nickel-plated, although most versions were chrome-plated.

Generous width is reminiscent of English club chairs and lends the chair a sense of comfort.

Bends in the steel give the impression of a single, continuous form.

WASILLY CHAIR

Marcel Breuer's masterpiece is made from nine pieces of tubular steel, which are bent, giving the frame the appearance of a continuous form. Screwed together, rather than welded, the chair is easy to dismantle.
1925. H:30 in (76 cm); W:30½ in (77.5 cm); D:27 in (68.5 cm).

BAUHAUS METAL WORKSHOP

From its inception, the Bauhaus metal workshop was primarily concerned with the different qualities of various metals—brass, silver, gold, copper—and with how they could be applied to Bauhaus design ideals. Under Marcel Breuer— head of the furniture workshop in Dessau from 1925—it followed that the technical properties of tubular steel would be examined and exploited in much the same way. 1928–29.

THE CANTILEVER

THE CANTILEVERED CHAIR WAS A FAVORITE OF MODERNIST DESIGNERS, ALTHOUGH IT IS UNCLEAR WHO FIRST HAD THE IDEA TO USE THE CANTILEVER PRINCIPLE IN CHAIR DESIGN.

The cantilever principle, whereby a structure's load is borne by a single mounting point, was used by many Modernist furniture designers, but there has been much debate—and litigation—to try to ascertain who employed the principle first. The attraction of the cantilever for Modernist designers is obvious. It reduces a chair's form to the minimum; it displays a one-upmanship on the age-old principle of the four-legged chair; plus, it has the visually arresting effect of making sitters appear to float on air.

Cantilever chair This chair is a Thonet reissue of Mart Stam's S33 cantilever chair. The chair has a chrome-plated, tubular-steel frame and a leather seat and back. *1926. H:33 in (84 cm); W:19⅝ in (50 cm); D:26¼ in (57 cm).*

Swinging tubular steel chair MR-10 By Ludwig Mies van der Rohe, this chair's frame is nickel-plated and the seat and back are cane. Made by Josef Müller of Berlin. *Late 1920s. H:32 in (80 cm); W:19¼ in (48 cm); D:26 in (65 cm). QU*

The first cantilevered steel chairs were shown at a *Die Wohnung* exhibition in Stuttgart in 1927: two by Mart Stam, a Dutchman, and two by Ludwig Mies van der Rohe, a German designer. It is most likely that Stam had the idea first, discussing it with Mies van der Rohe the previous year, before both went on to develop their own versions. Marcel Breuer, however, once claimed he was working on a design for a cantilevered steel chair as early as 1925, although it was not until 1927 (after the *Die Wohnung* show) that his version was exhibited.

To complicate matters further, when Mies van der Rohe applied for a patent it was discovered that an American, Harry Nolan, had registered a convoluted drawing of a metal cantilevered chair in 1922. Mies van der Rohe proved that Nolan's design would collapse the moment anyone sat on it and was awarded the patent.

The B33 chair This tubular-steel-framed chair has a canvas seat and back. Designed by Marcel Breuer c.1929. This example is a Thonet reissue from 2004. *H:33 in (84 cm); W:19½ in (49.5 cm); D:34 in (86 cm).*

wrote Gispen in 1977, "I simplified my designs and joined the train of thought of the Rationalists." Gispen's factory in Rotterdam, which still exists today, specialized in tubular-steel lamps.

While the Dutch and Germans saw tubular steel as a resolutely utilitarian material, it was used in a more stylized manner in France. René Herbst, Eileen Gray, and Le Corbusier all produced tubular-steel furniture in the 1920s and 30s that betrayed aesthetic, as well as Rational, concerns.

EMBRACED BY THE ELITE

Although clearly a material with its roots in industry, tubular steel initially proved more costly than wood, an irony that is often overlooked. Until the price of tubular-steel furniture fell in the late 1930s, it was sold almost exclusively to an affluent elite.

This trend was particularly apparent in Great Britain. By 1928 the lower-middle classes were being encouraged to buy tubular-steel furniture for its space-saving properties. Many people had been forced to downsize after World War I and were living in small homes ill-suited to older styles of furniture. This audience, however, proved resistant to tubular steel; it was the moneyed classes that were drawn to it.

Two British firms, PEL (Public Equipment Limited) and Cox and Co. began making tubular-steel furniture in the early 1930s, clearly basing their designs on works in the Thonet catalog. PEL's customers included Noel Coward, the Prince of Wales, and Lord Mountbatten, and by 1932, when the BBC employed Cox and Co. and PEL to refurnish their buildings, tubular steel was in vogue, albeit among a tiny minority. Widespread use of tubular steel was to come later, with the *Cabinet Maker* magazine reporting in 1935 that steel furniture "is being taken up by all sections of the community".

Although the late 1930s was a period of growth in sales of tubular-steel furniture, it was also a period of artistic decline. With Marcel Breuer and Mart Stam realizing the essential forms of tubular-steel furniture so early on, there was little scope for progress. By 1935, Stam was lamenting the endless bastardization of his, and Breuer's, ideas, expressing his wish for "all those macaroni-like steel monsters to disappear". His wish came true with the advent of World War II, which put a stop to the proliferation of tubular-steel designs. After 1945, tubular steel was used only sparingly, by designers who realized its moment had passed.

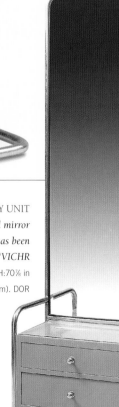

VANITY UNIT
This tubular-steel dressing table has a tall mirror above a small case with two drawers. It has been painted light blue and bears the label "VICHR A SPOL, PRAHA." Prague. c. 1930. H:70⅞ in (180 cm). DOR

SIDE TABLE
Marcel Breuer's model B12 side table has two black-painted wooden shelves—one flush with the top, the other a third of the way down. The table appears to be made of a continuous loop of steel. c. 1928. W:30 in (76 cm). DOR

SCANDINAVIA

SCANDINAVIA—USUALLY CONSIDERED to include Sweden, Denmark, Norway, Finland, and Iceland—experienced a very different history in the interwar years than other European nations did, and, as a result, produced a very different style of furniture.

The first thing to note is that the political situation in Scandinavia was relatively settled compared with much of what was happening in the rest of Europe. Industrialization, too, was slow to catch on in Scandinavia, and if you add this to a harsh climate and a deep, inherent reverence for the crafts, it becomes clear why the severe, iconoclastic forms of tubular-metal

furniture pioneered in Germany held no appeal for the Scandinavians.

A PREFERENCE FOR WOOD

Tubular steel was labeled "unsatisfactory from a human point of view" by Alvar Aalto, the foremost Scandinavian designer of the era (who also noted that metal furniture was particularly uncomfortable in the cold). It was wood, a material readily available from the forests that covered the region, which proved the most popular material for Scandinavian designers of the time.

There was an attempt at the beginning of the 1930s to introduce

to Scandinavia the sort of hard, industrial aesthetic that had taken root on the rest of the European continent. In 1930, the architect Gunnar Asplund put on an exhibition in Stockholm under the banner of Swedish Functionalism that showcased an angular style and synthetic materials, which, understandably, shocked the Scandinavian public. Asplund and his fellow exhibitors, many of whom had returned from studying and working abroad, were swiftly labeled "anti-Swedish," and the idea of Functionalism began to fade.

A GENTLER APPROACH

By the mid-1930s, Scandinavian designers had struck a balance between the bare, unadorned style of European Modernism and the organic, craft-based forms to which they were accustomed. What developed was an approach that came to be termed Soft Modernism, as epitomized by designers like Bruno Mathsson. Although Mathsson used natural

SAFARI CHAIR

The maple frame of this lightweight chair has no joints as such, but is held together simply by the leather seat and straps, which form the arms of the chair, and the slots that join the side struts together. Inspired by the traditional pieces originally made for the British military, the chair is collapsable and

easy to take apart. A market success from the time it was introduced, the Safari chair was handmade by the small furniture-making firm of Rudolf Rasmussen, which manufactured many of the Danish designer Kaare Klint's works. Wooden and canvas versions of the chair were also sold. By Kaare Klint. *1933. H:30½ in (77.5 cm); W:22 in (55.75 cm); D:25 in (63.5 cm).*

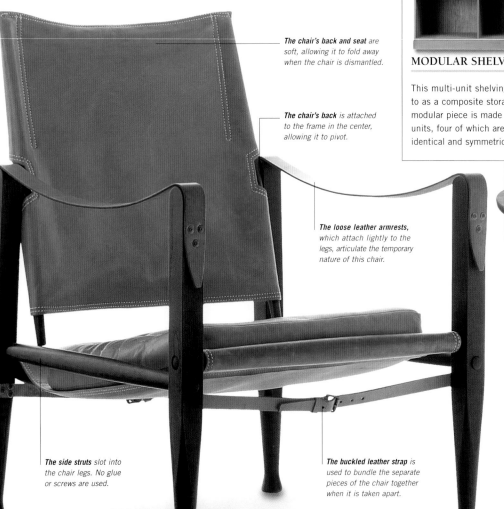

The chair's back and seat are soft, allowing it to fold away when the chair is dismantled.

The chair's back is attached to the frame in the center, allowing it to pivot.

The loose leather armrests, which attach lightly to the legs, articulate the temporary nature of this chair.

The side struts slot into the chair legs. No glue or screws are used.

The buckled leather strap is used to bundle the separate pieces of the chair together when it is taken apart.

MODULAR SHELVING

This multi-unit shelving system is referred to as a composite storage system. The modular piece is made up of five individual units, four of which are open and fitted with identical and symmetrical shelved interiors.

The whole storage system is supported by three base plinths, which are also of wood. The fifth unit is fronted with cupboard doors and is slightly deeper than the others. Designed by Mogens Koch. *1933. H:30 in (76 cm); W:30 in (76 cm); D:10⅞ in/14½ in (27.5 cm/37 cm).*

ANNIKA TABLE

This round magazine table, or occasional table, has a plain elm table top free of surface decoration. It is mounted on three bent-laminated beech legs. The legs taper slightly as they near the floor. Designed by Bruno Mathsson for the company Karl Mathsson. *1938. H:15¼ in (38 cm); D:26 in (65 cm). Bk*

materials and undulating lines, his furniture was undeniably Modern in its brazen display of its own construction and its lack of ornament.

Another thing to note about Mathsson is that the forms of his furniture were often inspired by ergonomics—the relationship between people and the equipment they use. This was a particularly Scandinavian trait, pioneered by Kaare Klint in Copenhagen in the 1920s. Klint and his students at the Royal Danish Academy of Fine Arts spent a great deal of time studying anthropomorphism; Klint used the information he gained to design ergonomic versions of archetypal forms of furniture.

The soft, sculptural style that we associate with Modern Scandinavian furniture, then, was partly inspired by the natural shapes that surrounded designers in their nonindustrialized environment. It was also informed by the study of human behavior and an insistence on using wood rather than metal. Most European and American designers came to learn of Soft Modernism through the well-traveled Alvar Aalto, and it was to have an increasingly apparent impact. Indeed, by the end of World War II, the tubular-steel designs pioneered in Germany, France, and Italy were shunned by a new generation of designers that favored the more humanistic approach of the Scandinavians.

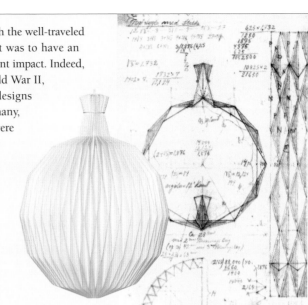

Fruit lantern This piece was designed by Kaare Klint. *1944.*

EVA CHAIR

This armless easy chair has a solid-birch seat frame; the underframe is bent laminated beech; the seat and back are a single piece of braided webbing. Bruno Mathsson. *1941. H:32¼ in (82 cm); W:19¼ in (49 cm); D:28 in (71 cm). Bk*

SMALL CHEST OF DRAWERS

Designed by Alvar Aalto, this chest of drawers has a birch frame and stands on wooden casters. Indentations in the drawers serve as handles. *1930. H:66 in (26.5 cm); W:15 in (38 cm); D:27½ in (68.5 cm). QU*

ALVAR AALTO

THE FINNISH DESIGNER ALVAR AALTO IS CREDITED WITH INTRODUCING THE USE OF PLYWOOD AND LAMINATED WOOD IN FURNITURE DESIGN, AN IDEA HE IS SAID TO HAVE GOTTEN FROM HIS LAMINATED CROSS-COUNTRY SKIS.

While across Europe and North America artists, architects, and designers proclaimed their visions for the future in manifestos, essays, and speeches, Alvar Aalto let his designs do the talking. Assisted by his wife, Aino, Aalto worked primarily with laminated wood and plywood. Unheard-of in Scandinavian furniture design before the Finn adopted them, these materials soon became inextricably linked with his name.

By 1931, two years after he started to experiment with plywood, Aalto produced the 41 chair. With the seat and back made from one piece of ply, it demonstrates Aalto's mastery of the material both formally and technically. The cantilevered 31 chair was another audacious display of his confidence with a form of furniture that was startlingly new.

Birch, which is abundant in Finland, was Aalto's wood of choice, and it's clear that the process of forming ply and laminated wood— which incorporates steaming the wood, then gently bending it— largely dictated the forms of Aalto's designs. Such was the couple's proficiency with plywood and laminated wood that in 1935 they launched their own company—Artek—to manufacture their designs, which are still produced in Finland today.

Aalto interior Riihitie House, Helsinki This was Alvar Aalto's residence for over 60 years—designed and furnished by Aalto and his wife. *1935–36.*

The rolling form of the chair's seat expresses the flexibility of laminated birch.

Paimio No. 41 The armchair's gently curved seat is molded plywood, suspended in a laminated birch frame. Designed for the Paimio Tuberculosis Sanatorium in Finland. *c. 1931. H:25¼ in (64 cm); W:26¾ in (60 cm); D:31½ in (80 cm). BonE*

The lacquering of the seat helps articulate the separate elements of seat and frame.

Slits in the seat back allow air to reach the back of the sitter's head, thus making it more hygienic.

The loops at the head and base of the seat give it a comfortable springiness.

BRITAIN

IN THE FIELD OF MODERN furniture design, Great Britain was considered more of a follower than a leader. In the late 19th century it had been home to the radical Arts and Crafts movement—which was itself of considerable influence on Modernist pioneers such as Alvar Aalto and Le Corbusier—but after this period the development of British furniture slowed down.

LITTLE PUBLIC INTEREST
In the latter half of the 1920s simple, solid-wood furniture, of the sort advocated by the Arts and Crafts Movement, was still relatively hard to come by. Industrial reproductions

of older, more ornate styles were preferred by the public, but this didn't stop a few shops—such as Heal's on London's Tottenham Court Road—from waving the flag for furniture of a more Modern bent. Perhaps the most notable designer of this style was the Cotswolds-based Gordon Russell, who worked prolifically on pieces that were pared down to their most basic form.

INTERNATIONAL INFLUENCES
The adoption by British designers of such new materials as plywood and tubular steel was a far from common occurrence. Tellingly, it tended to be designers who arrived in Great Britain

from abroad who were most open to the latest developments from overseas. Architects based in London, such as Serge Chermayeff and Berthold Lubetkin (both Russian-born) and the Hungarian-born Erno Goldfinger all experimented with plywood in the 1920s

Anglepoise lamp This articulated lamp allows light to be directed at will. The head and base swivel, and the lamp bends and flexes to obtain different positions. This is a Tecta reissue of George Cawardine's original 1932 design. *H:35½ in (90 cm). TEC*

The body of the desk is made of limed oak.

The upper section comprises open and closed storage.

The geometric shape reflects the fashions of the time.

SWOOPING ARMCHAIR

This lacquered plywood armchair by Gerald Summers is today considered an icon of Modern design. Summers succeeded in creating a unified design using just a single sheet of plywood. Only 120 chairs were produced before manufacturing was halted due to wartime rationing of materials. *1933–34. H:29 in (72.5 cm) W:24 in (60 cm); D:36 in (90 cm).*

CORNER DESK

This corner desk is made of limed oak and formed part of the "Signed Edition" Series, designed by Sir Ambrose Heal and manufactured by Heal's. The upper section of the desk consists of various storage areas, including three cupboards plus open storage. The lower section consists

of a deep writing surface above two pedestals that form a triangular arrangement with the back of the desk. Each pedestal contains a deep drawer at the base. This compact piece would have been ideal for the new urban homes where space was at a premium. This angular desk reflects the geometric fashions of the time. *1931. H:43¼ in (108 cm); W:36½ in (91.4 cm).*

OBJECT DESK

This is a Modernist interpretation of the single pedestal desk. The rectangular top is raised on four bow-fronted drawers at one end and fixed to a glass support at the

other. Additional stability is provided by a metal stretcher at the back of the desk. The curved wooden drawer fronts have off-set chromed handles. The piece was designed by Denham Maclaren *c.1929.*

and 1930s, although without the panache of their continental European counterparts.

Perhaps the most important designer working in Great Britain in the interwar years was Gerald Summers, a modest man whose lack of publicity skills meant that much of his furniture went unseen by the wider world. His celebrated Swooping armchair (1933–34), made from one piece of bent plywood, was a virtuoso effort that has rightly found a firm place in the history of Modern design. Also appearing to operate largely in isolation was Denham McLaren, a part-time designer who

was inspired by the elegance of French Modernism to produce pieces using plate glass and animal hides.

GRADUAL ACCEPTANCE
After 1935, when the political climate in Germany had become unbearable for many artists, architects, and designers, there was an influx of Bauhaus-trained designers into Great Britain. The most prominent of these was undoubtedly Marcel Breuer, who contributed designs both to Heal's and the newly established Isokon company. Others, such as Egon Riss and Hein Hockroth, also made their mark.

Slowly, the British attitude toward

the Modern style began to relax, and companies such as Morris of Glasgow and PEL (Practical Equipment Limited) began to manufacture furniture in tubular steel and bent plywood. The government promoted the style by publishing "The Production and Exhibition of Articles of Good Design and Everyday Life." The British people knew that the Modern style pointed the way toward the future, but they were nevertheless reluctant to accept it.

Further efforts to encourage the British to embrace Modern design were undertaken by the BBC, which not only commissioned

the forward-thinking Serge Chermayeff and Wells Coates to design their building's interiors, but broadcast discussions on contemporary design. Journals such as *Architectural Review* and *Building News* also reported enthusiastically on the developments in form and materials in countries across Europe. It was to be some time, however, before Great Britain could once again, after the innovations of the Arts and Crafts Movement, boast of being at the forefront of international furniture design.

THE ISOKON FLATS

THE LONDON-BASED ENTREPRENEUR JACK PRITCHARD AND HIS WIFE, MOLLY, GAVE THE CITY OF LONDON ITS FIRST LANDMARK MODERN BUILDING, THE ISOKON FLATS.

Jack and Molly Pritchard were firm believers in Modern design. In 1934 they commissioned the architect Wells Coates to build the defiantly Modern Isokon Flats, on Lawn Road, London. The flats soon became a beacon for those interested in the developments of the Modern style.

In 1935 the Pritchards persuaded Walter Gropius, the leader of the by-then-defunct Bauhaus, to move to London. Gropius became head of a new furniture-manufacturing company. Given the appropriately technical name Isokon (short for Isometric Unit Construction), the company would, it was hoped, teach the British public about the delights of Modern design.

The Pritchards, however, were not entirely confident of their customers' tastes and refused to use tubular steel, seeing it as too avant-garde. Bent plywood became Isokon's signature material, and, when Gropius brought Marcel Breuer to Britain, the man who had pioneered the use of tubular steel was instructed to work only in wood.

Breuer, who was fleeing Germany's Nazi regime, moved into the Isokon Flats in 1936 and soon set about designing

and installing what became known as the Isobar, so that people could have a drink while discussing the finer points of Modern design.

Breuer's Isokon Long Chair (1935–36) is perhaps the most celebrated piece of furniture to emerge from the Isokon factory, although Wells Coates and Egon Riss contributed successfully to the company, too. World War II forced Isokon into hibernation, but Jack Pritchard did revive the company in 1963, and it still survives, under the name of Isokon Plus, to this day.

MODEL Z SIDE TABLE

Designed by Gerald Summers, this piece is fashioned from bent and laminated plywood to form a Z-shaped occasional table. The two table tops are circular, positioned one above and to the left of the other. *c. 1936. H:17½ in (44.5 cm); W:21¾ in (55 cm).*

The Isokon Long Chair Marcel Breuer's chaise longue has a bent-laminated-birch and polished-shellac frame. *1935–36. H:29 in (74 cm); L:54 in (137 cm); W:24 in (61 cm). DOR*

Isokon Flats The building epitomized the Modernist desire for minimal living. The laundry facilities and restaurant made living spaces just that—doing away with cooking and washing areas.

OCCASIONAL TABLE

This two-tier circular-topped occasional table is made of oak and plywood, and the top is laminated with black bakelite. The legs of the two tiers form a continuous loop, creating the effect of one table inside another. The table was manufactured by Heal's. *c. 1932. H:26½ in (66 cm); Diam:24½ in (61 cm).*

UNITED STATES

DESPITE BEING A NATION largely defined by industry, the United States was surprisingly slow to adopt the Modern style in furniture. Indeed, in 1925, when asked by the committee of the Paris *Expositions des Arts Décoratifs et Industriels Modernes* to submit Modern designs for display, the Americans sheepishly admitted that they had nothing to show.

By the start of the 1930s a vogue had developed for streamlining (*see p.398*). This stylistic conceit was the United States' own take on

Modernism and was greeted with great enthusiasm by the American public.

Streamlined furniture was inspired by the trains, planes, cars, and ships that were causing such a stir in American society at the time. These vehicles were designed with curvaceous forms so as to offer less wind resistance; yet it was not the practical principle that appealed to designers, but the futuristic look of these forms of transportation.

Needless to say, many Americans, particularly the intelligentsia, sneered at streamlining. It was seen as a marketing ploy by companies eager to make

their goods appealing during the tough times of the Great Depression.

EUROPEAN INFLUENCES

A new style emerging at this time was the so-called International Style. The term was coined by Henry-Russell Hitchcock and Philip Johnson in their book of the same name. It referred to the austere architecture and design practiced by the likes of Le Corbusier and those associated with the Bauhaus. The Museum of Modern Art in New York City was a particularly active supporter of the International Style,

mounting exhibitions, such as "Machine Art" (1934), that promoted an approach to design that was based more on structural integrity than on formal flourishes and a belief that the form of a piece should be true to the nature of the materials from which it was made.

Meanwhile, designers on the West Coast quietly took on board the ideals of their European counterparts, while still maintaining their own sense of American style. One such designer, based in Los Angeles, was K.E.M. Weber, whose stated aim was to make "comfortable, hygienic, and beautiful furniture inexpensively." Weber's Airline

CHROME ARMCHAIR

The armchair frame is made of tubular chrome. In profile, the arms and legs form a Z shape. The seat cushion and back pad are upholstered in brushed fabric. Designed by Kem Weber for Lloyd. *c. 1930. H:31½ in (79 cm). SDR*

SIDE CHAIR

This side chair has an aluminum frame, which stands on an H-shaped base with hockey-puck feet. It is upholstered in oilcloth. Designed by Warren McArthur. *c. 1930. H:34¼ in (87 cm); W:16¾ in (42.5 cm); D:20 in (51 cm). SDR*

SINGLE-PEDESTAL DESK

The frame of this Warren McArthur single-pedestal desk is made from tubular steel. The rectangular, black-laminate top has a square shelf raised above it to the left-hand side. Below this are three drawers, also in black laminate, with circular pulls. *c. 1930. H:30¼ in (77 cm); W:49 in (124.5 cm); D:24 in (61 cm). SDR*

The circular seat and back add to the formal abstract appeal of the chair.

The color of the walnut wood and the painted metal reflects the brick color of the building for which the desk was designed.

The desk has a built-in lighting tube that illuminates the work surface.

The ribbed structure of the chair and desk is almost architectural.

The two work surface levels apply the cantilever principle.

The wastebasket is removable for easy emptying.

The chair stands on three legs to save space.

JOHNSON WAX 1 AND 2: DESK AND CHAIR

This desk has three wooden tops positioned at different heights and a painted steel structure. There are two drawers, a wastebasket, and two racks in the same color as the structure. The painted steel-tube chair has a tilted backrest, padded seat, and wooden armrests. The three legs terminate in brass feet. It was designed by Frank Lloyd Wright for the Johnson Wax building. *1936–39.*

The drawers swing, rather than slide, open to allow for their curved shape.

chair of 1935 displayed a modest, streamlined look and could be packed flat for easy transport.

Warren McArthur was another Los Angeles–based designer, one whose place in the history of American design was only asserted by academics in the 1980s. McArthur's tubular-steel and aluminum furniture grew from his interest in efficient manufacturing—indeed, so successful was his company that during World War II that he was enlisted to make aluminum seats for

Interior of the Johnson Wax Building Architect and furniture designer Frank Lloyd Wright designed the interior and furnishings of the Johnson Wax administrative building, which is located in Racine, Wisconsin.

bomber planes—although he also had a winning way with form.

A NEW DIRECTION

Also operating outside New York was the architect Frank Lloyd Wright. Although Lloyd Wright remained aloof from much of what was being discussed in the design world at the time, he still cast a long shadow on American furniture. By the 1930s, Lloyd Wright had rejected the heavy Arts and Crafts style that he had favored earlier and moved on to a lighter, sprightlier look. The desks and chairs Lloyd Wright designed for the Johnson Wax building (1936–39)

are a perfect example of his new approach. Like all of Lloyd Wright's furniture, they show an awareness of the function of furniture as a divider of interior space, although there is also a dynamic element that is clearly influenced by the streamlined style.

By 1940, the United States' infatuation with streamlining had waned. A new, organic style was beginning to arise that took more inspiration from Alvar Aalto than from sleek express trains. By the time Charles and Ray Eames began to assert their influence after World War II, the United States had come a long way from the humiliating no-show in Paris in 1925.

THE BUTTERFLY CHAIR

THROUGHOUT THE 20TH CENTURY, DESIGNERS REINVENTED ARCHETYPAL FORMS OF FURNITURE, NONE MORE SUCCESSFUL THAN THE BUTTERFLY CHAIR.

Also known as the A chair, the Hardoy chair, the Sling chair, and the Butterfly chair, the B.K.E. chair is named for its designers: Antonio Bonet, Juan Kurchan, and Jorge Ferrari-Hardoy, three architects who met while working for Le Corbusier.

In 1937, all three left for South America, where they set about updating a collapsible, canvas-and-wood British Army chair patented in the 19th century by J. B. Fenby, an English engineer.

It is unlikely that any of the three ever saw Fenby's chair, but they would have known either the Tripolina chair (a French adaptation) or the US No. 4, which was sold as a camping chair.

Regardless of the model they saw, the three made vital changes to its design: tubular steel replaced wood, making it lighter, and leather replaced canvas. In 1940, the Butterfly went into mass production; by 1945 it had sold millions.

SECTIONAL DAVENPORT

This three-piece sectional davenport has a narrow center section flanked on either side by two slightly wider ones. Essentially rectangular in form, its tubular-steel frame is exposed. The seats are raised from the floor, where the frame

makes an X-shaped support beneath each section. The back, side, and sprung seat cushions are upholstered in skunk skin and black leather. Inspiration must have come from Le Corbusier's *Gran Confort* (see pp.432–33). The piece was designed by Wolfgang Hoffmann. *1936. L:79½ in (202 cm). SDR*

The chair's tension comes only from the force exerted by the sitter's weight.

The leather cover of the chair is slipped onto the steel frame with no additional attachments.

The soft leather of the seat contrasts with the hard steel frame to articulate the simplicity of the chair's construction.

Two loops of bent steel are welded together to form the chair's frame.

The thin steel piping makes the chair appear almost bodiless.

Butterfly chair Designed in 1938, this Knoll Associates chair has a tubular frame and leather seat. *c. 1950s. H:34¼ in (90 cm); W:31 in (80 cm). BonBay*

LOUNGE CHAIR

This is a fine example of a Gilbert Rohde lounge chair. The angular, wooden frame rises vertically from the floor to make the uprights and reaches back horizontally to form the arms of the chair. The chair is upholstered in a dark brown woolen fabric. *H:31½ in (80 cm). SDR*

ITALY

MODERNISM IN ARCHITECTURE and furniture design first emerged in Italy in 1926 under the banner of *Razionalismo*, or Rationalism. Most prominent among the Rationalists, all of whom espoused a functional, pared-down approach to architecture and design, was Gruppo 7, a collective that included Luigi Figini, Gino Pollini, and Giuseppe Terragni.

Mussolini's government, whose rise to power coincided with the emergence of the Rationalists, initially embraced the nascent design style. Gruppo 7's

advocacy of industrial progress, clean living, and moral reform appeared to fit well with the Fascists' own ideals. Indeed, such was the relationship between the Rationalists and the Fascists that in 1934 Giuseppe Terragni completed both the building and the fixtures for the Fascist headquarters in Como, near Milan. Needless to say, the architecture was unremitcingly stark, with equally uncompromising furniture. Employing primarily tubular steel, Terragni

produced a range of tables and chairs that owed much to Marcel Breuer's work at the Bauhaus, although the furniture was more expressive in its lines than Breuer's deliberately anonymous-looking pieces.

THE USE OF TUBULAR STEEL
Italian designers would have seen the tubular-steel designs developed in Germany at the regular Triennial exhibitions, held for the first time in Monza in 1923. Ten years later, the

exhibitions were moved to Milan under the title of International Triennial of Decorative and Modern Industrial Art. The Triennials showcased the latest developments in design from Italy and across Europe. The idea of using tubular steel, which Italian designers first saw in 1930, struck a chord, since Italy was, in the interwar years, suffering a severe wood shortage. Mussolini's hard-line approach to rule had seen the country fall from favor with more liberal governments around

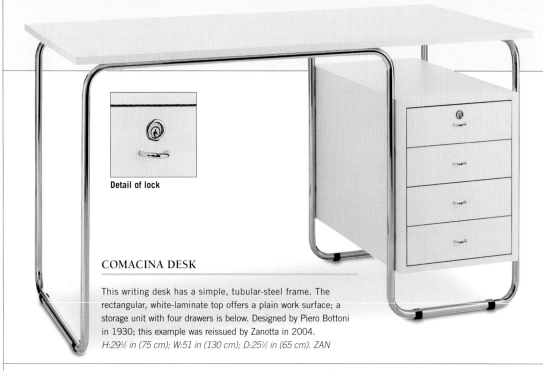

Detail of lock

COMACINA DESK

This writing desk has a simple, tubular-steel frame. The rectangular, white-laminate top offers a plain work surface; a storage unit with four drawers is below. Designed by Piero Bottoni in 1930; this example was reissued by Zanotta in 2004.
H:29½ in (75 cm); W:51 in (130 cm); D:25½ in (65 cm). ZAN

ARMCHAIR

The chair's frame is made from laminated beechwood. On each side, the arm and legs are one continuous loop of wood; joined beneath the seat by a cross-stretcher. The seat has a beech frame with a woven cane seat and back. Designed by Giuseppe Pagano.
1938. H:27⅞ in (71 cm); W:24 in (61 cm); D:26¾ in (68 cm).

OCCASIONAL TABLE

The most striking feature of this side, or occasional, table is its thick plate-glass top, which has a beveled edge. The circular glass table top collects light like a lens, producing a brilliant reflection below. The table top rests on a walnut support from which emerge four splayed legs that taper sharply toward the bottom. The legs are made of lacquered walnut. Designed by Pietro Chiesa, the table was manufactured by Fontana Arte. *c. 1950. H:19 in (48.25 cm); D:26 in (66 cm).*

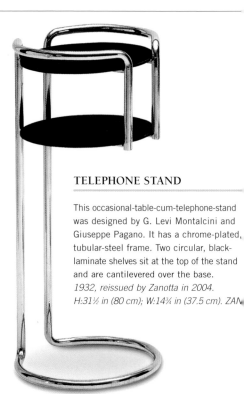

TELEPHONE STAND

This occasional-table-cum-telephone-stand was designed by G. Levi Montalcini and Giuseppe Pagano. It has a chrome-plated, tubular-steel frame. Two circular, black-laminate shelves sit at the top of the stand and are cantilevered over the base. *1932, reissued by Zanotta in 2004. H:31½ in (80 cm); W:14¾ in (37.5 cm). ZAN*

the world, and Italy was suffering under sanctions. As a result, tubular-steel designs by the likes of Terragni, Piero Bottoni, and Gabriele Mucchi were developed during these years, although they rarely met with popular success. Designed as prototypes for mass production, many designs of the era were only produced in significant numbers much later.

The Rationalists eventually fell out with the Fascists after Mussolini deemed their approach "too international"; Mussolini opted to support the Neoclassical style of the *Novecento* group. But where Hitler hounded all Modernist architects and designers from Germany, Mussolini took a far more lenient view. Indeed, the 1930s and 40s was a time in which many of Italy's most celebrated manufacturers and designers got their start. The likes of Cassina and Fontana Arte were not to gain fame until the 1950s, but they put down roots in the interwar period. Although the years 1925–45 were not the most distinguished in Italy's remarkable design history, they certainly paved the way for much of what was to come.

The lounge chair The Modernist era saw many pieces made for sanitoriums. The lounge chair was a favorite, with versions made that could be easily moved from inside to outside or transformed from a seat to a day bed.

Detail of leather straps

Tubular-steel frame

LOUNGE CHAIR

Made from tubular steel and slung fabric, this innovative piece can be used as a chair or a chaise longue, depending on which end it stands (*see above*). Designed by Battista and Gino Guidici. *1935. H:38 in (98 cm); L:45 in (113 cm); W:19½ in (49 cm). WKA*

FOLLIA CHAIR

The black-painted, rectilinear wooden seat and back of this Giuseppe Terragni chair are connected by chrome-plated spring supports. *1934, reissued by Zanotta in 2004. H:31½ in (80 cm); W:19⅝ in (50 cm); D:23⅝ in (60 cm). ZAN*

The cylindrical headrest is strapped to the chair to minimize bulk.

The armrest padding is kept to a bare minimum so as not to disturb the clean lines of the chair.

Simple, black upholstery covers the mattress on the footrest.

Tubular steel is used to form the chair's frame.

Cushioning on the ottoman is strapped to the tubular-steel base, accentuating the contrast of natural and synthetic materials.

The chair's seat appears suspended, giving it a sense of weightlessness.

GENNI LOUNGE CHAIR

This lounge chair's seat sits within a tubular-steel frame and is adjustable, with two positions. The upholstered mattress and headrest match the black elbow rests. The footstool echoes the chair's rectangular frame. It was reissued by Tecta in 2004. *H:32¼ in (82 cm) max.; W:16 in (41 cm); D:43 in (109 cm). Footstool: H:16 in (41 cm); W:17¾ in (45 cm) ; D:21⅔ in (55 cm).*

CHAIRS

AS FURNITURE PRODUCTION steadily shifted emphasis from craft-based manufacturing to industrial methods, the look of the chair changed dramatically. Ornament was doggedly erased from designs as structure became more important to the aesthetic look. Solid wood began to fall from favor (too expensive and inflexible) as molded plywood and tubular steel stepped into the spotlight.

Just as the notion of open-plan space was creeping into Western architecture, furniture was freed from fulfilling just one function. Chairs became increasingly ambiguous, with some made for indoor and outdoor use, and others equally at home in an office or dining room. Chairs became lighter, too, since they were frequently moved around the house.

With mass-production in mind, designers began to concentrate their efforts on fixtures. The aim became

to produce a chair made of a minimum number of components that fitted together easily and quickly. It's no surprise, then, that the cantilever chair became so popular, as the continuous loop of legs and base eradicated the need for numerous nuts and bolts.

While the structure of the chair became increasingly celebrated in its design, as opposed to any stylistic conceits, so the designer as an individual receded into the background. Industry became more important than art, as designers sought to express nothing more romantic than the manufacturing process.

The reason the chair dominated the focus of designers' efforts is because a person's emotional attachment is far greater to a chair than to, say, a shelving unit. If Modernist designers wanted to alter their audience's emotional and intellectual outlook, it was through the chair that they tried to do so.

CLUB CHAIR

The rectilinear frame is made from stained pearwood secured with brass fittings. The chair is upholstered in hand-woven woolen fabric. Peter Keler, Bauhaus Weimar. *1925*. H:27 in (69 cm); W:24½ in (62 cm); D:26¾ in (68 cm). WKA

AALTO-INSPIRED CHAIR

This armchair was inspired by a model made by Alvar Aalto. The chair's seat and back are made from a single sheet of laminated wood and sit within an oak open-arm frame. *H:30 in (76 cm) CA* **1**

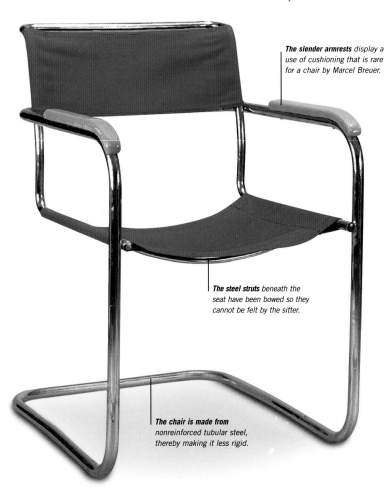

The slender armrests display a use of cushioning that is rare for a chair by Marcel Breuer.

The steel struts beneath the seat have been bowed so they cannot be felt by the sitter.

The chair is made from nonreinforced tubular steel, thereby making it less rigid.

EASY CHAIR

This easy chair comprises a series of square-section planks of pine, joined by wooden dowels. It has a slatted section on both seat and chair back. Designed by Hein Stolle. *c.1930. BonBay* **2**

LANDI CHAIR

Lightweight and durable, this stacking chair is made from pressed and bent aluminum. Each armrest and pair of legs is from one piece of aluminum. Hans Coray. *1938*. H: 29 in (76 cm); W:19 in (51 cm); D:21 in (55 cm). BonBay **2**

B34 CHAIR WITH ARMS

The frame of this cantilever chair is made from one continuous loop of tubular steel. Although the base looks as though it is all in contact with the floor, the side pieces bend slightly so that only the corners touch the floor—the idea

being that most floors are slightly uneven and the smallest change in level would make the chair wobble. This chair has arms with elbow supports, and a blue canvas seat and back. Designed by Marcel Breuer and produced by Thonet. *1928.* H:33½ in (85 cm); W:22⅖ in (57.5 cm); D:24¾ in (63 cm). Qu **1**

SIDE CHAIR

The seat and back of this early cantilevered chair are made of ebonized molded plywood and sit on a chrome-plated tubular-steel frame. The armrests are ebonized beech. Mart Stam for Thonet. *c. 1930. BonBay* **2**

ZIGZAG CHAIR

One of a pair, this chair has a tubular-steel frame reminiscent of Rietveld's Zigzag chair. The wooden seat is supported on steel rods and has a later vinyl cover. H: 32½ in (82.5 cm); W:16⅓ in (41.5 cm); D:25 in (63.5 cm). Qu **1**

LOUNGE CHAIR

One of a pair, this armchair has a tubular-chrome frame and seat with cushions upholstered in a dark brown, brushed fabric with red trim. The armrests are black-enameled. *H:34 in (86.5 cm). SDR* **1**

CANTILEVERED ARMCHAIR

Designed by Gilbert Rohde, this cantilevered armchair has a bright chrome base and black laminated armrests. The cushions are upholstered in ivory leather with a black trim. *H:37 in (94 cm). SDR* **1**

FREE SWINGER ARMCHAIR

The base of this chromed-steel cantilevered armchair from Austria is the only part of the structure that is exposed. The chair seat and back are filled with down and upholstered in sand-colored velour. *H:33½ in (84 cm). DOR* **3**

LAMINATED LOUNGE CHAIR

This chair has been made from one sheet of cut and molded laminated birch and resembles the Gerald Summers classic *(see p.438)*. The arms are fixed to the back with metal brackets. Hans Pieck. *1944. H:30 in (76 cm). BonBay* **4**

THE STACKING CHAIR

STILL FOUND IN CAFÉS WORLDWIDE, THIS ICONIC DESIGN IS PERHAPS THE FIRST STACKING CHAIR, AND CERTAINLY THE FIRST WIDESPREAD DESIGN, OF ITS KIND.

The origins of this chair, despite the efforts of numerous historians, have proved murky at best. The design is most likely to have been developed in France some time around 1925, specifically for the country's booming café culture. The chair bears a strong, albeit rather crude, resemblance to chairs designed by Emile-Jacques Ruhlmann, although it's doubtful whether the French high-society designer ever had a hand in its conception.

What is perhaps most impressive about the chair, apart from its stackability, is its economy of materials. The steel used is incredibly thin and, to give the legs rigidity, the steel has been subtly curved. To save further on metal, holes have been cut from the seat back. While the perfect low-cost, space-saving chair was to become something of a holy grail for 20th-century furniture designers, few ever bettered the chair design that first set the ball rolling.

BAUHAUS ARMCHAIR

This chair was designed by Erich Dieckmann for the Weimer Bauhaus, in collaboration with Ernst Mayo. Made from solid beech, it has a bowed back and slatted seat. *c. 1930. H:32½ in (81.5 cm); W:21 in (52.5 cm). WKA*

DINING CHAIR

This is one of a pair of stacking birch plywood dining chairs that were produced by Artek. The chair has a circular wooden seat and a pierced plywood back, supported on L-shaped plywood uprights. *c.1930s.*

The so-called Bistro chairs These have a pressed-steel frame and are painted red; with plywood seats. *c. 1926. H:32¼ in (82 cm). DOR* **3**

DIAGONAL CHAIR

This chrome-plated, tubular-steel chair is named after the supports between the seat back and legs. The arms, seat, and back are of laminated wood. W. H. Gispen. *c. 1927. H:32½ in (82.5 cm); W:21¼ in (54 cm). QU* **2**

SLATTED CHAIR

This Viennese chair has a tubular-steel frame and solid, stained-beech wooden slats for the seat and back. The arms have wooden armrests. One of a set of four. *1925. H:33¼ in (84.5 cm). DOR* **3**

TABLES

AS WITH MOST FORMS of furniture during the interwar period, tables were subjected to a radical process of reduction. All details deemed superfluous were stripped away to leave what designers considered to be a pure, practical form.

Marcel Breuer, the Hungarian-born student-turned-teacher at the Bauhaus, was the designer who most successfully achieved the desired, pared-down look. Utilizing tubular steel, a material that he is said to have borrowed from the bicycle-making industry, he produced tables that expressed little beyond their own function.

Eileen Gray's tubular-steel and glass side tables, now known as the E1027 tables in reference to the house for which she designed them, may not be as rudimentary as Breuer's tables, but they display more invention. The tops of the tables can be adjusted to sit at differing heights, and the table's stem

is placed at the side to allow the table top to come over an item of furniture (which, in Gray's case, was her own bed). Such versatility was to become a key feature in table design of the Modern era.

Since many designers in the interwar years were reacting to the excesses of the Art Nouveau style, most table tops were either a simple, unadorned circle or square. It wasn't until after World War II, with the advent of a more organic style, that this strict design principle was relaxed and irregular shapes came into use.

Glass, plywood, and tubular steel were always considered the most cutting-edge materials from which to make tables (due to their close association with industry), although some designers did use solid wood. If this was used, it was considered important to avoid all efforts to carve or decorate it, thereby keeping its surface as clean to the eye as possible.

GLASS DINING TABLE

Made of tubular steel, the frame of this table consists of a rectilinear base. At the top, at each end of the table, is a semicircular support for the glass table top that interlocks with the base. There are rubber pads on the supports, where they come into contact with the table top, to cushion the glass and prevent slippage. The glass top has been ground at the corners to produce smooth curves. Attributed to Emile Guillot and produced by Thonet, Paris. *1930. H:31¼ in (79 cm); W:47½ in (120.5 cm); D:28½ in (72.5 cm). WKA* **4**

BLACK-ENAMELED TABLE

The chrome-plated tubular-steel frame of this dining table offers a support for the black-enameled rectangular table top, before dropping to the floor in each corner to form the legs. Each leg is made from two parallel lengths of steel. As the legs reach the floor, they join in the center to form one single length of tubular steel below the table top. Designed by Wolfgang Hoffmann for Howell. *W:58 in (147.5 cm). SDR* **1**

The black-painted tops hide the wood grain and give the tables an industrial look.

The tables "nest" so as to save space in small apartments.

Chrome plating gives the tubular steel an alluring gleam.

NESTING TABLES

This series of four nesting tables fits neatly, one above the next, in a stack. They all have the same depth, but increase in width and height as they grow in size. Each table has a simple, rectilinear, chrome-plated tubular-steel frame and a black-painted wooden top. The top sits flush with the table frame. Designed by Marcel Breuer at Bauhaus Dessau in 1925–26, it is thought that they were initially designed as stools. This example was reissued by Tecta in 2004. *Largest table: H:23½ in (60 cm); W:26 in (66 cm); D:15 in (38 cm). TEC* **2**

EXTENSION DINING TABLE

This extension dining table was made in the US. The simple, straightforward design consists of a plain, rectangular wooden top with two pull-out leaves. The leaves, which are concealed underneath the table top, increase the table's width by 18 in (45 cm) on each side when extended. The top rests on a trestle base that ends in tubular-steel stretchers and bracket feet. Designed by Gilbert Rohde. *Closed: W:60 in (152.5 cm). SDR* **2**

SUNSHADE TABLE

This two-tiered end table is one of a pair. Each black laminate table top has a chrome trim. The smaller, top table sits flush with the tubular-steel frame, and the larger, bottom table is supported by the table base and legs. Designed by Gilbert Rohde for Troy. *W:17¾ in (45.5 cm). SDR* **1**

MODEL 91 TABLE

The rectangular top of this table is made from unlimed oak and has a black-linoleum surface. The corners have been slightly rounded. The table top rests on four rigid, chrome-plated tubular-steel legs. Designed by Marcel Breuer for Embru. *c.1933. W:48 in (120 cm). DOR* **4**

PALADAO DINING TABLE

This flip-top, wooden dining table has a simple rectangular top with rounded corners. It has two additional leaves for extending the table size and a fifth leg for extra support. The legs taper sharply as they reach the floor. Designed by Gilbert Rohde for Herman Miller. *H:36 in (91.5 cm). SDR* **1**

E1027 SIDE TABLES

These side tables are made from chrome-plated tubular steel, where the table's stand is placed to one side and can be adjusted to raise or lower the height of the circular glass table top to suit a range of purposes. Designed by Eileen Gray. *c. 1927. D:20 in (51 cm). DOR* **1**

CAFE TABLE

The square top of this table has a black-linoleum surface with a riveted, plate-steel surround. It rests on four chrome-plated tubular-steel legs, which bend to meet each other in the center above an X-shaped, tubular-steel base. The linoleum top is new. Produced by Thonet Mundus. *c. 1930. H:29½ in (75 cm). DOR* **3**

GAMES TABLE

The square, orange-laminate table top rests on a chrome-plated brass base. The base hinges in the center, making the table collapsible. At each corner is a swivel plate for holding a glass. Designed by Boris Lacroix. *c. 1930. H:27½ in (70 cm). DOR* **3**

BEECH SIDE TABLE

Designed and manufactured in Sweden, this small side or occasional table has a circular, white-laminate top above three bent-beech legs. The legs taper slightly as they reach the floor. Designed by Bruno Mathsson. *1936. D:17½ in (44.5 cm). SDR* **3**

ROSEWOOD CART

The circular, rosewood top of this cart table has hinged sides and rests on a chromium tripod base. The front wheels are also made from rosewood. The caster at the rear of the table is used to stabilize the cart. *H:22¼ in (56.5 cm); D:31½ in (80 cm). L&T*

BAUHAUS SOFA TABLE

The table's frame consists of a rectilinear, nickel-plated tubular-steel base, with a rectangle of tubular steel suspended below the circular, plate-glass table top. Designed by Marcel Breuer in 1929 and produced by Thonet. This example is a Tecta reissue from 2004. *H:23⅜ in (60 cm); D:31½ in (80 cm). TEC* **2**

MID-CENTURY MODERN
1945-1970

OPTIMISM AND WEALTH

IN THE AFTERMATH OF WORLD WAR II, THE UNITED STATES AND MUCH OF EUROPE EXPERIENCED NEW PROSPERITY AND OPTIMISM, WHICH FUELED THE GROWTH IN CONSUMERISM AND YOUTH CULTURE.

Pierre Paulin Tulip footstool This used new materials: the seat cove is vinyl and the base molded steel. *1965. W:29 in (73.5 cm).* FRE

THE PERIOD BETWEEN the end of World War II and the early 1960s was, on the whole, characterized by optimism and prosperity. Leading this boom was the United States, a country that had remained relatively unscathed during the war and would soon emerge as the world's dominant nation, not only economically but also culturally. Quick to fall in step behind the United States were many European countries, for whom the 1950s and 1960s were also an era of unprecedented progress.

In the immediate aftermath of the war, however, most nations were occupied with regeneration. A quiet desire to return to a normal way of life dominated, so that the late 1940s became a time of relative sobriety, as trade partnerships were gradually reestablished and industries rekindled.

The United States recovered from the ravages of war more quickly than most, and by the beginning of the 1950s its factories were achieving record levels of productivity, while technological innovations such as color television were helping to foster a sense of opportunity. It was in this atmosphere that artists such as Alexander Calder, Jackson Pollock, and Willem de Kooning established new forms of art, while Charles Eames and Eero Saarinen took the design world by storm. The United States, it seemed, was making its presence felt.

Between 1948 and 1951, with the introduction of the Marshall Plan, the United States used its considerable financial muscle to assist Europe in recovering from the war. This influx into Europe of nearly $13 billion dollars (close to $100 billion at present-day conversion rates) was the catalyst that many European nations needed to regain economic confidence. Italy, in particular, went on to enjoy a period of sustained industrial growth throughout the 1950s, while other nations, notably Germany and France, also prospered.

As the era of wartime frugality receded, a new consumer society bloomed in its place. Across the globe, buyers were beginning to demand greater choice, a trend that was stimulated by the growth of the mass media. The 1950s was the era that saw the explosion of youth culture, as a younger generation began to feel increasingly alienated from their elders. By 1961, when the first man orbited Earth in a spaceship, it was clear that a new age had begun.

John F. Kennedy, the youngest man ever to be elected president of the United States, seemed to symbolize this shift in the balance of power toward a new, forward-looking generation. Music, fashion, and furniture design of the time, not only in the United States but also across Europe, expressed an urgent mood of vitality.

By the end of the decade, however, cracks in this exciting culture were beginning to appear. President Kennedy was assassinated in 1963, the United States' involvement in the war in Vietnam was escalating out of control, crime rates were rising, and the realization was gradually dawning that many of the recreational drugs being used were not as harmless as was previously thought.

The heady feeling of liberation that had so characterized the 1950s and the early 1960s was fading, and an atmosphere of bitterness and resentment was slowly taking its place. Tensions flared up in many cities across the world—most notably in Paris during the riots of 1968—as the generation who had been raised during the prosperous years of the 1950s realized that much of their unfettered idealism had been misplaced.

The Kaufmann Desert House, Palm Springs, California Constructed of a series of horizontal planes that appear to float over glass walls, this is regarded as one of the finest examples of a Mid-Century Modern house in the United States. By Richard Neutra. *1946.*

TIMELINE 1945–1970

Cover of *Domus* magazine

1945 *Arts & Architecture* launches Case Study House. Designs by architects such as Richard Neutra and Pierre Koenig become icons.

1948 Gio Ponti edits *Domus*, the forum for debate on Modernist design.

Charles and Ray Eames design a molded-plastic armchair; it follows their innovations with plywood and precedes those with aluminum. The Museum of Modern Art (MoMA) organize International Competition for Low-Cost Furniture.

1949 R. Buckminster Fuller creates his strong, lightweight, low-cost geodesic dome.

1950 First MoMA Good

Design exhibition. *Hochschule für Gestaltung* opens in Ulm, Germany; it becomes the center for design education in Europe.

1951 Italian manufacturer Kartell introduces mass-produced plastic homewares. Black and White TV is widely available. Festival of Britain is held between May and September; the focus of the nationwide event is London.

Buckminster Fuller's Geodesic dome

1953 Osvaldo Borsani founds Tecno in Milan, producing luxurious furniture with an industrial aesthetic. Boeing 707, a military aircraft, is redesigned for civilian use. Air travel becomes more common.

1954 *Compasso D'Oro* launched by *La Rinascente* stores.

Interior of the Kaufman Desert House, Palm Springs
The interiors of the Kaufman House in California reflected the trends of the time in their use of wood, built-in furniture, and abstract patterns on the furnishing. A desert color palette is used throughout the interior, as well as the exterior. Designed by Richard Neutra. *1946.*

The Low Armchair Rod (LAR) chair This chair, by Charles and Ray Eames for The Herman Miller Furniture Company, has a fiberglass-reinforced, molded-plastic seat raised on a bent-wire frame. The American couple produced many iconic pieces in new materials. *1950. H:24 in (61 cm); W:24¾ in (63 cm); D:25¼ in (64 cm). WKA*

1955 Arne Jacobsen designs the hugely successful Series 7 chair.

1956 Alison and Peter Smithson's House of the Future designed for the "Ideal Homes" show in Britain.

1950s Bakelite television

1957 Achille and Pier Giacomo Castiglioni design the Sella stool, which uses a bicycle seat. The design predates the Pop designs of the next decade. The USSR launches

Sputnik, the first artificial satellite.

1958 Isamu Kenmochi's Rattan chair becomes the first Modern Japanese item of furniture to become popular in the West.

1959 The Mini, by Alec Issigonis, is

Arne Jacobsen's Series 7 chair

introduced. It is the first small-scale car to become a resounding success.

1962 André Courrèges designs the miniskirt.

1964 Herman Miller Furniture Company launches the Action Office furniture system by George Nelson and Robert Propst. Terence Conran opens Habitat, which carries European designs, in London.

1965 Cassina begin the *I Maestri* range, the first collection of Modernist reproductions.

1959 Austin Mini

1966 Archizoom and Superstudio founded in Florence, ushering in an intellectual, art-oriented approach to Italian design.

1968 Verner Panton presents color-saturated room sets at *Visiona* in Cologne.

1969 First human on the Moon.

MID-CENTURY MODERN FURNITURE

WORLD WAR II HALTED the development of furniture design. While some designers were in active service, others were in hiding, and many more were occupied with the war effort at home. For this reason, coupled with the prevailing sobriety of the post-war years, it was the pre-1945 Rational style that once again assumed center stage after the war.

There were, however, significant changes to what drove the post-war furniture industry, most of which stemmed from newly available manufacturing techniques. Pioneered for military purposes, most often by aircraft designers, processes such as aluminum-casting and innovative ways of bonding wood were embraced by designers and manufacturers.

RATIONALISM ON THE WANE
The increased scope that new techniques afforded designers soon led to a relaxation of the principles of Rationalism. The early work of American designers Charles and Ray Eames, for instance, clearly shows

that a looser, sculptural style—influenced by sculptors such as Constantin Brancusi—was emerging. The Eameses developed a technique for molding plywood in two directions—a method used in leg splints for injured servicemen during the war—and this lent their furniture an unprecedented three-dimensionality.

Of unparalleled popularity in the early 1950s—although Charles and Ray Eames' work was also well received—was Scandinavian furniture. In the 1930s, designers such as Alvar Aalto and Bruno Matthson had developed Soft Modernism, an aesthetic that was maintained in the post-war years. This gentle, ergonomically informed take on the severe look of Modernism struck a chord with both designers and consumers looking for comfort after the experiences of the war.

By the mid-1950s, many countries were experiencing a return to economic prosperity, which resulted in a welcome wave of optimism. It was in this atmosphere that the more extreme elements of the Rational style were phased out, as designers rebelled against the sober approach of previous generations.

This trend was most marked in Italy, where designers such as Gio Ponti and Carlo di Carli added a sensuous element to furniture design not seen since the heyday of Art Nouveau. In Britain, Alison and Peter Smithson presented their House of the Future (1956), a structure filled with (mostly fitted) furniture that was inspired as much by fantasy as by reality.

PLANNED OBSOLESCENCE
By the 1960s, a new spirit had overtaken the furniture industry. Many designers scrapped the ideal of making timeless designs and began creating work made for the moment. The concept of built-in obsolescence, which had emerged in the United States in the 1930s, resurfaced, as furniture with a limited lifespan was seen as making good economic sense.

Walnut sideboard This piece has a free-edge top above two sliding, spindle-front doors with pandanus cloth backing. Inside the sideboard are two interior shelves and four drawers. The case stands on a cross-plank base. Designed by George Nakashima (US). *H:77¼ in (197 cm). SDR*

Disposable furniture became a major craze, as did furniture in bright, attention-grabbing colors and shapes—often inspired by advertising. Early forms of plastic also allowed designers to experiment with new and daring shapes. At the forefront of this change was Italy, a nation giddy with its own economic success and willing to entertain radical ideas concerning furniture design and manufacturing.

Beneath all these new, seemingly spontaneous, explorations in material and form remained a strong underlying desire to make furniture that was both functional and articulate. Designers, in other words, still considered the comfort and desires of their users. This was to change as the 1960s wore on.

Anti-design was a term first used in Italy to describe the furniture being made by the likes of Superstudio and Archizoom. Disillusioned with what they perceived as a pervading culture of excess, many designers of the late 1960s made furniture that was deliberately awkward to use and look at. Shunning the Functionalism that had been in vogue since the 1920s, they made furniture that mocked the high-mindedness of Modernism. This antagonistic attitude, which grew as the economic and political outlook of Europe and the United States worsened, eventually developed into what we now call Postmodernism.

Egg chair This armchair is a good example of the trend for a more sculptural look and feel that characterizes many pieces from this period. The chair has a padded-leather seat and back over a fiberglass frame and is supported on an aluminum, star-shaped base. Designed by Arne Jacobsen for Fritz Hansen, Denmark. *1958. Bk*

PORTABLE TUBE CHAIR

Joe Colombo's innovative Tube chair consists of four polyurethane-foam-covered cylinders and six steel-and-rubber joints. Sold in a drawstring bag, the chair's components could be assembled any way the user chose. Made in 1969, the chair is a striking example of the rebellion against existing typologies of furniture design that occurred in the 1960s. Although he found an admirably logical solution to the problem of transporting furniture, Colombo appears to have been more concerned with creating a visually iconoclastic design than with providing comfortable seating.

Tube chair The four tubes that make up the chair are of arcipiuma plastic covered in foam and upholstered in vinyl. They fit within each other and come packaged in a duffel bag. Using a number of steel-and-rubber points, the user can make a range of different chairs to suit his or her needs. *1969. H:24 in (61 cm); W:24 in (61 cm); D:44 in (120 cm). WKA*

Duffel carrier bag Each tube component of this chair fits within the next one up in size, the whole being neatly packaged in a drawstring bag. *WKA*

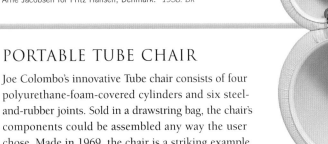

ALL-IN-ONE DESK

Produced in 1948 by The Herman Miller Furniture Company in Zeeland, Michigan, George Nelson's Home Office desk is a typical piece of Mid-Century Modern design, and the type of furniture design coming out of the United States at that time.

The lightweight look of Nelson's desk is achieved by raising much of the visual bulk of the object above the desk's thin, tubular-steel legs. The use of tubular steel, and the complete absence of surface decoration on the desk, illustrates the influence on Nelson of a previous generation of Modernist designers such as Marcel Breuer and Ludwig Mies van der Rohe.

NEW USE OF MATERIALS

Unlike the work of earlier Modernist designers, however, Nelson's desk differs in that it displays an eclectic use of both materials and form. Stylistic details such as the walnut veneer, the imitation-leather sliding doors, the beveled facade of the upper storage unit, and the splayed legs of the desk show how the purist attitude prevalent in the interwar years had begun to soften. The use of color, too, is further proof that designers such as Nelson were becoming more playful in their designs as they attempted to reflect the upbeat mood of the era.

Nelson's endeavors to incorporate a drawer, a shelving unit, a retractable wastepaper bin, a typewriter cabinet, and a desktop into a single piece of visually exciting furniture is emblematic of the progressive, can-do attitude that was a characteristic of much of American furniture design of the post-war years.

Home Office desk This writing desk has a hinged, walnut-veneer writing surface, below which is an aluminum wastepaper bin to one side and a typewriter cabinet to the other. Above the desktop are two sliding doors, each of which opens on to additional storage space. Designed by George Nelson for The Herman Miller Furniture Company. *1948.* H:41 in (103 cm); W:54¼ in (137 cm); D:28½ in (71 cm). QU

The doors slide open and shut neatly, rather than swinging open awkwardly.

Thin steel rods separate the upper storage unit from the desktop, lending the former a look of weightlessness.

The mustard-colored imitation leather adds further levity to the look of the desk.

The facade of the upper storage unit is beveled to add to the dynamism of the unit's appearance.

The walnut-veneered drawer appears to be suspended but is, in fact, supported by the tubular-steel legs.

The use of tubular steel maintains continuity with designs of the interwar years.

The desk's tubular-steel legs are splayed to increase the desk's sturdiness and give it a more informal appearance.

Perforations in the detachable aluminum container give it a lightweight look and distinguish it as a wastepaper basket.

ELEMENTS OF STYLE

After the austerity of the interwar years, a much more fleshed-out form of Modernism characterized furniture design in the late 1940s, the 1950s, and the 1960s. Reflecting the optimism of the era, as well as the greater variety of available materials and manufacturing techniques, furniture assumed a more playful appearance. The introduction of plastics and foam padding in the late 1950s took Modernism even farther from its Rationalist roots, as new colors and forms dictated new designs. By the end of the 1960s, the idea of Functionalism that had previously dominated 20th-century design was dying a very visible death, as designers overlooked practicality in favor of more experimental ideas.

Detail of wire table base

Metal-rod construction

The availability of increasingly narrow and lighter gauges of steel brought about a refinement in the use of metal in furniture design. Designers such as Harry Bertoia and Warren Platner produced lightweight wire furniture that was in keeping with the principles of Modernism: the exposed structure of metal-rod furniture provided the essence of its visual appeal.

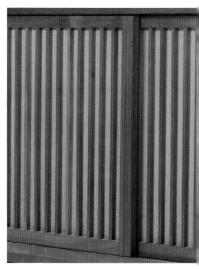

Japanese-inspired door front

Japanese influences

As international travel became easier and more commonplace during the late 1940s and early 1950s, design was opened up to new influences that had previously had little impact on Modernism. Of particular appeal to designers who adhered to the Modern aesthetic were the traditions of simplicity and clarity found in Japanese design.

Valet chair

Form and function

Designers of the 1940s and 1950s embraced many of the ideals of the Modernists, not least the idea that form should follow function. The form of this Hans Wegner chair relates to its function, the outstretched arms of the chair back mirroring those of the human form.

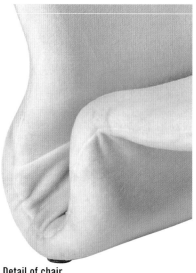

Detail of chair

Stretch fabrics

The development of new, elastic types of fabric allowed furniture designers of the 1960s to explore new forms. Most significantly, these fabrics allowed designers to stretch material over internal frameworks to create shapes that were no longer dictated by an object's structure. The clinging qualities of these new fabrics also did away with the need for upholstery.

Close-up of light fitting

Bold colors

As the purist tendencies that defined early Modernism ebbed away, designers began to use color to draw attention to their work. Although painted wood was still rejected (as too superficial), designers in the 1950s did use brilliantly colored upholstery. The introduction of plastics opened up new opportunities for the use of color, which many designers eagerly exploited.

Molded plastic table

Plastics
During the oil glut of the 1950s and 1960s, petroleum-based plastics became readily available and inexpensive materials for designers to use. It was only in the mid-1960s, however, that plastic furniture really took off, as designers made full use of new forms that could now be achieved by molding with these malleable new materials.

Detail of splayed-leg table

Splayed legs
In an attempt to distinguish their designs from the rigid creations of the Modernists, many furniture designers of the 1950s used splayed legs for their furniture. This stylistic detail, particularly prevalent among Italian furniture designs, gave desks, tables, and chairs an almost languid appearance that reflected the more relaxed mood of the post-war period.

Close-up of curved chair seat

Seats for slouching
The explosion of youth culture in the 1950s provoked an informal attitude in Western societies that was expressed in the way people sat. Younger generations no longer wanted to sit bolt upright, as their parents had encouraged them to do, and so started to slouch in their seats. Designers responded by creating chairs that users could drape themselves over comfortably.

Detail of abstract table base

Organic forms
New techniques for molding plywood and the availability of thinner, more malleable rods of steel encouraged a rash of shapely forms in post-war furniture design. Also influenced by the art of the Surrealists and the Abstract Expressionists, as well as the amoebic shapes associated with science, designers made pieces that were increasingly sculptural in form.

Detail of chair seat and back

Molded plywood
Although bent plywood had become popular in furniture design in the interwar years, it was only in the 1940s that a technique for flexing the material in more than one direction was perfected. Charles Eames and Eero Saarinen worked together to become early pioneers of molded plywood furniture, developing a style that used complex curves.

Aluminum wastepaper basket

Aluminum
This versatile material was widely used in the interiors of military transport vehicles, particularly in fighter planes, during World War II. Aluminum was in abundant supply during the 1940s and 1950s. Favored by designers because it is both durable and lightweight, aluminum was a commonly used material in post-war furniture design.

Linear shelving

Horizontal lines
As lifestyles became ever more informal during the post-war years, designers echoed this trend in their furniture using long, horizontal lines. The more relaxed look this gave the furniture they created was embraced by a young buying public eager to forget the stiff, unyielding style of domestic design that they had grown up with.

Foam-rubber cushions

Padding
Rubber padding was pioneered in Italy in the 1950s as an offshoot of the tire industry, while foam padding was developed at around the same time in Scandinavia. Produced by steaming polystyrene beads, which transformed into a foam under heat, the resulting substance could be applied to a framework and molded into whatever shape was required.

CHARLES AND RAY EAMES

REVOLUTIONIZING FURNITURE DESIGN WITH THEIR INNOVATIVE USE OF MATERIALS, THE EAMESES PRODUCED TIMELESS CLASSICS.

FEW NAMES LOOM larger in 20th-century furniture design than Charles and Ray Eames. This American husband and wife team, one an architect and former draftsman, the other an abstract expressionist painter, produced work that perfectly and eloquently expressed Modernism's aim of marrying industry and art. In the years between their meeting in 1940, at the Cranbrook Academy of Art in Michigan, and Charles's death in 1978, the couple revolutionized furniture design with pieces that are, with few exceptions, still top sellers.

NOVEL USE OF MATERIALS

The materials used in Charles and Ray Eames' furniture reveal their mission of "getting the most of the best to the greatest number of people for the least amount of money," which is why they turned to molded plywood, plastic, fiberglass, and aluminum. These materials were distinguished by their flexibility, affordability, and freshness.

Although Eames furniture is now considered timeless, the couple were ruthless innovators. It was a new technique for molding plywood (developed by Charles and Eero Saarinen) that set them on the path to dominating mid-century American design. Many designers had used molded plywood before, but none had been able to bend it in more than one direction.

A year after meeting, Charles and Ray moved to California to start the now-legendary Eames Office. Their first successful design was an unusual one— a leg splint, made from molded plywood and developed for the US Navy in 1942. Their careers took off when they embarked, in 1947, on a lifelong collaboration with the Herman Miller Furniture Company.

In the 1950s, Charles was at the helm of the Eames Office. He met with clients, developed concepts, and kept an eagle eye on the studio. Ray spent her time sourcing pictures, fabric swatches, and materials to inspire designs. If Charles was the technical obsessive, Ray's input was broader.

THE EAMES STYLE

Although they kept up with furniture developments, Charles and Ray Eames looked beyond their discipline for ideas. Their approach was nondogmatic; design was "a plan for arranging elements in such a way as to best accomplish a particular purpose." The roots of their democratic ideas can be traced to the Arts and Crafts Movement (*see pp.330-31; pp.336-37*), although

ESU-420N STORAGE UNIT
This storage unit is an early design by Charles and Ray Eames. The panels at the front are in beige, gray, black, and white masonite and fiberglass. The whole is supported on a steel frame in black. Made by the Herman Miller Furniture Company. c. 1951. H:58½ in (148.5 cm); W:47 in (119.5 cm); D:16 in (40.75 cm). R20

LAR (LOW ARMCHAIR ROD) CHAIR
The chair's seat is made from molded, fiberglass-reinforced polyester and is raised on a painted, steel-rod base. Manufactured by the Herman Miller Furniture Company. 1950. H:24 in (61 cm); W:24⅞ in (63 cm); D:25¼ in (64 cm). WKA

ROSEWOOD TABLE
In keeping with Charles and Ray Eames' desire to make multipurpose furniture, this table was sold as both a conference table and a dining table. It has a rosewood top and is raised on two chrome-plated steel columns terminating in splayed legs. The columns are joined by a flat stretcher. Manufactured by the Herman Miller Furniture Company. c. 1955. W:38 in (98 cm). SDR

CRANBROOK ACADEMY OF ART

A PROGRESSIVE ACADEMY THAT ENCOURAGED EXPERIMENTATION,
CRANBROOK DEEPLY INFLUENCED MODERN AMERICAN DESIGN.

Established in 1932, the Cranbrook Academy of Art turned out impressive graduates, including Charles and Ray Eames, Eero Saarinen, Harry Bertoia, David Rowland, Florence Knoll, and many others who were to make major contributions to Modern American furniture design.

The academy was founded by George and Ellen Booth. Both believed in the union of spiritual and artistic pursuits and spent considerable time and money developing an academic community in Bloomfield Hills, Michigan, that survives to this day.

Cranbrook was first led by the Finnish architect Eliel Saarinen. Visiting lecturers included Le Corbusier and Frank Lloyd Wright. Saarinen also invited Charles Eames to study there, and Eames soon became a tutor.

Experimentation was encouraged, especially between disciplines. In 1940, Charles Eames and Eero Saarinen submitted molded plywood designs to the Organic Design in Home Furnishing competition hosted by MoMA in New York and, to their great surprise, won. The victory marked their arrival into the world of American design.

The winning chair design Submitted by Charles Eames and Eero Saarinen for the Organic Design in Home Furnishing competition sponsored by MoMA, the chair has a molded-plywood frame covered in foam rubber and upholstered in red fabric. The splayed legs are in wood. It was designed in 1940.

Charles Eames (center) in the studio of the Cranbrook Academy of Art Having trained and worked as an architect, Charles came to Cranbrook to study and then went on to become a design instructor from 1939 to 1940. Ray studied weaving, ceramics, and metalwork at the academy. This photograph of Charles was taken in 1940.

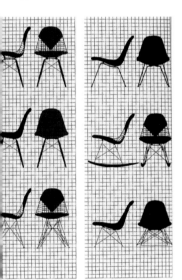

VERSATILE DESIGNS

The designs of Charles and Ray Eames displayed an unprecedented versatility. The same chair base design could be modified to become a rocking chair or a stacking chair, and could have seats made from a number of materials, including molded plywood and fiberglass-reinforced plastic.

LOUNGE CHAIR 670

The Eameses' interpretation of the English club chair is made up of three laminated-wood shells, which are attached to the metal frame. Each shell has a detachable, soft leather-upholstered cushion. The chair was (and still is) available with a matching ottoman. This original example is rosewood. Although no longer made in rosewood, the chair is still available in cherry and walnut. Made by the Herman Miller Furniture Company.

c. 1956. W:35 in (88 cm). DOR

the couple also admired Japanese architecture and Scandinavian design. Architects Mies van der Rohe and Le Corbusier also played a part in forming the Eames style.

Charles and Ray, who witnessed the Depression, were economical with materials, but never ignored comfort. Their Lounge Chair (1956) is perhaps the most convincing expression of comfort achieved by any seating design of the 20th century.

AN OPEN APPROACH TO DESIGN

Apart from furniture, Charles and Ray Eames also designed exhibitions and film sets. "What are the boundaries of design?" Charles was once asked, to which he replied, "What are the boundaries of problems?". This open approach to design was epitomized by their home near Santa Monica, California. Designed by Charles, Ray, and Eero Saarinen, the modular structure was intended to almost disappear; the aim was to accentuate the nature outside and the space within. Showcased in international magazines, it became the symbol of a new, unencumbered way of life.

It is easy to see why Charles and Ray Eames achieved iconic status. Their work was undertaken at a time before cynicism took hold, and optimism and invention pervade their designs. Ultimately, though, it was their ability to balance pragmatism and poetry that won them such an army of fans.

THE UNITED STATES

DURING THE FIRST half of the 20th century, the United States could rarely be described as being at the forefront of furniture design. By 1951, however, the British critic H. M. Dunnett was writing that there was "more evidence of a Modern Movement in America than there has been for 20 years." Dunnett went on to note that "contemporary designs in all sorts of materials and combinations have appeared. Solid wood, plywood, laminated wood and fabric, tube and solid steel, aluminum alloys, glass, Perspex [Plexiglas], and other plastics have all been used in a variety of ways [by American designers] to produce new forms."

EMBRACING MODERNITY
The United States' transformation from laggard to leading light in furniture design can be attributed to a fortuitous combination of factors, the most obvious of which was the country's unrivaled wealth. Suffering nothing like the devastation seen in Europe during the two world wars, US industrial infrastructure remained robust throughout the 1930s and 1940s. This background of economic success fueled a sense of self-belief, giving confidence to consumers and helping Americans to forge a new cultural identity that became the envy of their European counterparts. This

was an era in which Hollywood's movie industry blossomed and the abstract paintings and sculptures of American artists revolutionized the art world.

When it came to furniture design, it had taken the American consumer quite some time to warm to the Modern style (as H. M. Dunnett acknowledged). The catalyst for this acceptance was, first, the introduction of the softer, more approachable Scandinavian style of Modernism to the United States and, second, the arrival, in the late 1940s, of a new generation of homeowners.

A government program that subsidized the

buying of first homes created a new group of buyers who refused to fill their homes with the sort of reproduction furniture they associated with their parents.

Much was done to promote the Modern style, too, by institutions such as the Museum of Modern Art (MoMA) in New York City. MoMA had supported the designs of avant-garde European designers during the 1930s, and in the 1940s they pushed the idea of Good Design. Described in 1950 by Edgar Kaufmann, MoMA's director, as a "thorough merging of form and function...revealing a practical, uncomplicated, sensible beauty,"

The deep bowl seat resembles a nest.

Wire mesh was an unusual material for the time.

The chair's base is made from bent and welded steel rod.

The upholstery is unusual for a Bertoia wire-mesh design, which often used cushions.

SLIPPER CHAIR

This chair is upholstered in a striped-silk fabric in yellow, orange, and green; the legs are bleached mahogany. Designed by Edward Wormley for Dunbar. *H:30 in (76 cm). SDR*

CYCLONE TABLE

This dining table has a white-laminate top raised on a chrome-plated steel-wire column and cast-iron base. Designed by Isamu Noguchi for Knoll International. *H:48 in (122 cm). SDR*

BIRD CHAIR AND OTTOMAN

The Bird chair, so called because it resembles a bird with spread wings, has a high back and a diamond-shaped seat above a plastic-coated, steel-wire frame. It is fully upholstered with a removable black padded slip cover. The

ottoman has a rectangular pad on a wire frame of the same construction. Developed from the iconic Diamond chair, this chair and ottoman illustrate the sculptural quality of Bertoia's work. *1952. Chair: H:39 in (99 cm); W:39 in (99 cm); D:34 in (86.5 cm). Ottoman: H:17 in (43 cm); W:24 in (61 cm); D:17 in (43 cm). Bk*

GRASSHOPPER ARMCHAIR

With a laminated-birch frame and an upholstered seat and back, this armchair was designed by Eero Saarinen for Knoll International in 1946. This 1960s model has floral upholstery. *H:35 in (89 cm); W:29¼ in (74 cm); D:35 in (89 cm). QU*

Good Design was the focus of many competitions run by the museum.

Although open to designers around the globe, it was an American who made the most impact on these competitions. Charles Eames's first award in a MoMA competition was in 1940, for Organic Design in Home Furnishing, although he went on to win many more and, in 1946, secured a solo show at MoMA under the title New Furniture by Charles Eames.

DISTINCT AMERICAN STYLE
Charles Eames's work was way ahead of anything being produced in Europe. Along with Ray, his wife, and Eero Saarinen, a friend from the progressive Cranbrook Academy of Art in Michigan, he breathed new life into the American furniture industry.

Among the first to realize the potential of his and Ray's designs was George Nelson, who, in 1946, had just been appointed design director of The Herman Miller Furniture Company. Nelson was an accomplished designer in the Modern style himself, and by the 1950s Herman Miller had established itself, through the designs of Nelson and Charles and Ray Eames, at the forefront of the American furniture industry.

Another important manufacturer of this period was Knoll International, founded in New York in 1938. Hans Knoll, the son of the German furniture manufacturer Walter Knoll, came to the United States intent on introducing the sort of pared-down furniture he had seen so much of in his homeland and, at first, employed European designers exclusively. In 1945, however, Knoll met, and later married, Florence Schust, a graduate of the Cranbrook Academy of Art, who introduced him to the work of American designers such as Harry Bertoia and Isamu Noguchi. In deciding to produce their work, which used daring, sculptural forms and unusual materials such as metal rod, Knoll became a prominent force in the furniture industry and helped to establish a distinctive, American style of Modern design. Florence also designed a number of significant pieces for Knoll.

Across the country, designers began to take a more functional approach to furniture design. Although not quite as innovative as the work of the Eameses or Eero Saarinen, the furniture of designers such as Edward Wormley (whose work was produced in Indiana), Baldwin Kingrey (from Chicago), and George Nakashima (based in Pennsylvania) was, nonetheless, beautifully produced and distinctively American in its use of fluid forms.

COFFEE TABLE

The top of this table is fashioned from one piece of solid walnut and has a split-knot, free-edge top. The table is supported on two legs, also made of solid walnut, and is asymmetrical in both position and form. The wider end of the coffee table is supported on a free-form slab of walnut, and the narrower end is held up on a square-section, tapered leg. Designed by George Nakashima. *1965. W:50 in (127 cm). SDR*

CONFERENCE TABLE

The top of this conference table is made of rosewood. Rectangular in shape, the table top has slight bows to the long edges, making it somewhat wider at the center than at the edges. The table is supported on round steel legs, which are joined at each end by a metal stretcher and reinforced in the center by trestle-type supports. The conference table was designed by George Nelson for the Herman Miller Furniture Company. *W:103½ in (236 cm); D:43¼ in (110 cm). FRE*

HERMAN MILLER FURNITURE CO.

A CUTTING-EDGE FURNITURE-MAKER IN THE UNITED STATES, THE HERMAN MILLER FURNITURE COMPANY HELPED TO CREATE A DISTINCT AMERICAN STYLE.

The years between 1945 and 1960 were the glory days of 20th-century American furniture design, and no manufacturer was more prominent at the time than the Michigan-based Herman Miller Furniture Company. Founded as the Star Furniture Company in 1905, the company's name was changed in 1923 (after the chairman, D. J. De Pree, received a generous donation from his father-in-law, Mr. Herman Miller).

The company made furniture that imitated whatever historical style was in vogue. It was a precarious existence, and one that required De Pree to second-guess consumer tastes.

De Pree needed to change direction, and did so in 1930 when he staked the company's future on the Modern style, an aesthetic promoted by the Museum of Modern Art for its timeless, universal appeal. Designer Gilbert Rohde was given the task of reinvigorating the company, which he did with great success.

By 1946, the new design director, George Nelson, was pushing for cutting-edge style. Designers such as Charles Eames and Isamu Noguchi were employed to meet De Pree's demands for "durability, unity, integrity, and inevitability."

It is a testament to the standards of De Pree, who saw that innovation was worth little without quality, that many Herman Miller designs of the 1940s and 1950s still remain in production today.

Action Office Developed by Robert Propst and George Nelson in the 1960s, this was the world's first open-plan office system. Elements could be combined and recombined as needs changed.

AUSTRALIA

LIKE MUCH OF Europe and the United States, Australia enjoyed economic growth in the 1950s and 1960s. Industrial expansion was the driving force behind this era of affluence, and more and more Australians enjoyed the luxury of a disposable income.

Eager to capture some of these riches, canny entrepreneurs began to import the latest furniture designs from Europe and the United States and sell them to this new breed of consumer. Realizing that there was a thirst for cutting-edge products, a number of Australian designers also began to work in the Modern style that was such a success overseas.

A NEW GENERATION

One of the first Australian designers to look to the future for inspiration was Douglas Snelling. His Saran chairs, launched in 1947, incorporated parachute webbing and ushered in a new, experimental era in Australian furniture design. From 1947 to 1955, Snelling worked with the Sydney-based company Functional Products to produce furniture that was spare in style and concise in craftsmanship.

More flamboyant in his approach to design was the Melbourne designer Grant Featherston. Featherston's designs for a House of the Future in 1949 declared his intention to take Australian furniture into uncharted territory. His plywood Contour chair of 1951 was so advanced that no local manufacturer could put it into production, forcing Featherston to make it himself. Featherston created different versions of the chair, giving it arms, a rocking base, and leather upholstery. Clearly influenced by the designs of Charles and Ray Eames, the Contour chair became an icon of Australian design.

THE USE OF PLASTICS

In 1966, Featherston began to collaborate with his wife, Mary, a designer from Britain focusing on the use of plastics. Their chair for the Australian pavilion at the 1967 Montreal Expo was a polystyrene shell covered in polyurethane foam. The Expo Mark II Sound chair was so named because it had speakers in the back, although when it went on the market, this feature was gone. In the 1960s and early 1970s the Featherstons contributed as much to the field of plastic furniture design as any European or American designer.

Also based in Melbourne was Kjell Grant, a designer whose cantilevered Montreal chair (designed for the Montreal Expo) was, he claimed, inspired by tractor seats, although many

Buttons not only tighten the fabric but also perform a decorative function.

The high back gives the chair a sense of grandeur.

The curved seat and back are designed to make the user feel enclosed.

The chair base is made of solid wood.

The tapered legs of the base are typical of the period.

R152 CONTOUR CHAIR

Devoted to promoting a philosophy of good design, Grant Featherston designed the R152 Contour chair. This striking chair offered a comfortable but sleek alternative to the over-stuffed, bulky lounge suites popular during the pre-war era. The flexibility of the plywood frame provided Featherston with the opportunity to experiment with bending wood without compromising on strength, and this chair clearly demonstrates how seating furniture can be molded to accommodate the human form. This example is covered in the original blue vinyl fixed with buttons. The chair was manufactured by Emerson Brothers. *c. 1952.*

EXPO MARK II SOUND CHAIR

The Expo Mark II Sound chair is made of a polystyrene shell covered in polyurethane foam. It was designed by Grant and Mary Featherston and made by Aristoc Industries, Melbourne. *1967.*

RONDO CHAIR

Originally designed for an Olivetti showroom in 1956 and still in production, this Rondo chair has splayed legs. Versions with a tulip base or a six-star base are also made. The molded shell base is covered in foam. By Gordon Andrews.

COFFEE TABLE

This maple-wood coffee table has a free-form table top with rounded, organic curves; there are no right angles on the piece. The four legs of the coffee table, also in maple, are splayed and tapered, which adds to the elegance of the piece by lifting the focus away from the ground. The piece was designed by the architect and furniture designer Douglas Snelling and manufactured by Functional Products of Sydney. *1955.*

saw its springy form as reminiscent of the kangaroo. Selected by the Museum of Modern Art in New York for its permanent collection, the Montreal chair was one of the first Australian designs to attract worldwide attention.

SPARKING INTEREST AT HOME
In Sydney, the interior designer Marion Hall Best was introducing locals to the

delights of Modern design. In the late 1950s and 1960s, Hall Best opened a showroom stocked with works by Charles and Ray Eames, Joe Colombo, Eero Aarnio, and Harry Bertoia, as well as by Sydney-born Gordon Andrews.

Andrews was a furniture designer and a graphic designer (he designed Australia's first decimal currency notes in 1966) who had worked

in Europe as a commercial artist in the 1930s. In the 1950s, he struck up a relationship with the Italian firm Olivetti to design its showrooms. It was while working on this project that he produced his most celebrated pieces—the Rondo chair (1956) and the

Gazelle chair (1957). Eager to pare furniture down to its most essential, Andrews complemented his Rationalist principles with a sharp eye for proportion. Of all the Australian designers of this period, Andrews was the most original.

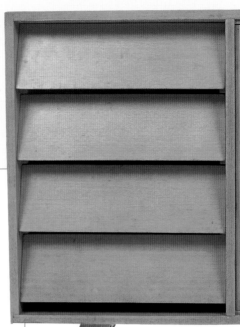

SPIDER CHAIR

The Spider is a beautifully proportioned swivel chair. The four-star base is in a brushed stainless steel. The chair also came in a lower seat height, for use as a casual chair for the home or office. Designed by Gordon Andrews. *1961.*

GAZELLE CHAIR

Called the Gazelle because of its thin, tapering gazelle-like legs, this chair is made of laminated plywood and cast aluminum. It is upholstered in a bright, woolen fabric. Designed by Gordon Andrews. *1957.*

SIDE CABINET

The largely plain front of this side cabinet has a simple, square wooden door handle and four drawers with slightly angled fronts. The wooden legs of the piece are splayed and taper toward the bottom. The cabinet was designed by Douglas Snelling. *c. 1954.*

LOUNGE CHAIR AND STOOL

Made from wood, metal, and synthetic Saran webbing, the chair is lightweight, because of the materials, and versatile, because of its simple color scheme and timeless fashioning. The Saran webbing distributes weight and tension evenly over the surface area and creates support without an upholstered or solid surface for the seat and backrest, showing that ergonomics were considered. Designed by Douglas Snelling for Functional Products. *c. 1957.*

TOWNHOUSE SUITE

Comprising a two-seater sofa and two single, matching armchairs with splayed legs, the Townhouse Suite is upholstered throughout in the original red, geometrically patterned fabric. This suite won an award in "The Australian Home Beautiful Second National Furniture Design Competition". The pieces were designed by Grant Featherston and manufactured by Emerson Brothers. *c. 1956.*

SCANDINAVIA

IN THE YEARS AFTER World War II, the profile of Scandinavian design soared. It is little surprise that such a brutal war had left people weary of the hard edges of early Modernism and more comfortable with the gentler forms of the Scandinavian style.

TRADITIONAL CRAFTSMANSHIP

It was something of a paradox that designers from the leading nations of furniture design in the immediate post-war period—Finland, Sweden, and, in particular, Denmark—worked primarily with traditional, rather than cutting-edge, manufacturing techniques. "Technically there was

nothing new in our work," reflected one of Denmark's foremost designers of the period, Hans Wegner, in 1983. "The philosophy behind it was not to make the process more complicated than necessary, but to show what we were able to do with our hands; to give the work a sense of spirit and make it look natural."

The aim for Scandinavian designers of the period was to distill design to its purest form. This is evidenced by the fact that the outstanding feature of Scandinavian furniture design in the late 1940s and early 1950s is the unsurpassed quality of its craftsmanship.

TEAK-STYLE FURNITURE

Scandinavians had long held a deep reverence for wood, since it not only provided for them financially, through exports (Scandinavians often referred to their forests at this time as "green gold"), but was also the material from which the iconic items of their culture—such as ships and skis— had been hewn.

Ironically, though, it was not an indigenous wood but one from East Asia that came to define Scandinavian design of the 1950s. Teak was inexpensive and readily available as a by-product of the military clearing exercises taking

place in Thailand and the Philippines during this period. The wood was hardy, easy to work with, and could be given an attractive satin finish. This propensity for working with teak wood is the reason why Scandinavian design of the post-war period was often referred to as the Teak style.

Finn Juhl, in particular, produced masterful examples of teak furniture in the late 1940s and early 1950s, often in a sculptural style that can be recognized as uniquely his. Inspired by the work of abstract painters and sculptors, his furniture designs have a freedom of form that distinguishes his output from the rather more

Right angles are kept to a minimum, as curves dominate the chair's appearance.

The muscular forms of the chair were inspired by primitive art.

Generous, convex armrests offer the user an image of comfort.

A slight swelling of the struts of the chair adds to the sculptural effect.

The chair's seat and back are detached, giving the illusion that the back is suspended in midair.

The front and back legs are turned.

TEAK CABINET

The top section of this cabinet has twin sliding doors enclosing open, shelved compartments. The deeper case beneath contains six long drawers, two of which are lined for silverware. The whole is supported on turned teak legs. Designed by Hans Wegner for Ry Mobler, Denmark. *H:71 in (180.5 cm). FRE*

CHIEFTAIN CHAIR

This chair is constructed from a teak frame and has a shaped-leather seat and back. The overall shape is largely curvaceous, with very few right angles. The back rail joins two dowel uprights, which also form the back legs. The armrests span the distance between the front and back

legs and the elbow rests are also of sculpted leather. The upholstered components of the chair are separated from its exposed frame—an idea that stemmed directly from the Modernist concepts of furniture design seen in the works of Gerrit Rietveld and Marcel Breuer. Designed by Finn Juhl for Niels Vodder, Denmark. *1949. H:38 in (96.5 cm); W:34 in (86 cm); D:39 in (99 cm). SDR*

TAMBOUR SIDEBOARD

This teak and teak-veneered sideboard has two long tambour doors at the front that open on to a fitted interior containing an arrangement of compartments and eight drawers. The sideboard is supported by a frame that has tapering legs attached to the outside of the case. Designed by Finn Juhl for Arne Vodder, Denmark. *1950s. W:81⅞ in (208 cm). DOR*

rigorous furniture designs produced by his contemporaries.

DEBT TO THE PAST

With the exception of Finn Juhl, the predominant Scandinavian approach to design in the post-war period was one of updating older forms of furniture. This was a trend initiated by Kaare Klint at the Royal Danish Academy of Fine Arts in the interwar years and continued with zeal by his students and followers. The Shaker chair (1944) by Borge Mogensen and the Chinese chair (1947) by Hans Wegner are two famous examples of Scandinavian furniture that clearly illustrate how the designers borrowed forms from bygone cultures.

No designer, though, was more diligent in his studies of past furniture types than Ole Wanscher. A student of Kaare Klint who eventually took over Klint's job at the Royal Danish Academy of Fine Arts, Wanscher compiled numerous books on the subject, including *Furniture Types* and *History of the Art of Furniture*. His designs were, unsurprisingly, heavily inspired by and indebted to past eras of furniture design, with 18th-century English and Egyptian furniture being of particular interest to him.

INTERNATIONAL APPEAL

The international acclaim bestowed upon Scandinavian furniture designers was due in large part to the timeless quality of their designs and the skill with which these designs were executed. In 1951, Finland took home the majority of medals at the Milan Triennale (an event that would later be referred to by the Finns as the Milan Miracle), while in the United States an ambitious exhibition entitled Design in Scandinavia proved so popular when it was first mounted in 1954 that it continued to tour the country (and Canada) for the next three years. The reason for the initial, and lasting, popularity of Scandinavian designs can be summed up by four words: integrity, reliability, beauty, and craftsmanship. Clearly, Scandinavian design represented to the public much that the world had been thirsting for after such a traumatic period in its history.

FLAG-HALYARD LOUNGE CHAIR

The tubular-steel frame is strung with flag halyard, and the chair has a sheepskin throw. By Hans Wegner. *1950. H:31¾ in (81 cm); W:41 in (104 cm); D:44 in (112 cm). BonBay*

OAK DAY BED

This day bed has a simple, rectangular oak frame raised on bracket legs. The single seat cushion and two back cushions are upholstered with buttoned fabric. Designed by Borge Mogensen for StoleFabrik, Denmark. *1950s. H:30 in (76 cm); W:77 in (195.5 cm); D:33 in (84 cm). R20*

WALNUT ARMCHAIR

This ladder-back armchair has outswept arms on turned supports. The dished seat has a squab cushion covered in ribbed fabric; the seat is raised on turned legs joined by stretchers. By Ole Wanscher for Fritz Hansen. *1946. BonBay*

THE CHAIR BY HANS WEGNER

ALTHOUGH IT INSPIRED COUNTLESS IMITATIONS, HANS WEGNER'S MODEL NO. JH 501 CHAIR REMAINS THE EPITOME OF FORM MEETING FUNCTION.

Despite its unassuming appearance, Hans Wegner's Model No. JH 501 chair (1949) enjoys a legendary reputation. It is often simply referred to as The Chair, and many commentators on Modern design have described it as the ultimate blend of function and form, and the era's most accomplished achievement.

First declared the most beautiful chair in the world in the late 1950s by the influential American magazine *House Beautiful*, The Chair was chosen by CBS to provide seating for the televised presidential debate in 1960 between John F. Kennedy and Richard Nixon.

The Chair's reputation was further enhanced by an exhibition in the 1970s that displayed it alongside 30 of the many imitations it had spawned. The copies fell short of matching the subtle refinement of the original, thus confirming once and for all the chair's superiority over all competitors.

Hans Wegner

The chair The teak chair's back rail elegantly joins the armrests, as though all pieces are one. *1950–60. H:30 in (76 cm); W:23 in (58.5 cm); D:21 in (53.5 cm). Bk*

ARNE JACOBSEN

CREATING AN AESTHETIC THAT COMBINED SOFT LINES WITH STRICT ATTENTION TO DETAIL, ARNE JACOBSEN DESIGNED SOME OF THE BIGGEST-SELLING PIECES OF THE 20TH CENTURY.

ARNE JACOBSEN RECEIVED his first international award for furniture design at 23, picking up a silver at the 1925 *Exposition des Arts Décoratifs et Industriels Modernes* in Paris. On his trip to France he also saw the *Pavilion de l'Esprit Nouveau* by the architect Le Corbusier. The minimalism of the building, and the way in which it eschewed craft in favor of technology, was to inform Jacobsen's designs for life.

Trained as a stonemason in Denmark, Jacobsen found the rigorous approach of Le Corbusier and Ludwig Mies van der Rohe (whose work he saw at *Die Wohnung* in Stuttgart in 1927) a revelation. "Clear, sane, readily comprehensible," was how he described their approach.

By the 1930s, Jacobsen had established himself as an architect in Denmark—his greatest achievement of this period being the Bella Vista estate in Copenhagen (1932–35)—but it was only after World War II that he asserted himself as a furniture designer. While most of his early designs were derived from Mies, Le Corbusier, and the Swedish Functionalist Gunnar Asplund, Jacobsen finally found his own style in the 1950s.

EGG TABLE
The egg-shaped top of this table is supported on three steel-rod legs with trestle supports and black-rubber-capped feet. Manufactured by Fritz Hansen.
W:45 in (114 cm). BonE

DROP CHAIR
The sculptural, polyurethane shell of this chair is covered in leather-upholstered foam and stands on copper-coated, tubular-steel legs. Manufactured by Fritz Hansen. 1958.
H:33¼ in (84.5 cm); W:18⅛ in (46 cm); D:21⅞ in (55.5 cm). QU

EXACTING DESIGN

The now-familiar Jacobsen aesthetic that emerged in the Ant chair (1952) was a combination of fluidity and precision. The defining feature of the Ant was its construction; it was made from two clearly defined parts: a base of three tubular-steel legs and a plywood seat shaped by steam. This logical approach made the chair easy to mass-produce. Designed for a factory cafeteria, the Ant's basic form would be referred to again and again by Jacobsen.

The influence of Eero Saarinen and Charles and Ray Eames is clear in the construction of the Ant's seat. Although not a pioneer of plywood designs, Jacobsen was as much a master of the material as the Eameses.

After completing the Ant, Jacobsen began work on his Series 7 chairs. Although similar in construction to the Ant, they had four legs, not three, and came in many styles. All with a curvilinear plywood seat, the Series 7 chairs were—and are—available with arms (3207), a swiveling base (3117), or both (3217), among other variants. The most successful chair is the most basic, the 3107, which by the end of the 20th century had sold over six million, making it, by some estimates, the most popular chair ever designed.

SWAN SOFA
This aluminum-framed sofa is upholstered in orange woolen fabric and has trestle bases with plastic-capped feet. Designed by Arne Jacobsen for Fritz Hansen. 1957. W:59¼ in (148 cm). L&T

BIOGRAPHY

Arne Jacobsen

1902 Born February 11 in Copenhagen.

1925 Awarded a silver medal for his chair design at the *Exposition des Arts Décoratifs et Industriels Modernes* in Paris.

1927 Travels to Stuttgart, to visit *Die Wohnung* exhibition.

1932–35 Designs the Bella Vista apartment complex and Bellevue recreation center on the outskirts of Copenhagen.

1952 Designs the Ant chair.

1955–61 Designs the Series 7 range of chairs.

1956–65 Designs the building and interior furnishings for the SAS Royal Hotel, Copenhagen.

1959 Designs the AJ lamp for Louis Poulsen.

1960–63 Designs the building and interior furnishings for St. Catherine's College, Oxford.

1961–78 Designs the Danish National Bank (completed after his death).

1971 Dies March 24 in Copenhagen.

THE COPENHAGEN SAS ROYAL HOTEL

COPENHAGEN'S FIRST SKYSCRAPER, THE JACOBSEN-DESIGNED SAS ROYAL HOTEL IS
KNOWN AS MUCH FOR ITS INTERIOR DESIGN AS FOR ITS ARCHITECTURE.

Many of Arne Jacobsen's most celebrated designs, from the Egg chair to the AJ pendant lamp, were designed for the SAS Royal Hotel in Copenhagen. Commissioned by SAS (Scandinavian Airlines System) and completed in 1960, the hotel was the Danish capital's first major skyscraper. The building consists of a two-story horizontal plinth attached to a 19-story tower. Such is the subtlety of Jacobsen's design that the tower appears to hover above the base.

Although admired for its architecture, the hotel is today rightly remembered for its interior design. With a legendary eye for detail, Jacobsen insisted that every element meet his strict standards—this is presumably why he designed so many of the fixtures himself.

As well as the famous Egg, Swan, and Drop chairs, he also designed the curtains, cutlery, and light fixtures. So fastidious was he that he even designed the door handles.

Today, many of Jacobsen's designs for the SAS Royal Hotel are available to buy. Sadly, the hotel has been stripped of many of its original fittings, although one room, 606, is still kept exactly as Jacobsen designed it.

The exterior of the SAS Royal Hotel Designed by Arne Jacobsen in 1960, the hotel highlights the fact that Jacobsen was not only an inspired interior designer, but also one of the great architects of the 20th century.

Room 606 in the SAS Royal Hotel Room 606 is on the sixth floor of the hotel and is the one remaining room in the building that has been left as Jacobsen intended. It gives an insight into the colors and shapes that were integral to Jacobsen's 1960s masterpiece.

PRACTICAL APPROACH

Although Jacobsen's designs were considered to epitomize the spirit of the new age, the designer himself was a remarkably conservative character. A lover of antiques, fine wine, and good cigars, he led a quiet life. His House of the Future, designed in 1929 with architect Flemming Lassen, might have been intended to cause a stir (it had a helicopter landing pad on the roof), but generally, Jacobsen considered himself a practical, rather than progressive, designer.

Almost all of Jacobsen's furniture designs were conceived for a specific space. The Ant, as mentioned, was designed for a cafeteria, while the Egg, Swan, and Drop chairs were made for the SAS Royal Hotel (*see box feature*). The latter three employed a new production technique, pioneered in Norway and licensed to Fritz Hansen, the manufacturer of Jacobsen's furniture designs. The technique involved steam-molding polystyrene beads—which transformed into foam under heat—onto a fiberglass base. The new process allowed Jacobsen to take his organic style to greater lengths, as the foam was as pliable as clay (or the wet plaster that he often used to make full-scale prototypes).

Jacobsen's last project to inspire a rash of furniture designs was his work on St. Catherine's College, Oxford (1960–63). Only available commercially since the 1980s, his designs displayed the same instinct for proportion, integrity of materials, and practicality of his previous work.

For the last decade of his life, Jacobsen concentrated on architecture and hardware design, although he did not abandon furniture design altogether. Never afraid to work with new materials and technology, he was, at the time of his death in 1971, designing an all-plastic office chair.

SERIES 7 CHAIR
The seat and back of this chair are made from a single sheet of shaped and molded plywood in black. The seat is supported on a tubular-steel base with rubber-capped feet. Designed for Fritz Hansen. H:30 in (76 cm). SDR

SCANDINAVIA: SECOND GENERATION

BY THE MID-1950S, the so-called Second Generation of Scandinavian designers had begun to make their mark. Whereas the First Generation—designers such as Hans Wegner, Borge Mogensen, and Ole Wanscher—had developed their distinctive style largely in isolation during World War II, the Second Generation enjoyed far greater exposure to developments elsewhere in the world, and this impacted greatly on their work.

INTERNATIONAL INFLUENCES

The experiments undertaken at the Cranbrook Academy of Art in Michigan, by Charles Eames and Eero Saarinen (who moved to the United States from Finland at the age of 13) were of critical interest to a young group of Scandinavian designers that included Arne Jacobsen and Poul Kjaerholm from Denmark, and Ilmari Tapiovaara and Antti Nurmesniemi from Finland. Some older designers, too, such as the lighting specialist Poul Henningsen, were also invigorated by what they saw happening overseas, prompting a change in tack for Scandinavian design.

What these designers saw in the work of their American counterparts was a more playful approach to form that inspired a new sculptural strain in Scandinavian design. Also of interest to the Scandinavians was the development of innovative techniques for molding plywood, which opened up possibilities for more sophisticated, sleeker shapes than were allowed by older, cruder techniques. Solid-wood furniture, it seemed, was losing its standing in Scandinavia.

The use of metal in furniture design had also been revolutionized by Americans. Whereas the early Modern designers of Europe had flaunted their use of steel, the American designers of the 1940s and 1950s used it sparingly and only where strictly necessary. The development of thinner steel rods also made it easier for designers to be more subtle in their use of metal, as designers such as Poul Kjaerholm proved. Earlier Scandinavian designers had rejected metal as too cold and clinical, but

The armrests curve subtly to create a soft, rounded outline.

The bright fabric shows that the chair was designed for a public space.

Stretched fabric over the chair's internal skeleton creates a soft silhouette.

The slightly angled back legs of the chair give it greater steadiness.

The legs are made of laminated birch, which is abundant in Scandinavia.

The crossbeam adds extra support to the chair's structure.

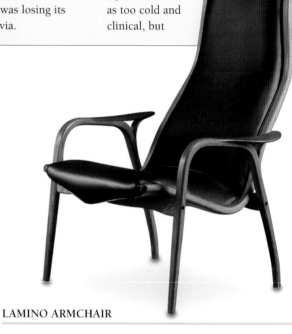

LAMINO ARMCHAIR

This ergonomically designed armchair has a bent, laminated frame made of oak and teak; the chair is upholstered in brown leather. An ottoman was available in the same design. Designed by Yngve Ekström for Swedese, Sweden. *1956. H:39¾ in (101 cm); W:27¼ in (69 cm); D:29½ in (75 cm). SDR*

HAMMOCK CHAISE LONGUE

Called the Hammock for its obvious similarities, this elegant chaise longue has a woven-cane seat and back supported by a polished-steel frame. The headrest is in black leather. Designed by Poul Kjaerholm for Fritz Hansen. *1965. BonE*

LULU CHAIR

The shell of this chair is made of case plastic. It is upholstered in a stretch fabric in bright orange-red; the slightly angled legs are made of birch and a crossbeam adds extra reinforcement and stability. The chair was designed for the restaurant of the Marski Hotel in Helsinki around 1960, but it was never mass produced, since the manufacturing process was too labor-intensive and, thus, made the chair too expensive for the wider market. Designed by Ilmari Tapiovaara for Asko, Finland. *R20* the Second Generation of designers saw that, shorn of its totemic value, steel used in moderation was immensely practical.

The work of the Second Generation is distinguished by svelte forms and experimentation with new materials. One can also point to the diminishing importance of hand-crafting, as new manufacturing techniques came to the fore. Where designers like Hans Wegner and Ole Wanscher were renowned as craftsmen (and were often referred to generically as cabinet-makers), Second Generation designers were categorized as industrial designers.

This shift was a reflection of a change in Scandinavian society as a whole. Industrialization had come late to the region, and it was only during the 1950s that Scandinavians acclimatized to life as an industrial, rather than a rural, society.

LARGE MANUFACTURERS

While small craft workshops had long formed the bedrock of the Scandinavian furniture industry, the late 1950s saw larger manufacturers play an ever more important role. Fritz Hansen, based in Copenhagen, was the most notable of this more ambitious and advanced breed of companies, and it was to produce

much of the work by Arne Jacobsen and, later in his career, Poul Kjaerholm.

When appraising the work of the leading Scandinavian designers of the 1950s and 1960s, it is interesting to note that only Ilmari Tapiovaara can be considered to have truly applied himself to the cause of low-cost, standardized furniture, a mission that many designers elsewhere in Europe and in the United States were pursuing. This fact is best explained by the relative affluence of Scandinavian countries during the second half of the 20th century.

Another factor of Scandinavian society that gave a further facet to their furniture design was the

advanced notions held, particularly in Denmark and Sweden, of sexual equality. In the United States and Europe, women furniture designers rarely rose to prominence during the post-war period, and if they did, they were often perceived to be riding on the coattails of their male partners (Ray Eames being an obvious example). In Scandinavia, however, female designers such as Nanna Ditzel and Grete Jalk (both Danish) acquired respectable reputations during the 1950s. In the mid-1950s, Ditzel became renowned for her designs for children's furniture, for which there was a particular need thanks to the post-war baby boom.

COFFEE TABLE

This two-tiered occasional, or coffee, table is made of teak. It has a rectangular top with slightly raised sides that create a dished effect. It is otherwise free of ornament or design; its simplicity highlights the beauty of the wood's natural grain. The table's top is raised on tapered dowel legs that are joined by a stretcher shelf underneath. The nine horizontal cross-slats form the open storage shelf. The table was designed by the Danish furniture designer Grete Jalk. *c. 1960. W:63½ in (161 cm). FRE*

LOUNGE CHAIR

Made of "folded" rather than bent plywood, this pine-laminate chair is constructed from two parts, which are secured together by two pairs of steel bolts. The piece was designed by Grete Jalk and produced by Poul Jeppeson. *1963.*

ARTICHOKE LAMP

This lamp takes its name from the several layers of overlapping, brushed-copper, leaflike elements that make up its form. Designed by Poul Henningsen for Firma Poulsen. *1958. H:30¾ in (78 cm); W:31½ in (80 cm). WKA*

PIRKKA DINING TABLE

The rectangular top of this dining table is made from two pieces of solid, varnished pine and is raised on solid-beech, black-lacquered dowel legs. The legs taper slightly and are joined by stretchers; trestle supports provide extra reinforcement. Designed by Ilmari Tapiovaara for Asko Ltd. & Laukaan Puu Ltd., Finland. *c. 1955. H:26½ in (67.5 cm); W:59 in (150 cm); D:27½ in (70 cm). DOR*

PK-41 FOLDING STOOL

This folding stool has a stretched-canvas seat pulled taut between two crisscrossed legs that are turned slightly to resemble propellers. The legs are formed from two rectangular pieces and are made from stainless steel. Designed by Poul Kjaerholm for E. Kold Christensen, Denmark. *1960s. H:16¾ in (42.5 cm); W:23 in (58.5 cm); D:17½ in (44.5 cm). Bk*

ITALY

OVER THREE MILLION HOUSES were destroyed in Italy during World War II. The impact on the country's factories, however, was not quite so devastating, and in the aftermath of the war, Italian industry, and its growing band of industrial designers, wasted little time in rebuilding a broken nation.

With the fall of Fascism, a new Socialist coalition government rose to power, and its ideologies were reflected by the Italian design industry. A 1946 exhibition by RIMA (*Riunione Italiane Mostre per l'Arredamento*) addressed concerns about how to furnish small living spaces, how to work with the limited

materials available in the post-war period, and how best to take advantage of recent developments in serial production. Architects and designers such as Franco Albini, Ernesto Rogers, and Studio BBPR all took their roles of providing for the impoverished working classes seriously; The Problems of the Least Privileged was the theme of the 1947 *Milan Triennale*.

A NEW CONFIDENCE
The 1950s, however, ushered in a new era for Italy. Thanks to generous aid from the United States and the commitment of a number of industrial

entrepreneurs, Italy was enjoying something of a boom. The Socialist government was dismantled and replaced by the capitalist Christian Democrats, and a new confidence buoyed both the country's producers and its consumers.

Designers responded to this new mood by bringing a more elegant, expressive edge to the Rationalist style that had dominated Italian design since the 1930s. Where architecture had been the most inspirational art form for designers before the war, it was now sculpture that dominated. *Domus* magazine, edited by Gio Ponti, ran large

features on Henry Moore, Alexander Calder, and other artists who employed an organic, abstract aesthetic.

Also much discussed in the pages of *Domus* magazine was the work of American designers such as George Nelson and Charles and Ray Eames. It was their experimentation with materials and forms that, as much as anything, prompted Italian designers to move on from the reductivist style of their predecessors.

This desk is modular, which makes it possible for the user to attach the lower table section to either side of the upper one, depending on preference.

The sheet steel of the desktop has been enameled to provide visual coherence.

Structural steel struts form the bulk of the desk, emphasizing the industrial nature of the design.

Drawer units are suspended, using the cantilever principle, to give a visually arresting effect.

Rubber fittings attached to the desk's legs give greater adhesion to the floor.

The gentle concave form of the seat is intended to make the chair more comfortable.

The chair's design is unusual in that the arms are attached to the seat, rather than the back.

The legs are made of steel rods, which were commonly used in furniture design of the 1950s and 1960s, largely replacing tubular steel.

LADY CHAIR

This upholstered armchair has a wooden frame and is covered in a red velour fabric. The foam-padded seat and back are raised on brass legs. Designed by Marco Zanuso for Arflex, Milan. *1951. H:30¾ in (78 cm). DOR*

SIDE CHAIR

The frame is made of stained and lacquered wood. With shaped uprights and a velour-covered, padded seat and back, the chair is raised on splayed, tapered legs. Designed by Carlo di Carli for Cassina. *1950. H:33⅛ in (84 cm). DOR*

ARCO DESK AND CHAIR

This writing desk and matching chair are part of a modular office system designed for Olivetti. The desk has wood-effect plastic table tops with molded edges. The smaller table top is designed to hold a typewriter. Gray-enameled, sheet-steel cabinets with filing drawers are suspended below the table tops; the cabinets are attached to the outer

leg supports of the desk. The angular frame of the table is made from black-enameled sheet- and structural-steel, and supports the desk on three pairs of splayed legs. The padded back, seat, and armrests of the chair are covered in a gray fabric; the whole is raised on an enameled, steel-rod frame. Designed by Studio BBPR for Olivetti and marked OLIVETTI ARREDAMENTI METALLICI. *1963. Desk: H:31¼ in (78 cm); W:72 in (180 cm); D:31¼ in (78 cm). QU*

Such was the beneficial economic situation and upbeat mood in Italy during the 1950s that a number of furniture manufacturers emerged who were willing to take risks with their designs. Firms such as Cassina, Zanotta, and Gavina gave designers like Ponti, Carlo di Carli, and the Castiglionis license to develop their own signature styles. These collaborations resulted in a fresh, adventurous language of design that was distinctly Italian.

FROM TIRES TO FURNITURE

Of all the unusual materials that were employed by the Italians during this period, it was perhaps rubber that best came to represent the country's new-found optimism and sense of daring. Used in vast quantities in the automobile industry, which was reaching its zenith in Italy at this time, it was a logical step that designers would begin using rubber in their furniture designs.

In 1950, Pirelli, the tire manufacturer, started an offshoot company called Arflex, which was dedicated to making furniture that used foam rubber in its construction.

Marco Zanuso was the most important designer to work for Arflex, and his Lady chair (1951)—whose forms were clearly inspired by abstract artists such as Calder and Jean Arp—gave elegant expression to an overtly industrial product.

Osvaldo Borsani was another designer who exploited the flexible qualities of rubber in his furniture designs. He founded his own company, Tecno, in 1953 and a year later he produced his famous P40 chair.

Technically advanced—rubber struts made it possible for the user to adjust the chair into over 450 positions—but also generously cushioned, the P40 chair was typical of the design of the era, being industrial and at the same time luxurious.

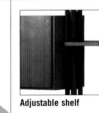
Adjustable shelf

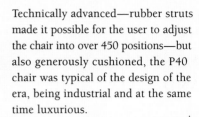

P40 RECLINER

This P40 recliner chair has a metal sectional frame with a polyurethane-foam seat and back; the padded seat and back are upholstered in a yellow fabric. Within the frame of the chair is a patented mechanism that makes it possible for the user to increase or decrease the angle between the seat and the backrest to suit his or her preference. The recliner can be set in an incredible 486 different positions. Designed by Osvaldo Borsani for Tecno. *1954. H:59 in (149 cm); D:35⅓ in (89.5 cm).*

SHELVING SYSTEM

Made of walnut and rosewood, the sections of this shelving system, model LB7, are held together by brass fittings. Four uprights support the three sections, two of which have one door cabinet each. The cabinets open onto internal, adjustable shelves. There is a drop-front cabinet, which becomes a writing table when opened, and ten adjustable shelves in total (seven are shown here). The system was designed by Franco Albini for Poggi. *1957. H:112 in (284.5 cm); W:134 in (340 cm); D:14 in (35.5 cm).*

CARLO MOLLINO

A HIGHLY ENERGETIC AND CHARISMATIC MAN, CARLO MOLLINO CREATED UNIQUE PLYWOOD FURNITURE DESIGNS IN THE TURINESE BAROQUE STYLE.

The success of Carlo Mollino's work in Italy during the 1950s can be attributed to two factors. First, one can point to the rise of a new generation of wealthy furniture buyers who were willing to purchase his bold, daring designs, and second—perhaps more importantly—the sheer force of Mollino's personality.

Such was Mollino's drive to succeed that he not only became one of Italy's foremost furniture-makers during the 1950s, but also went on to become a champion race-car driver, a stunt pilot, a pioneer of modern skiing techniques, and a celebrated photographer of erotic nudes.

Mollino's interest in the female form is clearly demonstrated in his curvaceous furniture designs, which were often made from bent plywood. All made by artisans in Turin, his biomorphic furniture conformed to a sumptuous style that later became known as Turinese Baroque.

Carlo Mollino

Minola apartment interior The sensual, organic furniture designs are an excellent example of Mollino's idiosyncratic and dramatic style. *1944–46.*

Day bed This piece is upholstered in velvet and has shaped and carved ebonized legs. *1944. H:26½ in (67 cm); W:66 in (168 cm); D:32 in (82 cm).*

GIO PONTI

IN A LONG AND VARIED CAREER, GIO PONTI
MANAGED TO CREATE WORKS IN MANY STYLES
AND ACROSS A RANGE OF DISCIPLINES.

THE CAREER OF GIOVANNI "Gio" Ponti spanned 60
years and encompassed many design styles. Evading
attempts to pin him down to a particular movement,
Ponti turned his considerable energy not only to
design, but also to architecture, painting, journalism,
and teaching. Although Ponti exerted significant
influence during every period in which he worked, it
was in the 1950s that his powers were at their peak.

A NEW OUTLOOK

In the aftermath of World War II, Italian architects
and designers focused on revitalizing their exhausted
nation. While many argued for the dogmatic,
Rationalist approach of the 1930s, Ponti believed that a
new outlook was needed. "I want works without labels
or adjectives," he wrote. "I want real, true, natural,
simple, and spontaneous things."

In 1952, Ponti answered his own call with perhaps
his most famous design, the *Superleggera* (or Super-

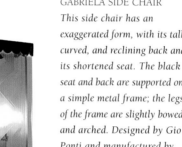

DINING TABLE
*This walnut dining table has a rectangular top that is raised
on turned, tapering legs, which terminate in brass caps. The
legs are joined by an H-stretcher. Designed by Gio Ponti for
Singer and Sons. 1954. W:64 in (162.5 cm). LOS*

GABRIELA SIDE CHAIR
*This side chair has an
exaggerated form, with its tall,
curved, and reclining back and
its shortened seat. The black
seat and back are supported on
a simple metal frame; the legs
of the frame are slightly bowed
and arched. Designed by Gio
Ponti and manufactured by
Walter Ponti. 1970. BonBay*

BIOGRAPHY

Gio Ponti

1891 Born in Milan.

1923 Becomes artistic
director of Richard
Ginori ceramics.

1928 Co-founds
Domus magazine.

1933 Made artistic
director of the company
Fontana Arte.

1936 Begins teaching at the *Politecnico di Milano*.

1936 Completes the Montecatini building in Milan.

1940 Meets Piero Fornasetti.

1945 Founds *Stile* magazine.

1948 Designs his celebrated espresso coffee
machine for La Pavoni.

1950 Begins his association with Cassina, the
manufacturer of the *Superleggera* chair (1952).

1953 Designs sets for La Scala opera house.

1954 Presents a desk design for Altamira in New
York that he proclaims his masterpiece.

1955 Completes the Villa Planchart in Caracas.

1956 Collaborates with Pier Luigi Nervi on the
Pirelli tower in Milan.

1972 Designs Denver Art Museum, Colorado.

1979 Dies in Milan.

FLOOR LAMP
*An early design, this floor lamp is made of a
tall, rectangular glass case and ten light bulbs
spaced in pairs and at intervals. It stands on a
round brass base. c. 1935. H:66⅛ in (168 cm). DOR*

SIDEBOARD
*This exotic wood veneer sideboard has
asymmetrical open shelves surrounding a
drop-front cabinet. The cabinet base has four
doors and tapered legs. W:78¾ in (200 cm). SDR*

SUPERLEGGERA CHAIR
This is Gio Ponti's take on the rustic chair. The frame has horizontal back slats between two uprights that continue to form the back legs. The dowel legs are joined by stretchers.
1952. H:32 in (81 cm); W:17 in (43 cm); D:16 in (40.5 cm). SDR

THE COVER OF DOMUS MAGAZINE.
Along with Gianni Mazzocchi, Gio Ponti founded this popular and influential architecture and design journal, which he edited from 1938 to 1941, and from 1948 until his death in 1979. The magazine featured the works of leading designers of the time.

Light) chair, which he described as "a chair-chair, an ordinary, modest, unqualified chair." Adapted from a rustic design he spotted in an Italian fishing village, the *Superleggera* is at once unpretentious and entirely civilized. In many ways the chair provides a parallel with Ponti's most celebrated architectural work of the 1950s, the Pirelli tower in Milan, a building he designed with the acclaimed engineer Pier Luigi Nervi. Nervi later wrote that he and Ponti "hunted out all superfluous weight," to achieve the final, sleek design. No doubt the same approach was taken with the *Superleggera* chair, as, at just 3½ lb (1.7 kg), it was the lightest chair in the world at the time.

Ponti produced the *Superleggera* for Cassina, a company with whom he collaborated for many years. Owner Cesare Cassina and Ponti shared a similar outlook on design, which Ponti described as "based on the most modern mechanical equipment blend with the human system, which ensures that people retain their predominance over machinery." It is a confusing aspect of Ponti's career that he embraced with equal measure the craft-based techniques of Italy and the industrial techniques of Germany and the United States. Indeed, he was as much at home designing car bodies for mass production as he was making unique pieces in ceramic.

LINEA ITALIANA
Credited with creating the concept of the *Linea Italiana*, a sophisticated idea of Italian design that was disseminated around the world, Ponti was also responsible for introducing the work of international artists, architects, and designers to Italy. In *Domus*, the journal he founded with Gianni Mazzocchi in 1928, Ponti published features on the furniture of Charles and Ray Eames and Arne Jacobsen, the art of Ben Nicholson and Jean Arp, and the architecture of Oscar Niemeyer and Luis Barragan. Under Ponti, *Domus*, which spoke to the enthusiast rather than the scholar, was a design journal whose influence was unprecedented.

In the late 1950s, Ponti's designs became even more ambitious. He had believed that furniture should be integrated into architecture as much as possible, but it was only later in his career that he explored this idea to the fullest. The concept of the "organized wall" was a particular favorite. This translated into either built-in or sprawling pieces of furniture that incorporated different types of shelving, lighting, and, often, drawers. His beds of this period, which have many in-built features, are some of his best-known designs, although other Ponti furniture from this era is equally impressive. In the 1960s and 1970s, Ponti continued to work with considerable zeal, shifting his style occasionally. It was only his death in 1979 that put an end to a long and fruitful career.

PONTI AND FORNASETTI

MANY OF PIERO FORNASETTI'S DESIGNS WERE USED IN GIO PONTI'S FURNITURE AND INTERIORS.

Piero Fornasetti (1913–88) was a child prodigy who displayed a remarkable talent for painting and drawing. At 17 he went to the *Accademia di Belle Arti di Brera* in Milan, but was soon expelled for rebelling against the school's strict, academic approach.

Fornasetti, however, continued to draw, and in 1940 his work caught the eye of Gio Ponti, who asked Fornasetti to produce patterns for his furniture. Modernism had, until this point, adhered to a policy of anti-decoration. When Ponti's works—richly embellished by the restless hand of Fornasetti—were presented, they caused a stir in the design community.

Fornasetti's designs drew from many sources, although he was clearly inspired by Classicism and the Surrealists (Giorgio de Chirico, in particular). Illusionism was a favorite theme, and many designs employed a trompe l'oeil effect.

Ponti and Fornasetti also worked together on interiors, most notably the Casino San Remo in 1950. By the time Fornasetti died in 1988, he had produced over 11,000 designs, all of which were variously applied to furniture (some by Ponti), ceramics, umbrellas, waistcoats, cars, bicycles, glass, and more. In 1970, he opened a shop in Milan to sell his work, and his son, Barnaba, runs it to this day.

A wood and metal bureau-bookcase The piece is decorated with a printed architectural scene in black on a cream background and finished with transparent lacquer. By Piero Fornasetti and Gio Ponti. c. 1950. H:87⅛ in (218 cm); W:32 in (80 cm); D:16½ in (41 cm). QU

BRITAIN

IN 1948, THE MODERN British furniture industry received a welcome boost when Clive Latimer and Robin Day's storage unit won the high-profile International Competition for Low-Cost Furniture Design run by the Museum of Modern Art in New York. Unfortunately, the jury's enthusiasm for their design was hardly reflected in their home country, where the public remained suspicious of the Modern style. The 1950s proved marginally better for Modern design in Britain, but it was not until the 1960s, with the emergence of an affluent youth market, that newer forms of furniture became more fashionable.

UTILITY FURNITURE

During the war years, people in Britain were given a taste of the stark Modern style through the government's program for Utility furniture. Run by designer Gordon Russell, the program promoted basic furniture designs that could be made in any number of available materials. Any company could put the designs into production and sell them at tax-free prices. Often made from low-grade hardboard, the only material plentiful during the era of rationing, they met with a mixed reaction from the public. While some admired Utility furniture for its practicality, others saw it as drab and dispiriting.

In the years immediately after the war, the British government attempted to raise the nation's spirits by staging an upbeat exhibition offering a gleaming vision of Britain's future. Britain Can Make It, staged at the Victoria & Albert Museum in London in 1946, drew huge crowds eager to see something fresh and new after years of enforced frugality.

One of the most talked-about designs on show was the BA chair (1945) by Ernest Race. Die-cast from surplus aluminum (a material used during the war to make bomb casings), over a quarter of a million BA chairs were sold.

Ernest Race went on to take a starring role in the 1951 Festival of Britain, an ambitious event organized in part by the recently established Council of Industrial Design (COID). Race produced innovative designs for the Festival, as did Robin Day and A. J. Milne. The broad range of Modern furniture designs created for the occasion proved that British designers had caught up with their American and European contemporaries in the bold use of metal rod and molded plywood.

Unfortunately, the popularity of the Festival of Britain proved something of

FESTIVAL OF BRITAIN, 1951

IN A COUNTRY STILL SUFFERING THE AFTEREFFECTS OF WAR, THE FESTIVAL OF BRITAIN PROVIDED A CHANCE TO LOOK FORWARD TO THE FUTURE.

Between May and September 1951, many British citizens found themselves participating in the nationwide Festival of Britain. The event was intended to raise the spirits of a nation still reeling from the war. Across Britain, new buildings were erected and old ones spruced up as exhibitions were mounted to present ideas on how to take Britain forward.

The focus of the festival was the South Bank of London's Thames River, where the Royal Festival Hall was built from concrete to a design by Leslie Martin. The Hall was furnished with designs by Robin

Day, while the South Bank's outdoor spaces were dotted with Ernest Race's steel-rod and plywood Antelope chairs.

As Britain attempted to put the austerity of the war years behind it, many stores put on special festival displays that eagerly embraced the event's forward-thinking spirit. Although originally intended to celebrate the centennial of the Great Exhibition of London, the Festival of Britain was an event that prompted people to consider the opportunities of the future, rather than the achievements of the past.

KANGAROO ROCKING CHAIR

The seat and back of this rocking chair are made of painted, bent-and-molded steel rods; it has a steel-rod and steel-strip frame. Designed for outdoor use by Ernest Race. *1952. H:28½ in (72.5 cm); W:22 in (56 cm); D:23¾ in (60.5 cm).*

BA CHAIR

This chair has an elegant, cast-aluminum frame with tapered legs. Among the first pieces of furniture to utilize war-surplus materials, it is by Ernest Race. *1945. H:28¾ in (73 cm); W:17½ in (44.5 cm); D:16¼ in (41.5 cm). RAC*

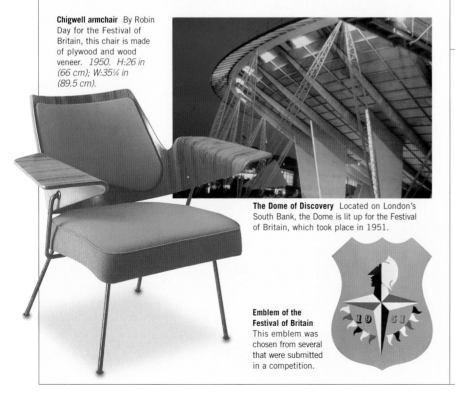

Chigwell armchair By Robin Day for the Festival of Britain, this chair is made of plywood and wood veneer. *1950. H:26 in (66 cm); W:35¼ in (89.5 cm).*

The Dome of Discovery Located on London's South Bank, the Dome is lit up for the Festival of Britain, which took place in 1951.

Emblem of the Festival of Britain This emblem was chosen from several that were submitted in a competition.

PLYMET PROTOTYPE CABINET

This sideboard has two cupboard doors on each side of a bank of drawers; the frame is birch veneer. The case is raised on splayed, aluminum legs. The use of cast- and sheet-aluminum gives a futuristic look. *1945–46. H:33¾ in (86 cm); W:54 in (135 cm); D:15¾ in (40 cm).*

a false start for Modern furniture in Britain, with the public seeing the style more as a novelty than as anything significant. Some manufacturing firms, such as Hille and Morris, did make a respectable profit selling Modern designs, but it seemed that the British public associated the style too closely with the Utility furniture imposed on them during the war. Indeed, as soon as an alternative to the Modern style arose, it was met with real enthusiasm.

CHEAP AND CHEERFUL
In 1959, Morris Motors launched the distinctive, Alec Issigonis–designed Mini, an impish-looking car that

became wildly popular, especially with young buyers. An undeniably contemporary (but approachable) design, it seemed to stimulate a suppressed desire among consumers for new, eye-catching objects that were far removed from the functional items of the past. By the mid-1960s, Carnaby Street, the King's Road, and Kensington in London had been colonized by colorful fashion boutiques such as Biba and Mary Quant, while a new homewares store, Habitat, offered a glimpse into the Continental lifestyle.

Furniture designers, too, responded in force to this new demand for cheap, cheerful goods (much to the irritation

of the COID, which was still trying to enforce a Modern style). The young RCA graduate Peter Murdoch developed a range of disposable paperboard furniture, while Bernard Holloway manufactured his Tom-o-Tom range in chipboard to make it "cheap enough to be expendable." Aligning itself with the brash aesthetic of the Pop movement, furniture design became colorful and cartoonlike. British artist Richard Hamilton gleefully described the characteristics of the Pop style as "popular (designed for a mass audience), transient (short-term

solution), expendable (easily forgotten), low-cost, mass-produced, young (aimed at youth), witty, sexy, gimmicky, glamorous, big business."

This ebullience, however, was not to last long; in the 1970s, much of the energy and excitement drained from the furniture industry in the face of increased economic difficulties.

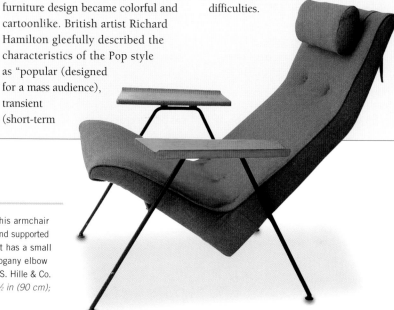

LOUNGER ARMCHAIR

The angular seat and back of this armchair are upholstered in green tweed and supported on a painted, steel-rod frame. It has a small cushion headrest and two mahogany elbow rests. Designed by Robin Day for S. Hille & Co. *1952. H:35½ in (90 cm); W:35½ in (90 cm); D:34 in (86.5 cm). MOU*

TRUNDLING TURK

This armchair has a lacquered wooden frame with chromed tubular-steel supports. The back, seat, and arms are upholstered and covered in fabrics of primary colors reminiscent of Modernist designs. The whole is raised on casters. Designed by Alison and Peter Smithson. *1953. H:23¼ in (59 cm); W:34¼ in (87 cm); D:32⅗ in (83 cm). TEC*

DINING TABLE

The rectangular top of this dining table is made from Formica, which has been decorated to give it the appearance of grained wood. The table is supported by four gray-painted legs, which form a T-section and taper slightly. Designed by Ernest Race. *W:45 in (114 cm). DN*

Black glass adds an element of sophistication to a warm and unpretentious design.

The solid beech links the design to many Scandinavian sideboards of this period.

The slim, rectangular shape of the drawers echoes the overall shape of the sideboard.

The use of mahogany for the sideboard's frame is a distinctly British detail.

The color of the brass hardware blends with the golden tones of the wood.

The frame has the same specifications as Latimer and Day's winning design.

SIDEBOARD

This solid, veneered, and inlaid beech and mahogany sideboard is part of a dining suite. An upper section contains three compartments behind sliding doors. Below is a glass shelf with two sliding drawers to one side of four short drawers. Designed by Robin Day for S. Hille & Co. *1949. H:49⅗ in (126 cm); W:72¾ in (185 cm); D:18⅔ in (47.5 cm).*

JAPAN

BETWEEN 1945 AND 1970, Japan underwent a radical transformation, changing from a predominantly rural nation into a formidable industrial superpower. The products most readily associated with industrial Japan are cars and electronic consumer goods, but the sweeping changes also affected the country's furniture industry.

A traditional Japanese home had contained relatively little furniture, with most people sitting on tatami mats and using minimal storage space. This lifestyle was typical until the 1950s, when Western ways, primarily learned from the American troops that occupied Japan between 1945 and 1952, began to exert an ever-increasing influence on Japanese society. "During the first few years of the occupation," historian Nobutaka Ike noted, "Japan was probably subjected to more Western influence than during the several decades that preceded it."

In the aftermath of World War II and the horrific devastation suffered by Japan during the war, attempts were made to revitalize the country. In particular, the government concentrated on the export market, and companies were encouraged to make their products more attractive to overseas markets. Before the war, Japan had made a name for producing competitively priced, but poorly made, imitations of Western products. In the post-war years a concerted effort was made to develop a more respectable reputation for both design and manufacturing, and to do this, it was acknowledged that the country needed to learn from the West.

BIRTH OF A JAPANESE STYLE
In the 1950s, the Japan Export and Trade Organization (known as JETRO) sent design students to Europe and the United States to study, on the understanding that they would return to work for Japanese companies. JETRO also flew in American and European designers to hold workshops in Japan as a distinctive, hybrid design style, which drew upon influences from both Japan and the West, began to emerge.

One of the earliest champions of this new aesthetic was Isamu Kenmochi, a Japanese designer who spent the late 1940s and early 1950s traveling across Europe and the United States (and keeping extensive journals). Although

taken by what he saw in the West, Kenmochi was also eager to maintain Japanese craft-based traditions. Creating furniture designs that owed an obvious debt to contemporary American and Scandinavian design, but still utilized Japanese construction techniques, Kenmochi's work met with considerable success.

In 1957, Kenmochi became one of the first recipients of the G-Mark prize, an award system created by the Japanese Promotions Council of the Ministry of Trade that was heavily reminiscent of the Good Design program run by the Museum of Modern Art in New York and the *Compasso D'Oro* awards of Italy. The G-Mark system made it clear that the Japanese authorities favored a type of design that was based on the Rationalist principles of European Modernism. In order to promote this essentially Western style, a number of design schools based on the Bauhaus model were set up across Japan.

EAST MEETS WEST
By the end of the 1950s, several Japanese furniture designers had begun to exploit the "East meets West" style with success. Sori Yanagi, who designed one of the first tape recorders for Sony, was one of the most prominent proponents of the style, and time has shown his Butterfly stool (1954) to be the most successful Japanese design of the period. Marrying advanced techniques for molding plywood and a particularly Japanese feeling for poetic form, the Butterfly stool still sells by the thousand every year.

The 1960s was a boom time for the Japanese electronics and automobile industries, but it was not a particularly distinguished time for furniture design. A relative late-comer to Modern design in the Western mold, Japan was hardly ready to embark on an exploration of new materials and forms in the way that countries such as Italy had done during the 1960s. Instead, the Japanese furniture industry consolidated its knowledge of design and manufacturing by continuing in the vein that it had established in the previous decade. It was not until the 1980s that Japanese design would be invigorated in the way that it had been in the post-war years.

The shape of the stool's seat resembles a butterfly in flight.

The stool's simple construction makes it easy to dismantle and transport.

The calligraphic shape of the stool also resembles a Japanese pictograph.

BUTTERFLY STOOL

The simple design of this butterfly stool is made from two sheets of laminated and molded beechwood, which are finished in a rosewood veneer. The two pieces are joined together by a single stretcher. The shape of the stool is said to have been inspired by a Japanese pictograph. Designed by Sori Yanagi in 1954, this example is a 2004 reissue from Tendo Mokko. *H:15¼ in (38.75 cm); W:16⅔ in (42 cm); D:12¼ in (31 cm). TDO*

ZAISU

This light, stackable, legless seat is made from beech with a zelkova veneer. A single piece of molded plywood forms an organic curve. The hole in the seat serves two purposes: first, to stop a cushion from sliding and second, to prevent the wood from warping. Designed by Kenji Fujimori in 1963, this example is a 2004 re-issue from Tendo Mokko. *H:15¾ in (40 cm); W:13 in (33 cm); D:19¼ in (49 cm). TDO*

PINE BENCH

This low bench in a light pine has a simple rectangular seat, which is molded and slightly curved in the middle to make it both more elegant and more comfortable to sit on.

The seat is supported at each end by gently tapered leg supports that have a groove down the center. Made of solid pine, the bench was designed by Riki Watanabe and produced by Tendo Mokko. *W:70 in (175 cm). FRE*

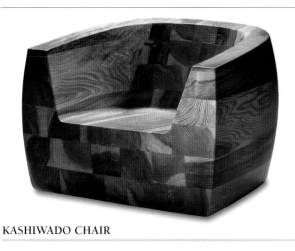

KASHIWADO CHAIR

This armchair, named after a famous sumo wrestler, is made from blocks of cedar trunk; the surface is finished with a sanding technique that reveals the wood's grains. Originally designed by Isamu Kenmochi in 1961, this 2004 model is from Tendo Mokko. *H:24¾ in (63 cm); W:33½ in (85 cm). TDO*

LOW TABLE

A modern take on a traditional Japanese form, this low beech table with a rosewood veneer has an indentation around the edge, called a *mizukaeshi* (water embankment). Designed by Isamu Kenmochi in 1968, this 2004 model is by Tendo Mokko. *H:13¼ in (33.5 cm); W:55⅛ in (140 cm). TDO*

SPOKE CHAIR

This oak chair has a rectangular rail above a tapering back. The spindles are supported on turned legs. The low seat is in line with traditional Japanese furniture. Designed by Katsuhei Toyoguchi in 1963, this 2004 model is from Tendo Mokko. *H:32⅝ in (83 cm); W:31⅛ in (81 cm); D:26¾ in (68 cm). TDO*

TENDO MOKKO

THE FIRST FURNITURE COMPANY IN JAPAN TO PRODUCE PLYWOOD FURNITURE, TENDO MOKKO INTRODUCED THE WORLD TO THE JAPANESE STYLE OF MODERNISM.

Fujitaro Oyama, president Tendo Mokko 1944–68

Most of the forward-thinking Japanese furniture designers of the 1950s worked with the fledgling manufacturer Tendo Mokko. A specialist in the use of plywood (*mokko* means woodwork), Tendo produced Sori Yanagi's Butterfly stool (1954), Isamu Kenmochi's Kashiwado chair (1961), and even a chair by Charlotte Perriand (1955), the French designer, who was a regular visitor to Japan.

Tendo Mokko started as little more than a cooperative of carpenters and cabinet-makers who came together in 1940 to make ammunition boxes and wooden decoy planes during the war. After the fighting ended, the group turned the cutting-edge skills they had developed to manufacturing furniture. Since they were the only furniture company in Japan at the time willing to work with plywood, it is no surprise that their services were sought out by a generation of young designers eager to utilize the manufacturing processes favored in Europe and America.

By the mid-1950s, Tendo Mokko was a thriving company with a strong export trade, especially to the United States. Indeed, it was Tendo's furniture collections of this decade that alerted the West to the fact that the Japanese could do Modernist design.

A German article on Japanese design, 1960s Proof that Japanese furniture designs were popular at the time in Western countries, this German design magazine featured furniture by Tendo Mokko in an issue from 1966.

MURAI STOOL

This stool is made of laminated, molded beech with a teak veneer. It has a minimal, geometric design. Designed by Reiko Tanabe in 1961, it received first place in the Tendo Concur Design awards. This is a 2004 model from Tendo Mokko. *H:14¼ in (36 cm); W:17¾ in (45 cm); D:17¼ in (43.5 cm). TDO*

FRANCE AND GERMANY

DESPITE BEING NEIGHBORING nations, France and Germany displayed stark differences in their attitudes toward Modern design. It was in Germany that Modernism started after World War I, while across the border new developments were met with deep-seated suspicion. Although the polarity of these attitudes was not as pronounced in the post-World War II era (many of the key figures of the Bauhaus had, after all, fled Germany), telling disparities remained.

In France, the appeal of Modernism had had little impact by the start of the 1950s. The country's Ministry of Commerce attempted to stimulate

interest in Rational design, in much the same way as Good Design was promoted in Britain and the United States. The government sponsored, for instance, the annual *Beauté de France* award, but such efforts inevitably failed. Jacque Tati's celebrated film *Mon Oncle* (1958) sums up the attitude of most French people to Modernist architecture and design, with its uproarious mockery of the style as pretentious, awkward, and uncomfortable.

DESIGNS FOR THE ELITE
Perhaps the main reason that Tati so mercilessly lampooned Modernism was because the style was so closely

associated with the bourgeoisie. French designers of the 1940s and 1950s adopted the minimalist Modern look not to provide inexpensive furniture for widespread use, as its pioneers had originally intended, but to sell to an affluent, educated elite. Designers such as Jacques Adnet, Jean Royere, and Serge Mouille had their designs made, often by hand, at great cost to clients who had reassuringly deep pockets. Adnet furnished luxurious ocean liners and presidential apartments, while Royere opened showrooms in the oil-rich nations of the Middle East.

The concern of French designers for the aesthetic, rather than the ideological, is apparent in the decorative effects that were incorporated into their designs. Displaying a prettiness rarely associated with Modernism was the work of Mathieu Matégot and Janette Laverrière, designers who did not cater strictly to an elite clientele, but who certainly ignored the needs of the poor. Matégot used perforated sheet metal to enliven his designs, while the Swiss-born Laverrière frequently produced work in enameled iron.

COFFEE TABLE

This coffee table has a square table top in rosewood; the table's tapering legs are made of hammered wrought iron. The legs are united by a tier underneath that is formed from pierced wrought iron. Designed in the style of Mathieu Matégot. *H:17¾ in (45 cm); W:19⅝ in (50 cm); D:19⅝ in (50 cm). CSB*

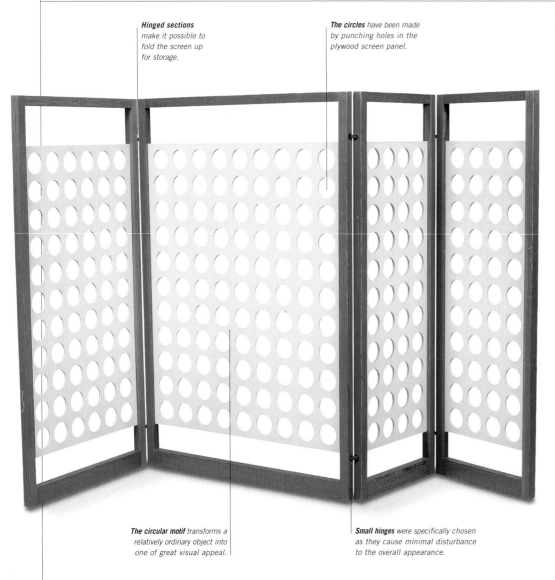

Hinged sections make it possible to fold the screen up for storage.

The circles have been made by punching holes in the plywood screen panel.

The circular motif transforms a relatively ordinary object into one of great visual appeal.

Small hinges were specifically chosen as they cause minimal disturbance to the overall appearance.

FOUR-PANEL SCREEN

This folding screen is made up of four separate panels, each of which is enclosed by a simple frame made of stained wood. The panels are of varying widths and are linked together with the use of small, unobtrusive hinges, so the screen can be folded flat easily for transport and

storage. The plywood panels that make up the screen have been perforated with symmetrical, round holes at regular intervals, adding to the visual attractiveness of the piece. All of the panels have a matt finish in white lacquer. The screen was designed by Egon Eiermann for the Chamber of Deputies in the Bundestag in Bonn, Germany. *1968. H:56 in (142 cm). DOR*

SIDE TABLE

This ash side table has a rectangular top above a single drawer with angle-cut sides. The table top is raised on square, tapering legs; the legs are joined by stretchers and united below by an undertier with a V-shaped magazine rack. Designed by Jean and Jacques Adnet. *c. 1950. H:24 in (61 cm); W:28¼ in (72.5 cm). CAL*

THE ULM SCHOOL

While designers in France were developing a luxuriant approach to Modernism, many of their German counterparts wanted to reduce design to its bare bones. In 1950, the *Hochschule für Gestaltung* (High School for Design) opened in Ulm, with Max Bill as its director. Following the lead of the Bauhaus (where Bill had studied), the Ulm school taught its students a clear, simple, functional style of design that aided mass production. Representative of this approach was Bill's Ulm stool (1954), an object so elementary in its construction that it hardly seems to have been designed at all.

The Ulm school was established largely with finances provided by the United States as part of the Marshall Plan. The influence of American money and American culture on Germany in the 1950s was to prove immensely important. Hollywood movies and American car culture captivated German youth, not least because of the stark contrast they provided to the archaic ideals of the Third Reich.

American furniture design was also a source of inspiration for German designers who found themselves indifferent to the strict, Rationalist principles being taught at Ulm. The more organic tendencies of Charles and Ray Eames, George Nelson, and others can be seen in the work of German designers such as Georg Leowald and Egon Eiermann and in-house designers of the Walter Knoll company.

It was Eiermann who was the most successful of these designers. Indeed, his smoothly shaped folding chair, the SE18, launched in 1953, became one of the biggest-selling wooden chairs of the decade. Also in demand as an architect, Eiermann proved that there was more to German design than austere Functionalism, a fact confirmed by the experimental designs produced in Germany during the 1960s.

ULM STOOL

Designed by Max Bill for the Ulm school, this rectilinear design with a simple stretcher could be used at whim as a stool, a table, a shelf, or a portable tray. *1954.* H:17⅓ in (44 cm); W:15½ in (39.5 cm); D:11½ in (29.5 cm).

DESK CHAIR

This chair has a molded plywood seat and back and is raised on a cast-metal pedestal that has a mechanism for adjusting the height. The inward-curving metal legs have rubber-padded feet. Designed by Egon Eiermann. *c. 1950. BonBay*

TULIP ARMCHAIR

This chair's one-piece seat and back has armrests that bend outward. It has a revolving metal base and detachable leather upholstery. Designed by Jorgen Kastholm and Preben Fabricius for Alfred Kill. *1964.* H:34¼ in (87 cm). *HERR*

BARREL CHAIR

The back and seat of this chair are made of one piece of alder bent plywood. It has a lacquered-beech frame with splayed legs. The added cushion is red. Designed by Pierre Guariche for Steiner, Paris. *c. 1954.* H:29½ in (75 cm). *DOR*

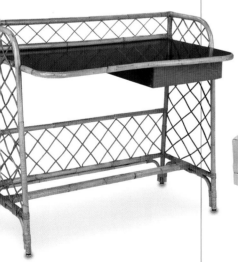

WRITING DESK

This writing desk has a bamboo frame and rattan trellis panels; the writing surface is made of lacquered wood. The piece was designed by Jean Royere. *c. 1952.* H:35 in (89 cm); W:41 in (104 cm); 20½ in (52 cm).

CONSTANZE BENCH

This is an early-1960s sofa bed with polished-steel, splayed-metal feet. The foam-padded seat and back are upholstered in buttoned, sand-colored fabric. The piece has a patented mechanism that allows it to be changed from a sofa into a bed. Designed by Johannes Spalt for Franz Wittman. H:27⅝ in (70 cm); W:68⅞ in (175 cm); D:27⅝ in (70 cm). *DOR*

EXPERIMENTS IN SEATING

BY CREATING NEW, INFORMAL SEATING THAT
GAVE THE USER FLEXIBILITY AND FREEDOM,
POST-WAR DESIGNERS REDEFINED THE CHAIR.

THE POST-WAR YEARS were a time of great experimentation. In 1946, the American designer Eero Saarinen began work on his Womb chair (*see p.500*). Commissioned by Hans and Florence Knoll, the Womb chair was one of the first designs that did not dictate how to sit. The user could sit on it, curl up in it, or slouch in it with his or her legs over the side. "The necessity of changing one's position is an important factor often forgotten in chair design," Saarinen pointed out, and for the next 25 years designers would become increasingly concerned with informal approaches to seating. Forms, materials, and processes were experimented with in a way that completely altered the topography of seating design.

Not long after the Womb chair went on the market in 1947, Charles Eames designed his own take on free-form seating. Eames was a collaborator of Saarinen's, and there was surely some friendly one-upmanship when he presented his La Chaise. Eames's biomorphic design was far more explicit in its suggestion of multiple seating positions than the Womb, and even did away with upholstery. Named after the French-American sculptor Gaston Lachaise, the design unashamedly celebrated the naked shape of its curvaceous fiberglass seat.

FORM FOLLOWS FUN

The malleability of fiberglass prompted many designers to explore more adventurous forms for furniture, and the strictly Rationalist principles that had guided Modern furniture design began to wane. George Nelson's Coconut chair (1955) was an early example of form following fun, rather than function. Resembling a cracked coconut shell, it predated the representational furniture that became popular a decade later, the most famous of which was the baseball-mitt-shaped Joe chair (named after baseball star Joe DiMaggio) by Gionatan De Pas, Donato D'Urbino, and Paulo Lomazzi.

This Italian trio also designed the inflatable Blow chair, another icon of the era. Portable, disposable, and inexpensive, the Blow—as well as the many cardboard chair designs of the period—was a rebellion against centuries of tradition that said furniture should be a carefully crafted and enduring feature of the home.

In 1967, Cesare Leonardi and Franca Stagi presented their celebrated Dondolo design, a sinuous, fiberglass chaise longue that rocked. An object best approached with caution by all but the bravest, the Dondolo was an intentional affront to accepted ideas of seating.

COCONUT CHAIR
Nelson's Coconut chair has a molded-plastic, fiberglass-reinforced shell that is raised on a four-legged, tubular-chrome base. The foam seat is upholstered in red fabric. Designed by George Nelson for the Herman Miller Furniture Company. 1955. H:33 in (84 cm); W:17½ in (44 cm); D:33 in (84 cm). SDR

HARP CHAIR
This chair has a solid ash frame with three curved legs and is reminiscent of Viking ships. The seat and back are made from taut flag line, which lends the chair a sculptural quality. Designed by Jorgen Hovelshov for Christensen & Larsen. 1968. H:51½ in (131 cm). SDR

LA CHAISE
The seat and back of the chair are made from molded fiberglass and are supported on five polished-steel rods that rise from an oak, cross-shaped base. Designed by Charles Eames. c. 1948. H:41⅓ in (150 cm). DOR

The lack of upholstery emphasizes the sculptural shape.

The seat comprises two fiberglass shells separated by a rubber disc.

Five iron rods attach the chair's seat to its base.

The chair's lightness is underscored by the hole in the back.

UP5 CHAIR

WITH ITS FORM REPRESENTING THE SHAPE OF A WOMAN, THE UP5 CHAIR WAS RADICAL
NOT ONLY IN APPEARANCE, BUT ALSO IN THE WAY IT WAS MADE AND PACKAGED.

Italian designer Gaetano Pesce's UP5 chair (1969) was not only radical in its peculiar, bulbous appearance, but also ground-breaking in the way it was made. First formed from high-density polyurethane foam and covered in stretch nylon, the chair was then put into a vacuum chamber and shrunk to 10 percent of its original size. The resulting form was then quickly heat-sealed between two airtight vinyl sheets and packed into an easily transportable box.

Once the box was taken home by the buyer, he or she would cut open the vinyl covering and watch as air seeped back into the chair, restoring it to its original voluminous shape.

The UP5 chair was one of a series of furniture items that Pesce designed for B&B Italia

utilizing this extraordinary process. Often referred to as *La Mamma* or *Donna*, the chair's shape "expressed my idea of woman," said Pesce. The UP6, a spherical footrest, represented a ball shackled to the woman by a chain—or in this case, a piece of elasticized cord (not shown).

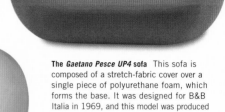

The *Gaetano Pesce UP4* sofa This sofa is composed of a stretch-fabric cover over a single piece of polyurethane foam, which forms the base. It was designed for B&B Italia in 1969, and this model was produced from 1970 to 1973. H:25 in (63.5 cm); W:64 in (162.5 cm); D:34 in (86.5 cm). R20

La Mamma (or *Donna*) foam lounge chair and matching ottoman Each piece is fully upholstered in a yellow, stretch-nylon fabric, which covers the polyurethane-foam structure. Both pieces bear the B&B Italia label. *1969.* H:40 in (110.5 cm); W:42 in (106.5 cm); D:68 in (173 cm). SDR

MALITTE SEATING SYSTEM

This seating system is made up of five sculpted polyurethane-foam blocks that stack up into a square wall when not in use. Four of the blocks are individual seats, while the fifth one serves as an ottoman. Designed by Roberto Matta. 1966. H:63 in (160 cm); W:63 in (160 cm); D:24¾ in (65 cm). WKA

LIFESTYLE SEATING

Designers of the 1960s often saw themselves as pioneers of a new, progressive lifestyle—a key reason for their experimentation with modes of seating. Andrea Branzi, a radical Italian designer, explained that his colleagues' work "undermines traditional relationships with the house and instead proposes objects with autonomous functions that should promote new types of behavior."

Roberto Matta's Malitte system (1966) was just the sort of autonomous object Branzi was referring to. Essentially a carved-up block of polyurethane foam, the Malitte separated into five ambiguous-looking elements, all of which could be sat on in various positions. Matta's Malitte was a long way from the conventional perception of the chair as an object with four legs, a seat, and a back.

"Followed to its extreme, furniture design would be a series of versatile, interchangeable, multipurpose cushions," mused British designer Max Clendinning at the beginning of the 1960s, and by the end of the decade his vision was close to becoming reality. The economic downturn of the 1970s, however, put an abrupt end to the idealistic experiments of avant-garde designers. While chair design would continue to prove an expansive playground for many, never again would there be such focus on sprawling, slouching, and slumping as there was in the 1950s and 1960s.

DONDOLO

This rocking chair is made from a single strip of molded, fiberglass-reinforced polyester. It is one of only about 50 that were designed by Cesare Leonardi and Franca Stagi. 1967. H:30½ in (76 cm); W:68 in (170 cm); D:15 in (37.5 cm). QU

1960s SCANDINAVIA

ON VISITING AN EXHIBITION of Scandinavian design in 1959, Danish designer Poul Henningsen declared that there were "many skills and much elegance" on display, "but not one dangerous object." Henningsen might have been infamous for his outspoken criticism of fellow designers, but there was some truth in his suggestion that much Scandinavian design of the late 1950s was produced purely with the aim "of being sold to America."

By the late 1950s, Scandinavian design had, in many ways, become a victim of its own success. So well-received was it worldwide that the furniture industry was unwilling to tamper with a winning formula. Luckily, a new generation of designers was emerging that was prepared to upset the status quo. Chief among them was the Dane Verner Panton.

A NEW GENERATION
In the early 1950s, Panton worked for Arne Jacobsen, and by the end of the decade he had taken his employer's tentative studies in sculptural form (chairs such as the Egg and the Swan) to new extremes. Panton's first solo project, a daring interior for a restaurant on the Danish island of Funen, where he grew up, was completed in 1958. Described by one newspaper as "the most untraditional restaurant in Denmark," it signaled the start of a new era in Scandinavian design.

Throughout the 1960s, Panton pushed the boundaries of design, both in terms of form and materials. His most outstanding achievement of the period was the Panton chair, a design that took over ten years to realize. This S-shaped cantilever chair, which was launched in 1967, used the new technique of injection molding and was manufactured by Vitra in Switzerland, where Panton was to move in the mid-1960s.

Working along similar lines was the Finnish designer Eero Aarnio. Like Panton, Aarnio was equally attuned to the brash demands of Pop culture and the more refined virtues of harmonious form and durable construction that traditionally characterize Scandinavian design. Aarnio's series of shapely seating designs, completed in the 1960s, have since become icons, appearing in many movies and photographs. His fiberglass Ball chair (1966) was even the subject of a feature in *The New York Times*, confirming the cultural and commercial success of his designs.

Yrjo Kukkapuro was another Finn who, like Aarnio, preferred plastics and fiberglass to wood. Kukkapuro's most distinguished design, the Carousel chair of 1964, was reputedly envisioned by the designer after he had fallen asleep in a bank of snow, having had one too many vodkas. On awakening, Kukkapuro realized how comfortable he had been and immediately took a mold of the impression his body had left in the snow, using the shape to make the Carousel chair.

THE LOST YEARS
Panton, Aarnio, and Kukkapuro were all fortunately supported by manufacturers who believed in their bold designs. Manufacturers like these were few and far between in Scandinavia during the 1960s, with most firms sticking to tried-and-trusted forms of furniture. In Sweden, for instance, it seems that no one was willing to take a chance on the audacious work of young designers, which is why the 1960s are now often referred to as the "lost years" of Swedish design.

The dining room of Verner Panton's home, Switzerland Verner Panton was a prolific designer whose commissions included a number of interiors. This room from his own home in Binningen is testament to the Pop style that was prevalent in the 1960s.

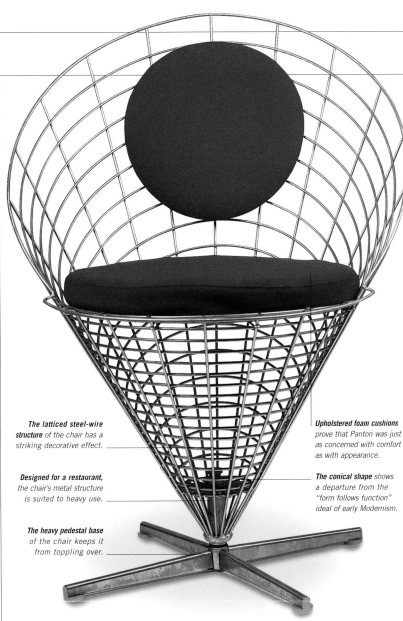

The latticed steel-wire structure of the chair has a striking decorative effect.

Designed for a restaurant, the chair's metal structure is suited to heavy use.

The heavy pedestal base of the chair keeps it from toppling over.

Upholstered foam cushions prove that Panton was just as concerned with comfort as with appearance.

The conical shape shows a departure from the "form follows function" ideal of early Modernism.

WIRE CONE CHAIR

The chromed, steel-wire frame of this chair is of conical form, centered at the chair's base and fanning out as it rises to make the seat and chair structure. The chair's seat and back have circular foam pads, which are covered in pink upholstery. The chair has a swivel action and stands on heavy cross-shaped feet made of chromed steel that form a sturdy base. Designed by Verner Panton for Plus-Linje, Denmark. *c. 1960. H:29¾ in (75.5 cm).*

SHELL FUN LAMP

This lamp is of mother-of-pearl-type discs hung from a ceiling fixture by metal chains. Designed by Verner Penton for J. Lüber, Switzerland. *1965. H:43½ in (110 cm); D:22 in (56 cm). DOR*

DRINKS CART

This lacquered wood, rolling bar has swiveling compartments for accessories, glassware, and bottles. Designed by Verner Panton. *1963. H:29½ in (74 cm); D:15½ in (39.5 cm).*

CONE TABLE

This occasional table is made from Formica, steel, and fabric. It is named for its cone-shaped support. Designed by Verner Paton and manufactured by Plus-Lijne, Denmark. *c. 1958. H:27½ in (70 cm); Diam:31¾ in (81 cm).*

ROUND TABLE

This green, circular table is made out of molded polyester; it is raised on a molded pedestal base made of the same material. Designed by Eero Aarnio for Asko Lahti, Finland. *1967–68. H:29½ in (75 cm); Diam:51¼ in (130 cm). DOR*

PONY CHAIR

This is an adult-sized chair that has been molded to resemble a pony. The chair has a foam body, feet, and ears over a tube frame. The entire piece is upholstered in black stretch fabric. Designed by Eero Aarnio. *H:34¼ in (87 cm); W:42⅛ in (107.5 cm); D:23⅛ in (59 cm). SDR*

BUBBLE CHAIR

Influenced by imagery of the Space Age, the frame of this chair is made from a hollow, transparent-plexiglass half-bubble attached to a chrome hoop and suspended from the ceiling by a metal chain. The gray leather-upholstered seat and chair back fit snugly within the half-bubble frame. Because the chair is made from transparent plexiglass and is fixed to the ceiling at a single point, it creates the impression that the user is floating in midair. Designed by Eero Aarnio for Asko Lahti, Finland. *1968. D:33½ in (85 cm). DOR*

CAROUSEL ARMCHAIR

The white fiberglass shell of the Carousel armchair's seat is raised on a swivel base, which is also made of white fiberglass. The chair has a molded seat and back that is upholstered and covered in a brownish-colored leather. The chair's edges are all slightly rounded. The chromed-steel spring to the rear of the seat connects the shell with the four-pronged base, and the chair has a rocking as well as a swiveling motion. The piece was designed by Yrjo Kukkapuro and produced by Haimi of Finland. *1965. BonE*

1960s FRANCE AND GERMANY

WHILE THE 1960s saw a backlash against the functionalism of Modern design in both France and Germany, the reaction was particularly vociferous in Germany.

Where 1960s French designers such as Pierre Paulin and Olivier Mourgue applied a contemporary twist to well-worn Rationalist principles, their German counterparts—such as Luigi Colani, Peter Raacke, and Helmut Batzner—were more forceful in breaking new ground. In 1968, Werner Nehls, a Munich architect, wrote of a "protest against the past, with its mechanistic, rational, puritanically utilitarian, soulless, inhuman way of forming the environment."

At the annual furniture fair in Cologne, experimental environments were constructed that offered fantastical visions, often inspired by spaceships, of the future. The most celebrated were the *Visiona* installations by the Dane Verner Panton, but many German designers presented similarly outlandish schemes.

German furniture design of the 1960s was not entirely based on fantasy. In 1966, Helmut Batzner accomplished the very real achievement of creating the first chair from a single piece of plastic. Called the Bofinger after the company that produced it, the chair had sold by the hundreds of thousands by the end of the decade.

SEX AND FURNITURE DESIGN

Although most of Europe and the United States was in the grip of a sexual revolution in the 1960s, Germans were particularly enchanted by free love. The German sex educationalist Oswalt Kolle became a popular figure, and the influence of his ideas extended even to furniture design. Although it had a short lifespan as a genre of furniture, the love seat—on which one was supposed to do more than sit—was for a time the focus of many German designers' attentions.

French designers were also letting their libidos drive designs, with Pierre Paulin creating a range of chairs sheathed in elasticated jersey—an idea inspired by the tight swimming suits favored by women on the Cote d'Azur.

Paulin's Mushroom (1963) and Tongue (1967) chairs were both without legs. The low-lying seats of these curvaceous chairs were supported by a frame of tubular steel and covered in foam and stretch fabric. Influenced by the organic shapes of American and Scandinavian designs of the 1950s, the chairs took the sculptural aesthetic to new heights.

The height and width of the chair's back envelop the user, shutting out the surrounding environment.

The glossy surface of the chair adds to the eye-catching nature of the chair's design.

The sculptural form of the chair shows that Rancillac was primarily an artist, rather than a furniture designer.

The chair's base is necessarily heavy to counterbalance the weight of the user.

Undulations in the surface provide support for the body and showcase new techniques for molding plastics.

The part of the chair intended to support the legs mimics the trunk of an elephant.

DJINN CHAIR

The seat and back of this chair are of fabric stretched over a polyurethane-and-metal frame on metal runners. Designed by Olivier Mourgue for Airborne and originally produced in 1965, this example is a later issue. *c. 1970. BonBay*

TULIP CHAIR

This armchair has a padded back, a seat with upswept arms, and a swiveling, aluminum, cross-shaped base. It is upholstered in teal snakeskin vinyl. Designed by Pierre Paulin for Artifort. *H:30 in (76 cm). SDR*

ELEPHANT CHAIR

Titled the Elephant, because of its obvious resemblance to an elephant's head and trunk, this lounge chair's body is formed from a single piece of bright scarlet fiberglass. The armrests bear a witty resemblance to an elephant's ears and the leg supports of the piece clearly mimic the trunk. Sculpturally fanciful but still functional, the chair's sturdy base is made of painted steel and is particularly heavy in order to provide a good sense of balance when used. Designed in 1966 by Bernard Rancillac and made in very limited quantities, this piece is a clear forerunner of the Pop-inspired pieces of the following decade. This version is one of a limited 1985 reissue that was manufactured by Michel Roudillon in France. *H:59⅛ in (150 cm); W:59⅛ in (150 cm); D:78¾ in (200 cm).*

Living room of the Bubble Place (*Le Palais Bulles*) Decorated in blues, the palace, with futuristic, round rooms and rotating floors, is on the French Riviera. By Pierre Cardin and Antti Lovag. *1970.*

Similar to Paulin's pieces were the 1960s designs of Olivier Mourgue. Mourgue's 1965 Djinn series (seen in the 1968 movie *2001: A Space Odyssey*) reflected his view that functionalism was not the only goal of design, since "one must pursue visual poetry too."

In 1968, inspired by the solidarity of the student riots in Paris, Mourgue produced his Bouloum chaise longue. Its anthropomorphic design, based on the outline of a friend, was an early expression of wit in Modern design and brought the discipline closer to art.

It was in the 1960s that many artists began to experiment with furniture design as a means of artistic expression. Pop artists Claes Oldenburg, Eduardo Paolozzi, and Bernard Rancillac all included furniture within their *oeuvre*, as the association of furniture with functionalism began to fade.

LUIGI COLANI

A DESIGNER WHO WOULD ANTICIPATE THE CULT OF CELEBRITY,
LUIGI COLANI EMBODIED THE ANTI-RATIONALISM OF THE 1960s.

Luigi Colani

Gleefully pointing out to anyone who would listen that he always refused to use a ruler, Luigi Colani epitomized the anti-Rationalist spirit that was characteristic of much German design in the 1960s.

Born Lutz Colani in Berlin in 1928, Colani changed his name from Lutz to Luigi in an effort to make himself sound less German. It is not surprising, therefore, that Colani studied and lived abroad. He studied aerodynamics at the Sorbonne in Paris, and then worked for the Douglas Aircraft Company in California for a short time.

In the late 1950s, Colani returned to his homeland, where he immediately caused a sensation with his futuristic automobile and motorcycle designs. Widely published (but rarely built), these sleek, podlike vehicle designs

reflected Colani's twin fascinations with space travel and the female form.

It was not until the mid-1960s, however, that Colani turned his restless talents to domestic designs. Always eager to operate at the cutting edge, Colani used the latest forms of plastic available at the time to produce his eccentrically shaped furniture. In 1968, Colani created a ball-shaped kitchen capsule for Poggenpohl, and in 1973 he designed his most famous piece of furniture, the Colani seat, which can be sat upon in a variety of different ways.

Colani's idiosyncratic design style, which he has applied to a wide range of products from everyday objects such as teapots and chairs to quirky jewelry and small jet airplanes, allied to his carefully crafted public persona, anticipated the cult of the celebrity personality that would become commonplace within the design community in the decades to come.

TV-Relax couch This couch by Luigi Colani has a buttoned seat and back that are of an organic form, stretching out to create a leg rest. The piece is upholstered in a saffron-colored stretch fabric. *1969. W:67 in (170 cm). DOR*

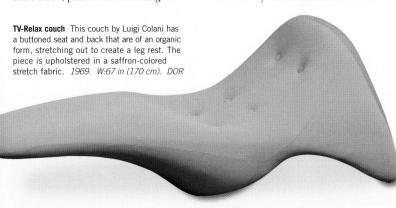

WRITING DESK

This desk has a top made of fiberglass-reinforced plastic. Made in one piece, the surface has been molded to provide a flat surface for writing at the front and compartments for equipment at the back. The rectangular top is raised on a white-painted metal frame. Designed by Marc Berthier for FDAN, France. *c. 1967. H:26⅓ in (67 cm); W:43 in (109 cm); D:70 in (27.5 cm). DOR*

SINGLE-PEDESTAL DESK

This single-pedestal desk has a free-form top that is made of laminate and extends over a bank of drawers. The entire piece is raised on a tubular, black-painted metal frame, while the desktop is supported by a single pedestal. Simple, unobtrusive grooves in the tops of the drawers serve as drawer handles. The piece is designed by Pierre Paulin for Mobilor. *H:29¼ in (74.5 cm); W:47 in (119.5 cm); D:24 in (61 cm). SDR*

POP INTERIOR

CONTRASTING SHAPES, TEXTURE, AND COLOR WERE VITAL
COMPONENTS OF INTERIORS OF THIS PERIOD AND RESULTED
IN FRESH, FUN, FUNCTIONAL, AND STYLISH SPACES.

FROM THE LATE 1950S, European design was dominated by
a reaction against the dogma of the Modernists. Pop, and its
successor Postmodernism, share an irreverent sense of irony
that infused the interior design of this period with humor.

OPEN-PLAN LIVING

A preference for open-plan living developed in the 1960s
as large loft and warehouse spaces in New York and
London were reinvented as housing developments.
Inhabitants of these large formless spaces used portable
screens and panels to subdivide space into manageable
sections, and furniture was positioned to create wall-less
boundaries within the living spaces. Zones could also
be demarcated by texture or bold colors, which were
inspired by Pop Art, as well as clever lighting that made
use of lamps and ceiling lights to illuminate specific areas.

Rooms of this period also benefited from technologies
developed for the war effort, which resulted in new
materials such as fiberglass. As these materials became
available to the consumer market, they gave designers
more scope to experiment and create surprising interiors.

COLOR, SHAPE, AND TEXTURE

This Normandy farmhouse was built in the 1970s and
furnished with pieces from the 1960s and 1970s. The owner
moved to the area from San Francisco, and brought the
cutting-edge tastes of the United States to this quiet corner of
rural France. The pieces in this room sum up the move away
from the functional designs of the Modernist era in favor
of bold, sculptural, fun shapes. Primarily monochrome,
the room takes its color from the bold yellow and
red of the seating. The bright red Alfa sofas are by
Zanotta. The ceiling provides a focal point as
the chaotic contours interrupt light from the
recessed lamps and conceal multicolored
lights. The white plastic dome of the side
lamp is echoed in the table base, the wall
lamp, and even the metal sculpture that
stands in the far corner of the room,
providing some sense of continuity.

Pantella table lamp Designed by Verner Panton
for Louis Poulsen in Denmark, this lamp has a
white, half-spherical acrylic lampshade above
a white-lacquered, trumpet-shaped base. *H:27½ in
(70 cm); Diam:19⅝ in (50 cm).*

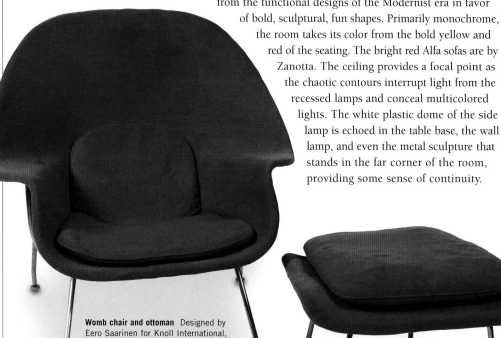

Womb chair and ottoman Designed by
Eero Saarinen for Knoll International,
these pieces have molded fiberglass-
reinforced polyester upholstered with red
latex covered foam, supported on tubular
steel frames. *1948–1950. H:35 in
(89 cm); W:39 in (100 cm) (chair). WKA*

1960s ITALY

BY THE BEGINNING of the 1960s, Italian design had become synonymous worldwide with sophisticated style. The terms *Bel Designo* and *Linea Italiana* had emerged to define the practical but elegant designs of figures such as Gio Ponti and Marco Zanuso. The 1964 Milan Triennale's theme of Leisure (in 1947 the theme was "The Problems of the Least Privileged") summed up the comfortable, assured attitude of the Italian furniture industry at the time.

ANTI-DESIGN EMERGES

The industry was hit by a rude shock in 1965. Trade unions demanded significant wage rises for workers and export trade began to suffer. At the same time, a small group of designers, who saw the prevailing notions of taste and luxury as elitist and out of touch with everyday life, began to question the self-satisfied nature of the industry.

From the mid-1960s, a rebellion revolutionized the Italian design industry, as designers turned toward more populist aesthetics. The work of the American Pop artists began to exert a major influence, and the use of plastic—a new, inexpensive material—was embraced wholeheartedly.

Chief among the exponents of Anti-Design, or Radical Design, as it came to be known, were Archizoom and Superstudio, two groups of architects and designers who formed in Florence in 1966. That they preferred a group

identity to using their individual names showed their distaste for the egotism and money-grabbing that they perceived to be gripping the industry.

Not quite as extreme as these groups, but still intent on injecting a more democratic, inclusive element into Italian design, was Joe Colombo. Although his designs were still rooted in the Rationalist principles of Functionalism, they also showed a desire by Colombo to communicate with, as opposed to dictating to, his users. Other designers such as Anna Castelli Ferrieri and Vico Magistretti also took this tack during the 1960s, often employing plastic, a material that inspired new and playful forms.

MOVING FORWARD

By the end of the 1960s, with the Italian economy near collapse, much of the unity and confidence of the country's design industry had dissolved into disharmony. Advocates of *Bel Designo* were being challenged by those involved with Anti-Design, resulting in something of a crisis of identity. A period of great creativity, however, arose from this chaos and enabled Italy to maintain its status as the most important European nation in the field of design.

Apartment of Joe Colombo, Milan The interior has two coordinated living machines, Rotoliving and Cabriolet bed, which synthesized day-time and night-time environments. They were the result of Colombo's research into living habitats. *1969–70.*

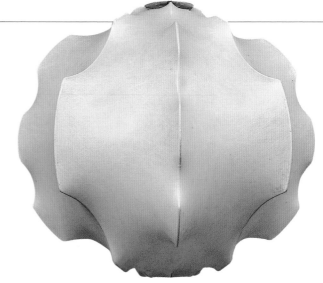

ORGANIC LAMP

This large, sculptural hanging lamp is organic in form, which explains where it received its name. The body of the lamp, which looks as if it could take its shape from nature, is made from a stiff fiberglass shell that is suspended on a wire frame. The cream-colored pendant lamp was designed by the renowned lighting designers Achille and Pier Giacomo Castiglioni. *c. 1968. DOR*

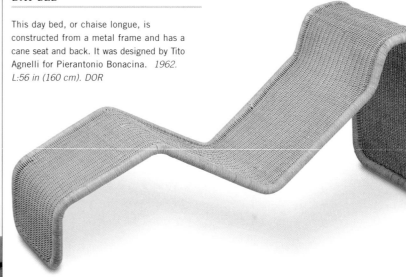

DAY BED

This day bed, or chaise longue, is constructed from a metal frame and has a cane seat and back. It was designed by Tito Agnelli for Pierantonio Bonacina. *1962. L:56 in (160 cm). DOR*

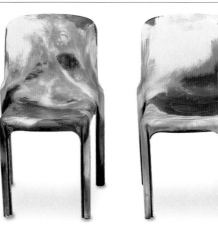

SELENE CHAIRS

Each of these stacking chairs has been formed from a single piece of injection-molded plastic; a camouflage-type color scheme has been used. The square-section legs have indents to give them greater strength. These three chairs were originally part of a set of four. Designed by Vico Magistretti for Studio Artemide, Milan. *1967–68. H:29½ in (75 cm); W:18½ in (47 cm); D:19½ in (50 cm). DOR*

The six bays of this seating design encourage the sitters to be sociable.

The fiberglass base of the seating "livingscape" has been painted white to give it a more immediate visual impact.

The sheer size of the seating design makes it almost architectural in appearance.

The fake leopard skin is a conscious use of kitsch and was intended as an affront to "good taste."

SAFARI LIVINGSCAPE

This modular, so-called "livingscape" has a fiberglass frame in four sections, which fit together to make a large, square-shaped seating area lined with textile-covered latex upholstery. Each individual seat is a petal of a flower-shaped form and is covered in fake leopard skin, as is the floor of the structure. Designed by Archizoom Associates for Poltronova. *1967–68. H:29½ in (75 cm); W:84⅓ in (214 cm); D:100 in (254 cm). DOR*

THE ELDA CHAIR

IN THE BRIEF TIME THAT HE WORKED AS A FURNITURE DESIGNER, JOE COLOMBO CREATED MANY TREND-SETTING AND TECHNICALLY ADVANCED PIECES, THE MOST NOTABLE OF WHICH IS THE LEATHER-AND-FIBERGLASS ELDA CHAIR.

Although Joe Colombo died tragically of heart failure in 1971, at the age of just 41, he produced an astonishing number of ground-breaking designs during his short career. The Elda armchair, designed for his wife of the same name, is one of Colombo's most recognizable pieces of furniture design and is typical in being both technologically and aesthetically advanced.

Cocooning the user in his or her own private world, the chair's sheer presence was a radical leap from the polite designs of his predecessors. Made from fiberglass, it was also the most ambitious use of this material that the furniture industry had seen.

The chair's thick, twisting cushions, which add to its womb-like appeal, are designed to hook on to the fiberglass base, so that they can be removed easily for cleaning. A further feature of the chair is the rotating base that enables the user to have a 360-degree view of his or her surroundings.

The futuristic styling of the chair has brought it to the attention of numerous film-set dressers, and, perhaps most notably, the Elda chair crops up more than once in villains' lairs in James Bond movies. Although Colombo never lived to see his designs on the big screen, he would no doubt have approved since, when younger, he changed his given name of Cesare to Joe because he thought it made him sound more like a Hollywood movie star.

COMPONIBILI STORAGE UNITS

This sectional system works in any home or office environment. The units have a base, door, and top. Designed by Anna Castelli Ferrieri for Kartell. *1969. H:23 in (58.5 cm); Diam:12½ in (32 cm).*

The Elda chair The chair has a molded, fiberglass-reinforced plastic shell with a black leather-upholstered seat. *1963–65. H:39⅖ in (100 cm); W:39⅖ in (100 cm); D:36⅝ in (93 cm). WKA*

One of Joe Columbo's sketches of the Elda chair This drawing illustrates how the rotating mechanism allowed the user to make a full 360-degree turn. *WKA*

POKER CARD TABLE

The table top of this card table is white plastic, covered in green baize with a leather trim. The legs are stainless steel. Designed by Joe Colombo in 1968; this example is a 2004 Zanotta re-issue. *H:27½ in (70 cm); W:38⅝ in (98 cm). ZAN*

CASTIGLIONI BROTHERS

THE CASTIGLIONI BROTHERS CREATED A STYLE THAT COMBINED A REVERENCE FOR EVERYDAY OBJECTS, PROVOCATIVE WIT, AND A RATIONALIST APPROACH TO FUNCTION.

BORN THE SONS of a sculptor in Milan, the Castiglioni brothers—Livio, Pier Giacomo, and Achille—grew up to dominate post-World War II Italian design. Designing everything from vacuum cleaners to table lamps and restaurants, the prolific brothers provided a bridge between the hard-edged Rationalists who came before them and the playful Postmodernists who were to follow.

It was the youngest brother, Achille, who would eventually gain the greatest prominence, but it was the eldest, Livio, who first brought the family to the public's attention, when he created, along with Luigi Caccia Dominioni and Pier Giacomo, the first Italian radio made using Bakelite.

By 1945, Achille, like his brothers, had graduated from the *Politecnico* in Milan and all three were working in the same studio. A modest door handle and a set of plywood hotel furniture were their first projects. Although trained in architecture, the brothers always favored furniture and industrial design.

BIOGRAPHY

Achille, Pier Giacomo, and Livio Castiglioni

1939 Livio and Pier Giacomo collaborate with Luigi Caccia Dominioni to create the Bakelite Phonola radio.

1945 The three brothers begin working together.

1947 Achille exhibits at the Milan Triennale and is involved in the exhibition until his death in 2002.

1952 Livio stops working with his brothers.

1956 The three brothers become founding members of the *Associazone per il Designo Industriale* (ADI).

1957 Exhibit *Colors and Forms of the Home Today*.

1960 Splugenbrau restaurant in Milan designed.

1962 Arco and Toio floor lamps designed for the lighting manufacturer Flos.

1969 Livio designs the Serpentine Boalum lamp with Gianfranco Frettini.

1970 Achille begins teaching at *Turin Politecnico*.

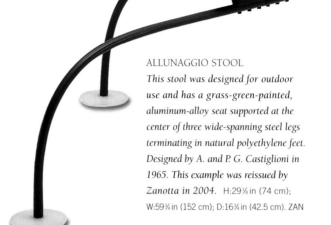

ALLUNAGGIO STOOL
This stool was designed for outdoor use and has a grass-green-painted, aluminum-alloy seat supported at the center of three wide-spanning steel legs terminating in natural polyethylene feet. Designed by A. and P. G. Castiglioni in 1965. This example was reissued by Zanotta in 2004. H:29⅛ in (74 cm); W:59¾ in (152 cm); D:16¾ in (42.5 cm). ZAN

SERVO RANGE
These pieces are from the A. and P. G. Castiglioni Servo range: the Servopluvio umbrella stand is on the left and the Servofumo ashtray on the right. Other items include a coat stand, a towel stand, a book stand, and a service table. 1961–1986. ZAN

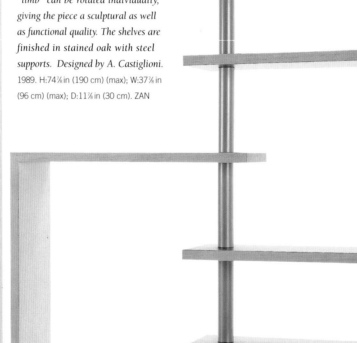

JOY SHELVING
This shelf unit comprises a number of honeycomb core uprights and shelves, with steel reinforcements inside. Each "limb" can be rotated individually, giving the piece a sculptural as well as functional quality. The shelves are finished in stained oak with steel supports. Designed by A. Castiglioni. 1989. H:74⅞ in (190 cm) (max); W:37⅞ in (96 cm) (max); D:11⅞ in (30 cm). ZAN

COMPASSO D'ORO AWARDS

CREATED BY GIO PONTI AND ALDO BORLETTI, THE *COMPASSO D'ORO* AWARDS BECAME THE MOST COVETED AND PRESTIGIOUS AWARDS IN 20TH-CENTURY FURNITURE DESIGN.

Between 1955 and 1994, the Castiglionis accumulated nine first prizes and 13 special mentions at the annual *Compasso d'Oro* (Golden Compass) awards. They collected awards for—among other things—a chair, a hospital bed, headphones, and an espresso machine.

The *Compasso d'Oro* awards were first distributed in 1954 and were soon to become the foremost accolades in Italian design, generating international attention for the products selected. The idea of designer Gio Ponti and Aldo Borletti, owner of *La Rinascente* department stores in Milan, the *Compasso d'Oro* awards were intended "to encourage industrialists and craftsmen to raise their production standards from both a technological and an aesthetic standpoint."

Although initially only products sold or distributed by *La Rinascente* qualified, it was not long before the remit of the awards was widened. By 1967, the awards were no longer associated with *La Rinascente* at all, administered instead by the *Associazone per il Designo Industriale* (ADI). Although their credibility was somewhat damaged in the 1980s amid accusations of cronyism, no award in 20th-century design was more prestigious.

Luminator floor lamp This steel lamp is based on a photographer's indirect lights. The tube is just wide enough to fit the bulb socket. Designed by A. and P. G. Castiglioni in 1955, this is a 1994 reissue by Flos. *H:51¼in (130 cm); W:6 in (15 cm); D:6 in (15 cm).*

Arco floor lamp Inspired by a street lamp, this ceiling lamp does not require holes in the ceiling, as light is projected away from the marble base. Designed by A. and P. G. Castiglioni for Flos. *1962. H:95 in (241 cm); W:78⅝ in (200 cm); D:11½ in (29 cm).*

CASTIGLIONI STYLE

The first time a distinctive Castiglioni style emerged was in 1950, with the design of the Leonardo and Bramante trestle tables. Fashioned after craftsmen's tables, they were an early example of Achille's magpie eye. Spotting the practical qualities of the trestle table, the Castiglionis tinkered with the archetypal design to make it their own. Naming the functional tables after two great figures of the Renaissance was a typical touch of wit—reminding us that even great accomplishments begin as sketches made on the humble trestle table.

In 1952, Livio parted company with his brothers. Around this time, too, Achille and Pier Giacomo's talent for lighting design began to gain full expression. In 1955, their Luminator standard lamp won a *Compasso D'Oro* award, while the Bulbo hanging lamp of 1957 showed a poetic use of industrial processes.

Perhaps the high point of their career in lighting design was 1962, when two of their most celebrated lights were produced by Flos. The Arco floor lamp, inspired by streetlights, has become an icon of 20th-century design, while the Toio lamp is a great example of the brothers' invention and resourcefulness. Though workmanlike in appearance, the lamp's ingenious application of car headlights and fishing-rod rings is an homage to the beauty of everyday designs.

OBJETS TROUVÉS

Pier Giacomo and Achille's reverence for anonymous objects was such that their studio was littered with such items, and Achille even had a wooden eel-fishing boat in his apartment. "I put it there as an *objet trouvé*," he explained, referring to the tradition initiated by Marcel Duchamp when he combined a stool and a bicycle wheel in an artwork in 1913.

The Castiglionis' most celebrated works in this tradition were shown to a shocked public in 1957. In an exhibit entitled Colors and Forms of the Home Today, they filled a room with "old" designs (such as Thonet bentwood chairs) and the latest Castiglioni creations. The latter included the Mezzadro stool, which incorporated a tractor seat, and the Sella stool, which had a leather bicycle seat. Although humorous, provocative designs, they were accomplished with such finesse, and with such a sober, Rationalist approach to function, that the joke is entirely convincing.

Pier Giacomo's death in 1968 left Achille to work on his own. His designs always inspired outrage and admiration in equal measure, and no design polarized opinions more than the Primate stool (1970). Demanding an Eastern seating position of folding the calves under the thighs, the Primate was praised by some for its daring, ergonomic approach and damned by others for its odd, toiletlike appearance.

"A design stems from the urge to create a rapport with the unknown person who will use the object," wrote Achille in 1992, and, love them or loathe them, Castiglioni designs always touch a nerve.

MEZZADRO STOOL

This stool has a shaped and perforated aluminum-alloy seat on a single, chromium-plated steel stem, with a steam-treated beech footrest. Designed by A. and P. G. Castiglioni in 1957, this example was reissued by Zanotta in 2004. H:20 in (51 cm); W:19⅓ in (49 cm); D:20 in (51 cm). ZAN

PRIMATE STOOL

The user sits on the top section of this stool with his or her knees resting on the lower section. The pieces are joined by a stainless-steel arm. The base of the stool is made from painted polystyrene. Designed by Achille Castiglioni in 1970, this example was reissued by Zanotta in 2004. H:18½ in (47 cm); W:19¾ in (50 cm); D:31½ in (80 cm). ZAN

1960s UNITED STATES

WHILE THE FORGING of a strong, coherent identity characterized American furniture design of the 1950s, the next decade was far foggier. The Rational, yet sculptural, style developed by Charles and Ray Eames, Eero Saarinen, and others in the 1950s would continue to meet with success during the 1960s, although there were also dissenters who tried to break the hegemony of the aesthetic referred to today as Mid-Century Modern.

Critically and commercially, companies such as the Herman Miller Furniture Company and Knoll were riding high at the start of the 1960s. From humble beginnings, they had risen to international prominence and, understandably, were unwilling to jeopardize this. The relentless invention of the early 1950s waned in the 1960s, as many American furniture companies attempted to consolidate their success by concentrating on the contract (or business) market and exports.

Figureheads of the 1950s turned their talents toward such areas as office furniture (George Nelson's Action Office range, 1964) and airport seating (the Eames Tandem system, 1964). A number of young designers took the corporate path, with David Rowland producing the triumphantly Rationalist 40/4 chair in 1964 (a stack of 40 stood 4 feet tall) and Charles Pollock (brother of Jackson) creating a range of stylish, if sober, executive seating.

American design was becoming stifled, it seemed, by the size of its furniture companies, which were unable to respond to the immediate demands of the market. While many European nations, whose furniture industries often consisted of networks of small companies, were turning out furniture in garish colors and outlandish shapes, this was rarely true of the United States.

FREE-FORM STYLE
The urge to explore a decorative, abstract style was not entirely absent in the United States, however. The work of designers such as Isamu Noguchi (IN50 coffee table), George Nelson (Coconut chair), and Eero Saarinen (Pedestal range) had, to a large extent, cleared the way for the loose, free-form style that swept the furniture world in the 1960s.

Perhaps the most eloquent exponent of the more whimsical style of the 1960s

was Warren Platner. His collection of steel-rod furniture for Knoll, called simply the Platner range, was launched in 1966 to great acclaim. "I felt there was room for the kind of decorative, gentle kind of design that appeared in a period style like Louis XV… but with a Rational base," Platner wrote, summing up his own take on furniture design.

American designers wanting to employ a daring and idiosyncratic style were, as a rule, ignored by the large manufacturers in the 1960s. Dismissed as superficial, designers such as Wendell Castle, Vladimir Kagan, and Erwine and Estelle Laverne had to produce their designs themselves, or seek out small companies with whom they might collaborate. Castle's amorphous furniture designs, made from fiberglass and plastics, were eventually put into limited production by Beylerian of New York, while the Lavernes' work, often distinguished by the use of clear acrylic, was produced by their own company, Laverne Originals. In Los Angeles, Charles Hollis Jones was also experimenting with the decorative possibilities of clear acrylic, producing custom furniture and lighting for clients such as Frank Sinatra, Tennessee Williams, and Diana Ross.

POSTMODERNISM
While the world of American furniture design seemed confused during the 1960s, there was a growing school of thought that insisted that this should be celebrated. Writing about the discipline of architecture, Robert Venturi and Denise Scott Brown published "Complexity and Contradiction in Architecture" in 1966, a text that argued the case for pluralism. The idea that a clear, universal design style should be avoided at all costs, as Venturi and Scott Brown outlined, would provide the basis of Postmodernism, a style that was to develop fully in the next decade.

THE PLATNER RANGE

The round table has a plate-glass table top raised on a spindle-shaped base, which is made out of nickel-plated steel rods. The four chairs have walnut tops and padded seats with removable, velvet-covered cushions. Designed by Warren Platner for Knoll, these pieces make up part of a range of furniture that is referred to simply as the Platner range. *1966. Table: H:28 in (71 cm); D:41½ in (105 cm). QU*

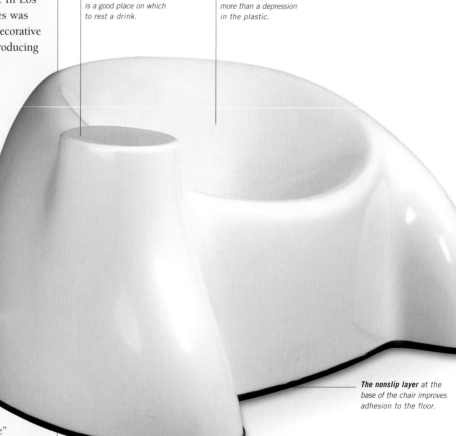

The Castle chair's turret *is a good place on which to rest a drink.*

The chair's seat *is nothing more than a depression in the plastic.*

The nonslip layer *at the base of the chair improves adhesion to the floor.*

CASTLE ARMCHAIR

Designer Wendell Castle achieved the organic, amorphous form of the Castle armchair through the use of white, fiberglass-reinforced polyester. The base of the armchair is trimmed in black rubber all around the base. The limited-edition piece was distributed by Beylerian of New York. This particular chair bears the artist's initials on the inside. *1969. H:33⅞ in (86 cm); W:46½ in (118 cm); D:35½ in (90 cm). QU*

MAILBOX TABLE LAMP

The mailbox-shaped lampshade of this table lamp is made from a single, bowed piece of acrylic. The thin, tubular stand and the base are made of steel. The lamp was designed by Charles Hollis Jones. *1963. H:23 in (58.5 cm); W:13¾ in (35 cm); D:9 in (23 cm).*

CLOUD SOFA

This curvaceous, biomorphic sofa with a low back is fully upholstered in a finely woven fabric that has an undulating pattern in red, pink, and gray. Three matching scatter cushions complete the ensemble. The sofa is raised on casters. *W:116 in (294.5 cm). SDR*

LILY CHAIR

This is a Lucite Lily chair, which was part of the Invisible Group series designed by Erwine and Estelle Laverne. The entire seat, including the molded base, is transparent. A fuzzy, white seat-pad completes the chair. *1957. H:37 in (94 cm); W:28 in (71 cm); D:27 in (68.5 cm). SDR*

GATELEG DINING TABLE

This wooden, drop-leaf, gateleg dining table is a 20th-century interpretation of a late 16th-century form and is a fine example of Vladimir Kagan's organic design style. The table has an oblong table top with rounded corners and is supported by a seven-legged wooden base. The angular, splayed design of the legs is characteristic of Kagan's work, and is a feature that Kagan applied to his seating furniture as well as his table designs. *Fully extended: H:29½ in (75 cm); W:66½ in (169 cm); D:42 in (106.5 cm). SDR*

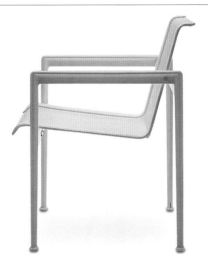

TWO-DOOR CABINET

This two-door, cherry-wood cabinet has contoured door fronts decorated with an ebony inlay. The doors open on to an interior fitted with a mirror, four shelves, and four small drawers, each of which has an ivory-enameled pull. The case stands on black cylindrical feet. Designed by Vladimir Kagan. *H:34 in (86.5 cm). SDR*

OUTDOOR DINING CHAIR

The chair's die-cast frame is made of extruded aluminum and finished in an outdoor epoxy-polyester coating. The polyester mesh seats are impregnated with polyvinyl chloride (PVC) for outdoor use. Designed by Richard Schultz. *1966. H:29 in (74 cm); D:24½ in (62 cm).*

40/4 STACKING CHAIR

One of the most famous and functional 20th-century chairs, this ultra-compact stacking chair was so named because the 40/4 stacks 40 chairs in 4 feet (1.2 m). The chair has a chrome frame and a metal seat and back. Designed by David Rowland. *1964. H:30 in (76 cm); W:19¼ in (49 cm); D:21½ in (54.5 cm).*

COFFEE TABLES

THE SUDDEN SURGE IN popularity of the coffee table in the post-war years can be directly attributed to the rise of the television. The presence of a television set in a house tended to pull families away from the dining room at mealtimes and into the living room, where the coffee table proved the ideal object on which people could place their plates.

Such was the increased traffic in the living room, thanks to the TV, that the most popular style of coffee table quickly became one on which you couldn't hurt your shins—that is, one without sharp corners. The classic coffee table with a curvaceous top—of which Isamu Noguchi's IN50 table (1944) is an early, and particularly eloquent, example—soon ousted the traditional dining table as the most gathered-around item of furniture in the house. More

conventional homeowners often preferred a rectangular table to one that had an irregular shape, but it was the novelty of the latter that attracted young buyers.

Also prized for its unusual appearance was the glass-topped coffee table. Making objects appear as if they were floating on air, the glass table top became a common feature of many coffee tables in the late 1940s and early 1950s.

As plastics began to be more widely used in furniture design of the mid-1960s, it was inevitable that plastic (usually fiberglass) coffee tables should appear on the market. By this time, however, the three-piece living-room suite that usually surrounded the coffee table was rapidly going out of fashion, and with it went much of the appeal of the coffee table.

MOLAR TABLE

This black fiberglass table is reminiscent of a molar tooth. From a range designed by Wendell Castle (US). *c. 1969.* H:15½ in (39.5 cm); W:40 in (101.5 cm); D:34 in (86.5 cm). SDR **4**

GLASS-TOPPED TABLE

This table has a thick, clear-glass, circular top above a patinated bronze, ribbonlike base. Produced by Dunbar (US). *1965.* W:42 in (107 cm). SDR **2**

TABLE WITH DRAWERS

This coffee table has a birch top above three narrow drawers; it is raised on brass legs joined by brass stretchers. Designed by Paul McCobb for Calvin (US). *W:66 in (167.5 cm).* FRE **1**

The plate-glass table top allows a good view of the table's sculptural base.

The table has two levels of glass in order to maximize the use of space.

A simple system of screws holds all the pieces of the table together.

Short legs raise the plywood from the ground, giving the table a poised appearance.

The sinuous curves of the base are typical of Mollino's idiosyncratic style.

The plywood frame is perforated to ensure that the table is both physically and visually light.

ARABESCO TABLE

This table has a perforated plywood frame, which has been veneered with varnished beech wood. The frame is bent to provide a magazine rack below the plate-glass table top. Both the table

top and lower glass shelf have an asymmetrical, sinuous form. The frame is fixed to the glass top by stainless-steel screws. Designed by Carlo Mollino in 1949, Italy. This example is a 2004 re-issue by Zanotta. *H:17¾ in (45 cm); W:50¾ in (129 cm); D:20⅞ in (53 cm).* ZAN

DUNBAR COFFEE TABLE

This American-designed coffee table has a rectangular, ½-in- (1-cm-) thick, smoky-glass top above a patinated bronze cruciform base. *c. 1965.* W:46¼ in (117 cm). SDR **2**

ORGANIC SOFA TABLE

This cherry-wood table, with its curved table top, is raised on splayed legs. It is finished in black laminate. Germany. *c. 1950.* H:19⅔ in (50 cm); W:51½ in (131 cm); D:18½ in (47 cm). DOR **2**

AMOEBIC TABLE

This table has a free-form top in thick laminated wood. The table was so named because of its amorphous and amoeba-like shape. The table top is raised on four screw-in, black dowel-legs. The table is signed by the American designer Lawrence Kelley. *1973. W:64½ in (163.5 cm). FRE* ❶

SLAB TABLE

The top of this coffee table is formed from a single slab of solid walnut. The table's most striking characteristic is its free-form, organic shape, which is in keeping with the choice of material. The coffee table is supported by two asymmetrically formed legs, which are positioned at different angles. The legs are also made of solid walnut. Designed by George Nakashima (US). *1956. W:56 in (132 cm). FRE* ❷

COFFEE TABLE

The thin, rectangular top of this coffee table rests on square-section legs with brass caps. The legs are not situated one in each corner, but arranged at the corners of the rear edge and in the center of the front edge. Stretchers add stability. Designed by Edward Wormley for Dunbar (US). *c. 1955. W:60 in (152.5 cm). LOS* ❸

WOOD AND BRASS TABLE

This American-made coffee table has a rectangular, wooden table top raised on four black-laminated, square-section legs, which terminate in brass caps. A brass frame, which mirrors the dimensions of the table top, runs inside the four legs. Designed by Harvey Probber. *c. 1960. W:70½ in (179 cm). LOS* ❸

KNOLL COFFEE TABLE

Stark and simple in design, this black and white coffee table, which was manufactured by Knoll International of New York, is made with a rectangular, white-laminate table top. The table top is supported on an angular metal base and metal legs. The base and legs are finished in a black enameling. *W:45 in (114 cm). SDR* ❶

DANISH ROSEWOOD TABLE

The rectangular top of this otherwise unadorned rosewood coffee table has a tile inset on one side. The tile is patterned in an abstract design in olive green and teal blue. The table is raised on turned and tapering legs. Designed and manufactured by Georg Jensen, Denmark. *H:20 in (51 cm); W:59 in (150 cm); D:31 in (79 cm). SDR* ❶

NOGUCHI IN50

This coffee table is made up of just three pieces: a ¾-in- (2-cm-) thick, three-sided, plate-glass top and two solid, curved, legs in ebonized wood. The legs interlock to form a stable support. Designed by Isamu Noguchi for the Herman Miller Furniture Company. *1944. H:23 in (58.5 cm); W:44½ in (113 cm); D:39¾ in (101 cm). QU* ❸

TEAK COFFEE TABLE

This Danish-made, teak-and-glass coffee table is made from just three pieces. The base is formed from two conjoined, cruciform teak frames that are rounded and upturned slightly at the edges. It supports a free-form, asymmetrically shaped glass table top. *c. 1960. H:15½ in (39 cm). FRE* ❶

SIDEBOARDS

SUCH WAS THE DESTRUCTION caused by machines during World War II that many designers instinctively turned their backs on industrial processes and embraced the more traditional values of craftsmanship instead. The sideboard was a piece of furniture particularly well suited to displaying what a talented craftsman could do, and so, during the late 1940s, the wooden sideboard emerged as a prominent form of furniture.

Sideboards and credenzas, rather than upright cabinets, were favored during this period, since they fitted well with the current vogue for low-lying, clutter-free interiors. Their horizontal form, too, spoke of dynamism in a way that the towering storage units of earlier eras never did.

With applied surface decoration still frowned upon, designers of Modern sideboards made the most of the pleasing patterns of wood grains, with the composition of handles and doors

also adding to the overall visual effect. Popular woods of the time included teak, rosewood, oak, and palisander, with brass often employed for handles. Short, sometimes tapered, legs were a common feature at the base of sideboards, as they lent them a lightweight look (and reflected the widespread use of similar supports in architecture of the time).

It was sideboards by the Scandinavian designers that were initially much in demand after the war, although it wasn't long before American furniture designers—and, to a lesser extent, Italian and British designers—were also producing sideboards of note. With the onset of the 1960s, however, and specifically with the arrival of plastics, the sideboard fell from favor, as a new generation of designers rejected anything they perceived as being too old-fashioned.

TEAK SIDEBOARD

This teak sideboard from the Netherlands has a rectangular top above two sets of double doors, each of which encloses a shelved interior, and two drawers. The case is raised on square-section, enameled-metal uprights. Designed by Cees Braakman and produced by Patsoe as part of the U + N range of furniture. *c. 1959. W:90¼ in (229 cm). BonBay* **2**

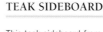

NAKASHIMA SIDEBOARD

This black walnut and grass cloth sideboard was made in the United States. The rectangular case has two sliding doors flanked by another cupboard door, a fitted interior, and three walnut feet. Designed by George Nakashima. *c. 1966. W:84 in (213.5 cm). FRE* **5**

The horizontal shape of the unit is offset by the vertical grain of the wood.

Discreet circular recesses make it easy to slide the doors back and forth.

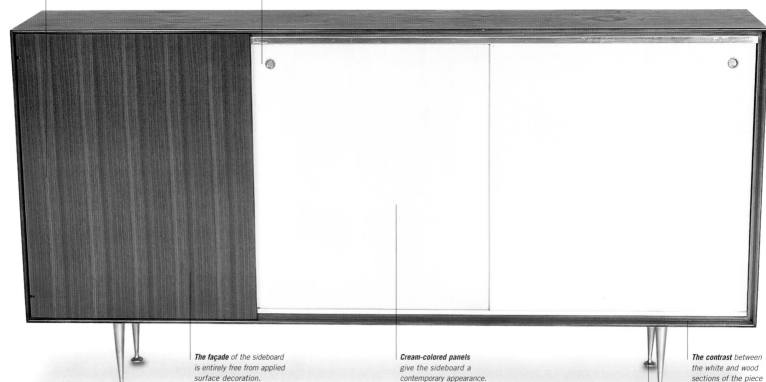

The façade of the sideboard is entirely free from applied surface decoration.

Cream-colored panels give the sideboard a contemporary appearance.

The contrast between the white and wood sections of the piece adds visual effect.

The use of metal for the legs gives the sideboard a somewhat industrial look.

THIN-EDGE SIDEBOARD

This walnut-veneer sideboard has one walnut cabinet that flanks two cream-colored sliding doors. The doors open to reveal three shelves. The case is supported by tapered, aluminum legs. Without any surface decoration, the sideboard's only visual effect is the contrast between the wood and white sections and the natural effect of the wood grain. The piece was designed by George Nelson for the Herman Miller Furniture Company. *1950s. H:33¼ in (84.5 cm); W:67¼ in (71 cm); D:12 in (30.5 cm). SDR* **3**

TEAK SIDEBOARD

This teak, rectilinear sideboard has two doors and four graduated drawers. The handles are small, polished-steel pulls and the case stands on steel supports. Designed by John and Sylvia Reid for Stag Furniture, UK. *1959. H:27½ in (170 cm); W:54 in (137 cm); D:15 in (45.75 cm)* . FRE **3**

NINE-DRAWER BUFFET

This buffet has three long drawers flanked on each side by three short drawers, all with rosewood fronts and brass ring pulls. The ebonized-oak frame is raised on short, square-section legs. Designed by Edward Wormley for Dunbar (US). *W:69¼ in (176 cm)*. SDR **2**

FOUR-DOOR SIDEBOARD

This rosewood-veneer sideboard has a rectangular top above veneer doors: sliding outer doors and a hinged inner pair. Each door has a small indent for a handle. Designed by Borge Mogensen, Denmark. *c. 1958. W:93¾ in (238 cm)*. DOR **3**

WALNUT CREDENZA

The top of this Japanese walnut credenza has a free-form edge. Below is a rectangular case with two sliding doors, each with a recessed rectangular pull. The interior of the cabinet has four drawers on one side and three adjustable shelves on the other. *W:72 in (183 cm)*. SDR **2**

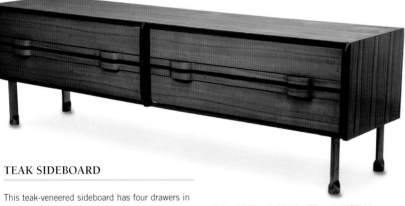

TEAK SIDEBOARD

This teak-veneered sideboard has four drawers in a rectangular case and steel legs terminating in wooden feet. Attributed to Gianfranco Frattini, Italy. *1950s. H:21⅛ in (53 cm); W:71⅛ in (178 cm); D:16⅞ in (42 cm)*. QU **1**

541 CABINET

This elm-veneer sideboard has a rectangular case and four sliding doors in matching veneer; the strap handles are in leather. The case stands on six metal legs. Designed by Florence Knoll for Knoll International (US). *c. 1952. W:70⅞ in (180 cm)*. DOR **3**

LACQUERED BUFFET

This ivory-lacquered buffet cabinet has five doors that conceal a set of interior drawers and shelves. The large ring pulls are in brass, and decorative brass studs are applied to the front and sides of the piece, while the top is free of ornamentation. Designed by Tommi Parzinger (US). *W:82 in (208)*. SDR **4**

WOVEN-FRONT SIDEBOARD

Made of oak and Brazilian rosewood, this Danish sideboard has two sliding doors. The doors are fronted with woven panels within a narrow frame and have recessed oval pulls. The leg supports are rectangular. Designed by Hans Wegner for Ry Mobler. *1966. H:30⅞ in (78.5 cm); W:78¾ in (200 cm); D:19¼ in (49 cm)*. Bk **2**

LIGHTING

IN THE FIRST HALF of the 20th century, lighting design was a separate discipline from furniture design, with designers rarely straddling the boundary between the two. The post-war generation of designers, however, considered both to be branches of industrial design.

The greatest draw of lighting design was the scope for decorative expression it allowed. As Achille Castiglioni, one of the most celebrated designers of the period, put it, "the interest [in lighting design] was not so much centered on solving the problems of lighting... as on emphasizing the decorative qualities of fixtures when they are without light." Italy led the way in post-war lighting, with companies such as O-Luce, Fontana Arte, and Stilnovo.

Initially, the preferred look was one of elegance, symmetry, and restraint. By the 1960s, however, the Space Age and science were influencing lighting design. Spherical forms (imitating planets, fusing nuclei, or DNA) became popular, and plastics were favored. Many designers were so taken with the decorative possibilities of lighting design that they made little attempt to articulate the function of the objects they designed. Others followed the "form follows function" mantra of Modernism, but with tongues firmly in cheeks. An essentially functional area of design in 1945, electric lighting lost its aura of naivety as designers realized it could be exploited to great decorative effect.

KD24 TABLE LAMP

The orange plastic cover of this lamp stands on a white plastic base. The cover and base curves mirror one another. Designed by Joe Colombo for Kartell, Italy. *1968. H:5¾ in (14.5 cm). DOR* **2**

TABLE LAMP

This adjustable table lamp has a painted, anodized-aluminum and steel frame. Designed by A. B. Reid and manufactured by Troughton and Young, UK. *1946. H:19 in (48.5 cm).*

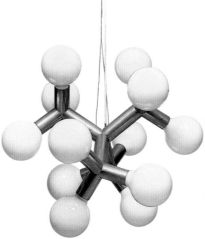

ATOMIC CHANDELIER

This atom-shaped lamp has 12 opaque-glass bulbs mounted on chromium-plated metal tubes. Designed by J. T. Kalmar, Austria. *1969. Diam:25¼ in (64 cm). DOR* **2**

METAL CEILING LIGHT

This six-bulb light with opaque bulbs is mounted on a tube-metal, atom-shaped frame; it is brass-coated and patinated. Italy. *1950s. H:43⅓ in (110 cm); Diam:23⅔ in (60 cm). DOR* **2**

The glass was specially blown to the designer's specifications.

The bulb is a bulb within a bulb.

The lamp was available with either clear glass (as shown here) or frosted glass.

The aluminum base has been polished for striking effect.

BULB FLOOR LAMP

This huge floor lamp in the shape of an electric light bulb is one of several designs on this popular theme—this particular example has a large, clear bulb of blown glass that stands on a screw base made of polished aluminum. The wit expressed in the piece was typical of lighting designs of the 1960s. The lamp was designed by Ingo Maurer, Germany. *1966. H:21¼ in (54 cm); D:15½ in (34 cm). DOR* **2**

PIPISTRELLO TABLE LAMP

The four-section shade is methacrylate; the metal stand has a height-adjustable, telescopic steel rod. Designed by Gae Aulenti for Martinelli Luce, Italy. *1965–66. Diam:21¼ in (54 cm). DOR* **2**

ARTELUCE CEILING LIGHT

The gray-enameled tin shade is suspended on a nickel-plated rod. The shades can be rotated to change the light's direction. Italy. *c. 1950. H:30⅓ in (77 cm); Diam:22¾ in (58 cm). DOR* **1**

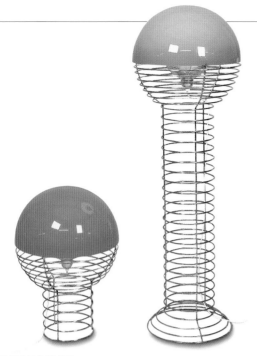

TABLE LAMPS

Each of these lamps has a brightly colored, half-spherical plastic lampshade that sits atop a chrome-plated, springlike wire base. Designed by Verner Panton for J.Lube, Switzerland. *1972. Small lamp: H:21⅗ in (55 cm); Diam:15¾ in (40 cm). DOR* **2**

RING LIGHT

This plastic wall light has a series of brightly colored, raised-and-molded concentric circles set within a square plastic tile. Designed by Verner Panton for Louis Poulsen, Denmark. *1969–70. H:16½ in (42 cm); W:24⅓ in (62 cm); D:9½ in (24 cm). DOR* **3**

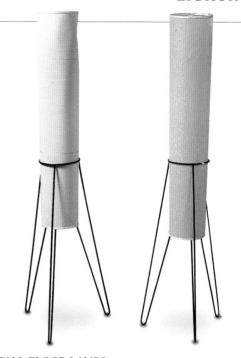

TALL FLOOR LAMPS

These tall floor-standing lamps have silk (left) and parchment (right) lampshades supported on three-legged, black-lacquered metal bases. Produced by Knoll International (US). *1950s. H:49¼ in (125 cm). DOR* **1**

FLAMINGO FLOOR LAMP

This lamp is made of flexible brass rods raised on a cast-iron stand. The aluminum shade is brown and eggplant. Designed by Karl Hagenauer, Austria. *1950s. H:50 in (127.5 cm). DOR* **3**

WOODEN FLOOR LAMP

This floor lamp has a white-lacquered wooden shade over a metal frame. Designed by Paolo Portoghesi for Casa Papanice, Italy. *1969. H:68⅞ in (175 cm). DOR* **4**

SAN REMO FLOOR LAMP

This lamp's ivory-colored, enameled metal stand sprouts plexiglass palm leaves. Designed by Archizoom Associates, Italy. *1968. H:85 in (160 cm); Diam:37½ in (95 cm). DOR* **4**

GIUNONE FLOOR LAMP

This white-lacquered, aluminum-and-metal floor lamp has four swiveling reflectors. Designed by Vico Magistretti for Artemide, Italy. *1970. H:81⅛ in (206 cm); Diam:42⅛ in (70 cm). DOR* **3**

CHAIRS AND STOOLS

THE IMPORTANCE OF THE chair in relation to other forms of furniture reached an all-time high in the post-war period. In 1953, George Nelson compiled his classic and economically titled *Chairs* and wrote in the book's introduction that "every truly original idea—every innovation in design, every new application of materials, every technical invention for furniture—seems to find its most important expression in a chair."

The key innovations to affect chair design at the time were, first, the breakthrough that made it possible to bend plywood in more than one direction and, second, the development of protean forms of plastic. Both of these developments allowed designers to experiment with more expressive forms, the result being that chairs became increasingly sculptural in shape. A heightened interest in ergonomics also helped to usher in the era of organic seating design.

As furniture designers gained confidence in using new materials and techniques, they increasingly began to challenge established beliefs about chair design. The idea of a four-legged chair, for instance, became outmoded, as designers opted for either three legs, a pedestal base (innovated by Eero Saarinen), or, in the 1960s, legless chairs that sat low to the ground. While some of these designs were legitimate responses to changes in lifestyle—formal social occasions, for example, were on the decline—others were produced purely to provoke.

STOOLS AND SIDE TABLE

Manufactured in the United States, each of the two stools of this three-piece set has a circular, polished-walnut seat that is fixed to a three-legged, black-enameled metal frame.

The third part of the set is the matching table, which has a square, black-laminate table top that is supported on a frame similar to the chair frames. Designed by Florence Knoll for Knoll International. *c. 1950. H:15 in (38 cm). DOR* **1**

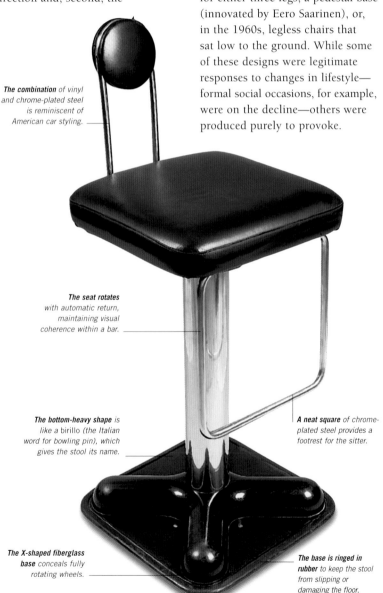

The combination of vinyl and chrome-plated steel is reminiscent of American car styling.

The seat rotates with automatic return, maintaining visual coherence within a bar.

The bottom-heavy shape is like a birillo (the Italian word for bowling pin), which gives the stool its name.

The X-shaped fiberglass base conceals fully rotating wheels.

A neat square of chrome-plated steel provides a footrest for the sitter.

The base is ringed in rubber to keep the stool from slipping or damaging the floor.

BIRILLO BAR STOOL

This unusual-looking bar stool has a chromium-plated, tubular-steel and steel-plate frame. The small, round backrest and the square seat are both upholstered and covered in black vinyl. A chrome-plated footrest hangs from the front of the seat. The stool is raised on a single column that terminates in a black, cross-shaped base made of fiberglass. The piece was designed by Joe Colombo for Zanotta, Italy. *1969–70. H:41⅓ in (105 cm); W:18½ in (47 cm); D:19⅔ in (50 cm). DOR* **2**

ROCKING STOOL

This rocking stool has a seat made of teak, which is supported by a chrome-plated wire shaft on a circular base. Designed by Isamu Noguchi for Knoll International (US). *H:11½ in (29.5 cm). SDR* **1**

LAMBDA CHAIR

This Italian chair has been made from a sheet of punched and molded tin, which was then finished in red lacquer. The tapering legs terminate in rubber feet. *1963. H:39⅛ in (76.5 cm). DOR* **3**

TULIP CHAIR

This armchair has a molded white-fiberglass shell on an enameled white base; the seat's slip cover is of a woven red fabric. Designed by Eero Saarinen for Knoll International. *1956. H:32 in (81 cm). FRE* **1**

PRETZEL CHAIR

The rail and arms are made from one piece of plywood bent into a pretzel shape. The seat has vinyl upholstery. Designed by George Nelson for the Herman Miller Furniture Company. *1957. H:30½ in (77.5 cm). FRE* **2**

VICARIO CHAIR

Molded from one piece of plastic, this chair has a squared back above a wide, rectangular seat; indents in the square-section legs add strength. Designed by Vico Magistretti, Italy. *c. 1970.* H:25 in (63.5 cm); W:28 in (71 cm). *BonBay* **1**

CHINESE CHAIR

This chair was so named because its design is based on that of ancient Chinese chairs. It has a light, oak-and-plywood frame with a woven-rope seat. Designed by Hans Wegner for Fritz Hansen, Denmark. *1943.* H:31 in (79 cm). *BonE* **1**

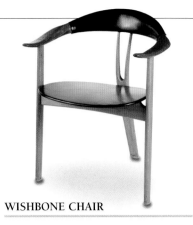

WISHBONE CHAIR

The top rail of this chair curves around to form the armrests, while the backrest is of black leather. A wishbone-shaped back splat continues down to form a back leg. The seat is a glossy black. *c. 1960.* H:29 in (73.5 cm). *LOS* **3**

FIBERGLASS CHAIR

Part of the Fiberglass Group of chairs, this armchair has a free-form seat in ivory with a cut-out back, on a steel pedestal base. Designed by Erwine and Estelle Laverne (US). H:29½ in (75 cm); W:24 in (61 cm); D:20 in (51 cm). *SDR* **2**

SIDE CHAIR

This mahogany side chair has a slender, curved crest rail and two tapering backposts. The leather-upholstered seat cushion has a webbed seat support and is raised on tapering legs. Denmark. H:31¾ in (80.5 cm). *DRA* **1**

SIDE CHAIR

This side chair has a plywood seat and back supported on a painted metal frame that terminates in metal feet. The chair was designed by Egon Eiermann, Germany. *1948.* *BonBay* **2**

ZITHER CHAIR

The chair has several turned back rails between two tapering supports. The solid maple seat has molded edges and rests on a wrought-iron base. Designed by Paul McCobb (US). H:34 in (86.5 cm); W:18 in (45.5 cm); D:19 in (48 cm). *LOS* **1**

GRAND PRIX CHAIR

This chair's seat and back are made from a single sheet of bent, laminated beech that is covered in black leather. The shaped and tapered legs are of teak. Designed by Arne Jacobsen for Fritz Hansen, Denmark. H:31 in (77.5 cm). *FRE* **1**

SWIVEL CHAIR

The armchair has a seat shell of white plastic, protruding armrests, and a suspended chair back. The base is plasticized metal. Designed by Luigi Colani, Germany. *c. 1969.* H:33 in (84 cm); W:25⅖ in (65 cm); D:22½ in (57 cm). *DOR* **2**

SKANDIA CHAIR

This rosewood stacking chair has a seat and back made from a series of single slats molded to fit the shape of the sitter. The legs are chromium-plated steel-rod. Designed by Hans Brattrud for Hove Mobler, Denmark. *1957.* *DN* **2**

POLYPROP CHAIR

The body of this extremely popular stackable chair is a white, injection-molded shell; it stands on tubular-steel supports. Designed by Robin Day and manufactured by Hille. *1962–63.* **1**

NIKKE CHAIR

This bent-plywood stacking chair is of teak veneer, and is raised on enameled steel legs. Designed by Tapio Wirkkala, Finland. *c. 1950s.* H:32½ in (82 cm); W:17⅓ in (44 cm); D:21¼ in (54 cm). **1**

LOUNGE CHAIRS

THE INCREASING DOMINANCE of the television within households meant that, more than ever, the living room had become the focus of many homes. With the fashion for built-in storage units forcing shelving into the background, coupled with the demise of the imposing dining table, it was left to the lounge chair to assume center stage.

The lounge chair was produced in an incredible variety of shapes and sizes in the post-war years and made in a diverse range of materials. The early trend of the mid-1940s was for lounge chairs of modest, minimal form. The most celebrated of these was the LCW by Charles and Ray Eames. This was a molded plywood chair that many consider to be the most complete achievement of the Modern era. A "completely integrated and harmonious expression of form, function, and materials" was how design critics Charlotte and Peter Fiell put it.

As the economic situation in countries across the globe brightened during the 1950s, however, the plush, generously proportioned armchair came back into favor. Colorful, and even patterned, upholstery became increasingly common, as people were eager to put the austerity of the war years behind them.

The development in the mid-1950s of foam and rubber padding offered new opportunities for designers, who could now make chairs that were soft, yet sleek. Stretch fabrics also increased the possibilities of lithe outlines, as the appearance of lounge chairs became increasingly refined. In the mid-1960s, the availability of new plastics blew the field of chair design wide open once again, although this new material ultimately had less impact on lounge chairs than on other types of chair design.

WOMB CHAIR

The Womb chair takes its name from the womblike form of the sculpted seat. The armchair's seat is made from a fiberglass shell, and the chair is upholstered in foam padding and covered in turquoise fabric.

The seat is raised on a varnished steel-rod frame. The armchair comes with a matching ottoman on a similar frame. The pair were designed by Eero Saarinen for Knoll International, US. *1950s. Armchair: H:37¼ in (96 cm); W:33¼ in (84.5 cm); D:40⅓ in (102.5 cm). QU* **3**

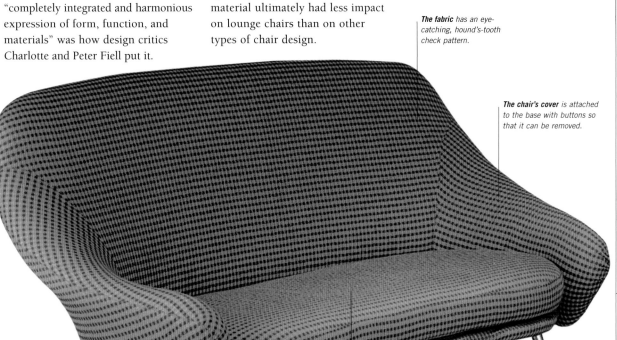

The fabric has an eye-catching, hound's-tooth check pattern.

The chair's cover is attached to the base with buttons so that it can be removed.

Latex foam upholstery ensures that the chair is comfortable.

The steel legs are brass-plated to give a richer visual effect.

Balls stop the chair legs from slipping on or digging into the floor.

MARTINGALA SOFA

This two-seater sofa has a high, upholstered back and sculptural, down-swept arms. The low arms give the impression that the piece is compact and takes up very little space; the narrow, tapered legs also add to this overall sense of lightness. The sofa has a steel frame with band stretchers and foam upholstery that is covered in red and black checkered fabric. The seat cushion is made from polyurethane foam and polyester fiber. The frame is raised on brass-plated legs that end in black-rubber, knob-shaped end fittings. Originally produced as a suite with two matching armchairs, the sofa was designed by Marco Zanuso for Arflex, Italy. *1954. H:34 in (86.5 cm); W:58 in (147.25 cm); D:32 in (81 cm). QU* **5**

WOODPECKER CHAIR

This armchair has a steel-rod frame with a coil-sprung upholstered seat. The black-painted legs have ball feet and support wooden armrests. Designed by Ernest Race. *c. 1952. H:26 in (66 cm); W:26¼ in (66.5 cm); D:22½ in (57 cm). R20*

GILDA ARMCHAIR

This Italian armchair has an oak-dyed ash frame with bronzed-brass hardware and a leather seat and back. Designed by Carlo Mollino in 1954, this is a 2004 Zanotta reissue. *H:36⅔ in (93 cm); W:31 in (79 cm); D: 44½ in (113 cm). ZAN*

SADIMA ARMCHAIR

This armchair has a foam base and a removable stretch fabric cover. It is raised on an ivory-colored polyester base. Designed by Luigi Colani and distributed by Sadima, Germany. c. 1970. H:27¼ in (69 cm). DOR **3**

P32 ARMCHAIR

This armchair has an adjustable, swiveling frame on a black-painted steel base. The foam seat is upholstered in yellow-green wool fabric. Designed by Osvaldo Borsani for Tecno, Italy. H:32⅔ in (83 cm); W:32¼ in (82 cm). WKA **3**

BOBO SEAT

This monoblock seating unit is made from polyurethane foam. It was intended for use as either a lounge chair or a sofa when more than one piece was side by side. Designed by Cini Boeri, Italy. 1967. H:23⅔ in (60 cm). SDR **1**

RELAX ARMCHAIR

This plush armchair has a spring seat-support; its frame and seat cushion are upholstered in brown mohair. The chair is supported on cylindrical, blonde-wood feet. Designed by Jean Royere, France. 1940s. H:40 in (101.5 cm). SDR **4**

EGG CHAIR

This chair has a flattened ovoid form and is made of fiberglass. The hinged lid opens to reveal an upholstered seat. Designed by Peter Ghyczy for Reuter Produkts, Germany. 1968. H:38½ in (98 cm); W:30 in (76 cm); D:35 in (89 cm). L&T **2**

DIAMOND ARMCHAIR

The chair's seat and back are made of sculpted, black-vinyl-coated wire mesh; they are raised on enameled supports. Designed by Harry Bertoia for Knoll International. 1952. H:28¼ in (71.75 cm); W:45 in (140 cm); D:31½ in (80 cm). L&T

PLATNER ARMCHAIR

This chromium-framed armchair has a leather-padded back and arms and a mesh support. The leather cushion rests on a mesh base. Designed by Warren Platner for Knoll International. c. 1966. H:28½ in (72.5 cm). L&T **1**

PK-20 EASY CHAIR

This easy chair has a cane seat and back on a cantilevered steel frame. It has a matt, chrome-plated spring-steel base. Designed by Poul Kjaerholm for Fritz Hansen, Denmark. 1967. H:33 in (84 cm); W:26¾ in (68 cm). Bk **2**

HIGH-BACK AIRCHAIR

This lounge chair has an angular seat and back, raised on flaring wooden legs. The upholstery is burgundy damask and the trim is brocade. Designed by Ico Parisi, Italy. H:44 in (120 cm); W:28 in (71 cm); D:35 in (89 cm). SDR **3**

NO 53 EASY CHAIR

This chair has a teak frame with horn-shaped arms and brass hardware. It is upholstered in green fabric. Designed by Finn Juhl, Denmark. 1953. H:29¼ in (74.25 cm); W:28 in (71 cm); D:25½ in (63.5 cm). SDR **2**

SUPERCOMFORT CHAIR

This lounge chair has an unusual rosewood-faced plywood frame. Its padded seat, back, and removable armrests are covered in black leather. Designed by Joe Colombo and produced by Comfort, Denmark. c. 1964. BonBay **3**

BAMSE ARMCHAIR

The *Bamse* "Papa Bear" armchair has a high upholstered-and-buttoned back and down-sweeping arms. The square upholstered seat with a cushion is raised on splayed teak legs. c. 1951. H:38¾ in (98.5 cm). Bk **1**

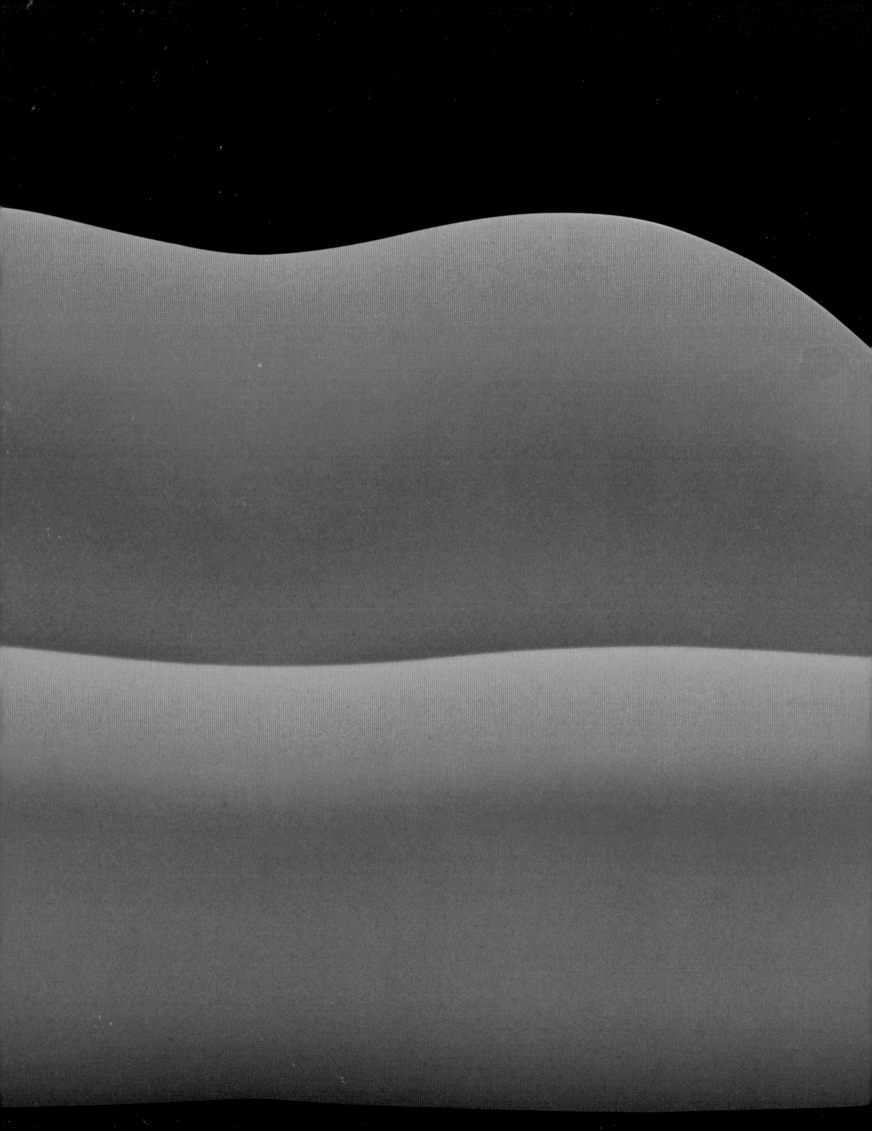

POSTMODERN AND CONTEMPORARY
1970 ONWARD

SOCIAL UNEASE

CHARACTERIZED BY INCREASED CYNICISM AND INDIVIDUALISM, THE LATE 20TH CENTURY ALSO SAW RAPID TECHNOLOGICAL ADVANCES, LEADING TO IMPROVED COMMUNICATION OF THOUGHTS AND IDEAS.

BY THE TIME THE 1970S arrived, the swinging 60s were losing momentum. Interest rates and inflation were rising, and unemployment figures were spiraling out of control. To add to the global sense of gloom, scientists were ringing warning bells about the damage that people were doing to the environment.

Against this backdrop, a crippling blow was dealt to the West by a group of oil-rich Arab nations. In 1973, in reaction to the West's support for Israel, oil supplies from the Middle East were cut, sparking a worldwide energy crisis. As the industries of the United States, Europe, and Japan struggled with the domino effect of the oil embargo, consumer confidence plummeted, and by 1975 a global recession was underway.

The utopian visions of a mechanized future, touted by Modernist architects and designers since the 1920s, were finally laid to rest during the 1970s, as a deep cynicism began to course through contemporary culture. Punks, conceptual artists, and satirical writers were all coming to the same nihilistic conclusions.

Such was the sense of disillusionment that when economies did begin to pick up again at the start of the 1980s, there was little of the communal spirit of optimism that characterized the boom years of the mid-century. Rather, there was a more self-interested attitude of "grab what you can." Such predatory instincts were only encouraged by the governments of Britain and the United States, led by Margaret Thatcher and Ronald Reagan, respectively, who made much of the economic necessity for a strong entrepreneurial and capitalist culture.

POSTMODERNISM COMES INTO FOCUS

In the 1980s, the concept of Postmodernism—an idea that had been gaining momentum since the 1960s—came firmly into focus. The subject of much discussion by everyone from philosophers to fashion designers, Postmodernism was characterized by a loss of faith in the forward momentum of Modernism. Culture had reached a cul-de-sac, or so

Postmodernists believed, and the only appropriate response was to plunder the past.

By the end of the decade, however, consumers had grown tired of the seeming anarchy of revivalist styles that were rampaging across all areas of design, while the economic crash of 1987 had dealt a blow to the culture of greed. The discovery of a hole in the ozone layer and the Chernobyl disaster of 1986 forced environmental issues back onto the international agenda. The 1990s, then, were greeted with a rather chastened outlook.

Table by Michèle de Lucchi This table, designed for Memphis, is animal-like in form. A circular, laminated table top emerges from the rectangular "body" on a thin, blue-painted steel "neck." The four steel legs have flat feet. *1983. H:23¾ in (60.5 cm); W:18½ in (47 cm); D:25 in (63.5 cm). MAP*

Perhaps the most significant cultural trend of the 1990s was driven by advances in both the computer and telecommunications industries. Through portable phones and via the Internet it now became possible to remain in close proximity to both home and office when physically distanced from them. The increased ease of communication also had the effect of turning the wheels of culture ever faster. With ideas and images being disseminated like quicksilver across the mass media, cultural developments seemed to come and go in the blink of an eye. Since the arrival of the new millennium, keeping up with current cultural trends has become increasingly onerous.

Centre Georges Pompidou, Paris The bright blue utility pipes and shiny metal frame give this Postmodern building a visually anarchic exterior. Completed in 1977, it marked a move away from the streamlined aesthetic that had dominated Modernism.

TIMELINE 1970–ONWARD

1970 Shiro Kuramata designs his Irregular Forms chest of drawers for Fujiko.

1973 Recession begins across Europe following OPEC oil-price rises.

1976 Mario Bellini designs the Cab chair; its steel skeleton and removable leather skin

signify a move away from the desire to achieve pure form. The Punk movement gains global attention and highlights young people's growing frustration and desire to dismantle the old order.

1977 Completion of the Richard Rogers– and Renzo

Ettore Sottsass chair

Piano–designed Pompidou Center in Paris.

1980 The launch of MTV, a 24-hour music channel that gives voice to an energetic youth culture.

1981 Memphis, a design group led by Ettore Sottsass, shows its first furniture collection in Milan. Ron Arad, an Israeli designer, opens his studio,

Apple Mac

called One Off Ltd., in London and creates unique pieces of furniture using inexpensive, industrial materials.

1982 The first fax machines and domestic camcorders first become available in Japan.

1984 Apple launches its Mac computer with mouse, revolutionizing the industry.

St. Martin's Lane Hotel French designer Philippe Starck has captured the energy, fun, and color of the age in his design for the St. Martin's Lane Hotel, London—one of the Schrager group of hotels. The hotel lobby is an eclectic mix of Postmodern and period-style furniture and decor, creating a truly contemporary effect. Typical features of the age are the muted gold-beige colors with occasional bright splashes, combined with the free-form shapes of the furniture.

Felt Chair This armchair has a reinforced fiberglass body supported on a polished aluminum leg. It was designed by Marc Newson for Cappellini. *1994. H:34 in (86 cm); W:26½ in (67 cm); D:41⅔ in (106 cm). SCP*

1985 Driade, an Italian furniture manufacturer, produces the first chair designs by Philippe Starck. A hole is discovered in the ozone layer.

1986 A Soviet nuclear reactor at Chernobyl in Russia explodes.

1987 The American stock market crashes.

1989 The Vitra Design Museum opens in Germany; its collection is almost entirely made up of

Philippe Starck chair

20th-century objects. Terence Conran's Design Museum opens in London. Jasper Morrison's Plywood chair signifies a shift away from a brash, energetic aesthetic to something a little more restrained. The Berlin Wall comes down.

1991 The Single European Market lifts trade restrictions within the EEC.

1993 Droog, a Netherlands-based design collective, debuts at the Milan Furniture fair.

1994 The Channel tunnel opens between England and France.

1997 Frank Gehry's Guggenheim Museum opens in Bilbao, Spain. The first adult mammal—a sheep called Dolly—is successfully cloned. Microsoft becomes the most valuable company in the world.

2000 Issey Miyake's Parisian A-Poc store is designed by French brothers Ronan and

Guggenheim Museum in Bilbao

Erwan Bouroullec. The estimated number of worldwide Internet users reaches 295 million.

POST-1970 FURNITURE

AS EARLY AS 1966, ROBERT VENTURI, an American architect and theorist, aired the ideas that would eventually become known as Postmodernism. In his influential text *Complexity and Contradiction in Architecture*, Venturi wrote of his admiration for "elements which are hybrid rather than 'pure,' compromising rather than 'clean,' distorted rather than 'straightforward,' ambiguous rather than 'articulated'." Venturi was boldly rebelling against Modernism's zealous drive for refinement. It was not until the 1980s that Postmodernism became the dominant theme of design, however.

During the 1970s two broad strands of design existed. The first strand was widely labeled "Anti-Design." Most prominently pursued in Italy, designers of this persuasion took furniture to ever more extremes in order to express their frustration with what they perceived to be a damagingly dysfunctional society. Although some designers, such as Studio 65, claimed their use of bright, clashing colors and kitsch, cartoonlike forms was an attempt to achieve popular appeal, others, such as Global Tools, insisted that the sheer oddness of their designs would deter buyers, forcing them to make furniture of their own.

The second strand of design to emerge during the 1970s was one that many people at the time referred to as "High Tech" (after a book of the same name by Joan Kron and Suzanne Slesin). This predominantly American trend was a return to the severe, rational principles of early Modernism, prompted by the belt-tightening going on within the furniture industry. Designers also claimed that their pursuit of timeless, durable designs would counter the culture of disposability that scientists had warned was destroying the planet.

THE HEYDAY OF POSTMODERNISM

The defining movement in furniture design of the early 1980s was Memphis. Although based in Milan, Memphis was a loose collective of international designers who nonetheless developed a highly distinctive style. Purposefully combining both expensive and inexpensive materials, as well as borrowing decorative motifs from various ethnic cultures and periods of history, the Memphis look was an attention-grabbing, highly eclectic (and entirely Postmodern) aesthetic that fitted well with

Little Beaver armchair and ottoman Both these pieces are made of laminated cardboard. Designed by Frank Gehry for Vitra, they form part of his "Experimental Edges" series, which exploited the expressive qualities of corrugated cardboard. This example is marked with a brass tag showing it to be No.54 out of the 100 made. *1987. Chair: H:32 in (81 cm); W:33½ in (85 cm); D:38 in (96.5 cm). SDR*

the 1980s trend for conspicuous consumption. Memphis products were part furniture, part art, and part fashion accessory. Any consideration for practicalities was purely perfunctory.

By the end of the decade, a new, rather more cool and calm look was beginning to emerge in furniture design. Designers from Japan, Belgium, Britain, and Italy all subscribed to the determinedly international style described variously as "New Minimalism," "Late Modern," or simply "Dematerialization." Unadorned furniture designs became the order of the day, with materials such as clear acrylic and wicker finding favor. As the 1990s progressed, however, designers quickly recovered their sense of adventure as a healthy injection of humor entered the furniture industry. Droog, another loose collective of designers, led the way with a witty take on design that often incorporated the use of found objects.

In the 1990s, computers became an essential tool for many designers, who could now develop their work on-screen rather than going through the laborious process of drawing up designs and making models. Many furniture designs acquired the smooth, technical appearance that had long defined the look of electronic consumer goods but had only lately entered the lexicon of furniture design.

Delo-Lindo table A witty twist on an existing form, designers Delo-Lindo have incorporated two canvas magazine bags into the corner of their coffee table.

Mendini's Lassu chair This archetypal chair form perched on top of a plinth was burned for art's sake by Mendini in 1974.

THE ROLE OF ART

Art and furniture design might have been bedfellows for centuries, but by the 1970s it had become, in some cases, virtually impossible to distinguish the two. "The main characteristics [of new design]," wrote the designer and theorist Alessandro Mendini in 1978, "is to regard objects not in their functional capacity but to think in terms of their expressivity." Four years earlier, Mendini had made the same point with actions rather than words, by setting fire to a chair placed on a plinth.

While designers at the end of the century were veering ever closer to the territories of art, a number of artists were flirting heavily with furniture design.

American Pop artist Claes Oldenburg was one of the first to adopt the language of furniture design for his sculptures, believing it would allow his art to communicate with a far wider audience.

Throughout the 1970s and 1980s, various artists produced functional furniture designs, the most prominent being the American artists Donald Judd and Richard Artschwager. In the 1990s, the trend continued as British furniture manufacturer SCP launched their "Please Touch" collection, a range of furniture designed by artists, including Rachel Whiteread, Julian Opie, and Richard Wentworth.

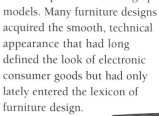

MODULAR COLORED CUBES

Like many furniture designs produced in the final few decades of the 20th century, Massimo Morozzi's *Paesaggi Italiani* storage system (1996) is visually exhilarating (*Paesaggi Italiani* translates as "Italian Landscapes") but entirely rudimentary from a functional standpoint. It illustrates perfectly that it was aesthetic and conceptual concerns, as opposed to practical ones, that dominated the thoughts of many designers of this era.

During the late 1960s, Morozzi was a member of the radical architecture and design group Archizoom, a flamboyant, Florence-based collective that played

a pivotal role in the development of Anti-Design (*see p.452*). Attempting to puncture the high-minded idealism and restraint that had long been associated with Modernism, the pioneers of "Anti-Design" can be seen as proto-Postmodernists.

Like many storage systems designed in the 1990s, the pixel-like *Paesaggi Italiani* is modular, meaning that it can assume innumerable shapes and sizes. The boxes, too, are available in a broad palette of colors, allowing the whims of the owner to dictate the ultimate appearance of the *Paesaggi Italiani*. This surrendering

of the design initiative to the consumer—who, theoretically, is an amateur—is a gesture entirely in keeping with the spirit of Anti-Design. The disco-lights effect of the colored cubes can also be considered as a mockery of the stern, perfectionist streak that characterized much Modernist design.

Paesaggi Italiani **storage system** This modular furniture system functions as a room divider on one side and as a storage system on the other. It is made of colored, lacquered, translucent plastic and is available in up to 75 colors. It is also available in any arrangement of size and shape to order.

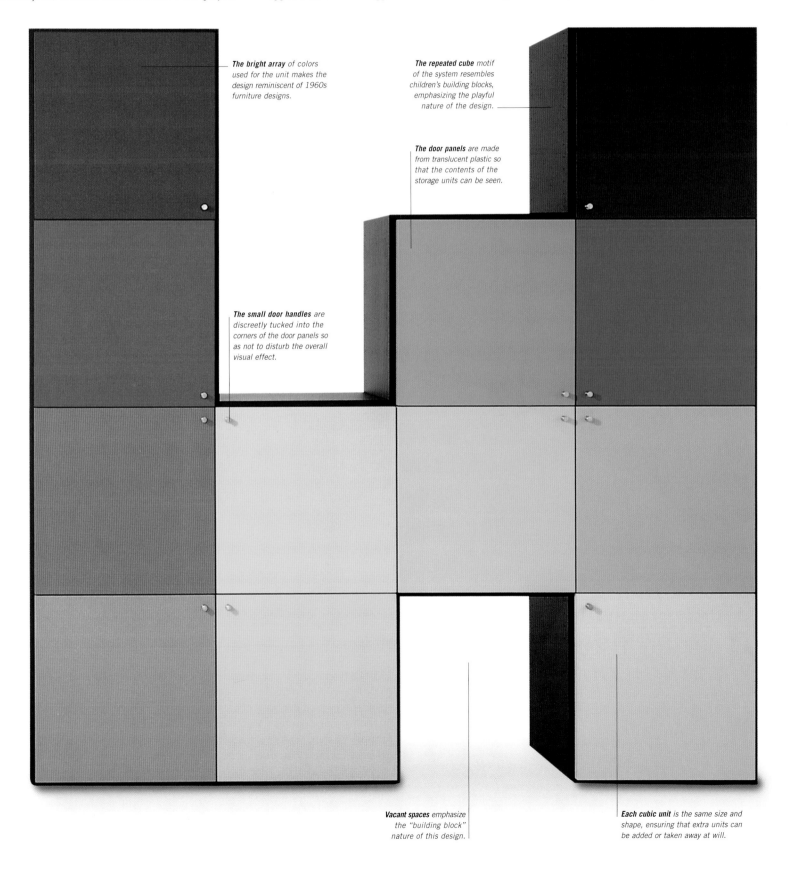

The bright array of colors used for the unit makes the design reminiscent of 1960s furniture designs.

The repeated cube motif of the system resembles children's building blocks, emphasizing the playful nature of the design.

The door panels are made from translucent plastic so that the contents of the storage units can be seen.

The small door handles are discreetly tucked into the corners of the door panels so as not to disturb the overall visual effect.

Vacant spaces emphasize the "building block" nature of this design.

Each cubic unit is the same size and shape, ensuring that extra units can be added or taken away at will.

ELEMENTS OF STYLE

The emergence of Postmodernism in the late 1970s led furniture designers of this period to become less concerned with function and structure and more fascinated by the communicative qualities of furniture's surface. With aesthetic and conceptual matters increasingly occupying designers during the 1980s and 1990s, materials and forms were often used for ornamental, rather than practical purposes. In an effort to divert attention toward the more ideological message of their work, many designers turned their backs on the ostentatious use of technologies, preferring to utilize rudimentary materials and construction techniques. Some designers (particularly those with a training in architecture) did embrace a more sophisticated, structural style that was variously labeled "High Tech" or "Matt Black." The 1990s also saw a return of interest in the technological aesthetic as the possibilities of computer-aided design and production became too enticing to ignore.

Easy Edges stool by Frank Gehry

Asymmetry

In order to demonstrate their rejection of the strict, rational ideals that had defined the Modern era, many Postmodern designers incorporated an awkward asymmetry into their work. Often this was expressed through color, but, more daringly, it was also expressed through form.

Plastic-laminated cabinet

Plastic laminates

Widely used during the 1980s to cover wooden furniture, plastic laminates were often exotically patterned. Their attention-grabbing nature emphasized the fact that function was of minor concern to designers—it was surface decoration that they were interested in. Plastic-covered wood was a gleeful Postmodern riposte to the "truth to materials" mantra of earlier decades.

Injection-molded chair

Injection-molding

While designers had largely tired of using plastic during the 1970s and 1980s, the material did return to popularity in the 1990s as increasingly sophisticated techniques for molding were developed. High-pressure injection-molding allowed greater precision of forms and prompted a spate of sculptural designs similar to those seen in the revolutionary 1960s.

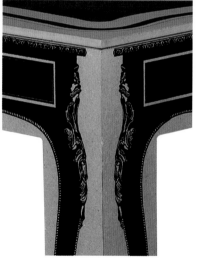

MDF *bureau plat*

Humor

As designers' interest in structure and engineering waned during the 1980s, an increasingly mischievous streak entered furniture design. While Postmodern designers of the 1980s often made esoteric jokes—as in the table above, printed with an 18th-century table design—there was a growing seam of softer humor in the 1990s that often incorporated anthropomorphism.

Detail of glass dining table

Minimalism

After the visually cacophonous Postmodern movement, many designers reverted to a quieter style of design at the end of the 1980s. Glass and clear acrylic became popular materials among designers during the 1990s, as did the use of untreated wood and brushed metals. This look was sometimes referred to as "Late Modern" by commentators.

Marble table base

Marble

Marble symbolized permanence, purity, and the high ideals of Classical antiquity to Postmodern designers, who frequently challenged such symbolism by combining it with more lowly materials, such as plastic, glass, or garishly painted wood. The attractive veining of marble was also appreciated at a time when surface decoration was once again in favor.

Rover car seat

Recycling

Increased awareness of environmental issues during the 1970s meant that by the 1980s, recycling was a common and much-discussed activity. It was not only for environmental reasons, however, that designers of the 1980s and 1990s recycled found objects in their furniture. As with Ron Arad's car seat, above, it was also a celebration of the defiantly anti-corporate DIY spirit.

Queen Anne back splat

Appropriation

As designers began to lose faith in the forward momentum of Modernism, they increasingly looked to the past for inspiration. Postmodern designers habitually borrowed motifs from bygone styles of furniture design, although, unlike many Modernists who did the same thing, they were not interested in their structural qualities, merely the symbolic message they conveyed.

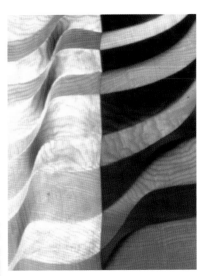

Detail of carved chest of drawers

Handcrafts

The demise of the Modern machine aesthetic, and the subsequent fall from favor of plastics, opened the door for a return of handcrafts in the late 1970s. Increased affluence in the 1980s also meant that many people in the UK and the United States had the disposable income to spend on laboriously wrought objects that were, more often than not, enormously expensive.

Comic table leg

Cartoon look

Cartoons were an important source of inspiration for Pop artists of the 1960s, who appreciated their popular, anti-intellectual appeal. Designers picked up on this influence in the early 1970s, and Postmodern designers of the 1980s enjoyed the provocative irony of translating an essentially two-dimensional cartoonlike look into a three-dimensional piece of furniture.

CD chest

Casters

Casters became an increasingly common feature of office furniture from the 1970s onward as the rigidity of office environments was steadily relaxed. Postmodern designers also applied casters to items of domestic furniture in an attempt to question the values of permanence and universalism preached by followers of Modernist principles.

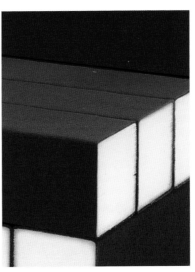

Modular seating

Modular furniture

Modular seating systems had become fashionable during the 1960s. In the 1990s, designers tentatively returned to this theme, although it was in shelving design that modularity became an enduring feature. Modular furniture had always been associated with a technical aesthetic, but by the 1990s designers had lent a degree of lyricism to the modular look in terms of color and materials.

Brightly upholstered chair

Color

During the 1980s, when communication became just as important as function in furniture design, designers became increasingly enthusiastic about the decorative use of color in their pieces. This trend continued, in part, well into the 1990s, although designers of this decade toned down earlier Postmodern designers' exuberant use of pattern.

MEMPHIS AND ALCHIMIA

THE GROUP OF DESIGNERS WHO FORMED MEMPHIS IN 1980 BUILT ON THE IDEAS OF MENDINI'S STUDIO ALCHIMIA, TO DEFINE POSTMODERNISM IN FURNITURE DESIGN.

IN APRIL 1981, A MOTLEY GROUP of designers by the name of Memphis showed their work to the public for the very first time. The exhibition, held in a small showroom in Milan at a time when most of the world's furniture industry was in the city for the annual *Salone del Mobile*, was a sensation. Roadblocks choked the streets surrounding the showroom as thousands of people clamored to catch a glimpse of what the Memphis group described as the "New International Style."

Led by Ettore Sottsass, a designer who had played an active role in the Anti-Design scene of the 1960s and 1970s, Memphis was the latest, and most persuasive, attempt by Italian designers to snuff out the flame of Modernism. "Memphis tries to separate the object from the idea of functionalism," said Sottsass. "It is an ironic approach to the Modern notion of philosophical pureness. In other words, a table may need four legs to function, but no one can tell me that the four legs have to look the same."

MULTICULTURAL MELTING POT

The appearance of Memphis furniture was frenetic, characterful, and saturated with color. Although no explicit allusions were made to bygone, popular, or primitive cultures, it was obvious that the Memphis group had an enthusiasm for all three. Indeed, the name Memphis—taken from the title of a Bob Dylan song that was playing when the group first met—was chosen for its associations with both rock 'n' roll and ancient Egypt (of which Memphis was the capital). The multicultural, melting-pot character of Memphis was asserted further by the fact that the group's designers, which included Sottsass, Michele de Lucchi, Michael Graves, and George J. Sowden, hailed from a broad range of nations—Italy, Spain, Japan, Austria, Britain, France, and the United States.

One notable absentee from the Memphis group was Alessandro Mendini. It was Mendini's Studio Alchimia, founded in Milan in 1976, that laid much of the ground on which Memphis was to build. In 1978, Mendini introduced a series of designs (or "redesigns" as he called them) to illustrate his ideas on "Banal Design" (*see p.512*), the most celebrated of which is the Proust armchair (1978). Mendini based his chair on an 18th-century French form, but covered it with dabs of color similar to those in pointillist paintings.

SUPER LAMP
Designed by Martine Bedin, this molded plastic light stands on four rubber wheels, so it can move around. The six naked light bulbs all screw into different-colored sockets. 1981. H:14 in (35.5 cm); W:24 in (61 cm); D:7 in (18 cm). MAP

D'ANTIBES CABINET
George Sowden's two-door cabinet has four tall, square-section legs. Made of plastic-laminated wood, it is brightly colored, with red door frames, blue feet, and patterned panels on the sides. 1981. H:63 in (160 cm); W:23⅗ in (60 cm); D:15¾ in (40 cm). MAP

The slanted bookends are reminiscent of Aztec architecture.

CARLTON BOOKCASE
Designed by Ettore Sottsass, this bookcase is one of the most iconic Postmodern pieces. The symmetrical unit has plastic-laminated shelves and compartments above a small central case with two drawers. It also works as a room divider. 1981. H:78 in (198 cm); W:75 in (190.5 cm); D:13 in (33 cm). MAP

The bookshelves are laminated with brightly colored plastic.

POST-MEMPHIS

MANY OF THE ORIGINAL MEMBERS OF THE MEMPHIS GROUP WENT ON TO FORM THEIR OWN SUCCESSFUL COMPANIES, WHILE POST DESIGN CONTINUES TO KEEP THE MEMPHIS SPIRIT ALIVE.

By the time Memphis disbanded in 1988, the original members had become major players within the design industry and many went on to form their own companies. Ettore Sottsass and his Sottsass Associati company completed a number of private houses in locations as far-flung as Singapore and Hawaii. He also continued to work with great success on smaller-scale, more personal projects. Michele De Lucchi, meanwhile, adopted a more modest and rational style. Focusing on industrial design and architecture, De Lucchi went on to run the multi-award-winning company AMDL.

Michael Graves, whose ambitious and highly stylized aesthetic made him one of the most talked-about members of Memphis, continued to work as an architect and designer in much the same vein. At the end of the 1990s and into the 21st century, Graves's work once again came under the spotlight as his designs for Target, the national chain of low-cost homeware stores, met with great critical and commercial success. He now carries out regular commissions for Alessi.

Memphis Milano, the manufacturing arm of Memphis, continues to produce and sell the group's older designs. In 1997, Memphis Milano's managing director, Alberto Albrichi, founded Post Design, a company dedicated to keeping the Memphis spirit alive. In Post Design's prominent gallery space in Milan, exhibitions are held of new collections by Sottsass and other ex-Memphis members, as well as the work of younger generations of designers, such as Johanna Grawunder and Pierre Charpin, whose work developed from the Memphis style.

Pierre Charpin Bookshelf Designed for Post Design, this bookshelf is made of red-dyed maple, with an arrangement of open shelves and compartments. Although restrained in appearance, the influence of Sottsass's work is clear. *1998. H:89 in (226 cm); W:44⅓ in (112.5 cm); D:15⅓ in (39 cm). MAP*

Just as ancient alchemists attempted to turn base ingredients into gold, Mendini and his fellow members of Studio Alchimia (which included Sottsass for a short period) sought to transform elements of popular culture into products of high design. Studio Alchimia's "bau. haus" collection of 1979 was, of course, ironically titled; rather than the refined, rational designs of the sort produced in Dessau, the furniture on show was a frenzied blend of Dada, Cubist, and Pop art influences.

IMPROVISATION AND COMMUNICATION
While Mendini's attitude toward design was essentially an academic one, Sottsass always espoused a more instinctive, sensual approach. The unorthodox forms of much Memphis furniture demonstrate the importance that the group placed on improvization and free-association, as opposed to more rigorous, ideological thinking.

Sottsass has described Memphis design as "a way of discussing life," and communication was of far greater concern to Memphis designers than practicality. In an effort to create the maximum communicative impact with their furniture, Memphis designers often used eccentrically patterned plastic laminates (usually applied to a base made from chipboard).

Such was the attention-grabbing effect of Memphis furniture that it soon became an international phenomenon, proving particularly popular in the United States and Japan. Realizing the commercial potential of Memphis design, Ernesto Gismondi, the director of the Artemide lighting firm, financed the foundation of a manufacturing company dedicated to producing the group's furniture. This company, Memphis Milano, still exists to this day.

BRANZI'S *STAZIONE* SIDEBOARD
This sideboard has a rectilinear case supported at one end on four square-section legs and at the other by a single columnar leg. The piece combines a range of storage options: small drawers; top-opening cupboards; and D-end open shelves. 1979.

PROUST ARMCHAIR
Designed by Alessandro Mendini for Cappellini, this armchair was inspired by Louis XV furniture. The elaborately carved wooden frame is painted in the style of the French pointillist painter Paul Signac, and upholstered in matching multicolored fabric. 1978.

ITALY

IN 1972, THE MUSEUM of Modern Art in New York held the landmark exhibition "Italy: The New Domestic Landscape—Achievements and Problems in Italian Design." A remarkably diverse exhibition, it was accompanied by a catalog in which the curator, Emilio Ambasz, identified three emerging strands of Italian design: "Conformist," "Reformist," and "Contesting." The "Contesting" trend (rooted in the late-1960s Anti-Design movement) dominated the 1970s, while the 1980s—with Ettore Sottsass and the Memphis group

attempting to stimulate and educate the Italian consumer—was labeled "Reformist." The 1990s, a decade when professionalism reigned in Italian design, was described by Ambasz as "Conformist."

By the time Ambasz's exhibition was held in New York, groups such as Archizoom, Superstudio, and Gruppo Strum had already begun to question the central tenets of Modernism. Their brand of brash, provocative Pop design had been developed during the late 1960s, and had become increasingly confrontational.

BANAL DESIGN
The dominant voice in Italian furniture design in the latter half of the 1970s belonged to Alessandro Mendini. A tireless *agent provocateur*, Mendini introduced to the furniture industry the concept of "Banal Design," in many ways a more cynical development of Anti-Design. With "Banal design," Mendini posited the rather apocalyptic idea that, since the walls of Modernism were coming crumbling down, there would soon

Interior of the Una Hotel Vittoria in Florence Designed by Fabio Novembre, this hotel interior creates a regenerating atmosphere. The restaurant's long, graceful "S"-shaped table and colorful Renaissance - inspired light invite guests to socialize. *2003.*

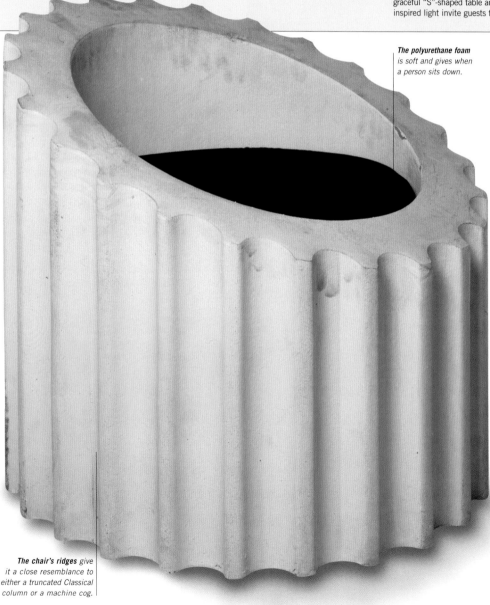

The polyurethane foam is soft and gives when a person sits down.

The chair's ridges give it a close resemblance to either a truncated Classical column or a machine cog.

ATTICA CHAIR

This simple chair was made by Gufram from flexible polyurethane foam. It is small in size, emphasizing the fact that it is a chair designed for perching on rather than lounging in. The polyurethane has been modeled to look like a fluted Ionic column and is cut on the diagonal to provide the backrest and arms of the chair. The pure white color of the foam chair makes it look as if it were made from heavy stone, marble, or alabaster and the elastic paint that covers the polyurethane makes the chair splash-proof, so that it can be washed easily. The chair's name is taken from the ancient Greek territory of Attica, a reference to the chair's columnar form. *1972.* H:27½ in (70 cm); Diam:26 in (66 cm). Bonbay

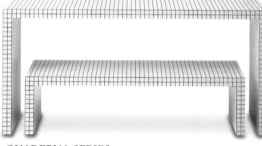

QUADERNA SERIES

This console table and bench each have a honeycomb core frame that has been covered with white plastic laminate. The tile-effect design is a silk-screen print with a black grid pattern. Designed by Superstudio for Zanotta, they are still available. *1970.* Table: H:33 in (84 cm); W:71¼ in (180 cm); D:16½ in (42 cm). ZAN

543 BROADWAY CHAIR

This chair has a bright orange translucent resin seat and back on a stainless tubular-steel frame. Each of the nylon feet incorporates a metal spring, which adjusts to the posture of the sitter. The chair was designed by Gaetano Pesce for Bernini. *1993.* H:17¾ in (45 cm); W:19¾ in (50 cm); D:15⅓ in (39 cm). SDR

be only a vacuous world in which designers could operate. The task of furniture designers in the future, then, would comprise little more than buffing up old designs found in the rubble of the past.

Mendini's extreme theories can be defined as Postmodern, although his nihilism is somewhat at odds with the American Postmodern attitude, which was far more celebratory in its appropriation of past styles. Soon, however, Mendini's dogmatic approach was eclipsed by that of the Memphis group (see pp.510–11). The sheer effusiveness of the Memphis furniture of the early 1980s signaled the end of the essentially destructive, antagonistic streak that had coursed through Italian design since the late 1960s.

GROWING COMMERCIALISM

At the start of the 1990s, much of the passion and excitement that had fueled Italian furniture design for the last 20 years had abated as a new wave of professionalism swept into the industry. Many companies that had operated at the cutting edge during the 1960s and 1970s (for example, B&B Italia, Poltrona Frau, and Cassina) had by now become thriving businesses and were accordingly less willing to court controversy. A few manufacturers, such as Cappellini and Edra, did continue to produce daring and flamboyant furniture, but their collections were often dominated by non-Italian designers.

Perhaps the most successful Italian furniture designers of the 1990s were Piero Lissoni and Antonio Citterio, both of whom adopted a succinct, technologically sophisticated style that favored "precision" over experimentation. "Design should search for an unequivocal result based on the relationship between production techniques, form, and functionality," Lissoni has said.

By the beginning of the 21st century, Italy had become the undoubted commercial capital of the global furniture industry, with the annual *Salone del Mobile* in Milan established as the premier international event in the furniture design calendar. In terms of its creative reputation, however, Italy had lost much of its gloss.

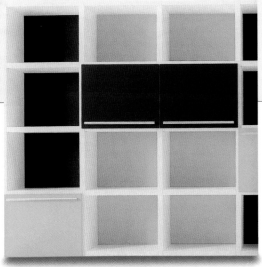

SISTEMA STORAGE SYSTEM

This very versatile range of storage units was designed by Piero Lissoni for Cappellini. It comes in modules, which can be stacked on top of each other or joined side by side. It is available in numerous finishes. *H:12½–36¼ in (32–92 cm); W:11¾in–35½ in (30–90 cm); D:11¾in–23⅔ in (30–60 cm).* VIA

REEF SEATING SYSTEM

This sofa has no armrests, but each end of the seat can be tilted in two different positions, converting them into head supports or armrests. Designed by Piero Lissoni for Cassina, the upholstered foam seat is raised on an exposed painted-steel frame. *2001. H:23¾ in (60.5 cm); L:118 in (300 cm); D:33⅓ in (84.5 cm).* CAS

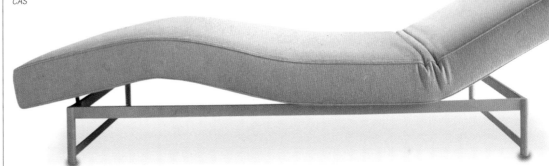

CAB CHAIR

This armchair has an enameled-steel skeletal frame over which the leather upholstery has been zipped. The leather functions as a supporting material. The padded polyurethane foam seat is also upholstered in leather. It was designed by Mario Bellini. *1977. H:20½ in (52 cm); W:32¼ in (82 cm); D:18½ in (47 cm).*

TORSO ARMCHAIR

Designed by Paolo Deganello, this armchair has an asymmetric, fabric-upholstered back and a leather-upholstered seat, which rises at the sides to form arms. The seat is raised on short, enameled legs. *1972. H:45½ in (150.5 cm); W:43 in (90 cm); D:34 in (86.5 cm).* SDR

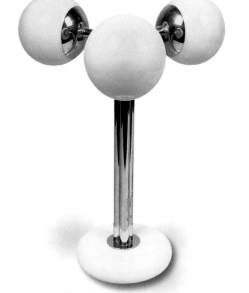

POLARIS TABLE LAMP

This rare Polaris table lamp has three azure glass balls on a chrome stand with a Carrara marble base. When the light is turned on, the balls appear to be white. It was designed by Superstudio for Design Centre and manufactured by Poltronova. *1969. H:19⅔ in (50 cm); D:19⅔ in (50 cm).* DOR

FRANCE

THE 1970S WERE QUIET years for French furniture design. Pierre Paulin and Pascal Mourgue, two designers who had established their reputations during the 1960s, continued to produce their familiar, ribbonlike designs, but beyond this, little of real consequence came to light.

One of the earliest significant events in French furniture design during the 1980s was the "New Barbarians" exhibition in 1981, a showcase of work by Elisabeth Garouste and Mattia Bonetti. Inspired by France's colonial past, Garouste's and Bonetti's designs liberally employed tribal motifs and materials to imbue their furniture with a sense of exoticism. Labeled "neo-primitivism" at the time, it was not a look that lasted for long.

INNOVATIVE DESIGN

In 1981, the government set up VIA (*Valorisation de l'Innovation dans l'Ameublement*) to support innovations in French furniture design. One of the first beneficiaries was Martin Szekely. The Parisian designer's cool, geometric designs, such as the Pi chaise longue of 1983, helped establish a more serene design style. Also resisting the excesses of the Postmodern style was architect Jean Nouvel. During the 1980s, Nouvel produced numerous furniture designs in a spare, unforgiving style.

Running counter to Nouvel's strict, rational style was the work of a

"designer-maker" who met with considerable success during the 1980: André Dubreuil. A master craftsman who spent much of his time in London, Dubreuil lent an air of Gallic elegance to Britain's "Craft Revival" scene (*see p.518*).

The 1980s was also the decade that saw the emergence of Philippe Starck, a designer who masterfully combined both the rational and more flamboyant tendencies of French design. Amazingly prolific in output, Starck's design style was clear, concise, and, more often than not, came with a witty twist.

Such was Starck's phenomenal worldwide success that by the end of the decade he was able to run a heavily staffed studio in Paris. During the late 1980s and early 1990s, this served as something of a finishing school for young French designers. Matali Crasset and Christophe Pillet are the most notable of Starck's *enfants*. Both functionalists at heart, they go to considerable lengths to enliven their essentially practical designs with the use of energetic color and engaging forms.

A NEW DIVERSITY

In the face of such a hegemony over the French design world, it was only natural that a small band of designers should rebel against Starck's influence in the mid-1990s. Designers such as Pierre Charpin and Delo Lindo developed an instinctive, experimental style that brought a new diversity to the world of French design.

By the end of the 1990s, talk about French design centered on two young brothers from Brittany, Ronan and Erwan Bouroullec. The Bouroullecs' urbane style owed much to the measured aesthetic of the British designer Jasper Morrison. The international success of the Bouroullecs, coupled with the strength in depth of the Parisian design scene, proved that at the end of the millennium, French furniture design was thriving.

The interior of the Hi Hotel in Nice Designed in an innovative and contemporary style by Matali Crasset, the simple, functional furniture and pastel shades create an inviting atmosphere that does not overwhelm. *2003.*

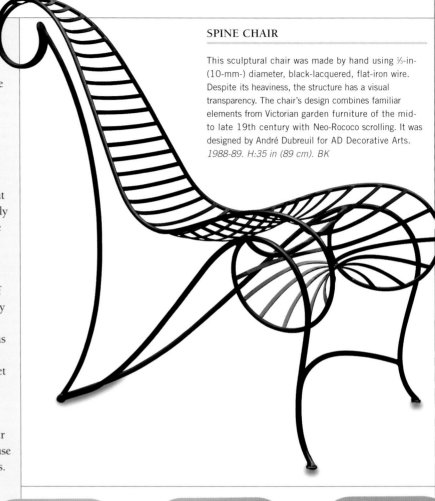

SPINE CHAIR

This sculptural chair was made by hand using ⅓-in-(10-mm-) diameter, black-lacquered, flat-iron wire. Despite its heaviness, the structure has a visual transparency. The chair's design combines familiar elements from Victorian garden furniture of the mid-to late 19th century with Neo-Rococo scrolling. It was designed by André Dubreuil for AD Decorative Arts. *1988-89. H:35 in (89 cm). BK*

BRICK BOOKSHELF

This modular bookcase system is made up of a number of honeycomb-shaped plywood shelves stacked one on top of the other. They have a white matt lacquer finish and are held in place by plywood book-stops. Available in a range of different colors, the system was designed by Ronan and Erwan Bouroullec for Cappellini. The brothers are considered to be among the best industrial designers of recent years. They are gifted at taking concepts and traditional forms and giving them a truly contemporary feel. Their designs look simple, yet are extremely modern, and they never lose sight of the ultimate purpose of a piece. *2001. Basic module: H:19¾ in (50 cm); W:118 in (300 cm); D:15¾ in (40 cm). SCP*

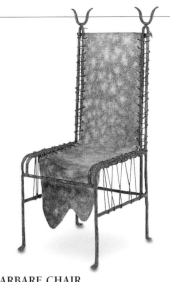

BARBARE CHAIR

This chair, designed by Elisabeth Garouste and Mattia Bonetti for Neotu, is inspired by African tribal art. Animal hide laced onto the patinated steel frame creates the chair's back and seat. *1981. H:46 in (117 cm); D:22 in (59 cm).*

A small **"connection"** links the two chairs and acts as an interconnecting table.

The low seats suggest that the chairs are meant primarily for informal use.

The contrasting colors articulate the simple structure of the design.

Splayed back legs give the chairs greater stability.

INTERFACE SEATING

Designed by Matali Crasset specifically for the ultra-contemporary Hi Hotel in Nice, these modular armchairs come with "connections" and can be arranged to offer a variety of different permutations of seating arrangements. Some of them are even designed to take laptop computers. They are made of brightly colored polyurethane-coated fabric over high-density foam and have brushed stainless-steel square-section legs. *2003. H:45¼ in (115 cm); W:22⅞ in (58 cm); D:29½ in (75 cm). MCP*

DELO-LINDO TABLE

The square table tops are raised on L-section legs. The designers have added a surreal touch with their use of warped perspective. The tables were designed by Delo-Lindo for Ligne Roset.

PHILIPPE STARCK

INTERIOR DESIGNER, ARCHITECT, AND FURNITURE AND PRODUCT DESIGNER PHILIPPE STARCK ROSE TO PROMINENCE IN THE 1980s, AND HIS BOLD DESIGNS REMAIN INFLUENTIAL TODAY.

Born in Paris in 1949, Starck became something of a household name during the 1980s and 1990s because of his unrivaled talent for self-promotion and his knack for producing slick, commercial products that retained a strong sense of individual charm.

Starck first rose to prominence in 1969 when, at just 20, he became the art director of the furniture arm of the Pierre Cardin empire. Starck spent much of the 1970s designing and furnishing

Philippe Starck

nightclubs, and it was not until 1982, when he completed the interior design scheme for President Mitterrand's private apartments in the Elysée Palace in Paris, that he received the international attention he craved.

During the 1980s and early 1990s, Starck was prolific, designing projects for everything from a mail-order house to organic food, but it was his furniture and lighting designs that won him the most plaudits. He produced such era-defining designs as the WW stool for Vitra (1990) and the Ara lamp for Flos (1988). Often blending primitive imagery (the Ara lamp resembles a bull's horn) with references to high-brow culture (the WW stool was originally designed for the art-house film director Wim Wenders), Starck has managed to stimulate the appetites of a remarkably broad audience.

Paramount Hotel interior The interior of this "cheap chic" hotel in New York is full of the witty and whimsical touches so characteristic of Starck's bold Postmodern design style.

The WW Stool This stool exemplifies the streamlined, elongated horn motif that Starck often uses. The stool has a varnished sand-cast aluminum frame with a pale green enamel finish. *1990. H:38¾ in (98.5 cm); W:21 in (53 cm). BK*

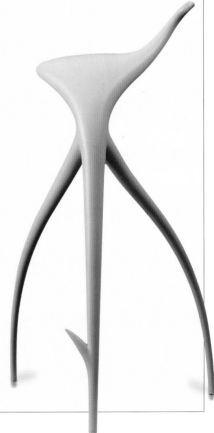

BRITAIN

AT THE HEIGHT OF the boom in 1960s youth culture, there was no hipper place to be than London. This enviable reputation stood the city in good stead for the next 30 years, as ambitious young artists and designers continued to flock there from abroad, in an attempt to establish themselves at the very cutting edge of creative culture.

DESIGN INFLUENCES

Those arriving during the 1970s, however, found themselves in a very different Britain from that of the 1960s. A more earnest atmosphere pervaded the 1970s, with the work of OMK, a design group founded by the

Polish-born Jerzy Olejnik, Bryan Morrison, and Rodney Kinsman, typical of the era. "It is irresponsible to design things that don't last," Kinsman stated, alluding to the 1960s obsession with ephemeral furniture. "You can't just rely on color or some formal gimmick, there has to be something deeper." OMK's most successful design was the Omkstack chair (1971), a concise steel

stacking chair that paved the way for a new, technical aesthetic in British furniture design.

The "High-Tech" look continued to prove popular with architects and designers well into the 1980s. Architects Eva Jiricna (born in Czechoslovakia) and Norman Foster, both of whom also produced furniture, became associated with a style that celebrated the magnificence of industry.

Not all British designers subscribed to this macho, machine-inspired aesthetic. In 1979, the Crafts Council was

launched in London to support designers who practiced a more hand-crafted style. The attitude of these Craft Revival designers (*see pp.518–19*) was similar to the DIY approach of the punk movement.

In 1979, Margaret Thatcher came to power and began to foster a society of capitalist enterprise. In this climate, a generation of "designer-makers" was born, a group that branched out on its own, producing limited editions of experimental work. Ron Arad, who had moved to Britain from Israel, formed One Off Ltd. and spent the 1980s making rough-edged hunks of furniture from discarded industrial

MINI-BOOKWORM SHELF

Designed by Ron Arad, this thin, sheet-steel bookshelf comes tightly coiled in its packaging and is supplied with a number of wall brackets so that users can design a bookshelf to suit their needs. *1993. L:198⅛ in (495.5 cm). QU*

MAGIS WAGON

This small table on wheels was designed by Michael Young for Magis. Its sand-blasted, die-cast aluminum frame on red translucent polyurethane wheels supports an injection-molded translucent polyurethane tray. *2003. H:11 in (28 cm); W:26¾ in (68 cm); D:26¾ in (68 cm). CRB*

The orange-red varnish anticipates the rust that will set in if the chair is left outside.

The flat steel back and seat provide a visual contrast with the tubular steel legs and arms.

Circular discs provide a space on which to place drinks.

The designer's notes have been incorporated as a feature of this design, emphasizing the honesty of its construction.

The deep seat of the chair encourages users to sit quietly and ponder, as the chair's name suggests.

THINKING MAN'S CHAIR

The frame of this easy chair is made from orange-red varnished metal tubes, and the seat and back are composed of contrasting flat metal bars. Each arm has a tray for holding a glass, and this design feature, combined with the deep seat, makes it a chair in which a thinking man could comfortably settle. The

incorporation of designer's notes, which are written on the chair parts, is reminiscent of the desire for honesty of construction, which has its roots in Modernism. The chair was designed by Jasper Morrison shortly after he left the RCA. *1986. H:27½ in (70 cm); W:22½ in (57 cm); D:35½ in (90 cm). SCP*

NEMO CHAIR

This armchair has a molded Lloyd Loom seat and back raised on a chromed-steel frame. The thin, tapering legs emphasize the lightness of the design. It was designed by Studio Dillon and manufactured by Lloyd Loom of Spalding. *1999. H:29 in (73.5 cm); W:31 in (79 cm); D:25¾ in (65.5 cm). DIL*

Creek Vean House, Cornwall This house was designed in a "High-Tech" style by Richard Rogers and Norman Foster and won an award in 1970.

materials. Tom Dixon also employed recycled materials, albeit with rather more elegance, to make items of furniture for his "Creative Salvage" company. The architects Nigel Coates and Zaha Hadi were intent on making a name for themselves, too, and began designing experimental furniture.

CONFIDENCE IN DESIGN
By the early 1990s, London seemed to have rediscovered its cutting edge, as confidence within the British design industry ran high. In 1989, Terence Conran opened the Design Museum in London. Numerous bar, restaurant, and hotel owners began employing designers to inject energy and glamour into their buildings' interiors. The design departments of London colleges, such as the RCA (*see below*) and Central St. Martins, were also the focus of much international attention.

With such an enthusiastic audience, British designers of the 1990s no longer needed to make such blunt, attention-seeking statements with their furniture. Instead, a smoother, more subtle and refined style developed, with Jasper Morrison the undisputed master. Arad and Dixon also began to tone down their designs, adopting a far more commercial approach.

Many designers chose to work together rather than alone. The mid-1990s saw groups such as El Ultimo Grito, Inflate, and Azumi emerge and adopt a modest, light-hearted approach to furniture design. By the millennium, much of the optimistic spirit that had drained from the British design industry in the 1970s had been restored.

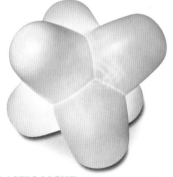

PLASTIC LIGHT
This white plastic light in the shape of a "jack" was designed by Tom Dixon for Eurolounge. Different lights can be stacked on top of one another. The light can also be used as a stool. *1997. H:23½ in (60 cm); W:23½ in (60 cm).*

SHIPSHAPE
This self-contained storage unit is made from laminated birch. It can also be used as a seat or side table. It was designed for Isokon Plus by Shin & Tomoko Azumi. *2003. H:15¾ in (40 cm); W:17¾ in (45 cm); D:11⅗ in (29.5 cm). ISO*

OMKSTACK CHAIR
This stackable chair has a tubular-steel frame supporting a polished, perforated sheet-steel back and seat, and stands on rubber feet. It was designed by Rodney Kinsman and manufactured by OMK. *1972. BouE*

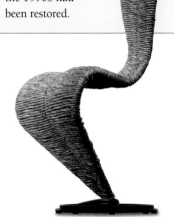

S-CHAIR
The metal frame of this chair is covered in woven marsh straw, emphasizing the organic feel of the structure. It was designed by Tom Dixon for Cappellini. *1985. H:39⅓ in (100 cm); W:16½ in (42 cm); D:20½ in (52 cm). SCP*

THE LEADING ROLE OF THE RCA
ALTHOUGH IN EXISTENCE SINCE 1837, IT WAS ONLY DURING THE 1980S AND 1990S THAT THE ROYAL COLLEGE OF ART COULD REALLY CLAIM TO BE ONE OF THE MOST IMPORTANT INSTITUTIONS IN THE WORLD FOR THE TEACHING OF DESIGN.

The RCA is a college that concentrates solely on postgraduate studies, and since 1948 it has focused mainly on preparing students for future professional practice. Disciplines taught at the RCA include fine art, fashion, vehicle design, animation, architecture, and, of course, industrial design and furniture design.

While Britain lagged somewhat behind world developments in furniture design during much of the early part of the 20th century, it began to forge an identity as a hotbed of creativity during the 1960s and 1970s, thanks in large part to the progressive teaching taking place at institutions such as the Architectural Association, the RCA, and the Central School of Art and Design. In response to this reputation, many of the most talented graduates from across the world flocked to London in order to pursue their postgraduate studies.

By the late 1980s, many of the most prominent figures of Britain's prospering design scene were graduates of the RCA, and alumni like Jasper Morrison, Jane Dillon, James Irvine, and Ross Lovegrove only helped to attract an even higher caliber of graduates to the college.

In the mid-1990s, by now referring to itself as an "ideas factory," the RCA consolidated its already robust reputation by appointing furniture designer Ron Arad as Professor of Furniture Design and architect Nigel Coates as Professor of Architecture and Interiors; both continued to uphold the tradition of progressive teaching.

Air chair by Jasper Morrison This chair was made from a single piece of gas-injected polypropylene. Designed by one of the RCA's most famous students, it was produced by Magis in Italy.

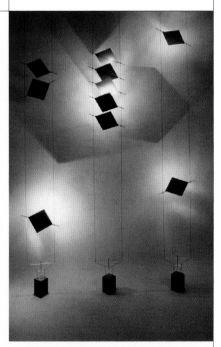

Aero lamp by Ralph Ball Since graduating from the RCA in 1980, Ralph Ball has achieved critical and commercial success for his work both as a lighting designer and as a furniture designer. *1979.*

CRAFT AND TECHNOLOGY

TWO DISTINCT STRANDS OF FURNITURE DESIGN EXISTED IN THE 1970S AND 1980S—"HIGH TECH" AND CRAFT REVIVAL. IN THE 1990S, COMPUTER TECHNOLOGY FACILITATED THEIR FUSION.

THE 1970S WAS A DECADE when fractures began to appear within the furniture design industry. While some designers argued for a more vital, hands-on approach to design, others continued to pursue the Modernist dream of a functional, mechanized future.

Sophisticated computer technology was still some way off. The stark "High-Tech" style of the 1970s had little to do with computers and more to do with construction and engineering. Its development was partly a response to manufacturers' demands for a skeletal style that scrimped on materials and was simple to mass-produce. In Switzerland, the architect Mario Botta (an ex-employee of Le Corbusier) began producing furniture from perforated sheet steel that resembled machine parts, while in Britain, Rodney Kinsman worked on a range of terse, rational designs, also made in metal. In 1986, Norman Foster produced the ultimate "High-Tech" furniture range for Tecno—the Nomos system. Designed for use in open-plan offices, the gleaming glass and steel tables looked like majestic feats of civil engineering rather than humble office desks.

CRAFT-BASED STYLES

Running counter to the "High-Tech" style was the Craft Revival movement. In the United States in the early 1980s, Wendell Castle, Sam Maloof, and Tage Frid worked in a highly contrived Postmodern style, often employing trompe l'oeil effects. Using a laborious, painstaking method to produce off-hand, jokey objects was self-consciously ironic. In Britain, John Makepeace led the Craft Revival movement. He set up the Parnham House Workshops in Dorset in 1977 and produced meticulously crafted objects, often ornamental in style, that sold for vast sums of money. Makepeace's Ebony and Nickel Silver chair (1978) was typical of his approach: it was constructed of 2,000 separate pieces of ebony.

In the late 1980s, a very different facet of the craft-based trend emerged. Designers in London, such as Fred Baier, Ron Arad, Tom Dixon, and Danny Lane, began to self-produce defiantly rough-and-ready furniture. This movement, labeled the "Salvage Look," the "Big Bang" style, or "Neo-Brutalism," was raw, energetic, and, to an extent, political. Incorporating discarded manhole covers, smashed glass, old car seats, and rusted steel, these new iconoclastic furniture designs were the equivalent of Vivienne Westwood's punk outfits.

DOLLY FOLDING CHAIR
Designed by Antonio Citterio for Kartell, this folding chair combines elegance and lightness with a sophisticated and solid plastic structural system. The arms of the chair are integral to the frame design rather than being separate, as in regular chair designs. The chair is available in a variety of colors, and has a padded, wooden, or plastic seat.

CHAISE LONGUE "SOFT"
Werner Aisslinger's sensuous design uses high-tech materials: the chaise longue has an aluminum alloy frame and a blue "TechnoGel®" seat cushion. The design and materials combine to give the piece a lightweight, transparent appearance. ZAN

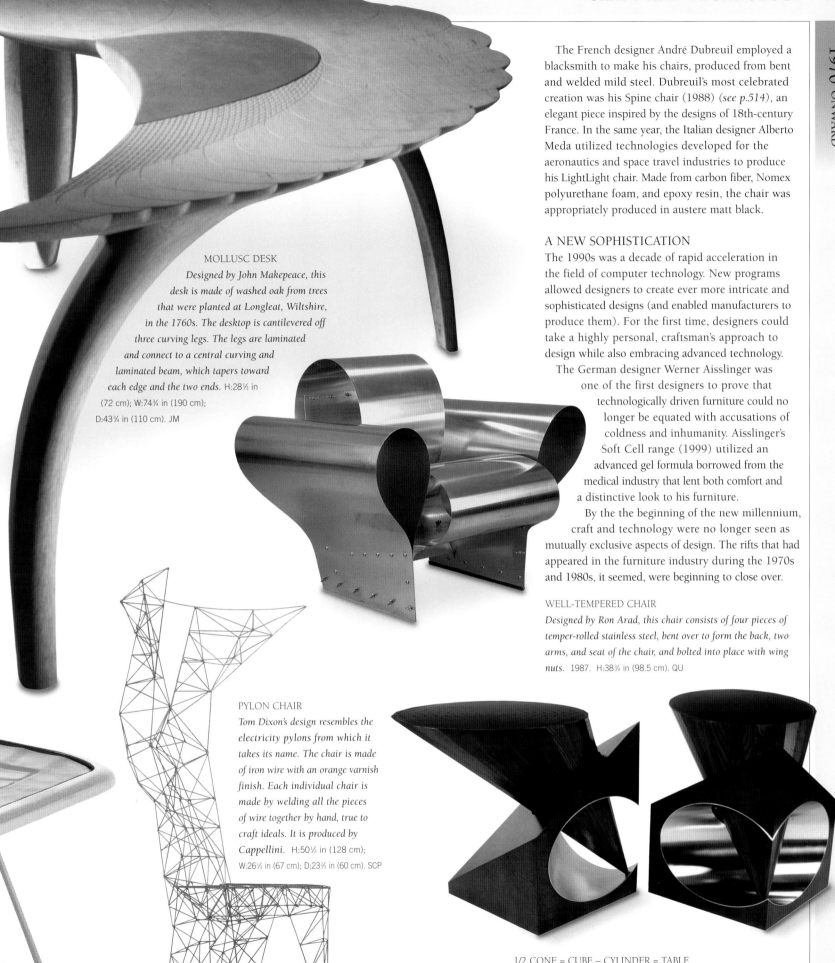

The French designer André Dubreuil employed a blacksmith to make his chairs, produced from bent and welded mild steel. Dubreuil's most celebrated creation was his Spine chair (1988) *(see p.514)*, an elegant piece inspired by the designs of 18th-century France. In the same year, the Italian designer Alberto Meda utilized technologies developed for the aeronautics and space travel industries to produce his LightLight chair. Made from carbon fiber, Nomex polyurethane foam, and epoxy resin, the chair was appropriately produced in austere matt black.

A NEW SOPHISTICATION

The 1990s was a decade of rapid acceleration in the field of computer technology. New programs allowed designers to create ever more intricate and sophisticated designs (and enabled manufacturers to produce them). For the first time, designers could take a highly personal, craftsman's approach to design while also embracing advanced technology.

The German designer Werner Aisslinger was one of the first designers to prove that technologically driven furniture could no longer be equated with accusations of coldness and inhumanity. Aisslinger's Soft Cell range (1999) utilized an advanced gel formula borrowed from the medical industry that lent both comfort and a distinctive look to his furniture.

By the the beginning of the new millennium, craft and technology were no longer seen as mutually exclusive aspects of design. The rifts that had appeared in the furniture industry during the 1970s and 1980s, it seemed, were beginning to close over.

MOLLUSC DESK
Designed by John Makepeace, this desk is made of washed oak from trees that were planted at Longleat, Wiltshire, in the 1760s. The desktop is cantilevered off three curving legs. The legs are laminated and connect to a central curving and laminated beam, which tapers toward each edge and the two ends. H:28⅓ in (72 cm); W:74¾ in (190 cm); D:43¾ in (110 cm). JM

WELL-TEMPERED CHAIR
Designed by Ron Arad, this chair consists of four pieces of temper-rolled stainless steel, bent over to form the back, two arms, and seat of the chair, and bolted into place with wing nuts. 1987. H:38¾ in (98.5 cm). QU

PYLON CHAIR
Tom Dixon's design resembles the electricity pylons from which it takes its name. The chair is made of iron wire with an orange varnish finish. Each individual chair is made by welding all the pieces of wire together by hand, true to craft ideals. It is produced by Cappellini. H:50⅓ in (128 cm); W:26⅓ in (67 cm); D:23⅗ in (60 cm). SCP

1/2 CONE = CUBE – CYLINDER = TABLE
This unique pair of tables was made by Fred Baier. Each one is formed from an oak cylinder, a burr myrtle cube, and a nickel silver cylinder. They are said to be the first furniture to interpret the minus key in three-dimensional form. H:21⅗ in (55 cm). FB

EUROPE

DURING THE 1970S, 1980s, and 1990s, furniture designers became itinerant to a remarkable degree, with designers from across the globe being drawn to established centers of design, such as London, Milan, and Amsterdam, like moths to a flame. By the 1990s, it had become common practice for aspiring designers from less-established design nations to educate themselves and build up a reputation abroad (often moving from city to city) before moving back to the country of their birth.

Despite many of its key protagonists being inveterate globetrotters, one of the most interesting aspects of Postmodern design was the fact that

it championed regional styles together with a combination of Classical motifs, often with unconventional materials. Typifying this is the Czech-born designer Borek Sipek who moved restlessly between Germany, the Netherlands, and Czechoslovakia in the late 1970s and 1980s, yet whose work consistently referred to the Baroque traditions of his homeland.

Also exemplary of this paradoxical Postmodern trend was Mario Botta, a Swiss architect and designer who worked for periods in Italy, France, and Japan during the 1980s, but still remained true to the innately Swiss spirit of technical engineering.

NEW DESIGN HOT SPOTS

As Postmodernism spread across the world of furniture design in the 1980s, nations with a rich history of functional Modernism began to fall from prominence. Although there were a few notable exceptions, such as Stefan Wewerka (who combined Bauhaus principles with an astute knowledge of art practice and ergonomics) and Peter Maly, Germany made little contribution to furniture design during the 1980s, and the same is true of the Scandinavian countries.

Spain, which has a rather thin history of Modern design,

emerged strongly in the 1980s, with Barcelona becoming a particular hot spot for contemporary design. Oscar Tusquets Blanca and Javier Mariscal represented the more exuberant spirit of Spanish design, while Jorge Pensi and Patricia Urquiola followed a more functional path.

Despite having designers like Gerrit Rietveld and Mart Stam, who were key to the development of the early Modern style, the Netherlands made little impact on the world of furniture design during

CD CHEST

This industrial-looking chest for storing CDs is made from welded and lacquered steel with industrial glass panels. The upper section of the chest is hinged and rises up to reveal a large storage area. Below this are six drawers for CDs. The case is open to the rear and stands on casters. It was designed by Götz Bury in cooperation with Franz West, Germany. *1992. H:37⅓ in (95.5 cm). POR*

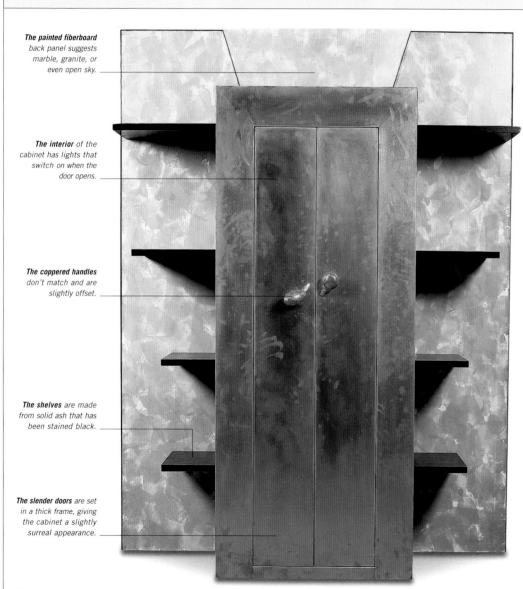

The painted fiberboard back panel suggests marble, granite, or even open sky.

The interior of the cabinet has lights that switch on when the door opens.

The coppered handles don't match and are slightly offset.

The shelves are made from solid ash that has been stained black.

The slender doors are set in a thick frame, giving the cabinet a slightly surreal appearance.

PO-LAM WARDROBE

This surreal Postmodern wardrobe was designed by Borek Sipek for Franz Leitner Interior Design, Austria. It has a copper central section within a fiberboard frame. The central section forms the wardrobe and has a wide frame, slender doors, and asymmetrical handles all made from untreated copper. The primed and

painted, shelved back panel is made from fiberboard with a marble-effect finish. Both the graduated shelves on the back panel and the fitted interior of the wardrobe are made of black-stained ash—a mainstay of Postmodern design. Lights inside the cabinet switch on when the doors are opened. The "keystone" element at the top gives the piece an architectural quality. *1990. H:86⅔ in (220 cm). DOR*

ARMCHAIR

This armchair was designed by Mario Botta. It has a black-lacquered aluminum frame, and the front legs and arms are shaped as huge hollow cylinders. The circular back and seat are made of vinyl-upholstered foam, in a black and white chevron design. *1980s. H:36 in (91.5 cm); W:38½ in (98 cm); D:41 in (104 cm). SDR*

the postwar years. During the 1980s and 1990s, however, Dutch design flourished as the Dutch became the leading proponents of a dry, gently conceptual style typified by the work of Droog, a collective of designers based in Amsterdam. Droog (which translates as "dry") summed up much of the non-dogmatic, playful attitude of late-1990s European design. "We certainly don't see our designs as the definitive solution to a problem, or the one true direction to take," said Droog's Remmy Ramakers. "Our designs are just the door to any number of possibilities."

Konstantin Grcic can also be considered a quintessentially 1990s

designer. Grcic's stated aim of making "furniture that everyone understands immediately" illustrates a very different attitude from that shown by many more willfully avant-garde designers of earlier decades. Born in Germany in 1965, Grcic followed the typical pattern of many designers of his generation by studying abroad in London—where he worked for a short time with Jasper Morrison—before returning home to Munich to set up his own office.

Apartment by Günther Domenig This apartment in the village of Steindorf in Austria is very anti-purist in style and goes against the grain of the clean lines espoused by Modernism. It also illustrates a very personal rather than universal approach to design.

PRADO DESK

This desk has a simple, rectangular frame made from solid American oak, and a flat oak-veneered work surface. It is a contemporary interpretation of a kneehole desk. Below the desktop are two shaped shelves, which span the entire width of the desk and have a curved cut-out to allow the sitter to pull up a chair. The back and sides of the desk are open and there is a shallow drawer beneath the desktop. The desk is raised on casters. It was designed by Konstantin Grcic for SCP. *H:30 in (76 cm); W:65 in (165 cm); D:31½ in (80 cm). SCP*

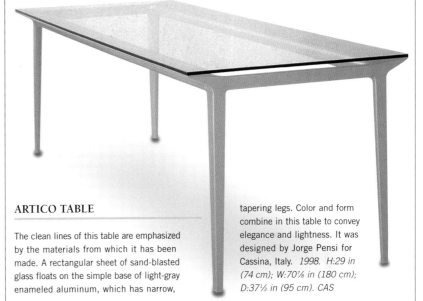

ARTICO TABLE

The clean lines of this table are emphasized by the materials from which it has been made. A rectangular sheet of sand-blasted glass floats on the simple base of light-gray enameled aluminum, which has narrow, tapering legs. Color and form combine in this table to convey elegance and lightness. It was designed by Jorge Pensi for Cassina, Italy. *1998. H:29 in (74 cm); W:70⅞ in (180 cm); D:37⅓ in (95 cm). CAS*

THREE-LEGGED CHAIR

This black-lacquered beech chair has a flat upholstered seat, a shaped back rail to allow the sitter to sit sideways or facing forward, and three legs. Designed by Stefan Wewerka for Tecta. *1979. H:30 in (76 cm); W:24⅛ in (62 cm). DOR*

"85 LAMPS" CHANDELIER

This chandelier uses 85 15-watt light bulbs at the end of narrow, flexible wire stems, which are knotted together to form a ball of the 85 plugs. Designed by Rody Graumans for Droog Design. *1993. H:43⅓ in (110 cm); W:27½ in (70 cm). DRO*

BENCH FOR TWO

Designed by Nanna Ditzel and produced by Fredericia furniture, this bench is made from solid maple and ¹⁄₁₆-in- (1.2-mm-) thick airplane plywood. The whole piece is covered with a silk-screen print design of concentric circles. In 1990, it was awarded a gold medal at the International Furniture Design Competition, Asahikawa, Japan. *1989.*

THE AMERICAS

ALTHOUGH THE IDEAS that would eventually go by the name of Postmodernism were first mooted in the late 1960s, there was something of a hiatus in their development during the early 1970s. This was a period when theorizing was put to one side in favor of more immediate concerns. The most important design book of these years was Victor Papanek's *Design in the Real World*, published in New York.

In 1970, the US Environmental Agency was founded in response to increasing concerns for the planet in the face of escalating consumerism. American designers of the early 1970s attempted to become more responsible in their approach to design by moving away from the use of plastics and favoring more natural materials. The most celebrated example of this environmentally conscious outlook was Frank Gehry's 1972 collection of furniture: "Easy Edges." Made from biodegradable cardboard, Gehry's ingenious designs were intentionally inexpensive (selling for $35–$100). At the end of the decade, Gehry returned to working with cardboard, but this time his "Experimental Edges" collection sold for much higher prices.

BRASH DESIGN

During the early 1980s, environmental concerns seemed to slip from the United States' agenda as a culture of conspicuous consumption was ushered in. Wall Street traders were making millions on junk bonds while consumer confidence returned with a vengeance. Against a background of such rampant demand, the bold ideas of Postmodernism once again rose to the surface. Bright, brash, and self-consciously smart, the aesthetic espoused

Gehry House Frank Gehry's own house is a deconstructivist remodeling of a suburban Californian house. Chain-link, plywood, and corrugated aluminum have been used on top of the house's original wood frame. The haphazard look is deliberate. *1978.*

STRAP CHAIR

This chair, which is part of an experimental line of furniture, has a light, box-like maple frame. It uses polypropylene strapping tape to create a lightweight, three-dimensional web as a minimal yet comfortable seating surface. It was designed by Boym Partners. *2000. H:31 in (76 cm). BOY*

LANDSCAPE CHAISE

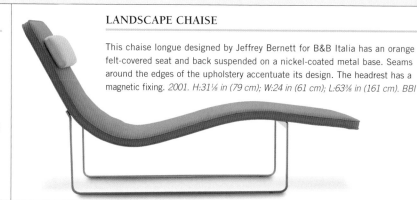

This chaise longue designed by Jeffrey Bernett for B&B Italia has an orange felt-covered seat and back suspended on a nickel-coated metal base. Seams around the edges of the upholstery accentuate its design. The headrest has a magnetic fixing. *2001. H:31⅛ in (79 cm); W:24 in (61 cm); L:63⅜ in (161 cm). BBI*

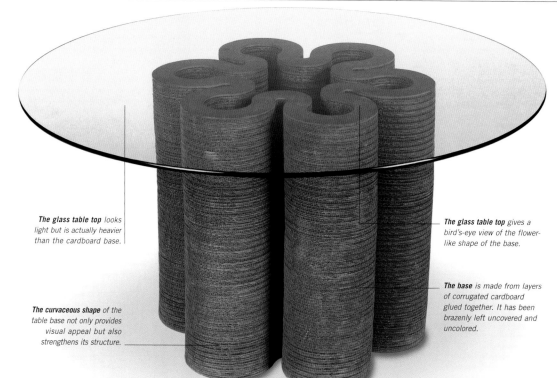

The glass table top looks light but is actually heavier than the cardboard base.

The curvaceous shape of the table base not only provides visual appeal but also strengthens its structure.

The glass table top gives a bird's-eye view of the flower-like shape of the base.

The base is made from layers of corrugated cardboard glued together. It has been brazenly left uncovered and uncolored.

DAISY TABLE

This extremely rare dining table has a circular, plate glass top raised on a six-cylinder corrugated cardboard base. The six-cylinder base is constructed of many layers of compressed and laminated corrugated cardboard to give it stability. The nature of the material means it is easy to shape and gives a singularly sculptural quality to the furniture. Although the cardboard was an ecological choice, the table was not as durable as those made of plastic at the same time. Designed by Frank Gehry, this table was just one of 14 designs from the "Easy Edges" series aimed at producing contemporary furniture at affordable prices. *c. 1972. H:23 in (58.5 cm); Diam:48 in (220 cm). SDR*

PLAZA DRESSING TABLE

Designed by Michael Graves for Memphis Milano, this Postmodern dressing table is made from plastic-laminated wood. It has an architectural upper section with crystal mirrors above six drawers, raised on a flared plinth. It comes with matching stool. *1981. H:89 in (226 cm); W:55⅛ in (140 cm); D:21¼ in (54 cm). MAP*

by the likes of Robert Venturi and Michael Graves perfectly fitted the mood of 1980s America. "Less is a bore," proclaimed Venturi, perverting Ludwig Mies van der Rohe's famous statement, "Less is more."

In 1979, Knoll International commissioned Venturi to design a series of showroom interiors and nine chair designs that embodied the American Postmodern style. Venturi's Queen Anne chair was based on an 18th-century English design, but the reference was only surface-deep. On closer scrutiny the bent laminated wood chair looked more like a stage prop than a chair fit for a queen.

CRAFT AND ENVIRONMENT
The 1980s also saw a revival of interest in traditional crafts, with American designers such as Wendell Castle and Sam Maloof producing one-of-a-kind, hugely labor-intensive objects in a highly personal style. Often referred to as the "Woodcraft" movement, their designs bore strong similarities to the work of the British Craft Revival designers of the same period.

This hands-on approach to design and production continued to flourish in the 1990s, although since the 1980s economic bubble had now burst, there was a greater emphasis on low-cost (often recycled) materials. Constantin Boym, who often worked with his wife Laurene Leon, was a leading exponent of this style, producing impressive collections of furniture from low-grade steel and cheap packaging materials.

In 1995, the Museum of Modern Art in New York, celebrated the resourcefulness of designers such as the Boyms in an exhibition entitled "Mutant Materials in Contemporary Design." This show reflected the desire of many American furniture and product designers to work with more ecologically sound materials.

Postmodernism fell from favor at the end of the 1980s as consumers deemed it too cerebral and complex. Emerging to fill the void was the work of the ebullient Karim Rashid. Taking his cue from the French designer Philippe Starck—in both his larger-than-life personality and his sensual design style—Rashid's work was a hit with buyers. Rashid's furniture was bright, bubbly, and designed to bring a smile to the face of its users, rather than the knowing smirk favored by fans of Postmodernism.

QUEEN ANNE CHAIR

This modern take on the Queen Anne chairs of the early 18th century by Robert Venturi for Knoll International, has a carved top rail, a solid, vase-shaped splat, and cabriole legs. It is made from bentwood laminates and plastic-laminated veneer. *1984. H:38½ in (98 cm). KNO*

POWERPLAY CHAIR

This chair is made up of wafer-thin strips of laminated maple, bent and woven to create a rigid form. The seat back strips have been bent back, while the seat has been woven. It was designed by Frank Gehry and manufactured by Knoll International. *1990–92. BonE*

CAMPANA BROTHERS

"BRAZIL IS OUR GREAT FOUNTAIN OF INSPIRATION," THE CAMPANA BROTHERS ONCE STATED, EXPLAINING WHY THEY HAVE NEVER MOVED FROM SÃO PAULO.

Humberto and Fernando Campana first established a design office together in 1983, Humberto having previously studied as a lawyer and Fernando as an architect. The brothers' scant experience of designing and making furniture forced the pair to utilize rudimentary construction techniques, while their lack of financial resources led to a preference for inexpensive, easily available materials for their pieces.

Transforming these seeming impediments into a positive feature of their work, the Campana brothers were, by the mid-1990s, attracting attention from beyond South America. Indeed, in 1998, the Museum of Modern Art in New York became so taken by the obvious ingenuity and humanity that pervaded the Campanas' work that they showcased their work in an installation entitled "Projects 66."

Perhaps the most startling of the Campanas' designs is the *Favela*, a chair designed in 1991 that pays homage to the homebuilders of Brazil's shanty towns. Constructed from scraps of wood, apparently put together at random, the design was taken on by the Italian manufacturer Edra 12 years later and sold (with great success) to the company's affluent European clientele.

Banquette chair This handmade, limited-edition chair is made from a compilation of stuffed toy sharks and dolphins on a metal base. *2004. H:25 in (63.5 cm); W:41 in (104 cm); D:37 in (94 cm).*

The *Favela* armchair This chair is made from many pieces of natural wood, glued and nailed together in a way similar to that in which the shacks of the *favelas*, or shanty towns, are built in Brazil. Because each chair is made by hand, no two are exactly the same. *1991.*

"Ideal House" This installation was created by the Campana brothers for the 2004 Cologne furniture fair. The brothers called this "spontaneous architecture," giving the impression it is built from found objects rather than being a planned design.

The Edra Sushi chair This chair is made by rolling up different materials and squeezing them into a large flexible tube. The part left uncovered forms a multicolored seat. *H:25½ in (65 cm); W:37½ in (95 cm).*

The Corallo chair This chair, designed for Edra, has a large seat formed out of an irregular structure of hand-bent steel wire with a coral-pink epoxy paint finish. *H:35½ in (90 cm); W:55 in (140 cm); D:39½ in (100 cm).*

JAPAN

BY THE 1970S, THE EFFORTS that the
Japanese furniture industry had made
to align itself with Western society
(and thus benefit from selling to a
thriving Western market) were reaping
rewards. Indeed, so comprehensively
had Japanese designers caught up
with their Western counterparts that
when Postmodernism emerged as a
dominant trend in design, the Japanese
were among its leading exponents.

In 1972, Arata Isozaki produced his
Marilyn chair, a protean Postmodern
design that borrowed from an unlikely
spectrum of sources. The chair's
curvaceous back was based on the
shapely form of Marilyn Monroe,
while the overall shape was clearly
derived from the chair designs of
the early-20th-century Glaswegian
designer Charles Rennie Mackintosh
(see pp.364–65). The very particular
craftsmanship was typically Japanese.

Also establishing a name for himself
during the 1970s was Shiro Kuramata,
a designer whose work was at once
lyrical and highly rational. Kuramata
gave industrial materials a grace and
sense of humanity that few designers
had ever previously achieved. It has
been pointed out that Kuramata's
furniture designs are as much objects
for contemplation as they are for
practical use.

At the start of the 1980s, a prosperous
decade for Japan, the work of Japanese
designers began to attract worldwide

attention. In 1981, the recently
formed Memphis group, based in
Milan, invited Isozaki, Kuramata, and
Masanori Umeda to contribute designs
to its latest collection. Meanwhile,
Ettore Sottsass traveled to Tokyo
in 1982; the Italian designer was
given a hero's welcome by a Japanese
public that had become enthusiastic
consumers of Western design. By the
1990s, Japan would be considered the
most important market in the world
for progressive design.

Mutual appreciation between the
worlds of Japanese and European
design in the 1980s and 1990s meant
that many Japanese designers worked
for European manufacturers, while
numerous European designers plied
their trade in Japan.

Making sure he had a foot in both
camps was Toshiyuki Kita, a designer
who kept offices in both Osaka and
Milan. Kita's most celebrated design
is his Wink chair for Cassina (1980),
a distinctly Postmodern design that
conflated several disparate references
into one object. While the bright
colors and Mickey Mouse ears of the
chair are redolent of Pop culture, the
chair's technical construction echoes
the achievements of early Modernism.
The enveloping nature of the chair is
reminiscent of aircraft or car seats.

WESTERN INFLUENCE
Sadly, during the 1990s, Japan
became increasingly enamored
with Western culture, and most
of its talented young designers
moved abroad. Manufacturers in
Japan began to collaborate ever
more with European designers, such
as Philippe Starck and Marc Newson.
Masanori Umeda did produce a
successful series of Flower chairs during
the 1990s (a reminder of Japan's natural
beauty in an increasingly technological
age) but Japanese furniture design of the
1990s showed little of the vitality that
it had displayed in the 1980s. Indeed,
when Shiro Kuramata died in 1991, it
became painfully clear that there were
few furniture designers left in Japan
who could ever hope to replicate the
international impact of his work.

The Museum of Modern Art, Texas This museum in
Fort Worth was designed in 2002 by Tadao Ando.
Five long, flat-roofed concrete and glass pavilions,
supported by 40-ft- (12-m-) high, Y-shaped columns
are reflected in the water of the adjacent pond.

BOOKSHELF

This simple but striking bookcase is made from
matt-white-lacquered strips of wood, which are
arranged vertically and horizontally to provide
a large number of boxed compartments that
graduate in size. The largest box is in the bottom
left-hand corner and the boxes grow smaller
toward the top right corner. The red crosses are
not part of the piece. It was designed by Shiro
Kuramata for Cappellini. *H:100 in (254 cm);
W:99⅓ in (252.5 cm); D:15¾ in (40 cm). SCP*

WINK ARMCHAIR

The base of this chair by Toshiyuki Kita can
be tilted forward to form a chaise longue. The
headrest is divided into two parts, each with an
independent reclining position; side knobs adjust
the back. The chair has a steel frame and fabric
or leather upholstery. *1980. H:40¼ in (102 cm);
W:32¾ in (83 cm); D:35½ in (90 cm) (min);
H:33½ in (85 cm); D:78¾ in (200 cm) (max). CAS*

KICK TABLE

This low table by Toshiyuki Kita has an ovoid wooden top with a red-lacquered surface. The table top is supported on a dark gray enameled steel base, which is regulated by a glass cylinder so that the height can be adjusted, and raised on casters. *1983. H:15¾-20¾ in (40–52.5 cm); W:19¾ in (50 cm); D:19¾ in (50 cm). CAS*

AKI BIKI CANTA

This swivel armchair is one of three variations on a theme designed by Toshiyuki Kita. Each chair has an upholstered swivel seat on a fixed steel base but a slightly different configuration. The Biki (shown here) has a backrest with arms. *2000. H:26¾ in (68 cm); W:28⅓ in (72 cm); D:26¾ in (68 cm).*

SING SING SING

Designed by Shiro Kuramata for XO, this chair has a cantilevered frame made from coated steel. The seat and back of the chair are made from wire mesh, which has been welded in place. The chair's slight spring adds to its comfort. *1985. H:34⅔ in (88 cm); W:20½ in (52 cm); D:25⅓ in (64.5 cm). QU*

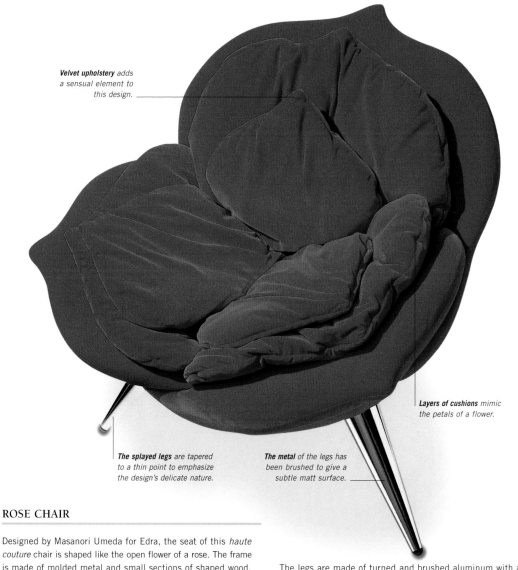

Velvet upholstery adds a sensual element to this design.

Layers of cushions mimic the petals of a flower.

The splayed legs are tapered to a thin point to emphasize the design's delicate nature.

The metal of the legs has been brushed to give a subtle matt surface.

ROSE CHAIR

Designed by Masanori Umeda for Edra, the seat of this *haute couture* chair is shaped like the open flower of a rose. The frame is made of molded metal and small sections of shaped wood. The velvet, petal-shaped cushions, which form the padding, are handmade. They are filled with polyurethane foam and Dacron®.

The legs are made of turned and brushed aluminum with a kiln-dried transparent finish coating. *H:31½ in (80 cm); W:35½ in (90 cm); D:32¼ in (82 cm).*

MARILYN CHAIR

This chair has a solid birch frame with a bent, laminated wood back and a leather-covered, upholstered seat. Seen from the side, the chair is a representation of Marilyn Monroe's figure. From the front it is clear that the designer, Arata Isozaki, was inspired by Charles Rennie Mackintosh. *1972. H:55 in (140 cm); W:60⅔ in (54 cm); D:60¾ in (54.5 cm). TDO*

MARC NEWSON

A PROLIFIC AND PASSIONATE DESIGNER WHO EMPLOYS THE LATEST COMPUTERIZED TECHNIQUES, MARC NEWSON DRAWS INSPIRATION FOR HIS SCULPTURAL DESIGNS FROM THE 1950S AND 1960S.

MARC NEWSON'S WORK embodies many of the paradoxes that prevailed in 1990s design. His work often alludes to the culture of his home country, Australia, yet most of his designs have been created in Tokyo, Paris, and London. Newson often employs the latest computerized design and manufacturing techniques, but also retains a great appreciation of natural materials and traditional handcrafts. While his designs take the pursuit of sculptural form to unprecedented heights, Newson's work is underpinned by an essentially conservative approach to function.

Newson likes to describe his works as "naive." By this he means that they are not driven by any grand concepts or ideologies. Indeed, more often than not, Newson has admitted, they are the result of absent-minded doodles. "I approach my designs in a fairly subliminal way," he once said, "which is lucky because I don't have time to think about it too much!" For this unencumbered approach to design, Newson believes that he has his education in Australia to thank. At the Sydney College of Arts, he studied jewelry and sculpture, rather than industrial or furniture design, and the lack of an entrenched design culture in Australia allowed him to pursue his own particular path.

LEVER HOUSE RESTAURANT, NEW YORK
Newson transformed the 6,500-square-foot (604-square-meter), subterranean, windowless restaurant at Lever House with his design. His use of hexagons and curved surfaces gives the room a retro 1950s feel, while the use of blonde oak and mirrored glass adds light. 2003

EMBRYO CHAIR
This armchair, manufactured by Cappellini, has three legs made from chromed tubular steel. The polyurethane foam padding is covered with bi-elastic fabric. 1988. H:31 in (78.7 cm); W:33 in (83.8 cm); D:34 in (86.4 cm).

ORGONE LOUNGE CHAIR
This lounge chair designed for Cappellini is made entirely from fiberglass and is available in a range of bright colors. It has an organic, flowing form, and stands on three tapering legs. 1992. H:19⅗ in (50 cm); W:71¼ in (181 cm). BK

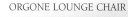

WOODEN CHAIR
This elegant chair, created for Cappellini, is constructed from extremely long strips of bent beech heartwood. Each strip has been looped back on itself to provide the seat back, seat, and support in one. H:29½ in (75 cm); W:29½ in (75 cm); L:39⅓ in (100 cm).

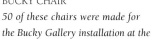

BUCKY CHAIR
50 of these chairs were made for the Bucky Gallery installation at the Cartier Contemporary Art Foundation in Paris. Each chair has a sculptural fiberglass shell electrostatically upholstered in flock and can be stacked (as shown above). 1995.

FORD DESIGN VICE PRESIDENT J. MAYS (LEFT), MARC NEWSON, AND THE FORD 021C CONCEPT VEHICLE
The Ford 021C concept vehicle, created by Newson, was displayed at the Tokyo Motor Show press preview in Makuhari on October 20, 1999.

021C CONCEPT FORD
Built around elements of Ford's next-generation small car platform, this car was, according to Mays, designed "to bring some fun back to the Tokyo Motor Show." 1999.

Newson's first major success as a designer was the exhibition in 1986 of his Lockheed Lounge at the Roslyn Oxley Gallery in Sydney. An organically-shaped chaise longue, encased in riveted aluminum panels, the Lockheed Lounge resembles a 1940s aircraft fuselage beaten into the shape of a Surrealist sculpture. Newson himself described it as "a giant glob of mercury." The design was widely featured in international design magazines and, by 1989, Newson was working in Japan for Teruo Kurosaki, whose company *Idée* had established a worldwide reputation for innovative furniture design.

The beginning of the 1990s saw Newson much in demand by European furniture manufacturers. Cappellini was his most enthusiastic suitor, and many of Newson's most notable designs would be produced by this Italian manufacturer. Such was the interest in Newson's work in Europe that he moved to Paris in 1992. References to the beach culture of Sydney, however, consistently cropped up in his work, as can be seen in the surfboard-shaped Orgone chaise longue. The hourglass shape of the Orgone became a much-used motif in Newson's work, and was one that he employed for the tire treads and floor carpets of his astonishing concept car for Ford. Designed by Newson in 1999, at Ford's research center in Turin, the 021C car catapulted his career to a whole new level. Soon Newson was working on designs for watches, bicycles, airplanes, clothing ranges, and much more.

CAPPELLINI

WITH AN EXACTING EYE FOR DESIGN COUPLED WITH THE COURAGE TO BACK NEW TALENT AND A GIFT FOR PROMOTION, GIULIO CAPPELLINI CATAPULTED A VAST NUMBER OF DESIGNERS TO FAME.

Giulio Cappellini

The list of designers that have collaborated with the Italian manufacturer Cappellini reads like a *Who's Who* of 1990s design. Marc Newson, Jasper Morrison, Piero Lissoni, Tom Dixon, Fabio Novembre, Konstantin Grcic, Werner Aisslinger, Karim Rashid, and Christophe Pillet have all had their designs produced in Cappellini's small but well-resourced factory in Arosio, north of Milan.

As well as having an exacting eye for design, and the courage to employ raw talent, Cappellini was also something of a master at generating public and media attention. Cappellini promoted his designers as personalities and produced lavish, high-concept catalogs. He also ensured that his stand at the annual *Salone del Mobile* in Milan was the most conspicuous.

Cappellini has said that the two qualities he values most in furniture designs are "purity and vitality." Because of his essentially classicist views, most Cappellini products have clean lines and rich, monochrome

surfaces. This is not to say that Cappellini was afraid of indulging the more fantastic whims of designers; he just insisted that any innovations be driven by structural logic. Eager to steer clear of what he described as the "saturated" aesthetic of Postmodernism, Cappellini gave a wide berth to anything approximating academic theory.

In 1997, the company—in its 50th year and at the height of its success—opened a chain of stores in the exclusive shopping areas of Vienna, New York, São Paulo, and Paris. Sadly, however, Giulio Cappellini was affected by the financial pressure that everyone was feeling at the end of the 1990s and, at the turn of the century, he sold a controlling stake in the company to the Poltrona Frau group.

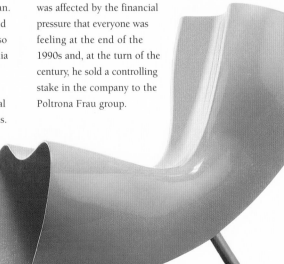

Felt Chair This armchair has a lacquer finish, making it suitable for outdoor use. The design was also produced with fabric upholstery, such as felt and leather, for indoor use. Designed for Cappellini by Marc Newson. *1994. H:34 in (86 cm); W:26½ in (67 cm).*

INSPIRED USE OF TECHNOLOGY

Despite such high-flying commissions, however, Newson continued to pursue the production of furniture. By the end of the decade, he was working with Benjamin de Haan, an architect who introduced the designer to many cutting-edge computer technologies. The recent development of Rapid Prototyping—a process whereby a computer drawing can be immediately realized in plastic without the need for making intermediate models or molds—perfectly suited Newson's impulsive approach to design.

Although Newson was using up-to-the-minute technologies, he continued to turn to the recent past for inspiration. Newson was fascinated with the forms and mechanics associated with the early developments of space travel, while he has often cited the quick-witted work of Achille Castiglioni and the domes of Buckminster Fuller as antecedents of his distinctive style. And when Newson was handed his first sizable paycheck, he bought an Aston Martin DB4, one of the most celebrated car designs of the 1950s.

The facility with which Newson ranges across vast territories of design—his sinuous style can be seen in everything from hair-dryers to entire restaurants—marks him out as one of the most distinguished talents of the 20th century, alongside Carlo Mollino, Raymond Loewy, Ettore Sottsass, and Philippe Starck.

OFFICE FURNITURE

DURING THE MID-1960S, many office environments underwent a radical change. Places that had previously resembled either vast classrooms or rabbit warrens now became intricate, open-plan spaces furnished with modular office-furniture systems.

These changes were first initiated in Germany—where the new look was described as the *Bürolandschaft* or "Office Landscape"—and in the United States, where George Nelson and Robert Propst had devised the ground-breaking Action Office scheme (1964).

The 1970s, then, were boom years for the newly revitalized office-furniture industry. Companies such as Herman Miller, Inc. in the United States and Vitra in Germany began to invest large sums of money in researching and developing office-furniture systems.

Flexibility soon became the key word in office-furniture design, as chairs were given swiveling seats and put on casters, and modular shelving systems became increasingly common. Ergonomics, too, was another much-

discussed subject as a growing percentage of the world's workforce was sitting down at desks rather than standing on the factory floor.

The arrival, in the late 1970s, of computers as a common feature of the office environment proved another spur for designers to rethink office furniture (the launch of the Apple Mac in 1984 changed the meaning of the word "desktop"). In the 1980s, personal computers allowed more people to work from home, prompting many spare bedrooms to be transformed into "home offices." This sparked a temporary move away from the technical aesthetic of office furniture.

The development of hot-desking in the 1990s further deformalized the office environment. In hot-desking offices, desks became little more than the equivalent of car parking spaces and were thus stripped of drawers and other storage spaces. By this time, too, the increased memory capacities of computers reduced the need for expansive filing systems.

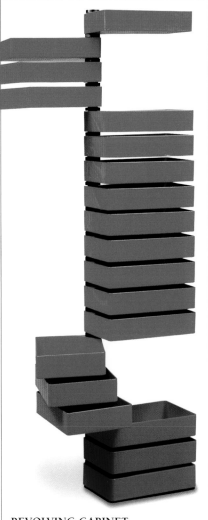

REVOLVING CABINET

Designed by Shiro Kuramata for Cappellini, this innovative filing system has 20 drawers, each of which rotates around a single vertical metal bar. *H:72¾ in (185 cm); W:14¼ in (36 cm); D:9⅞ in (25 cm). BK* **3**

STORAGE UNIT

This Postmodern storage unit was designed by Gaetano Pesce. It has an ebonized frame and two banks of 13 "mailbox" compartments with hinged fronts in polychromed wood. *1991. H:65¾ in (167 cm); W:24¼ in (61.5 cm). SDR* **1**

The tray is raised and swivels, so it is easy to reach papers inside it.

The shelving units are on casters so they can be moved around the office.

The shelving units are backed with wood, bringing a natural element into the office.

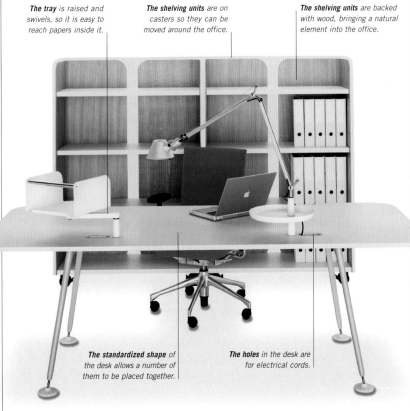

The standardized shape of the desk allows a number of them to be placed together.

The holes in the desk are for electrical cords.

VITRA ATM

Vitra's Advanced Table Module (ATM) was designed with practicality uppermost in mind. The look is simple and restrained but with carefully detailed features. The table has an eased edge for comfort, and discreet slots for

cables and accessories. It accommodates various accessories that organize the desktop, such as lamps, file trays, plates, and paper boxes, and it can fit together neatly with other tables to form multiple work stations. A mobile unit provides storage and helps to define the broader office landscape. *2003*

CORNER TABLE

This table forms part of the Sedus reception room furniture designed by the Australian architect Peter Wilson (*see also his Corner Chair, opposite*). The low table has a square, plate-glass top, and is supported on a

chromed-steel frame, which has an asymmetrical cross-shaped base and four large, black, padded feet. The angular asymmetry of the design gives the table a certain quirky personality of its own. *H:15¾ in (40 cm); W:27½ in (70 cm); D:27½ in (70 cm). SED*

ARCHIMOON CLASSIC

Philippe Starck's version of the classic desk lamp makes use of clean lines and a smooth aluminum finish. The lamp folds and pivots to direct light as needed. *H:22½ in (57 cm); D:27 in (68.5 cm).*

JOYN OFFICE SYSTEM

Designed by Ronan and Erwan Bouroullec for Vitra, this system provides a flexible series of work stations. It has a rectangular table top and a number of movable screens that can be slotted into the table to form enclosed compartments. *2002. The dimensions vary according to the model. VIT*

CORNER CHAIR

This asymmetric, upholstered chair is part of a range of reception furniture. The two-tone leather seat is supported on an asymmetrical chromed-steel frame. *H:33½ in (85 cm); W:23¾ in (60.5 cm); D:23⅔ in (60 cm). SED*

AERON OFFICE CHAIR

This swivel chair has a recycled aluminum- and fiberglass-reinforced frame with a mesh seat and back. It is raised on casters. It was designed by Donald Chadwick and William Stumpf for Herman Miller, Inc. *1992. L&T* **1**

OLIVETTI

OLIVETTI PLAYED A KEY ROLE IN THE DEVELOPMENT OF THE WHOLE OFFICE ENVIRONMENT THROUGHOUT THE 20TH CENTURY.

Olivetti's products, from Camillo Olivetti's first typewriter design in 1908 to its pioneering laptop computers of the 1980s, were always at the cutting edge of product design. And Olivetti's own offices were always at the forefront of ideas regarding office environment design.

In 1939, the designers Gino Pollini and Luigi Figini designed the company's offices and production plant in strict Rationalist style, furnishing the interiors with tubular-steel chairs. At this time, Marcello Nizzoli was the company's design director, producing a series of radically advanced typewriter designs.

In 1958, Ettore Sottsass took over Nizzoli's role and stamped his own unique spirit on Olivetti. The company's offices were soon furnished with bright, ergonomically advanced chairs, and Olivetti's product range was revamped. The portable Valentine typewriter that Sottsass designed with Perry A. King in 1969 caught the zeitgeist of an on-the-go

The Olivetti Establishment in Ivrea, Italy This large and open-plan, Rationalist-style office space was designed by Luigi Figini and Gino Pollino.

lifestyle, appearing more of a fashion accessory than a working tool.

During the 1970s and 1980s, Olivetti ensured that it kept pace with technological advances, and was one of the first manufacturers of personal computers (PCs) and fax machines.

KANT DESK

This white-laminate, birch plywood desk has a rectangular work surface that dips toward the back to create a bookshelf. This is a basic model to which a number of accessories can be added, including banks of drawers suspended from the desktop and a monitor panel. *2002. H:29¼ in (74 cm); W:63 in (160 cm); D:41⅓ in (105 cm). NHM* **2**

Olivetti furniture designed by Ettore Sottsass This office shows some of the technically innovative products that Sottsass designed, such as the ergonomic chairs and the pop-inspired Valentine typewriter. *1970–71.*

Synthesis 45 desk chair This injection-molded plastic chair, designed by Ettore Sottsass, is brightly colored and has a chunky silhouette. The chair was intended to appeal to young office workers. *1970–71.*

CHAIRS

THE 1970S WERE a decade when many designers finally relinquished their visions of a brave new world: no matter how many outlandish seating systems they devised, they realized that they could do little to alter natural human behavior.

In the face of such a sobering realization, the four-legged chair with a seat and back made a determined comeback. From the mid-1970s onward, designers worried less about challenging the archetypal form of a chair and concentrated instead on the chair's more superficial appearance. The chair became regarded as a canvas for communication. "Chairs present potent declarations about their designers," wrote the critic John Pile in 1990. "When sitting on a chair we are in touch not only with the object but also its human creator."

Plastic, a material that had opened up so many new vistas in the world of chair design, was largely rejected by

designers during the 1970s and 1980s. High oil prices had made it a more expensive material to use and designers had a greater awareness of plastic's negative ecological impact.

Wood returned as a favored material, although it was often painted or laminated, and high-grade woods were rarely used. Unusual materials, such as wicker, cork, cardboard, bamboo, and recycled frying pans (in the case of designer Tom Dixon) were also experimented with in an effort by designers not only to find more environmentally friendly alternatives to plastic but also to give their chairs greater communicative impact.

The upsurge of Postmodernism in the late 1970s and 1980s had a riotous effect on design, and chairs were covered in colored paint and patterned laminates. The 1990s, however, saw this bluster stripped away, as a more restrained style was adopted by furniture designers.

LAZY CHAIRS

Each of these lounge seats has a fabric sleeve slipped over a stainless steel frame and can be converted from an armchair into a chaise longue in one single movement. The chairs were designed for outdoor and indoor use and are still available in a range of materials, including leather, some of which are easy to remove from the frame. The chairs were designed by Patricia Urquiola for B&B Italia. *2003. Chair: H:26¾ in (68 cm); W:32¼ in (82 cm); D:42½ in (108 cm); Chaise longue: H:32¼ in (82 cm); W:32¼ in (82 cm); D:42½ in (113 cm). B&B*

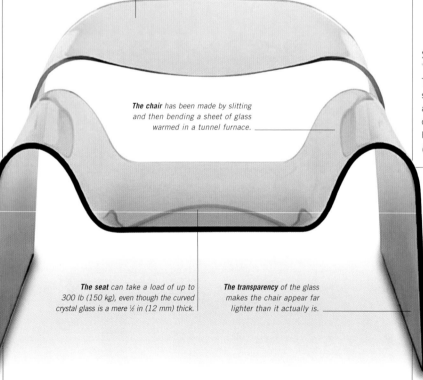

The glass has been gently twisted to create a flat back.

The chair has been made by slitting and then bending a sheet of glass warmed in a tunnel furnace.

The seat can take a load of up to 300 lb (150 kg), even though the curved crystal glass is a mere ½ in (12 mm) thick.

The transparency of the glass makes the chair appear far lighter than it actually is.

GHOST CHAIR

This chair is made from a single piece of molded glass that has been slit along its length and molded, while hot, to take its shape. The chair's form echoes the traditional British club chair (also adapted by Marcel Breuer for his Wassily chair).

While the chair's construction, combined with the transparency of the ½-in- (12-mm-) thick glass, make it look light, it can in fact take a load of up to 300 lb (150 kg). The chair was designed by Cini Boeri and Tomu Katayanagi and produced by Fiam. *1987. H:26¾ in (68 cm); W:37½ in (95 cm); D:29½ in (75 cm). BonBay* ④

SPAGHETTI CHAIR

This armchair has a tubular-steel frame supporting four tan leather slings. The four legs are straight and the back uprights and seat rail curve gently. It was designed by Giandomenico Belotti. *1979. H:28 in (71 cm); W:26¾ in (68 cm); D:23¼ in (59 cm). BonE* ①

NON 2000

This square-framed chair was molded in PUR rubber in one step. It has an inner steel frame with spring bands in the seat and can be used indoors and out. It is produced by Komplot Design. *2000. H:30⅓ in (77 cm); W:17⅓ in (44 cm); D:15⅓ in (39 cm). KAL*

FRED BAIER ARMCHAIR

This plywood and sycamore Postmodern armchair is stained red, purple, and yellow and then lacquered. It is a contemporary version of the smoker's bow, a type of Windsor chair. Four pairs exist, each in a unique colorway. Designed by Tim Wells. *1983. H:21⅔ in (55 cm). FB* ③

TOK CHAIR

The back rail and legs of this three-legged armchair are made from a single piece of bent wood. The leather seat and triangular backrest are raised on steel supports. The rear support is splayed at the bottom to form the back foot. *H:30¾ in (77 cm); W:21⅛ in (53 cm).* ②

ASTON CHAIR

This chair, designed by Linley, is a 21st-century interpretation of a gentleman's club chair, and its fluid shape is inspired by car upholstery. The chair is available in a variety of fabrics, including leather and silk, and in colors that range from white, cream, and black to bright red and electric blue. *2001.*

KARTELL ARMCHAIR

This chair has a black injection-molded frame with a curved backrest and a deep seat that slopes down toward the backrest. The seat and rounded arms of the chair are supported on L-section legs, so shaped for extra strength. It was designed by Gae Aulenti for Kartell. *BonE* **1**

FELTRI CHAIR

This armchair is made of thick wool felt and the lower section is impregnated with thermostatic resin to stiffen it. The seat back and seat cushion are quilted and sewn together with polyester padding. It was designed by Gaetano Pesce for Cassina. *1987. H:51¼ in (130 cm); W:28¾ in (73 cm); D:26 in (66 cm).*

IL CAPRICCIO DI UGO

This is a steel-framed armchair with a fabric-upholstered foam seat and armrests, raised on tubular-steel legs. The armrests fold down so that they can be used as trays. It was designed by Matali Crasset, France. *1997. H:30⅓ in (77 cm); W:24¾ in (63 cm) (closed), 43 in (109 cm) (open); D:24¾ in (63 cm). MCP*

VINE CHAIR

This chair is made from limewood, which has been carved and painted to simulate a seat and back made of vine leaves and legs resembling tree trunks. It was designed by John Makepeace. *H:33½ in (85 cm); W:19¾ in (50 cm); D:19¾ in (50 cm). JM* **6**

MAPLE DINING CHAIR

This solid maple dining chair is one of a set of 10. The chair has a cane back panel and a curved seat, which is raised on square-section legs. Designed by Studio Dillon for a private client. *2001. H:31½ in (80 cm); W:17¾ in (45 cm) D:19⅔ in (50 cm). DIL*

METAMORPHIC FURNITURE

SMALLER LIVING SPACES COMBINED WITH A FOCUS ON FUNCTION BY DESIGNERS LED TO THE DEVELOPMENT OF TRANSFORMABLE FURNITURE.

The Japanese have long been used to compact living spaces. During the 1980s and 1990s, however, compact living also became a key issue in cities across Europe and the United States as spiraling house prices forced people to inhabit ever-smaller spaces. With people considering how to make the most of such restricted room, the production of multifunctional furniture seemed like a logical idea. The 1990s saw a revival of interest in the functional aspects of furniture by designers, who found the idea of multi-purpose furniture particularly appealing. Designers of the 1990s took a more playful

approach to function than their Modern predecessors, and many worked on transformable furniture designs.

Typical of this type of design was French designer Matali Crasset's Teo (1999), a stool that could be dismantled to provide its owner with a mattress. Other notable multifunctional furniture designs of this decade included the Armchair–Table (1998) and the Wire Frame Reversible Bench (1999), both by Shin and Tomoko Azumi, who were brought up in Japan. While the former design is self-explanatory, the latter is best described as a bench that, when flipped over, becomes a chaise longue.

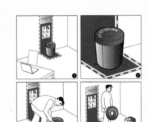

AFRICA CHAIR

One of a pair designed by Tobia and Afra Scarpa, this chair has a two-piece cherrywood back and a black leather-upholstered seat. Its simple frame has a cross-stretcher for extra stability. The chair back extends to become the back leg. It is manufactured by Maxalto. *1975.* **1**

BIBLIOTHÈQUE

This is one of a set of four limited-edition Richard Rogers and Renzo Piano bibliothèque dining chairs. It has a wire-mesh seat and adjustable back supported on four steel-rod uprights, with a tan-leather drop-in seat pad. *Late 1970s. Bonbay* **3**

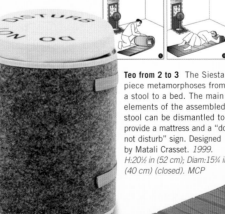

Teo from 2 to 3 The Siesta piece metamorphoses from a stool to a bed. The main elements of the assembled stool can be dismantled to provide a mattress and a "do not disturb" sign. Designed by Matali Crasset. *1999. H:20½ in (52 cm); Diam:15¾ in (40 cm) (closed). MCP*

TABLES

THE POPULARITY OF the coffee table during the 1940s, 1950s, and, to a lesser extent, the 1960s and 1970s, meant that the large, often cumbersome dining table was left somewhat by the wayside.

During the 1980s, however, the dining table enjoyed something of a revival in elite circles. This was a decade of conspicuous consumption, and an expansive, authoritative dining table served well as a status symbol. Not only did it declare that the owner had no pressing need to economize on space, it also gave the message that they were continually holding fashionable dinner parties.

Ownership of a dining table sent out much the same message in the 1990s. However, by now it was considered lacking in taste to flaunt objects of

obvious value. Dining tables, then, became simple in form and increasingly produced in understated materials, such as glass, blonde wood, and brushed metal.

The 1990s also saw an increasing trend for "loft living." The conversion of many ex-industrial buildings and warehouses into residential dwellings during this decade allowed for large, open-plan spaces in which the coffee table—usually seen squeezed between the television set and the sofa— seemed rather inappropriate. It was the rather more footloose occasional table, then, that began to enjoy a boom in popularity. Since ingenuity was a much-admired feature in furniture design during the 1990s, occasional tables often came in nesting sets of three.

PLATE-GLASS TABLE

This large, architectural-looking table has a heavily structured frame made from matt anodized aluminum. The trestle-type legs support a detachable, rectangular plate-glass top. The table's color and form give it an industrial look. It was designed by André Kiskan & Andreas Freund, Austria. *1985. H:30 in (76 cm); W:87½ in (220 cm); D:47 in (109 cm). DOR* **3**

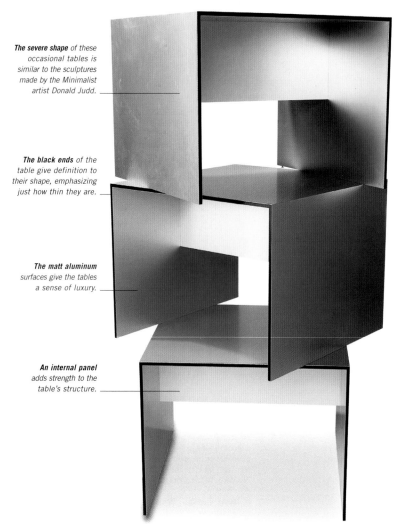

The severe shape of these occasional tables is similar to the sculptures made by the Minimalist artist Donald Judd.

The black ends of the table give definition to their shape, emphasizing just how thin they are.

The matt aluminum surfaces give the tables a sense of luxury.

An internal panel adds strength to the table's structure.

T60 TABLES

This set of three Antonio Citterio T60 tables is produced by B&B Italia. Each table is made from a single sheet of aluminum with a satin finish, which has been molded into an upside-down "U" shape. The table top is square and there is a central reinforcing element between the legs, which is also made of aluminum. Each outside edge has a ½-in- (10-mm-) thick black border that emphasizes the clean, straight lines and geometric form of the tables. *c. 1998. W:23½ in (59.5 cm). FRE* **1**

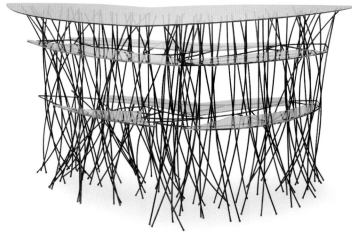

FREE-STANDING BAR

This intriguing bar has a curved plate-glass table top supported on numerous black-lacquered iron rods. Two lower levels of glass shelving have been added. These levels are each made of several pieces of glass, making it look as if they have been pierced by the iron rods. The bar was designed by B.R.A.N.D. (Boris Brochard & Rudolf Weber), Austria. B.R.A.N.D. was founded in 1983 with an initial symbolic event in which old furniture was burned in order to create space. *c. 1985. H:46 in (117 cm); W:96½ in (245 cm). DOR* **4**

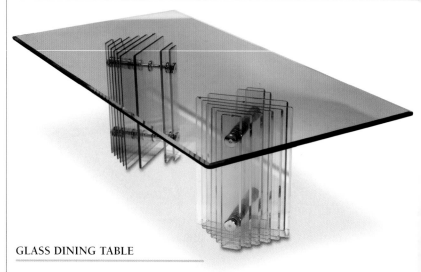

GLASS DINING TABLE

This table is almost all glass. The thick plate-glass top is supported on two large, square-section legs. Each leg is made up of nine vertical sheets of plate glass, which graduate in size, and have been joined together with steel bolts, spaced apart, to form a solid-looking leg. The table is typical of the quieter style of design at the end of the 1980s, which is sometimes referred to as "Late Modern." *W:96 in (244 cm). FRE* **2**

MY 082

This table has a white rectangular table top raised on a black injection-molded polypropylene frame with slender, tapering legs. The design is also available with a brown, green, orange, or gray frame. It was designed for Magis by the English designer Michael Young, who is known for his use of expressive colors. *2001. H:27¾ in (70.5 cm); W:58⅔ in (149 cm); D:26¾ in (68 cm). CRB*

ROOK TABLE

The rectangular top of this table is made from white-laminated beech. It is supported on a solid beech frame with rectangular-section, splayed legs. Versions of this table are also made with beech veneer or reinforced glass tops. It was designed by Konstantin Grcic for SCP. *H:29⅛ in (74 cm); W:75¼ in (190 cm); D:33½ in (85 cm). SCP*

CONSOLE TABLE

This simple, rectilinear console table has a maple table top and sides of equal depth. The sides are joined by a turned stretcher for extra stability. Below the table top are four pull-out steel units. It is produced by Zanotta of Italy, which is a recognized leader in Italian industrial design and produces designs by internationally famous designers and architects. *W:46¼ in (117.5 cm). FRE* 1

LENS TABLES

The tops and sides of these tables are made from sheets of crystal glass with a special film inserted between them, to give a semi-transparent, almost kaleidoscope effect. These cubes are made on a simple steel frame and can be used on their own or placed one over the other. Designed by Patricia Urquiola, the tables are manufactured by B&B Italia. *H:16⅛ in (43 cm); W:16⅞ in (43 cm); D:16⅞ in (43 cm). B&B*

TABLE TABLE

This contemporary center table by Clementine Hope has an 18th-century-style table printed on a square-section, medium-density fiberboard (MDF) frame. The witty take on the French *bureau plat* that is printed on the table includes typical 18th-century features, such as cabriole legs, ormolu mounts, Rococo escutcheons, and a leather-inset top. *H:30 in (76 cm); W:63 in (160 cm). L&T* 1

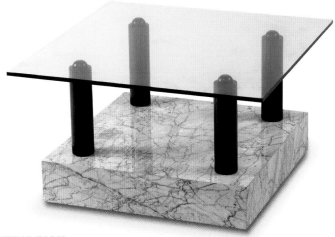

CENTRAL PARK

This table has a square glass top supported on four plastic-coated steel columns. The base of the table is made from a deep square of figured white marble, which forms a stark contrast with the black plastic above it. The table was designed by Ettore Sottsass, the leading member of the Memphis group. The group's main aim was to revive Radical design and break down the barriers between high and low design. The table was manufactured by Knoll International. *1982. BonE* 1

ANATOMY OF FURNITURE

Furniture is constantly evolving, and has been since the ancient civilizations of Egypt, Greece, and Rome. As time has gone by, advances in technology, the discovery of new materials, and the changing fashions of each era have done much to influence the construction, shape, and ornament of the prevailing furniture forms that we are familiar with today. From the mortise-and-tenon joints of the Middle Ages to complex welds of the Industrial Age, and from traditional horsehair stuffing to electrostatic flock upholstery, there have been countless changes in the way furniture is made.

This book has demonstrated, chapter by chapter, how the three basic forms—chairs, tables, and case pieces—have developed since 1600 to the present day: how pieces have become generally lighter and smaller in shape; how hand-crafted pieces differ from their machine-made counterparts; and how social and political events have influenced the various styles. The sheer diversity of design over the last 400 hundred years may lead to confusion when it comes to terminology. However, despite the many guises of the three basic forms, they all share common structural characteristics, many of which are outlined here.

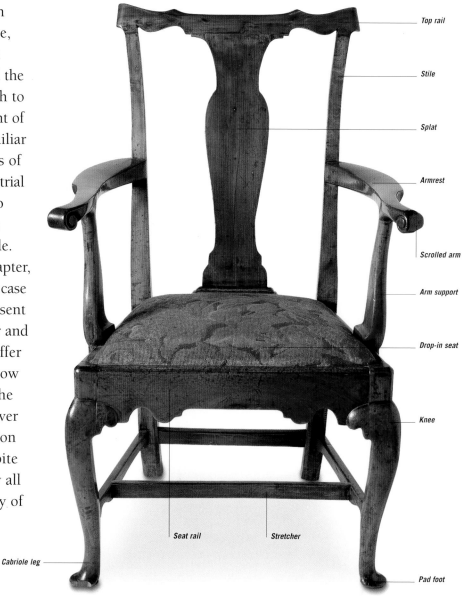

Top rail

Stile

Splat

Armrest

Scrolled arm

Arm support

Drop-in seat

Knee

Seat rail   Stretcher

Cabriole leg

Pad foot

Open armchair
This George II open armchair is made from solid walnut—the wood of choice in England for the first quarter of the 18th century. Typical features of the period are the use of solid wood, the wide, drop-in seat, and stiles that are a continuation of the back legs. The shaped top rail and solid, vase-shaped splat were also fairly common features at the time. *BonR*

Frieze

Drawer

Cock-beading

Stile

Serpentine front

Ring handle

Apron

Splayed bracket foot

Bow-front chest of drawers
Chests of drawers were in common usage from the end of the 17th century, usually for storing clothes. This George III chest of drawers is made from mahogany—the timber that superseded walnut in popularity in England from the mid-18th century. Typical features are the bow-fronted, graduated drawers, the crossbanding, and the brass ring handles. The serpentine apron and splayed feet were also common features of this period. *NA*

Drop leaf

Gateleg

Stretcher

Flattened bun foot

Frieze drawer

Baluster-turned leg

Gateleg table

The gateleg dates back to the end of the 16th century and has been made in various styles since then, but it was at its most popular in the 17th century. This example, made from yellow pine, was made in the southern colonies of America between 1690 and 1740. The defining features of a gateleg table are the drop leaves, supported on legs that swing out from the center, and the stretchers that connect the legs. *SP*

Cornice

Frieze

Drawer

Escutcheon

Crossbanding

Drop handle

Plinth

Apron

Cup-and-vase leg

Bun foot

Stretcher

Frieze

Decorative roundel

Cornice

Door panel

Drop handle

Bracket foot

Linen press

Large case pieces for the storage of household linen were popular from the 17th century onward, often with two doors, as in the French armoire or German *Schrank*. Later, they had two doors above a set of drawers, as here. This Georgian example is made from mahogany. Typical features of the period include the dentiled cornice, the paneled doors, and the square bracket feet. *L&T*

High chest of drawers

The high chest of drawers, or highboy, was popular in Britain and America during the early 18th century, and usually consisted of an upper chest of drawers supported on a lower, tablelike form with long legs. This example was made in Boston. Typical features include the tiger maple and burr maple veneer, the cup-and-vase legs, and the flat, shaped stretchers. *KEN*

USEFUL ADDRESSES

The Furniture History Society
1 Mercedes Cottages, St John's Road
Haywards Heath RH16 4EH
United Kingdom
Tel: 011 44 1444 413845
Fax: 011 44 1444 413845
Email: furniturehistorysociety
@hotmail.com

MUSEUMS AND GALLERIES

Australia
Powerhouse Museum
500 Harris Street Ultimo
PO Box: K346 Haymarket
Sydney NSW 1238
Tel: 011 61 2 92170111
www.phm.gov.au

Austria
Museen der Stadt Wien
Karlsplatz, A-1040 Vienna
Tel: 011 43 1 5058747
www.museum-vienna.at

Österreichisches Museum
für Angewandte Kunst
Stubenring 5, A-1010 Vienna
Tel: 011 43 1 711360

Belgium
Musée Horta
Amerikaans Straate/rue Américaine
23-35, 1060 Brussels
Tel: 011 32 2 5371692
www.hortamuseum.be

Denmark
The National Museum of Denmark
Frederiksholms Kanal 12
DK 1220 Copenhagen K
Tel: 011 45 3313 4411
www.natmus.dk

Egypt
Egyptian Museum
Tahrir Square, Cairo
www.egyptianmuseum.gov.eg

Finland
Alvar Aalto Museum
Alvar Aallon katu 7, Jyväskylä
Tel: 011 358 14 624809
www.alvaraalto.fi/museum

Designmuseo
Korkeavuorenkatu 23, 00130 Helsinki
Tel: 011 358 9 6220540
www.designmuseum.fi

National Museum of Finland
Mannerheimintie 34, Helsinki
Tel: 011 358 9 40509544
www.nba.fi

France
Musée des Arts Décoratifs
Palais du Louvre
107 rue de Rivoli, 75001 Paris
Tel: 011 33 1 44 55 57 50
www.paris.org

Musée de L'École de Nancy
36-38 rue de Sergent Blandan
54000 Nancy
Tel: 011 33 3 83 85 30 72
Email:menancy@mairie-nancy.fr

Musée du Louvre
Pyramide-Cour Napoléon, A.P. 34
36 quai du Louvre, 75058 Paris
Tel: 011 33 1 40 20 50 50
www.paris.org

Germany
Bauhaus
Gropiusallee 38, 06846 Dessau
Tel: 011 49 340 6508251
www.bauhaus-dessau.de

Germanisches Nationalmuseum
Kartäusergasse 1, D - 90402 Nürnberg
Tel: 011 49 911 13310
www.gnm.de

Staatliche Kunstsammlungen Dresden
Dresdner Residenzschloss
Taschenberg 2, 01067 Dresden
Tel: 011 49 3 51/49 142000
www.skd-dresden.de

Vitra Design Museum
Charles-Eames-str. 1
D-79576 Weil-am-Rhein
www.design-museum.de

Italy
Museo di Palazzo Davanzati
Via di Porta Rossa 13
50122 Florence

Netherlands
Rijksmuseum, Jan Luijkenstraat 1
Amsterdam
Tel: 011 31 20 6747000
www.rijksmuseum.nl

Norway
Kunstindustrimuseet
Besøksadresse: St. Olavs gate 1, Oslo

Tel: 011 47 22 036540
Email: info@nasjonalmuseet.no

Museet for samtidskunst
Bankplassen 4, Oslo
Tel: 011 47 22 862210
www.nasjonalmuseet.no

Spain
Casa Museu Gaudi
Parc Guell–Carretera del Carmel
08024 Barcelona
Tel: 011 34 93 2193811
www.casamuseugaudi.com

Museo Art Nouveau y Art Deco
Calle Gibralta 14, 37008 Salamanca
Tel: 011 34 92 3121425
www.museocasalis.org

Russia
State Hermitage Museum
Palace Embankment
38 Dvortsovaya Naberezhnaya
St Petersburg
Tel: 011 7 812 1109625
www.hermitagemuseum.org

South Africa
Stellenbosch Museum
Ryneveld Street, Stellenbosch, 7599
Tel: 011 27 21 8872902/8872937
Email: stelmus@mweb.co.za

Sweden
National Museum
Södra Blasieholmshamnen, Stockholm
Tel: 011 46 8 51954300
www.nationalmuseum.se

United Kingdom
American Museum
Claverton Manor, Bath BA2 7BD
Tel: 011 44 1225 460503
www.americanmuseum.org

Cheltenham Art Gallery and Museum
Clarence Street, Cheltenham GL50 3JT
Tel: 011 44 1242 237431
www.cheltenhammuseum.org.uk

Design Museum
Shad Thames, London SE1 2YD
Tel: 011 44 870 8339955
www.designmuseum.org

Geffrye Museum
Kingsland Road, London E2 8EA
Tel: 011 44 20 7739 9893
www.geffrye-museum.org.uk

Glasgow School of Art,
167 Renfrew Street, Glasgow G3 6RQ
Tel: 011 44 141 3534500

Hunterian Museum and Art Gallery
and Mackintosh House Gallery
82 Hillhead Street
University of Glasgow
Glasgow G12 8QQ
Tel: 011 44 141 3305431
www.hunterian.gla.ac.uk

Millinery Works Gallery
85-87 Southgate Road, London N1 3JS
Tel: 011 44 20 7359 2019
www.millineryworks.co.uk

Victoria and Albert Museum
Cromwell Road, London SW7 2RL
Tel: 011 44 20 7942 2000
www.vam.ac.uk

The Wallace Collection
Hertford House, Manchester Square
London W1U 3BN
Tel: 011 44 20 7563 9500
www.wallacecollection.org

William Morris Gallery
Walter House, Lloyd Park, Forest Road
London E17 4PP
Tel: 011 44 20 8527 3782
www.lbwf.gov.uk/wmg/home.htm

United States
Crabtree Farm
PO Box 218
Lake Bluff, IL 60044
Tel: (312) 391-8565

Delaware Art Museum
2301 Kentmere Parkway
Wimington, DE 19806
Tel: (303) 571-9590
www.delart.org

The DeWitt Wallace Decorative Arts
Museum
The Colonial Williamsburg
Foundation, P.O. Box 1776
Williamsburg, VA 23187
Tel: (757) 229-1000
www.colonialwilliamsburg.org

Elbert Hubbard Roycroft Museum
PO BOX 472, 363 Oakwood Avenue
East Aurora, NY 14052
Tel: (716) 652-4735
www.roycrofter.com/museum.htm

John Paul Getty Museum
Getty Center
Los Angeles, CA 90049-1687
Tel: (310) 440-7300
www.getty.edu

The Metropolitan Museum of Art
1000 Fifth Avenue
New York, NY 10028-0198
Tel: (212)535-7710
www.metmuseum.org

Museum of Fine Arts, Boston
Avenue of the Arts
465 Huntington Avenue
Boston, MA 02115-5597
Tel: (617) 267-9300
www.mfa.org

The Museum of Modern Art
11 West 53rd Street
New York, NY 10019-5497
Tel: (212) 708-9400
www.moma.org

Stickley Museum
300 Orchard Street
Fayetteville, NY 13104
Tel: (315) 682-5500
www.stickleymuseum.org

Winterthur Museum
Winterthur, DE 19735
Tel: (800) 448-3883
www.winterthur.org

The Wolfsonian Museum of Modern
Art and Design
1001 Washington Avenue
Miami Beach, FL 33139
www.wolfsonian.org

HISTORIC BUILDINGS

Austria

Schönbrunn Palace
Schönbrunner Schloßstrasse 47
Vienna
www.schoenbrunn.at

Belgium

Hôtel Solvay
224 avenue Louise
1050 Brussels

Denmark

Rosenborg Castle
Øster Voldgade 4, Copenhagen
Tel: 00 45 3315 3286
www.rosenborg-slot.dk;

France

Château de Fontainebleau
77300 Fontainebleau
Tel: 00 33 1 60 71 50 70
www.musee-chateau-fontainebleau.fr

Château de Malmaison
Avenue du château
92 500 Rueil-Malmaison
Tel: 011 33 1 41 29 05 55
www.chateau-malmaison.fr

Château de Versailles
834-78008 Versailles
www.chateauversailles.fr

Germany

Neue Rezidenz, Bamberg
Domplatz 8, 96049 Bamberg
Tel: 011 49 951 519390
www.schloesser.bayern.de

Charlottenhof
Sansoucci Park, Potsdam
Tel: 011 49 331 9694223

Schloß Charlottenburg
Spandauer Damm 20
Luisenplatz Berlin 14059
Tel: 011 49 33 19694202
www.schlosscharlottenburg.de

Schloß Nymphenburg
Eingang 19, 80638 München
Tel: 011 49 89 179080
www.schloesser.bayern.de

Italy

Pitti Palace
Piazza Pitti 1. 50125 Florence
www.polomuseale.firenze.it

Reale Palace
Piazza Castello, Turin
Tel: 011 39 11 4361455

Portugal

Palacio Nacional de Queluz
Queluz, Lisbon
Tel: 011 351 214 343860

Russia

Summer Palace
Letny Sad, 191186 St. Petersburg
www.saint-petersburg.com

Spain

Palacio Nacional Madrid
Calle Bailén, 28071 Madrid
Tel: 011 34 91 4548800
www.patrimonionacional.es

Sweden

Drottningholm Palace
178 02 Drottningholm
Tel: 011 46 8 4026280
www.royalcourt.se

Gripsholm Castle
Box 14
647 21 Marifred
Tel: 011 46 159 10194
www.royalcourt.se

Stockholm Palace
Slottsbacken
Tel: 011 46 8 4026130
www.royalcourt.se

United Kingdom

Castle Howard
York, North Yorkshire Y060 7DA
Tel: 011 44 1653 648444
www.castlehoward.co.uk

Georgian House
7 Charlotte Square
Edinburgh EH2 4DR
Tel: 011 44 131 2263318
Email: thegeorgianhouse@nts.org.uk

Harewood House
Moor House
Harewood Estate, Harewood
Leeds LS17 9LQ
Tel: 011 44 113 2181010
www.harewood.org

Hill House (The)
Upper Colquhoun Street
Helensburgh, Glasgow G84 9AJ
Tel: 011 44 1436 673900

Kedleston Hall
Derby DE22 5JH
Tel: 011 44 1332 842191
www.nationaltrust.org.uk

Knole
Sevenoaks, Kent TN15 ORP
Tel: 011 44 1732 462100
www.nationaltrust.org.uk

Lotherton Hall
Lotherton Lane, Aberford
Leeds LS25 3EB
Tel: 011 44 113 2813259
www.leedsgov.co.uk

Osborne House
Isle of Wight
Tel: 011 44 1983 200022
www.english-heritage.org.uk

The Red House
Red House Lane, Bexleyheath DA6 8JF
Tel: 011 44 1494 755588
www.nationaltrust.org.uk

The Royal Pavilion
Brighton BN1 1EE
Tel: 011 44 1273 290900
www.royalpavilion.org.co.uk

Temple Newsam House
Temple Newsam, Leeds LS15 0AD
Tel: 011 44 113 2647321
www.leedsgov.co.uk

Standen
West Hoathly Road, East Grinstead
Sussex RH19 4NE
Tel: 011 44 1342 323029
www.nationaltrust.org.uk

Syon House
Syon Park, London
Tel: 011 44 20 8560 0882
www.syonpark.co.uk

United States

Canterbury Shaker Village
Canterbury, NH 03224
www.shakers.org

Craftsman Farms
2352 Rte. 10 West, #5
Morris Plains, Parsippany, NJ 07950
Tel: (973) 540-1165
Email: craftsmanfarms@att.net

Gamble House
4 Westmoreland Place
Pasadena, CA 91103
Tel: (626) 793-3334
www.gamblehouse.org

Hancock Shaker Village
Route 20
Pittsfield, MA 01201
Tel: (413) 443-0188
www.hancockshakervillage.org

Marston House
3525 Seventh Avenue
San Diego, CA 92103
Tel: (619) 298-3142

Nathaniel Russell House
51 Meeting Street
Charleston, SC 29402
Tel: (843) 723-1159
www.historiccharleston.org

FURTHER READING

Arts Council of Great Britain (The), *The Age of Neo-Classicism*, London, 1972.

Aslin, Elizabeth, *Nineteenth Century English Furniture*, Faber & Faber, London, 1962.

Aronson, Joseph, *The Encyclopedia of Furniture*, Clarkson Potter/Publishers, New York, 1965.

Baarsen, Reinier, *Dutch Furniture, 1600-1800*, Rijksmuseum, Amsterdam, 1993.

Baarsen, Reinier, *17th-century Cabinets*, Rijksmuseum, Amsterdam, 2000.

Baarsen, Reinier, *German Furniture*, Rijksmuseum, Amsterdam, 1998.

Baker, Fiona and Keith, *20th Century Furniture*, Carlton Books, London, 2003.

Baker, Hollis S., *Furniture in the Ancient World*, The Connoisseur, London, 1966.

Beard, Geoffrey, *The Work of Robert Adam*, Bloomsbury Books, London, 1978.

Beckerdite, Luke (ed), *American Furniture 2001*, University Press of New England, Lebanon, New Hampshire, 2001.

Bowett, Adam, *English Furniture, 1660-1714, From Charles II to Queen Anne*, Antique Collector's Club, Woodbridge, 2002.

Brackett, Oliver, *English Furniture Illustrated: A Pictorial Review of English Furniture from Chaucer to Queen Victoria*, The Macmillan Company, New York, 1950.

Byne, Arthur, *Spanish Interiors and Furniture*, William Helburn, Inc., New York, 1922.

Chippendale, Thomas, *The Gentleman & Cabinet-Maker's Director*, Reprint of the Third Edition 1762, Dover Publications Inc., New York, 1966.

Clemmensen, Tove, *Danish Furniture of the Eighteenth Century*, Gyldendalske Boghandel Nordisk Forlag, Copenhagen, 1948.

Delaforce, Angela, *Art & Patronage in Eighteenth Century Portugal*, Cambridge University Press, New York, 2002.

Downs, Joseph, *American Furniture, Queen Anne and Chippendale Periods*, The Macmillian Company, New York, 1952.

Edwards, Clive, *Encyclopedia of Furniture Materials, Trades and Techniques*, Ashgate Publishing Limited, Aldershot, 2000.

Edwards, Clive D., *Eighteenth-Century Furniture*, Manchester University Press, Manchester, 1996.

Edwards, I.E.S. et al., *Tutankhamun: His Tomb and Its Treasures*, The Metropolitan Museum of Art and Alfred A. Knopf, Inc., New York, 1976.

Eidelberg, Martin (ed), *Design, 1935-1965: What Modern Was*, Harry N. Abrams Inc., New York, 2001.

Escritt, Stephen, *Art Nouveau*, Phaidon Press Limited, London, 2002.

Fisher, Volker (ed), *Design Now: Industry or Art*, Prestel Verlag, Munich, 1989.

Fairbanks, Jonathan L. and Trent, Robert F., *New England Begins: The Seventeenth Century*, Museum of Fine Arts, Boston, 1982.

Fales, Jr., Dean A., *American Painted Furniture 1660-1880*, E.P. Dutton and Company, Inc., New York, 1972.

Fastnedge, Ralph, *Shearer Furniture Designs from the Cabinet-Makers' London Book of Prices 1788*, Alec Tiranti, London, 1962.

Fiell, Charlotte and Peter, *1,000 Chairs*, Benedikt Taschen Verlag, Cologne, 2000.

Fiell, Charlotte and Peter, *Scandinavian Design*, Benedikt Taschen Verlag, Cologne, 2002.

Fischer, Felice and Hiesinger, Kathryn B., *Japanese Design: A Survey Since 1950*, Philadelphia Museum of Art in association with Harry N. Abrams Inc., New York, 1995.

Forman, Benno M., *American Seating Furniture, 1630-1730*, W.W. Norton & Company, New York, 1988.

Galissa, Rafael Doménech and Luis Pérez Bueno, *Antique Spanish Furniture, Meubles Antiguos Españoles*, The Archive Press, New York, 1965.

Garnett, Oliver, *Living in Style: A Guide to Historic Decoration & Ornament*, National Trust Enterprises Ltd, London, 2002.

Gilbert, Christopher, *The Life and Works of Thomas Chippendale*, Studio Vista/Christie's, London, 1978.

Greene Bowman, Leslie, *American Arts and Crafts: Virtue in Design*, Los Angeles County Museum of Art with Bulfinch, Little, Brown & Co., Boston, 1990.

Greenhalgh, Paul (ed), *Art Nouveau 1890-1914*, V&A Publications, London, 2000.

Gusler, Wallace B., *Furniture of Williamsburg and Eastern Virginia, 1710-1790*, Virginia Museum, Richmond, Virginia, 1979.

Gruber, Alain (ed), *The History of Decorative Arts, The Renaissance and Mannerism in Europe*, Abbeville Press, Publishers, London, 1994.

Harris, Eileen, *The Furniture of Robert Adam*, Academy Editions, London, 1973.

Hayward, Helena, *World Furniture: An Illustrated History*, Hamlyn Publishing Group Limited, London, 1982.

Heckscher, Morrison H. and Greene Bowman, Leslie, *American Rococo, 1750-1775: Elegance in Ornament*, Harry N. Abrams Inc., New York, 1992.

Hepplewhite, George, *The Cabinet-Maker and Upholsterer's Guide, The Third Edition of 1794*, Reprint, Dover Publications Inc., New York, 1969.

Hiesinger, Kathryn B., *Design since 1945*, Philadelphia Museum of Art, Philadelphia, 1983.

Honour, Hugh, *Cabinet Makers and Furniture Designers*, Hamlyn Publishing Group Limited, London, 1972.

Hornor, William MacPherson, Jr., *Philadelphia Furniture*, Philadelphia, 1935.

Hunter, George Leland, *Italian Furniture and Interiors*, William Helburn Inc., New York.

Hurst, Ronald L. and Prown, Jonathan, *Southern Furniture 1680-1830: The Colonial Williamsburg Collection*, The Colonial Williamsburg Foundation in association with Harry N. Abrams Inc., New York, 1997.

Huth, Hans, *Roentgen Furniture, Abraham and David Roentgen: European Cabinet-makers*, Sotheby Parke Bernet, London and New York, 1974.

Ince, William and Mayhew, John, *The Universal System of Household Furniture, Le Système Universel de Garniture de Maison, 1759-1762*, in parts, Reprint, Quadrangle Books, Chicago, 1960.

Jaffer, Amin, *Furniture from British India and Ceylon*, V&A Publications, London, 2001.

Jobe, Brock, et al., *Portsmouth Furniture, Masterworks from the New Hampshire Seacoast*, University Press of New England, Lebanon, New Hampshire, 1993.

Jobe, Brock and Myrna Kaye, *New England Furniture, The Colonial Era*, Houghton Mifflin Company, Boston, 1984.

Ketchum, Jr, William C., *The Antique Hunter's Guide: American Furniture Chests, Cupboards, Desks & Other Pieces*, revised by Elizabeth von Habsburg, Black Dog & Leventhal Publishers, New York, 2000.

Klein, Dan, McClelland, Nancy A., and Haslam, Malcolm, *In the Deco Style*, Thames and Hudson, London, 2003.

Kirk, John T., *American Furniture: Understanding Styles, Construction and Quality*, Harry N. Abrams Inc., New York, 2000.

Lessard, Michael, *Antique Furniture of Québec, Four Centuries of Furniture Making*, trans. Jane Macaulay and Alison McGain, McClelland & Stewart, Ltd, The Canadian Publishers, Québec, 2002.

Levenson, Jay A. (ed), *The Age of the Baroque in Portugal*, National Gallery of Art, Yale University Press, Washington, New Haven and London, 1993.

Massey, Anne, *Interior Design of the 20th Century*, Thames and Hudson, London, 2001.

Miller, Judith, *The Illustrated Dictionary of Antiques and Collectibles*, Marshall Publishing Ltd, London, 2001.

Muir Whitehill, Walter (ed), *Boston Furniture of the Eighteenth Century*, University Press of Virginia, Charlottesville, 1986.

Neuhart, John and Marilyn, *Eames Design*, Harry N. Abrams Inc., New York, 1989.

Neumann, Claudie, *Design Directory: Italy*, Universe Publishing, New York, 1999.

Oates, Phyllis Bennett, *The Story of Western Furniture*, The Herbert Press Limited, London, 1981.

O'Brien, Patrick K. (ed), *Atlas of World History, from the Origins of Humanity to the Year 2000*, George Philip Ltd, London 1999.

Ostergard, Derek E., *Bent Wood and Metal Furniture: 1850-1946*, University of Washington Press, Seattle, Washington, 1987.

Payne, Christopher (ed), *Sotheby's Concise Encyclopedia of Furniture*, Conran Octopus, London, 1989.

Polano, Sergio, *Achille Castiglioni: Complete Works*, Phaidon Press, London, 2002.

Pradère, Alexandre, *French Furniture Makers, The Art of the ébéniste from Louis XIV to the Revolution*, Sotheby's Publications, Philip Wilson Publishers Ltd, London, 1989.

Puig, Francis J. and Conforti Michael (ed), *The American Craftsman and the European Tradition 1620-1820*, University Press of New England, Lebanon, New Hampshire, 1989.

Radice, Barbara, *Memphis: Research, Experiences, Failures and Successes of New Design*, Thames and Hudson, London, 1995.

Rayner, Geoffrey et al., *Austerity to Affluence: British Art and Design 1945-1962*, Merrell Holberton Publishers in association with The Fine Art Society, London, 1997

Riccardi-Cubitt, Monique, *The Art of the Cabinet*, Thames and Hudson, London, 1992.

Sack, Albert, *The New Fine Points of Early American Furniture*, Crown Publishers Inc., New York, 1993.

Sassone, Adriana Boidi et al., *Furniture from Rococo to Art Deco*, Evergreen (imprint of Benedikt Taschen Verlag), Cologne, 2000.

Schmitz, Dr. Herman, *The Encyclopaedia of Furniture*, Ernest Benn Limited, London, 1926.

Schwartz, Marvin D., *The Antique Hunter's Guide: American Furniture Tables, Chairs, Sofas & Beds*, revised by Elizabeth von Habsburg, Black Dog & Leventhal Publishers, New York, 2000.

Sembach, Klaus-Jurgen et al, *Twentieth-Century Furniture Design*, Taschen, Cologne, 1991.

Sheraton, Thomas, *The Cabinet-Maker and Upholsterer's Drawing-Book*, 1793 Reprint, Dover Publications Inc., New York, 1972.

Sheraton, Thomas, *Cabinet Dictionary*, Reprint, Praeger Publishers, New York, 1970.

Symonds, R.W., *Furniture Making in Seventeenth and Eighteenth Century England: An Outline for Collectors*, The Connoisseur, London, 1955.

Symonds, R.W., *Veneered Walnut Furniture, 1660-1760*, Alec Tiranti Ltd., London, 1952.

Symonds, R.W. and Whineray, B.B., *Victorian Furniture*, Country Life Ltd., London, 1965.

Van der Kemp, Gerald, Hoog, Simone, Meyer, Daniel, *Versailles, The Chateau, The Gardens, and Trianon*, Editions d'Art Lys, Vilo Inc., New York, 1984.

Van Onselen, Lennox, E., *Cape Antique Furniture*, Howard Timmins, Cape Town, South Africa, 1959.

Verlet, Pierre, *French Furniture and Interior Decoration of the 18th Century*, Barrie and Rockliff, London, 1967.

Ward-Jackson, *English Furniture Designs of the Eighteenth Century*, Victoria and Albert Museum, London, 1984.

Watson, Sir Francis, *The History of Furniture*, William Morrow & Company Inc., New York, 1976.

Whitechapel Art Gallery, *Modern Chairs: 1918-1970*, London, 1970.

Whitehead, John, *The French Interior in the Eighteenth Century*, Dutton Studio Books, New York, 1993.

Wilk, Christopher (ed), *Western Furniture 1350 to the Present Day*, Philip Wilson Publishers in association with The Victoria and Albert Museum, London, 1996.

Wright, Louis B. et al., *The Arts in America: The Colonial Period*, Charles Scribner's Sons, New York, 1966.

DEALER CODES

Some of the pieces of furniture shown in this book are followed by a letter code. These codes identify the dealers or auction houses that are either selling or have sold the piece, or the museum that houses the piece. Inclusion in this book does not constitute or imply a contract or a binding offer on the part of any contributing dealer or auction house to supply or sell the pieces illustrated, or similar items, at the price stated.

2RA
2R Antiquités
Cité des Antiquaires
117, boulevard Stalingrad
69100 Lyon-Villeurbane, France
Tel: 011 33 4 78 93 11 08
E-mail: finzi.laurence@wanadoo.fr

ADE
Art Deco Etc
73 Upper Gloucester Road
Brighton BN1 3LQ, UK
Tel: 011 44 1273 329268
E-mail: johnclark@artdecoetc.co.uk

AME
American Museum
Claverton Manor, Claverton
Bath BA2 7BD, UK
Tel: 011 44 1225 460503
www.americanmuseum.org

AMH
Auktionsgalerie am Hofgarten
Jean-Paul-Str. 18
95444 Bayreuth, Germany
Tel: 011 49 92167447
Fax: 011 49 92158330

ANB
Antiquités Bonneton
Cité des Antiquaires
117, boulevard Stalingrad
69100 Lyon-Villeurbanne, France
Tel: 011 33 4 78 94 23 36
E-mail: bonneton@wanadoo.fr
www.antiquités-bonneton.com

AR
Anne Rogers Private Collection

B&B
B&B Italia
Strada Provinciale 32, no. 15
22060 Novedrate, Italy
Tel: 011 39 31 795343
Fax: 011 39 31 795224
E-mail: beb@bebitalia.it
www.bebitalia.it

B&I
Burden & Izett
180 Duane Street
New York, NY 10013
Tel: (212) 941-8247
Fax: (212) 431-5018
www.burdenandizett.net

BAM
Bamfords Ltd
The Old Picture Palace
133 Dale Road, Matlock
Derbyshire DE4 3LT, UK
Tel: 011 44 1629 574460
www.bamfords-auctions.com

BAR
Dreweatt Neate, Bristol
(formerly Bristol Auction Rooms)
St John's Place, Apsley Road
Clifton, Bristol BS8 2ST
Tel: 011 44 117 9737201
Fax: 011 44 117 9735671
www.dnfa.com/bristol

BDL
Bernard and S Dean Levy
24 East 84th Street
New York, NY 10028
Tel: (212) 628-7088

BEA
Beaussant Lefèvre
32, rue Drouot, 75009 Paris, France
Tel: 011 33 1 47 70 40 00
Fax: 011 33 1 47 70 62 40
www.beaussant-lefevre.auction.fr

BK
Bukowskis
Arsenalsgatan 4, Box 1754
111 87 Stockholm, Sweden

BL
Blanchard
86/88 Pimlico Road
London SW1W 8PL, UK
Tel: 011 44 20 7823 6310
Fax: 011 44 20 7823 6303

BMN
Auktionshaus Bergmann
Möhrendorfestraße 4
91056 Erlangen, Germany
Tel: 011 49 9131 450666
Fax: 011 49 9131 450204
www.auction-bergmann.de

BonBay
Bonhams, Bayswater
10 Salem Road
London W2 4DL, UK
Tel: 011 44 20 7313 2727
Fax: 011 44 20 7313 2703
www.bonhams.com

BonE
Bonhams, Edinburgh
65 George Street
Edinburgh EH2 2JL, UK
Tel: 011 44 131 225 2266
Fax: 011 44 131 220 2547
www.bonhams.com

BONS
Bonhams, Bond Street
101 New Bond Street
London W1S 1SR, UK
Tel: 011 44 20 7629 6602
Fax: 011 44 20 7629 8876
www.bonhams.com

BOY
Boym Partners Inc
131 Varick Street 915
New York, NY 10013
Tel: (212) 807-8210
www.boym.com

BRU
Brunk Auctions
Post Office Box 2135
Ashville, NC 28802
Tel: (828) 254-6846
Fax: (828) 254-6545
www.brunkauctions.com

BW
Biddle & Webb of Birmingham
Icknield Square,
Ladywood, Middleway
Birmingham B16 0PP, UK
Tel: 011 44 121 4558042
Fax: 011 44 121 4549615
www.biddleandwebb.co.uk

CA
Chiswick Auctions
1-5 Colville Road,
London W3 8BL, UK
Tel: 011 44 20 8992 4442
Fax: 011 44 20 8896 0541
www.chiswickauctions.co.uk

CAL
Calderwood Gallery
1622 Spruce Street
Philadelphia, PA
Tel: (215) 546-5357
Fax: (215) 546-5234
www.calderwoodgallery.com

CAS
Cassina SPA
Via Busnelli 1, Meda,
MI 20036, Italy
www.cassina.it

Cato
Lennox Cato
1 The Square, Church Street
Edenbridge, Kent TN8 5BD, UK
Tel: 011 44 1732 865988
E-mail:cato@lennoxcato.com
www.lennoxcato.com

CCA
Christopher Clarke
The Fosseway, Stow on the Wold
Gloucestershire, GL54 1JS, UK
Tel: 011 44 1451 830476
www.antiques-in-england.com

CdK
Caroline de Kerangal
Tel: 011 44 20 8394 1619 (UK)
E-mail:kerangal@aol.com

CRB
Magis Spa, Via Magnadola 15,
31045 Motta di Livenza, Italy
Tel: 011 39 0422 862650
Fax: 011 39 0422 862653
www.magisdesign.com

CSB
Chenu Scrive Berard
Hôtel des Ventes Lyon Presqu'île
Groupe Ivoire, 6, rue Marcel Rivière
69002 Lyon, France
Tel: 011 33 4 72 77 78 01
Fax: 011 33 4 72 56 30 07
www.chenu-scrive.com

DC
Delage-Creuzet
La Cité des Antiquaires
117, boulevard de Stalingrad
69100 Lyon-Villeurbanne, France
Tel: 011 33 4 78 89 70 21

DIL
Studio Dillon
28 Canning Cross
London SE5 8BH, UK
Tel: 011 44 20 7274 3430
E-mail: studiodillon@btinternet.com

DL
David Love
10 Royal Parade
Harrogate HG1 2SZ, UK
Tel: 011 44 1423 565797
Fax: 011 44 1423 525567

DN
Dreweatt Neate
Donnington Priory Salerooms
Donnington, Newbury
Berkshire RG14 2JE, UK
Tel: 011 44 1635 553553
Fax: 011 44 1635 553599
E-mail: donnington@dnfa.com
www.dnfa.com/donnington

DOR
Palais Dorotheum
Dorotheergasse 17
A-1010 Vienna,
Austria
E-mail: kundendienst@dorotheum.at
www.dorotheum.com

DP
David Pickup
115 High St, Burford
Oxfordshire, OX18 4RG, UK
Tel: 011 44 1993 822555

DRA
David Rago Auctions
333 North Main Street
Lambertville, NJ 08530
Tel: (609) 397-9374
Fax: (609) 397-9377
E-mail: info@ragoarts.com
www.ragoarts.com

DRO
Droog Design
Staalstraat 7a-7b
1011 JJ Amsterdam
Netherlands
Tel: 011 31 20 5235050
press@droogdesign.nl
www.droogdesign.nl

EDP
Etude de Provence
Hôtel des Ventes du Palais
25-27, rue Breteuil
13006, Marseille, France
Tel: 011 33 4 96 110 110
Fax: 011 33 4 96 110 111
www.etudedeprovence.com

EGU
Jaime Equigren
Posadas 1487 - (1011),
Buenos Aires, Argentina
Tel: 011 54 1 148162787

EIL
Eileen Lane Antiques
150 Thompson Street
New York, NY 10012
Tel: (212) 475-2988
Fax: (212) 673-8669
www.EileenLaneAntiques.com

EP
Elaine Phillips Antiques
1 & 2 Royal Parade
Harrogate, North Yorkshire, UK
Tel: 011 44 1423 569745

EVE
Evergreen Antiques
1249 Third Avenue
New York, NY 10021
Tel: (212) 744-5664
Fax: (212) 744-5666
www.evergreenantiques.com

FB
Fred Baier
5A High Street, Pewsey
Wiltshire SN9 5AE, UK
Tel: 011 44 1672 564892
www.fredbaier.com

FRE
Freeman's
1808 Chestnut Street
Philadelphia, PA 19103
Tel: (215) 563-9275
Fax: (215) 563-8236
www.freemansauction.com

GAL
Gallery 532
142 Duane Street
New York, NY 10013, USA
Tel: (212) 964 1282
Fax: (212) 571 4691
www.gallery532.com

GDG
Geoffrey Diner Gallery
1730 21st Street NW
Washington, DC 20009
Tel: (202) 483-5005
www.dinergallery.com

GK
Gallerie Koller
Hardturmstrasse 102,
Postfach, 8031 Zürich, Switzerland
Tel: 011 41 1 4456363
Fax: 011 41 1 2731966
E-mail: office@galeriekoller.ch
www.galeriekoller.ch

GorB
Gorringes, Bexhill

Terminus Road, Bexhill-on-Sea
East Sussex TN39 3LR, UK
Tel: 011 44 1424 212994
Fax: 011 44 1424 224035
bexhill@gorringes.co.uk
www.gorringes.co.uk

GorL
Gorringes, Lewes
15 North Street, Lewes
East Sussex BN7 2PD, UK
Tel: 011 44 1273 472503
Fax: 011 44 1273 479559
www.gorringes.co.uk

GYG
Gallery Yves Gastou
12 rue Bonaparte
75006 Paris, France
Tel: 011 33 1 53 73 00 10
Fax: 011 33 1 53 73 00 12

HAD
Henry Adams
Baffins Hall, Baffins Lane, Chichester
West Sussex PO19 1UA, UK
Tel: 011 44 1243 532223
Fax: 011 44 1243 532299
E-mail: enquiries@henryadams.co.uk
www.henryadamsfineart.co.uk

HamG
Dreweatte Neate
(Formerly Hamptons)
Baverstock House,
93 High Street, Godalming,
Surrey GU7 1AL, UK
Tel: 011 44 1483 423567
Fax: 011 44 1483 426392
E-mail: godalming@dnfa.com
www.dnfa.com/godalming

HERR
Herr Auctions
WG Herr Art & Auction House
Friesenwall 35
50672 Cologne, Germany
Tel: 011 49 221 254548
Fax: 011 49 221 2706742
www.herr-auktionen.de

HL
Harris Lindsay
67 Jermyn Street
London SW1Y 6NY, UK
Tel: 011 44 20 7839 5767
Fax: 011 44 20 7839 5768
www.harrislindsay.com

HS
Hansen Sørensen
Vesterled 19
DK-6950 Ringkøbing, Denmark

Tel: 011 45 97 324508
Fax: 011 45 97 324502
www.hansensorensen.com

ISO
Isokon Plus
Turnham Green Terrace Mews
London W4 1QU, UK
E-mail: info@isokonplus.com
www.isokonplus.com

JAZ
Jazzy
34 Church Street
London NW8 8EP, UK
Tel: 011 44 20 7724 0837
Fax: 011 44 20 7724 0837
www.jazzyartdeco.com

JK
John King
74 Pimlico Road
London SW1W 8LS, UK
Tel: 011 44 20 7730 0427
Fax: 011 44 20 7730 2515

JM
John Makepeace
Designers and furniture makers
Farrs, Beaminster DT8 3NB, UK
Tel: 011 44 1308 862204
Fax: 011 44 1308 863806
www.johnmakepeace.com

JR
Madame Jacqueline Robert
Cité des Antiquaires
117, boulevard Stalingrad
69100 Lyon-Villeurbane, France
Tel: 011 33 4 78 94 92 45

KAL
Källemo AB
Box 605 SE-331 26 Värnamo, Sweden
Tel: 011 46 370 15000
Fax: 011 46 370 15060
www.kallemo.se

KAU
Auktionshaus Kaupp
Schloss Sulzburg, Hauptstrasse 62
79295 Sulzburg, Germany
Tel: 011 49 7634 50380
Fax: 011 49 7634 503850
E-mail: auktionen@kaupp.de
www.kaupp.de

KEN
Leigh Keno American Antiques
127 East 69th Street
New York, NY 10021
Tel: (212) 734-2381
Fax: (212) 734-0707

KNO
Knoll Inc
76 Ninth Avenue, 11th Floor
New York, NY 10011
Tel: (212) 343-4128
www.knoll.com

LM
Lili Marleen
52 White Street
New York, NY 10013
Tel: (212) 219-0006
Fax: (212) 219-1246
www.lilimarleen.net

LOS
Lost City Arts
18 Cooper Square
New York, NY 10003
Tel: (212) 375-0500
Fax: (212) 375-9342
www.lostcityarts.com

LOT
Lotherton Hall
Lotherton Hall, Lotherton Lane
Aberford, Leeds LS25 3EB, UK
Tel: 011 44 113 2813259
www.leeds.gov.uk/lothertonhall

LPZ
Lempertz
Neumarkt 3
50667 Cologne, Germany
Tel: 011 49 221 9257290
Fax: 011 49 221 9257296
E-mail: info@lempertz.com
www.lempertz.com

LR
Ligne Roset
B.P. 9, 01470 Brioird, France
www.ligne-roset.com

MACK
Macklowe Gallery
667 Madison Avenue
New York, NY 10021
Tel: (212) 644-6400
Fax: (212) 755-6143
E-mail: email@macklowegallery.com

MAL
Mallett
141 New Bond Street
London W1S 2BS, UK
Tel: 011 44 20 7499 7411
Fax: 011 44 20 7495 3179
E-mail: antiques@mallett.co.uk

MAP
Memphis srl
Via Olivetti, 9

20010 Pregnan Milanese, Milan, Italy
Tel: 011 39 02 93290663
Fax: 011 39 02 93591202
E-mail: memphis.milano@tiscalinet.it
www.memphis-milano.it

MAR
Marc Menzoyan
Cité des Antiquaires
117 boulevard Stalingrad
69100 Lyon-Villeurbane, France
Tel: 011 33 4 78 81 50 81

MCP
Matali Crasset Productions
26 rue du Buisson Saint Louis
F-75010 Paris, France
Tel: 011 33 1 42 40 99 89
Fax: 011 33 1 42 40 99 98
E-mail: matali.crasset@wanadoo.fr
www.matalicrasset.com

MJM
Marc Matz Antiques
366.5 Broadway
Cambridge, MA 02139
Tel: (617) 460-6200
www.marcmatz@aol.com

MLL
Mallams
Bocardo House, 24a St Michaels' St,
Oxford OX1 2EB, UK
Tel: 011 44 1865 241358
www.mallams.co.uk

MOD
Moderne Gallery
111 North 3rd Street
Philadelphia, PA 19106
Tel: (215) 923-8536
RAibel@aol.com
www.modernegallery.com

MOU
Mouvements Modernes
68 rue Jean Jacques Rousseau
75001 Paris, France
Tel: 011 33 1 45 08 08 82

MSM
Modernism Gallery
1622 Ponce de Leon Boulevard
Coral Gables, FL 33134
Tel: (305) 442-8743
Fax: (305) 443-3074
E-mail: artdeco@modernism.com
www.modernism.com

NA
Northeast Auctions
93 Pleasant Street
Portsmouth, NH 03801

Tel: (603) 433-8400
Fax: (603) 433-0415
www.northeastauctions.com

NAG
Nagel
Neckarstrasse 189-191
70190 Stuttgart, Germany
Tel: 011 49 711 649690
Fax: 011 49 711 64969696
E-mail: contact@auction.de
www.auction.de

NOA
Norman Adams Ltd
8-10 Hans Road
London SW3 1RX, UK
Tel: 011 44 20 7589 5266
Fax: 011 44 20 7589 1968
E-mail: antiques@normanadams.com
www.normanadams.com

OVM
Otto von Mitzlaff
Prinzessinnen-Haus
63607 Wächtersbach, Germany
Tel: 011 49 6053 3927
Fax: 011 49 6053 3364

PAR
Partridge Fine Arts Plc
144-146 New Bond Street
London W1S 2PF, UK
Tel: 011 44 20 7629 0834
Fax: 011 44 20 7495 6266
www.partridgeplc.com

PER
Perkins
195 Highland (Main Street)/
PO Box 1331
Haliburton, Ontario, K0M IS0
Tel: (705) 455-9003
Fax: (705) 455-9003
E-mail: perkins.group@sympatico.ca
www.perkinsantiques.com

PHB
Philip H. Bradley Co. Antiques
1101 East Lancaster Avenue
Downingtown, PA 19335
Tel: (610) 269-0427
Fax: (610) 269-2872
E-mail: antique2@bellatlantic.net

PIL
Salle des Ventes Pillet
1, rue de la Libération
B. P. 23, 27480 Lyons la Forêt,
France
Tel: 011 33 2 32 49 60 64
Fax: 011 33 2 32 49 14 88
www.pillet.auction.fr

POOK (P&P)
Pook and Pook
463 East Lancaster Avenue
Downingtown PA 19335
Tel: (610) 269-4040
Fax: (610) 269-9274
E-mail: info@pookandpook.com
www.pookandpook.com

PRA
Pier Rabe Antiques
141 Dorp Street, Stellenbosch 7600
South Africa
Tel: 011 27 21 8839730
Fax: 011 27 21 8839452
E-mail: jomarie@mweb.co.za

PST
Patricia Stauble Antiques
180 Main Street, PO Box 265
Wiscasset, ME 04578
Tel: (207) 882-6341

PUR
Puritan Values
The Dome, St Edmund's Road
Southwold, Suffolk IP18 6BZ, UK
Tel: 011 44 1502 722211
E-mail: sales@puritanvalues.com

PV
Patrick Valentin
Antiquités -Décoration
Cité des Antiquaires
117, boulevard Stalingrad
69100 Lyon-Villeurbanne, France
Tel: 011 33 4 78 91 75 67

QU
Quittenbaum
Hohenstaufenstraße 1
D-80801, Munich, Germany
Tel: 011 49 89 3300756
Fax: 011 49 89 33007577
E-mail: dialog@quittenbaum.de

R20
R20th Century
82 Franklin Street
New York, NY 10013
Tel: (212) 343-7979
Fax: (212) 343-0226
www.r20thcentury.com

RAC
Race Furniture Ltd
Burton Industrial Park
Burton-on-the-Water
Gloucestershire GL54 2HQ, UK
Tel: 011 44 1451 821446
Fax: 011 44 1451 821686
E-mail: enquiries@racefurniture.com
www.racefurniture.com

RGA
Richard Gardner Antiques
Swan House, Market Square,
Petworth GU28 0AH, UK
Tel: 011 44 1798 343411

ROS
Rosebery
74-76 Knight's Hill
London SE27 0JD, UK
Tel: 011 44 20 8761 2522
Fax: 011 44 20 8761 2524
www.roseberys.co.uk

RY
Robert Young Antiques
68 Battersea Bridge Road
London SW11 3AG, UK
Tel: 011 44 20 7228 7847
Fax: 011 44 20 7585 0489
www.robertyoungantiques.com

S&K
Sloans & Kenyon
4605 Bradley Boulevard
Bethesda, MD 20815
Tel: (301) 634-2330
E-mail: info@sloansandkenyon.com
www.sloansandkenyon.com

SBA
Senger Bamberg
Karolinenstr. 8 und 1
D-96049 Bamberg, Germany
Tel: 011 49 951 54030

SCP
SCP Limited
135-139 Curtain Road
London EC2A 3BX, UK
Tel: 011 44 20 7739 1869
Fax: 011 44 20 7729 4224
E-mail: info@scp.co.uk
www.scp.co.uk

SDR
Sollo:Rago Modern Auctions
333 North Main Street
Lambertville, NJ 08530
Tel: (609) 397-9374
Fax: (609) 397-9377
E-mail: info@ragoarts.com
www.ragoarts.com

SED
Sedus
Sedus Stoll Aktiengesellschaft
Brückenstraße 15
D-79761 Waldshut, Germany
Tel: 011 49 7751 84278
Fax: 011 49 7751 84285
E-mail: HorstHug@sedus.de
www.sedus.de

SG
Sidney Gecker
226 West 21st Street
New York, NY 10011
Tel: (212) 929-8789

SI
Da Silva Interiors
Stand G095, Alfies Antiques Market
13 Church Street, London NW8 BDT,
UK
Tel: 011 44 20 7723 0449
www.alfiesantiques.com

SK
Skinner
63 Park Plaza
Boston, MA 02116
357 Main Street
Bolton, MA 01740
Tel: (617) 350-5400
Fax: (617) 350-5429
www.skinnerinc.com

SLK
Schlapka
Gabelsbergerstrasse 9
80333 Munich, Germany
Tel: 011 49 89 288617
E-mail: schlapka@schlapka.de
www.schlapka.de

SOO
Sotheby's Olympia
London W14, UK

SOT
Sotheby's
1334 York Avenue
New York, NY 10021

SP
Sumpter Priddy, Inc.
601 S. Washington Street
Alexandria, VA 22314
Tel: (703) 299-0800
Fax: (703) 299-9688
stp@sumpterpriddy.com
www.sumpterpriddy.com

SS
Spencer Swaffer Antiques
30 High Street, Arundel
West Sussex BN18 9AB, UK
Tel: 011 44 1903 882132
Fax: 011 44 1903 884564
www.spencerswaffer.com

SWA
Swann Galleries
104 East 25th Street
New York, New York 10010
Tel: (212) 254-4710

Fax: (212) 979-1017
E-mail: nlowry@swanngalleries.com
www.swanngalleries.com

SWT
Swing Time
St. Apern-Strasse 66-68
50667 Cologne, Germany
Tel: 011 49 221 2573181
Fax: 011 49 221 2573184
E-mail: artdeco@swing-time.com
www.swing-time.com

TDG
The Design Gallery
5 The Green, Westerham
Kent, TN16 1AS, UK
Tel: 011 44 1959 561234
E-mail: sales@designgallery.co.uk
www.designgallery.co.uk

TDO
Tendo Mokko
1-3-10 Midaregawa
Tendo, Yamagata, Japan
Tel: 011 81 23 6533121
Fax: 011 81 23 6533454
www.tendo-mokko.co.jp

TEC
Tecta
D-37697 Lauenförde, Germany
Tel: 011 49 5273 37890
Fax: 011 49 5273 378933
www.tecta.de

TNH
Temple Newsam House
Temple Newsam House
Leeds L515 0AE, UK
Tel: 011 44 113 2647321
www.leeds.gov.uk/templenewsam

VH
Van Ham
Schönhauser Strasse 10-16
50968 Cologne, Germany
Tel: 011 49 221 9258620
Fax: 011 49 221 9258624
E-mail: info@van-ham.com
www.van-ham.com

VIA
Viaduct
1-10 Summer Street
London EC1R 5BD, UK
Tel: 011 44 20 7239 9260
www.viaduct.co.uk

VIT
Vitra Management AG
Klünenfeldstrasse 22
CH-4127 Birsfelden

Switzerland
Tel: 011 41 61 3771726
Fax: 011 41 61 3772726
www.vitra.com

VZ
Von Zezschwitz
Friedrichstrasse 1a
80801 Munich, Germany
Tel: 011 49 89 3898930
Fax: 011 49 89 38989325
E-mail: info@von-zezschwitz.de
www.von-zezschwitz.de

WAD
Waddington's
111 Bathurst Street
Toronto, Ontario M5V 2R1
Tel: (416) 504-9100
Fax: (416) 504-0033
www.waddingtons.ca

WIL
Wilfried Wegiel
Cité des Antiquaires
117, boulevard Stalingrad
69100 Lyon-Villeurbane, France
E-mail: wilfriedwegiel@aol.com

WKA
Wiener Kunst Auktionen
Palais Kinsky
Freyung 4, 1010 Vienna, Austria
Tel: 011 43 1 5324200
Fax: 011 43 1 53242009
E-mail: office@imkinsky.com
www.palais-kinsky.com

WROB
Junnaa & Thomi Wroblewski
78 Marylebone High Street
Box 39, London W1U 5AP, UK
Tel: 011 44 20 7499 7793
Fax: 011 44 20 7499 7793
E-mail: junnaa@wroblewski.eu.com

WW
Woolley and Wallis
51-61 Castle Street, Salisbury
Wiltshire SP1 3SU, UK
Tel: 011 44 1722 424500
Fax: 011 44 1722 424508

ZAN
Zanotta
Via Vittorio Veneto, 57
20054 Nova Milanese, Italy
Tel: 011 39 362 4981
Fax: 011 39 362 451038
E-mail: zanottaspa@zanotta.it
www.zanotta.it

GLOSSARY

Acanthus A Mediterranean plant, *Acanthus spinosus*, with fleshy, scalloped leaves. From antiquity, it was widely used for carved ornament, such as decorative moldings, and Corinthian and Composite capitals. In the 18th century, it was a popular motif for furniture and metalwork.

Aluminum A lightweight, silvery-white metal extracted from bauxite, used by furniture designers after World World II, and favored for its malleability and rust-resistance.

Amaranth A South American tropical hardwood used for veneering since the 18th century. It is purple in color when first cut, and ages to a rich, dark brown. It is also known as purpleheart and palisander.

Amboyna A decorative hardwood, varying in color from light reddish-brown to orange, with a mottled figure and tightly curled grain. It was often used for veneering in the late 18th and early 19th centuries.

Anthemion With origins in ancient Greece and Rome, this is a fanlike decorative motif resembling the honeysuckle leaf and flower. It was used as a repeated motif for banding on Neoclassical friezes and cornices toward the end of the 18th century.

Apron The frieze rail of a table, the base of the framework of a piece of case furniture, or a shaped, sometimes carved, piece of wood beneath the seat rail of a chair. It is also known as a skirt.

Arabesque Stylized foliage arranged in a swirling, interlaced pattern and combining flowers and tendrils with spirals and zigzags. It originated in the Middle East and was popular in Europe until the early 17th century.

Armoire A French term for a storage cupboard for clothing and household linen. It usually has two large doors and interior shelving.

Astragal A molding, semicircular in cross-section, often used as glazing bars for bookcases.

Aubusson tapestry Tapestries made in Aubusson, France, which was granted the title of royal manufactory in 1665. They were generally less expensive than tapestries produced at the Gobelins factory in Paris.

Bail handle First used from about 1690, this is a loop-shaped handle suspended from two knobs, sometimes mounted on a backplate.

Bakelite A revolutionary synthetic plastic invented by L. H. Baekeland in 1909. This robust, nonflammable, and attractive plastic became popular in the 1920s and 1930s and is associated with Art Deco.

Ball foot A round, turned foot used on oak and walnut case furniture and chairs during the late 17th and early 18th centuries.

Baluster A short post or pillar, such as a table leg, or one in a series supporting a rail and forming a balustrade. Usually bulbous in shape, the form was inspired by Classical vases and has been used since the Renaissance.

Banding A decorative strip of veneer in a contrasting wood. Generally used around the edge of drawer fronts, table tops, and panels. With crossbanding, the contrasting wood runs at right angles to the main veneer. In feather, or herringbone banding, two narrow strips of contrasting veneer run diagonally in opposite directions, thus forming a chevron pattern.

Beading A decorative Neoclassical border, often used on case furniture, which has applied or embossed beads of the same size used in a single row, or alternating with elongated beads, in which case it is known as bead and reel.

Beech A pale timber with a fine, straight grain, native to Great Britain and Europe. It is easy to carve and was popular in France in the 18th century, often carved and gilded, and in Britain during the Regency period, when it was sometimes painted to resemble more expensive woods.

Bellflower *See* Husk motif.

Bentwood A technique perfected by Michael Thonet in Austria in the mid-19th century for producing bentwood furniture. It involves bending solid or laminated wood over steam to make curved sections for table and chair frames.

Bergère A French term for an informal, deep-seated chair of generous proportions. It usually has a caned or upholstered back and sides and a squab cushion.

Birch A northern European wood with a golden color, sometimes with a hint of red. It was used in its solid form for chairs and other small pieces in Russia and Scandinavia from the late 18th century onward.

Bird's-eye maple An attractive wood from northern Europe and North America that has a characteristic light-brown figuring of tiny rings that resemble a bird's eyes. It was very popular as a veneer in the late 18th and early 19th centuries.

Blackamoor A life-sized carved figure of a black slave in brightly colored clothes. Originating in Venice, blackamoors were used as pedestal supports for *torchères* and similar pieces from the 18th century.

Boiserie A French term for wood paneling elaborately carved with foliage, then painted and gilded. It was fashionable in the wealthy residences of France in the 17th and early 18th centuries, and was often complemented with furniture of a matching design.

Bolection A molding, usually with an S-shaped cross-section, used to cover the joint between two elements whose surfaces are not level and often found as a framework around panels.

Bombé A French term used to describe a chest with swelling, convex sides. The term is usually applied to case furniture, such as commodes. The style was popular during the Régence period in early-18th-century France.

Bonheur-du-jour A French term for a small, delicate lady's writing desk that has a flat writing surface with tiered drawers and compartments at the back. It was first seen in the mid-18th century.

Boulle marquetry A technique named after André-Charles Boulle that involves the elaborate inlay of brass into tortoiseshell or ebony and vice versa. The process was applied to high-quality furniture—usually made in matching pairs—from the late 17th century onward.

Bow front The front of a piece of case furniture that curves outward.

Bracket foot A foot used on case pieces from the late 17th century onward, made of two brackets that have been mitered and joined together at right angles.

Breakfront The front of a piece of case furniture, on which a squared center section protrudes farther than the sections at either side.

Buffet A French term for a large, heavy display cupboard with open shelves, used for displaying silverware in the 16th and 17th centuries.

Bun foot A round foot, flattened at the top and bottom, that was first used on case pieces in the late 17th century and then became popular again in the early 19th century.

Bureau A French term for a fall-front or cylinder-top writing desk.

Bureau-bookcase A case piece made in two sections, with a writing desk in the lower section and a smaller, glazed or paneled section—usually with two doors—above it.

Bureau plat A French term for a flat-topped writing desk. It often has a tooled leather insert on the writing surface and a single drawer in the shallow frieze below it.

Burr wood A growth on a tree trunk, also known as burlwood, slices of which reveal elaborate figuring ideal for decorative veneering.

Cabriole leg A furniture leg with two curves forming an attenuated S-shape, like an animal leg. Popular in the early 18th century, it was often used on chairs and terminated in a claw-and-ball or stylized paw foot.

Canapé A French term for a sofa: an upholstered seat with a back and arms, for two or more people.

Cane A lightweight, durable material first imported from the Far East in the late 17th century. Taken from the rattan tree, it was woven to make seats and chair backs.

Cantilever chair A chair with no back legs, in which the weight of the seat is supported by the front legs and base of the chair alone. It was popular with Modernist designers, who made models in tubular steel.

Carcass The term used to describe the shell of a piece of case furniture before the drawers, doors, shelves, or feet have been added.

Card table A small table designed for playing cards, first seen at the end of the 17th century. The top is usually lined with baize, and it has compartments for playing pieces.

Cartouche A panel or tablet in the form of a scroll with curled edges, sometimes bearing an inscription, monogram, or coat of arms, and used as a decorative feature.

Caryatid An architectural column in the form of a full-length figure that is used as a support for furniture. It originated in ancient Greece and was used during the 16th, late 18th, and early 19th centuries.

Case furniture A general term for any storage piece, including chests, bookcases, presses, and wardrobes.

Cassone An Italian term for a low chest or coffer made in Italy in the 15th and 16th centuries.

Caster A small wheel used at the end of a leg to make it easy to move heavy pieces of furniture.

Casting The process of making a solid form from a molten liquid, such as brass or bronze.

Chaise longue A French term for an upholstered day bed that has a high support at one end. It is also known as a *récamier* or a day bed.

Chamfer A term describing a beveled corner, usually on case pieces, and also referred to as canted.

Chest-on-chest A case piece in two sections, one above the other, each of which has drawers.

Cheval glass A freestanding mirror supported on a four-legged frame. The mirror can be tilted to provide a full-length reflection.

Chevron A zigzag decorative motif, popular in Art Deco design.

Chiffonnier From the French term *chiffonière*, this is a small side cabinet with drawers. A *table en chiffonière* has longer legs and a shelf below the drawers.

Chinoiserie A decorative style, popular in the early 18th century, in which fanciful, exotic motifs derived from Chinese originals were applied to European furniture.

Chrome A silvery metal usually plated on a base metal such as steel. Introduced commercially in the 1920s, it was used by designers for tubular-steel furniture because of its good rust-resistance and high sheen.

Claw-and-ball foot A termination for furniture legs that was popular in the early 18th century. It was said to be based on Chinese examples of a dragon claw clasping a pearl.

Cloven hoof See Hoof foot.

Coffer A low trunk, usually made of wood and known as far back as ancient times. It was popular until the 18th century, when it was superseded by the chest of drawers.

Coiffeuse A French term for a dressing table.

Columnar Having the shape of, constructed with, or having columns.

Commode A French term for a chest with deep drawers. The form was first seen in the late 17th century.

Console table A table that has two legs supporting its front, while its back is fixed to a wall.

Corbel A wooden bracket attached to an upright and used to support a horizontal feature, such as an arm on a chair, from below.

Cornice A decorative, molded projection that crowns a piece of furniture, particularly tall cupboards or display cabinets.

Crest rail See Top rail.

Crossbanding See Banding.

C-scroll A decorative, carved or applied Classical ornament in the shape of a C, developed during the Rococo period. (*See also* S-Scroll.)

Damask A rich, woven silk, linen, or cotton fabric with a satin weave, imported to Europe from Syria from the 15th century and used for furnishings from the 16th century.

Davenport A small desk with a sloping writing surface that usually has a bank of drawers in one side.

Day bed See Chaise longue.

Demi-lune A French term for a half-moon shape.

Dentil pattern An ornamental feature of Classical architecture, dentils are small rectangular blocks, resembling teeth, that run beneath a cornice.

Dovetail A joint, used from the end of the 17th century, in which two pieces of wood are joined together at right angles. Each piece of wood has a row of fan-shaped teeth, which interlock at the joint.

Dowel A small, headless wooden pin used in furniture construction to join two pieces of wood. Each piece of wood to be joined has a round hole, the size of the dowel, into which the dowel is inserted and glued.

Dresser A large piece of case furniture, popular since the 17th century, that has a shelved upper section. The lower section usually has a central cupboard flanked by drawers or open shelves.

Dressing table A small table with an arrangement of drawers for holding a lady's or gentleman's personal accessories. The term has been in use since the 17th century.

Drop front See Fall front.

Drop-in seat A removable chair seat that has been made separately and then "dropped" into the seat frame.

Drum table A writing table, used in the late 18th and early 19th centuries, that has a round, drum-shaped, leather-covered top and is supported on a central column on a tripod or pedestal base.

Ébéniste The French term for a cabinet-maker, in use from the 17th century and derived from the word for ebony. *Ébénistes* specialized in veneered pieces of furniture.

Ebonized wood Wood that has been stained black in imitation of ebony. It was popular in the late 18th and late 19th centuries.

Ebony A native hardwood from the Indian subcontinent that is black and heavy with a smooth, tight grain. It was popular as a veneer in late 17th-century Europe.

Elm A European and North American hardwood, red-brown in color, used largely for country furniture. It was popular as a veneer (burr elm) in the late 18th and early 19th centuries.

Enamel A colored, opaque composition derived from glass, sometimes used as a decorative inlay on pieces of furniture.

Encoignure A French term for a small corner cupboard, which often has a graduated shelved interior and short legs. It first appeared in France in the early 18th century.

Escutcheon A protective and usually ornamental keyhole plate, which is sometimes in the shape of a shield.

Estampille A French term to describe the stamp on French furniture made by cabinet-makers, and bearing their name, initials, or monogram. The practice was compulsory under the guild system in Paris 1751–91.

Étagère The French term for a set of shelves, which was first used in the late 18th century. It is usually free-standing, with two to three shelves.

Fall front The hinged, flat front of a desk or bureau that falls forward to form a writing surface. It is also sometimes known as a drop front.

Fauteuil A French term for a large, upholstered open armchair, first used at the Court of Louis XIV, and popular in the 18th century.

Faux A French word meaning "false," used to describe a paint effect that imitates the appearance of another material, such as wood (*faux bois*) or marble (*faux marbre*).

Feather banding *See* Banding.

Festoon A Classical decorative motif in the form of a garland of fruit and flowers tied with ribbons. It was first used on furniture during the early 17th century, and then again from the late 18th century onward.

Fiberglass A strong, lightweight, and versatile material made from matted glass fibers bonded with a synthetic resin. Fiberglass was popularized for making furniture by Charles and Ray Eames in the 1950s.

Fielded panel A raised wooden panel with beveled edges that sits within a flat outer frame.

Figuring A term denoting the natural grain of any piece of cut wood.

Filigree An arrangement of twisted gold and silver wire soldered into openwork forms or two-dimensional panels and used as decoration.

Finial A decorative turned or carved ornament surmounting a prominent terminal on a chair, a bed, or a case piece, often taking the form of an urn, an acorn, or a pinecone.

Fluting Parallel lines of shallow, concave molding running from the top to the bottom of a column, the opposite of reeding. Fluting was frequently used on table legs in Neoclassical furniture.

Foliate Shaped like a leaf.

Formica A material made from laminated plastic sheets containing melamine. Durable and easy to clean, it was popular for table tops in the 1950s and 60s.

Fretwork Originally Chinese, this is carved decoration consisting of a number of intersecting, often geometric lines, with perforated spaces between them. Fretwork was often used on Chippendale furniture in the Chinoiserie or Gothic styles.

Frieze A Classical term used to describe the horizontal strip that supports a table top, or the cornice on a piece of case furniture.

Fumed A term used to describe a technique popular with designers of the Arts and Crafts Movement, in which a chemical was used to darken the natural color of a wood, usually oak, to make it look older.

Gadrooning A row of concave or convex flutes used along the edge of a surface to make it more decorative. Originally a Classical motif, it was popular throughout the 18th century and was applied to chests, highboys, chairs, and tables.

Gallery A small metal or wooden railing around the edge of a tray, table, or cabinet, which was popular from the mid-18th century onward.

Galuchat *See* Shagreen.

Gateleg table First seen in the late 16th century, this is a table with hinged leaves. When raised, the leaves are supported on pivoting legs joined together by stretchers.

Gesso A composition of gypsum (plaster of Paris) and size, and sometimes linseed oil and glue. Gesso was used as a base for elaborately carved and gilded decoration on furniture during the 17th and early 18th centuries.

Gilding A decorative finish in which gold is applied to wood, leather, silver, ceramics, or glass. The process involves laying gold leaf or powdered gold (or silver) onto a base, such as gesso. Parcel gilding is the term used when only part of the object has been gilded.

Giltwood Wood that has been gilded.

Girandole An Italian term for an ornate giltwood candleholder that was popular with 18th-century Rococo and Neoclassical designers.

Goût grec A French term describing the renewed interest in ancient Greece and Rome that resulted in the Neoclassical style of the late 18th and early 19th centuries.

Greek key A decorative band of interlocking, geometric, hook-shaped forms. Originally a Classical motif, it was used on Neoclassical furniture.

Gros point A French term for an embroidery stitch in which the sewing thread crosses two threads of the base fabric before the stitch is completed. (See also *Petit point.*)

Grotesque A type of ornament, popular during the Renaissance, in which real and mythical beasts, human figures, flowers, scrolls, and candelabra were linked together, often in vertical panels.

Guéridon A French term for a small, stand or table, first seen in the 17th century, that was usually ornately carved and embellished.

Guilloche A decorative motif that takes the form of a continuous band of strands that are twisted or braided together. First seen in Classical architecture, the motif was popular with Neoclassical designers.

Hairy paw foot Originating in ancient Greece and revived during the late 18th and early 19th centuries, this is a leg terminal shaped like a hairy animal's paw, usually a lion's paw.

Hall chair A simple, high-backed chair first seen in the 18th century, and used as a waiting chair in the hallway or corridor of a grand house.

Herringbone banding *See* Banding.

Highboy An American term for a chest-on-chest, a form made throughout the northern colonies/states from about 1710 onward. It was often made with a matching lowboy—a low dressing table or writing table in the same style.

Hoof foot First seen in ancient Egypt, this is a leg terminal shaped like the hoof of a goat or ram. It was used in Europe from the late 17th century to the end of the 18th century and is also known as a cloven hoof.

Husk motif A stylized ornament in the shape of a husk of corn, which was popular in the late 18th century, when it was used repeatedly to form festoons or swags. It is known as a bellflower in the United States.

Inlay A decorative technique in which different-colored woods or exotic materials, such as mother-of-pearl, ivory, and bone, are pieced into the solid wood surface or veneer of a piece of furniture.

Intarsia First used in the 14th century, this is an Italian term for a pictorial type of marquetry. It was often used for decorative paneling on furniture in Renaissance Italy and 16th-century Germany.

Ivory A durable, cream-colored material, usually from elephant tusks. It was used as a decorative inlay on 17th-century furniture and on some French Art Deco pieces.

Japanning A decorative technique, dating from the 17th century, in which furniture is coated with layers of colored varnish in imitation of true Chinese or Japanese lacquer.

Jardinière A French term for a large ornamental vessel, usually ceramic, for holding cut flowers or for growing plants. It was was popular in Europe from the 17th century onward.

Kas A Dutch term for a large provincial clothes cupboard that originated in the Low Countries in the 17th century and was introduced into North America by Dutch settlers in the 18th and early 19th centuries.

Kingwood A Brazilian hardwood introduced to Europe in the late 17th century and often used for marquetry and banding.

Klismos chair A chair with a broad, curved top rail and concave saber legs that originated in ancient Greece and was popular in Greek Revival furniture of around 1800.

Kneehole desk A desk with a top that is supported on two banks of drawers on either side of a kneehole, a central recess for the sitter's knees. First seen in late-17th-century France and the Low Countries, it remains a popular form to this day.

Lacca povera An Italian term, meaning "poor man's lacquer," that describes a form of decoupage, in which sheets of engravings were colored, cut, and pasted onto the prepared surface of a piece of furniture, then varnished to produce a high-gloss finish. The technique originated in Venice in the 1750s.

Lacquerwork A technique originating in the Far East, in which resin, made from the sap of the *Rhus* tree, is applied to furniture in many layers in order to produce a smooth, lustrous, hard-wearing finish.

Ladder-back chair A country chair with a back made up of a number of horizontal rails, like the rungs of a ladder, between the uprights. It usually has a rush seat and was one of the chairs made by the Shakers.

Lamination A process in which thin sheets of wood are glued together with the grain at right angles. Lamination was first used as far back as the mid-19th century by John Henry Belter in the United States, and was then used to make plywood in the 20th century.

Library table A large writing table designed to stand in the center of a library. It was popular during the late 18th and early 19th centuries.

Limed oak A process, introduced in the early 20th century, in which oak is treated with lime, producing white streaks on its surface.

Linen press A large cupboard or cabinet for storing linen.

Lion's-paw foot A leg terminal carved in the shape of a lion's paw, a popular Regency and Empire motif.

Lopers A pair of sliding runners that are pulled forward to support the lid of a fall-front desk when it is open.

Lowboy *See* Highboy.

Lyre motif A Neoclassical motif based on the ancient Greek musical instrument and used as an ornamental shape or decoration for chair backs and table supports.

Mahogany A Central and South American hardwood imported into Europe in large quantities from 1730. It is reddish-brown in color, with a tight grain.

Maple A European hardwood, pale in color, which was used in marquetry during the 17th and 18th centuries. It was sometimes stained black to resemble ebony, a much more expensive wood.

Marquetry A decorative veneer made up of shaped pieces of wood in different colors that are pieced together to form a pattern or picture. The technique was perfected by the Dutch, who produced fine examples of floral marquetry during the 16th century. In seaweed marquetry, used on chests of drawers and cabinets in the late 17th century, richly figured timbers, such as holly and boxwood, were used to create a seaweed effect. *See also* Parquetry.

Mask A decorative motif representing the head of a human, a god, an animal, bird, or monster. Originally a Classical motif, it was also used during the Renaissance and on Neoclassical furniture.

Medallion An ornamental relief set within a circular or oval frame.

Menuisier A French term for a joiner or skilled craftsman who produced small pieces made of plain wood (as compared to an *ébéniste*, who specialized in veneered pieces).

Metamorphic furniture Furniture that has been designed for more than one purpose, such as a chair that can change into a set of library steps.

Molding A strip of wood applied to the surface of a piece of furniture to add decorative detail or to conceal a joint. Mouldings were used from the 18th century onward.

Mortise and tenon An early type of joint in which one piece of wood has a projection (tenon) that fits snugly into a hole (mortise) in a second piece. The joint may also be pegged, using a dowel that passes through holes drilled in both pieces of wood, to make the joint more secure.

Mother-of-pearl A pale, shiny, iridescent material found lining some seashells, and used as a decorative inlay on furniture.

Mount A collective term for brass, ormolu, or bronze decorative details that were applied to furniture made in the late 17th and 18th centuries, particularly in France. Initially applied to provide protection from knocks, and wear and tear, mounts eventually became purely decorative.

Oak A native European and North American hardwood that produces a light, honey-colored timber. Oak has been used to make furniture since the Middle Ages, and was the favorite timber of the 19th-century Arts and Crafts furniture-makers.

Occasional table A small table that can be used for different purposes and moved from room to room.

Ogee molding A form of molding, originally used in Gothic architecture, that has a shallow, S-shaped curve in cross-section.

Ormolu An English term derived from the French term *or moulu*, meaning "ground gold," denoting a process of gilding bronze for decorative mounts.

Oyster veneer Late-17th- and early-18th-century veneer made from diagonal cross-sections of small pieces of wood arranged to produce a repeating pattern of small rings.

Pad foot A popular terminal for a cabriole leg, this is a rounded foot that rests on a circular base.

Padouk A heavy, reddish hardwood that was imported by the Dutch and Portuguese from East Asia, and was often used as a component of veneers during the 18th century.

Palladian A restrained Classical style of architecture and decorative features that was derived from the works of the Italian architect Andrea Palladio (1518–80).

Palmette A Classical decorative motif that is based on the fanlike shape of a palm leaf. It was widely used as ornament on Neoclassical furniture in the late 18th century.

Papier mâché A lightweight material made from dampened paper and paste, which can be molded into any shape. Popular in furniture-making in the 18th and 19th centuries, pieces were often gilded, painted, japanned, and then varnished for decorative effect.

Parcel gilding *See* Gilding.

Parquetry A decorative veneer made up of a mosaic of small pieces of wood in contrasting colors pieced together to form a geometric pattern. A variation of marquetry, it was used on walnut-veneered furniture in the 18th century and with consummate skill on Louis XV furniture.

Patera An oval or circular ornament on a flat surface, which is often decorated with a floral design, a rosette, or fluting. Paterae were popular with Neoclassical designers.

Patina A sheen on the surface of metal and furniture, the result of years of handling and a gradual buildup of dirt and polish.

Pedestal table A round or square table raised on a single central pillar or column, often with a tripartite base. This type of table was popular in Great Britain in the 18th century.

Pediment An architectural term for the triangular gable found above the portico of a Greek temple, a feature adopted in Europe from the 16th century onward and applied to the tops of case pieces of furniture, such as bookcases and highboys. Furniture pediments were created in a variety of different shapes.

Pegged joint A joint in which two pieces of wood are held together by pegs driven through drilled holes.

Pembroke table A small table, often with an elaborately inlaid table top, that has two frieze drawers, two drop leaves, and is usually on legs with casters. It was made in Great Britain from the mid-18th century onward.

Penwork A technique in which the entire surface of a piece of furniture is japanned black before being worked with an intricate, decorative pattern of white japanning.

Petit point A French term for an embroidery stitch in which the sewing thread crosses one thread of the base fabric before the stitch is completed. (See also *Gros point.*)

Pier A term for the area of a wall between two windows, doors, or other openings in a room.

Pier glass A tall, narrow mirror designed to hang between two windows, often above a pier table.

Pier table A small table designed to stand against a pier (*see above*). It was popular from the 17th century onward and was often paired with a pier glass of the same design.

Pietra dura An Italian term for an expensive form of inlay using semi-precious stones, such as jasper and lapis lazuli, to create decorative panels for cabinets and table tops. First evident in Italy during the Renaissance, the technique was very popular during the 17th century.

Pilaster An architectural term for a flattened column attached to the surface of a case piece of furniture as a form of decoration, rather than for support. Pilasters usually flank cupboard doors or drawers, and are often topped with capitals.

Pine An inexpensive, light-colored, straight-grained softwood, used predominantly for drawer linings and the backboards of furniture.

Plastic A synthetic material, first popularized in the 1920s, that can be molded into shape while soft, then set into a rigid form.

Plywood A composite wood made of several layers of laminated wood laid at right angles to each other. The flexibility of thin plywood was useful in forming curved pieces of furniture in the 1920s and 1930s.

Polyurethane foam A synthetic substance used to fill seat cushions and backs, introduced in the 1960s.

Porcelain A mixture of china clay and china stone that becomes hard, translucent, and white when fired.

Pressed glass Glass that has been shaped by being pressed in a mold. The technique was developed in the United States in the 1820s.

Pressed steel Steel that has been shaped by being pressed in a mold, a technique that was developed in the mid-20th century.

Putto An Italian term for "cherub" or "boy," which denotes a motif widely used during the Renaissance and, in particular, during the 17th century.

Quatrefoil A Gothic decorative motif, often used in tracery, of four asymmetrical leaves resembling a four-leafed clover. Similar motifs with three leaves (trefoil) and five leaves (cinquefoil) are also common.

Rail A horizontal strip of wood on a furniture frame, such as those joining the legs of a table or chair, or the piece of wood joining the uprights of a chair back.

Récamier See Chaise longue.

Reeding Parallel convex molding running from the top to the bottom of a column, the opposite of fluting. Reeding was used from the late 18th century onward as decoration on table and chair legs.

Relief Carved, molded, or stamped decorative features that rise above the surface of a piece of furniture. Prominent patterns are known as high relief and less prominent patterns as low relief.

Reverse-painted An image that has been painted in reverse on the inner surface of glass.

Ribbon back A term that describes chair backs that have been carved to look like ribbons tied in bows. A popular design during the mid-18th century, it was a typical feature of the Chippendale chair.

Rocaille A French term meaning "rockwork," which denotes the asymmetrical rock and shell forms characteristic of the Rococo style.

Rosette Of ancient origin, this is a decorative motif in the shape of a rose, which is often used as a disc ornament or as a circular patera.

Rosewood A rich reddish-brown hardwood with an even grain, richly marked with dark stripes. It was used from the 18th century onward as a veneer, during the Regency period in solid form for whole pieces of furniture, and became popular again in the mid-20th century.

Saber leg A leg with a gentle concave curve, predominantly seen on chairs, that was widely used on Regency, Empire, and Federal furniture during the first half of the 19th century.

Sabot A metal shoe-fitting at the bottom of a cabriole leg.

Saddle seat A wooden seat that is raised at the center and scooped away at the sides and back, to look like a saddle. It is a common feature of Windsor chairs.

Satinwood A fine-grained, golden-yellow exotic hardwood used for fine-cut veneers. It was very popular in Great Britain during the late 18th and early 19th centuries

Scagliola A plasterlike substance, to which color pigments and small pieces of stone such as granite, marble, and alabaster are added so that once set, it can be polished to look like marble or *pietra dura*.

Scalloped A term used to describe a wavy edge or border resembling the edge of a scallop shell.

Schrank A German term for a cupboard, generally associated with the large, heavy, two-door cupboards of the 17th and early 18th centuries.

Sconce A candleholder designed to be mounted on a wall. It has an arm or bracket for holding the candle and a backplate for reflecting the light of the candle around a room.

Scroll foot A foot that terminates in a scroll or spiral form. It was usually seen on a cabriole leg and was fashionable in the mid-18th century.

Seat rail See Rail.

Seaweed marquetry See Marquetry.

Secrétaire A French term for a large cabinet in two sections, popular in the late 18th century. The lower section has a fall front that drops down to provide a writing surface and reveals a number of pigeonholes and drawers. Above this there is usually a bookcase or glazed cabinet.

Secrétaire à abattant A French term for a freestanding writing cabinet. It often has a slim drawer beneath the top, and a fall-front writing surface. Below that, there is an arrangement of drawers or cupboards. The form was popular in France during the late 18th century.

Semainier A French term for a tall, narrow chest with seven drawers, one for each day of the week, which was first made in the 18th century.

Serpentine A wavy or undulating surface. A commode with a serpentine front has a protruding central section and concave ends. Serpentine stretchers are curved cross-stretchers.

Settee A seat for two or more people, with a low back and open arms. Sometimes made with an upholstered seat, the settee was more comfortable than a settle and was seen in various forms in Europe from the 17th century onward.

Settle A wooden chest or bench with a high back and open arms. First made in the Middle Ages, the form was revived by the Arts and Crafts Movement in the late 19th century.

Shagreen Shark or ray skin, used by some 17th- and 18th-century designers as an inlay, and revived in the work of Art Deco designers in the early 20th century. It is also known by the French term *galuchat*.

Shell motif The scallop shell was a popular Rococo decorative motif, appearing on the knees of cabriole legs and at the center of aprons on American Queen Anne case pieces.

Sofa A fully upholstered seat for two or more people, a less formal version of the settee. It was made from the late 17th century onward.

Sofa table A long, narrow table with a drop leaf at either end and drawers. Designed to stand behind a sofa, it was popular during the late 18th and early 19th centuries.

Spade foot A rectangular, tapered foot, similar in shape to a spade, usually seen on table legs from the end of the 18th century onward.

Sphinx An ancient Egyptian form that has the head of a woman, the body of a lion, and wings. It was popularized by Napoleon during the Empire period and again by Art Deco designers in the 20th century.

Spindle A thin piece of wood turned on a lathe and used as an upright on a chair. Large numbers of spindles sometimes form the uprights of a gallery on a case piece of furniture.

Splat The flat, vertical, central part of a chair back. Back splats can be either solid or pierced, and are usually shaped. They are important indicators of period styles.

Squab cushion A removable cushion for a chair, sofa, or settee.

S-scroll A decorative carved or applied Classical ornament in the shape of an S, developed during the Rococo period. (*See* C-Scroll.)

Stainless steel *See* Steel.

Steel A hard, durable metal, made of a combination of iron and carbon. First used in various forms on 16th- and 17th-century furniture, it was adopted by 20th-century designers in modified forms, such as tubular steel, chromed steel, and stainless steel (a noncorrosive alloy of steel, nickel, and chrome).

Strapwork A form of ornament that looks like a scrolling pattern of bands or straps. Originating in the work of an Italian Mannerist painter, it became very popular in the late 16th and early 17th centuries and was often applied to furniture.

Streamlined A term borrowed from engineering and used to describe American Art Deco furniture with smooth, clean-lined shapes in the 1920s and 1930s.

Stretcher A rod or bar extending between two legs of a chair or table.

Stringing Narrow lines of inlay on a piece of furniture, used to create a simple, decorative border around drawer fronts or table tops. It was popular in the late 18th century.

Stuffover Upholstery that covers the entire wooden frame of a sofa or chair, so that none of it is visible.

Sunburst motif First popularized by Louis XIV in the late 16th and early 17th centuries, the motif of the sun surrounded by rays was later used in stylized form by Art Deco designers.

Swag A Classical decorative motif of a hanging garland of fruit, husks, flowers, or laurel leaves. Swags often featured in inlays or formed part of a frieze on a table. They were widely used on Neoclassical furniture.

Tabouret A French term for a low, upholstered footstool that was originally shaped like a drum.

Tambour A flexible, slatted, sliding shutter on a roll-top desk, made of thin strips of wood laid side by side and glued to a canvas backing.

Teak A heavy, deep-brown, oily hardwood used to make furniture since the 18th century. It was much favored by Scandinavian designers during the 1950s and 1960s.

Tenon *See* Mortise and tenon.

Thuyawood A native African reddish-brown hardwood, with a bird's-eye figure. It was popular as a veneer during the 18th and 19th centuries.

Tilt-top table A table with a top that has been hinged to its base on one side, so that it can be tilted into a vertical position, allowing the table to be stored flat against a wall.

Tongue and groove A wood joint in which a tongue along one side of a strip of wood fits into a groove along an adjoining strip of wood.

Tooling A technique of decorating leather either by embossing, gilding, or incising, often seen as the border of a leather insert on a writing table.

Top rail The highest horizontal bar on the back of a chair. It is also sometimes called a crest rail.

Torchère A French term for a lamp- or candlestand, usually a tall table with a small top supported on a column. *Torchères* were popular in the 17th and early 18th centuries.

Tortoiseshell A shiny, translucent material made from the shells of the hawksbill turtle. Tortoiseshell can be heat-molded, carved, and colored, and was used for inlays, particularly in 17th- and 18th-century Boulle marquetry. Today, tortoiseshell is usually imitated in celluloid.

Tracery A delicate, latticelike form of decoration based on the elaborate shapes of Gothic church windows.

Trefoil *See* Quatrefoil.

Trestle table A simple form of large dining table in which flat boards, usually made of oak, rest on one, two, or more trestles (pairs of splayed legs). Trestle tables were in wide use from the Middle Ages to the 17th century.

Tripod table A small, occasional pedestal table supported by three splayed legs. The form was popular in late 18th-century furniture.

Tubular steel Lightweight and strong hollow steel tubes, which can be bent into any shape. Favored for its durable, easy-to-clean qualities and its industrial appeal, it was widely used by Modernist designers during the first half of the 20th century.

Vargueño One of the most popular types of furniture in Spain during the 16th and 17th centuries, this is a writing cabinet on a chest or stand. It usually has a drop front and is elaborately carved or decorated.

Veneer A thin layer of fine wood that is applied to the surface of a carcass made of a coarser, cheaper wood, for decorative effect. Veneers were widely used from the second half of the 17th century onward.

Verdigris A green or bluish chemical deposit that forms on copper, brass, or bronze after a period of time.

Verre églomisé A French term for a technique of decorating glass, in which the back of the glass is covered in a layer of gold or silver leaf, and a design is then etched or engraved on the leaf. The technique was used during the 18th century.

Vinyl A revolutionary plastic with great durability and flexibility that was developed during the 1940s. It was primarily used by furniture designers in the 1950s and 1960s for covering chair seats.

Vitruvian scroll A wavelike series of scrolls used as a decorative motif—carved, painted, or gilded—on friezes. Originating as Classical ornament, it was widely used on Neoclassical furniture in the late 18th and early 19th centuries.

Volute A Classical motif, this is a spiraling scroll, thought to resemble the horns of a ram. Used since the Renaissance, the motif was popularized in Neoclassical design.

Walnut A European and North American native hardwood that produces a rich brown timber when cut. Walnut was popular in Europe, both in the solid and as a veneer, from the mid-17th to the early 18th century. Burr walnut, which is highly figured, was frequently used as a decorative veneer.

Wickerwork Known since ancient times, this is made by weaving rods of cane or willow together to form a flat, durable surface, ideal for making seats for chairs.

Windsor chair A country chair with a bentwood back and a wooden seat, into which the chair legs are pegged. An early 18th-century form, the chair was first made around the town of Windsor in England.

Worktable A small table that was often fitted with drawers or shelves and a hanging bag used for storing needlework and sewing materials. It was popular during the 18th century.

Zopfstil The late 18th-century German term for Neoclassicism, which takes its name from Classical braided friezes and festoons—*Zopf* means "braid" in German.

INDEX

Page numbers in *italic* refer to illustrations

ACKNOWLEDGMENTS

AUTHORS' ACKNOWLEDGMENTS

The authors would like to thank the following people for their substantial contributions to the production of this book:

Photographer Graham Rae for his patience, humor and wonderful photography as well as John McKenzie, Andy Johnson, Byron Slater, and Adam Gault for additional photography.

All of the dealers, auction houses and private collectors for kindly allowing us to photograph their collections, and for taking the time to provide a wealth of information about the pieces.

The team at DK, especially Angela Wilkes and Karla Jennings for all their skill and dedication to the project, and Corinne Asghar for her invaluable support. Thanks also to Lee Riches, Sarah Smithies, Kathryn Wilkinson, and Anna Plucinska.

Also special thanks to Anna Southgate, Dan Dunlavey, Jessica Bishop, Karen Morden, Alexandra Barr, and Sandra Lange at the Price Guide Company (UK) for their editorial contribution and help with sourcing information. Thanks also to Digital Image Coordinator Ellen Sinclair and consultants John Wainwright, Martine Franke, Nicolas Tricaud de Montonnière, Keith Baker, Silas Currie, and Matthew Smith who helped so much with the planning of the book.

We would also like to thank the following for their help in the execution of this book: Pierre Bergé et Associés, Paris; Lynda Cain, Samuel T Freeman and Co, Philadelphia; Maison de Ventes Chenu Scrive Bérard, Lyon; Sean Clarke, Christopher Clarke Antiques, Stow on the Wold, Gloucestershire; Dr Graham Dry, Von Zezschwitz, Munich; Judith Elsdon, Curator, The American Museum, Bath; John Mackie, Lyon and Turnbull, Edinburgh; Lucy Morton, Partridge Fine Arts plc, London; Ron and Debra Pook, Pook and Pook Inc, Lancaster, PA; Sebastian Pryke, Lyon and Turnbull, Edinburgh; Jo-Marie Rabe, Pier Rabe Antiques, Stellenbosch, South Africa; Paul Roberts, Lyon and Turnbull, Edinburgh; Rossini, Paris; J. Thomas Savage, Sotheby's Institute of Art, New York; Renee Taylor, Northeast Auctions, Portsmouth, New Hampshire; Anthony Well-Cole, Temple Newsam House, Leeds; Lee Young, Samuel T Freeman and Co, Philadelphia.

A special thank you to Partridge Fine Arts plc, London.

PUBLISHER'S ACKNOWLEDGMENTS

Dorling Kindersley would like to thank Amber Tokeley, Dawn Henderson, and Simon Adams for editorial contribution, Simon Murrell, Simon Oon, Steve Knowlden, and Katie Eke for design contribution, Richard Dabb and Fergus Muir for digital images coordination, Caroline Hunt for proofreading, and Dorothy Frame for compiling the index.

PICTURE CREDITS

The publisher would like to thank the following for their kind permission to reproduce their photographs:

Abbreviations key: t-top, b-bottom, r-right, l-left, c-centre, a-above, f-far

2 www.bridgeman.co.uk: Wallace Collection, London, UK (clb). 3 Sotheby's Picture Library, London (br). 4-5 Fritz Hansen A/S. 6 The Metropolitan Museum of Art: Gift of Mrs Russell Sage, 1909. 7 Fritz Hansen A/S (bl); The Metropolitan Museum of Art: Gift of Mrs Russell Sage, 1909 (br). 8 Réunion Des Musées Nationaux Agence Photographique: Blot/Lewandowski (bc). 10 www.bridgeman.co.uk: Museum of Fine Arts, Houston, Texas, USA (bcr). 14 akg-images: Rabatti - Domingie (tr); The Metropolitan Museum of Art: Fletcher Fund 1930 (tl). 18 The Art Archive: Egyptian Museum Cairo/Dagli Orti. 20 Corbis: Archivo Iconografico, S.A. (bc); The Metropolitan Museum of Art: 1992/Rogers Fund, 1930 (cl). 20 Topfoto.co.uk (tr). 21 The Ancient Egypt Picture Library (crb); Corbis: Roger Wood (t); The Art Archive: Musée du Louvre Paris/Dagli Orti (bc). 22 Corbis: Araldo de Luca (cl, tr); Dave Bartruff (br); The Art Archive: Cyprus Museum Nicosia/Dagli Orti (bl); Photo Scala, Florence (bc); 23 DK Images: The British Museum (c). 24 akg-images: François Guénet (cl). Alamy Images: Jon Arnold Images (bc, br); www.bridgeman.co.uk: National Palace Museum, Taipei, Taiwan, (bl). Trustees of the V&A (tr). 25 akg-images: François Guénet (r). www.bridgeman.co.uk: Biblioteca Nazionale, Turin, Italy, (br). Christie's Images Ltd: (tl). 26 akg-images: Museo del Prado/Erich Lessing (tr). Corbis: McPherson Colin (l). The Art Archive: Bodleian Library Oxford/ The Bodleian Library (br). 27 Alamy Images: Andre Jenny (cfl). The Art Archive: San Angelo in Formis Capua Italy/Dagli Orti (A) (bl). The Metropolitan Museum of Art: Gift of George Blumenthal, 1941 (t). 28 The Metropolitan Museum of Art: Harris Brisbane Dick Fund, 1958 (cl). Scala Art Resource: Palazzo Pitti, Florence, Italy (bl). V&A Images: Daniel McGrath (tr). 29 akg-images: Nimatallah, Vatican Museums (bl). www.bridgeman.co.uk: (br). The Metropolitan Museum of Art: Fletcher Fund 1930 (c); Rogers Fund, 1939 (t). 30 akg-images: National Museum Stockholm (bc). Corbis: Bettmann (bl); Sandro Vannini (cl). 31 www.bridgeman.co.uk: Eglise Saint-Laurent, Salon-de-Provence, France (br). DK Images: Centre des Monuments Nationaux (bl). Germanisches Nationalmuseum: (t). 32 Réunion Des Musées Nationaux Agence Photographique: Blot/Lewandowski. 34 Christie's Images Ltd: (tr). 35 Christie's Images Ltd: (l). Corbis: Adam Woolfitt (tr). DK Images: l'Etablissement Public du Musée et du Domaine National de Versailles (bc). 36 www.bridgeman.co.uk: Philip Mould, Historical Portraits Ltd, London, UK, (br). Staatliche Museen zu Berlin-Preussischer Kulturbesitz Kunstgewerbemuseum: (tr). Sotheby's Picture Library, London: (l). 37 akg-images: Rabatti - Domingie. 38 www.bridgeman.co.uk: Museum of Fine Arts, Houston, Texas, USA, Gift of Mr & Mrs Harris Masterson III (tc); Haddon Hall, Bakewell, Derbyshire, UK (l). Christie's Images Ltd: (bl). Staatliche Museen zu Berlin-Preussischer Kulturbesitz Kunstgewerbemuseum: (br). Sotheby's Picture Library, London: (tr). 39 The Art Archive: Dagli Orti (tcl). National Trust Photographic Library: (tl). Réunion Des Musées Nationaux Agence Photographique: (tcr). V&A Images: (bcl). 40 Archivi Alinari: Seat Archive (cl). Corbis: Araldo de Luca (bc, br). The Art Archive: Museo Civico Belluno/Dagli Orti (c). Sotheby's Picture Library, London: (bl). 41 akg-images: Rabatti-Domingie (bl, cl). Photo Scala, Florence: (tr). Sotheby's Picture Library, London: (cr). 42 DK Images: Natural History Museum (tr). National Trust Photographic Library: (b, c). 43 akg-images: (tl); Galleria degli Uffizi/Rabatti-Domingie (b). 44 akg-images: (tr). Christie's Images Ltd: (r). Rijksmuseum Foundation, Amsterdam: (l). 45 www.bridgeman.co.uk: Private Collection, The Stapleton Collection (cr). Rijksmuseum Foundation, Amsterdam: (bl, cl). 46 Christie's Images Ltd: (br). State Hermitage, St Petersburg: (cr).

Kinsky Auction House, Vienna: (cl). 48 V&A Images: (tr). 49 www.bridgeman.co.uk: Partridge Fine Arts, London, UK (tl). V&A Images: (bl). 52 Christie's Images Ltd: (cr, cr). V&A Images: (l). 53 Réunion Des Musées Nationaux Agence Photographique: (bl, tl). 54 Réunion Des Musées Nationaux Agence Photographique: (br, cla). 55 Réunion Des Musées Nationaux Agence Photographique: Blot/Lewandowski (bc). 56 Christie's Images Ltd: (cr). Sotheby's Picture Library, London: (br). 57 Christie's Images Ltd: (bl, br). Sotheby's Picture Library, London: (cl). 58 www.bridgeman.co.uk: Museum of Fine Arts, Houston, Texas, USA, Gift of Mr & Mrs Harris Masterson III (bl). The Metropolitan Museum of Art: Purchase, Joseph Pulitzer Bequest, 1940 (br). Winterthur Museum: (tr). 59 Museum Of Fine Arts, Boston: (bl). The Metropolitan Museum of Art: Rogers Fund 1909 (cr). Winterthur Museum: (cl). 60 Sotheby's Picture Library, London: (bl, cl). 61 State Hermitage, St Petersburg: (tc). 62 Christie's Images Ltd: (tc, tr). The Metropolitan Museum of Art: Ruth and Victoria Blumka Fund, 1955 (bl). Sotheby's Picture Library, London: (cr). 63 Sotheby's Picture Library, London: (br, tc, tl, tr). 64 akg-images: (tr). Christie's Images Ltd: (br, cr). V&A Images: (bl). 65 Christie's Images Ltd: (bl, br). State Hermitage, St Petersburg: (cr). Sotheby's Picture Library, London: (cl). 66 www.bridgeman.co.uk: Haddon Hall, Bakewell, Derbyshire, UK (br); Muncaster Castle, Ravenglass, Cumbria, UK (tr). The Art Archive: Museo Franz Mayer Mexico/Dagli Orti (tcr). V&A Images: (bc, bl). 67 The Art Archive: (tcl, tr). Sotheby's Picture Library, London: (bl). V&A Images: (bcr). Winterthur Museum: (bcl, tl). 68 Trustees of the V&A. 70 Alamy Images: SCPhotos (cl). 71 Alamy Images: Bildarchiv Monheim GmbH (bc, bcr). www.bridgeman.co.uk: Palacio Nacional, Queluz, Portugal (t); Palacio Nacional, Queluz, Portugal, (tr). 74 www.bridgeman.co.uk: Wallace Collection, London, UK (l). 78 The Metropolitan Museum of Art: (l). 79 Corbis: Massimo Listri (tl). 80 Christie's Images Ltd: (br). Palazzo del Quirinale: (cbr). 82 Christie's Images Ltd: (br). The Metropolitan Museum of Art: 1995 (cr). 83 Christie's Images Ltd: (car, tr). 84 Christie's Images Ltd: (br, bcr) 85 The Metropolitan Museum of Art: (bl, cfl). 86 Alamy Images: Bildarchiv Monheim GmbH (cfl, tl). 86-87 Alamy Images: Bildarchiv Monheim GmbH (t, c). 88 Christie's Images Ltd: (br). 89 Christie's Images Ltd: (tl). 90 Quinta Das Cruzes Museum: (bl). Sotheby's Picture Library, London: (br, cfl). 91 www.bridgeman.co.uk: Palacio Nacional, Queluz, Portugal (tl). Sotheby's Picture Library, London: (br). 93 Dansk Folkemuseums Billedsaunling: (c). 95 www.bridgeman.co.uk: (br). 96 akg-images. 97 Christie's Images Ltd: J Vardy (bl). 97 British Architectural Library, RIBA, London: (cfl). 98 Earl and Countess of Harewood and the Trustees of the Harewood House Trust: (tl). 98-99 Earl and Countess of Harewood and the Trustees of the Harewood House Trust. 99 Dover Publications: (cr). 104 The Metropolitan Museum of Art: (cfl); John Stewart Kennedy Fund, 1918 (cl). 105 The Metropolitan Museum of Art: (br); John Stewart Kennedy Fund (r). 107 Christie's Images Ltd: (r, cr). 110 The Metropolitan Museum of Art: (tr). 111 Sotheby's Picture Library, London: (cfr). 112 The Metropolitan Museum of Art: (bc, bl). 115 Mallett: (tc). 119 Reunion Des Musees Nationaux: Musee du Louvre, Paris/Daniel Arnaudet (tc). Réunion Des Musées Nationaux Agence Photographique: (tcr). 122 Mallett. 124 Corbis: Angelo Hornak (cl). Dover Publications: (bl). 125 Corbis: Adam Woolfitt (t). 130 Sotheby's Picture Library, London: (bl). 132 www.bridgeman.co.uk: (ca). 133 www.bridgeman.co.uk: Museo Archeologico Nazionale, Naples, Italy (ca). 138 Dover Publications: (c, tr). 139 British Library, London: (br). Christie's Images Ltd: (bc). Dover Publications: (tc, tcl). Sotheby's Picture Library, London: (tcr).

142 State Hermitage, St Petersburg: (cfl). Sotheby's Picture Library, London: (tr). 143 Christie's Images Ltd: (c). 144 Christie's Images Ltd: (car, cra). 145 The Metropolitan Museum of Art: The Annenberg Foundation Gift 2002 (bcr, br, cbr). 150 Dover Publications: (tr). 152 Christie's Images Ltd: (br, ca). Corbis: Bettmann (clb). 153 National Trust Photographic Library: (tl). 154 Trustees of the V&A: (cl). 155 Kungl Husgeradskammaren: Alexis Daflos (tl). 157 Pernille Klemp, Kunstindustrimuseet, Denmark: (br). 158 Institut Amatiller D'art Hispànic (Arxiu MAS): (tr). Sotheby's Picture Library, London: (br). 159 Christie's Images Ltd: (c). Institut Amatiller D'art Hispànic (Arxiu MAS): (br). 163 The Charleston Museum: (tl). Colonial Williamsburg Foundation: (br). 166 Alamy Images: Bildarchiv Monheim GmbH (bl). Dover Publishing: (br). 167 Christie's Images Ltd: (tl). 169 Dover Publications: (br). 174 Sotheby's Picture Library, London: (bcr, br). 185 Dover Publications: (cr). 186 Christie's Images Ltd: (bl). 187 Dover Publications: (bl). 189 Dover Publications: Gentleman & Cabinet-Maker's Director by Thomas Chippendale (br). 190-191 V&A Images. 192 akg-images: Laurent Lecat (tr). Alamy Images: Mervyn Rees (cl). 193 Corbis: Bojan Brecelj (t). 201 www.bridgeman.co.uk: Private Collection, Agnew's, London, UK (c). 203 Sotheby's Picture Library, London: (bl). 204 Photo Scala, Florence: Palazzo Pitti, Florence, Italy (bl). 205 Christie's Images Ltd: (car, tr). 206 Corbis: (tr). 213 Ullstein Bild: (tl). 215 akg-images: (br). Sotheby's Picture Library, London: (bc). 217 Alamy Images: Bildarchiv Monheim GmbH (tl). 223 Sotheby's Picture Library, London: (cr). 224 Christie's Images Ltd: (tr). Sotheby's, Inc., New York: (br). 225 Christie's Images Ltd: (tl, tr). 229 Corbis: Peter Harholdt (bl). Dover Publications: (bcr). 230-231 William Struhs: Historic Charleston Foundation. 232 Christie's Images Ltd: (l). 237 Corbis: Raymond Gehman (tc). 257 Dover Publications: (r). 260 Trustees of the V&A. 262 Alamy Images: Bildarchiv Monheim GmbH (cfl). Palais Dorotheum: (bl). 263 The English Heritage Photo Library: Nigel Corrie (c). 264 Trustees of the V&A. 265 Sotheby's Picture Library, London. 268 www.bridgeman.co.uk: New York Historical Society, New York, USA (br). 269 Corbis: Hulton-Deutsch Collection (bc). 271 Corbis: Archivo Iconografico, S.A. (tl). 272 Réunion Des Musées Nationaux Agence Photographique: Arnaudet (tl). 273 Sotheby's Picture Library, London: (br). 276 National Trust Photographic Library: (tr). 277 Mary Evans Picture Library: (bl). Trustees of the V&A: (br). 279 National Trust Photographic Library: Andreas von Einsiedel (tl). 281 Corbis: Hulton-Deutsch Collection (tl). 284 Corbis: Araldo de Luca (tr); Philadelphia Museum of Art (cr). Gebrüder Thonet GmbH: (tc). 285 Palais Dorotheum: (tl). The Falcon Companies: (c). Gebrüder Thonet GmbH: (tc). 288 Christie's Images Ltd: (br, cr). Index Fototeca: (tr). 291 Sotheby's Picture Library, London: (bl, br). 292 Christie's Images Ltd: (bl, br). State Hermitage, St Petersburg: (cra). 293 akg-images: State Hermitage, Russia (tr). State Hermitage, St Petersburg: (tc, tl). Mallett: (br). 294 Corbis: G.E. Kidder Smith (bl). 295 Indiana State Museum and Historic Sites: (br). 296 www.belterfurniture.net: Larry Kemper (cl). Corbis: Peter Harholdt (bc). 297 www.bridgeman.co.uk: Metropolitan Museum of Art, New York, USA (cl). 298 Sotheby's Picture Library, London: (bl, br). 299 Sotheby's Picture Library, London: (bl, br). 301 Mallett: (br). Sotheby's Picture Library, London: (cra). 302 Sotheby's Picture Library, London: (cr). 303 Sotheby's Picture Library, London: (bl). 309 Sotheby's Picture Library, London: (br). 316 The Art Archive: (cr). Mary Evans Picture Library: (tr). 317 Christie's Images Ltd: (tc). Corbis: (bc). 318 www.bridgeman.co.uk: Private Collection, The Stapleton Collection. 320 Corbis: Robert Landau (cl). Dover Publications: (bl).

321 Arcaid.co.uk: Richard Bryant (tr). Corbis: Bettmann (bl). 322 Cheltenham Art Gallery & Museums: (br). 324 www.bridgeman.co.uk: Private Collection, The Fine Art Society, London, UK (bl). 325 www.bridgeman.co.uk: Private Collection, The Fine Art Society, London, UK (br). 328 Corbis: Massimo Listri (bcr, bl, br). 329 Corbis: Peter Harholdt (tr). 330 www.bridgeman.co.uk: The Fine Art Society, London, UK, (l). Trustees of the V&A: Pip Barnard (cr, tr). 331 The Advertising Archive: (cbl). 332 Corbis: Bettmann (tr). 334 The Interior Archive: Fritz von der Schulenburg (tr). 336 Alamy Images: Arcaid (tr). 339 www.bridgeman.co.uk: (br). 339 The Craftsman Farms Foundation, Parsipanny, New Jersey: (tl). 346-347 The Art Archive: Nicolas Sapieha. 348 Corbis: Andrea Jemolo (cl). 349 Archives d'Architecture Moderne: (t). 353 DK Images: ADAGP, Paris and DACS, London 2005 (bcl). 354 Getty Images: Hulton Archive (tr). 355 Van Gogh Museum, Amsterdam: (bcl, tcl). V&A Images: (bcr). 359 The Art Archive: Bibliothèque des Arts Décoratifs Paris/Dagli Orti (bcr); Dagli Orti (bcl). 360 akg-images: DACS (bl). Réunion Des Musées Nationaux Agence Photographique: (tr). 361 Christie's Images Ltd: DACS (tl, tr). Réunion Des Musées Nationaux Agence Photographique: (tc). 362 Réunion Des Musées Nationaux Agence Photographique: P. Schmidt (tr). The Wolfsonian - Florida International University: (bl, br, tc). 363 Corbis: Massimo Listri (tl). DK Images: Judith Miller/DACS (cl, r). Photo Scala, Florence: Museum of Modern Art (MoMA), New York, USA (bc). 364 akg-images: (tr). www.bridgeman.co.uk: Private Collection, The Fine Art Society, London, UK (bcl, bcr). 367 Alamy Images: Arcaid (tl). 372 akg-images: Sotheby's/DACS (cr). DK Images: Judith Miller/DACS (bl). 373 DK Images: Judith Miller/DACS (bcr, bl). Réunion Des Musées Nationaux Agence Photographique: Herve Lewandowski/ DACS (cl). 374 DK Images: Judith Miller/DACS (tr). 375 The Falcon Companies: (bc). 376 akg-images: (tr). 377 akg-images: Sotheby's (cr, tl). Sotheby's Picture Library, London: (bl). 384 Trustees of the V&A. 386 akg-images: (bl). Arcaid.co.uk: (cl). Corbis: Bettmann (bc). 387 Alamy Images: Michael Booth (t). 391 DK Images: Judith Miller/DACS (bcr). 393 DK Images: ADAGP, Paris and DACS, London 2005 (br); Judith Miller (bc); Judith Miller/DACS (cl, cr). Réunion Des Musées Nationaux Agence Photographique: (tl). 394 DK Images: ADAGP, Paris and DACS, London 2005 (tr). 395 DK Images: ADAGP, Paris and DACS, London 2005 (cr). 397 Corbis: Angelo Hornak (tl). 400 Corbis: Peter Aprahamian (bl). 402 Réunion Des Musées Nationaux Agence Photographique: (bl, cl). 402-403 Réunion Des Musées Nationaux Agence Photographique. 406 Kyoto National Museum: Suzuki Masaya (bl). 407 Corbis: Robert Holmes (tl). Kyoto National Museum: Ban-ura Shizue (cl); Tokuriki Yasuno (bl). Phillips de Pury & Company: (bc, br). 409 The Advertising Archive: (cb). Savoy Hotel: (t). 412 DK Images: ADAGP, Paris and DACS, London 2005 (tr). 416 Trustees of the V&A. 418 Corbis: Edifice/DACS (cl). 419 DK Images: Neil Estern (br). Centraal Museum, Utrecht: DACS (c). Wright: DACS (r). 420 Artek: (cfl). 421 Réunion Des Musées Nationaux Agence Photographique: Jean-Claude Planchet/DACS. 422-423 DK Images: FCL/ADAGP, Paris and DACS, London 2005. 423 Wright: (tcr). 424 DK Images: DACS 2005 (bl). Centraal Museum, Utrecht: (l). Wright: (br); DACS (tr). 425 akg-images: © 2005 Mondrian/Holtzman Trust c/o HCR International Warrenton Virginia (ca). DK Images: DACS 2005 (b). 426 akg-images: (br). www.bridgeman.co.uk: Private Collection, Roger-Viollet, Paris; (cl). 427 Tecnolumen GmbH & Co. KG: DACS (bl). 429 Christie's Images Ltd: (br). Corbis: Bettmann. DK Images: DACS 2005 (bc, bl). 431 Christie's Images Ltd: (cr). ClassiCon GmbH: (bc, c). V&A Images: (br). 432 akg-images: (cb). Cassina: DACS (ca). Réunion Des Musées Nationaux Agence Photographique: Michele Bellot/Estate Brassai (tr). 433 Charlotte Perriand Archive, Paris: DACS (ADAGP) (tr). 434 Bauhaus-archive: (b). Institut Fur Stadtgeschichte

Frankfurt: (tr). 436 Bukowskis: (t). Dansk Moebelkunst: (bl). 437 Alvar Aalto Museum, Finland: Maija Holma/Alvar Aalto Foundation (bc). 437 Artek: Alvar Aalto Foundation (br). Le Klint: (t, tr). 438 Trustees of the V&A: (br). Vitra Design Museum: Thomas Dix (cr). 439 www.bridgeman.co.uk: Private Collection, Fine Art Society and Target Gallery, London (br). Isokon: Pritchard Papers, University of East Anglia (bc). Phillips de Pury & Company: (cr). 440 Trustees of the V&A: DACS (bl, br). 441 Corbis: Farrell Grehan (tl). 442 Réunion Des Musées Nationaux Agence Photographique: Georges Meguerditchian/Centre Georges Pompidou (cfr). Wright: (bl). 448-449 Palais Dorotheum. 450 Alamy Images: Arcaid (cl). Editoriale Domus S.p.a.: (bl). 451 Arcaid.co.uk: Alan Weintraub (t). 457 Cranbrook Archives: (tr). Vitra Design Museum: (c). 459 Herman Miller: (br). 460 Powerhouse Musuem, Sydney: Mary Featherston (c); Christopher Snelling (bc); Estate of Gordon Andrews (cr). Sotheby's Australia: Mary Featherston (bl). 461 Powerhouse Musuem, Sydney: Christopher Snelling (bl, bc); Estate of Gordon Andrews (c, cl). Sotheby's Australia: Christopher Snelling (tr); Mary Featherston (br). 463 PP Mobler ApS: (bc). 464 www.arne-jacobsen.com: Strüwing (tr). 465 www.arne-jacobsen.com: Strüwing (t). Rezidor SAS Hospitality, Denmark: (bl). 467 Christie's Images Ltd: (c). 469 Christie's Images Ltd: (br). Casa Mollino: Archivio Aldo Ballo (crb). Wright: (cl, cr). Zanotta Spa: (bc). 470 Getty Images: (cl). 471 Editoriale Domus S.p.A: (tc). 472 www.bridgeman.co.uk: Museum of London, UK (bc). Target Gallery: (bl, br, car). 473 Target Gallery: (br). 477 Wright: (bl). Zanotta Spa: DACS (cl). 480 Palais Dorotheum: (tr). Verner Panton Design: (bl). Wright: (br). 481 Dansk Moebelkunst: (tl). 482 Phillips de Pury & Company: DACS (l). 483 Colani Design Germany: (l). Corbis: Eric Robert (tl). 485 Jacqui Small: Simon Upton. 486 Studio Joe Colombo: (bl). 487 Kartell Spa: (cr). 488 Achille Castiglioni srl: (cl). 489 Flos S.p.A: (c, cr). 491 B&B Italia Spa: (bc). V&A Images: (br). Wright: (tl). 495 Wright: (tl). 496 Target Gallery: (tr). 500 Target Gallery: (cfr). 502 Edra Spa. 505 Cappellini Design Spa: (cl). Cassina: (cl). DK Images: The Sean Hunter Collection, Courtesy of the Guggenheim Museum, Bilbao (br). St Martins Lane Hotel, London: Todd Eberle (c). 506 Vitra Design Museum: (br). 507 Edra Spa. 510 SowdenDesign: George J. Sowden (tr). Wright: (b). 511 Andrea Branzi: (bl). Cappellini Design Spa: (bl). 512 Alberto Ferrero: Una Hotel Vittoria (tr). 513 Cappellini Design Spa: (cl). Cassina: (cfr). 514 View Pictures: Christian Michel (bl). 515 Christie's Images Ltd: (tr). Corbis: Yann Arthus-Bertrand (cbr). Paramount Hotel New York: (bl). 516 Jasper Morrison Ltd: James Mortimer (bl). Magis spa: (cr). 517 Alamy Images: Arcaid (tl). Cappellini Design Spa: (r). Tom Dixon: (cl). Magis spa: (bc). Studioball: (br). 518 Kartell Spa: (tr). 519 Cappellini Design Spa: (bl). 521 Alamy Images: mediacolor's (tr). Frederica Furniture: (br). 522 Edifice: (tr). 523 Edra Spa: (br, cl, cr). Ingmar Kurth + Constantin Meyer: (bc). www.mossonline.com: (tr). 524 Arcaid.co.uk: John Edward Linden (bl). Cassina: (br). 525 Cassina: (tl); Studio Uno (tc). Edra Spa: (bl). 526 Cappellini Design Spa: (bl). Lever House Restaurant: (ca). Marc Newson Ltd: (br, crb). Wright: (tr). 527 Cappellini Design Spa: (bc, cl). Corbis: Reuters (tl). Ford Motor Company Ltd: (c). 528 Vitra Management AG: Hans Hansen (bl). 529 Archivi Alinari: Florence (cr). Flos S.p.A: (tl). Assoc. Archivio Storico Olivetti: (bc). Vitra Management AG: (tr). Wright: (br). 531 Cassina: (tcr). Linley: (tl).